Wiley Loose-Leaf Print Edition

# SURVEY OF ACCOUNTING

SECOND EDITION

kimmel
weygandt

team for success

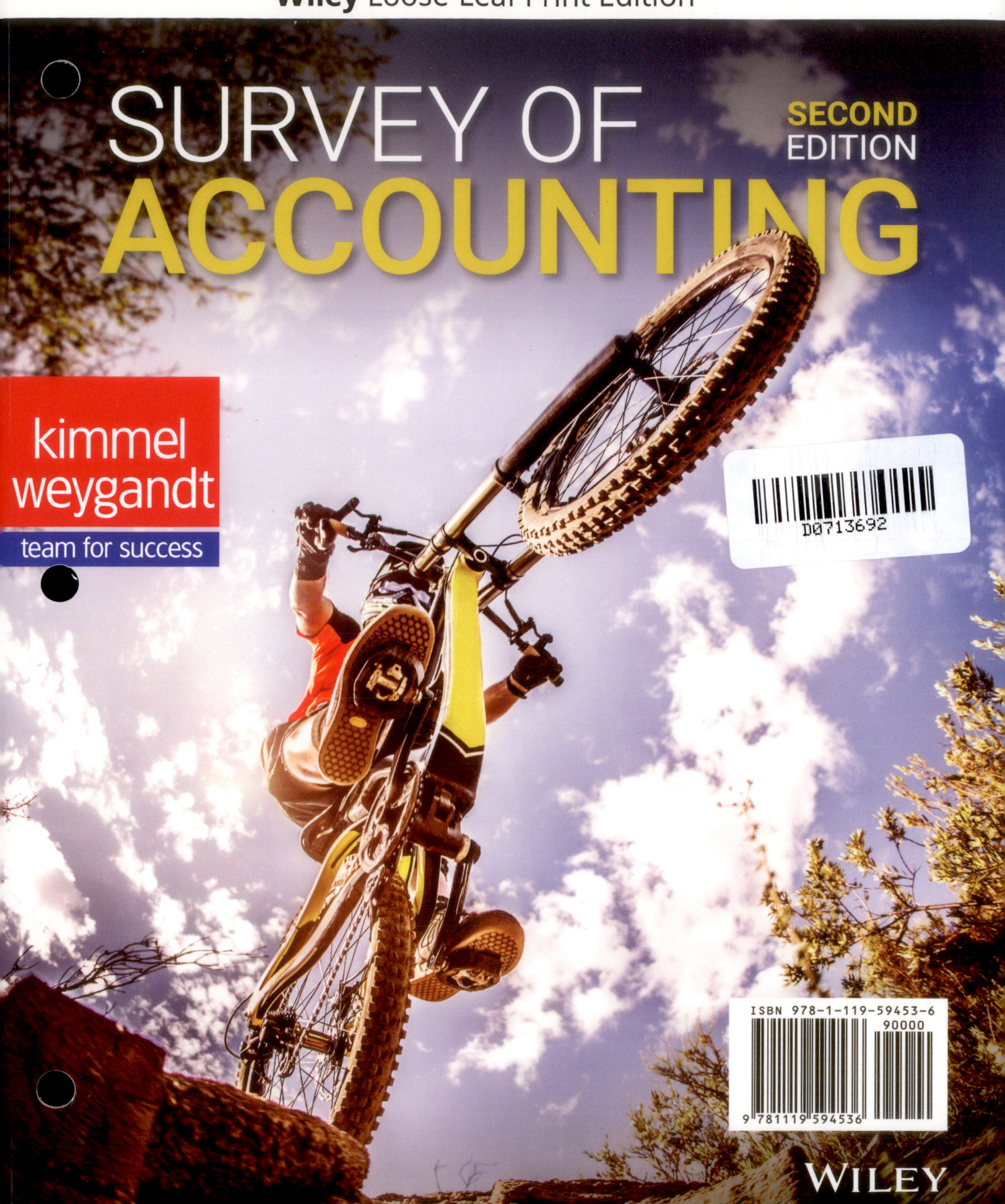

ISBN 978-1-119-59453-6

90000

9 781119 594536

**WILEY**

## Account Classification and Presentation

| Account Title | Classification | Financial Statement |
| --- | --- | --- |
| **A** | | |
| Accounts Payable | Current Liability | Balance Sheet |
| Accounts Receivable | Current Asset | Balance Sheet |
| Accumulated Depreciation—Buildings | Plant Asset—Contra | Balance Sheet |
| Accumulated Depreciation—Equipment | Plant Asset—Contra | Balance Sheet |
| Administrative Expenses | Operating Expense | Income Statement |
| Advertising Expense | Operating Expense | Income Statement |
| Allowance for Doubtful Accounts | Current Asset—Contra | Balance Sheet |
| Amortization Expense | Operating Expense | Income Statement |
| **B** | | |
| Bad Debt Expense | Operating Expense | Income Statement |
| Bonds Payable | Long-Term Liability | Balance Sheet |
| Buildings | Plant Asset | Balance Sheet |
| **C** | | |
| Cash | Current Asset | Balance Sheet |
| Common Stock | Stockholders' Equity | Balance Sheet |
| Copyrights | Intangible Asset | Balance Sheet |
| Cost of Goods Sold | Cost of Goods Sold | Income Statement |
| **D** | | |
| Debt Investments | Current Asset/Long-Term Investment | Balance Sheet |
| Depreciation Expense | Operating Expense | Income Statement |
| Discount on Bonds Payable | Long-term Liability—Contra | Balance Sheet |
| Dividend Revenue | Other Income | Income Statement |
| Dividends | Temporary account closed to Retained Earnings | Retained Earnings Statement |
| Dividends Payable | Current Liability | Balance Sheet |
| **E** | | |
| Equipment | Plant Asset | Balance Sheet |
| **F** | | |
| Freight-Out | Operating Expense | Income Statement |
| **G** | | |
| Gain on Disposal of Plant Assets | Other Income | Income Statement |
| Goodwill | Intangible Asset | Balance Sheet |
| **I** | | |
| Income Summary | Temporary account closed to Retained Earnings | Not Applicable |
| Income Tax Expense | Income Tax Expense | Income Statement |
| Income Taxes Payable | Current Liability | Balance Sheet |
| Insurance Expense | Operating Expense | Income Statement |
| Interest Expense | Other Expense | Income Statement |
| Interest Payable | Current Liability | Balance Sheet |
| Interest Receivable | Current Asset | Balance Sheet |
| Interest Revenue | Other Income | Income Statement |
| Inventory | Current Asset | Balance Sheet (1) |

*(continued)*

# Account Classification and Presentation *(continued)*

| Account Title | Classification | Financial Statement |
|---|---|---|
| **L** | | |
| Land | Plant Asset | Balance Sheet |
| Loss on Disposal of Plant Assets | Other Expense | Income Statement |
| **M** | | |
| Maintenance and Repairs Expense | Operating Expense | Income Statement |
| Mortgage Payable | Long-term Liability | Balance Sheet |
| **N** | | |
| Notes Payable | Current Liability/ Long-term Liability | Balance Sheet |
| **P** | | |
| Patents | Intangible Asset | Balance Sheet |
| Paid-in Capital in Excess of Par Value—Common Stock | Stockholders' Equity | Balance Sheet |
| Paid-in Capital in Excess of Par Value—Preferred Stock | Stockholders' Equity | Balance Sheet |
| Preferred Stock | Stockholders' Equity | Balance Sheet |
| Premium on Bonds Payable | Long-term Liability—Contra | Balance Sheet |
| Prepaid Insurance | Current Asset | Balance Sheet |
| Prepaid Rent | Current Asset | Balance Sheet |
| **R** | | |
| Rent Expense | Operating Expense | Income Statement |
| Retained Earnings | Stockholders' Equity | Balance Sheet and Retained Earnings Statement |
| **S** | | |
| Salaries and Wages Expense | Operating Expense | Income Statement |
| Salaries and Wages Payable | Current Liability | Balance Sheet |
| Sales Discounts | Revenue—Contra | Income Statement |
| Sales Returns and Allowances | Revenue—Contra | Income Statement |
| Sales Revenue | Revenue | Income Statement |
| Selling Expenses | Operating Expense | Income Statement |
| Service Revenue | Revenue | Income Statement |
| Stock Investments | Current Asset/Long-Term Investment | Balance Sheet |
| Supplies | Current Asset | Balance Sheet |
| Supplies Expense | Operating Expense | Income Statement |
| **T** | | |
| Treasury Stock | Stockholders' Equity | Balance Sheet |
| **U** | | |
| Unearned Service Revenue | Current Liability | Balance Sheet |
| Utilities Expense | Operating Expense | Income Statement |

(1) If a periodic system is used, Inventory also appears on the income statement in the calculation of cost of goods sold.

The following is a sample chart of accounts. It does not represent a comprehensive chart of all the accounts used in this text but rather those accounts that are commonly used. This sample chart of accounts is for a company that generates both service revenue and sales revenue. It uses the perpetual approach to inventory.

## Chart of Accounts

| Assets | Liabilities | Stockholders' Equity | Revenues | Expenses |
|---|---|---|---|---|
| Cash | Notes Payable | Common Stock | Service Revenue | Administrative Expenses |
| Accounts Receivable | Accounts Payable | Paid-in Capital in Excess of Par Value—Common Stock | Sales Revenue | Amortization Expense |
| Allowance for Doubtful Accounts | Unearned Service Revenue | Preferred Stock | Sales Discounts | Bad Debt Expense |
| Interest Receivable | Salaries and Wages Payable | Paid-in Capital in Excess of Par Value—Preferred stock | Sales Returns and Allowances | Cost of Goods Sold |
| Inventory | Interest Payable | Treasury Stock | Interest Revenue | Depreciation Expense |
| Supplies | Dividends Payable | Retained Earnings | Gain on Disposal of Plant Assets | Freight-Out |
| Prepaid Insurance | Income Taxes Payable | Dividends | | Income Tax Expense |
| Prepaid Rent | Bonds Payable | Income Summary | | Insurance Expense |
| Land | Discount on Bonds Payable | | | Interest Expense |
| Equipment | Premium on Bonds Payable | | | Loss on Disposal of Plant Assets |
| Accumulated Depreciation—Equipment | Mortgage Payable | | | Maintenance and Repairs Expense |
| Buildings | | | | Rent Expense |
| Accumulated Depreciation—Buildings | | | | Salaries and Wages Expense |
| Copyrights | | | | Selling Expenses |
| Goodwill | | | | Supplies Expense |
| Patents | | | | Utilities Expense |

# WileyPLUS

**WileyPLUS** gives you the freedom of mobility and provides a clear path to your course material and assignments, helping you stay engaged and on track.

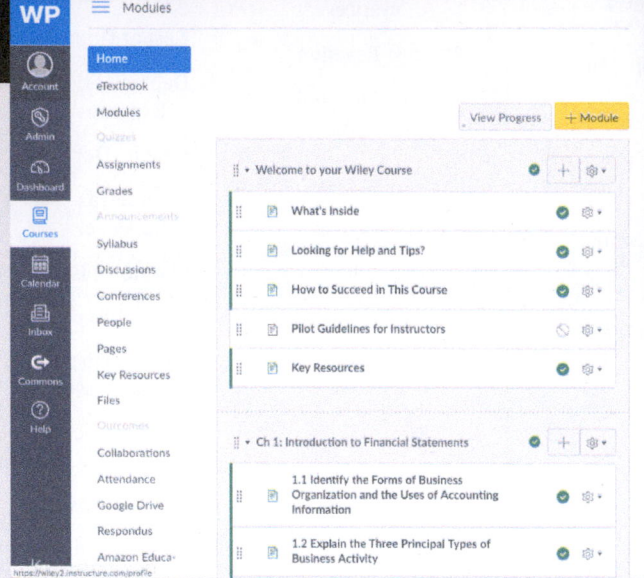

When course materials are presented in an organized way, you are more likely to stay focused, develop mastery, and participate in class. WileyPLUS provides you a clear path through the course material.

Starting with Wiley's quality curated content and adaptive practice questions, you can quickly access material most relevant to your course and understand topics that are most challenging to you. This easy-to-use, intuitive interface saves you time, helps you stay on track, and keeps you motivated throughout your course.

 ### Customized Content

Your course has been customized with videos, documents, pages, and relevant links to keep you motivated.

 ### Interactive eTextbook

You can easily search content, highlight and take notes, access instructor's notes and highlights, and read offline.

 ### Adaptive Practice Questions

Quickly identify areas that are most challenging for you and then focus on material most relevant to your needs.

 ### Linear Design and Organization

Course modules organized by learning objective include eTextbook content, videos, animations, interactives, and practice questions.

 ### Calendar

The course calendar syncs with other features—like assignments and syllabus—so any updates from your instructor will immediately appear.

 ### Student App

You can view due dates, submit assignments, read material, and communicate with your instructor all from your phone.

## www.wileyplus.com/student-register

# Survey of Accounting

**Second Edition**

# Survey of Accounting

**Second Edition**

**PAUL D. KIMMEL PhD, CPA**
University of Wisconsin—Madison
Madison, Wisconsin

**JERRY J. WEYGANDT PhD, CPA**
University of Wisconsin—Madison
Madison, Wisconsin

**WILEY**

## DEDICATED TO

the Wiley sales representatives who sell our texts and service
our adopters in a professional and ethical manner,
and to Merlynn and Enid.

| | |
|---|---|
| DIRECTOR AND VICE PRESIDENT | Michael McDonald |
| EXECUTIVE EDITOR | Zoe Craig |
| INSTRUCTIONAL DESIGN LEAD | Ed Brislin |
| INSTRUCTIONAL DESIGNER | Matthew Origoni |
| DIRECTOR OF MARKETING | Karolina Zarychta Honsa |
| MARKETING MANAGER | Christina Koop |
| EDITORIAL SUPERVISOR | Terry Ann Tatro |
| EDITORIAL ASSISTANT | Megan Joseph |
| SENIOR CONTENT MANAGER | Dorothy Sinclair |
| SENIOR PRODUCTION EDITOR | Rachel Conrad |
| SENIOR DESIGNER | Joanna Vieria |
| COVER IMAGE | ©wundervisuals/Getty Images |

This text was typeset in 9.5/12 STIX Two Text at Lumina Datamatics, Inc. and printed and bound by Quad Graphics. The cover was printed by Quad Graphics.

Founded in 1807, John Wiley & Sons, Inc. has been a valued source of knowledge and understanding for more than 200 years, helping people around the world meet their needs and fulfill their aspirations. Our company is built on a foundation of principles that include responsibility to the communities we serve and where we live and work. In 2008, we launched a Corporate Citizenship Initiative, a global effort to address the environmental, social, economic, and ethical challenges we face in our business. Among the issues we are addressing are carbon impact, paper specifications and procurement, ethical conduct within our business and among our vendors, and community and charitable support. For more information, please visit our website: www.wiley.com/go/citizenship.

ISBN-13: 9781119591344

The inside back cover will contain printing identification and country of origin if omitted from this page. In addition, if the ISBN on the cover differs from the ISBN on this page, the one on the cover is correct.

**Library of Congress Cataloging-in-Publication Data**

Names: Kimmel, Paul D., author. | Weygandt, Jerry J., author.
Title: Survey of accounting / Paul D. Kimmel, PhD, CPA, University of
  Wisconsin—Milwaukee, Jerry J. Weygandt, PhD, CPA, University of
  Wisconsin--Madison.
Description: Second edition. | Hoboken, NJ : John Wiley & Sons, Inc.,
  [2020] | Includes index.
Identifiers: LCCN 2019046240 (print) | LCCN 2019046241 (ebook) | ISBN
  9781119594536 (paperback) | ISBN 9781119610830 (adobe pdf) | ISBN
  9781119591344 (epub)
Subjects: LCSH: Accounting.
Classification: LCC HF5636 .K564 2020 (print) | LCC HF5636 (ebook) | DDC
  657—dc23
LC record available at https://lccn.loc.gov/2019046240
LC ebook record available at https://lccn.loc.gov/2019046241

Printed in America.

SKY10036114_092122

# Brief Contents

## Available in WileyPLUS and Wiley Custom:

# From the Authors

Dear Student,

**Why This Course?** Remember your biology course in high school? Did you have one of those "invisible man" models (or maybe something more high-tech than that) that gave you the opportunity to look "inside" the human body? This accounting course offers something similar. To understand a business, you have to understand the financial insides of a business organization. An accounting course will help you understand the essential financial components of businesses. Whether you are looking at a large multinational company like **Apple** or **Starbucks**, or a single-owner software consulting business or coffee shop, knowing the fundamentals of accounting will help you understand what is happening. As an employee, a manager, an investor, a business owner, or a director of your own personal finances—any of which roles you will have at some point in your life—you will make better decisions for having taken this course.

> "Whether you are looking at a large multinational company like **Apple** or **Starbucks**, or a single-owner software consulting business or coffee shop, knowing the fundamentals of accounting will help you understand what is happening."

**Why This Text?** Your instructor has chosen this text for you because of the authors' trusted reputation. The authors have worked hard to write a text that is engaging, timely, and accurate.

**How to Succeed?** We've asked many students and many instructors whether there is a secret for success in this course. The nearly unanimous answer turns out to be not much of a secret: "Do the homework." This is one course where doing is learning. The more time you spend on the homework assignments—using the various tools that this text provides—the more likely you are to learn the essential concepts, techniques, and methods of accounting. Besides the text itself, WileyPLUS also offers various support resources.

Good luck in this course. We hope you enjoy the experience and that you put to good use throughout a lifetime of success the knowledge you obtain in this course. We are sure you will not be disappointed.

Paul D. Kimmel
Jerry J. Weygandt

# Author Commitment

**JERRY J. WEYGANDT, PhD, CPA**, is Arthur Andersen Alumni Emeritus Professor of Accounting at the University of Wisconsin—Madison. He holds a Ph.D. in accounting from the University of Illinois. Articles by Professor Weygandt have appeared in *The Accounting Review, Journal of Accounting Research, Accounting Horizons, Journal of Accountancy*, and other academic and professional journals. These articles have examined such financial reporting issues as accounting for price-level adjustments, pensions, convertible securities, stock option contracts, and interim reports. Professor Weygandt is the author of other accounting and financial reporting texts and is a member of the American Accounting Association, the American Institute of Certified Public Accountants, and the Wisconsin Society of Certified Public Accountants. He has served on numerous committees of the American Accounting Association and as a member of the editorial board of *The Accounting Review*; he also has served as President and Secretary-Treasurer of the American Accounting Association. In addition, he has been actively involved with the American Institute of Certified Public Accountants and has been a member of the Accounting Standards Executive Committee (AcSEC) of that organization. He has served on the FASB task force that examined the reporting issues related to accounting for income taxes and served as a trustee of the Financial Accounting Foundation. Professor Weygandt has received the Chancellor's Award for Excellence in Teaching and the Beta Gamma Sigma Dean's Teaching Award. He is on the board of directors of M & I Bank of Southern Wisconsin. He is the recipient of the Wisconsin Institute of CPA's Outstanding Educator's Award and the Lifetime Achievement Award. In 2001 he received the American Accounting Association's Outstanding Educator Award.

**PAUL D. KIMMEL, PhD, CPA**, received his bachelor's degree from the University of Minnesota and his doctorate in accounting from the University of Wisconsin. He taught at U.W.—Milwaukee for over 25 years and now teaches at U.W.—Madison. He has public accounting experience with Deloitte & Touche (Minneapolis). He was the recipient of the UWM School of Business Advisory Council Teaching Award, the Reggie Taite Excellence in Teaching Award and a three-time winner of the Outstanding Teaching Assistant Award at the University of Wisconsin. He is also a recipient of the Elijah Watts Sells Award for Honorary Distinction for his results on the CPA exam. He is a member of the American Accounting Association and the Institute of Management Accountants and has published articles in *The Accounting Review, Accounting Horizons, Review of Accounting Studies, Advances in Management Accounting, Managerial Finance, Issues in Accounting Education, Journal of Accounting Education*, as well as other journals. His research interests include accounting for financial instruments and innovation in accounting education. He has published papers and given many presentations regarding accounting instruction, and helped prepare a catalog of critical thinking resources for the Federated Schools of Accountancy.

# New to This Edition

## Chapter-by-Chapter Changes

**Chapter 1: Introduction to Financial Statements**
- **New** discussion of importance of data analytics to users of accounting information.

**Chapter 2: A Further Look at the Balance Sheet**
- **New** chapter organization so that it is now completely focused on the balance sheet, with profitability ratios covered in a later chapter.

**Chapter 3: The Accounting Information System**
- **New** Accounting Across the Organization box on consequences of **Hain Celestial Group** failing to provide earnings information due to revenue recognition issues.
- **New** in-chapter and end-of-chapter DO IT! on financial statement preparation.

**Chapter 4: Accrual Accounting Concepts**
- **New** section on the five-step revenue recognition process, with detailed example and illustration as well as corresponding end-of-chapter material.
- **New** in-chapter DO ITs on adjustments for supplies expense and insurance expense, adjustments for accrued interest, and preparing financial statements.

**Chapter 5: Fraud, Internal Control, and Cash**
- **New** section on how data analytics helps improve internal controls.

**Chapter 6: Merchandising Operations and the Multiple-Step Income Statement**
- **New chapter**—previously "Recording and Analyzing Merchandising Transactions, Receivables, and Inventory"— now solely focused on merchandise operations and income statements.
- This chapter now has separate, expanded sections on inventory systems, recording purchases, and recording sales. (Cost flow assumptions and recognizing receivables are covered in Chapter 7.)
- **New** section on how companies use data analytics to improve business decision-making regarding their policies on credit sales, sales returns and allowances, and sales discounts.

**Chapter 7: Reporting and Analyzing Inventory and Receivables**
- **New chapter** (previously part of Chapter 6) focused on classifying and determining inventory, applying cost flow methods and analyzing their financial effects, recognizing and valuing inventory, and statement presentation and analysis of inventory.

- **New** section on data analytics and receivables management.
- **New** Comprehensive Accounting Cycle Review problem.

**Chapter 8: Reporting and Analyzing Long-Lived Assets**
- In-chapter DO IT! expanded to include practice of return on assets calculation.
- **New** Comprehensive Accounting Cycle Review problem.

**Chapter 9: Reporting and Analyzing Liabilities and Stockholders' Equity**
- **New** People, Planet, and Profit Insight box on how the use of green bonds has increased now that companies have guidelines on how to disclose and report on the green-bond proceeds.
- **New** Investor Insight box on how companies' dividend payments can affect investment decisions.
- Expanded discussion of how net income is recorded in Retained Earnings, including journal entries.

**Chapter 10: Financial Analysis: The Big Picture**
- **New** presentation of discontinued operations on the income statement (previously on the statement of comprehensive income) as well as format of the statement of comprehensive income.
- **New** section on how data analytics can assist in improving valuation models.
- Chapter appendix on comprehensive example of ratio analysis now moved as last part of Ratio Analysis section.

**Chapter 11: Managerial Accounting**
- **New** Management Insight boxes on (1) how **Inditex**'s value chain allows it to be more competitive and (2) why **DPR Construction** is run by an eight-person committee instead of a CEO.

**Chapter 12: Job Order Costing**
- **New chapter** on non-debit-credit analysis of job order cost systems.
- Includes job order for service companies.

**Chapter 13: Cost-Volume-Profit**
- **New** Management Insight box on increased use of automated labor in warehouses.
- **New** Appendix 13A: Regression Analysis, with end-of-chapter assignments.

**Chapter 14: Incremental Analysis**
- **New** Management Insight box on how car manufacturers such as **General Motors** decide whether to make or buy batteries for electric vehicles.

### Chapter 15: Budgetary Planning

- **New** expanded discussions within the production and direct materials budget sections to increase student understanding.
- **New** increased detail and explanation about cash budgets, to increase student understanding.
- **New** Management Insight box on use of zero-based budgeting by companies, including **Kraft Heinz**.

### Chapter 16: Budgetary Control and Responsibility Accounting

- **New** Management Insight box on how a company's reward system depends on employee responsibilities.
- Revised illustration on types of responsibility centers for better visual understanding.

### Chapter 17: Standard Costs and Balanced Scorecard

- Added discussion to analysis of variances, for improved understanding.

### Chapter 18: Planning for Capital Investments

- **New** People, Planet, and Profit Insight box on private investors building their own wind farms to manufacture electricity as a profit source.

### Appendices

- Replaced Appendix C (VF Corporation) with more student-friendly financial statements for **Under Armour**.
- **New Appendices** F (Activity-Based Costing), G (CVP Analysis: Additional Considerations), and H (Pricing).

# Proven Pedagogical Features

*Survey of Accounting, Second Edition,* provides a simple and practical introduction to financial accounting. It explains accounting concepts without the use of debits and credits, while also emphasizing the importance of decision-making, including the use of data analytics.

**In this new edition, all content has been carefully reviewed and revised to ensure maximum student understanding.** At the same time, the time-tested features that have proven to be of most help to students have been retained, such as the following.

## Financial Statement Transaction Illustrations

Throughout the text, carefully crafted illustrations demonstrate the analysis of business transactions. Each illustration shows the effect that a transaction has on (1) the basic accounting equation, (2) individual accounts, (3) the balance sheet and the income statement, and (4) cash.

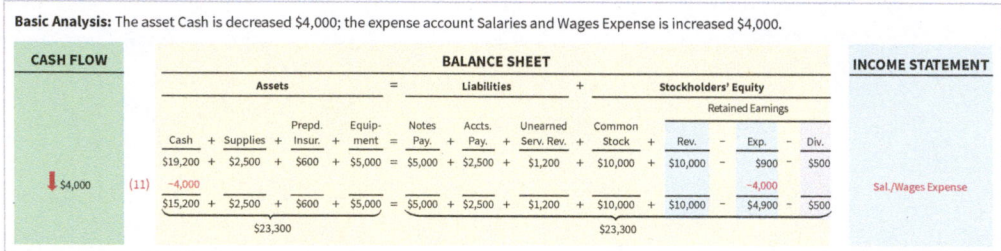

## Infographic Learning

Over half of the text is visual, providing students alternative ways of learning about accounting.

**ILLUSTRATION 4.3** Accrual- versus cash-basis accounting

| | 2021 | 2022 |
|---|---|---|
| **Activity** | Purchased paint, painted building, paid employees | Received payment for work done in 2021 |
| **Accrual basis** | Revenue $80,000<br>Expense 50,000<br>Net income $30,000 | Revenue $ 0<br>Expense 0<br>Net income $ 0 |
| **Cash basis** | Revenue $ 0<br>Expense 50,000<br>Net loss $(50,000) | Revenue $80,000<br>Expense 0<br>Net income $80,000 |

# Real-World Decision-Making and Data Analytics

Real-world examples, which illustrate engaging situations in companies, are provided throughout the text. In addition, the text also discusses how managers are increasingly relying on data analytics to make decisions using accounting information.

---

**Investor Insight**   Apple Inc.

PhotoAlto/James Hardy/Getty Images, Inc.

### Reporting Revenue Accurately

Until recently, electronics manufacturer **Apple** was required to spread the revenues from iPhone sales over the two-year period following the sale of the phone. Accounting standards required this because Apple was obligated to provide software updates after the phone was sold. Since Apple had service obligations after the initial date of sale, it was forced to spread the revenue over a two-year period. As a result, the rapid growth of iPhone sales was not fully reflected in the revenue amounts reported in Apple's income statement. A new accounting standard now enables Apple to report much more of its iPhone revenue at the point of sale. It was estimated that under the new rule revenues would have been about 17% higher and earnings per share almost 50% higher.

**In the past, why was it argued that Apple should spread the recognition of iPhone revenue over a two-year period, rather than recording it upfront? (Go to WileyPLUS for this answer and additional questions.)**

---

# Data Analytics and Credit Sales

Increased access to ever larger amounts of data about customers, suppliers, products, and virtually every other aspect of a business has resulted in a greater reliance by companies on data analytics to support business decisions. Credit sales, sales returns and allowances, and sales discounts all provide rich opportunities for the use of data analytics.

- Effectively analyzing data regarding current as well as potential customers can help a company expand its sales base while minimizing the risk of unpaid receivables.
- In recent years, companies such as **Best Buy**, **REI**, and **Costco** have all refined their customer return policies, sometimes with unique rules for specific product types, as a result of data analytics applied to their data on product returns.

---

# DO IT! Exercises

DO IT! Exercises in the body of the text prompt students to stop and review key concepts. They outline the Action Plan necessary to complete the exercise as well as show a detailed solution.

---

**ACTION PLAN**

- Insurance expense is the amount of insurance used during the period. This is determined by dividing the balance in Prepaid Insurance by the number of remaining months covered by the policy to get the monthly expense. Then multiply by the number of months.
- Supplies expense is determined by subtracting the ending balance of supplies from the unadjusted balance in supplies to determine the amount of supplies used.

**DO IT! 2  |  Adjustments for Deferrals—Supplies Expense and Insurance Expense**

**Part 1:** Ranier Corp. started business on October 1, 2022. On October 1, it purchased a 2-year insurance policy for $3,600 as well as supplies for $490. On November 15, Ranier purchased additional supplies for $610. On December 31, the company had supplies of $200 on hand.

1. What was the amount of insurance expense that would be recorded in a quarterly adjustment on December 31?
2. What was the amount of supplies expense that would be recorded in a quarterly adjustment on December 31?

**Solution**

1. The amount of insurance used during the quarter is $450 [($3,600 ÷ 24) × 3].
2. The amount of supplies used during the quarter is $900 [($490 + $610) − $200].

Related exercise material: **BE4.4, BE4.5, BE4.6, BE4.7, and DO IT! 4.2.**

# Decision Tools

Accounting concepts that are useful for management decision-making are highlighted throughout the text. A summary of Decision Tools is included in each chapter as well as a practice exercise and solution called Using the Decision Tools.

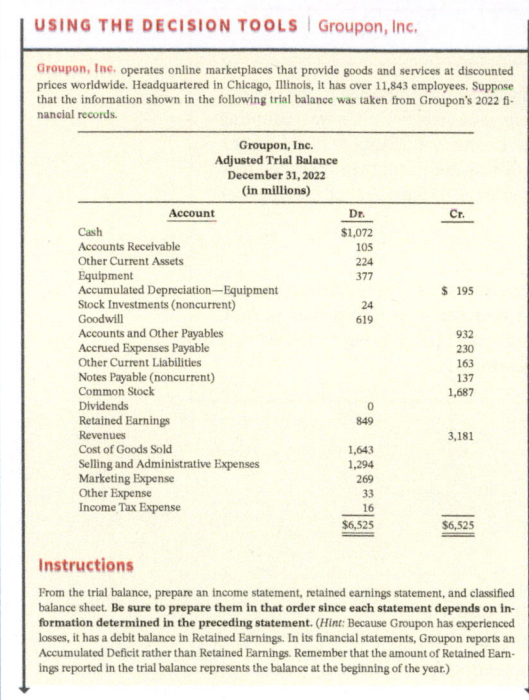

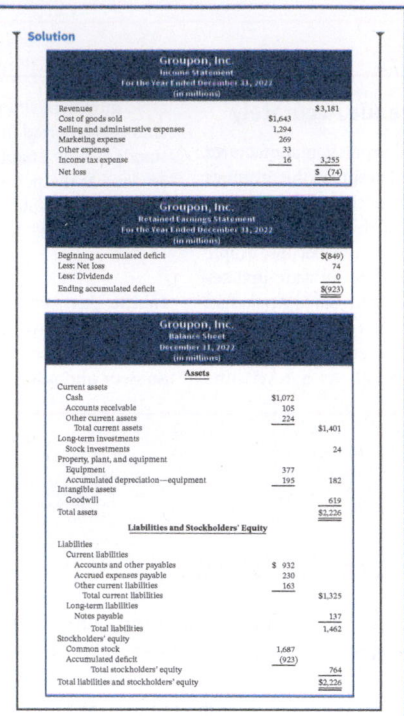

# Review and Practice

Each chapter concludes with a Review and Practice section which includes a review of learning objectives, Decision Tools review, key terms glossary, practice multiple-choice questions with annotated solutions, practice brief exercises with solutions, practice exercises with solutions, and a practice problem with a solution.

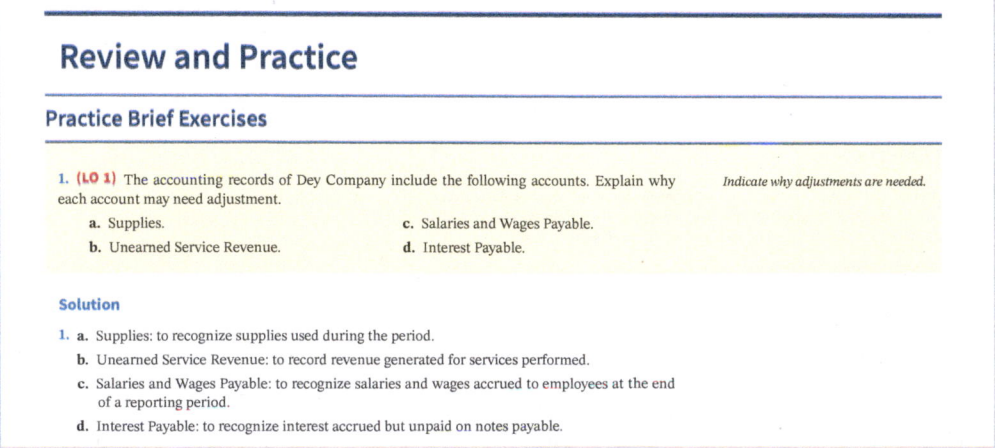

Digital study tools in the *Survey of Accounting* WileyPLUS course include the following.

## Real-World Company Videos

Real-world company videos feature both small businesses and larger companies to help students apply content and see how business owners apply concepts from the text in the real world.

## Solution Walkthrough Videos

Solution Walkthrough Videos are available as question assistance and help students develop problem-solving techniques. These videos walk students through solutions step-by-step and are based on the most regularly assigned exercises and problems in the text.

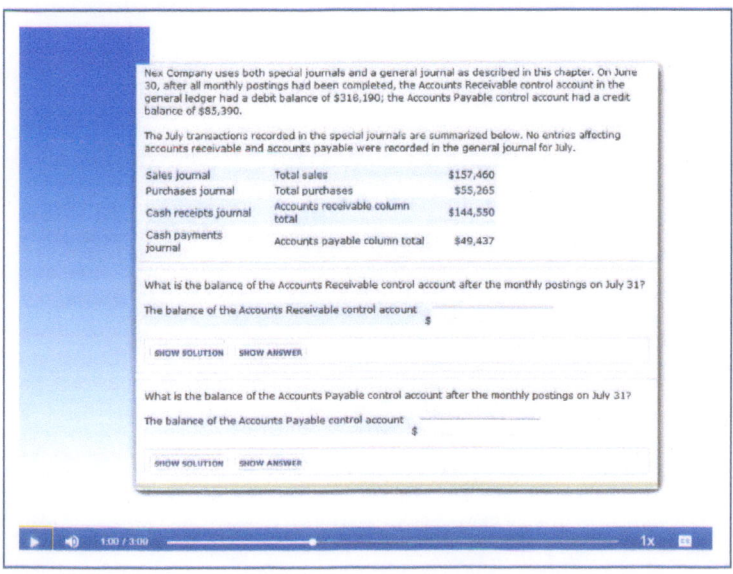

# Interactive Tutorials

Interactive tutorials are voice-guided reviews of topics in each learning objective. Check points in the tutorials require students to review and solve simple self-assessment exercises.

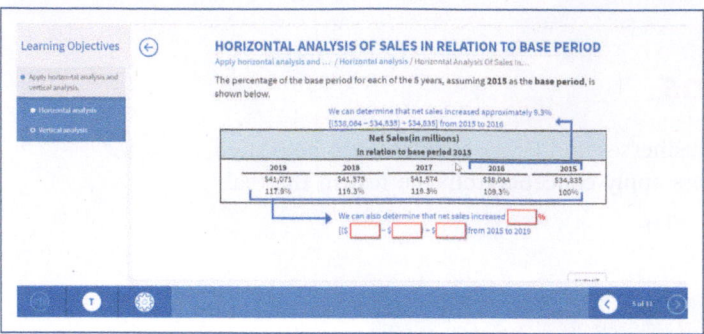

In addition, other WileyPLUS learning opportunities include the following.

- **Cookie Creations** is a continuing case that spans across chapters and shows how a small business grows.
- **Wiley Accounting Updates** (wileyaccountingupdates.com) provide faculty and students with weekly curated news articles and suggested discussion questions.
- **Flashcards and Crossword Puzzles** help students study and master basic vocabulary and concepts.
- **Student Practice** quickly and effectively assesses student understanding of the material they have just covered.
- **Adaptive Practice** helps students quickly understand what they know and what they do not know, and provides opportunities for practice to effectively prepare for class or quizzes and exams.
- **New Test Bank Questions** require students to analyze transactions using the tabular analysis in the text.

# Contents

## 6  Merchandising Operations and the Multiple-Step Income Statement  6-1

## 7  Reporting and Analyzing Inventory and Receivables  7-1

## 8  Reporting and Analyzing Long-Lived Assets  8-1

## 9  Reporting and Analyzing Liabilities and Stockholders' Equity  9-1

## Available in WileyPLUS and Wiley Custom:

# Acknowledgments

*Survey of Accounting, Second Edition,* has benefited greatly from those who have sent comments by letter or e-mail, ancillary authors, and proofers. We greatly appreciate the constructive suggestions and innovative ideas of reviewers and the creativity and accuracy of the ancillary authors and checkers.

Heather Altman, *University of Arizona*
Ellen Bartley, *St. Joseph's College*
LuAnn Bean, *Florida Institute of Technology*
Swati Bhandarkar, *University of Georgia*
Mike Bitter, *Stetson University*
Jack Borke, *University of Wisconsin—Platteville*
Elizabeth Briggs, *Louisiana State University*
C. Catherine Chiang, *Elon University*
Sandee Cohen, *Columbia College—Chicago*
Cari Edison, *Baylor University*
Jim Emig, *Villanova University*
Larry Falcetto, *Emporia State University*
Charmaine Felder, *Brandman University*
Vicki Greshik, *University of Jamestown*
Heidi Hansel, *Kirkwood Community College*
Coby Harmon, *University of California—Santa Barbara*
James Holland, *Virginia Commonwealth University*
Maggie Houston, *Wright State University*
Kimberly Hurt, *Central Community College*
Rebecca Hutchins, *Appalachian State University*
Constance Hylton, *George Mason University*
Surya Janakiraman, *University of Texas—Dallas*
Joseph Lipari, *Montclair State University*
Cynthia Lovick, *Austin Community College*

Lisa Ludlum, *Western Illinois University*
Kirk Lynch, *Sandhills Community College*
Anthony Masino, *East Tennessee State University*
Laura McNally, *Pacific University—Oregon*
William Miller, *University of Wisconsin—Eau Claire*
Jill Misuraca, *University of Tampa*
Kenneth Muccino, *Central Connecticut State University*
Barb Muller, *Arizona State University*
Roshelle Overton, *Central New Mexico Community College*
Yvonne Phang, *Borough of Manhattan Community College*
Jean Price, *Marshall University*
Laura Prosser, *Black Hills State University*
Reza Rafi, *University of Phoenix*
Carol Rogers, *Central New Mexico Community College*
Timothy Schultz
Lloyd Seaton, *Northern Colorado University*
Sherri Silverberg, *University of Arizona*
Kathleen Simons, *Bryant University*
Alice Sineath, *Forsyth Technical Community College*
Lynn Stallworth, *Appalachian State University*
Jill Trucke, *University of Nebraska—Lincoln*
Ski Vanderlann, *Delta College*
Sheila Viel, *University of Wisconsin—Milwaukee*
Dick Wasson, *Southwestern College*
Bruce Wright, *Loyalist College*
James Yang, *Montclair State University*
Melanie Yon
Lori Grady Zaher, *Bucks County Community College*
Ally Zimmerman, *Florida State University*

We appreciate the exemplary support and commitment given to us by editor Zoe Craig, director of marketing Karolina Zarychta Honsa, lead product designer Ed Brislin, product designer Matthew Origoni, editorial supervisor Terry Ann Tatro, designer Joanna Vieria, indexer Steve Ingle, senior production editor Rachel Conrad, and Julie Perry at Lumina. All of these professionals provided innumerable services that helped the text take shape.

We appreciate suggestions and comments from users—instructors and students alike. You can send your thoughts and ideas about the text to us via email at: *AccountingAuthors@ yahoo.com.*

**Paul D. Kimmel**
Madison, Wisconsin

**Jerry J. Weygandt**
Madison, Wisconsin

## CHAPTER 1

My Good Images/Shutterstock.com.

# Introduction to Financial Statements

## Chapter Preview

How do you start a business? How do you determine whether your business is making or losing money? How should you finance expansion—should you borrow, should you issue stock, should you use your own funds? How do you convince banks to lend you money or investors to buy your stock? Success in business requires making countless decisions, and decisions require financial information.

The purpose of this chapter is to show you what role accounting plays in providing financial information.

The **Chapter Preview** describes the purpose of the chapter and highlights major topics.

The **Feature Story** helps you picture how the chapter topic relates to the real world of accounting and business.

## Feature Story

### Knowing the Numbers

Many students who take this course do not plan to be accountants. If you are in that group, you might be thinking, "If I'm not going to be an accountant, why do I need to know accounting?" Well, consider this quote from Harold Geneen, the former chairman of **IT&T**: "To be good at your business, you have to know the numbers—cold." In business, accounting and financial statements are the means for communicating the numbers. If you don't know how to read financial statements, you can't really know your business.

Knowing the numbers is sometimes even a matter of corporate survival. Consider the story of **Columbia Sportswear Company**, headquartered in Portland, Oregon. Gert Boyle's family fled Nazi Germany when she was 13 years old and then purchased a small hat company in Oregon, Columbia Hat Company. In 1971, Gert's husband, who was then running the company, died suddenly of a heart attack. Gert took over the small, struggling company with help from her son Tim, who was then a senior at the University of Oregon. Somehow, they kept the company afloat. Today, Columbia has more than 4,000 employees and annual sales in excess of $1 billion. Its brands include Columbia, Mountain Hardwear, Sorel, and Montrail.

Columbia doesn't just focus on financial success. Several of its factories continue to participate in a project to increase health awareness of female factory workers in developing countries. Columbia is also a founding member of the Sustainable Apparel Coalition, which strives to reduce the environmental and social impact of the apparel industry. In addition, the company monitors all of the independent factories that produce its products to ensure that they comply with the company's Standards of Manufacturing Practices. These standards address such issues as forced labor, child labor, harassment, wages and benefits, health and safety, and the environment.

Employers such as Columbia Sportswear generally assume that managers in all areas of the company are "financially literate." To help prepare you for that, in this text you will learn how to read and prepare financial statements, and how to use key tools to evaluate financial results using basic data analytics.

# Chapter Outline

The **Chapter Outline** presents the chapter's topics and subtopics, as well as practice opportunities.

| LEARNING OBJECTIVES | REVIEW | PRACTICE |
|---|---|---|
| **LO 1** Identify the forms of business organization and the uses of accounting information. | • Forms of business organization<br>• Users and uses of financial information<br>• Ethics in financial reporting | **DO IT! 1** Business Organization Forms |
| **LO 2** Explain the three principal types of business activity. | • Financing activities<br>• Investing activities<br>• Operating activities | **DO IT! 2** Business Activities |
| **LO 3** Describe the four financial statements and how they are prepared. | • Income statement<br>• Retained earnings statement<br>• Balance sheet<br>• Statement of cash flows<br>• Interrelationships of statements<br>• Annual report elements | **DO IT! 3a** Financial Statements<br>**DO IT! 3b** Components of Annual Reports |

**Go to the Review and Practice section at the end of the chapter for a targeted summary and practice applications with solutions.**

**Visit WileyPLUS for additional tutorials and practice opportunities.**

# Business Organization and Accounting Information Uses

### LEARNING OBJECTIVE 1
Identify the forms of business organization and the uses of accounting information.

Suppose you graduate with a business degree and decide you want to start your own business. But what kind of business? You enjoy working with people, especially teaching them new skills. You also spend most of your free time outdoors, kayaking, backpacking, skiing, rock climbing, and mountain biking. You think you might be successful in opening an outdoor guide service where you grew up, in the Sierra Nevada mountains.

# Forms of Business Organization

Your next decision is to determine the organizational form of your business. You have three choices—sole proprietorship, partnership, or corporation.

## Sole Proprietorship

You might choose the sole proprietorship form for your outdoor guide service.

- A business owned by one person is a **sole proprietorship**.
- It is **simple to set up** and **gives you control** over the business.

Small owner-operated businesses such as barber shops, law offices, and auto repair shops are often sole proprietorships, as are farms and small retail stores.

## Partnership

Another possibility is for you to join forces with other individuals to form a partnership.

- A business owned by two or more persons associated as partners is a **partnership**.
- Partnerships often are formed because one individual does not have **enough economic resources** or other **unique skills or resources** to initiate or expand the business.

You and your partners should formalize your duties and contributions in a written partnership agreement. Retail and service-type businesses, including professional practices (lawyers, doctors, architects, and certified public accountants), often organize as partnerships.

## Corporation

As a third alternative, you might organize as a corporation.

- A business organized as a separate legal entity owned by stockholders is a **corporation**.
- Investors in a corporation receive shares of stock to indicate their ownership claim.

Buying stock in a corporation is often more attractive than investing in a partnership because shares of stock are **easy to sell** (transfer ownership). Selling a proprietorship or partnership interest is much more involved. Also, individuals can become **stockholders** by investing relatively small amounts of money (see **Alternative Terminology**). Therefore, it is **easier for corporations to raise funds**. Successful corporations often have thousands of stockholders, and their stock is traded on organized stock exchanges like the **New York Stock Exchange**. Many businesses start as sole proprietorships or partnerships and eventually incorporate.

Other factors to consider in deciding which organizational form to choose are **taxes and legal liability**. If you choose a sole proprietorship or partnership, you generally receive more favorable tax treatment than a corporation. However, proprietors and partners are personally liable for all debts and legal obligations of the business; corporate stockholders are not. In other words, corporate stockholders generally pay higher taxes but have no personal legal liability. We will discuss these issues in more depth in a later chapter.

## Hybrid Forms

Finally, while sole proprietorships, partnerships, and corporations represent the main types of business organizations, hybrid forms are now allowed in all states.

- Hybrid business forms combine the tax advantages of partnerships with the limited liability of corporations.
- Probably the most common among these hybrids types are limited liability companies (LLCs) and subchapter S corporations (these forms are discussed extensively in business law classes).

**Sole Proprietorship**
-Simple to establish
-Owner-controlled
-Tax advantages

**Partnership**
-Simple to establish
-Shared control
-Broader skills and resources
-Tax advantages

**Corporation**
-Easier to transfer ownership
-Easier to raise funds
-No personal liability

**ALTERNATIVE TERMINOLOGY**

**Stockholders are sometimes called *shareholders*.**

**Alternative Terminology** notes present synonymous terms that you may come across in practice.

The combined number of proprietorships and partnerships in the United States far exceeds the number of corporations. However, the revenue produced by corporations is many times greater. Most of the largest businesses in the United States—for example, **Coca-Cola**, **ExxonMobil**, **General Motors**, **Citigroup**, and **Microsoft**—are corporations. Because the majority of U.S. business is done by corporations, the emphasis in this text is on the corporate form of organization.

# Users and Uses of Financial Information

The purpose of financial information is to provide inputs for decision-making. **Accounting** is the information system that identifies, records, and communicates the economic events of an organization to interested users.

Accounting software systems collect vast amounts of data about the economic events experienced by a company and about the parties with whom the company engages, such as suppliers and customers. Business decision-makers take advantage of this wealth of data by using data analytics to make more informed business decisions.

- **Data analytics** involves analyzing data, often employing both software and statistics, to draw inferences.
- As both data access and analytical software improve, the use of data analytics to support decisions is becoming increasingly common at virtually all types of companies (see **Helpful Hint**).

**Users** of accounting information can be divided broadly into two groups: internal users and external users.

## Internal Users

**Internal users** of accounting information are managers who plan, organize, and run a business. These include **marketing managers**, **production supervisors**, **finance directors**, **and company officers**. In running a business, managers must answer many important questions, as shown in **Illustration 1.1**.

**ILLUSTRATION 1.1** Questions that internal users ask

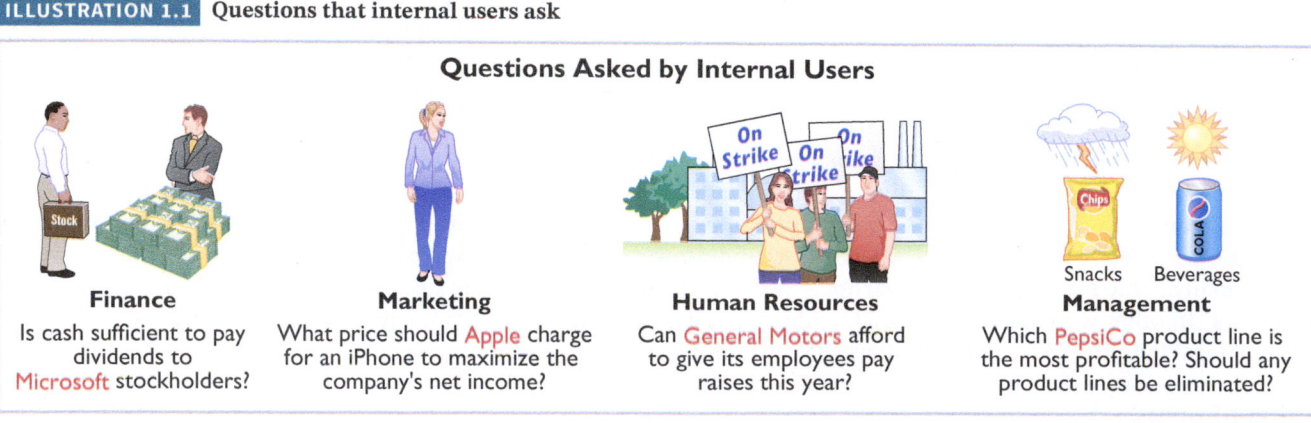

**Questions Asked by Internal Users**

**Finance**
Is cash sufficient to pay dividends to Microsoft stockholders?

**Marketing**
What price should Apple charge for an iPhone to maximize the company's net income?

**Human Resources**
Can General Motors afford to give its employees pay raises this year?

**Management**
Which PepsiCo product line is the most profitable? Should any product lines be eliminated?

To answer these and other questions, you need detailed information on a timely basis. For internal users, accounting provides internal reports, such as financial comparisons of operating alternatives, projections of income from new sales campaigns, and forecasts of cash needs for the next year. In addition, companies present summarized financial information in the form of financial statements.

**Accounting Across the Organization** boxes show applications of accounting information in various business functions.

## Accounting Across the Organization   Clif Bar & Company

iStock.com/Dan Moore

### Owning a Piece of the Bar

The original Clif Bar® energy bar was created in 1990 after six months of experimentation by Gary Erickson and his mother in her kitchen. The company has approximately 1,000 employees and was named one of Landor's Breakaway Brands®. One of **Clif Bar & Company**'s proudest moments was the creation of an employee stock ownership plan (ESOP). This plan gives its employees 20% ownership of the company.

The ESOP also resulted in Clif Bar enacting an open-book management program, including the commitment to educate all employee-owners about its finances. Armed with basic accounting knowledge, employees are more aware of the financial impact of their actions, which leads to better decisions.

**What are the benefits to the company and to the employees of making the financial statements available to all employees? (Go to WileyPLUS for this answer and additional questions.)**

## External Users

There are several types of **external users** of accounting information. **Investors** (owners) use accounting information to make decisions to buy, hold, or sell stock. **Creditors,** such as suppliers and bankers, use accounting information to evaluate the risks of selling on credit or lending money. Some questions that investors and creditors may ask about a company are shown in **Illustration 1.2**.

**ILLUSTRATION 1.2**   **Questions that external users ask**

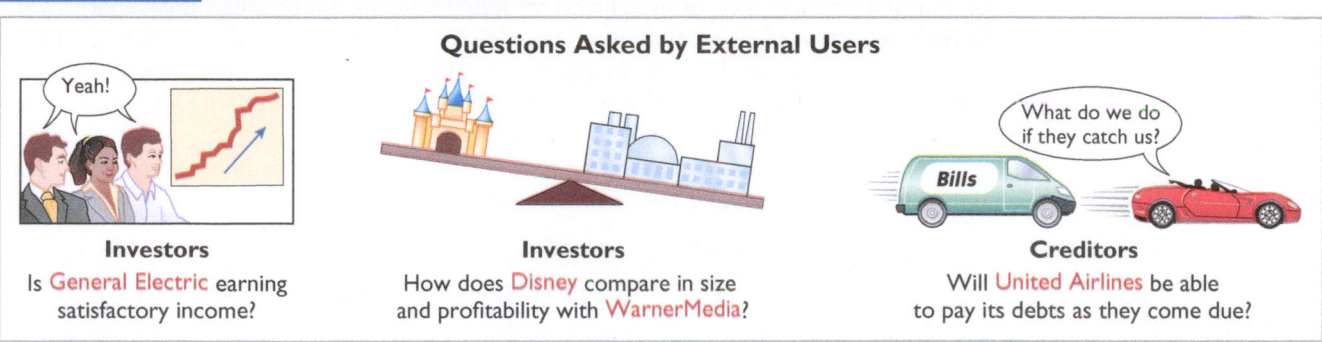

The information needs and questions of other external users vary considerably.

- **Taxing authorities**, such as the Internal Revenue Service, want to know whether the company complies with the tax laws.
- **Customers** are interested in whether a company like **General Motors** will be able to honor product warranties and otherwise support its product lines.
- **Labor unions**, such as the Major League Baseball Players Association, want to know whether the owners have the ability to pay increased wages and benefits.
- **Regulatory agencies**, such as the Securities and Exchange Commission or the Federal Trade Commission, want to know whether the company is operating within prescribed rules.

For example, **Enron**, **Dynegy**, **Duke Energy**, and other big energy-trading companies reported record profits at the same time as California was paying extremely high prices for energy and suffering from blackouts. This disparity caused regulators to investigate the energy traders to make sure that the profits were earned by legitimate and fair practices.

## Accounting Across the Organization

iStock.com/Josef Volavka

### Spinning the Career Wheel

How will the study of accounting help you? A working knowledge of accounting is desirable for virtually every field of business. Some examples of how accounting is used in business careers include the following.

**General management:** Managers of **Ford Motors**, **Massachusetts General Hospital**, **California State University–Fullerton**, a **McDonald's** franchise, and a **Trek** bike shop all need to understand accounting data in order to make wise business decisions.

**Marketing:** Marketing specialists at **Procter & Gamble** must be sensitive to costs and benefits, which accounting helps them quantify and understand. Making a sale is meaningless unless it is a profitable sale.

**Finance:** Do you want to be a banker for **Citicorp**, an investment analyst for **Goldman Sachs**, or a stock broker for **Merrill Lynch**? These fields rely heavily on accounting knowledge to analyze financial statements. In fact, it is difficult to get a good job in a finance function without two or three courses in accounting.

**Real estate:** Are you interested in being a real estate broker for **Prudential Real Estate**? Because a third party—the bank—is almost always involved in financing a real estate transaction, brokers must understand the numbers involved: Can the buyer afford to make the payments to the bank? Does the cash flow from an industrial property justify the purchase price? What are the tax benefits of the purchase?

**How might accounting help you? (Go to WileyPLUS for this answer and additional questions.)**

# Ethics in Financial Reporting

People won't gamble in a casino if they think it is "rigged." Similarly, people won't "play" the stock market if they think stock prices are rigged. At one time, the financial press was full of articles about financial scandals at **Enron**, **WorldCom**, **HealthSouth**, and **AIG**. As more scandals came to light, a mistrust of financial reporting in general seemed to be developing.

One article in the *Wall Street Journal* noted that "repeated disclosures about questionable accounting practices have bruised investors' faith in the reliability of earnings reports, which in turn has sent stock prices tumbling." Imagine trying to carry on a business or invest money if you could not depend on the financial statements to be honestly prepared. Information would have no credibility. There is no doubt that a sound, well-functioning economy depends on accurate and dependable financial reporting.

United States regulators and lawmakers were very concerned that the economy would suffer if investors lost confidence in corporate accounting because of unethical financial reporting.

**ETHICS NOTE**

Circus-founder P.T. Barnum is alleged to have said, "Trust everyone, but cut the deck." What Sarbanes-Oxley does is to provide measures that (like cutting the deck of playing cards) help ensure that fraud will not occur.

Ethics Notes help sensitize you to some of the ethical issues in accounting.

- Congress passed the **Sarbanes-Oxley Act (SOX)** to reduce unethical corporate behavior and decrease the likelihood of future corporate scandals (see **Ethics Note**).
- As a result of SOX, top management must now certify the accuracy of financial information.
- In addition, penalties for fraudulent financial activity are much more severe.
- Also, SOX increased both the independence of the outside auditors who review the accuracy of corporate financial statements and the oversight role of boards of directors.

Effective financial reporting depends on sound ethical behavior. To sensitize you to ethical situations and to give you practice at solving ethical dilemmas, we address ethics in a number of ways in this text.

1. A number of the *Feature Stories* and other parts of the text discuss the central importance of ethical behavior to financial reporting.
2. *Ethics Insight boxes* and marginal *Ethics Notes* highlight ethics situations and issues in actual business settings.
3. Many of the *People, Planet, and Profit Insight boxes* focus on ethical issues that companies face in measuring and reporting social and environmental issues.
4. At the end of each chapter, an *Ethics Case* simulates a business situation and asks you to put yourself in the position of a decision-maker in that case.

When analyzing these various ethics cases and your own ethical experiences, you should apply the three steps outlined in **Illustration 1.3.**

**ILLUSTRATION 1.3**   **Steps in analyzing ethics cases**

### Solving an Ethical Dilemma

**1. Recognize an ethical situation and the ethical issues involved.**
Use your personal ethics to identify ethical situations and issues. Some businesses and professional organizations provide written codes of ethics for guidance in some business situations.

**2. Identify and analyze the principal elements in the situation.**
Identify the **stakeholders**— persons or groups who may be harmed or benefited. Ask the question: What are the responsibilities and obligations of the parties involved?

**3. Identify the alternatives, and weigh the impact of each alternative on various stakeholders.**
Select the most ethical alternative, considering all the consequences. Sometimes there will be one right answer. Other situations involve more than one right solution; these situations require you to evaluate each alternative and select the best one.

**Insight** boxes provide examples of business situations from various perspectives—ethics, investor, international, and corporate social responsibility. Guideline answers to the critical thinking questions, as well as additional questions, are available in **WileyPLUS**.

### Ethics Insight   Dewey & LeBoeuf LLP

Alliance Images/
Shutterstock.com

#### I Felt the Pressure—Would You?

"I felt the pressure." That's what some of the employees of the now-defunct law firm of **Dewey & LeBoeuf LLP** indicated when they helped to overstate revenue and use accounting tricks to hide losses and cover up cash shortages. These employees worked for the former finance director and former chief financial officer (CFO) of the firm. Here are some of their comments:

- "I was instructed by the CFO to create invoices, knowing they would not be sent to clients. When I created these invoices, I knew that it was inappropriate."

- "I intentionally gave the auditors incorrect information in the course of the audit."

What happened here is that a small group of lower-level employees over a period of years carried out the instructions of their bosses. Their bosses, however, seemed to have no concern about unethical practices as evidenced by various e-mails with one another in which they referred to their financial manipulations as accounting tricks, cooking the books, and fake income.

**Sources:** Ashby Jones, "Guilty Pleas of Dewey Staff Detail the Alleged Fraud," *Wall Street Journal* (March 28, 2014); and Sara Randazzo, "Dewey CFO Escapes Jail Time in Fraud Case Sentencing," *Wall Street Journal* (October 10, 2017).

**Why did these employees lie, and what do you believe should be their penalty for these lies? (Go to WileyPLUS for this answer and additional questions.)**

**DO IT!** exercises prompt you to stop and review the key points you have just studied. The **Action Plan** offers you tips about how to approach the problem.

### DO IT! 1 | Business Organization Forms

In choosing the organizational form for your outdoor guide service, you should consider the pros and cons of each. Identify each of the following organizational characteristics with the organizational form or forms with which it is associated.

1. Easier to raise funds.
2. Simple to establish.
3. No personal legal liability.
4. Tax advantages.
5. Easier to transfer ownership.

**ACTION PLAN**

- **Know which organizational form best matches the business type, size, and preferences of the owner(s).**

**Solution**

1. Easier to raise funds: Corporation.
2. Simple to establish: Sole proprietorship and partnership.
3. No personal legal liability: Corporation.
4. Tax advantages: Sole proprietorship and partnership.
5. Easier to transfer ownership: Corporation.

Related exercise material: **BE1.1 and DO IT! 1.1.**

# The Three Types of Business Activity

**LEARNING OBJECTIVE 2**
Explain the three principal types of business activity.

All businesses are involved in three types of activity—financing, investing, and operating. For example, consider Gert Boyle's parents, the founders of **Columbia Sportswear**.

1. The Boyles obtained cash through **financing** (from personal savings and outside sources like banks) to start and grow their business.
2. The family then **invested** the cash in equipment to run the business, such as sewing equipment and delivery vehicles.
3. Once this equipment was in place, they could begin the **operating** activities of making and selling clothing.

The **accounting information system** keeps track of the results of each of the various business activities—financing, investing, and operating. Let's look at each type of business activity in more detail.

## Financing Activities

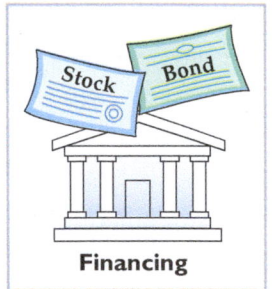

**Financing**

It takes money to make money. The two primary sources of outside funds for corporations are borrowing money (debt financing) and issuing (selling) shares of stock in exchange for cash (equity financing).

Columbia Sportswear may borrow money in a variety of ways. For example, it can take out a loan at a bank or borrow directly from investors by issuing debt securities called bonds. Persons or entities to whom Columbia owes money are its **creditors**.

- Amounts owed to creditors—in the form of debt and other obligations—are called **liabilities**.
- Specific names are given to different types of liabilities, depending on their source. Columbia may have a **note payable** to a bank for the money borrowed to purchase delivery trucks.
- Debt securities sold to investors that must be repaid at a particular date some years in the future are **bonds payable**.

Corporations also obtain funds by selling shares of stock to investors. **Common stock** is the term used to describe the total amount paid in by stockholders for the shares they purchase.

The claims of creditors differ from those of stockholders. If you loan money to a company, you are one of its creditors. In lending money, you specify a payment schedule (e.g., payment at the end of three months). As a creditor, you have a legal right to be paid at the agreed time. In the event of nonpayment, you may legally force the company to sell property to pay its debts. In the case of financial difficulty, creditor claims must be paid before stockholders' claims.

Stockholders, on the other hand, have no claim to corporate cash until the claims of creditors are satisfied. Suppose you buy a company's stock instead of loaning it money. You have no legal right to expect any payments from your stock ownership until all of the company's creditors are paid amounts currently due. However, many corporations make payments to stockholders on a regular basis as long as there is sufficient cash to cover required payments to creditors. These cash payments to stockholders are called **dividends**.

# Investing Activities

Once the company has raised cash through financing activities, it uses that cash in investing activities. Investing activities involve the purchase of the resources a company needs in order to operate. A growing company purchases many resources, such as computers, delivery trucks, furniture, and buildings.

**Investing**

- Resources owned by a business are called **assets**.
- Different types of assets are given different names; Columbia Sportswear's sewing equipment is a type of asset referred to as **property**, **plant**, **and equipment** (see **Alternative Terminology**).
- **Cash** is one of the more important assets owned by Columbia or any other business.
- If a company has excess cash that it does not need for a while, it might choose to invest in securities (stocks or bonds) of other corporations, a type of asset referred to as **investments**.

**ALTERNATIVE TERMINOLOGY**

Property, plant, and equipment is sometimes called *fixed assets*.

# Operating Activities

Once a business has the assets it needs to get started, it begins operations. Columbia Sportswear is in the business of selling outdoor clothing and footwear. It sells TurboDown jackets, Millennium snowboard pants, Sorel® snow boots, Bugaboots™, rainwear, and anything else you might need to protect you from the elements. We call amounts earned from the sale of these products **revenues**.

**Operating**

- **Revenue** is the increase in assets or decrease in liabilities resulting from the sale of goods or the performance of services in the normal course of business; Columbia records revenue when it sells a footwear product.
- Revenues arise from different sources and are identified by various names depending on the nature of the business; Columbia's primary source of revenue is the sale of sportswear (but it also generates interest revenue on debt securities held as investments).
- Sources of revenue common to many businesses are **sales revenue**, **service revenue**, and **interest revenue**.

The company purchases its longer-lived assets through investing activities as described earlier. Other assets with shorter lives, however, result from operating activities.

- **Supplies** are assets used in day-to-day operations (rather than sold to customers).
- Goods available for future sales to customers are assets called **inventory**.
- The right to receive money in the future is called an **account receivable**. If Columbia sells goods to a customer and does not receive cash immediately, then the company has a right to expect payment from that customer in the near future.

Before Columbia can sell a single Sorel® boot, it must purchase wool, rubber, leather, metal lace loops, laces, and other materials. It then must process, wrap, and ship the finished product. It also incurs costs like salaries, rents, and utilities. All of these costs, referred to as **expenses**, are necessary to produce and sell the product.

- In accounting language, **expenses** are the cost of assets consumed or services used in the process of generating revenues.
- Expenses take many forms and are identified by various names depending on the type of asset consumed or service used.

For example, Columbia keeps track of these types of expenses: **cost of goods sold** (such as the cost of materials), **selling expenses** (such as the cost of salespersons' salaries), **marketing expenses** (such as the cost of advertising), **administrative expenses** (such as the salaries of administrative staff, and telephone and heating costs incurred at the corporate office), **interest expense** (amounts of interest paid on various debts), and **income tax expense** (corporate taxes paid to the government).

Columbia may also have liabilities arising from these expenses.

- For example, Columbia may purchase goods on credit from suppliers. The obligations to pay for these goods are called **accounts payable**.
- Additionally, Columbia may have **interest payable** on the outstanding amounts owed to the bank.
- It may also have **wages payable** to its employees and **sales taxes payable**, **property taxes payable**, and **income taxes payable** to the government.

Columbia compares the revenues of a period with the expenses of that period to determine whether it earned a profit. When revenues exceed expenses, **net income** results. When expenses exceed revenues, a **net loss** results.

---

**ACTION PLAN**

- Classify each item based on its economic characteristics. Proper classification of items is critical if accounting is to provide useful information.

## DO IT! 2 | Business Activities

Classify each item as an asset, liability, common stock, revenue, or expense.

1. Cost of renting property.
2. Truck purchased.
3. Notes payable.
4. Issuance of ownership shares.
5. Amount recorded from performing services.
6. Amounts owed to suppliers.

### Solution

1. Cost of renting property: Expense.
2. Truck purchased: Asset.
3. Notes payable: Liability.
4. Issuance of ownership shares: Common stock.
5. Amount recorded from performing services: Revenue.
6. Amounts owed to suppliers: Liability.

Related exercise material: **BE1.3, DO IT! 1.2, and E1.4.**

# The Four Financial Statements

**LEARNING OBJECTIVE 3**
Describe the four financial statements and how they are prepared.

Assets, liabilities, expenses, and revenues are of interest to users of accounting information. This information is arranged in the format of four different **financial statements**, which form the backbone of financial accounting (see **International Note**):

1. To show how successfully your business performed during a period of time, you report its revenues and expenses in an **income statement**.
2. To indicate how much of previous income was distributed to you and the other owners of your business in the form of dividends, and how much was retained in the business to allow for future growth, you present a **retained earnings statement**.
3. To present a picture at a point in time of what your business owns (its assets) and what it owes (its liabilities), you prepare a **balance sheet**.
4. To show where your business obtained cash during a period of time and how that cash was used, you present a **statement of cash flows**.

To introduce you to these statements, we have prepared the financial statements for your outdoor guide service, Sierra Corporation, after your first month of operations. To summarize, you officially started your business in Truckee, California, on October 1, 2022. Sierra provides guide services in the Lake Tahoe area of the Sierra Nevada mountains. Its promotional materials describe outdoor day trips, such as rafting, snowshoeing, and hiking, as well as multi-day backcountry experiences. To minimize your initial investment, at this point the company has limited outdoor equipment for customer use. Instead, your customers either bring their own equipment or rent equipment through local outfitters. The financial statements for Sierra's first month of business are provided in the following pages.

## Income Statement

The **income statement** reports a company's revenues and expenses and resulting net income or loss for a period of time (see **Decision Tools**). To indicate that its income statement reports the results of operations for a **specific period of time**, Sierra Corporation dates the income statement "For the Month Ended October 31, 2022." The income statement lists the company's revenues followed by its expenses. Finally, Sierra determines the net income (or net loss) by deducting expenses from revenues. Sierra's income statement is shown in **Illustration 1.4** (see **Helpful Hint**). Congratulations, you are already showing a profit!

> **International Note**
> The primary types of financial statements required by International Financial Reporting Standards (IFRS) and U.S. generally accepted accounting principles (GAAP) are the same. Neither IFRS nor GAAP is very specific regarding format requirements for the primary financial statements. However, in practice, some format differences do exist in presentations commonly employed by IFRS companies as compared to GAAP companies.

> **Decision Tools**
> The income statement helps users determine if the company's operations are profitable.

**ILLUSTRATION 1.4**
Sierra Corporation's income statement

> **HELPFUL HINT**
> The financial statement heading identifies the company, the type of statement, and the time period covered. Sometimes, another line indicates the unit of measure, e.g., "in thousands" or "in millions."

### Sierra Corporation
#### Income Statement
#### For the Month Ended October 31, 2022

| | | |
|---|---:|---:|
| Revenues | | |
| Service revenue | | $10,600 |
| Expenses | | |
| Salaries and wages expense | $5,200 | |
| Rent expense | 900 | |
| Supplies expense | 1,500 | |
| Depreciation expense | 40 | |
| Interest expense | 50 | |
| Insurance expense | 50 | |
| Total expenses | | 7,740 |
| Net income | | $ 2,860 |

Why are financial statement users interested in net income?

- **Investors are interested in a company's past net income because it provides useful information for predicting future net income.** Investors buy and sell stock based on their beliefs about a company's future performance. If investors believe that Sierra will be successful in the future and that this will result in a higher stock price, they will buy its stock.

- Creditors also use the income statement to predict future earnings. When a bank loans money to a company, it believes that it will be repaid in the future. If it didn't think it would be repaid, it wouldn't loan the money. Therefore, prior to making the loan the bank loan officer uses the income statement as a source of information to predict whether the company will be profitable enough to repay its loan.

- Thus, reporting a strong profit will make it easier for Sierra to raise additional cash either by issuing shares of stock or borrowing.

**Amounts received from issuing stock are not revenues, and amounts paid out as dividends are not expenses.** As a result, they are not reported on the income statement. For example, Sierra Corporation does not treat as revenue the $10,000 of cash received from issuing new stock (see Illustration 1.7), nor does it regard as a business expense the $500 of dividends paid (see Illustration 1.5) (see **Ethics Note**).

---

**ACTION PLAN**

- **Report the revenues and expenses for a period of time in an income statement.**

## DO IT! 3a | Financial Statements—The Income Statement

**Part 1:** CSU Corporation began operations on January 1, 2022. The following information is available for CSU on December 31, 2022.

| | | | | | |
|---|---|---|---|---|---|
| Accounts receivable | $ 1,800 | Retained earnings | $ 0 | Supplies expense | $ 200 |
| Accounts payable | 2,000 | Equipment | 16,000 | Cash | 1,400 |
| Rent expense | 9,000 | Insurance expense | 1,000 | Dividends | 600 |
| Notes payable | 5,000 | Service revenue | 17,000 | | |
| Common stock | 10,000 | Supplies | 4,000 | | |

Prepare an income statement.

### Solution

**CSU Corporation**
**Income Statement**
**For the Year Ended December 31, 2022**

| | | |
|---|---|---|
| Revenues | | |
| Service revenue | | $17,000 |
| Expenses | | |
| Rent expense | $9,000 | |
| Insurance expense | 1,000 | |
| Supplies expense | 200 | |
| Total expenses | | 10,200 |
| Net income | | $ 6,800 |

Related exercise material: **BE1.6, BE1.7, BE1.8, DO IT! 1.3a, E1.5, E1.6, E1.10, E1.11, E1.12, E1.14, and E1.15.**

# Retained Earnings Statement

If Sierra Corporation is profitable, at the end of each period it must decide what portion of profits to pay to shareholders in dividends. In theory, it could pay all of its current-period profits, but few companies do this. Why? Because they want to retain part of the profits to allow for further expansion. High-growth companies, such as **Google** and **Facebook**, often pay no dividends. **Retained earnings** is the net income retained in the corporation.

The **retained earnings statement** shows the amounts and causes of changes in retained earnings for a specific time period (see **Decision Tools**). The time period is the same as that covered by the income statement. The beginning retained earnings amount appears on the first line of the statement. Then, the company adds net income and deducts dividends to determine the retained earnings at the end of the period. If a company has a net loss, it deducts (rather than adds) that amount in the retained earnings statement. **Illustration 1.5** presents Sierra's retained earnings statement (see **Helpful Hint**).

<table>
<tr><th colspan="2">Sierra Corporation<br>Retained Earnings Statement<br>For the Month Ended October 31, 2022</th></tr>
<tr><td>Retained earnings, October 1</td><td>$   0</td></tr>
<tr><td>Add: Net income</td><td>2,860</td></tr>
<tr><td></td><td>2,860</td></tr>
<tr><td>Less: Dividends</td><td>500</td></tr>
<tr><td>Retained earnings, October 31</td><td>$2,360</td></tr>
</table>

By monitoring the retained earnings statement, financial statement users can evaluate dividend payment practices.

- Some investors seek companies, such as **Dow Chemical**, that have a history of paying high dividends.
- Other investors seek companies, such as **Amazon.com**, that reinvest earnings to increase the company's growth instead of paying dividends.
- Lenders monitor their corporate customers' dividend payments because any money paid in dividends reduces a company's ability to repay its debts.

**Decision Tools**

The retained earnings statement helps users determine the company's policy toward dividends and growth.

**ILLUSTRATION 1.5**

**Sierra Corporation's retained earnings statement**

**HELPFUL HINT**

The heading of this statement identifies the company, the type of statement, and the time period covered by the statement.

---

## DO IT! 3a | Financial Statements—The Retained Earnings Statement

**Part 2:** CSU Corporation began operations on January 1, 2022. The following information is available for CSU on December 31, 2022.

| | | | | | | | |
|---|---|---|---|---|---|---|---|
| Accounts receivable | $ 1,800 | Retained earnings | $ 0 | Supplies expense | $ 200 |
| Accounts payable | 2,000 | Equipment | 16,000 | Cash | 1,400 |
| Rent expense | 9,000 | Insurance expense | 1,000 | Dividends | 600 |
| Notes payable | 5,000 | Service revenue | 17,000 | | |
| Common stock | 10,000 | Supplies | 4,000 | | |

Prepare a retained earnings statement. Refer to **DO IT! 3a Part 1** for net income.

**ACTION PLAN**

- Show the amounts and causes (net income and dividends) of changes in retained earnings during the period in the retained earnings statement.

### Solution

<table>
<tr><th colspan="2">CSU Corporation<br>Retained Earnings Statement<br>For the Year Ended December 31, 2022</th></tr>
<tr><td>Retained earnings, January 1</td><td>$   0</td></tr>
<tr><td>Add: Net income</td><td>6,800</td></tr>
<tr><td></td><td>6,800</td></tr>
<tr><td>Less: Dividends</td><td>600</td></tr>
<tr><td>Retained earnings, December 31</td><td>$6,200</td></tr>
</table>

Related exercise material: **BE1.7, BE1.10, DO IT! 1.3a, E1.5, E1.6, E1.7, E1.9, E1.12, E1.13, and E1.14.**

# Balance Sheet

The **balance sheet** reports assets and claims to assets at a specific **point** in time (see **Decision Tools**). Claims to assets are subdivided into two categories: claims of creditors and claims of owners. As noted earlier, claims of creditors are called **liabilities**. The owners' claim to assets is called **stockholders' equity**.

Illustration 1.6 shows the relationship among the categories on the balance sheet in equation form. This equation is referred to as the **basic accounting equation**.

**ILLUSTRATION 1.6**

**Basic accounting equation**

$$\text{Assets} = \text{Liabilities} + \text{Stockholders' Equity}$$

This relationship is where the name "balance sheet" comes from. Assets must balance with the claims to assets.

As you can see from looking at Sierra Corporation's balance sheet in **Illustration 1.7**, the balance sheet presents the company's financial position as of a specific date—in this case, October 31, 2022 (see **Helpful Hint**). It lists assets first. Assets are listed in the order of their liquidity, that is, how quickly they could be converted to cash. Assets are followed by liabilities and stockholders' equity (see **Alternative Terminology**). Stockholders' equity is comprised of two parts: (1) common stock and (2) retained earnings. As noted earlier, common stock results when the company sells new shares of stock; retained earnings is the net income retained in the corporation. Sierra has common stock of $10,000 and retained earnings of $2,360, for total stockholders' equity of $12,360.

**ALTERNATIVE TERMINOLOGY**

Liabilities are also referred to as *debt*.

**ILLUSTRATION 1.7**

**Sierra Corporation's balance sheet**

**HELPFUL HINT**

The heading of a balance sheet must identify the company, the statement, and the date.

## Sierra Corporation
### Balance Sheet
### October 31, 2022

**Assets**

| | | |
|---|---|---|
| Cash | | $15,200 |
| Accounts receivable | | 200 |
| Supplies | | 1,000 |
| Prepaid insurance | | 550 |
| Equipment, net | | 4,960 |
| Total assets | | $21,910 |

**Liabilities and Stockholders' Equity**

| | | |
|---|---|---|
| Liabilities | | |
| Notes payable | $ 5,000 | |
| Accounts payable | 2,500 | |
| Unearned service revenue | 800 | |
| Salaries and wages payable | 1,200 | |
| Interest payable | 50 | |
| Total liabilities | | $ 9,550 |
| Stockholders' equity | | |
| Common stock | 10,000 | |
| Retained earnings | 2,360 | |
| Total stockholders' equity | | 12,360 |
| Total liabilities and stockholders' equity | | $21,910 |

Creditors analyze a company's balance sheet to determine the likelihood that they will be repaid.

- Creditors carefully evaluate the nature of the company's assets and liabilities.

- In operating Sierra's guide service, the balance sheet will be used to determine whether cash on hand is sufficient for immediate cash needs.

- The balance sheet will also be used to evaluate the relationship between debt and stockholders' equity to determine whether the company has a satisfactory proportion of debt and common stock financing.

## DO IT! 3a | Financial Statements—The Balance Sheet

**ACTION PLAN**

- Present the assets and claims to those assets (liabilities and equity) at a specific point in time in the balance sheet.

**Part 3:** CSU Corporation began operations on January 1, 2022. The following information is available for CSU on December 31, 2022.

| | | | | | | | |
|---|---|---|---|---|---|---|---|
| Accounts receivable | $ 1,800 | Retained earnings | $    0 | Supplies expense | $  200 |
| Accounts payable | 2,000 | Equipment | 16,000 | Cash | 1,400 |
| Rent expense | 9,000 | Insurance expense | 1,000 | Dividends | 600 |
| Notes payable | 5,000 | Service revenue | 17,000 | | |
| Common stock | 10,000 | Supplies | 4,000 | | |

Prepare a balance sheet. Refer to **DO IT! 3a Part 2** for the ending balance in Retained Earnings.

### Solution

**CSU Corporation**
**Balance Sheet**
**December 31, 2022**

**Assets**

| | |
|---|---|
| Cash | $ 1,400 |
| Accounts receivable | 1,800 |
| Supplies | 4,000 |
| Equipment | 16,000 |
| Total assets | $23,200 |

**Liabilities and Stockholders' Equity**

| | | |
|---|---|---|
| Liabilities | | |
| Notes payable | $ 5,000 | |
| Accounts payable | 2,000 | |
| Total liabilities | | $ 7,000 |
| Stockholders' equity | | |
| Common stock | 10,000 | |
| Retained earnings | 6,200 | |
| Total stockholders' equity | | 16,200 |
| Total liabilities and stockholders' equity | | $23,200 |

Related exercise material: **BE1.5, BE1.6, BE1.7, BE1.8, BE1.9, BE1.10, DO IT! 1.3a, E1.8, E1.12, E1.13, and E1.18.**

# Statement of Cash Flows

**Decision Tools**

The statement of cash flows helps users determine if the company generates enough cash from operations to fund its investing activities.

The primary purpose of a **statement of cash flows** is to provide financial information about the cash receipts and cash payments of a business for a specific period of time (see **Decision Tools**). To help investors, creditors, and others in their analysis of a company's cash position, the statement of cash flows reports the cash effects of a company's **operating**, **investing**, and **financing** activities. In addition, the statement shows the net increase or decrease in cash during the period, and the amount of cash at the end of the period.

Users are interested in the statement of cash flows because they want to know what is happening to a company's most important resource. The statement of cash flows provides answers to these simple but important questions:

- Where did cash come from during the period?
- How was cash used during the period?
- What was the change in the cash balance during the period?

The statement of cash flows for Sierra Corporation, in **Illustration 1.8**, shows that cash increased $15,200 during the month (see **Helpful Hint**). This increase resulted because operating activities (services to clients) increased cash $5,700, and financing activities increased cash $14,500. Investing activities used $5,000 of cash for the purchase of equipment.

**ILLUSTRATION 1.8**

Sierra Corporation's statement of cash flows

**HELPFUL HINT**

The heading of this statement identifies the company, the type of statement, and the time period covered by the statement. Negative numbers are shown in parentheses.

### Sierra Corporation
#### Statement of Cash Flows
#### For the Month Ended October 31, 2022

| | | |
|---|---:|---:|
| Cash flows from operating activities | | |
| Cash receipts from operating activities | $11,200 | |
| Cash payments for operating activities | (5,500) | |
| Net cash provided by operating activities | | $ 5,700 |
| Cash flows from investing activities | | |
| Purchased office equipment | (5,000) | |
| Net cash used by investing activities | | (5,000) |
| Cash flows from financing activities | | |
| Issuance of common stock | 10,000 | |
| Issuance of note payable | 5,000 | |
| Payment of dividend | (500) | |
| Net cash provided by financing activities | | 14,500 |
| Net increase in cash | | 15,200 |
| Cash at beginning of period | | 0 |
| Cash at end of period | | $15,200 |

## People, Planet, and Profit Insight

iStock.com/Marek Uliasz

### Beyond Financial Statements

Should we expand our financial statements beyond the income statement, retained earnings statement, balance sheet, and statement of cash flows? Some believe we should take into account ecological and social performance, in addition to financial results, in evaluating a company. The argument is that a company's responsibility lies with anyone who is influenced by its actions. In other words, a company should be interested in benefiting many different parties, instead of only maximizing stockholders' interests.

A socially responsible business does not exploit or endanger any group of individuals. It follows fair trade practices, provides safe environments for workers, and bears responsibility for environmental damage. Granted, measurement of these factors is difficult. How to report this information is also controversial. But many interesting and useful efforts are underway. Throughout this text, we provide additional insights into how companies are attempting to meet the challenge of measuring and reporting their contributions to society, as well as their financial results, to stockholders.

**Why might a company's stockholders be interested in its environmental and social performance? (Go to WileyPLUS for this answer and additional questions.)**

## Interrelationships of Statements

**Illustration 1.9** shows the financial statements of Sierra Corporation (see **Helpful Hints**).

ILLUSTRATION 1.9

Sierra Corporation's financial statements

## Sierra Corporation
### Income Statement
### For the Month Ended October 31, 2022

| | | |
|---|---:|---:|
| Revenues | | |
| Service revenue | | $10,600 |
| Expenses | | |
| Salaries and wages expense | $5,200 | |
| Rent expense | 900 | |
| Supplies expense | 1,500 | |
| Depreciation expense | 40 | |
| Interest expense | 50 | |
| Insurance expense | 50 | |
| Total expenses | | 7,740 |
| Net income | | $ 2,860 |

**HELPFUL HINT**

Note that final sums are double-underlined.

## Sierra Corporation
### Retained Earnings Statement
### For the Month Ended October 31, 2022

| | |
|---|---:|
| Retained earnings, October 1 | $ 0 |
| Add: Net income | 2,860 |
| | 2,860 |
| Less: Dividends | 500 |
| Retained earnings, October 31 | $2,360 |

**HELPFUL HINT**

The arrows in this illustration show the interrelationships of the four financial statements.

## Sierra Corporation
### Balance Sheet
### October 31, 2022

**Assets**

| | | |
|---|---:|---:|
| Cash | | $15,200 |
| Accounts receivable | | 200 |
| Advertising supplies | | 1,000 |
| Prepaid insurance | | 550 |
| Equipment, net | | 4,960 |
| Total assets | | $21,910 |

**Liabilities and Stockholders' Equity**

| | | |
|---|---:|---:|
| Liabilities | | |
| Notes payable | $ 5,000 | |
| Accounts payable | 2,500 | |
| Unearned service revenue | 800 | |
| Salaries and wages payable | 1,200 | |
| Interest payable | 50 | |
| Total liabilities | | $ 9,550 |
| Stockholders' equity | | |
| Common stock | 10,000 | |
| Retained earnings | 2,360 | |
| Total stockholders' equity | | 12,360 |
| Total liabilities and stockholders' equity | | $21,910 |

## Sierra Corporation
### Statement of Cash Flows
### For the Month Ended October 31, 2022

| | | |
|---|---:|---:|
| Cash flows from operating activities | | |
| Cash receipts from operating activities | $11,200 | |
| Cash payments for operating activities | (5,500) | |
| Net cash provided by operating activities | | $ 5,700 |
| Cash flows from investing activities | | |
| Purchased office equipment | (5,000) | |
| Net cash used by investing activities | | (5,000) |
| Cash flows from financing activities | | |
| Issuance of common stock | 10,000 | |
| Issuance of note payable | 5,000 | |
| Payment of dividend | (500) | |
| Net cash provided by financing activities | | 14,500 |
| Net increase in cash | | 15,200 |
| Cash at beginning of period | | 0 |
| Cash at end of period | | $15,200 |

**HELPFUL HINT**

Negative amounts are presented in parentheses.

Because the results on some financial statements become inputs to other statements, the statements are interrelated. These interrelationships can be seen in Sierra's financial statements, as follows.

1. The retained earnings statement uses the results of the income statement. Sierra reported net income of $2,860 for the period. Net income is added to the beginning amount of retained earnings to determine ending retained earnings.

2. The balance sheet and retained earnings statement are also interrelated. **Sierra reports the ending amount of $2,360 on the retained earnings statement as the retained earnings amount on the balance sheet.**

3. Finally, the statement of cash flows relates to information on the balance sheet. The statement of cash flows shows how the Cash account changed during the period. It shows the amount of cash at the beginning of the period, the sources and uses of cash during the period, and the $15,200 of cash at the end of the period. The ending amount of cash shown on the statement of cash flows must agree with the amount of cash on the balance sheet.

Study these interrelationships carefully. **To prepare financial statements, you must understand the sequence in which these amounts are determined and how each statement impacts the next.**

---

**ACTION PLAN**

- **Report the revenues and expenses for a period of time in an income statement.**
- **Show the amounts and causes (net income and dividends) of changes in retained earnings during the period in the retained earnings statement.**
- **Present the assets and claims to those assets (liabilities and equity) at a specific point in time in the balance sheet.**

## DO IT! 3a | Financial Statements

**Part 4:** BRB Corporation began operations on January 1, 2022. The following information is available for BRB on December 31, 2022.

| | | | | | |
|---|---|---|---|---|---|
| Accounts receivable | $ 1,600 | Retained earnings | $   0 | Supplies expense | $  300 |
| Accounts payable | 3,000 | Equipment | 21,000 | Cash | 2,400 |
| Rent expense | 7,000 | Insurance expense | 2,000 | Dividends | 700 |
| Notes payable | 4,000 | Service revenue | 21,000 | | |
| Common stock | 12,000 | Supplies | 5,000 | | |

Prepare an income statement, a retained earnings statement, and a balance sheet.

### Solution

**BRB Corporation**
**Income Statement**
**For the Year Ended December 31, 2022**

| | | |
|---|---|---|
| Revenues | | |
| Service revenue | | $21,000 |
| Expenses | | |
| Rent expense | $7,000 | |
| Insurance expense | 2,000 | |
| Supplies expense | 300 | |
| Total expenses | | 9,300 |
| Net income | | $11,700 |

**BRB Corporation**
**Retained Earnings Statement**
**For the Year Ended December 31, 2022**

| | | |
|---|---|---|
| Retained earnings, January 1 | | $   0 |
| Add: Net income | | 11,700 |
| | | 11,700 |
| Less: Dividends | | 700 |
| Retained earnings, December 31 | | $11,000 |

---

**BRB Corporation**
**Balance Sheet**
**December 31, 2022**

<u>**Assets**</u>

| | | |
|---|---:|---:|
| Cash | | $ 2,400 |
| Accounts receivable | | 1,600 |
| Supplies | | 5,000 |
| Equipment | | 21,000 |
| Total assets | | $30,000 |

<u>**Liabilities and Stockholders' Equity**</u>

| | | |
|---|---:|---:|
| Liabilities | | |
| Notes payable | $ 4,000 | |
| Accounts payable | 3,000 | |
| Total liabilities | | $ 7,000 |
| Stockholders' equity | | |
| Common stock | 12,000 | |
| Retained earnings | 11,000 | |
| Total stockholders' equity | | 23,000 |
| Total liabilities and stockholders' equity | | $30,000 |

---

Related exercise material: **BE1.5, BE1.6, BE1.7, BE1.8, BE1.9, BE1.10, DO IT! 1.3a, E1.5, E1.6, E1.7, E1.8, E1.9, E1.10, E1.11, E1.12, E1.13, E1.14, E1.15, and E1.18.**

# Elements of an Annual Report

Publicly traded U.S. companies must provide shareholders with an **annual report**. The annual report always includes the financial statements introduced in this chapter. The annual report also includes other important information such as a management discussion and analysis section, notes to the financial statements, and an independent auditor's report. No analysis of a company's financial situation and performance is complete without a review of these items.

## Management Discussion and Analysis

The **management discussion and analysis (MD&A)** section presents management's views on the company's:

- Ability to pay near-term obligations.
- Ability to fund operations and expansion.
- Results of operations.

Management must highlight favorable or unfavorable trends and identify significant events and uncertainties that affect these three factors. This discussion obviously involves a number of subjective estimates and opinions. A brief excerpt from the MD&A section of **Columbia Sportswear**'s annual report, which addresses its liquidity requirements, is presented in **Illustration 1.10**.

---

**Columbia Sportswear Company**
**Management's Discussion and Analysis of**
**Seasonality and Variability of Business**

Our operations are affected by seasonal trends typical in the outdoor apparel and footwear industry and have historically resulted in higher sales and profits in the third and fourth calendar quarters. This pattern has resulted primarily from the timing of shipments of fall season products to wholesale customers in the third and fourth quarters and proportionally higher sales in our direct-to-consumer channels in the fourth quarter, combined with an expense base that is spread more consistent throughout the year. We believe that our liquidity requirements for at least the next 12 months will be adequately covered by existing cash, cash provided by operations and existing short-term borrowing arrangements.

**ILLUSTRATION 1.10**

**Columbia Sportswear's management discussion and analysis**

**Real World**

## Notes to the Financial Statements

Explanatory notes and supporting schedules accompany every set of financial statements and are an integral part of the statements. The **notes to the financial statements** clarify the financial statements and provide additional detail. Information in the notes does not have to be quantifiable (numeric). Examples of notes are:

- Descriptions of the significant accounting policies and methods used in preparing the statements.
- Explanations of uncertainties and contingencies.
- Various statistics and details too voluminous to be included in the statements.

The notes are essential to understanding a company's operating performance and financial position.

**Illustration 1.11** is an excerpt from the notes to **Columbia Sportswear**'s financial statements. It describes the methods that the company uses to account for revenues.

**ILLUSTRATION 1.11**

**Notes to Columbia Sportswear's financial statements**

**Real World**

| **Columbia Sportswear Company** |
| :---: |
| **Notes to Financial Statements** |
| **Revenue Recognition** |
| We record wholesale, distributor, e-commerce and licensed product revenues when title passes and the risks and rewards of ownership have passed to the customer. Title generally passes upon shipment to or upon receipt by the customer depending on the terms of sale with the customer. Retail store revenues are recorded at the time of sale. |

## Auditor's Report

An **auditor's report** is prepared by an independent outside auditor. It states the auditor's opinion as to the fairness of the presentation of the financial position and results of operations and their conformance with generally accepted accounting principles.

An **auditor** is an accounting professional who conducts an independent examination of a company's financial statements. Only accountants who meet certain criteria and thereby attain the designation **certified public accountant (CPA)** may perform audits.

- If the auditor is satisfied that the financial statements provide a fair representation of the company's financial position and results of operations in accordance with generally accepted accounting principles, then the auditor expresses an **unqualified opinion**.
- If the auditor expresses anything other than an unqualified opinion, then readers should only use the financial statements with caution.
- That is, without an unqualified opinion, we cannot have complete confidence that the financial statements give an accurate picture of the company's financial health.

For example, **Blockbuster LLC**'s auditor at one time stated that its financial situation raised "substantial doubt about the Company's ability to continue as a going concern."

**Illustration 1.12** is an excerpt from the auditor's report from Columbia Sportswear's 2016 annual report. Columbia received an unqualified opinion from its auditor, **Deloitte & Touche**.

**ILLUSTRATION 1.12**
**Excerpt from auditor's report on Columbia Sportswear's financial statements**

Real World

## Columbia Sportswear Company
### Excerpt from Auditor's Report

In our opinion, such consolidated financial statements present fairly, in all material respects, the financial position of Columbia Sportswear Company and subsidiaries as of December 31, 2016 and 2015, and the results of their operations and their cash flows for each of the three years in the period ended December 31, 2016, in conformity with accounting principles generally accepted in the United States of America. Also, in our opinion, such financial statement schedules, when considered in relation to the basic consolidated financial statements taken as a whole, present fairly, in all material respects, the information set forth therein.

## DO IT! 3b | Components of Annual Reports

**ACTION PLAN**

- Realize that financial statements provide information about a company's performance and financial position.
- Be familiar with the other elements of the annual report in order to gain a fuller understanding of a company.

State whether each of the following items is most closely associated with the management discussion and analysis (MD&A), the notes to the financial statements, or the auditor's report.

1. Descriptions of significant accounting policies.
2. Unqualified opinion.
3. Explanations of uncertainties and contingencies.
4. Description of ability to fund operations and expansion.
5. Description of results of operations.
6. Certified public accountant (CPA).

### Solution

1. Descriptions of significant accounting policies: Notes.
2. Unqualified opinion: Auditor's report.
3. Explanations of uncertainties and contingencies: Notes.
4. Description of ability to fund operations and expansion: MD&A.
5. Description of results of operations: MD&A.
6. Certified public accountant (CPA): Auditor's report.

Related exercise material: **BE1.11, DO IT! 1.3b, and E1.21.**

## USING THE DECISION TOOLS | Under Armour, Inc.

**Using the Decision Tools** comprehensive exercises ask you to apply business information and the decision tools presented in the chapter. Most of these exercises are based on the companies highlighted in the Feature Story.

There is a good chance that you are wearing one of **Under Armour, Inc.**'s products right now. Under Armour is a competitor to **Columbia Sportswear**. Suppose that you are considering investing in shares of Under Armour's common stock.

### Instructions

Answer these questions related to your decision whether to invest.

a. What financial statements should you evaluate?
b. What should these financial statements tell you?
c. Do you care if the financial statements have been audited? Explain.
d. Appendix B contains financial statements for Columbia, and Appendix C contains those for Under Armour. You can make many comparisons between Columbia and Under Armour in terms of their respective results from operations and financial position. Compare their respective total assets, total revenues, and net cash provided by operating activities for 2018.

### Solution

a. Before you invest, you should evaluate the income statement, retained earnings statement, balance sheet, and statement of cash flows.

b. You would probably be most interested in the income statement because it summarizes past performance and thus gives an indication of future performance. The retained earnings statement provides a record of the company's dividend history. The balance sheet reveals the relationship between assets and liabilities. The statement of cash flows reveals where the company is getting and spending its cash. This is especially important for a company that wants to grow.

c. You would want audited financial statements. These statements indicate that a CPA (certified public accountant) has examined and expressed an opinion that the statements present fairly the financial position and results of operations of the company. Investors and creditors should not make decisions without studying audited financial statements.

d. Many interesting comparisons can be made between the two companies (all numbers are in thousands). Columbia is smaller, with total assets of $2,368,721 versus $4,245,022 for Under Armour, and it has lower revenue—$2,802,326 versus $5,193,185 for Under Armour. In addition, Columbia's net cash provided by operating activities of $289,569 is less than Under Armour's $628,230. However, while useful, these basic measures are not enough to determine whether one company is a better investment than the other. In later chapters, you will learn tools that will allow you to compare the relative profitability and financial health of these and other companies.

The **Review and Practice** section provides opportunities for students to review key concepts and terms as well as complete multiple-choice questions, brief exercises, exercises, and a comprehensive problem. Detailed solutions are also included.

# Review and Practice

## Learning Objectives Review

### 1   Identify the forms of business organization and the uses of accounting information.

A sole proprietorship is a business owned by one person. A partnership is a business owned by two or more people associated as partners. A corporation is a separate legal entity for which evidence of ownership is provided by shares of stock.

Internal users are managers who need accounting information to plan, organize, and run business operations. The primary external users are investors and creditors. Investors (stockholders) use accounting information to decide whether to buy, hold, or sell shares of a company's stock. Creditors (suppliers and bankers) use accounting information to assess the risk of granting credit or loaning money to a business. Other groups who have an indirect interest in a business are taxing authorities, customers, labor unions, and regulatory agencies.

### 2   Explain the three principal types of business activity.

Financing activities involve collecting the necessary funds to support the business. Investing activities involve acquiring the resources necessary to run the business. Operating activities involve putting the resources of the business into action to generate a profit.

### 3   Describe the four financial statements and how they are prepared.

An income statement presents the revenues and expenses of a company for a specific period of time. A retained earnings statement summarizes the changes in retained earnings that have occurred for a specific period of time. A balance sheet reports the assets, liabilities, and stockholders' equity of a business at a specific date. A statement of cash flows summarizes information concerning the cash inflows (receipts) and outflows (payments) for a specific period of time.

Assets are resources owned by a business. Liabilities are the debts and obligations of the business. Liabilities represent claims of creditors on the assets of the business. Stockholders' equity represents the claims of owners on the assets of the business. Stockholders' equity is subdivided into two parts: common stock and retained earnings. The basic accounting equation is Assets = Liabilities + Stockholders' Equity.

Within the annual report, the management discussion and analysis provides management's interpretation of the company's results and financial position as well as a discussion of plans for the future. Notes to the financial statements provide additional explanation or detail to make the financial statements more informative. The auditor's report expresses an opinion as to whether the financial statements present fairly the company's results of operations and financial position.

## Decision Tools Review

| Decision Checkpoints | Info Needed for Decision | Tool to Use for Decision | How to Evaluate Results |
|---|---|---|---|
| Are the company's operations profitable? | Income statement | The income statement reports a company's revenues and expenses and resulting net income or loss for a period of time. | If the company's revenues exceed its expenses, it will report net income; otherwise, it will report a net loss. |
| What is the company's policy toward dividends and growth? | Retained earnings statement | The retained earnings statement reports how much of this year's income the company paid out in dividends to shareholders. | A company striving for rapid growth will pay a low (or no) dividend. |
| Does the company rely primarily on debt or stockholders' equity to finance its assets? | Balance sheet | The balance sheet reports the company's resources and claims to those resources; there are two types of claims: liabilities and stockholders' equity. | Compare the amount of debt versus the amount of stockholders' equity to determine whether the company relies more on creditors or owners for its financing. |
| Does the company generate sufficient cash from operations to fund its investing activities? | Statement of cash flows | The statement of cash flows shows the amount of net cash provided or used by operating activities, investing activities, and financing activities. | Compare the amount of net cash provided by operating activities with the amount of net cash used by investing activities. Any deficiency in cash from operating activities must be made up with cash from financing activities. |

## Glossary Review

**Accounting** The information system that identifies, records, and communicates the economic events of an organization to interested users. (p. 1-4).

**Annual report** A report prepared by corporate management that presents financial information including financial statements, a management discussion and analysis section, notes, and an independent auditor's report. (p. 1-19).

**Assets** Resources owned by a business. (p. 1-9).

**Auditor's report** A report prepared by an independent outside auditor stating the auditor's opinion as to the fairness of the presentation of the financial position and results of operations and their conformance with generally accepted accounting principles. (p. 1-20).

**Balance sheet** A financial statement that reports the assets and claims to those assets at a specific point in time. (p. 1-14).

**Basic accounting equation** Assets = Liabilities + Stockholders' Equity. (p. 1-14).

**Certified public accountant (CPA)** An individual who has met certain criteria and is thus allowed to perform audits of corporations. (p. 1-20).

**Common stock** Term used to describe the total amount paid in by stockholders for the shares they purchase. (p. 1-8).

**Corporation** A business organized as a separate legal entity owned by stockholders. (p. 1-3).

**Dividends** Payments of cash from a corporation to its stockholders. (p. 1-9).

**Expenses** The cost of assets consumed or services used in the process of generating revenues. (p. 1-10).

**Income statement** A financial statement that reports a company's revenues and expenses and resulting net income or net loss for a specific period of time. (p. 1-11).

**Liabilities** Amounts owed to creditors in the form of debts and other obligations. (p. 1-8).

**Management discussion and analysis (MD&A)** A section of the annual report that presents management's views on the company's ability to pay near-term obligations, its ability to fund operations and expansion, and its results of operations. (p. 1-19).

**Net income** The amount by which revenues exceed expenses. (p. 1-10).

**Net loss** The amount by which expenses exceed revenues. (p. 1-10).

**Notes to the financial statements** Notes that clarify information presented in the financial statements and provide additional detail. (p. 1-20).

**Partnership** A business owned by two or more persons associated as partners. (p. 1-3).

**Retained earnings** The amount of net income retained in the corporation. (p. 1-12).

**Retained earnings statement** A financial statement that summarizes the amounts and causes of changes in retained earnings for a specific time period. (p. 1-13).

**Revenue** The increase in assets or decrease in liabilities resulting from the sale of goods or the performance of services in the normal course of business. (p. 1-9).

**Sarbanes-Oxley Act (SOX)** Regulations passed by Congress to reduce unethical corporate behavior. (p. 1-6).

**Sole proprietorship** A business owned by one person. (p. 1-3).

**Statement of cash flows** A financial statement that provides financial information about the cash receipts and cash payments of a business for a specific period of time. (p. 1-15).

**Stockholders' equity** The owners' claim to assets. (p. 1-14).

## Practice Multiple-Choice Questions

**1. (LO 1)** Which is **not** one of the three forms of business organization?

    **a.** Sole proprietorship.     **c.** Partnership.

    **b.** Creditorship.     **d.** Corporation.

**2. (LO 1)** Which is an advantage of corporations relative to partnerships and sole proprietorships?

    **a.** Lower taxes.

    **b.** Harder to transfer ownership.

    **c.** Reduced legal liability for investors.

    **d.** Most common form of organization.

**3. (LO 1)** Which statement about users of accounting information is **incorrect**?

    **a.** Management is considered an internal user.

    **b.** Taxing authorities are considered external users.

    **c.** Present creditors are considered external users.

    **d.** Regulatory authorities are considered internal users.

**4. (LO 1)** Which of the following did **not** result from the Sarbanes-Oxley Act?

    **a.** Top management must now certify the accuracy of financial information.

    **b.** Penalties for fraudulent activity increased.

    **c.** Independence of auditors increased.

    **d.** Tax rates on corporations increased.

**5. (LO 2)** Which is **not** one of the three primary business activities?

    **a.** Financing.     **c.** Advertising.

    **b.** Operating.     **d.** Investing.

**6. (LO 2)** Which of the following is an example of a financing activity?

    **a.** Issuing shares of common stock.

    **b.** Selling goods on account.

    **c.** Buying delivery equipment.

    **d.** Buying inventory.

**7. (LO 2)** Net income will result during a time period when:

    **a.** assets exceed liabilities.

    **b.** assets exceed revenues.

    **c.** expenses exceed revenues.

    **d.** revenues exceed expenses.

**8. (LO 3)** The financial statements for Macias Corporation contained the following information.

| | |
|---|---|
| Accounts receivable | $ 5,000 |
| Sales revenue | 75,000 |
| Cash | 15,000 |
| Salaries and wages expense | 20,000 |
| Rent expense | 10,000 |

What was Macias Corporation's net income?

    **a.** $60,000.     **c.** $65,000.

    **b.** $15,000.     **d.** $45,000.

**9. (LO 3)** What section of a statement of cash flows indicates the cash spent on new equipment during the past accounting period?

    **a.** The investing activities section.

    **b.** The operating activities section.

    **c.** The financing activities section.

    **d.** The statement of cash flows does not give this information.

**10. (LO 3)** Which statement presents information as of a specific point in time?

    **a.** Income statement.

    **b.** Balance sheet.

    **c.** Statement of cash flows.

    **d.** Retained earnings statement.

**11. (LO 3)** Which financial statement reports assets, liabilities, and stockholders' equity?

    **a.** Income statement.

    **b.** Retained earnings statement.

    **c.** Balance sheet.

    **d.** Statement of cash flows.

**12. (LO 3)** Stockholders' equity represents:

    **a.** claims of creditors.

    **b.** claims of employees.

    **c.** the difference between revenues and expenses.

    **d.** claims of owners.

**13. (LO 3)** As of December 31, 2022, Rockford Corporation has assets of $3,500 and stockholders' equity of $1,500. What are the liabilities for Rockford as of December 31, 2022?

    **a.** $1,500.     **c.** $2,500.

    **b.** $1,000.     **d.** $2,000.

**14. (LO 3)** The element of a corporation's annual report that describes the corporation's accounting methods is/are the:

    **a.** notes to the financial statements.

    **b.** management discussion and analysis.

    **c.** auditor's report.

    **d.** income statement.

**15. (LO 3)** The element of the annual report that presents an opinion regarding the fairness of the presentation of the financial position and results of operations is/are the:

    **a.** income statement.

    **b.** auditor's opinion.

    **c.** balance sheet.

    **d.** comparative statements.

## Solutions

**1. b.** Creditorship is not a form of business organization. The other choices are incorrect because (a) sole proprietorship, (c) partnership, and (d) corporation are all forms of business organization.

**2. c.** An advantage of corporations is that investors are not personally liable for debts of the business. The other choices are incorrect because (a) lower taxes, (b) harder to transfer ownership, and (d) most common form of organization are not true of corporations.

**3. d.** Regulatory authorities are considered external, not internal, users. The other choices are true statements.

**4. d.** The Sarbanes-Oxley Act (SOX) was created to reduce unethical corporate behavior and decrease the likelihood of future corporate scandals, not to address tax rates. The other choices are incorrect because (a) top management must now certify the accuracy of financial information, (b) penalties for fraudulent activity increased, and (c) increased independence of auditors all resulted from SOX.

**5. c.** Advertising is a type of operating activity. The other choices are incorrect because (a) financing, (b) operating, and (d) investing are the three primary business activities.

**6. a.** Issuing shares of common stock is a financing activity. The other choices are incorrect because (b) selling goods on account is an operating activity, (c) buying delivery equipment is an investing activity, and (d) buying inventory is an operating activity.

**7. d.** When a company earns more revenues than expenses, it will report net income during a time period. The other choices are incorrect because (a) assets and liabilities are on the balance sheet, not the income statement; (b) assets are on the balance sheet, not the income statement; and (c) net income results when revenues exceed expenses, not when expenses exceed revenues.

**8. d.** Net income = Sales revenue ($75,000) − Salaries and wages expense ($20,000) − Rent expense ($10,000) = $45,000. The other choices are therefore incorrect.

**9. a.** The investing activities section of the statement of cash flows provides information about property, plant, and equipment accounts, not (b) the operating activities section or (c) the financing activities section. Choice (d) is incorrect as the statement of cash flows does provide this information.

**10. b.** The balance sheet presents information as of a specific point in time. The other choices are incorrect because the (a) income statement, (c) statement of cash flows, and (d) retained earnings statement all cover a period of time.

**11. c.** The balance sheet is a formal presentation of the accounting equation, such that Assets = Liabilities + Stockholders' Equity, not the (a) income statement, (b) retained earnings statement, or (d) statement of cash flows.

**12. d.** Stockholders' equity represents claims of owners. The other choices are incorrect because (a) claims of creditors and (b) claims of employees are liabilities. Choice (c) is incorrect because the difference between revenues and expenses is net income.

**13. d.** Using the accounting equation, liabilities can be computed by subtracting stockholders' equity from assets, or $3,500 − $1,500 = $2,000, not (a) $1,500, (b) $1,000, or (c) $2,500.

**14. a.** The corporation's accounting methods are described in the notes to the financial statements, not in the (b) management discussion and analysis, (c) auditor's report, or (d) income statement.

**15. b.** The element of the annual report that presents an opinion regarding the fairness of the presentation of the financial position and results of operations is the auditor's opinion, not the (a) income statement, (c) balance sheet, or (d) comparative statements.

## Practice Brief Exercises

**1. (LO 3)** At the beginning of the year, Ortiz Company had total assets of $900,000 and total liabilities of $440,000. Answer the following questions.

*Use basic accounting equation.*

a. If total assets decreased $100,000 during the year and total liabilities increased $80,000 during the year, what is the amount of stockholders' equity at the end of the year?

b. During the year, total liabilities decreased $100,000 during the year and stockholders' equity increased $200,000. What is the amount of total assets at the end of the year?

c. If total assets increased $50,000 during the year and stockholders' equity increased $60,000 during the year, what is the amount of total liabilities at the end of the year?

### Solution

**1. a.** ($900,000 − $440,000) − $100,000 − $80,000 = $280,000 stockholders' equity

   **b.** $900,000 − $100,000 + $200,000 = $1,000,000 total assets

   **c.** $440,000 − $60,000 + $50,000 = $430,000 total liabilities

**2. (LO 3)** Indicate whether the following items would appear on the income statement (IS), balance sheet (BS), or retained earnings statement (RES).

*Determine where items appear on financial statements.*

a. _____ Common stock.

b. _____ Cash.

c. _____ Salaries and wages expense.

d. _____ Service revenue.

e. _____ Accounts payable.

### Solution

2. **a.** __BS__ Common stock.
   **b.** __BS__ Cash.
   **c.** __IS__ Salaries and wages expense.
   **d.** __IS__ Service revenue.
   **e.** __BS__ Accounts payable.

*Prepare a balance sheet.*

**3. (LO 3)** Presented below in alphabetical order are balance sheet items for Feagler Company at December 31, 2022. Prepare a balance sheet following the format of Illustration 1.7.

| | |
|---|---:|
| Accounts receivable | $12,500 |
| Cash | 38,000 |
| Common stock | 5,000 |
| Notes payable | 40,000 |
| Retained earnings | 5,500 |

### Solution

3.

**Feagler Company**
**Balance Sheet**
**December 31, 2022**

**Assets**

| | | |
|---|---:|---:|
| Cash | | $38,000 |
| Accounts receivable | | 12,500 |
| Total assets | | $50,500 |

**Liabilities and Stockholders' Equity**

| | | |
|---|---:|---:|
| Liabilities | | |
|   Notes payable | $40,000 | |
|     Total liabilities | | $40,000 |
| Stockholders' equity | | |
|   Common stock | 5,000 | |
|   Retained earnings | 5,500 | |
|     Total stockholders' equity | | 10,500 |
| Total liabilities and stockholders' equity | | $50,500 |

*Determine where items appear on financial statements.*

**4. (LO 3)** Identify whether the following items would appear on the balance sheet (BS) or income statement (IS) of a corporation.

**a.** _____ Income taxes payable.       **f.** _____ Service revenue.

**b.** _____ Cost of goods sold.       **g.** _____ Depreciation expense.

**c.** _____ Supplies.       **h.** _____ Prepaid insurance.

**d.** _____ Notes payable.       **i.** _____ Interest payable.

**e.** _____ Salaries and wages expense.

### Solution

4. **a.** __BS__ Income taxes payable.
   **b.** __IS__ Cost of goods sold.
   **c.** __BS__ Supplies.
   **d.** __BS__ Notes payable.
   **e.** __IS__ Salaries and wages expense.
   **f.** __IS__ Service revenue.
   **g.** __IS__ Depreciation expense.
   **h.** __BS__ Prepaid insurance.
   **i.** __BS__ Interest payable.

# Practice Exercises

**1. (LO 3)** The following items and amounts were taken from Ricardo Inc.'s 2022 income statement and balance sheet.

*Prepare an income statement.*

| | | | | |
|---|---|---|---|---|
| Cash | $ 84,700 | | Inventory | $ 64,618 |
| Retained earnings | 123,192 | | Accounts receivable | 88,419 |
| Cost of goods sold | 483,854 | | Sales revenue | 693,485 |
| Salaries and wages expense | 125,000 | | Income taxes payable | 6,499 |
| Prepaid insurance | 7,818 | | Accounts payable | 49,384 |
| Interest expense | 994 | | Service revenue | 8,998 |

**Instructions**

Prepare an income statement for Ricardo Inc. for the year ended December 31, 2022.

## Solution

1.

**Ricardo Inc.**
**Income Statement**
**For the Year Ended December 31, 2022**

| | | |
|---|---|---|
| Revenues | | |
| Sales revenue | $693,485 | |
| Service revenue | 8,998 | |
| Total revenues | | $702,483 |
| Expenses | | |
| Cost of goods sold | 483,854 | |
| Salaries and wages expense | 125,000 | |
| Interest expense | 994 | |
| Total expenses | | 609,848 |
| Net income | | $ 92,635 |

**2. (LO 3)** Cozy Bear is a private camping ground near the Mountain Home Recreation Area. It has compiled the following financial information as of December 31, 2022.

*Compute net income and prepare a balance sheet.*

| | | | | |
|---|---|---|---|---|
| Service revenue (from camping fees) | $148,000 | | Dividends | $ 9,000 |
| Sales revenue (from general store) | 35,000 | | Bonds payable | 50,000 |
| Accounts payable | 16,000 | | Expenses during 2022 | 135,000 |
| Cash | 18,500 | | Supplies | 12,500 |
| Equipment | 129,000 | | Common stock | 40,000 |
| | | | Retained earnings (1/1/2022) | 15,000 |

**Instructions**

**a.** Determine net income from Cozy Bear for 2022.

**b.** Prepare a retained earnings statement and a balance sheet for Cozy Bear as of December 31, 2022.

## Solution

| | | |
|---|---|---|
| 2. **a.** | Service revenue | $148,000 |
| | Sales revenue | 35,000 |
| | Total revenue | 183,000 |
| | Expenses | 135,000 |
| | Net income | $ 48,000 |

b.

| Cozy Bear<br>**Retained Earnings Statement**<br>For the Year Ended December 31, 2022 | |
|---|---:|
| Retained earnings, January 1 | $15,000 |
| Add: Net income | 48,000 |
| | 63,000 |
| Less: Dividends | 9,000 |
| Retained earnings, December 31 | $54,000 |

**Cozy Bear**

**Balance Sheet**

**December 31, 2022**

**Assets**

| | |
|---|---:|
| Cash | $ 18,500 |
| Supplies | 12,500 |
| Equipment | 129,000 |
| Total assets | $160,000 |

**Liabilities and Stockholders' Equity**

| | | |
|---|---:|---:|
| Liabilities | | |
| Accounts payable | $16,000 | |
| Bonds payable | 50,000 | |
| Total liabilities | | $ 66,000 |
| Stockholders' equity | | |
| Common stock | 40,000 | |
| Retained earnings | 54,000 | |
| Total stockholders' equity | | 94,000 |
| Total liabilities and stockholders' equity | | $160,000 |

# Practice Problem

*Prepare financial statements.*

**(LO 3)** Jeff Andringa, a former college hockey player, quit his job and started Ice Camp, a hockey camp for kids ages 8 to 18. Eventually, he would like to open hockey camps nationwide. Jeff has asked you to help him prepare financial statements at the end of his first year of operations. He relates the following facts about his business activities.

In order to get the business off the ground, Jeff decided to incorporate. He sold shares of common stock to a few close friends, as well as bought some of the shares himself. He initially raised $25,000 through the sale of these shares. In addition, the company took out a $10,000 loan at a local bank.

Ice Camp purchased, for $12,000 cash, a bus for transporting kids. The company also bought hockey goals and other miscellaneous equipment with $1,500 cash. The company earned camp tuition of $100,000 during the year but had collected only $80,000 of this amount. Thus, at the end of the year, its customers still owed $20,000. The company rents time at a local rink for $50 per hour. Total rink rental costs during the year were $8,000, insurance was $10,000, salary expense was $20,000, and supplies used totaled $9,000, all of which were paid in cash. The company incurred $800 in interest expense on the bank loan, which it still owed at the end of the year.

The company paid dividends during the year of $5,000 cash. The balance in the corporate bank account at December 31, 2022, was $49,500.

## Instructions

Using the format of the Sierra Corporation statements in this chapter, prepare an income statement, retained earnings statement, balance sheet, and statement of cash flows. (*Hint:* Prepare the statements in the order stated to take advantage of the flow of information from one statement to the next, as shown in Illustration 1.9.)

## Solution

### Ice Camp
### Income Statement
### For the Year Ended December 31, 2022

| | | |
|---|---:|---:|
| Revenues | | |
| Service revenue | | $100,000 |
| Expenses | | |
| Salaries and wages expense | $20,000 | |
| Insurance expense | 10,000 | |
| Supplies expense | 9,000 | |
| Rent expense | 8,000 | |
| Interest expense | 800 | |
| Total expenses | | 47,800 |
| Net income | | $ 52,200 |

### Ice Camp
### Retained Earnings Statement
### For the Year Ended December 31, 2022

| | |
|---|---:|
| Retained earnings, January 1, 2022 | $ 0 |
| Add: Net income | 52,200 |
| | 52,200 |
| Less: Dividends | 5,000 |
| Retained earnings, December 31, 2022 | $47,200 |

### Ice Camp
### Balance Sheet
### December 31, 2022

**Assets**

| | | |
|---|---:|---:|
| Cash | | $49,500 |
| Accounts receivable | | 20,000 |
| Equipment ($12,000 + $1,500) | | 13,500 |
| Total assets | | $83,000 |

**Liabilities and Stockholders' Equity**

| | | |
|---|---:|---:|
| Liabilities | | |
| Notes payable | $10,000 | |
| Interest payable | 800 | |
| Total liabilities | | $10,800 |
| Stockholders' equity | | |
| Common stock | 25,000 | |
| Retained earnings | 47,200 | |
| Total stockholders' equity | | 72,200 |
| Total liabilities and stockholders' equity | | $83,000 |

| Ice Camp | | |
| --- | --- | --- |
| **Statement of Cash Flows** | | |
| **For the Year Ended December 31, 2022** | | |
| Cash flows from operating activities | | |
| Cash receipts from operating activities | $80,000 | |
| Cash payments for operating activities | (47,000) | |
| Net cash provided by operating activities | | $33,000 |
| Cash flows from investing activities | | |
| Purchase of equipment | (13,500) | |
| Net cash used by investing activities | | (13,500) |
| Cash flows from financing activities | | |
| Issuance of common stock | 25,000 | |
| Issuance of notes payable | 10,000 | |
| Dividends paid | (5,000) | |
| Net cash provided by financing activities | | 30,000 |
| Net increase in cash | | 49,500 |
| Cash at beginning of period | | 0 |
| Cash at end of period | | $49,500 |

# WileyPLUS

Brief Exercises, DO IT! Exercises, Exercises, Problems, and many additional resources are available for practice in WileyPLUS.

# Questions

**1.** What are the three basic forms of business organizations?

**2.** What are the advantages to a business of being formed as a corporation? What are the disadvantages?

**3.** What are the advantages to a business of being formed as a partnership or sole proprietorship? What are the disadvantages?

**4.** "Accounting is ingrained in our society and is vital to our economic system." Do you agree? Explain.

**5.** Who are the internal users of accounting data? How does accounting provide relevant data to the internal users?

**6.** Who are the external users of accounting data? Give examples.

**7.** What are the three main types of business activity? Give examples of each activity.

**8.** Listed here are some items found in the financial statements of Finzelberg. Indicate in which financial statement(s) each item would appear.

    **a.** Service revenue.

    **b.** Equipment.

    **c.** Advertising expense.

    **d.** Accounts receivable.

    **e.** Common stock.

    **f.** Interest payable.

**9.** Why would a bank want to monitor the dividend payment practices of the corporations to which it lends money?

**10.** "A company's net income appears directly on the income statement and the retained earnings statement, and it is included indirectly in the company's balance sheet." Do you agree? Explain.

**11.** What is the primary purpose of the statement of cash flows?

**12.** What are the three main categories of the statement of cash flows? Why do you think these categories were chosen?

**13.** What is retained earnings? What items increase the balance in retained earnings? What items decrease the balance in retained earnings?

**14.** What is the basic accounting equation?

**15. a.** Define the terms assets, liabilities, and stockholders' equity.

    **b.** What items affect stockholders' equity?

**16.** Which of these items are liabilities of White Glove Cleaning Service?

    **a.** Cash.     **f.** Equipment.

    **b.** Accounts payable.     **g.** Salaries and wages payable.

    **c.** Dividends.

    **d.** Accounts receivable.     **h.** Service revenue.

    **e.** Supplies.     **i.** Rent expense.

**17.** How are each of the following financial statements interrelated? (a) Retained earnings statement and income statement. (b) Retained earnings statement and balance sheet. (c) Balance sheet and statement of cash flows.

**18.** What is the purpose of the management discussion and analysis section (MD&A)?

**19.** Why is it important for financial statements to receive an unqualified auditor's opinion?

**20.** What types of information are presented in the notes to the financial statements?

**21.** The accounting equation is Assets = Liabilities + Stockholders' Equity. Appendix A reproduces **Apple**'s financial statements. Replacing words in the equation with dollar amounts, what is Apple's accounting equation at September 29, 2018?

## Brief Exercises

**BE1.1 (LO 1), K** Match each of the following forms of business organization with a set of characteristics: sole proprietorship (SP), partnership (P), corporation (C).

*Describe forms of business organization.*

a. _____ Shared control, tax advantages, increased skills and resources.

b. _____ Simple to set up and maintains control with owner.

c. _____ Easier to transfer ownership and raise funds, no personal liability.

**BE1.2 (LO 1), K** Match each of the following types of evaluation with one of the listed users of accounting information.

*Identify users of accounting information.*

1. Trying to determine whether the company complied with tax laws.

2. Trying to determine whether the company can pay its obligations.

3. Trying to determine whether an advertising proposal will be cost-effective.

4. Trying to determine whether the company's net income will result in a stock price increase.

5. Trying to determine whether the company should employ debt or equity financing.

a. _____ Investors in common stock.       d. _____ Chief Financial Officer.

b. _____ Marketing managers.              e. _____ Internal Revenue Service.

c. _____ Creditors.

**BE1.3 (LO 2), K** Indicate to which business activity, operating activity (O), investing activity (I), or financing activity (F), each item relates.

*Classify items by activity.*

a. _____ Cash received from customers.

b. _____ Cash paid to stockholders (dividends).

c. _____ Cash received from issuing new common stock.

d. _____ Cash paid to suppliers.

e. _____ Cash paid to purchase a new office building.

**BE1.4 (LO 3), C** Presented below are a number of transactions. Determine whether each transaction affects common stock (C), dividends (D), revenues (R), expenses (E), or does not affect stockholders' equity (NSE). Provide titles for the revenues and expenses.

*Determine effect of transactions on stockholders' equity.*

a. Costs incurred for advertising.

b. Cash received for services performed.

c. Costs incurred for insurance.

d. Amounts paid to employees.

e. Cash distributed to stockholders.

f. Cash received in exchange for allowing the use of the company's building.

g. Costs incurred for utilities used.

h. Cash purchase of equipment.

i. Cash received from investors.

*Prepare a balance sheet.*

**BE1.5 (LO 3), AP** In alphabetical order below are balance sheet items for Karol Company at December 31, 2022. Prepare a balance sheet following the format of Illustration 1.7.

| | |
|---|---|
| Accounts payable | $65,000 |
| Accounts receivable | 71,000 |
| Cash | 22,000 |
| Common stock | 18,000 |
| Retained earnings | 10,000 |

*Determine where items appear on financial statements.*

**BE1.6 (LO 3), K Eskimo Pie Corporation** markets a broad range of frozen treats, including its famous Eskimo Pie ice cream bars. The following items were taken from a recent income statement and balance sheet. In each case, identify whether the item would appear on the balance sheet (BS) or income statement (IS).

a. _____ Income tax expense.

b. _____ Inventory.

c. _____ Accounts payable.

d. _____ Retained earnings.

e. _____ Equipment.

f. _____ Sales revenue.

g. _____ Cost of goods sold.

h. _____ Common stock.

i. _____ Accounts receivable.

j. _____ Interest expense.

*Determine proper financial statement.*

**BE1.7 (LO 3), K** Indicate which statement you would examine to find each of the following items: income statement (IS), balance sheet (BS), retained earnings statement (RES), or statement of cash flows (SCF).

a. Revenue during the period.

b. Supplies on hand at the end of the year.

c. Cash received from issuing new bonds during the period.

d. Total debts outstanding at the end of the period.

*Use basic accounting equation.*

**BE1.8 (LO 3), AP** Use the basic accounting equation to answer these questions.

a. The liabilities of Lantz Company are $90,000 and the stockholders' equity is $230,000. What is the amount of Lantz's total assets?

b. The total assets of Salley Company are $170,000 and its stockholders' equity is $80,000. What is the amount of its total liabilities?

c. The total assets of Brandon Co. are $800,000 and its liabilities are equal to one-fourth of its total assets. What is the amount of Brandon's stockholders' equity?

*Use basic accounting equation.*

**BE1.9 (LO 3), AP** At the beginning of the year, Morales Company had total assets of $800,000 and total liabilities of $500,000. (Treat each item independently.)

a. If total assets increased $150,000 during the year and total liabilities decreased $80,000, what is the amount of stockholders' equity at the end of the year?

b. During the year, total liabilities increased $100,000 and stockholders' equity decreased $70,000. What is the amount of total assets at the end of the year?

c. If total assets decreased $80,000 and stockholders' equity increased $110,000 during the year, what is the amount of total liabilities at the end of the year?

*Identify assets, liabilities, and stockholders' equity.*

**BE1.10 (LO 3), K** Indicate whether each of these items is an asset (A), a liability (L), or part of stockholders' equity (SE).

a. Accounts receivable.

b. Salaries and wages payable.

c. Equipment.

d. Supplies.

e. Common stock.

f. Notes payable.

*Determine required parts of annual report.*

**BE1.11 (LO 3), K** Which is **not** a required part of an annual report of a publicly traded company?

a. Statement of cash flows.

b. Notes to the financial statements.

c. Management discussion and analysis.

d. All of these are required.

## DO IT! Exercises

**DO IT! 1.1 (LO 1), C** Identify each of the following organizational characteristics with the business organizational form or forms with which it is associated.

*Identify benefits of business organization forms.*

  **a.** Easier to transfer ownership.

  **b.** Easier to raise funds.

  **c.** More owner control.

  **d.** Tax advantages.

  **e.** No personal legal liability.

**DO IT! 1.2 (LO 2), K** Classify each item as an asset, liability, common stock, revenue, or expense.

*Classify financial statement elements.*

  **a.** Issuance of ownership shares.

  **b.** Land purchased.

  **c.** Amounts owed to suppliers.

  **d.** Bonds payable.

  **e.** Amount recorded from selling a product.

  **f.** Cost of advertising.

**DO IT! 1.3a (LO 3), AP** Gray Corporation began operations on January 1, 2022. The following information is available for Gray on December 31, 2022.

*Prepare financial statements.*

| | | | |
|---|---|---|---|
| Accounts payable | $ 5,000 | Notes payable | $ 7,000 |
| Accounts receivable | 2,000 | Rent expense | 10,000 |
| Advertising expense | 4,000 | Retained earnings | ? |
| Cash | 3,100 | Service revenue | 25,000 |
| Common stock | 15,000 | Supplies | 1,900 |
| Dividends | 2,500 | Supplies expense | 1,700 |
| Equipment | 26,800 | | |

Prepare an income statement, a retained earnings statement, and a balance sheet for Gray Corporation.

**DO IT! 1.3b (LO 3), K** Indicate whether each of the following items is most closely associated with the management discussion and analysis (MD&A), the notes to the financial statements, or the auditor's report.

*Identify components of annual reports.*

  **a.** Description of ability to pay near-term obligations.

  **b.** Unqualified opinion.

  **c.** Details concerning liabilities, too voluminous to be included in the statements.

  **d.** Description of favorable and unfavorable trends.

  **e.** Certified public accountant (CPA).

  **f.** Descriptions of significant accounting policies.

## Exercises

**E1.1 (LO 1, 2, 3), K** Here is a list of words or phrases discussed in this chapter:

*Match items with descriptions.*

  **1.** Corporation

  **2.** Creditor

  **3.** Accounts receivable

  **4.** Partnership

  **5.** Stockholder

  **6.** Common stock

  **7.** Accounts payable

  **8.** Auditor's opinion

### Instructions

Match each word or phrase with the best description of it.

  _____ **a.** An expression about whether financial statements conform with generally accepted accounting principles.

  _____ **b.** A business that raises money by issuing shares of stock.

  _____ **c.** The portion of stockholders' equity that results from receiving cash from investors.

  _____ **d.** Obligations to suppliers of goods.

  _____ **e.** Amounts due from customers.

  _____ **f.** A party to whom a business owes money.

  _____ **g.** A party that invests in common stock.

  _____ **h.** A business that is owned jointly by two or more individuals but does not issue stock.

*Match items with descriptions.*

**E1.2 (LO 1, 2, 3), K** The following terms or phrases are discussed in this chapter.

1. Certified public accountant (CPA)
2. Management discussion and analysis (MD&A)
3. Revenue
4. Dividends
5. Stockholders' equity
6. Net loss
7. Sole proprietorship
8. Basic accounting equation
9. Expenses
10. Liabilities
11. Sarbanes-Oxley Act (SOX)

### Instructions

Match each term or phrase to its description below.

a. _____ Assets = Liabilities + Stockholders' Equity.

b. _____ An individual who has met certain criteria and is thus allowed to perform audits of corporations.

c. _____ Payments of cash from a corporation to its stockholders.

d. _____ The cost of assets consumed or services used in the process of generating revenues.

e. _____ Amounts owed to creditors in the form of debts and other obligations.

f. _____ A section of the annual report that presents management's views on the company's ability to pay near-term obligations, its ability to fund operations and expansion, and its results of operations.

g. _____ The amount by which expenses exceed revenues.

h. _____ The increase in assets or decrease in liabilities resulting from the sale of goods or the performance of services in the normal course of business.

i. _____ Regulations passed by Congress to reduce unethical corporate behavior.

j. _____ A business owned by one person.

k. _____ The owners' claim to assets.

*Identify business activities.*

**E1.3 (LO 2), C** All businesses are involved in three types of activities—financing, investing, and operating. Listed below are the names and descriptions of companies in several different industries.

**Abitibi-Consolidated Inc.**—manufacturer and marketer of newsprint
**California State University—Northridge Student Union**—university student union
**Oracle Corporation**—computer software developer and retailer
**Aquilini Investment Group**—owner of the Vancouver Canucks ice hockey team
**Grant Thornton LLP**—professional accounting and business advisory firm
**Southwest Airlines**—low-cost airline

### Instructions

a. For each of the above companies, provide examples of (1) a financing activity, (2) an investing activity, and (3) an operating activity that the company likely engages in.

b. Which of the activities that you identified in (a) are common to most businesses? Which activities are not?

*Classify accounts.*

**E1.4 (LO 2, 3), C** The Bonita Vista Golf & Country Club details the following accounts in its financial statements.

| | |
|---|---|
| Accounts payable | \_\_\_\_\_ |
| Accounts receivable | \_\_\_\_\_ |
| Equipment | \_\_\_\_\_ |
| Sales revenue | \_\_\_\_\_ |
| Service revenue | \_\_\_\_\_ |
| Inventory | \_\_\_\_\_ |
| Mortgage payable | \_\_\_\_\_ |
| Supplies expense | \_\_\_\_\_ |
| Rent expense | \_\_\_\_\_ |
| Salaries and wages expense | \_\_\_\_\_ |

### Instructions

Classify each of the accounts as an asset (A), liability (L), stockholders' equity (SE), revenue (R), or expense (E) item.

**E1.5 (LO 3), AP** This information relates to Benser Co. for the year 2022.

*Prepare income statement and retained earnings statement.*

| | |
|---|---:|
| Retained earnings, January 1, 2022 | $67,000 |
| Advertising expense | 1,800 |
| Dividends | 6,000 |
| Rent expense | 10,400 |
| Service revenue | 58,000 |
| Utilities expense | 2,400 |
| Salaries and wages expense | 30,000 |

**Instructions**

Prepare an income statement and a retained earnings statement for the year ending December 31, 2022.

**E1.6 (LO 3), AP** Suppose the following information was taken from the 2022 financial statements of pharmaceutical giant **Merck & Co.** (All dollar amounts are in millions.)

*Prepare income statement and retained earnings statement.*

| | |
|---|---:|
| Retained earnings, January 1, 2022 | $43,698.8 |
| Cost of goods sold | 9,018.9 |
| Selling and administrative expenses | 8,543.2 |
| Dividends | 3,597.7 |
| Sales revenue | 38,576.0 |
| Research and development expense | 5,845.0 |
| Income tax expense | 2,267.6 |

**Instructions**

a. After analyzing the data, prepare an income statement and a retained earnings statement for the year ending December 31, 2022.

b. Suppose that Merck decided to reduce its research and development expense by 50%. What would be the short-term implications? What would be the long-term implications? How do you think the stock market would react?

**E1.7 (LO 3), AP** Presented here is information for Zheng Inc. for 2022.

*Prepare a retained earnings statement.*

| | |
|---|---:|
| Retained earnings, January 1 | $130,000 |
| Service revenue | 400,000 |
| Total expenses | 175,000 |
| Dividends | 65,000 |

**Instructions**

Prepare the 2022 retained earnings statement for Zheng Inc.

**E1.8 (LO 3), AP** The following information is available for Randall Inc.

*Prepare a balance sheet.*

| | | | |
|---|---:|---|---:|
| Accounts receivable | $ 2,400 | Cash | $ 6,250 |
| Accounts payable | 3,700 | Supplies | 3,760 |
| Interest payable | 580 | Unearned service revenue | 850 |
| Salaries and wages expense | 4,500 | Service revenue | 40,920 |
| Notes payable | 31,500 | Salaries and wages payable | 745 |
| Common stock | 50,700 | Depreciation expense | 670 |
| Inventory | 2,840 | Equipment (net) | 108,200 |

**Instructions**

Using the information above, prepare a balance sheet as of December 31, 2022. (*Hint:* Solve for the missing retained earnings amount.)

**E1.9 (LO 3), AN** Consider each of the following independent situations.

*Interpret financial data.*

a. The retained earnings statement of Lee Corporation shows dividends of $68,000, while net income for the year was $75,000.

b. The statement of cash flows for Steele Corporation shows that cash provided by operating activities was $10,000, cash used in investing activities was $110,000, and cash provided by financing activities was $130,000.

**Instructions**

For each company, provide a brief discussion interpreting these financial data. For example, you might discuss the company's financial health or its apparent growth philosophy.

*Identify financial statement components and prepare income statement.*

**E1.10 (LO 3), AP** The following items and amounts were taken from Lonyear Inc.'s 2022 income statement and balance sheet.

| | | | | |
|---|---|---:|---|---:|
| _____ | Cash | $ 84,700 | _____ Accounts receivable | $ 88,419 |
| _____ | Retained earnings | 123,192 | _____ Sales revenue | 584,951 |
| _____ | Cost of goods sold | 438,458 | _____ Notes payable | 6,499 |
| _____ | Salaries and wages expense | 115,131 | _____ Accounts payable | 49,384 |
| _____ | Prepaid insurance | 7,818 | _____ Service revenue | 4,806 |
| _____ | Inventory | 64,618 | _____ Interest expense | 1,882 |

**Instructions**

a. In each, case, identify on the blank line whether the item is an asset (A), liability (L), stockholders' equity (SE), revenue (R), or expense (E) item.

b. Prepare an income statement for Lonyear Inc. for the year ended December 31, 2022.

*Identify financial statement components and prepare income statement.*

**E1.11 (LO 3), AP** The following items and amounts were taken from Familia Inc.'s 2022 income statement and balance sheet, the end of its first year of operations.

| | | | | |
|---|---|---:|---|---:|
| _____ | Interest expense | $ 2,200 | _____ Equipment, net | $54,700 |
| _____ | Interest payable | 700 | _____ Depreciation expense | 3,200 |
| _____ | Notes payable | 11,800 | _____ Supplies | 4,100 |
| _____ | Sales revenue | 44,300 | _____ Common stock | 26,800 |
| _____ | Cash | 2,900 | _____ Supplies expense | 900 |
| _____ | Salaries and wages expense | 15,600 | | |

**Instructions**

a. In each case, identify on the blank line whether the item is an asset (A), liability (L), stockholders' equity (SE), revenue (R), or expense (E) item.

b. Prepare an income statement for Familia Inc. for December 31, 2022.

*Calculate missing amounts.*

**E1.12 (LO 3), AN** Here are incomplete financial statements for Donavan, Inc.

**Donavan, Inc.**
**Balance Sheet**

| **Assets** | | | **Liabilities and Stockholders' Equity** | |
|---|---:|---|---|---:|
| Cash | $ 7,000 | | Liabilities | |
| Inventory | 10,000 | | Accounts payable | $ 5,000 |
| Buildings (net) | 45,000 | | Stockholders' equity | |
| Total assets | $62,000 | | Common stock | (a) |
| | | | Retained earnings | (b) |
| | | | Total liabilities and | |
| | | | stockholders' equity | $62,000 |

**Income Statement**

| | |
|---|---:|
| Revenues | $85,000 |
| Cost of goods sold | (c) |
| Salaries and wages expense | 10,000 |
| Net income | $ (d) |

**Retained Earnings Statement**

| | |
|---|---:|
| Beginning retained earnings | $12,000 |
| Add: Net income | (e) |
| Less: Dividends | 5,000 |
| Ending retained earnings | $27,000 |

**Instructions**

Calculate the missing amounts.

**E1.13 (LO 3), AN** Here are incomplete financial statements for Oway Corporation.

*Calculate missing amounts.*

### Oway Corporation
### Balance Sheet

| Assets | | Liabilities and Stockholders' Equity | |
|---|---|---|---|
| Cash | $ 29,000 | Liabilities | |
| Supplies | (a) | Notes payable | $22,000 |
| Equipment (net) | 65,000 | Stockholders' equity | |
| Total assets | $ (b) | Common stock | 38,000 |
| | | Retained earnings | (c) |
| | | Total liabilities and stockholders' equity | $ (d) |

### Income Statement

| | |
|---|---|
| Revenues | $53,000 |
| Depreciation expense | (e) |
| Salaries and wages expense | 10,000 |
| Interest expense | 1,000 |
| Net income | $25,000 |

### Retained Earnings Statement

| | |
|---|---|
| Beginning retained earnings | $ (f) |
| Add: Net income | (g) |
| Less: Dividends | 6,000 |
| Ending retained earnings | $37,000 |

**Instructions**

Calculate the missing amounts.

**E1.14 (LO 3), AP** Otay Lakes Park is a private camping ground near the Mount Miguel Recreation Area. It has compiled the following financial information as of December 31, 2022.

*Compute net income and prepare a retained earnings statement and balance sheet.*

| | | | |
|---|---|---|---|
| Service revenue (from camping fees) | $132,000 | Dividends | $ 9,000 |
| Sales revenue (from general store) | 25,000 | Notes payable | 50,000 |
| Accounts payable | 11,000 | Expenses during 2022 | 126,000 |
| Cash | 8,500 | Supplies | 5,500 |
| Equipment | 114,000 | Common stock | 40,000 |
| | | Retained earnings (1/1/2022) | 5,000 |

**Instructions**

a. Determine Otay Lakes Park's net income for 2022.

b. Prepare a retained earnings statement and a balance sheet for Otay Lakes Park as of December 31, 2022.

c. Upon seeing this income statement, Walt Jones, the campground manager, immediately concluded, "The general store is more trouble than it is worth—let's get rid of it." The marketing director isn't so sure this is a good idea. What do you think?

**E1.15 (LO 3), AP Kellogg Company** is the world's leading producer of ready-to-eat cereal and a leading producer of grain-based convenience foods such as frozen waffles and cereal bars. Suppose the following items were taken from its 2022 income statement and balance sheet. (All dollars are in millions.)

*Identify financial statement components and prepare an income statement.*

| | | | |
|---|---|---|---|
| ____ Retained earnings | $5,481 | ____ Bonds payable | $ 4,835 |
| ____ Cost of goods sold | 7,184 | ____ Inventory | 910 |
| ____ Selling and administrative expenses | 3,390 | ____ Sales revenue | 12,575 |
| | | ____ Accounts payable | 1,077 |
| ____ Cash | 334 | ____ Common stock | 105 |
| ____ Notes payable | 44 | ____ Income tax expense | 498 |
| ____ Interest expense | 295 | | |

**Instructions**

a. In each case, identify whether the item is an asset (A), liability (L), stockholders' equity (SE), revenue (R), or expense (E).

b. Prepare an income statement for Kellogg Company for the year ended December 31, 2022.

*Prepare a statement of cash flows.*

**E1.16 (LO 3), AP** This information is for Williams Corporation for the year ended December 31, 2022.

| | |
|---|---:|
| Cash received from lenders | $20,000 |
| Cash received from customers | 50,000 |
| Cash paid for new equipment | 28,000 |
| Cash dividends paid | 8,000 |
| Cash paid to suppliers | 16,000 |
| Cash balance 1/1/22 | 12,000 |

**Instructions**

a. Prepare the 2022 statement of cash flows for Williams Corporation.

b. Suppose you are one of Williams' creditors. Referring to the statement of cash flows, evaluate Williams' ability to repay its creditors.

*Prepare a statement of cash flows.*

**E1.17 (LO 3), AP** Suppose the following data are derived from the 2022 financial statements of **Southwest Airlines**. (All dollars are in millions.) Southwest has a December 31 year-end.

| | |
|---|---:|
| Cash balance, January 1, 2022 | $1,390 |
| Cash paid for repayment of debt | 122 |
| Cash received from issuance of common stock | 144 |
| Cash received from issuance of long-term debt | 500 |
| Cash received from customers | 9,823 |
| Cash paid for property and equipment | 1,529 |
| Cash paid for dividends | 14 |
| Cash paid for repurchase of common stock | 1,001 |
| Cash paid for goods and services | 6,978 |

**Instructions**

a. After analyzing the data, prepare a statement of cash flows for Southwest Airlines for the year ended December 31, 2022.

b. Discuss whether the company's net cash provided by operating activities was sufficient to finance its investing activities. If it was not, how did the company finance its investing activities?

*Correct an incorrectly prepared balance sheet.*

**E1.18 (LO 3), AP** Wayne Holtz is the bookkeeper for Beeson Company. Wayne has been trying to get the balance sheet of Beeson Company to balance. It finally balanced, but now he's not sure it is correct.

**Beeson Company**
**Balance Sheet**
**December 31, 2022**

| Assets | | Liabilities and Stockholders' Equity | |
|---|---:|---|---:|
| Cash | $18,000 | Accounts payable | $16,000 |
| Supplies | 9,500 | Accounts receivable | (12,000) |
| Equipment | 40,000 | Common stock | 40,000 |
| Dividends | 8,000 | Retained earnings | 31,500 |
| Total assets | $75,500 | Total liabilities and | |
| | | stockholders' equity | $75,500 |

**Instructions**

Prepare a correct balance sheet.

*Classify items as assets, liabilities, and stockholders' equity and prepare accounting equation.*

**E1.19 (LO 3), AP** Suppose the following items were taken from the balance sheet of **Nike, Inc.** (All dollars are in millions.)

| | | | | |
|---|---:|---|---|---:|
| 1. Cash | $2,291.1 | | 7. Inventory | $2,357.0 |
| 2. Accounts receivable | 2,883.9 | | 8. Income taxes payable | 86.3 |
| 3. Common stock | 2,874.2 | | 9. Equipment | 1,957.7 |
| 4. Notes payable | 342.9 | | 10. Retained earnings | 5,818.9 |
| 5. Buildings | 3,759.9 | | 11. Accounts payable | 2,815.8 |
| 6. Mortgage payable | 1,311.5 | | | |

## Instructions

Perform each of the following.

a. Classify each of these items as an asset, liability, or stockholders' equity, and determine the total dollar amount for each classification.

b. Determine Nike's accounting equation by calculating the value of total assets, total liabilities, and total stockholders' equity.

c. To what extent does Nike rely on debt versus equity financing?

**E1.20 (LO 3), AN** The summaries of data from the balance sheet, income statement, and retained earnings statement for two corporations, Walco Corporation and Gunther Enterprises, are presented as follows for 2022.

*Use financial statement relationships to determine missing amounts.*

|  | Walco Corporation | Gunther Enterprises |
|---|---|---|
| Beginning of year |  |  |
| Total assets | $110,000 | $150,000 |
| Total liabilities | 70,000 | (d) |
| Total stockholders' equity | (a) | 70,000 |
| End of year |  |  |
| Total assets | (b) | 180,000 |
| Total liabilities | 120,000 | 55,000 |
| Total stockholders' equity | 60,000 | (e) |
| Changes during year in retained earnings |  |  |
| Dividends | (c) | 5,000 |
| Total revenues | 215,000 | (f) |
| Total expenses | 165,000 | 80,000 |

## Instructions

Determine the missing amounts. Assume all changes in stockholders' equity are due to changes in retained earnings.

**E1.21 (LO 3), K** The annual report provides financial information in a variety of formats, including the following.

*Classify various items in an annual report.*

Management discussion and analysis (MD&A)
Financial statements
Notes to the financial statements
Auditor's opinion

## Instructions

For each of the following, state in what area of the annual report the item would be presented. If the item would probably not be found in an annual report, state "Not disclosed."

a. The total cumulative amount received from stockholders in exchange for common stock.

b. An independent assessment concerning whether the financial statements present a fair depiction of the company's results and financial position.

c. The interest rate that the company is being charged on all outstanding debts.

d. Total revenue from operating activities.

e. Management's assessment of the company's results.

f. The names and positions of all employees hired in the last year.

# Problems

**P1.1 (LO 1), C** **Writing** Presented below are five independent situations.

*Determine forms of business organization.*

a. Three physics professors at MIT have formed a business to improve the speed of information transfer over the Internet for stock exchange transactions. Each has contributed an equal amount of cash and knowledge to the venture. Although their approach looks promising, they are concerned about the legal liabilities that their business might confront.

b. Bob Colt, a college student looking for summer employment, opened a bait shop in a small shed at a local marina.

c. Alma Ortiz and Jaime Falco each owned separate shoe manufacturing businesses. They have decided to combine their businesses. They expect that within the coming year they will need significant funds to expand their operations.

d. Alice, Donna, and Sam recently graduated with marketing degrees. They have been friends since childhood. They have decided to start a consulting business focused on marketing sporting goods over the Internet.

e. Don Rolls has developed a low-cost GPS device that can be implanted into pets so that they can be easily located when lost. He would like to build a small manufacturing facility to make the devices and then sell them to veterinarians across the country. Don has no savings or personal assets. He wants to maintain control over the business.

**Instructions**

In each case, explain what form of organization the business is likely to take—sole proprietorship, partnership, or corporation. Give reasons for your choice.

*Identify users and uses of financial statements.*

**P1.2 (LO 3), C** Writing Financial decisions often place heavier emphasis on one type of financial statement over the others. Consider each of the following hypothetical situations independently.

a. **The North Face** is considering extending credit to a new customer. The terms of the credit would require the customer to pay within 30 days of receipt of goods.

b. An investor is considering purchasing common stock of **Amazon.com**. The investor plans to hold the investment for at least 5 years.

c. **JPMorgan Chase** is considering extending a loan to a small company. The company would be required to make interest payments at the end of each year for 5 years, and to repay the loan at the end of the fifth year.

d. The president of **Campbell Soup** is trying to determine whether the company is generating enough cash to increase the amount of dividends paid to investors in this and future years, and still have enough cash to buy equipment as it is needed.

**Instructions**

In each situation, state whether the decision-maker would be most likely to place primary emphasis on information provided by the income statement, balance sheet, or statement of cash flows. In each case provide a brief justification for your choice. Choose only one financial statement in each case.

*Prepare an income statement, retained earnings statement, and balance sheet; discuss results.*

**P1.3 (LO 3), AP** On June 1, 2022, Elite Service Co. was started with an initial investment in the company of $22,100 cash. Here are the assets, liabilities, and common stock of the company at June 30, 2022, and the revenues and expenses for the month of June, its first month of operations:

| | | | |
|---|---|---|---|
| Cash | $ 4,600 | Notes payable | $12,000 |
| Accounts receivable | 4,000 | Accounts payable | 500 |
| Service revenue | 7,500 | Supplies expense | 1,000 |
| Supplies | 2,400 | Maintenance and repairs expense | 600 |
| Advertising expense | 400 | Utilities expense | 300 |
| Equipment | 26,000 | Salaries and wages expense | 1,400 |
| Common stock | 22,100 | | |

**Check figures** provide a key number to let you know you are on the right track.

a. Net income    $ 3,800
   Ret. earnings  $ 2,400
   Tot. assets    $37,000

During June, the company issued no additional stock but paid dividends of $1,400.

**Instructions**

a. Prepare an income statement and a retained earnings statement for the month of June and a balance sheet at June 30, 2022.

b. Briefly discuss whether the company's first month of operations was a success.

c. Discuss the company's decision to distribute a dividend.

*Prepare an income statement, retained earnings statement, and balance sheet.*

**P1.4 (LO 3), AP** Reese Inc., a provider of consulting services, was founded on October 1, 2022. At the end of the first month of operations, the company decided to prepare an income statement, retained earnings statement, and balance sheet using the following information.

| | | | |
|---|---|---|---|
| Accounts payable | $ 3,300 | Supplies | $ 2,460 |
| Interest expense | 410 | Supplies expense | 380 |
| Equipment (net) | 48,200 | Depreciation expense | 270 |
| Salaries and wages expense | 2,500 | Service revenue | 20,920 |
| Bonds payable | 21,500 | Salaries and wages payable | 445 |
| Unearned service revenue | 4,065 | Common stock | 9,100 |
| Accounts receivable | 1,300 | Interest payable | 140 |
| Cash | 3,950 | | |

End. retained earnings $17,360

**Instructions**

Using the information, prepare an income statement and retained earnings statement for the month of October 2022 and a balance sheet as of October 31, 2022.

**P1.5 (LO 3), AP** Presented below is selected financial information for Rojo Corporation for December 31, 2022.

*Determine items included in a statement of cash flows, prepare the statement, and comment.*

| | | | |
|---|---|---|---|
| Inventory | $ 25,000 | Cash paid to purchase equipment | $ 12,000 |
| Cash paid to suppliers | 104,000 | Equipment | 40,000 |
| Buildings | 200,000 | Service revenue | 100,000 |
| Common stock | 50,000 | Cash received from customers | 132,000 |
| Cash dividends paid | 7,000 | Cash received from issuing | |
| Cash at beginning of period | 9,000 | common stock | 22,000 |

**Instructions**

**a.** Prepare the statement of cash flows for Rojo Corporation.

a. Net cash increase $31,000

**b.** Comment on the adequacy of net cash provided by operating activities to fund the company's investing activities and dividend payments.

**P1.6 (LO 3), AN** **Writing** Micado Corporation was formed on January 1, 2022. At December 31, 2022, Miko Liu, the president and sole stockholder, decided to prepare a balance sheet, which appeared as follows.

*Comment on proper accounting treatment and prepare a corrected balance sheet.*

**Micado Corporation**
**Balance Sheet**
**December 31, 2022**

| Assets | | Liabilities and Stockholders' Equity | |
|---|---|---|---|
| Cash | $20,000 | Accounts payable | $30,000 |
| Accounts receivable | 50,000 | Notes payable | 15,000 |
| Inventory | 36,000 | Boat loan | 22,000 |
| Boat | 24,000 | Stockholders' equity | 63,000 |

Miko willingly admits that she is not an accountant by training. She is concerned that her balance sheet might not be correct. She has provided you with the following additional information.

**1.** The boat actually belongs to Miko, not to Micado Corporation. However, because she thinks she might take customers out on the boat occasionally, she decided to list it as an asset of the company. To be consistent, she also listed as a liability of the corporation her personal loan that she took out at the bank to buy the boat.

**2.** The inventory was originally purchased for $25,000, but due to a surge in demand Miko now thinks she could sell it for $36,000. She thought it would be best to record it at $36,000.

**3.** Included in the accounts receivable balance is $10,000 that Miko loaned to her brother 5 years ago. Miko included this in the receivables of Micado Corporation so she wouldn't forget that her brother owes her money.

**Instructions**

**a.** Comment on the proper accounting treatment of the three items above.

**b.** Provide a corrected balance sheet for Micado Corporation. (*Hint:* To get the balance sheet to balance, adjust stockholders' equity.)

b. Tot. assets $85,000

# Expand Your Critical Thinking

## Financial Reporting Problem: Apple Inc.

**CT1.1** The financial statements of **Apple Inc.** are presented in Appendix A.

**Instructions**

Refer to Apple's financial statements and answer the following questions.

**a.** What were Apple's total assets at September 29, 2018? At September 30, 2017?

**b.** How much cash (and cash equivalents) did Apple have on September 29, 2018?

**c.** What amount of accounts payable did Apple report on September 29, 2018? On September 30, 2017?

**d.** What were Apple's net sales in the year ending September 29, 2018? In the year ending September 30, 2017? In the year ending September 24, 2016?

**e.** What is the amount of the change in Apple's net income from 2017 to 2018?

## Comparative Analysis Problem:

## Columbia Sportswear Company vs. Under Armour, Inc.

**CT1.2** **Columbia Sportswear Company**'s financial statements are presented in Appendix B. Financial statements of **Under Armour, Inc.** are presented in Appendix C.

### Instructions

a. Based on the information in these financial statements, determine the following for each company.

   1. Total liabilities at December 31, 2018.

   2. Net property, plant, and equipment at December 31, 2018.

   3. Net cash provided or (used) in investing activities for 2018.

   4. Net income for 2018.

b. What conclusions concerning the two companies can you draw from these data?

## Interpreting Financial Statements

**CT1.3** **Xerox** was not having a particularly pleasant year. The company's stock price had already fallen in the previous year from $60 per share to $30. Just when it seemed things couldn't get worse, Xerox's stock fell to $4 per share. The data below were taken from the statement of cash flows of Xerox. (All dollars are in millions.)

| | | |
|---|---:|---:|
| Cash used in operating activities | | $ (663) |
| Cash used in investing activities | | (644) |
| Financing activities | | |
| Dividends paid | $ (587) | |
| Net cash received from issuing debt | 3,498 | |
| Cash provided by financing activities | | 2,911 |

### Instructions

Analyze the information, and then answer the following questions.

a. If you were a creditor of Xerox, what reaction might you have to the above information?

b. If you were an investor in Xerox, what reaction might you have to the above information?

c. If you were evaluating the company as either a creditor or a stockholder, what other information would you be interested in seeing?

d. Xerox decided to pay a cash dividend. This dividend was approximately equal to the amount paid in the previous year. Discuss the issues that were probably considered in making this decision.

## Real-World Focus

**CT1.4** You can easily search the Internet to find summary information about companies. This information includes basic descriptions of the company's location, activities, industry, financial health, and financial performance.

### Instructions

Go to the **Yahoo! Finance** website, type in a company name, and then use the links (such as Financials) to locate the information necessary to answer the following questions.

a. What is the company's net income? Over what period was this measured?

b. What is the company's total sales? Over what period was this measured?

c. What is the company's industry?

d. What are the names of four companies in this industry?

e. Choose one of the competitors. What is this competitor's name? What is its total sales? What is its net income?

**CT1.5** The June 1, 2017, issue of the *Wall Street Journal* includes an article by Michael Rapoport entitled "Coming Soon: What Auditors Really Think About Company Numbers." It provides a discussion about changes to be made to the auditor's report.

**Instructions**

Read the article and answer the following questions.

**a.** What does the current auditor's report primarily focus on?

**b.** What will the new report provide beyond the current report? What are some examples of items that might be discussed?

**c.** How would the requirements of the new report compare to the requirements of auditor reports in other countries?

**d.** What criteria must be met in order for an item to be disclosed in the new report?

## Decision-Making Across the Organization

**CT1.6** Sylvia Ayala recently accepted a job in the production department at **Johnson & Johnson**. Before she starts work, she decides to review the company's annual report to better understand its operations.

The content and organization of corporate annual reports have become fairly standardized. Excluding the public relations part of the report (pictures, products, etc.), the following are the traditional financial portions of the annual report:

- Financial Highlights
- Letter to the Stockholders
- Management's Discussion and Analysis
- Financial Statements
- Notes to the Financial Statements
- Management's Responsibility for Financial Reporting
- Management's Report on Internal Control over Financial Reporting
- Report of Independent Registered Public Accounting Firm
- Selected Financial Data

The official SEC filing of the annual report is called a **Form 10-K**, which often omits the public relations pieces found in most standard annual reports.

**Instructions**

Use Johnson & Johnson's 10-K report dated December 31, 2018, to answer the following questions.

**a.** What CPA firm performed the audit of Johnson & Johnson's financial statements?

**b.** What was the amount of Johnson & Johnson's basic earnings per share in 2018?

**c.** What are the company's international sales to customers in 2018?

**d.** What are the sales to customers in 2017?

**e.** How many shares of common stock have been authorized?

**f.** How much cash was spent on additions to property, plant, and equipment in 2018?

**g.** Over what life does the company depreciate its buildings?

**h.** What was the value of inventory in 2018?

## Communication Activity

**CT1.7** Marci Ling is the bookkeeper for Samco Company, Inc. Marci has been trying to get the company's balance sheet to balance. She finally got it to balance, but she still isn't sure that it is correct.

**Samco Company, Inc.**
**Balance Sheet**
**For the Month Ended December 31, 2022**

| Assets | | Liabilities and Stockholders' Equity | |
|---|---|---|---|
| Equipment | $18,000 | Common stock | $12,000 |
| Cash | 9,000 | Accounts receivable | (6,000) |
| Supplies | 1,000 | Dividends | (2,000) |
| Accounts payable | (4,000) | Notes payable | 10,000 |
| Total assets | $24,000 | Retained earnings | 10,000 |
| | | Total liabilities and stockholders' equity | $24,000 |

### Instructions

Explain to Marci Ling in a memo (a) the purpose of a balance sheet, and (b) why this balance sheet is incorrect and what she should do to correct it.

### Ethics Case

**CT1.8** Rules governing the investment practices of individual certified public accountants prohibit them from investing in the stock of a company that their firm audits. The Securities and Exchange Commission (SEC) became concerned that some accountants were violating this rule. In response to an SEC investigation, **PricewaterhouseCoopers** fired 10 people and spent $25 million educating employees about the investment rules and installing an investment tracking system.

### Instructions

Answer the following questions.

   **a.** Why do you think rules exist that restrict auditors from investing in companies that are audited by their firms?

   **b.** Some accountants argue that they should be allowed to invest in a company's stock as long as they themselves aren't involved in working on the company's audit or consulting. What do you think of this idea?

   **c.** Today, a very high percentage of publicly traded companies are audited by only four very large public accounting firms. These firms also do a high percentage of the consulting work that is done for publicly traded companies. How does this fact complicate the decision regarding whether CPAs should be allowed to invest in companies audited by their firm?

   **d.** Suppose you were a CPA and you had invested in **IBM** when IBM was not one of your firm's clients. Two years later, after IBM's stock price had fallen considerably, your firm won the IBM audit contract. You will be involved in working with the IBM audit. You know that your firm's rules require that you sell your shares immediately. If you do sell immediately, you will sustain a large loss. Do you think this is fair? What would you do?

   **e.** Why do you think PricewaterhouseCoopers took such extreme steps in response to the SEC investigation?

## All About You

**CT1.9** Some people are tempted to make their finances look worse to get college financial aid. Companies sometimes also manage their financial numbers in order to accomplish certain goals. Earnings management is the planned timing of revenues, expenses, gains, and losses to smooth out bumps in net income. In managing earnings, companies' actions vary from being within the range of ethical activity, to being both unethical and illegal attempts to mislead investors and creditors.

### Instructions

Provide responses for each of the following questions.

   **a.** Discuss whether you think each of the following actions (adapted from the **FinAid** website) to increase the chances of receiving financial aid is ethical.

       **1.** Spend down the student's assets and income first, before spending parents' assets and income.

       **2.** Accelerate necessary expenses to reduce available cash. For example, if you need a new car, buy it before applying for financial aid.

       **3.** State that a truly financially dependent child is independent.

       **4.** Have a parent take an unpaid leave of absence for long enough to get below the "threshold" level of income.

   **b.** What are some reasons why a **company** might want to overstate its earnings?

   **c.** What are some reasons why a **company** might want to understate its earnings?

   **d.** Under what circumstances might an otherwise ethical person decide to illegally overstate or understate earnings?

## CHAPTER 2

Brooks Kraft/Corbis News/Getty Images

# A Further Look at the Balance Sheet

## Chapter Preview

If you are thinking of purchasing **Best Buy** stock, or any stock, how can you decide what the shares are worth? If you manage **Columbia Sportswear**'s credit department, how should you determine whether to extend credit to a new customer? If you are a financial executive at **Alphabet Inc.** (**Google**), how do you decide whether your company is generating adequate cash to expand operations without borrowing? Your decision in each of these situations will be influenced by a variety of considerations. One of them should be your careful analysis of a company's financial statements. The reason: Financial statements offer relevant, representationally faithful information that will help you in your decision-making.

In this chapter, we take a closer look at the balance sheet and introduce some useful ways for evaluating the information provided by it. We begin by introducing the classified balance sheet.

# Feature Story

## Just Fooling Around?

Two early pioneers in providing investment information online to the public were Tom and David Gardner, brothers who created an online investor website called **The Motley Fool**. The name comes from Shakespeare's *As You Like It*. The fool in Shakespeare's play was the only one who could speak unpleasant truths to kings and queens without being killed. Tom and David view themselves as 21st-century "fools," revealing the "truths" of the stock market to the small investor, who they feel has been taken advantage of by Wall Street insiders. The Motley Fool's online bulletin board enables investors to exchange information and insights about companies.

Critics of these bulletin boards contend that they are simply high-tech rumor mills that cause investors to bid up stock prices to unreasonable levels. For example, the stock of **Pair-Gain Technologies** jumped 32% in a single day as a result of a bogus takeover rumor on an investment bulletin board. Some observers are concerned that small investors—ironically, the very people the Gardner brothers are trying to help—will be hurt the most by misinformation and intentional scams.

To show how these bulletin boards work, suppose that you had $10,000 to invest. You were considering **Best Buy Company**, the largest seller of electronics equipment in the United States. You scanned the Internet investment bulletin boards and found messages posted by two different investors. Here are excerpts from actual postings:

> *TMPVenus:* "Where are the prospects for positive movement for this company? Poor margins, poor management, astronomical P/E!"
>
> *broachman:* "I believe that this is a LONG TERM winner, and presently at a good price."

One says sell, and one says buy. Whom should you believe? If at that time you had taken "broachman's" advice and purchased the stock, the $10,000 you invested would have been worth over $300,000 five years later. Best Buy was one of America's best-performing stocks during that five-year period of time.

Rather than getting swept away by rumors, investors must sort out the good information from the bad. One thing is certain—as information services such as The Motley Fool increase in number, gathering information will become even easier. Evaluating it will be the harder task.

# Chapter Outline

| LEARNING OBJECTIVES | REVIEW | PRACTICE |
|---|---|---|
| **LO 1** Identify the sections of a classified balance sheet. | • Current assets<br>• Long-term investments<br>• Property, plant, and equipment<br>• Intangible assets<br>• Current liabilities<br>• Long-term liabilities<br>• Stockholders' equity | **DO IT! 1a** Assets Section of Classified Balance Sheet<br><br>**DO IT! 1b** Balance Sheet Classifications |
| **LO 2** Use ratios to evaluate a company's balance sheet. | • Ratio analysis<br>• Using a classified balance sheet | **DO IT! 2** Ratio Analysis |

**Go to the Review and Practice section at the end of the chapter for a targeted summary and practice applications with solutions.**

**Visit WileyPLUS for additional tutorials and practice opportunities.**

# The Classified Balance Sheet

**LEARNING OBJECTIVE 1**

Identify the sections of a classified balance sheet.

You learned that a balance sheet presents a snapshot of a company's financial position at a point in time. It lists individual asset, liability, and stockholders' equity items. However, to improve users' understanding of a company's financial position, companies often use a **classified** balance sheet instead.

- A **classified balance sheet** groups together similar assets and similar liabilities, using a number of standard classifications and sections.
- This is useful because items within a group have similar economic characteristics.

A classified balance sheet generally contains the standard classifications listed in **Illustration 2.1**.

| Assets | Liabilities and Stockholders' Equity |
|---|---|
| Current assets | Current liabilities |
| Long-term investments | Long-term liabilities |
| Property, plant, and equipment | Stockholders' equity |
| Intangible assets | |

**ILLUSTRATION 2.1**

**Standard balance sheet classifications**

These groupings help financial statement readers determine such things as:

1. Whether the company has enough assets to pay its debts as they come due.
2. The claims of short- and long-term creditors on the company's total assets.

Many of these groupings can be seen in the balance sheet of Franklin Corporation shown in **Illustration 2.2** (see **Helpful Hint**). In the sections that follow, we explain each of these groupings.

## Current Assets

**Current assets** are defined as follows.

- Assets that a company expects to convert to cash or use up within one year or its operating cycle, whichever is longer. In Illustration 2.2, Franklin Corporation had current assets of $22,100.
- For most businesses, the cutoff for classification as current assets is one year from the balance sheet date.

For example, accounts receivable are current assets because the company will collect them and convert them to cash within one year. Supplies is a current asset because the company expects to use the supplies in operations within one year.

Some companies use a period longer than one year to classify assets and liabilities as current because they have an operating cycle longer than one year.

- The **operating cycle** of a company is the average time required to go from cash to cash in producing revenue—to purchase inventory, sell it on account, and then collect cash from customers.
- For most businesses, this cycle takes less than a year, so they use a one-year cutoff.
- But for some businesses, such as vineyards or airplane manufacturers, this period may be longer than a year.

**Except where noted, we will assume that companies use one year to determine whether an asset or liability is current or long-term.**

**ILLUSTRATION 2.2**
**Classified balance sheet**

**HELPFUL HINT**
**Recall that the accounting equation is Assets = Liabilities + Stockholders' Equity.**

## Franklin Corporation
**Balance Sheet**
**October 31, 2022**

| | | | |
|---|---|---|---|
| **Assets** | | | |
| **Current assets** | | | |
| Cash | | $ 6,600 | |
| Debt investments | | 2,000 | |
| Accounts receivable | | 7,000 | |
| Notes receivable | | 1,000 | |
| Inventory | | 3,000 | |
| Supplies | | 2,100 | |
| Prepaid insurance | | 400 | |
| Total current assets | | | $22,100 |
| **Long-term investments** | | | |
| Stock investments | | 5,200 | |
| Investment in real estate | | 2,000 | 7,200 |
| **Property, plant, and equipment** | | | |
| Land | | 10,000 | |
| Equipment | $24,000 | | |
| Less: Accumulated depreciation—equipment | 5,000 | 19,000 | 29,000 |
| **Intangible assets** | | | |
| Patents | | | 3,100 |
| Total assets | | | $61,400 |
| **Liabilities and Stockholders' Equity** | | | |
| **Current liabilities** | | | |
| Notes payable | | $11,000 | |
| Accounts payable | | 2,100 | |
| Unearned sales revenue | | 900 | |
| Salaries and wages payable | | 1,600 | |
| Interest payable | | 450 | |
| Total current liabilities | | | $16,050 |
| **Long-term liabilities** | | | |
| Mortgage payable | | 10,000 | |
| Notes payable | | 1,300 | |
| Total long-term liabilities | | | 11,300 |
| Total liabilities | | | 27,350 |
| **Stockholders' equity** | | | |
| Common stock | | 14,000 | |
| Retained earnings | | 20,050 | |
| Total stockholders' equity | | | 34,050 |
| Total liabilities and stockholders' equity | | | $61,400 |

**Companies list current assets in order of liquidity, that is, the order in which they expect to convert them into cash** *(follow this rule when doing your homework).* For example, inventory is less liquid than accounts receivable because inventory is often sold on account; that account receivable must then be collected to convert it to cash. Common types of current assets, listed in order of liquidity, are:

1. Cash.
2. Investments (such as short-term U.S. government securities).
3. Receivables (accounts receivable, notes receivable, and interest receivable).
4. Inventories.
5. Prepaid expenses (insurance and supplies).

**Illustration 2.3** presents the current assets of **Southwest Airlines Co.** in a recent year.

**ILLUSTRATION 2.3**
**Current assets section**

**Real World**

| Southwest Airlines Co. | |
| --- | --- |
| Balance Sheet (partial) | |
| (in millions) | |
| **Current assets** | |
| Cash and cash equivalents | $1,680 |
| Short-term investments | 1,625 |
| Accounts receivable | 546 |
| Inventories | 337 |
| Prepaid expenses and other current assets | 310 |
| Total current assets | $4,498 |

As explained later in the chapter, a company's current assets are important in assessing its short-term debt-paying ability.

# Long-Term Investments

**Long-term investments** generally include the following (see **Alternative Terminology**).

- Investments in stocks and bonds of other corporations that are held for more than one year.
- Long-term assets such as land or buildings that a company is not currently using in its operating activities.
- Long-term notes receivable.

**ALTERNATIVE TERMINOLOGY**

Long-term investments are often referred to simply as *investments*.

In Illustration 2.2, Franklin Corporation reported total long-term investments of $7,200 on its balance sheet.

**Alphabet Inc.** reported long-term investments on its balance sheet in a recent year as shown in **Illustration 2.4**.

**ILLUSTRATION 2.4**
**Long-term investments section**

**Real World**

| Alphabet Inc. | |
| --- | --- |
| Balance Sheet (partial) | |
| (in millions) | |
| **Long-term investments** | |
| Non-marketable investments | $5,183 |

# Property, Plant, and Equipment

**Property, plant, and equipment** is defined as follows.

- Assets with relatively long useful lives that are currently used in operating the business (see **Alternative Terminology**).
- This category includes land, buildings, equipment, delivery vehicles, and furniture.

**ALTERNATIVE TERMINOLOGY**

Property, plant, and equipment is sometimes called *fixed assets* or *plant assets*.

In Illustration 2.2, Franklin Corporation reported property, plant, and equipment of $29,000.

Notice that in Illustration 2.2, Franklin Corporation subtracts Accumulated Depreciation—Equipment from the Equipment account. **Depreciation** is the allocation of the cost of an asset to a number of years. Companies do this by systematically assigning a portion of an asset's cost as an expense each year (rather than expensing the full purchase price in the year of purchase). The assets that the company depreciates are reported on the balance sheet at cost less accumulated depreciation, often referred to as book value. The **accumulated depreciation** account shows the total amount of depreciation that the company has expensed thus far in the asset's life. In Illustration 2.2, Franklin Corporation reported accumulated depreciation of $5,000, so the book value of the equipment is $19,000 ($24,000 – $5,000).

Illustration 2.5 presents the property, plant, and equipment of **Cooper Tire & Rubber Company** in a recent year. *In your homework, present each accumulated depreciation account immediately below the related plant asset, as shown in Illustration 2.2 for Franklin Corporation.*

**ILLUSTRATION 2.5**

**Property, plant, and equipment section**

**Real World**

| Cooper Tire & Rubber Company | | |
|---|---|---|
| **Balance Sheet (partial)** | | |
| **(in thousands)** | | |
| **Property, plant, and equipment** | | |
| Land and land improvements | $ 47,767 | |
| Buildings | 282,960 | |
| Machinery and equipment | 1,742,449 | |
| Molds, cores, and rings | 224,662 | $2,297,838 |
| Less: Accumulated depreciation | | 1,433,611 |
| | | $ 864,227 |

# Intangible Assets

Many companies have assets that do not have physical substance and yet often are very valuable:

**HELPFUL HINT**
Sometimes intangible assets are reported under a broader heading called *"Other assets."*

- We call these assets **intangible assets** (see **Helpful Hint**).
- One common intangible is goodwill.
- Other intangibles include patents, copyrights, and trademarks or trade names that give the company **exclusive right** of use for a specified period of time.

In Illustration 2.2, Franklin Corporation reported intangible assets of $3,100.

Illustration 2.6 shows the intangible assets adapted from the balance sheet of media and theme park giant **The Walt Disney Company** in a recent year.

**ILLUSTRATION 2.6**

**Intangible assets section**

**Real World**

| The Walt Disney Company | |
|---|---|
| **Balance Sheet (partial)** | |
| **(in millions)** | |
| **Intangible assets and goodwill** | |
| Character/franchise intangibles and copyrights | $ 5,829 |
| Other amortizable intangible assets | 893 |
| Accumulated amortization | (1,635) |
| Net amortizable intangible assets | 5,087 |
| FCC licenses | 624 |
| Trademarks | 1,218 |
| Other indefinite lived intangible assets | 20 |
| | 6,949 |
| Goodwill | 27,810 |
| | $34,759 |

## DO IT! 1a | Assets Section of Classified Balance Sheet

Baxter Hoffman recently received the following information related to Hoffman Corporation's December 31, 2022, balance sheet.

| | | | |
|---|---|---|---|
| Prepaid insurance | $ 2,300 | Inventory | $3,400 |
| Cash | 800 | Accumulated depreciation— | |
| Equipment | 10,700 | equipment | 2,700 |
| Debt investments (long-term) | 2,100 | Accounts receivable | 1,100 |
| | | Trademarks | 4,700 |

Prepare the assets section of Hoffman Corporation's classified balance sheet.

**ACTION PLAN**

- Present current assets first. Current assets are cash and other resources that the company expects to convert to cash or use up within one year.
- Present current assets in the order in which the company expects to convert them into cash.
- Subtract accumulated depreciation—equipment from equipment to determine net equipment.

### Solution

**Hoffman Corporation**
**Balance Sheet (partial)**
**December 31, 2022**

**Assets**

| | | |
|---|---|---|
| Current assets | | |
| Cash | $ 800 | |
| Accounts receivable | 1,100 | |
| Inventory | 3,400 | |
| Prepaid insurance | 2,300 | |
| Total current assets | | $ 7,600 |
| Long-term investments | | |
| Debt investments | | 2,100 |
| Property, plant, and equipment | | |
| Equipment | 10,700 | |
| Less: Accumulated depreciation—equipment | 2,700 | 8,000 |
| Intangible assets | | |
| Trademarks | | 4,700 |
| Total assets | | $22,400 |

Related exercise material: **BE2.2, DO IT! 2.1a, E2.3, and E2.4.**

# Current Liabilities

In the liabilities and stockholders' equity section of the balance sheet, the first grouping is current liabilities.

- **Current liabilities** are obligations that the company is to pay within the next year or operating cycle, whichever is longer.
- Common examples are accounts payable, salaries and wages payable, notes payable, unearned revenue, interest payable, and income taxes payable.
- Also included as current liabilities are current maturities of long-term obligations—payments to be made within a year of the balance sheet date on long-term obligations.

In Illustration 2.2, Franklin Corporation reported five different types of current liabilities, for a total of $16,050.

**Illustration 2.7** shows the current liabilities section adapted from the balance sheet of **Alphabet Inc.** in a recent year.

| Alphabet Inc. | |
|---|---|
| **Balance Sheet (partial)** | |
| **(in millions)** | |
| **Current liabilities** | |
| Accounts payable | $ 1,931 |
| Short-term debt | 3,225 |
| Accrued compensation and benefits | 3,539 |
| Accrued expenses and other current liabilities | 10,313 |
| Income taxes payable, net | 302 |
| Total current liabilities | $19,310 |

# Long-Term Liabilities

**Long-term liabilities (long-term debt)** are:

- Obligations that a company expects to pay **after** one year.
- Liabilities in this category include bonds payable, mortgages payable, long-term notes payable, lease liabilities, and pension liabilities.

Many companies report long-term debt maturing after one year as a single amount in the balance sheet and show the details of the debt in notes that accompany the financial statements. Others list the various types of long-term liabilities. In Illustration 2.2, Franklin Corporation reported long-term liabilities of $11,300.

**Illustration 2.8** shows the long-term liabilities that **Nike, Inc.** reported in its balance sheet in a recent year.

| Nike, Inc. | |
|---|---|
| **Balance Sheet (partial)** | |
| **(in millions)** | |
| **Long-term liabilities** | |
| Bonds payable | $5,474 |
| Deferred income taxes and other | 1,907 |
| Total long-term liabilities | $7,381 |

# Stockholders' Equity

Stockholders' equity consists of two parts: common stock and retained earnings.

- Companies record as **common stock** the investments of assets into the business by the stockholders (see **Alternative Terminology**).
- They record as **retained earnings** the income retained for use in the business.
- These two parts, combined, make up **stockholders' equity** on the balance sheet.

In Illustration 2.2, Franklin Corporation reported common stock of $14,000 and retained earnings of $20,050.

## DO IT! 1b | Balance Sheet Classifications

The following financial statement items were taken from the financial statements of Callahan Corp.

_____ Salaries and wages payable
_____ Service revenue
_____ Interest payable
_____ Goodwill
_____ Debt investments (short-term)
_____ Mortgage payable (due in 3 years)
_____ Investment in real estate

_____ Equipment
_____ Accumulated depreciation—equipment
_____ Depreciation expense
_____ Retained earnings
_____ Unearned service revenue

Match each of the items to its proper balance sheet classification, shown below. If the item would not appear on a balance sheet, use "NA."

Current assets (CA)
Long-term investments (LTI)
Property, plant, and equipment (PPE)
Intangible assets (IA)

Current liabilities (CL)
Long-term liabilities (LTL)
Stockholders' equity (SE)

**ACTION PLAN**

- Analyze whether each financial statement item is an asset, liability, or stockholders' equity item.
- Determine if asset and liability items are current or long-term.

### Solution

| | |
|---|---|
| CL | Salaries and wages payable |
| NA | Service revenue |
| CL | Interest payable |
| IA | Goodwill |
| CA | Debt investments (short-term) |
| LTL | Mortgage payable (due in 3 years) |

| | |
|---|---|
| LTI | Investment in real estate |
| PPE | Equipment |
| PPE | Accumulated depreciation—equipment |
| NA | Depreciation expense |
| SE | Retained earnings |
| CL | Unearned service revenue |

Related exercise material: **BE2.1, BE2.3, DO IT! 2.1b, E2.1, E2.2, E2.5,** and **E2.6.**

# Analyzing the Balance Sheet Using Ratios

**LEARNING OBJECTIVE 2**

Use ratios to evaluate a company's balance sheet.

We previously introduced the four financial statements. We discussed how these statements provide information about a company's performance and financial position. Here, we extend this discussion by showing you specific tools that you can use to analyze financial statements in order to make a more meaningful evaluation of a company.

## Ratio Analysis

**Ratio analysis** expresses the relationship among selected items of financial statement data. A **ratio** expresses the mathematical relationship between one quantity and another. For analysis of the primary financial statements, we classify ratios as shown in **Illustration 2.9**.

**ILLUSTRATION 2.9**

**Financial ratio classifications**

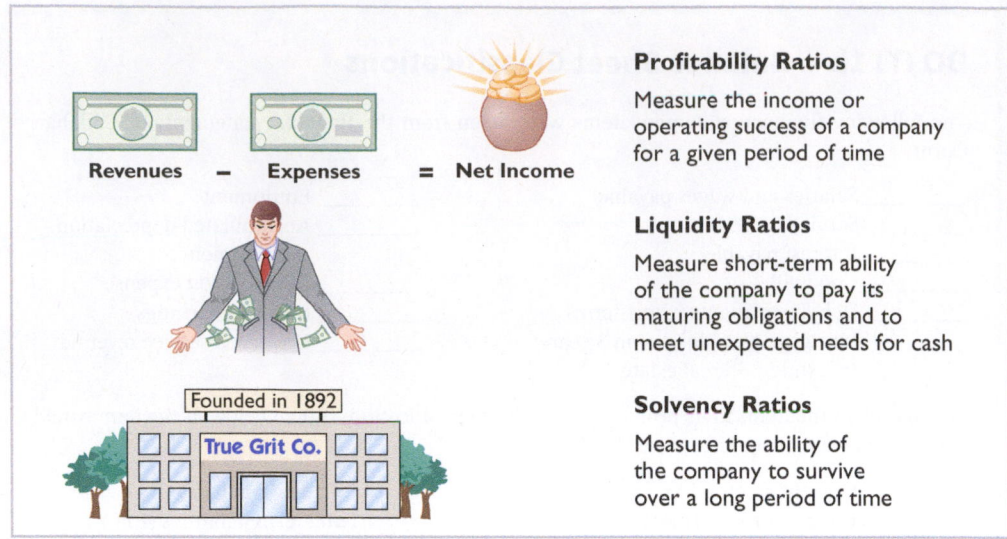

A single ratio by itself is not very meaningful. Accordingly, in this and the following chapters, we will use various comparisons to shed light on company performance:

1. **Intracompany comparisons** covering two years for the same company.
2. **Industry-average comparisons** based on average ratios for particular industries.
3. **Intercompany comparisons** based on comparisons with a competitor in the same industry.

Next, we use some ratios and comparisons to analyze the balance sheet of **Best Buy**.

# Using a Classified Balance Sheet

You can learn a lot about a company's financial health by evaluating the relationship between its various assets and liabilities. **Illustration 2.10** provides a simplified balance sheet for **Best Buy**.

**ILLUSTRATION 2.10**

**Best Buy's balance sheet**

**Real World**

| Best Buy Co., Inc. | | |
|---|---|---|
| Balance Sheets (in millions) | | |
| | **January 28, 2017** | **January 30, 2016** |
| **Assets** | | |
| Current assets | | |
| Cash and cash equivalents | $ 2,240 | $ 1,976 |
| Short-term investments | 1,681 | 1,305 |
| Receivables | 1,347 | 1,162 |
| Merchandise inventories | 4,864 | 5,051 |
| Other current assets | 384 | 392 |
| Total current assets | 10,516 | 9,886 |
| Property and equipment | 8,143 | 8,107 |
| Less: Accumulated depreciation | 5,850 | 5,761 |
| Net property and equipment | 2,293 | 2,346 |
| Other assets | 1,047 | 1,287 |
| Total assets | $13,856 | $13,519 |

| | January 28, 2017 | January 30, 2016 |
|---|---|---|
| **Liabilities and Stockholders' Equity** | | |
| Current liabilities | | |
| Accounts payable | $ 4,984 | $ 4,450 |
| Unredeemed gift card liabilities | 427 | 409 |
| Accrued liabilities | 865 | 802 |
| Accrued income taxes | 26 | 128 |
| Accrued compensation payable | 358 | 384 |
| Other current liabilities | 462 | 752 |
| Total current liabilities | 7,122 | 6,925 |
| Long-term liabilities | | |
| Long-term debt | 1,321 | 1,339 |
| Other long-term liabilities | 704 | 877 |
| Total long-term liabilities | 2,025 | 2,216 |
| Total liabilities | 9,147 | 9,141 |
| Stockholders' equity | | |
| Common stock | 31 | 32 |
| Retained earnings and other | 4,678 | 4,346 |
| Total stockholders' equity | 4,709 | 4,378 |
| Total liabilities and stockholders' equity | $13,856 | $13,519 |

**ILLUSTRATION 2.10**
*(continued)*

## Liquidity

Suppose you are a banker at **Citigroup** considering lending money to Best Buy, or you are a sales manager at **Apple** interested in selling computers and cell phones to Best Buy on credit.

- You would be concerned about Best Buy's **liquidity**—its ability to pay obligations expected to become due within the next year or operating cycle.
- You would look closely at the relationship of its current assets to current liabilities.

**Working Capital**   One measure of liquidity is **working capital**, which is the difference between the amounts of current assets and current liabilities (see **Illustration 2.11**).

**Working Capital = Current Assets − Current Liabilities**

**ILLUSTRATION 2.11**
**Working capital**

- When current assets exceed current liabilities, working capital is positive. When this occurs, there is a greater likelihood that the company will pay its liabilities.
- When working capital is negative, a company might not be able to pay short-term creditors, and the company might ultimately be forced into bankruptcy.

Best Buy had working capital in 2017 of $3,394 million ($10,516 million − $7,122 million).

**Current Ratio**   **Liquidity ratios** measure the short-term ability of the company to pay its maturing obligations and to meet unexpected needs for cash.

- One liquidity ratio is the **current ratio**, computed as current assets divided by current liabilities (see **Decision Tools**).
- The current ratio is a more dependable indicator of liquidity than working capital.
- Two companies with the same amount of working capital may have significantly different current ratios.

**Decision Tools**

The current ratio helps users determine if a company can meet its near-term obligations.

**Illustration 2.12** shows the 2017 and 2016 current ratios for **Best Buy** and for competitor **hhgregg**.

| Current Ratio = $\dfrac{\text{Current Assets}}{\text{Current Liabilities}}$ | | |
|---|---|---|
| **Best Buy**<br>($ in millions) | | **hhgregg** |
| **2017** | **2016** | **2017** |
| $\dfrac{\$10,516}{\$7,122} = 1.48:1$ | 1.43:1 | 1.51:1 |

What does the ratio actually mean? Best Buy's 2017 current ratio of 1.48:1 means that for every dollar of current liabilities, Best Buy has $1.48 of current assets. Best Buy's current ratio increased in 2017. Best Buy's current ratio is very similar to that of hhgregg.

One potential weakness of the current ratio is that it does not take into account the **composition** of the current assets.

- A satisfactory current ratio does not disclose whether a portion of the current assets is tied up in slow-moving inventory.

- The composition of the current assets matters because a dollar of cash is more readily available to pay the bills than is a dollar of inventory.

For example, suppose a company's cash balance declined while its merchandise inventory increased substantially. If inventory increased because the company is having difficulty selling its products, then the current ratio might not fully reflect the reduction in the company's liquidity (see **Ethics Note**).

**ETHICS NOTE**

A company that has more current assets than current liabilities can increase the ratio of current assets to current liabilities by using cash to pay off some current liabilities. This gives the appearance of being more liquid. Do you think this move is ethical?

## Accounting Across the Organization    REL Consultancy Group

iStock.com/Jorge Salcedo

### Can a Company Be Too Liquid?

There actually is a point where a company can be too liquid—that is, it can have too much working capital. While it is important to be liquid enough to be able to pay short-term bills as they come due, a company does not want to tie up its cash in extra inventory or receivables that are not earning the company money.

By one estimate from the **REL Consultancy Group**, the thousand largest U.S. companies had cumulative excess working capital of $1.017 trillion in a recent year. This was an 18% increase, which REL said represented a "deterioration in the management of operations." Given that managers throughout a company are interested in improving profitability, it is clear that they should have an eye toward managing working capital. They need to aim for a "Goldilocks solution"—not too much, not too little, but just right.

More recently, a different study found that companies reduced the number of days it took to convert working capital into cash received from customers from 37.1 days down to 35.7 days.

**Sources:** Maxwell Murphy, "The Big Number," *Wall Street Journal* (November 9, 2011); and Tatyana Shumsky and Nina Trentmann, "Finance Chiefs Look to Free Up Working Capital Ahead of Rate Increases," *Wall Street Journal* (August 21, 2017).

**What can various company managers do to ensure that working capital is managed efficiently to maximize net income? (Go to WileyPLUS for this answer and additional questions.)**

## DO IT! 2 | Ratio Analysis—Working Capital and Current Ratio

**Part 1:** Listed below are assets and liabilities of Steno Corporation for 2021 and 2022. Each is listed in alphabetical order.

| Assets | 2022 | 2021 | Liabilities | 2022 | 2021 |
|---|---|---|---|---|---|
| Accounts receivable | $ 1,600 | $ 1,400 | Accounts payable | $ 2,900 | $ 3,200 |
| Cash | 900 | 800 | Bonds payable | 21,000 | 28,000 |
| Equipment (net) | 42,000 | 40,000 | Notes payable (current) | 1,200 | 1,500 |
| Inventory | 3,800 | 3,200 | Notes payable (long-term) | 4,000 | 4,200 |
| Land | 22,000 | 22,000 | | | |
| Supplies | 400 | 500 | | | |

Steno reported net income of $48,000 for 2022 and $42,000 for 2021.

**a.** Compute total current assets and total current liabilities for each year.

**b.** Compute working capital and the current ratio for each year. (Round to two decimal places.)

**c.** Comment on the change in the company's liquidity.

### Solution

**a.** Current assets      2022: ($1,600 + $900 + $3,800 + $400) = $6,700
2021: ($1,400 + $800 + $3,200 + $500) = $5,900

     Current liabilities      2022: ($2,900 + $1,200) = $4,100
2021: ($3,200 + $1,500) = $4,700

**b.** Working capital      2022: ($6,700 – $4,100) = $2,600
2021: ($5,900 – $4,700) = $1,200

     Current ratio      2022: ($6,700 ÷ $4,100) = 1.63:1
2021: ($5,900 ÷ $4,700) = 1.26:1

**c.** The company's working capital and current ratio increased. This suggests that its liquidity, i.e., its ability to pay its short-term obligations, improved.

Related exercise material: **BE2.6, E2.8, and E2.9.**

**ACTION PLAN**

- **Current assets are expected to be converted to cash or used within one year or operating cycle, whichever is longer. Current liabilities are expected to be paid within one year or operating cycle, whichever is longer.**

- **Use the formula for the current ratio: Current assets ÷ Current liabilities.**

## Solvency

Now suppose that instead of being a short-term creditor, you are interested in either buying Best Buy's stock or extending the company a long-term loan.

- Long-term creditors and stockholders are interested in a company's **solvency**—its ability to pay interest as it comes due and to repay the balance of a debt due at its maturity.

- **Solvency ratios** measure the ability of the company to survive over a long period of time.

**Debt to Assets Ratio** The **debt to assets ratio** is one measure of solvency. It is calculated by dividing total liabilities (both current and long-term) by total assets. It measures the percentage of total financing provided by creditors rather than stockholders (see **Helpful Hint**).

- Debt financing is more risky than equity financing because debt must be repaid at specific points in time, whether the company is performing well or not.

- Thus, the higher the percentage of debt financing, the riskier the company.

The higher the percentage of total liabilities (debt) to total assets, the greater the risk that the company may be unable to pay its debts as they come due. **Illustration 2.13** shows the debt to assets ratios for **Best Buy** and **hhgregg**.

**HELPFUL HINT**

Some users evaluate solvency using a ratio of liabilities divided by stockholders' equity. The higher this "debt to equity" ratio is, the lower the company's solvency.

**ILLUSTRATION 2.13**

**Debt to assets ratio**

$$\text{Debt to Assets Ratio} = \frac{\text{Total Liabilities}}{\text{Total Assets}}$$

| Best Buy ($ in millions) | | hhgregg |
|---|---|---|
| **2017** | **2016** | **2017** |
| $\dfrac{\$9,147}{\$13,856} = 66\%$ | 68% | 69% |

The 2017 ratio of 66% means that every dollar of assets was financed by 66 cents of debt. Best Buy's ratio is similar to hhgregg's ratio of 69%. The higher the ratio, the more reliant the company is on debt financing. This means that a company with a high debt to assets ratio has a lower equity "buffer" available to creditors if the company becomes insolvent. Thus, from the creditors' point of view, a high ratio of debt to assets is undesirable (see **Decision Tools**).

**Decision Tools**

The debt to assets ratio helps users determine if a company can meet its long-term obligations.

The adequacy of this ratio is often judged in light of the company's net income.

- Note that while Best Buy and hhgregg relied on debt financing in a roughly equal fashion, hhgregg went bankrupt.
- This is largely explained by the fact that hhgregg's income was insufficient to pay its debt obligations as they came due.
- Generally, companies with relatively stable earnings, such as public utilities, can support higher debt to assets ratios than can cyclical companies with widely fluctuating earnings, such as many high-tech companies.

In later chapters, you will learn additional ways to evaluate solvency.

---

## Investor Insight    When Debt Is Good

iStock.com/David Crockett

Debt financing differs greatly across industries and companies. Here are some debt to assets ratios for selected companies in a recent year:

| | Debt to Assets Ratio |
| --- | --- |
| Google | 23% |
| Nike | 41% |
| Microsoft | 48% |
| ExxonMobil | 48% |
| General Motors | 74% |

**Discuss the difference in the debt to assets ratio of Microsoft and General Motors. (Go to WileyPLUS for this answer and additional questions.)**

---

**ACTION PLAN**

- Use the formula for the debt to assets ratio: Total liabilities ÷ Total assets.

## DO IT! 2 | Ratio Analysis—Debt to Assets Ratio

**Part 2:** Listed below are assets and liabilities of Steno Corporation for 2021 and 2022. Each is listed in alphabetical order.

| Assets | 2022 | 2021 | Liabilities | 2022 | 2021 |
| --- | --- | --- | --- | --- | --- |
| Accounts receivable | $ 1,600 | $ 1,400 | Accounts payable | $ 2,900 | $ 3,200 |
| Cash | 900 | 800 | Bonds payable | 21,000 | 28,000 |
| Equipment (net) | 42,000 | 40,000 | Notes payable (current) | 1,200 | 1,500 |
| Inventory | 3,800 | 3,200 | Notes payable (long-term) | 4,000 | 4,200 |
| Land | 22,000 | 22,000 | Total liabilities | $29,100 | $36,900 |
| Supplies | 400 | 500 | | | |
| Total assets | $70,700 | $67,900 | | | |

Steno reported net income of $48,000 for 2022 and $42,000 for 2021.

**a.** Compute the debt to assets ratio for each year. (Round to two decimal places.)

**b.** Comment on the change in the company's solvency.

### Solution

Debt to assets ratio     2022: ($29,100 ÷ $70,700) = 41%
2021: ($36,900 ÷ $67,900) = 54%

**b.** The company's debt to assets ratio decreased. This suggests that its solvency, i.e., its ability to pay interest and principal on its debts as they come due, has improved.

Related exercise material: **BE2.7, DO IT! 2.2, and E2.10.**

## USING THE DECISION TOOLS | Tweeter Home Entertainment

In this chapter, we evaluated a home electronics giant, **Best Buy**. **Tweeter Home Entertainment** sold consumer electronics products from 154 stores on the East Coast under various names. It specialized in products with high-end features. Tweeter filed for bankruptcy in June 2007 and was acquired by another company in July 2007. Financial data for Tweeter, prior to its bankruptcy, are provided below.

| | September 30 | |
| --- | --- | --- |
| **(amounts in millions)** | **2006** | **2005** |
| Current assets | $146.4 | $158.2 |
| Total assets | 258.6 | 284.0 |
| Current liabilities | 107.1 | 119.0 |
| Total liabilities | 190.4 | 201.1 |
| Total common stockholders' equity | 68.2 | 82.9 |
| Net income (loss) | (16.5) | (74.4) |
| Net cash provided (used) by operating activities | 15.6 | (26.7) |
| Capital expenditures (net) | 17.4 | 22.2 |
| Dividends paid | 0.0 | 0.0 |
| Weighted-average shares of common stock (millions) | 25.2 | 24.6 |

## Instructions

Using the data provided, answer the following questions and discuss how these results might have provided an indication of Tweeter's financial troubles.

1. Calculate the current ratio for Tweeter for 2006 and 2005 and discuss its liquidity position.
2. Calculate the debt to assets ratio for Tweeter for 2006 and 2005 and discuss its solvency.
3. Best Buy's accounting year-end was February 28, 2006; Tweeter's was September 30, 2006. How does this difference affect your ability to compare their profitability?

## Solution

1. Current ratio:

   2006:   $146.4 ÷ $107.1 = 1.37:1      2005:   $158.2 ÷ $119.0 = 1.33:1

   Tweeter's liquidity improved slightly from 2005 to 2006, but in both years it would most likely have been considered inadequate. In 2006, Tweeter had only $1.37 in current assets for every dollar of current liabilities. Sometimes larger companies, such as Best Buy, can function with lower current ratios because they have alternative sources of working capital. But a company of Tweeter's size would normally want a higher ratio.

2. Debt to assets ratio:

   2006:   $190.4 ÷ $258.6 = 73.6%      2005:   $201.1 ÷ $284.0 = 70.8%

   Tweeter's solvency, as measured by its debt to assets ratio, worsened from 2005 to 2006. Its ratio of 73.6% meant that every dollar of assets was financed by 73.6 cents of debt. For a retailer, this is extremely high reliance on debt. This low solvency suggests Tweeter's ability to meet its debt payments was questionable.

3. Tweeter's income statement covers 7 months not covered by Best Buy's. Suppose that the economy changed dramatically during this 7-month period, either improving or declining. This change in the economy would be reflected in Tweeter's income statement but would not be reflected in Best Buy's income statement until the following March, thus reducing the usefulness of a comparison of the income statements of the two companies.

# Review and Practice

## Learning Objectives Review

**1  Identify the sections of a classified balance sheet.**

In a classified balance sheet, companies classify assets as current assets; long-term investments; property, plant, and equipment; and intangibles. They classify liabilities as either current or long-term. A stockholders' equity section shows common stock and retained earnings.

**2  Use ratios to evaluate a company's balance sheet.**

Ratio analysis expresses the relationship among selected items of financial statement data. Liquidity ratios, such as the current ratio, measure the short-term ability of a company to pay its maturing obligations and to meet unexpected needs for cash. Solvency ratios, such as the debt to assets ratio, measure the ability of a company to survive over a long period. Profitability ratios measure aspects of the operating success of a company for a given period of time.

## Decision Tools Review

| Decision Checkpoints | Info Needed for Decision | Tool to Use for Decision | How to Evaluate Results |
|---|---|---|---|
| Can the company meet its near-term obligations? | Current assets and current liabilities | $\text{Current ratio} = \dfrac{\text{Current assets}}{\text{Current liabilities}}$ | Higher ratio suggests favorable liquidity. |
| Can the company meet its long-term obligations? | Total liabilities and total assets | $\text{Debt to assets ratio} = \dfrac{\text{Total liabilities}}{\text{Total assets}}$ | Lower value suggests favorable solvency. |

## Glossary Review

**Classified balance sheet** A balance sheet that groups together similar assets and similar liabilities, using a number of standard classifications and sections. (p. 2-3).

**Current assets** Assets that a company expects to convert to cash or use up within one year or the operating cycle, whichever is longer. (p. 2-3).

**Current liabilities** Obligations that a company expects to pay within the next year or operating cycle, whichever is longer. (p. 2-7).

**Current ratio** A measure of liquidity computed as current assets divided by current liabilities. (p. 2-11).

**Debt to assets ratio** A measure of solvency calculated as total liabilities divided by total assets. It measures the percentage of total financing provided by creditors. (p. 2-13).

**Intangible assets** Assets that do not have physical substance. (p. 2-6).

**Liquidity** The ability of a company to pay obligations that are expected to become due within the next year or operating cycle. (p. 2-11).

**Liquidity ratios** Measures of the short-term ability of a company to pay its maturing obligations and to meet unexpected needs for cash. (p. 2-11).

**Long-term investments** Generally, (1) investments in stocks and bonds of other corporations that a company holds for more than one year;

(2) long-term assets, such as land and buildings, not currently being used in the company's operations; and (3) long-term notes receivable. (p. 2-5).

**Long-term liabilities (long-term debt)** Obligations that a company expects to pay after one year. (p. 2-8).

**Operating cycle** The average time required to purchase inventory, sell it on account, and then collect cash from customers—that is, go from cash to cash. (p. 2-3).

**Property, plant, and equipment** Assets with relatively long useful lives that are currently used in operating the business. (p. 2-5).

**Ratio** An expression of the mathematical relationship between one quantity and another. (p. 2-9).

**Ratio analysis** A technique that expresses the relationship among selected items of financial statement data. (p. 2-9).

**Solvency** The ability of a company to pay interest as it comes due and to repay the balance of debt due at its maturity. (p. 2-13).

**Solvency ratios** Measures of the ability of a company to survive over a long period of time. (p. 2-13).

**Working capital** The difference between the amounts of current assets and current liabilities. (p. 2-11).

## Practice Multiple-Choice Questions

**1. (LO 1)** In a classified balance sheet, assets are usually classified as:

  **a.** current assets; long-term assets; property, plant, and equipment; and intangible assets.

  **b.** current assets; long-term investments; property, plant, and equipment; and common stock.

  **c.** current assets; long-term investments; tangible assets; and intangible assets.

  **d.** current assets; long-term investments; property, plant, and equipment; and intangible assets.

**2. (LO 1)** Current assets are listed:

  **a.** by order of expected conversion to cash.

  **b.** by importance.

  **c.** by longevity.

  **d.** alphabetically.

**3. (LO 1)** The correct order of presentation in a classified balance sheet for the following current assets is:

  **a.** accounts receivable, cash, prepaid insurance, inventory.

  **b.** cash, inventory, accounts receivable, prepaid insurance.

  **c.** cash, accounts receivable, inventory, prepaid insurance.

  **d.** inventory, cash, accounts receivable, prepaid insurance.

**4. (LO 1)** A company has purchased a tract of land. It expects to build a production plant on the land in approximately 5 years. During the 5 years before construction, the land will be idle. The land should be reported as:

  **a.** property, plant, and equipment.

  **b.** land expense.

  **c.** a long-term investment.

  **d.** an intangible asset.

**5. (LO 1)** The balance in retained earnings is **not** affected by:

  **a.** net income.

  **b.** net loss.

  **c.** issuance of common stock.

  **d.** dividends.

**6. (LO 2)** Which is an indicator of solvency?

  **a.** Current ratio.

  **b.** Working capital.

  **c.** Debt to assets ratio.

  **d.** Both current ratio and working capital.

**7. (LO 2)** A company will be able to support a higher debt to assets ratio if:

  **a.** its net income fluctuates significantly from year to year.

  **b.** its net income is relatively stable from year to year.

  **c.** it has a large amount of accounts receivable.

  **d.** it has a large amount of inventory.

**8. (LO 2)** Which of these measures is an evaluation of a company's ability to pay current liabilities?

  **a.** Total assets.

  **b.** Current ratio.

  **c.** Both total assets and current ratio.

  **d.** None of the answer choices are correct.

**9. (LO 2)** The following ratios are available for Reilly Inc. and O'Hare Inc.

| | Current Ratio | Debt to Assets Ratio |
| --- | --- | --- |
| Reilly Inc. | 2:1 | 75% |
| O'Hare Inc. | 1.5:1 | 40% |

Compared to O'Hare Inc., Reilly Inc. has:

  **a.** higher liquidity, higher solvency, and higher profitability.

  **b.** lower liquidity, higher solvency, and higher profitability.

  **c.** higher liquidity, lower solvency, and higher profitability.

  **d.** higher liquidity and lower solvency, but profitability cannot be compared based on information provided.

### Solutions

**1. d.** Assets are classified as current assets; long-term investments; property, plant, and equipment; and intangible assets. The other choices are incorrect because (a) long-term assets includes long-term investments; property, plant, and equipment; and intangible assets; (b) common stock refers to the equity of the firm and is not an asset; and (c) while tangible assets describes property, plant, and equipment, it is better to use the more common terminology of property, plant, and equipment.

**2. a.** Current assets should be listed by order of expected conversion to cash (liquidity), not (b) by importance, (c) by longevity, or (d) alphabetically.

**3. c.** The correct order of presentation for current assets is cash, accounts receivable, inventory, and then prepaid insurance. The other choices are therefore incorrect.

**4. c.** Land or buildings that are currently not used in operations are considered to be long-term investments. The other choices are incorrect because (a) this classification is for property, plant, and equipment used in operations; (b) land is never expensed; and (d) intangible assets have no physical existence and are used in the production of income.

**5. c.** Issuance of common stock has no impact on retained earnings. The other choices are incorrect because (a) net income increases retained earnings, (b) net loss decreases retained earnings, and (d) dividends decrease retained earnings.

**6. c.** Debt to assets ratio is a measure of solvency. The other choices are incorrect because (a) the current ratio and (b) working capital are both measures of liquidity.

**7. b.** A company will be able to support a higher debt to assets ratio if its net income is relatively stable from year-to-year as opposed to

(a) fluctuating. Since both (c) accounts receivable and (d) inventory are current assets, they have more influence on a company's short-term debt-paying ability than its ability to borrow in the long-term.

**8. b.** The current ratio measures liquidity. Higher current ratios indicate higher liquidity. The other choices are incorrect because (a) total assets indicates the size of a company, not its ability to pay its current liabilities; (c) one of these answers is incorrect; and (d) there is a correct answer.

**9. d.** Reilly Inc. has higher liquidity as it has a higher current ratio, and lower solvency due to its higher debt to assets ratio. However, profitability cannot be compared across companies using the ratios provided. The other choices are therefore incorrect.

## Practice Brief Exercises

*Prepare the current assets section of a balance sheet.*

**1. (LO 1)** A list of financial statement items for Miguel Company includes the following: Accounts Receivable $25,000, Prepaid Insurance $7,000, Cash $8,000, Supplies $11,000, and Stock Investments (short-term) $14,000. Prepare the current assets section of the balance sheet, listing the accounts in proper sequence.

### Solution

1.

| Miguel Company | |
|---|---|
| **Balance Sheet (partial)** | |
| Current assets | |
| Cash | $ 8,000 |
| Stock investments | 14,000 |
| Accounts receivable | 25,000 |
| Supplies | 11,000 |
| Prepaid insurance | 7,000 |
| Total current assets | $65,000 |

*Classify accounts on balance sheet.*

**2. (LO 1)** The following are the major balance sheet classifications:

Current assets (CA)            Current liabilities (CL)
Long-term investments (LTI)    Long-term liabilities (LTL)
Property, plant, and equipment (PPE)   Stockholders' equity (SE)
Intangible assets (IA)

Match each of the following accounts to its proper balance sheet classification.

_____ Prepaid insurance                    _____ Unearned service revenue
_____ Notes payable (short-term)           _____ Debt investments (short-term)
_____ Equipment                            _____ Accumulated depreciation—equipment
_____ Mortgage payable                     _____ Stock investments (long-term)
_____ Copyrights                           _____ Salaries and wages payable

### Solution

2.

__CA__ Prepaid insurance                      __CL__ Unearned service revenue
__CL__ Notes payable (short-term)             __CA__ Debt investments (short-term)
__PPE__ Equipment                             __PPE__ Accumulated depreciation—equipment
__LTL__ Mortgage payable                      __LTI__ Stock investments (long-term)
__IA__ Copyrights                             __CL__ Salaries and wages payable

**3. (LO 2)** Maison Inc. reported the following selected information at December 31.

*Calculate liquidity and solvency ratios.*

|  | **2022** |
|---|---|
| Total current assets | $ 45,584 |
| Total assets | 278,000 |
| Total current liabilities | 32,560 |
| Total liabilities | 189,040 |
| Net cash provided by operating activities | 48,500 |

Calculate (a) the current ratio and (b) the debt to assets ratio for December 31, 2022. The company paid dividends of $7,250 and spent $14,400 on capital expenditures.

**Solution**

**3. a.** Current ratio $= \dfrac{\text{Current assets}}{\text{Current liabilities}} = \dfrac{\$45,584}{\$32,560} = 1.40{:}1$

**b.** Debt to assets ratio $= \dfrac{\text{Total liabilities}}{\text{Total assets}} = \dfrac{\$189,040}{\$278,000} = 68.0\%$

## Practice Exercises

**1. (LO 1)** Suppose the following information (in thousands of dollars) is available for **H. J. Heinz Company**—famous for ketchup and other fine food products—for the year ended April 30, 2022.

*Prepare assets section of a classified balance sheet.*

| Prepaid insurance | $  168,182 | Buildings | $4,344,269 |
|---|---|---|---|
| Land | 56,007 | Cash | 617,687 |
| Goodwill | 4,411,521 | Accounts receivable | 1,161,481 |
| Trademarks | 723,243 | Accumulated depreciation— | |
| Inventory | 1,378,216 | buildings | 2,295,563 |

**Instructions**

Prepare the assets section of a classified balance sheet, listing the items in proper sequence and including a statement heading.

**Solution**

**1.**

### H. J. Heinz Company
#### Balance Sheet (partial)
#### April 30, 2022
#### (in thousands)

**Assets**

| | | | |
|---|---|---|---|
| Current assets | | | |
| Cash | | $  617,687 | |
| Accounts receivable | | 1,161,481 | |
| Inventory | | 1,378,216 | |
| Prepaid insurance | | 168,182 | |
| Total current assets | | | $ 3,325,566 |
| Property, plant, and equipment | | | |
| Land | | 56,007 | |
| Buildings | $4,344,269 | | |
| Less: Accumulated depr.—buildings | 2,295,563 | 2,048,706 | 2,104,713 |
| Intangible assets | | | |
| Goodwill | | 4,411,521 | |
| Trademarks | | 723,243 | 5,134,764 |
| Total assets | | | $10,565,043 |

*Compute and interpret various ratios.*

**2. (LO 2)** Suppose the following data were taken from the 2022 and 2021 financial statements of **American Eagle Outfitters**. (All dollars are in thousands.)

|  | 2022 | 2021 |
|---|---|---|
| Current assets | $1,020,834 | $1,189,108 |
| Total assets | 1,867,680 | 1,979,558 |
| Current liabilities | 376,178 | 464,618 |
| Total liabilities | 527,216 | 562,246 |
| Net income | 400,019 | 387,359 |
| Net cash provided by operating activities | 464,270 | 749,268 |
| Capital expenditures | 250,407 | 225,939 |
| Dividends paid on common stock | 80,796 | 61,521 |
| Weighted-average shares outstanding | 216,119 | 222,662 |

**Instructions**

Perform each of the following.

 **a.** Calculate the current ratio for each year.

 **b.** Calculate the debt to assets ratio for each year.

 **c.** Discuss American Eagle's solvency in 2022 versus 2021.

**Solution**

2.

|  | 2022 | 2021 |
|---|---|---|
| **a.** Current ratio | $\dfrac{\$1,020,834}{\$376,178} = 2.71{:}1$ | $\dfrac{\$1,189,108}{\$464,618} = 2.56{:}1$ |
| **b.** Debt to assets ratio | $\dfrac{\$527,216}{\$1,867,680} = 28.2\%$ | $\dfrac{\$562,246}{\$1,979,558} = 28.4\%$ |

 **c.** Using the debt to assets ratio as a measure of solvency shows little change for American Eagle Outfitters. Its debt to assets ratio decreased slightly from 28.4% for 2021 to 28.2% for 2022, indicating a very small increase in solvency for 2022.

# Practice Problem

*Prepare financial statements.*

**(LO 1)** The following are items taken from the income statement and balance sheet of Bargain Electronics, Inc. for the year ended December 31, 2022. Certain items have been combined for simplification. (Amounts are given in thousands.)

| | |
|---|---|
| Notes payable (due in 3 years) | $    50.5 |
| Cash | 141.1 |
| Salaries and wages expense | 2,933.6 |
| Common stock | 454.9 |
| Accounts payable | 922.2 |
| Accounts receivable | 723.3 |
| Equipment, net | 921.0 |
| Cost of goods sold | 9,501.4 |
| Income taxes payable | 7.2 |
| Interest expense | 1.5 |
| Mortgage payable | 451.5 |
| Retained earnings | 1,336.3 |
| Inventory | 1,636.5 |
| Sales revenue | 12,456.9 |
| Debt investments (short-term) | 382.6 |
| Income tax expense | 30.5 |
| Goodwill | 202.7 |
| Notes payable (due in 6 months) | 784.6 |

**Instructions**

Prepare an income statement and a classified balance sheet using the items listed. Do not use any item more than once.

**Solution**

## Bargain Electronics, Inc.
### Income Statement
**For the Year Ended December 31, 2022**
*(in thousands)*

| | | |
|---|---:|---:|
| Revenues | | |
| Sales revenue | | $12,456.9 |
| Expenses | | |
| Cost of goods sold | $9,501.4 | |
| Salaries and wages expense | 2,933.6 | |
| Interest expense | 1.5 | |
| Income tax expense | 30.5 | |
| Total expenses | | 12,467.0 |
| Net loss | | $ (10.1) |

## Bargain Electronics, Inc.
### Balance Sheet
**December 31, 2022**
*(in thousands)*

### Assets

| | | |
|---|---:|---:|
| Current assets | | |
| Cash | $ 141.1 | |
| Debt investments | 382.6 | |
| Accounts receivable | 723.3 | |
| Inventory | 1,636.5 | |
| Total current assets | | $2,883.5 |
| Equipment, net | | 921.0 |
| Goodwill | | 202.7 |
| Total assets | | $4,007.2 |

### Liabilities and Stockholders' Equity

| | | |
|---|---:|---:|
| Current liabilities | | |
| Notes payable | $ 784.6 | |
| Accounts payable | 922.2 | |
| Income taxes payable | 7.2 | |
| Total current liabilities | | $1,714.0 |
| Long-term liabilities | | |
| Mortgage payable | 451.5 | |
| Notes payable | 50.5 | 502.0 |
| Total liabilities | | 2,216.0 |
| Stockholders' equity | | |
| Common stock | 454.9 | |
| Retained earnings | 1,336.3 | |
| Total stockholders' equity | | 1,791.2 |
| Total liabilities and stockholders' equity | | $4,007.2 |

# WileyPLUS

Brief Exercises, DO IT! Exercises, Exercises, Problems, and many additional resources are available for practice in WileyPLUS.

## Questions

1. What is meant by the term operating cycle?

2. Define current assets. What basis is used for ordering individual items within the current assets section?

3. Distinguish between long-term investments and property, plant, and equipment.

4. How do current liabilities differ from long-term liabilities?

5. Identify the two parts of stockholders' equity in a corporation and indicate the purpose of each.

6. **a.** Geena Lowe believes that the analysis of financial statements is directed at two characteristics of a company: liquidity and profitability. Is Geena correct? Explain.

   **b.** Are short-term creditors, long-term creditors, and stockholders primarily interested in the same characteristics of a company? Explain.

7. Name ratios useful in assessing (a) liquidity and (b) solvency.

8. Tom Dawes, the founder of Footwear Inc., needs to raise $500,000 to expand his company's operations. He has been told that raising the money through debt will increase the riskiness of his company much more than issuing stock. He doesn't understand why this is true. Explain it to him.

9. What do these classes of ratios measure?

   **a.** Liquidity ratios.

   **b.** Profitability ratios.

   **c.** Solvency ratios.

10. Holding all other factors constant, indicate whether each of the following signals generally good or bad news about a company.

    **a.** Increase in the current ratio.

    **b.** Increase in the debt to assets ratio.

11. What was Apple's largest current asset, largest current liability, and largest item under "Assets" at September 29, 2018?

## Brief Exercises

*Classify accounts on balance sheet.*

**BE2.1 (LO 1), K** The following are the major balance sheet classifications:

Current assets (CA)                      Current liabilities (CL)
Long-term investments (LTI)              Long-term liabilities (LTL)
Property, plant, and equipment (PPE)     Stockholders' equity (SE)
Intangible assets (IA)

Match each of the following accounts to its proper balance sheet classification.

\_\_\_\_\_ Accounts payable                 \_\_\_\_\_ Income taxes payable
\_\_\_\_\_ Accounts receivable              \_\_\_\_\_ Investment in long-term bonds
\_\_\_\_\_ Accumulated depreciation         \_\_\_\_\_ Land
\_\_\_\_\_ Buildings                        \_\_\_\_\_ Inventory
\_\_\_\_\_ Cash                             \_\_\_\_\_ Patent
\_\_\_\_\_ Goodwill                         \_\_\_\_\_ Supplies

*Prepare the current assets section of a balance sheet.*

**BE2.2 (LO 1), AP** A list of financial statement items for Chin Company includes the following: accounts receivable $14,000, prepaid insurance $2,600, cash $10,400, supplies $3,800, and debt investments (short-term) $8,200. Prepare the current assets section of the balance sheet listing the items in the proper sequence.

*Identify the order of asset classifications.*

**BE2.3 (LO 1), K** Place a number, 1 through 7, in front of each of the following balance sheet categories to designate the order in which they are to be presented in a classified balance sheet.

\_\_\_\_\_ Long-term investments            \_\_\_\_\_ Current assets
\_\_\_\_\_ Current liabilities             \_\_\_\_\_ Long-term liabilities
\_\_\_\_\_ Stockholders' equity            \_\_\_\_\_ Property, plant, and equipment
\_\_\_\_\_ Intangible assets

*Prepare liability and stockholders' equity section of classified balance sheet.*

**BE2.4 (LO 1), AP** Alberta Company had the following account balances on December 31, 2022.

| Retained earnings | $54,500 | Common stock | $76,100 |
|---|---|---|---|
| Notes payable | 15,900 | Interest payable | 3,200 |
| Bonds payable | 24,900 | Accounts payable | 8,200 |

**Instructions**

Prepare the liability and stockholders' equity section of a classified balance sheet in good form as of December 31, 2022. Assume that $2,900 of the note payable will be paid during 2023.

**BE2.5 (LO 1), AP** Suppose the following items were taken from the 2022 financial statements of **Texas Instruments, Inc.** (All dollars are in millions.)

*Prepare a classified balance sheet.*

| | | | |
|---|---|---|---|
| Common stock | $2,826 | Accumulated depreciation— | |
| Prepaid rent | 164 | equipment | $3,547 |
| Equipment | 6,705 | Accounts payable | 1,459 |
| Stock investments (long-term) | 637 | Patents | 2,210 |
| Debt investments (short-term) | 1,743 | Notes payable (long-term) | 810 |
| Income taxes payable | 128 | Retained earnings | 6,896 |
| Cash | 1,182 | Accounts receivable | 1,823 |
| | | Inventory | 1,202 |

**Instructions**

Prepare a classified balance sheet in good form as of December 31, 2022.

**BE2.6 (LO 2), AP** These selected condensed data are taken from a recent balance sheet of **Bob Evans Farms** (in millions of dollars).

*Calculate liquidity ratios.*

| | |
|---|---|
| Cash | $ 29.3 |
| Accounts receivable | 20.5 |
| Inventory | 28.7 |
| Other current assets | 24.0 |
| Total current assets | $102.5 |
| Total current liabilities | $201.2 |

Compute working capital and the current ratio.

**BE2.7 (LO 2), AP** Ross Music Inc. reported the following selected information at March 31.

*Calculate liquidity and solvency ratios.*

| | **2022** |
|---|---|
| Total current assets | $262,787 |
| Total assets | 439,832 |
| Total current liabilities | 293,625 |
| Total liabilities | 376,002 |
| Net cash provided by operating activities | 62,300 |

Calculate (a) the current ratio and (b) the debt to assets ratio.

## DO IT! Exercises

**DO IT! 2.1a (LO 1), AP** Mylar Corporation has collected the following information related to its December 31, 2022, balance sheet.

*Prepare assets section of balance sheet.*

| | | | |
|---|---|---|---|
| Accounts receivable | $22,000 | Equipment | $180,000 |
| Accumulated depreciation—equipment | 50,000 | Inventory | 58,000 |
| Cash | 13,000 | Supplies | 7,000 |

Prepare the assets section of Mylar Corporation's balance sheet.

**DO IT! 2.1b (LO 1), K** The following financial statement items were taken from the financial statements of Gomez Corp.

*Classify financial statement items by balance sheet classification.*

| | |
|---|---|
| ____ Trademarks | ____ Inventory |
| ____ Notes payable (current) | ____ Accumulated depreciation |
| ____ Interest revenue | ____ Land |
| ____ Income taxes payable | ____ Common stock |
| ____ Debt investments (long-term) | ____ Advertising expense |
| ____ Unearned sales revenue | ____ Mortgage payable (due in 3 years) |

Match each of the financial statement items to its proper balance sheet classification as follows.

| | |
|---|---|
| Current assets (CA) | Current liabilities (CL) |
| Long-term investments (LTI) | Long-term liabilities (LTL) |
| Property, plant, and equipment (PPE) | Stockholders' equity (SE) |
| Intangible assets (IA) | |

If the item would not appear on the balance sheet, use "NA."

*Compute ratios and analyze.*

**DO IT! 2.2 (LO 2), AN** Listed below are assets and liabilities of Reliable Corporation for the years 2021 and 2022. Each is listed in alphabetical order.

| Assets | 2022 | 2021 | Liabilities | 2022 | 2021 |
|---|---|---|---|---|---|
| Accounts receivable | $ 1,700 | $ 2,400 | Accounts payable | $ 3,900 | $ 3,000 |
| Cash | 900 | 1,200 | Bonds payable | 31,000 | 26,000 |
| Equipment (net) | 44,000 | 50,000 | Notes payable (current) | 2,200 | 1,600 |
| Inventory | 3,700 | 4,200 | Notes payable (long-term) | 5,000 | 4,000 |
| Land | 22,000 | 22,000 | Total liabilities | $42,100 | $34,600 |
| Supplies | 400 | 700 | | | |
| Total assets | $72,700 | $80,500 | | | |

Reliable reported net income of $48,000 for 2022 and $42,000 for 2021.

a. Compute total current assets and total current liabilities for each year.

b. Compute working capital and the current ratio for each year. (Round to two decimal places.)

c. Compute the debt to assets ratio for each year. (Round to two decimal places.)

d. Comment on the change in the company's liquidity and solvency.

# Exercises

*Classify accounts on balance sheet.*

**E2.1 (LO 1), K** The following are the major balance sheet classifications.

Current assets (CA)              Current liabilities (CL)
Long-term investments (LTI)      Long-term liabilities (LTL)
Property, plant, and equipment (PPE)   Stockholders' equity (SE)
Intangible assets (IA)

**Instructions**

Classify each of the following financial statement items taken from Ming Corporation's balance sheet.

_____ Accounts payable                  _____ Income taxes payable
_____ Accounts receivable               _____ Inventory
_____ Accumulated depreciation—         _____ Stock investments (to be sold in 7 months)
        equipment                       _____ Land (in use)
_____ Buildings                         _____ Mortgage payable
_____ Cash                              _____ Supplies
_____ Interest payable                  _____ Equipment
_____ Goodwill                          _____ Prepaid rent

*Classify financial statement items by balance sheet classification.*

**E2.2 (LO 1), K** The following are the major balance sheet classifications.

Current assets (CA)              Current liabilities (CL)
Long-term investments (LTI)      Long-term liabilities (LTL)
Property, plant, and equipment (PPE)   Stockholders' equity (SE)
Intangible assets (IA)

**Instructions**

Classify each of the following financial statement items.

_____ Prepaid advertising               _____ Patents
_____ Equipment                         _____ Bonds payable
_____ Trademarks                        _____ Common stock
_____ Salaries and wages payable        _____ Accumulated depreciation—
_____ Income taxes payable                      equipment
_____ Retained earnings                 _____ Unearned sales revenue
_____ Accounts receivable               _____ Inventory
_____ Land (held for future use)

*Prepare assets section of balance sheet.*

**E2.3 (LO 1), AP** Suppose the following items were taken from the December 31, 2022, assets section of the **Boeing Company** balance sheet. (All dollars are in millions.)

| | | | |
|---|---|---|---|
| Inventory | $16,933 | Patents | $12,528 |
| Notes receivable—due after | | Buildings | 21,579 |
| December 31, 2023 | 5,466 | Cash | 9,215 |
| Notes receivable—due before | | Accounts receivable | 5,785 |
| December 31, 2023 | 368 | Debt investments (short-term) | 2,008 |
| Accumulated depreciation—buildings | 12,795 | | |

**Instructions**

Prepare the assets section of a classified balance sheet, listing the current assets in order of their liquidity.

*Prepare assets section of a classified balance sheet.*

**E2.4 (LO 1), AP** Suppose the following information (in thousands of dollars) is available for **H. J. Heinz Company**—famous for ketchup and other fine food products—at April 30, 2022.

| | | | |
|---|---|---|---|
| Prepaid insurance | $ 125,765 | Buildings | $4,033,369 |
| Land | 76,193 | Cash | 373,145 |
| Goodwill | 3,982,954 | Accounts receivable | 1,171,797 |
| Trademarks | 757,907 | Accumulated depreciation— | |
| Inventory | 1,237,613 | buildings | 2,131,260 |

**Instructions**

Prepare the assets section of a classified balance sheet, listing the items in proper sequence and including a statement heading.

*Prepare a classified balance sheet.*

**E2.5 (LO 1), AP** These items are taken from the financial statements of Longhorn Co. at December 31, 2022.

| | |
|---|---|
| Buildings | $105,800 |
| Accounts receivable | 12,600 |
| Prepaid insurance | 3,200 |
| Cash | 11,840 |
| Equipment | 82,400 |
| Land | 61,200 |
| Insurance expense | 780 |
| Depreciation expense | 5,300 |
| Interest expense | 2,600 |
| Common stock | 60,000 |
| Retained earnings (January 1, 2022) | 40,000 |
| Accumulated depreciation—buildings | 45,600 |
| Accounts payable | 9,500 |
| Notes payable | 93,600 |
| Accumulated depreciation—equipment | 18,720 |
| Interest payable | 3,600 |
| Service revenue | 14,700 |

**Instructions**

Prepare a classified balance sheet. Assume that $13,600 of the note payable will be paid in 2023.

*Prepare a classified balance sheet.*

**E2.6 (LO 1), AP** The following items are taken from the financial statements of Carmen Co. at December 31, 2022.

| | |
|---|---|
| Land | $195,600 |
| Accounts receivable | 21,700 |
| Supplies | 9,200 |
| Cash | 11,840 |
| Equipment | 82,400 |
| Buildings | 261,200 |
| Land improvements | 45,780 |
| Notes receivable (due in 2023) | 5,300 |
| Accumulated depreciation—land improvements | 12,600 |
| Common stock | 75,000 |
| Retained earnings (December 31, 2022) | 495,000 |
| Accumulated depreciation—buildings | 32,600 |
| Accounts payable | 9,500 |
| Mortgage payable | 93,600 |
| Accumulated depreciation—equipment | 18,720 |
| Interest payable | 3,600 |
| Income taxes payable | 14,700 |
| Patents | 46,700 |
| Investments in stock (long-term) | 71,500 |
| Debt investments (short-term) | 4,100 |

*Prepare financial statements.*

### Instructions

Prepare a classified balance sheet. Assume that $9,100 of the mortgage payable will be paid in 2023.

**E2.7 (LO 1), AP** These financial statement items are for Fairview Corporation at year-end, July 31, 2022.

| | |
|---|---:|
| Salaries and wages payable | $ 2,080 |
| Salaries and wages expense | 57,500 |
| Supplies expense | 15,600 |
| Equipment | 18,500 |
| Accounts payable | 4,100 |
| Service revenue | 66,100 |
| Rent revenue | 8,500 |
| Notes payable (due in 2025) | 1,800 |
| Common stock | 16,000 |
| Cash | 29,200 |
| Accounts receivable | 9,780 |
| Accumulated depreciation—equipment | 6,000 |
| Dividends | 4,000 |
| Depreciation expense | 4,000 |
| Retained earnings (beginning of the year) | 34,000 |

### Instructions

a. Prepare an income statement and a retained earnings statement for the year. Fairview Corporation did not issue any new stock during the year.

b. Prepare a classified balance sheet at July 31.

*Compute liquidity ratios and compare results.*

**E2.8 (LO 2), AP Nordstrom, Inc.** operates department stores in numerous states. Selected financial statement data (in millions of dollars) for a recent year follow.

| | End of Year | Beginning of Year |
|---|---:|---:|
| Cash and cash equivalents | $ 72 | $ 358 |
| Receivables (net) | 1,942 | 1,788 |
| Merchandise inventory | 900 | 956 |
| Other current assets | 303 | 259 |
| Total current assets | $3,217 | $3,361 |
| Total current liabilities | $1,601 | $1,635 |

### Instructions

a. Compute working capital and the current ratio at the beginning of the year and at the end of the year.

b. Did Nordstrom's liquidity improve or worsen during the year?

c. Using the data in the chapter, compare Nordstrom's liquidity with that of **Best Buy**.

*Compute liquidity measures and discuss findings.*

**E2.9 (LO 2), AP** The chief financial officer (CFO) of Myeneke Corporation requested that the accounting department prepare a preliminary balance sheet on December 30, 2022, so that the CFO could get an idea of how the company stood. He knows that certain debt agreements with its creditors require the company to maintain a current ratio of at least 2:1. The preliminary balance sheet is as follows.

**Myeneke Corp.**
**Balance Sheet**
**December 30, 2022**

| Current assets | | | Current liabilities | | |
|---|---:|---:|---|---:|---:|
| Cash | $25,000 | | Accounts payable | $ 20,000 | |
| Accounts receivable | 30,000 | | Salaries and wages payable | 10,000 | $ 30,000 |
| Prepaid insurance | 5,000 | $ 60,000 | Long-term liabilities | | |
| Equipment (net) | | 200,000 | Notes payable | | 80,000 |
| Total assets | | $260,000 | Total liabilities | | 110,000 |
| | | | Stockholders' equity | | |
| | | | Common stock | 100,000 | |
| | | | Retained earnings | 50,000 | 150,000 |
| | | | Total liabilities and stockholders' equity | | $260,000 |

**Instructions**

a. Calculate the current ratio and working capital based on the preliminary balance sheet.

b. Based on the results in (a), the CFO requested that $20,000 of cash be used to pay off the balance of the Accounts Payable account on December 31, 2022. Calculate the new current ratio and working capital after the company takes these actions.

c. Discuss the pros and cons of the current ratio and working capital as measures of liquidity.

d. Was it unethical for the CFO to take these steps?

**E2.10 (LO 2), AP** Suppose the following data were taken from the 2022 and 2021 financial statements of **American Eagle Outfitters**. (All numbers, including share data, are in thousands.)

*Compute and interpret solvency ratios.*

|  | **2022** | **2021** |
|---|---|---|
| Current assets | $   925,359 | $1,020,834 |
| Total assets | 1,963,676 | 1,867,680 |
| Current liabilities | 401,763 | 376,178 |
| Total liabilities | 554,645 | 527,216 |
| Net income | 179,061 | 400,019 |

**Instructions**

Perform each of the following.

a. Calculate the current ratio for each year.

b. Calculate the debt to assets ratio for each year.

c. Discuss American Eagle's solvency in 2022 versus 2021.

# Problems

**P2.1 (LO 1), AP** Suppose the following items are taken from the 2022 balance sheet of **Yahoo! Inc.** (All dollars are in millions.)

*Prepare a classified balance sheet.*

| | |
|---|---|
| Goodwill | $3,927 |
| Common stock | 6,283 |
| Equipment | 1,737 |
| Accounts payable | 152 |
| Patents | 234 |
| Stock investments (long-term) | 3,247 |
| Accounts receivable | 1,061 |
| Prepaid rent | 233 |
| Debt investments (short-term) | 1,160 |
| Retained earnings | 6,108 |
| Cash | 2,292 |
| Notes payable (long-term) | 734 |
| Unearned sales revenue | 413 |
| Accumulated depreciation—equipment | 201 |

**Instructions**

Prepare a classified balance sheet for Yahoo! Inc. as of December 31, 2022.

| Tot. current assets | $4,746 |
|---|---|
| Tot. assets | $13,690 |

*Prepare financial statements.*

**P2.2 (LO 1), AP** These items are taken from the financial statements of Martin Corporation for 2022.

| | |
|---|---:|
| Retained earnings (beginning of year) | $31,000 |
| Utilities expense | 2,000 |
| Equipment | 66,000 |
| Accounts payable | 18,300 |
| Cash | 10,100 |
| Salaries and wages payable | 3,000 |
| Common stock | 12,000 |
| Dividends | 12,000 |
| Service revenue | 68,000 |
| Prepaid insurance | 3,500 |
| Maintenance and repairs expense | 1,800 |
| Depreciation expense | 3,600 |
| Accounts receivable | 11,700 |
| Insurance expense | 2,200 |
| Salaries and wages expense | 37,000 |
| Accumulated depreciation—equipment | 17,600 |

**Instructions**

Net income $21,400
Tot. assets $73,700

Prepare an income statement, a retained earnings statement, and a classified balance sheet as of December 31, 2022.

*Prepare financial statements.*

**P2.3 (LO 1), AP** You are provided with the following information for Lazuris Enterprises, effective as of its April 30, 2022, year-end.

| | |
|---|---:|
| Accounts payable | $ 834 |
| Accounts receivable | 810 |
| Accumulated depreciation—equipment | 670 |
| Cash | 1,270 |
| Common stock | 900 |
| Cost of goods sold | 1,060 |
| Depreciation expense | 335 |
| Dividends | 325 |
| Equipment | 2,420 |
| Income tax expense | 165 |
| Income taxes payable | 135 |
| Insurance expense | 210 |
| Interest expense | 400 |
| Inventory | 967 |
| Land | 3,100 |
| Mortgage payable | 3,500 |
| Notes payable (due March 31, 2023) | 61 |
| Prepaid insurance | 60 |
| Retained earnings (beginning) | 1,600 |
| Salaries and wages expense | 700 |
| Salaries and wages payable | 222 |
| Sales revenue | 5,100 |
| Stock investments (short-term) | 1,200 |

**Instructions**

a. Net income $2,230
b. Tot. current assets $4,307
   Tot. assets $9,157

**a.** Prepare an income statement and a retained earnings statement for Lazuris Enterprises for the year ended April 30, 2022.

**b.** Prepare a classified balance sheet for Lazuris Enterprises as of April 30, 2022.

**P2.4 (LO 2), AN** Comparative financial statement data for Loeb Corporation and Bowsh Corporation, two competitors, appear below. All balance sheet data are as of December 31, 2022.

*Compute ratios; comment on relative liquidity and solvency.*

| | Loeb Corporation 2022 | Bowsh Corporation 2022 |
|---|---|---|
| Net sales | $1,800,000 | $620,000 |
| Cost of goods sold | 1,175,000 | 340,000 |
| Operating expenses | 283,000 | 98,000 |
| Interest expense | 9,000 | 3,800 |
| Income tax expense | 85,000 | 36,000 |
| Current assets | 407,200 | 190,336 |
| Plant assets (net) | 532,000 | 139,728 |
| Current liabilities | 66,325 | 33,716 |
| Long-term liabilities | 108,500 | 40,684 |

**Instructions**

a. Comment on the relative liquidity of the companies by computing working capital and the current ratio for each company for 2022.

b. Comment on the relative solvency of the companies by computing the debt to assets ratio for each company for 2022.

**P2.5 (LO 2), AP** The following are financial statements of Ohara Company.

*Compute and interpret liquidity and solvency ratios.*

**Ohara Company**
**Income Statement**
**For the Year Ended December 31, 2022**

| | |
|---|---|
| Net sales | $2,218,500 |
| Cost of goods sold | 1,012,400 |
| Selling and administrative expenses | 906,000 |
| Interest expense | 78,000 |
| Income tax expense | 69,000 |
| Net income | $ 153,100 |

**Ohara Company**
**Balance Sheet**
**December 31, 2022**

**Assets**

| | |
|---|---|
| Current assets | |
| Cash | $ 60,100 |
| Debt investments | 84,000 |
| Accounts receivable (net) | 169,800 |
| Inventory | 145,000 |
| Total current assets | 458,900 |
| Plant assets (net) | 575,300 |
| Total assets | $1,034,200 |

**Liabilities and Stockholders' Equity**

| | |
|---|---|
| Current liabilities | |
| Accounts payable | $ 160,000 |
| Income taxes payable | 35,500 |
| Total current liabilities | 195,500 |
| Bonds payable | 200,000 |
| Total liabilities | 395,500 |
| Stockholders' equity | |
| Common stock | 350,000 |
| Retained earnings | 288,700 |
| Total stockholders' equity | 638,700 |
| Total liabilities and stockholders' equity | $1,034,200 |

**Instructions**

a. Compute the following values and ratios for 2022. (We provide the results from 2021 for comparative purposes.)

1. Working capital. (2021: $160,500)

2. Current ratio. (2021: 1.65:1)

3. Debt to assets ratio. (2021: 31.0%)

b. Using your calculations from part (a), discuss changes from 2021 in liquidity and solvency.

*Compute and interpret liquidity and solvency ratios.*

**P2.6 (LO 2), AP** Writing Condensed balance sheet and income statement data for Danke Corporation are presented as follows.

**Danke Corporation**
**Balance Sheets**
**December 31**

|  | 2022 | 2021 |
|---|---|---|
| **Assets** | | |
| Cash | $ 28,000 | $ 20,000 |
| Receivables (net) | 70,000 | 62,000 |
| Other current assets | 90,000 | 73,000 |
| Long-term investments | 62,000 | 60,000 |
| Property, plant, and equipment (net) | 510,000 | 470,000 |
| Total assets | $760,000 | $685,000 |
| **Liabilities and Stockholders' Equity** | | |
| Current liabilities | $ 75,000 | $ 70,000 |
| Long-term liabilities | 80,000 | 90,000 |
| Common stock | 330,000 | 300,000 |
| Retained earnings | 275,000 | 225,000 |
| Total liabilities and stockholders' equity | $760,000 | $685,000 |

**Danke Corporation**
**Income Statements**
**For the Years Ended December 31**

|  | 2022 | 2021 |
|---|---|---|
| Sales revenue | $750,000 | $680,000 |
| Cost of goods sold | 440,000 | 400,000 |
| Operating expenses (including income taxes) | 240,000 | 220,000 |
| Net income | $ 70,000 | $ 60,000 |

**Instructions**

Compute these values and ratios for 2021 and 2022.

a. Working capital.

b. Current ratio.

c. Debt to assets ratio.

d. Based on the ratios calculated, discuss briefly the improvement or lack thereof in financial position from 2021 to 2022 of Danke Corporation.

**P2.7 (LO 2), AP** Selected financial data of two competitors, **Target** and **Walmart**, are presented here. (All dollars are in millions.) Suppose the data were taken from the 2022 financial statements of each company.

*Compute ratios and compare liquidity and solvency for two companies.*

| | Target (1/31/22) | Walmart (1/31/22) |
|---|---|---|
| | Income Statement Data for Year | |
| Net sales | $64,948 | $401,244 |
| Cost of goods sold | 44,157 | 306,158 |
| Selling and administrative expenses | 16,389 | 76,651 |
| Interest expense | 894 | 2,103 |
| Other income | 28 | 4,213 |
| Income taxes | 1,322 | 7,145 |
| Net income | $ 2,214 | $ 13,400 |

| | Target | Walmart |
|---|---|---|
| | Balance Sheet Data (End of Year) | |
| Current assets | $17,488 | $ 48,949 |
| Noncurrent assets | 26,618 | 114,480 |
| Total assets | $44,106 | $163,429 |
| Current liabilities | $10,512 | $ 55,390 |
| Long-term liabilities | 19,882 | 42,754 |
| Total stockholders' equity | 13,712 | 65,285 |
| Total liabilities and stockholders' equity | $44,106 | $163,429 |

**Instructions**

For each company, compute these values and ratios.

   **a.** Working capital.

   **b.** Current ratio.

   **c.** Debt to assets ratio.

   **d.** Compare the liquidity and solvency of the two companies.

# Expand Your Critical Thinking

## Financial Reporting Problem: Apple Inc.

**CT2.1** The financial statements of **Apple Inc.** are presented in Appendix A.

**Instructions**

Answer the following questions using the financial statements and the notes to the financial statements.

   **a.** What were Apple's total current assets at September 29, 2018, and September 30, 2017?

   **b.** Are the assets included in current assets listed in the proper order? Explain.

   **c.** How are Apple's assets classified?

   **d.** What were Apple's current liabilities at September 29, 2018, and September 30, 2017?

## Comparative Analysis Problem:
## Columbia Sportswear Company vs. Under Armour, Inc.

**CT2.2** The financial statements of **Columbia Sportswear Company** are presented in Appendix B. Financial statements of **Under Armour, Inc** are presented in Appendix C.

**Instructions**

   **a.** For each company, calculate the following values for 2018.

      **1.** Working capital.

      **2.** Current ratio.

      **3.** Debt to assets ratio.

   **b.** Based on your findings above, discuss the relative liquidity and solvency of the two companies.

## Interpreting Financial Statements

**CT2.3** Suppose the following information was reported by **Gap, Inc.**

|  | 2022 | 2021 | 2020 | 2019 | 2018 |
|---|---|---|---|---|---|
| Total assets (millions) | $7,065 | $7,985 | $7,564 | $7,838 | $8,544 |
| Working capital | $1,831 | $2,533 | $1,847 | $1,653 | $2,757 |
| Current ratio | 1.87:1 | 2.19:1 | 1.86:1 | 1.68:1 | 2.21:1 |
| Debt to assets ratio | .42:1 | .39:1 | .42:1 | .45:1 | .39:1 |

**a.** Determine the overall percentage decrease in Gap's total assets from 2018 to 2022. What was the average decrease per year?

**b.** Comment on the change in Gap's liquidity. Does working capital or the current ratio appear to provide a better indication of Gap's liquidity?

**c.** Comment on the change in Gap's solvency during this period.

## Real-World Focus

**CT2.4** You can use the Internet to identify summary liquidity, solvency, and profitability information about companies, and compare this information across companies in the same industry.

### Instructions

Select a well-known company and then go to the **Yahoo! Finance** website to locate information to answer the following questions.

**a.** What is the company's name? What was the company's current ratio and debt to equity ratio (a variation of the debt to assets ratio)?

**b.** What is the company's industry?

**c.** What is the name of a competitor? What is the competitor's current ratio and its debt to equity ratio?

**d.** Based on these measures, which company is more liquid? Which company is more solvent?

**CT2.5** The Feature Story described the dramatic effect that investment bulletin boards are having on the investment world. This exercise will allow you to evaluate a bulletin board discussing a company of your choice.

### Instructions

Go to the **Yahoo! Finance** website. Type in a company name (or use the index to find it) and then use the Conversations tab to answer the following questions.

**a.** State the nature of each of these messages (e.g., offering advice, criticizing company, predicting future results, ridiculing other people who have posted messages).

**b.** For those messages that expressed an opinion about the company, was evidence provided to support the opinion?

**c.** What effect do you think it would have on bulletin board discussions if the participants provided their actual names? Do you think this would be a good policy?

## Decision-Making Across the Organization

**CT2.6** As a financial analyst in the planning department for Erin Industries, Inc., you must develop ratios from the comparative financial statements. This information is to be used to convince creditors that, despite a slight decline in sales, Erin Industries is liquid and solvent, and it deserves their continued support.

Here are the data requested and the computations developed from the financial statements:

|  | 2022 | 2021 |
|---|---|---|
| Current ratio | 3.1 | 2.1 |
| Working capital | Up 22% | Down 7% |
| Debt to assets ratio | 0.60 | 0.70 |
| Net income | Up 32% | Down 8% |

### Instructions

Erin Industries asks you to prepare brief comments stating how each of these items supports the argument that its financial health is improving. The company wishes to use these comments to support presentation of data to its creditors. With the class divided into groups, prepare the comments as requested, giving the implications and the limitations of each item regarding Erin's financial well-being.

## Communication Activity

**CT2.7** B. P. Palmer is the chief executive officer of Future Products. Palmer is an expert engineer but a novice in accounting.

### Instructions

Write a letter to B. P. Palmer that explains (a) the three main types of ratios; (b) examples of liquidity and solvency ratios, how they are calculated, and what they measure; and (c) the bases for comparison in analyzing Future Products' financial statements.

## All About You

**CT2.8** Every company needs to plan in order to move forward. Its top management must consider where it wants the company to be in 3 to 5 years. Like a company, you need to think about where you want to be 3 to 5 years from now, and you need to start taking steps now in order to get there.

### Instructions

Provide responses to each of the following items.

a. Where would you like to be working in 3 to 5 years? Describe your plan for getting there by identifying 5 to 10 specific steps that you need to take in order to get there.

b. In order to get the job you want, you will need a résumé. Your résumé is the equivalent of a company's annual report. It needs to provide relevant and representationally faithful information about your past accomplishments so that employers can decide whether to "invest" in you. Do a search on the Internet to find a good résumé format. What are the basic elements of a résumé?

c. A company's annual report provides information about a company's accomplishments. In order for investors to use the annual report, the information must provide a faithful representation; that is, users must have faith that the information is accurate and believable. How can you provide assurance that the information on your résumé is a faithful representation of your accomplishments?

d. Prepare a résumé assuming that you have accomplished the 5 to 10 specific steps you identified in part (a). Also, provide evidence that would give assurance that the information is a faithful representation of your accomplishments.

## Considering People, Planet, and Profit

**CT2.9** Auditors provide a type of certification of corporate financial statements. Certification is used in many other aspects of business as well. For example, it plays a critical role in the sustainability movement. The February 7, 2012, issue of the *New York Times* contained an article by S. Amanda Caudill entitled "Better Lives in Better Coffee," which discusses the role of certification in the coffee business.

### Instructions

Read the article and answer the following questions.

a. The article mentions three different certification types that coffee growers can obtain from three different certification bodies. Using financial reporting as an example, what potential problems might the existence of multiple certification types present to coffee purchasers?

b. According to the author, which certification is most common among coffee growers? What are the possible reasons for this?

c. What social and environmental benefits are coffee certifications trying to achieve? Are there also potential financial benefits to the parties involved?

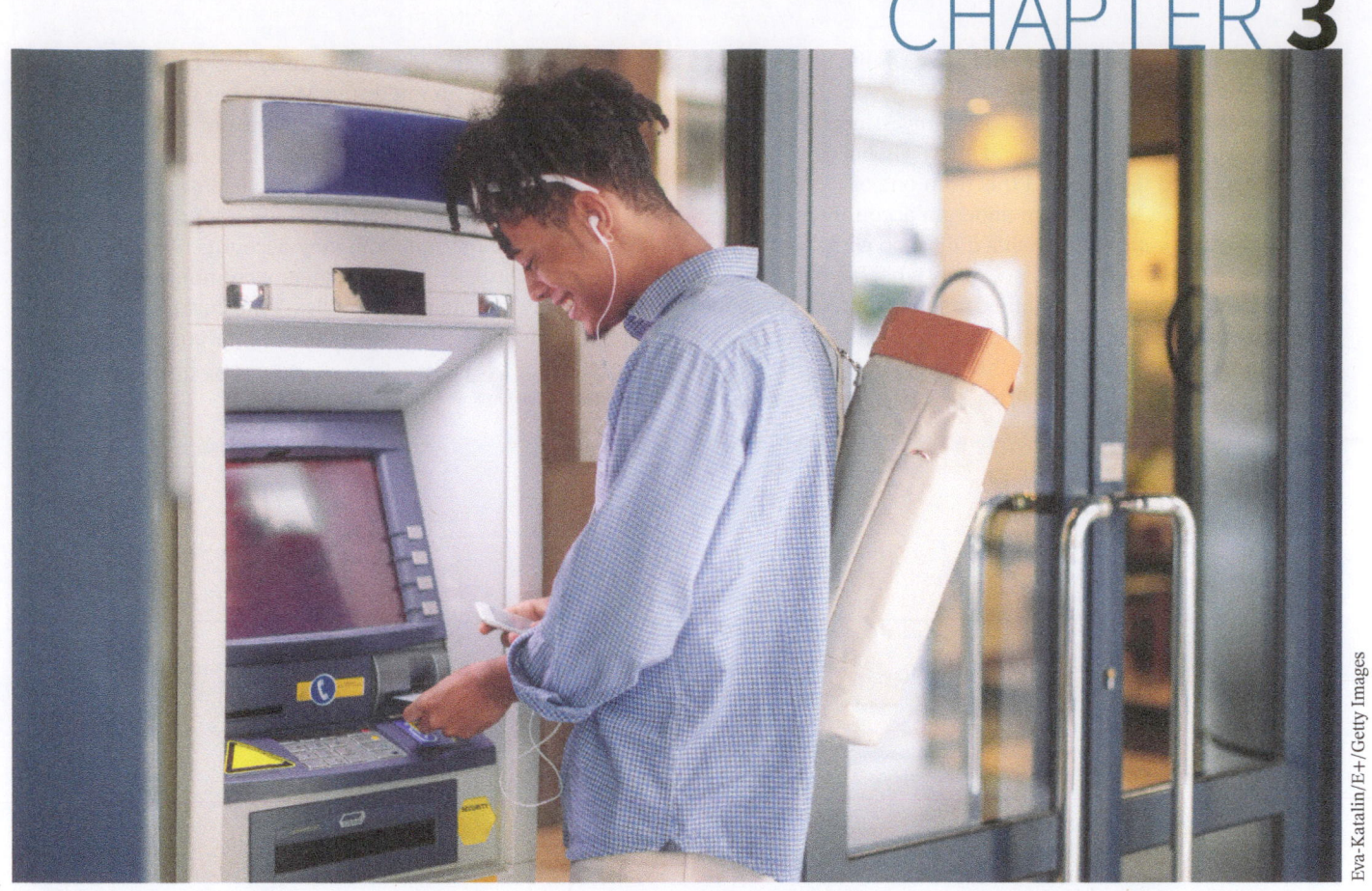

## CHAPTER 3

Eva-Katalin/E+/Getty Images

# The Accounting Information System

## Chapter Preview

As indicated in the Feature Story, a reliable information system is a necessity for any company. The purpose of this chapter is to explain and illustrate the features of an accounting information system.

## Feature Story

### Accidents Happen

How organized are you financially? Take a short quiz. Answer yes or no to each question:

- Does your wallet contain so many cash machine receipts that you've been declared a walking fire hazard?

- Do you wait until your debit card is denied before checking the status of your funds?

- Do you verify the accuracy of your bank account about as often as you clean the space behind your refrigerator?

If you think it is hard to keep track of the many transactions that make up *your* life, imagine how difficult it is for a big corporation to do so. Not only that, but now consider how important it is for a big company to have good accounting records, especially if it has control of *your* life savings. **MF Global Holdings Ltd** was such a company. As a large investment broker, it held billions of dollars of investments for clients. If you had your life savings invested at MF Global, you might be slightly displeased if you heard this from one of its representatives: "You know, I kind of remember an account for someone with a name like yours—now what did we do with that?"

Unfortunately, that is almost exactly what happened to MF Global's clients shortly before it filed for bankruptcy. During the days immediately following the bankruptcy filing, regulators and auditors struggled to piece things together. In the words of one regulator, "Their books are a disaster . . . we're trying to

figure out what numbers are real numbers." One company that considered buying an interest in MF Global walked away from the deal because it "couldn't get a sense of what was on the balance sheet." That company said the information that should have been instantly available instead took days to produce.

It now appears that MF Global did not properly segregate customer accounts from company accounts. And, because of its sloppy recordkeeping, customers were not protected when the company had financial troubles. Total customer losses were approximately $1 billion. As you can see, accounting matters!

**Source:** S. Patterson and A. Lucchetti, "Inside the Hunt for MF Global Cash," *Wall Street Journal Online* (November 11, 2011).

## Chapter Outline

| LEARNING OBJECTIVES | REVIEW | PRACTICE |
|---|---|---|
| **LO 1** Discuss financial reporting concepts. | • The standard-setting environment<br>• Qualities of useful information<br>• Assumptions in financial reporting<br>• Principles in financial reporting<br>• Cost constraint | **DO IT! 1** Financial Accounting Concepts and Principles |
| **LO 2** Analyze the effect of business transactions on the basic accounting equation. | • Accounting transactions<br>• Analyzing transactions<br>• Summary of transactions<br>• Preparing financial statements | **DO IT! 2a** Transaction Analysis<br>**DO IT! 2b** Financial Statement Preparation |

**Go to the Review and Practice section at the end of the chapter for a targeted summary and exercises with solutions.**

**Visit WileyPLUS for additional tutorials and practice opportunities.**

# Financial Reporting Concepts

### LEARNING OBJECTIVE 1
Discuss financial reporting concepts.

In Chapters 1 and 2, you learned about the four financial statements and some basic ways to interpret those statements. Now we will discuss concepts that underlie these financial statements. It would be unwise to make business decisions based on financial statements without understanding the implications of these concepts.

# The Standard-Setting Environment

How does **Best Buy** decide on the type of financial information to disclose? What format should it use? How should it measure assets, liabilities, revenues, and expenses? Accounting professionals at Best Buy and all other U.S. companies get guidance from a set of accounting standards that have authoritative support, referred to as **generally accepted accounting principles (GAAP)**.

Standard-setting bodies, in consultation with the accounting profession and the business community, determine these accounting standards.

- The **Securities and Exchange Commission (SEC)** is the agency of the U.S. government that oversees U.S. financial markets and accounting standard-setting bodies.

- The **Financial Accounting Standards Board (FASB)** is the primary accounting standard-setting body in the United States.

- The **International Accounting Standards Board (IASB)** issues standards called **International Financial Reporting Standards (IFRS)**, which have been adopted by many countries outside of the United States (see **International Note**). Today, the FASB and IASB are working closely together to minimize the differences in their standards. Foreign companies that wish to have their shares traded on U.S. stock exchanges no longer have to prepare reports that conform with GAAP, as long as their reports conform with IFRS.

- The **Public Company Accounting Oversight Board (PCAOB)** determines auditing standards and reviews the performance of auditing firms.

> **International Note**
>
> Over 115 countries use international standards. For example, all countries in the European Union follow IFRS.

## International Insight

Pool Interagences/
Gamma-Rapho/
Getty Images

### The Korean Discount

If you think that accounting standards don't matter, consider past events in South Korea. For many years, international investors complained that the financial reports of South Korean companies were inadequate and inaccurate. Accounting practices there often resulted in huge differences between stated revenues and actual revenues. Because investors did not have faith in the accuracy of the numbers, they were unwilling to pay as much for the shares of these companies relative to shares of comparable companies in different countries. This difference in share price was often referred to as the "Korean discount."

In response, Korean regulators adopted international accounting standards. This change was motivated by a desire to "make the country's businesses more transparent" in order to build investor confidence and spur economic growth. Many other Asian countries, including China, India, and Japan, have either adopted international standards or created standards that are based on the international standards.

**Source:** Evan Ramstad, "End to 'Korea Discount'?" *Wall Street Journal* (March 16, 2007).

**What is meant by the phrase "make the country's businesses more transparent"? Why would increasing transparency spur economic growth? (Go to WileyPLUS for this answer and additional questions.)**

# Qualities of Useful Information

Recently, the FASB and IASB completed the first phase of a joint project in which they developed a conceptual framework to serve as the basis for future accounting standards. The framework begins by stating that the primary objective of financial reporting is to provide financial information that is **useful** to investors and creditors for making decisions about providing capital. According to the FASB, useful information should possess two fundamental qualities, relevance and faithful representation, as shown in **Illustration 3.1**.

**ILLUSTRATION 3.1**
**Fundamental qualities of useful information**

**Relevance** Accounting information has **relevance** if it would make a difference in a business decision. Information is considered relevant if it provides information that has **predictive value**, that is, helps provide accurate expectations about the future, and has **confirmatory value**, that is, confirms or corrects prior expectations. **Materiality** is a company-specific aspect of relevance. An item is material when its **size** makes it likely to influence the decision of an investor or creditor.

**Faithful Representation** **Faithful representation** means that information accurately depicts what really happened. To provide a faithful representation, information must be **complete** (nothing important has been omitted), **neutral** (is not biased toward one position or another), and **free from error**.

## Enhancing Qualities

In addition to the two fundamental qualities, the FASB and IASB also describe a number of enhancing qualities of useful information. These include **comparability**, **verifiability**, **timeliness**, and **understandability**.

- In accounting, **comparability** results when different companies use the same accounting principles.

- Another type of comparability is consistency. **Consistency** means that a company uses the same accounting principles and methods from year to year.

- Information is **verifiable** if independent observers, using the same methods, obtain similar results. As noted in Chapter 1, certified public accountants (CPAs) perform audits of financial statements to verify their accuracy.

- For accounting information to have relevance, it must be **timely**. That is, it must be available to decision-makers before it loses its capacity to influence decisions. The SEC requires that large public companies provide their annual reports to investors within 60 days of their year-end.

- Information has the quality of **understandability** if it is presented in a clear and concise fashion, so that reasonably informed users of that information can interpret it and comprehend its meaning.

## Accounting Across the Organization

iStock.com/Skip Odonnell

### What Do These Companies Have in Common?

Another issue related to comparability is the accounting time period. An accounting period that is one-year long is called a **fiscal year**. But a fiscal year need not match the calendar year. For example, a company could **end** its fiscal year on April 30 rather than on December 31.

Why do companies choose the particular year-ends that they do? For example, why doesn't every company use December 31 as its accounting year-end? Many companies choose to end their accounting year when inventory or operations are at a low point. This is advantageous because compiling accounting information requires much time and effort by managers, so they would rather do it when they aren't as busy operating the business. Also, inventory is easier and less costly to count when its volume is low.

Some companies whose year-ends differ from December 31 are **Delta Air Lines**, June 30; **The Walt Disney Company**, September 30; and **Dunkin' Donuts, Inc.**, October 31. In the notes to its financial statements, **Best Buy** states that its accounting year-end is the Saturday nearest the end of January.

**What problems might Best Buy's year-end create for analysts? (Go to WileyPLUS for this answer and additional questions.)**

# Assumptions in Financial Reporting

To develop accounting standards, the FASB relies on some key assumptions, as shown in **Illustration 3.2** (see **Ethics Note**). These include assumptions about the monetary unit, economic entity, periodicity, and going concern.

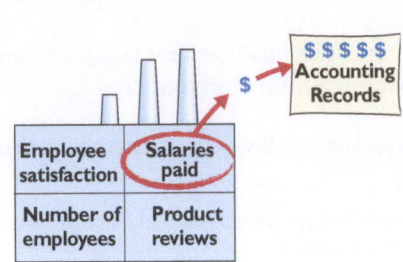

**Monetary Unit Assumption**   The **monetary unit assumption** requires that only those things that can be expressed in money are included in the accounting records. This means that certain important information needed by investors, creditors, and managers, such as customer satisfaction, is not reported in the financial statements. This assumption relies on the monetary unit remaining relatively stable in value.

**Economic Entity Assumption**   The **economic entity assumption** states that every economic entity can be separately identified and accounted for. In order to assess a company's performance and financial position accurately, it is important to not blur company transactions with personal transactions (especially those of its managers) or transactions of other companies.

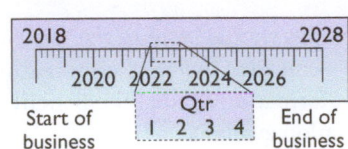

**Periodicity Assumption**   Notice that the income statement, retained earnings statement, and statement of cash flows all cover periods of one year, and the balance sheet is prepared at the end of each year. The **periodicity assumption** states that the life of a business can be divided into artificial time periods and that useful reports covering those periods can be prepared for the business.

**Going Concern Assumption**   The **going concern assumption** states that the business will remain in operation for the foreseeable future. Of course, many businesses do fail, but in general it is reasonable to assume that the business will continue operating.

**ILLUSTRATION 3.2**
**Key assumptions in financial reporting**

# Principles in Financial Reporting

## Measurement Principles

GAAP generally uses one of two measurement principles, the historical cost principle or the fair value principle. Selection of which principle to follow generally relates to trade-offs between relevance and faithful representation.

**Historical Cost Principle**   The **historical cost principle** (or cost principle) dictates that companies record assets at their cost. This is true not only at the time the asset is purchased but also over the time the asset is held. For example, if land that was purchased for $30,000 increases in value to $40,000, it continues to be reported at $30,000.

**Fair Value Principle** The **fair value principle** indicates that assets and liabilities should be reported at fair value (the price that would be received if an asset was sold or the amount that would be required to be paid to settle a liability). Fair value information may be more useful than historical cost for certain types of assets and liabilities. For example, certain investment securities are reported at fair value because market price information is often readily available for these types of assets.

In choosing between cost and fair value, the FASB uses two qualities that make accounting information useful for decision-making—relevance and faithful representation.

- In determining which measurement principle to use, the FASB weighs the factual nature of cost figures versus the relevance of fair value.

- In general, the FASB indicates that most assets must follow the historical cost principle because market values may not be representationally faithful.

- Only in situations where assets are actively traded, such as investment securities, is the fair value principle applied.

## Full Disclosure Principle

The **full disclosure principle** requires that companies disclose all circumstances and events that would make a difference to financial statement users. If an important item cannot reasonably be reported directly in one of the four types of financial statements, then it should be discussed in notes that accompany the statements.

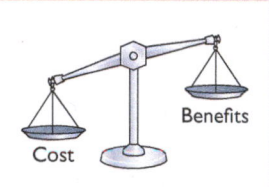

# Cost Constraint

Providing information is costly. In deciding whether companies should be required to provide a certain type of information, accounting standard-setters consider the **cost constraint**. It weighs the cost that companies will incur to provide the information against the benefit that financial statement users will gain from having the information available.

---

**ACTION PLAN**

- **Understand the need for conceptual guidelines in accounting.**

- **List the characteristics of useful financial information.**

- **Review the assumptions, principles, and constraint that comprise the guidelines in accounting.**

## DO IT! 1 | Financial Accounting Concepts and Principles

The following items guide the FASB when it creates accounting standards.

| | |
|---|---|
| Relevance | Periodicity assumption |
| Faithful representation | Going concern assumption |
| Comparability | Historical cost principle |
| Consistency | Full disclosure principle |
| Monetary unit assumption | Materiality |
| Economic entity assumption | |

Match each item above with a description below.

1. _____ The ability to easily evaluate one company's results relative to another's.

2. _____ A belief that a company will continue to operate for the foreseeable future.

3. _____ The judgment concerning whether an item is large enough to matter to decision-makers.

4. _____ The reporting of all information that would make a difference to financial statement users.

5. _____ The practice of preparing financial statements at regular intervals.

6. _____ The quality of information that indicates the information makes a difference in a decision.

7. _____ A belief that items should be reported on the balance sheet at the price that was paid to acquire the item.

8. _____ A company's use of the same accounting principles and methods from year to year.

9. _____ The requirement that a company must keep separate accounting records from personal accounting records.

10. _____ The desire to minimize errors and bias in financial statements.

11. _____ Reporting only those things that can be measured in dollars.

### Solution

1. Comparability
2. Going concern assumption
3. Materiality
4. Full disclosure principle
5. Periodicity assumption
6. Relevance
7. Historical cost principle
8. Consistency
9. Economic entity assumption
10. Faithful representation
11. Monetary unit assumption

Related exercise material: **BE3.2, BE3.3, BE3.4, BE3.5, DO IT! 3.1, E3.1, and E3.2.**

# Using the Accounting Equation to Analyze Transactions

**LEARNING OBJECTIVE 2**

Analyze the effect of business transactions on the basic accounting equation.

The system of collecting and processing transaction data and communicating financial information to decision-makers is known as the **accounting information system**. Factors that shape an accounting information system include:

- The nature of the company's business.
- The types of transactions.
- The size of the company.
- The volume of data.
- The information demands of management and others.

Most businesses use computerized accounting systems—sometimes referred to as electronic data processing (EDP) systems. These systems handle all the steps involved in the recording process, from initial data entry to preparation of the financial statements. In order to remain competitive, companies continually improve their accounting systems to provide accurate and timely data for decision-making. For example, in an annual report, **Tootsie Roll Industries** stated, "We also invested in additional processing and data storage hardware during the year. We view information technology as a key strategic tool, and are committed to deploying leading-edge technology in this area." In addition, many companies have upgraded their accounting information systems in response to the requirements of Sarbanes-Oxley.

In this chapter, in order to emphasize the underlying concepts and principles, we focus on a manual accounting system. The accounting concepts and principles do not change whether a system is computerized or manual.

# Accounting Transactions

To use an accounting information system, you need to know which economic events to recognize (record). Not all events are recorded and reported in the financial statements. For example, suppose **General Motors** hired a new employee and purchased a new computer. Are these events entered in its accounting records? The first event would not be recorded, but the second event would.

- We call economic events that require recording in the financial statements **accounting transactions**.
- An accounting transaction occurs when assets, liabilities, or stockholders' equity items change as a result of some economic event.
- The purchase of a computer by **General Motors**, the payment of rent by **Microsoft**, and the sale of a multi-day guided trip by Sierra Corporation are examples of events that change a company's assets, liabilities, or stockholders' equity.

**Illustration 3.3** summarizes the decision process companies use to decide whether or not to record economic events.

**ILLUSTRATION 3.3**  **Transaction identification process**

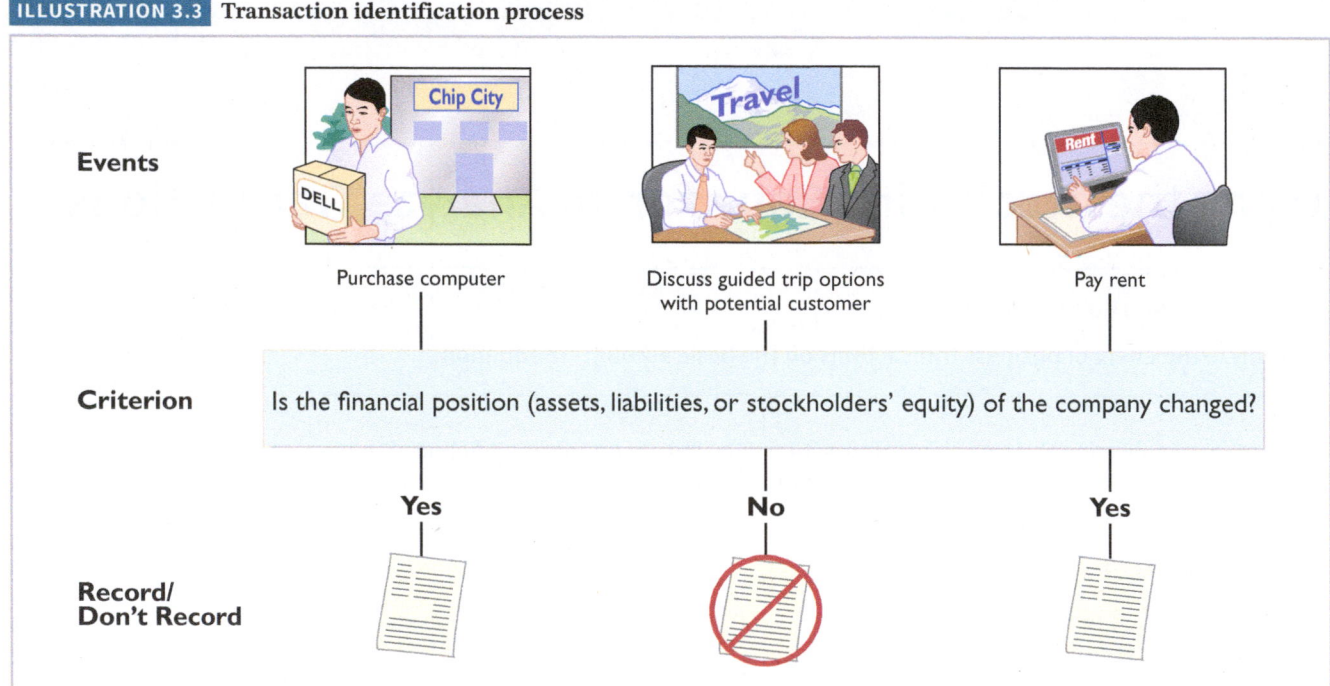

# Analyzing Transactions

**Decision Tools**

The accounting equation is used to determine if an accounting transaction has occurred.

In Chapter 1, you learned the basic accounting equation:

$$\textbf{Assets} = \textbf{Liabilities} + \textbf{Stockholders' Equity}$$

In this chapter, you will learn how to analyze transactions in terms of their effect on assets, liabilities, and stockholders' equity. **Transaction analysis** is the process of identifying the specific effects of economic events on the accounting equation (see **Decision Tools**).

**The accounting equation must always balance.** Each transaction has a dual (double-sided) effect on the equation. For example, if an individual asset is increased, there must be a corresponding:

- Decrease in another asset, *or*
- Increase in a specific liability, *or*
- Increase in stockholders' equity.

Two or more items could be affected when an asset is increased. For example, if a company purchases a computer for $10,000 by paying $6,000 in cash and signing a note for $4,000, one asset (equipment) increases $10,000, another asset (cash) decreases $6,000, and a liability (notes payable) increases $4,000. The result is that the accounting equation remains in balance—assets increased by a net $4,000 and liabilities increased by $4,000, as the following shows.

| Assets | = | Liabilities | + | Stockholders' Equity |
|---|---|---|---|---|
| +$10,000 | | +$4,000 | | |
| − 6,000 | | | | |
| $ 4,000 | = | $4,000 | | |

Chapter 1 presented the financial statements for Sierra Corporation for its first month. You should review those financial statements at this time. To illustrate how economic events affect the accounting equation, we will examine events affecting Sierra during its first month.

In order to analyze the transactions for Sierra, we will expand the basic accounting equation to better illustrate the impact of transactions on stockholders' equity.

- Recall from the balance sheets in Chapters 1 and 2 that stockholders' equity is comprised of two parts: common stock and retained earnings.
- Common stock is affected when the company issues new shares of stock in exchange for cash.
- Retained earnings is increased when the company recognizes revenue, and decreased when the company incurs expenses or pays dividends.

**Illustration 3.4** shows the expanded equation.

**ILLUSTRATION 3.4**   **Expanded accounting equation**

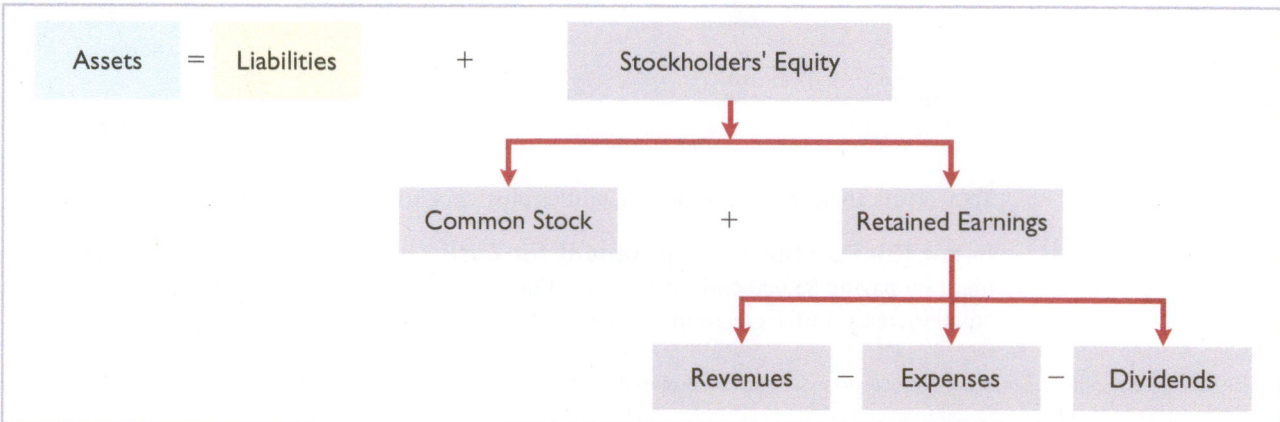

To demonstrate the effect that each transaction has on particular financial statements, we analyze each of Sierra's transactions using the tabular analysis shown in **Illustration 3.5**.

- Amounts that are reported on the balance sheet are shaded in yellow, income statement items in blue, and dividends (shown on the statement of retained earnings) in gray.
- Explanations for income statement items are reported in the blue section on the right-hand side.
- The green section on the left-hand side indicates whether cash flows increased, decreased, or were not affected.

**ILLUSTRATION 3.5** Tabular analysis of transactions

| CASH FLOW | BALANCE SHEET | | | | | | | INCOME STATEMENT |
|---|---|---|---|---|---|---|---|---|
| | Assets | = | Liabilities | + | Stockholders' Equity | | | |
| | | | | | | Retained Earnings | | |
| | | | | | Common Stock + | Rev. – | Exp. – Div. | |

### Event (1). Investment of Cash by Stockholders

On October 1, cash of $10,000 is invested in the business by investors in exchange for $10,000 of common stock. This event is an accounting transaction that results in an increase in both assets and stockholders' equity.

**Basic Analysis:** The asset Cash is increased $10,000; stockholders' equity (specifically Common Stock) is increased $10,000.

| CASH FLOW | BALANCE SHEET | | | | | | | INCOME STATEMENT |
|---|---|---|---|---|---|---|---|---|
| | Assets | = | Liabilities | + | Stockholders' Equity | | | |
| | | | | | | Retained Earnings | | |
| | Cash | = | | | Common Stock + | Rev. – | Exp. – Div. | |
| ⬆ $10,000 (1) | +$10,000 | | | | +$10,000 | | | No effect |

The equation is in balance after the issuance of common stock. Keeping track of the source of each change in stockholders' equity is essential for later accounting activities. In particular, items recorded in the revenue and expense columns are used for the calculation of net income.

### Event (2). Note Issued in Exchange for Cash

On October 1, Sierra borrowed $5,000 from Castle Bank by signing a 3-month, 12%, $5,000 note payable. This transaction results in an equal increase in assets and liabilities. The specific effect of this transaction and the cumulative effect of the first two transactions are as follows.

**Basic Analysis:** The asset Cash is increased $5,000; the liability Notes Payable is increased $5,000.

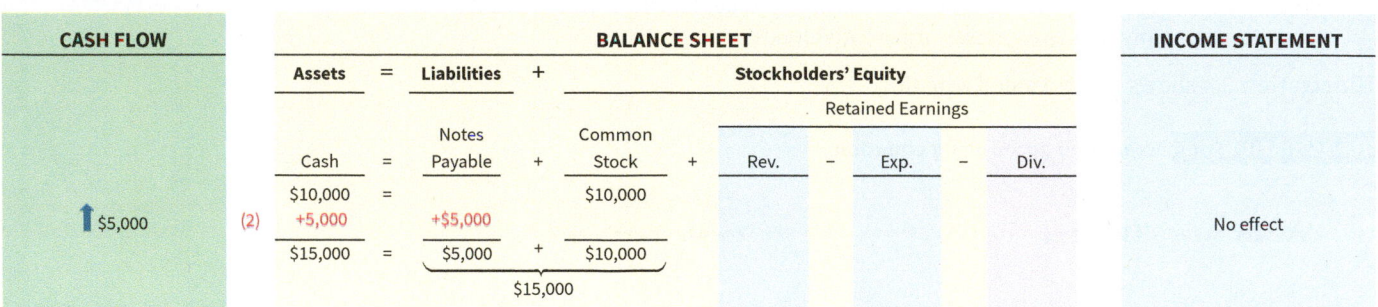

Total assets are now $15,000, and liabilities plus stockholders' equity also total $15,000.

### Event (3). Purchase of Equipment for Cash

On October 2, Sierra purchased equipment by paying $5,000 cash to Superior Equipment Sales Co. This transaction results in an equal increase and decrease in Sierra's assets.

**Basic Analysis:** The asset Equipment is increased $5,000; the asset Cash is decreased $5,000.

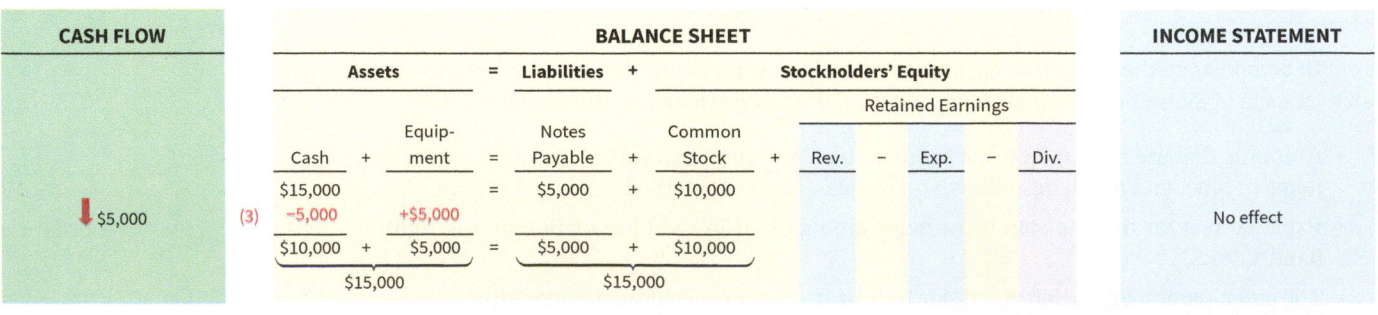

The balance in total assets did not change; one asset account decreased by the same amount that another increased. The total assets are still $15,000, and liabilities plus stockholders' equity also still total $15,000.

### Event (4). Receipt of Cash in Advance from Customer  On October 2, Sierra received a $1,200 cash advance from R. Knox, a client. Sierra received cash (an asset) for guide services for multi-day trips that it expects to complete in the future.

- Although Sierra received cash, **it does not record revenue until it has performed the work**.
- In some industries, such as the magazine and airline industries, customers are expected to prepay. These companies have a liability to the customer until they deliver the magazines or provide the flight.
- When the company eventually provides the product or service, it records the revenue.

Since Sierra received cash prior to performance of the service, Sierra has a liability for the work due.

**Basic Analysis:** The asset Cash is increased $1,200; the liability Unearned Service Revenue is increased $1,200 because the service has not been performed yet. That is, when an advance payment is received, unearned revenue (a liability) should be recorded in order to recognize the obligation that exists.

| CASH FLOW | | BALANCE SHEET | | | | | | | | | | INCOME STATEMENT |
|---|---|---|---|---|---|---|---|---|---|---|---|---|
| | | **Assets** | = | **Liabilities** | + | | | **Stockholders' Equity** | | | | |
| | | | | | | | | | Retained Earnings | | | |
| | | Cash + Equip-ment = | Notes Pay. + | Unearned Serv. Rev. + | Common Stock + | Rev. | – | Exp. | – | Div. | | |
| | | $10,000 + $5,000 = $5,000 | | | + $10,000 | | | | | | | |
| ↑$1,200 | (4) | +1,200 | | +$1,200 | | | | | | | | No effect |
| | | $11,200 + $5,000 = $5,000 + | | $1,200 + | $10,000 | | | | | | | |
| | | $16,200 | | $16,200 | | | | | | | | |

### Event (5). Services Performed for Cash  On October 3, Sierra received $10,000 in cash (an asset) from Copa Company for guide services performed for a corporate event. Guide service is the principal revenue-producing activity of Sierra. **Revenue increases stockholders' equity.** This transaction, then, increases both assets and stockholders' equity.

**Basic Analysis:** The asset Cash is increased $10,000; the revenue account Service Revenue is increased $10,000.

| CASH FLOW | | BALANCE SHEET | | | | | | | | | | INCOME STATEMENT |
|---|---|---|---|---|---|---|---|---|---|---|---|---|
| | | **Assets** | = | **Liabilities** | + | | | **Stockholders' Equity** | | | | |
| | | | | | | | | | Retained Earnings | | | |
| | | Cash + Equip-ment = | Notes Pay. + | Unearned Serv. Rev. + | Common Stock + | Rev. | – | Exp. | – | Div. | | |
| | | $11,200 + $5,000 = $5,000 + | | $1,200 + | $10,000 | | | | | | | |
| ↑$10,000 | (5) | +10,000 | | | | +$10,000 | | | | | | Service Revenue |
| | | $21,200 + $5,000 = $5,000 + | | $1,200 + | $10,000 + | $10,000 | | | | | | |
| | | $26,200 | | $26,200 | | | | | | | | |

Often companies perform services "on account." That is, they perform services for which they are paid at a later date.

- Revenue, however, is recorded when services are performed.
- Therefore, revenues would increase when services are performed, even though cash has not been received.
- Instead of receiving cash, the company receives a different type of asset, an **account receivable**.
- Accounts receivable represent the right to receive payment at a later date.

Suppose that Sierra had performed these services on account rather than for cash. This event would be reported using the accounting equation as:

| Assets | = | Liabilities | + | Stockholders' Equity | |
|---|---|---|---|---|---|
| Accounts Receivable = | | | | Revenues | |
| +$10,000 | | | | +$10,000 | Service Revenue |

Later, when Sierra collects the $10,000 from the customer, Accounts Receivable decreases by $10,000, and Cash increases by $10,000.

| | Assets | | = | Liabilities | + | Stockholders' Equity |
|---|---|---|---|---|---|---|
| | | Accounts | | | | |
| Cash | + | Receivable | | | | |
| +$10,000 | | −$10,000 | | | | |

Note that in this case, revenues are not affected by the collection of cash. Instead Sierra records an exchange of one asset (Accounts Receivable) for a different asset (Cash).

---

**ACTION PLAN**

- **Analyze the tabular analysis to determine the nature and effect of each transaction.**
- **Keep the accounting equation in balance.**
- **Remember that a change in an asset will require a change in another asset, in a liability, or in stockholders' equity.**

## DO IT! 2a | Transaction Analysis

**Part 1:** A tabular analysis of the transactions made by Roberta Mendez & Co., a certified public accounting firm, for the month of August is shown below. Each change in revenues or expenses is explained.

| | Assets | | = | Liabilities + | | Stockholders' Equity | | | |
|---|---|---|---|---|---|---|---|---|---|
| | | | | Accounts | | Common | | Retained Earnings | |
| | Cash | + Equipment | = | Payable | + | Stock | + Revenues | − Expenses | |
| 1. | +$25,000 | | | | | +$25,000 | | | |
| 2. | | +$7,000 | | +$7,000 | | | | | |
| 3. | +8,000 | | | | | | +$8,000 | | Service Revenue |
| 4. | −850 | | | −850 | | | | | |
| | $32,150 + | $7,000 | = | $6,150 | + | $25,000 + | $8,000 | | |
| | $39,150 | | | | | $39,150 | | | |

Describe each transaction that occurred for the month.

### Solution

1. The company issued shares of stock to stockholders for $25,000 cash.
2. The company purchased $7,000 of equipment on account.
3. The company received $8,000 of cash in exchange for services performed.
4. The company paid $850 for accounts payable due.

Related exercise material: **BE3.6, BE3.7, BE3.8, BE3.9, BE3.10, BE3.11, DO IT! 3.2, E3.3, E3.4, E3.5, and E3.6.**

---

**Event (6). Payment of Rent** On October 3, Sierra paid its office rent for the month of October in cash, $900. This rent payment is a transaction that results in a decrease in an asset, cash, as well as a decrease in stockholders' equity (see **Helpful Hint**).

Rent is a cost incurred by Sierra in its effort to generate revenues.

- It is treated as an expense because it pertains only to the current month.
- **Expenses decrease stockholders' equity.**

Sierra records the rent payment by decreasing cash and increasing expenses to maintain the balance of the accounting equation.

**HELPFUL HINT**

Since expenses reduce stockholders' equity, we must enter expenses as negatives.

- Note that a minus sign is placed in front of the $900 rent expense. **Since expenses reduce stockholders' equity, we must enter expenses as negatives.**
- This keeps the basic accounting equation in balance.

**Basic Analysis:** The expense account Rent Expense is increased $900 because the payment pertains only to the current month; the asset Cash is decreased $900.

| CASH FLOW | | | | BALANCE SHEET | | | | | | | | | | | INCOME STATEMENT |
|---|---|---|---|---|---|---|---|---|---|---|---|---|---|---|---|
| | | | **Assets** | = | | **Liabilities** | + | | | **Stockholders' Equity** | | | | | |
| | | | | | | | | | | | | Retained Earnings | | | |
| | | | Equip- | | Notes | Unearned | | Common | | | | | | | |
| | | Cash + | ment | = | Pay. + | Serv. Rev. | + | Stock | + | Rev. | – | Exp. | – | Div. | |
| | | $21,200 + | $5,000 | = | $5,000 + | $1,200 | + | $10,000 | + | $10,000 | | | | | |
| ↓$900 | (6) | −900 | | | | | | | | | | −$900 | | | Rent Expense |
| | | $20,300 + | $5,000 | = | $5,000 + | $1,200 | + | $10,000 | + | $10,000 | – | $900 | | | |
| | | $25,300 | | | | | | $25,300 | | | | | | | |

### Event (7). Purchase of Insurance Policy for Cash

On October 4, Sierra paid $600 for a one-year insurance policy that will expire next year on September 30. Payments of expenses that will benefit more than one accounting period are identified as assets called prepaid expenses or prepayments.

**Basic Analysis:** The asset Cash is decreased $600; the asset Prepaid Insurance is increased $600.

| CASH FLOW | | | | | BALANCE SHEET | | | | | | | | | | | INCOME STATEMENT |
|---|---|---|---|---|---|---|---|---|---|---|---|---|---|---|---|---|
| | | | | **Assets** | | = | | **Liabilities** | + | | | **Stockholders' Equity** | | | | |
| | | | | | | | | Unearned | | | | Retained Earnings | | | | |
| | | | Prepaid | Equip- | | Notes | Serv. | | Common | | | | | | | |
| | | Cash + | Insurance + | ment | = | Pay. + | Rev. | + | Stock | + | Rev. | – | Exp. | – | Div. | |
| | | $20,300 | | + $5,000 | = | $5,000 + | $1,200 | + | $10,000 | + | $10,000 | – | $900 | | | |
| ↓$600 | (7) | −600 | +$600 | | | | | | | | | | | | | No effect |
| | | $19,700 + | $600 | + $5,000 | = | $5,000 + | $1,200 | + | $10,000 | + | $10,000 | – | $900 | | | |
| | | | $25,300 | | | | | | $25,300 | | | | | | | |

The balance in total assets did not change; one asset account decreased by the same amount that another increased.

### Event (8). Purchase of Supplies on Account

On October 5, Sierra purchased an estimated three months of supplies on account from Aero Supply for $2,500. In this case, "on account" means that the company receives goods or services that it will pay for at a later date. This transaction increases both an asset (Supplies) and a liability (Accounts Payable).

**Basic Analysis:** The asset Supplies is increased $2,500; the liability Accounts Payable is increased $2,500.

| CASH FLOW | | | | | | BALANCE SHEET | | | | | | | | | | | | INCOME STATEMENT |
|---|---|---|---|---|---|---|---|---|---|---|---|---|---|---|---|---|---|---|
| | | | | **Assets** | | = | | **Liabilities** | | + | | | **Stockholders' Equity** | | | | | |
| | | | | | | | | | | | | | | Retained Earnings | | | | |
| | | | | Prepd. | Equip- | | Notes | Accounts | Unearned | | Common | | | | | | | |
| | | Cash + | Supplies + | Insur. + | ment | = | Pay. + | Payable | + Serv. Rev. + | | Stock | + | Rev. | – | Exp. | – | Div. | |
| | | $19,700 | | + $600 | + $5,000 | = | $5,000 | | + $1,200 | + | $10,000 | + | $10,000 | – | $900 | | | |
| No effect | (8) | | +$2,500 | | | | | +$2,500 | | | | | | | | | | No effect |
| | | $19,700 + | $2,500 + | $600 | + $5,000 | = | $5,000 + | $2,500 + | $1,200 | + | $10,000 | + | $10,000 | – | $900 | | | |
| | | | $27,800 | | | | | | $27,800 | | | | | | | | | |

### Event (9). Hiring of New Employees

On October 9, Sierra hired four new employees to begin work on October 15. Each employee will receive a weekly salary of $500 for a five-day work week, payable every two weeks. Employees will receive their first paychecks on October 26. On the date Sierra hires the employees, there is no effect on the accounting equation because the assets, liabilities, and stockholders' equity of the company have not changed.

**Basic Analysis :** An accounting transaction has not occurred. There is only an agreement that the employees will begin work on October 15. (See Event (11) for the first payment.)

**HELPFUL HINT**

Since dividends reduce stockholders' equity, we must enter dividends as negatives. Thus, we place a minus sign in front of the $500 dividend, as shown in the analysis.

**Event (10). Payment of Dividend** On October 20, Sierra paid a $500 cash dividend. **Dividends are a reduction of stockholders' equity but not an expense** (see **Helpful Hint**). Dividends are not included in the calculation of net income. Instead, a dividend is a distribution of the company's assets to its stockholders, which is presented in the retained earnings statement.

Note that a minus sign is placed in front of the $500 dividend.

- **Since dividends reduce stockholders' equity, we must enter dividends as negative.**
- This keeps the basic accounting equation in balance.

**Basic Analysis:** The Dividends account is increased $500; the asset Cash is decreased $500.

| CASH FLOW | | | BALANCE SHEET | | | | | | | | | | | | | | | INCOME STATEMENT |
|---|---|---|---|---|---|---|---|---|---|---|---|---|---|---|---|---|---|---|
| | | | Assets | | | | = | Liabilities | | | + | Stockholders' Equity | | | | | | |
| | | | | | | | | | | | | | | Retained Earnings | | | | |
| | | | Cash | + Supplies + | Prepd. Insur. + | Equip- ment | = | Notes Pay. + | Accts. Pay. + | Unearned Serv. Rev. + | | Common Stock + | Rev. | − | Exp. | − | Div. | |
| | | | $19,700 + | $2,500 + | $600 + | $5,000 | = | $5,000 + | $2,500 + | $1,200 + | | $10,000 + | $10,000 | − | $900 | | | No effect |
| ↓ $500 | (10) | | −500 | | | | | | | | | | | | | | −$500 | |
| | | | $19,200 + | $2,500 + | $600 + | $5,000 | = | $5,000 + | $2,500 + | $1,200 + | | $10,000 + | $10,000 | − | $900 | − | $500 | |
| | | | | | $27,300 | | | | | | | | $27,300 | | | | | |

**Event (11). Payment of Cash for Employee Salaries** Employees have worked two weeks, earning $4,000 in salaries, which were paid on October 26. Salaries and Wages Expense is an expense that reduces stockholders' equity. In this transaction, both assets and stockholders' equity are reduced.

**Basic Analysis:** The asset Cash is decreased $4,000; the expense account Salaries and Wages Expense is increased $4,000.

| CASH FLOW | | | BALANCE SHEET | | | | | | | | | | | | | | | INCOME STATEMENT |
|---|---|---|---|---|---|---|---|---|---|---|---|---|---|---|---|---|---|---|
| | | | Assets | | | | = | Liabilities | | | + | Stockholders' Equity | | | | | | |
| | | | | | | | | | | | | | | Retained Earnings | | | | |
| | | | Cash | + Supplies + | Prepd. Insur. + | Equip- ment | = | Notes Pay. + | Accts. Pay. + | Unearned Serv. Rev. + | | Common Stock + | Rev. | − | Exp. | − | Div. | |
| | | | $19,200 + | $2,500 + | $600 + | $5,000 | = | $5,000 + | $2,500 + | $1,200 + | | $10,000 + | $10,000 | − | $900 | − | $500 | |
| ↓ $4,000 | (11) | | −4,000 | | | | | | | | | | | | −4,000 | | | Sal./Wages Expense |
| | | | $15,200 + | $2,500 + | $600 + | $5,000 | = | $5,000 + | $2,500 + | $1,200 + | | $10,000 + | $10,000 | − | $4,900 | − | $500 | |
| | | | | | $23,300 | | | | | | | | $23,300 | | | | | |

## Accounting Across the Organization   Hain Celestial Group

Keith Homan/ Shutterstock .com

### It Starts with the Transaction

Recording financial transactions in a company's records should be straightforward. If a company determines that a transaction involves revenue, it records revenue. If it has an expense, then it records an expense. However, sometimes this is difficult to do. For example, for more than a year, **Hain Celestial Group** (an organic food company) did not provide income information to investors and regulators. The reason was that the company discovered revenue irregularities and said it could not release financial results until it determined when and how to record revenue for certain transactions. When Hain missed four deadlines for reporting earnings information, the food company suffered a 34% drop in its stock price. As one analyst noted, it was hard to fathom why a seemingly simple revenue recognition issue took one year to resolve.

In other situations, outright fraud may occur. For example, regulators charged **Obsidian Energy** for fraudulently moving millions of dollars in expenses from operating expenses to asset accounts. By understating reported operating expenses, Obsidian made it appear that it was efficiently managing its costs as well as increasing its income.

These examples demonstrate that "getting the basic transaction right" is the foundation for relevant and representationally faithful financial statements. Incorrect or inappropriate transactions lead to distortions in the financial statements.

**Sources:** Shawn Tully, "The Mystery of Hain Celestial's Accounting," *Fortune.com* (August 20, 2016); and Kelly Cryderman, "U.S. Charges Obsidian, Formerly Penn West, with Accounting Fraud," *The Globe and Mail* (June 28, 2017).

**Why is it important for companies to record financial transactions completely and accurately? (Go to WileyPLUS for this answer and additional questions.)**

## DO IT! 2a | Transaction Analysis

**Part 2:** A tabular analysis of transactions made by Roberta Mendez & Co., a certified public accounting firm, for the month of August is shown below. Each change in revenues or expenses is explained.

| | Assets | | = Liabilities + | | Stockholders' Equity | | | | |
|---|---|---|---|---|---|---|---|---|---|
| | Cash + | Accounts Receivable = | | Common Stock + | Retained Earnings Revenues − | Expenses − | Dividends | | |
| 1. | +$9,200 | | | | +$9,200 | | | | Service Revenue |
| 2. | | +$7,400 | | | +7,400 | | | | Service Revenue |
| 3. | −900 | | | | | | −$900 | | |
| 4. | −1,250 | | | | | −$1,250 | | | Sal./Wages Exp. |
| | $7,050 + | $7,400 = | | + | $16,600 − | $1,250 | −$900 | | |
| | | $14,450 | | | $14,450 | | | | |

Describe each transaction that occurred for the month.

**ACTION PLAN**
- Analyze the tabular analysis to determine the nature and effect of each transaction.
- Keep the accounting equation in balance.
- Remember that a change in an asset will require a change in another asset, in a liability, or in stockholders' equity.

### Solution

1. The company performed services for $9,200 cash.
2. The company performed services worth $7,400 on account.
3. The company paid $900 in dividends to stockholders.
4. The company paid $1,250 to employees for salaries and wages.

Related exercise material: **BE3.6, BE3.7, BE3.8, BE3.9, BE3.10, BE3.11, DO IT! 3.2a, E3.3, E3.4, E3.5, and E3.6.**

# Summary of Transactions

**Illustration 3.6** summarizes the transactions of Sierra Corporation to show their cumulative effect on the basic accounting equation. It includes the transaction number in the first column on the left. The right-most column shows the specific effect of any transaction that affects revenues or expenses. Remember that Event (9) did not result in a transaction, so nothing is recorded for that event. The illustration demonstrates three important points:

1. Each transaction is analyzed in terms of its effect on assets, liabilities, and stockholders' equity.
2. The two sides of the equation must always be equal.
3. The cause of each change in revenues or expenses must be indicated.

**ILLUSTRATION 3.6** Summary of transactions

| | BALANCE SHEET | | | | | | | | | | INCOME STATEMENT |
|---|---|---|---|---|---|---|---|---|---|---|---|
| | Assets | | | | = Liabilities | | | + Stockholders' Equity | | | |
| | | | | | | | | | Retained Earnings | | |
| | Cash + | Supplies + | Prepd. Insur. + | Equip- ment = | Notes Pay. + | Accts. Pay. + | Unearned Serv. Rev. + | Common Stock + | Rev. − | Exp. − Div. | |
| (1) | +$10,000 | | | | | | | +$10,000 | | | |
| (2) | +5,000 | | | | +$5,000 | | | | | | |
| (3) | −5,000 | | | +$5,000 | | | | | | | |
| (4) | +1,200 | | | | | | +$1,200 | | | | |
| (5) | +10,000 | | | | | | | | +$10,000 | | Service Revenue |
| (6) | −900 | | | | | | | | | −$900 | Rent Expense |
| (7) | −600 | | +$600 | | | | | | | | |
| (8) | | +$2,500 | | | | +$2,500 | | | | | |
| (9) | | | | | | | | | | | |
| (10) | −500 | | | | | | | | | −$500 | |
| (11) | −4,000 | | | | | | | | | −4,000 | Sal./Wages Expense |
| | $15,200 + | $2,500 + | $600 + | $5,000 = | $5,000 + | $2,500 + | $1,200 + | $10,000 + | $10,000 − | $4,900 − $500 | |
| | | $23,300 | | | | | $23,300 | | | | |

# Preparing Financial Statements

Companies prepare financial statements from the summarized accounting data. For example, **Illustration 3.7** shows the financial statements of Sierra Corporation, based on the summary of transactions shown in Illustration 3.6. Looking at Illustration 3.7, you may notice that the amounts in these statements differ from those in Illustration 1.9. The reason these numbers do not agree is because the financial statements in Chapter 1 are based on adjusted numbers. Additional adjustments are required at the end of the accounting period before the financial statements can be finalized. We show the necessary adjustments for Sierra in Chapter 4.

**ILLUSTRATION 3.7** Financial statements and their interrelationships

### Sierra Corporation
#### Income Statement
#### For the Month Ended October 31, 2022

| | | |
|---|---:|---:|
| Revenues | | |
| Service revenue | | $10,000 |
| Expenses | | |
| Salaries and wages expense | $4,000 | |
| Rent expense | 900 | |
| Total expenses | | 4,900 |
| Net income | | $ 5,100 |

### Sierra Corporation
#### Retained Earnings Statement
#### For the Month Ended October 31, 2022

| | |
|---|---:|
| Retained earnings, October 1 | $ 0 |
| Add: Net income | 5,100 |
| | 5,100 |
| Less: Dividends | 500 |
| Retained earnings, October 31 | $4,600 |

### Sierra Corporation
#### Balance Sheet
#### October 31, 2022

**Assets**

| | | |
|---|---:|---:|
| Current assets | | |
| Cash | $15,200 | |
| Supplies | 2,500 | |
| Prepaid insurance | 600 | |
| Total current assets | | $18,300 |
| Equipment | | 5,000 |
| Total assets | | $23,300 |

**Liabilities and Stockholders' Equity**

| | | |
|---|---:|---:|
| Current liabilities | | |
| Notes payable | $ 5,000 | |
| Accounts payable | 2,500 | |
| Unearned service revenue | 1,200 | |
| Total current liabilities | | $ 8,700 |
| Stockholders' equity | | |
| Common stock | 10,000 | |
| Retained earnings | 4,600 | |
| Total stockholders' equity | | 14,600 |
| Total liabilities and stockholders' equity | | $23,300 |

In addition, note that the statements shown in Illustration 3.7 are interrelated as follows.

1. Net income of $5,100 on the **income statement** is added to the beginning balance of retained earnings in the **retained earnings statement**.

2. Retained earnings of $4,600 at the end of the reporting period shown in the **retained earnings statement** is reported on the **balance sheet**.

Be sure to carefully examine the format and content of each statement in Illustration 3.7. We describe the essential features of each in the following sections.

## Income Statement

The income statement reports the success or profitability of the company's operations over a specific period of time. For example, Sierra Corporation's income statement is dated "For the Month Ended October 31, 2022." It is prepared from the data appearing in the revenue and expense columns of Illustration 3.6.

- The heading of the statement identifies the company, the type of statement, and the time period covered by the statement.
- The income statement lists revenues first, followed by expenses.
- The statement shows net income (or net loss). When revenues exceed expenses, a **net income** results. When expenses exceed revenues, a **net loss** results.

Note that the income statement does not include investment and dividend transactions between the stockholders and the business in measuring net income. For example, as explained earlier, the cash dividend from Sierra Corporation was not regarded as a business expense. This type of transaction is considered a reduction of retained earnings, which causes a decrease in stockholders' equity.

## Retained Earnings Statement

Sierra Corporation's retained earnings statement reports the changes in retained earnings for a specific period of time. The time period is the same as that covered by the income statement ("For the Month Ended October 31, 2022"). Data for the preparation of the retained earnings statement come from the retained earnings columns of the tabular summary (Illustration 3.6) and from the income statement (Illustration 3.7).

- The first line of the statement shows the beginning retained earnings amount, followed by net income and dividends.
- The retained earnings ending balance is the final amount on the statement.
- The information provided by this statement indicates the reasons why retained earnings increased or decreased during the period. If there is a net loss, it is deducted in the retained earnings statement.

## Classified Balance Sheet

Sierra Corporation's balance sheet reports the assets, liabilities, and stockholders' equity at a specific date (October 31, 2022). The company prepares the balance sheet from the column headings and the month-end data shown in the last line of the tabular summary (Illustration 3.6).

- The balance sheet lists current assets before equipment.
- Total assets must equal total liabilities and stockholders' equity.

## DO IT! 2b | Financial Statements Preparation

The following summary tabular analysis was prepared for Polar Corporation as of December 31, 2022.

| | | Assets | | | = | Liabilities | + | | | Stockholders' Equity | | | | |
|---|---|---|---|---|---|---|---|---|---|---|---|---|---|---|
| Cash | + | Accts. Rec. | + | Supplies | = | Accts. Pay. | + | Notes Pay. | + | Common Stock | + | Retained Earnings | | |
| $890 | + | $1,310 | + | $6,167 | = | $957 | + | $2,100 | + | $1,000 | + | $1,420 | | |
| | | | | | | | | | | | + | Rev. − Exp. − Div. | | |
| | | | | | | | | | | | | | | +$300 |
| | | | | | | | | | | | | +$4,900 | | Service Revenue |
| | | | | | | | | | | | | | −$700 | Rent Exp. |
| | | | | | | | | | | | | | −540 | Sal./Wages Exp. |
| | | | | | | | | | | | | | −470 | Supplies Exp. |
| Bal. $890 | | $1,310 | | $6,167 | | $957 | | $2,100 | | $1,000 | | $4,900 | $1,710 | $300 |

Prepare an income statement, a retained earnings statement, and a classified balance sheet for Polar Corporation for the year ended December 31, 2022. The balance in Retained Earnings is $1,420 as of January 1, 2022.

### ACTION PLAN

- Report the revenues and expenses for a period of time in an income statement.
- Show the amounts and causes (net income and dividends) of changes in retained earnings during the period in the retained earnings statement.
- Present the assets and claims to those assets (liabilities and equity) at a specific point in time in the balance sheet.

### Solution

**Polar Corporation**
**Income Statement**
**For the Year Ended December 31, 2022**

| | | |
|---|---|---|
| Revenues | | |
| Service revenue | | $4,900 |
| Expenses | | |
| Salaries and wages expense | $540 | |
| Rent expense | 700 | |
| Supplies expense | 470 | |
| Total expenses | | 1,710 |
| Net income | | $3,190 |

**Polar Corporation**
**Retained Earnings Statement**
**For the Year Ended December 31, 2022**

| | |
|---|---|
| Retained earnings, January 1 | $1,420 |
| Add: Net income | 3,190 |
| | 4,610 |
| Less: Dividends | 300 |
| Retained earnings, December 31 | $4,310 |

**Polar Corporation**
**Balance Sheet**
**December 31, 2022**

**Assets**

| | | |
|---|---|---|
| Current assets | | |
| Cash | $ 890 | |
| Accounts receivable | 1,310 | |
| Supplies | 6,167 | |
| Total current assets | | $8,367 |

**Liabilities and Stockholders' Equity**

| | | |
|---|---|---|
| Current liabilities | | |
| Notes payable | $2,100 | |
| Accounts payable | 957 | |
| Total current liabilities | | $3,057 |
| Stockholders' equity | | |
| Common stock | 1,000 | |
| Retained earnings | 4,310 | |
| Total stockholders' equity | | 5,310 |
| Total liabilities and stockholders' equity | | $8,367 |

Related exercise material: **DO IT! 3.2b, E3.7, E3.8, and E3.9.**

## USING THE DECISION TOOLS | Kansas Farmers' Vertically Integrated Cooperative, Inc.

The **Kansas Farmers' Vertically Integrated Cooperative, Inc. (K-VIC)** was formed by over 200 northeast Kansas farmers in the late 1980s. Its purpose is to process raw materials, primarily grain and meat products grown by K-VIC's members, into end-user food products and then to distribute the products nationally. Profits not needed for expansion or investment are returned to the members annually, on a pro rata basis, according to the fair value of the grain and meat products received from each farmer.

Assume that the following summary tabular analysis was prepared for K-VIC at the end of its first year of operations (amounts in millions).

| | | Assets | | | | | = | Liabilities | | | + | | | Stockholders' Equity | | | | |
|---|---|---|---|---|---|---|---|---|---|---|---|---|---|---|---|---|---|---|
| | | Accts. | | | | | | Accts. | | Mort. | | | | Retained Earnings | | | | |
| | Cash | + | Rec. | + | Inven. | + | Equip. | = | Pay. | + | Pay. | + | Rev. | − | Exp. | − | Div. | |
| | $32 | + | $712 | + | $1,291 | + | $538 | = | $747 | + | $873 | + | | | | | | |
| | | | | | | | | | | | | +$4,563 | | | | | Sales Revenue |
| | | | | | | | | | | | | | | −$2,384 | | | Cost of Goods Sold |
| | | | | | | | | | | | | | | −651 | | | Sal./Wages Exp. |
| | | | | | | | | | | | | | | −500 | | | Main./Repairs Exp. |
| Bal. | $32 | + | $712 | + | $1,291 | + | $538 | = | $747 | + | $873 | + | $4,563 | − | $3,535 | − | $0 | |

$2,573                                    $2,648

Because the tabular analysis is not in balance, you have checked with various people responsible for entering accounting data and have discovered the following.

1. The purchase of 35 new trucks, costing $7 million and paid for with cash, was not recorded.

2. A data entry clerk accidentally deleted the account name for an account with a balance of $472 million, so the amount was added to the Mortgage Payable account.

3. December cash sales revenue of $75 million increased the Sales Revenue account, but the other half of the transaction was not recorded.

4. $50 million of Salaries and Wages Expense was mistakenly charged to Maintenance and Repairs Expense.

## Instructions

Answer these questions.

**a.** Which mistake(s) caused the tabular analysis to be out of balance?

**b.** Should all of the items be corrected? Explain.

**c.** What is the name of the account the data entry clerk deleted?

**d.** Make the necessary corrections and prepare a correct summary tabular analysis.

## Solution

a. Only mistake #3 has caused the accounting equation in the tabular summary to be out of balance.

b. All of the items should be corrected. The misclassification error (mistake #4) on the salaries expense would not affect bottom-line net income, but it does affect the amounts reported in the two expense accounts.

c. There is no Common Stock account, so that must be the account that was deleted by the data entry clerk.

d.

| | | Assets | | | = | Liabilities | | | + | | Stockholders' Equity | | | |
|---|---|---|---|---|---|---|---|---|---|---|---|---|---|---|
| | | Accts. | | | | Accts. | Mort. | | | Com. | | Retained Earnings | | |
| | Cash + | Rec. + | Inven. + | Equip. = | | Pay. + | Pay. + | | | Stock + | Rev. − | Exp. − | Div. | |
| | $32 + | $712 + | $1,291 + | $538 = | | $747 + | $873 | | | | | | | |
| | | | | | | | | | | | +$4,563 | | | Sales Revenue |
| | | | | | | | | | | | | −$2,384 | | Cost of Goods Sold |
| | | | | | | | | | | | | −651 | | Sal./Wages Exp. |
| | | | | | | | | | | | | −500 | | Main./Repairs Exp. |
| Bal. | $32 + | $712 + | $1,291 + | $538 = | | $747 + | $873 + | | | $ 0 + | $4,563 − | $3,535 − | $0 | |
| 1 | −$7 | | | +$7 | | | | | | | | | | |
| 2 | | | | | | | −$472 | | | +$472 | | | | |
| 3 | +75 | | | | | | | | | | | | | |
| 4 | | | | | | | | | | | | +$50 | | Sal./Wages Exp. |
| | | | | | | | | | | | | −50 | | Main./Repairs Exp. |
| Adj. Bal. | $100 + | $712 + | $1,291 + | $545 = | | $747 + | $401 + | | | $472 + | $4,563 − | $3,535 − | $0 | |

$2,648      $2,648

# Review and Practice

## Learning Objectives Review

### 1  Discuss financial reporting concepts.

Generally accepted accounting principles are a set of rules and practices recognized as a general guide for financial reporting purposes. The basic objective of financial reporting is to provide information that is useful for decision-making.

To be judged useful, information should have the primary characteristics of relevance and faithful representation. In addition, useful information is comparable, consistent, verifiable, timely, and understandable.

The **monetary unit assumption** requires that companies include in the accounting records only transaction data that can be expressed in terms of money. The **economic entity assumption** states that economic events can be identified with a particular unit of accountability. The **periodicity assumption** states that the economic life of a business can be divided into artificial time periods and that meaningful accounting reports can be prepared for each period.

The **going concern assumption** states that the business will continue in operation for the foreseeable future.

The **historical cost principle** states that companies should record assets at their cost. The **fair value principle** indicates that assets and liabilities should be reported at fair value. The **full disclosure principle** requires that companies disclose circumstances and events that matter to financial statement users.

The **cost constraint** weighs the cost that companies incur to provide a type of information against its benefit to financial statement users.

### 2  Analyze the effect of business transactions on the basic accounting equation.

Each business transaction must have a dual effect on the accounting equation. For example, if an individual asset is increased, there must be a corresponding (a) decrease in another asset, or (b) increase in a specific liability, or (c) increase in stockholders' equity.

## Decision Tools Review

| Decision Checkpoints | Info Needed for Decision | Tool to Use for Decision | How to Evaluate Results |
|---|---|---|---|
| Has an accounting transaction occurred? | Details of the event | Accounting equation | If the event affects assets, liabilities, or stockholders' equity, then record as a transaction. |

## Glossary Review

**Accounting information system** The system of collecting and processing transaction data and communicating financial information to decision-makers. (p. 3-7).

**Accounting transactions** Events that require recording in the financial statements because they affect assets, liabilities, or stockholders' equity. (p. 3-8).

**Comparability** Ability to compare the accounting information of different companies because they use the same accounting principles. (p. 3-4).

**Consistency** Use of the same accounting principles and methods from year to year within a company. (p. 3-4).

**Cost constraint** Constraint that weighs the cost that companies will incur to provide the information against the benefit that financial statement users will gain from having the information available. (p. 3-6).

**Economic entity assumption** An assumption that every economic entity can be separately identified and accounted for. (p. 3-5).

**Fair value principle** Accounting principle that states that assets and liabilities should be reported at fair value (the price that would be received if an asset was sold or the amount that would be required to be paid to settle a liability). (p. 3-6).

**Faithful representation** Information that accurately depicts what really happened and is complete, neutral, and free from error. (p. 3-4).

**Financial Accounting Standards Board (FASB)** The primary accounting standard-setting body in the United States. (p. 3-3).

**Full disclosure principle** Accounting principle that dictates that companies disclose circumstances and events that make a difference to financial statement users. (p. 3-6).

**Generally accepted accounting principles (GAAP)** A set of accounting standards that have substantial authoritative support and which guide accounting professionals. (p. 3-3).

**Going concern assumption** The assumption that the company will continue in operation for the foreseeable future. (p. 3-5).

**Historical cost principle** Accounting principle that states that companies should record assets at their cost. (p. 3-5).

**International Accounting Standards Board (IASB)** An accounting standard-setting body that issues standards adopted by many countries outside of the United States. (p. 3-3).

**International Financial Reporting Standards (IFRS)** Accounting standards, issued by the IASB, that have been adopted by many countries outside of the United States. (p. 3-3).

**Materiality** Whether an item is large enough to likely influence the decision of an investor or creditor. (p. 3-4).

**Monetary unit assumption** An assumption that requires that only those things that can be expressed in money are included in the accounting records. (p. 3-5).

**Periodicity assumption** An assumption that the life of a business can be divided into artificial time periods and that useful reports covering those periods can be prepared for the business. (p. 3-5).

**Public Company Accounting Oversight Board (PCAOB)** The group charged with determining auditing standards and reviewing the performance of auditing firms. (p. 3-3).

**Relevance** The quality of information that indicates the information makes a difference in a decision. (p. 3-4).

**Securities and Exchange Commission (SEC)** The agency of the U.S. government that oversees U.S. financial markets and accounting standard-setting bodies. (p. 3-3).

**Timely** Information that is available to decision-makers before it loses its capacity to influence decisions. (p. 3-4).

**Understandability** Information presented in a clear and concise fashion so that users can interpret it and comprehend its meaning. (p. 3-4).

**Verifiable** The quality of information that occurs when independent observers, using the same methods, obtain similar results. (p. 3-4).

## Practice Multiple-Choice Questions

1. **(LO 1)** Generally accepted accounting principles are:
   a. a set of standards and rules that are recognized as a general guide for financial reporting.
   b. usually established by the Internal Revenue Service.
   c. the guidelines used to resolve ethical dilemmas.
   d. fundamental truths that can be derived from the laws of nature.

2. **(LO 1)** What organization issues U.S. accounting standards?
   a. Financial Accounting Standards Board.
   b. International Accounting Standards Committee.
   c. International Auditing Standards Committee.
   d. None of the answer choices is correct.

3. **(LO 1)** What is the primary criterion by which accounting information can be judged?
   a. Consistency.
   b. Predictive value.
   c. Usefulness for decision-making.
   d. Comparability.

4. **(LO 1)** Neutrality is an ingredient of:

| | Faithful Representation | Relevance |
|---|---|---|
| a. | Yes | Yes |
| b. | No | No |
| c. | Yes | No |
| d. | No | Yes |

5. **(LO 1)** The characteristic of information that evaluates whether it is large enough to impact a decision.
   a. Comparability.       c. Cost.
   b. Materiality.          d. Consistency.

6. **(LO 2)** The effects on the basic accounting equation of performing services for cash are to:
   a. increase assets and decrease stockholders' equity.
   b. increase assets and increase stockholders' equity.
   c. increase assets and increase liabilities.
   d. increase liabilities and increase stockholders' equity.

**7. (LO 2)** Genesis Company buys a $900 machine on credit. This transaction will affect the:

    **a.** income statement only.

    **b.** balance sheet only.

    **c.** income statement and retained earnings statement only.

    **d.** income statement, retained earnings statement, and balance sheet.

**8. (LO 2)** Which of the following events is **not** recorded in the accounting records?

    **a.** Equipment is purchased on account.

    **b.** An employee is terminated.

    **c.** A cash investment is made into the business.

    **d.** Company pays dividend to stockholders.

**9. (LO 2)** During 2022, Gibson Company assets decreased $50,000 and its liabilities decreased $90,000. Its stockholders' equity therefore:

    **a.** increased $40,000.

    **b.** decreased $140,000.

    **c.** decreased $40,000.

    **d.** increased $140,000.

## Solutions

**1. a.** All U.S. companies get guidance from a set of rules and practices that have authoritative support, referred to as generally accepted accounting principles (GAAP). Standard-setting bodies, in consultation with the accounting profession and the business community, determine these accounting standards. The other choices are incorrect because GAAP (b) is not established by the Internal Revenue Service, (c) is not intended to provide guidance in resolving ethical dilemmas, and (d) is created by people and can evolve over time, unlike laws of nature, such as those in physics and chemistry.

**2. a.** The Financial Accounting Standards Board (FASB) is the organization that issues U.S. accounting standards, not the (b) International Accounting Standards Committee or (c) International Auditing Standards Committee. Choice (d) is wrong as there is a correct answer.

**3. c.** Usefulness for decision-making is the primary criterion by which accounting information can be judged. The other choices are incorrect because (a) consistency, (b) predictive value, and (d) comparability all help to make accounting information more useful but are not the primary criteria by which accounting information is judged.

**4. c.** Neutrality is an ingredient of faithful representation but not relevance. The other choices are therefore incorrect.

**5. b.** Materiality evaluates whether information is large enough to impact a decision, not (a) comparability, (c) cost, or (d) consistency.

**6. b.** When services are performed for cash, assets are increased and stockholders' equity is increased. The other choices are therefore incorrect.

**7. b.** When equipment is purchased on credit, assets are increased and liabilities are increased. These are both balance sheet accounts. The other choices are incorrect because neither the income statement nor the retained earnings statement is affected.

**8. b.** Termination of an employee is not a recordable event in the accounting records. The other choices all represent events that are recorded.

**9. a.** Since assets decreased by $50,000 and liabilities decreased by $90,000, stockholders' equity has to increase by $40,000 to keep the accounting equation balanced. The other choices are therefore incorrect.

## Practice Brief Exercises

*Determine effect of transactions on basic accounting equation.*

**1. (LO 2)** Presented below are three economic events. Create a table with rows (a), (b), and (c), and columns for assets, liabilities, and stockholders' equity. In each column, indicate whether the event increased (+), decreased (−), or had no effect (NE) on assets, liabilities, and stockholders' equity.

    **a.** Paid amount owed on accounts payable.

    **b.** Purchased equipment on account.

    **c.** Incurred expenses on account.

### Solution

| 1. | | Assets | Liabilities | Stockholders' Equity |
|---|---|---|---|---|
| | **a.** | − | − | NE |
| | **b.** | + | + | NE |
| | **c.** | NE | + | − |

**2. (LO 2)** Presented below are three transactions. Mark each transaction as affecting common stock (C), dividends (D), revenue (R), or expense (E), or not affecting stockholders' equity (NSE).

*Determine effect of transactions on stockholders' equity.*

_____ **a.** Received cash for services previously performed on account.

_____ **b.** Paid cash for rent cost incurred.

_____ **c.** Paid cash to stockholders.

### Solution

**2.** _NSE_ **a.** Received cash for services previously performed on account.

_E_ **b.** Paid cash for rent cost incurred.

_D_ **c.** Paid cash to stockholders.

**3. (LO 2)** During 2022, Rain Corp. entered into the following transactions.

*Determine effect of transactions on basic accounting equation.*

**1.** Purchased equipment for $31,000 by issuing a note.

**2.** Received $960 from tenant for rent.

**3.** Paid $520 for supplies previously purchased on account.

**4.** Performed services on account for $12,500.

Using the following tabular analysis, show the effect of each transaction on the accounting equation. Put explanations for changes to revenues or expenses in the right-hand margin. For retained earnings, use separate columns for revenues, expenses, and dividends if necessary. Use Illustration 3.6 as a model.

| Assets | | | | = | Liabilities | | + | Stockholders' Equity | | | | |
|---|---|---|---|---|---|---|---|---|---|---|---|---|
| | | | | | | | | Common | Retained Earnings | | | |
| Cash | + Receivable | + Supplies | + Equip. | = | Accts. Pay. | + Notes Pay. | + | Stock | + Rev. | – Exp. | – Div. | |

### Solution

**3.**

| Assets | | | | = | Liabilities | | + | Stockholders' Equity | | | | |
|---|---|---|---|---|---|---|---|---|---|---|---|---|
| | | | | | | | | Common | Retained Earnings | | | |
| Cash | + Receivable | + Supplies | + Equip. | = | Accts. Pay. | + Notes Pay. | + | Stock | + Rev. | – Exp. | – Div. | |
| **1.** | | | +$31,000 | | | +$31,000 | | | | | | |
| **2.** +$960 | | | | | | | | | +$960 | | | Rent Revenue |
| **3.** −520 | | | | | −$520 | | | | | | | |
| **4.** | +$12,500 | | | | | | | | +12,500 | | | Service Revenue |

---

# Practice Exercises

**1. (LO 2)** Legal Services Inc. was incorporated on July 1, 2022. During the first month of operations, the following transactions occurred.

*Use tabular presentation to record transactions.*

**1.** Stockholders invested $10,000 in cash in exchange for common stock of Legal Services Inc.

**2.** Paid $800 for July rent on office space.

**3.** Purchased office equipment on account $3,000.

**4.** Performed legal services for clients for cash $1,500.

**5.** Borrowed $700 cash from a bank on a note payable.

**6.** Performed legal services for client on account $2,000.

**7.** Paid monthly expenses: salaries $500, utilities $300, and advertising $100.

### Instructions

Prepare a tabular summary of the transactions. Include margin explanations for any changes in revenues or expenses.

**Solution**

**1.**

| Trans-action | | Assets | | | = | Liabilities | | + | | Stockholders' Equity | | | | |
|---|---|---|---|---|---|---|---|---|---|---|---|---|---|---|
| | Cash | + | Accounts Receivable | + Equipment | = | Notes Payable | + Accounts Payable | + | Common Stock | + | Retained Earnings | | | |
| | | | | | | | | | | | Rev. | − Exp. | − Div. | |
| (1) | +$10,000 | | | | | | | | +$10,000 | | | | | |
| (2) | −800 | | | | | | | | | | | −$800 | | Rent Expense |
| (3) | | | | +$3,000 | | | +$3,000 | | | | | | | |
| (4) | +1,500 | | | | | | | | | | +$1,500 | | | Service Revenue |
| (5) | +700 | | | | | +$700 | | | | | | | | |
| (6) | | | +$2,000 | | | | | | | | +2,000 | | | Service Revenue |
| (7) | −500 | | | | | | | | | | | −500 | | Sal./Wages Exp. |
| | −300 | | | | | | | | | | | −300 | | Utilities Expense |
| | −100 | | | | | | | | | | | −100 | | Advertising Expense |
| | $10,500 | + | $2,000 | + $3,000 | = | $700 | + $3,000 | + | $10,000 | + | $3,500 | − $1,700 | + $0 | |

$15,500          $15,500

---

*Use tabular presentation to record transactions.*

**2. (LO 2)** Presented below is information related to Conan Real Estate Agency.

Oct. 1 Arnold Conan begins business as a real estate agent with a cash investment of $18,000 in exchange for common stock.

2 Hires an administrative assistant.

3 Purchases office equipment for $1,700, on account.

6 Sells a house and lot for B. Clinton; bills B. Clinton $4,200 for realty services performed.

27 Pays $900 on the balance related to the transaction of October 3.

30 Pays the administrative assistant $2,800 in salary for October.

**Instructions**

Prepare a tabular summary of the transactions. Include margin explanations for any changes in revenues or expenses.

---

**Solution**

**2.**

| Oct. | | Assets | | | = | Liabilities | + | | Stockholders' Equity | | | | |
|---|---|---|---|---|---|---|---|---|---|---|---|---|---|
| | Cash | + | Accounts Receivable | + Equipment | = | Accounts Payable | + | Common Stock | + | Retained Earnings | | | |
| | | | | | | | | | | Rev. | − Exp. | − Div. | |
| 1 | +$18,000 | | | | | | | +$18,000 | | | | | |
| 3 | | | | +$1,700 | | +$1,700 | | | | | | | |
| 6 | | | +$4,200 | | | | | | | +$4,200 | | | Service Revenue |
| 27 | −900 | | | | | −900 | | | | | | | |
| 30 | −2,800 | | | | | | | | | | −$2,800 | | Sal./Wages Exp. |
| | $14,300 | + | $4,200 | + $1,700 | = | $ 800 | + | $18,000 | + | $4,200 | − $2,800 | + $0 | |

$20,200          $20,200

---

# WileyPLUS

Brief Exercises, DO IT! Exercises, Exercises, Problems, and many additional resources are available for practice in WileyPLUS.

## Questions

1. **a.** What are generally accepted accounting principles (GAAP)?

   **b.** What body provides authoritative support for GAAP?

2. **a.** What is the primary objective of financial reporting?

   **b.** Identify the characteristics of useful accounting information.

3. Merle Hawkins, the president of Pathway Company, is pleased. Pathway substantially increased its net income in 2022 while keeping its unit inventory relatively the same. Jon Dietz, chief accountant, cautions Merle, however. Dietz says that since Pathway changed its method of inventory valuation, there is a consistency problem and it is difficult to determine whether Pathway is better off. Is Dietz correct? Why or why not?

4. What is the distinction between comparability and consistency?

5. Describe the constraint inherent in the presentation of accounting information.

6. Your roommate believes that accounting standards are uniform throughout the world. Is your roommate correct? Explain.

7. Wanda Roberts is president of Best Texts. She has no accounting background. Wanda cannot understand why fair value is not used as the basis for all accounting measurement and reporting. Discuss.

8. What is the economic entity assumption? Give an example of its violation.

9. Describe the accounting information system.

10. Can a business enter into a transaction that affects only the left side of the basic accounting equation? If so, give an example.

11. Are the following events recorded in the accounting records? Explain your answer in each case.

   **a.** A major stockholder of the company dies.

   **b.** Supplies are purchased on account.

   **c.** An employee is fired.

   **d.** The company pays a cash dividend to its stockholders.

12. Indicate how each business transaction affects the basic accounting equation.

   **a.** Paid cash for janitorial services.

   **b.** Purchased equipment for cash.

   **c.** Issued common stock to investors in exchange for cash.

   **d.** Paid an account payable in full.

## Brief Exercises

**BE3.1 (LO 1), K** Indicate whether each statement is true or false. If the statement is false, indicate how to correct the statement.

*Recognize generally accepted accounting principles.*

   **a.** GAAP is a set of rules and practices established by accounting standard-setting bodies to serve as a general guide for financial reporting purposes.

   **b.** Substantial authoritative support for GAAP usually comes from two standard-setting bodies: the FASB and the IRS.

**BE3.2 (LO 1), K** The accompanying chart shows the qualitative characteristics of useful accounting information. Fill in the blanks.

*Identify characteristics of useful information.*

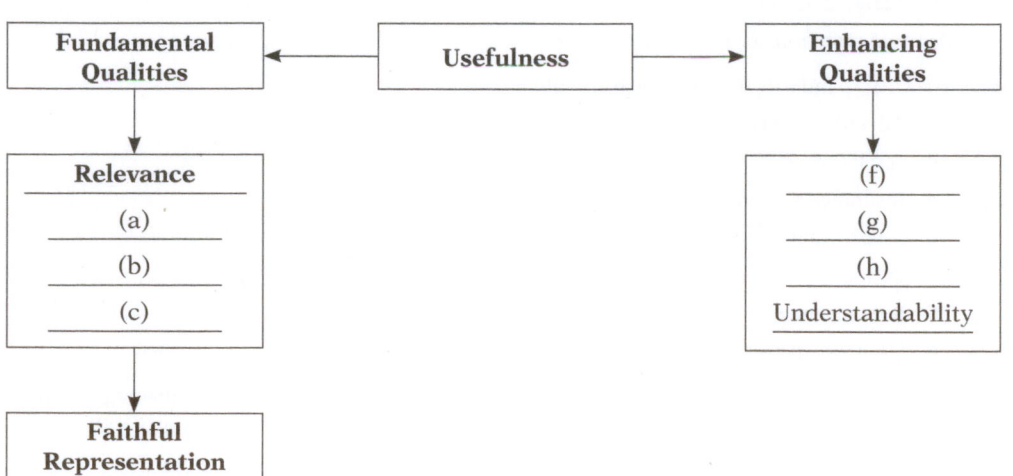

*Identify characteristics of useful information.*

**BE3.3 (LO 1), K** Given the characteristics of useful accounting information, complete each of the following statements.

    **a.** For information to be _____, it should have predictive and confirmatory value.

    **b.** _____ means that information accurately depicts what really happened.

    **c.** _____ means using the same accounting principles and methods from year to year within a company.

*Identify characteristics of useful information.*

**BE3.4 (LO 1), K** Here are some qualitative characteristics of useful accounting information:

    **1.** Predictive value    **3.** Verifiable

    **2.** Neutral    **4.** Timely

Match each qualitative characteristic to one of the following statements.

_____ **a.** Accounting information should help provide accurate expectations about future events.

_____ **b.** Accounting information cannot be selected, prepared, or presented to favor one set of interested users over another.

_____ **c.** The quality of information that occurs when independent observers, using the same methods, obtain similar results.

_____ **d.** Accounting information must be available to decision-makers before it loses its capacity to influence their decisions.

*Define full disclosure principle.*

**BE3.5 (LO 1), K** The full disclosure principle dictates that:

    **a.** financial statements should disclose all assets at their cost.

    **b.** financial statements should disclose only those events that can be measured in dollars.

    **c.** financial statements should disclose all events and circumstances that would matter to users of financial statements.

    **d.** financial statements should not be relied on unless an auditor has expressed an unqualified opinion on them.

*Determine effect of transactions on basic accounting equation.*

**BE3.6 (LO 2), C** Presented below are three economic events. Create a table with rows (a), (b), and (c), and columns for assets, liabilities, and stockholders' equity. In each column, indicate whether the event increased (+), decreased (−), or had no effect (NE) on assets, liabilities, and stockholders' equity.

    **a.** Purchased supplies on account.

    **b.** Received cash for performing a service.

    **c.** Expenses paid in cash.

*Determine effect of transactions on basic accounting equation.*

**BE3.7 (LO 2), C** Presented below are three economic events. Create a table with rows (a), (b), and (c), and columns for assets, liabilities, and stockholders' equity. In each column, indicate whether the event increased (+), decreased (−), or had no effect (NE) on assets, liabilities, and stockholders' equity.

    **a.** Stockholders invested cash in the business for common stock.

    **b.** Paid a cash dividend.

    **c.** Received cash from a customer who had previously been billed for services performed.

*Classify items affecting stockholders' equity.*

**BE3.8 (LO 2), C** Indicate the effect each account has on Retained Earnings.

_____ **a.** Advertising expense.

_____ **b.** Service revenue.

_____ **c.** Insurance expense.

_____ **d.** Salaries and wages expense.

_____ **e.** Dividends.

_____ **f.** Rent revenue.

_____ **g.** Utilities expense.

*Determine effect of transactions on stockholders' equity.*

**BE3.9 (LO 2), C** Presented below are three transactions. Mark each transaction as affecting common stock (C), dividends (D), revenue (R), or expense (E), or not affecting stockholders' equity (NSE).

_____ **a.** Received cash for services performed.

_____ **b.** Paid cash to purchase equipment.

_____ **c.** Paid employee salaries.

**BE3.10 (LO 2), AP** During 2022, Manion Corp. entered into the following transactions.

*Determine effect of transactions on basic accounting equation.*

1. Borrowed $60,000 by issuing a note.

2. Paid $9,000 cash dividend to stockholders.

3. Received $13,000 cash from a previously billed customer for services performed.

4. Purchased supplies on account for $3,100.

Using the following tabular analysis, show the effect of each transaction on the accounting equation. Put explanations for changes to revenues or expenses in the right-hand margin. For retained earnings, use separate columns for revenues, expenses, and dividends if necessary. Use Illustration 3.6 as a model.

| Assets | | | = | Liabilities | | + | Stockholders' Equity | | | | | |
|---|---|---|---|---|---|---|---|---|---|---|---|---|
| | Accounts | | | Accounts | Notes | | Common | | Retained Earnings | | | |
| Cash + | Receivable + | Supplies = | | Payable + | Payable + | | Stock + | | Rev. − | Exp. | − | Div. |

**BE3.11 (LO 2), AP** During 2022, Rostock Company entered into the following transactions.

*Determine effect of transactions on basic accounting equation.*

1. Purchased equipment for $286,176 cash.

2. Issued common stock to investors for $137,590 cash.

3. Purchased inventory of $68,480 on account.

Using the following tabular analysis, show the effect of each transaction on the accounting equation. Put explanations for changes to revenues or expenses in the right-hand margin. For retained earnings, use separate columns for revenues, expenses, and dividends if necessary. Use Illustration 3.6 as a model.

| Assets | | | = | Liabilities | + | Stockholders' Equity | | | | | |
|---|---|---|---|---|---|---|---|---|---|---|---|
| | | | | Accounts | | Common | | Retained Earnings | | | |
| Cash + | Inventory + | Equipment = | | Payable + | | Stock + | | Rev. − | Exp. | − | Div. |

# DO IT! Exercises

**DO IT! 3.1 (LO 1), K** The following characteristics, assumptions, principles, and constraint guide the FASB when it creates accounting standards.

*Identify financial accounting concepts and principles.*

a. Relevance

b. Faithful representation

c. Comparability

d. Consistency

e. Monetary unit assumption

f. Economic entity assumption

g. Periodicity assumption

h. Going concern assumption

i. Historical cost principle

j. Full disclosure principle

k. Materiality

l. Cost constraint

Match each item above with a description below.

1. _____ Items not easily quantified in dollar terms are not reported in the financial statements.

2. _____ Accounting information must be complete, neutral, and free from error.

3. _____ Personal transactions are not mixed with the company's transactions.

4. _____ The cost to provide information should be weighed against the benefit that users will gain from having the information available.

5. _____ A company's use of the same accounting principles from year to year.

6. _____ Assets are recorded and reported at original purchase price.

7. _____ Accounting information should help users predict future events, and should confirm or correct prior expectations.

8. _____ The life of a business can be divided into artificial segments of time.

9. _____ The reporting of all information that would make a difference to financial statement users.

10. _____ The judgment concerning whether an item's size makes it likely to influence a decision-maker.

11. _____ Assumes a business will remain in operation for the foreseeable future.

12. _____ Different companies use the same accounting principles.

*Prepare tabular analysis.*

**DO IT! 3.2a (LO 2), AP** Transactions made by Mickelson Co. for the month of March are shown below. Prepare a tabular analysis that shows the effects of these transactions on the expanded accounting equation, similar to that shown in Illustration 3.6. Use the following column headings: Cash, Accounts Receivable, Accounts Payable, Common Stock, and Retained Earnings (Revenues, Expenses, and Dividends).

1. The company performed $20,000 of services for customers on account.
2. The company received $20,000 in cash from customers who had been billed for services [in transaction (1)].
3. The company received a bill for $1,800 of advertising but will not pay it until a later date.
4. Mickelson Co. paid a cash dividend of $3,000.

*Prepare financial statements*

**DO IT! 3.2b (LO 2), AP** The following summary tabular analysis was prepared for Vortex Corporation as of December 31, 2022.

| | Assets | | | | = | Liabilities | | | + | Stockholders' Equity | | | | |
|---|---|---|---|---|---|---|---|---|---|---|---|---|---|---|
| Cash | + | Accts. Rec. | + Supplies + | Equip. | = | Accts. Pay. | + | Notes Pay. | + | Common Stock | + | Retained Earnings | | |
| $480 | + | $648 | + $295 + | $10,657 | = | $270 | + | $800 | + | $5,000 | + | $965 | | |
| | | | | | | | | | | + | Rev. | − Exp. | − Div. | |
| | | | | | | | | | | | +$8,715 | | | Service Revenue |
| | | | | | | | | | | | | −$190 | | Utilities Exp. |
| | | | | | | | | | | | | −2,860 | | Sal./Wages Exp. |
| | | | | | | | | | | | | −370 | −$250 | Main./Repairs Exp. |
| $480 | | $648 | $295 | $10,657 | | $270 | | $800 | | $5,000 | | $8,715 | $3,420 | $250 |

Prepare an income statement, a retained earnings statement, and a classified balance sheet for the year ended December 31, 2022. The balance in Retained Earnings is $965 as of January 1, 2022.

# Exercises

*Identify accounting assumptions and principles.*

**E3.1 (LO 1), K** Presented below are assumptions and principles discussed in this chapter.

1. Full disclosure principle
2. Going concern assumption
3. Monetary unit assumption
4. Periodicity assumption
5. Historical cost principle
6. Economic entity assumption

**Instructions**

Identify by number the accounting assumption or principle that is described below. Do not use a number more than once.

_____ a. Belief that a company will remain in operation for the foreseeable future.

_____ b. Indicates that personal and business recordkeeping should be separately maintained.

_____ c. Only those items that can be expressed in money are included in the accounting records.

_____ d. Separates financial information into time periods for reporting purposes.

_____ e. Measurement basis used when a reliable estimate of fair value is not available.

_____ f. Dictates that companies should report all circumstances and events that make a difference to financial statement users.

*Identify the assumption or principle that has been violated.*

**E3.2 (LO 1), C** Lopez Co. had three major business transactions during 2022.

a. Reported at its fair value of $260,000 merchandise inventory with a cost of $208,000.

b. The president of Lopez Co., Victor Lopez, purchased a truck for personal use and increased the company's equipment account.

c. Lopez Co. wanted to make its 2022 income look better, so it added 2 more weeks to its income statement reporting period (a 54-week year). Previous years were 52 weeks.

**Instructions**

In each situation, identify the assumption or principle that has been violated, if any, and discuss what the company should have done.

*Analyze the effect of transactions on assets, liabilities, and stockholders' equity.*

**E3.3 (LO 2), C** Keystone Computer Timeshare Company entered into the following transactions during May 2022.

1. Purchased computers for $20,000 from Data Equipment on account.
2. Paid $3,000 cash for May rent on storage space.

3. Received $15,000 cash from customers for contracts billed in April.

4. Performed computer services for Ryan Construction Company for $2,700 cash.

5. Paid Midland Power Co. $11,000 cash for energy usage in May.

6. Stockholders invested an additional $32,000 in the business.

7. Paid Data Equipment for the computers purchased in (1) above.

8. Incurred advertising expense for May of $840 on account.

### Instructions

Indicate with the appropriate letter whether each of the above transactions results in:

a. An increase in assets and a decrease in assets.

b. An increase in assets and an increase in stockholders' equity.

c. An increase in assets and an increase in liabilities.

d. A decrease in assets and a decrease in stockholders' equity.

e. A decrease in assets and a decrease in liabilities.

f. An increase in liabilities and a decrease in stockholders' equity.

g. An increase in stockholders' equity and a decrease in liabilities.

**E3.4 (LO 2), C** Selected transactions for Thyme Advertising Company, Inc. are listed here.   *Analyze the effect of transactions.*

1. Issued common stock to investors in exchange for cash received from investors.

2. Paid monthly rent.

3. Received cash from customers when service was performed.

4. Billed customers for services performed.

5. Paid dividend to stockholders.

6. Incurred advertising expense on account.

7. Received cash from customers billed in (4).

8. Purchased additional equipment for cash.

9. Purchased equipment on account.

### Instructions

Describe the effect of each transaction on assets, liabilities, and stockholders' equity. For example, the first answer is (1) Increase in assets and increase in stockholders' equity.

**E3.5 (LO 2), AP** Brady Company, a computer services company, entered into these transactions during   *Analyze the effect of transactions on assets, liabilities, and stockholders' equity.*
May 2022, its first month of operations.

1. Stockholders invested $40,000 in the business in exchange for common stock of the company.

2. Purchased computers for office use (recorded as Equipment) for $30,000 from Ladd Co. on account.

3. Paid $4,000 cash for May rent on storage space.

4. Performed computer services worth $19,000 on account.

5. Performed computer services for Wharton Construction Company for $5,000 cash.

6. Paid Western States Power Co. $8,000 cash for energy usage in May.

7. Paid Ladd Co. for the computers purchased in (2).

8. Incurred advertising expense for May of $1,300 on account.

9. Received $12,000 cash from customers for contracts billed in (4).

### Instructions

Using the following tabular analysis, show the effect of each transaction on the accounting equation. Put explanations for changes to revenues or expenses in the right-hand margin. Use Illustration 3.6 as a model.

| Assets | | | = | Liabilities | + | Stockholders' Equity | | | | |
|---|---|---|---|---|---|---|---|---|---|---|
| | Accounts | | | Accounts | | Common | | Retained Earnings | | |
| Cash + | Receivable + | Equipment | = | Payable | + | Stock | + | Revenues − | Expenses − | Dividends |

*Determine effect of transactions on basic accounting equation.*

**E3.6 (LO 2), AP** During 2022, its first year of operations as a delivery service, Persimmon Corp. entered into the following transactions.

1. Issued shares of common stock to investors in exchange for $100,000 in cash.
2. Borrowed $45,000 by issuing a note.
3. Purchased delivery trucks for $60,000 cash.
4. Performed services for customers for $16,000 cash.
5. Purchased supplies for $4,700 on account.
6. Paid rent of $5,200.
7. Performed services on account for $10,000.
8. Paid salaries of $28,000.
9. Paid a dividend of $11,000 to shareholders.

**Instructions**

Using the following tabular analysis, show the effect of each transaction on the accounting equation. Put explanations for changes to revenues or expenses in the right-hand margin. Use Illustration 3.6 as a model.

| Assets | | | | = | Liabilities | | + | Stockholders' Equity | | | | |
|---|---|---|---|---|---|---|---|---|---|---|---|---|
| | Accounts | | Equip- | | Accounts | Notes | | Common | | Retained Earnings | | |
| Cash + | Receivable + | Supplies + | ment = | | Payable + | Payable + | | Stock + | Revenues − | Expenses − | Dividends | |

*Analyze transactions and compute net income.*

**E3.7 (LO 2), AP** A tabular analysis of the transactions made during August 2022 by Wolfe Company during its first month of operations is shown below. Each change in revenues or expenses is explained.

| | Assets | | | | = Liabilities + | | Stockholders' Equity | | | | |
|---|---|---|---|---|---|---|---|---|---|---|---|
| | | Accounts | | Equip- | Accounts | Common | | Retained Earnings | | | |
| | Cash + | Receivable + | Supplies + | ment = | Payable + | Stock + | Rev. − | Exp. − | Div. | | |
| 1. | +$20,000 | | | | | +$20,000 | | | | | |
| 2. | −1,000 | | | +$5,000 | +$4,000 | | | | | | |
| 3. | −750 | | +$750 | | | | | | | | |
| 4. | +4,100 | +$5,400 | | | | | +$9,500 | | | | Serv. Rev. |
| 5. | −1,500 | | | | −1,500 | | | | | | |
| 6. | −2,000 | | | | | | | | −$2,000 | | Div. |
| 7. | −800 | | | | | | | −$800 | | | Rent Exp. |
| 8. | +450 | −450 | | | | | | | | | |
| 9. | −3,000 | | | | | | | −3,000 | | | Sal./Wages Exp. |
| 10. | | | | | +300 | | | −300 | | | Util. Exp. |

**Instructions**

a. Describe each transaction.
b. Determine how much stockholders' equity increased for the month.
c. Prepare an income statement for the month of August 2022.

*Analyze transactions and prepare financial statements.*

**E3.8 (LO 2), AP** An analysis of the August 2022 transactions made by Foley & Co., a certified public accounting firm, for its first month of operations is shown below. Each change in revenues or expenses is explained.

| | Assets | | | | = Liabilities + | | Stockholders' Equity | | | | |
|---|---|---|---|---|---|---|---|---|---|---|---|
| | | Accounts | | Equip- | Accounts | Common | | Retained Earnings | | | |
| | Cash + | Receivable + | Supplies + | ment = | Payable + | Stock + | Rev. − | Exp. − | Div. | | |
| 1. | +$15,000 | | | | | +$15,000 | | | | | |
| 2. | −2,000 | | | +$5,000 | +$3,000 | | | | | | |
| 3. | −750 | | +$750 | | | | | | | | |
| 4. | +4,900 | +$4,500 | | | | | +$9,400 | | | | Serv. Rev. |
| 5. | −1,500 | | | | −1,500 | | | | | | |
| 6. | −2,000 | | | | | | | | −$2,000 | | |
| 7. | −850 | | | | | | | −$850 | | | Rent Exp. |
| 8. | +450 | −450 | | | | | | | | | |
| 9. | −3,900 | | | | | | | −3,900 | | | Sal./Wages Exp. |
| 10. | | | | | +500 | | | −500 | | | Util. Exp. |

**Instructions**

  **a.** Describe each transaction.

  **b.** Determine how much stockholders' equity increased for the month.

  **c.** Prepare an income statement and a retained earnings statement for August and a classified balance sheet at August 31, 2022.

**E3.9 (LO 2), AP** The accounts of Rapid Delivery Service contain the following balances on July 31, 2022.    *Prepare financial statements.*

| | | | |
|---|---:|---|---:|
| Accounts Receivable | $13,400 | Prepaid Insurance | $ 2,200 |
| Accounts Payable | 8,400 | Service Revenue | 15,500 |
| Cash | 12,424 | Dividends | 700 |
| Equipment | 59,360 | Common Stock | 40,000 |
| Maintenance and Repairs Expense | 1,958 | Salaries and Wages Expense | 7,428 |
| Insurance Expense | 900 | Salaries and Wages Payable | 820 |
| Notes Payable (due 2025) | 28,450 | Retained Earnings (July 1, 2022) | 5,200 |

**Instructions**

Prepare an income statement, a retained earnings statement, and a classified balance sheet for the month of July 2022.

# Problems

**P3.1 (LO 1), E** `Writing` A friend of yours, Saira Ortiz, recently completed an undergraduate degree in science and has just started working with a biotechnology company. Saira tells you that the owners of the business are trying to secure new sources of financing which are needed in order for the company to proceed with development of a new healthcare product. Saira said that her boss told her that the company must put together a report to present to potential investors.

    Saira thought that the company should include in this package the detailed scientific findings related to the Phase I clinical trials for this product. She said, "I know that the biotech industry sometimes has only a 10% success rate with new products, but if we report all the scientific findings, everyone will see what a sure success this is going to be! The president was talking about the importance of following some set of accounting principles. Why do we need to look at some accounting rules? What they need to realize is that we have scientific results that are quite encouraging, some of the most talented employees around, and the start of some really great customer relationships. We haven't made any sales yet, but we will. We just need the funds to get through all the clinical testing and get government approval for our product. Then these investors will be quite happy that they bought in to our company early!"

*Comment on the objectives and qualitative characteristics of financial reporting.*

**Instructions**

  **a.** What is accounting information? Explain to Saira what is meant by generally accepted accounting principles.

  **b.** Comment on how Saira's suggestions for what should be reported to prospective investors conforms to the qualitative characteristics of accounting information. Do you think that the things that Saira wants to include in the information for investors will conform to financial reporting guidelines?

**P3.2 (LO 2), AP** On April 1, Wonder Travel Agency Inc. was established. These transactions were completed during the month.

*Analyze transactions and compute net income.*

  **1.** Stockholders invested $30,000 cash in the company in exchange for common stock.

  **2.** Paid $900 cash for April office rent.

  **3.** Purchased office equipment for $3,400 cash.

  **4.** Purchased $200 of advertising for the month in the *Chicago Tribune*, on account.

  **5.** Paid $500 cash for office supplies.

  **6.** Performed services worth $12,000. Cash of $3,000 is received from customers, and the balance of $9,000 is billed to customers on account.

  **7.** Paid $400 cash dividend.

  **8.** Paid *Chicago Tribune* amount due in transaction (4).

  **9.** Paid employees' salaries $1,800.

  **10.** Received $9,000 in cash from customers billed previously in transaction (6).

### Instructions

a. Cash        $34,800
    Total assets    $38,700

**a.** Prepare a tabular analysis of the transactions using these column headings: Cash, Accounts Receivable, Supplies, Equipment, Accounts Payable, Common Stock, and Retained Earnings (with separate columns for Revenues, Expenses, and Dividends). Include margin explanations for any changes in revenues or expenses.

**b.** From an analysis of the Retained Earnings columns, compute the net income or net loss for April.

*Analyze transactions and prepare financial statements.*

**P3.3 (LO 2), AP** Nona Curry started her own consulting firm, Curry Consulting Inc., on May 1, 2022. The following transactions occurred during the month of May.

| | | |
|---|---|---|
| May | 1 | Stockholders invested $15,000 cash in the business in exchange for common stock. |
| | 2 | Paid $600 for office rent for the month. |
| | 3 | Purchased $500 of supplies on account. |
| | 5 | Paid $150 to advertise for the month in the *County News*. |
| | 9 | Performed services for customer for $1,400 cash. |
| | 12 | Paid $200 cash dividend. |
| | 15 | Performed $4,200 of services on account. |
| | 17 | Paid $2,500 for employee salaries. |
| | 20 | Paid for the supplies purchased on account on May 3. |
| | 23 | Received a cash payment of $1,200 for services performed on account on May 15. |
| | 26 | Borrowed $5,000 from the bank on a note payable. |
| | 29 | Purchased office equipment for $2,000 paying $200 in cash and the balance on account. |
| | 30 | Paid $180 for utilities. |

### Instructions

a. Cash        $18,270
    Total assets    $23,770

**a.** Show the effects of the previous transactions on the accounting equation using the following format. Include margin explanations for any changes in revenues or expenses. Assume the note payable is to be repaid within the year.

| | Assets | | | | = | Liabilities | | + | Stockholders' Equity | | | |
|---|---|---|---|---|---|---|---|---|---|---|---|---|
| Date | Cash + | Accounts Receivable + | Supplies + | Equipment = | | Notes Payable + | Accounts Payable + | | Common Stock + | Revenues − | Retained Earnings Expenses − | Dividends |

b. Net income     $2,170

**b.** Prepare an income statement and a retained earnings statement for the month of May 2022.

**c.** Prepare a classified balance sheet at May 31, 2022.

*Analyze transactions and prepare financial statements.*

**P3.4 (LO 2), AP** Bindy Crawford created a corporation providing legal services, Bindy Crawford Inc., on July 1, 2022. On July 31 the balance sheet showed Cash $4,000, Accounts Receivable $2,500, Supplies $500, Equipment $5,000, Accounts Payable $4,200, Common Stock $6,200, and Retained Earnings $1,600. During August, the following transactions occurred.

| | | |
|---|---|---|
| Aug. | 1 | Collected $1,100 of accounts receivable due from customers. |
| | 4 | Paid $2,700 cash for accounts payable due. |
| | 9 | Performed services worth $5,400, of which $3,600 is collected in cash and the balance is due in September. |
| | 15 | Purchased additional office equipment for $4,000, paying $700 in cash and the balance on account. |
| | 19 | Paid salaries $1,400, rent for August $700, and advertising expenses $350. |
| | 23 | Paid a cash dividend of $700. |
| | 26 | Borrowed $5,000 from American Federal Bank; the money was borrowed on a 4-month note payable. |
| | 31 | Incurred utility expenses for the month on account $380. |

### Instructions

a. Cash        $7,150

**a.** Prepare a tabular analysis of the August transactions beginning with July 31 balances. Because there is a beginning retained earnings amount, set up your tabular analysis similar to the one shown in **DO IT! 2b**. Include margin explanations for any changes in revenues or expenses.

b. Net income     $2,570
    Ret. earnings   $3,470

**b.** Prepare an income statement for August, a retained earnings statement for August, and a classified balance sheet at August 31.

**P3.5 (LO 2), AP** Fredonia Repair Inc. was started on May 1. A summary of May transactions is presented below.

*Analyze transactions and compute net income.*

1. Stockholders invested $10,000 cash in the business in exchange for common stock.
2. Purchased equipment for $5,000 cash.
3. Paid $400 cash for May office rent.
4. Paid $300 cash for supplies.
5. Incurred $250 of advertising costs in the *Beacon News* on account.
6. Performed repair services for customer for $4,700 cash.
7. Paid a $700 cash dividend.
8. Paid part-time employee salaries $1,000.
9. Paid utility bills $140.
10. Performed repair services worth $1,100 on account.
11. Collected cash of $120 for services billed in transaction (10).

**Instructions**

a. Prepare a tabular analysis of the transactions using the following column headings: Cash, Accounts Receivable, Supplies, Equipment, Accounts Payable, Common Stock, and Retained Earnings (with separate columns for Revenues, Expenses, and Dividends). Include margin explanations for any changes in revenues or expenses. Revenue is called Service Revenue.

a. Total assets      $13,560

b. From an analysis of the Retained Earnings columns, compute the net income or net loss for May.

b. Net income      $4,010

**P3.6 (LO 2), AP** On August 31, 2022, the balance sheet of La Brava Veterinary Clinic showed Cash $9,000, Accounts Receivable $1,700, Supplies $600, Equipment $6,000, Accounts Payable $3,600, Common Stock $13,000, and Retained Earnings $700. During September, the following transactions occurred.

*Analyze transactions and prepare financial statements.*

1. Paid $2,900 cash for accounts payable due.
2. Collected $1,300 of accounts receivable.
3. Purchased additional equipment for $2,100, paying $800 in cash and the balance on account.
4. Performed services worth $7,300, of which $2,500 is collected in cash and the balance is due in October.
5. Paid a $400 cash dividend.
6. Paid salaries $1,700, rent for September $900, and advertising expense $200.
7. Incurred utilities expense for month on account $170.
8. Received $10,000 from Capital Bank on a 6-month note payable.

**Instructions**

a. Prepare a tabular analysis of the September transactions beginning with August 31 balances. Because there is a beginning retained earnings amount, set up your tabular analysis similar to the one shown in **DO IT! 2b**. Include margin explanations for any changes in revenues or expenses.

a. Ending cash      $15,900

b. Prepare an income statement for September, a retained earnings statement for September, and a classified balance sheet at September 30.

b. Net income      $4,330
   Total assets      $29,800

**P3.7 (LO 2), AP** Nancy Tercek started a delivery service, Tercek Deliveries, on June 1, 2022. The following transactions occurred during the month of June.

*Analyze transactions and prepare financial statements.*

June  1  Stockholders invested $10,000 cash in the business in exchange for common stock.
     2  Purchased a used van for deliveries for $14,000. Nancy paid $2,000 cash and signed a note payable for the remaining balance.
     3  Paid $500 for office rent for the month.
     5  Performed $4,800 of services for customer on account.
     9  Declared and paid $300 in cash dividends.
    12  Purchased supplies for $150 on account.
    15  Received a cash payment of $1,250 for services performed on June 5.
    17  Purchased gasoline for $100 on account.
    20  Performed services for customer for $1,500 cash.
    23  Made a cash payment of $500 on the note payable.
    26  Paid $250 for utilities.
    29  Paid for the gasoline purchased on account on June 17.
    30  Paid $1,000 for employee salaries.

**Instructions**

a. Total assets      $25,800

**a.** Show the effects of the previous transactions on the accounting equation using the following format.

| | | Assets | | | = | Liabilities | | + | | Stockholders' Equity | | |
|---|---|---|---|---|---|---|---|---|---|---|---|---|
| Date | Cash + | Accounts Receivable + | Supplies + | Equipment = | | Notes Payable + | Accounts Payable + | | Common Stock + | Revenues − | Retained Earnings Expenses − | Dividends |

Include margin explanations for any changes in revenues or expenses in your analysis.

b. Net income      $4,450

c. Cash      $8,100

**b.** Prepare an income statement and a retained earnings statement for the month of June.

**c.** Prepare a classified balance sheet at June 30, 2022.

# Expand Your Critical Thinking

## Financial Reporting Problem: Apple Inc.

**CT3.1** The financial statements of **Apple Inc.** in Appendix A contain the following selected accounts, all in thousands of dollars.

| | |
|---|---|
| Common Stock | $ 40,201 |
| Accounts Payable | 55,888 |
| Accounts Receivable | 23,186 |
| Selling, General, and Administrative Expenses | 16,705 |
| Inventories | 3,956 |
| Net Property, Plant, and Equipment | 41,304 |
| Net Sales | 265,595 |

**Instructions**

a. Identify the probable other account in the transaction and the effect on that account when:

    1. Accounts Receivable is decreased.

    2. Accounts Payable is decreased.

    3. Inventories is increased.

b. Identify the other account(s) that ordinarily would be involved when:

    1. Common Stock is increased.

    2. Property, Plant, and Equipment is increased.

## Comparative Analysis Problem:

## Columbia Sportswear Company vs. Under Armour, Inc.

**CT3.2** The financial statements of **Columbia Sportswear Company** are presented in Appendix B. Financial statements of **Under Armour, Inc.** are presented in Appendix C.

**Instructions**

Based on the information contained in these financial statements, identify the other account ordinarily involved when:

a. Accounts Receivable is increased.

b. Notes Payable is decreased.

c. Equipment is increased.

d. Prepaid Insurance is increased.

## Interpreting Financial Statements

**CT3.3** **Chieftain International, Inc.**, is an oil and natural gas exploration and production company. A recent balance sheet reported $208 million in assets with only $4.6 million in liabilities, all of which were short-term accounts payable.

During the year, Chieftain expanded its holdings of oil and gas rights, drilled 37 new wells, and invested in expensive 3-D seismic technology. The company generated $19 million cash from operating activities and paid no dividends. It had a cash balance of $102 million at the end of the year.

### Instructions

a. Name at least two advantages to Chieftain from having no long-term debt. Can you think of disadvantages?

b. What are some of the advantages to Chieftain from having this large a cash balance? What is a disadvantage?

c. Why do you suppose Chieftain has the $4.6 million balance in accounts payable, since it appears that it could have made all its purchases for cash?

## Real-World Focus

**CT3.4** This activity provides information about career opportunities for CPAs.

### Instructions

Search the Internet for "Start here go places" to access free accounting resources for future CPAs and then answer the following questions.

a. Where do CPAs work?

b. What skills does a CPA need?

c. What is the salary range for a CPA at a large firm during the first three years? What is the salary range for chief financial officers at large corporations?

**CT3.5** The January 27, 2011, edition of the *New York Times* contains an article by Richard Sandomir entitled "N.F.L. Finances, as Seen Through Packers' Records." The article discusses the fact that the **Green Bay Packers** are the only NFL team that publicly publishes its annual report.

### Instructions

Read the article and answer the following questions.

a. Why are the Green Bay Packers the only professional football team to publish and distribute an annual report?

b. Why is the football players' labor union particularly interested in the Packers' annual report?

c. In addition to the players' labor union, what other outside party might be interested in the annual report?

d. Even though the Packers' revenue increased in recent years, the company's operating profit fell significantly. How does the article explain this decline?

## Ethics Case

**CT3.6** At one time, **Boeing** closed a giant deal to acquire another manufacturer, **McDonnell Douglas**. Boeing paid for the acquisition by issuing shares of its own stock to the stockholders of McDonnell Douglas. In order for the deal not to be revoked, the value of Boeing's stock could not decline below a certain level for a number of months after the deal.

During the first half of the year, Boeing suffered significant cost overruns because of inefficiencies in its production methods. Had these problems been disclosed in the quarterly financial statements during the first and second quarters of the year, the company's stock most likely would have plummeted, and the deal would have been revoked. Company managers spent considerable time debating when the bad news should be disclosed. One public relations manager suggested that the company's problems be revealed on the date of either Princess Diana's or Mother Teresa's funeral, in the hope that it would be lost among those big stories that day. Instead, the company waited until October 22 of that year to announce a $2.6 billion write-off due to cost overruns. Within one week, the company's stock price had fallen 20%, but by this time the McDonnell Douglas deal could not be reversed.

**Instructions**

Answer the following questions.

a. Who are the stakeholders in this situation?

b. What are the ethical issues?

c. What assumptions or principles of accounting are relevant to this case?

d. Do you think it is ethical to try to "time" the release of a story so as to diminish its effect?

e. What would you have done if you were the chief executive officer of Boeing?

f. Boeing's top management maintains that it did not have an obligation to reveal its problems during the first half of the year. What implications does this have for investors and analysts who follow Boeing's stock?

## All About You

**CT3.7** In their annual reports to stockholders, companies must report or disclose information about all liabilities, including potential liabilities related to environmental clean-up. There are many situations in which you will be asked to provide personal financial information about your assets, liabilities, revenues, and expenses. Sometimes you will face difficult decisions regarding what to disclose and how to disclose it.

**Instructions**

Suppose that you are putting together a loan application to purchase a home. Based on your income and assets, you qualify for the mortgage loan, but just barely. How would you address each of the following situations in reporting your financial position for the loan application? Provide responses for each of the following questions.

a. You signed a guarantee for a bank loan that a friend took out for $20,000. If your friend doesn't pay, you will have to pay. Your friend has made all of the payments so far, and it appears he will be able to pay in the future.

b. You were involved in an auto accident in which you were at fault. There is the possibility that you may have to pay as much as $50,000 as part of a settlement. The issue will not be resolved before the bank processes your mortgage request.

c. The company at which you work isn't doing very well, and it has recently laid off employees. You are still employed, but it is quite possible that you will lose your job in the next few months.

# Accrual Accounting Concepts

## Chapter Preview

As indicated in the Feature Story, making adjustments is necessary to avoid misstatement of revenues and expenses such as those at **Groupon**. In this chapter, we introduce you to the accrual accounting concepts that make such adjustments possible.

## Feature Story

### Keeping Track of Groupons

Who doesn't like buying things at a discount? That's why it's not surprising that three years after it started as a company, **Groupon, Inc.** was estimated to be worth $16 billion. This translates into an average increase in value of almost $15 million per day.

Now consider that Groupon had previously been estimated to be worth even more than that. What happened? Well, accounting regulators and investors began to question the way that Groupon had accounted for some of its transactions.

Groupon sells coupons ("Groupons"), so how hard can it be to account for that? It turns out that accounting for coupons is not as easy as you might think.

First, consider what happens when Groupon makes a sale. Suppose it sells a Groupon for $30 for Highrise Hamburgers. When it receives the $30 from the customer, it must turn over half of that amount ($15) to Highrise Hamburgers. So should Groupon record revenue for the full $30 or just $15? Until recently, Groupon recorded the full $30. But, in response to an SEC ruling on the issue, Groupon now records revenue of $15 instead. This caused Groupon to restate its previous financial statements. This restatement reduced annual revenue by $312.9 million.

A second issue is a matter of timing. When should Groupon record this $15 revenue? Should it record the revenue when it sells the Groupon, or must it wait until the customer uses the Groupon at Highrise Hamburgers? The accounting becomes even more complicated when you consider the company's loyalty programs. Groupon offers free or discounted Groupons to its subscribers for doing things such as referring new customers or participating in promotions. These Groupons are to be used for future purchases, yet the company must record the expense at the time the customer receives the Groupon.

Finally, Groupon, like all other companies, relies on many estimates in its financial reporting. For example, Groupon reports that "estimates are utilized for, but not limited to, stock-based compensation, income taxes, valuation of acquired goodwill and intangible assets, customer refunds, contingent liabilities and the depreciable lives of fixed assets." It notes that "actual results could differ materially from those estimates." So, next time you use a coupon, think about what that means for the company's accountants!

## Chapter Outline

| LEARNING OBJECTIVES | REVIEW | PRACTICE |
|---|---|---|
| **LO 1** Explain the accrual basis of accounting and the reasons for adjustments. | • Revenue recognition principle<br>• Expense recognition principle<br>• Accrual vs. cash basis<br>• Need for adjustments<br>• Types of adjustments | **DO IT! 1** Timing Concepts |
| **LO 2** Prepare adjustments for deferrals. | • Prepaid expenses<br>• Unearned revenues | **DO IT! 2** Adjustments for Deferrals |
| **LO 3** Prepare adjustments for accruals. | • Accrued revenues<br>• Accrued expenses<br>• Summary of basic relationships | **DO IT! 3** Adjustments for Accruals |
| **LO 4** Prepare financial statements from adjusted amounts. | • Preparing financial statements from adjusted tabular summary | **DO IT! 4** Preparing Financial Statements |

**Go to the Review and Practice section at the end of the chapter for a targeted summary and exercises with solutions.**

**Visit WileyPLUS for additional tutorials and practice opportunities.**

# Accrual-Basis Accounting and Adjustments

### LEARNING OBJECTIVE 1

Explain the accrual basis of accounting and the reasons for adjustments.

Businesses need feedback about how well they are performing during a period of time.

- Management usually wants monthly reports on financial results, most large corporations are required to present quarterly and annual financial statements to stockholders, and the Internal Revenue Service requires all businesses to file annual tax returns.
- **Accounting divides the economic life of a business into artificial time periods.** As indicated in Chapter 3, this is the **periodicity assumption**.
- **Accounting time periods are generally a month, a quarter, or a year** (see **Helpful Hint**).
- Companies often report using the calendar year (i.e., January 1 to December 31) but sometimes choose a different 12-month period (e.g., August 1 to July 31).

Many business transactions affect more than one of these arbitrary time periods. For example, a new building purchased by **Citigroup** or a new airplane purchased by **Delta Air Lines** will be used for many years. It would not make sense to expense the full cost of the building or the airplane at the time of purchase because each will be used for many subsequent periods. Instead, companies allocate the cost to the periods of use.

Determining the amount of revenues and expenses to report in a given accounting period can be difficult. Proper reporting requires an understanding of the nature of the company's business. Two principles are used as guidelines: the revenue recognition principle and the expense recognition principle.

# The Revenue Recognition Principle

When a company agrees to perform a service or sell a product to a customer, it has a performance obligation.

- The **revenue recognition principle** requires that companies **recognize revenue in the accounting period in which the performance obligation is satisfied**.
- A company satisfies its performance obligation by performing a service or providing a good to a customer.

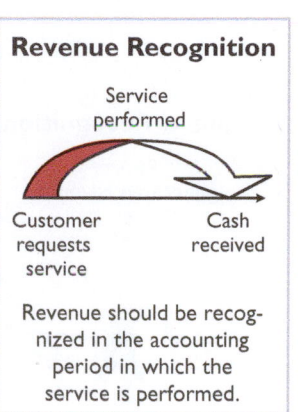

**Revenue Recognition**

Service performed

Customer requests service

Cash received

Revenue should be recognized in the accounting period in which the service is performed.

To illustrate, assume Conrad Dry Cleaners cleans clothing on June 30 for $500, but customers do not claim and pay for their clothes until the first week of July. Under the revenue recognition principle, Conrad records revenue in June when it satisfies its performance obligation, which is when it performs the service, not in July when it receives the cash. At June 30, Conrad would report a receivable on its balance sheet and revenue in its income statement for the service performed. The effect on the accounting equation for the June and July transactions would be as follows.

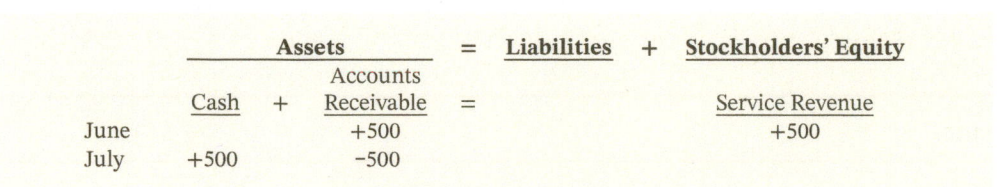

|  | Assets | | = | Liabilities | + | Stockholders' Equity |
|---|---|---|---|---|---|---|
|  | Cash | + | Accounts Receivable | = |  | Service Revenue |
| June |  |  | +500 | = |  | +500 |
| July | +500 |  | −500 |  |  |  |

## Five-Step Revenue Recognition Process—Sierra Corporation Example

Revenue recognition results from a five-step process. This process can best be illustrated with an example. Assume that Sierra Corporation signs a contract with the Lewis family to provide guide services for a one-week backpacking trip for $1,500. **Illustration 4.1** shows the five steps that Sierra follows to recognize revenue.

As indicated, Step 5 is when Sierra recognizes revenue related to providing the guide services to the Lewis family. At this point, Sierra completes the trip and satisfies its performance obligation.

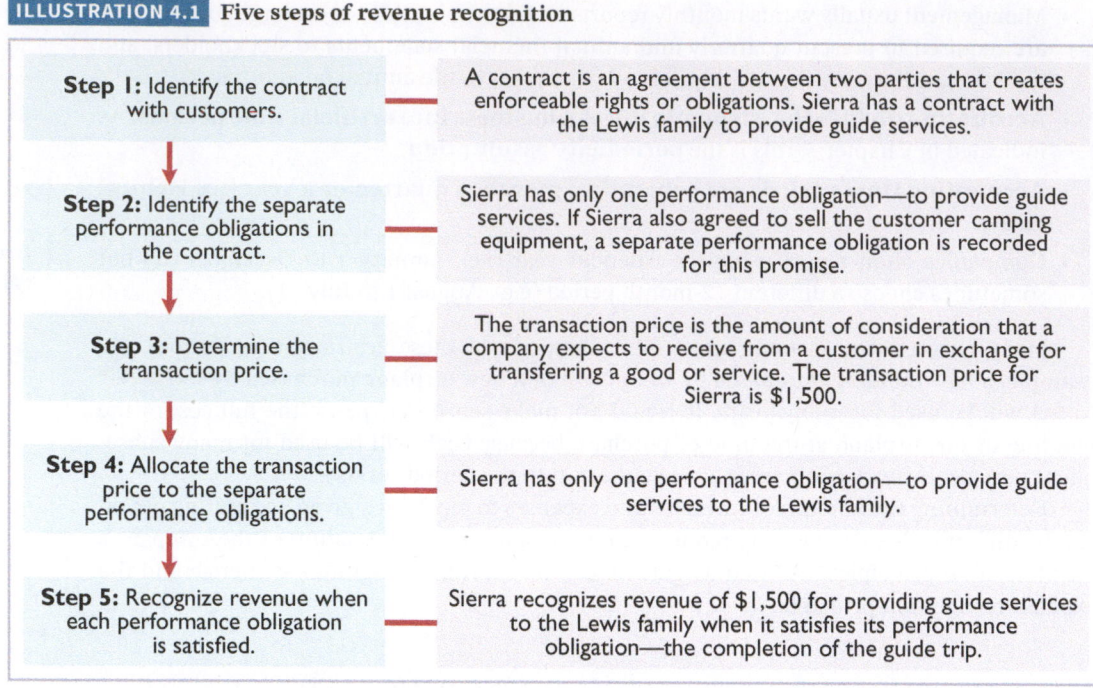

**ILLUSTRATION 4.1**  Five steps of revenue recognition

| | |
|---|---|
| **Step 1:** Identify the contract with customers. | A contract is an agreement between two parties that creates enforceable rights or obligations. Sierra has a contract with the Lewis family to provide guide services. |
| **Step 2:** Identify the separate performance obligations in the contract. | Sierra has only one performance obligation—to provide guide services. If Sierra also agreed to sell the customer camping equipment, a separate performance obligation is recorded for this promise. |
| **Step 3:** Determine the transaction price. | The transaction price is the amount of consideration that a company expects to receive from a customer in exchange for transferring a good or service. The transaction price for Sierra is $1,500. |
| **Step 4:** Allocate the transaction price to the separate performance obligations. | Sierra has only one performance obligation—to provide guide services to the Lewis family. |
| **Step 5:** Recognize revenue when each performance obligation is satisfied. | Sierra recognizes revenue of $1,500 for providing guide services to the Lewis family when it satisfies its performance obligation—the completion of the guide trip. |

## The Expense Recognition Principle

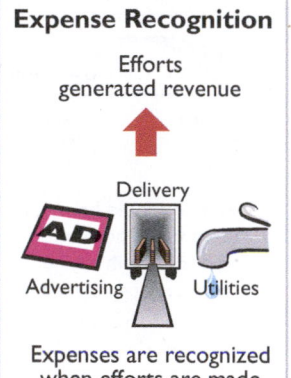

**Expense Recognition**

Efforts generated revenue

↑

Delivery

Advertising    Utilities

Expenses are recognized when efforts are made to generate revenue.

In recognizing expenses, a simple rule is followed: "Let the expenses follow the revenues." Thus, expense recognition is tied to revenue recognition.

- The practice of expense recognition is referred to as the **expense recognition principle**.
- It requires that companies recognize expenses in the period in which they make efforts (consume assets or incur liabilities) to generate revenue.

Applied to the Conrad Dry Cleaners example, this means that the salary expense Conrad incurred in performing the dry cleaning service on June 30 should be reported in the same period in which it recognizes the service revenue. The critical issue in expense recognition is determining when the expense makes its contribution to revenue. This may or may not be the same period in which the expense is paid. If Conrad does not pay the salary incurred on June 30 until July, it would report salaries and wages payable on its June 30 balance sheet.

---

**Investor Insight**    Apple Inc.

PhotoAlto/James Hardy/Getty Images, Inc.

### Reporting Revenue Accurately

Until recently, electronics manufacturer **Apple** was required to spread the revenues from iPhone sales over the two-year period following the sale of the phone. Accounting standards required this because Apple was obligated to provide software updates after the phone was sold. Since Apple had service obligations after the initial date of sale, it was forced to spread the revenue over a two-year period. As a result, the rapid growth of iPhone sales was not fully reflected in the revenue amounts reported in Apple's income statement. A new accounting standard now enables Apple to report much more of its iPhone revenue at the point of sale. It was estimated that under the new rule revenues would have been about 17% higher and earnings per share almost 50% higher.

**In the past, why was it argued that Apple should spread the recognition of iPhone revenue over a two-year period, rather than recording it upfront? (Go to WileyPLUS for this answer and additional questions.)**

Illustration 4.2 shows the relationships in revenue and expense recognition (see Decision Tools).

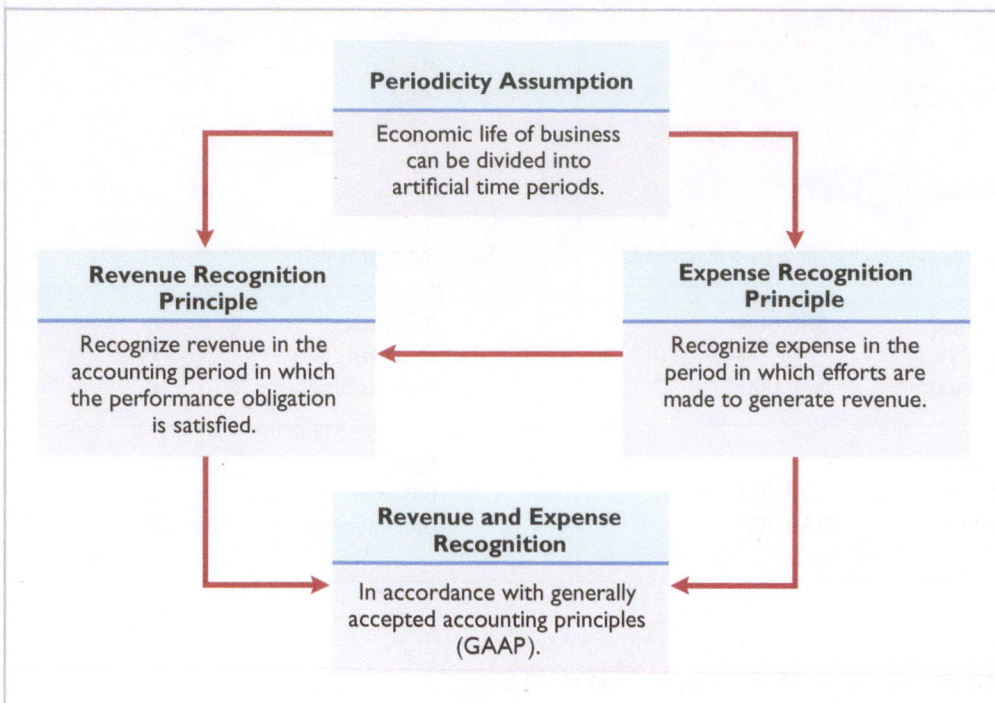

**ILLUSTRATION 4.2**
GAAP relationships in revenue and expense recognition

**Decision Tools**

The revenue recognition principle and the expense recognition principle help to ensure that companies report the correct amount of revenues and expenses in a given period.

# Accrual versus Cash Basis of Accounting

Accrual-basis accounting means that transactions that change a company's financial statements are recorded **in the periods in which the events occur**, even if cash was not exchanged (see International Note). For example, using the accrual basis means that companies recognize revenues when they perform the services (the revenue recognition principle), even if cash was not received. Likewise, under the accrual basis, companies recognize expenses when incurred (the expense recognition principle), even if cash was not paid.

An alternative to the accrual basis is the cash basis. Under cash-basis accounting, companies record revenue at the time they receive cash. They record an expense at the time they pay out cash.

**International Note**

Although different accounting standards are often used by companies in other countries, the accrual basis of accounting is central to all of these standards.

- The cash basis seems appealing due to its simplicity, but it often produces misleading financial statements. For example, it fails to record revenue for a company that has performed services but has not yet received payment.
- As a result, the cash basis may not reflect revenue in the period that a performance obligation is satisfied.
- **Cash-basis accounting is not in accordance with generally accepted accounting principles (GAAP).**

Illustration 4.3 compares accrual-based numbers and cash-based numbers. Suppose that Fresh Colors paints a large building in 2021. In 2021, it incurs and pays total expenses (salaries and paint costs) of $50,000. It bills the customer $80,000 but does not receive payment until 2022. On an accrual basis, Fresh Colors reports $80,000 of revenue during 2021 because that is when it performed the service. The company matches expenses of $50,000 to the $80,000 of revenue. Thus, 2021 net income is $30,000 ($80,000 − $50,000). The $30,000 of net income reported for 2021 indicates the profitability of Fresh Colors' efforts during that period.

If Fresh Colors instead used cash-basis accounting, it would report $50,000 of expenses in 2021 and $80,000 of revenues during 2022. As shown in Illustration 4.3, it would report a loss of $50,000 in 2021 and net income of $80,000 in 2022. Clearly, the cash-basis measures are misleading because the financial performance of the company would be misstated for both 2021 and 2022.

**ILLUSTRATION 4.3** Accrual- versus cash-basis accounting

| | 2021 | 2022 |
|---|---|---|
| **Activity** | Purchased paint, painted building, paid employees | Received payment for work done in 2021 |
| **Accrual basis** | Revenue $80,000<br>Expense 50,000<br>Net income $30,000 | Revenue $ 0<br>Expense 0<br>Net income $ 0 |
| **Cash basis** | Revenue $ 0<br>Expense 50,000<br>Net loss $(50,000) | Revenue $80,000<br>Expense 0<br>Net income $80,000 |

# The Need for Adjustments

In order for revenues to be recorded in the period in which the performance obligations are satisfied and for expenses to be recognized in the period in which they are incurred, companies make adjustments. **Adjustments are changes made to accounts at the end of the accounting period to ensure that the revenue recognition and expense recognition principles are followed.**

Adjustments are necessary because the first pulling together of the transaction data may not contain up-to-date and complete data. This is true for several reasons:

1. Some events are not recorded daily because it is not efficient to do so. Examples are the use of supplies and the earning of wages by employees.

2. Some costs are not recorded during the accounting period because these costs expire with the passage of time rather than as a result of recurring daily transactions. Examples are charges related to the use of buildings and equipment, rent, and insurance.

3. Some items may be unrecorded. An example is a utility service bill that will not be received until the next accounting period.

**HELPFUL HINT**

When doing homework, make sure each adjustment includes one income statement account and one balance sheet account.

**Adjustments are required every time a company prepares financial statements.** The company analyzes each account to determine whether it is complete and up-to-date for financial statement purposes. **Every adjustment will include one income statement account and one balance sheet account** (see **Helpful Hint**).

# Types of Adjustments

Adjustments are classified as either deferrals or accruals. As **Illustration 4.4** shows, each of these classes has two subcategories.

**ILLUSTRATION 4.4**

Categories of adjustments

**Deferrals:**
1. **Prepaid expenses:** Expenses paid in cash before they are used or consumed.
2. **Unearned revenues:** Cash received before services are performed.

*(continues)*

| Accruals: |
|---|
| 1. **Accrued revenues:** Revenues for services performed but not yet received in cash or recorded. |
| 2. **Accrued expenses:** Expenses incurred but not yet paid in cash or recorded. |

**ILLUSTRATION 4.4**

*(continued)*

Subsequent sections give examples of each type of adjustment. Each example is based on the October 31 summary of Sierra Corporation's transactions from Chapter 3. It is reproduced in **Illustration 4.5**.

**ILLUSTRATION 4.5**   **Unadjusted summary of transactions**

|  | BALANCE SHEET |||||||||||||| INCOME STATEMENT |
|---|---|---|---|---|---|---|---|---|---|---|---|---|---|---|
|  | Assets |||| = | Liabilities ||| + | Stockholders' Equity |||||
|  |  |  |  |  |  |  |  | Unearned |  |  | Retained Earnings ||||
|  |  |  | Prepd. | Equip- |  | Notes | Accts. | Serv. |  | Common |  |  |  |  |
|  | Cash | + Supplies + | Insur. + | ment | = Pay. | + Pay. | + | Rev. | + Stock | + | Rev. | − Exp. | − Div. |  |
| (1) | +$10,000 |  |  |  |  |  |  |  | +$10,000 |  |  |  |  |  |
| (2) | +5,000 |  |  |  | +$5,000 |  |  |  |  |  |  |  |  |  |
| (3) | −5,000 |  |  | +$5,000 |  |  |  |  |  |  |  |  |  |  |
| (4) | +1,200 |  |  |  |  |  |  | +$1,200 |  |  |  |  |  |  |
| (5) | +10,000 |  |  |  |  |  |  |  |  |  | +$10,000 |  |  | Service Revenue |
| (6) | −900 |  |  |  |  |  |  |  |  |  |  | −$900 |  | Rent Expense |
| (7) | −600 |  |  | +$600 |  |  |  |  |  |  |  |  |  |  |
| (8) |  | +$2,500 |  |  |  | +$2,500 |  |  |  |  |  |  |  |  |
| (9) |  |  |  |  |  |  |  |  |  |  |  |  |  |  |
| (10) | −500 |  |  |  |  |  |  |  |  |  |  |  | −$500 |  |
| (11) | −4,000 |  |  |  |  |  |  |  |  |  |  | −4,000 |  | Sal./Wages Expense |
|  | $15,200 + | $2,500 + | $600 + | $5,000 | = $5,000 | + $2,500 | + | $1,200 | + $10,000 | + | $10,000 | − $4,900 | − $500 |  |
|  | $23,300 |||||  |  |  | $23,300 |  |  |  |  |  |

We assume that Sierra uses an accounting period of one month. Thus, monthly adjustments are made. The adjustments are made on October 31.

---

## DO IT! 1 | Timing Concepts

Below is a list of concepts in the left column, with descriptions of the concepts in the right column. There are more descriptions provided than concepts. Match the description of the concept to the concept.

1. _____ Accrual-basis accounting.
2. _____ Calendar year.
3. _____ Periodicity assumption.
4. _____ Expense recognition principle.

a. Daily transactions.

b. Efforts (expenses) should be matched with results (revenues).

c. Accountants divide the economic life of a business into artificial time periods.

d. Companies record revenues when they receive cash and record expenses when they pay out cash.

e. An accounting time period that starts on January 1 and ends on December 31.

f. Companies record transactions in the period in which the events occur.

**ACTION PLAN**

- Review the terms identified.
- Study carefully the revenue recognition principle, the expense recognition principle, and the periodicity assumption.

### Solution

**1.** f   **2.** e   **3.** c   **4.** b

Related exercise material: **BE4.1, BE4.3, DO IT! 4.1, E4.1, E4.2, E4.3, E4.4, and E4.5.**

# Adjustments for Deferrals

---

**LEARNING OBJECTIVE 2**

Prepare adjustments for deferrals.

---

To defer means to postpone or delay.

- Deferrals are costs or revenues that are recognized at a date later than the point when cash was originally exchanged.
- Companies make adjustments for deferred expenses to record the expenses that were incurred during the period.
- Companies also make adjustments for deferred revenues to record services performed during the period.

The two types of deferrals are prepaid expenses and unearned revenues.

## Prepaid Expenses

Companies record payments of expenses that will benefit more than one accounting period as assets. These **prepaid expenses** or **prepayments** are expenses paid in cash before they are used or consumed. When expenses are prepaid, an asset account is increased to show the service or benefit that the company will receive in the future. Examples of common prepayments are insurance, supplies, advertising, and rent. In addition, companies make prepayments when they purchase buildings and equipment.

- **Prepaid expenses are costs that expire either with the passage of time** (e.g., rent and insurance) **or through use** (e.g., supplies).
- It would be impractical and is unnecessary to record the expiration of these costs daily. Accordingly, companies postpone the recognition of such cost expirations until they prepare financial statements.
- At each statement date, they make adjustments to record the expenses applicable to the current accounting period and to show the remaining amounts in the asset accounts.

Prior to adjustment, assets are overstated and expenses are understated. Therefore, as shown in **Illustration 4.6**, **an adjustment for prepaid expenses results in an increase to an expense account and a decrease to an asset account**.

**ILLUSTRATION 4.6**

Adjustment for prepaid expenses

| | | **Prepaid Expenses** | | | | |
|---|---|---|---|---|---|---|
| **Assets** | = | **Liabilities** | + | **Stockholders' Equity** | | |
| Asset Account | = | | + | Revenues | − | Expenses |
| Decrease | | | | | | Increase |

Let's look in more detail at some specific types of prepaid expenses, beginning with supplies.

### Supplies

The purchase of supplies, such as paper and envelopes, results in an increase to an asset account. During the accounting period, the company uses supplies.

- Rather than record supplies expense as the supplies are used, companies recognize supplies expense at the **end** of the accounting period.
- At the end of the accounting period, the company counts the remaining supplies.

- The difference between the unadjusted balance in the Supplies (asset) account and the actual cost of supplies on hand represents the supplies used (an expense) for that period.

Recall from Chapter 3 that Sierra Corporation purchased supplies costing $2,500 on October 5. Sierra recorded the purchase by increasing the asset Supplies. This account shows a balance of $2,500 as of October 31. A physical count of the inventory at the close of business on October 31 reveals that $1,000 of supplies are still on hand. Thus, the cost of supplies used is $1,500 ($2,500 – $1,000). This use of supplies decreases an asset, Supplies. It also decreases stockholders' equity by increasing an expense account, Supplies Expense. This is shown in **Illustration 4.7**.

**Supplies**

Oct. 5

Supplies purchased;
record asset

Oct. 31
Supplies used;
record supplies expense

**ILLUSTRATION 4.7**   **Adjustment for supplies**

**Basic Analysis:** The expense Supplies Expense is increased $1,500. Since it reduces stockholders' equity, it is entered as a negative. This keeps the equation in balance. The asset Supplies is decreased $1,500.

**Equation Analysis:**

| Assets | = | Liabilities | + | Stockholders' Equity |
|---|---|---|---|---|
| Supplies | | | | Supplies Expense |
| –$1,500 | = | | | –$1,500 |

**Post-Adjustment Tabular Analysis:**

| | | | BALANCE SHEET | | | | | | | | | | | INCOME STATEMENT |
|---|---|---|---|---|---|---|---|---|---|---|---|---|---|---|
| | | **Assets** | | | = | **Liabilities** | | | + | **Stockholders' Equity** | | | | |
| | | | | | | | | | | | | **Retained Earnings** | | |
| | Cash + | Sup-plies + | Prepd. Insur. + | Equip. = | Notes Pay. + | Accts. Pay. + | Unearn. Serv. Rev. + | Common Stock + | Rev. – | Exp. – | Div. | | | |
| Unadj. Bal. | 15,200 + | 2,500 + | 600 + | 5,000 = | 5,000 + | 2,500 + | 1,200 + | 10,000 + | 10,000 – | 4,900 – | 500 | | | |
| (A1) | | –1,500 | | | | | | | | –1,500 | | | | Supplies Expense |
| Bal. | 15,200 + | 1,000 + | 600 + | 5,000 = | 5,000 + | 2,500 + | 1,200 + | 10,000 + | 10,000 – | 6,400 – | 500 | | | |
| | | $21,800 | | | | | | $21,800 | | | | | | |

After adjustment, the asset account Supplies shows a balance of $1,000, which is equal to the cost of supplies on hand at the statement date. In addition, Supplies Expense shows a balance of $1,500, which equals the cost of supplies used in October. **If Sierra does not make the adjustment, October expenses will be understated and net income overstated by $1,500. Moreover, both assets and stockholders' equity will be overstated by $1,500 on the October 31 balance sheet** (see **Helpful Hint**).

**HELPFUL HINT**

Due to their nature, adjustments have **no effect** on cash flows. As a result, we do not show the cash flow effects as we did in Chapter 3.

## Insurance

Companies purchase insurance to protect themselves from losses due to fire, theft, and unforeseen events. Insurance must be paid in advance, often for multiple months.

- The cost of insurance (premiums) paid in advance is recorded as an increase in the asset account Prepaid Insurance.
- At the financial statement date, companies increase Insurance Expense and decrease Prepaid Insurance for the cost of insurance that has expired during the period.

On October 4, Sierra Corporation paid $600 for a one-year fire insurance policy. Coverage began on October 1. Sierra recorded the payment by increasing Prepaid Insurance. This account shows a balance of $600 on October 31. Insurance of $50 ($600 ÷ 12) expires each month. The expiration of prepaid insurance decreases an asset, Prepaid Insurance. It also decreases stockholders' equity by increasing an expense account, Insurance Expense.

As shown in **Illustration 4.8**, the asset Prepaid Insurance shows a balance of $550, which represents the unexpired cost for the remaining 11 months of coverage. At the same time, the balance in Insurance Expense equals the insurance cost that expired in October. **If Sierra does not make this adjustment, October expenses are understated by $50 and net income is overstated by $50. Moreover, both assets and stockholders' equity will be overstated by $50 on the October 31 balance sheet.**

**Insurance**

Oct. 4

Insurance
1 year policy
$600

Insurance purchased;
record asset

| Insurance Policy | | | |
|---|---|---|---|
| Oct $50 | Nov $50 | Dec $50 | Jan $50 |
| Feb $50 | March $50 | April $50 | May $50 |
| June $50 | July $50 | Aug $50 | Sept $50 |
| **Insurance = $600/year** | | | |

Oct. 31
Insurance expired;
record insurance expense

**ILLUSTRATION 4.8** **Adjustment for insurance**

**Basic Analysis:** The expense Insurance Expense is increased $50. Since it reduces stockholders' equity, it is entered as a negative. The asset Prepaid Insurance is decreased $50.

**Equation Analysis:**

| Assets | = | Liabilities | + | Stockholders' Equity |
|---|---|---|---|---|
| Prepaid Insurance | | | | Insurance Expense |
| −$50 | = | | | −$50 |

**Post-Adjustment Tabular Analysis:**

| | BALANCE SHEET | | | | | | | | | | | | | | | | INCOME STATEMENT |
|---|---|---|---|---|---|---|---|---|---|---|---|---|---|---|---|---|---|
| | **Assets** | | | | = | **Liabilities** | | | + | **Stockholders' Equity** | | | | | | | |
| | | | | | | | | | | | | **Retained Earnings** | | | | | |
| | Cash + | Sup-plies + | Prepd. Insur. + | Equip. = | | Notes Pay. + | Accts. Pay. + | Unearn. Serv. Rev. + | | Common Stock + | Rev. − | | Exp. − | | Div. | | |
| Bal. | 15,200 + | 1,000 + | 600 + | 5,000 = | | 5,000 + | 2,500 + | 1,200 + | | 10,000 + | 10,000 − | | 6,400 − | | 500 | | |
| (A2) | | | −50 | | | | | | | | | | −50 | | | | Insurance Expense |
| Bal. | 15,200 + | 1,000 + | 550 + | 5,000 = | | 5,000 + | 2,500 + | 1,200 + | | 10,000 + | 10,000 − | | 6,450 − | | 500 | | |
| | | $21,750 | | | | | | | | $21,750 | | | | | | | |

---

**ACTION PLAN**

- Insurance expense is the amount of insurance used during the period. This is determined by dividing the balance in Prepaid Insurance by the number of remaining months covered by the policy to get the monthly expense. Then multiply by the number of months.

- Supplies expense is determined by subtracting the ending balance of supplies from the unadjusted balance in supplies to determine the amount of supplies used.

## DO IT! 2 | Adjustments for Deferrals—Supplies Expense and Insurance Expense

**Part 1:** Ranier Corp. started business on October 1, 2022. On October 1, it purchased a 2-year insurance policy for $3,600 as well as supplies for $490. On November 15, Ranier purchased additional supplies for $610. On December 31, the company had supplies of $200 on hand.

1. What was the amount of insurance expense that would be recorded in a quarterly adjustment on December 31?

2. What was the amount of supplies expense that would be recorded in a quarterly adjustment on December 31?

### Solution

1. The amount of insurance used during the quarter is $450 [($3,600 ÷ 24) × 3].
2. The amount of supplies used during the quarter is $900 [($490 + $610) − $200].

Related exercise material: **BE4.4, BE4.5, BE4.6, BE4.7, and DO IT! 4.2.**

---

## Depreciation

A company typically owns a variety of assets that have long lives, such as buildings, equipment, and motor vehicles. The period of service for which the company plans to use the asset is referred to as the **useful life** of the asset. Because a building is expected to be of service for many years, it is recorded as an asset, rather than an expense, on the date it is acquired.

- As explained in Chapter 2, companies record such assets **at cost**, as required by the historical cost principle.
- To follow the expense recognition principle, companies allocate a portion of this cost as an expense during each period of the asset's useful life.
- **Depreciation** is the process of allocating the cost of an asset to expense over its useful life.

**Need for Adjustment** The acquisition of a long-lived asset is essentially a long-term prepayment for the use of an asset.

- An adjustment for depreciation is needed to recognize the cost that has been used (an expense) during the period and to report the unused cost (an asset) at the end of the period.

- One very important point to understand: **Depreciation is an allocation concept, not a valuation concept.** That is, depreciation **allocates an asset's cost to the periods in which it is used.**

- **Depreciation does not attempt to report the actual change in the value of the asset.**

For Sierra Corporation, assume that depreciation on the equipment is $480 a year, or $40 per month. As shown in **Illustration 4.9**, rather than decrease the asset account directly, Sierra instead increases Accumulated Depreciation—Equipment.

- Accumulated Depreciation is called a **contra asset account**.

- Such an account is offset against an asset account on the balance sheet. Thus, the Accumulated Depreciation—Equipment account offsets the asset Equipment.

- This account keeps track of the total amount of depreciation expense taken over the life of the asset.

To keep the accounting equation in balance, Sierra decreases stockholders' equity by increasing an expense account, Depreciation Expense.

**Depreciation**

Oct. 2

Equipment purchased;
record asset

| Equipment | | | |
|---|---|---|---|
| Oct $40 | Nov $40 | Dec $40 | Jan $40 |
| Feb $40 | March $40 | April $40 | May $40 |
| June $40 | July $40 | Aug $40 | Sept $40 |
| **Depreciation = $480/year** | | | |

Oct. 31
Depreciation recognized;
record depreciation expense

**ILLUSTRATION 4.9**    **Adjustment for depreciation**

**Basic Analysis:** The expense Depreciation Expense is increased $40. Since it reduces stockholders' equity, it is entered as a negative. This keeps the equation in balance. The contra asset Accumulated Depreciation—Equipment is increased $40. Since it reduces assets, it is entered as a negative.

| Equation Analysis: | Assets | = | Liabilities | + | Stockholders' Equity |
|---|---|---|---|---|---|
| | Accumulated Depreciation—Equipment | | | | Depreciation Expense |
| | −$40 | = | | | −$40 |

**Post-Adjustment Tabular Analysis:**

| | | | | | | | | | BALANCE SHEET | | | | | | | | | | | INCOME STATEMENT |
|---|---|---|---|---|---|---|---|---|---|---|---|---|---|---|---|---|---|---|---|---|
| | | Assets | | | | | | = | Liabilities | | | + | Stockholders' Equity | | | | | | | |
| | | Sup- | | Prepd. | | | Acc. Depr.— | | Notes | Accts. | Unearn. Serv. | | Com. | | Retained Earnings | | | | | |
| | Cash | plies | Insur. | Equip. | − | Equip. | = | Pay. | Pay. | Rev. | Stock | Rev. | − | Exp. | − | Div. | | |
| Bal. | 15,200 + | 1,000 + | 550 + | 5,000 − | | 0 | = | 5,000 + | 2,500 + | 1,200 + | 10,000 + | 10,000 − | | 6,450 − | | 500 | | |
| (A3) | | | | | | −40 | | | | | | | | −40 | | | Depr. Expense |
| Bal. | 15,200 + | 1,000 + | 550 + | 5,000 − | | 40 | = | 5,000 + | 2,500 + | 1,200 + | 10,000 + | 10,000 − | | 6,490 − | | 500 | | |
| | | | $21,710 | | | | | | | | $21,710 | | | | | | | |

The balance in the Accumulated Depreciation—Equipment account will increase $40 each month, and the balance in Equipment remains $5,000.

**Statement Presentation**    As noted above, Accumulated Depreciation—Equipment is a contra asset account. It is offset against Equipment on the balance sheet. A theoretical alternative to using a contra asset account would be to decrease the asset account by the amount of depreciation each period. But using the contra account is preferable for a simple reason: It discloses both the original cost of the equipment and the total cost that has expired to date. Thus, in the balance sheet, Sierra deducts Accumulated Depreciation—Equipment from the related asset account, as shown in **Illustration 4.10**.

| | |
|---|---|
| Equipment | $5,000 |
| Less: Accumulated depreciation—equipment | 40 |
| | **$4,960** |

**ILLUSTRATION 4.10**
**Balance sheet presentation of accumulated depreciation**

**Book value** is the difference between the cost of any depreciable asset and its related accumulated depreciation (see **Alternative Terminology**). In Illustration 4.10, the book value of the equipment at the balance sheet date is $4,960.

- The book value and the fair value of the asset are generally two different values.
- As noted earlier, **the purpose of depreciation is not valuation but a means of cost allocation.**

Depreciation expense identifies the portion of an asset's cost that expired during the period (in this case, in October). **Without this adjustment, total assets, total stockholders' equity, and net income are overstated by $40 and depreciation expense is understated by $40.** **Illustration 4.11** summarizes the accounting for prepaid expenses.

**ILLUSTRATION 4.11**

Accounting for prepaid expenses

| | **Accounting for Prepaid Expenses** | | |
|---|---|---|---|
| **Examples** | **Reason for Adjustment** | **Accounts Before Adjustment** | **Adjustment** |
| Insurance, supplies, advertising, rent, depreciation | Prepaid expenses originally recorded in asset accounts have been used. | Assets overstated. Expenses understated. | Increase expenses. Decrease assets (or increase contra assets). |

# Unearned Revenues

**Unearned Revenues**

Oct. 2  Thank you in advance for your work

I will finish by Dec. 31

$1,200

Cash is received in advance; liability is recorded

Oct. 31
Some service has been performed; some revenue is recorded

Companies record cash received before services are performed by increasing a liability account called **unearned revenues**. In other words, the **company has a performance obligation** to transfer a service to one of its customers. Items like rent, magazine subscriptions, and customer deposits for future service may result in unearned revenues. Airlines such as **United**, **American**, and **Delta**, for instance, treat receipts from the sale of tickets as unearned revenue until the flight service is provided.

Unearned revenues are the opposite of prepaid expenses. Indeed, unearned revenue on the books of one company is likely to be a prepaid expense on the books of the company that has made the advance payment. For example, if identical accounting periods are assumed, a landlord will have unearned rent revenue when a tenant has prepaid rent.

When a company receives payment for services to be performed in a future accounting period, it increases an unearned revenue account.

- Unearned revenue is a liability account used to recognize the obligation that exists.
- The company subsequently recognizes revenue when it performs the service. During the accounting period, it is not practical to record these revenues daily as the company performs services.
- Instead, the company delays recognition of revenue until the adjustment process. The company then makes an adjustment to record the revenue for services performed during the period and to show the liability that remains at the end of the accounting period.

Prior to adjustment, liabilities are typically overstated and revenues are understated. Therefore, as shown in **Illustration 4.12**, the adjustment for unearned revenues results in a decrease to a liability account and an increase to a revenue account.

**ILLUSTRATION 4.12**

Adjustment for unearned revenues

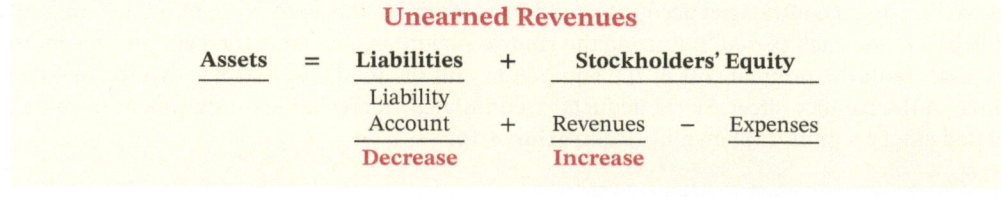

**Unearned Revenues**

| Assets | = | Liabilities | + | Stockholders' Equity | | |
|---|---|---|---|---|---|---|
| | | Liability Account | + | Revenues | − | Expenses |
| | | **Decrease** | | **Increase** | | |

Sierra Corporation received $1,200 on October 2 from R. Knox for guide services for multi-day trips expected to be completed by December 31. Sierra recorded the payment as an increase to Unearned Service Revenue. This liability account shows a balance of $1,200 as of October 31. From an evaluation of the service Sierra performed for Knox during October, the company determines that it should recognize $400 of revenue in October. The liability (Unearned Service Revenue) is therefore decreased and stockholders' equity (Service Revenue) is increased.

As shown in **Illustration 4.13**, the liability Unearned Service Revenue now shows a balance of $800. That amount represents the remaining guide services Sierra is obligated to perform in the future. Service Revenue shows total revenue for October of $10,400. **Without this adjustment, revenues and net income are understated by $400 in the income statement. Moreover, liabilities are overstated and stockholders' equity is understated by $400 on the October 31 balance sheet.**

---

**ILLUSTRATION 4.13**  **Service revenue accounts after adjustment**

**Basic Analysis:** The liability Unearned Service Revenue is decreased $400; the revenue Service Revenue is increased $400.

**Equation Analysis:**

| Assets | = | Liabilities | + | Stockholders' Equity |
|---|---|---|---|---|
| | | Unearned Service Revenue | | Service Revenue |
| | | −$400 | | +$400 |

**Post-Adjustment Tabular Analysis:**

| | | | | | | | | | | | | | BALANCE SHEET | | | | | | | | | | | | INCOME STATEMENT |
|---|---|---|---|---|---|---|---|---|---|---|---|---|---|---|---|---|---|---|---|---|---|---|---|---|---|---|
| | | | Assets | | | | | | = | | Liabilities | | + | | Stockholders' Equity | | | | | | | | | | | |
| | | | | | | | | Acc. | | | | | Unearn. | | Com. | | Retained Earnings | | | | | | | | |
| | | Sup- | | Prepd. | | | | Depr.— | | Notes | Accts. | | Serv. | | | | | | | | | | | | |
| | Cash | + plies | + Insur. | + Equip. | − | Equip. | = Pay. | + Pay. | + | Rev. | + Stock | + | Rev. | − | Exp. | − | Div. | | | | | | | | |
| Bal. | 15,200 | + 1,000 | + 550 | + 5,000 | − 40 | = 5,000 | + 2,500 | + | 1,200 | + 10,000 | + 10,000 | − 6,490 | − 500 | | | | | | | | | | | | | |
| (A4) | | | | | | | | | | −400 | | +400 | | | | | | | | | | | | Service Revenue | |
| Bal. | 15,200 | + 1,000 | + 550 | + 5,000 | − 40 | = 5,000 | + 2,500 | + | 800 | + 10,000 | + 10,400 | − 6,490 | − 500 | | | | | | | | | | | | | |
| | | | $21,710 | | | | | | | | $21,710 | | | | | | | | | | | | | | |

---

**Illustration 4.14** summarizes the accounting for unearned revenues.

**Accounting for Unearned Revenues**

| Examples | Reason for Adjustment | Accounts Before Adjustment | Adjustment |
|---|---|---|---|
| Rent, magazine subscriptions, customer deposits for future service | Unearned revenues recorded in liability accounts are now recognized as revenue for services performed. | Liabilities overstated. Revenues understated. | Decrease liabilities. Increase revenues. |

**ILLUSTRATION 4.14**

**Accounting for unearned revenues**

---

## Accounting Across the Organization    Best Buy

iStock.com/Skip Odonnell

### Turning Gift Cards into Revenue

Those of you who are marketing majors (and even most of you who are not) know that gift cards are among the hottest marketing tools in merchandising today. Customers purchase gift cards and give them to someone for later use. In a recent year, gift-card sales were expected to exceed $124 billion.

Although these programs are popular with marketing executives, they create accounting questions. Should revenue be recorded at the time the gift card is sold, or when it is exercised? How should expired gift cards be accounted for? In a recent balance sheet, **Best Buy** reported unearned revenue related to gift cards of $427 million.

**Source:** "2014 Gift Card Sales to Top $124 Billion, but Growth Slowing," *PRNewswire* (December 10, 2014).

**Suppose that Robert Jones purchases a $100 gift card at Best Buy on December 24, 2021, and gives it to his wife, Mary Jones, on December 25, 2021. On January 3, 2022, Mary uses the card to purchase $100 worth of CDs. When do you think Best Buy should recognize revenue and why? (Go to WileyPLUS for this answer and additional questions.)**

## ACTION PLAN

- Make adjustments at the end of the period for revenues recognized and expenses incurred in the period.
- Don't forget to make adjustments for deferrals. Failure to adjust for deferrals leads to overstatement of the asset or liability and understatement of the related expense or revenue.

## DO IT! 2 | Adjustments for Deferrals—Prepaid Expenses and Unearned Revenues

**Part 2:** A partial tabular summary of transactions for Hammond, Inc. on March 31, 2022, includes these accounts before adjustments are prepared.

| | | Assets | | | = | Liabilities | + | Stockholders' Equity | | |
|---|---|---|---|---|---|---|---|---|---|---|
| Prepaid Insur. | + Supplies | + | Equip- ment | − | Acc. Depr.— Equip. | = | Unearned Serv. Rev. | + | Rev. | − Exp. |
| 3,600 | 2,800 | | 25,000 | | −5,000 | | 9,200 | | | |

An analysis of the accounts shows the following.

1. Insurance expires at the rate of $100 per month.
2. Supplies on hand total $800.
3. The equipment depreciates $200 a month.
4. During March, services were performed for $4,000 of the unearned service revenue reported.

Prepare a tabular summary to record the adjustments for the month of March. Include an explanation for each adjustment.

### Solution

| | | | Assets | | | | = | Liabilities | + | Stockholders' Equity | | | |
|---|---|---|---|---|---|---|---|---|---|---|---|---|---|
| | Prepaid Insur. | + | Supplies | + | Equip- ment | − | Acc. Depr.— Equip. | = | Unearned Serv. Rev. | + | Rev. | − | Exp. | |
| | 3,600 | | 2,800 | | 25,000 | | −5,000 | | 9,200 | | | | | |
| 1. | −100 | | | | | | | | | | | | −100 | Insurance Exp. |
| 2. | | | −2,000 | | | | | | | | | | −2,000 | Supplies Exp. |
| 3. | | | | | | | −200 | | | | | | −200 | Depreciation Exp. |
| 4. | | | | | | | | | −4,000 | | +4,000 | | | Service Rev. |

Related exercise material: **BE4.4, BE4.5, BE4.6, BE4.7, and DO IT! 4.2.**

---

# Adjustments for Accruals

## Accrued Revenues

Oct. 31

My fee is $200

Revenue and receivable are recorded for unbilled services

Nov. 10

$200

Cash is received; receivable is reduced

### LEARNING OBJECTIVE 3
Prepare adjustments for accruals.

The second category of adjustments is **accruals**.

- Prior to an accrual adjustment, the revenue account (and the related asset account) or the expense account (and the related liability account) is understated.
- Thus, the adjustment for accruals will **increase both a balance sheet and an income statement account**.

## Accrued Revenues

Revenues for services performed but not yet recorded at the statement date are **accrued revenues**. Accrued revenues may accumulate (accrue) with the passing of time, as in the case of interest revenue. These are unrecorded because the earning of interest does not involve daily transactions. Companies do not record interest revenue on a daily basis because it is often impractical to do so. Accrued revenues also may result from services that have been performed but not yet billed nor collected, as in the case of commissions and fees. These may be unrecorded because only a portion of the total service has been performed and the clients won't be billed until the service has been completed.

An adjustment records the receivable that exists at the balance sheet date and the revenue for the services performed during the period. Prior to adjustment, both assets and revenues are understated. As shown in **Illustration 4.15**, **an adjustment for accrued revenues results in an increase to an asset account and an increase to a revenue account** (see **Helpful Hint**).

**HELPFUL HINT**

For accruals, there may have been no prior transaction recorded, and the accounts requiring adjustment may have zero balances prior to adjustment.

**ILLUSTRATION 4.15**
Adjustment for accrued revenues

### Accrued Revenues

| Assets | = | Liabilities | + | Stockholders' Equity | | |
|---|---|---|---|---|---|---|
| Asset Account | = | | + | Revenues | − | Expenses |
| **Increase** | | | | **Increase** | | |

In October, Sierra Corporation performed guide services worth $200 that were not billed to clients on or before October 31. Because these services were not billed, they were not recorded. The accrual of unrecorded service revenue increases an asset account, Accounts Receivable. It also increases stockholders' equity by increasing a revenue account, Service Revenue, as shown in **Illustration 4.16**.

**ILLUSTRATION 4.16** **Adjustment for accrued revenue**

**Basic Analysis:** The asset Accounts Receivable is increased $200; the revenue Service Revenue is increased $200.

**Equation Analysis:**

| Assets | = | Liabilities | + | Stockholders' Equity |
|---|---|---|---|---|
| Accounts Receivable | = | | | Service Revenue |
| +$200 | | | | +$200 |

**Post-Adjustment Tabular Analysis:**

| | | | | BALANCE SHEET | | | | | | | | | | | INCOME STATEMENT |
|---|---|---|---|---|---|---|---|---|---|---|---|---|---|---|---|
| | | **Assets** | | | = | | **Liabilities** | | + | | **Stockholders' Equity** | | | | |
| | | | | | | Acc. | | | Unearn. | | | Retained Earnings | | | |
| | Accts. | Sup- | Prepd. | | | Depr.— | Notes | Accts. | Serv. | Com. | | | | | |
| Cash + | Rec. + | plies + | Insur. + | Equip. − | | Equip. = | Pay. + | Pay. + | Rev. + | Stock + | Rev. − | Exp. − | Div. | | |
| Bal. 15,200 + | 0 + | 1,000 + | 550 + | 5,000 − | | 40 = | 5,000 + | 2,500 + | 800 + | 10,000 + | 10,400 − | 6,490 − | 500 | | |
| (A5) | +200 | | | | | | | | | | +200 | | | | Service Revenue |
| 15,200 + | 200 + | 1,000 + | 550 + | 5,000 − | | 40 = | 5,000 + | 2,500 + | 800 + | 10,000 + | 10,600 − | 6,490 − | 500 | | |
| | | $21,910 | | | | | | | | $21,910 | | | | | |

The asset Accounts Receivable shows that clients owe Sierra $200 at the balance sheet date. The balance of $10,600 in Service Revenue represents the total revenue for services Sierra performed during the month ($10,000 + $400 + $200). **Without the adjustment, assets and stockholders' equity on the balance sheet and revenues and net income on the income statement are understated.**

On November 10, Sierra receives cash of $200 for the services performed in October. The company records the collection of the receivables by an increase to Cash and a decrease to Accounts Receivable.

| Assets | | | = | Liabilities | + | Stockholders' Equity | | | |
|---|---|---|---|---|---|---|---|---|---|
| | | | | | | Retained Earnings | | | |
| Cash + | Accounts Receivable | = | | | + | Rev. − | Exp. − | Div. | |
| +200 | −200 | | | | | | | | |

Illustration 4.17 summarizes the accounting for accrued revenues.

| | Accounting for Accrued Revenues | | |
|---|---|---|---|
| Examples | Reason for Adjustment | Accounts Before Adjustment | Adjustment |
| Interest, rent, services | Services performed but not yet received in cash or recorded. | Assets understated. Revenues understated. | Increase assets. Increase revenues. |

## Accrued Expenses

Expenses incurred but not yet paid or recorded at the statement date are called **accrued expenses**. Interest, taxes, utilities, and salaries are common examples of accrued expenses.

Companies make adjustments for accrued expenses to record the obligations that exist at the balance sheet date and to recognize the expenses that apply to the current accounting period (see **Ethics Note**). Prior to adjustment, both liabilities and expenses are understated. Therefore, as shown in **Illustration 4.18**, **an adjustment for accrued expenses results in an increase to an expense account and an increase to a liability account**.

**Accrued Expenses**

$$\underline{Assets} \quad = \quad \underline{Liabilities} \quad + \quad \underline{Stockholders'\ Equity}$$

| Liability Account | + | Revenues | − | Expenses |
|---|---|---|---|---|
| Increase | | | | Increase |

Let's look in more detail at some specific types of accrued expenses, beginning with accrued interest.

### Accrued Interest

Sierra Corporation signed a three-month note payable in the amount of $5,000 on October 1. The note requires Sierra to pay interest at an annual rate of 12%.

The amount of the interest recorded is determined by three factors:

1. The face value of the note.

2. The interest rate, which is always expressed as an annual rate.

3. The length of time the note is outstanding.

For Sierra, the total interest due on the $5,000 note at its maturity date three months in the future is $150 ($5,000 × 12% × $\frac{3}{12}$), or $50 for one month. **Illustration 4.19** shows the formula for computing interest and its application to Sierra for the month of October (see **Helpful Hint**).

| Face Value of Note | × | Annual Interest Rate | × | Time in Terms of One Year | = | Interest |
|---|---|---|---|---|---|---|
| $5,000 | × | 12% | × | $\frac{1}{12}$ | = | $50 |

As **Illustration 4.20** shows, the accrual of interest at October 31 increases a liability account, Interest Payable. It also decreases stockholders' equity by increasing an expense account, Interest Expense.

Interest Expense shows the interest charges for the month of October. Interest Payable shows the amount of interest the company owes at the statement date. Sierra will not pay the interest until the note comes due at the end of three months. Companies use the Interest Payable account, instead of Notes Payable, to disclose the two different types of obligations—interest and principal—in the accounts and statements. **Without this adjustment, liabilities and interest expense are understated, and net income and stockholders' equity are overstated.**

**ILLUSTRATION 4.20**   **Adjustment for accrued interest**

**Basic Analysis:** The expense Interest Expense is increased $50. Since it reduces stockholders' equity, it is entered as a negative. The liability Interest Payable is increased $50. The sum of the positive and negative values keeps the equation in balance.

**Equation Analysis:**

| | Assets | = | Liabilities | + | Stockholders' Equity |
|---|---|---|---|---|---|
| | | | Interest Payable | | Interest Expense |
| | | | +$50 | | −$50 |

**Post-Adjustment Tabular Analysis:**

| | | | | | | BALANCE SHEET | | | | | | | | | | | | | INCOME STATEMENT |
|---|---|---|---|---|---|---|---|---|---|---|---|---|---|---|---|---|---|---|---|
| | | | Assets | | | | = | | Liabilities | | | + | | Stockholders' Equity | | | | | |
| | | | | | | Acc. | | | | | Unearn. | | | | Retained Earnings | | | | |
| | | Accts. | Sup- | Prepd. | | Depr.— | Notes | Accts. | Int. | Serv. | Com. | | | | | |
| | Cash | + Rec. | + plies | + Insur. | + Equip. | − Equip. | = Pay. | + Pay. | + Pay. | + Rev. | + Stock | + Rev. | − Exp. | − Div. | |
| Bal. | 15,200 | + 200 | + 1,000 | + 550 | + 5,000 | − 40 | = 5,000 | + 2,500 | | + 800 | + 10,000 | + 10,600 | − 6,490 | − 500 | |
| (A6) | | | | | | | | | +50 | | | | −50 | | Interest Expense |
| | 15,200 | + 200 | + 1,000 | + 550 | + 5,000 | − 40 | = 5,000 | + 2,500 | + 50 | + 800 | + 10,000 | + 10,600 | − 6,540 | − 500 | |

$21,910 — $21,910

---

## DO IT! 3 | Adjustments for Accruals—Accrued Interest

**Part 1:** Ranier Corp. started business on October 1, 2022. On October 1 it signed a 6-month note payable in the amount of $8,000. The annual rate of interest on the note is 8%. What is the amount of interest expense that Ranier Corp. would record for the quarter ended on December 31, 2022?

### Solution

The amount of interest expense is $160 ($8,000 × .08 × $\frac{3}{12}$).

Related exercise material: **BE4.8, DO IT! 4.3, E4.8, E4.9, E4.11, and E4.12.**

**ACTION PLAN**

- Interest expense is determined by multiplying the face amount of the note payable times the annual interest rate times the time in terms of one year.

---

## Accrued Salaries

Companies pay for some types of expenses, such as employee salaries and wages, after the services have been performed. Sierra paid salaries on October 26 for its employees' first two weeks of work; the next payment of salaries will not occur until November 9. As **Illustration 4.21** shows, three working days remain in October (October 29–31).

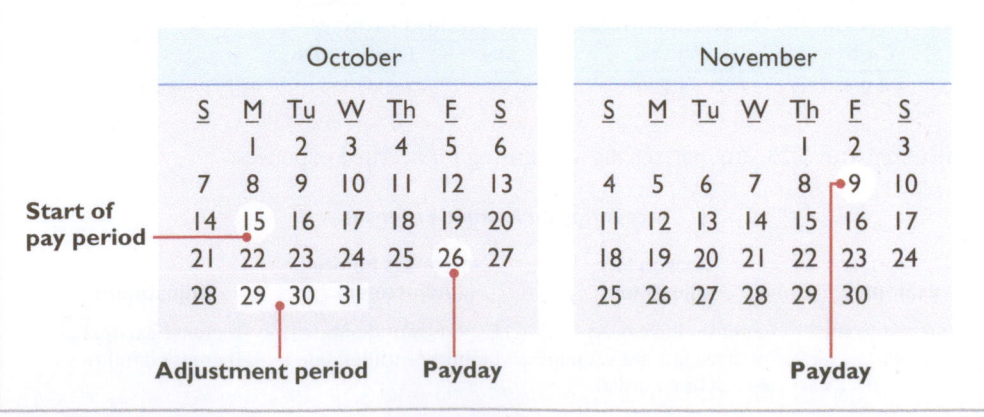

**ILLUSTRATION 4.21**

**Calendar showing Sierra Corporation's pay periods**

At October 31, the salaries for these three days represent an accrued expense and a related liability to Sierra. The employees receive total salaries of $2,000 for a five-day work week, or $400 per day. Thus, accrued salaries at October 31 are $1,200 ($400 × 3). This accrual increases a liability, Salaries and Wages Payable. It also decreases stockholders' equity by increasing an expense account, Salaries and Wages Expense, as shown in **Illustration 4.22**.

**ILLUSTRATION 4.22**  **Adjustment for accrued salaries**

**Basic Analysis:** The expense Salaries and Wages Expense is increased $1,200. Since it reduces stockholders' equity, it is entered as a negative. The liability Salaries and Wages Payable is increased $1,200.

**Equation Analysis:**

| Assets | = | Liabilities | + | Stockholders' Equity |
|---|---|---|---|---|
| | | Salaries and Wages Payable | | Salaries and Wages Expense |
| | | +$1,200 | | −$1,200 |

**Post-Adjustment Tabular Analysis:**

| | | | | | | BALANCE SHEET | | | | | | | | | | INCOME STATEMENT |
|---|---|---|---|---|---|---|---|---|---|---|---|---|---|---|---|---|
| | | | Assets | | | | = | | Liabilities | | | | + | Stockholders' Equity | | |
| | | | | | Acc. | | | | | Unearn. | Sal./ | | | Retained Earnings | | |
| | Accts. | Sup- | Prepd. | | Depr.— | Notes | Accts. | Int. | Serv. | Wages | Com. | | | | | |
| Cash | + Rec. | + plies | + Insur. | + Equip. | − Equip. | = Pay. | + Pay. | + Pay. | + Rev. | + Pay. | + Stock | + Rev. | − Exp. | − Div. | | |
| Bal. 15,200 | + 200 | + 1,000 | + 550 | + 5,000 | − 40 | = 5,000 | + 2,500 | + 50 | + 800 | | + 10,000 | + 10,600 | − 6,540 | − 500 | | |
| (A7) | | | | | | | | | | +1,200 | | | −1,200 | | Sal./Wages Expense |
| Bal. 15,200 | + 200 | + 1,000 | + 550 | + 5,000 | − 40 | = 5,000 | + 2,500 | + 50 | + 800 | + 1,200 | + 10,000 | + 10,600 | − 7,740 | − 500 | | |
| | | $21,910 | | | | | | | | $21,910 | | | | | | |

Notice the effects of the adjustment:

- After this adjustment, the balance in Salaries and Wages Expense of $5,200 (13 days × $400) is the actual salary expense for October. (The employees worked 13 days in October after beginning work on October 15.)
- The balance in Salaries and Wages Payable of $1,200 is the amount of the liability for salaries Sierra owes as of October 31.
- **Without the $1,200 adjustment for salaries, Sierra's expenses are understated $1,200 and its liabilities are understated $1,200.**

Sierra pays salaries every two weeks. Consequently, the next payday is November 9, when the company will again pay total salaries of $4,000. The payment consists of $1,200 of salaries and wages payable at October 31 plus $2,800 of salaries and wages expense for November (7 working days as shown in the November calendar × $400). On November 9, Sierra eliminates the liability for Salaries and Wages Payable that was recorded in the October 31 adjustment, and it records the proper amount of Salaries and Wages Expense for the period between November 1 and November 9.

| Assets | = | Liabilities | + | Stockholders' Equity | |
|---|---|---|---|---|---|
| | | Salaries and Wages | | Retained Earnings | |
| Cash | | Payable | | Rev. − Exp. − Div. | |
| −4,000 | = | −1,200 | + | −2,800 | Sal./Wages Exp. |

**Illustration 4.23** summarizes the accounting for accrued expenses.

**ILLUSTRATION 4.23**

**Accounting for accrued revenues**

| Accounting for Accrued Expenses | | | |
|---|---|---|---|
| Examples | Reason for Adjustment | Accounts Before Adjustment | Adjustment |
| Interest, rent, salaries | Expenses have been incurred but not yet paid in cash or recorded. | Expenses understated. Liabilities understated. | Increase expenses. Increase liabilities. |

---

### People, Planet, and Profit Insight

iStock.com/Nathan Gleave

#### Got Junk?

Do you have an old computer or two in your garage? How about an old TV that needs replacing? Many people do. Approximately 163,000 computers and televisions become obsolete **each day**. Yet, in a recent year, only 11% of computers were recycled. It is estimated that 75% of all computers ever sold are sitting in storage somewhere, waiting to be disposed of. Each of these old TVs and computers is loaded with lead, cadmium, mercury, and other toxic chemicals. If you have one of these electronic gadgets, you have a responsibility, and a probable cost, for disposing of it. Companies have the same problem, but their discarded materials may include lead paint, asbestos, and other toxic chemicals.

**What accounting issue might this cause for companies? (Go to WileyPLUS for this answer and additional questions.)**

---

## Summary of Basic Relationships

**Illustration 4.24** summarizes the four basic types of adjustments. Take some time to study and analyze the adjustments. Be sure to note that **each adjustment affects one balance sheet account and one income statement account**.

**ILLUSTRATION 4.24**

**Summary of adjustments**

| Type of Adjustment | Accounts Before Adjustment | Adjustment |
|---|---|---|
| Prepaid expenses | Assets overstated. Expenses understated. | Increase expenses. Decrease assets (or increase contra assets). |
| Unearned revenues | Liabilities overstated. Revenues understated. | Decrease liabilities. Increase revenues. |
| Accrued revenues | Assets understated. Revenues understated. | Increase assets. Increase revenues. |
| Accrued expenses | Expenses understated. Liabilities understated. | Increase expenses. Increase liabilities. |

**Illustration 4.25** summarizes the adjustments for Sierra Corporation on October 31 to show their cumulative effect on the basic accounting equation.

**ILLUSTRATION 4.25**   **Tabular summary of adjustments**

| | | | BALANCE SHEET | | | | | | | | | | | INCOME STATEMENT |
|---|---|---|---|---|---|---|---|---|---|---|---|---|---|---|
| | **Assets** | | | | | = | **Liabilities** | | | + | **Stockholders' Equity** | | | |
| | Cash + | Accts. Rec. + | Sup-plies + | Prepd. Insur. + | Equip. − | Acc. Depr.—Equip. = | Notes Pay. + | Accts. Pay. + | Int. Pay. + | Unearn. Serv. Rev. + | Sal./ Wages Pay. + | Com. Stock + | Rev. − | Exp. − Div. | |
| Bal. | 15,200 + | 0 + | 2,500 + | 600 + | 5,000 − | 0 = | 5,000 + | 2,500 + | 0 + | 1,200 + | 0 + | 10,000 + | 10,000 − | 4,900 − 500 | |
| (A1) | | −1,500 | | | | | | | | | | | | −1,500 | Supplies Expense |
| (A2) | | | −50 | | | | | | | | | | | −50 | Insurance Expense |
| (A3) | | | | | | −40 | | | | | | | | −40 | Depr. Expense |
| (A4) | | | | | | | | | | −400 | | | +400 | | Service Revenue |
| (A5) | | +200 | | | | | | | | | | | +200 | | Service Revenue |
| (A6) | | | | | | | | | +50 | | | | | −50 | Interest Expense |
| (A7) | | | | | | | | | | | +1,200 | | | −1,200 | Sal./Wages Expense |
| Bal. | 15,200 + | 200 + | 1,000 + | 550 + | 5,000 − | 40 = | 5,000 + | 2,500 + | 50 + | 800 + | 1,200 + | 10,000 + | 10,600 − | 7,740 − 500 | |

Retained Earnings

$21,910          $21,910

Illustration 4.25 includes the adjustment number in the first column on the left. The right-most column shows the specific effect on revenues and expenses.

## ACTION PLAN

- Make adjustments at the end of the period to recognize revenue for services performed and for expenses incurred.

- Don't forget to make adjustments for accruals. Adjustments for accruals will increase both a balance sheet and an income statement account.

### DO IT! 3 | Adjustments for Accruals—Accrued Salaries, Interest, and Utilities

**Part 2:** Micro Computer Services Inc. began operations on August 1, 2022. At the end of August 2022, management attempted to prepare monthly financial statements. The following information relates to August.

1. At August 31, the company owed its employees $800 in salaries that will be paid on September 1.

2. On August 1, the company borrowed $30,000 from a local bank on a 15-year mortgage. The annual interest rate is 10%.

3. Revenue for services performed but unrecorded for August totaled $1,100.

Indicate how adjustments for these three situations would affect the accounting equation by completing the following table, which includes a sample accrual for a utility bill received September 1 for services received during August 2022.

|  | Assets | = | Liabilities | + | Stockholders' Equity (Rev. | – | Exp.) |
|---|---|---|---|---|---|---|---|
| Sample | No effect | = | Increase | + | No effect | – | Increase |
| 1. |  |  |  |  |  |  |  |
| 2. |  |  |  |  |  |  |  |
| 3. |  |  |  |  |  |  |  |

### Solution

|  | Assets | = | Liabilities | + | Stockholders' Equity (Rev. | – | Exp.) |
|---|---|---|---|---|---|---|---|
| 1. | No effect | = | Increase | + | No effect | – | Increase |
| 2. | No effect | = | Increase | + | No effect | – | Increase |
| 3. | Increase | = | No effect | + | Increase | – | No effect |

Related exercise material: **BE4.8, DO IT! 4.3, E4.8, E4.9, E4.10, E4.11, and E4.12.**

# Preparing Financial Statements

### LEARNING OBJECTIVE 4

Prepare financial statements from adjusted amounts.

After adjusting the accounts, the adjusted balances for each account can be determined in a tabular analysis by summing each column. **Companies can then prepare financial statements directly from the details provided in the tabular summary of transactions and adjustments.** Illustration 4.26 presents the relationships between the data in the tabular summary of Sierra Corporation and the corresponding financial statements. As **Illustration 4.26** shows:

- Companies prepare the income statement from the revenue and expense accounts.

- Similarly, they derive the retained earnings statement from the Retained Earnings account, the Dividends account, and the net income (or net loss) shown in the income statement.

- Companies then prepare the balance sheet from the asset, liability, and stockholders' equity accounts.

- They obtain the amount reported for retained earnings on the balance sheet from the ending balance in the retained earnings statement.

**ILLUSTRATION 4.26**  **Preparation of financial statements from tabular summary**

| | Cash | + Accs. Rec. | + Sup-plies | + Prepd. Insur. | + Equip. | − Acc. Depr. Equip. | = Notes Pay. | + Accts. Pay. | + Int. Pay. | + Unearn. Serv. Rev. | + Sal./Wag. Pay. | + Com. Stock | + Rev. | − Exp. | − Div. | INCOME STATEMENT |
|---|---|---|---|---|---|---|---|---|---|---|---|---|---|---|---|---|
| (1) | 10,000 | | | | | | | | | | | 10,000 | | | | |
| (2) | 5,000 | | | | | | 5,000 | | | | | | | | | |
| (3) | −5,000 | | | | 5,000 | | | | | | | | | | | |
| (4) | 1,200 | | | | | | | | | 1,200 | | | | | | |
| (5) | 10,000 | | | | | | | | | | | | 10,000 | | | Service Revenue |
| (6) | −900 | | | | | | | | | | | | | −900 | | Rent Expense |
| (7) | −600 | | | 600 | | | | | | | | | | | | |
| (8) | | | 2,500 | | | | | 2,500 | | | | | | | | |
| (10) | −500 | | | | | | | | | | | | | | −500 | |
| (11) | −4,000 | | | | | | | | | | | | | −4,000 | | Sal./Wages Expense |
| Adj. | | | | | | | | | | | | | | | | |
| (A1) | | | −1,500 | | | | | | | | | | | −1,500 | | Supplies Expense |
| (A2) | | | | −50 | | | | | | | | | | −50 | | Insurance Expense |
| (A3) | | | | | | 40 | | | | | | | | −40 | | Depr. Expense |
| (A4) | | | | | | | | | | −400 | | | 400 | | | Service Revenue |
| (A5) | | 200 | | | | | | | | | | | 200 | | | Service Revenue |
| (A6) | | | | | | | | | 50 | | | | | −50 | | Interest Expense |
| (A7) | | | | | | | | | | | 1,200 | | | −1,200 | | Sal./Wages Expense |
| Bal. | 15,200 | + 200 | + 1,000 | + 550 | + 5,000 | − 40 | = 5,000 | + 2,500 | + 50 | + 800 | + 1,200 | + 10,000 | + 10,600 | − 7,740 | − 500 | |

Assets: $21,910        Liabilities + Stockholders' Equity: $21,910

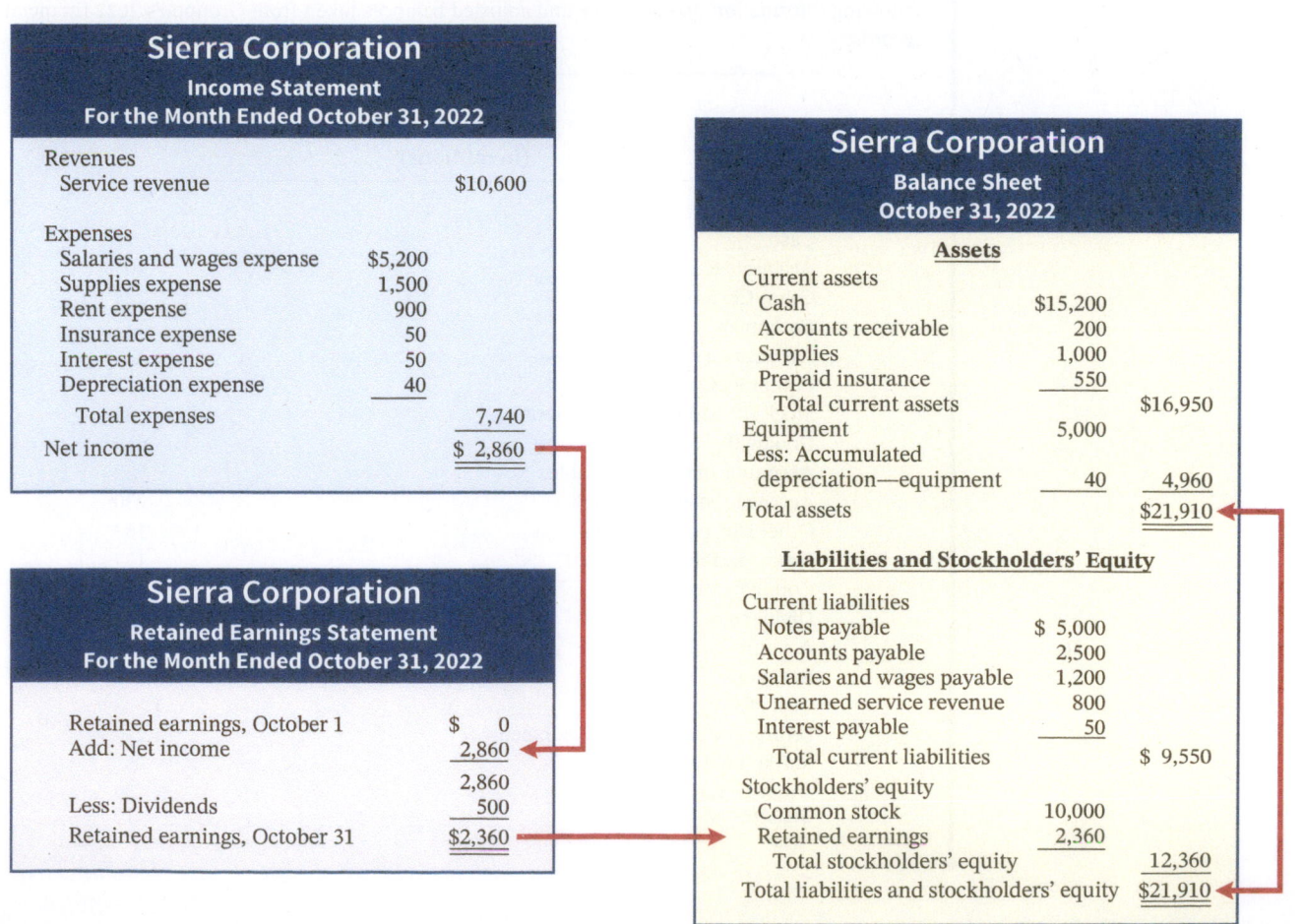

**Sierra Corporation**
**Income Statement**
**For the Month Ended October 31, 2022**

| | | |
|---|---|---|
| Revenues | | |
| Service revenue | | $10,600 |
| Expenses | | |
| Salaries and wages expense | $5,200 | |
| Supplies expense | 1,500 | |
| Rent expense | 900 | |
| Insurance expense | 50 | |
| Interest expense | 50 | |
| Depreciation expense | 40 | |
| Total expenses | | 7,740 |
| Net income | | $ 2,860 |

**Sierra Corporation**
**Retained Earnings Statement**
**For the Month Ended October 31, 2022**

| | | |
|---|---|---|
| Retained earnings, October 1 | | $    0 |
| Add: Net income | | 2,860 |
| | | 2,860 |
| Less: Dividends | | 500 |
| Retained earnings, October 31 | | $2,360 |

**Sierra Corporation**
**Balance Sheet**
**October 31, 2022**

**Assets**

| | | |
|---|---|---|
| Current assets | | |
| Cash | $15,200 | |
| Accounts receivable | 200 | |
| Supplies | 1,000 | |
| Prepaid insurance | 550 | |
| Total current assets | | $16,950 |
| Equipment | 5,000 | |
| Less: Accumulated depreciation—equipment | 40 | 4,960 |
| Total assets | | $21,910 |

**Liabilities and Stockholders' Equity**

| | | |
|---|---|---|
| Current liabilities | | |
| Notes payable | $ 5,000 | |
| Accounts payable | 2,500 | |
| Salaries and wages payable | 1,200 | |
| Unearned service revenue | 800 | |
| Interest payable | 50 | |
| Total current liabilities | | $ 9,550 |
| Stockholders' equity | | |
| Common stock | 10,000 | |
| Retained earnings | 2,360 | |
| Total stockholders' equity | | 12,360 |
| Total liabilities and stockholders' equity | | $21,910 |

**ACTION PLAN**
- Revenues and expenses are reported in the income statement.
- Dividends and net income are reported in the retained earnings statement.
- Asset, liability, and equity accounts are reported in the balance sheet.

## DO IT! 4 | Preparing Financial Statements

Indicate in which financial statement or statements each of the following adjusted account balances would be presented.

| | |
|---|---|
| Interest Revenue | Accounts Payable |
| Unearned Service Revenue | Depreciation Expense |
| Retained Earnings (beginning) | Accumulated Depreciation—Buildings |
| Supplies | Supplies Expense |
| Dividends | Cash |

### Solution

Income Statement:  Interest Revenue, Depreciation Expense, Supplies Expense.

Retained Earnings Statement:  Retained Earnings (beginning), Dividends.

Balance Sheet:  Unearned Service Revenue, Supplies, Accounts Payable, Accumulated Depreciation—Buildings, Cash.

Related exercise material: **BE4.10, BE4.11, BE4.12, DO IT! 4.4, and E4.18.**

## USING THE DECISION TOOLS | Groupon, Inc.

**Groupon, Inc.** operates online marketplaces that provide goods and services at discounted prices worldwide. Headquartered in Chicago, Illinois, it has over 11,843 employees. Suppose that the following information lists accounts and adjusted balances taken from Groupon's 2022 financial records.

**Groupon, Inc.**
**December 31, 2022**
**(in millions)**

| Account | |
|---|---:|
| Cash | $1,072 |
| Accounts Receivable | 105 |
| Other Current Assets | 224 |
| Equipment | 377 |
| Accumulated Depreciation— Equipment | 195 |
| Stock Investments (noncurrent) | 24 |
| Goodwill | 619 |
| Accounts and Other Payables | 932 |
| Accrued Expenses Payable | 230 |
| Other Current Liabilities | 163 |
| Notes Payable (noncurrent) | 137 |
| Common Stock | 1,687 |
| Dividends | 0 |
| Accumulated Deficit | 849 |
| Revenues | 3,181 |
| Cost of Goods Sold | 1,643 |
| Selling and Administrative Expenses | 1,294 |
| Marketing Expense | 269 |
| Other Expense | 33 |
| Income Tax Expense | 16 |

## Instructions

Using this information, prepare an income statement, retained earnings statement, and classified balance sheet. **Be sure to prepare them in that order since each statement depends
on information determined in the preceding statement.** (*Hint:* Note that because Groupon
has experienced losses, Groupon reports an Accumulated Deficit rather than Retained Earnings.
Remember that the amount of the Accumulated Deficit reported represents the balance at the
beginning of the year.)

### Solution

**Groupon, Inc.**
**Income Statement**
**For the Year Ended December 31, 2022**
**(in millions)**

| | | |
|---|---:|---:|
| Revenues | | $3,181 |
| Cost of goods sold | $1,643 | |
| Selling and administrative expenses | 1,294 | |
| Marketing expense | 269 | |
| Other expense | 33 | |
| Income tax expense | 16 | 3,255 |
| Net loss | | $ (74) |

**Groupon, Inc.**
**Retained Earnings Statement**
**For the Year Ended December 31, 2022**
**(in millions)**

| | |
|---|---:|
| Beginning accumulated deficit | $ (849) |
| Less: Net loss | 74 |
| Less: Dividends | 0 |
| Ending accumulated deficit | $ (923) |

**Groupon, Inc.**
**Balance Sheet**
**December 31, 2022**
**(in millions)**

**Assets**

| | | |
|---|---:|---:|
| Current assets | | |
| Cash | $1,072 | |
| Accounts receivable | 105 | |
| Other current assets | 224 | |
| Total current assets | | $1,401 |
| Long-term investments | | |
| Stock investments | | 24 |
| Property, plant, and equipment | | |
| Less: Equipment | 377 | |
| Less: Accumulated | | |
| depreciation—equipment | 195 | 182 |
| Intangible assets | | |
| Goodwill | | 619 |
| Total assets | | $2,226 |

| Liabilities and Stockholders' Equity | | |
|---|---|---|
| **Liabilities** | | |
| Current liabilities | | |
| Accounts and other | | |
| payables | $ 932 | |
| Accrued expenses | | |
| payable | 230 | |
| Other current liabilities | 163 | |
| Total current liabilities | | $1,325 |
| Long-term liabilities | | |
| Notes payable | | 137 |
| Total liabilities | | 1,462 |
| **Stockholders' equity** | | |
| Common stock | 1,687 | |
| Accumulated deficit | (923) | |
| Total stockholders' equity | | 764 |
| Total liabilities and stockholders' equity | | $2,226 |

# Review and Practice

## Learning Objectives Review

### 1 Explain the accrual basis of accounting and the reasons for adjustments.

The revenue recognition principle dictates that companies recognize revenue when a performance obligation has been satisfied. The expense recognition principle dictates that companies recognize expenses in the period when the companies make efforts to generate those revenues.

Under the cash basis, companies record events only in the periods in which the companies receive or pay cash. Accrual-based accounting means that companies record, in the periods in which the events occur, events that change the companies' financial statements even if cash has not been exchanged.

Companies make adjustments at the end of an accounting period. These adjustments ensure that companies record revenues in the period in which the performance obligation is satisfied and that companies recognize expenses in the period in which they are incurred. The major types of adjustments are prepaid expenses, unearned revenues, accrued revenues, and accrued expenses.

### 2 Prepare adjustments for deferrals.

Deferrals are either prepaid expenses or unearned revenues. Companies make adjustments for deferrals at the statement date to record the portion of the deferred item incurred as an expense (prepaid expenses) or satisfied by performance of services (unearned revenues).

### 3 Prepare adjustments for accruals.

Accruals are either accrued revenues or accrued expenses. Adjustments for accruals record revenues for services performed and expenses incurred in the current accounting period that have not yet been recognized in the accounting period.

### 4 Prepare financial statements from adjusted amounts.

After adjusting the accounts, the adjusted balances for each account can be determined in a tabular analysis by summing each column. The income statement can then be prepared from the revenue and expense accounts. The retained earnings statement is then prepared from the Retained Earnings account, Dividends account, and the net income (or net loss) shown in the income statement. The balance sheet is prepared from the asset, liability, and stockholders' equity accounts, and the ending balance in Retained Earnings from the retained earnings statement.

## Decision Tools Review

| Decision Checkpoints | Info Needed for Decision | Tool to Use for Decision | How to Evaluate Results |
|---|---|---|---|
| At what point should the company record revenue? | Need to understand the nature of the company's business | Record revenue in the period in which the performance obligation is satisfied. | Recognizing revenue too early overstates current period revenue; recognizing it too late understates current period revenue. |
| At what point should the company record expenses? | Need to understand the nature of the company's business | Record expenses in the period in which efforts are made to generate revenue. | Recognizing expenses too early overstates current period expense; recognizing them too late understates current period expense. |

## Glossary Review

**Accrual-basis accounting** Accounting basis in which companies record, in the periods in which the events occur, transactions that change the companies' financial statements, even if cash was not exchanged. (4-5).

**Accrued expenses** Expenses incurred but not yet paid in cash or recorded. (4-16).

**Accrued revenues** Revenues for services performed but not yet received in cash or recorded. (4-14).

**Adjustments** Changes made to accounts at the end of an accounting period to ensure that the revenue recognition and expense recognition principles are followed. (4-6).

**Book value** The difference between the cost of a depreciable asset and its related accumulated depreciation. (4-12).

**Cash-basis accounting** Accounting basis in which a company records revenue only when it receives cash and an expense only when it pays cash. (4-5).

**Contra asset account** An account that is offset against an asset account on the balance sheet. (4-11).

**Depreciation** The process of allocating the cost of an asset to expense over its useful life. (4-10).

**Expense recognition principle** The principle that companies recognize expenses in the period in which they make efforts (consume assets or incur liabilities) to generate revenue. (4-4).

**Fiscal year** An accounting period that is one-year long. (4-3, in margin).

**Periodicity assumption** An assumption that the economic life of a business can be divided into artificial time periods. (4-3).

**Prepaid expenses (prepayments)** Expenses paid in cash before they are used or consumed. (4-8).

**Revenue recognition principle** The principle that companies recognize revenue in the accounting period in which the performance obligation is satisfied. (4-3).

**Unearned revenues** Cash received and a liability recorded before services are performed. (4-12).

**Useful life** The length of service of a productive asset. (4-10).

## Practice Multiple-Choice Questions

1. **(LO 1)** What is the periodicity assumption?
   a. Companies should recognize revenue in the accounting period in which services are performed.
   b. Companies should match expenses with revenues.
   c. The economic life of a business can be divided into artificial time periods.
   d. The fiscal year should correspond with the calendar year.

2. **(LO 1)** Which principle dictates that efforts (expenses) be recorded with accomplishments (revenues)?
   a. Expense recognition principle.
   b. Historical cost principle.
   c. Periodicity principle.
   d. Revenue recognition principle.

3. **(LO 1)** Which one of these statements about the accrual basis of accounting is **false**?

   a. Companies record events that change their financial statements in the period in which events occur, even if cash was not exchanged.
   b. Companies recognize revenue in the period in which the performance obligation is satisfied.
   c. This basis is in accordance with generally accepted accounting principles.
   d. Companies record revenue only when they receive cash and record expense only when they pay out cash.

4. **(LO 1)** Adjustments are made to ensure that:
   a. expenses are recognized in the period in which they are incurred.
   b. revenues are recorded in the period in which the performance obligation is satisfied.
   c. balance sheet and income statement accounts have correct balances at the end of an accounting period.
   d. All of the answer choices are correct.

**5. (LO 2, 3)** Each of the following is a major type (or category) of adjustment **except**:

  a. prepaid expenses.    c. accrued expenses.

  b. accrued revenues.    d. unearned expenses.

**6. (LO 2)** The unadjusted account balances show Supplies $1,350 and Supplies Expense $0. If $600 of supplies are on hand at the end of the period, the adjustment:

  a. increases Supplies $600 and increases Supplies Expense $600.

  b. increases Supplies $750 and increases Supplies Expense $750.

  c. increases Supplies Expense $750 and decreases Supplies $750.

  d. increases Supplies Expense $600 and decreases Supplies $600.

**7. (LO 2)** Adjustments for unearned revenues:

  a. decrease liabilities and increase revenues.

  b. increase liabilities and increase revenues.

  c. increase assets and increase revenues.

  d. decrease revenues and decrease assets.

**8. (LO 2)** Adjustments for prepaid expenses:

  a. decrease assets and increase revenues.

  b. decrease expenses and increase assets.

  c. decrease assets and increase expenses.

  d. decrease revenues and increase assets.

**9. (LO 2)** Queenan Company computes depreciation on delivery equipment at $1,000 for the month of June. The adjustment to record this depreciation:

  a. increases Depreciation Expense $1,000 and increases Accumulated Depreciation—Queenan Company $1,000.

  b. increases Depreciation Expense $1,000 and increases Equipment $1,000.

  c. increases Depreciation Expense $1,000 and increases Accumulated Depreciation—Equipment $1,000.

  d. increases Equipment Expense $1,000 and increases Accumulated Depreciation—Equipment $1,000.

**10. (LO 3)** Adjustments for accrued revenues:

  a. increase assets and increase liabilities.

  b. increase assets and increase revenues.

  c. decrease assets and decrease revenues.

  d. decrease liabilities and increase revenues.

**11. (LO 3)** Colleen Mooney earned a salary of $400 for the last week of September. She will be paid on October 1. The adjustment for Colleen's employer at September 30 is:

  a. No adjustment is required.

  b. increase Salaries and Wages Expense $400 and increase Salaries and Wages Payable $400.

  c. increase Salaries and Wages Expense $400 and decrease Cash $400.

  d. decrease Salaries and Wages Payable $400 and decrease Cash $400.

## Solutions

**1. c.** The periodicity assumption states that the economic life of a business can be divided into artificial time periods. The other choices are incorrect because (a) this statement describes the revenue recognition principle, (b) this statement describes the expense recognition principle, and (d) the periodicity assumption states that the life of a business can be divided into artificial time periods, not that the fiscal year and calendar year must coincide.

**2. a.** The expense recognition principle dictates that companies recognize expense in the period in which they make efforts to generate revenue. The other choices are incorrect because (b) the historical cost principle states that when assets are purchased, they should be recorded at cost; (c) the periodicity assumption states that the life of a business can be divided into artificial time periods; and (d) the revenue recognition principle states that revenue should be recorded in the period in which the performance obligation is satisfied.

**3. d.** If companies record revenue only when they receive cash and record expense only when they pay out cash, they are using the cash basis of accounting. The other choices are true statements about accrual-basis accounting.

**4. d.** Adjustments are made to ensure that expenses are recognized in the period in which they are incurred, that revenues are recorded in the period in which the performance obligation is satisfied, and that balance sheet and income statement accounts have correct balances at the end of an accounting period. Although choices (a), (b), and (c) are correct, choice (d) is the best answer.

**5. d.** Unearned expenses are not a major type of adjustment. Choices (a) prepaid expenses, (b) accrued revenues, and (c) accrued expenses are all major types of adjustments.

**6. c.** The adjustment increases Supplies Expense for $750 ($1,350 – $600) and decreases Supplies for $750. The other choices are therefore incorrect.

**7. a.** Adjustments for unearned revenues decrease liabilities and increase revenues. The other choices are therefore incorrect.

**8. c.** Adjustments for prepaid expenses decrease assets and increase expenses. The other choices are therefore incorrect.

**9. c.** The adjustment increases Depreciation Expense and increases Accumulation Depreciation—Equipment. The other choices are incorrect because (a) the contra asset account title includes the asset being depreciated, not the company name; (b) the increase should be to the contra asset account, not the asset; and (d) the increase should be to Depreciation Expense, not Equipment Expense.

**10. b.** When the adjustment is made for accrued revenues, an asset account (usually Accounts Receivable) is increased and a revenue account is increased. The other choices are therefore incorrect.

**11. b.** The adjustment should increase Salaries and Wages Expense $400 and increase Salaries and Wages Payable for $400. Choice (a) is incorrect because if an adjustment is not made, the amount of money owed (liability) that is shown on the balance sheet will be understated and the amount of salaries and wages expense will also be understated. Choices (c) and (d) are incorrect because adjustments never affect cash.

# Practice Brief Exercises

**1. (LO 1)** The accounting records of Dey Company include the following accounts. Explain why each account may need adjustment.

*Indicate why adjustments are needed.*

    **a.** Supplies.

    **b.** Unearned Service Revenue.

    **c.** Salaries and Wages Payable.

    **d.** Interest Payable.

### Solution

**1. a.** Supplies: to recognize supplies used during the period.

    **b.** Unearned Service Revenue: to record revenue generated for services performed.

    **c.** Salaries and Wages Payable: to recognize salaries and wages accrued to employees at the end of a reporting period.

    **d.** Interest Payable: to recognize interest accrued but unpaid on notes payable.

**2. (LO 2)** At the end of its first year, a tabular summary of transactions for Rayburn Company before adjustments include the following selected account information.

*Prepare adjustment for depreciation.*

| | Assets | | = Liabilities + | Stockholders' Equity | | | |
|---|---|---|---|---|---|---|---|
| | Equip. − | Acc. Depr.—Equip. = | | Com. Stock + | Rev. − | Exp. (Depr.) − | Div. |
| Bal. | 40,000 | 0 | | | | 0 | |

Depreciation for the year is estimated to be $8,000. Record the adjustment for depreciation in the tabular summary and indicate the adjusted balance in each account.

### Solution

**2.**

| | Assets | | = Liabilities + | Stockholders' Equity | | | |
|---|---|---|---|---|---|---|---|
| | Equip. − | Acc. Depr.—Equip. = | | Com. Stock + | Rev. − | Exp. (Depr.) − | Div. |
| Bal. | 40,000 | 0 | | | | 0 | |
| Dec. 31 | | −8,000 | | | | −8,000 | |
| Adj. Bal. | 40,000 | −8,000 | | | | −8,000 | |

**3. (LO 3)** You are asked to prepare the following accrued adjustments at December 31.

*Prepare adjustments for accruals.*

    **a.** Services performed but not paid or recorded are $4,200.

    **b.** Utility expenses incurred but not paid are $660.

    **c.** Salaries and wages earned by employees of $3,000 are unpaid.

Use the following account titles: Accounts Payable, Accounts Receivable, Service Revenue, Salaries and Wages Expense, Salaries and Wages Payable, and Utilities Expense.

### Solution

**3.**

| | Assets = | Liabilities | | + | Stockholders' Equity | | | | |
|---|---|---|---|---|---|---|---|---|---|
| Adjustment | Accts. Rec. = | Accts. Pay. + | Sal./Wages Pay. + | | Com. Stock + | Rev. − | Exp. − | Div. | |
| a. | 4,200 | | | | | 4,200 | | | Service Revenue |
| b. | | 660 | | | | | −660 | | Utilities Expense |
| c. | | | 3,000 | | | | −3,000 | | Sal./Wages Expense |

**4. (LO 1, 2, 3)** Blair Company has the following balance sheet accounts. Identify the accounts that may require adjustment. For each account that requires adjustment, indicate (a) the type of

*Analyze balance sheet accounts that may require adjustment.*

adjustment (prepaid expense, unearned revenue, accrued revenue, or accrued expense) and (b) the related account in the adjustment.

Accounts Receivable          Interest Payable
Supplies                     Unearned Service Revenue
Prepaid Insurance

### Solution

4.

| Account | Type of Adjustment | Related Account |
|---|---|---|
| Accounts Receivable | Accrued Revenue | Service Revenue |
| Supplies | Prepaid Expense | Supplies Expense |
| Prepaid Insurance | Prepaid Expense | Insurance Expense |
| Interest Payable | Accrued Expense | Interest Expense |
| Unearned Service Revenue | Unearned Revenue | Service Revenue |

*Prepare an income statement from adjusted accounts.*

**5. (LO 4)** Harmony Company has the following adjusted accounts at December 31, 2022: Cash $12,000, Retained Earnings $22,000, Dividends $3,000, Service Revenue $41,000, Rent Expense $900, Salaries and Wages Expense $6,000, Supplies Expense $700, and Depreciation Expense $1,800. Prepare an income statement for the year.

### Solution

5.

**Harmony Company**
**Income Statement**
**For the Year Ended December 31, 2022**

| | | |
|---|---|---|
| Revenues | | |
| Service revenue | | $41,000 |
| Expenses | | |
| Salaries and wages expense | $6,000 | |
| Rent expense | 900 | |
| Depreciation expense | 1,800 | |
| Supplies expense | 700 | |
| Total expenses | | 9,400 |
| Net income | | $31,600 |

## Practice Exercise

*Prepare correct income statement.*

**(LO 2, 3, 4)** The income statement of Bragg Co. for the month of July 2022 shows net income of $1,400 based on Service Revenue $5,500, Salaries and Wages Expense $2,300, Supplies Expense $1,200, and Utilities Expense $600. In reviewing the statement, you discover the following.

1. Insurance expired during July of $450 was omitted.

2. Supplies expense includes $300 of supplies that are still on hand at July 31.

3. Depreciation on equipment of $180 was omitted.

4. Accrued but unpaid salaries and wages at July 31 of $400 were not included.

5. Services performed but unrecorded totaled $600.

### Instructions

Prepare a correct income statement for July 2022.

### Solution

| Bragg Co. |
| :-: |
| **Income Statement** |
| **For the Month Ended July 31, 2022** |

| | | |
| :--- | ---: | ---: |
| Revenues | | |
| Service revenue ($5,500 + $600) | | $6,100 |
| Expenses | | |
| Salaries and wages expense ($2,300 + $400) | $2,700 | |
| Supplies expense ($1,200 − $300) | 900 | |
| Utilities expense | 600 | |
| Insurance expense | 450 | |
| Depreciation expense | 180 | |
| Total expenses | | 4,830 |
| Net income | | $1,270 |

## Practice Problem

**(LO 2, 3)** Terry Thomas and a group of investors incorporated the Green Thumb Lawn Care Corporation on April 1. At April 30, a tabular summary of transactions shows the following balances.

*Prepare adjustments from selected data.*

| | Assets | | | | | = | Liabilities | | | + | Stockholders' Equity | | | |
| :--- | ---: | ---: | ---: | ---: | ---: | :-: | ---: | ---: | ---: | :-: | ---: | ---: | ---: | ---: |
| | | Accts. | Prepd. | | Acc. Depr.— | | Notes | Unearn. Serv. | Int. | | Com. | | Retained Earnings | |
| | Cash + | Rec. + | Insur. + | Equip. − | Equip. = | | Pay. + | Rev. + | Pay. + | | Stock + | Rev. − | Exp. − | Div. |
| Bal. | 11,800 + | 500 + | 3,600 + | 28,000 − | 0 = | | 20,000 + | 4,200 + | 0 + | | 18,000 + | 2,800 − | 1,100 − | 0 |

$43,900          $43,900

Analysis reveals the following additional data pertaining to these accounts.

1. Prepaid insurance is the cost of a 2-year insurance policy, effective April 1.

2. Depreciation on the equipment is $500 per month.

3. The note payable is dated April 1. It is a 6-month, 6% note.

4. Seven customers paid for the company's 6-month lawn service package of $600 beginning in April. These customers received the first month of services in April.

5. Lawn services performed for other customers but not billed at April 30 totaled $1,500.

### Instructions

Prepare the adjustments and record in the tabular summary with explanations for the month of April.

### Solution

| | Assets | | | | | = | Liabilities | | | + | Stockholders' Equity | | | | |
| :--- | ---: | ---: | ---: | ---: | ---: | :-: | ---: | ---: | ---: | :-: | ---: | ---: | ---: | ---: | :--- |
| | | Accts. | Prepd. | | Acc. Depr.— | | Notes | Unearn. Serv. | Int. | | Com. | | Retained Earnings | | |
| | Cash + | Rec. + | Insur. + | Equip. − | Equip. = | | Pay. + | Rev. + | Pay. + | | Stock + | Rev. − | Exp. − | Div. | |
| Bal. | 11,800 + | 500 + | 3,600 + | 28,000 − | 0 = | | 20,000 + | 4,200 + | 0 + | | 18,000 + | 2,800 − | 1,100 − | 0 | |
| Adj. | | | | | | | | | | | | | | | |
| (A1) | | | −150 | | | | | | | | | | −150 | | Ins. Exp. |
| (A2) | | | | | −500 | | | | | | | | −500 | | Depr. Exp. |
| (A3) | | | | | | | | | +100 | | | | −100 | | Int. Exp. |
| (A4) | | | | | | | | −700 | | | | +700 | | | Ser. Rev. |
| (A5) | | +1,500 | | | | | | | | | | +1,500 | | | Ser. Rev. |
| Bal. | 11,800 + | 2,000 + | 3,450 + | 28,000 − | 500 = | | 20,000 + | 3,500 + | 100 + | | 18,000 + | 5,000 − | 1,850 − | 0 | |

$44,750          $44,750

# WileyPLUS

Brief Exercises, DO IT! Exercises, Exercises, Problems, and many additional resources are available for practice in WileyPLUS.

## Questions

**1. a.** How does the periodicity assumption affect an accountant's analysis of accounting transactions?

**b.** Explain the term fiscal year.

**2.** Identify and state two generally accepted accounting principles that relate to adjusting the accounts.

**3.** Max Wilson, a lawyer, accepts a legal engagement in March, performs the work in April, and is paid in May. If Wilson's law firm prepares monthly financial statements, when should it recognize revenue from this engagement? Why?

**4.** Max Wilson, a lawyer, accepts a legal engagement in March, performs the work in April, and is paid in May. Wilson pays no costs in March, $2,500 in April, and $2,200 in May (incurred in April). How much expense should the firm deduct from revenues in the month when it recognizes the revenue? Why?

**5.** "The historical cost principle of accounting requires adjustments." Do you agree? Explain.

**6.** Why might the financial information from unadjusted accounts not be up-to-date and complete?

**7.** Distinguish between the two categories of adjustments and identify the types of adjustments applicable to each category.

**8.** What types of accounts does a company increase or decrease in a prepaid expense adjustment?

**9.** "Depreciation is a process of valuation that results in the reporting of the fair value of the asset." Do you agree? Explain.

**10.** Explain the differences between depreciation expense and accumulated depreciation.

**11.** Steele Company purchased equipment for $15,000. By the current balance sheet date, the company had depreciated $7,000. Indicate the balance sheet presentation of the data.

**12.** What types of accounts are increased or decreased in an unearned revenue adjustment?

**13.** Abe Technologies provides maintenance service for computers and office equipment for companies throughout the Northeast. The sales manager is elated because she closed a $300,000, 3-year maintenance contract on December 29, 2021, two days before the company's year-end. "Now we will hit this year's net income target for sure," she crowed. The customer is required to pay $100,000 on December 29 (the day the deal was closed). Two more payments of $100,000 each are also required on December 29, 2022 and 2023. Discuss the effect that this event will have on the company's financial statements.

**14.** BeneMart, a large national retail chain, is nearing its fiscal year-end. It appears that the company is not going to hit its revenue and net income targets. The company's marketing manager, Ed Mellon, suggests running a promotion selling $50 gift cards for $45. He believes that this would be very popular and would enable the company to meet its targets for revenue and net income. What do you think of this idea?

**15.** Whistler Corp. performed services for a customer but has not received payment nor has it recorded any information related to the work. Which of the following types of accounts are involved in the adjustment: (a) asset, (b) liability, (c) revenue, or (d) expense? For the accounts selected, indicate whether they would be increased or decreased in the adjustment.

**16.** A company fails to recognize an expense incurred but not paid. Indicate which of the following types of accounts is increased or decreased in the adjustment: (a) asset, (b) liability, (c) revenue, or (d) expense.

**17.** A company makes an accrued revenue adjustment for $780 and an accrued expense adjustment for $510. How much was net income understated or overstated prior to these adjustments? Explain.

**18.** On January 9, a company pays $6,200 for salaries, of which $1,100 was reported as Salaries and Wages Payable on December 31. Indicate all accounts increased or decreased as well as dollar amounts when payment occurs.

**19.** For each of the following items before adjustment, indicate the type of adjustment—prepaid expense, unearned revenue, accrued revenue, or accrued expense—that is needed to correct the misstatement. If an item could result in more than one type of adjustment, indicate each of the types.

    **a.** Assets are understated.

    **b.** Liabilities are overstated.

    **c.** Liabilities are understated.

    **d.** Expenses are understated.

    **e.** Assets are overstated.

    **f.** Revenue is understated.

**20.** One-half of the adjustment is given below. Indicate the account title for the other half of the adjustment.

    **a.** Salaries and Wages Expense is increased.

    **b.** Depreciation Expense is increased.

    **c.** Interest Payable is increased.

    **d.** Supplies is decreased.

    **e.** Accounts Receivable is increased.

    **f.** Unearned Service Revenue is decreased.

**21.** "An adjustment may affect more than one balance sheet or income statement account." Do you agree? Why or why not?

**22.** Which balance sheet account provides evidence that **Apple** records sales on an accrual basis rather than a cash basis? Explain.

**23. a.** What information do accrual-basis financial statements provide that cash-basis statements do not?

    **b.** What information do cash-basis financial statements provide that accrual-basis statements do not?

# Brief Exercises

**BE4.1 (LO 1), C** Transactions that affect earnings do not necessarily affect cash. Identify the effect, if any, that each of the following transactions would have upon cash and net income. The first transaction has been completed as an example.

*Identify impact of transactions on cash and net income.*

|  | Cash | Net Income |
|---|---|---|
| a. Purchased $100 of supplies for cash. | −$100 | $0 |

b. Recorded an adjustment to reflect the use of $20 of the above supplies.

c. Made sales of $1,300, all on account.

d. Received $800 from customers in payment of their accounts.

e. Purchased equipment for cash, $2,500.

f. Recorded depreciation of building for period used, $600.

**BE4.2 (LO 2, 3), C** The records of Melmann Company includes the following accounts. Explain why each account may require adjustment.

*Indicate why adjustments are needed.*

a. Prepaid Insurance.  c. Unearned Service Revenue.

b. Depreciation Expense.  d. Interest Payable.

**BE4.3 (LO 1), AN** Cortina Company accumulates the following adjustment data at December 31. Indicate (1) the type of adjustment (prepaid expense, accrued revenue, and so on) and (2) the status of the accounts before adjustment (for example, "assets understated and revenues understated").

*Identify the major types of adjustments.*

a. Supplies of $400 are on hand. Supplies account shows $1,600 balance.

b. Services performed but unbilled total $700.

c. Interest of $300 has accumulated on a note payable.

d. Rental services related to rent collected in advance totaling $1,100 have been provided.

**BE4.4 (LO 2), AP** A tabular summary of transactions for Lahey Advertising Company before adjustments includes the following selected account information.

*Prepare adjustment for supplies.*

| Assets | = | Liabilities | + | Stockholders' Equity | | | | | |
|---|---|---|---|---|---|---|---|---|---|
| Supplies | = |  |  | Com. Stock | + | Rev. | − | Exp. (Supplies.) | − Div. |
| Bal. 8,800 |  |  |  |  |  |  |  | 0 |  |

On December 31, there is $1,100 of supplies on hand. Record the adjustment for supplies in the tabular summary and indicate the adjusted balance in each account.

**BE4.5 (LO 2), AP** At the end of its first year, a tabular summary of transactions for Rayburn Company before adjustments include the following selected account information.

*Prepare adjustment for depreciation.*

| Assets | | = | Liabilities | + | Stockholders' Equity | | | | | |
|---|---|---|---|---|---|---|---|---|---|---|
| Equip. | − Acc. Depr.—Equip. | = |  |  | Com. Stock | + | Rev. | − | Exp. (Depr.) | − Div. |
| Bal. 22,000 | 0 |  |  |  |  |  |  |  | 0 |  |

Depreciation for the year is estimated to be $2,750. Record the adjustment for depreciation in the tabular summary and indicate the adjusted balance in each account.

**BE4.6 (LO 2), AP** On July 1, 2022, Ling Co. pays $12,400 to Marsh Insurance Co. for a 2-year insurance contract. Both companies have fiscal years ending December 31. For Ling Co., enter the July 1 transaction and the December 31 adjustment in the tabular summary that follows.

*Prepare adjustment for prepaid expense.*

| Assets | | | = | Liabilities | + | Stockholders' Equity | | | | | |
|---|---|---|---|---|---|---|---|---|---|---|---|
| Cash | + | Prepaid Insurance | = |  |  | Com. Stock | + | Rev. | − | Exp. | − Div. |
| Jul. 1 |  |  |  |  |  |  |  |  |  |  |  |
| Dec. 31 |  |  |  |  |  |  |  |  |  |  |  |
| Bal. |  |  |  |  |  |  |  |  |  |  |  |

*Prepare adjustment for unearned revenue.*

**BE4.7 (LO 2), AP** On July 1, 2022, Ling Co. pays $12,400 to Marsh Insurance Co. for a 2-year insurance contract. Both companies have fiscal years ending December 31. For Marsh Insurance Co., enter the July 1 transaction and the December 31 adjustment in the tabular summary that follows.

| | Assets | = | Liabilities | + | | Stockholders' Equity | | | | |
|---|---|---|---|---|---|---|---|---|---|---|
| | | | Unearned | | Com. | | | | | |
| | Cash | = | Serv. Rev. | + | Stock | + | Rev. | − | Exp. | − Div. |
| Jul. 1 | | | | | | | | | | |
| Dec. 31 | | | | | | | | | | |
| Bal. | | | | | | | | | | |

*Prepare adjustments for accruals.*

**BE4.8 (LO 3), AP** The bookkeeper for Tran Company asks you to record the following accrual adjustments at December 31 in the tabular summary that follows.

| Assets | = | Liabilities | | | + | | Stockholders' Equity | | | |
|---|---|---|---|---|---|---|---|---|---|---|
| Accounts | | Interest | | Sal./Wages | | Com. | | | | |
| Receivable | = | Payable | + | Payable | + | Stock | + | Rev. | − Exp. | − Div. |

Use these account titles: Service Revenue, Accounts Receivable, Interest Expense, Interest Payable, Salaries and Wages Expense, and Salaries and Wages Payable.

   **a.** Interest on notes payable of $300 is accrued.

   **b.** Services performed but unbilled total $1,700.

   **c.** Salaries of $780 earned by employees have not been recorded.

*Analyze balance sheet accounts that may require adjustment.*

**BE4.9 (LO 2, 3), AN** Woods Company includes the following balance sheet accounts. Identify the accounts that might require adjustment. For each account that requires adjustment, indicate (1) the type of adjustment (prepaid expense, unearned revenue, accrued revenue, or accrued expense) and (2) the related account in the adjustment.

   **a.** Accounts Receivable.                     **e.** Notes Payable.

   **b.** Prepaid Insurance.                        **f.** Interest Payable.

   **c.** Equipment.                                 **g.** Unearned Service Revenue.

   **d.** Accumulated Depreciation—Equipment.

*Prepare an income statement from adjusted account balances.*

**BE4.10 (LO 4), AP** The adjusted account balances of Levin Corporation at December 31, 2022, include the following accounts: Retained Earnings $17,200, Dividends $6,000, Service Revenue $32,000, Salaries and Wages Expense $14,000, Insurance Expense $1,800, Rent Expense $3,900, Supplies Expense $1,500, and Depreciation Expense $1,000. Prepare an income statement for the year.

*Determine net income and prepare a retained earnings statement from adjusted account balances.*

**BE4.11 (LO 4), AP** The adjusted account balances of Pepper Corp. at December 31, 2022, include the following accounts: Retained Earnings $21,000, Dividends $3,000, Service Revenue $45,000, Interest Revenue $3,100, Rent Expense $4,800, Depreciation Expense $2,500, and Salaries and Wage Expense $18,200. The balance in Retained Earnings is the balance of January 1, 2022. Determine net income and prepare a retained earnings statement for the year.

*Prepare a classified balance sheet from adjusted account balances.*

**BE4.12 (LO 4), AP** The following, listed in alphabetical order, are the adjusted accounts of Rainforest Inc. as of December 31, 2022: Accounts Payable $3,900, Accounts Receivable $1,700, Accumulated Depreciation—Equipment $6,000, Bonds Payable $31,000, Cash $1,300, Common Stock $20,000, Equipment $50,000, Notes Payable (current) $2,200, Inventory $3,700, Notes Payable (long term) $5,000, Land $26,000, Retained Earnings $15,000, and Supplies $400. Prepare a classified balance sheet in good form as of December 31, 2022.

*Identify financial statement for selected accounts.*

**BE4.13 (LO 4), K** The following selected accounts appear in the adjusted balances for Deane Company. Indicate the financial statement on which each account would be reported.

   **a.** Accumulated Depreciation.                **e.** Service Revenue.

   **b.** Depreciation Expense.                    **f.** Supplies.

   **c.** Retained Earnings (beginning).         **g.** Accounts Payable.

   **d.** Dividends.

## DO IT! Exercises

**DO IT! 4.1 (LO 1), C** A list of concepts is provided below in the left column, with descriptions of the concepts in the right column. There are more descriptions provided than concepts. Match the description to the concept.

*Identify timing concepts.*

1. _____ Cash-basis accounting.

2. _____ Fiscal year.

3. _____ Revenue recognition principle.

4. _____ Expense recognition principle.

a. Monthly and quarterly time periods.

b. Accountants divide the economic life of a business into artificial time periods.

c. Efforts (expenses) should be recognized in the period in which a company consumes assets or incurs liabilities to generate accomplishments (revenues).

d. Companies record revenues when they receive cash and record expenses when they pay out cash.

e. An accounting time period that is one year in length.

f. An accounting time period that starts on January 1 and ends on December 31.

g. Companies record transactions in the period in which the events occur.

h. Recognize revenue in the accounting period in which a performance obligation is satisfied.

**DO IT! 4.2 (LO 2), AP** A partial tabular summary of transactions for Umatilla, Inc. on March 31, 2022, includes the following accounts before adjustments.

*Prepare adjustments for deferrals.*

| | Assets | | | = | Liabilities | + | Stockholders' Equity | | |
|---|---|---|---|---|---|---|---|---|---|
| | Prepaid | | Acc. | | Unearned | | | | |
| Supplies + | Insur. + | Equip. − | Depr.— Equip. = | | Serv. Rev. + | | Rev. − | | Exp. |
| 2,500 | 2,400 | 30,000 | −4,800 | | 10,000 | | | | |

An analysis of the accounts shows the following.

1. Insurance expires at the rate of $300 per month.

2. Supplies on hand total $900.

3. The equipment depreciates $200 per month.

4. During March, services were performed for two-fifths of the unearned service revenue.

Prepare a tabular summary to record adjustments for the month of March. Include an explanation for each adjustment.

**DO IT! 4.3 (LO 3), AP** Jean Karns is the new owner of Jean's Computer Services. At the end of July 2022, her first month of ownership, Jean is trying to prepare monthly financial statements. She has the following information for the month.

*Prepare adjustments for accruals.*

1. At July 31, Jean owed employees $1,100 in salaries that the company will pay in August.

2. On July 1, Jean borrowed $20,000 from a local bank on a 10-year note. The annual interest rate is 9%.

3. Service revenue unrecorded in July totaled $1,600.

Indicate how adjustments for these three situations would affect the accounting equation by completing the following table, which includes a sample accrual for a utility bill received August 1 for services received during July 2022.

| | Assets | = | Liabilities | + | Stockholders' Equity | | |
|---|---|---|---|---|---|---|---|
| | | | | | (Rev. | − | Exp.) |
| Sample | No effect | = | Increase | + | No effect | | Increase |
| 1. | | | | | | | |
| 2. | | | | | | | |
| 3. | | | | | | | |

**DO IT! 4.4 (LO 4), C** Indicate in which financial statement each of the following adjusted account balances would be presented.

*Identify financial statements for selected accounts.*

| | |
|---|---|
| Service Revenue | Accounts Receivable |
| Notes Payable | Accumulated Depreciation |
| Common Stock | Utilities Expense |

## Exercises

*Identify point of revenue recognition.*

**E4.1 (LO 1), C** The following independent situations require professional judgment for determining when to recognize revenue from the transactions.

  **a.** **Southwest Airlines** sells you an advance-purchase airline ticket in September for your flight home in December.

  **b.** **Ultimate Electronics** sells you a home theater on a "no money down and full payment in three months" promotional deal.

  **c.** The **Toronto Blue Jays** sell season tickets online to games in the Skydome. Fans can purchase the tickets at any time, although the season doesn't officially begin until April. The major league baseball season runs from April through October.

  **d.** **RBC Financial Group** loans money on August 1. The loan and the interest are repayable in full in November.

  **e.** In August, a customer orders a sweater from the **Sears** website using a Sears credit card. The sweater arrives in September. Sears sends a bill in October and receives payment in October.

### Instructions

Identify when revenue should be recognized in each of the above situations.

*Identify accounting assumptions, principles, and constraint.*

**E4.2 (LO 1), K** These accounting concepts were discussed in this and previous chapters.

  1. Economic entity assumption.
  2. Expense recognition principle.
  3. Monetary unit assumption.
  4. Periodicity assumption.
  5. Historical cost principle.
  6. Materiality.
  7. Full disclosure principle.
  8. Going concern assumption.
  9. Revenue recognition principle.
  10. Cost constraint.

### Instructions

Identify by number the accounting concept that describes each situation below. Do not use a number more than once.

  _____ **a.** Is the rationale for why plant assets are not reported at liquidation value. (Do not use the historical cost principle.)

  _____ **b.** Indicates that personal and business recordkeeping should be separately maintained.

  _____ **c.** Ensures that all relevant financial information is reported.

  _____ **d.** Assumes that the dollar is the "measuring stick" used to report on financial performance.

  _____ **e.** Requires that accounting standards be followed for all items of **significant** size.

  _____ **f.** Separates financial information into time periods for reporting purposes.

  _____ **g.** Requires recognition of expenses in the same period as related revenues.

  _____ **h.** Indicates that fair value changes subsequent to purchase are not recorded in the accounts.

*Identify the violated assumption, principle, or constraint.*

**E4.3 (LO 1), C** Here are some accounting reporting situations.

  **a.** East Lake Company recognizes revenue at the end of the production cycle but before sale. The price of the product, as well as the amount that can be sold, is not certain.

  **b.** Hilo Company is in its fifth year of operation and has yet to issue financial statements. (Do not use the full disclosure principle.)

  **c.** Gomez, Inc. is carrying inventory at its original cost of $100,000. Inventory has a fair value of $110,000.

  **d.** Bly Hospital Supply Corporation reports only current assets and current liabilities on its balance sheet. Equipment and bonds payable are reported as current assets and current liabilities, respectively. Liquidation of the company is unlikely.

  **e.** Chieu Company has inventory on hand that cost $400,000. Chieu reports inventory on its balance sheet at its current fair value of $425,000.

  **f.** Toxy Syles, president of Classic Music Company, bought a computer for her personal use. She paid for the computer by using company funds and increased the "Computers" account.

## Instructions

For each situation, list the assumption, principle, or constraint that has been violated, if any. (Some were presented in earlier chapters.) List only one answer for each situation. Note "no violation" if no violation has occurred.

**E4.4 (LO 1, 2, 3), AP** Your examination of the records of a company that follows the cash basis of accounting tells you that the company's reported cash-basis earnings in 2022 are $33,640. If this firm had followed accrual-basis accounting practices, it would have reported the following year-end balances.

*Convert earnings from cash to accrual basis.*

|  | 2022 | 2021 |
|---|---|---|
| Accounts receivable | $3,400 | $2,800 |
| Supplies on hand | 1,300 | 1,460 |
| Unpaid wages owed | 2,000 | 2,400 |
| Other unpaid expenses | 1,400 | 1,100 |

## Instructions

Determine the company's net earnings on an accrual basis for 2022. Show all your calculations in an orderly fashion.

**E4.5 (LO 1), AP** In its first year of operations, Gomes Company recognized $28,000 in service revenue, $6,000 of which was on account and still outstanding at year-end. The remaining $22,000 was received in cash from customers.

*Determine cash-basis and accrual-basis earnings.*

The company incurred operating expenses of $15,800. Of these expenses, $12,000 were paid in cash; $3,800 was still owed on account at year-end. In addition, Gomes prepaid $2,400 for insurance coverage that would not be used until the second year of operations.

## Instructions

a. Calculate the first year's net earnings under the cash basis of accounting, and calculate the first year's net earnings under the accrual basis of accounting.

b. Which basis of accounting (cash or accrual) provides more useful information for decision-makers?

**E4.6 (LO 1, 2, 3, 4), AP** Franken Company, a ski tuning and repair shop, opened on November 1, 2021. The company carefully kept track of all its cash receipts and cash payments. The following information is available at the end of the ski season, April 30, 2022.

*Convert earnings from cash to accrual basis; prepare accrual-based financial statements.*

|  | Cash Receipts | Cash Payments |
|---|---|---|
| Issuance of common shares | $20,000 |  |
| Payment to purchase repair shop equipment |  | $ 9,200 |
| Payments to landlord |  | 1,225 |
| Newspaper advertising payment |  | 375 |
| Utility bill payments |  | 970 |
| Part-time helper's wage payments |  | 2,600 |
| Income tax payment |  | 5,500 |
| Cash receipts from ski and snowboard repair services | 32,150 |  |
| Subtotals | 52,150 | 19,870 |
| Cash balance |  | 32,280 |
| Totals | $52,150 | $52,150 |

The repair shop equipment was purchased on November 1 and has an estimated useful life of 4 years. Lease payments to the landlord are made at the beginning of each month. The amount of the payments to the landlord shown above includes a one-time security deposit of $175. The part-time helper is owed $420 at April 30, 2022, for unpaid wages. At April 30, 2022, customers owe Franken Company $540 for services they have received but have not yet paid for.

## Instructions

a. Prepare an accrual-basis income statement for the 6 months ended April 30, 2022.

b. Prepare the April 30, 2022, classified balance sheet.

**E4.7 (LO 1, 2, 3), C** Writing BizCon, a consulting firm, has just completed its first year of operations. The company's sales growth was explosive. To encourage clients to hire its services, BizCon offered 180-day financing—meaning its largest customers do not pay for nearly 6 months. Because BizCon is a new company, its equipment suppliers insist on being paid cash on delivery. Also, it had to pay up front for 2 years

*Identify differences between cash and accrual accounting.*

of insurance. At the end of the year, BizCon owed employees for one full month of salaries, but due to a cash shortfall, it promised to pay them the first week of next year.

**Instructions**

a. Explain how cash and accrual accounting would differ for each of the events listed above and describe the proper accrual accounting.

b. Assume that at the end of the year, BizCon reported a favorable net income, yet the company's management is concerned because the company is very short of cash. Explain how BizCon could have positive net income and yet run out of cash.

*Identify types of adjustments and accounts before adjustment.*

**E4.8 (LO 1, 2, 3), AN** Wang Company accumulates the following adjustment data at December 31.

a. Services performed but unbilled total $600.

b. Store supplies of $160 are on hand. The supplies account shows a $1,900 balance.

c. Utility expenses of $275 are unpaid.

d. Services performed of $490 collected in advance.

e. Salaries of $620 are unpaid.

f. Prepaid insurance totaling $400 has expired.

**Instructions**

For each item, indicate (1) the type of adjustment (prepaid expense, unearned revenue, accrued revenue, or accrued expense) and (2) the status of the accounts before adjustment (overstated or understated).

*Prepare adjustments from selected account data.*

**E4.9 (LO 2, 3), AP** A partial tabular summary for Howard Rental Agency on March 31 of the current year includes the accounts below before adjustments have been prepared.

| | | Assets | | | | | = | Liabilities | | | | | + | Stockholders' Equity | | | | |
|---|---|---|---|---|---|---|---|---|---|---|---|---|---|---|---|---|---|---|---|
| | | Prepd. | | | | Acc. Depr.— | | Int. | | Notes | | Unearn. Rent | | Com. | | Retained Earnings | | | |
| Sup. | + | Insur. | + | Equip. | − | Equip. | = | Pay. | + | Pay. | + | Rev. | + | Stock | + | Rev. | − | Exp. | − | Div. |
| Bal. 3,000 | | 3,600 | | 25,000 | | −8,400 | | | | 20,000 | | 12,400 | | | | | | | |

An analysis of the accounts shows the following.

1. The equipment depreciates $280 per month.

2. Half of the rental services related to unearned rent revenue was provided during the quarter.

3. Interest of $400 is accrued on the notes payable.

4. Supplies on hand total $850.

5. Insurance expires at the rate of $400 per month.

**Instructions**

Prepare a tabular summary to record adjustments at March 31, assuming that adjustments are made quarterly.

*Prepare adjustments.*

**E4.10 (LO 2, 3), AP** Al Medina, D.D.S., opened an incorporated dental practice on January 1, 2022. During the first month of operations, the following transactions occurred.

1. Performed services for patients who had dental plan insurance. At January 31, $760 of such services were completed but not yet billed to the insurance companies.

2. Utility expenses incurred but not paid prior to January 31 totaled $450.

3. Purchased dental equipment on January 1 for $80,000, paying $20,000 in cash and signing a $60,000, 3-year note payable (interest is paid each December 31). The equipment depreciates $400 per month. Interest is $500 per month.

4. Purchased a 1-year malpractice insurance policy on January 1 for $24,000.

5. Purchased $1,750 of dental supplies (recorded as increase to Supplies). On January 31, determined that $550 of supplies were on hand.

**Instructions**

Prepare adjustments on January 31 and record them in the tabular summary that follows.

| | | Assets | | | | | = | Liabilities | | | | | + | Stockholders' Equity | | | | |
|---|---|---|---|---|---|---|---|---|---|---|---|---|---|---|---|---|---|---|---|
| Accts. | | | | Prepd. | | Acc. Depr.— | | Accts. | | Int. | | | | Com. | | Retained Earnings | | | |
| Rec. | + | Supplies | + | Insur. | + | Equip. | − | Equip. | = | Pay. | + | Pay. | + | | | Stock | + | Rev. | − | Exp. | − | Div. |

**E4.11 (LO 2, 3), AP** The unadjusted tabular summary of transactions for Sierra Corp. is shown in Illustration 4.5. Instead of the adjustments shown in the text at October 31, assume the following adjustment data.

*Prepare adjustments.*

1. Supplies on hand at October 31 total $500.

2. Expired insurance for the month is $100.

3. Depreciation for the month is $75.

4. As of October 31, services worth $800 related to the previously recorded unearned revenue had been performed.

5. Services performed but unbilled (and no receivable has been recorded) at October 31 are $280.

6. Interest expense accrued at October 31 is $70.

7. Accrued salaries at October 31 are $1,400.

### Instructions

Prepare a tabular summary to record adjustments for the items above using the summary that follows.

| | | Assets | | | | | = | | Liabilities | | | + | | Stockholders' Equity | | |
|---|---|---|---|---|---|---|---|---|---|---|---|---|---|---|---|---|
| | | | | | | Acc. | | | | | Unearn. | Sal./ | | | Retained Earnings | | |
| | Accts. | Sup- | Prepd. | | | Depr.— | Notes | Accts. | Int. | Serv. | Wag. | Com. | | | | |
| Cash | + Rec. | + plies | + Insur. | + Equip. | − | Equip. | = Pay. | + Pay. | + Pay. | + Rev. | + Pay. | + Stock | + Rev. | − Exp. | − Div. |
| Bal. 15,200 | 0 | 2,500 | 600 | 5,000 | | 0 | 5,000 | 2,500 | 0 | 1,200 | 0 | 10,000 | 10,000 | 4,900 | 500 |

**E4.12 (LO 2, 3), AP** A partial tabular summary for Armour Lake Lumber Supply on July 31, 2022, includes the following accounts before adjustments have been prepared.

*Prepare adjustments from selected account data.*

| | Assets | | | | | | = | Liabilities | + | | Stockholders' Equity | | |
|---|---|---|---|---|---|---|---|---|---|---|---|---|---|
| Invest. | | | | | | Acc. | | Unearn. | | | | Retained Earnings | |
| Notes | Sup- | | Prepd. | | | Depr.— | | Serv. | | Com. | | | |
| Rec. | + plies | + | Rent | + Bldgs. | − | Bldgs. | = | Rev. | + | Stock | + Rev. | − Exp. | − Div. |
| Bal. 20,000 | 24,000 | | 3,600 | 250,000 | | −140,000 | | 11,500 | | | | | |

An analysis of the company's accounts shows the following.

1. The investment in the notes receivable earns interest at a rate of 6% per year.

2. Supplies on hand at the end of the month totaled $18,600.

3. The balance in Prepaid Rent represents 4 months of rent costs. Three months of rent remain unexpired at the end of July.

4. Employees were owed $3,100 related to unpaid salaries and wages.

5. Depreciation on buildings is $6,000 per year.

6. During the month, the company satisfied obligations worth $4,700 related to the Unearned Service Revenue.

7. Unpaid maintenance and repairs costs were $2,300.

### Instructions

Prepare a tabular summary to record adjustments on July 31 assuming that adjustments are made monthly. Use additional accounts as needed.

**E4.13 (LO 1, 2, 3, 4), AN** The income statement of Norski Co. for the month of July shows net income of $2,000 based on Service Revenue $5,500, Salaries and Wages Expense $2,100, Supplies Expense $900, and Utilities Expense $500. In reviewing the statement, you discover the following:

*Prepare a correct income statement.*

1. Insurance expired during July of $350 was omitted.

2. Supplies expense includes $200 of supplies that are still on hand at July 31.

3. Depreciation on equipment of $150 was omitted.

4. Accrued but unpaid wages at July 31 of $360 were not included.

5. Services performed but unrecorded totaled $700.

### Instructions

Prepare a correct income statement for July 2022.

**E4.14 (LO 1, 2, 3), AN** The following lists selected accounts and their adjusted balances for Ramon Company on January 31, 2022.

*Analyze adjusted data.*

| | | | |
|---|---|---|---|
| Insurance Expense | $ 520 | Service Revenue | $4,000 |
| Prepaid Insurance | 1,560 | Supplies | 700 |
| Salaries and Wages Expense | 1,800 | Supplies Expense | 950 |
| Salaries and Wages Payable | 1,060 | Unearned Service Revenue | 750 |

**Instructions**

Answer these questions, assuming the year begins January 1.

a. If the amount in Supplies Expense is equal to the January 31 adjustment and $300 of supplies were purchased in January, what was the balance in Supplies on January 1?

b. If the amount in Insurance Expense is equal to the January 31 adjustment and the original insurance premium was for 1 year, what was the total premium and when was the policy purchased?

c. If $2,500 of salaries were paid in January, what was the balance in Salaries and Wages Payable at December 31, 2021?

d. If $1,800 was received in January for services performed in January, what was the balance in Unearned Service Revenue at December 31, 2021? (Assume that Accounts Receivable had a zero balance on January 1.)

*Determine effect of adjustments.*

**E4.15 (LO 2, 3), AN** On December 31, 2022, Waters Company prepared an income statement and balance sheet, but failed to take into account three adjustments. The balance sheet showed total assets $150,000, total liabilities $70,000, and stockholders' equity $80,000. The incorrect income statement showed net income of $70,000.

The data for the three adjustments were:

1. Salaries and wages amounting to $10,000 for the last 2 days in December were not paid and not recorded. The next payroll will be in January.

2. Rent payments of $8,000 were received for two months in advance on December 1. The entire amount was recorded as Unearned Rent Revenue when received.

3. Depreciation expense for 2022 is $9,000.

**Instructions**

Complete the following table to correct the financial statement amounts shown (indicate deductions with parentheses).

| Item | Net Income | Total Assets | Total Liabilities | Stockholders' Equity |
|---|---|---|---|---|
| Incorrect balances | $70,000 | $150,000 | $70,000 | $80,000 |
| Effects of: | | | | |
| Salaries and Wages | _____ | _____ | _____ | _____ |
| Rent Revenue | _____ | _____ | _____ | _____ |
| Depreciation | _____ | _____ | _____ | _____ |
| Correct balances | ════════ | ════════ | ════════ | ════════ |

*Prepare adjustments for prepayments.*

**E4.16 (LO 2), AP** Action Quest Games Inc. adjusts its accounts annually. The following information is available for the year ended December 31, 2022.

1. Purchased a 1-year insurance policy on June 1 for $1,800 cash.

2. Paid $6,500 on August 31 for 5 months' rent in advance.

3. On September 4, received $3,600 cash in advance from a corporation to sponsor a game each month for a total of 9 months for the most improved students at a local school.

4. Signed a contract for cleaning services starting December 1 for $1,000 per month. Paid for the first 2 months on November 30. (*Hint:* Use the account Prepaid Cleaning to record prepayments.)

5. On December 5, received $1,500 in advance from a gaming club. Determined that on December 31, $475 of these games had not yet been played.

**Instructions**

a. Record each of the above transactions in the tabular summary that follows.

| Assets | | | | = | Liabilities | + | Stockholders' Equity | | |
|---|---|---|---|---|---|---|---|---|---|
| | Prepd. | Prepd. | Prepd. | | Unearn. | | Com. | Retained Earnings | |
| Cash + | Insur. + | Rent + | Clean. = | | Serv. Rev. | + | Stock + | Rev. – Exp. – | Div. |

b. For each of the above transactions, record the adjustment that is required on December 31 in the tabular summary from part (a). (*Hint:* Use the account Service Revenue for item 3 and Repairs and Maintenance Expense for item 4.)

*Prepare adjustments for accruals.*

**E4.17 (LO 3), AP** Greenock Limited has the following information available for accruals for the year ended December 31, 2022. The company adjusts its accounts annually.

1. The December utility bill for $425 was unrecorded on December 31. Greenock paid the bill on January 11.

2. Greenock is open 7 days a week and employees are paid a total of $3,500 every Monday for a 7-day (Monday–Sunday) workweek. December 31 is a Thursday, so employees will have worked 4 days (Monday, December 28–Thursday, December 31) that they have not been paid for by year-end. Employees will be paid next on January 4.

3. Greenock signed a $45,000, 5% bank loan on November 1, 2016, due in 2 years. Interest is payable on the first day of each following month. (For example, interest incurred during November would be paid on December 1.)

4. Greenock receives a fee from Pizza Shop next door for all pizzas sold to customers using Greenock's facility. The amount owed for December is $300, which Pizza Shop will pay on January 4. (*Hint:* Use the Service Revenue account.)

5. Greenock rented some of its unused warehouse space to a client for $6,000 a month, payable the first day of the following month. It received the rent for the month of December on January 2.

### Instructions

a. For each situation, record the adjustment required at December 31 using the tabular summary that follows. (Round all calculations to the nearest dollar.) After recording the final adjustment, total the columns.

| Assets | | = | Liabilities | | | | + | Stockholders' Equity | | | | | | | |
|---|---|---|---|---|---|---|---|---|---|---|---|---|---|---|---|
| | | | | | | | | | | Retained Earnings | | | | | |
| | | Accts. | Accts. | | Int. | Sal./Wag. | | Com. | | | | | | | |
| Cash | + | Rec. | = Pay. | + | Pay. | + Pay. | + | Stock | + | Rev. | − | Exp. | − | Div. | | |

b. For each situation, record the subsequent cash transaction in 2023 in the tabular summary from part (a). After recording the cash transactions, total the columns.

**E4.18 (LO 4), AP** Skolnick Co. was organized on April 1, 2022. The company prepares quarterly financial statements. The following adjusted balance amounts at June 30 are in alphabetical order.

*Prepare financial statements from adjusted accounts.*

| Account | Adjusted Bal. | Account | Adjusted Bal. |
|---|---|---|---|
| Accounts Payable | $ 1,510 | Prepaid Rent | $ 900 |
| Accounts Receivable | 600 | Rent Expense | 1,500 |
| Accumulated | | Rent Revenue | 800 |
| Depreciation—Equipment | 850 | Retained Earnings (April 1) | 0 |
| Cash | 6,700 | Salaries and Wages | |
| Common Stock | 14,000 | Expense | 9,400 |
| Depreciation Expense | 850 | Salaries and Wages Payable | 400 |
| Dividends | 600 | Service Revenue | 14,200 |
| Equipment | 15,000 | Supplies | 1,000 |
| Interest Expense | 50 | Supplies Expense | 200 |
| Interest Payable | 50 | Unearned Rent Revenue | 500 |
| Notes Payable (long-term) | 5,000 | Utilities Expense | 510 |

a. Prepare an income statement for the quarter ended June 30, 2022.

b. Prepare a retained earnings statement for the quarter ended June 30, 2022.

c. Prepare a classified balance sheet at June 30, 2022.

## Problems

**P4.1 (LO 1, 2, 3), AP** The following selected data are taken from the comparative financial statements of Yankee Curling Club. The club prepares its financial statements using the accrual basis of accounting.

*Record transactions on accrual basis; convert revenue to cash receipts.*

| September 30 | 2022 | 2021 |
|---|---|---|
| Accounts receivable for member dues | $ 15,000 | $ 19,000 |
| Unearned sales revenue | 20,000 | 23,000 |
| Service revenue (from member dues) | 151,000 | 135,000 |

Dues are billed to members based upon their use of the club's facilities. Unearned sales revenues arise from the sale of tickets to events, such as the Skins Game.

### Instructions

(*Hint:* You must analyze these data sequentially, as missing information must first be deduced before moving on.)

**a.** Use the tabular summary that includes selected accounts and balances to record the following events that took place during 2022.

| | Assets | | = | Liabilities | + | | Stockholders' Equity | | | |
|---|---|---|---|---|---|---|---|---|---|---|
| | | Accts. | = | Unearn. | + | Com. | | Retained Earnings | | |
| | Cash + | Rec. | = | Sales Rev. | + | Stock + | Rev. | – | Exp. | – Div. |
| Beg. Bal. | | 19,000 | | 23,000 | | | | | | |
| 1. | | | | | | | | | | |
| 2. | | | | | | | | | | |
| 3. | | | | | | | | | | |
| 4. | | | | | | | | | | |
| 5. | | | | | | | | | | |
| End. Bal. | | 15,000 | | 20,000 | | | | | | |

1. Dues receivable from members from 2021 were all collected during 2022.

2. During 2022, goods were provided for all of the unearned sales revenue at the end of 2021.

3. Additional tickets were sold for $44,000 cash during 2022; a portion of these were used by the purchasers during the year. The entire balance remaining in Unearned Sales Revenue relates to the upcoming Skins Game in 2022.

4. Dues of $151,000 for the 2021–2022 fiscal year were billed to members.

5. Dues receivable for 2022 (i.e., those billed in item 4 above) were partially collected.

*(b) Cash received $199,000*

**b.** Determine the amount of cash received by Yankee from the above transactions during the year ended September 30, 2022.

*Prepare adjustments.*

**P4.2 (LO 2, 3), AP** Len Kumar started his own consulting firm, Kumar Consulting, on June 1, 2022. The June transactions resulted in a tabular summary, with June 30 unadjusted balances shown here.

| | | Assets | | | | | | = | Liabilities | | | + | | Stockholders' Equity | | |
|---|---|---|---|---|---|---|---|---|---|---|---|---|---|---|---|---|
| | | Accts. | Sup- | Prepd. | | | Acc. Depr.— | | Accts. | Unearn. | Sal./Wag. | | Com. | | Retained Earnings | |
| | Cash + | Rec. + | plies + | Insur. + | Equip. | – | Equip. | = | Pay. + | Serv. Rev. + | Pay. | + | Stock + | Rev. | – Exp. | – Div. |
| Bal. | 6,850 + | 7,000 + | 2,000 + | 2,880 + | 15,000 | – | 0 | = | 4,230 + | 5,200 + | 0 | + | 22,000 + | 8,300 | – 6,000 | |

### Instructions

**a.** Record adjustments for the month of June that reflect the following data. Provide explanations for specific revenue and expense accounts in the rightmost column.

1. Supplies on hand at June 30 total $720.

2. A utility bill for $180 has not been recorded and will not be paid until next month.

3. The insurance policy is for a year.

4. Services were performed for $4,100 of unearned service revenue by the end of the month.

5. Salaries of $1,250 are accrued at June 30.

6. The equipment has a 5-year life with no salvage value and is being depreciated at $250 per month for 60 months.

7. Invoices representing $3,900 of services performed during the month have not been recorded as of June 30.

*(b) Service rev. $16,300*
*Total assets $35,860*

**b.** Find the adjusted balance for each column in the tabular summary. Prove that the expanded accounting equation balances.

*Prepare adjustments and financial statements.*

**P4.3 (LO 2, 3, 4), AP** The Moto Hotel opened for business on May 1, 2022. The May transactions resulted in a tabular summary, with May 31 unadjusted balances shown below in the first row. The $9,000 in the revenue column resulted from Rent Revenue. The $4,300 in the expense column includes Salaries and Wages $3,000, Utilities $800, and Advertising $500.

| | Assets | | | | | | = | Liabilities | | | | | + | Stockholders' Equity | | | |
|---|---|---|---|---|---|---|---|---|---|---|---|---|---|---|---|---|---|
| | | | | | Acc.<br>Depr.— | | | | | | Sal./ | Unearn. | | | Retained Earnings | | |
| | | Sup-<br>plies | Prepd.<br>Insur. | Land | Bldgs. - | Acc.<br>Depr.—<br>Bldgs. + | Equip. - | Acc.<br>Depr.—<br>Equip. = | Accts.<br>Pay. + | Int.<br>Pay. + | Wag.<br>Pay. + | Rent<br>Rev. + | Mortg.<br>Pay. + | Com.<br>Stock + | Rev. | – Exp. | – Div. |
| | Cash + | | | | | | | | | | | | | | | | |
| Unadj. Bal. | 2,500 + 2,600 + | 1,800 + | 15,000 + | 70,000 – | 0 | + 16,800 – | | 0 = 4,700 + | 0 + | 0 + | 3,300 + | 36,000 + | 60,000 + | 9,000 | – 4,300 | 0 | |

Adj.

(A1)

(A2)

(A3)

(A4)

(A5)

(A6)

Adj. Bal.

## Instructions

**a.** Record adjustments on May 31 that reflect the following data. Include explanations for each adjustment to revenue or expense.

1. Insurance expires at the rate of $450 per month.

2. A count of supplies shows $1,050 of unused supplies on May 31.

3. Annual depreciation is $3,600 on the building and $3,000 on equipment.

4. The mortgage interest rate is 6%. (The mortgage was taken out on May 1.)

5. Rental services related to unearned rent of $2,500 have been provided.

6. Salaries of $900 are accrued and unpaid at May 31.

**b.** Find the adjusted balance for each column in the tabular summary. Prove that the expanded accounting equation balances.

(b) Rent revenue     $11,500

**c.** Prepare an income statement and a retained earnings statement for the month of May and a classified balance sheet at May 31.

(c) Net income     $3,570

**P4.4 (LO 2, 3, 4), AP** Salt Creek Golf Inc. was organized on July 1, 2022. Quarterly financial statements are prepared. Information from the unadjusted and adjusted tabular summary on September 30, 2022, is shown as follows. The $14,800 in the revenue column includes Service Revenue: $14,100 and Rent Revenue: $700. The $10,170 in the expense column includes Salaries and Wages $8,800, Rent $900, and Utilities $470.

*Prepare adjustments and financial statements.*

| | Assets | | | | | | = | Liabilities | | | | | + | Stockholders' Equity | | | |
|---|---|---|---|---|---|---|---|---|---|---|---|---|---|---|---|---|---|
| | | Accts.<br>Rec. + | Sup-<br>plies + | Prepd.<br>Rent + | Equip. - | Acc.<br>Depr.—<br>Equip. = | | Notes<br>Pay. + | Accts.<br>Pay. + | Sal./<br>Wag.<br>Pay. + | Int.<br>Pay. + | Unearn.<br>Rent<br>Rev. + | | Com.<br>Stock + | Retained Earnings | | |
| | Cash + | | | | | | | | | | | | | | Rev. | – Exp. | – Div. |
| Unadj. Bal. | 6,700 + | 400 + | 1,200 + | 1,800 + | 15,000 – | 0 = | | 5,000 + | 1,070 + | 0 + | 0 + | 1,000 + | | 14,000 + | 14,800 | – 10,170 | – 600 |

Adj.

(A1)

(A2)

(A3)

(A4)

(A5)

(A6)

(A7)

| Adj. Bal. | 6,700 + | 1,000 + | 180 + | 900 + | 15,000 – | 350 = | | 5,000 + | 1,070 + | 600 + | 50 + | 800 + | | 14,000 + | 15,600 | – 13,090 | – 600 |

## Instructions

**a.** Record the adjustments that were made. Include an explanation for each adjustment to revenue or expense.

**b.** Prepare an income statement and a retained earnings statement for the 3 months ending September 30 and a classified balance sheet at September 30.

(b) Net income     $2,510
Tot. assets     $23,430

**c.** If the note bears interest at 12%, how many months has it been outstanding?

*Prepare adjustments.*

**P4.5 (LO 2, 3), AP** A review of the unadjusted balances for Lewis Company at December 31, 2022, produces these data pertaining to the preparation of annual adjustments.

1. Prepaid Insurance $15,200. The company has separate insurance policies on its buildings and its motor vehicles. Policy B4564 on the building was purchased on July 1, 2021, for $9,600. The policy has a term of 3 years. Policy A2958 on the vehicles was purchased on January 1, 2022, for $7,200. This policy has a term of 18 months.

2. Rent revenue $84,000

2. Unearned Rent Revenue $429,000. The company began subleasing office space in its new building on November 1. At December 31, the company had the following rental contracts that are paid in full for the entire term of the lease.

| Date | Term (in months) | Monthly Rent | Number of Leases |
|------|------------------|--------------|------------------|
| Nov. 1 | 9 | $5,000 | 5 |
| Dec. 1 | 6 | $8,500 | 4 |

3. Notes Payable $40,000. This balance consists of a note for 6 months at an annual interest rate of 7%, dated October 1.

4. Salaries and Wages Payable $0. There are eight salaried employees. Salaries are paid every Friday for the current week. Five employees receive a salary of $600 each per week, and three employees earn $700 each per week. Assume December 31 is a Wednesday. Employees do not work weekends. All employees worked the last 3 days of December.

**Instructions**

Record adjustments at December 31, 2022, for items 1 through 4 by completing the following tabular summary with selected unadjusted balances. Include an explanation for each adjustment to revenue or expense.

| Assets | = | Liabilities | | | | | + | Stockholders' Equity | | | | |
|--------|---|-------------|--|--|--|--|---|----------------------|--|--|--|--|
| | | | | | | | | | | Retained Earnings | | |
| Prepd. Insur. | = | Unearn. Rent Rev. | + | Notes Pay. | + | Sal./Wag. Pay. | + | Int. Pay. | + | Com. Stock | + | Rev. − Exp. − Div. |
| 15,200 | | 429,000 | | 40,000 | | 0 | | 0 | | | | |

*Prepare a corrected income statement.*

**P4.6 (LO 2, 3, 4), AN** Roadside Travel Court was organized on July 1, 2021, by Betty Johnson. Betty is a good manager but a poor accountant. From the unadjusted tabular summary, Betty prepared the following income statement for her fourth quarter, which ended June 30, 2022.

**Roadside Travel Court**
**Income Statement**
**For the Quarter Ended June 30, 2022**

| | | |
|--|--|--|
| Revenues | | |
|    Rent revenue | | $212,000 |
| Operating expenses | | |
|    Advertising expense | $ 3,800 | |
|    Salaries and wages expense | 80,500 | |
|    Utilities expense | 900 | |
|    Depreciation expense | 2,700 | |
|    Maintenance and repairs expense | 4,300 | |
|    Total operating expenses | | 92,200 |
| Net income | | $119,800 |

Betty suspected that something was wrong with the statement because net income had never exceeded $30,000 in any one quarter. Knowing that you are an experienced accountant, she asks you to review the income statement and other data.

You first look at the tabular summary. In addition to the account balances reported above in the income statement, it contains the following additional selected balances at June 30, 2022.

| | |
|--|--|
| Supplies | $ 8,200 |
| Prepaid Insurance | 14,400 |
| Notes Payable | 14,000 |

You then make inquiries and discover the following.

1. Roadside rental revenues include advanced rental payments received for summer occupancy, in the amount of $57,000.

2. There were $1,800 of supplies on hand at June 30.

3. Prepaid insurance resulted from the payment of a 1-year policy on April 1, 2022.

4. The mail in July 2022 brought the following bills: advertising for the week of June 24, $110; repairs made June 18, $4,450; and utilities for the month of June, $215.

5. Wage expense is $300 per day. At June 30, 4 days' wages have been incurred but not paid.

6. The note payable is a 6% note dated May 1, 2022, and due on July 31, 2022.

7. Income tax of $9,800 for the quarter is due in July but has not yet been recorded.

### Instructions

a. Prepare a correct income statement for the quarter ended June 30, 2022.

b. Explain to Betty the generally accepted accounting principles that she did not recognize in preparing her income statement and their effect on her results.

(a) Net income      $36,885

**P4.7 (LO 2, 3, 4), AP** Soho Equipment Repair began operating in September 2022. It prepares financial statements at the end of each month. On November 1, 2022, a tabular summary includes the following information. Note that Soho began the month with $3,000 in Retained Earnings. This balance represents the results of its first two months of business.

*Record transactions and adjustments, and prepare financial statements.*

| | | **Assets** | | | = | | **Liabilities** | | + | **Stockholders' Equity** | |
|---|---|---|---|---|---|---|---|---|---|---|---|
| | | | | Acc. | | | Unearn. | Sal./ | | | |
| | Accts. | Sup- | | Depr.— | Accts. | Serv. | Wag. | Com. | | |
| Cash + | Rec. + | plies + | Equip. - | Equip. = | Pay. + | Rev. + | Pay. + | Stock + | Retained Earnings |
| 11/1 Bal. 2,790 + | 2,910 + | 1,120 + | 10,000 - | 500 = | 2,300 + | 400 + | 620 + | 10,000 + | 3,000 |

During November, the following summary transactions were completed.

| Nov. | 8 | Paid $1,220 for salaries due employees, of which $600 is for November and $620 is for October salaries payable. |
|---|---|---|
| | 10 | Received $1,800 cash from customers in payment of account. |
| | 12 | Received $3,700 cash for services performed in November. |
| | 15 | Purchased store equipment on account $3,600. |
| | 17 | Purchased supplies on account $1,300. |
| | 20 | Paid creditors $2,500 of accounts payable due. |
| | 22 | Paid November rent $480. |
| | 25 | Paid salaries $1,000. |
| | 27 | Performed services on account worth $900 and billed customers. |
| | 29 | Received $750 from customers for services to be performed in the future. |

Adjustment data:

1. Supplies on hand are valued at $1,100.

2. Accrued salaries payable are $480.

3. Depreciation for the month is $250.

4. Services were performed to satisfy $500 of unearned service revenue.

### Instructions

Use the tabular summary below to complete the following.

| | Cash | + | Accts. Rec. | + | Sup-plies | + | Equip. | − | Acc. Depr.— Equip. | = | Accts. Pay. | + | Unearn. Serv. Rev. | + | Sal./ Wag. Pay. | + | Com. Stock | + | Retained Earnings |
|---|---|---|---|---|---|---|---|---|---|---|---|---|---|---|---|---|---|---|---|
| 11/1 Bal. | 2,790 | + | 2,910 | + | 1,120 | + | 10,000 | − | 500 | = | 2,300 | + | 400 | + | 620 | + | 10,000 | + | 3,000 |
| Transact. | | | | | | | | | | | | | | | | | | | Rev. − Exp. − Div. |
| Nov.   8 | | | | | | | | | | | | | | | | | | | |
| 10 | | | | | | | | | | | | | | | | | | | |
| 12 | | | | | | | | | | | | | | | | | | | |
| 15 | | | | | | | | | | | | | | | | | | | |
| 17 | | | | | | | | | | | | | | | | | | | |
| 20 | | | | | | | | | | | | | | | | | | | |
| 22 | | | | | | | | | | | | | | | | | | | |
| 25 | | | | | | | | | | | | | | | | | | | |
| 27 | | | | | | | | | | | | | | | | | | | |
| 29 | | | | | | | | | | | | | | | | | | | |
| Bal. | | | | | | | | | | | | | | | | | | | |
| Adj. | | | | | | | | | | | | | | | | | | | |
| (A1) | | | | | | | | | | | | | | | | | | | |
| (A2) | | | | | | | | | | | | | | | | | | | |
| (A3) | | | | | | | | | | | | | | | | | | | |
| (A4) | | | | | | | | | | | | | | | | | | | |
| Adj. Bal. | | | | | | | | | | | | | | | | | | | |

(d) Cash $3,840

(e) Net income $970

**a.** Record the November transactions. Include explanations for amounts in the revenue or expense column.

**b.** Compute the balance in each column after recording the November 29 transaction.

**c.** Record adjustments.

**d.** Compute the adjusted balance in each column.

**e.** Prepare an income statement and a retained earnings statement for November and a classified balance sheet at November 30.

## Expand Your Critical Thinking

### Financial Reporting Problem: Apple Inc.

**CT4.1** The financial statements of **Apple Inc.** are presented in Appendix A.

### Instructions

**a.** Using the consolidated income statement and balance sheet, identify items that may result in adjustments for deferrals.

**b.** Using the consolidated income statement, identify two items that may result in adjustments for accruals.

**c.** What was the amount of depreciation and amortization expense for 2018 and 2017? (You will need to examine the notes to the financial statements or the statement of cash flows.) Where were accumulated depreciation and amortization reported?

**d.** What was the cash paid for income taxes during 2018, reported at the bottom of the consolidated statement of cash flows? What was income tax expense (provision for income taxes) for 2018?

### Comparative Analysis Problem:

### Columbia Sportswear Company vs. Under Armour, Inc.

**CT4.2** The financial statements of **Columbia Sportswear Company** are presented in Appendix B. Financial statements of **Under Armour, Inc.** are presented in Appendix C.

**Instructions**

a. Identify two accounts on Columbia's balance sheet that provide evidence that Columbia uses accrual accounting. In each case, identify the income statement account that would be affected by the adjustment process.

b. Identify two accounts on Under Armour balance sheet that provide evidence that Under Armour uses accrual accounting (different from the two you listed for Columbia). In each case, identify the income statement account that would be affected by the adjustment process.

## Interpreting Financial Statements

**CT4.3** **Laser Recording Systems** produced disks for use in the home market. The following is an excerpt from Laser Recording Systems' financial statements (all dollars in thousands).

---

### Laser Recording Systems
#### Management Discussion

Accrued liabilities increased to $1,642 at January 31, from $138 at the end of the previous fiscal year. Compensation and related accruals increased $195 due primarily to increases in accruals for severance, vacation, commissions, and relocation expenses. Accrued professional services increased by $137 primarily as a result of legal expenses related to several outstanding contractual disputes. Other expenses increased $35, of which $18 was for interest payable.

---

**Instructions**

a. Can you tell from the discussion whether Laser Recording Systems has prepaid its legal expenses and is now making an adjustment to the asset account Prepaid Legal Expenses, or whether the company is handling the legal expense via an accrued expense adjustment?

b. Identify each of the adjustments Laser Recording Systems is discussing as one of the four types of possible adjustments discussed in the chapter. How is net income ultimately affected by each of the adjustments?

c. How did Laser Recording record the accrued interest?

## Real-World Focus

**CT4.4** You can use the internet to learn about the functions of the **Securities and Exchange Commission (SEC)**.

**Instructions**

Use the information at the SEC's website to answer the following questions.

a. What event spurred the creation of the SEC? Why was the SEC created?

b. What are the five divisions of the SEC? Briefly describe the purpose of each.

c. What are the responsibilities of the chief accountant?

## Decision-Making Across the Organization

**CT4.5** Abbey Park was organized on April 1, 2021, by Trudy Crawford. Trudy is a good manager but a poor accountant. Trudy used information from the unadjusted tabular summary to prepare the following income statement for the quarter that ended March 31, 2022.

**Abbey Park**
**Income Statement**
**For the Quarter Ended March 31, 2022**

| Revenues | | |
|---|---:|---:|
| Rent revenue | | $83,000 |
| Operating expenses | | |
| Advertising expense | $ 4,200 | |
| Salaries and wages expense | 27,600 | |
| Utilities expense | 1,500 | |
| Depreciation expense | 800 | |
| Maintenance and repairs expense | 2,800 | |
| Total operating expenses | | 36,900 |
| Net income | | $46,100 |

Trudy knew that something was wrong with the statement because net income had never exceeded $20,000 in any one quarter. Knowing that you are an experienced accountant, she asks you to review the income statement and other data.

You first look at the accounting records. In addition to the account balances reported in the income statement, the tabular summary contains these selected balances at March 31, 2022.

| | |
|---|---:|
| Supplies | $ 4,500 |
| Prepaid Insurance | 7,200 |
| Notes Payable | 20,000 |

You then make inquiries and discover the following.

1. Rent revenue includes advanced rentals for summer-month occupancy, $21,000.

2. There were $600 of supplies on hand at March 31.

3. Prepaid insurance resulted from the payment of a 1-year policy on January 1, 2022.

4. The mail on April 1, 2022, brought the following bills: advertising for week of March 24, $110; repairs made March 10, $1,040; and utilities $240.

5. Wage expense totals $290 per day. At March 31, 3 days' wages have been incurred but not paid.

6. The note payable is a 3-month, 7% note dated January 1, 2022.

### Instructions

With the class divided into groups, answer the following.

a. Prepare a correct income statement for the quarter ended March 31, 2022.

b. Explain to Trudy the generally accepted accounting principles that she did not follow in preparing her income statement and their effect on her results.

## Communication Activity

**CT4.6** On numerous occasions, proposals have surfaced to put the federal government on the accrual basis of accounting. This is no small issue because if this basis were used, it would mean that billions in unrecorded liabilities would have to be booked and the federal deficit would increase substantially.

### Instructions

a. What is the difference between accrual-basis accounting and cash-basis accounting?

b. Comment on why politicians prefer a cash-basis accounting system over an accrual-basis system.

c. Write a letter to your senators explaining why you think the federal government should adopt the accrual basis of accounting.

## Ethics Case

**CT4.7** Wells Company is a pesticide manufacturer. Its sales declined greatly this year due to the passage of legislation outlawing the sale of several of Wells' chemical pesticides. During the coming year, Wells will have environmentally safe and competitive replacement chemicals to replace these discontinued products. Sales in the next year are expected to greatly exceed those of any prior year. Therefore, the decline in this year's sales and profits appears to be a one-year aberration.

Even so, the company president believes that a large dip in the current year's profits could cause a significant drop in the market price of Wells' stock and make it a takeover target. To avoid this possibility, he urges Tim Allen, controller, to accrue every possible revenue and to defer as many expenses as possible in making this period's year-end adjustments. The president says to Tim, "We need the revenues this year, and next year we can easily absorb expenses deferred from this year. We can't let our stock price be hammered down!" Tim didn't get around to recording the adjustments until January 17, but he dated them December 31 as if they were recorded then. Tim also made every effort to comply with the president's request.

### Instructions

**a.** Who are the stakeholders in this situation?

**b.** What are the ethical considerations of the president's request and Tim's dating the adjustments December 31?

**c.** Can Tim accrue revenues and defer expenses and still be ethical?

## All About You

**CT4.8** Companies prepare balance sheets in order to know their financial position at a specific point in time. This enables them to make a comparison to their position at previous points in time and gives them a basis for planning for the future. In order to evaluate *your* financial position, you can prepare a personal balance sheet. Assume that you have compiled the following information regarding your finances. (*Hint:* Some of the items might not be used in your personal balance sheet.)

| | |
|---|---:|
| Amount owed on student loan balance (long-term) | $ 5,000 |
| Balance in checking account | 1,200 |
| Certificate of deposit (6-month) | 3,000 |
| Annual earnings from part-time job | 11,300 |
| Automobile | 7,000 |
| Balance on automobile loan (current portion) | 1,500 |
| Balance on automobile loan (long-term portion) | 4,000 |
| Home computer | 800 |
| Amount owed to you by younger brother | 300 |
| Balance in money market account | 1,800 |
| Annual tuition | 6,400 |
| Video and stereo equipment | 1,250 |
| Balance owed on credit card (current portion) | 150 |
| Balance owed on credit card (long-term portion) | 1,650 |

### Instructions

Prepare a personal balance sheet using the format you have learned for a classified balance sheet for a company. For the equity account, use M. Y. Own, Capital.

## CHAPTER 5

Tom Werner/DigitalVision/Getty Images

# Fraud, Internal Control, and Cash

## Chapter Preview

As the following Feature Story about recording cash sales at **Barriques** indicates, control of cash is important to ensure that fraud does not occur. Companies also need controls to safeguard other types of assets. For example, Barriques undoubtedly has controls to prevent the theft of food and supplies, and controls to prevent the theft of tableware and dishes from its kitchen.

In this chapter, we explain the essential features of an internal control system and how it prevents fraud. We also describe how those controls apply to a specific asset—cash. The applications include some controls with which you may be already familiar, such as the use of a bank.

## Feature Story

### Minding the Money in Madison

For many years, **Barriques** in Madison, Wisconsin, has been named the city's favorite coffeehouse. Barriques not only does a booming business in coffee but also has wonderful baked goods, delicious sandwiches, and a fine selection of wines.

"Our customer base ranges from college students to neighborhood residents as well as visitors to our capital city," says bookkeeper Kerry Stoppleworth, who joined the company shortly after it was founded in 1998. "We are unique because we have customers who come in early on their way to work for a cup of coffee and then will stop back after work to pick up a bottle of wine for dinner. We stay very busy throughout all three parts of the day."

Like most businesses where purchases are low-cost and high-volume, cash control has to be simple. "We use a computerized point-of-sale (POS) system to keep track of our inventory and allow us to efficiently ring through an order for a customer," explains Stoppleworth. "You can either scan a barcode for an item or enter in a code for items that don't have a barcode such as cups of coffee or bakery items." The POS system also automatically tracks sales by department and maintains electronic records of all the sales transactions that occur during the day.

"There are two POS stations at each store, and throughout the day any of the staff may operate them," says Stoppleworth. At the end of the day, each POS station is reconciled separately. The staff counts the cash in the drawer and enters this amount into the closing totals in the POS system. The POS system then compares the cash and credit amounts, less the cash being carried forward to the next day (the float), to the shift total in the electronic records. If there are discrepancies, a recount is done and the records are reviewed transaction by transaction to identify the problem. The staff then creates a deposit ticket for the cash less the float and puts this in a drop safe with the electronic record summary report for the manager to review and take to the bank the next day. Ultimately, the bookkeeper reviews all of these documents as well as the deposit receipt that the bank produces to make sure they are all in agreement.

As Stoppleworth concludes, "We keep the closing process and accounting simple so that our staff can concentrate on taking care of our customers and making great coffee and food."

# Chapter Outline

| LEARNING OBJECTIVES | REVIEW | PRACTICE |
|---|---|---|
| **LO 1** Define fraud and the principles of internal control. | • Fraud<br>• The Sarbanes-Oxley Act<br>• Internal control<br>• Principles of internal control activities<br>• Data analytics and internal controls<br>• Limitations of internal control | **DO IT! 1** Control Activities |
| **LO 2** Apply internal control principles to cash. | • Cash receipts controls<br>• Cash disbursements controls<br>• Petty cash fund | **DO IT! 2** Control over Cash Receipts |
| **LO 3** Identify the control features of a bank account. | • EFT system<br>• Bank statements<br>• Reconciling the bank account | **DO IT! 3** Bank Reconciliation |
| **LO 4** Explain the reporting of cash and the basic principles of cash management. | • Reporting cash<br>• Managing and monitoring cash<br>• Cash budgeting | **DO IT! 4a** Reporting Cash<br>**DO IT! 4b** Cash Budget |

**Go to the Review and Practice section at the end of the chapter for a targeted summary and practice applications with solutions.**

**Visit WileyPLUS for additional tutorials and practice opportunities.**

# Fraud and Internal Control

The Feature Story describes many of the internal control procedures used by **Barriques**. These procedures are necessary to discourage employees from fraudulent activities.

## Fraud

A **fraud** is a dishonest act by an employee that results in personal benefit to the employee at a cost to the employer. Examples of fraud reported in the financial press include the following.

- A bookkeeper in a small company diverted $750,000 of bill payments to a personal bank account over a three-year period.

- A shipping clerk with 28 years of service shipped $125,000 of merchandise to himself.

- A computer operator embezzled $21 million from **Wells Fargo Bank** over a two-year period.

- A church treasurer "borrowed" $150,000 of church funds to finance a friend's business dealings.

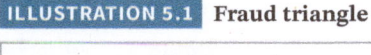

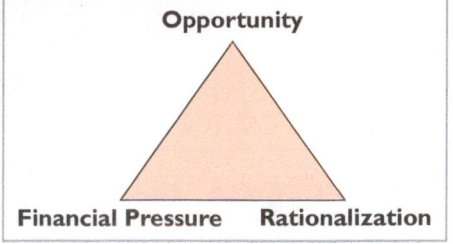

**ILLUSTRATION 5.1**  Fraud triangle

Why does fraud occur? The three main factors that contribute to fraudulent activity are depicted by the **fraud triangle** in **Illustration 5.1**.

The most important element of the fraud triangle is **opportunity**. For an employee to commit fraud, the workplace environment must provide opportunities that an employee can take advantage of. Opportunities occur when the workplace lacks sufficient controls to deter and detect fraud. For example, inadequate monitoring of employee actions can create opportunities for theft and can embolden employees because they believe they will not be caught.

A second factor that contributes to fraud is **financial pressure**. Employees sometimes commit fraud because of personal financial problems caused by too much debt. Or, they might commit fraud because they want to lead a lifestyle that they cannot afford on their current salary.

The third factor that contributes to fraud is **rationalization**. In order to justify their fraud, employees rationalize their dishonest actions. For example, employees sometimes justify fraud because they believe they are underpaid while the employer is making lots of money. Employees feel justified in stealing because they believe they deserve to be paid more.

## The Sarbanes-Oxley Act

What can be done to prevent or to detect fraud? After numerous corporate scandals came to light in the early 2000s, Congress addressed this issue by passing the **Sarbanes-Oxley Act (SOX)**.

- Under SOX, all publicly traded U.S. corporations are required to maintain an adequate system of internal control.

- Corporate executives and boards of directors must ensure that these controls are reliable and effective.

- Independent outside auditors must attest to the adequacy of the internal control system.

Companies that fail to comply are subject to fines, and company officers can be imprisoned. SOX also created the Public Company Accounting Oversight Board (PCAOB) to establish auditing standards and regulate auditor activity.

One poll found that 60% of investors believe that SOX helps safeguard their stock investments. Many say they would be unlikely to invest in a company that fails to follow SOX requirements. Although some corporate executives have criticized the time and expense involved in following SOX requirements, SOX appears to be working well. For example, the chief accounting officer of **Eli Lilly** noted that SOX triggered a comprehensive review of how the company documents its controls. This review uncovered redundancies and pointed out controls that needed to be added. In short, it added up to time and money well spent.

## Internal Control

**Internal control** is a process designed to provide reasonable assurance regarding the achievement of company objectives related to operations, reporting, and compliance. In more detail, the purposes of internal control are to safeguard assets, enhance the reliability of accounting records, increase efficiency of operations, and ensure compliance with laws and regulations. Internal control systems have five primary components as listed below.[1]

- **A control environment.** It is the responsibility of top management to make it clear that the organization values integrity and that unethical activity will not be tolerated. This component is often referred to as the "tone at the top."

- **Risk assessment.** Companies must identify and analyze the various factors that create risk for the business and must determine how to manage these risks.

- **Control activities.** To reduce the occurrence of fraud, management must design policies and procedures to address the specific risks faced by the company.

- **Information and communication.** The internal control system must capture and communicate all pertinent information both down and up the organization, as well as communicate information to appropriate external parties.

- **Monitoring.** Internal control systems must be monitored periodically for their adequacy. Significant deficiencies need to be reported to top management and/or the board of directors.

---

### People, Planet, and Profit Insight

iStock.com/Karl Dolenc

#### And the Controls Are . . .

Internal controls are important for an effective financial reporting system. The same is true for sustainability reporting. An effective system of internal controls for sustainability reporting will help in the following ways: (1) prevent the unauthorized use of data; (2) provide reasonable assurance that the information is accurate, valid, and complete; and (3) report information that is consistent with overall sustainability accounting policies. With these types of controls, users will have the confidence that they can use the sustainability information effectively.

Some regulators are calling for even more assurance through audits of this information. Companies that potentially can cause environmental damage through greenhouse gases, as well as companies in the mining and extractive industries, are subject to reporting requirements. And, as demand for more information in the sustainability area expands, the need for audits of this information will grow.

**Why is sustainability information important to investors? (Go to WileyPLUS for this answer and additional questions.)**

---

## Principles of Internal Control Activities

Each of the five components of an internal control system is important. Here, we will focus on one component, the control activities. The reason? These activities are the backbone of the company's efforts to address the risks it faces, such as fraud. The specific control activities used by a company will vary, depending on management's assessment of the risks faced. This assessment is heavily influenced by the size and nature of the company.

---

[1]The Committee of Sponsoring Organizations of the Treadway Commission, "Internal Control—Integrated Framework," *www.coso.org/documents/990025P_Executive_Summary_final_may20_e.pdf*; and Stephen J. McNally, "The 2013 COSO Framework and Sox Compliance," *Strategic Finance* (June 2013).

The six principles of control activities are as follows (see **Decision Tools**).

- Establishment of responsibility
- Segregation of duties
- Documentation procedures
- Physical controls
- Independent internal verification
- Human resource controls

We explain these principles in the following sections. You should recognize that they apply to most companies and are relevant to both manual and computerized accounting systems.

## Establishment of Responsibility

An essential principle of internal control is to assign responsibility to specific employees. **Control is most effective when only one person is responsible for a given task.**

To illustrate, assume that the cash on hand at the end of the day in a **Safeway** supermarket is $10 short of the cash entered in the cash register. If only one person has operated the register, the shift manager can quickly determine responsibility for the shortage. If two or more individuals have worked the register, it may be impossible to determine who is responsible for the error.

Many retailers solve this problem by having registers with multiple drawers. This makes it possible for more than one person to operate a register but still allows identification of a particular employee with a specific drawer. Only the signed-in cashier has access to his or her drawer.

Establishing responsibility often requires limiting access only to authorized personnel, and then identifying those personnel. For example, the automated systems used by many companies have mechanisms such as identifying passcodes that keep track of who recorded a transaction, entered a sale, or went into an inventory storeroom at a particular time. Use of identifying passcodes enables the company to establish responsibility by identifying the particular employee who carried out the activity.

It's your shift now. I'm turning in my cash drawer and heading home.

**Transfer of cash drawers**

## Anatomy of a Fraud

Maureen Frugali was a training supervisor for claims processing at Colossal Healthcare. As a standard part of the claims-processing training program, Maureen created fictitious claims for use by trainees. These fictitious claims were then sent to the accounts payable department. After the training claims had been processed, she was to notify Accounts Payable of all fictitious claims, so that they would not be paid. However, she did not inform Accounts Payable about every fictitious claim. She created some fictitious claims for entities that she controlled (that is, she would receive the payment), and she let Accounts Payable pay her.

**Total take: $11 million**

### The Missing Control

**Establishment of responsibility.** The healthcare company did not adequately restrict the responsibility for authorizing and approving claims transactions. The training supervisor should not have been authorized to create claims in the company's "live" system.

**Source:** Adapted from Wells, *Fraud Casebook* (2007), pp. 61–70.

## Segregation of Duties

Segregation of duties is indispensable in an internal control system. There are two common applications of this principle:

1. Different individuals should be responsible for related activities.
2. The responsibility for recordkeeping for an asset should be separate from the physical custody of that asset.

The rationale for segregation of duties is this: **The work of one employee should, without a duplication of effort, provide a reliable basis for evaluating the work of another employee.** For example, the personnel that design and program computerized systems should not be assigned duties related to day-to-day use of the system. Otherwise, they could design the system to benefit them personally and conceal the fraud through day-to-day use.

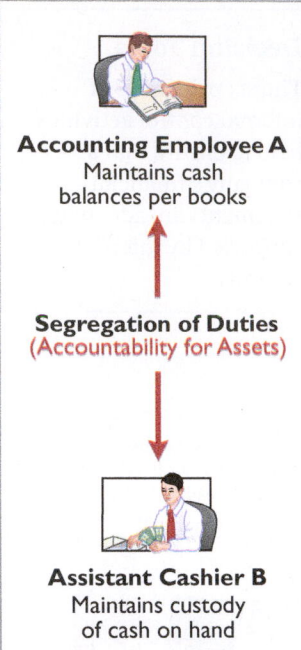

**Accounting Employee A**
Maintains cash
balances per books

**Segregation of Duties**
(Accountability for Assets)

**Assistant Cashier B**
Maintains custody
of cash on hand

**Segregation of Related Activities**   **Making one individual responsible for related activities increases the potential for errors and irregularities.**

**Purchasing Activities**   Companies should, for example, assign related **purchasing activities** to different individuals. Related purchasing activities include ordering merchandise, approving orders, receiving goods, authorizing payment, and paying for goods or services. Various frauds are possible when one person handles related purchasing activities:

- If a purchasing agent is allowed to order goods without obtaining supervisory approval, the likelihood of the purchasing agent receiving kickbacks from suppliers increases.
- If an employee who orders goods also handles the invoice and receipt of the goods, as well as payment authorization, he or she might authorize payment for a fictitious invoice.

These abuses are less likely to occur when companies divide the purchasing tasks.

**Sales Activities**   Similarly, companies should assign related **sales activities** to different individuals. Related selling activities include making a sale, shipping (or delivering) the goods to the customer, billing the customer, and receiving payment. Various frauds are possible when one person handles related sales activities:

- If a salesperson can make a sale without obtaining supervisory approval, he or she might make sales at unauthorized prices to increase sales commissions.
- A shipping clerk who also has access to accounting records could ship goods to himself.
- A billing clerk who handles billing and receipt could understate the amount billed for sales made to friends and relatives.

These abuses are less likely to occur when companies divide the sales tasks. The salespeople make the sale, the shipping department ships the goods on the basis of the sales order, and the billing department prepares the sales invoice after comparing the sales order with the report of goods shipped.

---

## Anatomy of a Fraud

Lawrence Fairbanks, the assistant vice-chancellor of communications at Aesop University, was allowed to make purchases of under $2,500 for his department without external approval. Unfortunately, he also sometimes bought items for himself, such as expensive antiques and other collectibles. How did he do it? He replaced the vendor invoices he received with fake vendor invoices that he created. The fake invoices had descriptions that were more consistent with the communications department's purchases. He submitted these fake invoices to the accounting department as the basis for their records and to the accounts payable department as the basis for payment.

### Total take: $475,000

#### The Missing Control

**Segregation of duties.** The university had not properly segregated related purchasing activities. Lawrence was ordering items, receiving the items, and receiving the invoice. By receiving the invoice, he had control over the documents that were used to account for the purchase and thus was able to substitute a fake invoice.

**Source:** Adapted from Wells, *Fraud Casebook* (2007), pp. 3–15.

---

**Segregation of Recordkeeping from Physical Custody**   The accountant should have neither physical custody of the asset nor access to it. Likewise, the custodian of the asset should not maintain or have access to the accounting records.

- **The custodian of the asset is not likely to convert the asset to personal use when one employee maintains the record of the asset, and a different employee has physical custody of the asset.**
- The separation of accounting responsibility from the custody of assets is especially important for cash and inventories because these assets are very vulnerable to fraud.

## Anatomy of a Fraud

Angela Bauer was an accounts payable clerk for Aggasiz Construction Company. Angela prepared and issued checks to vendors and reconciled bank statements. She perpetrated a fraud in this way: She wrote checks for costs that the company had not actually incurred (e.g., fake taxes). A supervisor then approved and signed the checks. Before issuing the check, though, Angela would "white-out" the payee line on the check and change it to personal accounts that she controlled. She was able to conceal the theft because she also reconciled the bank account. That is, nobody else ever saw that the checks had been altered.

**Total take: $570,000**

**The Missing Control**

**Segregation of duties.** Aggasiz Construction Company did not properly segregate recordkeeping from physical custody. Angela had physical custody of the checks, which essentially was control of the cash. She also had recordkeeping responsibility because she prepared the bank reconciliation.

**Source:** Adapted from Wells, *Fraud Casebook* (2007), pp. 100–107.

## Documentation Procedures

Documents provide evidence that transactions and events have occurred. For example, point-of-sale terminals are networked with a company's computing and accounting records, which results in direct documentation.

Similarly, a shipping document indicates that the goods have been shipped, and a sales invoice indicates that the company has billed the customer for the goods. By requiring signatures (or initials) on the documents, the company can identify the individual(s) responsible for the transaction or event. Companies should document transactions when they occur.

Companies should establish procedures for documents.

1. Whenever possible, companies should use **prenumbered documents**, **and all documents should be accounted for**. Prenumbering helps to prevent a transaction from being recorded more than once, or conversely, from not being recorded at all.

2. The control system should require that employees **promptly forward source documents to the accounting department**. **This control measure helps to ensure timely recording of the transaction** and contributes directly to the accuracy and reliability of the accounting records.

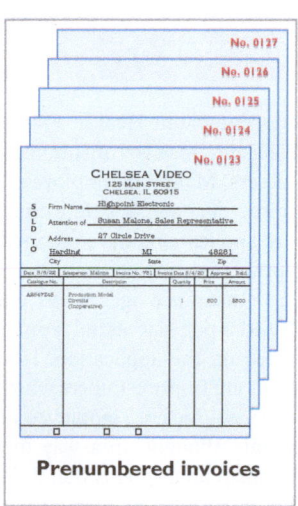

**Prenumbered invoices**

## Anatomy of a Fraud

To support their reimbursement requests for travel costs incurred, employees at Mod Fashions Corporation's design center were required to submit receipts. The receipts could include the detailed bill provided for a meal, the credit card receipt provided when the credit card payment is made, or a copy of the employee's monthly credit card bill that listed the item. A number of the designers who frequently traveled together came up with a fraud scheme: They submitted claims for the same expenses. For example, if they had a meal together that cost $200, one person submitted the detailed meal bill, another submitted the credit card receipt, and a third submitted a monthly credit card bill showing the meal as a line item. Thus, all three received a $200 reimbursement.

**Total take: $75,000**

**The Missing Control**

**Documentation procedures.** Mod Fashions should require the original, detailed receipt. It should not accept photocopies, and it should not accept credit card statements. In addition, documentation procedures could be further improved by requiring the use of a corporate credit card (rather than a personal credit card) for all business expenses.

**Source:** Adapted from Wells, *Fraud Casebook* (2007), pp. 79–90.

## Physical Controls

Use of physical controls is essential. **Physical controls** relate to the safeguarding of assets and enhance the accuracy and reliability of the accounting records. **Illustration 5.2** shows examples of these controls.

**ILLUSTRATION 5.2** Physical controls

**Physical Controls**

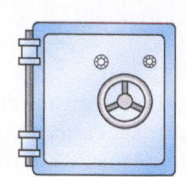     

| | | | | | |
|---|---|---|---|---|---|
| Safes, vaults, and safety deposit boxes for cash and business papers | Locked warehouses and storage cabinets for inventories and records | Computer facilities with passkey access or fingerprint or eyeball scans | Alarms to prevent break-ins | Television monitors and garment sensors to deter theft | Time clocks for recording time worked |

## Anatomy of a Fraud

At Centerstone Health, a large insurance company, the mailroom each day received insurance applications from prospective customers. Mailroom employees scanned the applications into electronic documents before the applications were processed. Once the applications were scanned, they could be accessed online by authorized employees.

Insurance agents at Centerstone Health earn commissions based upon successful applications. The sales agent's name is listed on the application. However, roughly 15% of the applications are from customers who did not work with a sales agent. Two friends—Alex, an employee in recordkeeping, and Parviz, a sales agent—thought up a way to perpetrate a fraud. Alex identified scanned applications that did not list a sales agent. After business hours, he entered the mailroom and found the hard-copy applications that did not show a sales agent. He wrote in Parviz's name as the sales agent and then rescanned the application for processing. Parviz received the commission, which the friends then split.

**Total take: $240,000**

**The Missing Control**

**Physical controls.** Centerstone Health lacked two basic physical controls that could have prevented this fraud. First, the mailroom should have been locked during nonbusiness hours, and access during business hours should have been tightly controlled. Second, the scanned applications supposedly could be accessed only by authorized employees using their passwords. However, the password for each employee was the same as the employee's user ID. Since employee user-ID numbers were available to all other employees, all employees knew each other's passwords. Thus, Alex could enter the system using another employee's password and access the scanned applications.

**Source:** Adapted from Wells, *Fraud Casebook* (2007), pp. 316–326.

### Independent Internal Verification

Most internal control systems provide for **independent internal verification**. This principle involves the review of data prepared by employees. To obtain maximum benefit from independent internal verification:

1. Companies should verify records periodically or on a surprise basis.
2. An employee who is independent of the personnel responsible for the information should make the verification.
3. Discrepancies and exceptions should be reported to a management level that can take appropriate corrective action.

Independent internal verification is especially useful in comparing recorded accountability with existing assets. The reconciliation of the electronic records with the cash in the point-of-sale terminal at **Barriques** is an example of this internal control principle. Other common examples are the reconciliation of a company's cash balance per books with the cash balance per bank, and the verification of the perpetual inventory records through a count of physical inventory. **Illustration 5.3** shows the relationship between this principle and the segregation of duties principle.

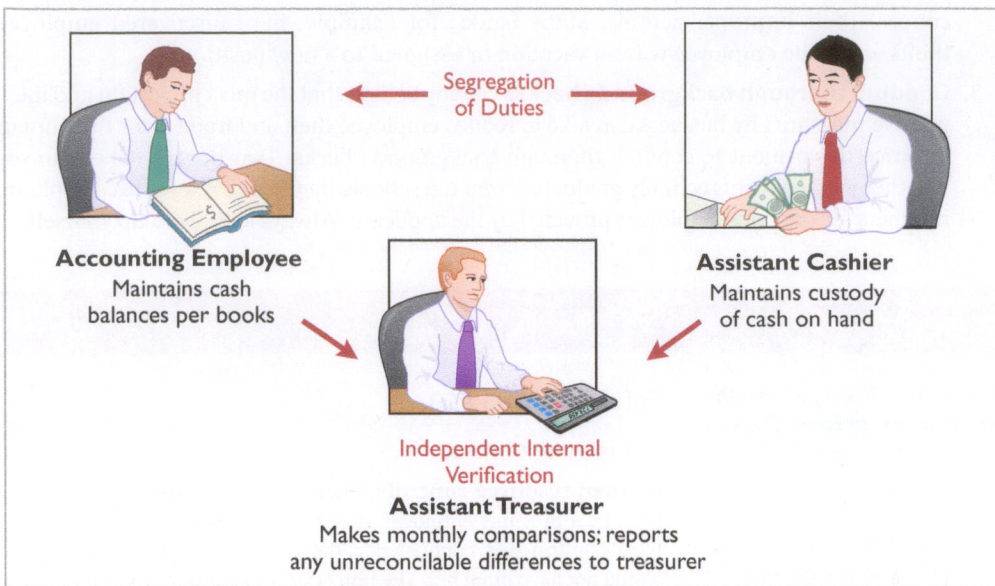

**ILLUSTRATION 5.3**
**Comparison of segregation of duties principle with independent internal verification principle**

## Anatomy of a Fraud

Bobbi Jean Donnelly, the office manager for Mod Fashions Corporation's design center, was responsible for preparing the design center budget and reviewing expense reports submitted by design center employees. Her desire to upgrade her wardrobe got the better of her, and she enacted a fraud that involved filing expense-reimbursement requests for her own personal clothing purchases. Bobbi Jean was able to conceal the fraud because she was responsible for reviewing all expense reports, including her own. In addition, she sometimes was given ultimate responsibility for signing off on the expense reports when her boss was "too busy." Also, because she controlled the budget, when she submitted her expenses, she coded them to budget items that she knew were running under budget, so that they would not catch anyone's attention.

**Total take: $275,000**

### The Missing Control

**Independent internal verification.** Bobbi Jean's boss should have verified her expense reports. When asked what he thought her expenses for a year were, the boss said about $10,000. At $115,000 per year, her actual expenses were more than 10 times what would have been expected. However, because he was "too busy" to verify her expense reports or to review the budget, he never noticed.

**Source:** Adapted from Wells, *Fraud Casebook* (2007), pp. 79–90.

Large companies often assign independent internal verification to internal auditors.

- **Internal auditors** are company employees who continuously evaluate the effectiveness of the company's internal control systems.
- They review the activities of departments and individuals to determine whether prescribed internal controls are being followed.
- They also recommend improvements when needed.

For example, **WorldCom** was at one time the second largest U.S. telecommunications company. The fraud that caused its bankruptcy (the largest ever when it occurred) involved billions of dollars. It was uncovered by an internal auditor.

## Human Resource Controls

Human resource control activities include the following.

1. **Bond employees who handle cash.** **Bonding** involves obtaining insurance protection against theft by employees. It contributes to the safeguarding of cash in two ways. First, the insurance company carefully screens all individuals before adding them to the policy and may reject risky applicants. Second, bonded employees know that the insurance company will vigorously prosecute all offenders.

2. **Rotate employees' duties and require employees to take vacations.** These measures deter employees from attempting thefts since they will not be able to permanently

If I take a vacation, they will know that I've been stealing.

conceal their improper actions. Many banks, for example, have discovered employee thefts when the employee was on vacation or assigned to a new position.

3. **Conduct thorough background checks.**   Many believe that the most important and inexpensive measure any business can take to reduce employee theft and fraud is for the human resource department to conduct thorough background checks. Two tips: (1) Check to see whether job applicants actually graduated from the schools they list. (2) Never use telephone numbers for previous employers provided by the applicant. Always look them up yourself.

---

## Anatomy of a Fraud

Ellen Lowry was the desk manager and Josephine Rodriguez was the head of housekeeping at the Excelsior Inn, a luxury hotel. The two best friends were so dedicated to their jobs that they never took vacations, and they frequently filled in for other employees. In fact, Ms. Rodriguez, whose job as head of housekeeping did not include cleaning rooms, often cleaned rooms herself, "just to help the staff keep up." These two "dedicated" employees, working as a team, found a way to earn a little more cash. Ellen, the desk manager, provided significant discounts to guests who paid with cash. She kept the cash and did not register the guests in the hotel's computerized system. Instead, she took the room out of circulation "due to routine maintenance." Because the room did not show up as being used, it did not receive a normal housekeeping assignment. Instead, Josephine, the head of housekeeping, cleaned the rooms during the guests' stay.

### Total take: $95,000

#### The Missing Control

**Human resource controls.** Ellen, the desk manager, had been fired by a previous employer after being accused of fraud. If the Excelsior Inn had conducted a thorough background check, it would not have hired her. The hotel fraud was detected when Ellen missed work for a few days due to illness. A system of mandatory vacations and rotating days off would have increased the chances of detecting the fraud before it became so large.

**Source:** Adapted from Wells, *Fraud Casebook* (2007), pp. 145–155.

---

## Accounting Across the Organization

### SOX Boosts the Role of Human Resources

Rawpixel Ltd/Alamy Stock Photo

Under SOX, a company needs to keep track of employees' degrees and certifications to ensure that employees continue to meet the specified requirements of a job. Also, to ensure proper employee supervision and proper separation of duties, companies must develop and monitor an organizational chart. When one corporation went through this exercise, it found that out of 17,000 employees, there were 400 people who did not report to anyone.

The corporation also had 35 people who reported to each other. In addition, if an employee complains of an unfair firing and mentions financial issues at the company, the human resource department must refer the case to the company audit committee and possibly to its legal counsel.

**Why would unsupervised employees or employees who report to each other represent potential internal control threats? (Go to WileyPLUS for this answer and additional questions.)**

---

# Data Analytics and Internal Controls

Data analytics has dramatically changed many aspects of internal control practices.

- In the past, internal and external auditors tended to rely heavily on investigations of period-end samples of transactions to identify potential violations.
- Now, rather than wait for a period-end sample, many companies employ continuous monitoring of virtually every transaction.
- As a result, spikes in certain types of activity or developing trends are more quickly identified and investigated.

Many different aspects of recording accounting transactions can be monitored continuously. For example, systems can automatically identify who recorded a transaction. This is important to ensure that segregation of duties is not violated, that is, that the transaction is only recorded by a current (as opposed to recently terminated) and authorized employee.

Large dollar amounts in risky areas can also be flagged and investigated quickly. Recipients of payments can be easily screened to ensure, for example, that bonus amounts are correctly determined based on results and bonus formulas, and that bonuses are only paid to employees who are designated for bonus payments. Similarly, vendor payments can be easily screened to ensure that payments only go to authorized vendors and that amounts are within an anticipated range. Sophisticated models can be used to continually estimate critical measures, and those estimates are then compared to actual results to identify outliers.

# Limitations of Internal Control

Companies generally design their systems of internal control to provide **reasonable assurance** of proper safeguarding of assets and reliability of the accounting records.

- The concept of reasonable assurance rests on the premise that the costs of establishing control procedures should not exceed their expected benefit (see **Helpful Hint**).
- For example, stores could eliminate shoplifting losses by having a security guard stop and search customers as they leave the store. But, store managers have concluded that the negative effects of such a procedure cannot be justified. Instead, they have attempted to control shoplifting losses by less costly procedures, such as using hidden cameras and store detectives to monitor customer activity, and installing sensor equipment at exits.

The **human element** often imposes limitations on internal control.

- A good system can become ineffective as a result of employee fatigue, carelessness, or indifference. For example, a receiving clerk may not bother to count goods received and may just "fudge" the counts.
- Occasionally, two or more individuals may work together to get around prescribed controls. Such **collusion** can significantly reduce the effectiveness of a system, eliminating the protection offered by segregation of duties.

The **size of the business** also may impose limitations on internal control.

- Small companies often find it difficult to segregate duties or to provide for independent internal verification.
- A study by the Association of Certified Fraud Examiners indicates that businesses with fewer than 100 employees are most at risk for employee theft.

In fact, 29% of frauds occurred at companies with fewer than 100 employees. The median loss at small companies was $154,000, which was nearly as high as the median fraud at companies with more than 10,000 employees ($160,000). A $154,000 loss can threaten the very existence of a small company.

**HELPFUL HINT**

Controls may vary with the risk level of the activity. For example, management may consider cash to be high risk and maintaining inventories in the stockroom as low risk. Thus, management would have stricter controls for cash.

---

## DO IT! 1 | Control Activities

Identify which control activity is violated in each of the following situations, and explain how the situation creates an opportunity for a fraud.

1. The person with primary responsibility for reconciling the bank account and making all bank deposits is also the company's accountant.
2. Wellstone Company's treasurer received an award for distinguished service because he had not taken a vacation in 30 years.
3. In order to save money spent on order slips and to reduce time spent keeping track of order slips, a local bar/restaurant does not buy prenumbered order slips.

### Solution

1. Violates the control activity of segregation of duties. Recordkeeping should be separate from physical custody. As a consequence, the employee could embezzle cash and record fraudulent transactions to hide the theft.
2. Violates the control activity of human resource controls. Key employees must take vacations. Otherwise, the treasurer, who manages the company's cash, might embezzle cash and use his position to conceal the theft.

**ACTION PLAN**

- Familiarize yourself with each of the control activities discussed.
- Understand the nature of the frauds that each control activity is intended to address.

**3.** Violates the control activity of documentation procedures. If prenumbered documents are not used, then it is virtually impossible to account for the documents. As a consequence, an employee could write up a dinner sale, receive the cash from the customer, and then throw away the order slip and keep the cash.

Related exercise material: **BE5.1, BE5.2, BE5.3, DO IT! 5.1, E5.1,** and **E5.2.**

# Cash Controls

**LEARNING OBJECTIVE 2**
Apply internal control principles to cash.

Cash is the one asset that is readily convertible into any other type of asset. It also is easily concealed and transported, and is highly desired.

- Because of these characteristics, **cash is the asset most susceptible to fraudulent activities**.
- In addition, because of the large volume of cash transactions, numerous errors may occur in executing and recording them.
- To safeguard cash and to ensure the accuracy of the accounting records for cash, effective internal control over cash is critical.

## Cash Receipts Controls

**Illustration 5.4** shows how the internal control principles explained earlier apply to cash receipts transactions. As you might expect, companies vary considerably in how they apply

**ILLUSTRATION 5.4**   Application of internal control principles to cash receipts

### Cash Receipts Controls

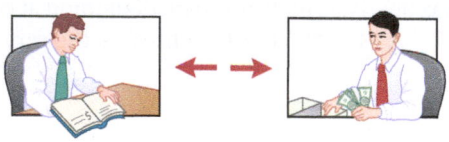

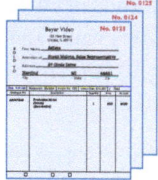

**Establishment of Responsibility**
Only designated personnel are authorized to handle cash receipts (cashiers)

**Segregation of Duties**
Different individuals receive cash, record cash receipts, and hold the cash

**Documentation Procedures**
Use remittance advice (mail receipts), cash register tapes or computer records, and deposit slips

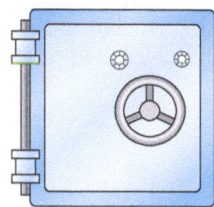

**Physical Controls**
Store cash in safes and bank vaults; limit access to storage areas; use cash registers or point-of-sale terminals

**Independent Internal Verification**
Supervisors count cash receipts daily; assistant treasurer compares total receipts to bank deposits daily

**Human Resource Controls**
Bond personnel who handle cash; require employees to take vacations; conduct background checks

these principles. To illustrate internal control over cash receipts, we will examine control activities for a retail store with both over-the-counter and mail receipts.

## Over-the-Counter Receipts

In retail businesses, control of over-the-counter receipts centers on cash registers that are visible to customers.

- A cash sale is entered in a cash register (or point-of-sale terminal), with the amount clearly visible to the customer. This activity prevents the sales clerk from entering a lower amount and pocketing the difference.
- The customer receives an itemized cash register receipt and is expected to count the change received. (One weakness at **Barriques** in the Feature Story is that customers are only given a receipt if requested.)
- The cash register's tape is locked in the register until a supervisor removes it. This tape accumulates the daily transactions and totals.

Alternatively, cash registers called point-of-sale terminals are often networked with the company's computers for direct recording in its records.

At the end of the clerk's shift, the clerk counts the cash and sends the cash and the count to the cashier. The cashier (or manager) counts the cash, prepares a deposit slip, and deposits the cash at the bank. The cashier also sends a duplicate of the deposit slip to the accounting department to indicate cash received. The supervisor removes the cash register tape and sends it to the accounting department as the basis for recording the cash received. (For point-of-sale systems, the accounting department receives information on daily transactions and totals through the computer network.) **Illustration 5.5** summarizes this process (see **Helpful Hint**).

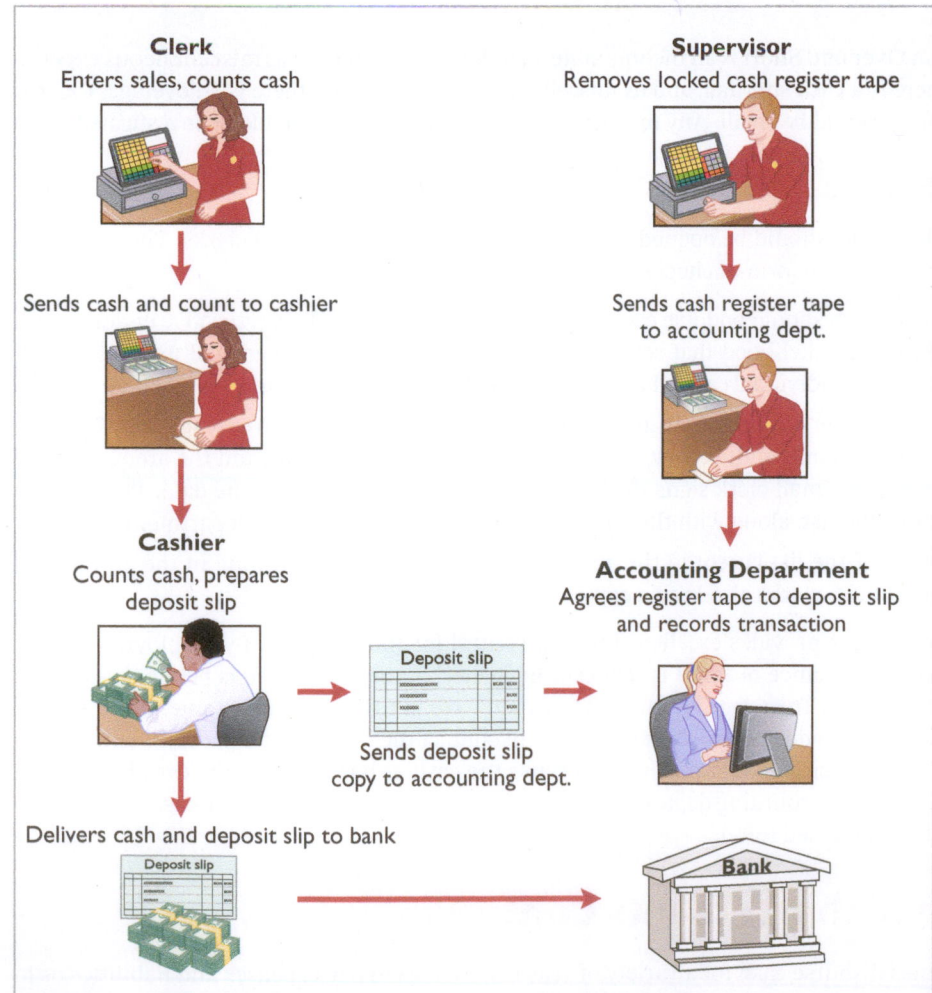

**ILLUSTRATION 5.5**

**Control of over-the-counter receipts**

**HELPFUL HINT**

Flowcharts such as this one enhance the understanding of the flow of documents, the processing steps, and the internal control procedures.

**Clerk**
Enters sales, counts cash

Sends cash and count to cashier

**Cashier**
Counts cash, prepares deposit slip

Sends deposit slip copy to accounting dept.

Delivers cash and deposit slip to bank

Deposit slip

**Supervisor**
Removes locked cash register tape

Sends cash register tape to accounting dept.

**Accounting Department**
Agrees register tape to deposit slip and records transaction

Deposit slip

**Bank**

This system for handling cash receipts uses an important internal control principle—segregation of recordkeeping from physical custody.

- The supervisor has access to the cash register tape but **not** to the cash.
- The clerk and the cashier have access to the cash but **not** to the register tape.
- In addition, the cash register tape provides documentation and enables independent internal verification.

Use of these three principles of internal control (segregation of recordkeeping from physical custody, documentation, and independent internal verification) provides an effective system of internal control. Any attempt at fraudulent activity should be detected unless there is collusion among the employees.

In some instances, the amount deposited at the bank will not agree with the cash recorded in the accounting records based on the cash register tape. These differences often result because the clerk hands incorrect change back to the retail customer. In this case, the difference between the actual cash and the amount reported on the cash register tape is reported in a Cash Over and Short account. For example, suppose that the cash register tape indicated sales of $6,956.20 but the amount of cash was only $6,946.10. A cash shortfall of $10.10 exists. To account for this cash shortfall and related cash, the company records the following.

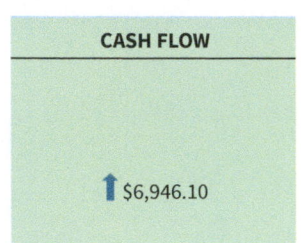
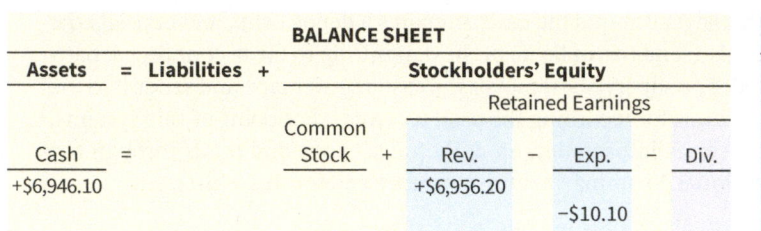

| CASH FLOW | BALANCE SHEET | | | | | | | INCOME STATEMENT |
|---|---|---|---|---|---|---|---|---|
| | **Assets** = **Liabilities** + | | **Stockholders' Equity** | | | | | |
| | | | | Retained Earnings | | | | |
| | | | Common | | | | | |
| | Cash = | | Stock + | Rev. | − | Exp. | − Div. | |
| ↑ $6,946.10 | +$6,946.10 | | | +$6,956.20 | | | | Sales Revenue |
| | | | | | | −$10.10 | | Cash Over/Short |

Cash Over and Short is an income statement item. It is reported as miscellaneous expense when there is a cash shortfall, and as miscellaneous revenue when there is an overage. Clearly, the amount should be small. Any material amounts in this account should be investigated.

### Mail Receipts

All mail receipts should be opened in the presence of at least two mail clerks. These receipts are generally in the form of checks.

- A mail clerk should endorse each check "For Deposit Only." This restrictive endorsement reduces the likelihood that someone could divert the check to personal use. Banks will not give an individual cash when presented with a check that has this type of endorsement.
- The mail clerks prepare, in triplicate, a list of the checks received each day. This list shows the name of the check issuer, the purpose of the payment, and the amount of the check. Each mail clerk signs the list to establish responsibility for the data. The original copy of the list, along with the checks, is then sent to the cashier's department.
- A copy of the list is sent to the accounting department for recording in the accounting records. The clerks also keep a copy.

This process provides excellent internal control for the company. By employing at least two clerks, the chance of fraud is reduced. Each clerk knows he or she is being observed by the other clerk(s). To engage in fraud, they would have to collude. The customers who submit payments also provide control because they will contact the company with a complaint if they are not properly credited for payment. Because the cashier has access to the cash but not the records, and the accounting department has access to the records but not the cash, neither can engage in undetected fraud.

## Cash Disbursements Controls

Companies disburse cash for a variety of reasons, such as to pay expenses and liabilities or to purchase assets. **Generally, internal control over cash disbursements is more effective**

**when companies pay by check or electronic funds transfer (EFT) rather than by cash.** One exception is **payments for incidental amounts that are paid out of petty cash**.

Companies generally issue checks only after following specified control procedures. **Illustration 5.6** shows how principles of internal control apply to cash disbursements.

**ILLUSTRATION 5.6**    **Application of internal control principles to cash disbursements**

## Cash Disbursements Controls

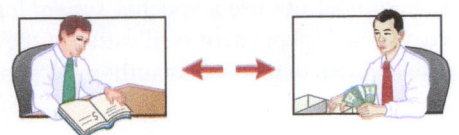

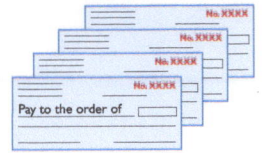

**Establishment of Responsibility**
Only designated personnel are authorized to sign checks (treasurer) and approve vendors

**Segregation of Duties**
Different individuals approve and make payments; check-signers do not record disbursements

**Documentation Procedures**
Use prenumbered checks and account for them in sequence; each check must have an approved invoice; require employees to use corporate credit cards for reimbursable expenses; stamp invoices "paid"

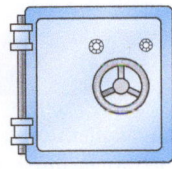

**Physical Controls**
Store blank checks in safes, with limited access; print check amounts by machine in indelible ink

**Independent Internal Verification**
Compare checks to invoices; reconcile bank statement monthly

**Human Resource Controls**
Bond personnel who handle cash; require employees to take vacations; conduct background checks

## Voucher System Controls

Most medium and large companies use vouchers as part of their internal control over cash disbursements. A **voucher system** is a network of approvals by authorized individuals, acting independently, to ensure that all disbursements by check are proper.

The system begins with the authorization to incur a cost or expense. It ends with the issuance of a check for the liability incurred. A **voucher** is an authorization form prepared for each expenditure. Companies require vouchers for all types of cash disbursements except those from petty cash.

- The starting point in preparing a voucher is to fill in the appropriate information about the liability on the face of the voucher. The vendor's invoice provides most of the needed information.

- Then, an employee in the accounts payable department records the voucher (in a **voucher register**) and files it according to the date on which it is to be paid. The company issues and sends a check on that date, and stamps the voucher "paid."

- The paid voucher is sent to the accounting department for recording (in a **check register**). A voucher system involves recording the liability when the voucher is issued and then later recording the payment of the liability that relates to the voucher.

The use of a voucher system, whether done manually or electronically, improves internal control over cash disbursements.

1. **The authorization process inherent in a voucher system establishes responsibility.** Each individual has responsibility to review the underlying documentation to ensure that it is correct.

2. **The voucher system keeps track of the documents that back up each transaction.** By keeping these documents in one place, a supervisor can independently verify the authenticity of each transaction.

Consider, for example, the case of Aesop University presented earlier in the "Anatomy of a Fraud" box. Aesop did not use a voucher system for transactions under $2,500. As a consequence, there was no independent verification of the documents, which enabled the employee to submit fake invoices to hide his unauthorized purchases.

# Petty Cash Fund

**ETHICS NOTE**

Petty cash funds are authorized and legitimate. In contrast, "slush" funds are unauthorized and hidden (under the table).

As you just learned, better internal control over cash disbursements is possible when companies make payments by check. However, using checks to pay small amounts is both impractical and a nuisance. For instance, a company would not want to write checks to pay for postage due, working lunches, or taxi fares. A common way of handling such payments, while maintaining satisfactory control, is to use a **petty cash fund** to pay relatively small amounts (see **Ethics Note**).

---

## Ethics Insight

iStock.com/Chris Fertnig

### How Employees Steal

Occupational fraud is using your own occupation for personal gain through the misuse or misapplication of the company's resources or assets. This type of fraud is one of three types:

1. **Asset misappropriation**, such as theft of cash on hand, fraudulent disbursements, false refunds, ghost employees, personal purchases, and fictitious employees. This fraud is the most common but the least costly.

2. **Corruption**, such as bribery, illegal gratuities, and economic extortion. This fraud generally falls in the middle between asset misappropriation and financial statement fraud as regards frequency and cost.

3. **Financial statement fraud**, such as fictitious revenues, concealed liabilities and expenses, improper disclosures, and improper asset values. This fraud occurs less frequently than other types of fraud, but it is the most costly.

The graph below shows the frequency and the median loss for each type of occupational fraud. (Note that the sum of percentages exceeds 100% because some cases of fraud involved more than one type.)

**Source:** *2016 Report to the Nations on Occupational Fraud and Abuse*, Association of Certified Fraud Examiners, p. 12.

**How can companies reduce the likelihood of occupational fraud? (Go to WileyPLUS for this answer and additional questions.)**

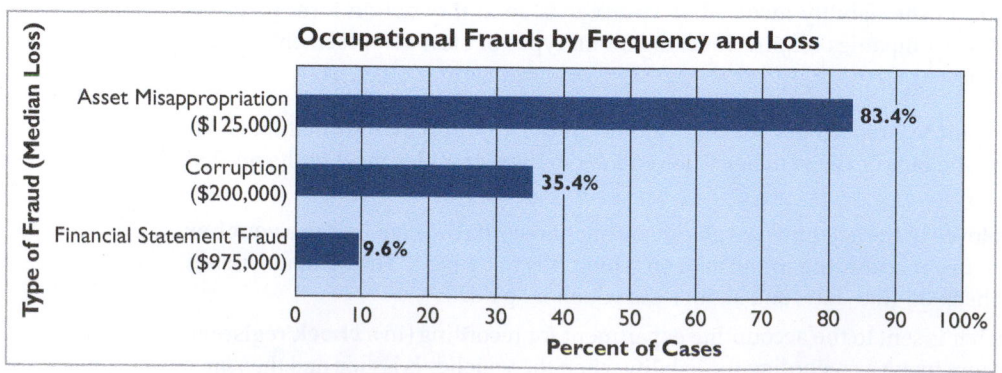

Occupational Frauds by Frequency and Loss

Type of Fraud (Median Loss):
- Asset Misappropriation ($125,000): 83.4%
- Corruption ($200,000): 35.4%
- Financial Statement Fraud ($975,000): 9.6%

Percent of Cases

## DO IT! 2 | Control over Cash Receipts

L. R. Cortez is concerned about the control over cash receipts in his fast food restaurant, Big Cheese. The restaurant has two cash registers. At no time do more than two employees take customer orders and enter sales. Work shifts for employees range from 4 to 8 hours. Cortez asks your help in installing a good system of internal control over cash receipts.

### Solution

Cortez should assign a separate cash register drawer to each employee at the start of each work shift, with register totals set at zero. Each employee should have access to only the assigned register drawer to enter all sales. Each customer should be given a receipt. At the end of the shift, the employee should do a cash count. A separate employee should compare the cash count with the register tape (or point-of-sale records) to be sure they agree. In addition, Cortez should install an automated point-of-sale system that would enable the company to compare orders entered in the register to orders processed by the kitchen.

Related exercise material: **BE5.4, BE5.5, BE5.6, DO IT! 5.2, E5.3, E5.4, and E5.5.**

**ACTION PLAN**

- Differentiate among the internal control principles of (1) establishing responsibility, (2) physical controls, and (3) independent internal verification.
- Design an effective system of internal control over cash receipts.

# Control Features of a Bank Account

**LEARNING OBJECTIVE 3**

Identify the control features of a bank account.

**The use of a bank contributes significantly to good internal control over cash.**

- A company safeguards its cash by using a bank as a depository and clearinghouse for checks received and checks written.
- The use of a bank checking account minimizes the amount of currency that must be kept on hand.
- It also facilitates control of cash because a double record is maintained of all bank transactions—one by the business and the other by the bank. The asset account Cash maintained by the company is the "flipside" of the bank's liability account for that company.
- A **bank reconciliation** is the process of comparing the bank's balance with the company's balance, and explaining the differences to make them agree.

Many companies have more than one bank account. For efficiency of operations and better control, national retailers like **Walmart** and **Target** often have regional bank accounts. Similarly, a company such as **ExxonMobil** with more than 100,000 employees may have a payroll bank account as well as one or more general bank accounts. In addition, a company may maintain several bank accounts in order to have more than one source for short-term loans.

## Electronic Funds Transfer (EFT) System

It is not surprising that companies and banks have developed approaches to transfer funds among parties without the use of paper (deposit tickets, checks, etc.).

- Such procedures, called **electronic funds transfers (EFTs)**, are disbursement systems that use wire, telephone, or computers to transfer cash from one location to another.
- Use of EFT is quite common. For example, many employees receive no formal payroll checks from their employers. Instead, employers send electronic payroll data to the appropriate banks.
- Also, companies now frequently make regular payments such as those for utilities, rent, and insurance by EFT.

EFT transactions normally result in better internal control since no cash or checks are handled by company employees. This does not mean that opportunities for fraud are eliminated. In fact, the same basic principles related to internal control apply to EFT transactions. For example, without proper segregation of duties and authorizations, an employee might be able to redirect electronic payments into a personal bank account and conceal the theft with fraudulent accounting records.

## Bank Statements

Each month, the company receives from the bank a **bank statement** showing its bank transactions and balances.[2] For example, the statement for Laird Company in **Illustration 5.7** shows the following.

1. Checks paid and other debits (such as debit card transactions or electronic funds transfers for bill payments) that reduce the balance in the depositor's account.
2. Deposits (by direct deposit, automated teller machine, or electronic funds transfer) and other credits that increase the balance in the depositor's account.
3. The account balance after each day's transactions (see **Helpful Hint**).

**ILLUSTRATION 5.7**

**Bank statement**

**HELPFUL HINT**

Essentially, the bank statement is a copy of the bank's records sent to the customer or made available online for review.

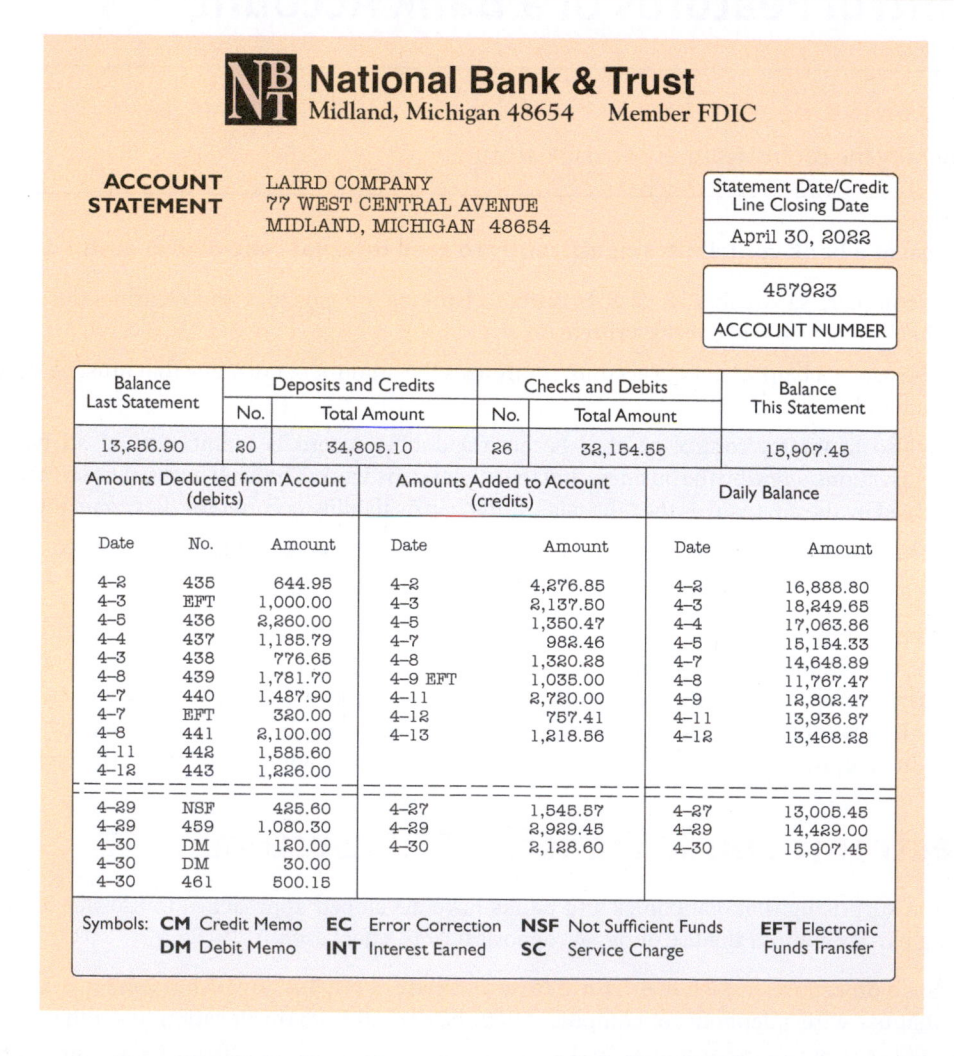

## National Bank & Trust
Midland, Michigan 48654     Member FDIC

**ACCOUNT STATEMENT**

LAIRD COMPANY
77 WEST CENTRAL AVENUE
MIDLAND, MICHIGAN  48654

Statement Date/Credit Line Closing Date

April 30, 2022

457923

ACCOUNT NUMBER

| Balance Last Statement | Deposits and Credits | | Checks and Debits | | Balance This Statement |
|---|---|---|---|---|---|
| | No. | Total Amount | No. | Total Amount | |
| 13,256.90 | 20 | 34,805.10 | 26 | 32,154.55 | 15,907.45 |

| Amounts Deducted from Account (debits) | | | Amounts Added to Account (credits) | | Daily Balance | |
|---|---|---|---|---|---|---|
| Date | No. | Amount | Date | Amount | Date | Amount |
| 4–2 | 435 | 644.95 | 4–2 | 4,276.85 | 4–2 | 16,888.80 |
| 4–3 | EFT | 1,000.00 | 4–3 | 2,137.50 | 4–3 | 18,249.65 |
| 4–5 | 436 | 2,260.00 | 4–5 | 1,350.47 | 4–4 | 17,063.86 |
| 4–4 | 437 | 1,185.79 | 4–7 | 982.46 | 4–5 | 15,154.33 |
| 4–3 | 438 | 776.65 | 4–8 | 1,320.28 | 4–7 | 14,648.89 |
| 4–8 | 439 | 1,781.70 | 4–9 EFT | 1,035.00 | 4–8 | 11,767.47 |
| 4–7 | 440 | 1,487.90 | 4–11 | 2,720.00 | 4–9 | 12,802.47 |
| 4–7 | EFT | 320.00 | 4–12 | 757.41 | 4–11 | 13,936.87 |
| 4–8 | 441 | 2,100.00 | 4–13 | 1,218.56 | 4–12 | 13,468.28 |
| 4–11 | 442 | 1,585.60 | | | | |
| 4–12 | 443 | 1,226.00 | | | | |
| 4–29 | NSF | 425.60 | 4–27 | 1,545.57 | 4–27 | 13,005.45 |
| 4–29 | 459 | 1,080.30 | 4–29 | 2,929.45 | 4–29 | 14,429.00 |
| 4–30 | DM | 120.00 | 4–30 | 2,128.60 | 4–30 | 15,907.45 |
| 4–30 | DM | 30.00 | | | | |
| 4–30 | 461 | 500.15 | | | | |

Symbols: **CM** Credit Memo   **EC** Error Correction   **NSF** Not Sufficient Funds   **EFT** Electronic Funds Transfer
**DM** Debit Memo   **INT** Interest Earned   **SC** Service Charge

[2]Our presentation assumes that a company makes all adjustments at the end of the month. In practice, a company may also update its records during the month as it reviews information from the bank regarding its account.

Remember that **bank statements are prepared from the *bank's* perspective**. For example, **every deposit the bank receives is an increase in the bank's liabilities (an account payable to the depositor)**. Therefore, in Illustration 5.7, National Bank and Trust **credits** to Laird Company every deposit it received from Laird. The reverse occurs when the bank "pays" a check issued by Laird Company on its checking account balance: Payment reduces the bank's liability and is therefore **debited** to Laird's account with the bank.

The bank statement lists in numerical sequence all paid checks along with the date the check was paid and its amount. Upon paying a check, the bank stamps the check "paid"; a paid check is sometimes referred to as a **canceled** check. In addition, the bank includes with the bank statement memoranda explaining other debits and credits it made to the depositor's account.

A check that is not paid by a bank because of insufficient funds in a bank account is called an **NSF check** (not sufficient funds).

- The bank uses a debit memorandum when a previously deposited customer's check "bounces" because of insufficient funds.
- In such a case, the customer's bank marks the check NSF (not sufficient funds) and returns it to the depositor's bank.
- The bank then debits (decreases) the depositor's account, as shown by the symbol NSF in Illustration 5.7, and sends the NSF check and debit memorandum to the depositor as notification of the charge.
- The NSF check creates an account receivable for the depositor and reduces cash in the bank account.

## Reconciling the Bank Account

Because the bank and the company maintain independent records of the company's checking account, you might assume that the respective balances will always agree. In fact, the two balances are seldom the same at any given time, and both balances differ from the "correct or true" balance. Therefore, it is necessary to make the balance per books and the balance per bank agree with the correct or true amount—a process called **reconciling the bank account**. The need for reconciliation has two causes:

1. **Time lags** that prevent one of the parties from recording the transaction in the same period.
2. **Errors** by either party in recording transactions.

Time lags occur frequently. For example, several days may elapse between the time a company pays by check and the date the bank pays the check. Similarly, when a company uses the bank's night depository to make its deposits, there will be a difference of one day between the time the company records the receipts and the time the bank does so. A time lag also occurs whenever the bank mails a debit or credit memorandum to the company.

You might think that if a company never writes checks (for example, if a small company uses only a debit card or electronic bill funds transfers), it does not need to reconcile its account.

- However, **the possibility of errors or fraud still necessitates periodic reconciliation**.
- The incidence of errors or fraud depends on the effectiveness of the internal controls maintained by the company and the bank.

Although bank errors are infrequent, either party could accidentally record a $450 check as $45 or $540. In addition, the bank might mistakenly charge a check drawn by C. D. Berg to the account of C. D. Burg.

### Reconciliation Procedure

In reconciling the bank account, it is customary to reconcile the balance per books and balance per bank to their adjusted (correct or true) cash balances.

- **To obtain maximum benefit from a bank reconciliation, an employee who has no other responsibilities related to cash should prepare the reconciliation.**
- When companies do not follow the internal control principle of independent internal verification in preparing the reconciliation, cash embezzlements may escape unnoticed.

For example, in the "Anatomy of a Fraud" box presented earlier, a bank reconciliation by someone other than Angela Bauer might have exposed her embezzlement.

**Illustration 5.8** shows the reconciliation process (see **Helpful Hint**). The starting point in preparing the reconciliation is to enter the balance per bank statement and balance per books on a schedule. The following steps should reveal all the reconciling items that cause the difference between the two balances.

**ILLUSTRATION 5.8**

**Bank reconciliation adjustments**

**HELPFUL HINT**

Deposits in transit and outstanding checks are reconciling items because of time lags.

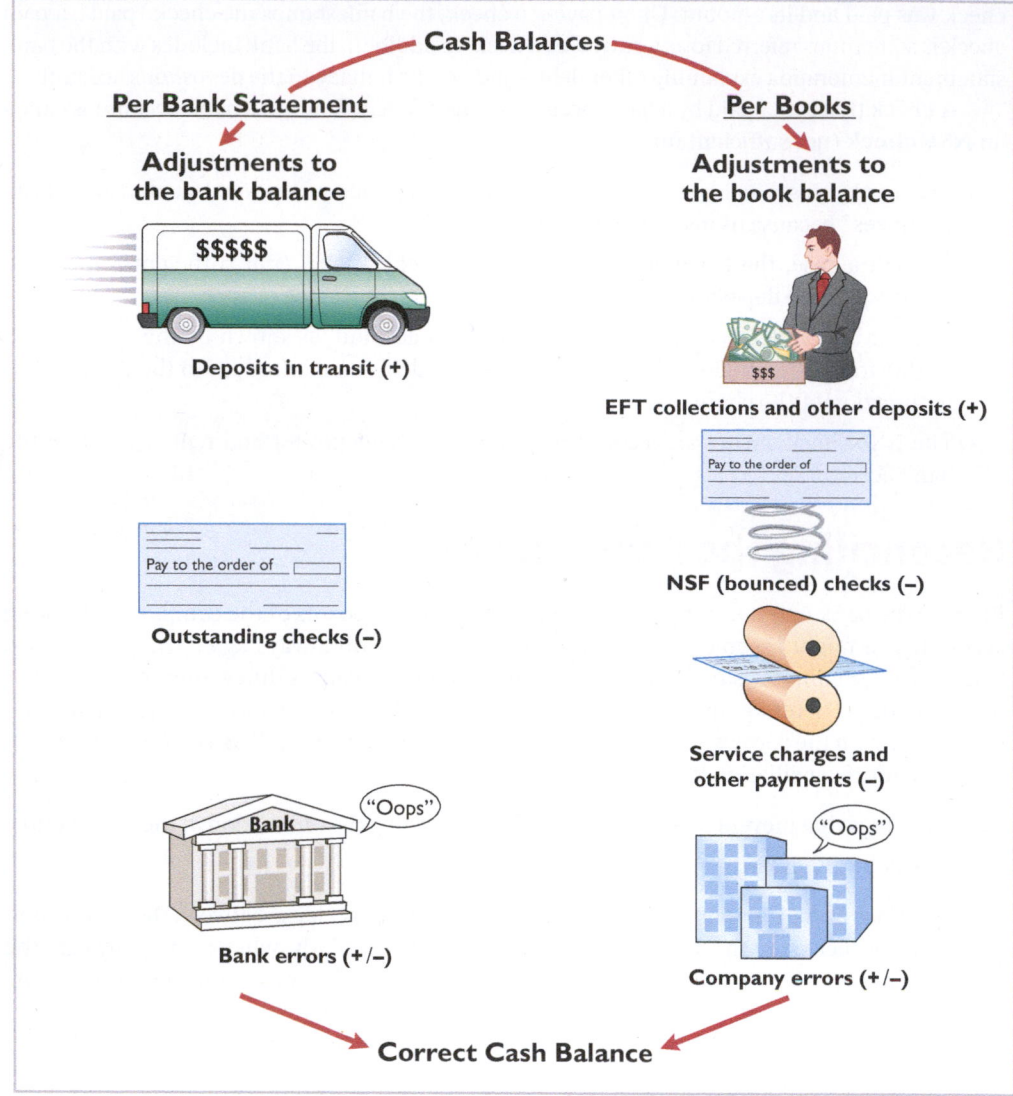

**Reconciling Items per Bank**   On the bank side of the reconciliation, the items to reconcile are deposits in transit (amounts added), outstanding checks (amounts deducted), and bank errors (if any). By adjusting the bank balance for these items, a company brings that balance up to date.

**Step 1   Deposits in transit (+).** Compare the individual deposits on the bank statement with the deposits in transit from the preceding bank reconciliation and with the deposits per company records or copies of duplicate deposit slips. Deposits recorded by the depositor that have not been recorded by the bank represent **deposits in transit**. Add these deposits to the balance per bank.

**Step 2   Outstanding checks (−).** Compare the paid checks shown on the bank statement or the paid checks returned with the bank statement with (a) checks outstanding from the preceding bank reconciliation, and (b) checks issued by the company that it recorded. Issued checks recorded by the company that have not been paid by the bank represent **outstanding checks**. Deduct outstanding checks from the balance per bank.

**Step 3   Bank errors (+/−).** Note any errors made by the bank that were discovered in the previous steps. For example, if the bank processed a deposit of $1,693 as $1,639 in error, the difference of $54 ($1,693 − $1,639) is added to the balance per bank on the bank reconciliation. All errors made by the bank are reconciling items in determining the adjusted cash balance per the bank.

**Reconciling Items per Books**   Reconciling items on the book side relate to amounts not yet recorded on the company's books and include adjustments from deposits and other amounts added, payments and other amounts deducted, and company errors (if any).

**Step 1   Other deposits (+).** Compare the other deposits on the bank statement with the company records. Any unrecorded amounts should be added to the balance per books. For example, if the bank statement shows electronic funds transfers from customers paying their accounts online, these amounts should be added to the balance per books on the bank reconciliation to update the company's records unless they had previously been recorded by the company.

**Step 2   Other payments (−).** Similarly, any unrecorded other payments should be deducted from the balance per books. For example, if the bank statement shows service charges (such as debit and credit card fees and other bank service charges), this amount is deducted from the balance per books on the bank reconciliation to make the company's records agree with the bank's records. **Normally, the company will already have recorded electronic payments.** However, if this has not been the case then these payments must be deducted from the balance per books on the bank reconciliation to make the company's records agree with the bank's records.

**Step 3   Book errors (+/−).** Note any errors made by the depositor that have been discovered in the previous steps. For example, say a company wrote check No. 443 to a supplier in the amount of $1,226 on April 12, but the accounting clerk recorded the check amount as $1,262. The error of $36 ($1,262 − $1,226) is added to the balance per books because the company reduced the balance per books by $36 too much when it recorded the check as $1,262 instead of $1,226. Only errors made by the company, not the bank, are included as reconciling items in determining the adjusted cash balance per books.

## Bank Reconciliation Illustrated

Illustration 5.7 presented the bank statement for Laird Company, which the company accessed online (see **Helpful Hint**). It shows a balance per bank of $15,907.45 on April 30, 2022. On this date the balance of cash per books is $11,709.45.

From the foregoing steps, Laird determines the following reconciling items for the bank.

**Step 1   Deposits in transit (+):** April 30 deposit (received by bank on May 1).                                                                                                    $2,201.40

**Step 2   Outstanding checks (−):** No. 453, $3,000.00; No. 457, $1,401.30; No. 460, $1,502.70.                                                                         5,904.00

**Step 3   Bank errors (+/−):** None.

Reconciling items per books are as follows.

**Step 1   Other deposits (+):** Unrecorded electronic receipt from customer on account on April 9 determined from the bank statement.                                  $1,035.00

**Step 2   Other payments (−):** The electronic payments on April 3 and 7 were previously recorded by the company when they were initiated. Unrecorded charges determined from the bank statement are as follows.

| | |
|---|---:|
| Returned NSF check on April 29 | 425.60 |
| Debit and credit card fees on April 30 | 120.00 |
| Bank service charges on April 30 | 30.00 |

**Step 3   Company errors (+):** Check No. 443 was correctly written by Laird for $1,226 and was correctly paid by the bank on April 12. However, it was recorded as $1,262 on Laird's books.                                                              36.00

**Illustration 5.9** shows Laird's bank reconciliation (see **Alternative Terminology**).

> **HELPFUL HINT**
>
> Note in the bank statement in Illustration 5.7 that the bank has paid checks No. 459 and 461, but check No. 460 is not listed. Thus, this check is outstanding. If a complete bank statement were provided, checks No. 453 and 457 also would not be listed. Laird obtains the amounts for these three checks from its cash payments records.

**ILLUSTRATION 5.9**
**Bank reconciliation**

**ILLUSTRATION 5.9**
**Bank reconciliation**

## Laird Company
### Bank Reconciliation
### April 30, 2022

| | | |
|---|---:|---:|
| Cash balance per bank statement | | $15,907.45 |
| Add: Deposits in transit | | 2,201.40 |
| | | 18,108.85 |
| Less: Outstanding checks | | |
| No. 453 | $3,000.00 | |
| No. 457 | 1,401.30 | |
| No. 460 | 1,502.70 | 5,904.00 |
| **Adjusted cash balance per bank** | | **$12,204.85** |
| | | |
| Cash balance per books | | $11,709.45 |
| Add: Electronic funds transfer received | $1,035.00 | |
| Error in recording check No. 443 | 36.00 | 1,071.00 |
| | | 12,780.45 |
| Less: NSF check | 425.60 | |
| Debit and credit card fees | 120.00 | |
| Bank service charge | 30.00 | 575.60 |
| **Adjusted cash balance per books** | | **$12,204.85** |

**ALTERNATIVE TERMINOLOGY**

The terms *adjusted cash balance, true cash balance,* and *correct cash balance* are used interchangeably.

## Bank Reconciliation Adjustments

The depositor (that is, the company) next must record each reconciling item used to determine the **adjusted cash balance per books**. If the company does not record these items, the Cash account will not show the correct balance. The adjustments for the Laird Company bank reconciliation on April 30 are as follows.

**Collection of Electronic Funds Transfer**  A payment of an account by a customer is recorded in the same way, whether the cash is received through the mail or electronically. The adjustment increases Cash and decreases Accounts Receivable $1,035.

| CASH FLOW | BALANCE SHEET | | | | | | | INCOME STATEMENT |
|---|---|---|---|---|---|---|---|---|
| | **Assets** | = **Liabilities** + | | **Stockholders' Equity** | | | | |
| | | | | | | Retained Earnings | | |
| | Cash + | Accounts Receivable = | | Common Stock + | Rev. − | Exp. − | Div. | |
| ⬆ $1,035 | +$1,035 | −$1,035 | | | | | | No effect |

**Book Error**  An examination of the cash disbursements records shows that check No. 443 was a payment on account to Andrea Company, a supplier. The correcting adjustment increases Cash and Accounts Payable $36.

| CASH FLOW | BALANCE SHEET | | | | | | | INCOME STATEMENT |
|---|---|---|---|---|---|---|---|---|
| | **Assets** | = **Liabilities** + | | **Stockholders' Equity** | | | | |
| | | | | | | Retained Earnings | | |
| | Cash = | Accounts Payable + | | Common Stock + | Rev. − | Exp. − | Div. | |
| ⬆ $36 | +$36 | +$36 | | | | | | No effect |

**NSF Check**  As indicated earlier, an NSF check becomes an accounts receivable to the depositor. The adjustment increases Accounts Receivable and decreases Cash $425.60.

| CASH FLOW | | BALANCE SHEET | | | | | | | | INCOME STATEMENT |
|---|---|---|---|---|---|---|---|---|---|---|
| | | **Assets** | **= Liabilities +** | | **Stockholders' Equity** | | | | | |
| | | | | | | | Retained Earnings | | | |
| | | Cash + | Accounts Receivable = | | Common Stock + | Rev. | – Exp. | – Div. | | |
| ↓ $425.60 | | –$425.60 | +$425.60 | | | | | | | No effect |

**Bank Charges Expense**   Fees for processing debit and credit card transactions normally increase the Bank Charges Expense account, as do bank service charges. We have chosen to combine and record these in a single adjustment, as the following shows, although they also could be recorded separately. The adjustment increases Bank Charge Expense and decreases Cash $150.

| CASH FLOW | | BALANCE SHEET | | | | | | | INCOME STATEMENT |
|---|---|---|---|---|---|---|---|---|---|
| | | **Assets** | **= Liabilities +** | | **Stockholders' Equity** | | | | |
| | | | | | | Retained Earnings | | | |
| | | Cash = | | Common Stock + | Rev. | – Exp. | – Div. | | |
| ↓ $150 | | –$150 | | | | –$150 | | | Bank Charge Exp. |

After Laird records these adjustments, the Cash account will appear as in **Illustration 5.10**. The adjusted cash balance should agree with the adjusted cash balance per books in the bank reconciliation in Illustration 5.9.

**ILLUSTRATION 5.10**   Adjusted balance in Cash account

| CASH FLOW | | | BALANCE SHEET | | | | | | | | INCOME STATEMENT |
|---|---|---|---|---|---|---|---|---|---|---|---|
| | | | **Assets** | | **= Liabilities +** | | **Stockholders' Equity** | | | | |
| | | | | | | | | Retained Earnings | | | |
| | | | Cash + | Accounts Receivable = | Accounts Payable + | Common Stock + | Rev. | – Exp. | – Div. | | |
| | | | $11,709.45 | | | | | | | | |
| | 1. | | +1,035 | –$1,035 | | | | | | | |
| | 2. | | +36 | | +$36 | | | | | | |
| | 3. | | –425.60 | +425.60 | | | | | | | |
| | 4. | | –150 | | | | | –$150 | | | Bank Charge Exp. |
| | | | $12,204.85 | | | | | | | | |

What adjustments does the bank record? If the company discovers any bank errors in preparing the reconciliation, it should notify the bank so the bank can make the necessary corrections on its records. The bank does not make any adjustments for deposits in transit or outstanding checks. Only when these items reach the bank will the bank record these items.

---

## Investor Insight

AP Images/Mary Altaffer

### Madoff's Ponzi Scheme

No recent fraud has generated more notoriety and rage than the one perpetrated by Bernard Madoff. Madoff was an elite New York investment fund manager who was highly regarded by securities regulators. Investors flocked to him because he delivered steady returns of between 10% and 15%, no matter whether the market was going up or going down. However, for many years, Madoff did not actually invest the cash that people gave to him. Instead, he was running a Ponzi scheme: He paid returns to existing investors using cash received from new investors. As long as the size of his investment fund continued to grow from new investments at a rate that exceeded the amounts that he needed to pay out in returns, Madoff was able to operate his fraud smoothly.

To conceal his misdeeds, Madoff fabricated false investment statements that were provided to investors. In addition, Madoff hired an auditor that never verified the accuracy of the investment records but automatically issued unqualified opinions each year. A competing fund manager warned the SEC a number of times over a nearly 10-year period that he thought Madoff was engaged in fraud. The SEC never aggressively investigated the allegations. Investors, many of which were charitable organizations, lost more than $18 billion. Madoff was sentenced to a jail term of 150 years.

**How was Madoff able to conceal such a giant fraud? (Go to WileyPLUS for this answer and additional questions.)**

**ACTION PLAN**

- **Understand the purpose of a bank reconciliation.**
- **Identify time lags and explain how they cause reconciling items.**

## DO IT! 3 | Bank Reconciliation

Sally Kist owns Linen Kist Fabrics. Sally asks you to explain how she should treat the following reconciling items when reconciling the company's bank account: (1) a debit memorandum for an NSF check, (2) a credit memorandum for an electronic funds transfer from one of the company's customers received by the bank, (3) outstanding checks, and (4) a deposit in transit.

### Solution

Sally should treat the reconciling items as follows.

1. NSF check: Deduct from balance per books.
2. Electronic funds transfer received by bank: Add to balance per books.
3. Outstanding checks: Deduct from balance per bank.
4. Deposit in transit: Add to balance per bank.

Related exercise material: **BE5.7, BE5.8, BE5.9, BE5.10, BE5.11, DO IT! 5.3, E5.6, E5.7, E5.8, E5.9, E5.10, E5.11, and E5.12.**

# Reporting Cash and Cash Management

> **LEARNING OBJECTIVE 4**
>
> Explain the reporting of cash and the basic principles of cash management.

## Reporting Cash

**Cash** consists of coins, currency (paper money), checks, money orders, and money on hand or on deposit in a bank or similar depository. Checks that are dated later than the current date (postdated checks) are not included in cash. Companies report cash in two different statements: the balance sheet and the statement of cash flows.

- The balance sheet reports the amount of cash available at a given point in time.
- The statement of cash flows shows the sources and uses of cash during a period of time.

In this section, we discuss some important points regarding the presentation of cash in the balance sheet.

When presented in a balance sheet, cash on hand, cash in banks, and petty cash are often combined and reported simply as **Cash**. Because it is the most liquid asset owned by the company, cash is listed first in the current assets section of the balance sheet.

### Cash Equivalents

Many companies use the designation "Cash and cash equivalents" in reporting cash. (See **Illustration 5.11** for an example.) **Cash equivalents** are short-term, highly liquid investments that are both:

1. Readily convertible to known amounts of cash.
2. So near their maturity that their market value is relatively insensitive to changes in interest rates. (Generally, only investments with maturities of three months or less qualify under this definition.)

| Delta Air Lines, Inc. | | |
| :--- | :--- | :--- |
| Balance Sheet (partial) | | |
| (in millions) | | |
| **Assets** | | |
| Current assets | | |
| Cash and cash equivalents | | $2,844 |
| Short-term investments | | 959 |
| Restricted cash | | 122 |

**ILLUSTRATION 5.11**
**Balance sheet presentation of cash**

Real World

Examples of cash equivalents are Treasury bills, commercial paper (short-term corporate notes), and money market funds (see **Ethics Note**). All typically are purchased with cash that is in excess of immediate needs.

Occasionally, a company will have a net negative balance in its bank account. In this case, the company should report the negative balance among current liabilities. For example, farm equipment manufacturer **Ag-Chem** at one time reported "Checks outstanding in excess of cash balances" of $2,145,000 among its current liabilities.

## Restricted Cash

A company may have **restricted cash**, cash that is not available for general use but rather is restricted for a special purpose (see **Decision Tools**). For example, landfill companies are often required to maintain a fund of restricted cash to ensure they will have adequate resources to cover closing and clean-up costs at the end of a landfill site's useful life. **McKesson Corp.** recently reported restricted cash of $962 million to be paid out as the result of investor lawsuits.

Cash restricted in use should be reported separately on the balance sheet as restricted cash.

- If the company expects to use the restricted cash within the next year, it reports the amount as a current asset. When this is not the case, it reports the restricted funds as a noncurrent asset.

- The FASB now requires that restricted cash be included with cash and cash equivalents when reconciling the beginning and ending amounts on a statement of cash flows.

Illustration 5.11 shows restricted cash reported in the financial statements of **Delta Air Lines** during a recent year. The company was required to maintain restricted cash as collateral to support insurance obligations related to workers' compensation claims. Delta did not have access to these funds for general use, and so it had to report them separately, rather than as part of cash and cash equivalents.

**ETHICS NOTE**

Recently, some companies were forced to restate their financial statements because they had too broadly interpreted which types of investments could be treated as cash equivalents. By reporting these items as cash equivalents, the companies made themselves look more liquid.

**Decision Tools**

Reporting restricted cash separately helps users determine the amount of cash available for a company's general use.

## DO IT! 4a | Reporting Cash

Indicate whether each of the following statements is true or false. If false, indicate how to correct the statement.

1. Cash and cash equivalents are comprised of coins, currency (paper money), money orders, and NSF checks.

2. Restricted cash is classified as either a current asset or noncurrent asset, depending on the circumstances.

3. A company may have a negative balance in its bank account. In this case, it should offset this negative balance against cash and cash equivalents on the balance sheet.

4. Because cash and cash equivalents often includes short-term investments, accounts receivable should be reported as the first item on the balance sheet.

**ACTION PLAN**

- **Understand how companies present cash and restricted cash on the balance sheet.**

- **Review the designations of cash equivalents and restricted cash, and how companies typically handle them.**

**Solution**

1. False. NSF checks should be reported as receivables, not cash and cash equivalents. **2.** True. **3.** False. Companies that have a negative balance in their bank accounts should report the negative balance as a current liability. **4.** False. Cash equivalents are readily convertible to known amounts of cash, and so near maturity (less than 3 months) that they are considered more liquid than accounts receivable and therefore are reported before accounts receivable on the balance sheet.

Related exercise material: **BE5.12, DO IT! 5.4a, and E5.13.**

# Managing and Monitoring Cash

Many companies struggle, not because they fail to generate sales, but because they cannot manage their cash. A real-life example of this is a clothing manufacturing company owned by Sharon McCollick. McCollick gave up a stable, high-paying marketing job with **Intel Corporation** to start her own company. Soon she had more orders from stores such as **JC Penney** and **Dayton Hudson** (now **Target**) than she could fill. Yet she found herself on the brink of financial disaster, owing three mortgage payments on her house and $2,000 to the IRS. Her company could generate sales, but it was not collecting cash fast enough to support its operations. The bottom line is that a business must have cash.[3]

A merchandising company's operating cycle is generally shorter than that of a manufacturing company. **Illustration 5.12** shows the cash-to-cash operating cycle of a merchandising operation.

**ILLUSTRATION 5.12**

**Operating cycle of a merchandising company**

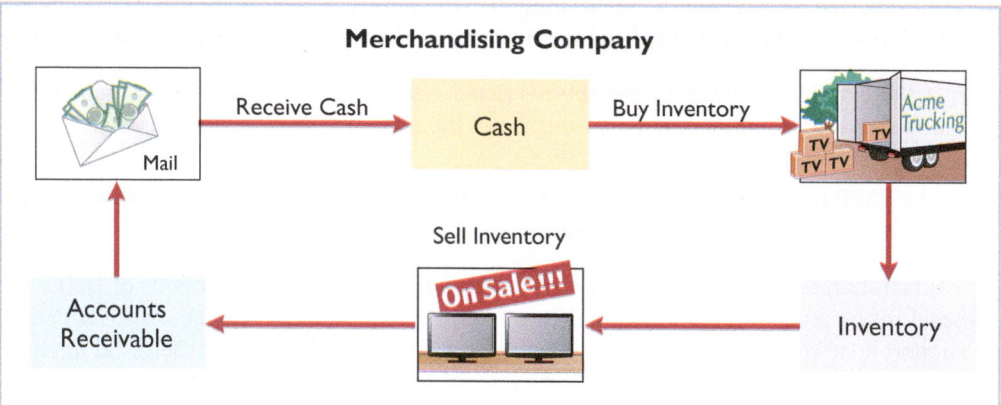

To understand cash management, consider the operating cycle of Sharon McCollick's clothing manufacturing company.

1. The company purchases cloth. Let's assume that it purchases the cloth on credit provided by the supplier, so the company owes its supplier money.

2. Employees convert the cloth to clothing. Now the company also owes its employees money.

3. The company sells the clothing to retailers, on credit. McCollick's company will have no money to repay suppliers or employees until it receives payments from customers.

In a manufacturing operation, there may be a significant lag between the original purchase of raw materials and the ultimate receipt of cash from customers.

---

[3]Adapted from T. Petzinger, Jr., "The Front Lines—Sharon McCollick Got Mad and Tore Down a Bank's Barriers," *Wall Street Journal* (May 19, 1995), p. B1.

Managing the often-precarious balance created by the ebb and flow of cash during the operating cycle is one of a company's greatest challenges. The objective is to ensure that a company has sufficient cash to meet payments as they come due, yet minimize the amount of non-revenue-generating cash on hand.

## Basic Principles of Cash Management

Management of cash is the responsibility of the company **treasurer**. Any company can improve its chances of having adequate cash by following five basic principles of cash management.

1. **Increase the speed of receivables collection.**   Money owed Sharon McCollick by her customers is money that she cannot use. The more quickly customers pay her, the more quickly she can use those funds. Thus, rather than have an average collection period of 30 days, she may want an average collection period of 15 days. However, she must carefully weigh any attempt to force her customers to pay earlier against the possibility that she may anger or alienate them. Perhaps her competitors are willing to provide a 30-day grace period. One common way to encourage customers to pay more quickly is to offer cash discounts for early payment.

2. **Keep inventory levels low.**   Maintaining a large inventory of cloth and finished clothing is costly. It ties up large amounts of cash, as well as warehouse space. Increasingly, companies are using techniques to reduce the inventory on hand, thus conserving their cash. Of course, if Sharon McCollick has inadequate inventory, she will lose sales. The proper level of inventory is an important decision.

3. **Monitor payment of liabilities.**   Sharon McCollick should monitor when her bills are due, so she avoids paying them too early. Let's say her supplier allows 30 days for payment. If she pays in 10 days, she has lost the use of that cash for 20 days. Therefore, she should use the full payment period. But, she should not pay late. This could damage her credit rating (and future borrowing ability). Also, late payments to suppliers can damage important supplier relationships and may even threaten a supplier's viability. McCollick's company also should conserve cash by taking cash discounts offered by suppliers, when possible (see **International Note**).

4. **Plan the timing of major expenditures.**   To maintain operations or to grow, all companies must make major expenditures. These often require some form of outside financing. To increase the likelihood of obtaining outside financing, Sharon McCollick should carefully consider the timing of major expenditures in light of her company's operating cycle. If at all possible, she should make any major expenditure when the company normally has excess cash—usually during the off-season.

5. **Invest idle cash.**   Cash on hand earns nothing. An important part of the treasurer's job is to ensure that the company invests any excess cash, even if it is only overnight. Many businesses, such as Sharon McCollick's clothing company, are seasonal. During her slow season, when she has excess cash, she should invest it.

    To avoid a cash crisis, it is very important that investments of idle cash be highly liquid and risk-free.

    - A **liquid investment** is one with a market in which someone is always willing to buy or sell the investment.

    - A **risk-free investment** means there is no concern that the party will default on its promise to pay its principal and interest.

For example, using excess cash to purchase stock in a small company because you heard that it was probably going to increase in value in the near term is totally inappropriate. First, the stock of small companies is often illiquid. Second, if the stock suddenly decreases in value, you might be forced to sell the stock at a loss in order to pay your bills as they come due. The most common form of liquid investments is interest-paying U.S. government securities.

**Illustration 5.13** summarizes these five principles of cash management.

### International Note

International sales complicate cash management. For example, if **Nike** must repay a Japanese supplier 30 days from today in Japanese yen, Nike will be concerned about how the exchange rate of U.S. dollars for yen might change during those 30 days. Often, corporate treasurers make investments known as *hedges* to lock in an exchange rate to reduce the company's exposure to exchange-rate fluctuation.

**ILLUSTRATION 5.13**
Five principles of sound cash management

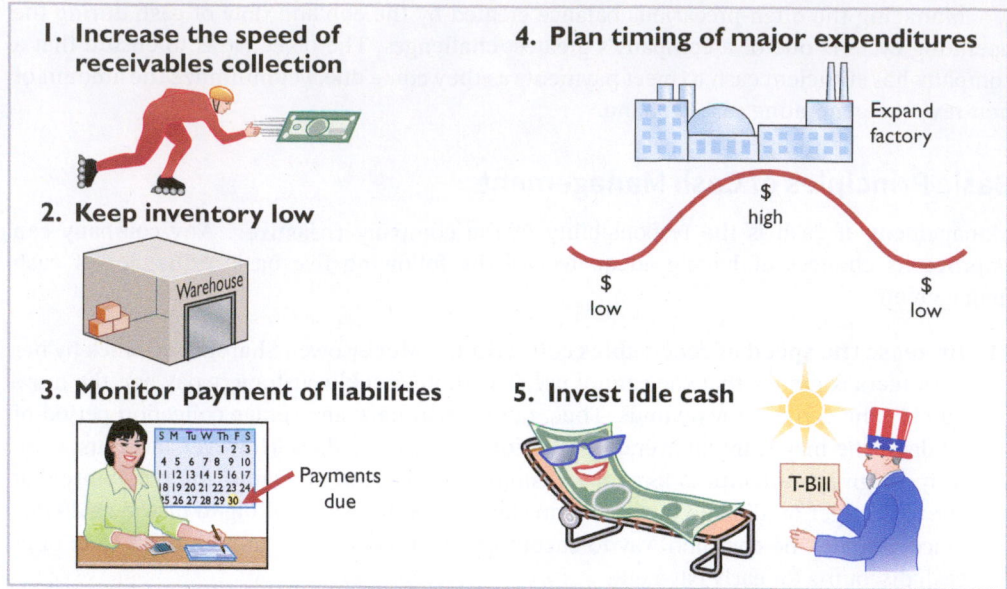

## Cash Budgeting

**Decision Tools**

The cash budget helps users determine if the company will be able to meet its projected cash needs.

Because cash is so vital to a company, **planning the company's cash needs** is a key business activity. It enables the company to plan ahead to cover possible cash shortfalls and to make investments of idle funds. The **cash budget** shows anticipated cash flows, usually over a one- to two-year period (see **Decision Tools**). In this section, we introduce the basics of cash budgeting. More advanced discussion of cash budgets and budgets in general is provided in managerial accounting texts.

As shown in **Illustration 5.14**, the cash budget contains three sections—cash receipts, cash disbursements, and financing—and the beginning and ending cash balances.

**ILLUSTRATION 5.14**
Basic form of cash budget

| Any Company | |
| --- | --- |
| **Cash Budget** | |
| Beginning cash balance | $X,XXX |
| Add: **Cash receipts** (itemized) | X,XXX |
| Total available cash | X,XXX |
| Less: **Cash disbursements** (itemized) | X,XXX |
| Excess (deficiency) of available cash over cash disbursements | X,XXX |
| **Financing** | |
| Add: Borrowings | X,XXX |
| Less: Repayments | X,XXX |
| Ending cash balance | $X,XXX |

1. The **Cash receipts** section includes expected receipts from the company's principal source(s) of cash, such as cash sales and collections from customers on credit sales. This section also shows anticipated receipts of interest and dividends, and proceeds from planned sales of investments, plant assets, and the company's capital stock.

2. The **Cash disbursements** section shows expected payments for inventory, labor, overhead, and selling and administrative expenses. It also includes projected payments for income taxes, dividends, investments, and plant assets. Note that it does not include depreciation since depreciation expense does not use cash.

3. The **Financing** section shows expected borrowings and repayments of borrowed funds plus interest. Financing is needed when there is a cash deficiency or when the cash balance is less than management's minimum required balance.

Companies must prepare multi-period cash budgets in sequence because the ending cash balance of one period becomes the beginning cash balance for the next period. In practice, companies often prepare cash budgets for the next 12 months on a monthly basis.

To minimize detail, we will assume that Hayes Company prepares an annual cash budget by quarters. Preparing a cash budget requires making some assumptions. For example, Hayes makes assumptions regarding collection of accounts receivable, sales of securities, payments for materials and salaries, and purchases of property, plant, and equipment. The accuracy of the cash budget is very dependent on the accuracy of these assumptions.

In **Illustration 5.15**, we present the cash budget for Hayes. The budget indicates that the company will need $3,000 of financing in the second quarter to maintain a minimum cash balance of $15,000. Since there is an excess of available cash over disbursements of $22,500 at the end of the third quarter, Hayes will repay the borrowing, plus $100 interest, in that quarter.

**ILLUSTRATION 5.15**
**Sample cash budget**

### Hayes Company
#### Cash Budget
#### For the Year Ending December 31, 2022

| | Quarter | | | |
| --- | --- | --- | --- | --- |
| | 1 | 2 | 3 | 4 |
| Beginning cash balance | $ 38,000 | $ 25,500 | $ 15,000 | $ 19,400 |
| Add: **Cash receipts** | | | | |
| Collections from customers | 168,000 | 198,000 | 228,000 | 258,000 |
| Sale of securities | 2,000 | 0 | 0 | 0 |
| Total receipts | 170,000 | 198,000 | 228,000 | 258,000 |
| Total available cash | 208,000 | 223,500 | 243,000 | 277,400 |
| Less: **Cash disbursements** | | | | |
| Inventory | 23,200 | 27,200 | 31,200 | 35,200 |
| Salaries | 62,000 | 72,000 | 82,000 | 92,000 |
| Selling and administrative expenses (excluding depreciation) | 94,300 | 99,300 | 104,300 | 109,300 |
| Purchase of truck | 0 | 10,000 | 0 | 0 |
| Income tax expense | 3,000 | 3,000 | 3,000 | 3,000 |
| Total disbursements | 182,500 | 211,500 | 220,500 | 239,500 |
| Excess (deficiency) of available cash over disbursements | 25,500 | 12,000 | 22,500 | 37,900 |
| **Financing** | | | | |
| Add: Borrowings | 0 | 3,000 | 0 | 0 |
| Less: Repayments—plus $100 interest | 0 | 0 | 3,100 | 0 |
| Ending cash balance | $ 25,500 | $ 15,000 | $ 19,400 | $ 37,900 |

**A cash budget contributes to more effective cash management.** For example, it can show when a company will need additional financing well before the actual need arises. Conversely, it can indicate when the company will have excess cash available for investments or other purposes.

## ACTION PLAN

- **Add the beginning cash balance to receipts to determine total available cash.**
- **Subtract disbursements to determine excess or deficiency.**
- **Compare excess or deficiency with desired minimum cash to determine borrowing needs.**

## DO IT! 4b | Cash Budget

Martian Company's management wants to maintain a minimum monthly cash balance of $15,000. At the beginning of March, the cash balance is $16,500, expected cash receipts for March are $210,000, and cash disbursements are expected to be $220,000. How much cash, if any, must Martian borrow to maintain the desired minimum monthly balance?

### Solution

| | |
|---|---:|
| Beginning cash balance | $ 16,500 |
| Add: Cash receipts for March | 210,000 |
| Total available cash | 226,500 |
| Less: Cash disbursements for March | 220,000 |
| Excess of available cash over cash disbursements | 6,500 |
| Financing | |
| Add: **Borrowings** | **8,500** |
| Ending cash balance | $ 15,000 |

To maintain the desired minimum cash balance of $15,000, Martian Company must borrow $8,500 of cash.

Related exercise material: **BE5.13, DO IT! 5.4b, E5.14, and E5.15.**

## USING THE DECISION TOOLS | Mattel Corporation

Presented below is hypothetical financial information for **Mattel Corporation** from the year ended December 31, 2021. Mattel is a toy manufacturing company, at one time named by *Fortune* magazine as one of the top 100 companies for which to work.

### Selected Financial Information
### Year Ended December 31, 2021
#### (in millions)

| | |
|---|---:|
| Net cash provided by operating activities | $325 |
| Capital expenditures | 162 |
| Dividends paid | 80 |
| Total expenses | 680 |
| Depreciation expense | 40 |
| Cash balance | 206 |

Also provided below are estimates of the company's sources and uses of cash during the year ended December 31, 2022. This information should be used to prepare a cash budget for 2022.

### Projected Sources and Uses of Cash
#### (in millions)

| | |
|---|---:|
| Beginning cash balance | $206 |
| Cash receipts from sales of product | 355 |
| Cash receipts from sale of short-term investments | 20 |
| Cash payments for inventory | 357 |
| Cash payments for selling and administrative costs | 201 |
| Cash payments for property, plant, and equipment | 45 |
| Cash payments for taxes | 17 |

Mattel's management believes it should maintain a balance of $200 million cash.

### Instructions

a. Using the hypothetical projected sources and uses of cash information presented above, prepare a cash budget for 2022 for Mattel Corporation.

b. Comment on the company's cash adequacy, and discuss steps that might be taken to improve its cash position.

## Solution

**a.**

**Mattel Corporation**
**Cash Budget**
**For the Year Ending December 31, 2022**
**(in millions)**

| | | |
|---|---:|---:|
| Beginning cash balance | | $206 |
| Add: Cash receipts | | |
| From sales of product | $355 | |
| From sale of short-term investments | 20 | 375 |
| Total available cash | | 581 |
| Less: Cash disbursements | | |
| Payments for inventory | 357 | |
| Payments for selling and administrative costs | 201 | |
| Payments for property, plant, and equipment | 45 | |
| Payments for taxes | 17 | |
| Total disbursements | | 620 |
| Excess (deficiency) of available cash over disbursements | | (39) |
| Financing | | |
| Add: **Borrowings** | | **239** |
| Ending cash balance | | $200 |

**b.** Using these hypothetical data, Mattel's cash position appears adequate. For 2022, Mattel is projecting a cash shortfall. This should be investigated. Its primary line of business is toys. Most toys are sold during December. We would expect Mattel's cash position to vary significantly during the course of the year. After the holiday season, once its customers have paid Mattel, it probably has a lot of excess cash. However, when it is making and selling its product but has not yet been paid, it may need to borrow to meet any temporary cash shortfalls.

If Mattel's management is concerned with its cash position, it could take the following steps. (1) Offer its customers cash discounts for early payment, such as 2/10, n/30. (2) Implement inventory management techniques to reduce the need for large inventories of such things as the plastics used to make its toys. (3) Carefully time payments to suppliers by keeping track of when payments are due, so as not to pay too early. (4) If it has plans for major expenditures, time those expenditures to coincide with its seasonal period of excess cash.

# Review and Practice

## Learning Objectives Review

### 1  Define fraud and the principles of internal control.

Fraud is a dishonest act by an employee that results in personal benefit to the employee at a cost to the employer. The fraud triangle refers to the three factors that contribute to fraudulent activity by employees: opportunity, financial pressure, and rationalization. Internal control consists of all the related methods and measures adopted within an organization to safeguard assets, enhance the reliability of accounting records, increase efficiency of operations, and ensure compliance with laws and regulations.

The principles of internal control are establishment of responsibility, segregation of duties, documentation procedures, physical controls, independent internal verification, and human resource controls.

### 2  Apply internal control principles to cash.

Internal controls over cash receipts include (a) designating only personnel such as cashiers to handle cash; (b) assigning the duties of receiving cash, recording cash, and having custody of cash to different individuals; (c) obtaining remittance advices for mail receipts, cash register tapes or computer records for over-the-counter receipts, and deposit slips for bank deposits; (d) using company safes and bank vaults to store cash with access limited to authorized personnel, and using cash registers or point-of-sale terminals in executing over-the-counter receipts; (e) making independent daily counts of register receipts and daily comparisons of total receipts with total deposits; and (f) conducting background checks and bonding personnel who handle cash, as well as requiring them to take vacations.

Internal controls over cash disbursements include (a) having only specified individuals such as the treasurer authorized to sign checks and approve vendors; (b) assigning the duties of approving items for payment, paying the items, and recording the payment to different individuals; (c) using prenumbered checks and accounting for all checks, with each check supported by an approved invoice; after payment, stamping each approved invoice "paid"; (d) storing blank checks in a safe or vault with access restricted to authorized personnel, and using a machine with indelible ink to imprint amounts on checks; (e) comparing each check with the approved invoice before issuing the check, and making monthly reconciliations of bank and book balances; and (f) bonding personnel who handle cash, requiring employees to take vacations, and conducting background checks.

### 3  Identify the control features of a bank account.

In reconciling the bank account, it is customary to reconcile the balance per books and the balance per bank to their adjusted balance.

The steps reconciling the Cash account are to determine deposits in transit and electronic funds transfers received by the bank, outstanding checks and electronic payments, errors by the depositor or the bank, and unrecorded bank memoranda.

### 4  Explain the reporting of cash and the basic principles of cash management.

Cash is listed first in the current assets section of the balance sheet. Companies often report cash together with cash equivalents. Cash restricted for a special purpose is reported separately as a current asset or as a noncurrent asset, depending on when the company expects to use the cash.

The basic principles of cash management include (a) increase the speed of receivables collection, (b) keep inventory levels low, (c) monitor the timing of payment of liabilities, (d) plan timing of major expenditures, and (e) invest idle cash.

The three main elements of a cash budget are the cash receipts section, cash disbursements section, and financing section.

## Decision Tools Review

| Decision Checkpoints | Info Needed for Decision | Tool to Use for Decision | How to Evaluate Results |
|---|---|---|---|
| Are the company's financial statements supported by adequate internal controls? | Auditor's report, management discussion and analysis, articles in financial press | The principles of internal control activities are (1) establishment of responsibility, (2) segregation of duties, (3) documentation procedures, (4) physical controls, (5) independent internal verification, and (6) human resource controls. | If any indication is given that these or other controls are lacking, use the financial statements with caution. |
| Is all of the company's cash available for general use? | Balance sheet and notes to financial statements | The company reports restricted cash in assets section of balance sheet. | A restriction on the use of cash limits management's ability to use those resources for general obligations. This might be considered when assessing liquidity. |
| Will the company be able to meet its projected cash needs? | Cash budget (typically available only to management) | The cash budget shows projected sources and uses of cash. If cash uses exceed internal cash sources, then the company must look for outside sources. | Two issues: (1) Are management's projections reasonable? (2) If outside sources are needed, are they available? |

## Glossary Review

**Bank reconciliation**  The process of comparing the bank's account balance with the company's balance, and explaining the differences to make them agree. (p. 5-17).

**Bank statement**  A statement received monthly from the bank that shows the depositor's bank transactions and balances. (p. 5-18).

**Bonding**  Obtaining insurance protection against theft by employees. (p. 5-9).

**Cash**  Resources that consist of coins, currency, checks, money orders, and money on hand or on deposit in a bank or similar depository. (p. 5-24).

**Cash budget**  A projection of anticipated cash flows, usually over a one- to two-year period. (p. 5-28).

**Cash equivalents**  Short-term, highly liquid investments that can be readily converted to a specific amount of cash and which are relatively insensitive to interest rate changes. (p. 5-24).

**Deposits in transit**  Deposits recorded by the depositor that have not been recorded by the bank. (p. 5-20).

**Electronic funds transfer (EFT)**  A disbursement system that uses wire, telephone, or computer to transfer cash from one location to another. (p. 5-17).

**Fraud**   A dishonest act by an employee that results in personal benefit to the employee at a cost to the employer. (p. 5-3).

**Fraud triangle**   The three factors that contribute to fraudulent activity by employees: opportunity, financial pressure, and rationalization. (p. 5-3).

**Internal auditors**   Company employees who continuously evaluate the effectiveness of the company's internal control systems. (p. 5-9).

**Internal control**   A process designed to provide reasonable assurance regarding the achievement of company objectives related to operations, reporting, and compliance. (p. 5-4).

**NSF check**   A check that is not paid by a bank because of insufficient funds in a bank account. (p. 5-19).

**Outstanding checks**   Checks issued and recorded by a company that have not been paid by the bank. (p. 5-20).

**Petty cash fund**   A cash fund used to pay relatively small amounts. (p. 5-16).

**Restricted cash**   Cash that is not available for general use but instead is restricted for a particular purpose. (p. 5-25).

**Sarbanes-Oxley Act (SOX)**   Law that requires publicly traded companies to maintain adequate systems of internal control. (p. 5-3).

**Treasurer**   Employee responsible for the management of a company's cash. (p. 5-27).

**Voucher**   An authorization form prepared for each expenditure in a voucher system. (p. 5-15).

**Voucher system**   A network of approvals by authorized individuals, acting independently, to ensure that all disbursements by check are proper. (p. 5-15).

## Practice Multiple-Choice Questions

1. **(LO 1)** Which of the following is **not** an element of the fraud triangle?

    **a.** Rationalization.

    **b.** Financial pressure.

    **c.** Segregation of duties.

    **d.** Opportunity.

2. **(LO 1)** Internal control is used in a business to:

    **a.** safeguard its assets.

    **b.** enhance the accuracy and reliability of its accounting records.

    **c.** ensure compliance with laws and regulations.

    **d.** All of these answer choices are correct.

3. **(LO 1)** The principles of internal control do **not** include:

    **a.** establishment of responsibility.

    **b.** documentation procedures.

    **c.** management responsibility.

    **d.** independent internal verification.

4. **(LO 1)** Physical controls do **not** include:

    **a.** safes and vaults to store cash.

    **b.** independent bank reconciliations.

    **c.** locked warehouses for inventories.

    **d.** bank safety deposit boxes for important papers.

5. **(LO 1)** Which of the following was **not** a result of the Sarbanes-Oxley Act?

    **a.** Companies must file financial statements with the Internal Revenue Service.

    **b.** All publicly traded companies must maintain adequate internal controls.

    **c.** The Public Company Accounting Oversight Board was created to establish auditing standards and regulate auditor activity.

    **d.** Corporate executives and boards of directors must ensure that controls are reliable and effective, and they can be fined or imprisoned for failure to do so.

6. **(LO 1)** Which of the following control activities is **not** relevant when a company uses a computerized (rather than manual) accounting system?

    **a.** Establishment of responsibility.

    **b.** Segregation of duties.

    **c.** Independent internal verification.

    **d.** All of these control activities are relevant to a computerized system.

7. **(LO 2)** Permitting only designated personnel such as cashiers to handle cash receipts is an application of the principle of:

    **a.** segregation of duties.

    **b.** establishment of responsibility.

    **c.** independent internal verification.

    **d.** human resource controls.

8. **(LO 2)** The use of prenumbered checks in disbursing cash is an application of the principle of:

    **a.** establishment of responsibility.

    **b.** segregation of duties.

    **c.** physical controls.

    **d.** documentation procedures.

9. **(LO 3)** The control features of a bank account do **not** include:

    **a.** having bank auditors verify the correctness of the bank balance per books.

    **b.** minimizing the amount of cash that must be kept on hand.

    **c.** providing a double record of all bank transactions.

    **d.** safeguarding cash by using a bank as a depository.

10. **(LO 3)** In a bank reconciliation, deposits in transit are:

    **a.** deducted from the book balance.

    **b.** added to the book balance.

    **c.** added to the bank balance.

    **d.** deducted from the bank balance.

**11. (LO 3)** The reconciling item in a bank reconciliation that will result in an adjustment by the depositor is:

   **a.** outstanding checks.    **c.** a bank error.

   **b.** deposit in transit.    **d.** bank service charges.

**12. (LO 4)** Which of the following items in a cash drawer at November 30 is **not** cash?

   **a.** Money orders.

   **b.** Coins and currency.

   **c.** An NSF check.

   **d.** A customer check dated November 28.

**13. (LO 4)** Which statement correctly describes the reporting of cash?

   **a.** Cash cannot be combined with cash equivalents.

   **b.** Restricted cash funds may be combined with cash.

   **c.** Cash is listed first in the current assets section.

   **d.** Restricted cash funds cannot be reported as a current asset.

**14. (LO 4)** Which of the following would **not** be an example of good cash management?

   **a.** Provide discounts to customers to encourage early payment.

   **b.** Invest temporary excess cash in stock of a small company.

   **c.** Carefully monitor payments so that payments are not made early.

   **d.** Employ just-in-time inventory methods to keep inventory low.

**15. (LO 4)** Which of the following is **not** one of the sections of a cash budget?

   **a.** Cash receipts section.

   **b.** Cash disbursements section.

   **c.** Financing section.

   **d.** Cash from operations section.

## Solutions

**1. c.** Segregation of duties is not an element of the fraud triangle. The other choices are elements of the fraud triangle.

**2. d.** Safeguarding a company's assets, enhancing the accuracy and reliability of its accounting records, and ensuring compliance with laws and regulations are all aspects of internal control.

**3. c.** Management responsibility is not one of the principles of internal control. The other choices are true statements.

**4. b.** Independent bank reconciliations are not a physical control. The other choices are true statements.

**5. a.** Filing financial statements with the IRS is not a result of the Sarbanes-Oxley Act (SOX); SOX focuses on the prevention or detection of fraud. The other choices are results of SOX.

**6. d.** Establishment of responsibility, segregation of duties, and independent internal verification are all relevant to a computerized system. Although choices (a), (b), and (c) are correct, choice (d) is the better answer.

**7. b.** Permitting only designated personnel to handle cash receipts is an application of the principle of establishment of responsibility, not (a) segregation of duties, (c) independent internal verification, or (d) human resource controls.

**8. d.** The use of prenumbered checks in disbursing cash is an application of the principle of documentation procedures, not (a) establishment of responsibility, (b) segregation of duties, or (c) physical controls.

**9. a.** Having bank auditors verify the correctness of the bank balance per books is not one of the control features of a bank account. The other choices are true statements.

**10. c.** Deposits in transit are added to the bank balance on a bank reconciliation, not (a) deducted from the book balance, (b) added to the book balance, or (d) deducted from the bank balance.

**11. d.** Because the depositor does not know the amount of the bank service charges until the bank statement is received, an adjustment must be made when the statement is received. The other choices are incorrect because (a) outstanding checks do not require an adjustment by the depositor because the checks have already been recorded in the depositor's books, (b) deposits in transit do not require an adjustment by the depositor because the deposits have already been recorded in the depositor's books, and (c) bank errors do not require an adjustment by the depositor, but the depositor does need to inform the bank of the error so it can be corrected.

**12. c.** An NSF check should not be considered cash. The other choices are true statements.

**13. c.** Cash is listed first in the current assets section. The other choices are incorrect because (a) cash and cash equivalents can be appropriately combined when reporting cash on the balance sheet, (b) restricted cash is not to be combined with cash when reporting cash on the balance sheet, and (d) restricted funds can be reported as current assets if they will be used within one year.

**14. b.** Investing excess cash to purchase stock in a small company is inappropriate because the stock of small companies is often not easily converted to cash. Choices (a) providing discounts to customers to encourage early payment, (c) carefully monitoring payments so that cash is held until just before the payment date of liabilities, and (d) keeping inventory levels low are all good cash management practices.

**15. d.** Cash from operations is not a section of a cash budget. Choices (a) cash receipts section, (b) cash disbursements section, and (c) financing section are all elements of a cash budget.

---

## Practice Brief Exercises

*Prepare partial bank reconciliation.*

**1. (LO 3)** At August 31, Saladino Company has the following bank information: cash balance per bank $5,200, outstanding checks $1,462, deposits in transit $1,211, and a bank debit memo $110. Determine the adjusted cash balance per bank at July 31.

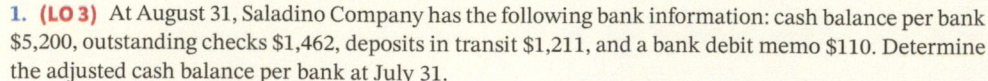

## Solution

1.

| | |
|---|---:|
| Cash balance per bank | $5,200 |
| Add: Deposits in transit | 1,211 |
| | 6,411 |
| Less: Outstanding checks | 1,462 |
| Adjusted cash balance per bank | $4,949 |

**2. (LO 4)** Zian Company has the following cash balances: Cash in Bank $18,762, Payroll Bank Account $8,000, Petty Cash $150, and Plant Expansion Fund Cash $30,000 to be used 2 years from now. Explain how each balance should be reported on the balance sheet.

*Explain the statement presentation of cash balances.*

## Solution

**2.** Zian Company should report Cash in Bank, Payroll Bank Account, and Petty Cash as current assets (usually combined as one Cash amount). Plant Expansion Fund Cash should be reported as a noncurrent asset, assuming the fund is not expected to be used during the next year.

**3. (LO 4)** The following information is available for Bohemia Company for the month of June: expected cash receipts $73,000, expected cash disbursements $81,000, and cash balance on June 1, $10,000. Management wishes to maintain a minimum cash balance of $11,000. Prepare a basic cash budget for the month of June.

*Prepare a cash budget.*

## Solution

3.

| Bohemia Company<br>Cash Budget<br>For the Month of June | |
|---|---:|
| Beginning cash balance | $10,000 |
| Add: Cash receipts | 73,000 |
| Total available cash | 83,000 |
| Less: Cash disbursements | 81,000 |
| Excess of available cash over cash disbursements | 2,000 |
| Add: Borrowings | 9,000 |
| Ending cash balance | $11,000 |

# Practice Exercises

**1. (LO 1, 2)** Listed below are five procedures followed by Shepherd Company.

*Indicate whether procedure is good or weak internal control.*

1. Total cash receipts are compared to bank deposits daily by someone who has no other cash responsibilities.

2. Time clocks are used for recording time worked by employees.

3. Employees are required to take vacations.

4. Any member of the sales department can approve credit sales.

5. Sam Hill ships goods to customers, bills customers, and receives payment from customers.

## Instructions

Indicate whether each procedure is an example of good internal control or of weak internal control. If it is an example of good internal control, indicate which internal control principle is being followed. If it is an example of weak internal control, indicate which internal control principle is violated. Use the table below.

| Procedure | IC Good or Weak? | Related Internal Control Principle |
|---|---|---|
| 1. | | |
| 2. | | |
| 3. | | |
| 4. | | |
| 5. | | |

### Solution

**1.**

| Procedure | IC Good or Weak? | Related Internal Control Principle |
|---|---|---|
| 1. | Good | Independent internal verification |
| 2. | Good | Physical controls |
| 3. | Good | Human resource controls |
| 4. | Weak | Establishment of responsibility |
| 5. | Weak | Segregation of duties |

*Prepare bank reconciliation and adjustments.*

**2. (LO 3)** The information below relates to the Cash account for Ansel Company.

Balance June 1—$17,450; Cash deposited—$64,000.

Balance June 30—$17,704; Checks written—$63,746.

The June bank statement shows a balance of $16,422 on June 30 and the following memoranda.

| Credits | | Debits | |
|---|---|---|---|
| Collection of $1,530 through electronic funds transfer | $1,530 | NSF check: Anne Adams | $425 |
| Interest earned on checking account | $35 | Safety deposit box rent | $55 |

At June 30, deposits in transit were $4,750, and outstanding checks totaled $2,383.

### Instructions

a. Prepare the bank reconciliation at June 30.

b. Prepare a tabular analysis for the adjustments at June 30, assuming (1) the NSF check was from a customer on account, and (2) no interest had been accrued on the note. Use the following column headings: Cash, Accounts Receivable, Revenues, and Expenses. Include margin explanations for any changes in revenues and expenses.

### Solution

**2. a.**

|  | Ansel Company Bank Reconciliation June 30 | |
|---|---|---|
| Cash balance per bank statement | | $16,422 |
| Add: Deposits in transit | | 4,750 |
| | | 21,172 |
| Less: Outstanding checks | | 2,383 |
| Adjusted cash balance per bank | | $18,789 |
| | | |
| Cash balance per books | | $17,704 |
| Add: Electronic funds transfer received | $1,530 | |
|     Interest earned | 35 | 1,565 |
| | | 19,269 |
| Less: NSF check | 425 | |
|     Safety deposit box rent | 55 | 480 |
| Adjusted cash balance per books | | $18,789 |

**b.**

| Assets | | = Liabilities + | Stockholders' Equity | | | |
|---|---|---|---|---|---|---|
| | Accounts | | Retained Earnings | | | |
| Cash + | Receivable = | | + Rev. − | Exp. − | Div. | |
| $1,530 | −$1,530 | | | | | |
| 35 | | | $35 | | | Interest Rev. |
| −425 | 425 | | | | | |
| −55 | | | | −$55 | | Bank Charges Exp. |

## Practice Problem

**(LO 3)** Trillo Company's bank statement for May 2022 shows these data.

*Prepare bank reconciliation and adjustments.*

| | | | |
|---|---|---|---|
| Balance May 1 | $12,650 | Balance May 31 | $14,280 |
| Debit memorandum: | | Credit memorandum: | |
| NSF check | 175 | Collection of electronic funds transfer | 505 |

The cash balance per books at May 31 is $13,319. Your review of the data reveals the following.

1. The NSF check was from Hup Co., a customer.

2. Outstanding checks at May 31 total $2,410.

3. Deposits in transit at May 31 total $1,752.

4. A Trillo Company check for $352 dated May 10 cleared the bank on May 25. This check, which was a payment on account, was recorded for $325.

### Instructions

a. Prepare a bank reconciliation at May 31.

b. Prepare a tabular analysis for the adjustments required by the reconciliation. Use the following column headings: Cash, Accounts Receivable, and Accounts Payable.

### Solution

**a.**

| | | |
|---|---|---|
| Cash balance per bank statement | | $14,280 |
| Add: Deposits in transit | | 1,752 |
| | | 16,032 |
| Less: Outstanding checks | | 2,410 |
| Adjusted cash balance per bank | | $13,622 |
| Cash balance per books | | $13,319 |
| Add: Electronic funds transfer received | | 505 |
| | | 13,824 |
| Less: NSF check | $175 | |
| Error in recording check ($352 − $325) | 27 | 202 |
| Adjusted cash balance per books | | $13,622 |

**b.**

| Assets | | = Liabilities + | Stockholders' Equity |
|---|---|---|---|
| | Accounts | Accounts | |
| Cash + | Receivable = | Payable | |
| $505 | −$505 | | |
| −175 | 175 | | |
| −27 | | $27 | |

# WileyPLUS

Brief Exercises, DO IT! Exercises, Exercises, Problems, and many additional resources are available for practice in WileyPLUS.

## Questions

**1.** A local bank reported that it lost $150,000 as the result of employee fraud. Ray Fairburn is not clear on what is meant by "employee fraud." Explain the meaning of fraud to Ray and give an example of fraud that might occur at a bank.

**2.** Fraud experts often say that there are three primary factors that contribute to employee fraud. Identify the three factors and explain what is meant by each.

**3.** Identify the five components of a good internal control system.

**4.** "Internal control is concerned only with enhancing the accuracy of the accounting records." Do you agree? Explain.

**5.** Discuss how the Sarbanes-Oxley Act has increased the importance of internal control to top managers of a company.

**6.** What principles of internal control apply to most businesses?

**7.** In the corner grocery store, all sales clerks make change out of one cash register drawer. Is this a violation of internal control? Why?

**8.** Branden Doyle is reviewing the principle of segregation of duties. What are the two common applications of this principle?

**9.** How do documentation procedures contribute to good internal control?

**10.** What internal control objectives are met by physical controls?

**11. a.** Explain the control principle of independent internal verification.

  **b.** What practices are important in applying this principle?

**12.** As the company accountant, explain the following ideas to the management of Ortiz Company.

  **a.** The concept of reasonable assurance in internal control.

  **b.** The importance of the human factor in internal control.

**13.** Discuss the human resources department's involvement in internal controls.

**14.** Robbins Inc. owns the following assets at the balance sheet date.

| | |
|---|---|
| Cash in bank—savings account | $ 8,000 |
| Cash on hand | 1,100 |
| Cash refund due from the IRS | 1,000 |
| Checking account balance | 12,000 |
| Postdated checks | 500 |

What amount should be reported as Cash in the balance sheet?

**15.** What principle(s) of internal control is (are) involved in making daily cash counts of over-the-counter receipts?

**16.** Assume that **Kohl's** installed new cash registers in its stores. How do cash registers improve internal control over cash receipts?

**17.** At Lazlo Wholesale Company, two mail clerks open all mail receipts. How does this strengthen internal control?

**18.** "To have maximum effective internal control over cash disbursements, all payments should be made by check." Is this true? Explain.

**19.** Pauli Company's internal controls over cash disbursements provide for the treasurer to sign checks imprinted by a checkwriter after comparing the check with the approved invoice. Identify the internal control principles that are present in these controls.

**20.** How do these principles apply to cash disbursements?

  **a.** Physical controls.

  **b.** Human resource controls.

**21.** What is the essential feature of an electronic funds transfer (EFT) procedure?

**22.** "The use of a bank contributes significantly to good internal control over cash." Is this true? Why?

**23.** Hank Cook is confused about the lack of agreement between the cash balance per books and the balance per bank. Explain the causes for the lack of agreement to Hank and give an example of each cause.

**24.** Identify the basic principles of cash management.

**25.** Trisha Massey asks for your help concerning an NSF check. Explain to Trisha (a) what an NSF check is, (b) how it is treated in a bank reconciliation, and (c) whether it will require an adjustment on the company's books.

**26. a.** Describe cash equivalents and explain how they are reported.

  **b.** How should restricted cash funds be reported on the balance sheet?

**27.** What was **Apple**'s balance in cash and cash equivalents at September 29, 2018? Did it report any restricted cash? How did Apple define cash equivalents?

## Brief Exercises

*Identify fraud triangle concepts.*

**BE5.1 (LO 1), C** Match each situation with the fraud triangle factor (opportunity, financial pressure, or rationalization) that best describes it.

  **a.** An employee's monthly credit card payments are nearly 75% of her monthly earnings.

  **b.** An employee earns minimum wage at a firm that has reported record earnings for each of the last 5 years.

   **c.** An employee has an expensive gambling habit.

   **d.** An employee has check-writing and -signing responsibilities for a small company, and is also responsible for reconciling the bank account.

**BE5.2 (LO 1), C** Pat Buhn is the new owner of Young Co. She has heard about internal control but is not clear about its importance for her business. Explain to Pat the four purposes of internal control, and give her one application of each purpose for Young Co.

*Explain the importance of internal control.*

**BE5.3 (LO 1), C** The internal control procedures in Dayton Company result in the following provisions. Identify the principles of internal control that are being followed in each case.

*Identify internal control principles.*

   **a.** Employees who have physical custody of assets do not have access to the accounting records.

   **b.** Each month, the assets on hand are compared to the accounting records by an internal auditor.

   **c.** A prenumbered shipping document is prepared for each shipment of goods to customers.

**BE5.4 (LO 2), C** Jolson Company has the following internal control procedures over cash receipts. Identify the internal control principle that is applicable to each procedure.

*Identify the internal control principles applicable to cash receipts.*

   **a.** All over-the-counter receipts are entered in cash registers.

   **b.** All cashiers are bonded.

   **c.** Daily cash counts are made by cashier department supervisors.

   **d.** The duties of receiving cash, recording cash, and having custody of cash are assigned to different individuals.

   **e.** Only cashiers may operate cash registers.

**BE5.5 (LO 2), AP** While examining cash receipts information, the accounting department determined the following information: opening cash balance $150, cash on hand $1,125.74, and cash sales per register tape $988.62. Prepare a tabular analysis of the required adjustment based upon the cash count sheet.

*Make adjustment using cash count sheet.*

**BE5.6 (LO 2), C** Tott Company has the following internal control procedures over cash disbursements. Identify the internal control principle that is applicable to each procedure.

*Identify the internal control principles applicable to cash disbursements.*

   **a.** Company checks are prenumbered.

   **b.** The bank statement is reconciled monthly by an internal auditor.

   **c.** Blank checks are stored in a safe in the treasurer's office.

   **d.** Only the treasurer or assistant treasurer may sign checks.

   **e.** Check-signers are not allowed to record cash disbursement transactions.

**BE5.7 (LO 3), C** Luke Roye is uncertain about the control features of a bank account. Explain the control benefits of (a) a checking account and (b) a bank statement.

*Identify the control features of a bank account.*

**BE5.8 (LO 3), C** The following reconciling items are applicable to the bank reconciliation for Forde Co. Indicate how each item should be shown on a bank reconciliation.

*Indicate location of reconciling items in a bank reconciliation.*

   **a.** Outstanding checks.

   **b.** Bank debit memorandum for service charge.

   **c.** Bank credit memorandum for collecting an electronic funds transfer.

   **d.** Deposit in transit.

**BE5.9 (LO 3), C** The following reconciling items are applicable to the bank reconciliation for Forde Co. Indicate (1) the items that will result in an adjustment to the depositor's records and (2) why the other items do not require adjustment.

*Identify reconciling items that require adjustments.*

   **a.** Outstanding checks.

   **b.** Bank debit memorandum for service charge.

   **c.** Bank credit memorandum for collecting an electronic funds transfer.

   **d.** Deposit in transit.

**BE5.10 (LO 3), AP** At July 31, Planter Company has this bank information: cash balance per bank $7,291, outstanding checks $762, deposits in transit $1,350, and a bank service charge $40. Determine the adjusted cash balance per bank at July 31.

*Prepare partial bank reconciliation.*

**BE5.11 (LO 3), AP** In the month of November, its first month in business, Fiesta Company Inc. wrote checks in the amount of $9,750. In December, checks in the amount of $11,762 were written. In November, $8,800 of these checks were presented to the bank for payment, and $10,889 in December. What is the amount of outstanding checks at the end of November? At the end of December?

*Analyze outstanding checks.*

*Explain the statement presentation of cash balances.*

**BE5.12 (LO 4), C** Spahn Company has these cash balances: cash in bank $12,742, payroll bank account $6,000, and plant expansion fund cash $25,000. Explain how each balance should be reported on the balance sheet.

*Prepare a cash budget.*

**BE5.13 (LO 4), AP** The following information is available for Bonkers Company for the month of January: expected cash receipts $59,000, expected cash disbursements $67,000, and cash balance on January 1, $12,000. Management wishes to maintain a minimum cash balance of $9,000. Prepare a basic cash budget for the month of January.

## DO IT! Exercises

*Identify violations of control activities.*

**DO IT! 5.1 (LO 1), C** Identify which control activity is violated in each of the following situations, and explain how the situation creates an opportunity for fraud or inappropriate accounting practices.

1. Once a month, the sales department sends sales invoices to the accounting department to be recorded.

2. Steve Nicoles orders merchandise for Binn Company; he also receives merchandise and authorizes payment for merchandise.

3. Several clerks at Draper's Groceries use the same cash register drawer.

*Design system of internal control over cash receipts.*

**DO IT! 5.2 (LO 2), C** Wes Unsel is concerned with control over mail receipts at Wooden Sporting Goods. All mail receipts are opened by Mel Blount. Mel sends the checks to the accounting department, where they are stamped "For Deposit Only." The accounting department records and deposits the mail receipts weekly. Wes asks your help in installing a good system of internal control over mail receipts.

*Explain treatment of items in bank reconciliation.*

**DO IT! 5.3 (LO 3), K** Ned Douglas owns Ned's Blankets. Ned asks you to explain how he should treat the following reconciling items when reconciling the company's bank account.

1. Outstanding checks.

2. A deposit in transit.

3. The bank charged to our account a check written by another company.

4. A debit memorandum for a bank service charge.

*Analyze statements about the reporting of cash.*

**DO IT! 5.4a (LO 4), AP** Indicate whether each of the following statements is true or false. If false, indicate how to correct the statement.

1. A company has the following assets at the end of the year: cash on hand $40,000, cash refund due from customer $30,000, and checking account balance $22,000. Cash and cash equivalents is therefore $62,000.

2. A company that has received NSF checks should report these checks as a current liability on the balance sheet.

3. Restricted cash that is a current asset is reported as part of cash and cash equivalents.

4. A company has cash in the bank of $50,000, petty cash of $400, and stock investments of $100,000. Total cash and cash equivalents is therefore $50,400.

*Prepare a cash budget.*

**DO IT! 5.4b (LO 4), AP** Stern Corporation's management wants to maintain a minimum monthly cash balance of $8,000. At the beginning of September, the cash balance is $12,270, expected cash receipts for September are $97,200, and cash disbursements are expected to be $115,000. How much cash, if any, must Stern borrow to maintain the desired minimum monthly balance? Determine your answer by using the basic form of the cash budget.

## Exercises

*Identify the principles of internal control.*

**E5.1 (LO 1), C** Bank employees use a system known as the "maker-checker" system. An employee will record a transaction, and then a supervisor will verify and approve it. These days, as all of a bank's accounts are computerized, the employee first enters a batch of transactions into the computer, and then the records are updated automatically after the supervisor approves them on the system.

Access to the computer system is password-protected and task-specific, which means that the computer system will not allow the employee to approve a transaction or the supervisor to record a transaction.

**Instructions**

Identify the principles of internal control inherent in the "maker-checker" procedure used by banks.

**E5.2 (LO 1), C** Ricci's Pizza operates strictly on a carryout basis. Customers pick up their orders at a counter where a clerk exchanges the pizza for cash. While at the counter, the customer can see other employees making the pizzas and the large ovens in which the pizzas are baked.

*Identify the principles of internal control.*

**Instructions**

Identify the six principles of internal control and give an example of each principle that you might observe when picking up your pizza. (*Note:* It may not be possible to observe all the principles.)

**E5.3 (LO 2), E** The following control procedures are used in Keaton Company for over-the-counter cash receipts.

*List internal control weaknesses over cash receipts and suggest improvements.*

1. Each store manager is responsible for interviewing applicants for cashier jobs. They are hired if they seem honest and trustworthy.
2. All over-the-counter receipts are registered by three clerks who share a cash register with a single cash drawer.
3. To minimize the risk of robbery, cash in excess of $100 is stored in an unlocked briefcase in the stockroom until it is deposited in the bank.
4. At the end of each day, the total receipts are counted by the cashier on duty and reconciled to the cash register total.
5. The company accountant makes the bank deposit and then records the day's receipts.

**Instructions**

a. For each procedure, explain the weakness in internal control and identify the control principle that is violated.
b. For each weakness, suggest a change in the procedure that will result in good internal control.

**E5.4 (LO 2), E** The following control procedures are used in Bunny's Boutique Shoppe for cash disbursements.

*List internal control weaknesses for cash disbursements and suggest improvements.*

1. Each week, 100 company checks are left in an unmarked envelope on a shelf behind the cash register.
2. The store manager personally approves all payments before she signs and issues checks.
3. The store purchases used goods for resale from people who bring items to the store. Since that can occur anytime that the store is open, all employees are authorized to purchase goods for resale by disbursing cash from the register. The purchase is documented by having the store employee write on a piece of paper a description of the item that was purchased and the amount that was paid. The employee then signs the paper and puts it in the register.
4. After payment, bills are "filed" in a paid invoice folder.
5. The company accountant prepares the bank reconciliation and reports any discrepancies to the owner.

**Instructions**

a. For each procedure, explain the weakness in internal control and identify the internal control principle that is violated.
b. For each weakness, suggest a change in the procedure that will result in good internal control.

**E5.5 (LO 2), E** At Martinez Company, checks are not prenumbered because both the purchasing agent and the treasurer are authorized to issue checks. Each signer has access to unissued checks kept in an unlocked file cabinet. The purchasing agent pays all bills pertaining to goods purchased for resale. Prior to payment, the purchasing agent determines that the goods have been received and verifies the mathematical accuracy of the vendor's invoice. After payment, the invoice is filed by vendor name and the purchasing agent then records the transaction. The treasurer pays all other bills following approval by authorized employees. After payment, the treasurer stamps all bills "paid," files them by payment date, and records the checks. Martinez Company maintains one checking account that is reconciled by the treasurer.

*Identify internal control weaknesses for cash disbursements and suggest improvements.*

**Instructions**

a. List the weaknesses in internal control over cash disbursements.
b. Identify improvements for correcting these weaknesses.

*Prepare bank reconciliation and adjustments.*

**E5.6 (LO 3), AP** Rachel Sells is unable to reconcile the bank balance at January 31. Rachel's reconciliation is shown as follows.

| | |
|---|---:|
| Cash balance per bank | $3,677.20 |
| Add: NSF check | 450.00 |
| Less: Bank service charge | 28.00 |
| Adjusted balance per bank | $4,099.20 |
| Cash balance per books | $3,975.20 |
| Less: Deposits in transit | 590.00 |
| Add: Outstanding checks | 770.00 |
| Adjusted balance per books | $4,155.20 |

**Instructions**

a. What is the proper adjusted cash balance per bank?

b. What is the proper adjusted cash balance per books?

c. Prepare a tabular analysis for the adjustments required to reach the adjusted cash balance per books. Use the following column headings: Cash, Accounts Receivable, Revenues, and Expenses. Include margin explanations for the changes in revenues and expenses.

*Determine outstanding checks.*

**E5.7 (LO 3), AP** At April 30, the bank reconciliation of Back 40 Company shows three outstanding checks: No. 254 $650, No. 255 $700, and No. 257 $410. The May bank statement and the May cash payments record are given here.

| Bank Statement Checks Paid | | | Cash Payments Record Checks Issued | | |
|---|---|---|---|---|---|
| **Date** | **Check No.** | **Amount** | **Date** | **Check No.** | **Amount** |
| 5-4 | 254 | $650 | 5-2 | 258 | $159 |
| 5-2 | 257 | 410 | 5-5 | 259 | 275 |
| 5-17 | 258 | 159 | 5-10 | 260 | 925 |
| 5-12 | 259 | 275 | 5-15 | 261 | 500 |
| 5-20 | 260 | 925 | 5-22 | 262 | 750 |
| 5-29 | 263 | 480 | 5-24 | 263 | 480 |
| 5-30 | 262 | 750 | 5-29 | 264 | 360 |

**Instructions**

Using Step 2 in the reconciliation procedure, list the outstanding checks at May 31.

*Prepare bank reconciliation and adjustments.*

**E5.8 (LO 3), AP** The following information pertains to Lance Company.

1. Cash balance per bank, July 31, $7,328.

2. July bank service charge not recorded by the depositor $38.

3. Cash balance per books, July 31, $7,364.

4. Deposits in transit, July 31, $2,700.

5. $2,016 collected for Lance Company in July by the bank through electronic funds transfer. The collection has not been recorded by Lance Company.

6. Outstanding checks, July 31, $686.

**Instructions**

a. Prepare a bank reconciliation at July 31, 2022.

b. Prepare a tabular analysis for the adjustments at July 31 on the books of Lance Company. Use the following column headings: Cash, Accounts Receivable, Revenues, and Expenses. Include margin explanations for the changes in revenues and expenses.

*Prepare bank reconciliation and adjustments.*

**E5.9 (LO 3), AP** This information relates to the Cash account for Howard Company.

Balance September 1—$16,500; Cash deposited—$64,000
Balance September 30—$17,600; Checks written—$62,800

The September bank statement shows a balance of $16,500 at September 30 and the following memoranda.

| Credits | | Debits | |
|---|---|---|---|
| Collection of electronic funds transfer | $1,830 | NSF check: H. Kane | $560 |
| Interest earned on checking account | 45 | Safety deposit box rent | 60 |

At September 30, deposits in transit were $4,738 and outstanding checks totaled $2,383.

### Instructions

a. Prepare the bank reconciliation at September 30, 2022.

b. Prepare a tabular analysis for the adjustments at September 30, assuming the NSF check was from a customer on account. Use the following column headings: Cash, Accounts Receivable, Revenues, and Expenses. Include margin explanations for the changes in revenues and expenses.

**E5.10 (LO 3), AP** The following information pertains to Raydon Company.

*Prepare bank reconciliation and adjustments.*

1. Cash balance per books, July 31, $8,768.

2. $2,023 collected from a customer for Raydon Company in July by the bank through electronic funds transfer. The collection has not been recorded by Raydon Company.

3. Cash balance per bank, July 31, $8,732.

4. July bank service charge not recorded by the depositor $45.

5. Outstanding checks, July 31, $1,486.

6. Deposits in transit, July 31, $3,500.

### Instructions

a. Prepare a bank reconciliation at July 31, 2022.

b. Prepare a tabular analysis of the adjustments at July 31 for Raydon Company.

**E5.11 (LO 3), AP** The cash records of Upton Company show the following.

*Compute deposits in transit and outstanding checks for two bank reconciliations.*

For July:

1. The June 30 bank reconciliation indicated that deposits in transit total $580. During July, the Cash account shows deposits of $16,900, but the bank statement indicates that only $15,600 in deposits were received during the month.

2. The June 30 bank reconciliation also reported outstanding checks of $940. During the month of July, Upton Company books show that $17,500 of checks were issued, yet the bank statement showed that $16,400 of checks cleared the bank in July.

For September:

3. In September, deposits per bank statement totaled $25,900, deposits per books were $26,400, and deposits in transit at September 30 were $2,200.

4. In September, cash disbursements per books were $23,500, checks clearing the bank were $24,000, and outstanding checks at September 30 were $2,100.

There were no bank debit or credit memoranda, and no errors were made by either the bank or Upton Company.

### Instructions

Answer the following questions.

a. In situation 1, what were the deposits in transit at July 31?

b. In situation 2, what were the outstanding checks at July 31?

c. In situation 3, what were the deposits in transit at August 31?

d. In situation 4, what were the outstanding checks at August 31?

**E5.12 (LO 3), AP** Perth Inc.'s bank statement from Main Street Bank at August 31, 2022, gives the following information.

*Prepare bank reconciliation and adjustments.*

| | | | | |
|---|---|---|---|---|
| Balance, August 1 | $18,400 | Bank debit memorandum: | | |
| August deposits | 71,000 | Safety deposit box fee | $ | 25 |
| Checks cleared in August | 68,678 | Service charge | | 50 |
| Bank credit memorandum: | | Balance, August 31 | | 20,692 |
| Interest earned | 45 | | | |

A summary of the Cash account for August shows the following: balance, August 1, $18,700; receipts $74,000; disbursements $73,570; and balance, August 31, $19,130. Analysis reveals that the only reconciling items on the July 31 bank reconciliation were a deposit in transit for $4,800 and outstanding checks of $4,500. In addition, you determine that there was an error involving a company check drawn in August: A check for $400 to a creditor on account that cleared the bank in August was recorded for $40.

### Instructions

a. Determine deposits in transit.

b. Determine outstanding checks. (*Hint:* You need to correct disbursements for the check error.)

c. Prepare a bank reconciliation at August 31.

d. Prepare a tabular analysis for the adjustments to be made by Perth Inc. at August 31. Use the following column headings: Cash, Accounts Payable, Revenues, and Expenses. Include margin explanations for the changes in revenues and expenses.

*Identify reporting of cash.*

**E5.13 (LO 4), AP** A new accountant at Wyne Inc. is trying to identify which of the following amounts should be reported as the current asset "Cash and cash equivalents" in the year-end balance sheet, as of April 30, 2022.

1. $60 of currency and coin in a locked box used for incidental cash transactions.

2. A $10,000 U.S. Treasury bill, due May 31, 2022.

3. $260 of April-dated checks that Wyne has received from customers but not yet deposited.

4. An $85 check received from a customer in payment of its April account, but postdated to May 1.

5. $2,500 in the company's checking account.

6. $4,800 in its savings account.

7. $75 of prepaid postage in its postage meter.

8. A $25 IOU from the company receptionist.

### Instructions

a. What balance should Wyne report as its "Cash and cash equivalents" balance at April 30, 2022?

b. In what account(s) and in what financial statement(s) should the items not included in "Cash and cash equivalents" be reported?

*Review cash management practices.*

**E5.14 (LO 4), C** Lance, Art, and Wayne have joined together to open a law practice but are struggling to manage their cash flow. They haven't yet built up sufficient clientele and revenues to support their legal practice's ongoing costs. Initial costs, such as advertising, renovations to their premises, and the like, all result in outgoing cash flow at a time when little is coming in. Lance, Art, and Wayne haven't had time to establish a billing system since most of their clients' cases haven't yet reached the courts, and the lawyers didn't think it would be right to bill them until "results were achieved."

Unfortunately, Lance, Art, and Wayne's suppliers don't feel the same way. Their suppliers expect them to pay their accounts payable within a few days of receiving their bills. So far, there hasn't even been enough money to pay the three lawyers, and they are not sure how long they can keep practicing law without getting some money into their pockets.

### Instructions

Can you provide any suggestions for Lance, Art, and Wayne to improve their cash management practices?

*Prepare a cash budget for two months.*

**E5.15 (LO 4), AP** Rigley Company expects to have a cash balance of $46,000 on January 1, 2022. These are the relevant monthly budget data for the first two months of 2022.

1. Collections from customers: January $71,000 and February $146,000.

2. Payments to suppliers: January $40,000 and February $75,000.

3. Wages: January $30,000 and February $40,000. Wages are paid in the month they are incurred.

4. Administrative expenses: January $21,000 and February $24,000. These costs include depreciation of $1,000 per month. All other costs are paid as incurred.

5. Selling expenses: January $15,000 and February $20,000. These costs are exclusive of depreciation. They are paid as incurred.

6. Sales of short-term investments in January are expected to realize $12,000 in cash. Rigley has a line of credit at a local bank that enables it to borrow up to $25,000. The company wants to maintain a minimum monthly cash balance of $20,000.

### Instructions

Prepare a cash budget for January and February.

## Problems

**P5.1 (LO 2), C** Gary Theater is in the Hoosier Mall. A cashier's booth is located near the entrance to the theater. Two cashiers are employed. One works from 1:00 to 5:00 P.M., the other from 5:00 to 9:00 P.M. Each cashier is bonded. The cashiers receive cash from customers and operate a machine that ejects serially numbered tickets. The rolls of tickets are inserted and locked into the machine by the theater manager at the beginning of each cashier's shift.

*Identify internal control weaknesses for cash receipts.*

After purchasing a ticket, the customer takes the ticket to a doorperson stationed at the entrance of the theater lobby some 60 feet from the cashier's booth. The doorperson tears the ticket in half, admits the customer, and returns the ticket stub to the customer. The other half of the ticket is dropped into a locked box by the doorperson.

At the end of each cashier's shift, the theater manager removes the ticket rolls from the machine and makes a cash count. The cash count sheet is initialed by the cashier. At the end of the day, the manager deposits the receipts in total in a bank night deposit vault located in the mall. In addition, the manager sends copies of the deposit slip and the initialed cash count sheets to the theater company treasurer for verification and to the company's accounting department. Receipts from the first shift are stored in a safe located in the manager's office.

### Instructions

**a.** Identify the internal control principles and their application to the cash receipts transactions of Gary Theater.

**b.** If the doorperson and cashier decided to collaborate to misappropriate cash, what actions might they take?

**P5.2 (LO 2), C** Blue Bayou Middle School wants to raise money for a new sound system for its auditorium. The primary fund-raising event is a dance at which the famous disc jockey Kray Zee will play classic and not-so-classic dance tunes. Grant Hill, the music and theater instructor, has been given the responsibility for coordinating the fund-raising efforts. This is Grant's first experience with fund-raising. He decides to put the eighth-grade choir in charge of the event; he will be a relatively passive observer.

*Identify internal control weaknesses in cash receipts and cash disbursements.*

Grant had 500 unnumbered tickets printed for the dance. He left the tickets in a box on his desk and told the choir students to take as many tickets as they thought they could sell for $5 each. In order to ensure that no extra tickets would be floating around, he told them to dispose of any unsold tickets. When the students received payment for the tickets, they were to bring the cash back to Grant, and he would put it in a locked box in his desk drawer.

Some of the students were responsible for decorating the gymnasium for the dance. Grant gave each of them a key to the money box and told them that if they took money out to purchase materials, they should put a note in the box saying how much they took and what it was used for. After 2 weeks, the money box appeared to be getting full, so Grant asked Lynn Dandi to count the money, prepare a deposit slip, and deposit the money in a bank account that Grant had opened.

The day of the dance, Grant wrote a check from the account to pay Kray Zee. The DJ said, however, that he accepted only cash and did not give receipts. So Grant took $200 out of the cash box and gave it to Kray. At the dance, Grant had Dana Uhler working at the entrance to the gymnasium, collecting tickets from students and selling tickets to those who had not pre-purchased them. Grant estimated that 400 students attended the dance.

The following day, Grant closed out the bank account, which had $250 in it, and gave that amount plus the $180 in the cash box to Principal Sanchez. Principal Sanchez seemed surprised that, after generating roughly $2,000 in sales, the dance netted only $430 in cash. Grant did not know how to respond.

### Instructions

Identify as many internal control weaknesses as you can in this scenario, and suggest how each could be addressed.

**P5.3 (LO 3), AP** On July 31, 2022, Keeds Company had a cash balance per books of $6,140. The statement from Dakota State Bank on that date showed a balance of $7,690.80. A comparison of the bank statement with the Cash account revealed the following facts.

*Prepare a bank reconciliation and adjustments.*

**1.** The bank service charge for July was $25.

**2.** The bank collected $1,520 for Keeds Company through electronic funds transfer.

3. The July 31 receipts of $1,193.30 were not included in the bank deposits for July. These receipts were deposited by the company in a night deposit vault on July 31.

4. Company check No. 2480 issued to L. Taylor, a creditor, for $384 that cleared the bank in July was incorrectly entered in the cash payments record on July 10 for $348.

5. Checks outstanding on July 31 totaled $1,860.10.

6. On July 31, the bank statement showed an NSF charge of $575 for a check received by the company from W. Krueger, a customer, on account.

**Instructions**

a. Adjusted cash bal.  $7,024.00

a. Prepare the bank reconciliation as of July 31.

b. Prepare a tabular analysis for the necessary adjustments at July 31. Use the following column headings: Cash, Accounts Receivable, Accounts Payable, Revenues, and Expenses. Include margin explanations for the revenues and expenses.

*Prepare a bank reconciliation and adjustments from detailed data.*

**P5.4 (LO 3), AP** The bank portion of the bank reconciliation for Bogalusa Company at October 31, 2022, is as follows.

**Bogalusa Company**
**Bank Reconciliation**
**October 31, 2022**

| | | |
|---|---|---|
| Cash balance per bank | | $12,367.90 |
| Add: Deposits in transit | | 1,530.20 |
| | | 13,898.10 |
| Less: Outstanding checks | | |

| Check Number | Check Amount | |
|---|---|---|
| 2451 | $1,260.40 | |
| 2470 | 684.20 | |
| 2471 | 844.50 | |
| 2472 | 426.80 | |
| 2474 | 1,050.00 | 4,265.90 |
| Adjusted cash balance per bank | | $ 9,632.20 |

The adjusted cash balance per bank agreed with the cash balance per books at October 31. The November bank statement showed the following checks and deposits.

**Bank Statement**

| | Checks | | | Deposits | |
|---|---|---|---|---|---|
| Date | Number | Amount | | Date | Amount |
| 11-1 | 2470 | $   684.20 | | 11-1 | $ 1,530.20 |
| 11-2 | 2471 | 844.50 | | 11-4 | 1,211.60 |
| 11-5 | 2474 | 1,050.00 | | 11-8 | 990.10 |
| 11-4 | 2475 | 1,640.70 | | 11-13 | 2,575.00 |
| 11-8 | 2476 | 2,830.00 | | 11-18 | 1,472.70 |
| 11-10 | 2477 | 600.00 | | 11-21 | 2,945.00 |
| 11-15 | 2479 | 1,750.00 | | 11-25 | 2,567.30 |
| 11-18 | 2480 | 1,330.00 | | 11-28 | 1,650.00 |
| 11-27 | 2481 | 695.40 | | 11-30 | 1,186.00 |
| 11-30 | 2483 | 575.50 | | Total | $16,127.90 |
| 11-29 | 2486 | 940.00 | | | |
| | Total | $12,940.30 | | | |

The cash records per books for November showed the following.

| | Cash Payments Record | | | | | | Cash Receipts Record | |
|---|---|---|---|---|---|---|---|---|
| **Date** | **Number** | **Amount** | **Date** | **Number** | **Amount** | | **Date** | **Amount** |
| 11-1 | 2475 | $1,640.70 | 11-20 | 2483 | $   575.50 | | 11-3 | $  1,211.60 |
| 11-2 | 2476 | 2,830.00 | 11-22 | 2484 | 829.50 | | 11-7 | 990.10 |
| 11-2 | 2477 | 600.00 | 11-23 | 2485 | 974.80 | | 11-12 | 2,575.00 |
| 11-4 | 2478 | 538.20 | 11-24 | 2486 | 940.00 | | 11-17 | 1,472.70 |
| 11-8 | 2479 | 1,705.00 | 11-29 | 2487 | 398.00 | | 11-20 | 2,954.00 |
| 11-10 | 2480 | 1,330.00 | 11-30 | 2488 | 800.00 | | 11-24 | 2,567.30 |
| 11-15 | 2481 | 695.40 | Total | | $14,469.10 | | 11-27 | 1,650.00 |
| 11-18 | 2482 | 612.00 | | | | | 11-29 | 1,186.00 |
| | | | | | | | 11-30 | 1,304.00 |
| | | | | | | | Total | $15,910.70 |

The bank statement contained two bank memoranda:

1. A credit of $2,242 for the collection for Bogalusa Company of an electronic funds transfer.

2. A debit for the printing of additional company checks $85.

At November 30, the cash balance per books was $11,073.80 and the cash balance per bank statement was $17,712.50. The bank did not make any errors, but **Bogalusa Company made two errors**.

### Instructions

a. Using the steps in the reconciliation procedure described in the chapter, prepare a bank reconciliation at November 30, 2022.

b. Prepare a tabular analysis for the adjustments based on the reconciliation. Use the following column headings: Cash, Accounts Receivable, Accounts Payable, Revenues, and Expenses. Include margin explanations for the changes in revenues and expenses. (*Note:* The correction of any errors pertaining to recording checks should be made to Accounts Payable. The correction of any errors relating to recording cash receipts should be made to Accounts Receivable.)

*a. Adjusted cash bal. $13,176.80*

**P5.5 (LO 3), AP** Timmins Company of Emporia, Kansas, spreads herbicides and applies liquid fertilizer for local farmers. On May 31, 2022, the company's Cash account showed a balance of $6,738.90.
  The bank statement from Emporia State Bank on that date showed the following balance.

*Prepare a bank reconciliation and adjustments.*

| | Emporia State Bank | |
|---|---|---|
| **Checks and Debits** | **Deposits and Credits** | **Daily Balance** |
| XXX | XXX | 5-31   6,968.00 |

A comparison of the details on the bank statement with the details in the Cash account revealed the following facts.

1. The statement included a debit memo of $40 for the printing of additional company checks.

2. Cash sales of $883.15 on May 12 were deposited in the bank. The cash receipts record and the deposit slip were incorrectly made for $933.15. The bank credited Timmins Company for the correct amount.

3. Outstanding checks at May 31 totaled $276.25, and deposits in transit were $1,880.15.

4. On May 18, the company issued check No. 1181 for $685 to H. Moses, on account. The check, which cleared the bank in May, was incorrectly recorded by Timmins Company for $658.

5. $2,690 was collected by the bank for Timmins Company on May 31 through electronic funds transfer.

6. Included with the canceled checks was a check issued by Tomins Company to C. Pernod for $360 that was incorrectly charged to Timmins Company by the bank.

7. On May 31, the bank statement showed an NSF charge of $380 for a check issued by Sara Ballard, a customer, to Timmins Company on account.

### Instructions

a. Prepare the bank reconciliation at May 31, 2022.

b. Prepare a tabular analysis for the necessary adjustments for Timmins Company at May 31, 2022. Use the following column headings: Cash, Accounts Receivable, Accounts Payable, Revenues, and Expenses. Include margin explanations for the changes in revenues and expenses.

*a. Adjusted cash bal.  $8,931.90*

*Prepare a comprehensive bank reconciliation and analyze theft and internal control deficiencies.*

**P5.6 (LO 1, 2, 3), E** Daisey Company is a very profitable small business. It has not, however, given much consideration to internal control. For example, in an attempt to keep clerical and office expenses to a minimum, the company has combined the jobs of cashier and bookkeeper. As a result, Bret Turrin handles all cash receipts, keeps the accounting records, and prepares the monthly bank reconciliations.

The balance per the bank statement on October 31, 2022, was $18,380. Outstanding checks were No. 62 for $140.75, No. 183 for $180, No. 284 for $253.25, No. 862 for $190.71, No. 863 for $226.80, and No. 864 for $165.28. Included with the statement was a credit memorandum of $185 indicating the bank collected funds for Daisey Company on October 25 through electronic funds transfer. This memorandum has not been recorded by Daisey.

The company's Cash account showed a balance of $21,877.72. The balance included undeposited cash on hand. Because of the lack of internal controls, Bret took for personal use all of the undeposited receipts in excess of $3,795.51. He then prepared the following bank reconciliation in an effort to conceal his theft of cash.

| | | |
|---|---:|---:|
| Cash balance per books, October 31 | | $21,877.72 |
| Add: Outstanding checks | | |
| No. 862 | $190.71 | |
| No. 863 | 226.80 | |
| No. 864 | 165.28 | 482.79 |
| | | 22,360.51 |
| Less: Undeposited receipts | | 3,795.51 |
| Unadjusted balance per bank, October 31 | | 18,565.00 |
| Less: Bank credit memorandum | | 185.00 |
| Cash balance per bank statement, October 31 | | $18,380.00 |

### Instructions

a. **Adjusted cash bal. $21,018.72**

a. Prepare a correct bank reconciliation. (*Hint:* Deduct the amount of the theft from the adjusted balance per books.)

b. Indicate the three ways that Bret attempted to conceal the theft and the dollar amount involved in each method.

c. What principles of internal control were violated in this case?

*Prepare a cash budget.*

**P5.7 (LO 4), AP** You are provided with the following information taken from Moynahan Inc.'s March 31, 2022, balance sheet.

| | |
|---|---:|
| Cash | $ 11,000 |
| Accounts receivable | 20,000 |
| Inventory | 36,000 |
| Property, plant, and equipment, net of depreciation | 120,000 |
| Accounts payable | 22,400 |
| Common stock | 150,000 |
| Retained earnings | 11,600 |

Additional information concerning Moynahan Inc. is as follows.

1. Gross profit is 25% of sales.

2. Actual and budgeted sales data:

| | |
|---|---|
| March (actual) | $46,000 |
| April (budgeted) | 70,000 |

3. Sales are both cash and credit. Cash collections expected in April are:

| | | |
|---|---|---|
| March | $18,400 | (40% of $46,000) |
| April | 42,000 | (60% of $70,000) |
| | $60,400 | |

4. Half of a month's purchases are paid for in the month of purchase and half in the following month. Cash disbursements expected in April are:

| | |
|---|---|
| Purchases March | $22,400 |
| Purchases April | 28,100 |
| | $50,500 |

5. Cash operating costs are anticipated to be $11,200 for the month of April.

6. Equipment costing $2,500 will be purchased for cash in April.

7. The company wishes to maintain a minimum cash balance of $9,000. An open line of credit is available at the bank. All borrowing is done at the beginning of the month, and all repayments are made at the end of the month. The interest rate is 12% per year, and interest expense is accrued at the end of the month and paid in the following month.

**Instructions**

Prepare a cash budget for the month of April. Determine how much cash Moynahan Inc. must borrow, or can repay, in April.

*Apr. borrowings        $1,800*

**P5.8 (LO 4), AP** Bastille Corporation prepares monthly cash budgets. Here are relevant data from operating budgets for 2022.

*Prepare a cash budget.*

| | January | February |
|---|---|---|
| Sales | $360,000 | $400,000 |
| Purchases | 120,000 | 130,000 |
| Salaries | 84,000 | 81,000 |
| Administrative expenses | 72,000 | 75,000 |
| Selling expenses | 79,000 | 88,000 |

All sales and purchases are on account. Budgeted collections and disbursement data are given below. All other expenses are paid in the month incurred. Administrative expenses include $1,000 of depreciation per month.

Other data.

1. Collections from customers: January $326,000; February $378,000.

2. Payments for purchases: January $110,000; February $135,000.

3. Other receipts: January: collection of December 31, 2016, notes receivable $15,000; February: proceeds from sale of securities $4,000.

4. Other disbursements: February $10,000 cash dividend.

The company's cash balance on January 1, 2022, is expected to be $46,000. The company wants to maintain a minimum cash balance of $40,000.

**Instructions**

Prepare a cash budget for January and February.

*Jan. 31 cash bal.        $43,000*

## Expand Your Critical Thinking

### Financial Reporting Problem: Apple Inc.

**CT5.1** The financial statements of **Apple Inc.** are presented in Appendix A. The company's complete annual report, including the notes to its financial statements, is available at its website.

**Instructions**

Using the financial statements and reports, answer these questions about Apple's internal controls and cash.

a. What comments, if any, are made about cash in the "Report of Independent Registered Public Accounting Firm"?

b. What data about cash and cash equivalents are shown in the consolidated balance sheet (statement of financial position)?

c. What activities are identified in the consolidated statement of cash flows as being responsible for the changes in cash during 2018?

d. How are cash equivalents defined in the Notes to Consolidated Financial Statements?

e. Read the section of the report titled "Management's Report on Internal Control Over Financial Reporting." Summarize the statements made in that section of the report.

## Comparative Analysis Problem:

## Columbia Sportswear Company vs. Under Armour, Inc.

**CT5.2** The financial statements of **Columbia Sportswear Company** are presented in Appendix B. Financial statements of **Under Armour, Inc.** are presented in Appendix C.

### Instructions

Answer the following questions for each company.

- **a.** What is the balance in cash and cash equivalents at December 31, 2018?
- **b.** What percentage of total assets does cash represent for each company over the last 2 years? Has it changed significantly for either company?
- **c.** How much cash was provided by operating activities during 2018?
- **d.** Comment on your findings in parts (a) through (c).

## Interpreting Financial Statements

**CT5.3** The international accounting firm **Ernst & Young** performed a global survey on fraud. The results of that survey are summarized in a report titled *Global Fraud Survey 2016*. You can find this report by doing an Internet search on the title.

### Instructions

Read the Overview section and then answer the following questions.

- **a.** What steps should businesses take to minimize risk?
- **b.** What percentage of survey respondents consider bribery and fraud to happen widely in their country?
- **c.** What percentage of finance team members said they would engage in unethical behavior to meet targets or protect corporate survival?

## Real-World Focus

**CT5.4** The **Financial Accounting Standards Board (FASB)** is a private organization established to improve accounting standards and financial reporting. The FASB conducts extensive research before issuing a "Statement of Financial Accounting Standards," which represents an authoritative expression of generally accepted accounting principles.

### Instructions

Go to the FASB website to answer the following questions.

- **a.** What are the 10 steps of the standard-setting process?
- **b.** What are the advisory groups that provide service to the FASB?
- **c.** What characteristics make the FASB's procedures an "open" decision-making process?

**CT5.5** The **Public Company Accounting Oversight Board (PCAOB)** was created as a result of the Sarbanes-Oxley Act. It has oversight and enforcement responsibilities over accounting firms in the United States.

### Instructions

Go to the PCAOB website to answer the following questions.

- **a.** What is the mission of the PCAOB?
- **b.** Briefly summarize its responsibilities related to inspections.
- **c.** Briefly summarize its responsibilities related to enforcement.

## Decision-Making Across the Organization

**CT5.6** **Alternative Distributor Corp.**, a distributor of groceries and related products, is headquartered in Medford, Massachusetts.

During a recent audit, Alternative Distributor Corp. was advised that existing internal controls necessary for the company to develop reliable financial statements were inadequate. The audit report stated that the current system of accounting for sales, receivables, and cash receipts constituted a material weakness. Among other items, the report focused on nontimely deposit of cash receipts, exposing

Alternative Distributor to potential loss or misappropriation, excessive past due accounts receivable due to lack of collection efforts, disregard of advantages offered by vendors for prompt payment of invoices, absence of appropriate segregation of duties by personnel consistent with appropriate control objectives, inadequate procedures for applying accounting principles, lack of qualified management personnel, lack of supervision by an outside board of directors, and overall poor recordkeeping.

### Instructions

**a.** Identify the principles of internal control violated by Alternative Distributor Corp.

**b.** Explain why managers of various functional areas in the company should be concerned about internal controls.

## Communication Activity

**CT5.7** As a new auditor for the CPA firm of Blacke and Whyte, you have been assigned to review the internal controls over mail cash receipts of Simon Company. Your review reveals that checks are promptly endorsed "For Deposit Only," but no list of the checks is prepared by the person opening the mail. The mail is opened either by the cashier or by the employee who maintains the accounts receivable records. Mail receipts are deposited in the bank weekly by the cashier.

### Instructions

Write a letter to Frank Simon, owner of Simon Company, explaining the weaknesses in internal control and your recommendations for improving the system.

## Ethics Cases

**CT5.8** Banks charge fees for "bounced" checks—that is, checks that exceed the balance in the account. It has been estimated that processing bounced checks costs a bank roughly $1.50 per check. Thus, the profit margin on bounced checks is very high. Recognizing this, some banks have started to process checks from largest to smallest. By doing this, they maximize the number of checks that bounce if a customer overdraws an account. For example, **NationsBank** (now **Bank of America**) projected a $14 million increase in fee revenue as a result of processing largest checks first. In response to criticism, banks have responded that their customers prefer to have large checks processed first, because those tend to be the most important. At the other extreme, some banks will cover their customers' bounced checks, effectively extending them an interest-free loan while their account is overdrawn.

### Instructions

Answer each of the following questions.

**a.** Carl Roen had a balance of $1,500 in his checking account at First National Bank on a day when the bank received the following five checks for processing against his account.

| Check Number | Amount | Check Number | Amount |
|---|---|---|---|
| 3150 | $ 35 | 3165 | $ 550 |
| 3162 | 400 | 3166 | 1,510 |
| | | 3169 | 180 |

Assuming a $30 fee assessed by the bank for each bounced check, how much fee revenue would the bank generate if it processed checks (1) from largest to smallest, (2) from smallest to largest, and (3) in order of check number?

**b.** Do you think that processing checks from largest to smallest is an ethical business practice?

**c.** In addition to ethical issues, what other issues must a bank consider in deciding whether to process checks from largest to smallest?

**d.** If you were managing a bank, what policy would you adopt on bounced checks?

**CT5.9** The National Fraud Information Center (NFIC) was originally established in 1992 by the National Consumers League, the oldest nonprofit consumer organization in the United States, to fight the growing menace of telemarketing fraud by improving prevention and enforcement. It maintains a website that provides many useful fraud-related resources.

### Instructions

Go to the NFIC website and find an item of interest to you. Write a short summary of your findings.

### All About You

**CT5.10** The print and electronic media are full of stories about potential security risks that can arise from your personal computer. It is important to keep in mind, however, that there are also many ways that your identity can be stolen other than from your computer. The federal government provides many resources to help protect you from identity thieves.

### Instructions

Search the Internet for "ID Theft Faceoff Game" and then complete the quiz provided there.

iStock.com/omgimages

# Merchandising Operations and the Multiple-Step Income Statement

## Chapter Preview

Merchandising is one of the largest and most influential industries in the United States. It is likely that a number of you will work for a merchandiser. Therefore, understanding the financial statements of merchandising companies is important. In this chapter, you will learn the basics about reporting merchandising transactions. In addition, you will learn how to prepare and analyze a commonly used form of the income statement—the multiple-step income statement.

## Feature Story

### Buy Now, Vote Later

Have you ever shopped for outdoor gear at an **REI (Recreational Equipment Incorporated)** store? If so, you might have been surprised if a salesperson asked if you were a member. A member? What do you mean a member? REI is a consumer cooperative, or "co-op" for short. To figure out what that means, consider this quote from the company's annual report:

> As a cooperative, the Company is owned by its members. Each member is entitled to one vote in

the election of the Company's Board of Directors. Since January 1, 2008, the nonrefundable, nontransferable, one-time membership fee has been $20. As of December 31, 2010, there were approximately 10.8 million members.

Voting rights? Now that's something you don't get from shopping at **Walmart**. REI members get other benefits as well, including sharing in the company's profits through a dividend at the end of the year. The more you spend, the bigger your dividend.

Since REI is a co-op, you might wonder whether management's incentives might be a little different. Management is still concerned about making a profit, as it ensures the long-term viability of the company. REI's members also want the company to be run efficiently, so that prices remain low. In order for its members to evaluate just how well management is doing, REI publishes an audited annual report, just like publicly traded companies do.

How well is this business model working for REI? Well, it has consistently been rated as one of the best places to work in the United States by *Fortune* magazine. Also, REI had sustainable business practices long before social responsibility became popular at other companies. The CEO's Stewardship Report states "we reduced the absolute amount of energy we use despite opening four new stores and growing our business; we grew the amount of FSC-certified paper we use to 58.4 percent of our total paper footprint—including our cash register receipt paper; we facilitated 2.2 million volunteer hours and we provided $3.7 million to more than 330 conservation and recreation nonprofits."

So, while REI, like other retailers, closely monitors its financial results, it also strives to succeed in other areas. And, with over 10 million votes at stake, REI's management knows that it has to deliver.

# Chapter Outline

| LEARNING OBJECTIVES | REVIEW | PRACTICE |
|---|---|---|
| **LO 1** Describe inventory systems and record purchases under a perpetual inventory system. | • Flow of costs<br>• Recording purchases under a perpetual inventory system<br>• Freight costs<br>• Purchase returns and allowances<br>• Purchase discounts<br>• Summary of purchasing transactions | **DO IT! 1** Purchase Transactions |
| **LO 2** Record sales under a perpetual inventory system. | • Recording sales<br>• Sales returns and allowances<br>• Sales discounts<br>• Data analytics and credit sales | **DO IT! 2** Sales Transactions |
| **LO 3** Prepare a multiple-step income statement. | • Format of the multiple-step income statement<br>• Components of the multiple-step income statement | **DO IT! 3** Multiple-Step Income Statement |
| **LO 4** Compute and analyze gross profit rate and profit margin. | • Gross profit rate<br>• Profit margin | **DO IT! 4** Gross Profit Rate and Profit Margin |

**Go to the Review and Practice section at the end of the chapter for a targeted summary and practice applications with solutions.**

**Visit WileyPLUS for additional tutorials and practice opportunities.**

# Merchandising Operations and Inventory Purchases

**REI**, **Walmart Inc.**, and **Amazon.com** are called merchandising companies because they buy and sell merchandise rather than perform services as their primary source of revenue.

- Merchandising companies that purchase and sell directly to consumers are called **retailers**.
- Merchandising companies that sell to retailers are known as **wholesalers**.
- For example, retailer **Walgreens** might buy goods from wholesaler **McKesson**. Retailer **Office Depot** might buy office supplies from wholesaler **United Stationers**.

The primary source of revenue for merchandising companies is the sale of merchandise, often referred to simply as **sales revenue** or **sales**. A merchandising company has two categories of expenses: cost of goods sold and operating expenses.

**Cost of goods sold** is the total cost of merchandise sold during the period. This expense is directly related to the revenue recognized from the sale of goods. **Illustration 6.1** shows the income measurement process for a merchandising company. The items in the two blue boxes are expense items that are unique to a merchandising company; they are not used by a service company.

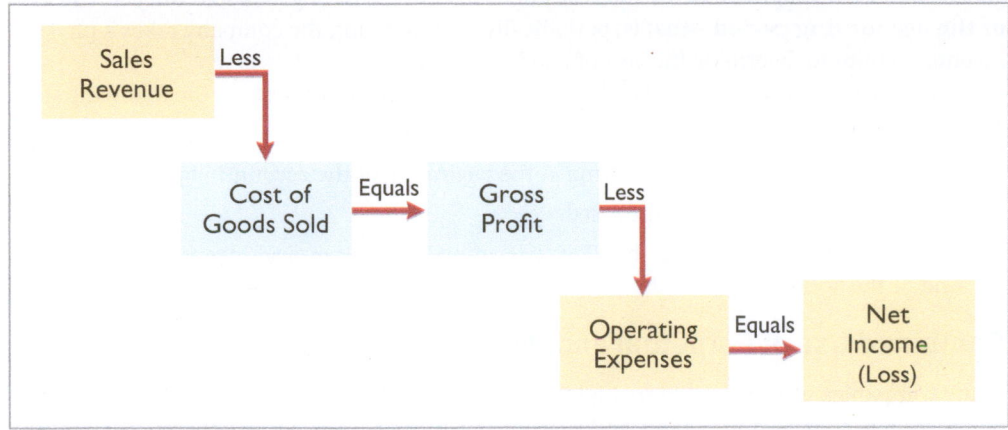

**ILLUSTRATION 6.1**

**Income measurement process for a merchandising company**

## Flow of Costs

The flow of costs for a merchandising company is as follows.

1. Beginning inventory plus the cost of goods purchased is the cost of goods available for sale.
2. As goods are sold, they are assigned to cost of goods sold.
3. Those goods that are not sold by the end of the accounting period represent ending inventory.

**Illustration 6.2** describes these relationships.

**ILLUSTRATION 6.2**
**Flow of costs**

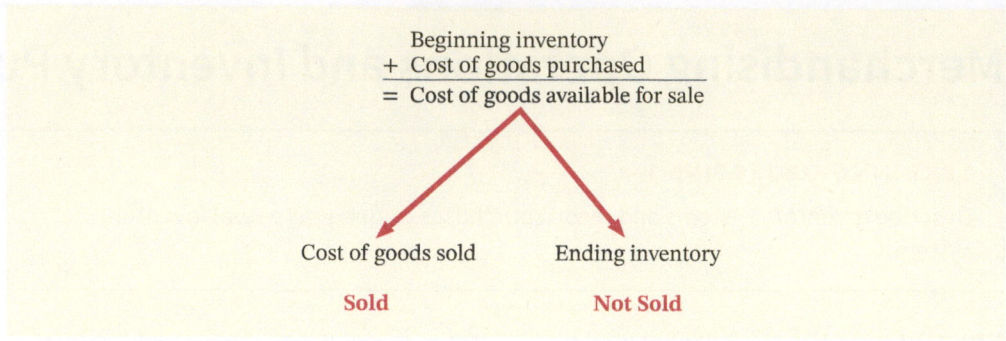

Companies use one of two systems to account for inventory: a **perpetual inventory system** or a **periodic inventory system**.

## Perpetual System

In a perpetual inventory system, companies keep detailed records of the cost of each inventory purchase and sale (see **Helpful Hint**). These records continuously—perpetually—show the inventory that should be on hand for every item. For example, a **Ford** dealership has separate inventory records for each automobile, truck, and van on its lot and showroom floor. Similarly, a **Kroger** grocery store uses bar codes and optical scanners to keep a daily running record of every box of cereal and every jar of jelly that it buys and sells. Under a perpetual inventory system, a company determines the cost of goods sold **each time a sale occurs**.

## Periodic System

In a periodic inventory system, companies do not keep detailed inventory records of the goods on hand throughout the period. They determine the cost of goods sold **only at the end of the accounting period**—that is, periodically. At that point, the company takes a physical inventory count to determine the cost of goods on hand.

To determine the cost of goods sold under a periodic inventory system, the following steps are necessary:

1. Determine the cost of goods on hand at the beginning of the accounting period.
2. Add to it the cost of goods purchased.
3. Subtract the cost of goods on hand as determined by the physical inventory count at the end of the accounting period.

## Combined Use of Perpetual and Periodic Systems

Many companies use both the perpetual approach and the periodic approach. They use a perpetual system to record purchases and sales of inventory on a day-to-day basis. Then, at the end of the period, they perform a physical count of their inventory, combined with the periodic approach, to determine the final values of ending inventory and cost of goods sold for reporting purposes.

**HELPFUL HINT**

Even under perpetual inventory systems, companies take a physical inventory count. This is done as a control procedure to verify inventory levels, in order to detect theft or "shrinkage."

---

### Investor Insight  Morrow Snowboards, Inc.

iStock.com/Ben Blankenburg

#### Improving Stock Appeal

Investors are often eager to invest in a company that has a hot new product. However, when snowboard maker **Morrow Snowboards, Inc.** issued shares of stock to the public for the first time, some investors expressed reluctance to invest in Morrow because of a number of accounting control problems. To reduce investor concerns, Morrow implemented a perpetual inventory system to improve its control over inventory. In addition, it stated that it would perform a physical inventory count every quarter until it felt that its perpetual inventory system was reliable.

**If a perpetual system keeps track of inventory on a daily basis, why do companies ever need to do a physical count? (Go to WileyPLUS for this answer and additional questions.)**

## Recording Purchases Under a Perpetual Inventory System

Companies may purchase inventory for cash or on account (credit). They normally record purchases when they receive the goods from the seller.

- Each purchase should be supported by a **purchase invoice**, which indicates the total purchase price and other relevant information; it provides written evidence of the transaction.
- Each cash purchase should be supported by a canceled check or a cash register receipt indicating the items purchased and amounts paid.
- Under a perpetual inventory system, companies record cash purchases by an increase in Inventory and a decrease in Cash.

For example, suppose Sauk Stereo received an invoice from PW Audio Supply dated May 4 for goods with a purchase price to Sauk Stereo of $3,800. Sauk Stereo increases Inventory and increases Accounts Payable. This event is recorded as follows.

| CASH FLOW | BALANCE SHEET | | | | | | | | | | INCOME STATEMENT |
|---|---|---|---|---|---|---|---|---|---|---|---|
| | **Assets** | **=** | **Liabilities** | **+** | | | **Stockholders' Equity** | | | | |
| | | | | | | Common | | Retained Earnings | | | |
| | Inventory | = | Accounts Payable | + | Stock | + | Rev. | − | Exp. | − | Div. | |
| No effect | +$3,800 | | +$3,800 | | | | | | | | | No effect |

Under the perpetual inventory system, companies record purchases of merchandise for sale in the Inventory account. Thus, **REI** would increase Inventory for clothing, sporting goods, and anything else purchased for resale to customers.

Not all purchases result in an increase to Inventory, however. Companies record purchases of assets acquired for use and not for resale, such as supplies, equipment, and similar items, as increases to specific asset accounts rather than to Inventory. For example, to record the purchase of materials used to make shelf signs or for cash register receipt paper, REI would increase Supplies.

## Freight Costs

The sales agreement should indicate who—the seller or the buyer—is to pay for transporting the goods to the buyer's place of business. When a common carrier such as a railroad, trucking company, or airline transports the goods, the carrier prepares a freight bill in accord with the sales agreement.

Freight terms are expressed as either FOB shipping point or FOB destination.

- The letters FOB mean **free on board**.
- Thus, **FOB shipping point** means that the seller places the goods free on board the carrier, and the buyer pays the freight costs.
- Conversely, **FOB destination** means that the seller places the goods free on board to the buyer's place of business, and the seller pays the freight.

**Illustration 6.3** illustrates these shipping terms.

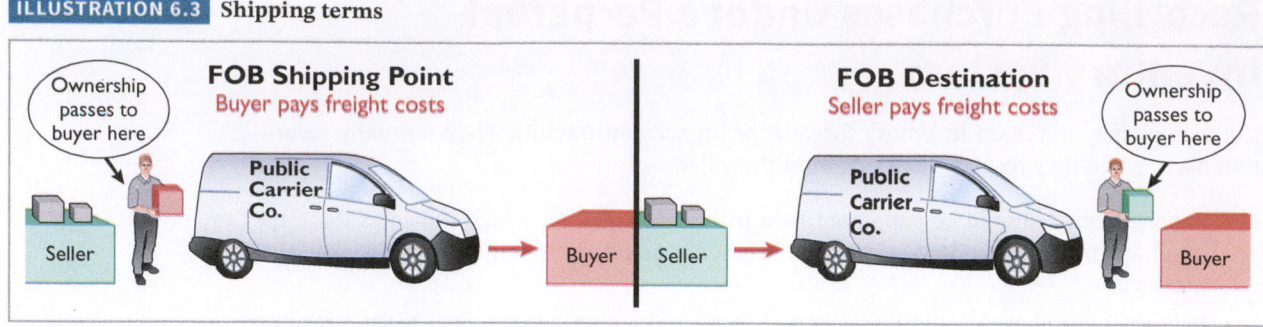

**ILLUSTRATION 6.3** Shipping terms

### Freight Costs Incurred by the Buyer

When the buyer incurs the transportation costs, these costs are considered part of the cost of purchasing inventory. Therefore, the buyer increases the Inventory account. For example, if Sauk Stereo (the buyer) pays Public Carrier Co. $150 for freight charges on May 6, the event is recorded by Sauk Stereo as follows.

| CASH FLOW | BALANCE SHEET | | | | | | | | | | INCOME STATEMENT |
|---|---|---|---|---|---|---|---|---|---|---|---|
| | Assets | | | = | Liabilities | + | Stockholders' Equity | | | | |
| | | | | | | | Common Stock | + | Retained Earnings | | |
| | Cash | + | Inventory | = | | | | | Rev. − Exp. − Div. | | |
| −$150 | −$150 | | +$150 | | | | | | | | No effect |

Thus, any freight costs incurred by the buyer are part of the cost of merchandise purchased.

- Inventory cost should include all costs to acquire the inventory, including freight necessary to deliver the goods to the buyer.
- Companies recognize these costs as cost of goods sold when inventory is sold.

### Freight Costs Incurred by the Seller

In contrast, **freight costs incurred by the seller on outgoing merchandise are an operating expense to the seller**. These costs increase an expense account titled Freight-Out (sometimes called Delivery Expense). For example, if a seller (PW Audio Supply) pays the $150 freight charges for Sauk Stereo's above purchase, the event is recorded by PW Audio Supply as follows.

| CASH FLOW | BALANCE SHEET | | | | | | | | INCOME STATEMENT |
|---|---|---|---|---|---|---|---|---|---|
| | Assets | = | Liabilities | + | Stockholders' Equity | | | | |
| | | | Accounts Payable | | Common Stock | + | Retained Earnings | | |
| | Cash | = | | + | | | Rev. − Exp. − Div. | | |
| −$150 | −$150 | = | | | | | −$150 | | Freight-Out |

When the seller pays the freight charges, the seller will usually establish a higher invoice price for the goods to cover the shipping expense.

## Purchase Returns and Allowances

A purchaser may be dissatisfied with the merchandise received because the goods are damaged or defective, of inferior quality, or do not meet the purchaser's specifications.

- The purchaser may return the goods to the seller for credit if the sale was made on credit, or for a cash refund if the purchase was for cash; this transaction is known as a **purchase return**.
- The purchaser may choose to keep the merchandise if the seller is willing to grant an allowance (deduction) from the purchase price; this transaction is known as a **purchase allowance**.

Assume that Sauk Stereo returned goods costing $300 to PW Audio Supply on May 8. Sauk Stereo records the returned merchandise by decreasing Accounts Payable and decreasing Inventory.

| CASH FLOW | BALANCE SHEET | | | | | | | | | INCOME STATEMENT |
|---|---|---|---|---|---|---|---|---|---|---|
| | Assets | = | Liabilities | + | | Stockholders' Equity | | | | |
| | | | | | | | Retained Earnings | | | |
| | | | Accounts | | Common | | | | | |
| | Inventory | = | Payable | + | Stock | + | Rev. − | Exp. − | Div. | |
| No effect | −$300 | | −$300 | | | | | | | No effect |

Because Sauk Stereo increased Inventory when the goods were received, Inventory is decreased when Sauk Stereo returns the goods.

Suppose instead that Sauk Stereo chose to keep the goods after being granted a $50 allowance (reduction in price). It would reduce Accounts Payable and reduce Inventory for $50.

# Purchase Discounts

The credit terms of a purchase on account may permit the buyer to claim a cash discount for prompt payment.

- The buyer calls this cash discount a **purchase discount**.
- This incentive offers advantages to both parties.
- The purchaser saves money, and the seller converts the accounts receivable into cash more quickly.

**Credit terms** specify the amount of the cash discount and time period in which it is offered. They also indicate the time period in which the purchaser is expected to pay the full invoice price. Suppose, for example, that Sauk Stereo's credit terms from PW Audio Supply are 2/10, n/30, which is read "two-ten, net thirty" (see **Helpful Hint**).

- This means that the buyer may take a 2% cash discount on the invoice price, less ("net of") any returns or allowances, if payment is made within 10 days of the invoice date (the **discount period**).
- Otherwise, the invoice price, less any returns or allowances, is due 30 days from the invoice date.
- Alternatively, the discount period may extend to a specified number of days following the month in which the sale occurs. For example, 1/10 EOM (end of month) means that a 1% discount is available if the invoice is paid within the first 10 days of the next month.

When the seller elects not to offer a cash discount for prompt payment, credit terms will specify only the maximum time period for paying the balance due. For example, the invoice may state the time period as n/30, n/60, or n/10 EOM. This means, respectively, that the buyer must pay the net amount in 30 days, in 60 days, or within the first 10 days of the next month.

When the buyer pays an invoice within the discount period, the amount of the discount decreases Inventory. Why? Because companies record inventory at cost, and by paying within the discount period, the buyer has reduced its cost. To illustrate, assume Sauk Stereo pays the balance due of $3,500 (gross invoice price of $3,800 less purchase returns and allowances of $300) on May 14, the last day of the discount period.

**HELPFUL HINT**

The term *net* in "net 30" means the remaining amount due after subtracting any sales returns and allowances and partial payments.

- Since the terms are 2/10, n/30, the cash discount is $70 ($3,500 × 2%) and Sauk Stereo pays $3,430 ($3,500 − $70).
- Sauk Stereo records its May 14 payment by decreasing Accounts Payable by the amount of the gross invoice price, reducing Inventory by the $70 discount, and reducing Cash by the net amount owed.

| CASH FLOW | BALANCE SHEET | | | | | | | | | INCOME STATEMENT |
|---|---|---|---|---|---|---|---|---|---|---|
| | Assets | | | = | Liabilities | + | Stockholders' Equity | | | |
| | | | | | | | | Retained Earnings | | |
| | Cash | + | Inventory | = | Accounts Payable | | Common Stock | + Rev. − Exp. − Div. | | |
| −$3,430 | −$3,430 | | −$70 | | −$3,500 | | | | | |

If Sauk Stereo failed to take the discount and instead made full payment of $3,500 on June 3, it would decrease Accounts Payable and decrease Cash for $3,500 each.

| CASH FLOW | BALANCE SHEET | | | | | | | | | INCOME STATEMENT |
|---|---|---|---|---|---|---|---|---|---|---|
| | Assets | | | = | Liabilities | + | Stockholders' Equity | | | |
| | | | | | | | | Retained Earnings | | |
| | Cash | + | Inventory | = | Accounts Payable | | Common Stock | + Rev. − Exp. − Div. | | |
| −$3,500 | −$3,500 | | | | −$3,500 | | | | | |

A merchandising company usually should take all available discounts. Passing up the discount may be viewed as **paying interest** for use of the money.

- For example, passing up the discount offered by PW Audio Supply would be comparable to Sauk Stereo paying an interest rate of 2% for the use of $3,500 for 20 days.
- This is the equivalent of an annual interest rate of 36.5% [2% × (365 ÷ 20)].

Obviously, it would be better for Sauk Stereo to borrow at prevailing bank interest rates of 6% to 10% than to lose the discount.

## Summary of Purchasing Transactions

The following tabular summary shows the effect of the previous transactions on Inventory:

1. Sauk Stereo originally purchased $3,800 worth of inventory on account for resale.
2. It paid $150 in freight charges.
3. It then returned $300 of goods.
4. It received a $70 discount off the balance owed because it paid within the discount period.

This results in a balance in Inventory of $3,580.

| CASH FLOW | BALANCE SHEET | | | | | | | | | INCOME STATEMENT |
|---|---|---|---|---|---|---|---|---|---|---|
| | Assets | | | = | Liabilities | + | Stockholders' Equity | | | |
| | | | | | | | | Retained Earnings | | |
| | Cash | + | Inventory | = | Accounts Payable | | Common Stock | + Rev. − Exp. − Div. | | |
| No effect | | | +$3,800 | | +$3,800 | | | | | No effect |
| −$150 | −$150 | | +150 | | | | | | | No effect |
| No effect | | | −300 | | −300 | | | | | No effect |
| −$3,450 | −3,430 | | −70 | | −3,500 | | | | | No effect |
| | −$3,580 | | +$3,580 | | $0 | | | | | |

## DO IT! 1 | Purchase Transactions

On September 5, De La Hoya Company buys merchandise on account from Junot Diaz Company. The purchase price of the goods paid by De La Hoya is $1,500, and the cost to Diaz Company was $800. On September 8, De La Hoya returns defective goods with a selling price of $200. Use a tabular summary to record the transactions on the books of De La Hoya Company.

### Solution

| Assets | | = Liabilities + | | Stockholders' Equity | | | |
|---|---|---|---|---|---|---|---|
| | | Accounts | Common | | Retained Earnings | | |
| Cash | + Inventory = | Payable | + Stock | + Rev. | – Exp. | – Div. | |
| | +$1,500 | +$1,500 | | | | | |
| | −200 | −200 | | | | | |

Related exercise material: **BE6.1, BE6.2, DO IT! 6.1, E6.1, E6.2, and E6.3.**

---

# Recording Sales Under a Perpetual Inventory System

**LEARNING OBJECTIVE 2**

Record sales under a perpetual inventory system.

In accordance with the revenue recognition principle, companies record sales revenue, like service revenue, when the performance obligation is satisfied. Typically, that performance obligation is satisfied when the goods are transferred from the seller to the buyer. At this point, the sales transaction is completed and the sales price is established.

Sales may be made on credit or for cash. Every sales transaction should be supported by a **business document** that provides written evidence of the sale. **Cash register documents** provide evidence of cash sales.

- A **sales invoice** provides support for each credit sale.
- The original copy of the invoice goes to the customer, and the seller keeps a copy for use in recording the sale.
- The invoice shows the date of sale, customer name, total sales price, and other relevant information.

## Recording Sales

For each sale, the seller:

1. Increases Accounts Receivable or Cash, as well as Sales Revenue (see **Helpful Hint**).
2. Increases Cost of Goods Sold and decreases Inventory. As a result, the Inventory account will show at all times the amount of inventory that should be on hand.

To illustrate a credit sales transaction, recall the earlier transaction where PW Audio Supply sold inventory to Sauk Stereo for $3,800. These goods had a cost to PW Audio Supply of $2,400. PW Audio Supply records the sale to Sauk Stereo as follows.

**HELPFUL HINT**

The merchandiser increases the Sales Revenue account only for sales of goods held for resale. Sales of assets not held for resale, such as equipment or land, decrease the asset account.

| CASH FLOW | BALANCE SHEET | | | | | | | | | | INCOME STATEMENT |
|---|---|---|---|---|---|---|---|---|---|---|---|
| | Assets | | | = | Liabilities | + | Stockholders' Equity | | | | |
| | Accounts Receivable | + | Inventory | = | | | Common Stock | + | Retained Earnings | | |
| | | | | | | | | | Rev.   −   Exp.   −   Div. | | |
| No effect | +$3,800 | | | | | | | | +$3,800 | | Sales Revenue |
| No effect | | | −$2,400 | | | | | | −$2,400 | | Cost of Goods Sold |

# Sales Returns and Allowances

Sometimes, a purchaser may be dissatisfied with the merchandise received because the goods are damaged or defective, of inferior quality, or do not meet the purchaser's specifications. In such cases, the seller either accepts goods back from a purchaser (a return) or grants a reduction in the purchase price (an allowance) so that the buyer will keep the goods; the seller records these as **sales returns and allowances**. To record credit for returned goods:

- The seller uses the Sales Returns and Allowances account. Sales Returns and Allowances is subtracted from sales revenue on the income statement to determine net sales.
- The company also decreases Accounts Receivable at the selling price.
- If goods are returned, Inventory is increased and Cost of Goods Sold is decreased for the cost of the goods.
- If the goods were defective, PW Audio Supply would then reduce the Inventory account to reflect their decline in value.

If PW Audio Supply received returned goods that had a selling price of $300 and a cost of $140, it would be recorded as follows.

| CASH FLOW | BALANCE SHEET | | | | | | | | | | INCOME STATEMENT |
|---|---|---|---|---|---|---|---|---|---|---|---|
| | Assets | | | = | Liabilities | + | Stockholders' Equity | | | | |
| | Accounts Receivable | + | Inventory | = | | | Common Stock | + | Retained Earnings | | |
| | | | | | | | | | Rev.   −   Exp.   −   Div. | | |
| No effect | −$300 | | | | | | | | −$300 | | Sales Returns and Allowances |
| No effect | | | +$140 | | | | | | +$140 | | Cost of Goods Sold |

## Anatomy of a Fraud

Holly Harmon was a cashier at a national superstore for only a short time when she began stealing merchandise using three methods. Under the first method, her husband or friends took UPC labels from cheaper items and put them on more expensive items. Holly then scanned the goods at the register. Using the second method, Holly scanned an item at the register but then voided the sale and left the merchandise in the shopping cart. A third approach was to put goods into large plastic containers. She scanned the plastic containers but not the goods within them. After Holly quit, a review of past surveillance tapes enabled the store to observe the thefts and to identify the participants.

**Total take: $12,000**

**The Missing Controls**

**Human resource controls.** A background check would have revealed Holly's previous criminal record. She would not have been hired as a cashier.

**Physical controls.** Software can flag high numbers of voided transactions or a high number of sales of low-priced goods. Random comparisons of video records with cash register records can ensure that the goods reported as sold on the register are the same goods that are shown being purchased on the video recording. Finally, employees should be aware that they are being monitored.

**Source:** Adapted from Wells, *Fraud Casebook* (2007), pp. 251–259.

# Sales Discounts

A seller may at times offer customers a cash discount—called by the seller a **sales discount**—for the prompt payment of the balance due. If a customer pays within the discount period, the Sales Discounts account is increased by the amount of the discount.

Continuing our example, PW Audio Supply records the cash receipt or May 14 from Sauk Stereo within the discount period as follows.

| CASH FLOW | BALANCE SHEET | | | | | | | | | INCOME STATEMENT |
|---|---|---|---|---|---|---|---|---|---|---|
| | **Assets** | | = | **Liabilities** | + | **Stockholders' Equity** | | | | |
| | | | | | | | | Retained Earnings | | |
| | | | | | | Common | | Rev. − | Exp. − Div. | |
| | Cash | + Accounts Receivable = | | | | Stock | + | | | |
| +$3,430 | +$3,430 | −$3,500 | | | | | | −$70 | | Sales Discounts |

Sales Discounts is subtracted from revenues on the income statement to determine net sales.

# Data Analytics and Credit Sales

Increased access to ever larger amounts of data about customers, suppliers, products, and virtually every other aspect of a business has resulted in a greater reliance by companies on data analytics to support business decisions. Credit sales, sales returns and allowances, and sales discounts all provide rich opportunities for the use of data analytics.

- Effectively analyzing data regarding current as well as potential customers can help a company expand its sales base while minimizing the risk of unpaid receivables.
- In recent years, companies such as **Best Buy**, **REI**, and **Costco** have all refined their customer return policies, sometimes with unique rules for specific product types, as a result of data analytics applied to their data on product returns.
- To achieve the optimal cost-benefit balance on sales discounts, companies statistically analyze past discount practices to determine how large the discount should be, how long the payment period should be, and other factors.

---

## DO IT! 2 | Sales Transactions

On September 20, De La Hoya Company sells on account merchandise with a cost of $750 to Marin Inc. for $1,100 cash. On September 25, De La Hoya receives returned goods from Marin that had a selling price of $200 and a cost of $150. Use a tabular summary to record the transactions for the books of De La Hoya Company.

**Solution**

| Assets | | = Liabilities + | | Stockholders' Equity | | | | |
|---|---|---|---|---|---|---|---|---|
| | | | Common | Retained Earnings | | | | |
| Accounts Receivable + | Inventory = | Accounts Payable + | Stock + | Rev. − | Exp. − | Div. | | |
| +$1,100 | | | | +$1,100 | | | Sales Rev. | |
| | −$750 | | | | −$750 | | Cost of Goods Sold | |
| −200 | | | | −200 | | | Sales Returns/Allow. | |
| | +150 | | | | +150 | | Cost of Goods Sold | |

Related exercise material: **BE6.3, BE6.4, DO IT! 6.2, E6.4, and E6.5.**

**ACTION PLAN**

- Seller records both the sale and the cost of goods sold at the time of the sale.
- When goods are returned, the seller records the return in Sales Returns and Allowances, and reduces Accounts Receivable.
- Any goods returned increase Inventory and reduce Cost of Goods Sold. Defective or damaged inventory is reduced to fair value (scrap value).

# Multiple-Step Income Statement

**LEARNING OBJECTIVE 3**
Prepare a multiple-step income statement.

## Format of the Multiple-Step Income Statement

A **multiple-step income statement** is often considered more useful than other formats because it highlights the components of net income. The **REI** income statement in **Illustration 6.4** is an example.

**ILLUSTRATION 6.4**

Multiple-step income statement

**Real World**

### Recreational Equipment, Inc.
#### Income Statements
#### (in thousands)

| | For the year ended | |
| --- | --- | --- |
| | December 31, 2016 | January 2, 2016 |
| Net sales | $2,557,543 | $2,423,221 |
| Cost of goods sold | 1,460,433 | 1,388,125 |
| **Gross profit** | 1,097,110 | 1,035,096 |
| Operating expenses | | |
| Payroll-related expenses | 494,820 | 478,474 |
| Occupancy, general and administrative | 420,898 | 381,147 |
| Total operating expenses | 915,718 | 859,621 |
| **Income from operations** | 181,392 | 175,475 |
| Other revenues and gains | | |
| Other revenues | -0- | -0- |
| Other expenses and losses | | |
| Patronage refunds and other | 121,401 | 121,853 |
| Income before income taxes | 59,991 | 53,622 |
| Income tax expense | 21,716 | 18,250 |
| **Net income** | $ 38,275 | $ 35,372 |

The multiple-step income statement has three important line items: gross profit, income from operations, and net income. They are determined as follows.

1. Subtract cost of goods sold from net sales to determine **gross profit**.
2. Deduct operating expenses from gross profit to determine **income from operations**.
3. Add or subtract the results of activities not related to operations to determine **net income**.

Note that companies report income tax expense in a separate section of the income statement before net income. The following discussion provides additional information about the components of a multiple-step income statement.

# Components of the Multiple-Step Income Statement

## Sales

The income statement for a merchandising company typically presents gross sales for the period. The company deducts sales returns and allowances and sales discounts from sales revenue in the income statement to arrive at **net sales**. **Illustration 6.5** shows the sales section of the income statement for PW Audio Supply.

**ILLUSTRATION 6.5**

Statement presentation of sales section

| PW Audio Supply, Inc. | | |
|---|---|---|
| **Income Statement (partial)** | | |
| **Sales** | | |
| Sales revenue | | $480,000 |
| Less: Sales returns and allowances | $12,000 | |
| Sales discounts | 8,000 | 20,000 |
| **Net sales** | | **$460,000** |

## Gross Profit

The excess of net sales over cost of goods sold is **gross profit** (see **Alternative Terminology**). It is determined by deducting **cost of goods sold** from net sales. As shown in Illustration 6.4, **REI** had a gross profit of $1,097 million for the year ended December 31, 2016. This computation uses **net sales**, which takes into account sales returns and allowances and sales discounts.

On the basis of the PW Audio Supply sales data presented in Illustration 6.5 (net sales of $460,000) and the cost of goods sold (assume a balance of $316,000), PW Audio Supply's gross profit is $144,000, computed as follows.

**ALTERNATIVE TERMINOLOGY**

Gross profit is sometimes referred to as *gross margin*.

| | |
|---|---|
| Net sales | $460,000 |
| Cost of goods sold | 316,000 |
| **Gross profit** | **$144,000** |

It is important to understand what gross profit is—and what it is not.

- Gross profit represents the **merchandising profit** of a company.
- Because operating expenses have not been deducted, it is **not a measure of the overall profit** of a company.

Nevertheless, comparisons of current gross profit with past amounts and rates and with those in the industry indicate the effectiveness of a company's purchasing and pricing policies.

## Operating Expenses

Operating expenses are the next component in measuring net income for a merchandising company. At REI, for example, operating expenses were about $916 million for the year ended December 31, 2016.

At PW Audio Supply, operating expenses were $114,000. The firm determines its income from operations by subtracting operating expenses from gross profit. Thus, income from operations is $30,000, as follows.

| | |
|---|---|
| Gross profit | $144,000 |
| **Operating expenses** | **114,000** |
| Income from operations | $ 30,000 |

## Nonoperating Activities and Income Tax Expense

**Nonoperating activities** consist of various revenues and expenses and gains and losses that are unrelated to the company's main line of operations.

- When nonoperating items are included, the label **Income from operations** (or Operating income) precedes them.
- This label clearly identifies the results of the company's normal operations, an amount determined by subtracting cost of goods sold and operating expenses from net sales.
- The results of nonoperating activities are shown in the categories **Other revenues and gains** and **Other expenses and losses**.

**Illustration 6.6** lists examples of each.

**ILLUSTRATION 6.6**

**Examples of nonoperating activities**

| Other Revenues and Gains |
|---|
| **Interest revenue** from notes receivable and marketable securities. |
| **Dividend revenue** from investments in capital stock. |
| **Rent revenue** from subleasing a portion of the store. |
| **Gain** from the sale of property, plant, and equipment. |

| Other Expenses and Losses |
|---|
| **Interest expense** on notes and loans payable. |
| **Casualty losses** from such causes as vandalism and accidents. |
| **Loss** from the sale or abandonment of property, plant, and equipment. |
| **Loss** from strikes by employees and suppliers. |

**ETHICS NOTE**

Companies manage earnings in various ways. Conagra Brands recorded a non-recurring gain for $186 million from the sale of Pilgrim's Pride stock to help meet an earnings projection for the quarter.

Nonoperating income is sometimes very significant. For example, in one quarter, Sears Holdings earned more than half of its net income from investment securities.

The distinction between operating and nonoperating activities is crucial to external users of financial data.

- These users view operating income as sustainable and many nonoperating activities as non-recurring.
- When forecasting next year's income, analysts put the most weight on this year's operating income and less weight on this year's nonoperating activities (see **Ethics Note**).

---

## Ethics Insight    IBM

ImageRite RF/Getty Images

### Disclosing More Details

Increased investor criticism and regulator scrutiny have forced many companies to improve the clarity of their financial disclosures. For example, **IBM** began providing more detail regarding its Other gains and losses. It had previously included these items in its selling, general, and administrative expenses, with little disclosure. For example, previously if IBM sold off one of its buildings at a gain, it included this gain in the selling, general, and administrative expense line item, thus reducing that expense. This made it appear that the company had done a better job of controlling operating expenses than it actually had.

As another example, when **eBay** recently sold the remainder of its investment in **Skype** to **Microsoft**, it reported a gain in Other revenues and gains of $1.7 billion. Since eBay's total income from operations was $2.4 billion, it was very important that the gain from the Skype sale not be buried in operating income.

**Why have investors and analysts demanded more accuracy in isolating Other gains and losses from operating items? (Go to WileyPLUS for this answer and additional questions.)**

---

Nonoperating activities are reported in the income statement immediately after operating activities. Included among Other revenues and gains in Illustration 6.7 are Interest Revenue and Gain on Disposal of Plant Assets. Included in Other expenses and losses are Interest Expense and Casualty Loss from Vandalism.

- The net amount resulting from Other revenues and gains and Other expenses and losses is added to or subtracted from Income from operations to arrive at Income before income taxes.
- This amount is then multiplied by the company's corporate income tax rate to arrive at **Income tax expense**.
- Income tax expense is subtracted from **Income before income taxes** to arrive at net income.

In **Illustration 6.7**, we have provided the multiple-step income statement of PW Audio Supply. This statement provides more detail than that of REI and thus is useful as a guide for homework. *For homework problems, use the multiple-step form of the income statement.*

**ILLUSTRATION 6.7**
**Multiple-step income statement**

### PW Audio Supply, Inc.
#### Income Statement
#### For the Year Ended December 31, 2022

| | | |
|---|---:|---:|
| **Sales** | | |
| Sales revenue | | $480,000 |
| Less: Sales returns and allowances | $12,000 | |
| Sales discounts | 8,000 | 20,000 |
| Net sales | | 460,000 |
| **Cost of goods sold** | | 316,000 |
| **Gross profit** | | 144,000 |
| **Operating expenses** | | |
| Salaries and wages expense | 64,000 | |
| Utilities expense | 17,000 | |
| Advertising expense | 16,000 | |
| Depreciation expense | 8,000 | |
| Freight-out | 7,000 | |
| Insurance expense | 2,000 | |
| Total operating expenses | | 114,000 |
| Income from operations | | 30,000 |
| **Other revenues and gains** | | |
| Interest revenue | 3,000 | |
| Gain on disposal of plant assets | 600 | 3,600 |
| **Other expenses and losses** | | |
| Interest expense | 1,800 | |
| Casualty loss from vandalism | 200 | 2,000 |
| Income before income taxes | | 31,600 |
| Income tax expense | | 10,100 |
| **Net income** | | $ 21,500 |

- Calculation of gross profit
- Calculation of income from operations
- Results of activities not related to operations

---

## DO IT! 3 | Multiple-Step Income Statement

The following information is available for Art Center Corp. for the year ended December 31, 2022.

| | | | |
|---|---:|---|---:|
| Other revenues and gains | $ 8,000 | Sales revenue | $462,000 |
| Other expenses and losses | 3,000 | Operating expenses | 187,000 |
| Cost of goods sold | 147,000 | Sales discounts | 20,000 |

Prepare a multiple-step income statement for Art Center Corp. The company has a tax rate of 25%.

**ACTION PLAN**

- Subtract cost of goods sold from net sales to determine gross profit.
- Subtract operating expenses from gross profit to determine income from operations.
- Add/subtract nonoperating items to income from operations to determine income before tax.
- Multiply the tax rate by income before tax to determine tax expense.

**Solution**

| Art Center Corp. Income Statement For the Year Ended December 31, 2022 | | |
| --- | --- | --- |
| Sales | | |
| Sales revenue | | $462,000 |
| Sales discounts | | 20,000 |
| Net sales | | 442,000 |
| Cost of goods sold | | 147,000 |
| Gross profit | | 295,000 |
| Operating expenses | | 187,000 |
| Income from operations | | 108,000 |
| Other revenues and gains | $8,000 | |
| Other expenses and losses | 3,000 | 5,000 |
| Income before income taxes | | 113,000 |
| Income tax expense | | 28,250 |
| Net income | | $ 84,750 |

Related exercise material: **BE6.5, BE6.6, BE6.7, DO IT! 6.3, E6.6, E6.7, E6.8, E6.9, and E6.10.**

# Gross Profit Rate and Profit Margin

**LEARNING OBJECTIVE 4**

Compute and analyze gross profit rate and profit margin.

## Gross Profit Rate

A company's gross profit may be expressed as a **percentage** by dividing the amount of gross profit by net sales. This is referred to as the **gross profit rate**. For PW Audio Supply, the gross profit rate is 31.3% ($144,000 ÷ $460,000).

Analysts generally consider the gross profit **rate** to be more informative than the gross profit **amount.**

**Decision Tools**

The gross profit rate helps companies decide if the prices of their goods are in line with changes in the cost of inventory.

- The gross profit rate expresses a more meaningful relationship between gross profit and net sales (see **Decision Tools**).

- For example, a gross profit amount of $1,000,000 may sound impressive.

- But if it was the result of sales of $100,000,000, the company's gross profit rate was only 1%.

**Illustration 6.8** demonstrates that gross profit rates differ greatly across industries.

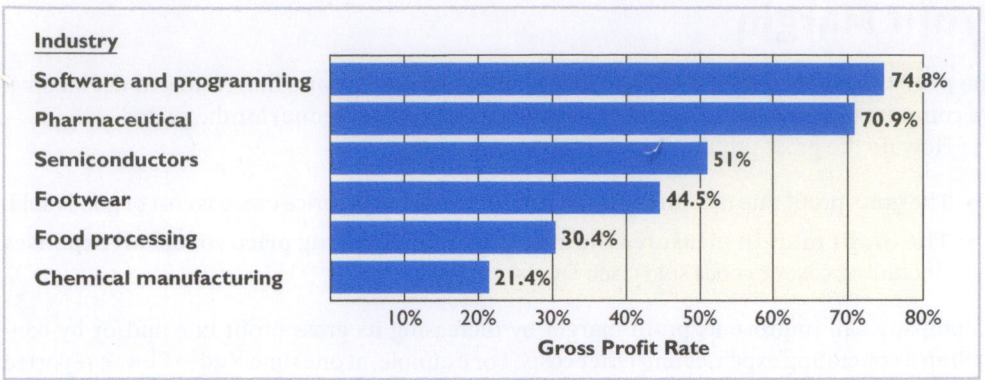

**ILLUSTRATION 6.8**
**Gross profit rate by industry**

A decline in a company's gross profit rate might have several causes.

- The company may have begun to sell products with a lower "markup"—for example, budget jeans versus designer jeans. Increased competition may have resulted in a lower selling price.

- Or, maybe the company was forced to pay higher prices to its suppliers and was not able to pass these costs on to its customers.

The gross profit rates for **REI** and **Dick's Sporting Goods** are presented in **Illustration 6.9**.

**ILLUSTRATION 6.9**
**Gross profit rate**

| $$\text{Gross Profit Rate} = \frac{\text{Gross Profit}}{\text{Net Sales}}$$ | | |
|---|---|---|
| REI ($ in thousands) | | Dick's Sporting Goods |
| 2016 | 2015 | 2016 |
| $\dfrac{\$1,097,110}{\$2,557,543} = 42.9\%$ | 42.7% | 29.9% |

REI's gross profit rate increased from 42.7% in 2015 to 42.9% in 2016. What might cause changes in REI's gross profit rate? When the economy changes, retailers also often adjust their selling prices. Changes in national weather patterns can also affect the amount of time people spend outdoors—and therefore impact their purchases of REI merchandise.

Why does REI's gross profit rate differ so much from that of Dick's Sporting Goods?

1. The gross profit rate often differs across retailers because of differences in the nature of their goods.
   - REI focuses on outdoor equipment, while Dick's also sells sporting goods and hunting gear.
   - The markup may differ significantly in these different product sectors.

2. Although REI and Dick's both sell outdoor equipment, the quality of the equipment they sell might differ.
   - If REI tends to sell more "high-end" goods compared to Dick's, its gross profit rate would tend to be higher.
   - Higher-quality goods often receive a higher markup, but the retailer also sells fewer of them.
   - In general, retailers adopt either a high-volume–low-margin approach (e.g., **Walmart**) or a low-volume–high-margin approach (e.g., **Saks Fifth Avenue**). The strategic choice is often revealed in differences in the companies' gross profit rates.

# Profit Margin

The **profit margin** measures the percentage of each dollar of sales that results in net income. We compute this ratio by dividing net income by net sales (revenue) for the period.

How do the gross profit rate and profit margin differ?

- The gross profit rate measures the margin by which selling price exceeds cost of goods sold.
- **The profit margin measures the extent by which selling price covers all expenses** (including cost of goods sold) (see **Decision Tools**).

A company can improve its profit margin by increasing its gross profit rate and/or by controlling its operating expenses and other costs. For example, at one time **Radio Shack** reported increased profit margins which it accomplished by closing stores and slashing costs. Eventually, however, it was forced to file for bankruptcy as sales continued to decline.

Profit margins vary across industries. Businesses with high turnovers, such as grocery stores (**Safeway** and **Kroger**) and discount stores (**Target** and **Walmart**), generally experience low profit margins. Low-turnover businesses, such as high-end jewelry stores (**Tiffany and Co.**) or major drug manufacturers (**Merck**), have high profit margins. **Illustration 6.10** shows profit margins from a variety of industries.

**ILLUSTRATION 6.10**

**Profit margins by industry**

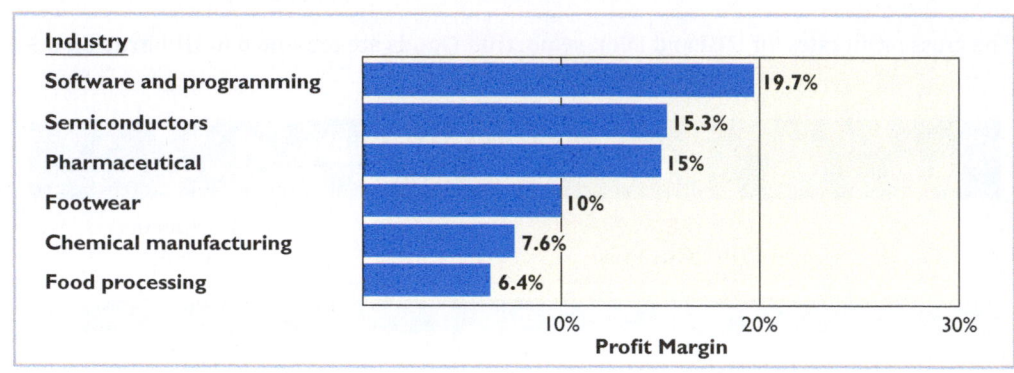

Profit margins for REI and Dick's Sporting Goods are presented in **Illustration 6.11**.

**ILLUSTRATION 6.11**

**Profit margin**

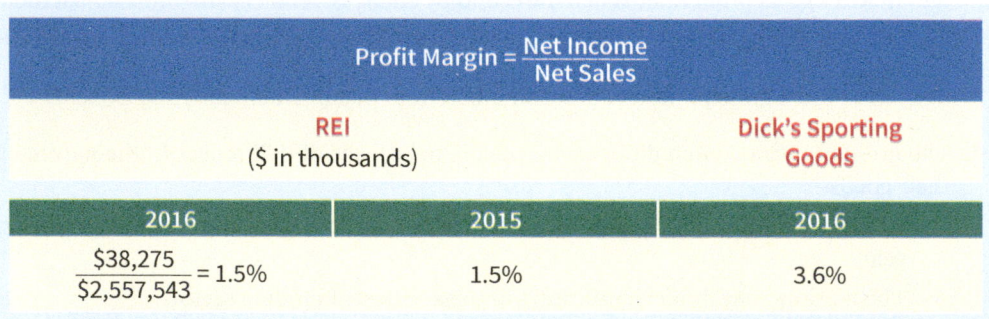

| | REI<br>($ in thousands) | | Dick's Sporting<br>Goods |
|---|---|---|---|
| | 2016 | 2015 | 2016 |
| | $\dfrac{\$38,275}{\$2,557,543} = 1.5\%$ | 1.5% | 3.6% |

REI's profit margin remained at 1.5% between 2015 and 2016. This means that the company generated 1.5¢ of profit on each dollar of sales. This constant profit margin occurred even though the gross profit rate increased.

A change in the profit margin can be caused by:

- A change in the gross profit rate.
- A change in the amount of operating expenses relative to sales.
- A change in the amount of other items (other revenues and gains, or other expenses and losses) relative to sales.

From Illustration 6.11, we know that REI's gross profit rate increased slightly. From analyzing the information in Illustration 6.4, we see that operating expenses as a percentage of sales increased from 35.5% ($859,621 ÷ $2,423,221) in 2015 to 35.8% ($915,718 ÷ $2,557,543) in 2016. This increase in operating expenses as a percentage of sales was offset by an increase in the gross profit rate from 42.7% ($1,035,096 ÷ $2,423,221) to 42.9% ($1,097,110 ÷ $2,557,543).

How does REI compare to its competitors? Its profit margin was lower than Dick's in 2016. Thus, its profit margin does not suggest exceptional profitability.

## DO IT! 4 | Gross Profit Rate and Profit Margin

Rachel Rose, Inc. reported the following in its 2022 and 2021 income statements.

|  | 2022 | 2021 |
|---|---|---|
| Net sales | $80,000 | $120,000 |
| Cost of goods sold | 40,000 | 60,000 |
| Operating expenses | 19,000 | 36,000 |
| Income tax expense | 3,000 | 4,000 |
| Net income | $18,000 | $ 20,000 |

Determine the company's gross profit rate and profit margin. Discuss the cause for changes in the ratios.

**ACTION PLAN**

- To determine gross profit rate, divide gross profit by net sales.
- To find profit margin, divide net income by net sales.

### Solution

|  | 2022 | 2021 |
|---|---|---|
| Gross profit rate | $\dfrac{(\$80,000 - \$40,000)}{\$80,000} = 50\%$ | $\dfrac{(\$120,000 - \$60,000)}{\$120,000} = 50\%$ |
| Profit margin | $\$18,000 \div \$80,000 = 22.5\%$ | $\$20,000 \div \$120,000 = 16.7\%$ |

The company's gross profit rate remained constant. However, its profit margin increased significantly due to a sharp decline in its operating costs as a percentage of sales, which declined from 30% ($36,000 ÷ $120,000) in 2021 to 23.8% ($19,000 ÷ $80,000) in 2022.

Related exercise material: **BE6.8, BE6.9, DO IT! 6.4, E6.11, and E6.12**.

## USING THE DECISION TOOLS | Mountain Equipment Cooperative

Like **REI**, **Mountain Equipment Cooperative (MEC)** is a retailer of outdoor equipment organized as a cooperative (though MEC sells *only* to its members, who pay a one-time fee of $5). Also like REI, MEC has a significant commitment to sustainability. Many of its stores employ state-of-the-art building techniques to minimize energy use, and it pledges 1% of annual sales revenue to environmental causes. Since MEC is a Canadian company, it follows International Financial Reporting Standards (IFRS) rather than U.S. GAAP, which means that some accounting differences would need to be addressed before you could make a thorough comparison of REI and MEC. Here are data for MEC.

|  | Year ended | |
|---|---|---|
| ($ in thousands) | 2/26/2017 | 12/27/2015 |
| Net income | $ (4,652) | $     53 |
| Sales revenue | 464,876 | 365,561 |
| Cost of goods sold | 318,803 | 255,757 |

## Instructions

Evaluate MEC's profit margin and gross profit rate for the years ended February 26, 2017, and December 27, 2015. (Note that the period ended 2/26/2017 was actually a 14-month period because the company changed its year-end from the last Sunday in December to the last Sunday in February). How do MEC's profit margin and gross profit rate compare to those of REI and Dick's Sporting Goods for 2016?

## Solution

| ($ in thousands) | Year ended | |
|---|---|---|
| | 2/26/2017 | 12/27/2015 |
| Profit margin | $\dfrac{\$(4,652)}{\$464,876} = -1.0\%$ | $\dfrac{\$53}{\$365,561} = 0.0\%$ |
| Gross profit rate | $\dfrac{\$146,073^*}{\$464,876} = 31.4\%$ | $\dfrac{\$109,804^{**}}{\$365,561} = 30.0\%$ |

*$464,876 − $318,803; **$365,561 − $255,757

MEC's profit margin (income per dollar of sales) was 0% in 2015 and then declined to a negative 1% in 2016. This is well below both REI's (1.5%) and Dick's (3.6%). Thus, MEC is not as effective at turning its sales into net income as these two competitors.

MEC's gross profit rate increased from 30.0% to 31.4%. This suggests that its ability to maintain its markup above its cost of goods sold increased during this period. MEC's gross profit rate of 31.4% is lower than REI's (42.9%) but slightly higher than Dick's (29.9%). Dick's gross profit is depressed by the fact that it sells many low-margin products. REI is superior to MEC both in its ability to maintain its markup above its costs of goods sold (its gross profit rate) and in its ability to control operating costs (its profit margin).

# Review and Practice

## Learning Objectives Review

### 1 Describe inventory systems and record purchases under a perpetual inventory system.

Because of the presence of inventory, a merchandising company has sales revenue, cost of goods sold, and gross profit. To account for inventory, a merchandising company must choose between a perpetual inventory system and a periodic inventory system.

The Inventory account is increased for all purchases of merchandise and for freight costs, and it is reduced for purchase discounts and purchase returns and allowances.

### 2 Record sales under a perpetual inventory system.

When inventory is sold, Accounts Receivable (or Cash) is increased and Sales Revenue is increased for the selling price of the merchandise. At the same time, Cost of Goods Sold is increased and Inventory is reduced for the cost of inventory items sold. Separate accounts are maintained for Sales Returns and Allowances and Sales

Discounts. These accounts are increased as needed to record returns, allowances, or discounts related to the sale. Net sales is computed by subtracting sales returns and allowances and sales discounts from sales revenue.

### 3 Prepare a multiple-step income statement.

A multiple-step income statement shows numerous steps in determining net income, including a calculation of gross profit, income from operations, results of nonoperating activities, income before income taxes, and income taxes.

### 4 Compute and analyze gross profit rate and profit margin.

Profitability is affected by gross profit, as measured by the gross profit rate, and by management's ability to control costs, as measured by the profit margin.

## Decision Tools Review

| Decision Checkpoints | Info Needed for Decision | Tool to Use for Decision | How to Evaluate Results |
| --- | --- | --- | --- |
| Is the price of goods keeping pace with changes in the cost of inventory? | Gross profit and net sales | $\text{Gross profit rate} = \dfrac{\text{Gross profit}}{\text{Net sales}}$ | Higher ratio suggests the average margin between selling price and inventory cost is increasing. Too high a margin may result in lost sales. |
| Is the company maintaining an adequate margin between sales and expenses? | Net income and net sales | $\text{Profit margin} = \dfrac{\text{Net income}}{\text{Net sales}}$ | Higher value suggests favorable return on each dollar of sales. |

## Glossary Review

**Cost of goods sold**   The total cost of merchandise sold during the period. (p. 6-3).

**FOB destination**   Freight terms indicating that ownership of goods remains with the seller until the goods reach the buyer. (p. 6-5).

**FOB shipping point**   Freight terms indicating that ownership of goods passes to the buyer when the public carrier accepts the goods from the seller. (p. 6-5).

**Gross profit**   The excess of net sales over the cost of goods sold. (p. 6-13).

**Gross profit rate**   Gross profit expressed as a percentage by dividing the amount of gross profit by net sales. (p. 6-16).

**Income tax expense**   The product of a company's income before income taxes and its corporate income tax rate. (p. 6-15).

**Net sales**   Sales less sales returns and allowances and sales discounts. (p. 6-13).

**Periodic inventory system**   An inventory system in which a company does not maintain detailed records of goods on hand throughout the period and determines the cost of goods sold only at the end of an accounting period. (p. 6-4).

**Perpetual inventory system**   A detailed inventory system in which a company maintains the cost of each inventory item, and the records continuously show the inventory that should be on hand. (p. 6-4).

**Profit margin**   Measures the percentage of each dollar of sales that results in net income, computed by dividing net income by net sales. (p. 6-18).

**Purchase allowance**   A deduction made to the selling price of merchandise, granted by the seller, so that the buyer will keep the merchandise. (p. 6-7).

**Purchase discount**   A cash discount claimed by a buyer for prompt payment of a balance due. (p. 6-7).

**Purchase invoice**   A document that provides support for each purchase. (p. 6-5).

**Purchase return**   A return of goods from the buyer to the seller for cash or credit. (p. 6-7).

**Sales discount**   A reduction given by a seller for prompt payment of a credit sale. (p. 6-11).

**Sales invoice**   A document that provides support for each sale. (p. 6-9).

**Sales returns and allowances**   Transactions in which the seller either accepts goods back from the purchaser (a return) or grants a reduction in the purchase price (an allowance) so that the buyer will keep the goods. (p. 6-10).

**Sales revenue**   Primary source of revenue for a merchandising company. (p. 6-3).

## Practice Multiple-Choice Questions

**1. (LO 1)** Which of the following statements about a periodic inventory system is **true**?

    a. Companies determine cost of goods sold only at the end of the accounting period.

    b. Companies continuously maintain detailed records of the cost of each inventory purchase and sale.

    c. The periodic system provides better control over inventories than a perpetual system.

    d. The increased use of computerized systems has increased the use of the periodic system.

**2. (LO 1)** When goods are purchased for resale by a company using a perpetual inventory system, it increases:

    a. Inventory.         c. Cost of Goods Sold.

    b. Purchases.       d. Sales Revenue.

**3. (LO 2)** To record the sale of goods for cash under a perpetual inventory system:

    a. record only cost of goods sold and reduction of inventory.

    b. record only the receipt of cash and the sales revenue.

    c. record the receipt of cash and sales revenue, and record the cost of goods sold and reduction of inventory.

    d. record the receipt of cash and reduction of inventory, and record the cost of goods sold and sales revenue.

**4. (LO 2)** Which sales accounts are subtracted from sales to determine net sales?

    a. Sales Discounts.

    b. Sales Returns and Allowances.

    c. Both Sales Discounts and Sales Returns and Allowances.

    d. None of the answer choices is correct.

**5. (LO 3)** Gross profit will result if:

a. operating expenses are less than net income.

b. net sales are greater than operating expenses.

c. net sales are greater than cost of goods sold.

d. operating expenses are greater than cost of goods sold.

**6. (LO 3)** If net sales are $400,000, cost of goods sold is $310,000, and operating expenses are $60,000, what is the gross profit?

a. $30,000.

b. $90,000.

c. $340,000.

d. $400,000.

**7. (LO 3)** The multiple-step income statement for a merchandising company shows each of these features **except**:

a. gross profit.

b. cost of goods sold.

c. a sales section.

d. an investing activities section.

**8. (LO 4)** Which of the following would affect the gross profit rate?

a. An increase in advertising expense.

b. A decrease in depreciation expense.

c. An increase in cost of goods sold.

d. A decrease in insurance expense.

**9. (LO 4)** The gross profit rate is equal to:

a. net income divided by sales.

b. cost of goods sold divided by sales.

c. net sales minus cost of goods sold, divided by net sales.

d. sales minus cost of goods sold, divided by cost of goods sold.

**10. (LO 4)** During the year ended December 31, 2022, Bjornstad Corporation had the following results: net sales $267,000, cost of goods sold $107,000, net income $92,400, operating expenses $55,400, and net cash provided by operating activities $108,950. What was the company's profit margin?

a. 40%.

c. 20.5%.

b. 60%.

d. 34.6%.

## Solutions

**1. a.** Under the periodic inventory system, cost of goods sold is determined only at the end of the accounting period. The other choices are incorrect because (b) detailed records of the cost of each inventory purchase and sale are maintained continuously when a perpetual, not periodic, system is used; (c) the perpetual system provides better control over inventories than a periodic system; and (d) the increased use of computerized systems has increased the use of the perpetual, not periodic, system.

**2. a.** Under a perpetual inventory system, when a company purchases goods for resale, purchases on account increase the Inventory account, not (b) Purchases or (c) Cost of Goods Sold. Choice (d) is incorrect because Sales Revenue is increased only when the goods are sold.

**3. c.** To record the sale of goods for cash under a perpetual inventory system, record the receipt of cash and sales revenue, and record the cost of goods sold and reduction of inventory. The other choices are incorrect because (a) only considers the recognition of the expense and ignores the revenue, (b) only considers the recognition of revenue and leaves out the expense or cost of merchandise sold, and (d) the receipt of cash and sales revenue, not reduction of inventory, are paired together, and the cost of goods sold and reduction of inventory, not sales revenue, are paired together.

**4. c.** Both Sales Discounts and Sales Returns and Allowances are subtracted from sales to determine net sales. Choices (a) and (b) are

both correct, but (c) is the better answer. Choice (d) is incorrect as there is a correct answer.

**5. c.** Gross profit will result if net sales are greater than cost of goods sold. The other choices are incorrect because (a) operating expenses and net income are not used in the computation of gross profit; (b) gross profit results when net sales are greater than cost of goods sold, not operating expenses; and (d) gross profit results when net sales, not operating expenses, are greater than cost of goods sold.

**6. b.** Gross profit = Net sales ($400,000) − Cost of goods sold ($310,000) = $90,000, not (a) $30,000, (c) $340,000, or (d) $400,000.

**7. d.** An investing activities section is not part of a multiple-step income statement (it is part of the statement of cash flows). Choices (a) gross profit, (b) cost of goods sold, and (c) a sales section are all features of a multiple-step income statement.

**8. c.** Gross profit rate = Gross profit ÷ Net sales. Therefore, any changes in sales revenue, sales returns and allowances, sales discounts, or cost of goods sold will affect the ratio. Changes in (a) advertising expense, (b) depreciation expense, or (d) insurance expense will not affect the computation of the gross profit rate.

**9. c.** Gross profit rate = Gross profit (Net sales − Cost of goods sold) ÷ Net sales. The other choices are therefore incorrect.

**10. d.** Net income ($92,400) ÷ Net sales ($267,000) = Profit margin of 34.6%, not (a) 40%, (b) 60%, or (c) 20.5%.

## Practice Brief Exercises

*Record purchase transactions.*

**1. (LO 1)** Use a tabular summary to record the following transactions on Robertson Company's books using a perpetual inventory system.

a. On March 2, Melky Company sold $800,000 of merchandise to Robertson Company, terms 2/10, n/30.

b. On March 6, Robertson Company returned $100,000 of the merchandise purchased on March 2.

c. On March 12, Robertson Company paid the balance due to Melky Company.

## Solution

**1.**

| | Assets | | = Liabilities | + | | Stockholders' Equity | | | | |
|---|---|---|---|---|---|---|---|---|---|---|
| | | | | | Common | | Retained Earnings | | | |
| | Cash | + Inventory | = Accts. Pay. | + | Stock | + | Rev. | − Exp. | − | Div. |
| **a.** | | +$800,000 | +$800,000 | | | | | | | |
| **b.** | | −100,000 | −100,000 | | | | | | | |
| **c.** | −$686,000 | −14,000 | −700,000 | | | | | | | |

**2. (LO 2)** Use a tabular summary to record the following transactions on Wendel Company's books using a perpetual inventory system.

*Record sales transactions.*

  **a.** On March 2, Wendel Company sold $70,000 of merchandise to Krista Company, terms 2/10, n/30. The cost of the merchandise sold was $46,000.

  **b.** On March 6, Krista Company returned $8,000 of the merchandise purchased on March 2. The cost of the merchandise returned was $5,400.

  **c.** On March 12, Wendel Company received the balance due from Krista Company.

## Solution

**2.**

| | | Assets | | | = Liabilities + | | Stockholders' Equity | | | | |
|---|---|---|---|---|---|---|---|---|---|---|---|
| | | Accounts | | | | Common | | Retained Earnings | | | |
| | Cash | Receivable | + Inventory | = | | Stock | + | Rev. | − Exp. | − Div. | |
| **a.** | +$70,000 | | | | | | | +$70,000 | | | Sales Revenue |
| | | | −$46,000 | | | | | | −$46,000 | | Cost of Goods Sold |
| **b.** | | −8,000 | | | | | | −8,000 | | | Sales Ret./Allow. |
| | | | +5,400 | | | | | | +5,400 | | Cost of Goods Sold |
| **c.** | +$60,760[1] | −62,000[2] | | | | | | | | −1,240[3] | Sales Discounts |

(1) $62,000 − $1,240
(2) $70,000 − $8,000
(3) $62,000 × 2%

**3. (LO 3, 4)** Assume Yoan Company has the following reported amounts: Sales revenue $400,000, Sales discounts $10,000, Cost of goods sold $234,000, and Operating expenses $60,000. Compute the following: (a) net sales, (b) gross profit, (c) income from operations, and (d) gross profit rate. (Round to one decimal place.)

*Compute net sales, gross profit, income from operations, and gross profit rate.*

## Solution

**3. a.** Net sales = $400,000 − $10,000 = $390,000

  **b.** Gross profit = $390,000 − $234,000 = $156,000

  **c.** Income from operations = $156,000 − $60,000 = $96,000

  **d.** Gross profit rate = $156,000 ÷ $390,000 = 40%

## Practice Exercises

**1. (LO 1, 2)** On June 10, Vareen Company purchased $8,000 of merchandise on account from Harrah Company. On June 25, Vareen sold 75% of the merchandise to Michel Company for $10,000 cash.

*Record purchase and sales transactions.*

### Instructions

Use a tabular summary to record the June 10 and 25 transactions for Vareen Company.

**Solution**

**1.**

| Assets | | = | Liabilities | + | | Stockholders' Equity | | | | |
|---|---|---|---|---|---|---|---|---|---|---|
| | | | | | Common | | Retained Earnings | | | |
| Cash | + Inventory | = | Accts. Pay. | + | Stock | + | Rev. | − Exp. | − Div. | |
| | +$8,000 | | +$8,000 | | | | | | | |
| +$10,000 | | | | | | | +$10,000 | | | Sales Revenue |
| | −6,000 | | | | | | | −$6,000 | | Cost of Goods Sold |

*Prepare a multiple-step income statement.*

**2. (LO 3)** In its income statement for the year ended December 31, 2022, Marten Company reported the following condensed data.

| | | | | |
|---|---:|---|---|---:|
| Interest expense | $ 70,000 | | Net sales | $2,200,000 |
| Operating expenses | 725,000 | | Interest revenue | 25,000 |
| Cost of goods sold | 1,300,000 | | Loss on disposal of plant assets | 17,000 |
| | | | Income tax expense | 10,000 |

**Instructions**

Prepare a multiple-step income statement.

**Solution**

**2.**

**Marten Company**
**Income Statement**
**For the Year Ended December 31, 2022**

| | | | |
|---|---:|---:|---:|
| Net sales | | | $2,200,000 |
| Cost of goods sold | | | 1,300,000 |
| Gross profit | | | 900,000 |
| Operating expenses | | | 725,000 |
| Income from operations | | | 175,000 |
| Other revenues and gains | | | |
|   Interest revenue | | $25,000 | |
| Other expenses and losses | | | |
|   Interest expense | $70,000 | | |
|   Loss on disposal of plant assets | 17,000 | 87,000 | (62,000) |
| Income before income taxes | | | 113,000 |
| Income tax expense | | | 10,000 |
| Net income | | | $ 103,000 |

# Practice Problem

*Prepare a multiple-step income statement.*

**(LO 3)** The adjusted balances for the year ended December 31, 2022, for Dykstra Company are shown as follows. The accounts are listed in alphabetical order.

| Account | Adjusted Balance |
|---|---:|
| Accounts Payable | $ 10,600 |
| Accounts Receivable | 11,100 |
| Accumulated Depreciation—Equipment | 18,000 |
| Advertising Expense | 12,000 |
| Cash | 14,500 |
| Common Stock | 70,000 |
| Cost of Goods Sold | 363,400 |

| Account | Adjusted Balance |
|---|---|
| Depreciation Expense | 9,000 |
| Dividends | 12,000 |
| Equipment | 95,000 |
| Freight-Out | 7,600 |
| Insurance Expense | 4,500 |
| Interest Expense | 3,600 |
| Interest Revenue | 2,500 |
| Inventory | 29,000 |
| Notes Payable | 25,000 |
| Prepaid Insurance | 2,500 |
| Rent Expense | 24,000 |
| Retained Earnings | 11,000 |
| Salaries and Wages Expense | 56,000 |
| Sales Discounts | 5,000 |
| Sales Returns and Allowances | 6,700 |
| Sales Revenue | 536,800 |
| Utilities Expense | 18,000 |

## Instructions

Prepare a multiple-step income statement for Dykstra Company. Assume a tax rate of 20%.

## Solution

### Dykstra Company
### Income Statement
### For the Year Ended December 31, 2022

| | | |
|---|---:|---:|
| Sales | | |
| Sales revenue | | $536,800 |
| Less: Sales returns and allowances | $ 6,700 | |
| Sales discounts | 5,000 | 11,700 |
| Net sales | | 525,100 |
| Cost of goods sold | | 363,400 |
| Gross profit | | 161,700 |
| Operating expenses | | |
| Salaries and wages expense | 56,000 | |
| Rent expense | 24,000 | |
| Utilities expense | 18,000 | |
| Advertising expense | 12,000 | |
| Depreciation expense | 9,000 | |
| Freight-out | 7,600 | |
| Insurance expense | 4,500 | |
| Total operating expenses | | 131,100 |
| Income from operations | | 30,600 |
| Other revenues and gains | | |
| Interest revenue | | 2,500 |
| Other expenses and losses | | |
| Interest expense | | 3,600 |
| Income before income taxes | | 29,500 |
| Income tax expense | | 5,900 |
| Net income | | $ 23,600 |

# WileyPLUS

Brief Exercises, DO IT! Exercises, Exercises, Problems, and many additional resources are available for practice in WileyPLUS.

## Questions

**1. a.** "The steps in the accounting cycle for a merchandising company differ from the steps in the accounting cycle for a service company." Do you agree or disagree?

**b.** Is the measurement of net income in a merchandising company conceptually the same as in a service company? Explain.

**2.** How do the components of revenues and expenses differ between a merchandising company and a service company?

**3.** Maria Lopez, CEO of Sales Bin Stores, is considering a recommendation made by both the company's purchasing manager and director of finance that the company should invest in a sophisticated new perpetual inventory system to replace its periodic system. Explain the primary difference between the two systems, and discuss the potential benefits of a perpetual inventory system.

**4. a.** Explain the income measurement process in a merchandising company.

**b.** How does income measurement differ between a merchandising company and a service company?

**5.** Waymon Co. has net sales of $100,000, cost of goods sold of $70,000, and operating expenses of $18,000. What is its gross profit?

**6.** Marie Ascot believes revenues from credit sales may be recorded before they are collected in cash. Do you agree? Explain.

**7.** What is the primary source document for recording (a) cash sales and (b) credit sales?

**8.** As the end of Smyle Company's fiscal year approached, it became clear that the company had considerable excess inventory. Marvin Ross, the head of marketing and sales, ordered salespeople to "add 20% more units to each order that you ship. The customers can always ship the extra back next period if they decide they don't want it. We've got to do it to meet this year's sales goal." Discuss the accounting implications of Marvin's action.

**9.** To encourage bookstores to buy a broader range of book titles and to discourage price discounting, the publishing industry allows bookstores to return unsold books to the publisher. This results in very significant returns each year. To ensure proper recognition of revenues, how should publishing companies account for these returns?

**10.** Mai Company has always provided its customers with payment terms of 1/10, n/30. Members of its sale force have commented that competitors are offering customers 2/10, n/45. Explain what these terms mean, and discuss the implications to Mai of switching its payment terms to those of its competitors.

**11.** Scribe Company reports net sales of $800,000, gross profit of $560,000, and net income of $230,000. What are its operating expenses?

**12.** In its year-end earnings announcement press release, Ransome Corp. announced that its earnings increased by $15 million relative to the previous year. This represented a 20% increase. Inspection of its income statement reveals that the company reported a $20 million gain under "Other revenues and gains" from the sale of one of its factories. Discuss the implications of this gain from the perspective of a potential investor.

**13.** Identify the distinguishing features of an income statement for a merchandising company.

**14.** What factors affect a company's gross profit rate—that is, what can cause the gross profit rate to increase and what can cause it to decrease?

**15.** Earl Massey, director of marketing, wants to reduce the selling price of his company's products by 15% to increase market share. He says, "I know this will reduce our gross profit rate, but the increased number of units sold will make up for the lost margin." Before this action is taken, what other factors does the company need to consider?

## Brief Exercises

*Record purchase transactions.*

**BE6.1 (LO 1), AP** Brandon purchased merchandise on account on April 5 for $5,100. On April 7, Brandon paid $50 of freight charges for the goods purchased on April 5. On April 8, Brandon returned goods purchased on April 5 for $100. Use a tabular summary to record these transactions.

*Record purchase transactions.*

**BE6.2 (LO 1), AP** Prepare a tabular summary to record the following transactions on Berry Company's books using a perpetual inventory system.

**a.** On September 3, Raven Company sold $700,000 of merchandise to Berry Company on account, terms 2/10, n/30. The cost of the merchandise sold was $430,000.

**b.** On September 6, Berry Company returned $90,000 of the merchandise purchased on March 2. The seller's cost of the merchandise returned was $60,000.

**c.** On September 13, Berry Company paid the balance due to Raven Company.

**BE6.3 (LO 1, 2), AP** Rita Company buys merchandise on account from Linus Company for $590. Rita sells the goods to Ellis for $900 cash. Use a tabular summary to record the transactions for Rita Company using a perpetual inventory system.

*Record perpetual inventory purchase and sale.*

**BE6.4 (LO 2), AP** Use a tabular summary to record the following transactions for Borst Company using a perpetual inventory system.

*Record sales transactions using a perpetual inventory system.*

a. On March 2, Borst Company sold $800,000 of merchandise to McLeena Company on account. The cost of the merchandise sold was $540,000.

b. On March 6, McLeena Company returned $140,000 of the merchandise purchased on March 2. The cost of the merchandise returned was $94,000.

c. On March 12, Borst Company received the balance due from McLeena Company.

**BE6.5 (LO 3), AP** Presented here are the components in Salas Company's income statement. Determine the missing amounts.

*Compute missing amounts in determining net income.*

| Sales Revenue | Cost of Goods Sold | Gross Profit | Operating Expenses | Net Income |
|---|---|---|---|---|
| $ 71,200 | (b) | $ 30,000 | (d) | $12,100 |
| $108,000 | $70,000 | (c) | (e) | $29,500 |
| (a) | $71,900 | $109,600 | $46,200 | (f) |

**BE6.6 (LO 3), AP** Barto Company provides this information for the month ended October 31, 2022: sales on credit $300,000, cash sales $150,000, sales discounts $5,000, and sales returns and allowances $19,000. Prepare the sales section of the income statement based on this information.

*Prepare sales section of income statement.*

**BE6.7 (LO 3), C** Explain where each of these items would appear on a multiple-step income statement: gain on disposal of plant assets, cost of goods sold, depreciation expense, and sales returns and allowances.

*Identify placement of items on a multiple-step income statement.*

**BE6.8 (LO 4), AP** Dublin Corporation reported net sales of $250,000, cost of goods sold of $150,000, operating expenses of $50,000, net income of $32,500, beginning total assets of $520,000, and ending total assets of $600,000. Calculate each of the following values and explain what they mean: (a) profit margin and (b) gross profit rate.

*Calculate profitability ratios.*

**BE6.9 (LO 4), AP** Garten Corporation reported net sales $800,000, cost of goods sold $520,000, operating expenses $210,000, and net income $68,000. Calculate the following values and explain what they mean: (a) profit margin and (b) gross profit rate.

*Calculate profitability ratios.*

## DO IT! Exercises

**DO IT! 6.1 (LO 1), AP** On October 5, Iverson Company buys merchandise on account from Lasse Company. The selling price of the goods is $5,000, and the cost to Lasse Company is $3,000. On October 8, Iverson returns defective goods with a selling price of $640 and a scrap value of $240. Use a tabular summary to record the transactions of Iverson Company, assuming a perpetual approach.

*Record transactions of purchasing company.*

**DO IT! 6.2 (LO 2), AP** On October 20, Iverson sells merchandise with a cost of $3,000 to Thom for $5,000 cash. On October 25, Iverson receives returned goods from Thom that had a selling price of $500 and a cost of $300. Use a tabular summary to record the transactions for Iverson Company using a perpetual inventory system.

*Record sales transactions.*

**DO IT! 6.3 (LO 3), AP** The following information is available for Berlin Corp. for the year ended December 31, 2022:

*Prepare a multiple-step income statement.*

| | | | |
|---|---|---|---|
| Other revenues and gains | $ 12,700 | Sales revenue | $592,000 |
| Other expenses and losses | 13,300 | Operating expenses | 186,000 |
| Cost of goods sold | 156,000 | Sales returns and allowances | 40,000 |

Prepare a multiple-step income statement for Berlin Corp. The company has a tax rate of 20%.

*Compute and analyze profitability ratios.*

**DO IT! 6.4 (LO 4), AN** Owen Wise, Inc. reported the following in its 2022 and 2021 income statements.

|  | **2022** | **2021** |
|---|---|---|
| Net sales | $150,000 | $120,000 |
| Cost of goods sold | 90,000 | 72,000 |
| Operating expenses | 44,000 | 20,000 |
| Income tax expense | 6,000 | 6,000 |
| Net income | $ 10,000 | $ 22,000 |

Determine the company's gross profit rate and profit margin for both years. Discuss the cause for changes in the ratios.

# Exercises

*Record purchase transactions.*

**E6.1 (LO 1), AP** This information relates to Rice Co.

1. On April 5, purchased merchandise from Jax Company for $28,000 on account.
2. On April 7, purchased equipment on account for $30,000.
3. On April 8, returned $3,600 of April 5 merchandise to Jax Company.
4. On April 15, paid the amount due to Jax Company in full.

**Instructions**

Prepare a tabular summary to record the transactions listed above for Rice Co. using a perpetual inventory system.

*Record purchase transactions.*

**E6.2 (LO 1), AP** Raison Co. had the following transactions during October.

1. On October 8, purchased merchandise on account from Baker Company for $17,000, terms 2/10, n/30.
2. On October 9, paid freight costs of $500 on merchandise purchased from Baker Company.
3. On October 11, returned $2,600 of October 8 merchandise to Baker Company.
4. On October 18, paid the amount due to Baker Company in full.

**Instructions**

Use a tabular summary to record the transactions listed above on Raison Co.'s books. Raison Co. uses a perpetual inventory system.

*Record purchase transactions.*

**E6.3 (LO 1), AP** On June 10, Pais Company purchased $9,000 of merchandise from McGiver Company, on account, terms 3/10, n/30. Pais pays the freight costs of $400 on June 11. Goods totaling $600 are returned to McGiver for credit on June 12. On June 19, Pais Company pays McGiver Company in full, less the purchase discount. Both companies use a perpetual inventory system.

**Instructions**

Use a tabular summary to record transaction on the books of Pais Company.

*Record sales transactions.*

**E6.4 (LO 2), AP** The following transactions are for Alonzo Company.

1. On December 3, Alonzo Company sold $500,000 of merchandise to Arte Co. on account. The cost of the merchandise sold was $330,000.
2. On December 8, Arte Co. returned $25,000 of merchandise purchased on December 3. The cost of the goods was $16,000.
3. On December 13, Alonzo Company received the balance due from Arte Co.

**Instructions**

Prepare a tabular summary to record these transactions for Alonzo Company using a perpetual inventory system.

*Prepare sales section of income statement.*

**E6.5 (LO 3), AP** The adjusted account balances of Doqe Company show these data pertaining to sales at the end of its fiscal year, October 31, 2022: Sales Revenue $900,000, Freight-Out $14,000, Sales Returns and Allowances $22,000, and Sales Discounts $13,500.

**Instructions**

Prepare the sales section of the income statement.

**E6.6 (LO 3), AP** The following is information for Lieu Co. for the month of January 2022.

*Prepare an income statement.*

| | | | |
|---|---|---|---|
| Cost of goods sold | $212,000 | Rent expense | $ 32,000 |
| Freight-out | 7,000 | Sales discounts | 8,000 |
| Insurance expense | 12,000 | Sales returns and allowances | 20,000 |
| Salaries and wages expense | 60,000 | Sales revenue | 370,000 |
| Income tax expense | 5,000 | | |

**Instructions**

Prepare an income statement using the format presented in Illustration 6.4.

**E6.7 (LO 3), AP** In its income statement for the year ended December 31, 2022, Darren Company reported the following condensed data.

*Prepare a multiple-step income statement.*

| | | | |
|---|---|---|---|
| Salaries and wages expense | $465,000 | Loss on disposal of plant assets | $ 83,500 |
| Cost of goods sold | 987,000 | Sales revenue | 2,210,000 |
| Interest expense | 71,000 | Income tax expense | 25,000 |
| Interest revenue | 65,000 | Sales discounts | 160,000 |
| Depreciation expense | 310,000 | Utilities expense | 110,000 |

**Instructions**

Prepare a multiple-step income statement.

**E6.8 (LO 3), AP** In its income statement for the year ended December 31, 2022, Laine Inc. reported the following condensed data.

*Prepare a multiple-step income statement.*

| | | | |
|---|---|---|---|
| Operating expenses | $ 725,000 | Interest revenue | $ 33,000 |
| Cost of goods sold | 1,256,000 | Loss on disposal of plant assets | 17,000 |
| Interest expense | 70,000 | Net sales | 2,200,000 |
| Income tax expense | 47,000 | | |

**Instructions**

Prepare a multiple-step income statement.

**E6.9 (LO 3), AP** The selected accounts from the Blue Door Corporation's accounting records are presented below for the year ended December 31, 2022:

*Prepare a multiple-step income statement.*

| | | | |
|---|---|---|---|
| Advertising expense | $ 55,000 | Interest revenue | $ 30,000 |
| Common stock | 250,000 | Inventory | 67,000 |
| Cost of goods sold | 1,085,000 | Rent revenue | 24,000 |
| Depreciation expense | 125,000 | Retained earnings | 535,000 |
| Dividends | 150,000 | Salaries and wages expense | 675,000 |
| Freight-out | 25,000 | Sales discounts | 8,500 |
| Income tax expense | 70,000 | Sales returns and | |
| Insurance expense | 15,000 | allowances | 41,000 |
| Interest expense | 70,000 | Sales revenue | 2,400,000 |

**Instructions**

Prepare a multiple-step income statement.

**E6.10 (LO 3, 4), AP** Financial information is presented here for two companies.

*Compute missing amounts and calculate profitability ratios.*

| | Yoste Company | Noone Company |
|---|---|---|
| Sales revenue | $90,000 | ? |
| Sales returns and allowances | ? | $ 5,000 |
| Net sales | 84,000 | 100,000 |
| Cost of goods sold | 58,000 | ? |
| Gross profit | ? | 40,000 |
| Operating expenses | 14,380 | ? |
| Net income | ? | 17,000 |

### Instructions

a. Fill in the missing amounts. Show all computations.

b. Calculate the profit margin and the gross profit rate for each company.

c. Discuss your findings in part (b).

*Prepare a multiple-step income statement and calculate profitability ratios.*

**E6.11 (LO 3, 4), AP** Suppose in its income statement for the year ended June 30, 2022, **The Clorox Company** reported the following condensed data (dollars in millions).

| | | | |
|---|---|---|---|
| Salaries and wages expense | $ 460 | Research and | |
| Depreciation expense | 90 |    development expense | $ 114 |
| Sales revenue | 5,730 | Income tax expense | 162 |
| Interest expense | 161 | Loss on disposal of plant assets | 46 |
| Advertising expense | 499 | Cost of goods sold | 3,104 |
| Sales returns and | | Rent expense | 105 |
|    allowances | 280 | Utilities expense | 60 |

### Instructions

a. Prepare a multiple-step income statement.

b. Calculate the gross profit rate and the profit margin and explain what each means.

c. Assume the marketing department has presented a plan to increase advertising expenses by $340 million. It expects this plan to result in an increase in both net sales and cost of goods sold of 25%. (*Hint:* Increase both sales revenue and sales returns and allowances by 25%.) Redo parts (a) and (b) and discuss whether this plan has merit. (Assume a tax rate of 20%, and round all amounts to whole dollars.)

## Problems

*Record purchase and sales transactions using a perpetual inventory system.*

**P6.1 (LO 1, 2), AP** Powell Warehouse distributes hardback books to retail stores and extends credit to all of its customers. During the month of June, the following merchandising transactions occurred.

| | | |
|---|---|---|
| June | 1 | Purchased books on account for $1,040 from Catlin Publishers. |
| | 3 | Sold books on account to Garfunkel Bookstore for $1,200. The cost of the merchandise sold was $720. |
| | 6 | Received $40 credit for books returned to Catlin Publishers. |
| | 9 | Paid Catlin Publishers in full. |
| | 15 | Received payment in full from Garfunkel Bookstore. |
| | 17 | Sold books on account to Bell Tower for $1,200. The cost of the merchandise sold was $730. |
| | 20 | Purchased books on account for $720 from Priceless Book Publishers. |
| | 24 | Received payment in full from Bell Tower. |
| | 26 | Paid Priceless Book Publishers in full. |
| | 28 | Sold books on account to General Bookstore for $1,300. The cost of the merchandise sold was $780. |
| | 30 | Granted General Bookstore $130 credit for books returned costing $80. |

### Instructions

Prepare a tabular summary to record the transactions for the month of June for Powell Warehouse using a perpetual inventory system.

*Record purchases and sales using a perpetual inventory system and prepare partial income statement.*

**P6.2 (LO 1, 2, 3), AP** At the beginning of the current season on April 1, the records of Granite Hills Pro Shop showed Cash $2,500, Inventory $3,500, and Common Stock $6,000. The following transactions occurred during April 2022.

| | | |
|---|---|---|
| Apr. | 5 | Purchased golf bags, clubs, and balls on account from Arnie Co. $1,500. |
| | 9 | Received credit from Arnie Co. for merchandise returned $200. |
| | 10 | Sold merchandise on account to members $1,340. The merchandise sold had a cost of $820. |
| | 12 | Purchased golf shoes, sweaters, and other accessories on account from Woods Sportswear $830. |
| | 14 | Paid Arnie Co. in full. |

Apr. 17  Received credit from Woods Sportswear for merchandise returned $30.
20  Made sales on account to members $810. The cost of merchandise sold was $550.
21  Paid Woods Sportswear in full.
30  Received payments on account from members $1,220.

**Instructions**

a. Prepare a tabular summary that includes the following accounts: Cash, Accounts Receivable, Inventory, Accounts Payable, Common Stock, Sales Revenue, Sales Returns and Allowances, and Cost of Goods Sold. Enter the beginning balances in the summary. Record the April transactions using a perpetual inventory system.

b. Prepare an income statement through gross profit for the month of April 2022.

*b.  Gross profit          $780*

**P6.3 (LO 1, 2), AP** Assume that on September 1, **Office Depot** had an inventory that included a variety of calculators. The company uses a perpetual inventory system. During September, these transactions occurred.

*Record purchase and sales transactions.*

Sept. 6  Purchased calculators from Dragoo Co. at a total cost of $1,650, on account, terms n/30.
9  Paid freight of $50 on calculators purchased from Dragoo Co.
10  Returned calculators to Dragoo Co. for $66 credit because they did not meet specifications.
12  Sold calculators costing $520 for $690 to Fryer Book Store, on account, terms n/30.
14  Granted credit of $45 to Fryer Book Store for the return of one calculator that was not ordered. The calculator cost $34.
20  Sold calculators costing $570 for $760 to Heasley Card Shop, on account, terms n/30.

**Instructions**

Prepare a tabular summary to record the transactions for the month of September for Office Depot using a perpetual inventory system.

**P6.4 (LO 3), AP** Wolford Department Store is located in midtown Metropolis. During the past several years, net income has been declining because suburban shopping centers have been attracting business away from city areas. At the end of the company's fiscal year on November 30, 2022, its accounting records included the following accounts and adjusted balances.

*Prepare financial statements.*

| | |
|---|---:|
| Accounts Payable | $ 26,800 |
| Accounts Receivable | 17,200 |
| Accumulated Depreciation—Equipment | 68,000 |
| Advertising Expense | 33,500 |
| Cash | 8,000 |
| Common Stock | 35,000 |
| Cost of Goods Sold | 614,300 |
| Freight-Out | 6,200 |
| Equipment | 157,000 |
| Depreciation Expense | 13,500 |
| Dividends | 12,000 |
| Gain on Disposal of Plant Assets | 2,000 |
| Income Tax Expense | 10,000 |
| Insurance Expense | 9,000 |
| Interest Expense | 5,000 |
| Inventory | 26,200 |
| Notes Payable | 43,500 |
| Prepaid Insurance | 6,000 |
| Rent Expense | 34,000 |
| Retained Earnings | 14,200 |
| Salaries and Wages Expense | 117,000 |
| Salaries and Wages Payable | 6,000 |
| Sales Returns and Allowances | 20,000 |
| Sales Revenue | 904,000 |
| Utilities Expense | 10,600 |

Additional data: Notes payable are due in 2026.

**Instructions**

Prepare a multiple-step income statement, a retained earnings statement, and a classified balance sheet.

*Net income          $ 32,900*
*Tot. assets          $146,400*

*Prepare a correct multiple-step income statement.*

**P6.5 (LO 3), AP** An inexperienced accountant prepared this condensed income statement for Simon Company, a retail firm that has been in business for a number of years.

**Simon Company**
**Income Statement**
**For the Year Ended December 31, 2022**

| | | |
|---|---|---:|
| Revenues | | |
| Net sales | | $850,000 |
| Other revenues | | 22,000 |
| | | 872,000 |
| Cost of goods sold | | 555,000 |
| Gross profit | | 317,000 |
| Operating expenses | | |
| Selling expenses | | 109,000 |
| Administrative expenses | | 103,000 |
| | | 212,000 |
| Net earnings | | $105,000 |

As an experienced, knowledgeable accountant, you review the statement and determine the following facts.

1. Net sales consist of sales $911,000, less freight-out on merchandise sold $33,000, and sales returns and allowances $28,000.

2. Other revenues consist of sales discounts $18,000 and rent revenue $4,000.

3. Selling expenses consist of salespersons' salaries $80,000, depreciation on equipment $10,000, advertising $13,000, and sales commissions $6,000. The commissions represent commissions paid. At December 31, $3,000 of commissions have been earned by salespersons but have not been paid. All compensation should be recorded as Salaries and Wages Expense.

4. Administrative expenses consist of office salaries $47,000, dividends $18,000, utilities $12,000, interest expense $2,000, and rent expense $24,000, which includes prepayments totaling $6,000 for the first quarter of 2023.

**Instructions**

*Net income*      *$67,500*

Prepare a correct detailed multiple-step income statement. Assume a 25% tax rate.

---

# Expand Your Critical Thinking

## Financial Reporting Problem: Apple Inc.

**CT6.1** The notes that accompany a company's financial statements provide informative details that would clutter the amounts and descriptions presented in the statements. Refer to the financial statements of **Apple Inc.** in Appendix A. Apple's complete annual report, including the notes to the financial statements, is available at the company's website.

**Instructions**

Answer the following questions. (Give the amounts in thousands of dollars, as shown in Apple's annual report.)

a. What did Apple report for the amount of inventories in its Consolidated Balance Sheet at September 29, 2018? At September 30, 2017?

b. Compute the dollar amount of change and the percentage change in inventories between 2017 and 2018. Compute inventory as a percentage of current assets for 2018.

c. What are the cost of sales reported by Apple for 2018, 2017, and 2016? Compute the ratio of cost of sales to net sales in 2018.

## Comparative Analysis Problem:

## Columbia Sportswear Company vs. Under Armour, Inc.

**CT6.2** The financial statements of **Columbia Sportswear Company** are presented in Appendix B. Financial statements of **Under Armour, Inc.** are presented in Appendix C.

### Instructions

**a.** Based on the information contained in these financial statements, determine the following values for each company.

    **1.** Profit margin for 2018.

    **2.** Gross profit for 2018.

    **3.** Gross profit rate for 2018.

    **4.** Income from operations for 2018.

    **5.** Percentage change in Income from operations from 2017 to 2018.

**b.** What conclusions concerning the relative profitability of the two companies can be drawn from these data?

## Interpreting Financial Statements

**CT6.3** Recently, it was announced that two giant French retailers, **Carrefour SA** and **Promodes SA**, would merge. A headline in the *Wall Street Journal* blared, "French Retailers Create New Walmart Rival." While **Walmart**'s total sales would still exceed those of the combined company, Walmart's international sales are far less than those of the combined company. This is a serious concern for Walmart, since its primary opportunity for future growth lies outside of the United States.

    Below are basic financial data for the combined corporation (in euros) and Walmart (in U.S. dollars). Even though their results are presented in different currencies, by employing ratios we can make some basic comparisons.

|  | Carrefour (in millions) | Walmart (in millions) |
|---|---|---|
| Sales revenue | €70,486 | $256,329 |
| Cost of goods sold | 54,630 | 198,747 |
| Net income | 1,738 | 9,054 |
| Total assets | 39,063 | 104,912 |
| Current assets | 14,521 | 34,421 |
| Current liabilities | 13,660 | 37,418 |
| Total liabilities | 29,434 | 61,289 |

### Instructions

Compare the two companies by answering the following.

**a.** Calculate the gross profit rate for each of the companies, and discuss their relative abilities to control cost of goods sold.

**b.** Calculate the profit margin, and discuss the companies' relative profitability.

**c.** Calculate the current ratio and debt to assets ratio for each of the two companies, and discuss their relative liquidity and solvency.

**d.** What concerns might you have in relying on this comparison?

## Real-World Focus

**CT6.4** No financial decision-maker should ever rely solely on the financial information reported in the annual report to make decisions. It is important to keep abreast of financial news. This activity demonstrates how to search for financial news on the Internet.

### Instructions

Search the Internet for an article on either **PepsiCo** or **Coca-Cola** that sounds interesting to you and that would be relevant to an investor in these companies, and then answer the following questions.

**a.** What was the source of the article (e.g., Reuters, Businesswire, Prnewswire)?

**b.** Assume that you are a personal financial planner and that some of your clients own stock in the company. Write a brief memo to these clients summarizing the article and explaining the implications of the article for their investment.

### Decision-Making Across the Organization

**CT6.5** Three years ago, Karen Suez and her brother-in-law Reece Jones opened Gigasales Department Store. For the first 2 years, business was good, but the following condensed income statement results for 2022 were disappointing.

**Gigasales Department Store**
**Income Statement**
**For the Year Ended December 31, 2022**

| | | |
|---|---:|---:|
| Net sales | | $700,000 |
| Cost of goods sold | | 560,000 |
| Gross profit | | 140,000 |
| Operating expenses | | |
| Selling expenses | $100,000 | |
| Administrative expenses | 20,000 | |
| | | 120,000 |
| Net income | | $ 20,000 |

Karen believes the problem lies in the relatively low gross profit rate of 20%. Reece believes the problem is that operating expenses are too high. Karen thinks the gross profit rate can be improved by making two changes. (1) Increase average selling prices by 15%; this increase is expected to lower sales volume so that total sales dollars will increase only 4%. (2) Buy merchandise in larger quantities and take all purchase discounts. These changes to purchasing practices are expected to increase the gross profit rate from its current rate of 20% to a new rate of 25%. Karen does not anticipate that these changes will have any effect on operating expenses.

Reece thinks expenses can be cut by making these two changes. (1) Cut 2023 sales salaries of $60,000 in half and give sales personnel a commission of 2% of net sales. (2) Reduce store deliveries to one day per week rather than twice a week; this change will reduce 2023 delivery expenses of $40,000 by 40%. Reece feels that these changes will not have any effect on net sales.

Karen and Reece come to you for help in deciding the best way to improve net income.

### Instructions

With the class divided into groups, answer the following.

a. Prepare a condensed income statement for 2023 assuming (1) Karen's changes are implemented and (2) Reece's ideas are adopted.

b. What is your recommendation to Karen and Reece?

c. Prepare a condensed income statement for 2023 assuming both sets of proposed changes are made.

d. Discuss the impact that other factors might have. For example, would increasing the quantity of inventory increase costs? Would a salary cut affect employee morale? Would decreased morale affect sales? Would decreased store deliveries decrease customer satisfaction? What other suggestions might be considered?

## Communication Activity

**CT6.6** The following events are presented in chronological order.

1. Aikan decides to buy a surfboard.
2. He calls Surfing Hawaii Co. to inquire about their surfboards.
3. Two days later, he requests that Surfing Hawaii Co. make him a surfboard.
4. Three days later, Surfing Hawaii Co. sends him a purchase order to fill out.
5. He sends back the purchase order.
6. Surfing Hawaii Co. receives the completed purchase order.
7. Surfing Hawaii Co. completes the surfboard.
8. Aikan picks up the surfboard.
9. Surfing Hawaii Co. bills Aikan.
10. Surfing Hawaii Co. receives payment from Aikan.

**Instructions**

In a memo to the president of Surfing Hawaii Co., answer the following questions.

   **a.** When should Surfing Hawaii Co. record the sale?

   **b.** Suppose that with his purchase order, Aikan is required to make a down payment. Would that change your answer to part (a)?

## Ethics Case

**CT6.7** Tabitha Andes was just hired as the assistant treasurer of Southside Stores, a specialty chain store company that has nine retail stores concentrated in one metropolitan area. Among other things, the payment of all invoices is centralized in one of the departments Tabitha will manage. Her primary responsibility is to maintain the company's high credit rating by paying all bills when due and to take advantage of all cash discounts.

Pete Wilson, the former assistant treasurer who has been promoted to treasurer, is training Tabitha in her new duties. He instructs Tabitha that she is to continue the practice of preparing all checks "net of discount" and dating the checks the last day of the discount period. "But," Pete continues, "we always hold the checks at least 4 days beyond the discount period before mailing them. That way we get another 4 days of interest on our money. Most of our creditors need our business and don't complain. And, if they scream about our missing the discount period, we blame it on the mailroom or the post office. We've only lost one discount out of every hundred we take that way. I think everybody does it. By the way, welcome to our team!"

**Instructions**

   **a.** What are the ethical considerations in this case?

   **b.** What stakeholders are harmed or benefited?

   **c.** Should Tabitha continue the practice started by Pete? Does she have any choice?

## All About You

**CT6.8** There are many situations in business where it is difficult to determine the proper period in which to record revenue. Suppose that after graduation with a degree in finance, you take a job as a manager at a consumer electronics store called FarWest Electronics. The company has expanded rapidly in order to compete with **Best Buy**.

FarWest has also begun selling gift cards. The cards are available in any dollar amount and allow the holder of the card to purchase an item for up to 2 years from the time the card is purchased. If the card is not used during those 2 years, it expires.

**Instructions**

At what point should the revenue from the gift cards be recognized? Include the reasoning to support your answer.

## CHAPTER 7

James Porter/Stone/Getty Images

# Reporting and Analyzing Inventory and Receivables

## Chapter Preview

We previously discussed the accounting for merchandise inventory using a perpetual inventory system. In this chapter, we explain the methods used to calculate the cost of inventory on hand at the balance sheet date and the cost of goods sold. We also discuss some of the decisions related to reporting and analyzing receivables. Because receivables are often a significant asset, companies must pay close attention to their receivables balances and manage them carefully.

## Feature Story

### "Where Is That Spare Bulldozer Blade?"

Let's talk inventory—big, bulldozer-size inventory. **Caterpillar Inc.** is the world's largest manufacturer of construction and mining equipment, diesel and natural gas engines, and

industrial gas turbines. It sells its products in over 200 countries, making it one of the most successful U.S. exporters. More than 70% of its productive assets are located domestically, and nearly 50% of its sales are foreign.

In the past, Caterpillar's profitability suffered, but today it is very successful. A big part of this turnaround can be attributed to effective management of its inventory. Imagine what it costs Caterpillar to have too many bulldozers sitting around in inventory—a situation the company definitely wants to avoid. Yet Caterpillar must also make sure it has enough inventory to meet demand.

At one time during a 7-year period, Caterpillar's sales increased by 100% while its inventory increased by only 50%. To achieve this proportional reduction in inventory while continuing to meet customers' needs, Caterpillar used a two-pronged approach. First, it completed a factory modernization program, which greatly increased its production efficiency. The program reduced by 60% the amount of inventory the company processes at any one time. It also reduced by an incredible 75% the time it takes to manufacture a part.

Second, Caterpillar dramatically improved its parts distribution system. It ships more than 100,000 items daily from its 23 distribution centers strategically located around the world (10 million square feet of warehouse space—remember, we're talking bulldozers). The company can virtually guarantee that it can get any part to anywhere in the world within 24 hours.

These changes led to record exports, profits, and revenues for Caterpillar. It would seem that things couldn't be better. But industry analysts, as well as the company's managers, thought otherwise. In order to maintain Caterpillar's position as the industry leader, management began another major overhaul of inventory production and inventory management processes. The goal: to cut the number of repairs in half, increase productivity by 20%, and increase inventory turnover by 40%.

In short, Caterpillar's ability to manage its inventory has been a key reason for its past success and will very likely play a huge part in its future profitability as well.

# Chapter Outline

| LEARNING OBJECTIVES | REVIEW | PRACTICE |
|---|---|---|
| **LO 1** Discuss how to classify and determine inventory. | • Classifying inventory<br>• Determining inventory quantities | **DO IT! 1** Rules of Ownership |
| **LO 2** Apply inventory cost flow methods and discuss their financial effects. | • Specific identification<br>• Cost flow assumptions<br>• Financial statement and tax effects of cost flow methods | **DO IT! 2** Cost Flow Methods |
| **LO 3** Explain how companies recognize and value receivables. | • Types of receivables<br>• Recognizing accounts receivable<br>• Valuing accounts receivable<br>• Data analytics and receivables management | **DO IT! 3** Bad Debt Expense |
| **LO 4** Explain the statement presentation and analysis of inventory. | • Presentation<br>• Analysis | **DO IT! 4** Inventory Turnover |

**Go to the Review and Practice section at the end of the chapter for a targeted summary and practice applications with solutions.**

**Visit WileyPLUS for additional tutorials and practice opportunities.**

# Classifying and Determining Inventory

Two important steps in the reporting of inventory at the end of the accounting period are the classification of inventory based on its degree of completion and the determination of inventory amounts.

## Classifying Inventory

How a company classifies its inventory depends on whether the firm is a merchandiser or a manufacturer. In a **merchandising** company, inventory consists of many different items. For example, in a grocery store, canned goods, dairy products, meats, and produce are just a few of the inventory items on hand. These items have two common characteristics:

1. They are owned by the company.
2. They are in a form ready for sale to customers in the ordinary course of business.

Thus, merchandisers need only one inventory classification, **merchandise inventory**, to describe the many different items that make up the total inventory.

In a **manufacturing** company, some inventory may not yet be ready for sale. As a result, manufacturers usually classify inventory into three categories (see **Helpful Hint**).

- **Finished goods inventory** is manufactured items that are completed and ready for sale.
- **Work in process** is that portion of manufactured inventory that has begun the production process but is not yet complete.
- **Raw materials** are the basic goods that will be used in production but have not yet been placed into production.

For example, **Caterpillar** classifies earth-moving tractors completed and ready for sale as **finished goods**. It classifies the tractors on the assembly line in various stages of production as **work in process**. The steel, glass, tires, and other components that are on hand waiting to be used in the production of tractors are identified as **raw materials**.

**HELPFUL HINT**

Regardless of the classification, companies report all inventories under Current Assets on the balance sheet.

## Determining Inventory Quantities

No matter whether they are using a periodic or perpetual inventory system, all companies need to determine inventory quantities at the end of the accounting period. If using a perpetual system, companies take a physical inventory for the following reasons:

1. To check the accuracy of their perpetual inventory records.
2. To determine the amount of inventory lost due to wasted raw materials, shoplifting, or employee theft.

Companies using a periodic inventory system take a physical inventory for **two different purposes**: to determine the inventory on hand at the balance sheet date, and to determine the cost of goods sold for the period.

Determining inventory quantities involves two steps: (1) taking a physical inventory of goods on hand and (2) determining the ownership of goods.

**ETHICS NOTE**

In a famous fraud, a salad oil company filled its storage tanks mostly with water. The oil rose to the top, so auditors thought the tanks were full of oil. The company also said it had more tanks than it really did: It repainted numbers on the tanks to confuse auditors.

## Taking a Physical Inventory

Companies take a physical inventory at the end of the accounting period. Taking a physical inventory involves actually counting, weighing, or measuring each kind of inventory on hand (see **Ethics Note**). In many companies, taking an inventory is a formidable task. Retailers such as **Target**, **True Value Hardware**, and **Home Depot** have thousands of different inventory items. An inventory count is generally more accurate when goods are not being sold or received during the counting. Consequently, companies often "take inventory" when the business is closed or when business is slow. Many retailers close early on a chosen day in January—after the holiday sales and returns, when inventories are at their lowest level—to count inventory. **Walmart Inc.**, for example, has a year-end of January 31.

## Determining Ownership of Goods

One challenge in computing inventory quantities is determining what inventory a company owns. To determine ownership of goods, two questions must be answered:

1. Do all of the goods included in the count belong to the company?
2. Does the company own any goods that were not included in the count?

### Ethics Insight   Leslie Fay

iStock.com/Greg Brookes

#### Falsifying Inventory to Boost Income

Managers at women's apparel maker **Leslie Fay** were convicted of falsifying inventory records to boost net income in an attempt to increase management bonuses. In another case, executives at **Craig Consumer Electronics** were accused of defrauding lenders by manipulating inventory records. The indictment said the company both classified "defective goods as new or refurbished" and claimed that it owned certain shipments "from overseas suppliers" when, in fact, either Craig did not own the shipments or the shipments did not exist.

**What effect does an overstatement of inventory have on a company's financial statements? (Go to WileyPLUS for this answer and additional questions.)**

**Goods in Transit**   A complication in determining ownership is **goods in transit** (on board a truck, train, ship, or plane) at the end of the period.

- The company may have purchased goods that have not yet been received.
- It may have sold goods that have not yet been delivered.
- To arrive at an accurate count, the company must determine ownership of these goods.

Goods in transit should be included in the inventory of the company that has legal title to the goods. Legal title is determined by the terms of the sale, as shown in **Illustration 7.1** and described below.

1. When the terms are **FOB (free on board) shipping point**, ownership of the goods passes to the buyer when the public carrier accepts the goods from the seller.
2. When the terms are **FOB destination**, ownership of the goods remains with the seller until the goods reach the buyer.

**ILLUSTRATION 7.1**   **Terms of sale**

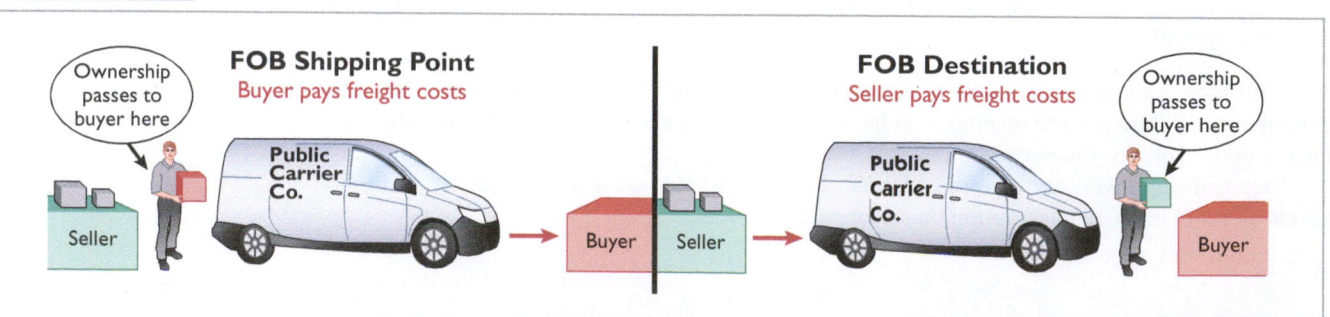

If goods in transit at the statement date are ignored, inventory quantities may be seriously miscounted. Assume, for example, that Hargrove Company has 20,000 units of inventory on hand on December 31. It also has the following goods in transit:

1. Sales of 1,500 units shipped December 31 FOB destination.
2. Purchases of 2,500 units shipped FOB shipping point by the seller on December 31.

Hargrove has legal title to both the 1,500 units sold and the 2,500 units purchased. If the company ignores the units in transit, it would understate inventory quantities by 4,000 units (1,500 + 2,500).

**Consigned Goods**   In some lines of business, it is common to hold the goods of other parties and try to sell the goods for them for a fee, but without taking ownership of the goods. These are called **consigned goods**.

For example, you might have a used car that you would like to sell.

- If you take the item to a dealer, the dealer might be willing to put the car on its lot and charge you a commission if it is sold.
- Under this agreement, the dealer **would not take ownership** of the car, which would still belong to you.
- Therefore, if an inventory count were taken, the car would not be included in the dealer's inventory because the dealer does not own it.

Many car, boat, and antique dealers sell goods on consignment to keep their inventory costs down and to avoid the risk of purchasing an item that they will not be able to sell. Today, even some large companies arrange a form of consignment agreement with their suppliers, rather than a traditional purchase, in order to keep their inventory levels low. For example, prior to filing bankruptcy, **Sports Authority** became embroiled in lawsuits with suppliers over goods that it was holding on consignment. A judge ruled that Sports Authority had to comply with the suppliers' wishes since the consigned goods belonged to the suppliers.

## Anatomy of a Fraud

Ted Nickerson, CEO of clock manufacturer Dally Industries, had expensive tastes. To support this habit, Ted took out large loans, which he collateralized with his shares of Dally Industries stock. If the price of Dally's stock fell, he was required to provide the bank with more shares of stock. To achieve target net income figures and thus maintain the stock price, Ted coerced employees in the company to alter inventory figures. Inventory quantities were manipulated by changing the amounts on inventory control tags after the year-end physical inventory count. For example, if a tag said there were 20 units of a particular item, the tag was changed to 220. Similarly, the unit costs that were used to determine the value of ending inventory were increased from, for example, $125 per unit to $1,250. Both of these fraudulent changes had the effect of increasing the amount of reported ending inventory. This reduced cost of goods sold and increased net income.

**Total take: $245,000**

### The Missing Control

**Independent internal verification.** The company should have spot-checked its inventory records periodically, verifying that the number of units in the records agreed with the amount on hand and that the unit costs agreed with vendor price sheets.

**Source:** Adapted from Wells, *Fraud Casebook* (2007), pp. 502–509.

## DO IT! 1 | Rules of Ownership

Hasbeen Company completed its inventory count. It arrived at a total inventory value of $200,000. As a new member of Hasbeen's accounting department, you have been given the information listed below. Discuss how this information affects the reported cost of inventory.

1. Hasbeen included in the inventory goods held on consignment for Falls Co., costing $15,000.
2. The company did not include in the count purchased goods of $10,000 which were in transit (terms: FOB shipping point).
3. The company did not include in the count sold inventory with a cost of $12,000 which was in transit (terms: FOB shipping point).

**ACTION PLAN**

- **Apply the rules of ownership to goods held on consignment.**
- **Apply the rules of ownership to goods in transit.**

**Solution**

The goods of $15,000 held on consignment should be deducted from the inventory count. The goods of $10,000 purchased FOB shipping point should be added to the inventory count. Sold goods of $12,000 which were in transit FOB shipping point should not be included in the ending inventory. Thus, inventory should be carried at $195,000 ($200,000 − $15,000 + $10,000).

Related exercise material: **BE7.1, BE7.2, DO IT! 7.1, E7.1, E7.2, and E7.3**.

# Inventory Methods and Financial Effects

> **LEARNING OBJECTIVE 2**
>
> Apply inventory cost flow methods and discuss their financial effects.

Inventory is accounted for at cost.

- Cost includes all expenditures necessary to acquire goods and place them in a condition ready for sale.
- For example, freight costs incurred to acquire inventory are added to the cost of inventory, but the cost of shipping goods to a customer is a selling expense.
- After a company has determined the quantity of units of inventory, it applies unit costs to the quantities to compute the total cost of the inventory and the cost of goods sold.

This process can be complicated if a company has purchased inventory items at different times and at different prices.

For example, assume that Crivitz TV Company purchases three identical 50-inch TVs on different dates at costs of $700, $750, and $800. During the year, Crivitz sold two TVs at $1,200 each. These facts are summarized in **Illustration 7.2**.

**ILLUSTRATION 7.2**

**Data for inventory costing example**

| **Purchases** | | | |
|---|---|---|---|
| February 3 | 1 TV | at | $700 |
| March 5 | 1 TV | at | $750 |
| May 22 | 1 TV | at | $800 |
| **Sales** | | | |
| June 1 | 2 TVs | for | $2,400 ($1,200 × 2) |

Cost of goods sold will differ depending on which two TVs the company sold. For example, it might be $1,450 ($700 + $750), or $1,500 ($700 + $800), or $1,550 ($750 + $800). In this section, we discuss alternative costing methods available to Crivitz.

## Specific Identification

If Crivitz can positively identify which particular units it sold and which are still in ending inventory, it can use the **specific identification method** of inventory costing. For example, if Crivitz sold the TVs it purchased on February 3 and May 22, then its cost of goods sold is $1,500 ($700 + $800), and its ending inventory is $750 (see **Illustration 7.3**). Using this method, companies can accurately determine ending inventory and cost of goods sold.

Specific identification requires that companies keep records of the original cost of each individual inventory item.

- Historically, specific identification was possible only when a company sold a limited variety of high-unit-cost items that could be identified clearly from the time of purchase

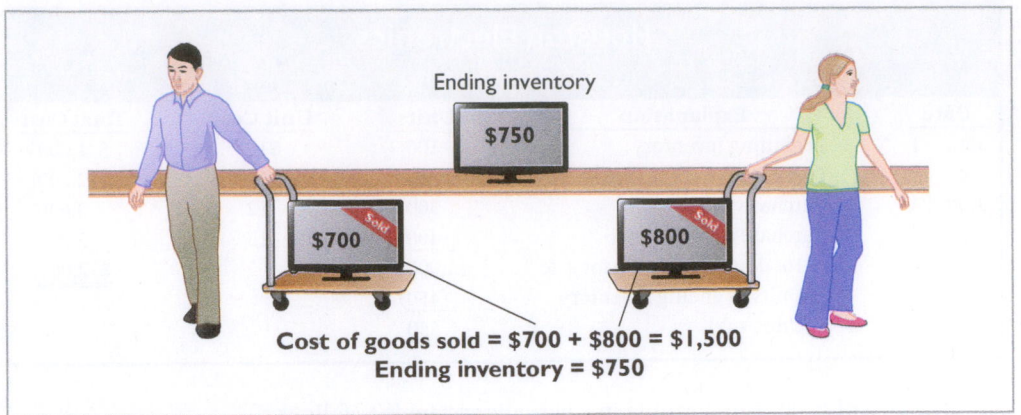

**ILLUSTRATION 7.3**
Specific identification method

through the time of sale. Examples of such products are cars, pianos, or expensive antiques (see **Ethics Note**).

- Today, bar coding, electronic product codes, and radio frequency identification make it theoretically possible to do specific identification with nearly any type of product. The reality is, however, that this practice is still relatively rare.

Instead, rather than keep track of the cost of each particular item sold, most companies make assumptions, called **cost flow assumptions**, about which units were sold.

## Cost Flow Assumptions

Because specific identification is often impractical, other cost flow methods are permitted. These differ from specific identification in that they **assume** flows of costs that may be unrelated to the physical flow of goods. There are three assumed cost flow methods:

1. First-in, first-out **(FIFO)**.
2. Last-in, first-out **(LIFO)**.
3. Average-cost.

**There is no accounting requirement that the cost flow assumption be consistent with the physical movement of the goods.** Company management selects the appropriate cost flow method.

To demonstrate the three cost flow methods, we will use a **periodic** inventory system.

- We assume a periodic system because **very few companies use perpetual LIFO, FIFO, or average-cost** to cost their inventory and related cost of goods sold.
- Instead, companies that use perpetual systems often use an assumed cost (called a standard cost) to record cost of goods sold at the time of sale.
- Then, at the end of the period when they count their inventory, they **recalculate cost of goods sold using periodic FIFO, LIFO, or average-cost** as shown in this chapter and adjust cost of goods sold to this recalculated number.[1]

To illustrate the three inventory cost flow methods, we will use the data for Houston Electronics' Astro condensers, shown in **Illustration 7.4**.

**ETHICS NOTE**

A major disadvantage of the specific identification method is that management may be able to manipulate net income. For example, it can boost net income by selling units purchased at a low cost, or reduce net income by selling units purchased at a high cost.

---

[1]Also, some companies use a perpetual system to keep track of units even though they do not use it to record cost of goods sold. In addition, firms that employ LIFO tend to use **dollar-value LIFO**, a method discussed in upper-level courses. FIFO periodic and FIFO perpetual give the same result. Therefore, companies should not incur the additional cost to use FIFO perpetual. Few companies use perpetual average-cost because of the added cost of recordkeeping. Finally, for instructional purposes, we believe it is easier to demonstrate the cost flow assumptions under the periodic system, which makes it more pedagogically appropriate.

**ILLUSTRATION 7.4**
**Data for Houston Electronics**

## Houston Electronics
### Astro Condensers

| Date | Explanation | Units | Unit Cost | Total Cost |
|------|-------------|-------|-----------|------------|
| Jan. 1 | Beginning inventory | 100 | $10 | $ 1,000 |
| Apr. 15 | Purchase | 200 | 11 | 2,200 |
| Aug. 24 | Purchase | 300 | 12 | 3,600 |
| Nov. 27 | Purchase | 400 | 13 | 5,200 |
| | Total units available for sale | 1,000 | | $12,000 |
| | Units in ending inventory | (450) | | |
| | Units sold | 550 | | |

The cost of goods sold formula in a periodic system is as follows.

$$\text{Beginning Inventory} \; + \; \text{Cost of Goods Purchased} \; - \; \text{Ending Inventory} \; = \; \text{Cost of Goods Sold}$$

Houston Electronics had a total of 1,000 units available to sell during the period (beginning inventory plus purchases). The total cost of these 1,000 units is $12,000, referred to as **cost of goods available for sale**. A physical inventory taken at December 31 determined that there were 450 units in ending inventory. Therefore, Houston sold 550 units (1,000 − 450) during the period. To determine the cost of the 550 units that were sold (the cost of goods sold):

- We assign a cost to the ending inventory and subtract that value from the cost of goods available for sale.

- The value assigned to the ending inventory **depends on which cost flow method we use.**

- No matter which cost flow assumption we use, though, the sum of cost of goods sold plus the cost of the ending inventory must equal the cost of goods available for sale—in this case, $12,000.

## First-In, First-Out (FIFO)

The **first-in, first-out (FIFO) method** assumes that the **earliest goods** purchased are the first to be sold.

- FIFO often parallels the actual physical flow of merchandise. That is, it generally is good business practice to sell the oldest units first.

- Under the FIFO method, therefore, the **costs** of the earliest goods purchased are the first to be recognized in determining cost of goods sold.

- This does not necessarily mean that the oldest units **are** sold first, but that the costs of the oldest units are **recognized** first. In a bin of nails at the hardware store, for example, no one really knows, nor would it matter, which nails are sold first.

**Illustration 7.5** shows the allocation of the cost of goods available for sale at Houston Electronics under FIFO (see **Helpful Hint**).

Under FIFO, since it is assumed that the first goods purchased were the first goods sold, ending inventory is based on the prices of the most recent units purchased (see **Helpful Hint**). That is, **under FIFO, companies obtain the cost of the ending inventory by taking the unit cost of the most recent purchase and working backward until all units of inventory have been costed**. In this example:

**HELPFUL HINT**

Another way of thinking about the calculation of FIFO ending inventory is the LISH assumption—last in still here.

1. Houston Electronics prices the 450 units of ending inventory using the **most recent** prices. The last purchase was 400 units at $13 on November 27.

2. The remaining 50 units are priced using the unit cost of the second most recent purchase, $12, on August 24.

3. Houston Electronics calculates cost of goods sold by subtracting the cost of the units **not sold** (ending inventory) from the cost of all goods available for sale.

ILLUSTRATION 7.5

**Allocation of costs—FIFO method**

## Cost of Goods Available for Sale

| Date | Explanation | Units | Unit Cost | Total Cost |
|------|-------------|-------|-----------|------------|
| Jan. 1 | Beginning inventory | 100 | $10 | $ 1,000 |
| Apr. 15 | Purchase | 200 | 11 | 2,200 |
| Aug. 24 | Purchase | 300 | 12 | 3,600 |
| Nov. 27 | Purchase | 400 | 13 | 5,200 |
| | Total | 1,000 | | **$12,000** |

## Step 1: Ending Inventory

| Date | Units | Unit Cost | Total Cost |
|------|-------|-----------|------------|
| Nov. 27 | 400 | $13 | $5,200 |
| Aug. 24 | 50 | 12 | 600 |
| Total | 450 | | **$5,800** |

## Step 2: Cost of Goods Sold

| | |
|---|---|
| Cost of goods available for sale | $12,000 |
| Less: Ending inventory | 5,800 |
| Cost of goods sold | **$ 6,200** |

HELPFUL HINT

Note the sequencing of the allocation: (1) compute ending inventory, and (2) determine cost of goods sold.

Illustration 7.6 demonstrates that companies also can calculate cost of goods sold by pricing the 550 units sold using the prices of the first 550 units acquired. Note that of the 300 units purchased on August 24, only 250 units are assumed sold. This agrees with our calculation of the cost of ending inventory, where 50 of these units were assumed unsold and thus included in ending inventory.

| Date | Units | Unit Cost | Total Cost |
|------|-------|-----------|------------|
| Jan. 1 | 100 | $10 | $1,000 |
| Apr. 15 | 200 | 11 | 2,200 |
| Aug. 24 | 250 | 12 | 3,000 |
| Total | 550 | | **$6,200** |

ILLUSTRATION 7.6

**Proof of cost of goods sold**

## DO IT! 2 | Cost Flow Methods—FIFO

**Part 1:** The accounting records of Shumway Ag Implements show the following data.

| | |
|---|---|
| Beginning inventory | 4,000 units at $3 |
| Purchases | 6,000 units at $4 |
| Sales | 7,000 units at $12 |

Determine the cost of goods sold during the period under a periodic inventory system using the FIFO method.

### Solution

Cost of goods available for sale = (4,000 × $3) + (6,000 × $4) = $36,000
Ending inventory = 10,000 − 7,000 = 3,000 units
Cost of goods sold (FIFO): $36,000 − (3,000 × $4) = $24,000

Related exercise material: **BE7.3, BE7.5, DO IT! 7.2, E7.4, E7.5, and E7.7.**

**ACTION PLAN**

- Determine cost of goods available for sale.
- Determine ending inventory units.
- Determine cost of ending inventory using cost of most recent purchase and working backward.
- Subtract cost of ending inventory from cost of goods available for sale.

## Last-In, First-Out (LIFO)

The **last-in, first-out (LIFO) method** assumes that the **latest goods** purchased are the first to be sold.

- LIFO seldom coincides with the actual physical flow of inventory. (Exceptions include goods stored in piles, such as coal or hay, where goods are removed from the top of the pile as they are sold.)
- Under the LIFO method, the **costs** of the latest goods purchased are the first to be recognized in determining cost of goods sold.

**Illustration 7.7** shows the allocation of the cost of goods available for sale at Houston Electronics under LIFO.

**ILLUSTRATION 7.7**

**Allocation of costs—LIFO method**

### Cost of Goods Available for Sale

| Date | Explanation | Units | Unit Cost | Total Cost |
|------|-------------|-------|-----------|------------|
| Jan.  1 | Beginning inventory | 100 | $10 | $ 1,000 |
| Apr. 15 | Purchase | 200 | 11 | 2,200 |
| Aug. 24 | Purchase | 300 | 12 | 3,600 |
| Nov. 27 | Purchase | 400 | 13 | 5,200 |
|  | Total | 1,000 |  | **$12,000** |

### Step 1: Ending Inventory

| Date | Units | Unit Cost | Total Cost |
|------|-------|-----------|------------|
| Jan.  1 | 100 | $10 | $1,000 |
| Apr. 15 | 200 | 11 | 2,200 |
| Aug. 24 | 150 | 12 | 1,800 |
| Total | 450 |  | **$5,000** |

### Step 2: Cost of Goods Sold

| | |
|---|---|
| Cost of goods available for sale | $12,000 |
| Less: Ending inventory | 5,000 |
| Cost of goods sold | **$ 7,000** |

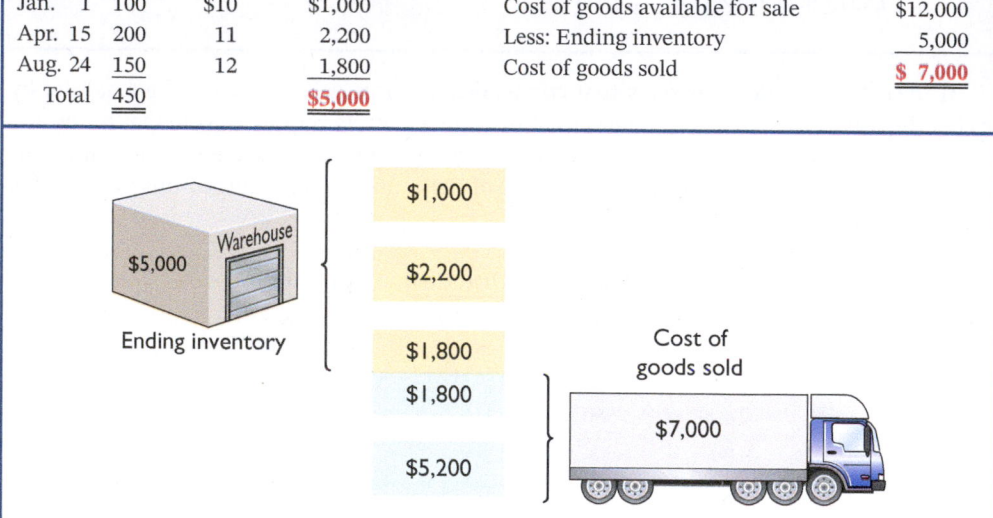

**HELPFUL HINT**

Another way of thinking about the calculation of LIFO ending inventory is the FISH assumption—first in still here.

Under LIFO, since it is assumed that the first goods sold were those that were most recently purchased, ending inventory is based on the prices of the oldest units purchased (see **Helpful Hint**). That is, **under LIFO, companies obtain the cost of the ending inventory by taking the unit cost of the earliest goods available for sale and working forward until all units of inventory have been costed**. In this example:

1.  Houston Electronics prices the 450 units of ending inventory using the **earliest** prices.
    - The first purchase was 100 units at $10 in the January 1 beginning inventory.
    - Then, 200 units were purchased at $11.
    - The remaining 150 units needed are priced at $12 per unit (August 24 purchase).

2. Houston Electronics calculates cost of goods sold by subtracting the cost of the units **not sold** (ending inventory) from the cost of all goods available for sale.

Illustration 7.8 demonstrates that companies also can calculate cost of goods sold by pricing the 550 units sold using the prices of the last 550 units acquired. Note that of the 300 units purchased on August 24, only 150 units are assumed sold. This agrees with our calculation of the cost of ending inventory, where 150 of these units were assumed unsold and thus included in ending inventory.

| Date | Units | Unit Cost | Total Cost |
|------|-------|-----------|------------|
| Nov. 27 | 400 | $13 | $5,200 |
| Aug. 24 | 150 | 12 | 1,800 |
| Total | 550 | | $7,000 |

**ILLUSTRATION 7.8**

**Proof of cost of goods sold**

Under a periodic inventory system, which we are using here, **all goods purchased during the period are assumed to be available for the first sale, regardless of the date of purchase**.

---

## DO IT! 2 | Cost Flow Methods—LIFO

**Part 2:** The accounting records of Shumway Ag Implements show the following data.

| | |
|---|---|
| Beginning inventory | 4,000 units at $3 |
| Purchases | 6,000 units at $4 |
| Sales | 7,000 units at $12 |

Determine the cost of goods sold during the period under a periodic inventory system using the LIFO method.

### Solution

Cost of goods available for sale = $(4,000 \times \$3) + (6,000 \times \$4) = \$36,000$
Ending inventory = $10,000 - 7,000 = 3,000$ units
Cost of goods sold (LIFO): $\$36,000 - (3,000 \times \$3) = \$27,000$

Related exercise material: **BE7.3, BE7.5, DO IT! 7.2, E7.4, E7.5, and E7.7.**

**ACTION PLAN**

- **Determine cost of goods available for sale.**
- **Determine ending inventory units.**
- **Determine cost of ending inventory using cost of earliest goods available for sale and working forward.**
- **Subtract cost of ending inventory from cost of goods available for sale.**

---

## Average-Cost

The **average-cost method** allocates the cost of goods available for sale on the basis of the **weighted-average unit cost** incurred. Illustration 7.9 presents the formula and a sample computation of the weighted-average unit cost.

| Cost of Goods Available for Sale | ÷ | Total Units Available for Sale | = | Weighted-Average Unit Cost |
|---|---|---|---|---|
| $12,000 | ÷ | 1,000 | = | $12 |

**ILLUSTRATION 7.9**

**Formula for weighted-average unit cost**

The company then applies the weighted-average unit cost to the units on hand to determine the cost of the ending inventory. Illustration 7.10 shows the allocation of the cost of goods available for sale at Houston Electronics using average-cost.

**Allocation of costs—average-cost method**

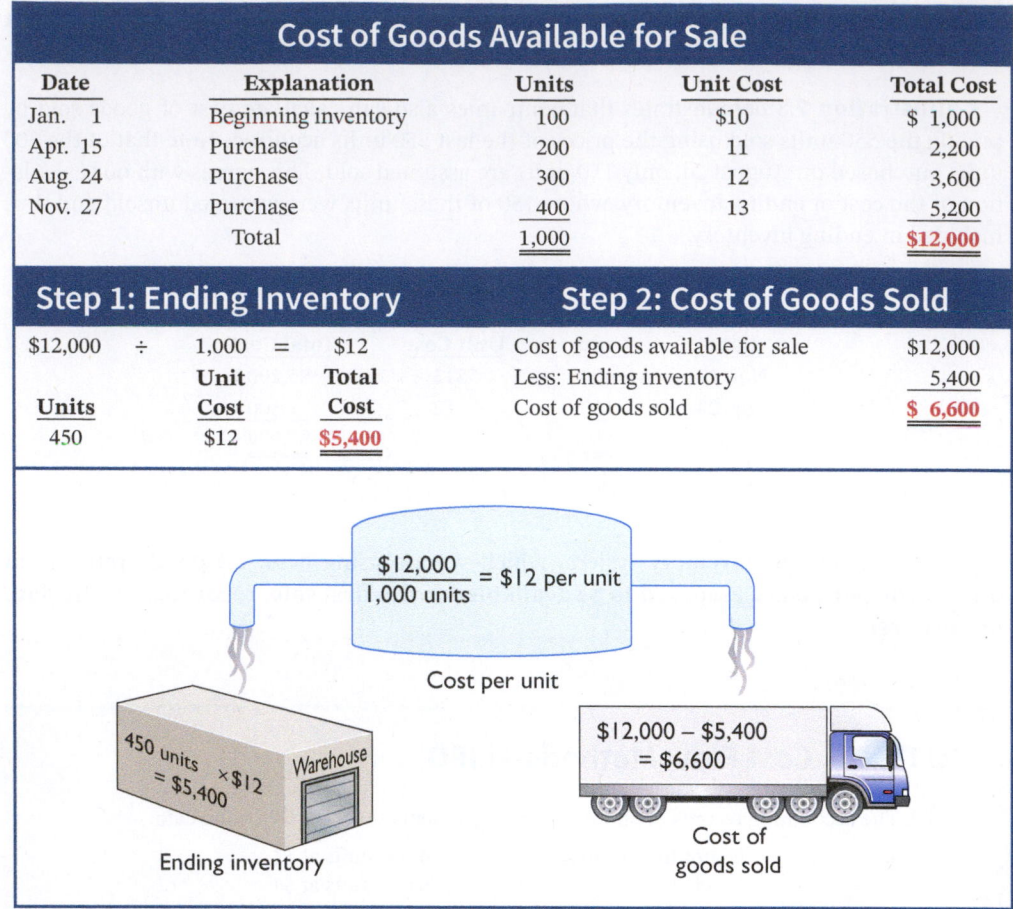

## Cost of Goods Available for Sale

| Date | Explanation | Units | Unit Cost | Total Cost |
|---|---|---|---|---|
| Jan.  1 | Beginning inventory | 100 | $10 | $ 1,000 |
| Apr. 15 | Purchase | 200 | 11 | 2,200 |
| Aug. 24 | Purchase | 300 | 12 | 3,600 |
| Nov. 27 | Purchase | 400 | 13 | 5,200 |
| | Total | 1,000 | | $12,000 |

### Step 1: Ending Inventory

$12,000 ÷ 1,000 = $12

| Units | Unit Cost | Total Cost |
|---|---|---|
| 450 | $12 | $5,400 |

### Step 2: Cost of Goods Sold

| | |
|---|---|
| Cost of goods available for sale | $12,000 |
| Less: Ending inventory | 5,400 |
| Cost of goods sold | $ 6,600 |

We can verify the cost of goods sold under this method by multiplying the units sold times the weighted-average unit cost (550 × $12 = $6,600).

- Note that this method does **not** use the average of the unit costs; that average is $11.50 ($10 + $11 + $12 + $13 = $46; $46 ÷ 4).

- The average-cost method instead uses the average **weighted by** the quantities purchased at each unit cost.

---

- **Determine cost of goods available for sale.**
- **Determine average cost by dividing cost of goods available for sale by total units available for sale.**
- **Multiply units sold by average cost per unit.**

## DO IT! 2 | Cost Flow Methods—Average-Cost

**Part 3:** The accounting records of Shumway Ag Implements show the following data.

| | |
|---|---|
| Beginning inventory | 4,000 units at $3 |
| Purchases | 6,000 units at $4 |
| Sales | 7,000 units at $12 |

Determine the cost of goods sold during the period under a periodic inventory system using the average-cost method.

### Solution

Cost of goods available for sale = (4,000 × $3) + (6,000 × $4) = $36,000
Ending inventory = 10,000 − 7,000 = 3,000 units
Average cost per unit: [(4,000 @ $3) + (6,000 @ $4)] ÷ 10,000 = $3.60
Ending inventory = 3,000 × $3.60 = $10,800
Cost of goods sold (average-cost): $36,000 − $10,800 = $25,200, or 7,000 × $3.60 = $25,200

Related exercise material: **BE7.4, BE7.5, DO IT! 7.2, E7.4, E7.5, and E7.7.**

# Financial Statement and Tax Effects of Cost Flow Methods

Each of the three assumed cost flow methods is acceptable for use. **Illustration 7.11** shows the use of the three cost flow methods in 500 large U.S. companies.

The reasons companies adopt different inventory cost flow methods are varied, but they usually involve one of three factors:

1. Income statement effects.
2. Balance sheet effects.
3. Tax effects (see **Decision Tools**).

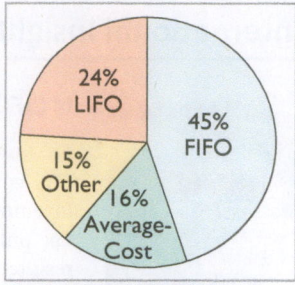

**Use of cost flow methods in major U.S. companies**

## Income Statement Effects

In periods of changing prices, the cost flow assumption can have significant impacts both on income and on evaluations of income, such as the following.

1. In a period of inflation, FIFO produces a higher net income because lower unit costs of the first units purchased are matched against revenue.
2. In a period of inflation, LIFO produces a lower net income because higher unit costs of the last goods purchased are matched against revenue.
3. If prices are falling, the results from the use of FIFO and LIFO are reversed. FIFO will report the lowest net income and LIFO the highest.
4. Regardless of whether prices are rising or falling, average-cost produces net income between FIFO and LIFO.

> **Decision Tools**
>
> Analyzing financial statement and tax effects helps users determine which inventory costing method best meets the company's objectives.

To management, higher net income is an advantage. It causes external users to view the company more favorably. In addition, management bonuses, if based on net income, will be higher. Therefore, when prices are rising (which is usually the case), companies tend to prefer FIFO because it results in higher net income.

Others believe that LIFO presents a more realistic net income number.

- LIFO matches the more recent costs against current revenues to provide a better measure of net income.
- During periods of inflation, many challenge the quality of non-LIFO earnings, noting that failing to match current costs against current revenues leads to an understatement of cost of goods sold and an overstatement of net income.
- As some indicate, net income computed using FIFO creates **"paper or phantom profits"**— that is, earnings that do not really exist.

## Balance Sheet Effects

A major advantage of the FIFO method is that in a period of inflation, the costs allocated to ending inventory will approximate the inventory's current cost.

- Conversely, a major shortcoming of the LIFO method is that in a period of inflation, the costs allocated to ending inventory may be significantly understated in terms of current cost.
- The understatement becomes greater over prolonged periods of inflation if the inventory includes goods purchased in one or more prior accounting periods.

For example, **Caterpillar** has used LIFO for more than 50 years. Its balance sheet shows ending inventory of $9,700 million. But the inventory's actual current cost if FIFO had been used is $12,189 million.

## Tax Effects

We have seen that both inventory on the balance sheet and net income on the income statement are higher when companies use FIFO in a period of inflation. Yet, many companies have selected LIFO. Why? The reason is that LIFO results in the lowest income taxes (because of lower net income) during times of rising prices (see **Helpful Hint**).

> **HELPFUL HINT**
>
> A tax rule, often referred to as the LIFO conformity rule, requires that if companies use LIFO for tax purposes they must also use it for financial reporting purposes. This means that if a company chooses the LIFO method to reduce its tax bills, it will also have to report lower net income in its financial statements.

---

### International Insight    ExxonMobil Corporation

Bloomberg/Getty Images

#### Is LIFO Fair?

**ExxonMobil Corporation**, like many U.S. companies, uses LIFO to value its inventory for financial reporting and tax purposes. In one recent year, this resulted in a cost of goods sold figure that was $5.6 billion higher than under FIFO. By increasing cost of goods sold, ExxonMobil reduces net income, which reduces taxes. Critics say that LIFO provides an unfair "tax dodge." As Congress looks for more sources of tax revenue, some lawmakers favor the elimination of LIFO. Supporters of LIFO argue that the method is conceptually sound because it matches current costs with current revenues. In addition, they point out that this matching provides protection against inflation.

International accounting standards do not allow the use of LIFO. Because of this, the net income of foreign oil companies such as **BP** and **Royal Dutch Shell** are not directly comparable to U.S. companies, which can make analysis difficult.

**Source:** David Reilly, "Big Oil's Accounting Methods Fuel Criticism," *Wall Street Journal* (August 8, 2006), p. C1.

**What are the arguments for and against the use of LIFO? (Go to WileyPLUS for this answer and additional questions.)**

---

# Reporting Receivables

**LEARNING OBJECTIVE 3**
Explain how companies recognize and value receivables.

The term **receivables** refers to amounts due from individuals and companies.

- Receivables are claims that are expected to be collected in cash.
- The management of receivables is a very important activity for any company that sells goods or services on credit.

Receivables are important because they represent one of a company's most liquid assets. For many companies, receivables are also one of the largest assets. For example, receivables represent 18.5% of the assets of **Nike**. **Illustration 7.12** lists receivables as a percentage of total assets for five other well-known companies in a recent year.

**ILLUSTRATION 7.12**

**Receivables as a percentage of assets**

| Company | Receivables as a Percentage of Total Assets |
|---|---|
| Ford Motor Company | 43.2% |
| General Electric (GE) | 41.5 |
| Minnesota Mining and Manufacturing Company (3M) | 12.7 |
| DuPont | 11.7 |
| Intel Corporation | 3.9 |

## Types of Receivables

The relative significance of a company's receivables as a percentage of its assets depends on various factors: its industry, the time of year, whether it extends long-term financing, and its credit policies. To reflect important differences among receivables, they are frequently classified as:

- **Accounts receivable**, which are amounts customers owe on account. They result from the sale of goods and services. Companies generally expect to collect accounts receivable within 30 to 60 days. They are usually the most significant type of claim held by a company.
- **Notes receivable**, which are a written promise (as evidenced by a formal instrument) for amounts to be received. The note normally requires the collection of interest and extends

for time periods of 60–90 days or longer. Notes and accounts receivable that result from sales transactions are often called **trade receivables**.

- **Other receivables**, which include nontrade receivables such as interest receivable, loans to company officers, advances to employees, and income taxes refundable. These do not generally result from the operations of the business. Therefore, they are generally classified and reported as separate items in the balance sheet (see **Ethics Note**).

# Recognizing Accounts Receivable

Recognizing accounts receivable is relatively straightforward.

- A service organization records a receivable when it performs a service on account.
- A merchandiser records accounts receivable at the point of sale of merchandise on account.
- When a merchandiser sells goods, it increases Accounts Receivable and increases Sales Revenue.

The seller may offer terms that encourage early payment by providing a discount. Discounts reduce sales revenue and accounts receivable. Sometimes a buyer might find some of the goods unacceptable and choose to return the unwanted goods. Sales returns also reduce revenues and receivables.

# Valuing Accounts Receivable

Once companies record receivables in the accounts, the next question is: How should they report receivables in the financial statements?

- Companies report accounts receivable on the balance sheet as an asset.
- Determining the **amount** to report is sometimes difficult because some receivables will become uncollectible.

Although each customer must satisfy the credit requirements of the seller before the credit sale is approved, inevitably some accounts receivable become uncollectible. For example, a corporate customer may not be able to pay because it experienced a sales decline due to an economic downturn. Similarly, individuals may be laid off from their jobs or be faced with unexpected hospital bills. The seller records these losses that result from extending credit as **Bad Debt Expense** (see **Alternative Terminology**). Such losses are a normal and necessary risk of doing business on a credit basis.

When U.S. home prices fell, home foreclosures rose, and the economy in general slowed as a result of the financial crisis of 2008, lenders experienced huge increases in their bad debt expense. For example, during one quarter **Wachovia**, a large U.S. bank now owned by **Wells Fargo**, increased bad debt expense from $108 million to $408 million. Similarly, **American Express** increased its bad debt expense by 70%.

Two methods are used in accounting for uncollectible accounts:

1. The direct write-off method.
2. The allowance method.

## Direct Write-Off Method for Uncollectible Accounts

Under the **direct write-off method**, when a company determines receivables from a particular company to be uncollectible, it charges the loss to Bad Debt Expense. Assume, for example, that Warden Co. writes off M. E. Doran's $200 balance as uncollectible on December 12. Warden records the write-off as follows.

| CASH FLOW | BALANCE SHEET | | | | | | | | INCOME STATEMENT |
|---|---|---|---|---|---|---|---|---|---|
| | **Assets** | **=** | **Liabilities** | **+** | **Stockholders' Equity** | | | | |
| | | | | | Common | | Retained Earnings | | |
| | Accounts | | | | Stock | Rev. | Exp. | Div. | |
| | Rec. | = | | + | | − | − | − | |
| No effect | −$200 | | | | | | −$200 | | Bad Debt Exp. |

Under this method:

- Bad debt expense will show only **actual losses** from uncollectibles.
- The company reports accounts receivable at its gross amount without any adjustment for estimated losses for bad debts.

Use of the direct write-off method can reduce the usefulness of both the income statement and balance sheet. Under the direct write-off method, companies often record bad debt expense in a period after the period in which they recorded the revenue. Thus, no attempt is made to align bad debt expense to sales revenue in the income statement. Nor does the company try to show accounts receivable in the balance sheet at the amount actually expected to be received. Consequently, unless a company expects bad debt losses to be insignificant, **the direct write-off method is not acceptable for financial reporting purposes.**

## Allowance Method for Uncollectible Accounts

The **allowance method** of accounting for bad debts involves estimating uncollectible accounts at the end of each period. This provides a closer relationship of expenses with revenues on the income statement.

- It ensures that receivables are stated at their cash (net) realizable value on the balance sheet.
- **Cash (net) realizable value** is the net amount a company expects to receive in cash from receivables; it excludes amounts that the company estimates it will not collect.

> **HELPFUL HINT**
>
> In this context, *material* means significant or important to financial statement users.

Estimated uncollectible receivables therefore reduce the amount of receivables reported on the balance sheet through use of the allowance method.

**Companies must use the allowance method for financial reporting purposes when bad debts are material in amount** (see **Helpful Hint**). It has three essential features:

> **HELPFUL HINT**
>
> Recall from the discussion of Accumulated Depreciation that a contra asset account is offset against an asset account on the balance sheet.

1. Companies **estimate** uncollectible accounts receivable and **match them against revenues** in the same accounting period in which the revenues are recorded.
2. Companies record estimated uncollectibles as an increase to Bad Debt Expense and an increase to Allowance for Doubtful Accounts through an adjustment at the end of each period. Allowance for Doubtful Accounts is a contra asset account to Accounts Receivable (see **Helpful Hint**).
3. Companies record actual uncollectibles by decreasing the Allowance for Doubtful Accounts and Accounts Receivable at the time the specific account is written off as uncollectible.

**Recording Estimated Uncollectibles**  To illustrate the allowance method, assume that in its first year of operations, Hampson Furniture has credit sales of $1,200,000 in 2022, of which $200,000 remains uncollected at December 31. The credit manager estimates that $12,000 of these receivables will prove uncollectible. The adjustment to record the estimated uncollectibles increases Bad Debt Expense and increases Allowance for Doubtful Accounts, as follows.

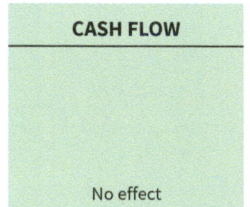
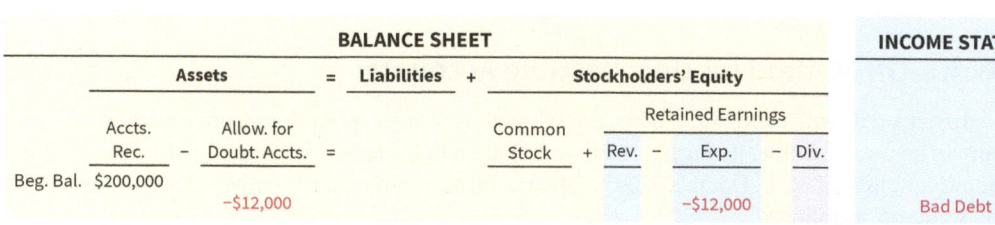

Companies report Bad Debt Expense in the income statement as an operating expense (usually as a selling expense). Thus, Hampson matches the estimated uncollectibles with sales in 2022 because the expense is recorded in the same year the company makes the sales.

Allowance for Doubtful Accounts shows the estimated amount of claims on customers that companies expect will become uncollectible in the future.

- Companies use a contra account instead of a direct reduction to Accounts Receivable because they do not know which customers will not pay.
- The balance in the allowance account will absorb the specific write-offs when they occur.
- The company deducts the allowance account from Accounts Receivable in the current assets section of the balance sheet, as shown in **Illustration 7.13**.

| Hampson Furniture | | |
|---|---|---|
| **Balance Sheet (partial)** | | |
| Current assets | | |
| Cash | | $ 14,800 |
| **Accounts receivable** | $200,000 | |
| **Less: Allowance for doubtful accounts** | 12,000 | 188,000 |
| Inventory | | 310,000 |
| Supplies | | 25,000 |
| Total current assets | | $537,800 |

**ILLUSTRATION 7.13**

**Presentation of allowance for doubtful accounts**

The amount of $188,000 in Illustration 7.13 represents the expected **cash realizable value** of the accounts receivable at the statement date.

**Recording the Write-Off of an Uncollectible Account**   Various methods are used to collect past-due accounts. When a company exhausts all means of collecting a past-due account and collection appears unlikely, the company writes off the account.

- In the credit card industry, it is standard practice to write off accounts that are 210 days past due.
- To prevent premature or unauthorized write-offs, authorized management personnel should formally approve each write-off.
- **To maintain segregation of duties, the employee authorized to write off accounts should not have daily responsibilities related to cash or receivables.**

To illustrate a receivables write-off, assume that the vice president of finance of Hampson Furniture on March 1, 2023, authorizes a write-off of the $500 balance owed by R. A. Ware. The write-off is recorded as follows.

| CASH FLOW | | BALANCE SHEET | | | | | | | | | INCOME STATEMENT |
|---|---|---|---|---|---|---|---|---|---|---|---|
| | | Assets | | = Liabilities + | | Stockholders' Equity | | | | | |
| | | | | | | | | Retained Earnings | | | |
| | | Accts. Receiv. | − | Allow. for Doubt. Accts. = | | Common Stock | + | Rev. − | Exp. | − Div. | |
| | Beg. Bal. | $200,000 | | −$12,000 | | | | | | | |
| | | −500 | | +500 | | | | | | | |
| No effect | End. Bal. | $199,500 | | −$11,500 | | | | | | | No effect |

The company does not increase Bad Debt Expense when the write-off occurs. **Under the allowance method, a company records every bad debt write-off to the allowance account and not to Bad Debt Expense.**

A write-off affects only balance sheet accounts. Cash realizable value in the balance sheet, therefore, remains the same before and after the write-off, as shown in **Illustration 7.14**.

| | Before Write-Off | After Write-Off |
|---|---|---|
| Accounts receivable | $200,000 | $199,500 |
| Less: Allowance for doubtful accounts | 12,000 | 11,500 |
| **Cash realizable value** | **$188,000** | **$188,000** |

**ILLUSTRATION 7.14**

**Cash realizable value comparison**

**Estimating the Allowance**  For Hampson Furniture in Illustration 7.13, the amount of the expected uncollectibles was given. However, in "real life," companies must estimate the amount of expected uncollectible accounts if they use the allowance method, generally using one of the following two methods:

1. The **percentage-of-receivables basis**, where management establishes a percentage relationship between the amount of receivables and expected losses from uncollectible accounts (see **Helpful Hint**). For an example of applying this method, see **DO IT! 3**.

2. **Aging the accounts receivable**, which is a schedule that classifies customer balances by the length of time they have been unpaid (see **Decision Tools**).

When the second method is used, after the company arranges the accounts by age, it determines the expected bad debt losses by applying percentages, based on past experience, to the totals of each category. The longer a receivable is past due, the less likely it is to be collected. As a result, the estimated percentage of uncollectible debts increases as the number of days past due increases. **Illustration 7.15** shows an aging schedule for Dart Company (see **Helpful Hint**). Note the increasing uncollectible percentages from 2% to 40%.

| | A | B | C | D | E | F | G |
|---|---|---|---|---|---|---|---|
| 1 | | | | | Number of Days Past Due | | |
| 2 | | | Not | | | | |
| 3 | Customer | Total | Yet Due | 1–30 | 31–60 | 61–90 | Over 90 |
| 4 | T. E. Adert | $ 600 | | $ 300 | | $ 200 | $ 100 |
| 5 | R. C. Bortz | 300 | $ 300 | | | | |
| 6 | B. A. Carl | 450 | | 200 | $ 250 | | |
| 7 | O. L. Diker | 700 | 500 | | | 200 | |
| 8 | T. O. Ebbet | 600 | | | 300 | | 300 |
| 9 | Others | 36,950 | 26,200 | 5,200 | 2,450 | 1,600 | 1,500 |
| 10 | | $39,600 | $27,000 | $5,700 | $3,000 | $2,000 | $1,900 |
| 11 | Estimated percentage uncollectible | | | 2% | 4% | 10% | 20% | 40% |
| 12 | Total estimated uncollectible accounts | $ 2,228 | $ 540 | $ 228 | $ 300 | $ 400 | $ 760 |
| 13 | | | | | | | |

Total estimated uncollectible accounts for Dart Company ($2,228) represent the existing customer claims expected to become uncollectible in the future.

- Thus, this amount represents the **required balance** in Allowance for Doubtful Accounts at the balance sheet date.

- Accordingly, **the amount of bad debt expense that should be recorded in the adjustment is the difference between the required balance and the existing balance in the allowance account**.

- The existing, unadjusted balance in Allowance for Doubtful Accounts is the net result of the beginning balance less the write-offs of specific accounts during the year.

For example, if the unadjusted balance in Allowance for Doubtful Accounts is $528, then an adjustment for $1,700 ($2,228 − $528) is necessary:

| CASH FLOW | | BALANCE SHEET | | | | | | | | INCOME STATEMENT |
|---|---|---|---|---|---|---|---|---|---|---|
| | | Assets | = | Liabilities | + | | Stockholders' Equity | | | |
| | | | | | | | | Retained Earnings | | |
| | Accts. Receiv. | Allow. for Doubt. Accts. | = | | | Common Stock | + Rev. − | Exp. | − Div. | |
| | Beg. Bal. $39,600 | −$528 −1,700 | | | | | | −$1,700 | | Bad Debt Exp. |
| No effect | Adj. Bal. | −$2,228 | | | | | | | | |

# Data Analytics and Receivables Management

Opportunities abound to improve receivables management through data analytics.

- Software packages promise increases in working capital, improved revenues, and enhanced customer relations.
- So-called visualization software, which presents data in sophisticated graph format, enables managers to more quickly identify issues and obtain a deeper understanding of the factors that influence successful receivables management.
- Use of such software helps identify which currencies, sales representatives, customers, product lines, or geographic regions need closer attention. This sometimes enables management to do a more granular investigation of the cash-to-cash cycle time to evaluate which product lines are meeting company goals.

Data analytics of receivables is particularly valuable for predictive analysis, which allows improved evaluation of customers' risk profiles. In many instances, the company can identify risky customers and take corrective action before problems arise. Software provided by companies such as **Workday** use artificial intelligence to forecast which customers are likely to pay late.

## Ethics Insight

### Cookie Jar Allowances

Christy Thompson/
Shutterstock.com

There are many pressures on companies to achieve earnings targets. For managers, poor earnings can lead to dismissal or lack of promotion. It is not surprising, then, that management may be tempted to look for ways to boost their earnings number.

One way a company can achieve greater earnings is to lower its estimate of what is needed in its Allowance for Doubtful Accounts (sometimes referred to as "tapping the cookie jar"). For example, suppose a company has an Allowance for Doubtful Accounts of $10 million and decides to reduce this balance to $9 million.

As a result of this change, Bad Debt Expense decreases by $1 million and earnings increase by $1 million.

Large banks such as **JPMorgan Chase**, **Wells Fargo**, and **Bank of America** recently decreased their Allowance for Doubtful Accounts by over $4 billion. These reductions came at a time when these big banks were still suffering from lower mortgage lending and trading activity, both of which lead to lower earnings. They justified these reductions in the allowance balances by noting that credit quality and economic conditions had improved. This may be so, but it sure is great to have a cookie jar that might be tapped when a boost in earnings is needed.

**How might investors determine that a company is managing its earnings? (Go to WileyPLUS for this answer and additional questions.)**

## DO IT! 3 | Bad Debt Expense

Brule Corporation has been in business for 5 years. The unadjusted balance at the end of the current year shows Accounts Receivable $30,000, Sales Revenue $180,000, and Allowance for Doubtful Accounts $500. Brule estimates bad debts to be 10% of accounts receivable. Record the adjustment to Allowance for Doubtful Accounts in a tabular summary.

### Solution

Brule should make the following adjustment to Allowance for Doubtful Accounts to bring it to a balance of $3,000 (10% × $30,000):

| | Assets | | = | Liabilities | + | Stockholders' Equity | | | | |
|---|---|---|---|---|---|---|---|---|---|---|
| | Accts. Receiv. | Allow. for Doubt. Accts. | | | | Common Stock | Retained Earnings | | | |
| | | | | | | | Rev. | Exp. | Div. | |
| Beg. Bal. | $30,000 | −$500 | | | | | +$180,000 | | | |
| | | −2,500 | | | | | | −$2,500 | | Bad Debt Exp. |
| Adj. Bal. | | −$3,000 | | | | | | | | |

Related exercise material: **BE7.10, BE7.11, DO IT! 7.3, E7.9, E7.10, and E7.11.**

### ACTION PLAN

- **Estimate the amount the company does not expect to collect.**
- **Consider the existing balance in the allowance account when using the percentage-of-receivables basis.**
- **Report receivables at their cash (net) realizable value—that is, the amount the company expects to collect in cash.**

# Inventory Presentation and Analysis

> **LEARNING OBJECTIVE 4**
> Explain the statement presentation and analysis of inventory.

## Presentation

Recall that inventory is classified in the balance sheet as a current asset immediately below receivables. In a multiple-step income statement, cost of goods sold is subtracted from net sales. There also should be disclosure of:

1. The major inventory classifications.
2. The cost method (FIFO, LIFO, or average-cost).

Walmart Inc., for example, in its January 31, 2017, balance sheet reported inventories of $43,046 million under current assets. The accompanying notes to the financial statements, as shown in Illustration 7.16, disclosed the following information.

**ILLUSTRATION 7.16**

Inventory disclosures by Walmart

Real World

---

### Walmart Inc.
#### Notes to the Financial Statements

**Note 1. Summary of Significant Accounting Policies**

**Inventories**

The Company values inventories at the lower of cost or market as determined primarily by the retail method of accounting, using the last-in, first-out ("LIFO") method for substantially all of the Walmart U.S. segment's inventories. The inventory at the Walmart International segment is valued primarily by the retail inventory method of accounting, using the first-in, first-out ("FIFO") method. The retail method of accounting results in inventory being valued at the lower of cost or market since permanent markdowns are immediately recorded as a reduction of the retail value of inventory. The inventory at the Sam's Club segment is valued using the LIFO method. At January 31, 2017 and 2016, the Company's inventories valued at LIFO approximate those inventories as if they were valued at FIFO.

---

## Analysis

For companies that sell goods, managing inventory levels can be one of the most critical tasks.

- Having too much inventory on hand costs the company money in storage costs, interest costs (on funds tied up in inventory), and costs associated with the obsolescence of technical goods (e.g., computer chips) or shifts in fashion (e.g., clothes).
- Having too little inventory on hand results in lost sales.

### Data Analytics and Inventory Management

Clearly, inventory management is an area that benefits from data analytics.

- Companies such as Walmart collect massive amounts of data about every inventory item and every customer.
- They analyze customer habits, buying patterns, and sales trends.
- Using sophisticated models that incorporate economic variables, weather patterns, and many other factors, they strive to optimize inventory levels to maximize sales while minimizing inventory holding costs.

Next, we discuss some issues related to evaluating inventory levels.

## Inventory Turnover

The **inventory turnover** is calculated as cost of goods sold divided by average inventory.

- It indicates the liquidity of inventory by measuring the number of times the average inventory "turns over" (is sold) during the year.
- Inventory turnover can be divided into 365 days to compute **days in inventory**, which indicates the average number of days inventory is held (see **Decision Tools**).

**Decision Tools**

Inventory turnover and days in inventory help users determine how long an item is in inventory.

High inventory turnover (low days in inventory) indicates the company has minimal funds tied up in inventory—that it has a minimal amount of inventory on hand at any one time. Although minimizing the funds tied up in inventory is efficient, too high an inventory turnover may indicate that the company is losing sales opportunities because of inventory shortages. For example, investment analysts at one time suggested that **Office Depot** had gone too far in reducing its inventory—they said they were seeing too many empty shelves. Thus, management should closely monitor this ratio to achieve the best balance between too much and too little inventory.

We have previously discussed the increasingly competitive environment of retailers, such as **Walmart** and **Target**. Walmart has implemented inventory management procedures as well as many technological innovations to improve the efficiency of its inventory management. The following data are available for Walmart at January 31, 2017 (labeled 2016), and January 31, 2016 (labeled 2015).

| (in millions) | 2016 | 2015 |
|---|---|---|
| Ending inventory | $ 43,046 | $44,469 |
| Cost of goods sold | 361,256 | |

**Illustration 7.17** presents the inventory turnovers and days in inventory for Walmart and Target, using data from the financial statements of those corporations for 2016 and 2015.

$$\text{Inventory Turnover} = \frac{\text{Cost of Goods Sold}}{\text{Average Inventory}}$$

$$\text{Days in Inventory} = \frac{365}{\text{Inventory Turnover}}$$

| Ratio | Walmart ($ in millions) 2016 | 2015 | Target 2016 |
|---|---|---|---|
| Inventory turnover | $\dfrac{\$361,256}{(\$43,046 + \$44,469) \div 2} = 8.3$ times | 8.1 times | 5.8 times |
| Days in inventory | $\dfrac{365 \text{ days}}{8.3} = 44.0$ days | 45.1 days | 62.9 days |

**ILLUSTRATION 7.17**

**Inventory turnover and days in inventory**

The calculations in Illustration 7.17 show that Walmart turns its inventory more frequently than Target (8.3 times for Walmart versus 5.8 times for Target). Consequently, the average time an item spends on a Walmart shelf is shorter (44.0 days for Walmart versus 62.9 days for Target).

This analysis suggests that Walmart is more efficient than Target in its inventory management. Walmart's sophisticated inventory tracking and distribution system allows it to keep minimum amounts of inventory on hand, while still keeping the shelves full of what customers are looking for.

Many other companies have also significantly lowered inventory levels and costs using **just-in-time (JIT) inventory** methods.

- Under a just-in-time method, companies manufacture or purchase goods only when needed.

- **Dell** is famous for having developed a system for making computers in response to individual customer requests. Even though it makes each computer to meet each customer's particular specifications, Dell is able to assemble the computer and put it on a truck in less than 48 hours.

- The success of the JIT system depends on reliable suppliers. By integrating its information systems with those of its suppliers, Dell reduced its inventories to nearly zero. This is a huge advantage in an industry where products become obsolete nearly overnight.

---

## Accounting Across the Organization    Sony

iStock.com/
Dmitry Kutlayev

### Too Many TVs or Too Few?

Financial analysts closely monitor the inventory management practices of companies. For example, some analysts following **Sony** expressed concern because the company built up its inventory of televisions in an attempt to sell 25 million liquid crystal display (LCD) TVs—a 60% increase over the prior year. A year earlier, Sony had cut its inventory levels so that its quarterly days in inventory was down to 38 days, compared to 61 days for the same quarter a year before

that. But in the next year, as a result of its inventory build-up, days in inventory rose to 59 days. Management said that it didn't think that Sony's inventory levels were too high. However, analysts were concerned that the company would have to engage in very heavy discounting in order to sell off its inventory. Analysts noted that the losses from discounting can be "punishing."

**Source:** Daisuke Wakabayashi, "Sony Pledges to Corral Inventory," *Wall Street Journal Online* (November 2, 2010).

**For Sony, what are the advantages and disadvantages of having a low days in inventory measure? (Go to WileyPLUS for this answer and additional questions.)**

---

### ACTION PLAN

- **To find the inventory turnover, divide cost of goods sold by average inventory.**
- **To determine days in inventory, divide 365 days by the inventory turnover.**

## DO IT! 4 | Inventory Turnover

Early in 2022, Westmoreland Company switched to a just-in-time inventory system. Its sales revenue, cost of goods sold, and inventory amounts for 2021 and 2022 are as follows.

|  | 2021 | 2022 |
|---|---|---|
| Sales revenue | $2,000,000 | $1,800,000 |
| Cost of goods sold | 1,000,000 | 910,000 |
| Beginning inventory | 290,000 | 210,000 |
| Ending inventory | 210,000 | 50,000 |

Determine the inventory turnover and days in inventory for 2021 and 2022. Discuss the changes in the amount of inventory, the inventory turnover and days in inventory, and the amount of sales across the two years.

### Solution

|  | 2021 | 2022 |
|---|---|---|
| Inventory turnover | $\dfrac{\$1,000,000}{(\$290,000 + \$210,000) \div 2} = 4$ | $\dfrac{\$910,000}{(\$210,000 + \$50,000) \div 2} = 7$ |
| Days in inventory | $365 \div 4 = 91.3$ days | $365 \div 7 = 52.1$ days |

The company experienced a very significant decline in its ending inventory as a result of the just-in-time inventory. This decline improved its inventory turnover and its days in inventory. However, its sales declined by 10%. It is possible that this decline was caused by the dramatic reduction in the amount of inventory that was on hand, which increased the likelihood of running out of specific types of inventory, referred to as "stock-outs." To determine the optimal inventory level, management must weigh the benefits of reduced inventory against the potential lost sales caused by stock-outs.

Related exercise material: **BE7.12, DO IT! 7.4, E7.12, and E7.13.**

## USING THE DECISION TOOLS | The Manitowoc Company

**The Manitowoc Company** is located in Manitowoc, Wisconsin. It has made a series of strategic acquisitions to grow and enhance its market-leading positions in each of its three business segments: (1) cranes and related products (crawler cranes, tower cranes, and boom trucks), (2) food service equipment (commercial ice-cube machines, ice-beverage dispensers, and commercial refrigeration equipment), and (3) marine operations (shipbuilding and ship-repair services). The company reported inventory of $644.5 million for 2014 and of $720.8 million for 2013. Here is the inventory note taken from the 2014 financial statements.

**The Manitowoc Company**
**Notes to the Financial Statements**

**Inventories:** The components of inventories at December 31, 2014, and December 31, 2013, are summarized as follows:

| (in millions) | 2014 | 2013 |
|---|---|---|
| Inventories—gross: | | |
| Raw materials | $226.2 | $259.0 |
| Work in process | 103.7 | 130.2 |
| Finished goods | 414.8 | 436.8 |
| Total inventories—gross | 744.7 | 826.0 |
| Excess and obsolete inventory reserve | (64.0) | (69.0) |
| Net inventories at FIFO cost | 680.7 | 757.0 |
| Excess of FIFO costs over LIFO value | (36.2) | (36.2) |
| Inventories—net (as reported on balance sheet) | $644.5 | $720.8 |

Manitowoc determines inventory cost using the first-in, first-out (FIFO) method to be approximately 84% and 87% of total inventory for 2014 and 2013, respectively. The remainder of the inventory is costed using the last-in, first-out (LIFO) method.

Additional facts for 2014 (amounts in millions):

| | |
|---|---|
| Current liabilities | $1,011.3 |
| Current assets (as reported) | 1,186.1 |
| Cost of goods sold | 2,900.4 |

## Instructions

Answer the following questions.

**a.** Why does the company report its inventory in three components?

**b.** Why might the company use two methods (LIFO and FIFO) to account for its inventory?

**c.** Calculate the inventory turnover and days in inventory using the LIFO inventory.

## Solution

**a.** The Manitowoc Company is a manufacturer, so it purchases raw materials and makes them into finished products. At the end of each period, it has some goods that have been started but are not yet complete (work in process).

By reporting all three components of inventory, a company reveals important information about its inventory position. For example, if amounts of raw materials have increased significantly compared to the previous year, we might assume the company is planning to step up production. On the other hand, if levels of finished goods have increased relative to last year and raw materials have declined, we might conclude that sales are slowing down—that the company has too much inventory on hand and is cutting back production.

**b.** Companies are free to choose different cost flow assumptions for different types of inventory. A company might choose to use FIFO for a product that is expected to decrease in price over time. One common reason for choosing a method other than LIFO is that many foreign countries do not allow LIFO; thus, the company cannot use LIFO for its foreign operations.

**c.** Inventory turnover $= \dfrac{\text{Cost of goods sold}}{\text{Average inventory}} = \dfrac{\$2,900.4}{(\$644.5 + \$720.8) \div 2} = 4.2$ times

Days in inventory $= \dfrac{365}{\text{Inventory turnover}} = \dfrac{365}{4.2} = 86.9$ days

# Review and Practice

## Learning Objectives Review

### 1 Discuss how to classify and determine inventory.

Merchandisers need only one inventory classification, merchandise inventory, to describe the different items that make up total inventory. Manufacturers, on the other hand, usually classify inventory into three categories: finished goods, work in process, and raw materials. To determine inventory quantities, manufacturers (1) take a physical inventory of goods on hand and (2) determine the ownership of goods in transit or on consignment.

### 2 Apply inventory cost flow methods and discuss their financial effects.

The primary basis of accounting for inventories is cost. Cost includes all expenditures necessary to acquire goods and place them in a condition ready for sale. Cost of goods available for sale includes (a) cost of beginning inventory and (b) cost of goods purchased. The inventory cost flow methods are specific identification and three assumed cost flow methods—FIFO, LIFO, and average-cost.

When prices are rising, the first-in, first-out (FIFO) method results in lower cost of goods sold and higher net income than the average-cost and the last-in, first-out (LIFO) methods. The reverse is true when prices are falling. In the balance sheet, FIFO results in an ending inventory that is closest to current value, whereas the inventory under LIFO is the farthest from current value. LIFO results in the lowest income taxes when prices are rising (because of lower taxable income).

### 3 Explain how companies recognize and value receivables.

Receivables are frequently classified as accounts, notes, and other. Accounts receivable are amounts customers owe on account. Notes receivable represent claims that are evidenced by formal instruments of credit. Other receivables include nontrade receivables such as interest receivable, loans to company officers, advances to employees, and income taxes refundable.

Companies record accounts receivable when they perform a service on account or at the point-of-sale of merchandise on account. Sales returns and allowances and cash discounts reduce the amount received on accounts receivable.

The two methods of accounting for uncollectible accounts are the allowance method and the direct write-off method. Under the allowance method, companies estimate uncollectible accounts as a percentage of receivables. This method emphasizes the cash realizable value of the accounts receivable. An aging schedule is frequently used with this approach.

### 4 Explain the statement presentation and analysis of inventory.

Inventory turnover is calculated as cost of goods sold divided by average inventory. It can be converted to average days in inventory by dividing 365 days by the inventory turnover. A higher inventory turnover or lower average days in inventory suggests that management is trying to keep inventory levels low relative to its sales level.

## Decision Tools Review

| Decision Checkpoints | Info Needed for Decision | Tool to Use for Decision | How to Evaluate Results |
|---|---|---|---|
| Which inventory costing method should be used? | Are prices increasing, or are they decreasing? | Income statement, balance sheet, and tax effects | Depends on objective. In a period of rising prices, income and inventory are higher and cash flow is lower under FIFO. LIFO provides opposite results. Average-cost can moderate the impact of changing prices. |
| Is the amount of past due accounts increasing? Which accounts require management's attention? | List of outstanding receivables and their due dates | Prepare an aging schedule showing the receivables in various stages: outstanding 0–30 days, 31–60 days, 61–90 days, and over 90 days. | Accounts in the older categories require follow-up: letters, phone calls, and possible renegotiation of terms. |
| How long is an item in inventory? | Cost of goods sold; beginning and ending inventory | $$\text{Inventory turnover} = \frac{\text{Cost of goods sold}}{\text{Average inventory}}$$ $$\text{Days in inventory} = \frac{365}{\text{Inventory turnover}}$$ | A higher inventory turnover or lower average days in inventory suggests that management is reducing the amount of inventory on hand, relative to cost of goods sold. |

## Glossary Review

**Accounts receivable**   Amounts customers owe on account. (p. 7-14).

**Aging the accounts receivable**   A schedule of customer balances classified by the length of time they have been unpaid. (p. 7-18).

**Allowance method**   A method of accounting for bad debts that involves estimating uncollectible accounts at the end of each period. (p. 7-16).

**Average-cost method**   An inventory costing method that uses the weighted-average unit cost to allocate the cost of goods available for sale to ending inventory and cost of goods sold. (p. 7-11).

**Bad Debt Expense**   The account in which the seller records losses resulting from extending credit. (p. 7-15).

**Cash (net) realizable value**   The net amount a company expects to receive in cash from receivables. (p. 7-16).

**Consigned goods**   Goods held for sale by one party although ownership of the goods is retained by another party. (p. 7-5).

**Days in inventory**   Measure of the average number of days inventory is held; calculated as 365 divided by inventory turnover. (p. 7-21).

**Direct write-off method**   A method of accounting for bad debts that involves charging receivable balances to Bad Debt Expense at the time receivables from a particular company are determined to be uncollectible. (p. 7-15).

**Finished goods inventory**   Manufactured items that are completed and ready for sale. (p. 7-3).

**First-in, first-out (FIFO) method**   An inventory costing method that assumes that the earliest goods purchased are the first to be sold. (p. 7-8).

**FOB destination**   Freight terms indicating that ownership of goods remains with the seller until the goods reach the buyer. (p. 7-4).

**FOB shipping point**   Freight terms indicating that ownership of goods passes to the buyer when the public carrier accepts the goods from the seller. (p. 7-4).

**Inventory turnover**   A ratio that indicates the liquidity of inventory by measuring the number of times average inventory is sold during the year; computed by dividing cost of goods sold by the average inventory. (p. 7-21).

**Just-in-time (JIT) inventory**   Inventory system in which companies manufacture or purchase goods only when needed. (p. 7-21).

**Last-in, first-out (LIFO) method**   An inventory costing method that assumes that the latest goods purchased are the first to be sold. (p. 7-10).

**Notes receivable**   Written promise (as evidenced by a formal instrument) for amounts to be received. (p. 7-14).

**Percentage-of-receivables basis**   A method of estimating the amount of bad debt expense whereby management establishes a percentage relationship between the amount of receivables and the expected losses from uncollectible accounts. (p. 7-18).

**Raw materials**   Basic goods that will be used in production but which have not yet been placed in production. (p. 7-3).

**Receivables** Amounts due from individuals and companies that are expected to be collected in cash. (p. 7-14).

**Specific identification method**   An actual physical-flow costing method in which particular items sold and items still in inventory are specifically costed to arrive at cost of goods sold and ending inventory. (p. 7-6).

**Trade receivables**   Notes and accounts receivable that result from sales transactions. (p. 7-15).

**Weighted-average unit cost**   Average cost that is weighted by the number of units purchased at each unit cost. (p. 7-11).

**Work in process**   That portion of manufactured inventory that has begun the production process but which is not yet complete. (p. 7-3).

## Practice Multiple-Choice Questions

1. **(LO 1)** When is a physical inventory usually taken?
   a. When the company has its greatest amount of inventory.
   b. When a limited number of goods are being sold or received.
   c. At the end of the company's fiscal year.
   d. Both when a limited number of goods are being sold or received, and at the end of the company's fiscal year.

2. **(LO 1)** Which of the following should **not** be included in the physical inventory of a company?
   a. Goods held on consignment from another company.
   b. Goods shipped on consignment to another company.
   c. Goods in transit from another company shipped FOB shipping point.
   d. All of the answer choices are correct.

3. **(LO 1)** As a result of a thorough physical inventory, Railway Company determined that it had inventory worth $180,000 at December 31, 2022. This count did not take into consideration the following facts. Rogers Consignment Store currently has goods worth $35,000 on its sales floor that belong to Railway but are being sold on consignment by Rogers. The selling price of these goods is $50,000. Railway purchased $13,000 of goods that were shipped on December 27, FOB destination, that will be received by Railway on January 3. Determine the correct amount of inventory that Railway should report.

   a. $230,000.
   b. $215,000.
   c. $228,000.
   d. $193,000.

4. **(LO 2)** Kam Company has the following units and costs.

   | | Units | Unit Cost |
   | --- | --- | --- |
   | Inventory, Jan. 1 | 8,000 | $11 |
   | Purchase, June 19 | 13,000 | 12 |
   | Purchase, Nov. 8 | 5,000 | 13 |

   If 9,000 units are on hand at December 31, what is the cost of the ending inventory under FIFO?

   a. $99,000.
   b. $108,000.
   c. $113,000.
   d. $117,000.

5. **(LO 2)** Kam Company has the following units and costs.

   | | Units | Unit Cost |
   | --- | --- | --- |
   | Inventory, Jan. 1 | 8,000 | $11 |
   | Purchase, June 19 | 13,000 | 12 |
   | Purchase, Nov. 8 | 5,000 | 13 |

   If 9,000 units are on hand at December 31, what is the cost of the ending inventory under LIFO?

   a. $113,000.
   b. $108,000.
   c. $99,000.
   d. $100,000.

**6. (LO 2)** Davidson Electronics has the following:

| | Units | Unit Cost |
|---|---|---|
| Inventory, Jan. 1 | 5,000 | $ 8 |
| Purchase, April 2 | 15,000 | 10 |
| Purchase, Aug. 28 | 20,000 | 12 |

If Davidson has 7,000 units on hand at December 31, the cost of ending inventory under the average-cost method is:

  **a.** $84,000.        **c.** $56,000.

  **b.** $70,000.        **d.** $75,250.

**7. (LO 2)** In periods of rising prices, LIFO will produce:

  **a.** higher net income than FIFO.

  **b.** the same net income as FIFO.

  **c.** lower net income than FIFO.

  **d.** higher net income than average-cost.

**8. (LO 2)** Cost of goods available for sale consists of two elements: beginning inventory and:

  **a.** ending inventory.

  **b.** cost of goods purchased.

  **c.** cost of goods sold.

  **d.** All of the answer choices are correct.

**9. (LO 2)** Considerations that affect the selection of an inventory costing method do **not** include:

  **a.** tax effects.

  **b.** balance sheet effects.

  **c.** income statement effects.

  **d.** perpetual versus periodic inventory system.

**10. (LO 3)** Receivables are frequently classified as:

  **a.** accounts receivable, company receivables, and other receivables.

  **b.** accounts receivable, notes receivable, and employee receivables.

  **c.** accounts receivable and general receivables.

  **d.** accounts receivable, notes receivable, and other receivables.

**11. (LO 3)** Accounts receivable are reported in the current assets section of the balance sheet at:

  **a.** cash (net) realizable value.

  **b.** net book value.

  **c.** lower-of-cost-or-market value.

  **d.** invoice cost.

**12. (LO 3)** Net credit sales for the month are $800,000. The accounts receivable balance is $160,000. The allowance is calculated as 7.5% of the receivables balance using the percentage-of-receivables basis. If Allowance for Doubtful Accounts has a balance of $5,000 before adjustment, what is the balance after adjustment?

  **a.** $12,000.        **c.** $17,000.

  **b.** $7,000.        **d.** $31,000.

**13. (LO 3)** An analysis and aging of the accounts receivable of Raja Company at December 31 reveal these data:

| | |
|---|---|
| Accounts receivable | $800,000 |
| Allowance for doubtful accounts per books before adjustment | 50,000 |
| Amounts expected to become uncollectible | 65,000 |

What is the cash realizable value of the accounts receivable at December 31, after adjustment?

  **a.** $685,000.        **c.** $800,000.

  **b.** $750,000.        **d.** $735,000.

**14. (LO 3)** Hughes Company has a balance of $5,000 in its Allowance for Doubtful Accounts before any adjustments are made at the end of the year. Based on review and aging of its accounts receivable at the end of the year, Hughes estimates that $60,000 of its receivables are uncollectible. The amount of bad debt expense which should be reported for the year is:

  **a.** $5,000.        **c.** $60,000.

  **b.** $55,000.        **d.** $65,000.

**15. (LO 4)** Which of these would cause inventory turnover to increase the most?

  **a.** Increasing the amount of inventory on hand.

  **b.** Keeping the amount of inventory on hand constant but increasing sales.

  **c.** Keeping the amount of inventory on hand constant but decreasing sales.

  **d.** Decreasing the amount of inventory on hand and increasing sales.

**16. (LO 4)** Carlos Company had beginning inventory of $80,000, ending inventory of $110,000, cost of goods sold of $285,000, and sales of $475,000. Carlos's days in inventory is:

  **a.** 73 days.        **c.** 102.5 days.

  **b.** 121.7 days.        **d.** 84.5 days.

## Solutions

**1. d.** A physical inventory is usually taken when a limited number of goods are being sold or received, and at the end of the company's fiscal year. Choice (a) is incorrect because a physical inventory count is usually taken when the company has the least, not greatest, amount of inventory. Choices (b) and (c) are correct, but (d) is the better answer.

**2. a.** Goods held on consignment should not be included because another company has title (ownership) to the goods. The other choices are incorrect because (b) goods shipped on consignment to another company and (c) goods in transit from another company shipped FOB shipping point should be included in a company's ending inventory. Choice (d) is incorrect because goods held on consignment from another company are not included in the physical inventory.

**3. b.** The inventory held on consignment by Rogers should be included in Railway's inventory balance at cost ($35,000). The purchased goods of $13,000 should not be included in inventory until January 3 because the goods are shipped FOB destination. Therefore, the correct amount of inventory is $215,000 ($180,000 + $35,000), not (a) $230,000, (c) $228,000, or (d) $193,000.

**4. c.** Under FIFO, ending inventory will consist of 5,000 units from the Nov. 8 purchase and 4,000 units from the June 19 purchase. Therefore, ending inventory is (5,000 × $13) + (4,000 × $12) = $113,000, not (a) $99,000, (b) $108,000, or (d) $117,000.

**5. d.** Under LIFO, ending inventory will consist of 8,000 units from the inventory at Jan. 1 and 1,000 units from the June 19 purchase. Therefore, ending inventory is (8,000 × $11) + (1,000 × $12) = $100,000, not (a) $113,000, (b) $108,000, or (c) $99,000.

**6. d.** Under the average-cost method, total cost of goods available for sale needs to be calculated in order to determine average cost per unit. The total cost of goods available is $430,000 = (5,000 × $8) + (15,000 × $10) + (20,000 × $12). The average cost per unit = ($430,000 ÷ 40,000 total units available for sale) = $10.75. Therefore, ending inventory is ($10.75 × 7,000) = $75,250, not (a) $84,000, (b) $70,000, or (c) $56,000.

**7. c.** In periods of rising prices, LIFO will produce lower net income than FIFO, not (a) higher than FIFO or (b) the same as FIFO. Choice (d) is incorrect because in periods of rising prices, LIFO will produce lower net income than average-cost. LIFO therefore charges the highest inventory cost against revenues in a period of rising prices.

**8. b.** Cost of goods available for sale consists of beginning inventory and cost of goods purchased, not (a) ending inventory or (c) cost of goods sold. Therefore, choice (d) is also incorrect.

**9. d.** Perpetual vs. periodic inventory system is not one of the factors that affect the selection of an inventory costing method. The other choices are incorrect because (a) tax effects, (b) balance sheet effects, and (c) income statement effects all affect the selection of an inventory costing method.

**10. d.** Receivables are frequently classified as accounts receivable, notes receivable, and other receivables. The other choices are incorrect because receivables are not frequently classified as (a) company receivables, (b) employee receivables, or (c) general receivables.

**11. a.** Accounts receivable are reported in the current assets section of the balance sheet at cash (net) realizable value, not (b) net book value, (c) lower-of-cost-or-market value, or (d) invoice cost.

**12. a.** The ending balance required in the allowance account is 7.5% × $160,000, or $12,000. Since there is already a balance of $5,000 in Allowance for Doubtful Accounts, the difference of $7,000 should be added, resulting in a balance of $12,000, not (b) $7,000, (c) $17,000, or (d) $31,000.

**13. d.** The cash realizable value of the accounts receivable is Accounts Receivable ($800,000) less the expected ending balance in Allowance for Doubtful Accounts after adjustments ($65,000) = $735,000, not (a) $685,000, (b) $750,000, or (c) $800,000.

**14. b.** After increasing Allowance for Doubtful Accounts by $55,000, the new balance will be the required balance of $60,000. This adjustment increases Bad Debt Expense and Allowance for Doubtful Accounts by $55,000, not (a) $5,000, (c) $60,000, or (d) $65,000.

**15. d.** Decreasing the amount of inventory on hand will cause the denominator to decrease, causing inventory turnover to increase. Increasing sales will cause the numerator of the ratio to increase (higher sales means higher COGS), thus causing inventory turnover to increase even more. The other choices are incorrect because (a) increasing the amount of inventory on hand causes the denominator of the ratio to increase while the numerator stays the same, causing inventory turnover to decrease; (b) keeping the amount of inventory on hand constant but increasing sales will cause inventory turnover to increase because the numerator of the ratio will increase (higher sales means higher COGS) while the denominator stays the same, which will result in a lesser inventory increase than decreasing amount of inventory on hand and increasing sales; and (c) keeping the amount of inventory on hand constant but decreasing sales will cause inventory turnover to decrease because the numerator of the ratio will decrease (lower sales means lower COGS) while the denominator stays the same.

**16. b.** Carlos's days in inventory = 365 ÷ Inventory turnover = 365 ÷ {$285,000 ÷ [($80,000 + $110,000) ÷ 2]} = 121.7 days, not (a) 73 days, (c) 102.5 days, or (d) 84.5 days.

## Practice Brief Exercises

**1. (LO 1)** Fylus Company took a physical inventory on December 31 and determined that goods costing $180,000 were on hand. Not included in the physical count were $18,000 of goods purchased from Rake Corporation, FOB destination, and $27,000 of goods sold to Shovel Company for $40,000, FOB destination. Both the Rake purchase and the Shovel sale were in transit year-end. What amount should Fylus report as its December 31 inventory?

*Determine ending inventory amount.*

### Solution

**1.** Physical inventory     $180,000
    Add: Goods sold to Shovel     27,000
    Fylus ending inventory     $207,000

The $18,000 of goods purchased from Rake are excluded from ending inventory because the terms are FOB destination, which means Fylus takes title at the time the goods are received. Goods sold to Shovel FOB destination means that the goods are still Fylus's until delivered.

**2. (LO 2)** In its first month of operations, Moncada Company made three purchases of merchandise in the following sequence: (1) 200 units at $7, (2) 300 units at $8, and (3) 150 units at $9. Assuming there are 220 units on hand, compute the cost of the ending inventory under the (a) FIFO method and (b) LIFO method. Moncada use a periodic inventory system.

*Compute ending inventory using FIFO and LIFO.*

### Solution

2. **a.** The ending inventory under FIFO consists of (150 units at $9) + (70 units at $8) for a total allocation of $1,910 ($1,350 + $560).

   **b.** The ending inventory under LIFO consists of (200 units at $7) + (20 units at $8) for a total allocation of $1,560 ($1,400 + $160).

*Record bad debt expense using percentage-of-receivables method.*

3. **(LO 3)** Sanchez Co. uses the percentage-of-receivables basis in 2022 to record bad debt expense. It estimates that 3% of accounts receivable will become uncollectible. Sales revenues are $900,000 for 2022, and sales returns and allowances are $50,000 at December 31, 2022. Accounts receivable has a balance of $139,000, and the allowance for doubtful accounts has a balance of $3,000. Use a tabular summary to record this information and to record bad debt expense in 2022.

### Solution

3.

| | Assets | | = | Liabilities | + | | Stockholders' Equity | | | |
|---|---|---|---|---|---|---|---|---|---|---|
| | Accts. Receiv. | − Allow. for Doubt. Accts. = | | | | Common Stock | + | Rev. | − Exp. | − Div. |
| Beg. Bal. | $139,000 | −$3,000 | | | | | | $900,000 | | |
| | | −1,170* | | | | | | | −$1,170 | Bad Debt Exp. |
| Adj. Bal. | | −$4,170 | | | | | | | | |

*($139,000 × 3%) − $3,000

*Compute inventory turnover and days in inventory.*

4. **(LO 4)** At December 31, 2022, the following information was available for Garcia Company: ending inventory $30,000, beginning inventory $42,000, cost of goods sold $240,000, and sales revenue $400,000. Calculate inventory turnover and days in inventory for Garcia Company.

### Solution

4. Inventory turnover: $\dfrac{\$240,000}{(\$30,000 + \$42,000) \div 2} = \dfrac{\$240,000}{\$36,000} = 6.67$

   Days in inventory: $\dfrac{365}{6.67} = 54.7$ days

## Practice Exercises

*Determine the correct inventory amount.*

1. **(LO 1)** Mika Sorbino, an auditor with Martinez CPAs, is performing a review of Sergei Company's inventory account. Sergei's did not have a good year and top management is under pressure to boost reported income. According to its records, the inventory balance at year-end was $650,000. However, the following information was not considered when determining that amount.

   1. Included in the company's count were goods with a cost of $200,000 that the company is holding on consignment. The goods belong to Bosnia Corporation.

   2. The physical count did not include goods purchased by Sergei with a cost of $40,000 that were shipped FOB shipping point on December 28 and did not arrive at Sergei's warehouse until January 3.

   3. Included in the inventory account was $15,000 of office supplies that were stored in the warehouse and were to be used by the company's supervisors and managers during the coming year.

   4. The company received an order on December 28 that was boxed and was sitting on the loading dock awaiting pick-up on December 31. The shipper picked up the goods on January 1 and

delivered them on January 6. The shipping terms were FOB shipping point. The goods had a selling price of $40,000 and a cost of $30,000. The goods were not included in the count because they were sitting on the dock.

5. On December 29, Sergei shipped goods with a selling price of $80,000 and a cost of $60,000 to Oman Sales Corporation FOB shipping point. The goods arrived on January 3. Oman Sales had only ordered goods with a selling price of $10,000 and a cost of $8,000. However, a Sergei's sales manager had authorized the shipment and said that if Oman wanted to ship the goods back next week, it could.

6. Included in the count was $30,000 of goods that were parts for a machine that the company no longer made. Given the high-tech nature of Sergei's products, it was unlikely that these obsolete parts had any other use. However, management would prefer to keep them on the books at cost, "since that is what we paid for them, after all."

### Instructions

Prepare a schedule to determine the correct inventory amount. Provide explanations for each item above, saying why you did or did not make an adjustment for each item.

### Solution

| | |
|---|---:|
| 1. Ending inventory—as reported | $650,000 |
|   1. Subtract from inventory: The goods belong to Bosnia Corporation. Sergei is merely holding them for Bosnia. | (200,000) |
|   2. Add to inventory: The goods belong to Sergei when they were shipped. | 40,000 |
|   3. Subtract from inventory: Office supplies should be carried in a separate account. They are not considered inventory held for resale. | (15,000) |
|   4. Add to inventory: The goods belong to Sergei until they are shipped (Jan. 1). | 30,000 |
|   5. Add to inventory: Oman Sales ordered goods with a cost of $8,000. Sergei should record the corresponding sales revenue of $10,000. Sergei's decision to ship extra "unordered" goods does not constitute a sale. The manager's statement that Oman could ship the goods back indicates that Sergei knows this overshipment is not a legitimate sale. The manager acted unethically in an attempt to improve Sergei's reported income by overshipping. | 52,000 |
|   6. Subtract from inventory: GAAP requires that inventory be valued at the lower of either its cost or the net amount that would be received upon sale. Obsolete parts should be adjusted from cost to zero if they have no other use. | (30,000) |
| Correct inventory | $527,000 |

---

**2. (LO 3)** The unadjusted balances of J.C. Cobb Company at the end of the current year show Accounts Receivable $150,000 and Sales Revenue $850,000.

*Record bad debts using two different bases.*

### Instructions

a. If J.C. Cobb uses the direct write-off method to account for uncollectible accounts, use a tabular summary to prepare the adjustment at December 31, assuming J.C. Cobb determines that M. Jack's $1,500 balance is uncollectible.

b. If Allowance for Doubtful Accounts has a balance of $2,400, use a tabular summary to prepare the adjustment at December 31, assuming bad debts are expected to be 10% of accounts receivable.

### Solution

**2. a.**

| | Assets | = Liabilities + | Stockholders' Equity | | | |
|---|---|---|---|---|---|---|
| | | | | Retained Earnings | | |
| | Accounts | | Common | | | |
| | Receivable = | | Stock + | Rev. − | Exp. − | Div. |
| Beg. Bal. | $150,000 | | | $850,000 | | |
| | −1,500 | | | | −$1,500 | Bad Debt Exp. |
| End. Bal. | $148,500 | | | | | |

**b.**

| | Assets | | = Liabilities + | Stockholders' Equity | | | |
|---|---|---|---|---|---|---|---|
| | | Allow. for | | | Retained Earnings | | |
| | Accts. | Doubt. | | Common | | | |
| | Receiv. − | Accts. = | | Stock + | Rev. − | Exp. − Div. | |
| Beg. Bal. | $150,000 | −$2,400 | | | $850,000 | | |
| | | −12,600* | | | | −$12,600 | Bad Debt Exp. |
| Adj. Bal. | | −$15,000 | | | | | |

*($150,000 × 10%) − $2,400

---

## Practice Problem

*Compute inventory and cost of goods sold using three cost flow methods in a perpetual inventory system.*

**(LO 2)** Englehart Company has the following inventory, purchases, and sales data for the month of March.

| Inventory: March 1 | 200 units @ $4.00 | $ 800 |
|---|---|---|
| Purchases: | | |
| March 10 | 500 units @ $4.50 | 2,250 |
| March 20 | 400 units @ $4.75 | 1,900 |
| March 30 | 300 units @ $5.00 | 1,500 |
| Sales: | | |
| March 15 | 500 units | |
| March 25 | 400 units | |

The physical inventory count on March 31 shows 500 units on hand.

### Instructions

Under a **periodic inventory system**, determine the cost of inventory on hand at March 31 and the cost of goods sold for March under (a) the first-in, first-out (FIFO) method; (b) the last-in, first-out (LIFO) method; and (c) the average-cost method. (For average-cost, carry cost per unit to three decimal places.)

### Solution

The cost of goods available for sale is $6,450:

| Inventory: March 1 | 200 units @ $4.00 | $ 800 |
|---|---|---|
| Purchases: | | |
| March 10 | 500 units @ $4.50 | 2,250 |
| March 20 | 400 units @ $4.75 | 1,900 |
| March 30 | 300 units @ $5.00 | 1,500 |
| Total cost of goods available for sale | | $6,450 |

**a.**                                  **FIFO Method**

Ending inventory:

| Date | Units | Unit Cost | Total Cost | |
|------|-------|-----------|-----------|---|
| Mar. 30 | 300 | $5.00 | $1,500 | |
| Mar. 20 | 200 | 4.75 | 950 | $ 2,450 |
| Cost of goods sold: $6,450 − $2,450 = | | | | $ 4,000 |

**b.**                                  **LIFO Method**

Ending inventory:

| Date | Units | Unit Cost | Total Cost | |
|------|-------|-----------|-----------|---|
| Mar.  1 | 200 | $4.00 | $  800 | |
| Mar. 10 | 300 | 4.50 | 1,350 | $ 2,150 |
| Cost of goods sold: $6,450 − $2,150 = | | | | $ 4,300 |

**c.**                                  **Average-Cost Method**

Weighted-average unit cost: $6,450 ÷ 1,400 = $4.607

| | |
|---|---|
| Ending inventory: 500 × $4.607 = | $2,303.50 |
| Cost of goods sold: $6,450 − $2,303.50 = | $4,146.50 |

# WileyPLUS

Brief Exercises, DO IT! Exercises, Exercises, Problems, and many additional resources are available for practice in WileyPLUS.

## Questions

**1.** "The key to successful business operations is effective inventory management." Do you agree? Explain.

**2.** An item must possess two characteristics to be classified as inventory. What are these two characteristics?

**3.** What is just-in-time inventory management? What are its potential advantages?

**4.** Your friend Will Juritz has been hired to help take the physical inventory in Byrd's Hardware Store. Explain to Will what this job will entail.

**5. a.** Bonita Company ships merchandise to Myan Corporation on December 30. The merchandise reaches the buyer on January 5. Indicate the terms of sale that will result in the goods being included in (1) Bonita's December 31 inventory and (2) Myan's December 31 inventory.

 **b.** Under what circumstances should Bonita Company include consigned goods in its inventory?

**6.** Nona Hat Shop received a shipment of hats for which it paid the wholesaler $2,940. The price of the hats was $3,000, but Nona was given a $60 cash discount and required to pay freight charges of $75. What amount should Nona include in inventory? Why?

**7.** What is the primary basis of accounting for inventories?

**8.** Ken McCall believes that the allocation of cost of goods available for sale should be based on the actual physical flow of the goods. Explain to Ken why this may be both impractical and inappropriate.

**9.** What is the major advantage and major disadvantage of the specific identification method of inventory costing?

**10.** "The selection of an inventory cost flow method is a decision made by accountants." Do you agree? Explain. Once a method has been selected, what accounting requirement applies?

**11.** Which assumed inventory cost flow method:

 **a.** Usually parallels the actual physical flow of merchandise?

 **b.** Divides cost of goods available for sale by total units available for sale to determine a unit cost?

 **c.** Assumes that the latest units purchased are the first to be sold?

**12.** In a period of rising prices, the inventory reported in Short Company's balance sheet is close to the current cost of the inventory, whereas King Company's inventory is considerably below its current cost. Identify the inventory cost flow method used by each company. Which company probably has been reporting the higher gross profit?

**13.** Mamosa Corporation has been using the FIFO cost flow method during a prolonged period of inflation. During the same time period,

Mamosa has been paying out all of its net income as dividends. What adverse effects may result from this policy?

**14.** Oscar Geer, a mid-level product manager for Theresa's Shoes, thinks his company should switch from LIFO to FIFO. He says, "My bonus is based on net income. If we switch it will increase net income and increase my bonus. The company would be better off and so would I." Is he correct? Explain.

**15.** Discuss the impact the use of LIFO has on taxes paid, cash flows, and the quality of earnings ratio relative to the impact of FIFO when prices are increasing.

**16.** What is the difference between an account receivable and a note receivable?

**17.** What are some common types of receivables other than accounts receivable or notes receivable?

**18.** What are the essential features of the allowance method of accounting for bad debts?

**19.** Lance Morrow cannot understand why the cash realizable value does not decrease when an uncollectible account is written off under the allowance method. Clarify this point for Lance.

**20.** Sarasota Company has a balance of $2,200 in Allowance for Doubtful Accounts before adjustment. The estimated uncollectibles under the percentage-of-receivables basis is $5,100. Explain the adjustment.

**21.** How are bad debts accounted for under the direct write-off method? What are the disadvantages of this method?

**22.** Under what circumstances might inventory turnover be too high—that is, what possible negative consequences might occur?

## Brief Exercises

*Identify items to be included in taking a physical inventory.*

**BE7.1 (LO 1), C** Peete Company identifies the following items for possible inclusion in the physical inventory. Indicate whether each item should be included or excluded from the inventory taking.

   **a.** 900 units of inventory shipped on consignment by Peete to another company.

   **b.** 3,000 units of inventory in transit from a supplier shipped FOB destination.

   **c.** 1,200 units of inventory sold but being held for customer pickup.

   **d.** 500 units of inventory held on consignment from another company.

*Determine ending inventory amount.*

**BE7.2 (LO 1), AN** Stallman Company took a physical inventory on December 31 and determined that goods costing $200,000 were on hand. Not included in the physical count were $25,000 of goods purchased from Pelzer Corporation, FOB, shipping point, and $22,000 of goods sold to Alvarez Company for $30,000, FOB destination. Both the Pelzer purchase and the Alvarez sale were in transit at year-end. What amount should Stallman report as its December 31 inventory?

*Compute ending inventory using FIFO and LIFO.*

**BE7.3 (LO 2), AP** In its first month of operations, McLanie Company made three purchases of merchandise in the following sequence: (1) 300 units at $6, (2) 400 units at $8, and (3) 600 units at $9. Assuming there are 200 units on hand at the end of the period, compute the cost of the ending inventory under (a) the FIFO method and (b) the LIFO method. McLanie uses a periodic inventory system.

*Compute the ending inventory using average-cost.*

**BE7.4 (LO 2), AP** In its first month of operations, McLanie Company made three purchases of merchandise in the following sequence: (1) 300 units at $6, (2) 400 units at $8, and (3) 600 units at $9. Assuming there are 200 units on hand at the end of the period, compute the cost of the ending inventory under the average-cost method. McLanie uses a periodic inventory system.

*Compute cost of goods sold using FIFO, LIFO, and average-cost.*

**BE7.5 (LO 2), AP** Sunnyside Marine Products began the year with 10 units of marine floats at a cost of $11 each. During the year, it made the following purchases: May 5, 30 units at $16; July 16, 15 units at $19; and December 7, 20 units at $23. Assuming there are 25 units on hand at the end of the period, determine the cost of goods sold under (a) FIFO, (b) LIFO, and (c) average-cost. Sunnyside uses the periodic approach.

*Explain the financial statement effect of inventory cost flow assumptions.*

**BE7.6 (LO 2), C** The management of Milque Corp. is considering the effects of various inventory-costing methods on its financial statements and its income tax expense. Assuming that the cost the company pays for inventory is increasing, which method will:

   **a.** Provide the highest net income?

   **b.** Provide the highest ending inventory?

   **c.** Result in the lowest income tax expense?

   **d.** Result in the most stable earnings over a number of years?

*Explain the financial statement effect of inventory cost flow assumptions.*

**BE7.7 (LO 2), AP** In its first month of operation, Hoffman Company purchased 100 units of inventory for $6, then 200 units for $7, and finally 140 units for $8. At the end of the month, 180 units remained. Compute the amount of phantom profit that would result if the company used FIFO rather than LIFO. Explain why this amount is referred to as phantom profit. The company uses the periodic method.

**BE7.8 (LO 2), C** For each of the following cases, state whether the statement is true for LIFO or for FIFO. Assume that prices are rising.

*Identify the impact of LIFO versus FIFO.*

a. Results in a higher quality of earnings ratio.

b. Results in higher phantom profits.

c. Results in higher net income.

d. Results in lower taxes.

e. Results in lower net cash provided by operating activities.

**BE7.9 (LO 3), C** The following are three receivables transactions. Indicate whether these receivables are reported as accounts receivable, notes receivable, or other receivables on a balance sheet.

*Identify different types of receivables.*

a. Advanced $10,000 to an employee.

b. Received a promissory note of $34,000 for services performed.

c. Sold merchandise on account for $60,000 to a customer.

**BE7.10 (LO 3), AP** Use a tabular summary to record the following transactions for Jarvis Co. (Omit recording cost of goods sold.)

*Record basic accounts receivable transactions.*

a. On July 1, Jarvis Co. sold merchandise on account to Stacey Inc. for $23,000.

b. On July 8, Stacey Inc. returned $2,400 of July 1 merchandise to Jarvis Co.

c. On July 11, Stacey Inc. paid for the merchandise.

**BE7.11 (LO 3), AP** At the end of 2021, Safer Co. has accounts receivable of $700,000 and an allowance for doubtful accounts of $25,000. On January 24, 2022, it is learned that the company's receivable from Madonna Inc. is not collectible and therefore management authorizes a write-off of $4,300.

*Record write-off and determine cash realizable value.*

a. Use a tabular summary to record the write-off. Enter 2021 amounts as beginning balances.

b. What is the cash realizable value of the accounts receivable (1) before the write-off and (2) after the write-off?

**BE7.12 (LO 4), AP** Suppose at December 31 of a recent year, the following information (in thousands) was available for sunglasses manufacturer **Oakley, Inc.**: ending inventory $155,377, beginning inventory $119,035, cost of goods sold $349,114, and sales revenue $761,865. Calculate the inventory turnover and days in inventory for Oakley, Inc. (Round inventory turnover to two decimal places.)

*Compute inventory turnover and days in inventory.*

## DO IT! Exercises

**DO IT! 7.1 (LO 1), AN** Sheldon Company just took its physical inventory on December 31. The count of inventory items on hand at the company's business locations resulted in a total inventory cost of $300,000. In reviewing the details of the count and related inventory transactions, you have discovered the following items that had not been considered.

*Apply rules of ownership to determine inventory cost.*

1. Sheldon has sent inventory costing $28,000 on consignment to Richfield Company. All of this inventory was at Richfield's showrooms on December 31.

2. The company did not include in the count inventory (cost, $20,000) that was sold on December 28, terms FOB shipping point. The goods were in transit on December 31.

3. The company did not include in the count inventory (cost, $13,000) that was purchased with terms of FOB shipping point. The goods were in transit on December 31.

Compute the correct December 31 inventory.

**DO IT! 7.2 (LO 2), AP** The accounting records of Ohm Electronics show the following data.

*Compute cost of goods sold under different cost flow methods.*

| | |
|---|---|
| Beginning inventory | 3,000 units at $5 |
| Purchases | 7,000 units at $7 |
| Sales | 8,400 units at $10 |

Determine cost of goods sold during the period under a periodic inventory system using (a) the FIFO method, (b) the LIFO method, and (c) the average-cost method. (Carry the unit cost to two decimal places.)

*Record uncollectible accounts.*

**DO IT! 7.3 (LO 3), AP** Mantle Company has been in business several years. At the end of the current year, the unadjusted balances show:

| | |
|---|---|
| Accounts Receivable | $ 310,000 |
| Sales Revenue | 2,200,000 |
| Allowance for Doubtful Accounts | 5,700 |

Bad debts are estimated to be 7% of receivables. Record adjustment to Allowance for Doubtful Accounts in a tabular summary.

*Compute inventory turnover and assess inventory level.*

**DO IT! 7.4 (LO 4), AN** Early in 2022, Fedor Company switched to a just-in-time inventory system. Its sales and inventory amounts for 2021 and 2022 are shown below.

| | **2021** | **2022** |
|---|---|---|
| Sales revenue | $3,120,000 | $3,713,000 |
| Cost of goods sold | 1,200,000 | 1,425,000 |
| Beginning inventory | 170,000 | 210,000 |
| Ending inventory | 210,000 | 90,000 |

Determine the inventory turnover and days in inventory for 2021 and 2022. Discuss the changes in the amount of inventory, the inventory turnover and days in inventory, and the amount of sales across the 2 years.

# Exercises

*Determine the correct inventory amount.*

**E7.1 (LO 1), AN** Umatilla Bank and Trust is considering giving Pohl Company a loan. Before doing so, it decides that further discussions with Pohl's accountant may be desirable. One area of particular concern is the Inventory account, which has a year-end balance of $275,000. Discussions with the accountant reveal the following.

1. Pohl shipped goods costing $55,000 to Hemlock Company FOB shipping point on December 28. The goods are not expected to reach Hemlock until January 12. The goods were not included in the physical inventory because they were not in the warehouse.

2. The physical count of the inventory did not include goods costing $95,000 that were shipped to Pohl FOB destination on December 27 and were still in transit at year-end.

3. Pohl received goods costing $25,000 on January 2. The goods were shipped FOB shipping point on December 26 by Yanice Co. The goods were not included in the physical count.

4. Pohl shipped goods costing $51,000 to Ehler of Canada FOB destination on December 30. The goods were received in Canada on January 8. They were not included in Pohl's physical inventory.

5. Pohl received goods costing $42,000 on January 2 that were shipped FOB destination on December 29. The shipment was a rush order that was supposed to arrive December 31. This purchase was included in the ending inventory of $275,000.

**Instructions**

Determine the correct inventory amount on December 31.

*Determine the correct inventory amount.*

**E7.2 (LO 1), AN** Farley Bains, an auditor with Nolls CPAs, is performing a review of Ryder Company's Inventory account. Ryder did not have a good year, and top management is under pressure to boost reported income. According to its records, the inventory balance at year-end was $740,000. However, the following information was not considered when determining that amount.

1. Included in the company's count were goods with a cost of $228,000 that the company is holding on consignment. The goods belong to Nader Corporation.

2. The physical count did not include goods purchased by Ryder with a cost of $40,000 that were shipped FOB shipping point on December 28 and did not arrive at Ryder's warehouse until January 3.

3. Included in the Inventory account was $17,000 of office supplies that were stored in the warehouse and were to be used by the company's supervisors and managers during the coming year.

4. The company received an order on December 29 that was boxed and was sitting on the loading dock awaiting pick-up on December 31. The shipper picked up the goods on January 1 and delivered them on January 6. The shipping terms were FOB shipping point. The goods had a selling price of $40,000 and a cost of $29,000. The goods were not included in the count because they were sitting on the dock.

5. Included in the count was $50,000 of goods that were parts for a machine that the company no longer made. Given the high-tech nature of Ryder's products, it was unlikely that these obsolete parts had any other use. However, management would prefer to keep them on the books at cost, "since that is what we paid for them, after all."

**Instructions**

Prepare a schedule to determine the correct inventory amount. Provide explanations for each item above, stating why you did or did not make an adjustment for each item.

**E7.3 (LO 1), C** Gato Inc. had the following inventory situations to consider at January 31, its year-end. *Identify items in inventory.*

a. Goods held on consignment for Steele Corp. since December 12.

b. Goods shipped on consignment to Logan Holdings Inc. on January 5.

c. Goods shipped to a customer, FOB destination, on January 29 that are still in transit.

d. Goods shipped to a customer, FOB shipping point, on January 29 that are still in transit.

e. Goods purchased FOB destination from a supplier on January 25 that are still in transit.

f. Goods purchased FOB shipping point from a supplier on January 25 that are still in transit.

g. Office supplies on hand at January 31.

**Instructions**

Identify which of the preceding items should be included in inventory. If the item should not be included in inventory, state in what account, if any, it should have been recorded.

**E7.4 (LO 2), AP** Mather sells a snowboard, EZslide, that is popular with snowboard enthusiasts. Below is information relating to Mather's purchases of EZslide snowboards during September. During the same month, 105 EZslide snowboards were sold. Mather uses a periodic inventory system. *Compute inventory and cost of goods sold using periodic FIFO, LIFO, and average-cost.*

| Date | Explanation | Units | Unit Cost | Total Cost |
|---|---|---|---|---|
| Sept. 1 | Inventory | 15 | $100 | $ 1,500 |
| 12 | Purchase | 45 | 102 | 4,590 |
| 19 | Purchase | 50 | 104 | 5,200 |
| 26 | Purchase | 20 | 105 | 2,100 |
| | Total | 130 | | $13,390 |

**Instructions**

Compute the ending inventory at September 30 and the cost of goods sold using the FIFO, LIFO, and average-cost methods. Prove the amount allocated to cost of goods sold under each method.

**E7.5 (LO 2), AP** Rusthe Inc. uses a periodic inventory system. Its records show the following for the month of May, in which 74 units were sold. *Calculate inventory and cost of goods sold using FIFO, LIFO, and average-cost in a periodic inventory system.*

| Date | Explanation | Units | Unit Cost | Total Cost |
|---|---|---|---|---|
| May 1 | Inventory | 30 | $ 8 | $ 240 |
| 15 | Purchase | 25 | 11 | 275 |
| 24 | Purchase | 45 | 13 | 585 |
| | Total | 100 | | $1,100 |

**Instructions**

Calculate the ending inventory at May 31 using the (a) FIFO, (b) LIFO, and (c) average-cost methods. Prove the amount allocated to cost of goods sold under each method.

**E7.6 (LO 2), AN** On December 1, Premium Electronics has three DVD players left in stock. All are identical, and all are priced to sell at $85. One of the three DVD players left in stock, with serial #1012, was purchased on June 1 at a cost of $52. Another, with serial #1045, was purchased on November 1 for $48. The last player, serial #1056, was purchased on November 30 for $40. *Calculate cost of goods sold using specific identification and FIFO periodic.*

**Instructions**

a. Calculate the cost of goods sold using the FIFO periodic inventory method, assuming that two of the three players were sold by the end of December, Premium Electronics' year-end.

b. If Premium Electronics used the specific identification method instead of the FIFO method, how might it alter its earnings by "selectively choosing" which particular players to sell to the two customers? What would Premium's cost of goods sold be if the company wished to minimize earnings? Maximize earnings?

c. Which inventory method, FIFO or specific identification, do you recommend that Premium use? Explain why.

*Compute inventory and cost of goods sold using periodic FIFO, LIFO, and average-cost.*

**E7.7 (LO 2), AP** Jeters Company uses a periodic inventory system and reports the following for the month of June.

| Date | | Explanation | Units | Unit Cost | Total Cost |
|---|---|---|---|---|---|
| June | 1 | Inventory | 100 | $4 | $ 400 |
| | 12 | Purchase | 400 | 6 | 2,400 |
| | 23 | Purchase | 250 | 8 | 2,000 |
| | 30 | Inventory | 230 | | |

**Instructions**

a. Compute the cost of the ending inventory and the cost of goods sold under (1) FIFO, (2) LIFO, and (3) average-cost. (Carry unit cost to two decimal places.)

b. Which costing method gives the highest ending inventory? The highest cost of goods sold? Why?

c. How do the average-cost values for ending inventory and cost of goods sold relate to ending inventory and cost of goods sold for FIFO and LIFO?

d. Explain why the average cost is not $6.

*Evaluate impact of LIFO and FIFO on cash flows and earnings quality.*

**E7.8 (LO 2), AP** The following comparative information is available for Rose Company for 2022.

| | LIFO | FIFO |
|---|---|---|
| Sales revenue | $86,000 | $86,000 |
| Cost of goods sold | 38,000 | 29,000 |
| Operating expenses | | |
| (including depreciation) | 27,000 | 27,000 |
| Depreciation | 10,000 | 10,000 |
| Cash paid for inventory purchases | 32,000 | 32,000 |

**Instructions**

a. Determine net income under each approach. Assume a 30% tax rate.

b. Determine net cash provided by operating activities under each approach. Assume that all sales were on a cash basis and that income taxes and operating expenses, other than depreciation, were on a cash basis.

*Record receivables transactions.*

**E7.9 (LO 3), AP** At the beginning of the current period, Rose Corp. had balances in Accounts Receivable of $200,000 and in Allowance for Doubtful Accounts of $9,000. During the period, it had net credit sales of $800,000 and collections of $763,000. It wrote off as uncollectible accounts receivable of $7,300. Uncollectible accounts are estimated to total $25,000 at the end of the period. (Omit recording cost of goods sold.)

**Instructions**

Enter the beginning balances for Accounts Receivable and Allowance for Doubtful Accounts in a tabular summary. Use the summary to record transactions (a), (b), and (c) below.

a. Record sales and collections during the period.

b. Record the write-off of uncollectible accounts during the period.

c. Record bad debt expense for the period.

d. Determine the ending balances in Accounts Receivable and Allowance for Doubtful Accounts.

e. What is the net realizable value of the receivables at the end of the period?

*Determine bad debt expense.*

**E7.10 (LO 3), AN** The records of Macarty Company at the end of the current year show Accounts Receivable $78,000, Credit Sales $810,000, and Sales Returns and Allowances $40,000.

**Instructions**

a. If Macarty uses the direct write-off method to account for uncollectible accounts and Macarty determines that Matisse's $900 balance is uncollectible, what will Macarty record as bad debt expense?

b. If Allowance for Doubtful Accounts has a balance of $1,100 and Macarty concludes bad debts are expected to be 10% of accounts receivable, what will Macarty record as bad debt expense?

**E7.11 (LO 3), AN** Godfreid Company has accounts receivable of $95,400 at March 31, 2022. At March 31, 2022, there is a $2,100 balance in Allowance for Doubtful Accounts prior to adjustment. The company uses the percentage-of-receivables basis for estimating uncollectible accounts. The company's estimates of bad debts are as shown below.

*Determine bad debt expense.*

| | Balance, March 31 | | Estimated Percentage |
| Age of Accounts | 2022 | 2021 | Uncollectible |
| --- | --- | --- | --- |
| Current | $65,000 | $75,000 | 2% |
| 1–30 days past due | 12,900 | 8,000 | 5 |
| 31–90 days past due | 10,100 | 2,400 | 30 |
| Over 90 days past due | 7,400 | 1,100 | 50 |
| | $95,400 | $86,500 | |

**Instructions**

a. Determine the total estimated uncollectibles.

b. Indicate the amount to record as bad debt expense on March 31, 2022.

c. Discuss the implications of the changes in the aging schedule from 2021 to 2022.

**E7.12 (LO 4), AP** Suppose this information is available for **PepsiCo, Inc.** for 2020, 2021, and 2022.

*Compute inventory turnover, days in inventory, and gross profit rate.*

| (in millions) | 2020 | 2021 | 2022 |
| --- | --- | --- | --- |
| Beginning inventory | $ 1,926 | $ 2,290 | $ 2,522 |
| Ending inventory | 2,290 | 2,522 | 2,618 |
| Cost of goods sold | 18,038 | 20,351 | 20,099 |
| Sales revenue | 39,474 | 43,251 | 43,232 |

**Instructions**

a. Calculate the inventory turnover for 2020, 2021, and 2022. (Round to one decimal place.)

b. Calculate the days in inventory for 2020, 2021, and 2022.

c. Calculate the gross profit rate for 2020, 2021, and 2022.

d. Comment on any trends observed in your answers to parts (a), (b), and (c).

**E7.13 (LO 4), AP** The following information is available for Zoe's Activewear Inc. for three recent fiscal years.

*Calculate inventory turnover, days in inventory, and gross profit rate.*

| | 2022 | 2021 | 2020 |
| --- | --- | --- | --- |
| Inventory (12/31) | $ 553,000 | $ 568,000 | $ 332,000 |
| Net sales | 1,948,000 | 1,725,000 | 1,311,000 |
| Cost of goods sold | 1,552,000 | 1,288,000 | 947,000 |

**Instructions**

a. Calculate the inventory turnover, days in inventory, and gross profit rate for 2022 and 2021.

b. Based on the ratios calculated in part (a), did Zoe's liquidity and profitability improve or deteriorate in 2022?

## Problems

**P7.1 (LO 1), AN** Pitt Limited is trying to determine the value of its ending inventory as of February 28, 2022, the company's year-end. The accountant counted everything that was in the warehouse as of February 28, which resulted in an ending inventory valuation of $48,000. However, she didn't know how to treat the following transactions so she didn't record them.

*Determine items and amounts to be recorded in inventory.*

a. On February 26, Pitt shipped to a customer goods costing $800. The goods were shipped FOB shipping point, and the receiving report indicates that the customer received the goods on March 2.

**b.** On February 26, Martine Inc. shipped goods to Pitt FOB destination. The invoice price was $350 plus $25 for freight. The receiving report indicates that the goods were received by Pitt on March 2.

**c.** Pitt had $500 of inventory at a customer's warehouse "on approval." The customer was going to let Pitt know whether it wanted the merchandise by the end of the week, March 4.

**d.** Pitt also had $400 of inventory at a Belle craft shop, on consignment from Pitt.

**e.** On February 26, Pitt ordered goods costing $750. The goods were shipped FOB shipping point on February 27. Pitt received the goods on March 1.

**f.** On February 28, Pitt packaged goods and had them ready for shipping to a customer FOB destination. The invoice price was $350 plus $25 for freight; the cost of the items was $280. The receiving report indicates that the goods were received by the customer on March 2.

**g.** Pitt had damaged goods set aside in the warehouse because they are no longer saleable. These goods originally cost $400 and, originally, Pitt expected to sell these items for $600.

### Instructions

For each of the above transactions, specify whether the item in question should be included in ending inventory, and if so, at what amount. For each item that is not included in ending inventory, indicate who owns it and what account, if any, it should have been recorded in.

*Determine cost of goods sold and ending inventory using FIFO, LIFO, and average-cost with analysis.*

**b. Cost of goods sold:**

| | |
|---|---|
| FIFO | $ 91,000 |
| LIFO | $103,500 |
| Average | $ 96,760 |

**P7.2 (LO 2), AP** Mullins Distribution markets CDs of numerous performing artists. At the beginning of March, Mullins had in beginning inventory 2,500 CDs with a unit cost of $6. During March, Mullins made the following purchases of CDs.

| | | | | |
|---|---|---|---|---|
| March 5 | 3,000 @ $7 | | March 21 | 5,000 @ $9 |
| March 13 | 3,500 @ $8 | | March 26 | 2,000 @ $10 |

During March, 12,000 units were sold. Mullins uses a periodic inventory system.

### Instructions

**a.** Determine the cost of goods available for sale.

**b.** Determine (1) the ending inventory and (2) the cost of goods sold under each of the assumed cost flow methods (FIFO, LIFO, and average-cost). Prove the accuracy of the cost of goods sold under the FIFO and LIFO methods. (*Note:* For average-cost, carry cost per unit to two decimal places.)

**c.** Which cost flow method results in (1) the highest inventory amount for the balance sheet and (2) the highest cost of goods sold for the income statement?

*Determine cost of goods sold and ending inventory using FIFO, LIFO, and average-cost in a periodic inventory system and assess financial statement effects.*

**b. Cost of goods sold:**

| | |
|---|---|
| FIFO | $13,000 |
| LIFO | $13,900 |
| Average | $13,500 |

**P7.3 (LO 2), AP** Vista Company Inc. had a beginning inventory of 100 units of Product RST at a cost of $7 per unit. During the year, purchases were:

| | | | | |
|---|---|---|---|---|
| Feb. 20 | 600 units at $8 | | Aug. 12 | 400 units at $10 |
| May 5 | 500 units at $9 | | Dec. 8 | 200 units at $11 |

Vista Company uses a periodic inventory system. Sales totaled 1,500 units.

### Instructions

**a.** Determine the cost of goods available for sale.

**b.** Determine the ending inventory and the cost of goods sold under each of the assumed cost flow methods (FIFO, LIFO, and average-cost). Prove the accuracy of the cost of goods sold under the FIFO and LIFO methods.

**c.** Which cost flow method results in the lowest inventory amount for the balance sheet? The lowest cost of goods sold for the income statement?

*Compute ending inventory, prepare income statements, and answer questions using FIFO and LIFO.*

**P7.4 (LO 2), AN** Writing The management of National Inc. asks your help in determining the comparative effects of the FIFO and LIFO inventory cost flow methods. For 2022, the accounting records show these data.

| | |
|---|---|
| Inventory, January 1 (10,000 units) | $ 35,000 |
| Cost of 120,000 units purchased | 468,500 |
| Selling price of 98,000 units sold | 750,000 |
| Operating expenses | 124,000 |

Units purchased consisted of 35,000 units at $3.70 on May 10, 60,000 units at $3.90 on August 15, and 25,000 units at $4.20 on November 20. Income taxes are 28%.

## Instructions

**a.** Prepare comparative condensed income statements for 2022 under FIFO and LIFO. (Show computations of ending inventory.)

**b.** Answer the following questions for management in the form of a business letter.

1. Which inventory cost flow method produces the inventory amount that most closely approximates the amount that would have to be paid to replace the inventory? Why?

2. Which inventory cost flow method produces the net income amount that is a more likely indicator of next period's net income? Why?

3. Which inventory cost flow method is most likely to approximate the actual physical flow of the goods? Why?

4. How much more cash will be available under LIFO than under FIFO? Why?

5. How much of the gross profit under FIFO is illusionary in comparison with the gross profit under LIFO?

*a. Gross profit:*

| | |
|---|---|
| FIFO | $378,800 |
| LIFO | $362,900 |

**P7.5 (LO 2), AP** You have the following information for Jewels Gems. Jewels uses the periodic method of accounting for its inventory transactions. Jewels only carries one brand and size of diamonds—all are identical. Each batch of diamonds purchased is carefully coded and marked with its purchase cost.

*Compare specific identification, FIFO, and LIFO under periodic method; use cost flow assumption to influence earnings.*

| | | |
|---|---|---|
| March | 1 | Beginning inventory 150 diamonds at a cost of $310 per diamond. |
| | 3 | Purchased 200 diamonds at a cost of $350 each. |
| | 5 | Sold 180 diamonds for $600 each. |
| | 10 | Purchased 330 diamonds at a cost of $375 each. |
| | 25 | Sold 390 diamonds for $650 each. |

## Instructions

**a.** Assume that Jewels Gems uses the specific identification cost flow method.

1. Demonstrate how Jewels could maximize its gross profit for the month by specifically selecting which diamonds to sell on March 5 and March 25.

2. Demonstrate how Jewels could minimize its gross profit for the month by selecting which diamonds to sell on March 5 and March 25.

**b.** Assume that Jewels uses the FIFO cost flow assumption. Calculate cost of goods sold. How much gross profit would Jewels report under this cost flow assumption?

**c.** Assume that Jewels uses the LIFO cost flow assumption. Calculate cost of goods sold. How much gross profit would the company report under this cost flow assumption?

**d.** Which cost flow method should Jewels Gems select? Explain.

*a. Gross profit:*

| | |
|---|---|
| Maximum | $162,500 |
| Minimum | $155,350 |

**P7.6 (LO 3), AP** At December 31, 2021, Suisse Imports reported this information on its balance sheet.

*Record transactions related to bad debt expense.*

| | |
|---|---|
| Accounts receivable | $600,000 |
| Less: Allowance for doubtful accounts | 37,000 |

During 2022, the company had the following transactions related to receivables.

| | | |
|---|---|---|
| 1. | Sales on account | $2,500,000 |
| 2. | Sales returns and allowances | 50,000 |
| 3. | Collections of accounts receivable | 2,200,000 |
| 4. | Write-offs of accounts receivable deemed uncollectible | 41,000 |

## Instructions

**a.** Prepare a tabular summary that includes the following accounts: Cash, Accounts Receivable, Allowance for Doubtful Accounts, Revenue, and Expense. Enter the January 1, 2022, balances in Accounts Receivable and Allowance for Doubtful Accounts.

**b.** Record transactions 1 through 4. (Omit recording cost of goods sold.)

**c.** Record bad debt expense for 2022, assuming that aging the accounts receivable indicates that estimated bad debts are $46,000.

**d.** Indicate how accounts receivable and the allowance for doubtful accounts will be reported on the December 31, 2022, balance sheet.

*b. A/R bal.          $809,000*

*Analyze transactions related to bad debt expense.*

→ Excel

**P7.7 (LO 3), AP** The following is an aging schedule for Bryan Company.

| Customer | Total | Not Yet Due | 1–30 | 31–60 | 61–90 | Over 90 |
|---|---|---|---|---|---|---|
| | | | Number of Days Past Due | | | |
| Accounts receivable | $262,000 | $107,000 | $49,000 | $28,000 | $40,000 | $38,000 |
| Estimated percentage uncollectible | | 3% | 7% | 12% | 24% | 60% |
| Total estimated bad debts | $ 42,400 | $ 3,210 | $ 3,430 | $ 3,360 | $ 9,600 | $22,800 |

At December 31, 2021, the unadjusted balance in Allowance for Doubtful Accounts is $8,000.

**Instructions**

a. Cash realizable value
$219,600

**a.** Indicate the amount of bad debt expense for the year ending December 31, 2021, and the cash realizable value of Accounts Receivable.

**b.** On January 5, 2022, a $600 customer balance originating in 2021 is judged uncollectible. Indicate the cash realizable value of Accounts Receivable after recognizing the January 5 write-off.

*Compute bad debt amounts.*

**P7.8 (LO 3), AP** Writing Here is information related to Morgane Company for 2022.

| | |
|---|---|
| Total credit sales | $1,500,000 |
| Accounts receivable at December 31 | 840,000 |
| Bad debts written off | 37,000 |

**Instructions**

**a.** What amount of bad debt expense will Morgane Company report if it uses the direct write-off method of accounting for bad debts?

b. Bad debt exp. $30,600

**b.** Assume that Morgane Company decides to estimate its bad debt expense based on 4% of accounts receivable. What amount of bad debt expense will the company record if Allowance for Doubtful Accounts has a balance of $3,000?

**c.** What is a weakness of the direct write-off method of reporting bad debt expense?

*Answer questions related to bad debts.*

**P7.9 (LO 3), AP** Writing At December 31, 2022, the records of Malone Company contained the following amounts before adjustment.

| | |
|---|---|
| Accounts Receivable | $180,000 |
| Allowance for Doubtful Accounts | 1,500 |

**Instructions**

**a.** What amount of bad debt expense will Malone Company report if its aging schedule indicates that $10,200 of accounts receivable will be uncollectible?

b. Bad debt exp. $0

**b.** During the next month, January 2023, a $2,100 account receivable is written off as uncollectible. What amount of bad debt expense will Malone Company report in January 2023?

**c.** Repeat part (b), assuming that Malone Company uses the direct write-off method instead of the allowance method in accounting for uncollectible accounts receivable.

**d.** What are the advantages of using the allowance method in accounting for uncollectible accounts as compared to the direct write-off method?

*Compute inventory turnover and days in inventory; compute current ratio.*

**P7.10 (LO 4), AP** Suppose this information (in millions) is available for the Automotive and Other Operations Divisions of **General Motors Corporation** for a recent year. General Motors uses the LIFO inventory method.

| | |
|---|---|
| Beginning inventory | $ 13,921 |
| Ending inventory | 14,939 |
| Current assets | 60,135 |
| Current liabilities | 70,308 |
| Cost of goods sold | 166,259 |
| Sales revenue | 178,199 |

**Instructions**

**a.** Calculate the inventory turnover and days in inventory. (Round to one decimal place.)

**b.** Calculate the current ratio.

## Comprehensive Accounting Cycle Review

**ACR7** Waylon Company began operating on October 1, 2022. It prepares monthly financial statements. A tabular summary including information as of December 1, 2022, is shown below in the instructions. Note that the Inventory balance of $1,800 is based on 3,000 units costing $0.60 per unit. Also, the $17,000 balance in Retained Earnings represents the results for the first two months of operations.

The following transactions occurred during December.

| Dec. 3 | Purchased 4,000 units of Inventory on account at a cost of $0.72 per unit. |
|---|---|
| 5 | Sold 4,400 units of inventory on account for $0.90 per unit. (Waylon sold 3,000 of the $0.60 units and 1,400 of the $0.72.) |
| 7 | Granted the December 5 customer $180 credit for 200 units of inventory returned costing $144. These units were returned to inventory. |
| 17 | Purchased 2,200 units of inventory for cash at $0.80 each. |
| 22 | Sold 2,000 unit of inventory on account for $0.95 per unit. (Waylon sold 2,000 of the $0.72 units.) |

Adjustment data:

1. Accrued salaries and wages payable $400.

2. Depreciation on equipment $200 per month.

3. Income tax expense was $215, to be paid next year.

### Instructions

**a.** Use the following tabular summary to complete the following.

| | Assets | | | | | = | Liabilities | | | + | Stockholders' Equity | |
|---|---|---|---|---|---|---|---|---|---|---|---|---|
| | Cash + | Accts. Rec. + | Inventory + | Equip. − | Accum. Depr.— Equip. = | | Accts. Pay. + | Income Taxes Pay. + | Sal./ Wages Pay. + | | Com. Stock + | Retained Earnings |
| 12/1/Bal. | $4,800 | $3,900 | $1,800 | $21,000 | −$1,500 | | $3,000 | | | | $10,000 | $17,000 |
| | | | | | | | | | | | | + Rev. − Exp. − Div. |
| Dec. 3 | | | | | | | | | | | | |
| 5 | | | | | | | | | | | | |
| 7 | | | | | | | | | | | | |
| 17 | | | | | | | | | | | | |
| 22 | | | | | | | | | | | | |
| Unadj. Bal. | | | | | | | | | | | | |
| Adj. | | | | | | | | | | | | |
| (A1) | | | | | | | | | | | | |
| (A2) | | | | | | | | | | | | |
| (A3) | | | | | | | | | | | | |
| Adj. Bal. | | | | | | | | | | | | |

1. Record the December transactions. Include explanations for amounts in the revenue or expense columns.

2. Compute the balance in each column after recording the December 22 transaction.

3. Record adjustments.

4. Compute the adjusted balance in each column.

5. Prepare an income statement and a retained earnings statement for December and a classified balance sheet at December 31.

**b.** Compute ending inventory and cost of goods sold under FIFO, assuming Waylon Company uses the periodic inventory system.

**c.** Compute ending inventory and cost of goods sold under LIFO, assuming Waylon Company uses the periodic inventory system.

## Expand Your Critical Thinking

### Financial Reporting Problem: Apple Inc.

**CT7.1** The notes that accompany a company's financial statements provide informative details that would clutter the amounts and descriptions presented in the statements. Refer to the financial statements of **Apple Inc.** in Appendix A. The complete annual report, including the notes to the financial statements, is available at the company's website.

#### Instructions

Answer the following questions. (Give the amounts in millions of dollars, as shown in Apple's annual report.)

a. What did Apple report for the amount of inventories in its Consolidated Balance Sheet at September 29, 2018? At September 30, 2017?

b. Compute the dollar amount of change and the percentage change in inventories between 2017 and 2018. Compute inventory as a percentage of current assets for 2018.

c. What are the cost of sales reported by Apple for 2018, 2017, and 2016? Compute the ratio of cost of sales to net sales in 2018.

### Comparative Analysis Problem:

### Columbia Sportswear Company vs. Under Armour, Inc.

**CT7.2** The financial statements of **Columbia Sportswear Company** are presented in Appendix B. Financial statements for **Under Armour, Inc.** are presented in Appendix C.

#### Instructions

a. Based on the information in the financial statements, compute these values for each company for the most recent year.

   1. Inventory turnover. (Use cost of goods sold or cost of sales and inventories.)

   2. Days in inventory.

b. What conclusions concerning the management of the inventory can you draw from these data?

### Interpreting Financial Statements

**CT7.3** Suppose the following information is from the 2022 annual report of **American Greetings Corporation** (all dollars in thousands).

| | Feb. 28, 2022 | Feb. 28, 2021 |
|---|---|---|
| Inventories | | |
|   Finished goods | $232,893 | $244,379 |
|   Work in process | 7,068 | 10,516 |
|   Raw materials and supplies | 49,937 | 43,861 |
| | 289,898 | 298,756 |
|     Less: LIFO reserve | 86,025 | 82,085 |
| Total (as reported) | $203,873 | $216,671 |
| Cost of goods sold | $809,956 | $780,771 |
| Current assets (as reported) | $561,395 | $669,340 |
| Current liabilities | $343,405 | $432,321 |

The notes to the company's financial statements also include the following information.

The last-in, first-out (LIFO) cost method is used for approximately 75% of the domestic inventories in 2022 and approximately 70% in 2021. The foreign subsidiaries principally use the first-in, first-out (FIFO) method. Display material and factory supplies are carried at average-cost.

#### Instructions

a. Define each of the following: finished goods, work in process, and raw materials.

b. What might be a possible explanation for why the company uses FIFO for its nondomestic inventories?

**c.** Calculate the company's inventory turnover and days in inventory for 2021 and 2022 using the "Total (as reported)" amounts. (The 2020 inventory was $182,618.) Discuss the implications of any change in the ratios.

## Real-World Focus

**CT7.4**  The October 31, 2017, issue of the *Wall Street Journal* includes an article by Suzanne Kapner entitled "Inside the Decline of Sears, the Amazon of the 20th Century."

### Instructions

Read the article and then answer the following questions.

**a.** Describe some of the steps that suppliers took in response to the decline of **Sears'** credit quality.

**b.** As its suppliers took the steps described in part (a), what were the implications for Sears' ability to compete as a retailer?

**c.** How did companies that provide factoring services respond to Sears' troubles?

## Decision-Making Across the Organization

**CT7.5**  Solar Electronics has enjoyed tremendous sales growth during the last 10 years. However, even though sales have steadily increased, the company's CEO, Dana Byrnes, is concerned about certain aspects of its performance. She has called a meeting with the corporate controller and the vice presidents of finance, operations, sales, and marketing to discuss the company's performance. Dana begins the meeting by making the following observations:

> We have been forced to take significant write-downs on inventory during each of the last three years because of obsolescence. In addition, inventory storage costs have soared. We rent four additional warehouses to store our increasingly diverse inventory. Five years ago inventory represented only 20% of the value of our total assets. It now exceeds 35%. Yet, even with all of this inventory, "stockouts" (measured by complaints by customers that the desired product is not available) have increased by 40% during the last three years. And worse yet, it seems that we constantly must discount merchandise that we have too much of.

Dana asks the group to review the following data and make suggestions as to how the company's performance might be improved.

| (in millions) | 2022 | 2021 | 2020 | 2019 |
|---|---|---|---|---|
| Inventory | | | | |
| Raw materials | $242 | $198 | $155 | $128 |
| Work in process | 116 | 77 | 49 | 33 |
| Finished goods | 567 | 482 | 398 | 257 |
| Total inventory | $925 | $757 | $602 | $418 |
| | | | | |
| Current assets | $1,800 | $1,423 | $1,183 | $841 |
| Total assets | $2,643 | $2,523 | $2,408 | $2,090 |
| Current liabilities | $600 | $590 | $525 | $420 |
| Sales revenue | $9,428 | $8,674 | $7,536 | $6,840 |
| Cost of goods sold | $6,328 | $5,474 | $4,445 | $3,557 |
| Net income | $754 | $987 | $979 | $958 |

### Instructions

Using the information provided, answer the following questions.

**a.** Compute the current ratio, gross profit rate, profit margin, inventory turnover, and days in inventory for 2020, 2021, and 2022.

**b.** Discuss the trends and potential causes of the changes in the ratios in part (a).

**c.** Discuss potential remedies to any problems discussed in part (b).

**d.** What concerns might be raised by some members of management with regard to your suggestions in part (c)?

## Communication Activity

**CT7.6**  In a discussion of dramatic increases in coffee-bean prices, a *Wall Street Journal* article noted the following fact about **Starbucks**.

Before this year's bean-price hike, Starbucks added several defenses that analysts say could help it maintain earnings and revenue. The company last year began accounting for its coffee-bean purchases by taking the average price of all beans in inventory.

Prior to this change, the company was using FIFO.

### Instructions

Your client, the CEO of Superior Coffee, Inc., read this article and sent you an e-mail requesting that you explain why Starbucks might have taken this action. Your response should explain what impact this change in accounting method has on earnings, why the company might want to do this, and any possible disadvantages of such a change.

## Ethics Cases

**CT7.7** Nixon Wholesale Corp. uses the LIFO cost flow method. In the current year, profit at Nixon is running unusually high. The corporate tax rate is also high this year, but it is scheduled to decline significantly next year. In an effort to lower the current year's net income and to take advantage of the changing income tax rate, the president of Nixon Wholesale instructs the plant accountant to recommend to the purchasing department a large purchase of inventory for delivery 3 days before the end of the year. The price of the inventory to be purchased has doubled during the year, and the purchase will represent a major portion of the ending inventory value.

### Instructions

a. What is the effect of this transaction on this year's and next year's income statement and income tax expense? Why?

b. If Nixon Wholesale had been using the FIFO method of inventory costing, would the president give the same directive?

c. Should the plant accountant order the inventory purchase to lower income? What are the ethical implications of this order?

**CT7.8** As its year-end approaches, it appears that Mendez Corporation's net income will increase 10% this year. The president of Mendez Corporation, nervous that the stockholders might expect the company to sustain this 10% growth rate in net income in future years, suggests that the controller increase the allowance for doubtful accounts to 4% of receivables in order to lower this year's net income. The president thinks that the lower net income, which reflects a 6% growth rate, will be a more sustainable rate of growth for Mendez Corporation in future years. The controller of Mendez Corporation believes that the company's yearly allowance for doubtful accounts should be 2% of receivables.

### Instructions

a. Who are the stakeholders in this case?

b. Does the president's request pose an ethical dilemma for the controller?

c. Should the controller be concerned with Mendez Corporation's growth rate in estimating the allowance? Explain your answer.

## All About You

**CT7.9** Credit card usage in the United States is substantial. Many startup companies use credit cards as a way to help meet short-term financial needs. The most common forms of debt for startups are use of credit cards and loans from relatives.

Suppose that you start up Fantastic Sandwich Shop. You invested your savings of $20,000 and borrowed $70,000 from your relatives. Although sales in the first few months are good, you see that you may not have sufficient cash to pay expenses and maintain your inventory at acceptable levels, at least in the short term. You decide you may need to use one or more credit cards to fund the possible cash shortfall.

### Instructions

a. Go to the Internet and find two sources that provide insight into how to compare credit card terms.

b. Develop a list, in descending order of importance, as to what features are most important to you in selecting a credit card for your business.

c. Examine the features of your present credit card. (If you do not have a credit card, select a likely one online for this exercise.) Given your analysis above, what are the three major disadvantages of your present credit card?

# Reporting and Analyzing Long-Lived Assets

## Chapter Preview

For airlines and many other companies, making the right decisions regarding long-lived assets is critical because these assets represent huge investments. The discussion in this chapter is in two parts: plant assets and intangible assets. **Plant assets** are the property, plant, and equipment (physical assets) that commonly come to mind when we think of what a company owns. **Intangible assets**, such as copyrights and patents, lack physical substance but can be extremely valuable and vital to a company's success.

## Feature Story

### A Tale of Two Airlines

So, you're interested in starting a new business. Have you thought about the airline industry? Today, the most profitable airlines in the industry are not well-known majors like **American Airlines** and **United**. In fact, most giant, older airlines seem to be either bankrupt or on the verge of bankruptcy. In a recent year, five major airlines representing 24% of total U.S. capacity were operating under bankruptcy protection.

Not all airlines are hurting. The growth and profitability in the airline industry today is found at relative newcomers like **Southwest Airlines** and **JetBlue Airways**. These and other newer airlines compete primarily on ticket prices. During a recent five-year period, the low-fare airline market share increased by 47%, reaching 22% of U.S. airline capacity.

Southwest was the first upstart to make it big. It did so by taking a different approach. It bought small, new, fuel-efficient planes. Also, instead of the "hub-and-spoke" approach used by the majors, it opted for direct, short hop, no frills flights. It was all about controlling costs—getting the most out of its efficient new planes.

JetBlue, founded by former employees of Southwest, was recently ranked as the number 1 airline in the United States by the airline rating company **SkyTrax**. Management initially attempted to differentiate JetBlue by offering amenities not found on other airlines, such as seatback entertainment systems, while adopting Southwest's low-fare model. This approach was successful during JetBlue's early years, as it enjoyed both profitability and rapid growth. However, more recently the company has had to take aggressive steps to rein in costs in order to return to profitability.

In the past, upstarts such as **ValuJet** chose a different approach. The company bought planes that were 20 to 30 years old (known in the industry as *zombies*), which allowed it to quickly add planes to its fleet. Valujet started with a $3.4 million investment and grew to be worth $630 million in its first three years.

But with high fuel costs, airlines are no longer in the market for old planes, which generally can't be operated efficiently. Today, success in the airline business comes from using the newest and most efficient equipment, and knowing how to get the most out of it.

# Chapter Outline

| LEARNING OBJECTIVES | REVIEW | PRACTICE |
|---|---|---|
| **LO 1** Explain the accounting for plant asset expenditures. | • Determining the cost of plant assets<br>• Expenditures during useful life | **DO IT! 1** Cost of Plant Assets |
| **LO 2** Apply depreciation methods to plant assets. | • Factors in computing depreciation<br>• Depreciation methods<br>• Revising depreciation<br>• Impairments | **DO IT! 2a** Straight-Line Depreciation<br>**DO IT! 2b** Revised Depreciation |
| **LO 3** Explain how to account for the disposal of plant assets. | • Sale of plant assets<br>• Retirement of plant assets | **DO IT! 3** Plant Asset Disposals |
| **LO 4** Identify the basic issues related to reporting intangible assets. | • Accounting for intangible assets<br>• Types of intangible assets | **DO IT! 4** Classification Concepts |
| **LO 5** Discuss how long-lived assets are reported and analyzed. | • Presentation<br>• Analysis | **DO IT! 5** Asset Turnover and Return on Assets |

**Go to the Review and Practice section at the end of the chapter for a targeted summary and practice applications with solutions.**

**Visit WileyPLUS for additional tutorials and practice opportunities.**

# Plant Asset Expenditures

**Plant assets** are resources that have physical substance (a definite size and shape), are used in the operations of a business, and are not intended for sale to customers.

- Plant assets are called various names—property, plant, and equipment; plant and equipment; and fixed assets.
- These assets are expected to be of service to the company for a number of years.
- Except for land, plant assets decline in service potential (ability to produce revenue) over their useful lives.

Plant assets are critical to a company's success because they determine the company's capacity and therefore its ability to satisfy customers. With too few planes, for example, **JetBlue Airways** and **Southwest Airlines** would lose customers to their competitors. But with too many planes, they would be flying with empty seats. Management must constantly monitor its needs and acquire assets accordingly. Failure to do so results in lost business opportunities or inefficient use of existing assets and, eventually, poor financial results.

It is important for a company to:

1. Keep assets in good operating condition.
2. Replace worn-out or outdated assets.
3. Expand its productive assets as needed.

The decline of rail travel in the United States can be traced in part to the failure of railroad companies to maintain and update their assets. Conversely, the growth of air travel in this country can be attributed in part to the general willingness of airline companies to follow these essential guidelines.

For many companies, investments in plant assets are substantial. **Illustration 8.1** shows the percentages of plant assets in relation to total assets in various companies in a recent year.

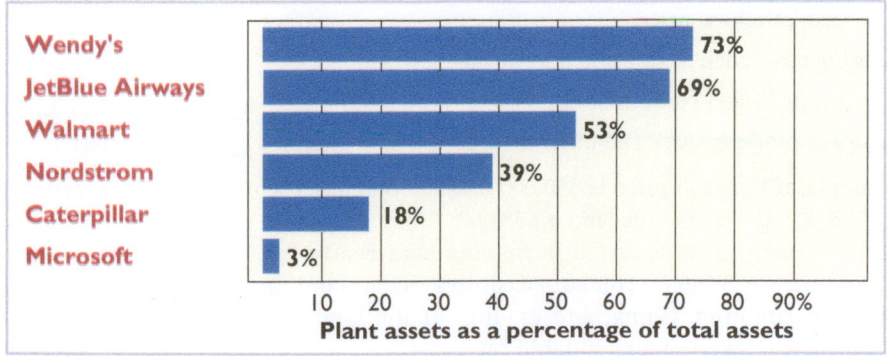

**ILLUSTRATION 8.1**

**Percentages of plant assets in relation to total assets**

## Determining the Cost of Plant Assets

The **historical cost principle** requires that companies record plant assets at cost. Thus, JetBlue Airways and Southwest Airlines record their planes at cost. **Cost consists of all expenditures necessary to acquire an asset and make it ready for its intended use.** For example, when **Boeing** buys equipment, the purchase price, freight costs paid by Boeing, and installation costs are all part of the cost of the equipment.

Determining which costs to include in a plant asset account and which costs not to include is very important.

- If a cost is not included in a plant asset account, then it must be expensed immediately.
- Such costs are referred to as **revenue expenditures**.
- On the other hand, costs that are not expensed immediately but are instead included in a plant asset account are referred to as **capital expenditures**. JetBlue reported capital expenditures of $1,074 million during 2017.

The distinction between revenue and capital expenditures is important; it has immediate, and often material, implications for the income statement. Some companies, in order to boost current income, have **improperly capitalized expenditures** that they should have expensed.

For example, suppose that a company improperly capitalizes to a building account $1,000 of maintenance costs incurred at the end of the year. That is, the costs are included in the asset account Buildings rather than being expensed immediately as Maintenance and Repairs Expense. If the company is allocating the cost of the building as an expense (depreciating it) over a 40-year life, then the maintenance cost of $1,000 will be incorrectly spread across 40 years instead of being expensed in the current year. As a result, the company will understate current-year expenses by approximately $1,000 and will overstate current-year income by approximately $1,000. Thus, determining which costs to capitalize and which to expense is very important.

Cost is measured by the cash paid in a cash transaction or by the **cash equivalent price** paid when companies use noncash assets in payment.

- **The cash equivalent price is equal to the fair value of the asset given up or the fair value of the asset received, whichever is more clearly determinable** (see **International Note**).
- Once cost is established, it becomes the basis of accounting for the plant asset over its useful life.
- Current fair value is not used to increase the recorded cost after acquisition.

We explain the application of the historical cost principle to each of the major classes of plant assets in the following sections.

> **International Note**
>
> IFRS is more flexible regarding asset valuation. Companies revalue to fair value when they believe this information is more relevant.

## Land

Companies often use land as a building site for a manufacturing plant or office site. The cost of land includes:

1. The cash purchase price.
2. Closing costs such as title and attorney fees.
3. Real estate broker commissions.
4. Accrued property taxes and other liens on the land assumed by the purchaser.

For example, if the cash price is $50,000 and the purchaser agrees to pay accrued property taxes of $5,000, the cost of the land is $55,000.

All necessary costs incurred in making land **ready for its intended use** increase the Land account. When a company acquires vacant land, its cost includes expenditures for clearing, draining, filling, and grading. If the land has a building on it that must be removed to make the site suitable for construction of a new building, the company includes all demolition and removal costs, less any proceeds from salvaged materials, in the Land account.

To illustrate, assume that Hayes Company acquires real estate at a cash cost of $100,000. The property contains an old warehouse that is removed at a net cost of $6,000 ($7,500 in costs less $1,500 proceeds from salvaged materials). Additional expenditures are for the attorney's fee $1,000 and the real estate broker's commission $8,000. Given these factors, the cost of the land is $115,000, computed as shown in **Illustration 8.2**.

**ILLUSTRATION 8.2**
**Computation of cost of land**

| Land | |
|---|---|
| Cash price of property | $100,000 |
| Net removal cost of warehouse | 6,000 |
| Attorney's fee | 1,000 |
| Real estate broker's commission | 8,000 |
| **Cost of land** | **$115,000** |

When Hayes records the acquisition, it increases Land and decreases Cash by $115,000.

## Land Improvements

**Land improvements** are structural additions with limited lives that are made to land, such as driveways, parking lots, fences, landscaping, and underground sprinklers.

- The cost of land improvements includes all expenditures necessary to make the improvements ready for their intended use. For example, the cost of a new company parking lot includes the amount paid for paving, fencing, and lighting. Thus, the company would record the total of all of these costs to Land Improvements.
- Land improvements have limited useful lives. Even when well-maintained, they will eventually need to be replaced.
- As a result, companies expense (depreciate) the cost of land improvements over their useful lives.

## Buildings

Buildings are facilities used in operations, such as stores, offices, factories, warehouses, and airplane hangars. Companies charge to the Buildings account all necessary expenditures relating to the purchase or construction of a building.

- When a building is **purchased**, such costs include the purchase price, closing costs (attorney's fees, title insurance, etc.), and real estate broker's commission.
- Costs to make the building ready for its intended use consist of expenditures for remodeling rooms and offices and replacing or repairing the roof, floors, electrical wiring, and plumbing.
- When a new building is **constructed**, its cost consists of the contract price plus payments made by the owner for architects' fees, building permits, and excavation costs.

In addition, companies add certain interest costs to the cost of a building. Interest costs incurred to finance a construction project are included in the cost of the asset when a significant period of time is required to get the asset ready for use. In these circumstances, interest costs are considered as necessary as materials and labor. However, the inclusion of interest costs in the cost of a constructed building is **limited to interest costs incurred during the construction period**. When construction has been completed, subsequent interest payments on funds borrowed to finance the construction are recorded as increases to Interest Expense.

## Equipment

**Equipment** includes assets used in operations, such as store check-out counters, office furniture, factory machinery, and delivery trucks. **JetBlue Airways**' equipment includes aircraft, in-flight entertainment systems, and trucks for ground operations.

- The cost of equipment consists of the cash purchase price, sales taxes, freight charges, and insurance during transit paid by the purchaser.
- It also includes expenditures required in assembling, installing, and testing the unit.
- However, companies treat as expenses the costs of motor vehicle licenses and accident insurance on company trucks and cars. Such items are **annual recurring expenditures and do not benefit future periods**.

- Two criteria apply in determining the cost of equipment:
    1. The frequency of the cost—one time or recurring.
    2. The benefit period—the life of the asset or one year.

To illustrate, assume that Lenard Company purchases a delivery truck on January 1 at a cash price of $22,000. Related expenditures are sales taxes $1,320, painting and lettering $500, motor vehicle license $80, and a three-year accident insurance policy $1,600. The cost of the delivery truck is $23,820, computed as shown in **Illustration 8.3**.

**ILLUSTRATION 8.3**

**Computation of cost of delivery truck**

| Delivery Truck | |
| --- | ---: |
| Cash price | $22,000 |
| Sales taxes | 1,320 |
| Painting and lettering | 500 |
| **Cost of delivery truck** | **$23,820** |

Lenard treats the cost of a motor vehicle license as an expense and the cost of an insurance policy as a prepaid asset. Thus, the company records the purchase of the truck and related expenditures as follows.

| CASH FLOW | BALANCE SHEET | | | | | | | | | | INCOME STATEMENT |
| --- | --- | --- | --- | --- | --- | --- | --- | --- | --- | --- | --- |
| | Assets | | | = Liabilities + | | Stockholders' Equity | | | | | |
| | | | | | | | | Retained Earnings | | | |
| | Cash + | Prepd. Insur. + | Equip- ment = | | | Common Stock + | Rev. − | Exp. − | Div. | | |
| ↓$25,500 | −$25,500 | +$1,600 | +$23,820 | | | | | −$80 | | | License Exp. |

For another example, assume Merten Company purchases factory machinery at a cash price of $50,000. Related expenditures are sales taxes $3,000, insurance during shipping $500, and installation and testing $1,000. The cost of the factory machinery is $54,500, computed as shown in **Illustration 8.4**.

**ILLUSTRATION 8.4**

**Computation of cost of factory machinery**

| Factory Machinery | |
| --- | ---: |
| Cash price | $50,000 |
| Sales taxes | 3,000 |
| Insurance during shipping | 500 |
| Installation and testing | 1,000 |
| **Cost of factory machinery** | **$54,500** |

| CASH FLOW | BALANCE SHEET | | | | | | | | | INCOME STATEMENT |
| --- | --- | --- | --- | --- | --- | --- | --- | --- | --- | --- |
| | Assets | | = Liabilities + | | Stockholders' Equity | | | | | |
| | | | | | | Retained Earnings | | | | |
| | Cash + | Equip- ment = | | | Common Stock + | Rev. − | Exp. − | Div. | | |
| ↓$54,500 | −$54,500 | +$54,500 | | | | | | | | No effect |

## Expenditures During Useful Life

During the useful life of a plant asset, a company may incur costs for ordinary repairs, additions, and improvements.

- **Ordinary repairs** are expenditures to maintain the operating efficiency and expected productive life of the unit.

- They usually are fairly small amounts that occur frequently throughout the service life, such as oil changes for motor vehicles, the painting of buildings, and the replacing of worn-out gears on factory machinery.
- Ordinary repairs are recorded as Maintenance and Repairs Expense as incurred.

In contrast, **additions and improvements** are costs incurred to **increase** the operating efficiency, productive capacity, or expected useful life of the plant asset.

- These expenditures are usually material in amount and occur infrequently during the period of ownership.
- Because the expenditures for additions and improvements increase the company's investment in productive facilities and are generally added to the plant asset affected, they are **capital expenditures**.
- The accounting for capital expenditures varies depending on the nature of the expenditure.

**Northwest Airlines** at one time spent $120 million to spruce up 40 jets. The improvements were designed to extend the lives of the planes, meet stricter government noise limits, and save money. The capital expenditure was expected to extend the life of the jets by 10 to 15 years and save about $560 million compared to the cost of buying new planes. The jets were, on average, 24 years old.

---

## Anatomy of a Fraud

Bernie Ebbers was the founder and CEO of the phone company **WorldCom**. The company engaged in a series of increasingly large, debt-financed acquisitions of other companies. These acquisitions made the company grow quickly, which made the stock price increase dramatically. However, because the acquired companies all had different accounting systems, WorldCom's financial records were a mess.

When WorldCom's performance started to flatten out, Bernie coerced WorldCom's accountants to engage in a number of fraudulent activities to make net income look better than it really was and thus prop up the stock price. One of these frauds involved treating $7 billion of line costs as capital expenditures. The line costs, which were rental fees paid to other phone companies to use their phone lines, had always been properly expensed in previous years. Capitalization delayed expense recognition to future periods and thus boosted current-period profits.

### Total take: $7 billion

#### The Missing Controls

**Documentation procedures.** The company's accounting system was a disorganized collection of non-integrated systems, which resulted from a series of corporate acquisitions. Top management took advantage of this disorganization to conceal its fraudulent activities.

**Independent internal verification.** A fraud of this size should have been detected by a routine comparison of the actual physical assets with the list of physical assets shown in the accounting records.

---

## DO IT! 1 | Cost of Plant Assets

Assume that Drummond Corp. purchases a delivery truck for $15,000 cash plus sales taxes of $900 and delivery costs of $500. The buyer also pays $200 for painting and lettering, $600 for an annual insurance policy, and $80 for a motor vehicle license. Explain how the company should account for each of these costs.

### Solution

The first four payments ($15,000 purchase price, $900 sales taxes, $500 delivery, and $200 painting and lettering) are expenditures necessary to make the truck ready for its intended use. Thus, the cost of the truck is $16,600. The payments for insurance and the license are operating expenses incurred annually during the useful life of the asset.

Related exercise material: **BE8.1, BE8.2, BE8.3, DO IT! 8.1, E8.1, E8.2, and E8.3.**

**ACTION PLAN**
- Identify expenditures made in order to get delivery equipment ready for its intended use.
- Expense operating costs incurred during the useful life of the equipment.

# Depreciation Methods

As explained in Chapter 4, **depreciation** is the process of allocating to expense the cost of a plant asset over its useful (service) life in a rational and systematic manner. Such cost allocation is designed to properly record expenses (efforts) with associated revenues (results) (see **Illustration 8.5**).

**ILLUSTRATION 8.5**

**Depreciation as a cost allocation concept**

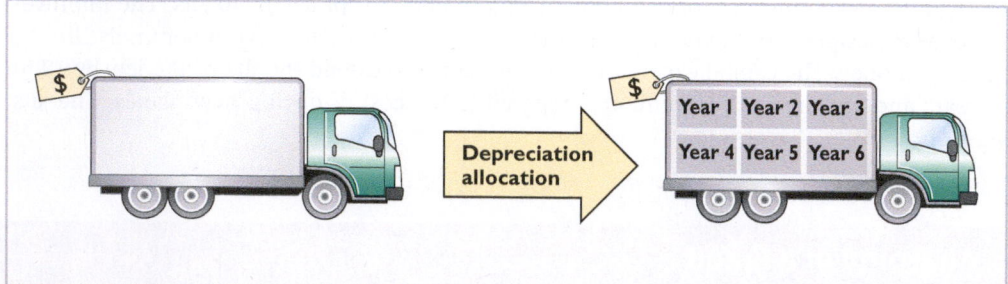

Depreciation affects the balance sheet through accumulated depreciation, which companies report as a deduction from plant assets. It affects the income statement through depreciation expense.

It is important to understand that **depreciation is a cost allocation process**, **not an asset valuation process**.

- No attempt is made to measure the change in an asset's fair value during ownership.
- Thus, the **book value**—cost less accumulated depreciation—of a plant asset may differ significantly from its **fair value**.
- In fact, if an asset is fully depreciated, it can have zero book value but still have a significant fair value.

**ETHICS NOTE**

When a business is acquired, proper allocation of the purchase price to various asset classes is important since different depreciation treatment can materially affect income. For example, buildings are depreciated, but land is not.

Depreciation applies to **three classes of plant assets**: land improvements, buildings, and equipment (see **Ethics Note**). Each of these classes is considered to be a **depreciable asset** because the usefulness to the company and the revenue-producing ability of each class decline over the asset's useful life. Depreciation **does not apply to land** because its usefulness and revenue-producing ability generally remain intact as long as the land is owned. In fact, in many cases, the usefulness of land increases over time because of the scarcity of good sites. Thus, **land is not a depreciable asset**.

During a depreciable asset's useful life, its revenue-producing ability declines because of:

- Wear and tear; a delivery truck that has been driven 100,000 miles will be less useful to a company than one driven only 800 miles.
- **Obsolescence**, which is the process by which an asset becomes out of date before it physically wears out. For example, many companies replace their computers long before they originally planned to do so because technological improvements make their old hardware obsolete.

**Recognizing depreciation for an asset does not result in the accumulation of cash for replacement of the asset.** The balance in Accumulated Depreciation represents the total amount of the asset's cost that the company has charged to expense to date; **it is not a cash fund**.

# Factors in Computing Depreciation

Three factors affect the computation of depreciation, as shown in **Illustration 8.6** (see **Helpful Hint**).

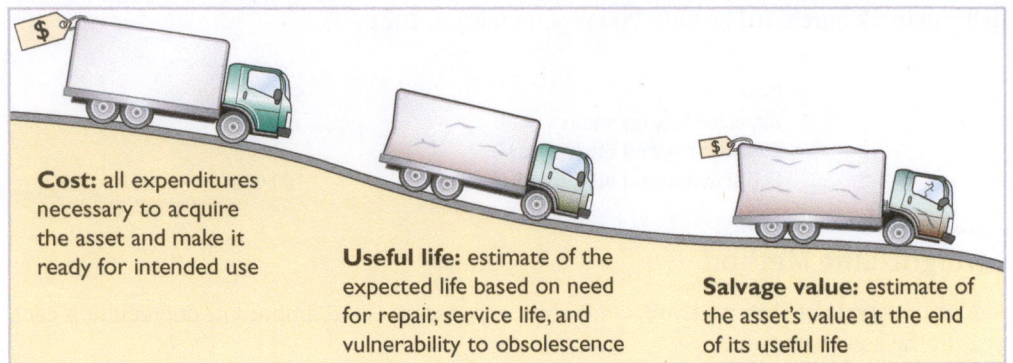

**ILLUSTRATION 8.6**

**Three factors in computing depreciation**

**HELPFUL HINT**

Depreciation expense is reported on the income statement. Accumulated depreciation is reported on the balance sheet as a deduction from plant assets.

**Cost:** all expenditures necessary to acquire the asset and make it ready for intended use

**Useful life:** estimate of the expected life based on need for repair, service life, and vulnerability to obsolescence

**Salvage value:** estimate of the asset's value at the end of its useful life

1. **Cost.** Earlier in the chapter, we explained the considerations that affect the cost of a depreciable asset. Remember that companies record plant assets at cost, in accordance with the historical cost principle.

2. **Useful life.** Useful life is an estimate of the expected productive life, also called service life, of the asset for its owner. Useful life may be expressed in terms of time, units of activity (such as machine hours), or units of output. Useful life is an estimate. In making the estimate, management considers such factors as the intended use of the asset, repair and maintenance policies, and vulnerability of the asset to obsolescence. The company's past experience with similar assets is often helpful in deciding on expected useful life.

3. **Salvage value.** Salvage value is an estimate of the asset's value at the end of its useful life for its owner. Companies may base the value on the asset's worth as scrap or on its expected trade-in value. Like useful life, salvage value is an estimate. In making the estimate, management considers how it plans to dispose of the asset and its experience with similar assets.

# Depreciation Methods

Although a number of methods exist, depreciation is generally computed using one of three methods:

1. Straight-line.
2. Declining-balance.
3. Units-of-activity.

Like the alternative inventory methods discussed in Chapter 7, each of these depreciation methods is acceptable under generally accepted accounting principles.

- Management selects the method it believes best measures an asset's contribution to revenue over its useful life.
- Once a company chooses a method, it should apply that method consistently over the useful life of the asset.
- Consistency enhances the ability to analyze financial statements over multiple years.

**Illustration 8.7** shows the distribution of the primary depreciation methods in a sample of the largest U.S. companies. Clearly, straight-line depreciation is the most widely used approach. In fact, because some companies use more than one method, **straight-line depreciation is used for some or all of the depreciation taken by more than 95% of U.S. companies**. For this reason, we illustrate procedures for straight-line depreciation and discuss the alternative depreciation

**ILLUSTRATION 8.7**

**Use of depreciation methods in major U.S. companies**

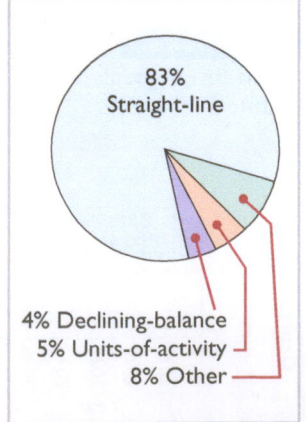

83% Straight-line

4% Declining-balance
5% Units-of-activity
8% Other

approaches only at a conceptual level. This coverage introduces you to the basic idea of depreciation as an allocation concept without entangling you in too much procedural detail. (Also, note that many calculators are preprogrammed to perform the basic depreciation methods.)

No matter what method is used, the total amount depreciated over the useful life of the asset is its depreciable cost. **Depreciable cost** is equal to the cost of the asset less its salvage value.

Our illustration of depreciation methods is based on the following data relating to a small delivery truck purchased by Bill's Pizzas on January 1, 2022.

| | |
|---|---|
| Cost | $13,000 |
| Expected salvage value | $1,000 |
| Estimated useful life (in years) | 5 |
| Estimated useful life (in miles) | 100,000 |

## Straight-Line Method

Under the **straight-line method**, companies expense an equal amount of depreciation each year of the asset's useful life.

- Management must choose the useful life of an asset based on its own expectations and experience.
- To compute the annual depreciation expense, we divide depreciable cost by the estimated useful life.
- As indicated above, depreciable cost represents the total amount subject to depreciation; it is calculated as the cost of the plant asset less its salvage value.

**Illustration 8.8** shows the computation of depreciation expense in the first year for Bill's Pizzas' delivery truck.

**ILLUSTRATION 8.8**

**Formula for straight-line method**

| Cost | − | Salvage Value | = | Depreciable Cost |
|---|---|---|---|---|
| $13,000 | − | $1,000 | = | $12,000 |

| Depreciable Cost | ÷ | Useful Life (in years) | = | Depreciation Expense |
|---|---|---|---|---|
| $12,000 | ÷ | 5 | = | $2,400 |

Alternatively, we can compute an annual **rate** at which the company depreciates the delivery truck. In this case, the rate is 20% (100% ÷ 5 years). When an annual rate is used under the straight-line method, the company applies the percentage rate to the depreciable cost of the asset, as shown in the **depreciation schedule** in **Illustration 8.9**.

**ILLUSTRATION 8.9**

**Straight-line depreciation schedule**

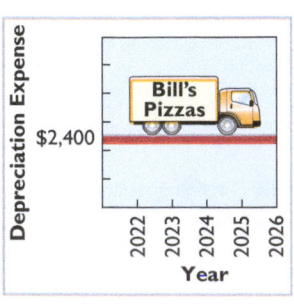

### Bill's Pizzas

| | Computation | | | Annual | End of Year | |
|---|---|---|---|---|---|---|
| Year | Depreciable Cost | × Depreciation Rate | = | Depreciation Expense | Accumulated Depreciation | Book Value |
| 2022 | $12,000 | 20% | | $ 2,400 | $ 2,400 | $10,600* |
| 2023 | 12,000 | 20 | | 2,400 | 4,800 | 8,200 |
| 2024 | 12,000 | 20 | | 2,400 | 7,200 | 5,800 |
| 2025 | 12,000 | 20 | | 2,400 | 9,600 | 3,400 |
| 2026 | 12,000 | 20 | | 2,400 | 12,000 | 1,000 |
| | | | Total | $12,000 | | |

*$13,000 − $2,400

Note that the depreciation expense of $2,400 is the same each year. The book value at the end of the useful life is equal to the estimated $1,000 salvage value.

What happens when an asset is purchased **during** the year, rather than on January 1 as in our example?

- In that case, it is necessary to **prorate the annual depreciation** for the portion of a year used.
- If Bill's Pizzas had purchased the delivery truck on April 1, 2022, the company would use the truck for 9 months in 2022.
- The depreciation for 2022 would be $1,800 ($12,000 × 20% × $\frac{9}{12}$ of a year).

As indicated earlier, the straight-line method predominates in practice. For example, such large companies as **Campbell Soup**, **Marriott**, and **General Mills** use the straight-line method. It is simple to apply, and it records expenses with associated revenues appropriately when the use of the asset is reasonably uniform throughout the service life. Generally, the types of assets that give equal benefits over their useful lives are those for which daily use does not affect productivity. Examples are office furniture and fixtures, buildings, warehouses, and garages for motor vehicles.

---

## DO IT! 2a | Straight-Line Depreciation

On January 1, 2022, Iron Mountain Ski Corporation purchased a new snow-grooming machine for $50,000. The machine is estimated to have a 10-year life with a $2,000 salvage value. Prepare a tabular summary to record depreciation on December 31, 2022, if Iron Mountain uses the straight-line method of depreciation.

**ACTION PLAN**

- Calculate depreciable cost (Cost − Salvage value).
- Divide the depreciable cost by the asset's estimated useful life.

### Solution

$$\text{Depreciation expense} = \frac{\text{Cost} - \text{Salvage value}}{\text{Useful life}} = \frac{\$50,000 - \$2,000}{10} = \$4,800$$

Iron Mountain would record the first year's depreciation as follows.

| | **Assets** | | **= Liabilities +** | | **Stockholders' Equity** | | | |
|---|---|---|---|---|---|---|---|---|
| | | Accum. | | | | Retained Earnings | | |
| | Equip- | Depr.— | | Common | | | | |
| | ment − | Equip. = | | Stock + | Rev. − | Exp. | − Div. | |
| Bal. | $50,000 | | | | | | | |
| Dec. 31 | | −$4,800 | | | | −$4,800 | | Deprec. Exp. |

Related exercise material: **BE8.4, DO IT! 8.2a, E8.4, and E8.5**.

---

## Declining-Balance Method

The **declining-balance method** computes depreciation expense using a constant rate applied to a declining book value.

- This method is called an **accelerated-depreciation method** because it results in higher depreciation in the early years of an asset's life than does the straight-line approach.
- However, because the total amount of depreciation (the depreciable cost) taken over an asset's life is the same **no matter what approach** is used, the declining-balance method produces a decreasing annual depreciation expense over the asset's useful life.
- In early years, declining-balance depreciation expense will exceed straight-line. In later years, it will be less than straight-line.

Managers might choose an accelerated approach if they think that an asset's utility will decline quickly.

Companies can apply the declining-balance approach at different rates, which result in varying speeds of depreciation. A common declining-balance rate is double the straight-line rate. Using that rate, the method is referred to as the **double-declining-balance method**.

If we apply the double-declining-balance method to Bill's Pizzas' delivery truck, assuming a five-year life, we get the pattern of depreciation shown in **Illustration 8.10**. Again, note that total depreciation over the life of the truck is $12,000, the depreciable cost.

**ILLUSTRATION 8.10**

Declining-balance depreciation schedule

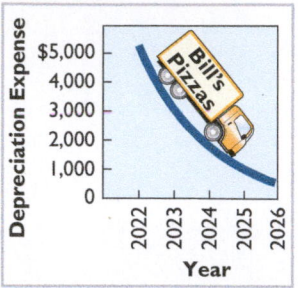

| | | End of Year | |
| Year | Annual Depreciation Expense | Accumulated Depreciation | Book Value |
|---|---|---|---|
| 2022 | $ 5,200 | $ 5,200 | $7,800 |
| 2023 | 3,120 | 8,320 | 4,680 |
| 2024 | 1,872 | 10,192 | 2,808 |
| 2025 | 1,123 | 11,315 | 1,685 |
| 2026 | 685 | 12,000 | 1,000 |
| Total | $12,000 | | |

*Bill's Pizzas*

## Units-of-Activity Method

As indicated earlier, useful life can be expressed in ways other than a time period. Under the **units-of-activity method**, useful life is expressed in terms of the total units of production or the use expected from the asset.

- The units-of-activity method is ideally suited to factory machinery: Companies can measure production in terms of units of output or in terms of machine hours used in operating the machinery.
- It is also possible to use the method for such items as delivery equipment (miles driven) and airplanes (hours in use).
- The units-of-activity method is generally not suitable for such assets as buildings or furniture because activity levels are difficult to measure for these assets.

Applying the units-of-activity method to the delivery truck owned by Bill's Pizzas, we first must know some basic information. Bill's expects to be able to drive the truck a total of 100,000 miles. **Illustration 8.11** shows depreciation over the five-year life based on an assumed mileage pattern.

**ILLUSTRATION 8.11**

Units-of-activity depreciation schedule

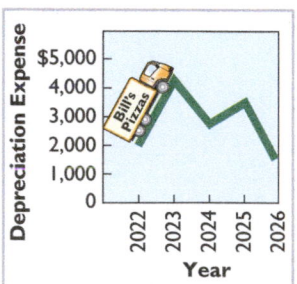

*Bill's Pizzas*

| | Units of Activity (miles) | Annual Depreciation Expense | End of Year | |
| Year | | | Accumulated Depreciation | Book Value |
|---|---|---|---|---|
| 2022 | 15,000 | $ 1,800 | $ 1,800 | $11,200 |
| 2023 | 30,000 | 3,600 | 5,400 | 7,600 |
| 2024 | 20,000 | 2,400 | 7,800 | 5,200 |
| 2025 | 25,000 | 3,000 | 10,800 | 2,200 |
| 2026 | 10,000 | 1,200 | 12,000 | 1,000 |
| Total | 100,000 | $12,000 | | |

As the name implies, under units-of-activity depreciation, the amount of depreciation is proportional to the activity that took place during that period. For example, the delivery truck was driven twice as many miles in 2023 as in 2022, and depreciation was exactly twice as much in 2023 as it was in 2022.

## Management's Choice: Comparison of Methods

**Illustration 8.12** compares annual and total depreciation expense for Bill's Pizzas under the three methods.

| Year | Straight-Line | Declining-Balance | Units-of-Activity |
|------|------|------|------|
| 2022 | $ 2,400 | $ 5,200 | $ 1,800 |
| 2023 | 2,400 | 3,120 | 3,600 |
| 2024 | 2,400 | 1,872 | 2,400 |
| 2025 | 2,400 | 1,123 | 3,000 |
| 2026 | 2,400 | 685 | 1,200 |
| | **$12,000** | **$12,000** | **$12,000** |

**ILLUSTRATION 8.12**

**Comparison of depreciation methods**

Note the following about Illustration 8.12:

- Annual depreciation expense varies considerably among the methods, but **total depreciation expense is the same ($12,000) for the five-year period**.
- Each method is acceptable in accounting because each recognizes the decline in service potential of the asset in a rational and systematic manner.

**Illustration 8.13** graphs the depreciation expense pattern under each method.

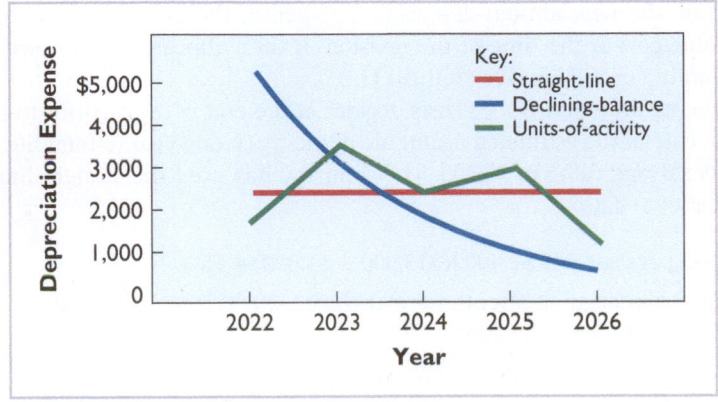

**ILLUSTRATION 8.13**

**Patterns of depreciation**

## Depreciation and Income Taxes

The Internal Revenue Service (IRS) allows corporate taxpayers to deduct depreciation expense when computing taxable income.

- However, the tax regulations of the IRS do not require the taxpayer to use the same depreciation method on the tax return that it uses in preparing financial statements (see **Helpful Hint**).
- Consequently, many large corporations use straight-line depreciation in their financial statements in order to maximize net income; at the same time, they use a special accelerated-depreciation method on their tax returns in order to minimize their income taxes.

For tax purposes, taxpayers must use on their tax returns either the straight-line method or a special accelerated-depreciation method called the **Modified Accelerated Cost Recovery System** (MACRS).

**HELPFUL HINT**

Depreciation per financial statements is usually different from depreciation per tax returns.

## Depreciation Disclosure in the Notes

Companies must disclose the choice of depreciation method in their financial statements or in related notes that accompany the statements. **Illustration 8.14** shows excerpts from the "Property and equipment" notes from the financial statements of **Southwest Airlines**.

**ILLUSTRATION 8.14**
**Disclosure of depreciation policies**

**Real World**

### Southwest Airlines
#### Notes to the Financial Statements

**Property and equipment** Depreciation is provided by the straight-line method to estimated residual values over periods generally ranging from 23 to 25 years for flight equipment.

From this note, we learn that Southwest Airlines uses the straight-line method to depreciate its planes over periods of 23 to 25 years.

## Revising Periodic Depreciation

Management should periodically review annual depreciation expense. If wear and tear or obsolescence indicates that annual depreciation is either inadequate or excessive, the company should change the depreciation expense amount.

When a change in an estimate is required, the company makes the change in **current and future years but not to prior periods**.

1. The company does not change previously recorded depreciation expense.

2. The company revises depreciation expense for current and future years.

**HELPFUL HINT**

Use a step-by-step approach: (1) determine new depreciable cost; (2) divide by remaining useful life.

The rationale for this treatment is that continual restatement of prior periods would adversely affect users' confidence in financial statements.

To determine the new annual depreciation expense, the company first computes the asset's depreciable cost at the time of the revision. It then allocates the revised depreciable cost to the remaining useful life (see **Helpful Hint**).

To illustrate, assume that Bill's Pizzas decides at the end of 2025 (prior to the year-end adjustments) to extend the estimated useful life of the truck one year (a total life of six years) and increase its salvage value to $2,200. The company has used the straight-line method to depreciate the asset to date.

- Depreciation per year was $2,400 [($13,000 − $1,000) ÷ 5].
- Accumulated depreciation after three years (2022–2024) is $7,200 ($2,400 × 3), and book value is $5,800 ($13,000 − $7,200).
- The new annual depreciation is $1,200, computed on December 31, 2025, as shown in **Illustration 8.15**.

**ILLUSTRATION 8.15**
**Revised depreciation computation**

| | | |
|---|---|---|
| Book value, 1/1/25 | $ 5,800 | |
| Less: New salvage value | 2,200 | |
| Depreciable cost | $ 3,600 | |
| Remaining useful life | 3 years | (2025–2027) |
| **Revised annual depreciation ($3,600 ÷ 3)** | **$ 1,200** | |

Bill's Pizzas does not record the change in estimate. On December 31, 2025, during the preparation of adjustments, it records depreciation expense of $1,200 instead of the amount recorded in previous years.

Companies must disclose in the financial statements significant changes in estimates. Although a company may have a legitimate reason for changing an estimated life, financial statement users should be aware that some companies might change an estimate simply to achieve financial statement goals. For example, extending an asset's estimated life reduces depreciation expense and increases current period income.

At one time, **AirTran Airways** (now owned by **Southwest Airlines**) increased the estimated useful lives of some of its planes from 25 to 30 years and increased the estimated lives of related aircraft parts from 5 years to 30 years. It disclosed that the change in estimate decreased its net loss for the year by approximately $0.6 million, or about $0.01 per share. Whether these changes were appropriate depends on how reasonable it is to assume that planes will continue to be used for a long time. Our Feature Story suggests that although in the past many planes lasted a long time, it is also clear that because of high fuel costs, airlines are now scrapping many of their old, inefficient planes.

# Impairments

As noted earlier, the book value of plant assets is rarely the same as the fair value. In instances where the value of a plant asset declines substantially, its fair value might fall materially below book value. This may happen because a machine has become obsolete, or the market for the product made by the machine has dried up or has become very competitive.

- A **permanent decline** in the fair value of an asset is referred to as an **impairment**.
- So as not to overstate the asset on the books, the company records a write-down, whereby the asset's cost is reduced to its new fair value during the year in which the decline in value occurs.

For example, **Disney** recorded a $200 million write-down on its action movie *John Carter*. Disney spent more than $300 million producing the film.

In the past, some companies **improperly** delayed recording losses on impairments until a year when it was "convenient" to do so—when the impact on the company's reported results was minimized. For example, in a year when a company has record profits, it can afford to write down some of its bad assets without hurting its reported results too much.

- The practice of timing the recognition of gains and losses to achieve certain income results is known as **earnings management**.
- Earnings management reduces earnings quality.
- To minimize earnings management, accounting standards now require immediate loss recognition on impaired assets.

Write-downs can create problems for users of financial statements. Critics of write-downs note that after a company writes down assets, its depreciation expense will be lower in all subsequent periods. Some companies improperly inflate asset write-downs in bad years, when they are going to report poor results anyway. (This practice is referred to as "taking a big bath.") Then in subsequent years, when the company recovers, its results will look even better because of lower depreciation expense.

---

## DO IT! 2b | Revised Depreciation

Chambers Corporation purchased a piece of equipment for $36,000. It estimated a 6-year life and $6,000 salvage value. Thus, straight-line depreciation was $5,000 per year [($36,000 − $6,000) ÷ 6]. At the end of year three (before the depreciation adjustment), it estimated the new total life to be 10 years and the new salvage value to be $2,000. Compute the revised depreciation.

**ACTION PLAN**

- Calculate depreciable cost.
- Divide depreciable cost by new remaining life.

### Solution

Original depreciation expense = [($36,000 − $6,000) ÷ 6] = $5,000
Accumulated depreciation after 2 years = 2 × $5,000 = $10,000
Book value = $36,000 − $10,000 = $26,000

| | |
|---|---:|
| Book value after 2 years of depreciation | $26,000 |
| Less: New salvage value | 2,000 |
| Depreciable cost | $24,000 |
| Remaining useful life | 8 years |
| Revised annual depreciation ($24,000 ÷ 8) | $ 3,000 |

Related exercise material: **BE8.6, DO IT! 8.2b, and E8.6**.

# Plant Asset Disposals

**LEARNING OBJECTIVE 3**

Explain how to account for the disposal of plant assets.

Companies dispose of plant assets that are no longer useful to them. **Illustration 8.16** shows the three ways in which companies make plant asset disposals.

**ILLUSTRATION 8.16** **Methods of plant asset disposal**

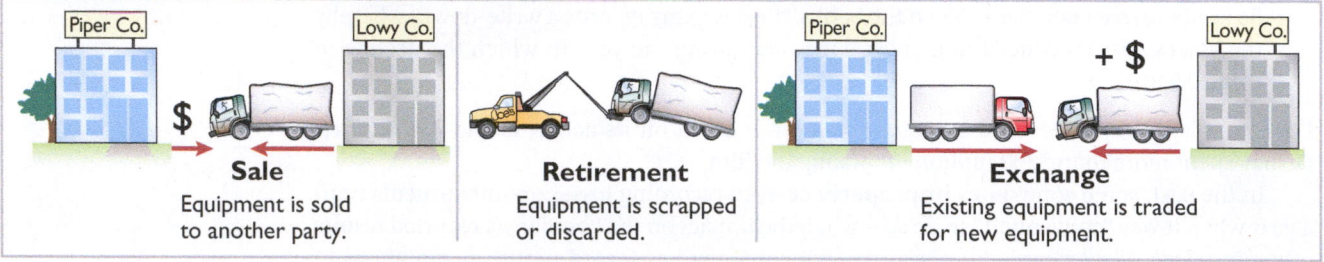

Whatever the disposal method, the company must:

1. Determine the book value of the plant asset at the time of disposal in order to determine the gain or loss. Recall that the book value is the difference between the cost of the plant asset and the accumulated depreciation to date.

2. Record depreciation for the fraction of the year to the date of disposal if the disposal does not occur on the first day of the year.

3. Eliminate the book value by reducing Accumulated Depreciation for the total depreciation associated with that asset to the date of disposal and reducing the asset account for the cost of the asset.

A gain or loss on disposal may need to be recorded, as discussed next.

## Sale of Plant Assets

In a disposal by sale, the company compares the book value of the asset with the proceeds received from the sale.

- If the proceeds from the sale **exceed** the book value of the plant asset, a **gain on disposal** occurs.

- If the proceeds from the sale **are less than** the book value of the plant asset sold, a **loss on disposal** occurs.

Only by coincidence will the book value and the fair value of the asset be the same at the time the asset is sold. Gains and losses on sales of plant assets are therefore quite common. As an example, **Delta Air Lines** at one time reported a $94 million gain on the sale of five **Boeing** B-727-200 aircraft and five **Lockheed** L-1011-1 aircraft.

### Gain on Sale

To illustrate a gain on sale of plant assets, assume that on July 1, 2022, Wright Company sells office furniture for $16,000 cash. The office furniture originally cost $60,000 and as of January 1, 2022, had accumulated depreciation of $41,000. Depreciation for the first six months of 2022 is $8,000. Wright records depreciation expense and updates accumulated depreciation to July 1 as follows.

| CASH FLOW | BALANCE SHEET | | | | | | | | | INCOME STATEMENT |
|---|---|---|---|---|---|---|---|---|---|---|
| | **Assets** | | = **Liabilities** + | | **Stockholders' Equity** | | | | | |
| | | Accum. | | | | | Retained Earnings | | | |
| | Equip- | Depr.— | | | Common | | | | | |
| | ment − | Equip. = | | | Stock + | Rev. | − | Exp. | − Div. | |
| | Bal. $60,000 | −$41,000 | | | | | | | | |
| No effect | | −8,000 | | | | | | −$8,000 | | Depreciation Exp. |

After the accumulated depreciation balance is updated, the company computes the gain or loss as the difference between the proceeds from sale and the book value at the date of disposal. Wright Company has a gain on disposal of $5,000, as computed in **Illustration 8.17**.

| | |
|---|---|
| Cost of office furniture | $60,000 |
| Less: Accumulated depreciation ($41,000 + $8,000) | 49,000 |
| Book value at date of disposal | 11,000 |
| Proceeds from sale | 16,000 |
| **Gain on disposal of plant asset** | **$ 5,000** |

**ILLUSTRATION 8.17**
**Computation of gain on disposal**

Wright records the sale and the gain on sale of the plant asset as follows.

| CASH FLOW | BALANCE SHEET | | | | | | | | | | INCOME STATEMENT |
|---|---|---|---|---|---|---|---|---|---|---|---|
| | **Assets** | | | = **Liabilities** + | | **Stockholders' Equity** | | | | | |
| | | | Accum. | | | | | Retained Earnings | | | |
| | | Equip- | Depr.— | | | Common | | | | | |
| | Cash + | ment − | Equip. = | | | Stock + | Rev. | − | Exp. − | Div. | |
| | Bal. | $60,000 | −$49,000 | | | | | | | | |
| ↑$16,000 | +$16,000 | −60,000 | +49,000 | | | | | +$5,000 | | | Gain on Disposal |

Companies report a gain on disposal of plant assets in the "Other revenues and gains" section of the income statement.

## Loss on Sale

Assume that instead of selling the office furniture for $16,000, Wright sells it for $9,000. In this case, Wright experiences a loss of $2,000, as computed in **Illustration 8.18**.

| | |
|---|---|
| Cost of office furniture | $60,000 |
| Less: Accumulated depreciation | 49,000 |
| Book value at date of disposal | 11,000 |
| Proceeds from sale | 9,000 |
| **Loss on disposal of plant asset** | **$ 2,000** |

**ILLUSTRATION 8.18**
**Computation of loss on disposal**

Wright records the sale and the loss on sale of the plant asset as follows.

| CASH FLOW | BALANCE SHEET | | | | | | | | | | INCOME STATEMENT |
|---|---|---|---|---|---|---|---|---|---|---|---|
| | **Assets** | | | = **Liabilities** + | | **Stockholders' Equity** | | | | | |
| | | | Accum. | | | | | Retained Earnings | | | |
| | | Equip- | Depr.— | | | Common | | | | | |
| | Cash + | ment ÷ | Equip. = | | | Stock + | Rev. − | | Exp. − | Div. | |
| | Bal. | $60,000 | −$49,000 | | | | | | | | |
| ↑$9,000 | +$9,000 | −60,000 | +49,000 | | | | | −$2,000 | | | Loss on Disposal |

Companies report a loss on disposal of the plant asset in the "Other expenses and losses" section of the income statement.

## Retirement of Plant Assets

Companies simply retire, rather than sell, some assets at the end of their useful lives. For example, some productive assets used in manufacturing may have very specific uses, and they consequently have no ready market when the company no longer needs them. In such a case, the asset is simply retired.

Companies record retirement of an asset as a special case of a disposal where no cash is received.

- They decrease Accumulated Depreciation for the full amount of depreciation taken over the life of the asset and decrease the asset account for the original cost of the asset.
- The loss (a gain is not possible on a retirement) is equal to the asset's book value on the date of retirement.[1]

---

**ACTION PLAN**

- Compare the asset's book value and its fair value to determine whether a gain or loss has occurred.
- Make sure that both the Equipment account and Accumulated Depreciation—Equipment are reduced upon disposal.

### DO IT! 3 | Plant Asset Disposals

Overland Trucking has an old truck that cost $30,000 and has accumulated depreciation of $16,000. Assume two different situations:

1. The company sells the old truck for $17,000 cash.
2. The truck is worthless, so the company simply retires it.

How should Overland record each scenario?

### Solution

**1.**

| | Assets | | | = | Liabilities | + | | Stockholders' Equity | | |
|---|---|---|---|---|---|---|---|---|---|---|
| | | | Accum. Depr.— | | | | Common | Retained Earnings | | |
| | Cash | + Equip-ment | − Equip. | = | | | Stock | + Rev. | − Exp. | − Div. |
| Bal. | | $30,000 | −$16,000 | | | | | | | |
| | +$17,000 | −30,000 | +16,000 | | | | | +$3,000 | | | Gain on Disposal |

**2.**

| | Assets | | | = | Liabilities | + | | Stockholders' Equity | | |
|---|---|---|---|---|---|---|---|---|---|---|
| | | | Accum. Depr.— | | | | Common | Retained Earnings | | |
| | Cash + | Equip-ment | − Equip. | = | | | Stock | + Rev. − | Exp. | − Div. |
| Bal. | | $30,000 | −$16,000 | | | | | | | |
| | | −30,000 | +16,000 | | | | | | −$14,000 | | Loss on Disposal |

Related exercise material: **BE8.7, BE8.8, DO IT! 8.3, E8.7, E8.8, and E8.9**.

---

# Intangible Assets

### LEARNING OBJECTIVE 4

Identify the basic issues related to reporting intangible assets.

**Intangible assets** are rights, privileges, and competitive advantages that result from ownership of long-lived assets that do not possess physical substance. Many companies' most valuable assets are intangible. Some widely known intangibles are **Microsoft**'s patents, **McDonald's** franchises, the trade name iPod, and **Nike**'s trademark "swoosh."

---

[1] More advanced courses discuss the accounting for exchanges, the third method of plant asset disposal.

As you will learn in this section, financial statements report numerous intangibles. Yet, many other financially significant intangibles are not reported.

- For example, according to its financial statements in a recent year, **Google** had total stockholders' equity of $22.7 billion.
- Its market value—the total market price of all its shares on that same date—was roughly $178.5 billion.
- Thus, its actual market value was about $155.8 billion greater than the amount reported for stockholders' equity on the balance sheet.

It is not uncommon for a company's reported book value to differ from its market value because balance sheets are reported at historical cost. But such an extreme difference seriously diminishes the usefulness of the balance sheet to decision-makers. In the case of Google, the difference is due to unrecorded intangibles. For many high-tech or so-called intellectual-property companies, most of their value is from intangibles, many of which are not reported under current accounting rules.

Intangibles may be evidenced by contracts, licenses, and other documents. Intangibles may arise from the following sources:

1. Government grants, such as patents, copyrights, licenses, trademarks, and trade names.
2. Acquisition of another business in which the purchase price includes a payment for goodwill.
3. Private monopolistic arrangements arising from contractual agreements, such as franchises and leases.

# Accounting for Intangible Assets

Companies record intangible assets at cost. Cost is comprised of all expenditures necessary for the company to acquire the right, privilege, or competitive advantage. Intangibles are categorized as having either a limited life or an indefinite life.

- If an intangible has a **limited life**, the company allocates its cost over the asset's useful life using a process similar to depreciation.
- The process of allocating to expense the cost of intangibles is referred to as **amortization**.
- The cost of intangible assets with **indefinite lives should not be amortized**.

To record amortization of an intangible asset, a company increases Amortization Expense and decreases the specific intangible asset. (Alternatively, some companies choose to increase a contra account, such as Accumulated Amortization. *For homework, you should directly decrease the specific intangible asset.*)

Intangible assets are typically amortized on a straight-line basis. For example, the legal life of a patent is 20 years. Companies **amortize the cost of a patent over its 20-year life or its useful life, whichever is shorter**. To illustrate the computation of patent amortization, assume that National Labs purchases a patent at a cost of $60,000 on June 30.

- If National estimates the useful life of the patent to be eight years, the annual amortization expense is $7,500 ($60,000 ÷ 8) per year.
- National records $3,750 ($7,500 $\times \frac{6}{12}$) of amortization for the six-month period ended December 31 as follows.

| CASH FLOW | BALANCE SHEET | | | | | | | | | INCOME STATEMENT |
|---|---|---|---|---|---|---|---|---|---|---|
| | Assets | = | Liabilities | + | Stockholders' Equity | | | | | |
| | | | | | | | Retained Earnings | | | |
| | | | | | Common | | | | | |
| | Patents | = | | | Stock | + | Rev. − | Exp. | − Div. | |
| | Bal. $60,000 | | | | | | | | | |
| No effect | −3,750 | | | | | | | −$3,750 | | Amortization Exp. |

When a company has significant intangibles, analysts should evaluate the reasonableness of the useful life estimates that the company discloses in the notes to its financial statements. In determining useful life, the company should consider obsolescence, inadequacy, and other factors. These may cause a patent or other intangible to become economically ineffective before the end of its legal life (see **Decision Tools**).

For example, suppose **Intel** obtained a patent on a new computer chip it had developed. The legal life of the patent is 20 years. From experience, however, we know that the useful life of a computer chip patent is rarely more than five years. Because new superior chips are developed so rapidly, existing chips become obsolete. Consequently, we would question the amortization expense of Intel if it amortized its patent on a computer chip for a life significantly longer than a five-year period. Amortizing an intangible over a period that is too long will understate amortization expense, overstate Intel's net income, and overstate its assets.

# Types of Intangible Assets

## Patents

A **patent** is an exclusive right issued by the U.S. Patent Office that enables the recipient to manufacture, sell, or otherwise control an invention for a period of 20 years from the date of the grant.

- The initial cost of a patent is the cash or cash equivalent price paid to acquire the patent.
- The saying "A patent is only as good as the money you're prepared to spend defending it" is very true. Most patents are subject to some type of litigation by competitors.

A well-known example is the patent infringement suit brought by **Amazon.com** against **Barnes & Noble.com** regarding its online shopping software. If the owner incurs legal costs in successfully defending the patent in an infringement suit, such costs are considered necessary to establish the validity of the patent. Thus, **the owner adds those costs to the Patents account and amortizes them over the remaining life of the patent**.

## Research and Development Costs

**Research and development costs** are expenditures that may lead to patents, copyrights, new processes, and new products (see **Helpful Hint**).

- Many companies spend considerable sums of money on research and development (R&D) in an ongoing effort to develop new products or processes. For example, in a recent year **Google** spent over $9.8 billion on research and development.
- There are uncertainties in identifying the extent and timing of the future benefits of these expenditures.
- As a result, companies usually record research and development costs **as an expense when incurred**, whether the R&D is successful or not.

To illustrate, assume that Laser Scanner Company spent $3 million on research and development that resulted in two highly successful patents. It spent $20,000 on legal fees for the patents. It can include the legal fees in the cost of the patents but cannot include the R&D costs in the cost of the patents. Instead, Laser Scanner records the R&D costs as an expense when incurred.

Many disagree with this accounting approach (see **International Note**). They argue that to expense these costs leads to understated assets and net income. Others argue that capitalizing these costs would lead to highly speculative assets on the balance sheet. It is difficult to determine who is correct.

## Copyrights

**Copyrights** are granted by the federal government and give the owner the exclusive right to reproduce and sell an artistic or published work.

- Copyrights last for the life of the creator plus 70 years. However, the useful life of a copyright generally is significantly shorter than its legal life.
- The cost of the copyright consists of the **cost of acquiring and defending it**. The cost may be only the small fee paid to the U.S. Copyright Office, or it may amount to a great deal more if a copyright is acquired from another party.

## Trademarks and Trade Names

A **trademark** or **trade name** is a word, phrase, jingle, or symbol that distinguishes or identifies a particular enterprise or product.

- Trade names like Wheaties, Monopoly, Sunkist, Kleenex, Coca-Cola, Big Mac, and Jeep create immediate product identification and generally enhance the sale of the product.
- The creator or original user may obtain the exclusive legal right to the trademark or trade name by registering it with the U.S. Patent Office.
- Such registration provides 20 years' protection and may be renewed indefinitely as long as the trademark or trade name is in use.

If a company purchases the trademark or trade name, the cost is the purchase price. If the company develops the trademark or trade name itself, the cost includes attorney's fees, registration fees, design costs, successful legal defense costs, and other expenditures directly related to securing it. Because trademarks and trade names have indefinite lives, they are not amortized.

---

### Accounting Across the Organization    Google

#### We Want to Own Glass

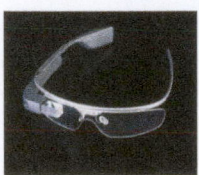

Hattanas/
Shutterstock.com

**Google**, which has trademarked the term "Google Glass," now wants to trademark the term "Glass." Why? Because the simple word Glass has marketing advantages over the term Google Glass. It is easy to remember and is more universal. Regulators, however, are balking at Google's request. They say that the possible trademark is too similar to other existing or pending software trademarks that contain the word "glass." Also, regulators suggest that the term Glass is merely descriptive and therefore lacks trademark protection. For example, regulators note that a company that makes salsa could not trademark the term "Spicy Salsa."

**BorderStylo LLC**, which developed a Web-browser extension called Write on Glass, has filed a notice of opposition to Google's request. Google is fighting back and has sent the trademark examiner a 1,928-page application defense.

**Source:** Jacob Gershman, "Google Wants to Own 'Glass'," *Wall Street Journal* (April 4, 2014), p. B5.

**If Google is successful in registering the term Glass, where will this trademark be reported on its financial statements? (Go to WileyPLUS for this answer and additional questions.)**

---

## Franchises

A **franchise** is a contractual arrangement under which the franchisor grants the franchisee the right to sell certain products, to perform specific services, or to use certain trademarks or trade names, usually within a designated geographic area.

- When you purchase a RAV4 from a **Toyota** dealer, fill up your tank at the corner **Shell** station, eat lunch at **Subway**, or make reservations at a **Marriott** hotel, you are dealing with franchises.
- Another type of franchise is a license; licenses granted by a governmental body permit a business to use public property in performing its services.
- Examples of licenses are the use of city streets for a bus line or taxi service; the use of public land for telephone, electric, and cable television lines; and the use of airwaves for radio or TV broadcasting.

In a recent license agreement, **Fox**, **CBS**, and **NBC** agreed to pay $27.9 billion for the right to broadcast **NFL** football games over an eight-year period.

Franchises and licenses may be granted for a definite period of time, or the time period may be indefinite or perpetual.

- **When a company incurs costs in connection with the acquisition of the franchise or license, it should recognize an intangible asset.**
- Companies record as **operating expenses** annual payments made under a franchise agreement in the period in which they are incurred.
- In the case of a limited life, a company amortizes the cost of a franchise (or license) as operating expense over the useful life. If the life is indefinite or perpetual, the cost is not amortized.

## Goodwill

Usually, the largest intangible asset that appears on a company's balance sheet is goodwill. **Goodwill** represents the value of all favorable attributes that relate to a company that are not attributable to any other specific asset.

- These favorable attributes include exceptional management, desirable location, good customer relations, skilled employees, high-quality products, fair pricing policies, and harmonious relations with labor unions.
- Goodwill is unique because unlike other assets such as investments, plant assets, and even other intangibles, which can be sold **individually** in the marketplace, goodwill can be identified only with the business **as a whole**.

If goodwill can be identified only with the business as a whole, how can it be determined? Certainly, many business enterprises have many of the factors cited above (exceptional management, desirable location, and so on). However, to determine the amount of goodwill in these situations would be difficult and very subjective. In other words, to recognize goodwill without an exchange transaction that puts a value on the goodwill would lead to subjective valuations that do not contribute to the reliability of financial statements. **Therefore, companies record goodwill only when there is an exchange transaction that involves the purchase of an entire business. When an entire business is purchased, goodwill is the excess of cost over the fair value of the net assets (assets less liabilities) acquired.**

In recording the purchase of a business, a company records:

1. The identifiable acquired assets and liabilities at their fair values.
2. Cash for the purchase price.
3. The difference as the cost of goodwill.

Goodwill is not amortized because it is considered to have an indefinite life. However, it must be written down if a company determines the value of goodwill has been permanently impaired.

## DO IT! 4 | Classification Concepts

Match the following terms or phrases with the statement most directly associated with it.

1. Copyright.
2. Intangible assets.
3. Research and development costs.
4. Amortization.
5. Franchise.

a. _____ The allocation to expense of the cost of an intangible asset over the asset's useful life.

b. _____ Rights, privileges, and competitive advantages that result from the ownership of long-lived assets that do not possess physical substance.

c. _____ An exclusive right granted by the federal government to reproduce and sell an artistic or published work.

d. _____ A right to sell certain products or services or to use certain trademarks or trade names within a designated geographic area.

e. _____ Costs incurred by a company that often lead to patents or new products. These costs must be expensed as incurred.

**ACTION PLAN**

- Know that the accounting for intangibles often depends on whether the item has a finite or indefinite life.

- Recognize the many similarities and differences between the accounting for plant assets and intangible assets.

### Solution

a. 4.    d. 5.

b. 2.    e. 3.

c. 1.

Related exercise material: **BE8.9, DO IT! 8.4, E8.11, E8.12, and E8.13.**

# Statement Presentation and Analysis

**LEARNING OBJECTIVE 5**

Discuss how long-lived assets are reported and analyzed.

## Presentation

Usually, companies show plant assets in the financial statements under "Property, plant, and equipment," and they show intangibles separately under "Intangible assets." **Illustration 8.19** shows a typical balance sheet presentation of long-lived assets.

When a plant asset is fully depreciated, the plant asset and related accumulated depreciation should continue to be reported on the balance sheet without further depreciation or adjustment until the asset is retired. Intangibles do not usually use a contra asset account like the contra asset account Accumulated Depreciation used for plant assets. Instead, companies record amortization of intangibles as a direct decrease to the asset account.

Either within the balance sheet or in the notes, companies should disclose:

- The balances of the major classes of assets, such as land, buildings, and equipment, and of accumulated depreciation by major classes or in total.

- The depreciation and amortization methods used and the amount of depreciation and amortization expense for the period.

*For homework purposes, use the format in Illustration 8.19 for preparing balance sheet information.*

**ILLUSTRATION 8.19**

**Presentation of property, plant, and equipment, and intangible assets**

## Artex Company
### Balance Sheet (partial)
### (in thousands)

| | | | |
|---|---|---:|---:|
| **Current assets** | | | |
| Cash | | $ 430 | |
| Accounts receivable | | 100 | |
| Inventory | | 910 | |
|   Total current assets | | | $ 1,440 |
| **Property, plant, and equipment** | | | |
| Land | | 920 | |
| Buildings | $7,600 | | |
| Less: Accumulated depreciation—buildings | 500 | 7,100 | |
| Equipment | 3,870 | | |
| Less: Accumulated depreciation—equipment | 620 | 3,250 | |
|   Total property, plant, and equipment | | | 11,270 |
| **Intangible assets** | | | |
| Patents | | 440 | |
| Trademarks | | 180 | |
| Goodwill | | 900 | 1,520 |
|   Total assets | | | $14,230 |

---

## People, Planet, and Profit Insight  BHP

iStock.com/Christian Uhrig

### Sustainability Report Please

Sustainability reports identify how the company is meeting its corporate social responsibilities. Many companies, both large and small, are now issuing these reports. For example, companies such as **Disney**, **Best Buy**, **Microsoft**, **Ford**, and **ConocoPhillips** issue these reports. Presented below is an adapted section of a recent **BHP** (a global mining, oil, and gas company) sustainability report on its environmental policies. These policies are to (1) take action to address the challenges of climate change, (2) set and achieve targets that reduce pollution, and (3) enhance biodiversity by assessing and considering ecological values and land-use aspects. Here is how BHP measures the success or failure of some of these policies:

| Social Responsibility | Target | Target Date |
|---|---|---|
| Safety | • Zero work-related fatalities.<br>• Year-on-year improvement of our total recordable injury frequency (TRIF). | Annual<br>Annual |
| Health | For our most material exposures of respirable silica, diesel particulate and coal mine dust, we will achieve a 50 percent reduction in the number of workers potentially exposed as compared with the FY2017 baseline. | 30 June 2022 |
| Community | Zero significant community events. | Annual |
| | Our social investment will contribute to improved quality of life in host communities and support achievement of the UN Sustainable Development Goals. We will invest not less than one percent of pre-tax profit (three-year rolling average) in meeting these objectives. | 30 June 2022 |
| | Regional Indigenous Peoples Plans will be developed, which support implementation of BHP's Indigenous Peoples Strategy. Plans will include all geographically relevant assets. | 30 June 2022 |
| Climate change | Maintain FY2022 greenhouse gas (GHG) emissions at or below FY2017 levels while we continue to grow our business. | 30 June 2022 |
| | **Longer-term goal:** In line with international commitments, BHP aims to achieve net-zero operational GHG emissions in the second half of this century. | The second half of this century. |

In addition to the environment, BHP has sections in its sustainability report that discuss people, safety, health, and community.

**Why do you believe companies issue sustainability reports? (Go to WileyPLUS for this answer and additional questions.)**

# Analysis

The presentation of financial statement information about plant assets enables decision-makers to analyze the company's use of its plant assets. We will use two measures to analyze plant assets: return on assets and asset turnover. We also show how profit margin relates to both.

## Return on Assets

An overall measure of profitability is the **return on assets** (see **Decision Tools**).

- This ratio is computed by dividing net income by average total assets. (Average assets are commonly calculated by adding the beginning and ending values of assets and dividing by 2.)
- Return on assets indicates the amount of net income generated by each dollar of assets.
- Thus, the higher the return on assets, the more profitable the company.

For example, consider the following information related to **JetBlue Airways**.

|  | JetBlue (in millions) |
|---|---|
| Net income, 2017 | $1,147 |
| Total assets, 12/31/17 | 9,781 |
| Total assets, 12/31/16 | 9,323 |
| Net sales, 2017 | 7,015 |

**Illustration 8.20** presents the return on assets of JetBlue Airways and Southwest Airlines.

$$\text{Return on Assets} = \frac{\text{Net Income}}{\text{Average Total Assets}}$$

| JetBlue Airways ($ in millions) | | Southwest Airlines |
|---|---|---|
| 2017 | 2016 | 2017 |
| $\dfrac{\$1,147}{(\$9,781 + \$9,323) \div 2} = 12.0\%$ | 8.4% | 14.4% |

**ILLUSTRATION 8.20**

**Return on assets for JetBlue and Southwest**

JetBlue's return on assets was less than Southwest's. At one time, the airline industry experienced financial difficulties as it attempted to cover high labor, fuel, and security costs while offering fares low enough to attract customers. Such difficulties were reflected in a low industry average for return on assets. In response, Southwest announced that it would not add additional planes beyond the 700 it already had until it met its investment-return targets. Instead, the company added seats to existing planes and replaced some smaller planes with larger ones.

## Accounting Across the Organization

Walter G Arce/Cal Sport Media/Topeka KS United States/Newscom

### Marketing ROI as Profit Indicator

Marketing executives use the basic finance concept underlying return on assets to determine "marketing return on investment (ROI)." They calculate *marketing ROI* as the profit generated by a marketing initiative divided by the investment in that initiative.

It can be tricky to determine what to include in the "investment" amount and how to attribute profit to a particular marketing initiative. However, many firms feel that measuring marketing ROI is worth the effort because it allows managers to evaluate the relative effectiveness of various programs. In addition, it helps quantify the benefits that marketing provides to the organization. In periods of tight budgets, the marketing ROI number can provide particularly valuable evidence to help a marketing manager avoid budget cuts.

**Source:** James O. Mitchel, "Marketing ROI," *LIMRA's MarketFacts Quarterly* (Summer 2004), p. 15.

**How does measuring marketing ROI support the overall efforts of the organization? (Go to WileyPLUS for this answer and additional questions.)**

## Asset Turnover

**Asset turnover** indicates how efficiently a company uses its assets to generate sales—that is, how many dollars of sales a company generates for each dollar invested in assets (see **Decision Tools**).

- It is calculated by dividing net sales by average total assets.
- When we compare two companies in the same industry, the one with the higher asset turnover is operating more efficiently. It is generating more sales per dollar invested in assets.

**Illustration 8.21** presents the asset turnovers for JetBlue Airways and Southwest Airlines.

**ILLUSTRATION 8.21**

**Asset turnovers for JetBlue and Southwest**

| Asset Turnover = $\dfrac{\text{Net Sales}}{\text{Average Total Assets}}$ | | |
|---|---|---|
| **JetBlue Airways** ($ in millions) | | **Southwest Airlines** |
| **2017** | **2016** | **2017** |
| $\dfrac{\$7,015}{(\$9,781 + \$9,323) \div 2} = 0.73$ times | 0.74 times | 0.92 times |

These asset turnover values tell us that for each dollar of assets, JetBlue generates sales of $0.73 and Southwest $0.92. Southwest is more successful in generating sales per dollar invested in assets. In recent years, airlines have reduced both the number of planes used and routes flown to try to pack more customers on a plane. This would increase the asset turnover.

Asset turnovers vary considerably across industries. During a recent year, the average asset turnover for electric utility companies was 0.34. The grocery industry had an average asset turnover of 2.89. Asset turnover values, therefore, are only comparable within—not between—industries.

## Profit Margin Revisited

In Chapter 6, you learned about **profit margin**.

- That ratio is calculated by dividing net income by net sales.
- It tells how effective a company is in turning its sales into income—that is, how much income each dollar of sales provides.

**Illustration 8.22** shows that return on assets can be computed as the product of profit margin and asset turnover.

**ILLUSTRATION 8.22**

**Composition of return on assets**

| Profit Margin | × | Asset Turnover | = | Return on Assets |
|---|---|---|---|---|
| $\dfrac{\text{Net Income}}{\text{Net Sales}}$ | × | $\dfrac{\text{Net Sales}}{\text{Average Total Assets}}$ | = | $\dfrac{\text{Net Income}}{\text{Average Total Assets}}$ |

This relationship has very important strategic implications for management. From Illustration 8.22, we can see that if a company wants to increase its return on assets, it can do so in two ways:

1. By increasing the margin it generates from each dollar of goods that it sells (the profit margin)
2. By increasing the volume of goods that it sells (the asset turnover).

For example, most grocery stores have very low profit margins, often in the range of one or two cents for every dollar of goods sold. Grocery stores, therefore, focus on asset turnover: They rely on high turnover to increase their return on assets. Alternatively, a store selling luxury goods, such as expensive jewelry, does not generally have a high turnover. Consequently, a seller of luxury goods focuses on having a high profit margin. Recently, **Apple** decided to offer a more expensive version of its popular iPhone. This new product would provide a higher margin but lower volume than Apple's less expensive version.

Let's evaluate the return on assets of JetBlue and Southwest for 2017 by evaluating its components—profit margin and asset turnover. See **Illustration 8.23**.

**ILLUSTRATION 8.23**

**Components of rate of return for JetBlue and Southwest**

|  | Profit Margin | × | Asset Turnover | = | Return on Assets |
|---|---|---|---|---|---|
| **JetBlue Airways** | 16.4% | × | 0.73 | = | 12.0% |
| **Southwest Airlines** | 15.7% | × | 0.92 | = | 14.4% |

JetBlue's return on asset of 12% versus Southwest's 14.4% means that JetBlue generates 12.0 cents of net income per each dollar invested in assets, while Southwest generates 14.4 cents. Illustration 8.23 reveals that although these two airlines have similar returns on assets, they achieve these returns in a slightly different fashion. First, JetBlue's profit margin of 16.4% versus Southwest's 15.7% means that for every dollar of sales, JetBlue generates approximately 16.4 cents of net income, while Southwest generates approximately 15.7 cents. Second, Jet-Blue's asset turnover of 0.73 means that it generates 73 cents of sales per each dollar invested in assets, while Southwest generates 92 cents. Therefore, in 2017, Southwest was more effective at generating sales from its assets, while JetBlue was better at deriving profit from its sales.

## DO IT! 5 | Asset Turnover and Return on Assets

Paramour Company reported net income of $180,000, net sales of $420,000, and had total assets of $460,000 on January 1, 2022, and total assets on December 31, 2022, of $540,000. Determine Paramour's asset turnover and return on assets for 2022.

### Solution

The asset turnover for Paramour Company is computed as follows.

| Net Sales | ÷ | Average Total Assets | = | Asset Turnover |
|---|---|---|---|---|
| $420,000 | ÷ | $\dfrac{\$460,000 + \$540,000}{2}$ | = | .84 times |

The return on assets for Paramour Company is computed as follows.

| Net Income | ÷ | Average Total Assets | = | Return on Assets |
|---|---|---|---|---|
| $180,000 | ÷ | $\dfrac{\$460,000 + \$540,000}{2}$ | = | 36.0% |

Related exercise material: **BE8.10, DO IT! 8.5, and E8.15**.

**ACTION PLAN**

- **Recognize that the asset turnover analyzes the productivity of a company's assets.**
- **Know the formula Net sales ÷ Average total assets = Asset turnover.**
- **Know the formula Net income ÷ Average total assets = Return on assets.**

**USING THE DECISION TOOLS** | Delta Air Lines

**Delta Air Lines, Inc.**, headquartered in Atlanta, Georgia, is one of the largest airlines in the world. It serves 342 destinations in 61 countries. Delta provided the following information in its 2016 annual report.

**Delta Air Lines, Inc.**
**Notes to the Financial Statements (partial)**

*Long-Lived Assets*

The following table summarizes our property and equipment:

| (in millions, except for estimated useful life) | Estimated Useful Life | December 31 2016 | December 31 2015 |
|---|---|---|---|
| Flight equipment | 20–32 years | $28,135 | $26,057 |
| Ground property and equipment | 3–40 years | 6,581 | 5,862 |
| Flight and ground equipment under capital leases | Shorter of lease term or estimated useful life | 1,056 | 1,112 |
| Advance payments for equipment | | 1,059 | 879 |
| Less: accumulated depreciation and amortization[1] | | (12,456) | (10,871) |
| Total property and equipment, net | | $24,375 | $23,039 |

[1]Includes accumulated amortization for flight and ground equipment under capital leases in the amount of $757 million and $782 million at December 31, 2016 and 2015, respectively.

We record property and equipment at cost and depreciate or amortize these assets on a straight-line basis to their estimated residual values over their estimated useful lives.

## Instructions

Use the information provided to answer the following questions.

**a.** What method does the company use to depreciate its aircraft? Over what period is the company depreciating these aircraft?

**b.** Compute the company's return on assets ratio, asset turnover ratio, and profit margin ratio for 2016 and 2015. Comment on your results.

| (in millions) | 2016 | 2015 |
|---|---|---|
| Net income (loss) | $ 4,373 | $ 4,526 |
| Net sales | 39,639 | 40,704 |
| Beginning total assets | 53,134 | 54,121 |
| Ending total assets | 51,261 | 53,134 |

## Solution

**a.** The company depreciates property and equipment using the straight-line approach. It depreciates aircraft over a 20–32-year life.

**b.**

| | 2016 | 2015 |
|---|---|---|
| Return on assets | $\dfrac{\$4,373}{(\$53,134 + \$51,261) \div 2} = 8.4\%$ | $\dfrac{\$4,526}{(\$54,121 + \$53,134) \div 2} = 8.4\%$ |
| Asset turnover | $\dfrac{\$39,639}{(\$53,134 + \$51,261) \div 2} = 0.76 \text{ times}$ | $\dfrac{\$40,704}{(\$54,121 + \$53,134) \div 2} = 0.76 \text{ times}$ |
| Profit margin | $\dfrac{\$4,373}{\$39,639} = 11.0\%$ | $\dfrac{\$4,526}{\$40,704} = 11.1\%$ |

Delta's return on assets, asset turnover, and profit margin ratios were virtually unchanged from 2015 to 2016.

# Review and Practice

## Learning Objectives Review

### 1  Explain the accounting for plant asset expenditures.

The cost of plant assets includes all expenditures necessary to acquire the asset and make it ready for its intended use. Once cost is established, a company uses that amount as the basis of accounting for the plant asset over its useful life.

### 2  Apply depreciation methods to plant assets.

Depreciation is the process of allocating to expense the cost of a plant asset over its useful (service) life in a rational and systematic manner. Depreciation is not a process of valuation, and it is not a process that results in an accumulation of cash. Depreciation reflects an asset's decreasing usefulness and revenue-producing ability, resulting from wear and tear and from obsolescence.

The formula for straight-line depreciation is:

$$\frac{\text{Cost} - \text{Salvage value}}{\text{Useful life (in years)}}$$

The expense patterns of the three depreciation methods are as follows.

| Method | Annual Depreciation Pattern |
| --- | --- |
| Straight-line | Constant amount |
| Declining-balance | Decreasing amount |
| Units-of-activity | Varying amount |

Companies make revisions of periodic depreciation in present and future periods, not retroactively.

### 3  Explain how to account for the disposal of plant assets.

The procedure for accounting for the disposal of a plant asset through sale or retirement is (a) eliminate the book value of the plant asset at the date of disposal; (b) record cash proceeds, if any; and (c) account for the difference between the book value and the cash proceeds as a gain or a loss on disposal.

### 4  Identify the basic issues related to reporting intangible assets.

Companies report intangible assets at their cost less any amounts amortized. If an intangible asset has a limited life, its cost should be allocated (amortized) over its useful life. Intangible assets with indefinite lives should not be amortized.

### 5  Discuss how long-lived assets are reported and analyzed.

Companies usually show plant assets under "Property, plant, and equipment"; they show intangibles separately under "Intangible assets." Either within the balance sheet or in the notes, companies disclose the balances of the major classes of assets, such as land, buildings, and equipment, and accumulated depreciation by major classes or in total. They describe the depreciation and amortization methods used, and disclose the amount of depreciation and amortization expense for the period.

Plant assets may be analyzed using return on assets and asset turnover. Return on assets consists of two components: asset turnover and profit margin.

## Decision Tools Review

| Decision Checkpoints | Info Needed for Decision | Tool to Use for Decision | How to Evaluate Results |
| --- | --- | --- | --- |
| Is the company's amortization of intangibles reasonable? | Estimated useful life of intangibles from notes to financial statements of this company and its competitors | If the company's estimated useful life significantly exceeds that of competitors or does not seem reasonable in light of the circumstances, the reason for the difference should be investigated. | Too high an estimated useful life will result in understating amortization expense and overstating net income. |
| Is the company using its assets effectively? | Net income and average total assets | $\text{Return on assets} = \dfrac{\text{Net income}}{\text{Average total assets}}$ | Higher value suggests favorable efficiency (use of assets). |
| How effective is the company at generating sales from its assets? | Net sales and average total assets | $\text{Asset turnover} = \dfrac{\text{Net sales}}{\text{Average total assets}}$ | Indicates the sales dollars generated per dollar of assets. A high value suggests the company is effective in using its resources to generate sales. |

## Glossary Review

**Accelerated-depreciation method** A depreciation method that produces higher depreciation expense in the early years than the straight-line approach. (p. 8-11).

**Additions and improvements** Costs incurred to increase the operating efficiency, productive capacity, or expected useful life of a plant asset. (p. 8-7).

**Amortization** The process of allocating to expense the cost of an intangible asset. (p. 8-19).

**Asset turnover** Indicates how efficiently a company uses its assets to generate sales; calculated as net sales divided by average total assets. (p. 8-26).

**Capital expenditures** Expenditures that increase the company's investment in plant assets. (p. 8-4).

**Cash equivalent price** An amount equal to the fair value of the asset given up or the fair value of the asset received, whichever is more clearly determinable. (p. 8-4).

**Copyright** An exclusive right granted by the federal government allowing the owner to reproduce and sell an artistic or published work. (p. 8-21).

**Declining-balance method** A depreciation method that applies a constant rate to the declining book value of the asset and produces a decreasing annual depreciation expense over the asset's useful life. (p. 8-11).

**Depreciable cost** The cost of a plant asset less its salvage value. (p. 8-10).

**Depreciation** The process of allocating to expense the cost of a plant asset over its useful life in a rational and systematic manner. (p. 8-8).

**Franchise** A contractual arrangement under which the franchisor grants the franchisee the right to sell certain products, to perform specific services, or to use certain trademarks or trade names, usually within a designated geographic area. (p. 8-21).

**Goodwill** The value of all favorable attributes that relate to a company that are not attributable to any other specific asset. (p. 8-22).

**Impairment** A permanent decline in the fair value of an asset. (p. 8-15).

**Intangible assets** Rights, privileges, and competitive advantages that result from the ownership of long-lived assets that do not possess physical substance. (p. 8-18).

**Ordinary repairs** Expenditures to maintain the operating efficiency and expected productive life of the asset. (p. 8-6).

**Patent** An exclusive right issued by the U.S. Patent Office that enables the recipient to manufacture, sell, or otherwise control an invention for a period of 20 years from the date of the grant. (p. 8-20).

**Plant assets** Resources that have physical substance, are used in the operations of a business, and are not intended for sale to customers. (p. 8-3).

**Research and development costs** Expenditures that may lead to patents, copyrights, new processes, and new products; must be expensed as incurred. (p. 8-20).

**Return on assets** A profitability measure that indicates the amount of net income generated by each dollar of assets; computed as net income divided by average total assets. (p. 8-25).

**Revenue expenditures** Expenditures that are immediately charged against revenues as an expense. (p. 8-4).

**Straight-line method** A depreciation method in which companies expense an equal amount of depreciation for each year of the asset's useful life. (p. 8-10).

**Trademark (trade name)** A word, phrase, jingle, or symbol that distinguishes or identifies a particular enterprise or product. (p. 8-21).

**Units-of-activity method** A depreciation method in which useful life is expressed in terms of the total units of production or use expected from the asset. (p. 8-12).

## Practice Multiple-Choice Questions

**1. (LO 1)** Corrieten Company purchased equipment and incurred these costs:

| | |
|---|---|
| Cash price | $24,000 |
| Sales taxes | 1,200 |
| Insurance during transit | 200 |
| Installation and testing | 400 |
| Total costs | $25,800 |

What amount should be recorded as the cost of the equipment?

**a.** $24,000.          **c.** $25,400.

**b.** $25,200.          **d.** $25,800.

**2. (LO 1)** Additions to plant assets are:

**a.** revenue expenditures.

**b.** added to the Maintenance and Repairs Expense account.

**c.** added to the Purchases account.

**d.** capital expenditures.

**3. (LO 2)** Depreciation is a process of:

**a.** valuation.          **c.** cash accumulation.

**b.** cost allocation.          **d.** appraisal.

**4. (LO 2)** Cuso Company purchased equipment on January 1, 2021, at a total invoice cost of $400,000. The equipment has an estimated salvage value of $10,000 and an estimated useful life of 5 years. What is the amount of accumulated depreciation at December 31, 2022, if the straight-line method of depreciation is used?

**a.** $80,000.          **c.** $78,000.

**b.** $160,000.          **d.** $156,000.

**5. (LO 2)** A company would minimize its depreciation expense the most in the first year of owning an asset if it used:

**a.** a high estimated life, a high salvage value, and declining-balance depreciation.

**b.** a low estimated life, a high salvage value, and straight-line depreciation.

**c.** a high estimated life, a high salvage value, and straight-line depreciation.

**d.** a low estimated life, a low salvage value, and declining-balance depreciation.

**6. (LO 2)** When there is a change in estimated depreciation:

**a.** previous depreciation should be corrected.

**b.** current and future years' depreciation should be revised.

c. only future years' depreciation should be revised.

d. None of the answer choices is correct.

**7. (LO 2)** Able Towing Company purchased a tow truck for $60,000 on January 1, 2022. It was originally depreciated on a straight-line basis over 10 years with an assumed salvage value of $12,000. On December 31, 2024, before an adjustment had been made, the company decided to change the remaining estimated life to 4 years (including 2024) and the salvage value to $2,000. What was the depreciation expense for 2024?

a. $6,000.                  c. $15,000.

b. $4,800.                  d. $12,100.

**8. (LO 3)** Bennie Razor Company has decided to sell one of its old manufacturing machines on June 30, 2022. The machine was purchased for $80,000 on January 1, 2018, and was depreciated on a straight-line basis for 10 years assuming no salvage value. If the machine was sold for $26,000, what was the amount of the gain or loss recorded at the time of the sale?

a. $18,000 loss.            c. $22,000 gain.

b. $54,000 loss.           d. $46,000 gain.

**9. (LO 4)** Pierce Company incurred $150,000 of research and development costs in its laboratory to develop a new product. It spent $20,000 in legal fees for a patent granted on January 2, 2022. On July 31, 2022, Pierce paid $15,000 for legal fees in a successful defense of the patent. What is the total amount that should be included as Patents, ignoring amortization, through July 31, 2022?

a. $150,000.               c. $185,000.

b. $35,000.                d. $170,000.

**10. (LO 4)** Indicate which one of these statements is **true**.

a. Since intangible assets lack physical substance, they need to be disclosed only in the notes to the financial statements.

b. Goodwill should be reported as a contra account in the stockholders' equity section.

c. Totals of major classes of assets can be shown in the balance sheet, with asset details disclosed in the notes to the financial statements.

d. Intangible assets are typically combined with plant assets and inventory and then shown in the property, plant, and equipment section.

**11. (LO 4)** If a company reports goodwill as an intangible asset on its books, what is the one thing you know with certainty?

a. The company is a valuable company worth investing in.

b. The company has a well-established brand name.

c. The company purchased another company.

d. The goodwill will generate a lot of positive business for the company for many years to come.

**12. (LO 4)** Which of the following statements is **false**?

a. If an intangible asset has a finite life, it should be amortized.

b. The amortization period of an intangible asset can exceed 20 years.

c. Goodwill is recorded only when a business is purchased.

d. Research and development costs are expensed when incurred, except when the research and development expenditures result in a successful patent.

**13. (LO 5)** Which of the following measures provides an indication of how efficient a company is in employing its assets?

a. Current ratio.          c. Debt to assets ratio.

b. Profit margin.          d. Asset turnover.

**14. (LO 5)** Lake Coffee Company reported net sales of $180,000, net income of $54,000, beginning total assets of $200,000, and ending total assets of $300,000. What was the company's asset turnover?

a. 0.90 times.             c. 0.72 times.

b. 0.20 times.             d. 1.39 times.

## Solutions

**1. d.** All of the costs ($1,200 + $200 + $400) in addition to the cash price ($24,000) should be included in the cost of the equipment because they were necessary expenditures to acquire the asset and make it ready for its intended use. The other choices are therefore incorrect.

**2. d.** When an addition is made to plant assets, it is intended to increase productive capacity, increase the assets' useful life, or increase the efficiency of the assets. This is called a capital expenditure. The other choices are incorrect because (a) additions to plant assets are not revenue expenditures because the additions will have a long-term useful life whereas revenue expenditures are minor repairs and maintenance that do not prolong the life of the assets; (b) additions to plant assets increase the Plant Assets account, not Maintenance and Repairs Expense, because the Maintenance and Repairs Expense account is used to record expenditures not intended to increase the life of the assets; and (c) additions to plant assets increase the Plant Assets account, not Purchases, because the Purchases account is used to record assets intended for resale (inventory).

**3. b.** Depreciation is a process of allocating the cost of an asset over its useful life, not a process of (a) valuation, (c) cash accumulation, or (d) appraisal.

**4. d.** Accumulated depreciation will be the sum of 2 years of depreciation expense. Annual depreciation for this asset is ($400,000 − $10,000) ÷ 5 = $78,000. The sum of 2 years' depreciation is therefore $156,000 ($78,000 + $78,000), not (a) $80,000, (b) $160,000, or (c) $78,000.

**5. c.** A high estimated life spreads the cost over a longer period of time, resulting in a smaller expense each year. The high salvage value limits the cost to be allocated. Straight-line depreciation yields a smaller depreciation charge in the first year than the declining-balance method. The other choices are therefore incorrect.

**6. b.** When there is a change in estimated depreciation, the current and future years' depreciation computation should reflect the new estimates. The other choices are incorrect because (a) previous years' depreciation should not be adjusted when new estimates are made for depreciation, and (c) when there is a change in estimated depreciation, the current and future years' depreciation computation should reflect the new estimates. Choice (d) is wrong because there is a correct answer.

**7. d.** First, calculate accumulated depreciation from January 1, 2022, through December 31, 2023, which is $9,600 {[($60,000 − $12,000) ÷ 10 years] × 2 years}. Next, calculate the revised depreciable cost, which is $48,400 ($60,000 − $9,600 − $2,000). Thus, the depreciation expense for 2024 is $12,100 ($48,400 ÷ 4), not (a) $6,000, (b) $4,800, or (c) $15,000.

**8. a.** First, the book value needs to be determined. The accumulated depreciation as of June 30, 2022, is $36,000 [($80,000 ÷ 10) × 4.5 years]. Thus, the cost of the machine less accumulated depreciation equals $44,000 ($80,000 − $36,000). The loss recorded at the time of sale is $18,000 ($26,000 − $44,000), not (b) $54,000, or a gain of (c) $22,000 or (d) $46,000.

**9. b.** Because the $150,000 was spent developing the patent rather than buying it from another firm, it is added to Research and Development Expense. Only the $35,000 spent on legal fees ($20,000 for granting patent and $15,000 for defense) can be added to Patents, not (a) $150,000, (c) $185,000, or (d) $170,000.

**10. c.** Reporting only totals of major classes of assets in the balance sheet is appropriate. Additional details can be shown in the notes to the financial statements. The other choices are false statements.

**11. c.** In order to report goodwill, a company must have entered into an exchange transaction that involves the purchase of another business. Choices (a) the company is a valuable company worth investing in, (b) the company has a well-established brand name, and (d) the goodwill will generate a lot of positive business for the company for many years to come are not necessarily valid assumptions.

**12. d.** Research and development (R&D) costs are expensed when incurred, regardless of whether the research and development expenditures result in a successful patent or not. The other choices are true statements.

**13. d.** The asset turnover indicates how efficiently a company is employing its assets. The other choices are incorrect because (a) the current ratio is an indicator of liquidity and the company's ability to pay its obligations when they come due, (b) the profit margin is an indicator of how profitable a company is, and (c) the debt to assets ratio indicates the proportion of assets that are financed by debt rather than by equity.

**14. c.** Asset turnover = Net sales ($180,000) ÷ Average total assets [($200,000 + $300,000) ÷ 2] = 0.72 times, not (a) 0.90, (b) 0.20, or (d) 1.39 times.

# Practice Brief Exercises

*Compute straight-line depreciation.*

**1. (LO 2)** Fulmer Company acquires a delivery truck at a cost of $50,000. The truck is expected to have a salvage value of $5,000 at the end of its 5-year useful life. Compute annual depreciation expense for the first and second years using the straight-line method.

### Solution

**1.** Depreciable cost is $45,000, ($50,000 − $5,000). With a 5-year useful life, annual depreciation is $9,000, ($45,000 ÷ 5). Under the straight-line method, depreciation is the same each year. Thus, depreciation is $9,000 for both the first and second years.

*Record disposal by sale.*

**2. (LO 3)** Giolito Company sells equipment on August 31, 2022, for $20,000 cash. The equipment originally cost $60,000 and as of January 1, 2022, had accumulated depreciation of $38,000. Depreciation for the first 8 months of 2022 is $6,000. Prepare a tabular summary to (a) update depreciation to August 31, 2022, and (b) record the sale of the equipment.

### Solution

**2.**

| | Assets | | | = | Liabilities | + | Stockholders' Equity | | | | | |
|---|---|---|---|---|---|---|---|---|---|---|---|---|
| | | | Accum. | | | | | | Retained Earnings | | | |
| | | Equip- | Depr.— | | | | Common | | | | | |
| | Cash | + ment | − Equip. | = | | | Stock | + Rev. | − | Exp. | − | Div. |
| Bal. | | $60,000 | − $38,000 | | | | | | | | | |
| a. | | | −6,000 | | | | | | | −$6,000 | | Dep. Exp. |
| b. | + $20,000 | −60,000 | + 44,000 | | | | | +$4,000 | | | | Gain on Disposal |

Calculations: Cost of equipment ... $60,000
Less: Accumulated depreciation ... 44,000*
Book value at date of disposal ... 16,000
Proceeds from sale ... 20,000
Gain on disposal ... $ 4,000

*$38,000 + $6,000

**3. (LO 4)** Lucas Company acquires a limited-life franchise for $200,000 on January 2, 2022. Its estimated useful life is 10 years. (a) Prepare a tabular summary to record amortization expense for the first year. (b) Show how this franchise is reported on the balance sheet at the end of the first year.

*Record amortization expense and prepare balance sheet presentation for intangibles.*

### Solution

**3. a.**

| Assets | = | Liabilities | + | | | Stockholders' Equity | | | | |
|---|---|---|---|---|---|---|---|---|---|---|
| | | | | | | | Retained Earnings | | | |
| | | | | Common | | | | | | |
| Franchises | = | | | Stock | + | Rev. | − | Exp. | − | Div. |
| Bal. $200,000 | | | | | | | | | | |
| −20,000 | | | | | | | −$20,000 | | | Amortization Exp. |

**b.** Intangible assets
   Franchises       $180,000

# Practice Exercises

**1. (LO 2)** Will Smith, the new controller of Alexandria Company, has reviewed the expected useful lives and salvage values of selected depreciable assets at the beginning of 2022. Here are his findings:

*Compute revised annual depreciation.*

| Type of Asset | Date Acquired | Cost | Accumulated Depreciation, Jan. 1, 2022 | Useful Life (in Years) Old | Proposed | Salvage Value Old | Proposed |
|---|---|---|---|---|---|---|---|
| Building | Jan. 1, 2014 | $900,000 | $172,000 | 40 | 50 | $40,000 | $47,600 |
| Warehouse | Jan. 1, 2016 | 120,000 | 27,600 | 25 | 20 | 5,000 | 3,600 |

All assets are depreciated by the straight-line method. Alexandria Company uses a calendar year in preparing annual financial statements. After discussion, management has agreed to accept Will's proposed changes. (The "Proposed" useful life is total life, not remaining life.)

### Instructions

Compute the revised annual depreciation on each asset in 2022. (Show computations.)

### Solution

**1.**

| | Type of Asset Building | Warehouse |
|---|---|---|
| Book value, 1/1/22 | $728,000 | $92,400 |
| Less: Salvage value | 47,600 | 3,600 |
| Depreciable cost (1) | $680,400 | $88,800 |
| Revised remaining useful life in years (2) | 42* | 14** |
| Revised annual depreciation (1) ÷ (2) | $16,200 | $6,343 |

*50 − 8; **20 − 6

**2. (LO 4)** Lake Company, organized in 2022, has the following transactions related to intangible assets.

*Record transactions related to intangible assets.*

| 1/2/22 | Purchased patent (8-year life) | $560,000 |
|---|---|---|
| 4/1/22 | Goodwill acquired when business purchased (indefinite life) | 360,000 |
| 7/1/22 | 10-year franchise; expiration date 7/1/2032 | 440,000 |
| 9/1/22 | Research and development costs | 185,000 |

### Instructions

Use a tabular summary to record these transactions. All costs incurred were for cash. Make the adjustments as of December 31, 2022, recording any necessary amortization and reflecting all balances accurately as of that date.

### Solution

2.

| Assets | | | | = Liabilities + | | | Stockholders' Equity | | | |
|---|---|---|---|---|---|---|---|---|---|---|

| | | | | | | | | | Retained Earnings | | |
|---|---|---|---|---|---|---|---|---|---|---|---|
| | | | | | | | Common | | | | |
| Cash | + | Patents | + Franchises + | Goodwill | = | | Stock | + Rev. − | Exp. | − Div. | |
| −$560,000 | | + $560,000 | | | | | | | | | |
| −360,000 | | | | + $360,000 | | | | | | | |
| −440,000 | | | +$440,000 | | | | | | | | |
| −185,000 | | | | | | | | | −$185,000 | | Res./Dev. Exp. |
| | | −70,000 | −22,000 | | | | | | −92,000* | | Amortization Exp. |

*($560,000 ÷ 8) + [($440,000 ÷ 10) × $\frac{1}{2}$]

Ending balances, 12/31/22:
Patents = $490,000 ($560,000 − $70,000)
Goodwill = $360,000
Franchises = $418,000 ($440,000 − $22,000)
R&D expense = $185,000
Amortization expense = $92,000

---

## Practice Problems

*Compute depreciation expense.*

**1. (LO 2)** DuPage Company purchases a factory machine at a cost of $18,000 on January 1, 2022. DuPage expects the machine to have a salvage value of $2,000 at the end of its 4-year useful life.

During its useful life, the machine is expected to be used 160,000 hours. Actual annual hourly use was 2022, 40,000; 2023, 60,000; 2024, 35,000; and 2025, 25,000.

### Instructions

Prepare a depreciation schedule for the straight-line method.

### Solution

1.

**Straight-Line Method**

| | Computation | | | Annual | End of Year | |
|---|---|---|---|---|---|---|
| Year | Depreciable Cost* | × | Depreciation Rate | = Depreciation Expense | Accumulated Depreciation | Book Value |
| 2022 | $16,000 | | 25% | $4,000 | $ 4,000 | $14,000** |
| 2023 | 16,000 | | 25% | 4,000 | 8,000 | 10,000 |
| 2024 | 16,000 | | 25% | 4,000 | 12,000 | 6,000 |
| 2025 | 16,000 | | 25% | 4,000 | 16,000 | 2,000 |

*$18,000 − $2,000
**$18,000 − $4,000

**2. (LO 3)** On January 1, 2019, Skyline Limousine Co. purchased a limousine at an acquisition cost of $28,000. Skyline depreciated the vehicle by the straight-line method using a 4-year service life and a $4,000 salvage value. The company's fiscal year ends on December 31.

*Record disposal of plant asset.*

### Instructions

Use a tabular summary to record the disposal of the limousine, assuming that it was:

a. Retired and scrapped with no salvage value on January 1, 2023.

b. Sold for $5,000 on July 1, 2022.

### Solution

2. a.

| Assets | | = | Liabilities + | Stockholders' Equity | | | | | |
|---|---|---|---|---|---|---|---|---|---|
| Equip- ment | Accum. Depr.— Equip. = | | | Common Stock + | Retained Earnings | | | | |
| | | | | | Rev. − | Exp. − | Div. | | |
| −$28,000 | +$24,000* | | | | | −$4,000 | | Loss on Disposal | |

*[($28,000 − $4,000) ÷ 4] × 4 years

b.

| Assets | | | = | Liabilities + | Stockholders' Equity | | | | |
|---|---|---|---|---|---|---|---|---|---|
| Cash + | Equip- ment − | Accum. Depr.— Equip. = | | | Common Stock + | Retained Earnings | | | |
| | | −$3,000 | | | | Rev. − | Exp. − | Div. | |
| +$5,000 | −$28,000 | +21,000** | | | | −$3,000* | | Depreciation Exp. | |
| | | | | | | −2,000 | | Loss on Disposal | |

*[($28,000 − $4,000) ÷ 4] × ½ year
**[($28,000 − $4,000) ÷ 4] × 3.5 years

# WileyPLUS

Brief Exercises, DO IT! Exercises, Exercises, Problems, and many additional resources are available for practice in WileyPLUS.

# Questions

1. Mrs. Harcross is uncertain about how the historical cost principle applies to plant assets. Explain the principle to Mrs. Harcross.

2. How is the cost for a plant asset measured in a cash transaction? In a noncash transaction?

3. Barrister Company acquires the land and building owned by Ansel Company. What types of costs may be incurred to make the asset ready for its intended use if Barrister Company wants to use only the land? If it wants to use both the land and the building?

4. Distinguish between ordinary repairs and capital expenditures during an asset's useful life.

5. In a recent newspaper release, the president of Magnusson Company asserted that something has to be done about depreciation. The president said, "Depreciation does not come close to accumulating the cash needed to replace the asset at the end of its useful life." What is your response to the president?

6. Melanie is studying for the next accounting examination. She asks your help on two questions: (a) What is salvage value? (b) How is salvage value used in determining depreciable cost under the straight-line method? Answer Melanie's questions.

7. Contrast the straight-line method and the units-of-activity method in relation to (a) useful life and (b) the pattern of periodic depreciation over useful life.

8. Contrast the effects of the three depreciation methods on annual depreciation expense.

9. In the fourth year of an asset's 5-year useful life, the company decides that the asset will have a 6-year service life. How should the revision of depreciation be recorded? Why?

10. How is a gain or a loss on the sale of a plant asset computed?

11. Marsh Corporation owns a machine that is fully depreciated but is still being used. How should Marsh account for this asset and report it in the financial statements?

12. What does **Apple** use as the estimated useful life on its buildings? On its machinery and equipment? (*Hint:* You will need to use the notes to Apple's financial statements, available at the company's website.)

**13.** What are the similarities and differences between depreciation and amortization?

**14.** During a recent management meeting, Bruce Dunn, director of marketing, proposed that the company begin capitalizing its marketing expenditures as goodwill. In his words, "Marketing expenditures create goodwill for the company which benefits the company for multiple periods. Therefore it doesn't make good sense to have to expense it as it is incurred. Besides, if we capitalize it as goodwill, we won't have to amortize it, and this will boost reported income." Discuss the merits of Bruce's proposal.

**15.** Warwick Company hires an accounting intern who says that intangible assets should always be amortized over their legal lives. Is the intern correct? Explain.

**16.** Goodwill has been defined as the value of all favorable attributes that relate to a business enterprise. What types of attributes could result in goodwill?

**17.** Kathy Malone, a business major, is working on a case problem for one of her classes. In this case problem, the company needs to raise cash to market a new product it developed. Doug Price, an engineering major, takes one look at the company's balance sheet and says, "This company has an awful lot of goodwill. Why don't you recommend that they sell some of it to raise cash?" How should Kathy respond to Doug?

**18.** Under what conditions is goodwill recorded? What is the proper accounting treatment for amortizing goodwill?

**19.** Often research and development costs provide companies with benefits that last a number of years. (For example, these costs can lead to the development of a patent that will increase the company's income for many years.) However, GAAP requires that such costs be recorded as an expense when incurred. Why?

**20.** Suppose in 2022 that **Campbell Soup Company** reported average total assets of $6,265 million, net sales of $7,586 million, and net income of $736 million. What was Campbell Soup's return on assets?

**21.** Cassy Dominic, a marketing executive for Fresh Views Inc., has proposed expanding its product line of framed graphic art by producing a line of lower-quality products. These would require less processing by the company and would provide a lower profit margin. Mel Joss, the company's CFO, is concerned that this new product line would reduce the company's return on assets. Discuss the potential effect on return on assets that this product might have.

**22.** Give an example of an industry that would be characterized by (a) a high asset turnover and a low profit margin, and (b) a low asset turnover and a high profit margin.

**23.** Peyton Corporation and Rogers Corporation operate in the same industry. Peyton uses the straight-line method to account for depreciation, whereas Rogers uses an accelerated method. Explain what complications might arise in trying to compare the results of these two companies.

**24.** Mesa Corporation uses straight-line depreciation for financial reporting purposes but an accelerated method for tax purposes. Is it acceptable to use different methods for the two purposes? What is Mesa Corporation's motivation for doing this?

**25.** You are comparing two companies in the same industry. You have determined that Gore Corp. depreciates its plant assets over a 40-year life, whereas Ross Corp. depreciates its plant assets over a 20-year life. Discuss the implications this has for comparing the results of the two companies.

## Brief Exercises

*Determine the cost of land.*

**BE8.1 (LO 1), AP** These expenditures were incurred by Dobbin Company in purchasing land: cash price $60,000, accrued taxes $5,000, attorney's fees $2,100, real estate broker's commission $3,300, and clearing and grading $3,500. What is the cost of the land?

*Determine the cost of a truck.*

**BE8.2 (LO 1), AP** Thoms Company incurs these expenditures in purchasing a truck: cash price $24,000, accident insurance (during use) $2,000, sales taxes $1,080, motor vehicle license $300, and painting and lettering $1,700. What is the cost of the truck?

*Distinguish between revenue expenditures versus capital expenditures.*

**BE8.3 (LO 1), C** Krieg Company had the following two transactions related to its delivery truck.

1. Paid $38 for an oil change.

2. Paid $400 to install special shelving units, which increase the operating efficiency of the truck.

What cost should be added to the delivery truck account?

*Compute straight-line depreciation.*

**BE8.4 (LO 2), AP** Gordon Chemicals Company acquires a delivery truck at a cost of $31,000 on January 1, 2022. The truck is expected to have a salvage value of $4,000 at the end of its 4-year useful life. Compute annual depreciation for the first and second years using the straight-line method.

*Compute depreciation and evaluate treatment.*

**BE8.5 (LO 2), AN** Ivy Company purchased land and a building on January 1, 2022. Management's best estimate of the value of the land was $100,000 and of the building $250,000. However, management told the accounting department to record the land at $230,000 and the building at $120,000. The building is being depreciated on a straight-line basis over 20 years with no salvage value. Why do you suppose management requested this accounting treatment? Is it ethical?

*Compute revised depreciation.*

**BE8.6 (LO 2), AP** On January 1, 2022, the Hermann Company records show Equipment $36,000 and Accumulated Depreciation $13,600. The depreciation resulted from using the straight-line method with a useful life of 10 years and a salvage value of $2,000. On this date, the company concludes that the equipment has a remaining useful life of only 2 years with the same salvage value. Compute the revised annual depreciation.

**BE8.7 (LO 3), AP** Prepare tabular summaries to record these transactions. (a) Echo Company retires its delivery equipment, which cost $41,000. Accumulated depreciation is also $41,000 on this delivery equipment. No salvage value is received. (b) Assume the same information as in part (a), except that accumulated depreciation for the equipment is $37,200 instead of $41,000.

*Prepare a tabular summary for disposal of plant assets.*

**BE8.8 (LO 3), AP** Antone Company sells office equipment on July 31, 2022, for $21,000 cash. The office equipment originally cost $72,000 and as of January 1, 2022, had accumulated depreciation of $42,000. Depreciation for the first 7 months of 2022 is $4,600. Prepare a tabular summary to (a) update depreciation to July 31, 2022, and (b) record the sale of the equipment.

*Prepare a tabular summary for sale of plant assets.*

**BE8.9 (LO 4), AP** Abner Company purchases a patent for $156,000 on January 2, 2022. Its estimated useful life is 6 years.

*Account for intangibles—patents.*

a. Compute amortization expense for the first year.

b. Show how this patent is reported on the balance sheet at the end of the first year.

**BE8.10 (LO 5), AP** Suppose in its 2022 annual report that **McDonald's Corporation** reports beginning total assets of $28.46 billion, ending total assets of $30.22 billion, net sales of $22.74 billion, and net income of $4.55 billion.

*Compute return on assets and asset turnover.*

a. Compute McDonald's return on assets.

b. Compute McDonald's asset turnover.

**BE8.11 (LO 5), AP** Suppose **Nike, Inc.** reported the following plant assets and intangible assets for the year ended May 31, 2022 (in millions): other plant assets $965.8, land $221.6, patents and trademarks (at cost) $515.1, machinery and equipment $2,094.3, buildings $974.0, goodwill (at cost) $193.5, accumulated amortization $47.7, and accumulated depreciation $2,298.0. Prepare a partial balance sheet for Nike for these items.

*Classification of long-lived assets on balance sheet.*

## DO IT! Exercises

**DO IT! 8.1 (LO 1), C** Hummer Company purchased a delivery truck. The total cash payment was $30,020, including the following items.

*Explain accounting for cost of plant assets*

| | |
|---|---|
| Negotiated purchase price | $24,000 |
| Installation of special shelving | 1,100 |
| Painting and lettering | 900 |
| Motor vehicle license | 180 |
| Two-year insurance policy | 2,400 |
| Sales tax | 1,440 |
| Total paid | $30,020 |

Explain how each of these costs would be accounted for.

**DO IT! 8.2a (LO 2), AP** On January 1, 2022, Salt Creek Country Club purchased a new riding mower for $15,000. The mower is expected to have a 10-year life with a $1,000 salvage value. Prepare a tabular summary to record depreciation expense on December 31, 2022, if Salt Creek uses straight-line depreciation.

*Calculate depreciation expense.*

**DO IT! 8.2b (LO 2), AP** Fordon Corporation purchased a piece of equipment for $50,000. It estimated an 8-year life and $2,000 salvage value. At the end of year 4 (before the depreciation adjustment), it estimated the new total life to be 10 years and the new salvage value to be $4,000. Compute the revised depreciation.

*Calculate revised depreciation*

**DO IT! 8.3 (LO 3), AP** Bylie Company has an old factory machine that cost $50,000. The machine has accumulated depreciation of $28,000. Bylie has decided to sell the machine.

*Prepare a tabular summary to record plant asset disposal.*

a. Prepare a tabular summary to record the sale of the machine for $25,000 cash.

b. Prepare a tabular summary to record the sale of the machine for $15,000 cash.

**DO IT! 8.4 (LO 4), C** Match the statement with the term most directly associated with it.

*Match intangible assets with concepts.*

| | |
|---|---|
| Goodwill | Amortization |
| Intangible assets | Franchise |
| Research and development costs | |

1. _____ Rights, privileges, and competitive advantages that result from the ownership of long-lived assets that do not possess physical substance.

2. _____ The allocation of the cost of an intangible asset to expense in a rational and systematic manner.

3. _____ A right to sell certain products or services, or use certain trademarks or trade names within a designated geographic area.

4. _____ Costs incurred by a company that often lead to patents or new products. These costs must be expensed as incurred.

5. _____ The excess of the cost of a company over the fair value of the net assets required.

*Calculate asset turnover and return on assets.*

**DO IT! 8.5 (LO 5), AP** For 2022, Sale Company reported beginning total assets of $300,000 and ending total assets of $340,000. Its net income for this period was $50,000, and its net sales were $400,000. Compute the company's asset turnover and return on assets for 2022.

# Exercises

*Determine cost of plant acquisitions.*

**E8.1 (LO 1), C** **Writing** The following expenditures relating to plant assets were made by Glenn Company during the first 2 months of 2022.

1. Paid $7,000 of accrued taxes at the time the plant site was acquired.

2. Paid $200 insurance to cover a possible accident loss on new factory machinery while the machinery was in transit.

3. Paid $850 sales taxes on a new delivery truck.

4. Paid $21,000 for parking lots and driveways on the new plant site.

5. Paid $250 to have the company name and slogan painted on the new delivery truck.

6. Paid $8,000 for installation of new factory machinery.

7. Paid $900 for a 2-year accident insurance policy on the new delivery truck.

8. Paid $75 motor vehicle license fee on the new truck.

## Instructions

a. Explain the application of the historical cost principle in determining the acquisition cost of plant assets.

b. List the numbers of the transactions, and opposite each indicate the account each expenditure would increase.

*Determine property, plant, and equipment costs.*

**E8.2 (LO 1), C** Adama Company incurred the following costs.

| | |
|---|---:|
| 1. Sales tax on factory machinery purchased | $ 5,000 |
| 2. Painting of and lettering on truck immediately upon purchase | 700 |
| 3. Installation and testing of factory machinery | 2,000 |
| 4. Real estate broker's commission on land purchased | 3,500 |
| 5. Insurance premium paid for 2-year insurance policy on new truck | 880 |
| 6. Cost of landscaping on property purchased | 7,200 |
| 7. Cost of paving parking lot for new building constructed | 17,900 |
| 8. Cost of clearing, draining, and filling land | 13,300 |
| 9. Architect's fees on self-constructed building | 10,000 |

## Instructions

Indicate the title of the account that would be increased for each expenditure.

*Determine acquisition costs of land.*

**E8.3 (LO 1), AP** On March 1, 2022, Boyd Company acquired real estate, on which it planned to construct a small office building, by paying $80,000 in cash. An old warehouse on the property was demolished at a cost of $8,200; the salvaged materials were sold for $1,700. Additional expenditures before construction began included $1,900 attorney's fee for work concerning the land purchase, $5,200 real estate broker's fee, $9,100 architect's fee, and $14,000 to put in driveways and a parking lot.

## Instructions

a. Determine the amount to be reported as the cost of the land.

b. For each cost not used in part (a), indicate the account to be increased.

**E8.4 (LO 2), C** Alysha Monet has prepared the following list of statements about depreciation.

*Understand depreciation concepts.*

1. Depreciation is a process of asset valuation, not cost allocation.

2. Depreciation provides for the proper matching of expenses with revenues.

3. The book value of a plant asset should approximate its fair value.

4. Depreciation applies to three classes of plant assets: land, buildings, and equipment.

5. Depreciation does not apply to a building because its usefulness and revenue-producing ability generally remain intact over time.

6. The revenue-producing ability of a depreciable asset will decline due to wear and tear and to obsolescence.

7. Recognizing depreciation on an asset results in an accumulation of cash for replacement of the asset.

8. The balance in accumulated depreciation represents the total cost that has been charged to expense since placing the asset in service.

9. Depreciation expense and accumulated depreciation are reported on the income statement.

10. Three factors affect the computation of depreciation: cost, useful life, and salvage value.

## Instructions

Identify each statement as true or false. If false, indicate how to correct the statement.

**E8.5 (LO 2), AP** Gotham Company purchased a new machine on October 1, 2022, at a cost of $90,000. The company estimated that the machine has a salvage value of $8,000. The machine is expected to be used for 70,000 working hours during its 8-year life.

*Determine straight-line depreciation for partial period.*

## Instructions

Compute the depreciation expense under the straight-line method for 2022 and 2023, assuming a December 31 year-end.

**E8.6 (LO 2), AN** Victor Mineli, the new controller of Santorini Company, has reviewed the expected useful lives and salvage values of selected depreciable assets at the beginning of 2022. Here are his findings:

*Compute revised annual depreciation.*

| Type of Asset | Date Acquired | Cost | Accumulated Depreciation, Jan. 1, 2022 | Useful Life (in Years) Old | Proposed | Salvage Value Old | Proposed |
|---|---|---|---|---|---|---|---|
| Building | Jan. 1, 2014 | $700,000 | $130,000 | 40 | 48 | $50,000 | $35,000 |
| Warehouse | Jan. 1, 2017 | 120,000 | 23,000 | 25 | 20 | 5,000 | 3,600 |

All assets are depreciated by the straight-line method. Santorini Company uses a calendar year in preparing annual financial statements. After discussion, management has agreed to accept Victor's proposed changes. (The "Proposed" useful life is total life, not remaining life.)

## Instructions

Compute the revised annual depreciation on each asset in 2022. (Show computations.)

**E8.7 (LO 3), AP** Thieu Co. has delivery equipment that cost $50,000 and has been depreciated $24,000.

*Prepare tabular summaries to record disposals of plant assets.*

## Instructions

Prepare a tabular summary to record the disposal under the following assumptions.

a. It was scrapped as having no value.

b. It was sold for $37,000.

c. It was sold for $20,000.

**E8.8 (LO 3), AP** Here are selected 2022 transactions of Akron Corporation.

*Record disposal of equipment.*

Jan.   1   Retired a piece of machinery that was purchased on January 1, 2012. The machine cost $62,000 and had a useful life of 10 years with no salvage value.

June 30   Sold a computer that was purchased on January 1, 2020. The computer cost $36,000 and had a useful life of 3 years with no salvage value. The computer was sold for $5,000 cash.

Dec. 31    Sold a delivery truck for $9,000 cash. The truck cost $25,000 when it was purchased on January 1, 2019, and was depreciated based on a 5-year useful life with a $4,000 salvage value.

**Instructions**

Prepare a tabular summary to record all transactions described on the above dates. Depreciation was last recorded on December 31, 2021. Update depreciation on assets disposed of, where applicable. Akron Corporation uses straight-line depreciation.

*Analyze equipment transactions and determine missing amounts.*

**E8.9 (LO 1, 2, 3), AN** The following is a tabular summary relating to equipment that was purchased for cash by a company on the first day of the current year. The equipment was depreciated on a straight-line basis with an estimated useful life of 10 years and a salvage value of $100. Part of the equipment was sold on the last day of the current year for cash proceeds.

| | Assets | | | = Liabilities + | Stockholders' Equity | | | | |
|---|---|---|---|---|---|---|---|---|---|
| | | | Accum. | | | Retained Earnings | | | |
| | | Equip- | Depr.— | | Common | | | | |
| | Cash + | ment | − Equip. = | | Stock | + Rev. | − Exp. | − Div. | |
| Jan. 1 | (a) | +$1,100 | | | | | | | |
| Dec. 31 | | | −$100 | | | | (b) | | |
| Dec. 31 | +$450 | −440 | +40 | | | | (c) | | |

**Instructions**

Use the information in the tabular summary to derive the missing amounts:

a. Purchase of equipment on January 1. What was the cash paid?

b. Depreciation recorded on December 31. What was the depreciation expense?

c. Sale of part of the equipment on December 31. What was the gain on disposal?

*Apply accounting concepts.*

**E8.10 (LO 1, 2, 3, 4), C** The following situations are independent of one another.

1. An accounting student recently employed by a small company doesn't understand why the company is only depreciating its buildings and equipment, but not its land. The student recorded depreciation expense for all the company's property, plant, and equipment for the current year-end.

2. The same student also thinks the company's amortization policy on its intangible assets is wrong. The company is currently amortizing its patents but not its goodwill. As a result, the student added goodwill to her adjustment for amortization at the end of the current year. She told a fellow employee that she felt she had improved the consistency of the company's accounting policies by making these changes.

3. The same company has a building still in use that has a zero book value but a substantial fair value. The student felt that this practice didn't benefit the company's users—especially the bank—and wrote the building up to its fair value. After all, she reasoned, you can write down assets if fair values are lower. Writing them up if fair value is higher is yet another example of the improved consistency that she has brought to the company's accounting practices.

**Instructions**

Explain whether or not the accounting treatment in each of the above situations is in accordance with generally accepted accounting principles. Explain what accounting principle or assumption, if any, has been violated and what the appropriate accounting treatment should be.

*Compute amortization expense.*

**E8.11 (LO 4), AN** These are selected 2022 transactions for Wyle Corporation:

Jan. 1    Purchased a copyright for $120,000. The copyright has a useful life of 6 years and a remaining legal life of 30 years.

Mar. 1    Purchased a patent with an estimated useful life of 4 years and a legal life of 20 years for $54,000.

Sept. 1    Purchased a small company and recorded goodwill of $150,000. Its useful life is indefinite.

**Instructions**

Indicate the amount of amortization expense on December 31, 2022, for Wyle Corporation.

*Record transactions for different intangibles; calculate amortization.*

**E8.12 (LO 4), AN** On January 1, 2022, Haley Company had a balance of $360,000 of goodwill on its balance sheet that resulted from the purchase of a small business in a prior year. The goodwill had an indefinite life. During 2022, the company had the following additional transactions.

Jan. 2    Purchased a patent (5-year life) $280,000.

July 1    Acquired a 9-year franchise; expiration date July 1, 2031, $540,000.

Sept. 1    Research and development costs $185,000.

## Instructions

a. Prepare a tabular summary to record the January 1 balance in the Goodwill account as well as the 2022 transactions related to intangibles. All costs incurred were for cash.

b. Record any necessary amortization as of December 31, 2022.

c. Indicate what the intangible asset account balances should be on December 31, 2022.

**E8.13 (LO 4), C** **Writing** **Alliance Atlantis Communications Inc.** changed its accounting policy to amortize broadcast rights over the contracted exhibition period, which is based on the estimated useful life of the program. Previously, the company amortized broadcast rights over the lesser of 2 years or the contracted exhibition period.

*Discuss implications of amortization period.*

## Instructions

Write a short memo to your client explaining the implications this has for the analysis of Alliance Atlantis's results.

**E8.14 (LO 2, 4), C** The questions listed below are independent of one another.

*Answer questions on depreciation and intangibles.*

## Instructions

Provide a brief answer to each question.

a. Why should a company depreciate its buildings?

b. How can a company have a building that has a zero reported book value but substantial fair value?

c. What are some examples of intangibles that you might find on your college campus?

d. Give some examples of company or product trademarks or trade names. Are trade names and trademarks reported on a company's balance sheet?

**E8.15 (LO 5), AP** Suppose during 2022 that **Federal Express** reported the following information (in millions): net sales of $35,497 and net income of $98. Its balance sheet also showed total assets at the beginning of the year of $25,633 and total assets at the end of the year of $24,244.

*Calculate asset turnover and return on assets.*

## Instructions

Calculate the (a) asset turnover and (b) return on assets.

# Problems

**P8.1 (LO 1), C** Peete Company was organized on January 1. During the first year of operations, the following plant asset expenditures and receipts were recorded in random order.

*Determine acquisition costs of land and building.*

### Expenditures

|   |   |   |
|---|---|---|
| 1. Excavation costs for new building | $ | 23,000 |
| 2. Architect's fees on building plans | | 33,000 |
| 3. Full payment to building contractor | | 640,000 |
| 4. Cost of real estate purchased as a plant site (land $255,000 and building $25,000) | | 280,000 |
| 5. Cost of parking lots and driveways | | 29,000 |
| 6. Accrued real estate taxes paid at time of purchase of real estate | | 3,170 |
| 7. Installation cost of fences around property | | 6,800 |
| 8. Cost of demolishing building to make land suitable for construction of new building | | 31,000 |
| 9. Real estate taxes paid for the current year on land | | 6,400 |
| | | $1,052,370 |

### Receipts

|   |   |   |
|---|---|---|
| 10. Proceeds from salvage of demolished building | $ | 12,000 |

**Instructions**

Analyze the transactions using the following table column headings. Enter the number of each transaction in the Item column, and enter the amounts in the appropriate columns. For amounts in the Other Accounts column, also indicate the account title.

Land   $302,170

*Record transactions related to purchase, sale, retirement, and depreciation.*

| Item | Land | Buildings | Other Accounts |
|------|------|-----------|----------------|

**P8.2 (LO 2, 3, 5), AP** At December 31, 2022, Arnold Corporation reported the following plant assets.

| | | |
|---|---|---|
| Land | | $ 3,000,000 |
| Buildings | $26,500,000 | |
| Less: Accumulated depreciation—buildings | 11,925,000 | 14,575,000 |
| Equipment | 40,000,000 | |
| Less: Accumulated depreciation—equipment | 5,000,000 | 35,000,000 |
| Total plant assets | | $52,575,000 |

During 2023, the following selected cash transactions occurred.

Apr. 1   Purchased land for $2,200,000.

May 1   Sold equipment that cost $600,000 when purchased on January 1, 2016. The equipment was sold for $170,000.

June 1   Sold land for $1,600,000. The land cost $1,000,000.

July 1   Purchased equipment for $1,100,000.

Dec. 31   Retired equipment that cost $700,000 when purchased on December 31, 2013. No salvage value was received.

**Instructions**

a. Prepare a tabular summary that includes the plant asset accounts and balances shown on the December 31, 2022, balance sheet.

b. Enter the 2023 transactions in the tabular summary from part (a). Arnold uses straight-line depreciation for buildings and equipment. The buildings are estimated to have a 40-year useful life and no salvage value; the equipment is estimated to have a 10-year useful life and no salvage value. Update depreciation on assets disposed of at the time of sale or retirement.

c. Record adjustments to accounts for depreciation for 2023.

d. Tot. plant assets   $50,037,500

d. Prepare the plant assets section of Arnold's balance sheet at December 31, 2023.

*Compute gains and losses for disposal of plant assets.*

**P8.3 (LO 3), AP** Pine Company had the following assets on January 1, 2022.

| Item | Cost | Purchase Date | Useful Life (in years) | Salvage Value |
|------|------|---------------|------------------------|---------------|
| Machinery | $71,000 | Jan. 1, 2012 | 10 | $ -0- |
| Forklift | 30,000 | Jan. 1, 2019 | 5 | -0- |
| Truck | 33,400 | Jan. 1, 2017 | 8 | 3,000 |

During 2022, each of the assets was removed from service. The machinery was retired on January 1. The forklift was sold on June 30 for $12,000. The truck was discarded on December 31. The company uses straight-line depreciation. All depreciation was up to date as of December 31, 2021.

**Instructions**

Loss on truck disposal   $10,600

Compute the gain or loss for each of the asset disposals that occurred in 2022. (*Hint:* Be sure to update depreciation for each asset from January 1, 2022, to disposal date.)

*Record property, plant, and equipment transactions; prepare partial balance sheet.*

**P8.4 (LO 1, 2, 3, 5), AP** At January 1, 2022, Youngstown Company reported the following property, plant, and equipment accounts:

| | |
|---|---|
| Accumulated depreciation—buildings | $ 62,200,000 |
| Accumulated depreciation—equipment | 54,000,000 |
| Buildings | 97,400,000 |
| Equipment | 150,000,000 |
| Land | 20,000,000 |

The company uses straight-line depreciation for buildings and equipment, its year-end is December 31, and it makes adjustments annually. The buildings are estimated to have a 40-year useful life and no salvage value; the equipment is estimated to have a 10-year useful life and no salvage value.

During 2022, the following selected transactions occurred:

Apr.  1   Purchased land for $4.4 million. Paid $1.1 million cash and issued a 3-year, 6% note payable for the balance. Interest on the note is payable annually each April 1.

May  1   Sold equipment for $300,000 cash. The equipment cost $2.8 million when originally
purchased on January 1, 2014.

June  1   Sold land for $3.6 million. Received $900,000 cash and accepted a 3-year, 5% note for
the balance. The land cost $1.4 million when purchased on June 1, 2016. Interest on the
note is due annually each June 1.

July  1   Purchased equipment for $2.2 million cash.

Dec. 31   Retired equipment that cost $1 million when purchased on December 31, 2012. No pro-
ceeds were received.

### Instructions

a. Prepare a tabular summary that includes the property, plant, and equipment balances as of
January 1, 2022.

b. Record the above transactions in the tabular summary from part (a).

c. Record any adjustments required at December 31.

d. Prepare the property, plant, and equipment section of the company's balance sheet at December 31.     *d.  Total PP&E      $138,575,000*

**P8.5  (LO 4, 5), AP**  The intangible assets section of Amato Corporation's balance sheet at December 31,
2022, is presented here.

*Record transactions related to
acquisition and amortization of
intangibles; prepare the intangible
assets section and note.*

| | |
|---|---|
| Patents ($60,000 cost less $6,000 amortization) | $54,000 |
| Copyrights ($36,000 cost less $25,200 amortization) | 10,800 |
| Total | $64,800 |

The patent was acquired in January 2022 and has a useful life of 10 years. The copyright was acquired
in January 2016 and also has a useful life of 10 years. The following cash transactions may have affected
intangible assets during 2023.

Jan.  2   Paid $46,800 legal costs to successfully defend the patent against infringement by another
company.

Jan.–June Developed a new product, incurring $230,000 in research and development costs. A pat-
ent was granted for the product on July 1, and its useful life is equal to its legal life. Legal
and other costs for the patent were $20,000.

Sept. 1   Paid $40,000 to a quarterback to appear in commercials advertising the company's
products. The commercials will air in September and October.

Oct.  1   Acquired a copyright for $200,000. The copyright has a useful life and legal life of
50 years.

### Instructions

a. Prepare a tabular summary that includes the intangible asset balances as of December 31, 2022.

b. Record the 2023 transactions in the tabular summary from part (a).

c. Record the 2023 amortization expense for intangible assets.

d. Prepare the intangible assets section of the balance sheet at December 31, 2023.     *d.  Tot. intangibles      $315,300*

e. Prepare the note to the financial statements on Amato Corporation's intangible assets as of December 31, 2023.

**P8.6  (LO 4), AN**  Due to rapid employee turnover in the accounting department, the following transactions involving intangible assets were improperly recorded by Inland Corporation.

*Correct errors in recording and
amortizing intangible assets.*

1. Inland developed a new manufacturing process, incurring research and development costs of
$160,000. The company also purchased a patent for $40,000. In early January, Inland capitalized
$200,000 as the cost of the patents. Patent amortization expense of $10,000 was recorded based on a
20-year useful life.

2. On July 1, 2022, Inland purchased a small company and as a result recorded goodwill of $80,000.
Inland recorded a half-year's amortization in 2022, based on a 20-year life ($2,000 amortization).
The goodwill has an indefinite life.

### Instructions

Indicate the account titles and amounts to increase or decrease to correct any errors made during 2022.

*Calculate and comment on return on assets, profit margin, and asset turnover.*

**P8.7 (LO 5), AN** Blythe Corporation and Jacke Corporation, two companies of roughly the same size, are both involved in the manufacture of shoe-tracing devices. Each company depreciates its plant assets using the straight-line approach. An investigation of their financial statements reveals the following information.

|  | **Blythe Corp.** | **Jacke Corp.** |
|---|---|---|
| Net income | $ 240,000 | $ 300,000 |
| Sales revenue | 1,150,000 | 1,200,000 |
| Total assets (average) | 3,200,000 | 3,000,000 |
| Plant assets (average) | 2,400,000 | 1,800,000 |
| Intangible assets (goodwill) | 300,000 | 0 |

**Instructions**

a. For each company, calculate these values:

   1. Return on assets.

   2. Profit margin.

   3. Asset turnover.

b. Based on your calculations in part (a), comment on the relative effectiveness of the two companies in using their assets to generate sales. What factors complicate your ability to compare the two companies?

## Comprehensive Accounting Cycle Review

**ACR8** Milo Corporation prepares monthly financial statements. The tabular summary shown in the instructions below reflects the results of January–November 2022. During December, the following transactions occurred:

Dec. 2 Paid cash for equipment with a purchase price of $16,000, plus $800 of sales tax.

     2 Milo sold for $4,500 equipment that originally cost $6,000. Accumulated depreciation on this equipment at January 1, 2022, was $2,160; 2022 depreciation expense prior to the sale of equipment was $990.

    15 Milo sold inventory for $75,000 cash that cost $52,500.

    23 Salaries and wages of $6,600 were paid.

Adjustment data:

1. The balance in prepaid insurance represents a 6-month policy with coverge beginning December 1, 2022.

2. The equipment owned prior to this year is being depreciated using the straight-line method over 5 years. The salvage value is 10% of cost.

3. The equipment purchased on December 2, 2022, is being depreciated using the straight-line method over 5 years, with a salvage value of $1,800.

4. The patent was acquired on January 1, 2022, and has a useful life of 8 years from that date.

5. Unpaid salaries at December 31, 2022, total $2,200.

| | | Assets | | | | | = | Liabilities | + | Stockholders' Equity | |
|---|---|---|---|---|---|---|---|---|---|---|---|
| | Cash | + Inventory + | Prepaid Insurance + | Equip. − | Accum. Depr.— Equip. | + Patents = | Accts. Pay. + | Sal./ Wages Pay. | + | Com. Stock + | Retained Earnings |
| 12/1/Bal. | $22,000 | $102,600 | $3,600 | $60,000 | $24,000 | $9,600 | $27,300 | | | $90,000 | $56,500 |
| | | | | | | | | | | | + Rev. − Exp. − Div. |
| Dec. 2 | | | | | | | | | | | |
| 2 | | | | | | | | | | | |
| 15 | | | | | | | | | | | |
| 23 | | | | | | | | | | | |
| Unadj. Bal. | | | | | | | | | | | |
| Adjustments | | | | | | | | | | | |
| (A1) | | | | | | | | | | | |
| (A2) | | | | | | | | | | | |
| (A3) | | | | | | | | | | | |
| (A4) | | | | | | | | | | | |
| (A5) | | | | | | | | | | | |
| Adj. Bal. | | | | | | | | | | | |

a. Use the tabular summary above to complete the following.

 1. Record the December transactions. Include explanations for amounts in the revenue and expense columns.

 2. Determine the unadjusted balance for each column.

 3. Record the December adjustments.

 4. Determine the adjusted balance for each column

b. Prepare an income statement and statement of retained earnings for the month of December 2022.

c. Prepare a December 31, 2022, balance sheet.

b. Net income    $12,600

c. Total assets    $188,600

# Expand Your Critical Thinking

## Financial Reporting Problem: Apple Inc.

**CT8.1** The financial statements of **Apple Inc.** are presented in Appendix A. The complete annual report, including the notes to the financial statements, is available at the company's website.

### Instructions

Answer the following questions.

a. What were the total cost and book value of property, plant, and equipment at September 29, 2018?

b. Using the notes to the financial statements, what method or methods of depreciation are used by Apple for financial reporting purposes?

c. What was the amount of depreciation and amortization expense for each of the 3 years 2016–2018? (*Hint:* Use the statement of cash flows.)

d. Using the notes to the financial statements, explain how Apple accounted for its intangible assets in 2018.

## Comparative Analysis Problem:
## Columbia Sportswear Company vs. Under Armour, Inc.

**CT8.2** The financial statements of **Columbia Sportswear Company** are presented in Appendix B. Financial statements of **Under Armour, Inc.** are presented in Appendix C. The complete annual reports, including the notes to the financial statements, are available at each company's respective website.

### Instructions

a. Based on the information in these financial statements and the accompanying notes and schedules, compute the following values for each company in 2018.

 1. Return on assets.

 2. Profit margin (use "Total Revenue").

 3. Asset turnover.

b. What conclusions concerning the management of plant assets can be drawn from these data?

## Interpreting Financial Statements

**CT8.3** The March 29, 2012, edition of the *Wall Street Journal Online* contains an article by Miguel Bustillo entitled, "Best Buy Forced to Rethink Big Box." The article explains how the 1,100 giant stores that enabled **Best Buy** to obtain its position as the largest retailer of electronics are now reducing the company's profitability and even threatening its survival. The problem is that many customers go to Best Buy stores to see items but then buy them for less from online retailers. As a result, Best Buy recently announced that it would close 50 stores and switch to smaller stores. However, some analysts think that these changes are not big enough.

 Suppose the following data were extracted from the 2022 and 2017 annual reports of Best Buy. (All amounts are in millions.)

| | 2022 | 2021 | 2017 | 2016 |
|---|---|---|---|---|
| Total assets at year-end | $17,849 | $18,302 | $11,864 | $10,294 |
| Net sales | 50,272 | | 30,848 | |
| Net income | 1,277 | | 1,140 | |

**Instructions**

Using the data above, answer the following questions.

a. How might the return on assets and asset turnover of Best Buy differ from an online retailer?

b. Compute the profit margin, asset turnover, and return on assets for 2022 and 2017.

c. Present the ratios calculated in part (b) in the equation format shown in Illustration 8.22.

d. Discuss the implications of the ratios calculated in parts (b) and (c).

## Real-World Focus

**CT8.4** A company's annual report identifies the amount of its plant assets and the depreciation method used.

### Instructions

Select a particular company, search for the investor relations site for the company, and then answer the following questions.

a. What is the name of the company?

b. At fiscal year-end, what is the net amount of its plant assets?

c. What is the accumulated depreciation?

d. Which method of depreciation does the company use?

**CT8.5** The November 16, 2011, edition of the *Wall Street Journal Online* contains an article by Maxwell Murphy entitled "The Big Number: 51."

### Instructions

Read the article and answer the following questions.

a. What do the 51 companies referred to in the title have in common? What implications does this have regarding the fair value of a company's assets?

b. What significance does the common trait referred to in part (a) have for a company's goodwill?

c. How does a company get to record goodwill on its books—that is, what must have occurred for goodwill to show up on a company's books?

d. If these companies write down their goodwill, will this reduce their cash?

## Decision-Making Across the Organization

**CT8.6** Brady Furniture Corp. is nationally recognized for making high-quality products. Management is concerned that it is not fully exploiting its brand power. Brady's production managers are also concerned because their plants are not operating at anywhere near full capacity. Management is currently consider-ing a proposal to offer a new line of affordable furniture.

Those in favor of the proposal (including the vice president of production) believe that, by offering these new products, the company could attract a clientele that it is not currently servicing. Also, it could operate its plants at full capacity, thus taking better advantage of its assets.

The vice president of marketing, however, believes that the lower-priced (and lower-margin) prod-uct would have a negative impact on the sales of existing products. The vice president believes that $10,000,000 of the sales of the new product will be from customers that would have purchased the more expensive product but switched to the lower-margin product because it was available. (This is often referred to as cannibalization of existing sales.) Top management feels, however, that even with canni-balization, the company's sales will increase and the company will be better off.

The following data are available.

| (in thousands) | Current Results | Proposed Results without Cannibalization | Proposed Results with Cannibalization |
|---|---|---|---|
| Sales revenue | $ 45,000 | $ 60,000 | $ 50,000 |
| Net income | 12,000 | 13,500 | 12,000 |
| Average total assets | 100,000 | 100,000 | 100,000 |

**Instructions**

a. Compute Brady's return on assets, profit margin, and asset turnover, both with and without the new product line.

b. Discuss the implications that your findings in part (a) have for Brady's decision.

c. Are there any other options that Brady should consider? What impact would each of these have on the above ratios?

## Communication Activity

**CT8.7** The chapter presented some concerns regarding the current accounting standards for research and development expenditures.

**Instructions**

Assume that you are either (a) the president of a company that is very dependent on ongoing research and development, writing a memo to the FASB complaining about the current accounting standards regarding research and development, or (b) the FASB member defending the current standards regarding research and development. Your memo should address the following questions.

1. By requiring expensing of R&D, do you think companies will spend less on R&D? Why or why not? What are the possible implications for the competitiveness of U.S. companies?

2. If a company makes a commitment to spend money for R&D, it must believe it has future benefits. Shouldn't these costs therefore be capitalized just like the purchase of any long-lived asset that you believe will have future benefits?

## Ethics Case

**CT8.8**  Clean Aire Anti-Pollution Company is suffering declining sales of its principal product, nonbiodegradable plastic cartons. The president, Wade Truman, instructs his controller, Kate Rollins, to lengthen asset lives to reduce depreciation expense. A processing line of automated plastic extruding equipment, purchased for $3.5 million in January 2022, was originally estimated to have a useful life of 8 years and a salvage value of $400,000. Depreciation has been recorded for 2 years on that basis. Wade wants the estimated life changed to 12 years total and the straight-line method continued. Kate is hesitant to make the change, believing it is unethical to increase net income in this manner. Wade says, "Hey, the life is only an estimate, and I've heard that our competition uses a 12-year life on their production equipment."

**Instructions**

a. Who are the stakeholders in this situation?

b. Is the proposed change in asset life unethical, or is it simply a good business practice by an astute president?

c. What is the effect of Wade's proposed change on income before taxes in the year of change?

## All About You

**CT8.9** A company's trade name is a very important asset to the company, as it creates immediate product identification. Companies invest substantial sums to ensure that their product is well-known to the consumer. Test your knowledge of who owns some famous brands and their impact on the financial statements.

**Instructions**

a. Provide an answer to the four multiple-choice questions below.

    1. Which company owns both Taco Bell and Pizza Hut?

        **a.** McDonald's.    **b.** CKE.    **c.** Yum Brands.    **d.** Wendy's.

    2. Dairy Queen belongs to:

        **a.** Breyers.    **b.** Berkshire Hathaway.    **c.** GE.    **d.** The Coca-Cola Company.

    3. Phillip Morris, the cigarette maker, is owned by:

        **a.** Altria.    **b.** GE.    **c.** Boeing.    **d.** ExxonMobil.

    4. AOL, a major Internet provider, belongs to:

        **a.** Microsoft.    **b.** Cisco.    **c.** NBC.    **d.** Verizon Communications.

b. How do you think the value of these brands is reported on the appropriate company's balance sheet?

iStock.com/monkeybusinessimages

# Reporting and Analyzing Liabilities and Stockholders' Equity

## Chapter Preview

Debt can threaten companies' very existence. Given this risk, why do companies sometimes choose to borrow money rather than issuing stock? Financing decisions are critical to a company's success and survival. In this chapter, we address fundamental issues related to debt and equity financing.

## Feature Story

### And Then There Were Two

Debt can help a company acquire the things it needs to grow. But, it is often the very thing that can also kill a company. A brief history of **Maxwell Car Company** illustrates the role of debt in the U.S. auto industry. In 1920, Maxwell Car Company was on the brink of financial ruin. Because it was unable to pay its bills, its creditors stepped in and took over. They hired a former **General Motors (GM)** executive named Walter Chrysler to reorganize the company. By 1925, he had taken over the company and renamed it Chrysler. By 1933, **Chrysler** was booming, with sales surpassing even those of **Ford**.

But the next few decades saw Chrysler make a series of blunders. By 1980, with its creditors pounding at the gates, Chrysler was again on the brink of financial ruin.

At that point, Chrysler brought in a former Ford executive named Lee Iacocca to save the company. Iacocca argued that the United States could not afford to let Chrysler fail because of the loss of jobs. He convinced the federal government to grant loan guarantees—promises that if Chrysler failed to pay its creditors, the government would pay them. Iacocca then streamlined operations and brought out some profitable products. Chrysler repaid all of its government-guaranteed loans by 1983, seven years ahead of the scheduled final payment.

To compete in today's global vehicle market, you must be big—really big. So in 1998, Chrysler merged with German automaker **Daimler-Benz** to form **DaimlerChrysler**. For a time, this left just two U.S.-based auto manufacturers—GM and Ford. But in 2007, DaimlerChrysler sold 81% of Chrysler to **Cerberus**, an investment group, to provide much-needed cash infusions to the automaker. In 2009, Daimler turned over its remaining stake to Cerberus. Three days later, Chrysler filed for bankruptcy.

The car companies are giants. GM and Ford typically rank among the top five U.S. firms in total assets. But GM and Ford accumulated truckloads of debt on their way to getting big. Although debt made it possible to get so big, the Chrysler story makes it clear that debt can also threaten a company's survival.

# Chapter Outline

| LEARNING OBJECTIVES | REVIEW | PRACTICE |
|---|---|---|
| **LO 1** Explain how to account for current liabilities. | • What is a current liability?<br>• Notes payable<br>• Sales taxes payable<br>• Unearned revenues<br>• Current maturities of long-term debt<br>• Payroll and payroll taxes payable | **DO IT! 1a** Current Liabilities<br>**DO IT! 1b** Wages and Payroll Taxes |
| **LO 2** Explain how to account for bonds. | • Issuing bonds at face value<br>• Discount or premium on bonds<br>• Issuing bonds at a discount<br>• Issuing bonds at a premium<br>• Redeeming bonds at maturity | **DO IT! 2** Bond Issuance |
| **LO 3** Explain how to account for the issuance of common and preferred stock, and the purchase of treasury stock. | • Stockholder rights<br>• Corporate capital<br>• Common stock<br>• Preferred stock<br>• Treasury stock | **DO IT! 3a** Issuance of Stock<br>**DO IT! 3b** Treasury Stock |
| **LO 4** Explain how to account for cash dividends. | • Cash dividends<br>• Dividend preferences | **DO IT! 4** Preferred Stock Dividends |
| **LO 5** Discuss how stockholders' equity is reported and analyzed. | • Balance sheet presentation of stockholders' equity<br>• Analysis of stockholders' equity<br>• Debt versus equity decision | **DO IT! 5** Analyzing Stockholders' Equity |

**Go to the Review and Practice section at the end of the chapter for a targeted summary and exercises with solutions.**

**Visit WileyPLUS for additional tutorials and practice opportunities.**

# Accounting for Current Liabilities

**LEARNING OBJECTIVE 1**

Explain how to account for current liabilities.

## What Is a Current Liability?

Liabilities are often defined as "creditors' claims on total assets" and as "existing debts and obligations." Companies must settle or pay these claims, debts, and obligations at some time in the future by transferring assets or services. The future date on which they are due or payable (the maturity date) is a significant feature of liabilities.

As explained in Chapter 2, a **current liability** is a debt that a company reasonably expects to pay:

1. From existing current assets or through the creation of other current liabilities.

2. Within one year or the operating cycle, whichever is longer.

Debts that do not meet both criteria are **long-term liabilities**.

Financial statement users want to know whether a company's obligations are current or long-term.

- A company that has more current liabilities than current assets often lacks liquidity, or short-term debt-paying ability.

- In addition, users want to know the types of liabilities a company has. If a company declares bankruptcy, a specific, predetermined order of payment to creditors exists.

Thus, the amount and type of liabilities are of critical importance.

The different types of current liabilities include notes payable, accounts payable, unearned revenues, and accrued liabilities such as taxes, salaries and wages, and interest. In the sections that follow, we discuss a few of the common types of current liabilities (see **Helpful Hint**).

**HELPFUL HINT**

In previous chapters, we explained the recording of accounts payable and adjustments for some current liabilities.

## Notes Payable

Companies record obligations in the form of written notes as **notes payable**.

- Companies often use notes payable instead of accounts payable because notes payable provide written documentation of the obligation in case legal remedies are needed to collect the debt.

- Companies frequently issue notes payable to meet short-term financing needs.

- Notes payable usually require the borrower to pay interest.

Notes are issued for varying periods of time. **Those due for payment within one year of the balance sheet date are usually classified as current liabilities.**

To illustrate the accounting for notes payable, assume that on September 1, 2022, Cole Williams Co. signs a $100,000, 12%, four-month note maturing on January 1 with First National Bank. When a company issues an interest-bearing note, the amount of assets it receives generally equals the note's face value. Cole Williams Co. therefore will receive $100,000 cash and record the transaction as follows.

| CASH FLOW | BALANCE SHEET | | | | INCOME STATEMENT |
|---|---|---|---|---|---|

**BALANCE SHEET** — first table:

| CASH FLOW | Assets = Liabilities + Stockholders' Equity | | | | | | | INCOME STATEMENT |
|---|---|---|---|---|---|---|---|---|
| | | Notes | | Common | | Retained Earnings | | |
| | Cash = | Payable + | | Stock + | Rev. – | Exp. – | Div. | |
| ↑$100,000 | +$100,000 | +$100,000 | | | | | | No effect |

Interest accrues over the life of the note, and the issuer must periodically record that accrual. If Cole Williams Co. prepares financial statements annually, it makes an adjustment at December 31 to recognize four months of interest expense and interest payable of $4,000 ($100,000 × 12% × $\frac{4}{12}$) as follows.

| CASH FLOW | Assets = Liabilities + Stockholders' Equity | | | | | | | INCOME STATEMENT |
|---|---|---|---|---|---|---|---|---|
| | | Interest | | Common | | Retained Earnings | | |
| | | Payable + | | Stock + | Rev. – | Exp. – | Div. | |
| No effect | | +$4,000 | | | | –$4,000 | | Interest Expense |

In the December 31 financial statements, the current liabilities section of the balance sheet will show notes payable $100,000 and interest payable $4,000. In addition, the company will report interest expense of $4,000 under "Other expenses and losses" in the income statement.

At maturity on January 1, Cole Williams Co. must pay the face value of the note ($100,000) plus $4,000 interest ($100,000 × 12% × $\frac{4}{12}$). The following illustration shows the December 31 balances and then the payment on January 1 for the note and accrued interest.

| CASH FLOW | Assets = Liabilities + Stockholders' Equity | | | | | | | | INCOME STATEMENT |
|---|---|---|---|---|---|---|---|---|---|
| | | Notes | Int. | Common | | Retained Earnings | | | |
| | Cash = | Pay. + | Pay. + | Stock + | Rev. – | Exp. – | Div. | | |
| ↓$104,000 | Dec. 31 Bal. | $100,000 | $4,000 | | | | | | |
| | Jan. 1 –$104,000 | –100,000 | –4,000 | | | | | | No effect |

# Sales Taxes Payable

Many of the products we purchase at retail stores are subject to sales taxes. Many states require sales taxes on purchases made on the Internet as well.

- Sales taxes are expressed as a percentage of the sales price.
- The selling company collects the tax from the customer when the sale occurs and periodically (usually monthly) remits the collections to the state's department of revenue.
- Collecting sales taxes is important. For example, the State of New York recently sued **Sprint Corporation** for $300 million for its alleged failure to collect sales taxes on phone calls.

**HELPFUL HINT**

Check your sales receipts from local retailers to see whether the sales tax is computed separately. For point-of-sales systems, the company receives sales information through the computer network.

Under most state laws, the selling company must enter separately on the cash register the amount of the sale and the amount of the sales tax collected (see **Helpful Hint**). (Gasoline sales are a major exception.) The company then uses the cash register readings to increase Sales Revenue and Sales Taxes Payable. For example, if the March 25 cash register readings for Cooley Grocery show sales of $10,000 and sales taxes of $600 (sales tax rate of 6%), its accounting records show the following.

| CASH FLOW | BALANCE SHEET | | | | | | | | | INCOME STATEMENT |
|---|---|---|---|---|---|---|---|---|---|---|
| | **Assets** | **=** | **Liabilities** | **+** | **Stockholders' Equity** | | | | | |
| | | | Sales | | | | Retained Earnings | | | |
| | | | Taxes | | Common | | | | | |
| | Cash | = | Payable | + | Stock | + | Rev. | – Exp. | – Div. | |
| ⬆$10,600 | +$10,600 | | +$600 | | | | +$10,000 | | | Sales Revenue |

When the company remits the taxes to the taxing agency, it decreases Sales Taxes Payable and decreases Cash. The company does not report sales taxes as an expense. It simply forwards to the government the amount paid by the customer. Thus, Cooley Grocery serves only as a **collection agent** for the taxing authority.

Sometimes companies do not enter sales taxes separately on the cash register. To determine the amount of sales in such cases, divide total receipts by 100% plus the sales tax percentage. For example, assume that Cooley Grocery enters total receipts of $10,600.

- Because the amount received from the sale is equal to the sales price (100%) plus 6% of sales, or 1.06 times the sales total, we can compute sales as follows: $10,600 ÷ 1.06 = $10,000.
- Thus, we can find the sales tax amount of $600 by either:
  1. Subtracting sales from total receipts ($10,600 − $10,000).
  2. Multiplying sales by the sales tax rate ($10,000 × 6%).

## Unearned Revenues

A magazine publisher such as **Sports Illustrated** collects cash when customers place orders for magazine subscriptions. An airline company such as **American Airlines** often receives cash when it sells tickets for future flights. Season tickets for concerts, sporting events, and theatre programs are also paid for in advance. How do companies account for unearned revenues that are received before goods are delivered or services are performed?

1. When the company receives an advance, it increases Cash and increases a current liability account identifying the source of the unearned revenue.
2. When the company recognizes revenue, it decreases the unearned revenue account and increases a revenue account.

To illustrate, assume that on August 6, Superior University sells 10,000 season football tickets at $50 each for its five-game home schedule. As each game is completed, Superior records the recognition of $100,000 ($500,000 ÷ 5) of revenue.

The sale of season tickets on August 6 and the completion of a game on September 1 are recorded as follows.

| CASH FLOW | | BALANCE SHEET | | | | | | | | | | INCOME STATEMENT |
|---|---|---|---|---|---|---|---|---|---|---|---|---|
| | | **Assets** | **=** | **Liabilities** | **+** | **Stockholders' Equity** | | | | | | |
| | | | | Unearned | | Common | | Retained Earnings | | | | |
| | | Cash | = | Ticket Rev. | + | Stock | + | Rev. | – Exp. | – Div. | | |
| ⬆$500,000 | Aug. 6 | +$500,000 | | +$500,000 | | | | | | | | No effect |
| No effect | Sept. 1 | | | −100,000 | | | | +$100,000 | | | | Ticket Revenue |

The account Unearned Ticket Revenue represents unearned revenue, and Superior reports it as a current liability. As the university recognizes revenue, it reclassifies the amount from unearned revenue to Ticket Revenue.

- Unearned revenue is material for some companies.
- In the airline industry, tickets sold for future flights often represent almost 50% of total current liabilities.
- At **United Air Lines**, unearned ticket revenue is its largest current liability, recently amounting to more than $1 billion.

**Illustration 9.1** shows specific unearned revenue and revenue accounts used in selected types of businesses.

**ILLUSTRATION 9.1**
**Unearned revenue and revenue accounts**

| Type of Business | Account Title | |
| --- | --- | --- |
| | **Unearned Revenue** | **Revenue** |
| Airline | Unearned Ticket Revenue | Ticket Revenue |
| Magazine publisher | Unearned Subscription Revenue | Subscription Revenue |
| Hotel | Unearned Rental Revenue | Rental Revenue |

# Current Maturities of Long-Term Debt

Companies often have a portion of long-term debt that comes due in the current year. As an example, assume that Wendy Construction issues a five-year, interest-bearing $25,000 note on January 1, 2021.

- This note specifies that each January 1, starting January 1, 2022, Wendy should pay $5,000 of the note.
- When the company prepares financial statements on December 31, 2021, it should report $5,000 as a current liability and $20,000 as a long-term liability. (The $5,000 amount is the portion of the note that is due to be paid within the next 12 months.)
- Companies often identify current maturities of long-term debt on the balance sheet as **long-term debt due within one year**. In a recent year, **General Motors** had $724 million of such debt.

It is not necessary to prepare an adjustment to recognize the current maturity of long-term debt. At the balance sheet date, all obligations due within one year are classified as current, and all other obligations are long-term.

---

**ACTION PLAN**

- Use the interest formula: Face value of note × Annual interest rate × Time in terms of one year.
- Divide total receipts by 100% plus the tax rate to determine sales; then, subtract sales from the total receipts.
- Determine what fraction of the total unearned rent should be recognized this year.

### DO IT! 1a | Current Liabilities

You and several classmates are studying for the next accounting exam. They ask you to answer the following questions.

1. If cash is borrowed on a $50,000, 6-month, 12% note on September 1, how much interest expense would be incurred by December 31?
2. The cash register total including sales taxes is $23,320, and the sales tax rate is 6%. What is the sales taxes payable?
3. If $15,000 is collected in advance on November 1 for 3 months' rent, what amount of rent revenue should be recognized by December 31?

#### Solution

1. $50,000 \times 12\% \times \frac{4}{12} = \$2,000$
2. $23,320 \div 1.06 = \$22,000$; $\$23,320 - \$22,000 = \$1,320$
3. $\$15,000 \times \frac{2}{3} = \$10,000$

Related exercise material: **BE9.2, BE9.3, BE9.4, DO IT! 9.1a, E9.1, E9.2, E9.3, and E9.5.**

---

# Payroll and Payroll Taxes Payable

Assume that Susan Alena works 40 hours this week for Pepitone Inc., earning a wage of $10 per hour. Will Susan receive a $400 check at the end of the week? Not likely.

- Pepitone is required to withhold amounts from her wages to pay various governmental authorities.
- For example, Pepitone will withhold amounts for FICA taxes (Social Security and Medicare)[1] and for federal and state income taxes.
- If these withholdings total $100, Susan will receive a check for only $300.

**Illustration 9.2** summarizes the types of payroll deductions that normally occur for most companies.

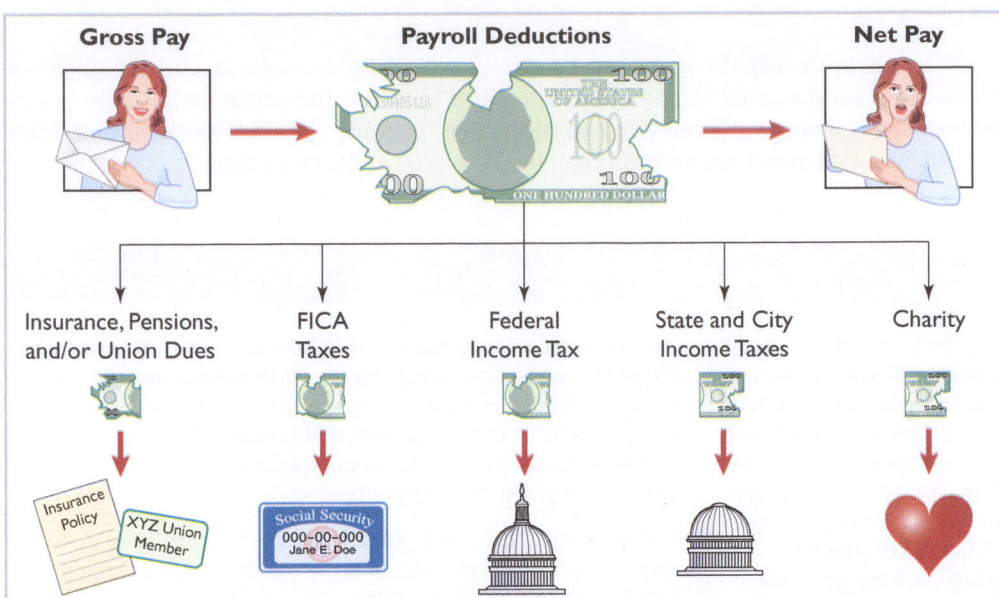

As a result of these deductions, companies withhold from employee paychecks amounts that must be paid to other parties. Pepitone therefore has incurred a liability to pay these third parties and must report this liability in its balance sheet.

As a second illustration, assume that Cargo Corporation records (1) its payroll for the week ended March 7 and (2) payment of this payroll as follows.

| CASH FLOW | | | BALANCE SHEET | | | | | | | | | | | INCOME STATEMENT |
|---|---|---|---|---|---|---|---|---|---|---|---|---|---|---|
| | | **Assets** = | | **Liabilities** | | | + | | **Stockholders' Equity** | | | | | |
| | | | FICA Tax. | Fed. Inc. Tax. | State Inc. Tax. | Sal./ Wages | | Com. | | Retained Earnings | | | | |
| | | Cash = | Pay. + | Pay. + | Pay. + | Pay. | + | Stock + | Rev. − | | Exp. | − Div. | | |
| No effect | (1) | | +$7,650 | +$21,864 | +$2,922 | +$67,564 | | | | | −$100,000 | | | Sal./Wages Exp. |
| ↓ $67,564 | (2) | −$67,564 | | | | −67,564 | | | | | | | | No effect |

In this case, Cargo reports $100,000 in salaries and wages expense. In addition, it reports liabilities for the salaries and wages payable as well as liabilities to governmental agencies. Rather than pay the employees $100,000, Cargo instead must withhold the taxes and make the tax payments directly. In summary, Cargo is essentially serving as a tax collector.

In addition to the liabilities incurred as a result of withholdings, employers also incur a second type of payroll-related liability.

- With every payroll, the employer incurs liabilities to pay various **payroll taxes** levied upon the employer.
- These payroll taxes include the **employer's share** of FICA taxes and state and federal unemployment taxes.

[1]Social Security and Medicare taxes are commonly called FICA taxes. In 1937, Congress enacted the Federal Insurance Contribution Act (FICA) whereby the employee and employer must make equal contributions. The recent combined Social Security and Medicare rate was 7.65%. *Our examples and homework use 7.65% as the FICA rate.*

Based on Cargo's $100,000 payroll, the company would record the employer's expense and liability for these payroll taxes as follows.

| CASH FLOW | | BALANCE SHEET | | | | | | | | INCOME STATEMENT |
|---|---|---|---|---|---|---|---|---|---|---|
| | Assets = | | Liabilities | | + | | Stockholders' Equity | | | |
| | | FICA Tax. Pay. + | Fed. Unemploy. Tax. Pay. + | State Unemploy. Tax. Pay. + | | Com. Stock + | Retained Earnings | | | |
| | | | | | | | Rev. – | Exp. – | Div. | |
| No effect | | +$7,650 | +$800 | +$5,400 | | | | –$13,850 | | Payroll Tax Expense |

Companies classify the payroll and payroll tax liability accounts as current liabilities because they must be paid to employees or remitted to taxing authorities periodically and in the near term. Taxing authorities impose substantial fines and penalties on employers if the withholding and payroll taxes are not computed correctly and paid on time.

## Anatomy of a Fraud

Art was a custodial supervisor for a large school district. The district was supposed to employ between 35 and 40 regular custodians, as well as 3 or 4 substitute custodians to fill in when regular custodians were absent. Instead, in addition to the regular custodians, Art "hired" 77 substitutes. In fact, almost none of these people worked for the district. Instead, Art submitted time cards for these people, collected their checks at the district office, and personally distributed the checks to the "employees." If a substitute's check was for $1,200, that person would cash the check, keep $200, and pay Art $1,000.

### Total take: $150,000

### The Missing Controls

**Human resource controls.** Thorough background checks should be performed. No employees should begin work until they have been approved by the Board of Education and entered into the payroll system. No employees should be entered into the payroll system until they have been approved by a supervisor. All paychecks should be distributed directly to employees at the official school locations by designated employees or direct-deposited into approved employee bank accounts.

**Independent internal verification.** Budgets should be reviewed monthly to identify situations where actual costs significantly exceed budgeted amounts.

**Source:** Adapted from Wells, *Fraud Casebook* (2007), pp. 164–171.

---

### ACTION PLAN

- Remember that wages earned are an expense to the company, but withholdings reduce the amount due to be paid to the employee.
- Payroll taxes are taxes the company incurs related to its employees.

## DO IT! 1b | Wages and Payroll Taxes

During the month of September, Lake Corporation's employees earned wages of $60,000. Withholdings related to these wages were $3,500 for FICA, $6,500 for federal income tax, and $2,000 for state income tax. Costs incurred for unemployment taxes were $90 for federal and $150 for state.

Prepare a tabular summary to record the September 30 (a) salaries and wages expense and salaries and wages payable, assuming that all September wages will be paid in October, and (b) the company's payroll tax expense.

### Solution

| | Assets = | | | | Liabilities | | + | | Stockholders' Equity | | | |
|---|---|---|---|---|---|---|---|---|---|---|---|---|
| | FICA Tax. Pay. + | Fed. Inc. Tax. Pay. + | State Inc. Tax. Pay. + | Sal./ Wages Pay. + | Fed. Unempl. Tax. Pay. + | State Unempl. Tax. Pay. + | | Common Stock + | Retained Earnings | | | |
| | | | | | | | | | Rev. – | Exp. – | Div. | |
| a. | +$3,500 | +$6,500 | +$2,000 | +$48,000 | | | | | | –$60,000 | | Sal./Wag. Exp. |
| b. | +3,500 | | | | +$90 | +$150 | | | | | –3,740 | Pay. Tax. Exp. |

Related exercise material: **BE9.5, BE9.6, BE9.7, DO IT! 9.1b,** and **E9.4.**

# Accounting for Bond Transactions

**Long-term liabilities** are obligations that a company expects to pay more than one year in the future. In this section, we explain the accounting for the principal types of obligations reported in the long-term liabilities section of the balance sheet. These obligations often are in the form of bonds or long-term notes.

**Bonds** are a form of interest-bearing note payable issued by corporations, universities, and governmental agencies.

- Bonds, like common stock, are sold in small denominations (usually $1,000 or multiples of $1,000).
- As a result, bonds attract many investors.
- When a corporation issues bonds, it is borrowing money.
- The person who buys the bonds (the bondholder) is investing in bonds.

A **bond certificate** is issued to the investor to provide evidence of the investor's claim against the company. The bond certificate provides information such as the name of the company that issued the bonds, the face value of the bonds, the maturity date of the bonds, and the contractual interest rate.

- The **face value** is the amount of principal due at the maturity date.
- The **maturity date** is the date that the final payment is due to the investor from the issuing company.
- The **contractual interest rate** is the rate used to determine the amount of cash interest the issuer pays and the investor receives. Usually, the contractual rate is stated as an annual rate (see **Alternative Terminology**).

A corporation records bond transactions when it issues (sells) or redeems (buys back) bonds. If bondholders sell their bond investments to other investors, the issuing corporation receives no further money on the transaction, **nor does the issuing corporation record the transaction** (although it does keep track of the names of bondholders in some cases).

Bonds may be issued at face value, below face value (discount), or above face value (premium).

- Bond prices for both new issues and existing bonds are quoted as **a percentage of the face value of the bond**.
- **Face value is usually $1,000.**
- Thus, a $1,000 bond with a quoted price of 97 means that the selling price of the bond is 97% of face value, or $970.

## Issuing Bonds at Face Value

To illustrate the accounting for bonds issued at face value, assume that Devor Corporation issues 100 five-year, 10%, $1,000 bonds dated January 1, 2022, at 100 (100% of face value). The sale is recorded as follows.

| CASH FLOW | BALANCE SHEET | | | | | | | | INCOME STATEMENT |
|---|---|---|---|---|---|---|---|---|---|
| | **Assets** = | **Liabilities** + | | **Stockholders' Equity** | | | | | |
| | | | | | | Retained Earnings | | | |
| | Cash = | Bonds Pay. + | Common Stock + | Rev. – | | Exp. – | | Div. | |
| ⬆ $100,000 | +$100,000 | +$100,000 | | | | | | | No effect |

Devor reports bonds payable in the long-term liabilities section of the balance sheet because the maturity date is January 1, 2027 (more than one year away).

Over the term (life) of the bonds, companies record bond interest.

- Interest on bonds payable is computed in the same manner as interest on notes payable, as explained earlier.
- If we assume that interest is payable annually on January 1 on the bonds described above, Devor accrues interest of $10,000 ($100,000 × 10% × $\frac{12}{12}$) on December 31.
- At December 31, Devor recognizes the $10,000 of interest expense incurred with the following adjustment.

| CASH FLOW | BALANCE SHEET | | | | | | | | | INCOME STATEMENT |
|---|---|---|---|---|---|---|---|---|---|---|
| | **Assets** = | **Liabilities** | | + | **Stockholders' Equity** | | | | | |
| | | | | | | | Retained Earnings | | | |
| | Cash = | Int. Pay. | Bonds Pay. + | Common Stock + | Rev. – | | Exp. – | Div. | | |
| | Bal. | | $100,000 | | | | | | | |
| No effect | Dec. 31 Adj. | +$10,000 | | | | | –$10,000 | | | Interest Expense |
| ⬇ $10,000 | Jan. 1 Payment –$10,000 | –10,000 | | | | | | | | No effect |

The company classifies **interest payable as a current liability** because it is scheduled for payment within the next year. When Devor pays the interest on January 1, 2023, it decreases Interest Payable and decreases Cash for $10,000. Devor records the payment on January 1 as shown above.

## Discount or Premium on Bonds

The previous example assumed that the contractual (stated) interest rate and the market (effective) interest rate paid on bonds were the same.

- As mentioned above, the **contractual interest rate** is the rate applied to the face (par) value to arrive at the interest paid in a year.
- The **market interest rate** is the rate investors demand for loaning funds to the corporation.
- When the contractual interest rate and the market interest rate are the same, **bonds sell at face value**.

However, market interest rates change daily. The type of bond issued, the state of the economy, current industry conditions, and the company's individual performance all affect market interest rates. As a result, the contractual and market interest rates often differ. To make bonds salable when the two rates differ, bonds sell below or above face value.

To illustrate, suppose that a company issues 10% bonds at a time when other bonds of similar risk are paying 12%.

- Investors will not be interested in buying the 10% bonds, so their value will fall below their face value.

- When a bond is sold for less than its face value, the difference between the face value of the bond and its selling price is called a **discount**.
- As a result of the decline in the bonds' selling price, the actual interest rate incurred by the company increases to the level of the current market interest rate (see **Helpful Hint**).

Conversely, if the market rate of interest is **lower than** the contractual interest rate, investors will have to pay more than face value for the bonds.

- That is, if the market rate of interest is 8% but the contractual interest rate on the bonds is 10%, the price on the bonds will be bid up.
- When a bond is sold for more than its face value, the difference between the face value and its selling price is called a **premium**.

**Illustration 9.3** shows these relationships graphically.

**HELPFUL HINT**

Bond prices *vary inversely* with changes in the market interest rate. As market interest rates decline, bond prices increase. When a bond is issued, if the market interest rate is below the contractual rate, the bond price is higher than the face value.

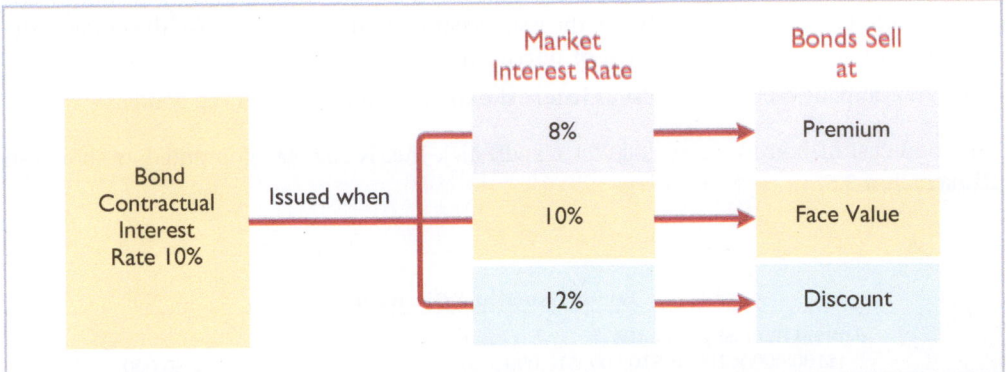

**ILLUSTRATION 9.3**
Interest rates and bond prices

Issuance of bonds at an amount different from face value is quite common. By the time a company prints the bond certificates and markets the bonds, it will be a coincidence if the market rate and the contractual rate are the same. Thus, the issuance of bonds at a discount does not mean that the financial strength of the issuer is suspect (see **Helpful Hint**). Conversely, the sale of bonds at a premium does not indicate that the financial strength of the issuer is exceptional.

**HELPFUL HINT**

Some bonds are sold at a discount by design. "Zero-coupon" bonds, which pay no interest, sell at a deep discount to face value.

## Issuing Bonds at a Discount

To illustrate the issuance of bonds at a discount, assume that on January 1, 2022, Candlestick Inc. sells $100,000, five-year, 10% bonds at 98 (98% of the $100,000 face value) with interest payable on January 1. The issuance is recorded as follows.

| CASH FLOW | BALANCE SHEET | | | | | | | | INCOME STATEMENT |
|---|---|---|---|---|---|---|---|---|---|
| | Assets | = | Liabilities | | + | Stockholders' Equity | | | |
| | | | | | | Common | Retained Earnings | | |
| | Cash | = | Bonds Pay. | – Disc. on Bonds Pay. | + | Stock | + Rev. – Exp. – Div. | | |
| ⬆ $98,000 | +$98,000 | | +$100,000 | –$2,000 | | | | | No effect |

Discount on Bonds Payable reduces liabilities.

- It is a **contra account**, which is **deducted from bonds payable** on the balance sheet as shown in **Illustration 9.4**.
- The $98,000 represents the **carrying (or book) value** of the bonds (see **Helpful Hint**).
- On the date of issue, this amount equals the market price of the bonds.

**HELPFUL HINT**

The carrying value (book value) of bonds issued at a discount is determined by subtracting the balance of the discount account from the balance of the Bonds Payable account.

**ILLUSTRATION 9.4**

Statement presentation of discount on bonds payable

| Candlestick Inc. | | |
|---|---|---|
| Balance Sheet (partial) | | |
| Long-term liabilities | | |
| Bonds payable | $100,000 | |
| Less: Discount on bonds payable | 2,000 | $98,000 |

The issuance of bonds below face value causes the total cost of borrowing to differ from the bond interest paid.

- That is, the issuing corporation not only must pay the contractual interest rate over the term of the bonds but also must pay the face value (rather than the issuance price) at maturity.
- Therefore, the difference between the issuance price and the face value of the bonds—the discount—is an **additional cost of borrowing**.
- The company records this cost as **interest expense** over the life of the bonds.

The total cost of borrowing $98,000 for Candlestick Inc. is $52,000, computed as shown in **Illustration 9.5**.

**ILLUSTRATION 9.5**

Computation of total cost of borrowing—bonds issued at discount

| Bonds Issued at a Discount | |
|---|---|
| Annual interest payments | |
| ($100,000 × 10% = $10,000; $10,000 × 5) | $50,000 |
| Add: Bond discount ($100,000 − $98,000) | 2,000 |
| **Total cost of borrowing** | **$52,000** |

Alternatively, we can compute the total cost of borrowing as shown in **Illustration 9.6**.

**ILLUSTRATION 9.6**

Alternative computation of total cost of borrowing—bonds issued at discount

| Bonds Issued at a Discount | |
|---|---|
| Principal at maturity | $100,000 |
| Annual interest payments ($10,000 × 5) | 50,000 |
| Cash to be paid to bondholders | 150,000 |
| Less: Cash received from bondholders | 98,000 |
| **Total cost of borrowing** | **$ 52,000** |

To follow the expense recognition principle, companies allocate bond discount to expense in each period in which the bonds are outstanding. This is referred to as **amortizing the discount**.

- Amortization of the discount **increases** the amount of interest expense reported each period.
- That is, after the company amortizes the discount, the amount of interest expense it reports in a period will exceed the contractual amount.

As shown in Illustration 9.5, for the bonds issued by Candlestick Inc., total interest expense will exceed the contractual interest by $2,000 over the life of the bonds.

As the discount is amortized, its balance declines. As a consequence, the carrying value of the bonds will increase, until at maturity the carrying value of the bonds equals their face amount. This is shown in **Illustration 9.7**.

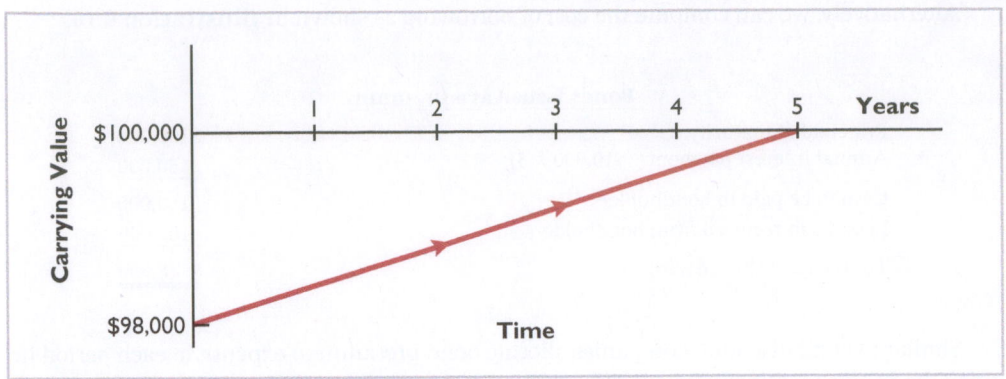

ILLUSTRATION 9.7
**Amortization of bond discount**

# Issuing Bonds at a Premium

We can illustrate the issuance of bonds at a premium by now assuming the Candlestick Inc. bonds described above sell at 102 (102% of the $100,000 face value) rather than at 98. The sale is recorded as follows.

| CASH FLOW | | BALANCE SHEET | | | | | | | | | | INCOME STATEMENT |
|---|---|---|---|---|---|---|---|---|---|---|---|---|
| | | **Assets** | **=** | **Liabilities** | | | **+** | **Stockholders' Equity** | | | | |
| | | | | | | | | | | Retained Earnings | | |
| | | | | Bonds | | Prem. on | | Common | | | | |
| | | Cash | = | Pay. | + | Bonds Pay. | + | Stock | + | Rev. − Exp. − Div. | | |
| ⬆ $102,000 | | +$102,000 | | $100,000 | | +$2,000 | | | | | | No effect |

Candlestick adds the premium on bonds payable **to the bonds payable** amount on the balance sheet, as shown in **Illustration 9.8** (see **Helpful Hint**).

ILLUSTRATION 9.8
**Statement presentation of bond premium**

| Candlestick Inc. | | |
|---|---|---|
| **Balance Sheet (partial)** | | |
| Long-term liabilities | | |
| Bonds payable | $100,000 | |
| Add: Premium on bonds payable | 2,000 | $102,000 |

> **HELPFUL HINT**
>
> Both a discount and a premium account are valuation accounts. A *valuation account* is one that is needed to value properly the item to which it relates.

The sale of bonds above face value causes the total cost of borrowing to be **less than the bond interest paid.**

- The borrower is not required to pay the bond premium at the maturity date of the bonds.
- Thus, the premium is considered to be **a reduction in the cost of borrowing** that reduces bond interest expense over the life of the bonds.

The total cost of borrowing $102,000 for Candlestick Inc. is $48,000, computed as in **Illustration 9.9**.

| Bonds Issued at a Premium | |
|---|---|
| Annual interest payments | |
| ($100,000 × 10% = $10,000; $10,000 × 5) | $50,000 |
| Less: Bond premium ($102,000 − $100,000) | 2,000 |
| **Total cost of borrowing** | **$48,000** |

Alternatively, we can compute the cost of borrowing as shown in **Illustration 9.10**.

**ILLUSTRATION 9.10**

Alternative computation of total cost of borrowing—bonds issued at a premium

| Bonds Issued at a Premium | |
| --- | --- |
| Principal at maturity | $100,000 |
| Annual interest payments ($10,000 × 5) | 50,000 |
| Cash to be paid to bondholders | 150,000 |
| Less: Cash received from bondholders | 102,000 |
| **Total cost of borrowing** | **$ 48,000** |

Similar to bond discount, companies allocate bond premium to expense in each period in which the bonds are outstanding. This is referred to as **amortizing the premium**.

- Amortization of the premium **decreases** the amount of interest expense reported each period.
- That is, after the company amortizes the premium, the amount of interest expense it reports in a period will be less than the contractual amount.

As shown in Illustration 9.9, for the bonds issued by Candlestick Inc., contractual interest will exceed the interest expense by $2,000 over the life of the bonds.

As the premium is amortized, its balance declines. As a consequence, the carrying value of the bonds will decrease, until at maturity the carrying value of the bonds equals their face amount. This is shown in **Illustration 9.11**.

**ILLUSTRATION 9.11**

Amortization of bond premium

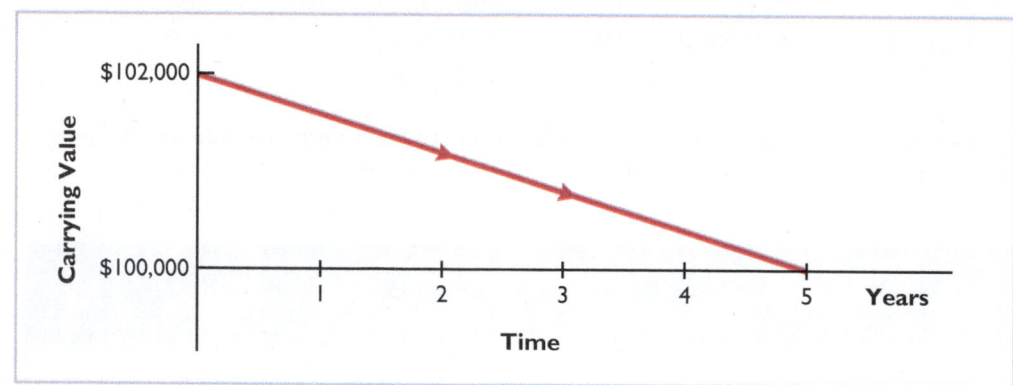

# Redeeming Bonds at Maturity

Regardless of the issue price of bonds, the book value of the bonds at maturity will equal their face value. Assuming that the company pays and records separately the interest for the last interest period, Candlestick records the redemption of its bonds at maturity as follows.

| CASH FLOW | | BALANCE SHEET | | | | | | | | INCOME STATEMENT |
| --- | --- | --- | --- | --- | --- | --- | --- | --- | --- | --- |
| | | Assets | = | Liabilities | + | Stockholders' Equity | | | | |
| | | | | | | | | Retained Earnings | | |
| | | | | Bonds | | Common | | | | |
| | | Cash | = | Pay. | + | Stock | + Rev. | − Exp. | − Div. | |
| | Bal. | | | $100,000 | | | | | | |
| ↓ $100,000 | Redemp. | −$100,000 | | −100,000 | | | | | | No effect |

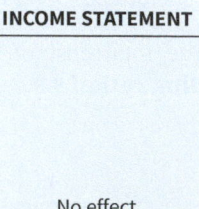

## People, Planet, and Profit Insight

### How About Some Green Bonds?

Green bonds are debt used to fund activities such as renewable-energy projects. For example, a company may use the proceeds from the sale of green bonds to clean up its manufacturing

CarpathianPrince/
Shutterstock.com

operations and cut waste (such as related to energy consumption).

The use of green bonds has taken off as companies now have guidelines as to how to disclose and report on these green-bond proceeds. These standardized disclosures provide transparency as to how these bonds are used and their effect on overall profitability.

Investors are taking a strong interest in these bonds. Investing companies are installing socially responsible investing teams and have started to integrate sustainability into their investment processes. The disclosures of how companies are using the bond proceeds help investors to make better financial decisions.

**Source:** Ben Edwards, "Green Bonds Catch On," *Wall Street Journal* (April 3, 2014), p. C5.

**Why might standardized disclosure help investors to better understand how proceeds from the sale or issuance of bonds are used? (Go to WileyPLUS for this answer and additional questions.)**

---

## DO IT! 2 | Bond Issuance

Giant Corporation issues $200,000 of bonds for $189,000. (a) Prepare a tabular summary to record the issuance of the bonds, and (b) show how the bonds would be reported on the balance sheet at the date of issuance.

**ACTION PLAN**

- **Record cash received, bonds payable at face value, and the difference as a discount or premium.**
- **Report discount as a deduction from bonds payable and premium as an addition to bonds payable.**

### Solution

a.

| Assets | = | Liabilities | | + | Stockholders' Equity | | | | | |
|---|---|---|---|---|---|---|---|---|---|---|
| | | | | | | | Retained Earnings | | | |
| Cash | = | Bonds Pay. | − Disc. on Bonds Pay. | + | Common Stock | + Rev. | − Exp. | − Div. | | |
| +$189,000 | | +$200,000 | −$11,000 | | | | | | | |

b.

| Long-term liabilities | | |
|---|---|---|
| Bonds payable | $200,000 | |
| Less: Discount on bonds payable | 11,000 | $189,000 |

Related exercise material: **BE9.8, BE9.9, BE9.10, DO IT! 9.2, E9.6, E9.7, E9.8, E9.9, E9.10, and E9.11.**

---

# Accounting for Common, Preferred, and Treasury Stock

### LEARNING OBJECTIVE 3

Explain how to account for the issuance of common and preferred stock, and the purchase of treasury stock.

A corporation is created by law.

- As a legal entity, a **corporation** has most of the rights and privileges of a person.
- The major exceptions relate to privileges that can be exercised only by a living person, such as the right to vote or to hold public office.
- Similarly, a corporation is subject to the same duties and responsibilities as a person. For example, it must abide by the law and it must pay taxes.

We can classify corporations in a variety of ways. Two common classifications are **by purpose** and **by ownership**. A corporation may be organized for the purpose of making a profit (such as **Facebook** or **General Motors**), or it may be a nonprofit charitable, medical, or educational corporation (such as **The Salvation Army** or the **American Cancer Society**). Classification by ownership differentiates publicly held and privately held corporations.

- A **publicly held corporation** may have thousands of stockholders, and its stock is traded on a national securities market such as the New York Stock Exchange. Examples are **IBM**, **Caterpillar**, and **General Electric (GE)**.
- A **privately held corporation**, often referred to as a closely held corporation, usually has only a few stockholders and does not offer its stock for sale to the general public.
- Privately held companies are generally much smaller than publicly held companies although some notable exceptions exist. For example, **Cargill Inc.**, a private corporation that trades in grain and other commodities, is one of the largest companies in the United States.

This chapter deals primarily with issues related to publicly held companies.

A corporation is formed by grant of a state **charter**. The charter is a document that describes:

1. The name and purpose of the corporation.
2. The types and number of shares of stock that are authorized to be issued.
3. The names of the individuals that formed the company.
4. The number of shares that these individuals agreed to purchase.

## Stockholder Rights

When chartered, the corporation begins selling shares of stock. When a corporation has only one class of stock, it is identified as **common stock**. Each share of common stock gives the stockholder the ownership rights listed in **Illustration 9.12**. The articles of incorporation or

**ILLUSTRATION 9.12**

**Ownership rights of stockholders**

**Stockholders have the right to:**

1. Vote in election of board of directors at annual meeting and vote on actions that require stockholder approval.

2. Share the corporate earnings through receipt of dividends if declared by board of directors.

   Dividends

3. Keep the same percentage ownership when new shares of stock are issued (**preemptive right**[2]).

   Before — 14%    New shares issued    After — 14%

4. Share in assets upon liquidation in proportion to their holdings. This is called a **residual claim** because owners are paid with assets that remain after all other claims have been paid.

   GON Corp. Going out of business → Lenders / Creditors → Stockholders

---

[2]A number of companies have eliminated the preemptive right because they believe it places an unnecessary and cumbersome demand on management. For example, **IBM**, by stockholder approval, has dropped its preemptive right for stockholders.

the by-laws state the ownership rights of a share of stock. Proof of stock ownership is evidenced by a printed or engraved form known as a **stock certificate**.

### Authorized Stock

**Authorized stock** is the amount of stock that a corporation is authorized to sell as indicated in its charter. If the corporation has sold all of its authorized stock, then it must obtain permission from the state to change its charter before it can issue additional shares.

### Issuance of Stock

A corporation can issue common stock **directly** to investors (see **International Note**). Alternatively, it can issue common stock **indirectly** through an investment banking firm that specializes in bringing securities to the attention of prospective investors. Direct issue is typical in closely held companies. Indirect issue is customary for a publicly held corporation.

### Par and No-Par Value Stocks

**Par value stock** is capital stock that has been assigned a value per share in the corporate charter.

- Years ago, par value determined the **legal capital** that must be retained in the business for the protection of corporate creditors.
- That amount is not available for withdrawal by stockholders.
- Thus, in the past, most states required the corporation to sell its shares at par or above.

However, the usefulness of par value as a device to protect creditors was limited because par value was often immaterial relative to the value of the company's stock in the securities markets—even at the time of issue. For example, **Facebook**'s par value is $0.000006 per share, yet its market price recently was $84. Thus, par has no relationship with market price. In the vast majority of cases, it is an immaterial amount. As a consequence, today many states do not require a par value. Instead, they use other means to protect creditors.

**No-par value stock** is capital stock that has not been assigned a value in the corporate charter.

- No-par value stock is fairly common today.
- For example, **Nike** and **Procter & Gamble** both have no-par stock.
- In many states, the board of directors assigns a **stated value** to the no-par shares.

> ### International Note
>
> U.S. and U.K. corporations raise most of their capital through millions of outside shareholders and bondholders. In contrast, companies in Germany, France, and Japan acquire financing mostly from large banks or other financial institutions. Consequently, in the latter environment, shareholders are somewhat less important.

## Corporate Capital

Owners' equity is identified by various names: **stockholders' equity**, **shareholders' equity**, or **corporate capital**. The stockholders' equity section of a corporation's balance sheet consists of two parts:

1. Paid-in (contributed) capital.
2. Retained earnings (earned capital).

The distinction between **paid-in capital** and **retained earnings** is important from both a legal and a financial point of view.

- Legally, corporations can make distributions of earnings (declare dividends) out of retained earnings in all states.
- However, in many states they cannot declare dividends out of paid-in capital.
- Management, stockholders, and others often look to retained earnings for the continued existence and growth of the corporation.

### Paid-in Capital

**Paid-in capital** is the total amount of cash and other assets paid in to the corporation by stockholders in exchange for capital stock. As noted earlier, when a corporation has only one class of stock, it is **common stock**.

### Retained Earnings

**Retained earnings** is net income that a corporation retains in the business. Net income increases Retained Earnings. Dividends reduce Retained Earnings.

## Accounting for Common Stock

Let's now look at how to account for new issues of common stock. The primary objectives in accounting for the issuance of common stock are to:

1. Identify the specific sources of paid-in capital.
2. Maintain the distinction between paid-in capital and retained earnings.

As shown below, **the issuance of common stock affects only paid-in capital accounts** (see **Helpful Hint**).

### Issuing Par Value Common Stock for Cash

As discussed earlier, par value does not indicate a stock's market price. The cash proceeds from issuing par value stock may be equal to, greater than, or less than par value. When a company issues common stock for cash, it records:

1. The par value of the shares in Common Stock.
2. The portion of the proceeds that is above or below par value in a separate paid-in capital account.

To illustrate, assume that Hydro-Slide, Inc. issues 1,000 shares of $1 par value common stock at par for cash. This transaction is recorded as follows.

> **HELPFUL HINT**
>
> Stock is sometimes issued in exchange for services (payment to attorneys or consultants, for example) or for noncash assets (land or buildings). The value recorded for the shares issued is determined by either the market price of the shares or the value of the good or service received, depending upon which amount the company can more readily determine.

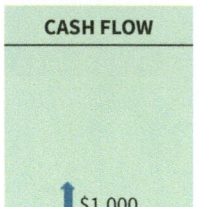
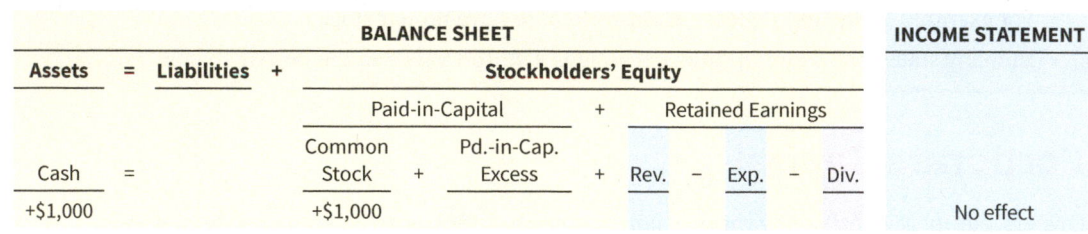

Now assume Hydro-Slide, Inc. issues an additional 1,000 shares of the $1 par value common stock for cash at $5 per share. The amount received above the par value, in this case $4 ($5 − $1), would be added to Paid-in Capital in Excess of Par Value. It is recorded as follows.

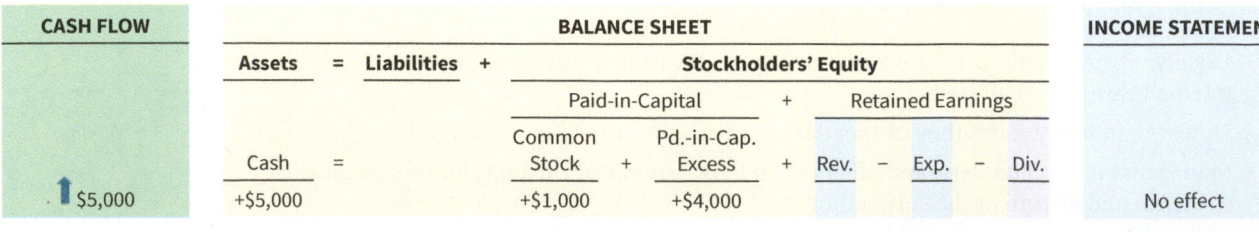

The total paid-in capital from these two transactions is $6,000. If Hydro-Slide, Inc. has retained earnings of $27,000, the stockholders' equity section of the balance sheet is as shown in **Illustration 9.13**.

**ILLUSTRATION 9.13**

**Stockholders' equity—paid-in capital in excess of par value**

### Hydro-Slide, Inc.
**Balance Sheet (partial)**

| | |
|---|---:|
| Stockholders' equity | |
| Paid-in capital | |
| Common stock | $ 2,000 |
| **Paid-in capital in excess of par value** | **4,000** |
| Total paid-in capital | 6,000 |
| Retained earnings | 27,000 |
| Total stockholders' equity | $33,000 |

Some companies issue no-par stock with a stated value.

- For accounting purposes, companies treat the stated value in the same way as the par value.
- For example, if in our Hydro-Slide example the stock was no-par stock with a stated value of $1, it would be recorded the same as for the par stock except the term "Par Value" would be replaced with "Stated Value."
- If a company issues no-par stock that does not have a stated value, then it increases the Common Stock account for the full amount received and there is no need for the Paid-in Capital in Excess of Stated Value account.

## Accounting for Preferred Stock

To appeal to a larger segment of potential investors, a corporation may issue an additional class of stock, called preferred stock.

- **Preferred stock** has contractual provisions that give it preference or priority over common stock in certain areas.
- Typically, preferred stockholders have a priority in relation to (1) dividends and (2) assets in the event of liquidation.
- However, they sometimes do not have voting rights.

**Facebook** had 543 million preferred shares held by investors at the end of 2011, prior to going public. Approximately 6% of U.S. companies have one or more classes of preferred stock.

Like common stock, companies issue preferred stock for cash or for noncash consideration.

- The recording of these transactions is similar to that for common stock.
- When a corporation has more than one class of stock, each paid-in capital account title should identify the stock to which it relates (e.g., Preferred Stock, Common Stock, Paid-in Capital in Excess of Par Value—Preferred Stock, and Paid-in Capital in Excess of Par Value—Common Stock).

Assume that Stine Corporation issues 10,000 shares of $10 par value preferred stock for $12 cash per share. The issuance is recorded as follows.

| CASH FLOW | | BALANCE SHEET | | | | | | | | | INCOME STATEMENT |
|---|---|---|---|---|---|---|---|---|---|---|---|
| | Assets | = | Liabilities | + | Stockholders' Equity | | | | | | |
| | | | | | Paid-in-Capital | | | | + | Retained Earnings | |
| | | | | Common Stock | + | Pd.-in-Cap. Common | + | Preferred Stock | + | Pd.-in-Cap. Preferred | + Rev. − Exp. − Div. | |
| ↑$120,000 | Cash = +$120,000 | | | | | | | +$100,000 | | +$20,000 | No effect |

Preferred stock has either a par value or no par value. In the stockholders' equity section of the balance sheet, companies show preferred stock first because of its dividend and liquidation preferences over common stock.

---

### Investor Insight  Facebook

EMMANUEL DUNAND/AFP/Getty Images

#### How to Read Stock Quotes

Organized exchanges trade the stock of publicly held companies at dollar prices per share established by the interaction between buyers and sellers. For each listed security, the financial press reports the high and low prices of the stock during the year, the total volume of stock traded on a given day, the high and low prices for the day, and the closing market price, with the net change for the day. **Facebook** is listed on the Nasdaq exchange. Here is a recent listing for Facebook:

These numbers indicate the following. The high and low market prices for the last 52 weeks have been $86.07 and $54.66. The trading volume for the day was 54,156,600 shares. The high, low, and closing prices for that date were $85.59, $83.11, and $84.63, respectively. The net change for the day was a decrease of $0.629 per share.

**For stocks traded on organized exchanges, how are the dollar prices per share established? What factors might influence the price of shares in the marketplace?** (Go to WileyPLUS for this answer and additional questions.)

| Stock | 52 Weeks High | Low | Volume | High | Low | Close | Net Change |
|---|---|---|---|---|---|---|---|
| Facebook | 86.07 | 54.66 | 54,156,600 | 85.59 | 83.11 | 84.63 | .629 |

---

### ACTION PLAN

- In issuing shares for cash, increase Common Stock for par value per share.
- Add any additional proceeds in excess of par to a separate paid-in capital account.

### DO IT! 3a | Issuance of Stock

Cayman Corporation begins operations on March 1 by issuing 100,000 shares of $1 par value common stock for cash at $12 per share. On March 28, Cayman issues 1,500 shares of $10 par value preferred stock for cash at $30 per share. Prepare a tabular summary to record the issuance of the common and preferred shares.

#### Solution

| | Assets | = | Liabilities + | | Stockholders' Equity | | | | | | |
|---|---|---|---|---|---|---|---|---|---|---|---|
| | | | | | Paid-in-Capital | | | | | + | Retained Earnings |
| | Cash | = | | Common Stock | + | Pd.-in-Cap. Common | + | Preferred Stock | + | Pd.-in-Cap. Preferred | + Rev. − Exp. − Div. |
| Mar. 1 | +$1,200,000 | = | | +$100,000 | | +$1,100,000 | | | | | |
| 28 | +45,000 | | | | | | | +$15,000 | | +$30,000 | |

Related exercise material: **BE9.13, BE9.14, BE9.15, DO IT! 9.3a, and E9.12.**

---

## Accounting for Treasury Stock

**Treasury stock** is a corporation's own stock that has been reacquired by the corporation and is being held for future use. A corporation may acquire treasury stock for various reasons:

1. To reissue the shares to officers and employees under bonus and stock compensation plans.

2. To increase trading of the company's stock in the securities market. Companies expect that buying their own stock will signal that management believes the stock is underpriced, which they hope will enhance its market price.

3. To have additional shares available for use in acquiring other companies.

4. To reduce the number of shares outstanding and thereby increase earnings per share.

A less frequent reason for purchasing treasury shares is to eliminate hostile shareholders by buying them out.

Many corporations have treasury stock. For example, in the United States approximately 65% of companies have treasury stock. During one quarter, companies in the **Standard & Poor's** 500-stock index spent a record of about $118 billion to buy treasury stock. In a recent year, **Nike** purchased more than 6 million treasury shares. At one point, stock repurchases were so substantial that a study by two Federal Reserve economists suggested that a sharp reduction in corporate purchases of treasury shares might result in a sharp drop in the value of the U.S. stock market.

## Purchase of Treasury Stock

The purchase of treasury stock is generally accounted for by the **cost method**.

- This method derives its name from the fact that the Treasury Stock account is maintained at the cost of shares purchased (see **Helpful Hint**).

- Under the cost method, **companies increase Treasury Stock by the price paid to reacquire the shares**.

- **Treasury Stock decreases by the same amount when the company later sells the shares.**

> **HELPFUL HINT**
>
> Treasury Stock is a contra stockholders' equity account.

To illustrate, assume that on January 1, 2022, the stockholders' equity section for Mead, Inc. has 100,000 shares of $5 par value common stock outstanding (all issued at par value) and retained earnings of $200,000. **Illustration 9.14** shows the stockholders' equity section of the balance sheet before purchase of treasury stock.

> **ILLUSTRATION 9.14**
>
> Stockholders' equity with no treasury stock

| Mead, Inc. | |
|---|---|
| **Balance Sheet (partial)** | |
| Stockholders' equity | |
|   Paid-in capital | |
|     Common stock, $5 par value, 400,000 shares authorized, | |
|       100,000 shares issued and outstanding | $500,000 |
|   Retained earnings | 200,000 |
|   Total stockholders' equity | $700,000 |

On February 1, 2022, Mead acquires 4,000 shares of its stock at $8 per share. It is recorded as follows.

| CASH FLOW | BALANCE SHEET | | | | | | INCOME STATEMENT |
|---|---|---|---|---|---|---|---|
| | Assets | = | Liabilities | + | Stockholders' Equity | | |
| | | | | | Paid-in-Capital | + Retained Earnings | |
| | | | | | Common Stock | Treasury Stock | |
| | Cash | = | | | | | |
| | Bal. | | | | $500,000 | +$200,000 | |
| ↓ $32,000 | Feb. 1  –$32,000 | | | | –$32,000 | | No effect |

The Treasury Stock account would increase by the cost of the shares purchased ($32,000). The original paid-in capital account, Common Stock, would not be affected because **the number of issued shares does not change**.

Companies show treasury stock as a deduction from total paid-in capital and retained earnings in the stockholders' equity section of the balance sheet. **Illustration 9.15** shows this presentation for Mead, Inc. Thus, the acquisition of treasury stock reduces stockholders' equity.

**ILLUSTRATION 9.15**

**Stockholders' equity with treasury stock**

| Mead, Inc. | |
| --- | --- |
| **Balance Sheet (partial)** | |
| Stockholders' equity | |
| Paid-in capital | |
| Common stock, $5 par value, 400,000 shares authorized, | |
| 100,000 shares issued, and 96,000 shares outstanding | $500,000 |
| Retained earnings | 200,000 |
| Total paid-in capital and retained earnings | 700,000 |
| **Less: Treasury stock (4,000 shares)** | **32,000** |
| Total stockholders' equity | $668,000 |

Company balance sheets disclose both the number of shares issued (100,000) and the number in the treasury (4,000).

- The difference is the number of shares of stock outstanding (96,000).
- The term **outstanding stock** means the number of shares of issued stock that are being held by stockholders.

In a bold (and some would say risky) move, **Reebok** at one time bought back nearly a third of its shares. This repurchase of shares dramatically reduced Reebok's available cash (see **Ethics Note**). In fact, the company borrowed significant funds to accomplish the repurchase. In a press release, management stated that it was repurchasing the shares because it believed that the stock was severely underpriced. The repurchase of so many shares was meant to signal management's belief in good future earnings.

Skeptics, however, suggested that Reebok's management repurchased the shares to make it less likely that the company would be acquired by another company (in which case Reebok's top managers would likely lose their jobs). Acquiring companies like to purchase companies with large cash reserves so they can pay off debt used in the acquisition. By depleting its cash through the purchase of treasury shares, Reebok became a less likely acquisition target.

**ETHICS NOTE**

The purchase of treasury stock reduces the cushion for creditors. To protect creditors, many states require that a portion of retained earnings equal to the cost of the treasury stock purchased be restricted from being paid as dividends.

**ACTION PLAN**

- **Record the purchase of treasury stock at cost.**
- **Report treasury stock as a deduction from stockholders' equity (contra account) at the bottom of the stockholders' equity section.**

## DO IT! 3b | Treasury Stock

Santa Anita Inc. purchases 3,000 shares of its $50 par value common stock for $180,000 cash on July 1. It expects to hold the shares in the treasury until resold. Prepare a tabular summary to record the treasury stock transaction.

**Solution**

| Assets | = | Liabilities | + | Stockholders' Equity | | | | | | |
| --- | --- | --- | --- | --- | --- | --- | --- | --- | --- | --- |
| | | | | Paid-in-Capital | | + | Retained Earnings | | | |
| | | | | Common Stock | − Treasury Stock | + | Rev. | − Exp. | − | Div. |
| Cash | = | | | | | | | | | |
| −$180,000 | | | | | −$180,000 | | | | | |

Related exercise material: **DO IT! 9.3b and E9.13.**

# Accounting for Cash Dividends

A **dividend** is a distribution by a corporation to its stockholders on a pro rata (proportional to ownership) **basis**.

- Pro rata means that if you own, say, 10% of the common shares, you will receive 10% of the dividend.
- Dividends can take four forms: cash, property, scrip (promissory note to pay cash), or stock.
- Cash dividends predominate in practice, although companies also declare stock dividends with some frequency.

Investors are very interested in a company's dividend practices. In the financial press, **dividends are generally reported quarterly as a dollar amount per share**. (Sometimes they are reported on an annual basis.) For example, the recent **quarterly** dividend rate was 24 cents per share for **Nike**, 22 cents per share for **GE**, and 25 cents per share for **Conagra Brands**. **Facebook** does not pay dividends.

## Cash Dividends

A **cash dividend** is a pro rata (proportional to ownership) distribution of cash to stockholders. Cash dividends are not paid on treasury shares. For a corporation to pay a cash dividend, it must have the following:

1. **Retained earnings.**   Payment of dividends from retained earnings is legal in all states. In addition, loan agreements frequently constrain companies to pay dividends only from retained earnings. Many states prohibit payment of dividends from legal capital. However, payment of dividends from paid-in capital in excess of par value is legal in some states.

2. **Adequate cash.**   Recently, Facebook had a balance in retained earnings of $6,099 million but a cash balance of only $4,315 million. If it had wanted to pay a dividend equal to its retained earnings, Facebook would have had to raise $1,784 million more in cash. It would have been unlikely to do this because it would not be able to pay this much in dividends in future years. In addition, such a dividend would completely deplete Facebook's balance in retained earnings, so it would not be able to pay a dividend in the next year unless it had positive net income.

3. **Declared dividends.**   The board of directors has full authority to determine the amount of income to distribute in the form of dividends. Dividends are not a liability until they are declared.

The amount and timing of a dividend are important issues for management to consider. The payment of a large cash dividend could lead to liquidity problems for the company. Conversely, a small dividend or a missed dividend may cause unhappiness among stockholders who expect to receive a reasonable cash payment from the company on a periodic basis. Many companies declare and pay cash dividends quarterly. On the other hand, a number of high-growth companies pay no dividends, preferring to conserve cash to finance future capital expenditures.

Investors monitor a company's dividend practices.

- Regular dividend boosts in the face of irregular earnings can be a warning signal. Companies with high dividends and rising debt may be borrowing money to pay shareholders.
- Low dividends may not be a negative sign because it may mean the company is reinvesting in itself, which may result in high returns through increases in the stock price.

Presumably, investors seeking regular dividends buy stock in companies that pay periodic dividends, and those seeking growth in the stock price (capital gains) buy stock in companies that retain their earnings rather than pay dividends.

### Recording Cash Dividends

Three dates are important in connection with dividends:

1. The declaration date.
2. The record date.
3. The payment date.

Companies record transactions on the declaration date and the payment date.

On the **declaration date**, the board of directors formally authorizes the cash dividend and announces it to stockholders.

- The declaration of a cash dividend **commits the corporation to a binding legal obligation**.
- Thus, the company must record the increase in Dividends and the increase in the liability Dividends Payable.

To illustrate, assume that on December 1, 2022, the directors of Media General declare a $0.50 per share cash dividend on 100,000 shares of $10 par value common stock. The dividend is $50,000 (100,000 × $0.50). The declaration is recorded as follows.

| CASH FLOW | BALANCE SHEET | | | | | | | | INCOME STATEMENT |
|---|---|---|---|---|---|---|---|---|---|
| | **Assets** | = | **Liabilities** | + | | | **Stockholders' Equity** | | |
| | | | | | Paid-in-Capital | + | | Retained Earnings | |
| | | | Dividends | | Common | | | | |
| | | | Payable | + | Stock | + | Rev. − Exp. − | Div. | |
| No effect | | | +$50,000 | | | | | −$50,000 | No effect |

Dividends Payable is a current liability. It will normally be paid within the next several months.

At the **record date**, the company determines ownership of the outstanding shares for dividend purposes (see **Helpful Hint**).

- The stockholders' records maintained by the corporation supply this information. For Media General, the record date is December 22.
- No accounting entry is required on this date.

On the **payment date**, the company makes cash dividend payments to the stockholders on record as of December 22. It also records the payment of the dividend. If January 20 is the payment date for Media General, the payment is recorded as follows.

| CASH FLOW | BALANCE SHEET | | | | | | | | INCOME STATEMENT |
|---|---|---|---|---|---|---|---|---|---|
| | | **Assets** | = | **Liabilities** | + | | **Stockholders' Equity** | | |
| | | | | | | Paid-in-Capital + | | Retained Earnings | |
| | | | | Dividends | | Common | | | |
| | | Cash | = | Payable | + | Stock + | Rev. − Exp. − | Div. | |
| | Bal. | | | $50,000 | | | | −$50,000 | |
| ↓$50,000 | Jan. 20 | −$50,000 | | −50,000 | | | | | No effect |

Note that payment of the dividend on the payment date reduces both current assets and current liabilities, but it has no effect on stockholders' equity. The cumulative effect of the **declaration and payment** of a cash dividend on a company's financial statements is to **decrease both stockholders' equity and total assets**.

# Dividend Preferences

**Preferred stockholders have the right to share in the distribution of corporate income before common stockholders.**

- For example, if the dividend rate on preferred stock is $5 per share, common shareholders cannot receive any dividends in the current year until preferred stockholders have received $5 per share.
- The first claim to dividends does not, however, **guarantee** dividends.
- Dividends depend on many factors, such as adequate retained earnings and availability of cash.

For preferred stock, companies state the per share dividend amount as a percentage of the par value of the stock or as a specified amount. For example, **EarthLink** specifies a 3% dividend.

Most preferred stocks have a preference on corporate assets if the corporation fails. This feature provides security for the preferred stockholder. The preference to assets may be for the par value of the shares or for a specified liquidating value. For example, **Commonwealth Edison** issued preferred stock that entitled the holders to receive $31.80 per share, plus accrued and unpaid dividends, in the event of involuntary liquidation. The liquidation preference is used in litigation pertaining to bankruptcy lawsuits involving the respective claims of creditors and preferred stockholders.

---

## Investor Insight

iStock.com/Palto

### What About Dividends?

If you have some excess dollars that you want to invest, you might consider stocks that pay dividends. According to data from the **Standard & Poor's (S&P)** Dow Jones Indices, dividend income made up 33% of the monthly return of the S&P 500 between 1926 and 2015. What that means is that dividends comprise one-third of the return to shareholders.

In addition, data from 1927 to 2014 indicate that dividend payers outperformed non-dividend payers, averaging 10.4% annual growth versus 8.5%. If you do not think that difference is much, the table indicates how an annual investment of $10,000 would grow at each of these rates.

| Growth Over | 8.5% Annual Growth Rate | 10.4% Annual Growth Rate |
|---|---|---|
| 10 years | $   161,000 | $   179,400 |
| 20 years | 524,900 | 661,800 |
| 30 years | 1,300,000 | 2,000,000 |

Some companies have strong dividend yields, such as **Ford Motor Company** and **AT&T**. Others have been increasing dividend payouts at a strong clip, such as **UPS**, **Microsoft**, and **Boeing**. Good luck in your future investing!

**Source:** Selena Maranjian, "Dividend Stocks in 2017: 7 Stats Everyone Should Know," *The Motley Fool* (December 14, 2016).

**What factors must management consider in deciding how large a dividend to pay? (Go to WileyPLUS for this answer and additional questions.)**

---

## Cumulative Dividend

Preferred stock contracts often contain a **cumulative dividend** feature.

- This feature stipulates that preferred stockholders must be paid both current-year dividends and any unpaid prior-year dividends before common stockholders are paid dividends.
- When preferred stock is cumulative, preferred dividends not declared that were supposed to be declared in a given period are called **dividends in arrears**.

To illustrate, assume that Scientific Leasing has 5,000 shares of 7%, $100 par value cumulative preferred stock outstanding. Each $100 share pays a $7 dividend (.07 × $100). The annual dividend is $35,000 (5,000 × $7 per share). If dividends are two years in arrears, preferred stockholders are entitled to receive in the current year the dividends as shown in **Illustration 9.16**.

**ILLUSTRATION 9.16**

**Computation of total dividends to preferred stock**

| | |
|---|---|
| Dividends in arrears ($35,000 × 2) | $ 70,000 |
| Current-year dividends | 35,000 |
| **Total preferred dividends** | **$105,000** |

No distribution can be made to common stockholders until Scientific Leasing pays this entire preferred dividend. In other words, companies cannot pay dividends to common stockholders while any preferred stock dividend is in arrears.

**Dividends in arrears are not considered a liability.**

- **No obligation exists until the board of directors formally "declares" that the corporation will pay a dividend.**
- However, companies should disclose in the notes to the financial statements the amount of dividends in arrears.
- Doing so enables investors to assess the impact of this potential obligation on the corporation's financial position.

The investment community does not look favorably upon companies that are unable to meet their dividend obligations. As a financial officer noted in discussing one company's failure to pay its cumulative preferred dividend for a period of time, "Not meeting your obligations on something like that is a major black mark on your record."

---

**ACTION PLAN**

- **Determine dividends on preferred shares by multiplying the dividend rate times the par value of the stock times the number of preferred shares.**
- **Understand the cumulative feature: If preferred stock is cumulative, then any missed dividends (dividends in arrears) and the current year's dividend must be paid to preferred stockholders before dividends are paid to common stockholders.**

## DO IT! 4 | Preferred Stock Dividends

MasterMind Corporation has 2,000 shares of 6%, $100 par value preferred stock outstanding at December 31, 2022. At December 31, 2022, the company declared a $60,000 cash dividend. Determine the dividend paid to preferred stockholders and common stockholders under each of the following scenarios.

1. The preferred stock is noncumulative, and the company has not missed any dividends in previous years.
2. The preferred stock is noncumulative, and the company did not pay a dividend in each of the two previous years.
3. The preferred stock is cumulative, and the company did not pay a dividend in each of the two previous years.

### Solution

1. The company has not missed past dividends and the preferred stock is noncumulative. Thus, the preferred stockholders are paid only this year's dividends. The dividend paid to preferred stockholders would be $12,000 (2,000 × .06 × $100). The dividend paid to common stockholders would be $48,000 ($60,000 − $12,000).

2. The preferred stock is noncumulative. Thus, past unpaid dividends do not have to be paid. The dividend paid to preferred stockholders would be $12,000 (2,000 × .06 × $100). The dividend paid to common stockholders would be $48,000 ($60,000 − $12,000).

3. The preferred stock is cumulative. Thus, dividends that have been missed (dividends in arrears) must be paid. The dividend paid to preferred stockholders would be $36,000 (3 × 2,000 × .06 × $100). Of the $36,000, $24,000 relates to dividends in arrears and $12,000 relates to the current dividend on preferred stock. The dividend paid to common stockholders would be $24,000 ($60,000 − $36,000).

Related exercise material: **DO IT! 9.4.**

# Presentation and Analysis of Stockholders' Equity

**LEARNING OBJECTIVE 5**
Discuss how stockholders' equity is reported and analyzed.

## Balance Sheet Presentation of Stockholders' Equity

In the stockholders' equity section of the balance sheet, companies report paid-in capital, retained earnings, accumulated other comprehensive income, and treasury stock. Within paid-in capital, two classifications are recognized:

1. **Capital stock**, which consists of preferred and common stock. Companies show preferred stock before common stock because of its preferential rights. They report information about the par value, shares authorized, shares issued, and shares outstanding for each class of stock.

2. **Additional paid-in capital**, which includes the excess of amounts paid in over par or stated value.

In some instances, unrealized gains and losses are not included in net income. Instead, these excluded items, referred to as other comprehensive income items, are reported as part of a more inclusive earnings measure called comprehensive income. Examples of other comprehensive income items include certain adjustments to pension plan assets, types of foreign currency gains and losses, and some gains and losses on investments.

- The items reported as other comprehensive income are closed each year to the **Accumulated Other Comprehensive Income** account.
- Thus, this account includes the cumulative amount of all previous items reported as other comprehensive income.
- This account can have either a positive or negative balance depending on whether or not accumulated gains exceed accumulated losses over the years.
- If accumulated losses exceed gains, then the company reports accumulated other comprehensive loss.

**Illustration 9.17** presents the stockholders' equity section of the balance sheet of Graber Inc. (see **International Note**). The stockholders' equity section for Graber Inc. includes most of the accounts discussed in this chapter. The disclosures pertaining to Graber's common stock indicate that 400,000 shares are issued, 100,000 shares are unissued (500,000 authorized less 400,000 issued), and 390,000 shares are outstanding (400,000 issued less 10,000 shares in treasury).

## Analysis of Stockholders' Equity

Investors are interested in both a company's dividend record and its earnings performance. Although those two measures are often parallel, that is not always the case. Thus, investors should investigate each one separately.

**International Note**

Like GAAP, under IFRS companies typically disclose separate categories of capital on the balance sheet. However, because of varying accounting treatments of certain transactions (such as treasury stock or asset revaluations), some categories used under IFRS vary from those under GAAP.

## Graber Inc.
### Balance Sheet (partial)

| | | |
|---|---:|---:|
| Stockholders' equity | | |
| Paid-in capital | | |
| Capital stock | | |
| 9% preferred stock, $100 par value, cumulative, 10,000 shares authorized, 6,000 shares issued and outstanding | | $ 600,000 |
| Common stock, no par, $5 stated value, 500,000 shares authorized, 400,000 shares issued, and 390,000 outstanding | | 2,000,000 |
| Total capital stock | | 2,600,000 |
| Additional paid-in capital | | |
| Paid-in capital in excess of par value—preferred stock | $ 30,000 | |
| Paid-in capital in excess of stated value—common stock | 1,050,000 | |
| Total additional paid-in capital | | 1,080,000 |
| Total paid-in capital | | 3,680,000 |
| Retained earnings | | 1,050,000 |
| Total paid-in capital and retained earnings | | 4,730,000 |
| Accumulated other comprehensive income | | 110,000 |
| Less: Treasury stock (10,000 common shares) | | 80,000 |
| Total stockholders' equity | | $4,760,000 |

## Dividend Record

One way that companies reward stock investors for their investment is to pay them dividends.

**Decision Tools**

The payout ratio helps users determine the portion of a company's earnings that it pays out in dividends.

- The **payout ratio** measures the percentage of earnings a company distributes in the form of cash dividends to common stockholders (see **Decision Tools**).
- It is computed by **dividing total cash dividends declared to common shareholders by net income**.

Using the following information, the payout ratio for **Nike** in 2016 and 2015 (years ended May 31, 2017 and 2016, respectively) is calculated in **Illustration 9.18**.

| | 2016 | 2015 |
|---|---:|---:|
| Dividends (in millions) | $1,133 | $1,022 |
| Net income (in millions) | 4,240 | 3,760 |

| Payout Ratio = | $\dfrac{\text{Cash Dividends Declared on Common Stock}}{\text{Net Income}}$ | |
|---|---|---|
| **($ in millions)** | **2016** | **2015** |
| Payout Ratio | $\dfrac{\$1,133}{\$4,240} = 26.7\%$ | $\dfrac{\$1,022}{\$3,760} = 27.2\%$ |

Nike's payout ratio was relatively constant at approximately 27%. Companies attempt to set their dividend rate at a level that will be sustainable.

Companies that have high growth rates are characterized by low payout ratios because they reinvest most of their net income in the business. Thus, a low payout ratio is not necessarily bad news.

- Companies that believe they have many good opportunities for growth, such as **Facebook**, will reinvest those funds in the company rather than pay dividends.
- However, low dividend payments, or a cut in dividend payments, might signal that a company has liquidity or solvency problems and is trying to conserve cash by not paying dividends.

Thus, investors and analysts should investigate the reason for low dividend payments. **Illustration 9.19** lists recent payout ratios of four well-known companies.

| Company | Payout Ratio |
|---------|--------------|
| Microsoft | 24.5% |
| Kellogg | 43.3% |
| Facebook | 0% |
| Walmart | 49.0% |

**ILLUSTRATION 9.19**

**Payout ratios of companies**

## Earnings Performance

Another way to measure corporate performance is through profitability.

- A widely used ratio that measures profitability from the common stockholders' viewpoint is **return on common stockholders' equity (ROE)** (see **Decision Tools**).
- This ratio shows how many dollars of net income a company earned for each dollar of common stockholders' equity.
- It is computed by dividing net income available to common stockholders (Net income – Preferred dividends) by average common stockholders' equity.
- Common stockholders' equity is equal to total stockholders' equity minus any equity from preferred stock.

> **Decision Tools**
>
> Return on common stockholders' equity helps users determine a company's return on its common stockholders' investment.

Using the previous information and the additional following information, **Illustration 9.20** shows **Nike**'s return on common stockholders' equity.

| (in millions) | 2016 | 2015 | 2014 |
|---------------|------|------|------|
| Preferred dividends | $  –0– | $  –0– | $  –0– |
| Common stockholders' equity | 12,407 | 12,258 | 12,707 |

**ILLUSTRATION 9.20**

**Nike's return on common stockholders' equity**

| Return on Common Stockholders' Equity = $\dfrac{\text{Net Income – Preferred Dividends}}{\text{Average Common Stockholders' Equity}}$ | | |
|---|---|---|
| ($ in millions) | 2016 | 2015 |
| Return on Common Stockholders' Equity | $\dfrac{\$4{,}240 - \$0}{(\$12{,}407 + \$12{,}258) \div 2} = 34.4\%$ | $\dfrac{\$3{,}760 - \$0}{(\$12{,}258 + \$12{,}707) \div 2} = 30.1\%$ |

From 2015 to 2016, Nike's return on common shareholders' equity increased. As a company grows larger, it becomes increasingly hard to sustain a high return. In Nike's case, since many believe the U.S. market for expensive sports shoes is saturated, it will need to grow either along new product lines, such as hiking shoes and golf equipment, or in new markets, such as Europe and Asia.

## Debt versus Equity Decision

When obtaining long-term capital, corporate managers must decide whether to issue bonds or to sell common stock. Bonds have three primary advantages relative to common stock, as shown in **Illustration 9.21**.

**ILLUSTRATION 9.21**

**Advantages of bond financing over common stock**

| Bond Financing | Advantages |
|---|---|
| Ballot | 1. **Stockholder control is not affected.** Bondholders do not have voting rights, so current owners (stockholders) retain full control of the company. |
| Tax Bill | 2. **Tax savings result.** Bond interest is deductible for tax purposes; dividends on stock are not. |
| $ / Stock | 3. **Return on common stockholders' equity may be higher.** Although bond interest expense reduces net income, return on common stockholders' equity often is higher under bond financing because no additional shares of common stock are issued. |

How does the debt versus equity decision affect the return on common stockholders' equity?

- **Illustration 9.22** shows that the return on common stockholders' equity is affected by the return on assets and the amount of leverage a company uses—that is, by the company's reliance on debt (often measured by the debt to assets ratio).

- **If a company wants to increase its return on common stockholders' equity, it can either increase its return on assets or increase its reliance on debt financing.**

**ILLUSTRATION 9.22**

**Components of the return on common stockholders' equity**

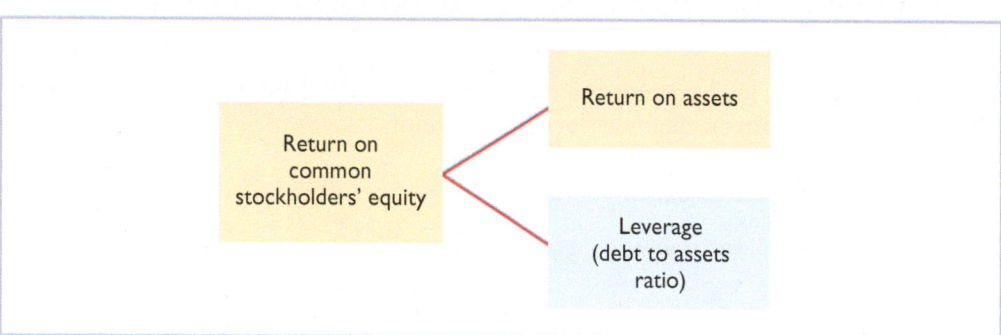

To illustrate the potential effect of debt financing on the return on common stockholders' equity, assume that Microsystems Inc. currently has 100,000 shares of common stock outstanding issued at $25 per share and no debt. It is considering two alternatives for raising an additional $5 million. Plan A involves issuing 200,000 shares of common stock at the current market price of $25 per share. Plan B involves issuing $5 million of 12% bonds at face value. Income before interest and taxes will be $1.5 million; income taxes are expected to be 30%. The alternative effects on the return on common stockholders' equity are shown in **Illustration 9.23**.

**ILLUSTRATION 9.23**

**Effects on return on common stockholders' equity of issuing debt**

|  | Plan A: Issue Stock | Plan B: Issue Bonds |
|---|---|---|
| Income before interest and taxes | $1,500,000 | $1,500,000 |
| Interest (12% × $5,000,000) | — | 600,000 |
| Income before income taxes | 1,500,000 | 900,000 |
| Income tax expense (30%) | 450,000 | 270,000 |
| Net income | $1,050,000 | $ 630,000 |
| Common stockholders' equity | $7,500,000 | $2,500,000 |
| Return on common stockholders' equity | 14% | 25.2% |

- Note that with long-term debt financing (bonds), net income is $420,000 ($1,050,000 − $630,000) less.

- However, the return on common stockholders' equity increases from 14% to 25.2% with the use of debt financing because net income is spread over a smaller amount of common stockholders' equity.

- **In general, as long as the return on assets rate exceeds the rate paid on debt, a company will increase the return on common stockholders' equity by the use of debt.**

After seeing this illustration, you might ask, why don't companies rely almost exclusively on debt financing rather than equity? Debt has one major disadvantage: **Debt reduces solvency. The company locks in fixed payments that it must make in good times and bad. The company must pay interest on a periodic basis and must pay the principal (face value) of the bonds at maturity.** A company with fluctuating earnings and a relatively weak cash position may experience great difficulty in meeting interest requirements in periods of low earnings. In the extreme, this can result in bankruptcy. With common stock financing, on the other hand, the company can decide to pay low (or no) dividends if earnings are low.

---

## DO IT! 5 | Analyzing Stockholders' Equity

On January 1, 2022, Siena Corporation purchased 2,000 shares of treasury stock. Other information regarding Siena Corporation is as follows.

|  | 2022 | 2021 |
|---|---|---|
| Net income | $110,000 | $110,000 |
| Dividends on preferred stock | $10,000 | $10,000 |
| Dividends on common stock | $1,600 | $2,000 |
| Common stockholders' equity, beginning of year | $400,000* | $500,000 |
| Common stockholders' equity, end of year | $400,000 | $500,000 |

*Adjusted for purchase of treasury stock.

(a) Compute return on common stockholders' equity for each year, and (b) discuss its change from 2021 to 2022.

**ACTION PLAN**

- Determine return on common stockholders' equity by dividing net income available to common stockholders by average common stockholders' equity.

### Solution

a.

|  | 2022 | 2021 |
|---|---|---|
| Return on common stockholders' equity | $\dfrac{(\$110,000 - \$10,000)}{(\$400,000 + \$400,000) \div 2} = 25\%$ | $\dfrac{(\$110,000 - \$10,000)}{(\$500,000 + \$500,000) \div 2} = 20\%$ |

b. Between 2021 and 2022, return on common stockholders' equity improved from 20% to 25%. While this would appear to be good news for the company's common stockholders, this increase should be carefully evaluated. It is important to note that net income did not change during this period. The increase in the ratio was due to the purchase of treasury shares, which reduced the denominator of the ratio. As the company repurchases its own shares, it becomes more reliant on debt and thus increases its risk.

Related exercise material: **BE9.20, DO IT! 9.5, E9.18, and E9.19.**

### USING THE DECISION TOOLS | adidas

**adidas** is one of **Nike**'s competitors. In such a competitive and rapidly changing environment, one wrong step can spell financial disaster.

### Instructions

The following facts are available from adidas's annual report. As a German company, adidas reports under International Financial Reporting Standards (IFRS). Using this information, evaluate its (a) payout ratio and (b) earnings per share and return on common stockholders' equity (ROE). (c) Compare the payout ratio and ROE with those for Nike for 2016 and 2015 (see Illustrations 9.18 and 9.20).

| (in millions) | 2016 | 2015 | 2014 |
|---|---|---|---|
| Dividends declared | €320 | €303 | |
| Net income | €1,017 | €634 | |
| Preferred dividends | 0 | 0 | |
| Shares outstanding at end of year | 201 | 200 | 204 |
| Common stockholders' equity | €6,472 | €5,666 | €5,625 |

### Solution

**a.** A measure to evaluate a company's dividend record is the payout ratio. For adidas, this measure in 2016 and 2015 is calculated as follows.

| | **2016** | **2015** |
|---|---|---|
| Payout ratio | $\dfrac{€320}{€1,017} = 31.5\%$ | $\dfrac{€303}{€634} = 47.8\%$ |

**b.** There are many measures of earnings performance. Some of those presented thus far in the text were earnings per share and the return on common stockholders' equity. These measures for adidas in 2016 and 2015 are calculated as follows.

| | **2016** | **2015** |
|---|---|---|
| Earnings per share | $\dfrac{€1,017 - 0}{(201 + 200) \div 2} = €5.07$ | $\dfrac{€634 - 0}{(200 + 204) \div 2} = €3.14$ |
| Return on common stockholders' equity | $\dfrac{€1,017 - 0}{(€6,472 + €5,666) \div 2} = 16.8\%$ | $\dfrac{€634 - 0}{(€5,666 + €5,625) \div 2} = 11.2\%$ |

**c.** Nike's payout ratio was 26.7%. adidas's payout ratio decreased from 2015 to 2016 but was still higher than Nike's ratio in 2016. This means that adidas paid a higher percentage of its earnings as dividends. Nike had a higher return on shareholders' equity (30.1% and 34.4%) during this 2-year period than adidas.

# Review and Practice

## Learning Objectives Review

**1** **Explain how to account for current liabilities.**

A current liability is a debt that a company can reasonably expect to pay (a) from existing current assets or through the creation of other current liabilities and (b) within one year or the operating cycle, whichever is longer. The major types of current liabilities are notes payable, accounts payable, sales taxes payable, unearned revenues, and accrued liabilities such as taxes, salaries and wages, and interest payable.

When a note payable is interest-bearing, the amount of assets received upon the issuance of the note is generally equal to the face value of the note, and interest expense is accrued over the life of the note. At maturity, the amount paid is equal to the face value of the note plus accrued interest.

Companies record sales taxes payable at the time the related sales occur. The company serves as a collection agent for the taxing authority. Sales taxes are not an expense to the company. Companies withhold employee withholding taxes and record them in appropriate liability accounts, until they remit these taxes to the governmental taxing authorities. Unearned revenues are initially recorded in an unearned revenue account. As a company recognizes revenue, a transfer from unearned revenue to revenue occurs. Companies report the current maturities of long-term debt as current liabilities in the balance sheet.

---

**2   Explain how to account for bonds.**

---

When companies issue bonds, they increase Cash for the cash proceeds and increase Bonds Payable for the face value of the bonds. In addition, they use the accounts Premium on Bonds Payable and Discount on Bonds Payable to show the bond premium and bond discount, respectively. Bond discount and bond premium are amortized over the life of the bond, which increases or decreases interest expense, respectively.

When companies redeem bonds at maturity, they decrease Cash and Bonds Payable for the face value of the bonds.

---

**3   Explain how to account for the issuance of common and preferred stock, and the purchase of treasury stock.**

---

When a company issues common stock or preferred stock for cash, it records (1) the par value of the shares in Common Stock or Preferred Stock and (2) the portion of the proceeds that is above par value in a separate paid-in capital account. When no-par common stock has a stated value, it is treated similarly to par value stock. When no-par common stock does not have a stated value, then a company increases Common Stock for the entire proceeds from the issue.

Companies generally use the cost method in accounting for treasury stock. Under this approach, a company records Treasury Stock at the price paid to reacquire the shares.

---

**4   Explain how to account for cash dividends.**

---

Companies record dividend transactions at the declaration date and the payment date. At the declaration date, both Dividends and Dividends Payable are increased.

Preferred stock has contractual provisions that give it priority over common stock in certain areas. Typically, preferred stockholders have a preference as to (1) dividends and (2) assets in the event of liquidation. However, they sometimes do not have voting rights.

---

**5   Discuss how stockholders' equity is reported and analyzed.**

---

In the stockholders' equity section of the balance sheet, companies report paid-in capital and retained earnings and identify specific sources of paid-in capital. Within paid-in capital, companies show two classifications: capital stock and additional paid-in capital. If a corporation has treasury stock, it deducts the cost of treasury stock from total paid-in capital and retained earnings to determine total stockholders' equity.

A company's dividend record can be evaluated by looking at what percentage of net income it chooses to pay out in dividends, as measured by the payout ratio (dividends divided by net income). Earnings performance is measured with the return on common stockholders' equity (income available to common stockholders divided by average common stockholders' equity).

## Decision Tools Review

| Decision Checkpoints | Info Needed for Decision | Tool to Use for Decision | How to Evaluate Results |
|---|---|---|---|
| What portion of its earnings does the company pay out in dividends? | Net income and total cash dividends on common stock | $$\text{Payout ratio} = \frac{\text{Cash dividends declared on common stock}}{\text{Net income}}$$ | A low ratio may suggest that the company is retaining its earnings for investment in future growth. |
| What is the company's return on common stockholders' investment? | Earnings available to common stockholders and average common stockholders' equity | $$\text{Return on common stockholders' equity} = \frac{\text{Net income} - \text{Preferred dividends}}{\text{Average common stockholders' equity}}$$ | A high measure suggests strong earnings performance from common stockholders' perspective. |

## Glossary Review

**Accumulated Other Comprehensive Income** An account that includes the cumulative amount of all previous items reported as other comprehensive income. (p. 9-27).

**Authorized stock** The amount of stock that a corporation is authorized to sell as indicated in its charter. (p. 9-17).

**Bond certificate** A legal document that indicates the name of the issuer, the face value of the bonds, and other data, such as the contractual interest rate and the maturity date of the bonds. (p. 9-9).

**Bonds** A form of interest-bearing notes payable issued by corporations, universities, and governmental agencies. (p. 9-9).

**Cash dividend** A pro rata (proportional to ownership) distribution of cash to stockholders. (p. 9-23).

**Charter** A document that describes a corporation's name and purpose, types of stock and number of shares authorized, names of individuals involved in the formation, and number of shares each individual has agreed to purchase. (p. 9-16).

**Contractual (stated) interest rate** Rate used to determine the amount of interest the issuer pays and the investor receives. (p. 9-9).

**Corporation** A company organized as a separate legal entity, with most of the rights and privileges of a person. (p. 9-15).

**Cumulative dividend** A feature of preferred stock entitling the stockholder to receive current and unpaid prior-year dividends before common stockholders receive any dividends. (p. 9-25).

**Current liability** A debt that a company reasonably expects to pay (1) from existing current assets or through the creation of other current liabilities, and (2) within one year or the operating cycle, whichever is longer. (p. 9-3).

**Declaration date** The date the board of directors formally authorizes the dividend and announces it to stockholders. (p. 9-24).

**Discount (on a bond)** The difference between the face value of a bond and its selling price when a bond is sold for less than its face value. (p. 9-11).

**Dividend** A distribution by a corporation to its stockholders on a pro rata (proportional to ownership) basis. (p. 9-23).

**Dividends in arrears** Preferred dividends that were supposed to be declared but were not declared during a given period. (p. 9-25).

**Face value** Amount of principal due at the maturity date of the bond. (p. 9-9).

**Legal capital** The amount of capital that must be retained in the business for the protection of corporate creditors. (p. 9-17).

**Long-term liabilities** Obligations that a company expects to pay more than one year in the future. (p. 9-9).

**Market interest rate** The rate investors demand for loaning funds to the corporation. (p. 9-10).

**Maturity date** The date on which the final payment on a bond is due from the bond issuer to the investor. (p. 9-9).

**No-par value stock** Capital stock that has not been assigned a value in the corporate charter. (p. 9-17).

**Notes payable** An obligation in the form of a written note. (p. 9-3).

**Outstanding stock** Capital stock that has been issued and is being held by stockholders. (p. 9-22).

**Paid-in capital** The amount stockholders paid in to the corporation in exchange for shares of ownership. (p. 9-18).

**Par value stock** Capital stock that has been assigned a value per share in the corporate charter. (p. 9-17).

**Payment date** The date cash dividend payments are made to stockholders. (p. 9-24).

**Payout ratio** A measure of the percentage of earnings a company distributes in the form of cash dividends to common stockholders. (p. 9-28).

**Preferred stock** Capital stock that has contractual preferences over common stock in certain areas. (p. 9-19).

**Premium (on a bond)** The difference between the selling price and the face value of a bond when a bond is sold for more than its face value. (p. 9-11).

**Privately held corporation** A corporation that has only a few stockholders and whose stock is not available for sale to the general public. (p. 9-16).

**Publicly held corporation** A corporation that may have thousands of stockholders and whose stock is traded on a national securities market. (p. 9-16).

**Record date** The date when the company determines ownership of outstanding shares for dividend purposes. (p. 9-24).

**Retained earnings** Net income that a company retains in the business. (p. 9-18).

**Return on common stockholders' equity (ROE)** A measure of profitability from the stockholders' point of view; computed by dividing net income minus preferred dividends by average common stockholders' equity. (p. 9-29).

**Stated value** The amount per share assigned by the board of directors to no-par stock. (p. 9-17).

**Treasury stock** A corporation's own stock that has been reacquired by the corporation and is being held for future use. (p. 9-20).

## Practice Multiple-Choice Questions

**1. (LO 1)** The time period for classifying a liability as current is one year or the operating cycle, whichever is:

    **a.** longer.        **c.** probable.

    **b.** shorter.        **d.** possible.

**2. (LO 1)** To be classified as a current liability, a debt must be expected to be paid within:

    **a.** 1 year.        **c.** 2 years.

    **b.** the operating cycle.    **d.** 1 year or the operating cycle, whichever is longer.

**3. (LO 1)** Ottman Company borrows $88,500 on September 1, 2022, from Farley State Bank by signing an $88,500, 12%, 1-year note. What is the accrued interest at December 31, 2022?

    **a.** $2,655.        **c.** $4,425.

    **b.** $3,540.        **d.** $10,620.

**4. (LO 1)** JD Company borrowed $70,000 on December 1 on a 6-month, 12% note. At December 31:

    **a.** neither the note payable nor the interest payable is a current liability.

    **b.** the note payable is a current liability but the interest payable is not.

    **c.** the interest payable is a current liability but the note payable is not.

    **d.** both the note payable and the interest payable are current liabilities.

**5. (LO 1)** Alexis Company has total proceeds from sales of $4,515. If the proceeds include sales taxes of 5%, what is the amount to be recorded in Sales Revenue?

    **a.** $4,000.        **c.** $4,289.25.

    **b.** $4,300.        **d.** The correct answer is not given.

**6. (LO 1)** When recording payroll:

    **a.** gross earnings are recorded as salaries and wages payable.

    **b.** net pay is recorded as salaries and wages expense.

    **c.** payroll deductions are recorded as liabilities.

    **d.** More than one of the answer choices are correct.

**7. (LO 1)** No Fault Insurance Company collected a premium of $18,000 for a 1-year insurance policy on April 1. What amount should No Fault report as a current liability for Unearned Insurance Premiums at December 31?

    **a.** $0.

    **b.** $4,500.

    **c.** $13,500.

    **d.** $18,000.

**8. (LO 1)** Employer payroll taxes do **not** include:

    **a.** federal unemployment taxes.

    **b.** state unemployment taxes.

    **c.** federal income taxes.

    **d.** FICA taxes.

**9. (LO 2)** The market interest rate:

    **a.** is the contractual interest rate used to determine the amount of cash interest paid by the borrower.

    **b.** is listed in the bond indenture.

    **c.** is the rate investors demand for loaning funds.

    **d.** More than one of the answer choices are correct.

**10. (LO 2)** Laurel Inc. issues 10-year bonds with a maturity value of $200,000. If the bonds are issued at a premium, this indicates that:

    **a.** the contractual interest rate exceeds the market interest rate.

    **b.** the market interest rate exceeds the contractual interest rate.

    **c.** the contractual interest rate and the market interest rate are the same.

    **d.** no relationship exists between the two rates.

**11. (LO 2)** On January 1, 2022, Kelly Corp. issues $200,000, 5-year, 7% bonds at face value. To record the issuance of the bonds, Kelly would:

    **a.** increase Cash for $14,000.

    **b.** decrease Bonds Payable for $200,000.

    **c.** increase Bonds Payable for $200,000.

    **d.** decrease Interest Expense of $14,000.

**12. (LO 2)** Prescher Corporation issued bonds that pay interest every July 1 and January 1. To accrue bond interest at December 31, Prescher would:

    **a.** decrease Interest Payable.

    **b.** decrease Cash.

    **c.** decrease Interest Expense.

    **d.** increase Interest Payable.

**13. (LO 3)** ABC Corp. issues 1,000 shares of $10 par value common stock at $12 per share. When the transaction is recorded, increases are made to:

    **a.** Common Stock $10,000 and Paid-in Capital in Excess of Stated Value $2,000.

    **b.** Common Stock $12,000.

    **c.** Common Stock $10,000 and Paid-in Capital in Excess of Par Value $2,000.

    **d.** Common Stock $10,000 and Retained Earnings $2,000.

**14. (LO 3)** Treasury stock may be repurchased:

    **a.** to reissue the shares to officers and employees under bonus and stock compensation plans.

    **b.** to signal to the stock market that management believes the stock is underpriced.

    **c.** to have additional shares available for use in the acquisition of other companies.

    **d.** More than one of the answer choices are correct.

**15. (LO 3)** Preferred stock may have priority over common stock **except** in:

    **a.** dividend preference.

    **b.** preference to assets in the event of liquidation.

    **c.** cumulative dividends.

    **d.** voting.

**16. (LO 3)** In the stockholders' equity section, the cost of treasury stock is deducted from:

    **a.** total paid-in capital and retained earnings.

    **b.** retained earnings.

    **c.** total stockholders' equity.

    **d.** common stock in paid-in capital.

**17. (LO 4)** U-Bet Corporation has 10,000 shares of 8%, $100 par value, cumulative preferred stock outstanding at December 31, 2022. No dividends were declared in 2020 or 2021. If U-Bet wants to pay $375,000 of dividends in 2022, common stockholders will receive:

    **a.** $0.

    **b.** $295,000.

    **c.** $215,000.

    **d.** $135,000.

**18. (LO 4)** Companies must record cash dividends on the:

    **a.** declaration date and the record date.

    **b.** record date and the payment date.

    **c.** declaration date, record date, and payment date.

    **d.** declaration date and the payment date.

**19. (LO 5)** The return on common stockholders' equity is usually increased by all of the following, **except**:

    **a.** an increase in the return on assets ratio.

    **b.** an increase in the use of debt financing.

    **c.** an increase in the company's stock price.

    **d.** an increase in the company's net income.

**20. (LO 5)** Thomas is nearing retirement and would like to invest in a stock that will provide a good steady income. Thomas should choose a stock with a:

    **a.** high current ratio.

    **b.** high dividend payout.

    **c.** high earnings per share.

    **d.** high price-earnings ratio.

**21. (LO 5)** Jackson Inc. reported net income of $186,000 during 2022 and paid dividends of $26,000 on common stock. It also paid dividends on its 10,000 shares of 6%, $100 par value, noncumulative preferred stock. Common stockholders' equity was $1,200,000 on January 1, 2022, and $1,600,000 on December 31, 2022. The company's return on common stockholders' equity for 2022 is:

    **a.** 10.0%.

    **b.** 9.0%.

    **c.** 7.1%.

    **d.** 13.3%.

**22. (LO 5)** If everything else is held constant, earnings per share is increased by:

    **a.** the payment of a cash dividend to common shareholders.

    **b.** the payment of a cash dividend to preferred shareholders.

    **c.** the issuance of new shares of common stock.

    **d.** the purchase of treasury stock.

## Solutions

**1. a.** The time period for classifying a liability as current is one year or the operating cycle, whichever is longer, not (b) shorter, (c) probable, or (d) possible.

**2. d.** To be classified as a current liability, a debt must be expected to be paid within 1 year or the operating cycle, whichever is longer. Choices (a) and (b) are both correct, but (d) is the better answer. Choice (c) is incorrect.

**3. b.** Accrued interest at 12/31/22 is computed as the face value ($88,500) times the interest rate (12%) times the portion of the year the debt was outstanding (4 months out of 12), or $3,540 ($88,500 × 12% × $\frac{4}{12}$), not (a) $2,655, (c) $4,425, or (d) $10,620.

**4. d.** A current liability is a debt the company reasonably expects to pay (1) from existing current assets or through the creation of other current liabilities, and (2) within the next year or the operating cycle, whichever is longer. Since both the interest payable and the note payable are expected to be paid within one year, they both will be considered current liabilities. The other choices are therefore incorrect.

**5. b.** Dividing the total proceeds ($4,515) by one plus the sales tax rate (1.05) will result in the amount of sales to be recorded in the Sales Revenue account of $4,300 ($4,515 ÷ 1.05). The other choices are therefore incorrect.

**6. c.** Payroll deductions are recorded as liabilities. The other choices are incorrect because (a) gross earnings are recorded as salaries and wages expense, and (b) net pay is recorded as salaries and wages payable. Choice (d) is wrong as there is only one correct answer.

**7. b.** The monthly premium is $1,500 ($18,000 ÷ 12). Because No Fault has recognized 9 months of insurance revenue (April 1–December 31), 3 months' insurance premium is still unearned. The amount that No Fault should report as Unearned Service Revenue is therefore $4,500 (3 months × $1,500), not (a) $0, (c) $13,500, or (d) $18,000.

**8. c.** Federal income taxes are a payroll deduction, not an employer payroll tax. The employer is merely a collection agent. The other choices are all included in employer payroll taxes.

**9. c.** The market interest rate is the rate investors demand for loaning funds to the corporation. The other choices are incorrect because (a) the rate on the bond certificate is used to determine the interest payments, (b) the contract interest rate is listed in the bond indenture, and (d) there is only one correct answer.

**10. a.** When bonds are issued at a premium, this indicates that the contractual interest rate is higher than the market interest rate. The other choices are incorrect because (b) when the market interest rate exceeds the contractual interest rate, bonds are sold at a discount; (c) when the contractual interest rate and the market interest rate are the same, bonds will be issued at par; and (d) the relationship between the market rate of interest and the contractual rate of interest determines whether bonds are issued at par, a discount, or a premium.

**11. c.** The issuance for the bonds includes an increase to Cash for $200,000 and an increase to Bonds Payable for $200,000. The other choices are therefore incorrect.

**12. d.** Since the interest has been accrued but not yet paid, it has to be recognized as an increase in expenses and liabilities. It would be recorded as an increase to Interest Expense and to Interest Payable. The other choices are incorrect because (a) an interest accrual will increase, not decrease, Interest Payable; (b) interest accruals do not affect Cash; and (c) an interest accrual will increase, not decrease, Interest Expense.

**13. c.** Common Stock should be increased for $10,000 and Paid-in Capital in Excess of Par Value should be increased for $2,000. The stock is par value stock, not stated value stock, and this excess is contributed, not earned, capital. The other choices are therefore incorrect.

**14. d.** Treasury stock may be repurchased to reissue the shares as part of bonus and stock compensation plans, to signal to the stock market that the stock is underpriced, and to have additional shares available for use in the acquisition of other companies. Choice (a), (b), (c) are all correct, but (d) is the best answer.

**15. d.** Preferred stock usually does not have voting rights and therefore does not have priority over common stock on this issue. The other choices are true statements.

**16. a.** The cost of treasury stock is deducted from total paid-in capital and retained earnings. The other choices are therefore incorrect.

**17. d.** The preferred stockholders will receive a total of $240,000 of dividends [dividends in arrears ($80,000 × 2 years) + current-year dividends ($80,000)]. If U-Bet wants to pay a total of $375,000 in 2022, then common stockholders will receive $135,000 ($375,000 − $240,000), not (a) $0, (b) $295,000, or (c) $215,000.

**18. d.** Dividends must be recorded on the declaration date and the payment date, but not the record date. The other choices are therefore incorrect.

**19. c.** An increase in the company's stock price has no effect on the return on common stockholders' equity. The other choices are incorrect because (a) an increase in a firm's return on assets, (b) an increase in a firm's use of debt financing, and (c) an increase in a firm's net income will all increase the return on common stockholders' equity.

**20. b.** Thomas should focus on a high dividend payout. The other choices are incorrect because a stock with a (a) high current ratio, (c) high earnings per share, or (d) high price-earnings ratio may or may not pay dividends on a consistent basis.

**21. b.** Return on common stockholders' equity is net income available to common stockholders divided by average common stockholders' equity. Net income available to common stockholders is net income less preferred dividends = $126,000 [$186,000 − (10,000 × .06 × $100)]. The company's return on common stockholders' equity for the year is therefore 9.0% {$126,000 ÷ [($1,200,000 + $1,600,000) ÷ 2]}, not (a) 10.0%, (c) 7.1%, or (d) 13.3%.

**22. d.** The purchase of treasury stock reduces the number of shares outstanding, which is the denominator of earnings per share (EPS). With a smaller denominator, EPS is larger. The other choices are incorrect because (a) the payment of a cash dividend to common stockholders does not affect the earnings or the number of outstanding shares, so EPS will stay the same; (b) the payment of a cash dividend to preferred stockholders will reduce the amount of earnings available to the common stockholders, thus reducing EPS; and (c) the issuance of new shares of common stock would not affect earnings but will increase the number of outstanding shares, thereby reducing EPS.

## Practice Brief Exercises

**1. (LO 1)** Amy Pond Discounts does not segregate sales and sales taxes at the time of sale. The register total for March 17 is $19,928. All sales are subject to a 6% sales tax. Compute sales taxes payable and record sales taxes payable and sales revenue.

*Compute and record sales taxes payable.*

### Solution

**1.** Sales tax payable:

Sales = $18,800 ($19,928 ÷ 1.06)

Sales taxes payable = $1,128 ($18,800 × 6%)

| Assets | = | Liabilities | + | | | Stockholders' Equity | | | | |
|---|---|---|---|---|---|---|---|---|---|---|
| | | | | | | | Retained Earnings | | | |
| | | Sales Taxes | | Common | | | | | | |
| Cash | = | Payable | + | Stock | + | Rev. | − | Exp. | − | Div. |
| +$19,928 | | +$1,128 | | | | +$18,800 | | | | Sales Revenue |

**2. (LO 1)** Ben Borke's regular hourly wage rate is $20, and he receives an hourly rate of $30 for work in excess of 40 hours. During a January pay period, Ben works 46 hours. Ben's federal income tax withholding is $123, he has no voluntary deductions, and the FICA tax rate is 7.65%. There are no state income taxes. Compute Ben's gross earnings and net pay for the pay period.

*Compute gross earnings and net pay.*

### Solution

**2.** Gross earnings:

| | | |
|---|---|---|
| Regular pay (40 × $20) | | $800.00 |
| Overtime pay (6 × $30) | | 180.00 |
| Gross earnings | | $980.00 |
| Less: FICA taxes payable ($980 × 7.65%) | $ 74.97 | |
| Federal income taxes payable | 123.00 | 197.97 |
| Net pay | | $782.03 |

**3. (LO 2)** Kahnle Corporation issued 300 7%, 5-year, $1,000 bonds dated January 1, 2022, at 100. Interest is paid each January 1. (a) Record the sale of these bonds on January 1, 2022. (b) Record the adjustment on December 31, 2022, for interest expense. (c) Record the January 1, 2023, transaction.

*Record bonds issued at face value.*

### Solution

**3.**

| | Assets | = | Liabilities | | + | | Stockholders' Equity | | | | |
|---|---|---|---|---|---|---|---|---|---|---|---|
| | | | Interest | Bonds | | Common | | Retained Earnings | | | |
| | Cash | = | Pay. | Pay. | + | Stock | + | Rev. | − | Exp. | − Div. |
| **a.** Jan. 1 | +$300,000 | | | +$300,000* | | | | | | | |
| **b.** Dec. 31 Adj. | | | +$21,000 | | | | | | | −$21,000 | Interest Expense |
| **c.** Jan. 1 Payment | −$21,000 | | −21,000** | | | | | | | | |

*300 × $1,000
**$300,000 × 7%

*Record issuance of par value common stock.*

**4. (LO 3)** On April 10, Leury Corporation issues 3,000 shares of $5 par value common stock for cash at $14 per share. Record the issuance of the stock.

### Solution

4.

| Assets | = | Liabilities | + | Stockholders' Equity | | | | | | |
|---|---|---|---|---|---|---|---|---|---|---|
| | | | | Paid-in-Capital | | | + | Retained Earnings | | |
| | | | | Common | | Pd.-in-Cap. | | | | |
| Cash | = | | | Stock | + | Excess | + Rev. | − Exp. | − Div. | |
| +$42,000* | | | | +$15,000** | | +$27,000*** | | | | |

*3,000 × $14
**3,000 × $5
***3,000 × $9

---

*Record treasury stock transactions.*

**5. (LO 3)** On June 1, Omar Corporation purchases 600 shares of its $5 par value common stock for the treasury at a cash price of $10 per share. Record the treasury stock transaction.

### Solution

5.

| | Assets | = | Liabilities | + | Stockholders' Equity | | | |
|---|---|---|---|---|---|---|---|---|
| | | | | | Paid-in-Capital | | + | Retained Earnings |
| | | | | | Common | Treasury | | |
| | Cash | = | | | Stock | − Stock | | |
| June 1 | −$6,000* | | | | | −$6,000 | | |

*600 × $10

---

*Record a cash dividend.*

**6. (LO 4)** Giovanni Corporation has 7,000 shares of common stock outstanding. It declares a $2 per share cash dividend on November 15 to stockholders of record on December 15. The dividend is paid on December 31. Record the declaration and payment of the cash dividend.

### Solution

6.

| | Assets | = | Liabilities | + | Stockholders' Equity | | | | | |
|---|---|---|---|---|---|---|---|---|---|---|
| | | | | | Paid-in-Capital | + | | Retained Earnings | | |
| | | | Dividends | | Common | | | | | |
| | Cash | = | Payable | + | Stock | + Rev. | − Exp. | − Div. | | |
| Nov. 15 | | | $14,000 | | | | | −$14,000* | | |
| Dec. 31 | −$14,000 | | −14,000 | | | | | | | |

*7,000 × $2

---

# Practice Exercises

*Record transactions for interest-bearing notes.*

**1. (LO 1)** On June 1, JetSet Company borrows $150,000 from First Bank on a 6-month, $150,000, 8% note.

### Instructions

Prepare a tabular summary to record:

   **a.** The transaction on June 1.

   **b.** The adjustment on June 30.

   **c.** The maturity (December 1), assuming monthly adjustments have been made through November 30.

   **d.** What was the total financing cost (interest expense)?

## Solution

**1.**

| | Assets | = | Liabilities | | | + | | Stockholders' Equity | | | |
|---|---|---|---|---|---|---|---|---|---|---|---|
| | | | Notes | | Interest | | Common | | Retained Earnings | | |
| | Cash | = | Pay. | + | Pay. | + | Stock | + Rev. | − Exp. | − Div. | |
| **a.** | +$150,000 | | +$150,000 | | | | | | | | |
| **b.** | | | | | +$1,000* | | | | −$1,000 | | Int. Exp. |
| **c.** | −156,000 | | −150,000 | | −6,000** | | | | | | |
| **d.** | $6,000 | | | | | | | | | | |

*$150,000 × .08 × $\frac{1}{12}$

**$150,000 × .08 × $\frac{6}{12}$

---

**2. (LO 2)** Global Airlines Company issued $900,000 of 8%, 10-year bonds on January 1, 2022, at face value. Interest is payable annually on January 1.

*Record transactions for bonds issued at face value.*

### Instructions

Prepare a tabular summary to record the following events.

a. The issuance of the bonds.

b. The accrual of interest on December 31.

c. The payment of interest on January 1, 2023.

d. The redemption of bonds at maturity, assuming interest for the last interest period has been paid and recorded.

## Solution

**2.**

| | Assets | = | Liabilities | | | + | | Stockholders' Equity | | | |
|---|---|---|---|---|---|---|---|---|---|---|---|
| | | | Int. | | Bonds | | Common | | Retained Earnings | | |
| | Cash | = | Pay. | + | Pay. | + | Stock | + Rev. | − Exp. | − Div. | |
| **a.** | +$900,000 | | | | +$900,000 | | | | | | |
| **b.** | | | +$72,000 | | | | | | −$72,000* | | Int. Exp. |
| **c.** | −72,000 | | −72,000 | | | | | | | | |
| **d.** | −900,000 | | | | −900,000 | | | | | | |

*$900,000 × 8%

---

**3. (LO 3)** Maci Co. had the following transactions during the current period.

*Record issuance of common and preferred stock and purchase of treasury stock.*

June 12   Issued 60,000 shares of $5 par value common stock for cash of $370,000.

July 11   Issued 1,000 shares of $100 par value preferred stock for cash at $112 per share.

Nov. 28   Purchased 2,000 shares of treasury stock for $70,000.

### Instructions

Prepare a tabular summary to record the transactions.

## Solution

**3.**

| | Assets | = Liabilities + | | | Stockholders' Equity | | | | | | | |
|---|---|---|---|---|---|---|---|---|---|---|---|---|
| | | | | | | Paid-in-Capital | | | | + | Retained Earnings | |
| | | | Preferred | | Common | Pd.-in-Cap. | Pd.-in-Cap. | Treasury | | | | |
| | Cash | = | Stock | + | Stock | + Preferred | + Common | − Stock | + Rev. | − Exp. | − Div. | |
| June 12 | +$370,000 | | | | +$300,000 | | +$70,000 | | | | | |
| July 11 | +112,000 | | +$100,000 | | | +$12,000 | | | | | | |
| Nov. 28 | −70,000 | | | | | | | −$70,000 | | | | |

*Record cash dividends.*

**4. (LO 4)** On January 1, Chong Corporation had 95,000 shares of no-par common stock issued and outstanding. The stock has a stated value of $5 per share. During the year, the following occurred.

| | |
|---|---|
| Apr. 1 | Issued 25,000 additional shares of common stock for $17 per share. |
| June 15 | Declared a cash dividend of $1 per share to stockholders of record on June 30. |
| July 10 | Paid the $1 cash dividend. |
| Dec. 1 | Issued 2,000 additional shares of common stock for $19 per share. |
| 15 | Declared a cash dividend on outstanding shares of $1.20 per share to stockholders of record on December 31. |

**Instructions**

Prepare a tabular summary and record the transactions on each of the three dividend dates.

**Solution**

4.

| | Assets | = | Liabilities | + | | Stockholders' Equity | | | | |
|---|---|---|---|---|---|---|---|---|---|---|
| | | | | | | Paid-in-Capital | + | | Retained Earnings | |
| | | | Dividends | | | Common | | | | |
| | Cash | = | Payable | + | | Stock | + Rev. − Exp. − | | | Div. |
| June 15 | | | +$120,000 | | | | | | | −$120,000* |
| July 10 | −$120,000 | | −120,000 | | | | | | | |
| Dec. 15 | | | +146,400 | | | | | | | −146,400** |

*(95,000 + 25,000) × $1
**(95,000 + 25,000 + 2,000) × $1.20

# Practice Problems

*Record issuance of bonds, interest accrual, and bond redemption.*

**1. (LO 2)** Snyder Software Inc. successfully developed a new spreadsheet program. However, to produce and market the program, the company needed additional financing. On January 1, 2021, Snyder borrowed money as follows.

1. Snyder issued $500,000, 11%, 10-year bonds. The bonds sold at face value and pay interest on January 1.

2. Snyder issued $1.0 million, 10%, 10-year bonds for $886,996.

**Instructions**

a. For the 11% bonds, prepare a tabular summary to record the following items.

   1. The issuance of the bonds on January 1, 2021.

   2. Accrue interest expense on December 31, 2021.

   3. The payment of interest on January 1, 2022.

b. For the 10-year, 10% bonds, prepare a tabular summary to record the following items.

   1. The issuance of the bonds on January 1, 2021.

   2. The redemption of the bonds on January 1, 2031.

**Solution**

1. a.

| | Assets | = | | Liabilities | | | + | | Stockholders' Equity | | | |
|---|---|---|---|---|---|---|---|---|---|---|---|---|
| | | | Int. | | Bonds | | | Common | | Retained Earnings | | |
| | Cash | = | Pay. | + | Pay. | | + | Stock | + Rev. − | Exp. | − Div. | |
| 1. | +$500,000 | | | | +$500,000 | | | | | | | |
| 2. | | | +$55,000* | | | | | | | −$55,000 | | Int. Exp. |
| 3. | −55,000 | | −55,000 | | | | | | | | | |

*$500,000 × .11

**b.**

| | Assets | = | Liabilities | | + | Stockholders' Equity | | |
|---|---|---|---|---|---|---|---|---|
| | | | Bonds | Disc. on | | Common | Retained Earnings | |
| | Cash | = | Pay. | − Bonds Pay. | + | Stock | + Rev. − Exp. − Div. | |
| 1. | +$886,996 | | +$1,000,000 | −$113,004 | | | | |
| 2. | −1,000,000 | | −1,000,000 | | | | | |

*Record transactions and prepare
stockholders' equity section.*

**2. (LO 3, 4, 5)** Rolman Corporation is authorized to issue 1,000,000 shares of $5 par value common stock. In its first year, the company has the following stock transactions.

| | |
|---|---|
| Jan. 10 | Issued 400,000 shares of stock at $8 per share. |
| Sept. 21 | Purchased 10,000 shares of common stock for the treasury at $9 per share. |
| Dec. 24 | Declared a cash dividend of 10 cents per share on common stock outstanding. |

**Instructions**

a. Prepare a tabular summary to record the transactions.

b. Prepare the stockholders' equity section of the balance sheet, assuming the company had retained earnings of $150,600 at December 31 and an accumulated other comprehensive loss of $105,000.

**Solution**

**2. a.**

| | Assets | = | Liabilities | + | Stockholders' Equity | | | | |
|---|---|---|---|---|---|---|---|---|---|
| | | | | | | Paid-in-Capital | | Retained Earnings | |
| | | | Dividends | | Common | Pd.-in-Cap. | Treasury | | |
| | Cash | = | Payable | + | Stock | + Common | − Stock | + Rev. − Exp. − | Div. |
| Jan. 10 | +$3,200,000[a] | | | | $2,000,000[b] | +$1,200,000 | | | |
| Sept. 21 | −90,000[c] | | | | | | −$90,000 | | |
| Dec. 24 | | | +$39,000[d] | | | | | | −$39,000 |

[a]400,000 × $8; [b]400,000 × $5; [c]10,000 × $9; [d](400,000 − 10,000) × $0.10

**b.**

### Rolman Corporation
#### Balance Sheet (partial)

| | |
|---|---|
| Stockholders' equity | |
| Paid-in capital | |
| Capital stock | |
| Common stock, $5 par value, 1,000,000 shares | |
| authorized, 400,000 shares issued, 390,000 outstanding | $2,000,000 |
| Additional paid-in capital | |
| Paid-in capital in excess of par value—common stock | 1,200,000 |
| Total paid-in capital | 3,200,000 |
| Retained earnings | 150,600 |
| Total paid-in capital and retained earnings | 3,350,600 |
| Accumulated other comprehensive loss | 105,000 |
| Less: Treasury stock (10,000 shares) | 90,000 |
| Total stockholders' equity | $3,155,600 |

# WileyPLUS

Brief Exercises, DO IT! Exercises, Exercises, Problems, and many additional resources are available for practice in WileyPLUS.

## Questions

**1.** Jenny Perez believes a current liability is a debt that can be expected to be paid in one year. Is Jenny correct? Explain.

**2.** Rayborn Company obtains $20,000 in cash by signing a 9%, 6-month, $20,000 note payable to First Bank on July 1. Rayborn's fiscal year ends on September 30. What information should be reported for the note payable in the annual financial statements?

**3. a.** Your roommate says, "Sales taxes are reported as an expense in the income statement." Do you agree? Explain.

   **b.** Leiana's Cafe has cash proceeds from sales of $8,550. This amount includes $550 of sales taxes. Use a tabular summary to record the proceeds.

**4.** Carolina University sold 9,000 season football tickets at $100 each for its five-game home schedule. What accounts should be increased or decreased (a) when the tickets are sold and (b) after each game?

**5.** Identify three taxes commonly withheld by the employer from an employee's gross pay.

**6. a.** Identify three taxes commonly paid by employers on employees' salaries and wages.

   **b.** Where in the financial statements does the employer report taxes withheld from employees' pay?

**7.** Identify the liabilities classified by **Apple** as current.

**8. a.** What are long-term liabilities? Give two examples.

   **b.** What is a bond?

**9.** Explain each of these important terms in issuing bonds:

   **a.** Face value.

   **b.** Contractual interest rate.

   **c.** Bond certificate.

**10.** Describe the two major obligations incurred by a company when bonds are issued.

**11.** Assume that Acorn Inc. sold bonds with a face value of $100,000 for $104,000. Was the market interest rate equal to, less than, or greater than the bonds' contractual interest rate? Explain.

**12.** Lee and Jay are discussing how the market interest rate of a bond is determined. Lee believes that the market interest rate of a bond is solely a function of the amount of the principal payment at the end of the term of a bond. Is he right? Discuss.

**13.** If a 6%, 10-year, $800,000 bond is issued at face value and interest is paid annually, what is the amount of the interest payment at the end of the first period?

**14.** If the Bonds Payable account has a balance of $700,000 and the Discount on Bonds Payable account has a balance of $36,000, what is the carrying value of the bonds?

**15.** What are the basic ownership rights of common stockholders in the absence of restrictive provisions?

**16.** A corporation has been defined as an entity separate and distinct from its owners. In what ways is a corporation a separate legal entity?

**17.** What are the two principal components of stockholders' equity?

**18.** The corporate charter of Gage Corporation allows the issuance of a maximum of 100,000 shares of common stock. During its first 2 years of operation, Gage sold 70,000 shares to shareholders and reacquired 4,000 of these shares. After these transactions, how many shares are authorized, issued, and outstanding?

**19.** Which is the better investment—common stock with a par value of $5 per share or common stock with a par value of $20 per share?

**20.** For what reasons might a company like **IBM** repurchase some of its stock (treasury stock)?

**21.** Monet, Inc. purchases 1,000 shares of its own previously issued $5 par common stock for $11,000. Assuming the shares are held in the treasury, what effect does this transaction have on (a) net income, (b) total assets, (c) total paid-in capital, and (d) total stockholders' equity?

**22. a.** What are the principal differences between common stock and preferred stock?

   **b.** Preferred stock may be cumulative. Discuss this feature.

   **c.** How are dividends in arrears presented in the financial statements?

**23.** Indicate how each of these accounts should be classified in the stockholders' equity section of the balance sheet.

   **a.** Common Stock.

   **b.** Paid-in Capital in Excess of Par Value.

   **c.** Retained Earnings.

   **d.** Treasury Stock.

   **e.** Paid-in Capital in Excess of Stated Value.

   **f.** Preferred Stock.

**24.** What three conditions must be met before a cash dividend is paid?

**25.** Three dates associated with Petrie Company's cash dividend are May 1, May 15, and May 31. Discuss the significance of each date and prepare a tabular analysis at each date.

**26.** Thom Inc.'s common stock has a par value of $1 and a current market price of $15. Explain why these amounts are different.

**27.** What is the formula for the payout ratio? What does it indicate?

**28.** Explain the circumstances under which debt financing will increase the return on common stockholders' equity.

**29.** Under what circumstances will the return on assets and the return on common stockholders' equity be equal?

**30.** Sauer Corp. has a return on assets of 12%. It plans to issue bonds at 8% and use the cash to repurchase stock. What effect will this have on its debt to assets ratio and on its return on common stockholders' equity?

# Brief Exercises

**BE9.1 (LO 1), C** Busch Company has these obligations at December 31: (a) a note payable for $100,000 due in 2 years, (b) a 10-year mortgage payable of $200,000 payable in ten $20,000 annual payments and (c) interest payable of $15,000 on the mortgage, and (d) accounts payable of $60,000. For each obligation, indicate whether it should be classified as a current liability, long-term liability, or both.

*Identify whether obligations are current liabilities.*

**BE9.2 (LO 1), AP** Hive Company borrows $90,000 on July 1 from the bank by signing a $90,000, 7%, 1-year note payable. Prepare a tabular summary to record (a) the proceeds of the note and (b) accrued interest at December 31, assuming adjustments are made only at the end of the year.

*Record an interest-bearing note payable.*

**BE9.3 (LO 1), AP** Greenspan Supply does not segregate sales and sales taxes at the time of sale. The register total for March 16 is $10,388. All sales are subject to a 6% sales tax. Compute sales taxes payable and prepare a tabular summary to record sales taxes payable and sales.

*Compute and record sales taxes payable.*

**BE9.4 (LO 1), AP** Bramble University sells 3,500 season basketball tickets at $80 each for its 10-game home schedule. Prepare a tabular summary to record (a) the sale of the season tickets and (b) the revenue recognized after playing the first home game.

*Record unearned revenues.*

**BE9.5 (LO 1), AP** Betsy Strand's regular hourly wage rate is $16, and she receives an hourly rate of $24 for work in excess of 40 hours. During a January pay period, Betsy works 47 hours. Betsy's federal income tax withholding is $95, and she has no voluntary deductions. Compute Betsy Strand's gross earnings and net pay for the pay period. Assume that the FICA tax rate is 7.65%. (Round calculations to two decimal places.)

*Compute gross earnings and net pay.*

**BE9.6 (LO 1), AP** Betsy Strand's regular hourly wage rate is $16, and she receives an hourly rate of $24 for work in excess of 40 hours. During a January pay period, Betsy works 47 hours. Betsy's federal income tax withholding is $95, and she has no voluntary deductions. Prepare a tabular summary for Betsy's employer to record (a) Betsy's pay for the period and (b) the payment of Betsy's wages. Use January 15 for the end of the pay period and the payment date. Assume that the FICA tax rate is 7.65%.

*Record a payroll and the payment of wages.*

**BE9.7 (LO 1), AP** Betsy Strand's regular hourly wage rate is $16, and she receives an hourly rate of $24 for work in excess of 40 hours. During a January pay period, Betsy works 47 hours. Betsy's federal income tax withholding is $95, and she has no voluntary deductions. Prepare a tabular summary to record the employer's payroll taxes for the period. Assume that the FICA tax rate is 7.65%. Ignore unemployment taxes.

*Record payroll taxes.*

**BE9.8 (LO 2), AP** Bridle Inc. issues $300,000, 10-year, 8% bonds at 98. Prepare a tabular summary to record the sale of these bonds on March 1, 2022.

*Record issuance of bonds.*

**BE9.9 (LO 2), AP** Ravine Company issues $400,000, 20-year, 7% bonds at 101. Prepare a tabular summary to record the sale of these bonds on June 1, 2022.

*Record issuance of bonds.*

**BE9.10 (LO 2), AP** Clooney Corporation issued 3,000 7%, 5-year, $1,000 bonds dated January 1, 2022, at face value. Interest is paid each January 1. Prepare a tabular summary to:

*Record bonds issued at face value.*

a. Record the sale of these bonds on January 1, 2022.

b. Adjust accounts on December 31, 2022, to record interest expense.

c. Record interest paid on January 1, 2023.

**BE9.11 (LO 2), AP** Presented here are long-term liability items for Stevens Inc. at December 31, 2022. Prepare the long-term liabilities section of the balance sheet for Stevens Inc.

*Prepare statement presentation of long-term liabilities.*

| | |
|---|---|
| Bonds payable (due 2026) | $700,000 |
| Notes payable (due 2024) | 80,000 |
| Discount on bonds payable | 28,000 |

**BE9.12 (LO 1, 2), AP** Presented here are liability items for O'Brian Inc. at December 31, 2022. Prepare the liabilities section of O'Brian's balance sheet.

*Prepare liabilities section of balance sheet.*

| | | | |
|---|---|---|---|
| Accounts payable | $157,000 | FICA taxes payable | $ 7,800 |
| Notes payable | 20,000 | Interest payable | 40,000 |
| (due May 1, 2023) | | Notes payable (due 2024) | 80,000 |
| Bonds payable (due 2026) | 900,000 | Income taxes payable | 3,500 |
| Unearned rent revenue | 240,000 | Sales taxes payable | 1,700 |
| Discount on bonds payable | 41,000 | | |

*Record issuance of par value common stock.*

**BE9.13 (LO 3), AP** On May 10, Pilar Corporation issues 2,500 shares of $5 par value common stock for cash at $13 per share. Prepare a tabular summary to record the issuance of the stock.

*Record issuance of no-par common stock.*

**BE9.14 (LO 3), AP** On June 1, Forrest Inc. issues 3,000 shares of no-par common stock at a cash price of $7 per share. Prepare a tabular summary to record the issuance of the shares.

*Record issuance of preferred stock.*

**BE9.15 (LO 3), AP** Layes Inc. issues 8,000 shares of $100 par value preferred stock for cash at $106 per share. Prepare a tabular summary to record the issuance of the preferred stock.

*Record cash dividend.*

**BE9.16 (LO 4), AP** Basse Corporation has 7,000 shares of common stock outstanding. It declares a $1 per share cash dividend on November 1 to stockholders of record on December 1. The dividend is paid on December 31. Prepare a tabular summary to record the declaration and payment of the cash dividend.

*Analyze impact of cash dividends and stock transactions.*

**BE9.17 (LO 3, 4), K** Indicate whether each of the following transactions would increase (+), decrease (−), or not affect (N/A) total assets, total liabilities, and total stockholders' equity.

| Transaction | Assets | Liabilities | Stockholders' Equity |
|---|---|---|---|
| **a.** Declared cash dividend. | | | |
| **b.** Paid cash dividend declared in (a). | | | |
| **c.** Issued shares of common stock for cash. | | | |
| **d.** Purchased shares of stock to hold as treasury stock. | | | |

*Prepare a stockholders' equity section.*

**BE9.18 (LO 5), AP** Sudz Corporation has these accounts at December 31: Common Stock, $10 par, 5,000 shares issued, $50,000; Paid-in Capital in Excess of Par Value $22,000; Retained Earnings $42,000; and Treasury Stock, 500 shares, $11,000. Prepare the stockholders' equity section of the balance sheet.

*Evaluate a company's dividend record.*

**BE9.19 (LO 5), C** Hans Miken, president of Miken Corporation, believes that it is a good practice for a company to maintain a constant payout of dividends relative to its earnings. Last year, net income was $600,000, and the corporation paid $120,000 in dividends. This year, due to some unusual circumstances, the corporation had income of $1,600,000. Hans expects next year's net income to be about $700,000. What was Miken Corporation's payout ratio last year? If it is to maintain the same payout ratio, what amount of dividends would it pay this year? Is this necessarily a good idea—that is, what are the pros and cons of maintaining a constant payout ratio in this scenario?

*Calculate the return on stockholders' equity.*

**BE9.20 (LO 5), AP** SUPERVALU, one of the largest grocery retailers in the United States, is headquartered near Minneapolis. Suppose the following financial information (in millions) was taken from the company's 2022 annual report: net sales $44,597, net income $393, beginning stockholders' equity $2,581, and ending stockholders' equity $2,887. There were no dividends paid on preferred stock. Compute the return on common stockholders' equity. (Round ratio calculation to two decimal places.) Provide a brief interpretation of your findings.

*Compare bond financing to stock financing.*

**BE9.21 (LO 5), AP** Emron Inc. is considering these two alternatives to finance its construction of a new $2 million plant:

1. Issuance of 200,000 shares of common stock at the market price of $10 per share.
2. Issuance of $2 million, 6% bonds at face value.

Complete the table and indicate which alternative is preferable.

| | Issue Stock | Issue Bonds |
|---|---|---|
| Income before interest and taxes | $1,500,000 | $1,500,000 |
| Interest expense from bonds | _____ | _____ |
| Income before income taxes | | |
| Income tax expense (30%) | _____ | _____ |
| Net income | $ _____ | $ _____ |
| Outstanding shares | _____ | 700,000 |
| Earnings per share | $ _____ | $ _____ |

# DO IT! Exercises

**DO IT! 9.1a (LO 1), AP** You and several classmates are studying for the next accounting exam. They ask you to answer the following questions:

*Answer questions about current liabilities.*

1. If cash is borrowed on a $60,000, 9-month, 10% note on August 1, how much interest expense would be incurred by December 31?

2. The cash register total including sales taxes is $42,000, and the sales tax rate is 5%. What is the sales taxes payable?

3. If $42,000 is collected in advance on November 1 for 6-month magazine subscriptions, what amount of subscription revenue should be recognized on December 31?

**DO IT! 9.1b (LO 1), AP** During the month of February, Hennesey Corporation's employees earned wages of $74,000. Withholdings related to these wages were $5,661 for FICA, $7,100 for federal income tax, and $1,900 for state income tax. Costs incurred for unemployment taxes were $110 for federal and $160 for state.

*Record payroll and payroll taxes.*

Prepare a tabular summary to record on February 28 (a) salaries and wages expense and salaries and wages payable assuming that all February wages will be paid in March and (b) the company's payroll tax expense.

**DO IT! 9.2 (LO 2), AP** Smiley Corporation issues $300,000 of bonds for $315,000. (a) Prepare a tabular summary to record the issuance of the bonds, and (b) show how the bonds would be reported on the balance sheet at the date of issuance.

*Record bond issuance and show balance sheet presentation.*

**DO IT! 9.3a (LO 3), AP** Beauty Island Corporation began operations on April 1 by issuing 55,000 shares of $5 par value common stock for cash at $13 per share. In addition, Beauty Island issued 1,000 shares of $1 par value preferred stock for $6 per share. Prepare a tabular summary to record the issuance of the common and preferred shares.

*Record issuance of stock.*

**DO IT! 9.3b (LO 3), AP** Dinosso Corporation purchased 2,000 shares of its $10 par value common stock for $76,000 on August 1. It will hold these in the treasury until resold. Prepare a tabular summary to record the treasury stock transaction.

*Record treasury stock transaction.*

**DO IT! 9.4 (LO 4), AP** Sparks Corporation has 3,000 shares of 8%, $100 par value preferred stock outstanding at December 31, 2022. At December 31, 2022, the company declared a $105,000 cash dividend. Determine the dividend paid to preferred stockholders and common stockholders under each of the following scenarios.

*Determine dividends paid to preferred and common stockholders.*

1. The preferred stock is noncumulative, and the company has not missed any dividends in previous years.

2. The preferred stock is noncumulative, and the company did not pay a dividend in each of the two previous years.

3. The preferred stock is cumulative, and the company did not pay a dividend in each of the two previous years.

**DO IT! 9.5 (LO 5), AP** On January 1, 2022, Vahsholtz Corporation purchased 5,000 shares of treasury stock. Other information regarding Vahsholtz Corporation is provided as follows.

*Compute return on stockholders' equity and discuss changes.*

| | 2022 | 2021 |
|---|---|---|
| Net income | $110,000 | $100,000 |
| Dividends on preferred stock | $ 30,000 | $ 30,000 |
| Dividends on common stock | $ 25,000 | $ 20,000 |
| Weighted-average number of common shares outstanding | 45,000 | 50,000 |
| Common stockholders' equity beginning of year | $750,000 | $600,000 |
| Common stockholders' equity end of year | $830,000 | $750,000 |

(a) Compute return on common stockholders' equity for each year, and (b) discuss the changes in each.

## Exercises

*Record interest-bearing notes.*

**E9.1 (LO 1), AP** Kelly Jones and Tami Crawford borrowed $15,000 on a 7-month, 8% note from Gem State Bank to open their business, JC's Coffee House. The money was borrowed on June 1, 2022, and the note matures January 1, 2023.

**Instructions**

a. Prepare a tabular summary to record the receipt of the funds from the loan.

b. Prepare a tabular summary to accrue the interest on June 30.

c. Assuming adjustments are made at the end of each month, determine the balance in the Interest Payable account at December 31, 2022.

d. Prepare a tabular summary to record the repayment of the loan on January 1, 2023.

*Record interest-bearing notes.*

**E9.2 (LO 1), AP** On June 1, Marchon Company Ltd. borrows $60,000 from Acme Bank on a 6-month, $60,000, 8% note. The note matures on December 1.

**Instructions**

a. Prepare a tabular summary to record the note issued on June 1.

b. Prepare a tabular summary to record adjustment on June 30.

c. Prepare a tabular summary to record the repayment at maturity (December 1), assuming monthly adjustments have been made through November 30.

d. What was the total financing cost (interest expense)?

*Record sales and related taxes.*

**E9.3 (LO 1), AP** In performing accounting services for small businesses, you encounter the following situations pertaining to cash sales.

1. Cerviq Company enters sales and sales taxes separately on its cash register. On April 10, the register totals are sales $22,000 and sales taxes $1,100.

2. Quartz Company does not segregate sales and sales taxes. Its register total for April 15 is $13,780, which includes a 6% sales tax.

**Instructions**

Prepare tabular summaries to record the sales transactions and related taxes for (a) Cerviq Company and (b) Quartz Company.

*Record payroll transactions.*

**E9.4 (LO 1), AP** During the month of March, Munster Company's employees earned wages of $64,000. Withholdings related to these wages were $4,896 for FICA, $7,500 for federal income tax, $3,100 for state income tax, and $400 for union dues. The company incurred no cost related to these earnings for federal unemployment tax but incurred $700 for state unemployment tax.

**Instructions**

a. Prepare a tabular summary to record salaries and wages expense and salaries and wages payable on March 31. Assume that wages earned during March will be paid during April.

b. Prepare a tabular summary to record the company's payroll tax expense.

*Record unearned subscription revenue.*

**E9.5 (LO 1), AP** Cassini Company Ltd. publishes a monthly sports magazine, *Fishing Preview*. Subscriptions to the magazine cost $28 per year. During November 2022, Cassini sells 6,300 subscriptions for cash, beginning with the December issue. Cassini prepares financial statements quarterly and recognizes subscription revenue at the end of the quarter. The company uses the accounts Unearned Subscription Revenue and Subscription Revenue. The company has a December 31 year-end.

**Instructions**

Prepare a tabular summary to record the following events.

a. Receipt of the subscriptions in November.

b. Adjustment at December 31, 2022, to record subscription revenue in December 2022.

*Record issuance of bonds and payment and accrual of interest.*

**E9.6 (LO 2), AP** On August 1, 2022, Gonzaga Corporation issued $600,000, 7%, 10-year bonds at face value. Interest is payable annually on August 1. Gonzaga's year-end is December 31.

## Instructions

Prepare a tabular summary to record the following events.

   **a.** The issuance of the bonds.

   **b.** The accrual of interest on December 31, 2022.

   **c.** The payment of interest on August 1, 2023.

**E9.7 (LO 2), AP** On January 1, Kirkland Company issued $300,000, 8%, 10-year bonds at face value. Interest is payable annually on January 1.

*Record issuance of bonds and payment and accrual of interest.*

## Instructions

Prepare a tabular summary to record the following events.

   **a.** The issuance of the bonds.

   **b.** The accrual of interest on December 31.

   **c.** The payment of interest on January 1.

**E9.8 (LO 2), AP** Arroyo Company issued $600,000, 10-year, 6% bonds at 103.

*Record issuance of bonds, provide balance sheet presentation, and explain cause of deviations from face value.*

## Instructions

   **a.** Prepare a tabular summary to record the sale of these bonds on January 1, 2022.

   **b.** Suppose the remaining Premium on Bonds Payable was $10,800 on December 31, 2025. Show the balance sheet presentation on this date.

   **c.** Explain why the bonds sold at a price above the face amount.

**E9.9 (LO 2), AP** Mobbe Company issued $500,000, 15-year, 7% bonds at 96.

*Record issuance of bonds, provide balance sheet presentation, and explain cause of deviations from face value.*

## Instructions

   **a.** Prepare a tabular summary to record the sale of these bonds on January 1, 2022.

   **b.** Suppose the remaining Discount on Bonds Payable was $12,000 on December 31, 2027. Show the balance sheet presentation on this date.

   **c.** Explain why the bonds sold at a price below the face amount.

**E9.10 (LO 2), AN** Assume that the following are independent situations recently reported in the *Wall Street Journal*.

*Record issuance of bonds.*

   **1.** **General Electric (GE)** 7% bonds, maturing January 28, 2023, were issued at 111.12.

   **2.** **Boeing** 7% bonds, maturing September 24, 2037, were issued at 99.08.

## Instructions

   **a.** Were GE and Boeing bonds issued at a premium or a discount?

   **b.** Explain how bonds, both paying the same contractual interest rate, could be issued at different prices.

   **c.** Prepare tabular summaries to record the issue of each of these two bonds, assuming each company issued $800,000 of bonds in total.

**E9.11 (LO 2), AP** Kale Company issued $350,000 of 8%, 20-year bonds on January 1, 2022, at face value. Interest is payable annually on January 1.

*Record issuance of bonds, payment of interest, and redemption at maturity.*

## Instructions

Prepare a tabular summary to record the following events.

   **a.** The issuance of the bonds.

   **b.** The accrual of interest on December 31, 2022.

   **c.** The payment of interest on January 1, 2023.

   **d.** The redemption of the bonds at maturity, assuming interest for the last interest period has been paid and recorded.

**E9.12 (LO 3), AP** During its first year of operations, Mona Corporation had these transactions pertaining to its common stock.

*Record issuance of common stock.*

   Jan. 10   Issued 30,000 shares for cash at $5 per share.
   July  1   Issued 60,000 shares for cash at $7 per share.

### Instructions

a. Prepare a tabular summary to record the transactions, assuming that the common stock has a par value of $5 per share.

b. Prepare a tabular summary to record the transactions, assuming that the common stock is no-par with a stated value of $1 per share.

*Record issuance of common stock and preferred stock and purchase of treasury stock.*

**E9.13 (LO 3), AP** Sagan Co. had these transactions during the current period.

| June 12 | Issued 80,000 shares of $1 par value common stock for cash of $300,000. |
| July 11 | Issued 3,000 shares of $100 par value preferred stock for cash at $106 per share. |
| Nov. 28 | Purchased 2,000 shares of treasury stock for $9,000. |

### Instructions

Prepare a tabular summary to record the Sagan Co. transactions.

*Record preferred stock transactions and indicate statement presentation.*

**E9.14 (LO 3, 5), AP** Penland Corporation is authorized to issue both preferred and common stock. The par value of the preferred is $50. During the first year of operations, the company had the following events and transactions pertaining to its preferred stock.

| Feb. 1 | Issued 40,000 shares for cash at $51 per share. |
| July 1 | Issued 60,000 shares for cash at $56 per share. |

### Instructions

a. Prepare a tabular summary to record the transactions.

b. Discuss the statement presentation of the accounts.

*Answer questions about stockholders' equity section.*

**E9.15 (LO 3, 4), C** The stockholders' equity section of Lachlin Corporation's balance sheet at December 31 is presented here.

---

**Lachlin Corporation**
**Balance Sheet (partial)**

---

| | |
|---|---:|
| Stockholders' equity | |
| Paid-in capital | |
| Preferred stock, cumulative, 10,000 shares authorized, | |
| 6,000 shares issued and outstanding | $ 600,000 |
| Common stock, no par, 750,000 shares authorized, | |
| 580,000 shares issued | 2,900,000 |
| Total paid-in capital | 3,500,000 |
| Retained earnings | 1,158,000 |
| Total paid-in capital and retained earnings | 4,658,000 |
| Less: Treasury stock (6,000 common shares) | 32,000 |
| Total stockholders' equity | $4,626,000 |

### Instructions

From a review of the stockholders' equity section, answer the following questions.

a. How many shares of common stock are outstanding?

b. Assuming there is a stated value, what is the stated value of the common stock?

c. What is the par value of the preferred stock?

d. If the annual dividend on preferred stock is $36,000, what is the dividend rate on preferred stock?

e. If dividends of $72,000 were in arrears on preferred stock, what would be the balance reported for retained earnings?

*Record cash dividends and indicate statement presentation.*

**E9.16 (LO 4), AP** On January 1, Graves Corporation had 60,000 shares of no-par common stock issued and outstanding. The stock has a stated value of $4 per share. During the year, the following transactions occurred.

| Apr. 1 | Issued 9,000 additional shares of common stock for $11 per share. |
| June 15 | Declared a cash dividend of $1.50 per share to stockholders of record on June 30. |
| July 10 | Paid the $1.50 cash dividend. |
| Dec. 1 | Issued 4,000 additional shares of common stock for $12 per share. |
| 15 | Declared a cash dividend on outstanding shares of $1.60 per share to stockholders of record on December 31. |

**Instructions**

a. Prepare a tabular summary to record the three dates that involved dividends.

b. How are dividends and dividends payable reported in the financial statements prepared at December 31?

**E9.17 (LO 5), AP** The following accounts appear in the records of Paisan Inc. at December 31, 2022. *Prepare a stockholders' equity section.*

| | |
|---|---|
| Common Stock (no-par, $1 stated value, 400,000 shares authorized, 250,000 shares issued) | $   250,000 |
| Paid-in Capital in Excess of Stated Value—Common Stock | 1,200,000 |
| Preferred Stock ($50 par value, 8%, 40,000 shares authorized, 14,000 shares issued) | 700,000 |
| Retained Earnings | 920,000 |
| Treasury Stock (9,000 common shares) | 64,000 |
| Paid-in Capital in Excess of Par Value—Preferred Stock | 24,000 |
| Accumulated Other Comprehensive Loss | 31,000 |

**Instructions**

Prepare the stockholders' equity section at December 31.

**E9.18 (LO 5), AN** The following financial information is available for Flintlock Corporation. *Calculate ratios to evaluate dividend and earnings performance.*

| (in millions) | 2022 | 2021 |
|---|---|---|
| Average common stockholders' equity | $2,532 | $2,591 |
| Dividends declared for common stockholders | 298 | 611 |
| Dividends declared for preferred stockholders | 40 | 40 |
| Net income | 504 | 555 |

**Instructions**

Calculate the payout ratio and return on common stockholders' equity for 2022 and 2021. Comment on your findings.

**E9.19 (LO 5), AN** Suppose the following financial information is available for **Walgreens**. *Calculate ratios to evaluate dividend and earnings performance.*

| (in millions) | 2022 | 2021 |
|---|---|---|
| Average common stockholders' equity | $13,622.5 | $11,986.5 |
| Dividends declared for common stockholders | 471 | 394 |
| Dividends declared for preferred stockholders | 0 | 0 |
| Net income | 2,006 | 2,157 |

**Instructions**

Calculate the payout ratio and return on common stockholders' equity for 2022 and 2021. Comment on your findings.

**E9.20 (LO 5), AN** Kojak Corporation decided to issue common stock and used the $300,000 proceeds to redeem all of its outstanding bonds on January 1, 2022. The following information is available for the company for 2022 and 2021. *Calculate ratios to evaluate profitability and solvency.*

| | 2022 | 2021 |
|---|---|---|
| Net income | $   182,000 | $   150,000 |
| Dividends declared for preferred stockholders | 8,000 | 8,000 |
| Average common stockholders' equity | 1,000,000 | 700,000 |
| Total assets | 1,200,000 | 1,200,000 |
| Current liabilities | 100,000 | 100,000 |
| Total liabilities | 200,000 | 500,000 |

**Instructions**

a. Compute the return on common stockholders' equity for both years.

b. Explain how it is possible that net income increased but the return on common stockholders' equity decreased.

c. Compute the debt to assets ratio for both years, and comment on the implications of this change in the company's solvency.

*Compare issuance of stock financing to issuance of bond financing.*

**E9.21 (LO 5), AN** Baja Airlines is considering these two alternatives for financing the purchase of a fleet of airplanes:

1. Issue 50,000 shares of common stock at $40 per share. (Cash dividends have not been paid, nor is the payment of any contemplated.)

2. Issue 12%, 10-year bonds at face value for $2,000,000.

It is estimated that the company will earn $800,000 before interest and taxes as a result of this purchase. The company has an estimated tax rate of 30% and has 90,000 shares of common stock outstanding prior to the new financing.

**Instructions**

Determine the effect on net income and earnings per share for (a) issuing stock and (b) issuing bonds. Assume the new shares or new bonds will be outstanding for the entire year.

# Problems

*Record current liabilities, adjustments, and current liabilities section.*

**P9.1 (LO 1), AP** On January 1, 2022, Romada Company's accounting records contained these liability accounts.

| | |
|---|---|
| Accounts Payable | $42,500 |
| Sales Taxes Payable | 6,600 |
| Unearned Service Revenue | 19,000 |

During January, the following selected transactions occurred.

| Jan. | 1 | Borrowed $18,000 in cash from Apex Bank on a 4-month, 5%, $18,000 note. |
|---|---|---|
| | 5 | Sold merchandise for cash totaling $6,254, which includes 6% sales taxes. |
| | 12 | Performed services for customers who had made advance payments of $10,000. (Record Service Revenue.) |
| | 14 | Paid state treasurer's department for sales taxes collected in December 2021, $6,600. |
| | 20 | Sold 500 units of a new product on credit at $48 per unit, plus 6% sales tax. |

During January, the company's employees earned wages of $70,000. Withholdings related to these wages were $5,355 for FICA, $5,000 for federal income tax, and $1,500 for state income tax. The company owed no money related to these earnings for federal or state unemployment tax. Assume that wages earned during January will be paid during February. Wages or payroll tax expense have not been recorded as of January 31.

**Instructions**

a. Prepare a tabular summary to record the January transactions and the adjustments on January 31 for the outstanding note payable and the salaries and wages expense and payroll tax expense.

b. Prepare the current liabilities section of the balance sheet at January 31, 2022. Assume no change in Accounts Payable.

*b. Tot. current liabilities $146,724*

*Record issuance of bonds, interest, balance sheet presentation, and bond redemption.*

**P9.2 (LO 1, 2), AP** On October 1, 2021, Kristal Corp. issued $700,000, 5%, 10-year bonds at face value. The bonds were dated October 1, 2021, and pay interest annually on October 1. Financial statements are prepared annually on December 31.

**Instructions**

a. Prepare a tabular summary to record the issuance of the bonds and the adjustments to record the accrual of interest on December 31, 2021.

b. Show the balance sheet presentation of bonds payable and bond interest payable on December 31, 2021.

c. Prepare a tabular summary to record the payment of interest on October 1, 2022.

d. Prepare a tabular summary to record redemption of the bonds on October 1, 2031, their maturity date.

*Record stock transactions and prepare paid-in capital section.*

**P9.3 (LO 3, 5), AP** Tidal Corporation was organized on January 1, 2022. It is authorized to issue 20,000 shares of 6%, $50 par value preferred stock and 500,000 shares of no-par common stock with a stated value of $1 per share. The following stock transactions were completed during the first year.

| Jan. | 10 | Issued 70,000 shares of common stock for cash at $4 per share. |
|---|---|---|
| Mar. | 1 | Issued 12,000 shares of preferred stock for cash at $53 per share. |
| May | 1 | Issued 120,000 shares of common stock for cash at $6 per share. |
| Sept. | 1 | Issued 5,000 shares of common stock for cash at $5 per share. |
| Nov. | 1 | Issued 3,000 shares of preferred stock for cash at $56 per share. |

## Instructions

**a.** Prepare a tabular summary to record the transactions.

**b.** Prepare the paid-in capital portion of the stockholders' equity section at December 31, 2022.

b.  Tot. paid-in
    capital          $1,829,000

**P9.4 (LO 3, 4, 5), AP** The stockholders' equity accounts of Cyrus Corporation on January 1, 2022, were as follows.

*Record transactions and prepare a stockholders' equity section; calculate ratios.*

| | |
|---|---:|
| Preferred Stock (7%, $100 par noncumulative, 5,000 shares authorized) | $ 300,000 |
| Common Stock ($4 stated value, 300,000 shares authorized) | 1,000,000 |
| Paid-in Capital in Excess of Par Value—Preferred Stock | 15,000 |
| Paid-in Capital in Excess of Stated Value—Common Stock | 480,000 |
| Retained Earnings | 688,000 |
| Treasury Stock (5,000 common shares) | 40,000 |

During 2022, the corporation had the following transactions and events pertaining to its stockholders' equity.

| | | |
|---|---|---|
| Feb. | 1 | Issued 5,000 shares of common stock for $30,000. |
| Mar. | 20 | Purchased 1,000 additional shares of common treasury stock at $7 per share. |
| Oct. | 1 | Declared a 7% cash dividend on preferred stock, payable November 1. |
| Nov. | 1 | Paid the dividend declared on October 1. |
| Dec. | 1 | Declared a $0.50 per share cash dividend to common stockholders of record on December 15, payable December 31, 2022. |
| | 31 | Paid the dividend declared on December 1. |

## Instructions

**a.** Prepare a tabular summary that includes the January 1, 2022, balances. Do not include the beginning balance in Retained Earnings in the tabular summary.

**b.** Record the 2022 transactions in the tabular summary.

**c.** Prepare the stockholders' equity section of the balance sheet at December 31, 2022. Include 2022 net income of $280,000 as an increase to the January 1, 2022, Retained Earnings.

c.  Tot. paid-in
    capital          $1,825,000

**d.** Calculate the payout ratio, earnings per share, and return on common stockholders' equity. (*Note:* Use the common shares outstanding on January 1 and December 31 to determine the average shares outstanding.)

**P9.5 (LO 3, 4, 5), AP** On December 31, 2021, Jons Company had 1,300,000 shares of $5 par common stock issued and outstanding. At December 31, 2021, stockholders' equity had the amounts listed here.

*Prepare a stockholders' equity section.*

| | |
|---|---:|
| Common Stock | $6,500,000 |
| Additional Paid-in Capital | 1,800,000 |
| Retained Earnings | 1,200,000 |

Transactions during 2022 and other information related to stockholders' equity accounts were as follows.

1. On January 10, 2022, issued at $107 per share 120,000 shares of $100 par value, 9% cumulative preferred stock.

2. On February 8, 2022, reacquired 15,000 shares of its common stock for $11 per share.

3. On May 9, 2022, declared the yearly cash dividend on preferred stock, payable June 10, 2022, to stockholders of record on May 31, 2022.

4. On June 8, 2022, declared a cash dividend of $1.20 per share on the common stock outstanding, payable on July 10, 2022, to stockholders of record on July 1, 2022.

5. Net income for the year was $3,600,000.

## Instructions

Prepare the stockholders' equity section of Jons' balance sheet at December 31, 2022.

Tot. stockholders'
equity          $23,153,000

**P9.6 (LO 3, 4, 5), AP** On January 1, 2022, Kimbel Inc. had these stockholders' equity balances.

*Prepare a stockholders' equity section.*

| | |
|---|---:|
| Common Stock, $1 par (2,000,000 shares authorized, 600,000 shares issued and outstanding) | $ 600,000 |
| Paid-in Capital in Excess of Par Value | 1,500,000 |
| Retained Earnings | 700,000 |
| Accumulated Other Comprehensive Income | 60,000 |

During 2022, the following transactions and events occurred.

1. Issued 50,000 shares of $1 par value common stock for $3 per share.

2. Issued 60,000 shares of common stock for cash at $4 per share.

3. Purchased 20,000 shares of common stock for the treasury at $3.80 per share.
4. Declared and paid a cash dividend of $207,000.
5. Earned net income of $410,000.
6. Had other comprehensive income of $17,000.

**Instructions**

Prepare the stockholders' equity section of the balance sheet at December 31, 2022.

*Tot. stockholders'*
*equity*      **$3,394,000**

*Evaluate a company's profitability and solvency.*

**P9.7 (LO 5), AN** Spahn Company manufactures backpacks. During 2022, Spahn issued bonds at 10% interest and used the cash proceeds to purchase treasury stock. The following financial information is available for Spahn Company for the years 2022 and 2021.

|  | 2022 | 2021 |
|---|---|---|
| Sales revenue | $ 9,000,000 | $ 9,000,000 |
| Net income | 2,240,000 | 2,500,000 |
| Interest expense | 500,000 | 140,000 |
| Tax expense | 670,000 | 750,000 |
| Dividends paid on common stock | 890,000 | 1,026,000 |
| Dividends paid on preferred stock | 300,000 | 300,000 |
| Total assets (year-end) | 14,500,000 | 16,875,000 |
| Average total assets | 15,687,500 | 17,763,000 |
| Total liabilities (year-end) | 6,000,000 | 3,000,000 |
| Avg. total common stockholders' equity | 9,400,000 | 14,100,000 |

**Instructions**

a. Use the information above to calculate the following ratios for both years: (1) return on assets, (2) return on common stockholders' equity, (3) payout ratio, and (4) debt to assets ratio.

b. Referring to your findings in part (a), discuss the changes in the company's profitability from 2021 to 2022.

c. Referring to your findings in part (a), discuss the changes in the company's solvency from 2021 to 2022.

d. Based on your findings in (b), was the decision to issue debt to purchase common stock a wise one?

# Expand Your Critical Thinking

## Financial Reporting Problem: Apple Inc.

**CT9.1** Refer to the financial statements of **Apple Inc.** in Appendix A.

**Instructions**

Answer the following questions.

a. What were Apple's total current liabilities at September 29, 2018? What was the increase/decrease in Apple's total current liabilities from the prior year?

b. How much were the accounts payable at September 29, 2018?

c. What were the components of total current liabilities on September 29, 2018 (other than accounts payable already discussed above)?

## Comparative Analysis Problem:
## Columbia Sportswear Company vs. Under Armour, Inc.

**CT9.2** The financial statements of **Columbia Sportswear Company** are presented in Appendix B. Financial statements of **Under Armour, Inc.** are presented in Appendix C.

**Instructions**

a. Based on the information in these financial statements, compute the 2018 return on common stockholders' equity, debt to assets ratio, and return on assets for each company.

b. What conclusions concerning the companies' profitability can be drawn from these ratios? Which company relies more on debt to boost its return to common shareholders?

c. Compute the payout ratio for each company. Which pays out a higher percentage of its earnings?

## Interpreting Financial Statements

**CT9.3** Marriott Corporation split into two companies: **Host Marriott Corporation** and **Marriott International**. Host Marriott retained ownership of the corporation's vast hotel and other properties, while Marriott International, rather than owning hotels, managed them. The purpose of this split was to free Marriott International from the "baggage" associated with Host Marriott, thus allowing it to be more aggressive in its pursuit of growth. The following information (in millions) is provided for each corporation for their first full year operating as independent companies.

|  | Host Marriott | Marriott International |
|---|---|---|
| Sales revenue | $1,501 | $8,415 |
| Net income | (25) | 200 |
| Total assets | 3,822 | 3,207 |
| Total liabilities | 3,112 | 2,440 |
| Common stockholders' equity | 710 | 767 |

### Instructions

a. The two companies were split by the issuance of shares of Marriott International to all shareholders of the previous combined company. Discuss the nature of this transaction.

b. Calculate the debt to assets ratio for each company.

c. Calculate the return on assets and return on common stockholders' equity for each company.

d. The company's debtholders were fiercely opposed to the original plan to split the two companies because the original plan had Host Marriott absorbing the majority of the company's debt. They relented only when Marriott International agreed to absorb a larger share of the debt. Discuss the possible reasons the debtholders were opposed to the plan to split the company.

## Real-World Focus

**CT9.4** Use the stockholders' equity section of an annual report and identify the major components.

### Instructions

Select a company of your choice and search the Internet for "investor relations" and the name of the company to find its most recent annual report. Then, answer the following questions.

a. What is the company's name?

b. What classes of capital stock has the company issued?

c. For each class of stock:

   1. How many shares are authorized, issued, and/or outstanding?

   2. What is the par value?

d. What are the company's retained earnings?

e. Has the company acquired treasury stock? How many shares?

## Decision-Making Across the Organization

**CT9.5** During a recent period, the fast-food chain **Wendy's International** purchased many treasury shares. This caused the number of shares outstanding to fall from 124 million to 105 million. The following information was drawn from the company's financial statements (in millions).

|  | Information for the Year After Purchase of Treasury Stock | Information for the Year Before Purchase of Treasury Stock |
|---|---|---|
| Net income | $ 193.6 | $ 123.4 |
| Total assets | 2,076.0 | 1,837.9 |
| Average total assets | 2,016.9 | 1,889.8 |
| Total common stockholders' equity | 1,029.8 | 1,068.1 |
| Average common stockholders' equity | 1,078.0 | 1,126.2 |
| Total liabilities | 1,046.3 | 769.9 |
| Average total liabilities | 939.0 | 763.7 |
| Interest expense | 30.2 | 19.8 |
| Income taxes | 113.7 | 84.3 |
| Cash provided by operations | 305.2 | 233.8 |
| Cash dividends paid on common stock | 26.8 | 31.0 |
| Preferred stock dividends | 0.0 | 0.0 |
| Average number of common shares outstanding | 109.7 | 119.9 |

### Instructions

Use the information provided to answer the following questions.

a. Compute earnings per share, return on common stockholders' equity, and return on assets for both years. Discuss the change in the company's profitability over this period.

b. Compute the dividend payout ratio. Also compute the average cash dividend paid per share of common stock (dividends paid divided by the average number of common shares outstanding). Discuss any change in these ratios during this period and the implications for the company's dividend policy.

c. Compute the debt to assets ratio. Discuss the change in the company's solvency.

d. Based on your findings in (a) and (c), discuss to what extent any change in the return on common stockholders' equity was the result of increased reliance on debt.

e. Does it appear that the purchase of treasury stock and the shift toward more reliance on debt were wise strategic moves?

## Communication Activity

**CT9.6** Earl Kent, your uncle, is an inventor who has decided to incorporate. Uncle Earl knows that you are an accounting major at U.N.O. In a recent letter to you, he ends with the question, "I'm filling out a state incorporation application. Can you tell me the difference among the following terms: (1) authorized stock, (2) issued stock, (3) outstanding stock, and (4) preferred stock?"

### Instructions

In a brief note, differentiate for Uncle Earl the four different stock terms. Write the letter to be friendly, yet professional.

## Ethics Case

**CT9.7** The R&D division of Pele Corp. has just developed a chemical for sterilizing the vicious Brazilian "killer bees" which are invading Mexico and the southern United States. The president of Pele is anxious to get the chemical on the market because Pele profits need a boost—and his job is in jeopardy because of decreasing sales and profits. Pele has an opportunity to sell this chemical in Central American countries, where the laws are much more relaxed than in the United States.

The director of Pele's R&D division strongly recommends further research in the laboratory to test the side effects of this chemical on other insects, birds, animals, plants, and even humans. He cautions the president, "We could be sued from all sides if the chemical has tragic side effects that we didn't even test for in the lab." The president answers, "We can't wait an additional year for your lab tests. We can avoid losses from such lawsuits by establishing a separate wholly owned corporation to shield Pele Corp. from such lawsuits. We can't lose any more than our investment in the new corporation, and we'll invest just the patent covering this chemical. We'll reap the benefits if the chemical works and is safe, and avoid the losses from lawsuits if it's a disaster." The following week, Pele creates a new wholly owned corporation called Cabo Inc., sells the chemical patent to it for $10, and watches the spraying begin.

### Instructions

a. Who are the stakeholders in this situation?

b. Are the president's motives and actions ethical?

c. Can Pele shield itself against losses of Cabo Inc.?

## All About You

**CT9.8** In response to the Sarbanes-Oxley Act, many companies have implemented formal ethics codes. Many other organizations also have ethics codes.

### Instructions

Obtain the ethics code from an organization that you belong to (e.g., student organization, business school, employer, or a volunteer organization). Evaluate the ethics code based on how clearly it identifies proper and improper behavior. Discuss its strengths, and how it might be improved.

## Considering People, Planet, and Profit

**CT9.9** The December 10, 2011, edition of *The Economist* contains an article entitled "Helping the Poor to Save: Small Wonder." This article discusses how many of the world's poorest people benefit from borrowing small amounts of money.

### Instructions

Read the article and answer the following questions. (The article can be accessed by doing an Internet search that includes the title of the article and magazine.)

a. What monthly rate of interest do people pay on the loans they borrow from the microfinance organizations described in the article? What would these rates be on an annualized basis?

b. The rates described in your answer to part (a) are very high. Explain how somebody can pay such high rates and yet still benefit from borrowing.

c. Describe the structure of the typical village savings and loan organization.

## CHAPTER 10

Bloomberg/Getty Images

# Financial Analysis: The Big Picture

## Chapter Preview

We can all learn an important lesson from Warren Buffett: Study companies carefully if you wish to invest. Do not get caught up in fads but instead find companies that are financially healthy. Using some of the basic decision tools presented in this text, you can perform a rudimentary analysis on any company and draw basic conclusions about its financial health. Although it would not be wise for you to bet your life savings on a company's stock relying solely on your current level of knowledge, we strongly encourage you to practice your new skills wherever possible. Only with practice will you improve your ability to interpret financial numbers.

Before we unleash you on the world of high finance, we present a few more important concepts and techniques as well as one more comprehensive review of corporate financial statements. We use all of the decision tools presented in this text to analyze a single company, with comparisons to a competitor and industry averages.

# Feature Story

## It Pays to Be Patient

A recent issue of *Forbes* magazine listed **Warren Buffett** as the second richest person in the world. His estimated wealth was $69 billion, give or take a few million. How much is $69 billion? If you invested $69 billion in an investment earning just 4%, you could spend $7.6 million per day—every day—forever.

So, how does Buffett spend his money? Basically, he doesn't! He still lives in the same house that he purchased in Omaha, Nebraska, in 1958 for $31,500. He still drives his own car (a Cadillac DTS). And, in case you were thinking that his kids are riding the road to Easy Street, think again. Buffett has committed to donate virtually all of his money to charity before he dies.

How did Buffett amass this wealth? Through careful investing. Buffett epitomizes a "value investor." He applies the basic techniques he learned in the 1950s from the great value investor Benjamin Graham. He looks for companies that have good long-term potential but are currently underpriced. He invests in companies that have low exposure to debt and that reinvest their earnings for future growth. He does not get caught up in fads or the latest trends.

For example, Buffett sat out on the dot-com mania in the 1990s. When other investors put lots of money into fledgling high-tech firms, Buffett didn't bite because he did not find dot-com companies that met his criteria. He didn't get to enjoy the stock price boom on the way up, but on the other hand, he didn't have to ride the price back down to Earth. When the dot-com bubble burst, everyone else was suffering from investment shock. Buffett swooped in and scooped up deals on companies that he had been following for years.

In 2012, the stock market had again reached near record highs. Buffett's returns had been significantly lagging the market. Only 26% of his investments at that time were in stock, and he was sitting on $38 billion in cash. One commentator noted that "if the past is any guide, just when Buffett seems to look most like a loser, the party is about to end."

If you think you want to follow Buffett's example and transform your humble nest egg into a mountain of cash, be warned. His techniques have been widely circulated and emulated, but never practiced with the same degree of success. You should probably start by honing your financial analysis skills. A good way for you to begin your career as a successful investor is to master the fundamentals of financial analysis discussed in this chapter.

**Source:** Jason Zweig, "Buffett Is Out of Step," *Wall Street Journal* (May 7, 2012).

# Chapter Outline

| LEARNING OBJECTIVES | REVIEW | PRACTICE |
|---|---|---|
| **LO 1** Apply the concepts of sustainable income and quality of earnings. | • Sustainable income<br>• Quality of earnings | **DO IT! 1** Unusual Items |
| **LO 2** Apply horizontal analysis and vertical analysis. | • Horizontal analysis<br>• Vertical analysis | **DO IT! 2** Horizontal Analysis |
| **LO 3** Analyze a company's performance using ratio analysis. | • Liquidity ratios<br>• Solvency ratios<br>• Profitability ratios<br>• Financial analysis and data analytics<br>• Comprehensive example | **DO IT! 3** Ratio Analysis |

**Go to the Review and Practice section at the end of the chapter for a targeted summary and practice applications with solutions.**

**Visit WileyPLUS for additional tutorials and practice opportunities.**

# Sustainable Income and Quality of Earnings

## Sustainable Income

The value of a company like **Google** is a function of the amount, timing, and uncertainty of its future cash flows. Google's current and past income statements are particularly useful in helping analysts predict these future cash flows. In using this approach, analysts must make sure that Google's past income numbers reflect its **sustainable income**, that is, do not include unusual (out-of-the-ordinary) revenues, expenses, gains, and losses.

- **Sustainable income** is, therefore, the most likely level of income to be obtained by a company in the future.
- Sustainable income differs from actual net income by the amount of unusual revenues, expenses, gains, and losses included in the current year's income. Determining sustainable income requires an understanding of discontinued operations, comprehensive income, and changes in accounting principle.
- Analysts are interested in sustainable income because it helps them derive an estimate of future earnings without the "noise" of unusual items.

## Discontinued Operations

**Discontinued operations** refers to the disposal of a **significant component** of a business, such as the elimination of a major class of customers or an entire activity (see **Decision Tools**). For example, to downsize its operations, **General Dynamics Corp.** sold its missile business to **Hughes Aircraft Co.** for $450 million. In its income statement, General Dynamics reported the sale in a separate section entitled "Discontinued operations."

A company reports the disposal of a significant component as follows.

- When a company has discontinued operations, the company should report on its income statement both income from continuing operations and income (or loss) from discontinued operations.
- **The income (loss) from discontinued operations consists of two parts: the income (loss) from operations** and **the gain (loss) on disposal of the component.**
- The income from continuing operations as well as the discontinued component are reported net of tax.

To illustrate, assume that during 2022 Acro Energy Inc. has income before income taxes of $800,000. During 2022, Acro discontinued and sold its unprofitable chemical division. The loss in 2022 from chemical operations (net of $60,000 taxes) was $140,000. The loss on disposal of the chemical division (net of $30,000 taxes) was $70,000. Assuming a 30% tax rate on income, **Illustration 10.1** shows Acro's income statement (see **Helpful Hint**).

Note that the statement uses the caption "Income from continuing operations" and adds a new section "Discontinued operations."

- **The new section reports both the operating loss and the loss on disposal net of applicable income taxes.**
- This presentation clearly indicates the separate effects of continuing operations and discontinued operations on net income.

> **Decision Tools**
>
> The discontinued operations section alerts users to the sale of any of a company's major components of its business.

**ILLUSTRATION 10.1**
**Income statement**

### Acro Energy Inc.
#### Income Statement (partial)
#### For the Year Ended December 31, 2022

| | | |
|---|---:|---:|
| Income before income taxes | | $800,000 |
| Income tax expense | | 240,000 |
| Income from continuing operations | | 560,000 |
| **Discontinued operations** | | |
| **Loss from operation of chemical division, net of $60,000 income tax savings** | **$140,000** | |
| **Loss from disposal of chemical division, net of $30,000 income tax savings** | **70,000** | **210,000** |
| Net income | | $350,000 |

---

## Investor Insight

iStock.com/Andrey Armiagov

### What Does "Non-Recurring" Really Mean?

Many companies incur restructuring charges as they attempt to reduce costs. They often label these items in the income statement as "non-recurring" charges, to suggest that they are isolated events, unlikely to occur in future periods. The question for analysts is, are these costs really one-time, "non-recurring events" or do they reflect problems that the company will be facing for many periods in the future? If they are one-time events, then they can be largely ignored when trying to predict future earnings.

But, some companies report "one-time" restructuring charges over and over again. For example, **Procter & Gamble** reported a restructuring charge in 12 consecutive quarters, and **Motorola** had "special" charges in 14 consecutive quarters. On the other hand, other companies have a restructuring charge only once in a 5- or 10-year period. There appears to be no substitute for careful analysis of the numbers that comprise net income.

**If a company takes a large restructuring charge, what is the effect on the company's current income statement versus future ones? (Go to WileyPLUS for this answer and additional questions.)**

## Comprehensive Income

Most revenues, expenses, gains, and losses are included in net income.

- However, as discussed in earlier chapters, certain gains and losses that bypass net income are reported as part of a more inclusive earnings measure called comprehensive income.
- **Comprehensive income** is the sum of net income and other comprehensive income items.[1]

**Illustration of Comprehensive Income** Accounting standards require that companies adjust most investments in stocks and bonds up or down to their market price at the end of each accounting period. For example, assume that during 2022, its first year of operations, Stassi Corporation purchased **IBM** bonds for $10,500 as an investment, which it intends to sell sometime in the future. At the end of 2022, Stassi was still holding the investment, but the bonds' market price was now $8,000. In this case, Stassi is required to reduce the recorded value of its IBM investment by $2,500. The $2,500 difference is an "unrealized" loss. A gain or loss is referred to as unrealized when an asset has experienced a change in value but the owner has not sold the asset. The sale of the asset results in "realization" of the gain or loss.

Should Stassi include this $2,500 unrealized loss in net income? It depends on whether Stassi classifies the IBM bonds as a trading security or an available-for-sale security.

---

[1]The FASB's Conceptual Framework describes comprehensive income as including all changes in stockholders' equity during a period except those changes resulting from investments by stockholders and distributions to stockholders.

- A **trading security** is bought and held primarily for sale in the near term to generate income on short-term price differences.
- Companies report unrealized losses on trading securities in the "Other expenses and losses" section of the income statement.
- The rationale: It is likely that the company will realize the unrealized loss (or an unrealized gain), so the company should report the loss (gain) as part of net income.

If Stassi did not purchase the investment for trading purposes, it is classified as available-for-sale.

- **Available-for-sale securities** are held with the intent of selling them sometime in the future.
- Companies do not include unrealized gains or losses on available-for-sale securities in net income.
- Instead, they report them as part of "Other comprehensive income," which is not included in net income.

**Format**   Companies report other comprehensive income in a separate statement of comprehensive income. For example, assuming that Stassi Corporation has a net income of $300,000 and a 20% tax rate, the unrealized loss would be reported below net income, net of tax, as shown in **Illustration 10.2**.

**ILLUSTRATION 10.2**

**Statement of comprehensive income**

| Stassi Corporation | |
|---|---|
| **Statement of Comprehensive Income** | |
| **For the Year Ended December 31, 2022** | |
| Net income | $300,000 |
| Other comprehensive income | |
| Unrealized loss on available-for-sale securities, | |
| net of $500 income tax savings | 2,000 |
| Comprehensive income | $298,000 |

Companies report the cumulative amount of other comprehensive income from all years as a separate component of stockholders' equity. To illustrate, assume Stassi has common stock of $3,000,000, retained earnings of $300,000, and accumulated other comprehensive loss of $2,000. (To simplify, we are assuming that this is Stassi's first year of operations. Since it has only operated for one year, the cumulative amount of other comprehensive income is this year's loss of $2,000.) **Illustration 10.3** shows the balance sheet presentation of the accumulated other comprehensive loss.

**ILLUSTRATION 10.3**

**Unrealized loss in stockholders' equity section**

| Stassi Corporation | |
|---|---|
| **Balance Sheet (partial)** | |
| Stockholders' equity | |
| Common stock | $3,000,000 |
| Retained earnings | 300,000 |
| Total paid-in capital and retained earnings | 3,300,000 |
| **Accumulated other comprehensive loss** | **(2,000)** |
| Total stockholders' equity | $3,298,000 |

Note that the presentation of the accumulated other comprehensive loss is similar to the presentation of the cost of treasury stock in the stockholders' equity section. (An unrealized gain would be added in this section of the balance sheet.)

**Income Statement and Statement of Comprehensive Income** As discussed, many companies report net income and other comprehensive income in separate statements, such as those shown for Pace Corporation in **Illustration 10.4**.

**ILLUSTRATION 10.4**

**Income statement and statement of comprehensive income**

| Pace Corporation | | |
|---|---|---|
| **Income Statement** | | |
| **For the Year Ended December 31, 2022** | | |
| Net sales | | $440,000 |
| Cost of goods sold | | 260,000 |
| Gross profit | | 180,000 |
| Operating expenses | | 110,000 |
| Income from operations | | 70,000 |
| Other revenues and gains | | 5,600 |
| Other expenses and losses | | 9,600 |
| Income before income taxes | | 66,000 |
| Income tax expense ($66,000 × 30%) | | 19,800 |
| Income from continuing operations | | 46,200 |
| **Discontinued operations** | | |
| Loss from operation of plastics division, net of income tax savings $18,000 ($60,000 × 30%) | $42,000 | |
| Gain on disposal of plastics division, net of $15,000 income taxes ($50,000 × 30%) | 35,000 | 7,000 |
| Net income | | $39,200 |

| Pace Corporation | |
|---|---|
| **Statement of Comprehensive Income** | |
| **For the Year Ended December 31, 2022** | |
| Net income | $39,200 |
| **Other comprehensive income** | |
| Unrealized gain on available-for-sale securities, net of income taxes ($15,000 × 30%) | 10,500 |
| **Comprehensive income** | $49,700 |

- The income statement presents the types of items usually found on this statement, such as net sales, cost of goods sold, operating expenses, and income taxes.

- The income statement and statement of comprehensive income show how companies report discontinued operations and other comprehensive income (highlighted in red).

## Changes in Accounting Principle

> **Decision Tools**
>
> Informing users of a change in accounting principle helps them determine the effect of this change on current and prior periods.

For ease of comparison, users of financial statements expect companies to prepare their statements on a basis **consistent** with the preceding period.

- A **change in accounting principle** occurs when the principle used in the current year is different from the one used in the preceding year (see **Decision Tools**).
- An example is a change in inventory costing methods (such as FIFO to average-cost).
- Accounting rules permit a change when management can show that the new principle is preferable to the old principle.

Companies report most changes in accounting principle retroactively.[2] That is, they report both the current period and previous periods using the new principle. As a result, the same principle applies in all periods. This treatment improves the ability to compare results across years.

---

**Investor Insight**    United Parcel Service (UPS)

Larry MacDougal/
Canadian Press Images

### More Frequent Ups and Downs

In the past, U.S. companies used a method to account for their pension plans that smoothed out the gains and losses on their pension portfolios by spreading gains and losses over multiple years. Many felt that this approach was beneficial because it reduced the volatility of reported net income. However, recently some companies have opted to adopt a method that comes closer to recognizing gains and losses in the period in which they occur. Some of the companies that have adopted this approach are **United Parcel Service (UPS)**, **Honeywell International**, **IBM**, **AT&T**, and **Verizon Communications**. The CFO at UPS said he favored the new approach because "events that occurred in prior years will no longer distort current-year results. It will result in better transparency by eliminating the noise of past plan performance." When UPS switched, it resulted in a charge of $827 million from the change in accounting principle.

**Source:** Bob Sechler and Doug Cameron, "UPS Alters Pension-Plan Accounting," *Wall Street Journal* (January 30, 2012).

**When predicting future earnings, how should analysts treat the one-time charge that results from a switch to the different approach for accounting for pension plans? (Go to WileyPLUS for this answer and additional questions.)**

---

# Quality of Earnings

The quality of a company's earnings is of extreme importance to analysts.

- A company that has a high **quality of earnings** provides full and transparent information that will not confuse or mislead users of the financial statements.
- Recent accounting scandals suggest that some companies are spending too much time managing their income and not enough time managing their business.

Here are some of the factors affecting quality of earnings.

## Alternative Accounting Methods

Variations among companies in the application of generally accepted accounting principles (GAAP) may hamper comparability and reduce quality of earnings. For example, suppose one company uses the FIFO method of inventory costing, while another company in the same industry uses LIFO. If inventory is a significant asset to both companies, it is unlikely that their current ratios are comparable. For example, if **General Motors Corporation** used FIFO instead of LIFO for inventory valuation, its inventories in a recent year would have been 26% higher, which significantly affects the current ratio (and other ratios as well).

In addition to differences in inventory costing methods, differences also exist in reporting such items as depreciation and amortization. Although these differences in accounting methods might be detectable from reading the notes to the financial statements, adjusting the financial data to compensate for the different methods is often difficult, if not impossible.

## Pro Forma Income

Companies whose stock is publicly traded are required to present their income statement following GAAP.

- In recent years, many companies have been also reporting a second measure of income, called pro forma income.

---

[2]An exception to the general rule is a change in depreciation methods. The effects of this change are reported in current and future periods. Discussion of this approach is left for more advanced courses.

- **Pro forma income** usually excludes items that the company thinks are unusual or non-recurring.
- For example, in a recent year, **Cisco Systems** (a high-tech company) reported a quarterly net loss under GAAP of $2.7 billion. Cisco reported pro forma income for the same quarter as a profit of $230 million.

This large difference in profits between GAAP income numbers and pro forma income is not unusual. For example, during one nine-month period, the 100 largest companies on the Nasdaq stock exchange reported a total pro forma income of $19.1 billion but a total loss as measured by GAAP of $82.3 billion—a difference of about $100 billion!

To compute pro forma income, companies generally exclude any items they deem inappropriate for measuring their performance. Many analysts and investors are critical of the practice of using pro forma income because these numbers often make companies look better than they really are. As the financial press noted, pro forma numbers might be called "earnings before bad stuff." Companies, on the other hand, argue that pro forma numbers more clearly indicate sustainable income because they exclude unusual and non-recurring expenses. "Cisco's technique gives readers of financial statements a clear picture of Cisco's normal business activities," the company said in a statement issued in response to questions about its pro forma income accounting.

Recently, the SEC provided some guidance on how companies should present pro forma information. Stay tuned: Everyone seems to agree that pro forma numbers can be useful if they provide insights into determining a company's sustainable income. However, many companies have abused the flexibility that pro forma numbers allow and have used the measure as a way to put their companies in a more favorable light.

## Improper Recognition

Because some managers feel pressure from Wall Street to continually increase earnings, they manipulate earnings numbers to meet these expectations. The most common abuse is the improper recognition of revenue. One practice that some companies use is called **channel stuffing**.

- Offering deep discounts, companies encourage customers to buy early (stuff the channel) rather than later.
- This boosts the seller's earnings in the current period, but it often leads to a disaster in subsequent periods because customers have no need for additional goods.

To illustrate, **Bristol-Myers Squibb** at one time indicated that it used sales incentives to encourage wholesalers to buy more drugs than they needed. As a result, the company had to issue revised financial statements showing corrected revenues and income.

Another practice is the improper capitalization of operating expenses. **WorldCom** capitalized over $7 billion of operating expenses in order to report positive net income. In other situations, companies fail to report all their liabilities. **Enron** promised to make payments on certain contracts if financial difficulty developed, but these guarantees were not reported as liabilities. In addition, disclosure was so lacking in transparency that it was impossible to understand what was happening at the company.

---

**ACTION PLAN**
- **Show discontinued operations and other comprehensive income net of tax.**

### DO IT! 1 | Unusual Items

In its proposed 2022 income statement, AIR Corporation reports income before income taxes $400,000, unrealized gain on available-for-sale securities $100,000, income taxes $120,000 (not including unusual items), loss from operation of discontinued flower division $50,000, and loss on disposal of discontinued flower division $90,000. The income tax rate is 30%. Prepare a correct partial income statement, beginning with "Income before income taxes," and a statement of comprehensive income.

**Solution**

| AIR Corporation | | |
|---|---|---|
| **Income Statement (partial)** | | |
| **For the Year Ended December 31, 2022** | | |
| Income before income taxes | | $400,000 |
| Income tax expense | | 120,000 |
| Income from continuing operations | | 280,000 |
| Discontinued operations | | |
| Loss from operation of flower division, | | |
| net of $15,000 income tax savings | $35,000 | |
| Loss on disposal of flower division, | | |
| net of $27,000 income tax savings | 63,000 | 98,000 |
| Net income | | $182,000 |

| AIR Corporation | |
|---|---|
| **Statement of Comprehensive Income** | |
| **For the Year Ended December 31, 2022** | |
| Net income | $182,000 |
| Other comprehensive income | |
| Unrealized gain on available-for-sale | |
| securities, net of $30,000 income taxes | 70,000 |
| Comprehensive income | $252,000 |

Related exercise material: **BE10.1, BE10.2, DO IT! 10.1, E10.1,** and **E10.2.**

# Horizontal Analysis and Vertical Analysis

> **LEARNING OBJECTIVE 2**
>
> Apply horizontal analysis and vertical analysis.

In assessing the financial performance of a company, investors are interested in the core or sustainable earnings of a company. In addition, investors are interested in making comparisons from period to period. Throughout this text, we have relied on three types of comparisons to improve the decision-usefulness of financial information:

1. **Intracompany basis.** Comparisons within a company are often useful to detect changes in financial relationships and significant trends. For example, a comparison of **Kellogg**'s current year's cash amount with the prior year's cash amount shows either an increase or a decrease. Likewise, a comparison of Kellogg's year-end cash amount with the amount of its total assets at year-end shows the proportion of total assets in the form of cash.

2. **Intercompany basis.** Comparisons with other companies provide insight into a company's competitive position. For example, investors can compare Kellogg's total sales for the year with the total sales of its competitors in the breakfast cereal area, such as **General Mills**.

3. **Industry averages.** Comparisons with industry averages provide information about a company's relative position within the industry. For example, financial statement readers can compare Kellogg's financial data with the averages for its industry compiled by financial rating organizations such as **Dun & Bradstreet**, **Moody's**, and **Standard & Poor's**, or with information provided on the Internet by organizations such as **Yahoo!** on its financial site.

We use three basic tools in financial statement analysis to highlight the significance of financial statement data:

1. Horizontal analysis.
2. Vertical analysis.
3. Ratio analysis.

In previous chapters, we relied primarily on ratio analysis, supplemented with some basic horizontal and vertical analysis. In the remainder of this section, we introduce more formal forms of horizontal and vertical analysis. In the next section, we review ratio analysis in some detail.

# Horizontal Analysis

**Horizontal analysis**, also known as trend analysis, is a technique for evaluating a series of financial statement data over a period of time (see **Decision Tools**). Its purpose is to determine the increase or decrease that has taken place, expressed as either an amount or a percentage. For example, here are recent net sales figures (in thousands) of Chicago Cereal Company:

| 2022 | 2021 | 2020 | 2019 | 2018 |
|------|------|------|------|------|
| $11,776 | $10,907 | $10,177 | $9,614 | $8,812 |

If we assume that 2018 is the base year, we can measure all percentage increases or decreases relative to this base-period amount with the formula shown in **Illustration 10.5**.

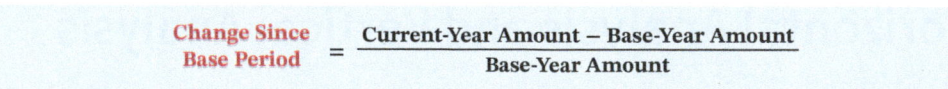

$$\text{Change Since Base Period} = \frac{\text{Current-Year Amount} - \text{Base-Year Amount}}{\text{Base-Year Amount}}$$

Using horizontal analysis, we can determine the following.

- Net sales for Chicago Cereal increased approximately 9.1% [($9,614 − $8,812) ÷ $8,812] from 2018 to 2019.
- Net sales increased by 33.6% [($11,776 − $8,812) ÷ $8,812] from 2018 to 2022.

Alternatively, we can express current-year sales as a percentage of the base period. To do so, we would divide the current-year amount by the base-year amount, as shown in **Illustration 10.6**.

$$\text{Current Results in Relation to Base Period} = \frac{\text{Current-Year Amount}}{\text{Base-Year Amount}}$$

Current-period sales expressed as a percentage of the base period for each of the five years, using 2018 as the base period, are shown in **Illustration 10.7**.

**Chicago Cereal Company**
Net Sales (in thousands)
Base Period 2018

| 2022 | 2021 | 2020 | 2019 | 2018 |
|------|------|------|------|------|
| $11,776 | $10,907 | $10,177 | $9,614 | $8,812 |
| 133.6% | 123.8% | 115.5% | 109.1% | 100% |

**ILLUSTRATION 10.7**
Horizontal analysis of net sales

The large increase in net sales during 2019 would raise questions regarding possible reasons for such a significant change. Chicago Cereal's 2019 notes to the financial statements explain that the company completed an acquisition of Elf Foods Company during 2019. This major acquisition would help explain the increase in sales highlighted by horizontal analysis.

To further illustrate horizontal analysis, we use the financial statements of Chicago Cereal Company. Its two-year condensed balance sheets for 2022 and 2021, showing dollar and percentage changes, are presented in **Illustration 10.8** (see **Helpful Hint**).

**Chicago Cereal Company**
Condensed Balance Sheets
December 31 (in thousands)

| | 2022 | 2021 | Increase (Decrease) during 2022 Amount | Percent |
|---|---|---|---|---|
| **Assets** | | | | |
| Current assets | $ 2,717 | $ 2,427 | $290 | 11.9 |
| Property assets (net) | 2,990 | 2,816 | 174 | 6.2 |
| Other assets | 5,690 | 5,471 | 219 | 4.0 |
| Total assets | $11,397 | $10,714 | $683 | 6.4 |
| **Liabilities and Stockholders' Equity** | | | | |
| Current liabilities | $ 4,044 | $ 4,020 | $ 24 | 0.6 |
| Long-term liabilities | 4,827 | 4,625 | 202 | 4.4 |
| Total liabilities | 8,871 | 8,645 | 226 | 2.6 |
| Stockholders' equity | | | | |
| Common stock | 493 | 397 | 96 | 24.2 |
| Retained earnings | 3,390 | 2,584 | 806 | 31.2 |
| Treasury stock (cost) | (1,357) | (912) | 445 | 48.8 |
| Total stockholders' equity | 2,526 | 2,069 | 457 | 22.1 |
| Total liabilities and stockholders' equity | $11,397 | $10,714 | $683 | 6.4 |

**ILLUSTRATION 10.8**
Horizontal analysis of balance sheets

**HELPFUL HINT**
When using horizontal analysis, be sure to examine both dollar amount changes and percentage changes. It is not necessarily bad if a company's earnings are growing at a declining rate. The amount of increase may be the same as or more than the base year, but the percentage change may be less because the base is greater each year.

The comparative balance sheets show that a number of changes occurred in Chicago Cereal's financial position from 2021 to 2022.

- In the assets section, current assets increased $290,000, or 11.9% ($290 ÷ $2,427), and property assets (net) increased $174,000, or 6.2%. Other assets increased $219,000, or 4.0%.
- In the liabilities section, current liabilities increased $24,000, or 0.6%, while long-term liabilities increased $202,000, or 4.4%.
- In the stockholders' equity section, we find that retained earnings increased $806,000, or 31.2%.

**Illustration 10.9** presents two-year comparative income statements of Chicago Cereal Company for 2022 and 2021, showing dollar and percentage changes (see **Helpful Hint**).

**HELPFUL HINT**

The increase in the Amount column of $99 results from adding and subtracting the amounts shown. In the Percent column, the 9.9% cannot be determined by adding and subtracting the percentages shown.

### Chicago Cereal Company
#### Condensed Income Statements
#### For the Years Ended December 31 (in thousands)

| | 2022 | 2021 | Increase (Decrease) during 2022 Amount | Increase (Decrease) during 2022 Percent |
|---|---|---|---|---|
| Net sales | $11,776 | $10,907 | $869 | 8.0 |
| Cost of goods sold | 6,597 | 6,082 | 515 | 8.5 |
| Gross profit | 5,179 | 4,825 | 354 | 7.3 |
| Selling and administrative expenses | 3,311 | 3,059 | 252 | 8.2 |
| Income from operations | 1,868 | 1,766 | 102 | 5.8 |
| Interest expense | 321 | 294 | 27 | 9.2 |
| Income before income taxes | 1,547 | 1,472 | 75 | 5.1 |
| Income tax expense | 444 | 468 | (24) | (5.1) |
| Net income | $ 1,103 | $ 1,004 | $ 99 | 9.9 |

Horizontal analysis of the income statements shows the following changes.

- Net sales increased $869,000, or 8.0% ($869 ÷ $10,907).
- Cost of goods sold increased $515,000, or 8.5% ($515 ÷ $6,082).
- Selling and administrative expenses increased $252,000, or 8.2% ($252 ÷ $3,059).
- Overall, gross profit increased 7.3% and net income increased 9.9%. The increase in net income can be attributed to the increase in net sales and a decrease in income tax expense.

The measurement of changes from period to period in percentages is relatively straightforward and quite useful. However, complications can result in making the computations. If an item has no value in a base year or preceding year and a value in the next year, no percentage change can be computed.

# Vertical Analysis

**Decision Tools**

Vertical analysis helps users compare relationships between financial statement items with those of last year or of competitors.

**Vertical analysis**, also called common-size analysis, is a technique for evaluating financial statement data that expresses each item in a financial statement as a **percentage of a base amount** (see **Decision Tools**). For example, on a balance sheet we might express current assets as 22% of total assets (total assets being the base amount). Or, on an income statement we might express selling expenses as 16% of net sales (net sales being the base amount).

Presented in **Illustration 10.10** are the comparative balance sheets of Chicago Cereal for 2022 and 2021, analyzed vertically. The base for the asset items is **total assets**, and the base for the liability and stockholders' equity items is **total liabilities and stockholders' equity**.

### Chicago Cereal Company
#### Condensed Balance Sheets
#### December 31 (in thousands)

| | 2022 Amount | 2022 Percent* | 2021 Amount | 2021 Percent* |
|---|---|---|---|---|
| **Assets** | | | | |
| Current assets | $ 2,717 | 23.8 | $ 2,427 | 22.6 |
| Property assets (net) | 2,990 | 26.2 | 2,816 | 26.3 |
| Other assets | 5,690 | 50.0 | 5,471 | 51.1 |
| Total assets | $11,397 | 100.0 | $10,714 | 100.0 |

ILLUSTRATION 10.10

*(continued)*

| | 2022 | | 2021 | |
|---|---|---|---|---|
| | Amount | Percent* | Amount | Percent* |
| **Liabilities and Stockholders' Equity** | | | | |
| Current liabilities | $ 4,044 | 35.5 | $ 4,020 | 37.5 |
| Long-term liabilities | 4,827 | 42.4 | 4,625 | 43.2 |
| Total liabilities | 8,871 | 77.9 | 8,645 | 80.7 |
| Stockholders' equity | | | | |
| Common stock | 493 | 4.3 | 397 | 3.7 |
| Retained earnings | 3,390 | 29.7 | 2,584 | 24.1 |
| Treasury stock (cost) | (1,357) | (11.9) | (912) | (8.5) |
| Total stockholders' equity | 2,526 | 22.1 | 2,069 | 19.3 |
| Total liabilities and stockholders' equity | $11,397 | 100.0 | $10,714 | 100.0 |

*Numbers have been rounded to total 100%.

In addition to showing the relative size of each category on the balance sheets, vertical analysis can show the percentage change in the individual asset, liability, and stockholders' equity items.

- Current assets increased $290,000 from 2021 to 2022, and they increased from 22.6% to 23.8% of total assets.
- Property assets (net) decreased from 26.3% to 26.2% of total assets.
- Other assets decreased from 51.1% to 50.0% of total assets.
- Retained earnings increased by $806,000 from 2021 to 2022, and total stockholders' equity increased from 19.3% to 22.1% of total liabilities and stockholders' equity.

This switch to a higher percentage of equity financing has two causes.

1. While total liabilities increased by $226,000, the percentage of liabilities declined from 80.7% to 77.9% of total liabilities and stockholders' equity.
2. Retained earnings increased by $806,000, from 24.1% to 29.7% of total liabilities and stockholders' equity.

Thus, the company shifted toward equity financing by relying less on debt and by increasing the amount of retained earnings.

Vertical analysis of the comparative income statements of Chicago Cereal, shown in **Illustration 10.11**, reveals the following.

ILLUSTRATION 10.11

**Vertical analysis of income statements**

| **Chicago Cereal Company** | | | | |
|---|---|---|---|---|
| **Condensed Income Statements** | | | | |
| **For the Years Ended December 31 (in thousands)** | | | | |
| | 2022 | | 2021 | |
| | Amount | Percent* | Amount | Percent* |
| Net sales | $11,776 | 100.0 | $10,907 | 100.0 |
| Cost of goods sold | 6,597 | 56.0 | 6,082 | 55.8 |
| Gross profit | 5,179 | 44.0 | 4,825 | 44.2 |
| Selling and administrative expenses | 3,311 | 28.1 | 3,059 | 28.0 |
| Income from operations | 1,868 | 15.9 | 1,766 | 16.2 |
| Interest expense | 321 | 2.7 | 294 | 2.7 |
| Income before income taxes | 1,547 | 13.2 | 1,472 | 13.5 |
| Income tax expense | 444 | 3.8 | 468 | 4.3 |
| Net income | $ 1,103 | 9.4 | $ 1,004 | 9.2 |

*Numbers have been rounded to total 100%.

- Cost of goods sold **as a percentage of net sales** increased from 55.8% to 56.0%, and selling and administrative expenses increased from 28.0% to 28.1%.
- Net income as a percentage of net sales increased from 9.2% to 9.4%. Chicago Cereal's increase in net income as a percentage of sales is due primarily to the decrease in income tax expense as a percentage of sales.

Vertical analysis also enables you to compare companies of different sizes. For example, one of Chicago Cereal's competitors is Giant Mills. Giant Mills' sales are 1,000 times larger than those of Chicago Cereal. Vertical analysis enables us to meaningfully compare the condensed income statements of Chicago Cereal and Giant Mills, as shown in **Illustration 10.12**.

**ILLUSTRATION 10.12**

**Intercompany comparison by vertical analysis**

| Condensed Income Statements <br> For the Year Ended December 31, 2022 | | | | |
|---|---|---|---|---|
| | Chicago Cereal (in thousands) | | Giant Mills, Inc. (in millions) | |
| | Amount | Percent* | Amount | Percent* |
| Net sales | $11,776 | 100.0 | $17,910 | 100.0 |
| Cost of goods sold | 6,597 | 56.0 | 11,540 | 64.4 |
| Gross profit | 5,179 | 44.0 | 6,370 | 35.6 |
| Selling and administrative expenses | 3,311 | 28.1 | 3,474 | 19.4 |
| Non-recurring charges and (gains) | 0 | — | (62) | (0.3) |
| Income from operations | 1,868 | 15.9 | 2,958 | 16.5 |
| Other expenses and revenues (including income taxes) | 765 | 6.5 | 1,134 | 6.3 |
| Net income | $ 1,103 | 9.4 | $ 1,824 | 10.2 |

*Numbers have been rounded to total 100%.

Although Chicago Cereal's net sales are much less than those of Giant Mills, vertical analysis eliminates the impact of this size difference for our analysis.

- Chicago Cereal has a higher gross profit percentage of 44.0%, compared to 35.6% for Giant Mills.
- But, Chicago Cereal's selling and administrative expenses are 28.1% of net sales, while those of Giant Mills are 19.4% of net sales.
- Looking at net income, we see that Chicago Cereal's net income as a percentage of net sales is 9.4%, compared to 10.2% for Giant Mills.

## Anatomy of a Fraud

Sometimes relationships between numbers can be used to detect fraud. Financial ratios that appear abnormal or statistical abnormalities in the numbers themselves can reveal fraud. For example, the fact that **WorldCom**'s line costs, as a percentage of either total expenses or revenues, differed very significantly from those of its competitors should have alerted people to the possibility of fraud. Or, consider the case of a bank manager, who cooperated with a group of his friends to defraud the bank's credit card department. The manager's friends would apply for credit cards and then run up balances of slightly less than $5,000. The bank had a policy of allowing bank personnel to write off balances of less than $5,000 without seeking supervisor approval.

The fraud was detected by applying statistical analysis based on Benford's Law. Benford's Law states that in a random collection of numbers, the frequency of lower digits (e.g., 1, 2, or 3) should be much higher than that of higher digits (e.g., 7, 8, or 9). In this case, bank auditors analyzed the first two digits of amounts written off. There was a spike at 48 and 49, which was not consistent with what would be expected if the numbers were random.

**Total take: Thousands of dollars**

**The Missing Control**

**Independent internal verification.** While it might be efficient to allow employees to write off accounts below a certain level, it is important that these write-offs be reviewed and verified periodi-

cally. Such a review would likely call attention to an employee with large amounts of write-offs, or in this case, write-offs that were frequently very close to the approval threshold.

**Source:** Mark J. Nigrini, "I've Got Your Number," *Journal of Accountancy Online* (May 1999).

---

## DO IT! 2 | Horizontal Analysis

Summary financial information for Rosepatch Company is as follows.

|  | December 31, 2022 | December 31, 2021 |
|---|---|---|
| Current assets | $234,000 | $180,000 |
| Plant assets (net) | 756,000 | 420,000 |
| Total assets | $990,000 | $600,000 |

Compute the amount and percentage changes in 2022 using horizontal analysis, assuming 2021 is the base year.

### Solution

|  | Increase in 2022 | |
|---|---|---|
|  | **Amount** | **Percent** |
| Current assets | $ 54,000 | 30% [($234,000 − $180,000) ÷ $180,000] |
| Plant assets (net) | 336,000 | 80% [($756,000 − $420,000) ÷ $420,000] |
| Total assets | $390,000 | 65% [($990,000 − $600,000) ÷ $600,000] |

Related exercise material: **BE10.4, BE10.6, BE10.7, BE10.9, DO IT! 10.2, E10.3, E10.5, and E10.6.**

**ACTION PLAN**

- **Find the percentage change by dividing the amount of the increase by the 2021 amount (base year).**

---

# Ratio Analysis

### LEARNING OBJECTIVE 3
Analyze a company's performance using ratio analysis.

**Ratio analysis** expresses the relationship among selected items of financial statement data (see **Decision Tools**).

- A **ratio** expresses the mathematical relationship between one quantity and another.
- The relationship is expressed in terms of either a percentage, a rate, or a simple proportion.

To illustrate, in a recent year, **Nike, Inc.** had current assets of $13,626 million and current liabilities of $3,926 million. We can find the relationship between these two measures by dividing current assets by current liabilities. The alternative means of expression are as follows.

**Decision Tools**

Ratio analysis helps users evaluate mathematical relationships between financial statement items and compare across years, competitors, and industry.

**Percentage:** Current assets are 347% of current liabilities.
**Rate:** Current assets are 3.47 times current liabilities.
**Proportion:** The relationship of current assets to liabilities is 3.47:1.

To analyze the primary financial statements, we can use ratios to evaluate liquidity, profitability, and solvency. **Illustration 10.13** describes these classifications.

**ILLUSTRATION 10.13**
**Financial ratio classifications**

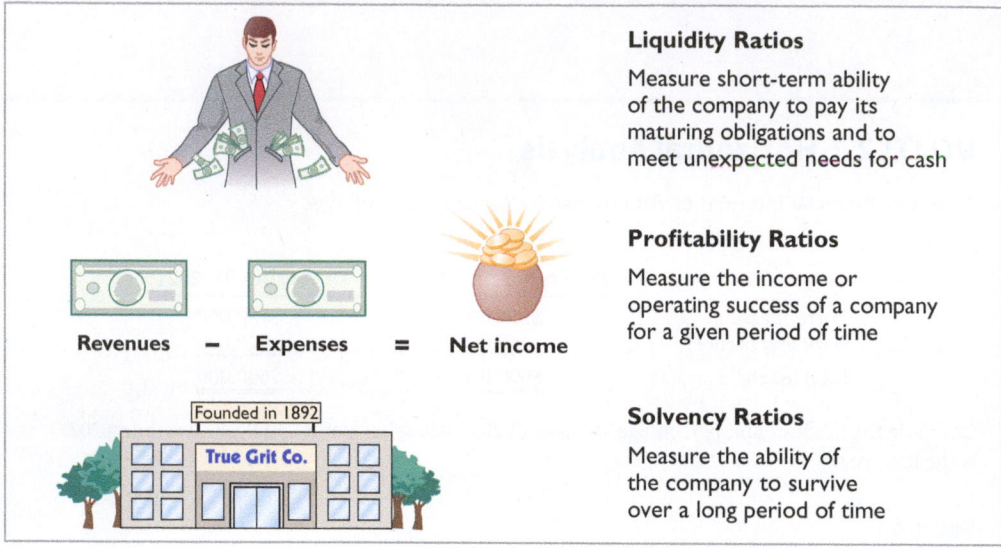

**Liquidity Ratios**

Measure short-term ability of the company to pay its maturing obligations and to meet unexpected needs for cash

**Revenues − Expenses = Net income**

**Profitability Ratios**

Measure the income or operating success of a company for a given period of time

Founded in 1892

True Grit Co.

**Solvency Ratios**

Measure the ability of the company to survive over a long period of time

Ratios can provide clues to underlying conditions that may not be apparent from individual financial statement components. However, a single ratio by itself is not very meaningful. Thus, in the discussion of ratios we will use the following types of comparisons.

1. **Intracompany comparisons** for two years for Chicago Cereal.
2. **Industry average comparisons** based on median ratios for the industry.
3. **Intercompany comparisons** based on Giant Mills as Chicago Cereal's principal competitor.

## Liquidity Ratios

**Liquidity ratios** (**Illustration 10.14**) measure the short-term ability of the company to pay its maturing obligations and to meet unexpected needs for cash. Short-term creditors such as bankers and suppliers are particularly interested in assessing liquidity.

**ILLUSTRATION 10.14**
**Summary of liquidity ratios**

**Liquidity Ratios**

| | |
|---|---|
| Working capital | Current assets − Current liabilities |
| Current ratio | $\dfrac{\text{Current assets}}{\text{Current liabilities}}$ |
| Inventory turnover | $\dfrac{\text{Cost of goods sold}}{\text{Average inventory}}$ |
| Days in inventory | $\dfrac{365 \text{ days}}{\text{Inventory turnover}}$ |
| Accounts receivable turnover | $\dfrac{\text{Net credit sales}}{\text{Average net accounts receivable}}$ |
| Average collection period | $\dfrac{365 \text{ days}}{\text{Accounts receivable turnover}}$ |

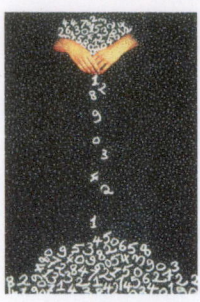
#### How to Manage the Current Ratio

The apparent simplicity of the current ratio can have real-world limitations because adding equal amounts to both the numerator and the denominator causes the ratio to decrease.

　　Assume, for example, that a company has $2,000,000 of current assets and $1,000,000 of current liabilities. Its current ratio is 2:1. If it purchases $1,000,000 of inventory on account, it will have $3,000,000 of current assets and $2,000,000 of current liabilities. Its current ratio decreases to 1.5:1. If, instead, the company pays off $500,000 of its current liabilities, it will have $1,500,000 of current assets and $500,000 of current liabilities. Its current ratio increases to 3:1. Thus, any trend analysis should be done with care because the ratio is susceptible to quick changes and is easily influenced by management.

**How might management influence a company's current ratio? (Go to WileyPLUS for this answer and additional questions.)**

## Solvency Ratios

Solvency ratios (**Illustration 10.15**) measure the ability of the company to survive over a long period of time. Long-term creditors and stockholders are interested in a company's long-run solvency, particularly its ability to pay interest as it comes due and to repay the balance of debt at its maturity.

**ILLUSTRATION 10.15**

**Summary of solvency ratios**

| Solvency Ratios | |
|---|---|
| Debt to assets ratio | $\dfrac{\text{Total liabilities}}{\text{Total assets}}$ |
| Times interest earned | $\dfrac{\text{Net income} + \text{Interest expense} + \text{Income tax expense}}{\text{Interest expense}}$ |
| Free cash flow | $\dfrac{\text{Net cash provided}}{\text{by operating activities}} - \dfrac{\text{Capital}}{\text{expenditures}} - \dfrac{\text{Cash}}{\text{dividends}}$ |

## Profitability Ratios

Profitability ratios (**Illustration 10.16**) measure the income or operating success of a company for a given period of time. A company's income, or lack of it, affects its ability to obtain debt and equity financing, its liquidity position, and its ability to grow. As a consequence, creditors and investors alike are interested in evaluating profitability. Profitability is frequently used as the ultimate test of management's operating effectiveness.

**ILLUSTRATION 10.16**

**Summary of profitability ratios**

| Profitability Ratios | |
|---|---|
| Earnings per share | $\dfrac{\text{Net income} - \text{Preferred dividends}}{\text{Weighted-average common shares outstanding}}$ |
| Price-earnings ratio | $\dfrac{\text{Market price per share}}{\text{Earnings per share}}$ |
| Gross profit rate | $\dfrac{\text{Gross profit}}{\text{Net sales}}$ |
| Profit margin | $\dfrac{\text{Net income}}{\text{Net sales}}$ |
| Return on assets | $\dfrac{\text{Net income}}{\text{Average total assets}}$ |
| Asset turnover | $\dfrac{\text{Net sales}}{\text{Average total assets}}$ |
| Payout ratio | $\dfrac{\text{Cash dividends declared on common stock}}{\text{Net income}}$ |
| Return on common stockholders' equity | $\dfrac{\text{Net income} - \text{Preferred dividends}}{\text{Average common stockholders' equity}}$ |

iStock.com/Ferran
Traite Soler

### High Ratings Can Bring Low Returns

**Moody's**, **Standard & Poor's**, and **Fitch** are three big firms that perform financial analysis on publicly traded companies and then publish ratings of the companies' creditworthiness. Investors and lenders rely heavily on these ratings in making investment and lending decisions. Some people feel that the collapse of the financial markets in 2008 was worsened by inadequate research reports and ratings provided by the financial rating agencies. Critics contend that the rating agencies were reluctant to give large companies low ratings because they feared that by offending them they would lose out on business opportunities. For example, the rating agencies gave many so-called mortgage-backed securities ratings that suggested that they were low risk. Later, many of these very securities became completely worthless. Steps have been taken to reduce the conflicts of interest that lead to these faulty ratings.

**Sources:** Aaron Lucchetti and Judith Burns, "Moody's CEO Warned Profit Push Posed a Risk to Quality of Ratings," *Wall Street Journal Online* (October 23, 2008); and Alan S. Binder, "A Better Way to Run Rating Agencies," *Wall Street Journal* (April 17, 2014).

**Why are credit rating agencies important to the financial markets? (Go to WileyPLUS for this answer and additional questions.)**

## Financial Analysis and Data Analytics

In the age of "Big Data," opportunities for investors to apply data analytics to financial data are boundless. Immense quantities and types of data are available to investors. Free financial data about corporations, for example, can be obtained from the SEC's Edgar database and other sources. Alternatively, database services such as Compustat and WorldScope sell financial and other information regarding a wide range of company and industry characteristics. In addition, each day massive amounts of trading data are collected from financial exchanges.

Professional analysts employ sophisticated computerized valuation models that use financial, nonfinancial, and trading data to identify investment opportunities.

- Since these valuation models frequently rely heavily on accounting data, it is important to have a sound understanding of the financial accounting standards on which the numbers used in the models are based.
- If you desire to someday use data analytics to evaluate companies, the accounting skills and financial analysis tools acquired in this course are a good start.

## Comprehensive Example of Ratio Analysis

In this section, we provide a comprehensive review of ratios used for evaluating the financial health and performance of a company. We use the financial information in **Illustrations 10.17** through **10.20** to calculate Chicago Cereal Company's 2022 ratios. You can use these data to review the computations.

**ILLUSTRATION 10.17**

Chicago Cereal Company's balance sheets

| Chicago Cereal Company | | |
|---|---|---|
| **Balance Sheets** | | |
| **December 31 (in thousands)** | | |
| | **2022** | **2021** |
| **Assets** | | |
| Current assets | | |
| Cash | $ 524 | $ 411 |
| Accounts receivable | 1,026 | 945 |
| Inventory | 924 | 824 |
| Prepaid expenses and other current assets | 243 | 247 |
| Total current assets | 2,717 | 2,427 |
| Property assets (net) | 2,990 | 2,816 |
| Intangibles and other assets | 5,690 | 5,471 |
| Total assets | $11,397 | $10,714 |

|  | 2022 | 2021 |
|---|---|---|
| **Liabilities and Stockholders' Equity** | | |
| Current liabilities | $ 4,044 | $ 4,020 |
| Long-term liabilities | 4,827 | 4,625 |
| Stockholders' equity—common | 2,526 | 2,069 |
| Total liabilities and stockholders' equity | $11,397 | $10,714 |

**ILLUSTRATION 10.17**

*(continued)*

## Chicago Cereal Company
### Condensed Income Statements
### For the Years Ended December 31 (in thousands)

|  | 2022 | 2021 |
|---|---|---|
| Net sales | $11,776 | $10,907 |
| Cost of goods sold | 6,597 | 6,082 |
| Gross profit | 5,179 | 4,825 |
| Selling and administrative expenses | 3,311 | 3,059 |
| Income from operations | 1,868 | 1,766 |
| Interest expense | 321 | 294 |
| Income before income taxes | 1,547 | 1,472 |
| Income tax expense | 444 | 468 |
| Net income | $ 1,103 | $ 1,004 |

**ILLUSTRATION 10.18**

Chicago Cereal Company's income statements

## Chicago Cereal Company
### Condensed Statements of Cash Flows
### For the Years Ended December 31 (in thousands)

|  | 2022 | 2021 |
|---|---|---|
| Cash flows from operating activities | | |
| Cash receipts from operating activities | $11,695 | $10,841 |
| Cash payments for operating activities | (10,192) | (9,431) |
| Net cash provided by operating activities | 1,503 | 1,410 |
| Cash flows from investing activities | | |
| Purchases of property, plant, and equipment | (472) | (453) |
| Other investing activities | (129) | 8 |
| Net cash used in investing activities | (601) | (445) |
| Cash flows from financing activities | | |
| Issuance of common stock | 163 | 218 |
| Issuance of debt | 2,179 | 721 |
| Reductions of debt | (2,011) | (650) |
| Payment of dividends | (475) | (450) |
| Repurchase of common stock and other items | (645) | (612) |
| Net cash provided (used) by financing activities | (789) | (773) |
| Increase (decrease) in cash and cash equivalents | 113 | 192 |
| Cash and cash equivalents at beginning of year | 411 | 219 |
| Cash and cash equivalents at end of year | $ 524 | $ 411 |

**ILLUSTRATION 10.19**

Chicago Cereal Company's statements of cash flows

**Additional information:**

|  | 2022 | 2021 |
|---|---|---|
| Weighted-average number of shares (thousands) | 418.7 | 418.5 |
| Stock price at year-end | $52.92 | $50.06 |

**ILLUSTRATION 10.20**

Additional information for Chicago Cereal Company

As indicated in the chapter, we can classify ratios into three types for analysis of the primary financial statements:

1. **Liquidity ratios.** Measures of the short-term ability of the company to pay its maturing obligations and to meet unexpected needs for cash.

2. **Solvency ratios.** Measures of the ability of the company to survive over a long period of time.

3. **Profitability ratios.** Measures of the income or operating success of a company for a given period of time.

As a tool of analysis, ratios can provide clues to underlying conditions that may not be apparent from an inspection of the individual components of a particular ratio. But, a single ratio by itself is not very meaningful. Accordingly, in this discussion we use the following three comparisons.

1. **Intracompany comparisons** covering two years for Chicago Cereal (using comparative financial information from Illustrations 10.17 through 10.20).

2. **Intercompany comparisons** using Giant Mills as one of Chicago Cereal's competitors.

3. **Industry average comparisons** based on **MSN.com** median ratios for manufacturers of flour and other grain mill products and comparisons with other sources. For some of the ratios that we use, industry comparisons are not available (denoted "na").

## Liquidity Ratios

Liquidity ratios measure the short-term ability of the company to pay its maturing obligations and to meet unexpected needs for cash.

- Short-term creditors such as bankers and suppliers are particularly interested in assessing liquidity.
- The measures used to determine the company's short-term debt-paying ability are the current ratio, the accounts receivable turnover, the average collection period, the inventory turnover, and days in inventory.

1. **Current ratio.** The **current ratio** expresses the relationship of current assets to current liabilities, computed by dividing current assets by current liabilities. It is widely used for evaluating a company's liquidity and short-term debt-paying ability. The 2022 and 2021 current ratios for Chicago Cereal and comparative data are shown in **Illustration 10.21**.

**ILLUSTRATION 10.21** Current ratio

| Ratio | Formula | Chicago Cereal | | Giant Mills | Industry Average |
|---|---|---|---|---|---|
| | | 2022 | 2021 | 2022 | |
| Current ratio | $\dfrac{\text{Current assets}}{\text{Current liabilities}}$ | $\dfrac{\$2,717}{\$4,044} = .67$ | .60 | .67 | 1.06 |

What do the measures tell us?

- Chicago Cereal's 2022 current ratio of .67 means that for every dollar of current liabilities, it has $0.67 of current assets. (We sometimes state such ratios as .67:1 to reinforce this interpretation.)
- Its current ratio—and therefore its liquidity—increased significantly in 2022.
- It is well below the industry average but the same as that of Giant Mills.

2. **Accounts receivable turnover.** Analysts can measure liquidity by how quickly a company converts certain assets to cash. A low value for the current ratio can sometimes be compensated for if some of the company's current assets are highly liquid.

How liquid, for example, are the receivables? The ratio used to assess the liquidity of the receivables is the **accounts receivable turnover**, which measures the number of times, on average, a company collects receivables during the period. The accounts receivable turnover is computed by dividing net credit sales (net sales less cash sales) by average net accounts receivable during the year. The accounts receivable turnover for Chicago Cereal is shown in **Illustration 10.22**.

**ILLUSTRATION 10.22** Accounts receivable turnover

| Ratio | Formula | Chicago Cereal 2022 | 2021 | Giant Mills 2022 | Industry Average |
|-------|---------|---------------------|------|------------------|------------------|
| Accounts receivable turnover | $\dfrac{\text{Net credit sales}}{\text{Average net accounts receivable}}$ | $\dfrac{\$11,776}{(\$1,026 + \$945) \div 2} = 11.9$ | 12.0 | 12.2 | 11.2 |

In computing the rate, we assumed that all Chicago Cereal's sales are credit sales.

- Its accounts receivable turnover declined slightly in 2022.
- The turnover of 11.9 times is higher than the industry average of 11.2 times, and slightly lower than Giant Mills' turnover of 12.2 times.
- A higher value suggests better liquidity because the receivables are being collected more quickly.

3. **Average collection period.**   A popular variant of the accounts receivable turnover converts it into an **average collection period** in days. This is done by dividing the accounts receivable turnover into 365 days. The average collection period for Chicago Cereal is shown in **Illustration 10.23**.

**ILLUSTRATION 10.23**   Average collection period

| Ratio | Formula | Chicago Cereal 2022 | 2021 | Giant Mills 2022 | Industry Average |
|-------|---------|---------------------|------|------------------|------------------|
| Average collection period | $\dfrac{365 \text{ days}}{\text{Accounts receivable turnover}}$ | $\dfrac{365}{11.9} = 30.7$ | 30.4 | 29.9 | 32.6 |

Chicago Cereal's 2022 accounts receivable turnover of 11.9 times is divided into 365 days to obtain approximately 31 days.

- This means that the average collection period for receivables is about 31 days.
- Its average collection period is slightly longer than that of Giant Mills and shorter than that of the industry.
- A shorter collection period means receivables are being collected more quickly and thus are more liquid.

Analysts frequently use the average collection period to assess the effectiveness of a company's credit and collection policies. The general rule is that the collection period should not greatly exceed the credit term period (i.e., the time allowed for payment, which is 30 days for many companies).

4. **Inventory turnover.**   The **inventory turnover** measures the number of times average inventory was sold during the period. Its purpose is to measure the liquidity of the inventory. A high measure indicates that inventory is being sold and replenished frequently. The inventory turnover is computed by dividing the cost of goods sold by the average inventory during the period. Unless seasonal factors are significant, average inventory can be computed from the beginning and ending inventory balances. Chicago Cereal's inventory turnover is shown in **Illustration 10.24**.

ILLUSTRATION 10.24 **Inventory turnover**

| Ratio | Formula | Chicago Cereal | | Giant Mills | Industry Average |
|---|---|---|---|---|---|
| | | 2022 | 2021 | 2022 | |
| Inventory turnover | $\dfrac{\text{Cost of goods sold}}{\text{Average inventory}}$ | $\dfrac{\$6,597}{(\$924 + \$824) \div 2} = 7.5$ | 7.9 | 7.4 | 6.7 |

Chicago Cereal's inventory turnover decreased slightly in 2022.

- The turnover of 7.5 times is higher than the industry average of 6.7 times and similar to that of Giant Mills.
- Generally, the faster the inventory turnover, the less cash is tied up in inventory and the less the chance of inventory becoming obsolete.
- A downside of high inventory turnover is that it sometimes results in lost sales because if a company keeps less inventory on hand, it is more likely to run out of inventory when it is needed.

5. **Days in inventory.** A variant of the inventory turnover is the **days in inventory**, which measures the average number of days inventory is held. The days in inventory for Chicago Cereal is shown in **Illustration 10.25**.

ILLUSTRATION 10.25 **Days in inventory**

| Ratio | Formula | Chicago Cereal | | Giant Mills | Industry Average |
|---|---|---|---|---|---|
| | | 2022 | 2021 | 2022 | |
| Days in inventory | $\dfrac{365 \text{ days}}{\text{Inventory turnover}}$ | $\dfrac{365}{7.5} = 48.7$ | 46.2 | 49.3 | 54.5 |

Chicago Cereal's 2022 inventory turnover of 7.5 divided into 365 is approximately 49 days.

- An average selling time of 49 days is faster than the industry average and similar to that of Giant Mills.
- However, inventory turnovers vary considerably among industries. For example, grocery store chains have a turnover of 10 times and an average selling period of 37 days. In contrast, jewelry stores have an average turnover of 1.3 times and an average selling period of 281 days.
- Within a company, there may even be significant differences in inventory turnover among different types of products. Thus, in a grocery store the turnover of perishable items such as produce, meats, and dairy products is faster than the turnover of soaps and detergents.

To conclude, nearly all of these liquidity measures suggest that Chicago Cereal's liquidity changed little during 2022. Its liquidity appears acceptable when compared to the industry as a whole and when compared to Giant Mills.

## Solvency Ratios

**Solvency ratios** measure the ability of the company to survive over a long period of time.

- Long-term creditors and stockholders are interested in a company's long-run solvency, particularly its ability to pay interest as it comes due and to repay the face value of debt at maturity.
- The debt to assets ratio and times interest earned provide information about debt-paying ability.
- In addition, free cash flow provides information about the company's solvency and its ability to pay additional dividends or invest in new projects.

**6. Debt to assets ratio.**   The **debt to assets ratio** measures the percentage of total financing provided by creditors. It is computed by dividing total liabilities (both current and long-term debt) by total assets. This ratio indicates the degree of financial leveraging. It also provides some indication of the company's ability to withstand losses without impairing the interests of its creditors. The higher the percentage of debt to assets, the greater the risk that the company may be unable to meet its maturing obligations. Thus, from the creditors' point of view, a low ratio of debt to assets is desirable. Chicago Cereal's debt to assets ratio is shown in **Illustration 10.26**.

**ILLUSTRATION 10.26**  Debt to assets ratio

| Ratio | Formula | Chicago Cereal | | Giant Mills | Industry Average |
|---|---|---|---|---|---|
| | | 2022 | 2021 | 2022 | |
| Debt to assets ratio | $\dfrac{\text{Total liabilities}}{\text{Total assets}}$ | $\dfrac{\$8,871}{\$11,397} = 78\%$ | 81% | 55% | 55% |

Chicago Cereal's 2022 ratio of 78% means that creditors have provided financing sufficient to cover 78% of the company's total assets.

- Alternatively, the ratio indicates says that the company would have to liquidate 78% of its assets at their book value in order to pay off all of its debts.

- Chicago Cereal's ratio is above the industry average of 55%, as well as that of Giant Mills.

- This suggests that it is less solvent than the industry average and Giant Mills. Chicago Cereal's solvency improved slightly during the year.

The adequacy of this ratio is often judged in light of the company's earnings. Generally, companies with relatively stable earnings, such as public utilities, have higher debt to assets ratios than cyclical companies with widely fluctuating earnings, such as many high-tech companies.

Another ratio with a similar meaning is the **debt to equity ratio**.

- It shows the relative use of borrowed funds (total liabilities) compared with resources invested by the owners.

- Because this ratio can be computed in several ways, be careful when making comparisons with it; debt may be defined to include only the noncurrent portion of liabilities, and intangible assets may be excluded from stockholders' equity (which would equal tangible net worth).

- If debt and assets are defined as above (all liabilities and all assets), then when the debt to assets ratio equals 50%, the debt to equity ratio is 1:1.

**7. Times interest earned.**   The **times interest earned** (also called interest coverage) indicates the company's ability to meet interest payments as they come due. It is computed by dividing the sum of net income, interest expense, and income tax expense by interest expense. Note that this ratio uses income before interest expense and income taxes because this amount represents what is available to cover interest. Chicago Cereal's times interest earned is shown in **Illustration 10.27**.

**ILLUSTRATION 10.27**  Times interest earned

| Ratio | Formula | Chicago Cereal | | Giant Mills | Industry Average |
|---|---|---|---|---|---|
| | | 2022 | 2021 | 2022 | |
| Times interest earned | $\dfrac{\text{Net Income} + \text{Interest expense} + \text{Income tax expense}}{\text{Interest expense}}$ | $\dfrac{\$1,103 + \$321 + \$444}{\$321} = 5.8$ | 6.0 | 9.9 | 5.5 |

For Chicago Cereal, the 2022 interest coverage was 5.8 times, which indicates that income before interest and taxes was 5.8 times the amount needed for interest expense.

- This is less than the rate for Giant Mills, but it slightly exceeds the rate for the industry.
- The debt to assets ratio decreased for Chicago Cereal during 2022, and its times interest earned held relatively constant.
- A low debt to assets ratio and high times interest earned suggest better solvency.

8. **Free cash flow.** One indication of a company's solvency, as well as of its ability to pay dividends or expand operations, is the amount of excess cash it generated after investing in capital expenditures and paying dividends. This amount is referred to as **free cash flow**. For example, if you generate $100,000 of net cash provided by operating activities but you spend $30,000 on capital expenditures and pay $10,000 in dividends, you have $60,000 ($100,000 − $30,000 − $10,000) to use either to expand operations, pay additional dividends, or pay down debt. Chicago Cereal's free cash flow is shown in **Illustration 10.28**.

**ILLUSTRATION 10.28** Free cash flow

| Ratio | Formula | | | Chicago Cereal 2021 | Chicago Cereal 2022 | Giant Mills 2022 | Industry Average |
|---|---|---|---|---|---|---|---|
| Free cash flow | Net cash provided by operating activities | − Capital expenditures | − Cash dividends | $1,503 − $472 − $475 = $556 (in thousands) | $507 | $895 (in millions) | na |

Chicago Cereal's free cash flow increased slightly from 2021 to 2022.

- During both years, the net cash provided by operating activities was more than enough to allow it to acquire additional productive assets and maintain dividend payments.
- It could have used the remaining cash to reduce debt if necessary.
- Given that Chicago Cereal is much smaller than Giant Mills, we would expect its free cash flow to be substantially smaller, which it is.

## Profitability Ratios

**Profitability ratios** measure the income or operating success of a company for a given period of time.

- A company's income, or the lack of it, affects its ability to obtain debt and equity financing, its liquidity position, and its ability to grow.
- As a consequence, creditors and investors alike are interested in evaluating profitability.
- Analysts frequently use profitability as the ultimate test of management's operating effectiveness.

The relationships among measures of profitability are very important. Understanding them can help management determine where to focus its efforts to improve profitability. **Illustration 10.29** diagrams these relationships. Our discussion of Chicago Cereal's profitability is structured around this diagram.

9. **Return on common stockholders' equity (ROE).** A widely used measure of profitability from the common stockholders' viewpoint is the **return on common stockholders' equity (ROE)**. This ratio shows how many dollars of net income the company earned for each dollar invested by the owners. It is computed by dividing net income minus any

**ILLUSTRATION 10.29**

**Relationships among profitability measures**

preferred dividends—that is, income available to common stockholders—by average common stockholders' equity. The return on common stockholders' equity for Chicago Cereal is shown in **Illustration 10.30**.

**ILLUSTRATION 10.30** Return on common stockholders' equity

| Ratio | Formula | Chicago Cereal | | Giant Mills | Industry |
| | | 2022 | 2021 | 2022 | Average |
|---|---|---|---|---|---|
| Return on common stockholders' equity | $\dfrac{\text{Net Income} - \text{Preferred dividends}}{\text{Average common stockholders' equity}}$ | $\dfrac{\$1,103 - \$0}{(\$2,526 + \$2,069) \div 2} = 48\%$ | 46% | 25% | 19% |

Chicago Cereal's 2022 return on common stockholders' equity is unusually high at 48%. The industry average is 19% and Giant Mills' return is 25%. In the subsequent sections, we investigate the causes of this high return.

10. **Return on assets.**   The return on common stockholders' equity is affected by two factors: the **return on assets** and the degree of leverage. The return on assets measures the overall profitability of assets in terms of the income earned on each dollar invested in assets. It is computed by dividing net income by average total assets. Chicago Cereal's return on assets is shown in **Illustration 10.31**.

**ILLUSTRATION 10.31** Return on assets

| Ratio | Formula | Chicago Cereal | | Giant Mills | Industry |
| | | 2022 | 2021 | 2022 | Average |
|---|---|---|---|---|---|
| Return on assets | $\dfrac{\text{Net income}}{\text{Average total assets}}$ | $\dfrac{\$1,103}{(\$11,397 + \$10,714) \div 2} = 10.0\%$ | 9.4% | 6.2% | 5.3% |

Chicago Cereal had a 10.0% return on assets in 2022. This rate is significantly higher than that of Giant Mills and the industry average.

Note that its rate of return on common stockholders' equity (48%) is substantially higher than its rate of return on assets (10%). The reason is that it has made effective use of **leverage**.

- **Leveraging** or **trading on the equity** at a gain means that the company has borrowed money at a lower rate of interest than the rate of return it earns on the assets it purchased with the borrowed funds.

- Leverage enables management to use money supplied by nonowners to increase the return to owners.
- A comparison of the rate of return on assets with the rate of interest paid for borrowed money indicates the profitability of trading on the equity.

For example, if you borrow money at 8% and your rate of return on assets is 11%, you are trading on the equity at a gain. Note, however, that trading on the equity is a two-way street. For example, if you borrow money at 11% and earn only 8% on it, you are trading on the equity at a loss.

Chicago Cereal earns more on its borrowed funds than it has to pay in interest. Thus, the return to stockholders exceeds the return on assets because of the positive benefit of leverage. Recall from our earlier discussion that Chicago Cereal's percentage of debt financing, as measured by the ratio of debt to assets (or debt to equity), was higher than Giant Mills' and the industry average. It appears that Chicago Cereal's high return on common stockholders' equity is due in part to its use of leverage.

11. **Profit margin.** The return on assets is affected by two factors, the first of which is the profit margin. The **profit margin**, or rate of return on sales, is a measure of the percentage of each dollar of sales that results in net income. It is computed by dividing net income by net sales for the period. Chicago Cereal's profit margin is shown in **Illustration 10.32**.

**ILLUSTRATION 10.32**

**Profit margin**

| Ratio | Formula | Chicago Cereal | | Giant Mills | Industry Average |
|---|---|---|---|---|---|
| | | 2022 | 2021 | 2022 | |
| Profit margin | $\dfrac{\text{Net income}}{\text{Net sales}}$ | $\dfrac{\$1,103}{\$11,776} = 9.4\%$ | 9.2% | 8.2% | 6.1% |

Chicago Cereal experienced a slight increase in its profit margin from 2021 to 2022 of 9.2% to 9.4%.

- Its profit margin was higher, indicating the company earned more profit out of each dollar of sales, than the industry average and that of Giant Mills.
- High-volume (high inventory turnover) businesses such as grocery stores and pharmacy chains generally have low profit margins.
- Low-volume businesses such as jewelry stores and airplane manufacturers have high profit margins.

12. **Asset turnover.** The other factor that affects the return on assets is the asset turnover. The **asset turnover** measures how efficiently a company uses its assets to generate sales. It is determined by dividing net sales by average total assets for the period. The resulting number shows the dollars of sales produced by each dollar invested in assets. **Illustration 10.33** shows the asset turnover for Chicago Cereal.

**ILLUSTRATION 10.33**

**Asset turnover**

| Ratio | Formula | Chicago Cereal | | Giant Mills | Industry Average |
|---|---|---|---|---|---|
| | | 2022 | 2021 | 2022 | |
| Asset turnover | $\dfrac{\text{Net sales}}{\text{Average total assets}}$ | $\dfrac{\$11,776}{(\$11,397 + \$10,714) \div 2} = 1.07$ | 1.02 | .76 | .87 |

The asset turnover shows that in 2022, Chicago Cereal generated sales of $1.07 for each dollar it had invested in assets.

- The ratio rose from 2021 to 2022.
- Its asset turnover is above the industry average and that of Giant Mills.
- Asset turnovers vary considerably among industries. The average asset turnover for utility companies is .45, for example, while the grocery store industry has an average asset turnover of 3.49.

In summary, Chicago Cereal's return on assets increased from 9.4% in 2021 to 10.0% in 2022. Underlying this increase was an increased profitability on each dollar of sales (as measured by the profit margin) and a rise in the sales-generating efficiency of its assets (as measured by the asset turnover). We can analyze the combined effects of profit margin and asset turnover on return on assets for Chicago Cereal as shown in **Illustration 10.34**.

**ILLUSTRATION 10.34**  **Composition of return on assets**

| Ratios: | Profit Margin | × | Asset Turnover | = | Return on Assets |
|---|---|---|---|---|---|
| | Net Income / Net Sales | × | Net Sales / Average Total Assets | = | Net Income / Average Total Assets |
| **Chicago Cereal** | | | | | |
| 2022 | 9.4% | × | 1.07 times | = | 10.1%* |
| 2021 | 9.2% | × | 1.02 times | = | 9.4% |

*Difference from value in Illustration 10.31 due to rounding.

13. **Gross profit rate.**   One factor that strongly influences the profit margin is the gross profit rate. The **gross profit rate** is determined by dividing gross profit (net sales less cost of goods sold) by net sales. This rate indicates a company's ability to maintain an adequate selling price above its cost of goods sold.

As an industry becomes more competitive, this ratio declines.

- For example, in the early years of the personal computer industry, gross profit rates were quite high.
- Today, because of increased competition and a belief that most brands of personal computers are similar in quality, gross profit rates have become thin.
- Analysts should closely monitor gross profit rates over time.

**Illustration 10.35** shows Chicago Cereal's gross profit rate.

| Ratio | Formula | Chicago Cereal 2022 | Chicago Cereal 2021 | Giant Mills 2022 | Industry Average |
|---|---|---|---|---|---|
| Gross profit rate | Gross profit / Net sales | $\dfrac{\$5,179}{\$11,776} = 44\%$ | 44% | 34% | 30% |

**ILLUSTRATION 10.35**

Gross profit rate

Chicago Cereal's gross profit rate remained constant from 2021 to 2022.

14. **Earnings per share (EPS).**   Stockholders usually think in terms of the number of shares they own or plan to buy or sell. Expressing net income earned on a per share basis provides a useful perspective for determining profitability. **Earnings per share** is a measure of the net income earned on each share of common stock. It is computed by dividing net income by the average number of common shares outstanding during the year.

The terms "net income per share" and "earnings per share" refer to the amount of net income applicable to each share of **common stock**. Therefore, when we compute earnings per share, if there are preferred dividends declared for the period, we must deduct them from net income to arrive at income available to the common stockholders. Chicago Cereal's earnings per share is shown in **Illustration 10.36**.

**Earnings per share**

| Ratio | Formula | Chicago Cereal | | Giant Mills | Industry Average |
|---|---|---|---|---|---|
| | | 2022 | 2021 | 2022 | |
| Earnings per share (EPS) | $\dfrac{\text{Net income} - \text{Preferred dividends}}{\text{Weighted-average common shares outstanding}}$ | $\dfrac{\$1,103 - \$0}{418.7} = \$2.63$ | $2.40 | $2.90 | na |

Note that no industry average is presented in Illustration 10.36.

- Industry data for earnings per share are not reported, and in fact the Chicago Cereal and Giant Mills ratios should not be compared.

- Such comparisons are not meaningful because of the wide variations in the number of shares of outstanding stock among companies.

- Chicago Cereal's earnings per share increased 23 cents per share in 2022. This represents a 9.6% increase from the 2021 EPS of $2.40.

15. **Price-earnings ratio.**  The **price-earnings ratio** is an oft-quoted statistic that measures the ratio of the market price of each share of common stock to the earnings per share. The price-earnings (P-E) ratio reflects investors' assessments of a company's future earnings. It is computed by dividing the market price per share of the stock by earnings per share. Chicago Cereal's price-earnings ratio is shown in **Illustration 10.37**.

**Price-earnings ratio**

| Ratio | Formula | Chicago Cereal | | Giant Mills | Industry Average |
|---|---|---|---|---|---|
| | | 2022 | 2021 | 2022 | |
| Price-earnings ratio | $\dfrac{\text{Market price per share}}{\text{Earnings per share}}$ | $\dfrac{\$52.92}{\$2.63} = 20.1$ | 20.9 | 24.3 | 35.8 |

At the end of 2022 and 2021, the market price of Chicago Cereal's stock was $52.92 and $50.06, respectively.

- In 2022, each share of Chicago Cereal's stock sold for 20.1 times the amount that was earned on each share.

- Chicago Cereal's price-earnings ratio is lower than Giant Mills' ratio of 24.3 and lower than the industry average of 35.8 times.

- Its lower P-E ratio suggests that the market is less optimistic about Chicago Cereal than about Giant Mills, but it might also signal that Chicago Cereal's stock is underpriced.

16. **Payout ratio.**  The **payout ratio** measures the percentage of earnings distributed in the form of cash dividends. It is computed by dividing cash dividends declared on common stock by net income. Companies that have high growth rates are characterized by low payout ratios because they reinvest most of their net income in the business. The payout ratio for Chicago Cereal is shown in **Illustration 10.38**.

**Payout ratio**

| Ratio | Formula | Chicago Cereal | | Giant Mills | Industry Average |
|---|---|---|---|---|---|
| | | 2022 | 2021 | 2022 | |
| Payout ratio | $\dfrac{\text{Cash dividends declared on common stock}}{\text{Net income}}$ | $\dfrac{\$475}{\$1,103} = 43\%$ | 45% | 54% | 37% |

The 2022 and 2021 payout ratios for Chicago Cereal are lower than that of Giant Mills (54%) but higher than the industry average (37%).

- A lower payout ratio means a company has chosen to pay out a lower percentage of its net income as dividends.

- Management has some control over the amount of dividends paid each year, and companies are generally reluctant to reduce a dividend below the amount paid in a previous year.

- The payout ratio will actually increase if a company's net income declines but the company keeps its total dividend payment the same. (Of course, unless the company returns to its previous level of profitability, maintaining this higher dividend payout ratio is probably not possible over the long run.)

Before drawing any conclusions regarding Chicago Cereal's dividend payout ratio, we should calculate this ratio over a longer period of time to evaluate any trends and also try to find out whether management's philosophy regarding dividends has changed recently. The "Selected Financial Data" section of Chicago Cereal's Management Discussion and Analysis shows that over a 5-year period, earnings per share rose 45%, while dividends per share grew only 19%.

In terms of the types of financial information available and the ratios used by various industries, what can be practically covered in this text gives you the "Titanic approach." That is, you are only seeing the tip of the iceberg compared to the vast databases and types of ratio analysis that are available on computers. The availability of information is not a problem. The real trick is to be discriminating enough to perform relevant analysis and select pertinent comparative data.

## DO IT! 3 | Ratio Analysis

**ACTION PLAN**

- Remember that the current ratio includes all current assets.
- Use average balances for turnover ratios like inventory, accounts receivable, and return on assets.

The condensed financial statements of John Cully Company, for the years ended June 30, 2022 and 2021, are presented as follows.

### John Cully Company
**Balance Sheets**
**June 30**

|  | (in thousands) | |
|---|---|---|
|  | **2022** | **2021** |
| **Assets** | | |
| Current assets | | |
| Cash and cash equivalents | $ 553.3 | $ 611.6 |
| Accounts receivable (net) | 776.6 | 664.9 |
| Inventory | 768.3 | 653.5 |
| Prepaid expenses and other current assets | 204.4 | 269.2 |
| Total current assets | 2,302.6 | 2,199.2 |
| Investments | 12.3 | 12.6 |
| Property, plant, and equipment (net) | 694.2 | 647.0 |
| Intangibles and other assets | 876.7 | 849.3 |
| Total assets | $3,885.8 | $3,708.1 |
| **Liabilities and Stockholders' Equity** | | |
| Current liabilities | $1,497.7 | $1,322.0 |
| Long-term liabilities | 679.5 | 637.1 |
| Stockholders' equity—common | 1,708.6 | 1,749.0 |
| Total liabilities and stockholders' equity | $3,885.8 | $3,708.1 |

| John Cully Company | | |
| --- | --- | --- |
| **Income Statements** | | |
| **For the Years Ended June 30** | | |
| | | **(in thousands)** |
| | **2022** | **2021** |
| Sales revenue | $6,336.3 | $5,790.4 |
| Costs and expenses | | |
| Cost of goods sold | 1,617.4 | 1,476.3 |
| Selling and administrative expenses | 4,007.6 | 3,679.0 |
| Interest expense | 13.9 | 27.1 |
| Total costs and expenses | 5,638.9 | 5,182.4 |
| Income before income taxes | 697.4 | 608.0 |
| Income tax expense | 291.3 | 232.6 |
| Net income | $ 406.1 | $ 375.4 |

Compute the following ratios for 2022 and 2021.

**a.** Current ratio.

**b.** Inventory turnover. (Inventory on 6/30/20 was $599.0.)

**c.** Profit margin.

**d.** Return on assets. (Assets on 6/30/20 were $3,349.9.)

**e.** Return on common stockholders' equity. (Stockholders' equity on 6/30/20 was $1,795.9.)

**f.** Debt to assets ratio.

**g.** Times interest earned.

### Solution

| | **2022** | **2021** |
| --- | --- | --- |
| **a.** Current ratio: | | |
| $2,302.6 ÷ $1,497.7 = | 1.5:1 | |
| $2,199.2 ÷ $1,322.0 = | | 1.7:1 |
| **b.** Inventory turnover: | | |
| $1,617.4 ÷ [($768.3 + $653.5) ÷ 2] = | 2.3 times | |
| $1,476.3 ÷ [($653.5 + $599.0) ÷ 2] = | | 2.4 times |
| **c.** Profit margin: | | |
| $406.1 ÷ $6,336.3 = | 6.4% | |
| $375.4 ÷ $5,790.4 = | | 6.5% |
| **d.** Return on assets: | | |
| $406.1 ÷ [($3,885.8 + $3,708.1) ÷ 2] = | 10.7% | |
| $375.4 ÷ [($3,708.1 + $3,349.9) ÷ 2] = | | 10.6% |
| **e.** Return on common stockholders' equity: | | |
| ($406.1 − $0) ÷ [($1,708.6 + $1,749.0) ÷ 2] = | 23.5% | |
| ($375.4 − $0) ÷ [($1,749.0 + $1,795.9) ÷ 2] = | | 21.2% |
| **f.** Debt to assets ratio: | | |
| ($1,497.7 + $679.5) ÷ $3,885.8 = | 56.0% | |
| ($1,322.0 + $637.1) ÷ $3,708.1 = | | 52.8% |
| **g.** Times interest earned: | | |
| ($406.1 + $13.9 + $291.3) ÷ $13.9 = | 51.2 times | |
| ($375.4 + $27.1 + $232.6) ÷ $27.1 = | | 23.4 times |

Related exercise material: **BE10.10, BE10.11, BE10.12, BE10.13, BE10.14, BE10.15, DO IT! 10.3, E10.7, E10.8, E10.9, E10.10, E10.11, E10.12, and E10.13.**

## USING THE DECISION TOOLS | Kellogg Company

In analyzing a company, you should always investigate an extended period of time in order to determine whether the condition and performance of the company are changing. The condensed financial statements of **Kellogg Company** for 2017 and 2016 are presented here.

**Kellogg Company, Inc.**
**Balance Sheets**
**December 30, 2017, and December 31, 2016**
**(in millions)**

| | 2017 | 2016 |
|---|---|---|
| **Assets** | | |
| Current assets | | |
| Cash | $ 281 | $ 280 |
| Accounts receivable (net) | 1,389 | 1,231 |
| Inventories | 1,217 | 1,238 |
| Other current assets | 149 | 191 |
| Total current assets | 3,036 | 2,940 |
| Property (net) | 3,716 | 5,166 |
| Other assets | 9,598 | 7,005 |
| Total assets | $16,350 | $15,111 |
| **Liabilities and Stockholders' Equity** | | |
| Current liabilities | $ 4,479 | $ 4,474 |
| Long-term liabilities | 9,643 | 8,711 |
| Stockholders' equity—common | 2,228 | 1,926 |
| Total liabilities and stockholders' equity | $16,350 | $15,111 |

**Kellogg Company, Inc.**
**Condensed Income Statements**
**For the Years Ended December 30, 2017, and December 31, 2016**
**(in millions)**

| | 2017 | 2016 |
|---|---|---|
| Net sales | $12,923 | $ 13,014 |
| Cost of goods sold | 7,901 | 8,259 |
| Gross profit | 5,022 | 4,755 |
| Selling and administrative expenses | 3,076 | 3,360 |
| Income from operations | 1,946 | 1,395 |
| Interest expense | 256 | 406 |
| Other income (expense), net | (16) | (62) |
| Income before income taxes | 1,674 | 927 |
| Income tax expense | 412 | 233 |
| Other earnings (loss) | 7 | 0 |
| Net income | $ 1,269 | $ 694 |

## Instructions

Compute the following ratios for Kellogg for 2017 and discuss your findings (2016 values are provided for comparison).

1. Liquidity:
   a. Current ratio (2016: .66:1).
   b. Inventory turnover (2016: 6.6 times).

2. Solvency:
   a. Debt to assets ratio (2016: 87%).
   b. Times interest earned (2016: 3.3 times).

3. Profitability:

   a. Return on assets (2016: 4.6%).

   b. Profit margin (2016: 5.3%).

   c. Return on common stockholders' equity (2016: 33%).

**Solution**

1. Liquidity

   a. Current ratio:

   2017: $\dfrac{\$3,036}{\$4,479} = .68{:}1$       2016:   .66:1

   b. Inventory turnover:

   2017: $\dfrac{\$7,901}{(\$1,217 + \$1,238) \div 2} = 6.4$ times       2016:   6.6 times

   We see that between 2016 and 2017, the current ratio increased, which suggests an increase in liquidity. The inventory turnover decreased, which suggests a decline in liquidity.

2. Solvency

   a. Debt to assets ratio:

   2017: $\dfrac{\$4,479 + \$9,643}{\$16,350} = 86\%$       2016:   87%

   b. Times interest earned:

   2017: $\dfrac{\$1,269 + \$256 + \$412}{\$256} = 7.6$ times       2016:   3.3 times

   Kellogg's debt to assets ratio decreased in 2017, and its times interest earned increased. Both changes suggest improved solvency.

3. Profitability

   a. Return on assets:

   2017: $\dfrac{\$1,269}{(\$16,350 + \$15,111) \div 2} = 8.1\%$       2016:   4.6%

   b. Profit margin:

   2017: $\dfrac{\$1,269}{\$12,923} = 9.8\%$       2016:   5.3%

   c. Return on common stockholders' equity:

   2017: $\dfrac{\$1,269}{(\$2,228 + \$1,926) \div 2} = 61\%$       2016:   33%

   Kellogg's return on assets, profit margin, and return on stockholders' equity increased. The company experienced a sharp increase in net income, while its total assets, sales, and equity were relatively constant.

# Review and Practice

## Learning Objectives Review

**1  Apply the concepts of sustainable income and quality of earnings.**

Sustainable income analysis is useful in evaluating a company's performance. Sustainable income is the most likely level of income to be obtained by the company in the future and omits unusual items. Discontinued operations and other comprehensive income are presented separately to highlight their unusual nature. Items below income from continuing operations must be presented net of tax.

A high quality of earnings provides full and transparent information that will not confuse or mislead users of the financial statements. Issues related to quality of earnings are (1) alternative accounting methods, (2) pro forma income, and (3) improper recognition.

**2   Apply horizontal analysis and vertical analysis.**

Horizontal analysis is a technique for evaluating a series of data over a period of time to determine the increase or decrease that has taken place, expressed as either a dollar amount or a percentage.

Vertical analysis is a technique that expresses each item in a financial statement as a percentage of a relevant total or a base amount.

**3   Analyze a company's performance using ratio analysis.**

Financial ratios are provided in Illustration 10.14 (liquidity), Illustration 10.15 (solvency), and Illustration 10.16 (profitability). Analysis is enhanced by intracompany, intercompany, and industry comparisons of these three classes of ratios.

## Decision Tools Review

| Decision Checkpoints | Info Needed for Decision | Tool to Use for Decision | How to Evaluate Results |
|---|---|---|---|
| Has the company sold any major components of its business? | Discontinued operations section of income statement | Anything reported in this section indicates that the company has discontinued a major component of its business. | If a major component has been discontinued, its results during the current period should not be included in estimates of future net income. |
| Has the company changed any of its accounting principles? | Effect of change in accounting principle on current and prior periods | Management indicates that the new principle is preferable to the old principle. Discussed in notes to financial statements. | Examine current and prior years' reported income, using new-principle basis to assess trends for estimating future income. |
| How do the company's financial position and operating results compare with those of the previous period? | Income statement and balance sheet | Comparative financial statements should be prepared over at least two years, with the first year reported being the base year. Changes in each line item relative to the base year should be presented both by amount and by percentage. This is called **horizontal analysis**. | Significant changes should be investigated to determine the reason for the change. |
| How do the relationships between items in this year's financial statements compare with those of last year or those of competitors? | Income statement and balance sheet | Each line item on the income statement should be presented as a percentage of net sales, and each line item on the balance sheet should be presented as a percentage of total assets or total liabilities and stockholders' equity. These percentages should be investigated for differences either across years in the same company or in the same year across different companies. This is called **vertical analysis**. | Any significant differences either across years or between companies should be investigated to determine the cause. |
| How do mathematical relationships between financial statement items compare to prior years, competitors, and industry? | Financial statements | Various ratios that measure liquidity, solvency, and profitability. | Significant differences from prior-year values, or from competitor or industry values, should be investigated to determine the cause. |

## Glossary Review

**Accounts receivable turnover** A measure of the liquidity of receivables; computed as net credit sales divided by average net accounts receivable. (p. 10-21).

**Asset turnover** A measure of how efficiently a company uses its assets to generate sales; computed as net sales divided by average total assets. (p. 10-26).

**Available-for-sale securities** Securities that are held with the intent of selling them sometime in the future. (p. 10-5).

**Average collection period** The average number of days that receivables are outstanding; calculated as accounts receivable turnover divided into 365 days. (p. 10-21).

**Change in accounting principle** Use of an accounting principle in the current year different from the one used in the preceding year. (p. 10-6).

**Comprehensive income** The sum of net income and other comprehensive income items. (p. 10-4).

**Current ratio** A measure used to evaluate a company's liquidity and short-term debt-paying ability; calculated as current assets divided by current liabilities. (p. 10-20).

**Days in inventory** A measure of the average number of days inventory is held; computed as inventory turnover divided into 365 days. (p. 10-22).

**Debt to assets ratio** A measure of the percentage of total financing provided by creditors; computed as total liabilities divided by total assets. (p. 10-23).

**Discontinued operations** The disposal of a significant component of a business. (p. 10-3).

**Earnings per share** The net income earned by each share of outstanding common stock; computed as net income less preferred dividends divided by the weighted-average common shares outstanding. (p. 10-27).

**Free cash flow** A measure of solvency. Cash remaining from operating activities after adjusting for capital expenditures and dividends paid. (p. 10-24).

**Gross profit rate** Gross profit expressed as a percentage of sales; computed as gross profit divided by net sales. (p. 10-27).

**Horizontal analysis** A technique for evaluating a series of financial statement data over a period of time to determine the increase (decrease) that has taken place, expressed as either a dollar amount or a percentage. (p. 10-10).

**Inventory turnover** A measure of the liquidity of inventory. Measures the number of times average inventory was sold during the period; computed as cost of goods sold divided by average inventory. (p. 10-21).

**Leveraging** Borrowing money at a lower rate of interest than can be earned by using the borrowed money; also referred to as *trading on the equity*. (p. 10-25).

**Liquidity ratios** Measures of the short-term ability of the company to pay its maturing obligations and to meet unexpected needs for cash. (p. 10-16).

**Payout ratio** A measure of the percentage of earnings distributed in the form of cash dividends; calculated as cash dividends declared on common stock divided by net income. (p. 10-28).

**Price-earnings (P-E) ratio** A comparison of the market price of each share of common stock to the earnings per share; computed as the market price of the stock divided by earnings per share. (p. 10-28).

**Profitability ratios** Measures of the income or operating success of a company for a given period of time. (p. 10-17).

**Profit margin** A measure of the net income generated by each dollar of sales; computed as net income divided by net sales. (p. 10-26).

**Pro forma income** A measure of income that usually excludes items that a company thinks are unusual or non-recurring. (p. 10-8).

**Quality of earnings** Indicates the level of full and transparent information that is provided to users of the financial statements. (p. 10-7).

**Ratio** The mathematical relationship between one quantity and another. The relationship may be expressed either as a percentage, a rate, or a simple proportion. (p. 10-15).

**Ratio analysis** A technique for evaluating financial statements that expresses the relationship between selected financial statement data. (p. 10-15).

**Return on assets** A profitability measure that indicates the amount of net income generated by each dollar of assets; calculated as net income divided by average total assets. (p. 10-25).

**Return on common stockholders' equity (ROE)** A measure of the dollars of net income earned for each dollar invested by the owners; computed as income available to common stockholders divided by average common stockholders' equity. (p. 10-24).

**Solvency ratios** Measures of the ability of a company to survive over a long period of time, particularly to pay interest as it comes due and to repay the balance of debt at its maturity. (p. 10-17).

**Sustainable income** The most likely level of income to be obtained by a company in the future. (p. 10-3).

**Times interest earned** A measure of a company's solvency and ability to meet interest payments as they come due; calculated as the sum of net income, interest expense, and income tax expense divided by interest expense. (p. 10-23).

**Trading on the equity** *See leveraging.* (p. 10-25).

**Trading securities** Securities bought and held primarily for sale in the near term to generate income on short-term price differences. (p. 10-5).

**Vertical analysis** A technique for evaluating financial statement data that expresses each item in a financial statement as a percentage of a base amount. (p. 10-12).

## Practice Multiple-Choice Questions

**1. (LO 1)** In reporting discontinued operations, the income statement should show in a special section:

   **a.** gains on the disposal of the discontinued component.

   **b.** losses on the disposal of the discontinued component.

   **c.** neither gains nor losses on the disposal of the discontinued component.

   **d.** both gains and losses on the disposal of the discontinued component.

**2. (LO 1)** Cool Stools Corporation has income before taxes of $400,000 and a loss on discontinued operations of $100,000. If the income tax rate is 25% on all items, the income statement should show income from continuing operations and discontinued operations, respectively, of

    **a.** $325,000 and $100,000.

    **b.** $325,000 and $75,000.

    **c.** $300,000 and $100,000.

    **d.** $300,000 and $75,000.

**3. (LO 1)** Which of the following would be considered an "Other comprehensive income" item?

    **a.** Gain on disposal of discontinued operations.

    **b.** Unrealized loss on available-for-sale securities.

    **c.** Loss related to flood.

    **d.** Net income.

**4. (LO 1)** Which situation below might indicate a company has a low quality of earnings?

    **a.** The same accounting principles are used each year.

    **b.** Revenue is recognized when the performance obligation is satisfied.

    **c.** Maintenance costs are capitalized and then depreciated.

    **d.** The company's P-E ratio is high relative to competitors.

**5. (LO 2)** In horizontal analysis, each item is expressed as a percentage of the:

    **a.** net income amount.

    **b.** stockholders' equity amount.

    **c.** total assets amount.

    **d.** base-year amount.

**6. (LO 2)** Adams Corporation reported net sales of $300,000, $330,000, and $360,000 in the years 2020, 2021, and 2022, respectively. If 2020 is the base year, what percentage do 2022 sales represent of the base?

    **a.** 77%.               **c.** 120%.

    **b.** 108%.            **d.** 130%.

**7. (LO 2)** The following schedule is a display of what type of analysis?

| | Amount | Percent |
|---|---|---|
| Current assets | $200,000 | 25% |
| Property, plant, and equipment | 600,000 | 75% |
| Total assets | $800,000 | |

    **a.** Horizontal analysis.    **c.** Vertical analysis.

    **b.** Differential analysis.    **d.** Ratio analysis.

**8. (LO 2)** In vertical analysis, the base amount for depreciation expense is generally:

    **a.** net sales.

    **b.** depreciation expense in a previous year.

    **c.** gross profit.

    **d.** fixed assets.

**9. (LO 3)** Which measure is an evaluation of a company's ability to pay current liabilities?

    **a.** Accounts receivable turnover.

    **b.** Current ratio.

    **c.** Both accounts receivable turnover and current ratio.

    **d.** None of the answer choices is correct.

**10. (LO 3)** Which measure is useful in evaluating the efficiency in managing inventories?

    **a.** Inventory turnover.

    **b.** Days in inventory.

    **c.** Both inventory turnover and days in inventory.

    **d.** None of the answer choices is correct.

**11. (LO 3)** Which of these is **not** a liquidity ratio?

    **a.** Current ratio.

    **b.** Asset turnover.

    **c.** Inventory turnover.

    **d.** Accounts receivable turnover.

**12. (LO 3)** Plano Corporation reported net income $24,000, net sales $400,000, and average assets $600,000 for 2022. What is the 2022 profit margin?

    **a.** 6%.              **c.** 40%.

    **b.** 12%.            **d.** 200%.

Use the following financial statement information as of the end of each year to answer Questions 13–17.

| | 2022 | 2021 |
|---|---|---|
| Inventory | $ 54,000 | $ 48,000 |
| Current assets | 81,000 | 106,000 |
| Total assets | 382,000 | 326,000 |
| Current liabilities | 27,000 | 36,000 |
| Total liabilities | 102,000 | 88,000 |
| Common stockholders' equity | 240,000 | 198,000 |
| Net sales | 784,000 | 697,000 |
| Cost of goods sold | 306,000 | 277,000 |
| Net income | 134,000 | 90,000 |
| Income tax expense | 22,000 | 18,000 |
| Interest expense | 12,000 | 12,000 |
| Dividends paid to preferred stockholders | 4,000 | 4,000 |
| Dividends paid to common stockholders | 15,000 | 10,000 |

**13. (LO 3)** Compute the days in inventory for 2022.

    **a.** 64.4 days.        **c.** 6 days.

    **b.** 60.8 days.        **d.** 24 days.

**14. (LO 3)** Compute the current ratio for 2022.

    **a.** 1.26:1.          **c.** 0.80:1.

    **b.** 3.0:1.           **d.** 3.75:1.

**15. (LO 3)** Compute the profit margin for 2022.

    **a.** 17.1%.          **c.** 37.9%.

    **b.** 18.1%.          **d.** 5.9%.

**16. (LO 3)** Compute the return on common stockholders' equity for 2022.

    **a.** 54.2%.          **c.** 61.2%.

    **b.** 52.5%.          **d.** 59.4%.

**17. (LO 3)** Compute the times interest earned for 2022.

    **a.** 11.2 times.      **c.** 14.0 times.

    **b.** 65.3 times.      **d.** 13.0 times.

## Solutions

**1. d.** Gains and losses from the operations of a discontinued segment and gains and losses on the disposal of the discontinued segment are shown in a separate section immediately after continuing operations in the income statement. Choices (a) and (b) are correct, but (d) is the better answer. Choice (c) is wrong as there is a correct answer.

**2. d.** Income tax expense = 25% × $400,000 = $100,000; therefore, income from continuing operations = $400,000 − $100,000 = $300,000. The loss on discontinued operations is shown net of tax, $100,000 × 75% = $75,000. The other choices are therefore incorrect.

**3. b.** Unrealized gains and losses on available-for-sale securities are part of other comprehensive income. The other choices are incorrect because (a) a gain on the disposal of discontinued operations is reported as an unusual item, (c) loss related to a flood is reported among other expenses and losses, and (d) net income is a separate line item.

**4. c.** Capitalizing and then depreciating maintenance costs suggests that a company is trying to avoid expensing certain costs by deferring them to future accounting periods to increase current-period income. The other choices are incorrect because (a) using the same accounting principles each year and (b) recognizing revenue when the performance obligation is satisfied is in accordance with GAAP. Choice (d) is incorrect because a high P-E ratio does not suggest that a firm has low quality of earnings.

**5. d.** Horizontal analysis converts each succeeding year's balance to a percentage of the base year amount, not (a) net income amount, (b) stockholders' equity amount, or (c) total assets amount.

**6. c.** The trend percentage for 2022 is 120% ($360,000 ÷ $300,000), not (a) 77%, (b) 108%, or (d) 130%.

**7. c.** The data in the schedule are a display of vertical analysis because the individual asset items are expressed as a percentage of total assets. The other choices are therefore incorrect. Horizontal analysis is a technique for evaluating a series of data over a period of time.

**8. a.** In vertical analysis, net sales is used as the base amount for income statement items, not (b) depreciation expense in a previous year, (c) gross profit, or (d) fixed assets.

**9. c.** Both the accounts receivable turnover and the current ratio measure a firm's ability to pay current liabilities. Choices (a) and (b) are correct but (c) is the better answer. Choice (d) is incorrect because there is a correct answer.

**10. c.** Both inventory turnover and days in inventory measure a firm's efficiency in managing inventories. Choices (a) and (b) are correct but (c) is the better answer. Choice (d) is incorrect because there is a correct answer.

**11. b.** Asset turnover is a measure of profitability. The other choices are incorrect because the (a) current ratio, (c) inventory turnover, and (d) accounts receivable turnover are all measures of a firm's liquidity.

**12. a.** Profit margin = Net income ($24,000) ÷ Net sales ($400,000) = 6%, not (b) 12%, (c) 40%, or (d) 200%.

**13. b.** Inventory turnover = Cost of goods sold ÷ Average inventory {$306,000 ÷ [($54,000 + $48,000) ÷ 2]} = 6 times. Thus, days in inventory = 60.8 (365 ÷ 6), not (a) 64.4, (c) 6, or (d) 24 days.

**14. b.** Current ratio = Current assets ÷ Current liabilities ($81,000 ÷ $27,000) = 3.0:1, not (a) 1.26:1, (c) 0.80:1, or (d) 3.75:1.

**15. a.** Profit margin = Net income ÷ Net sales ($134,000 ÷ $784,000) = 17.1%, not (b) 18.1%, (c) 37.9%, or (d) 5.9%.

**16. d.** Return on common stockholders' equity = Net income ($134,000) − Dividends to preferred stockholders ($4,000) ÷ Average common stockholders' equity [($240,000 + $198,000) ÷ 2] = 59.4%, not (a) 54.2%, (b) 52.5%, or (c) 61.2%.

**17. c.** Times interest earned = (Net income + Interest expense + Income tax expense) ÷ Interest expense [($134,000 + $12,000 + $22,000) ÷ $12,000] = 14.0 times, not (a) 11.2, (b) 65.3, or (d) 13.0 times.

## Practice Brief Exercises

*Prepare a discontinued operations section.*

**1. (LO 1)** On September 30, Reynaldo Corporation discontinued its operations in Africa. During the year, the operating income was $100,000 before taxes. On September 1, Reynaldo disposed of its African facilities at a pretax loss of $350,000. The applicable tax rate is 30%. Show the discontinued operations section of the income statement.

### Solution

**1.**

**Reynaldo Corporation**
**Income Statement (partial)**

| | | |
|---|---|---|
| Income from operations of discontinued division, net of $30,000 income taxes ($100,000 × 30%) | $ 70,000 | |
| Loss from disposal of discontinued division, net of $105,000 income tax savings ($350,000 × 30%) | (245,000) | $(175,000) |

*Prepare horizontal analysis.*

**2. (LO 2)** Using the following data from the comparative balance sheet of Alfredo Company, perform horizontal analysis.

| | December 31, 2022 | December 31, 2021 |
|---|---|---|
| Accounts payable | $ 300,000 | $ 200,000 |
| Common stock | 700,000 | 600,000 |
| Total liabilities and equity | 2,000,000 | 1,800,000 |

## Solution

**2.**

| | December 31, 2022 | December 31, 2021 | Increase or (Decrease) Amount | Increase or (Decrease) Percent* |
|---|---|---|---|---|
| Accounts payable | $   300,000 | $ 200,000 | $100,000 | 50% |
| Common stock | 700,000 | 600,000 | 100,000 | 17 |
| Total liabilities and stockholders' equity | 2,000,000 | 1,800,000 | 200,000 | 11 |

*$100 \div 200 = 50\%$; $100 \div 600 = 16.7\%$; $200 \div 1,800 = 11.1\%$

**3. (LO 3)** Gonzalez Company has beginning inventory of $400,000, cost of goods sold of $2,200,000, and days in inventory of 73. What is Gonzalez' inventory turnover and ending inventory?

*Calculate ratios.*

## Solution

**3.**   Days in inventory = 365 ÷ Inventory turnover
73 = 365 ÷ Inventory turnover.
Inventory turnover = 5 (365 ÷ 73)

Inventory turnover = Cost of goods sold ÷ Average inventory
5 = $2,200,000 ÷ Average inventory
Average inventory = $2,200,000 ÷ 5 = $440,000.

Since beginning inventory is $400,000, ending inventory must be $480,000:
($400,000 + $480,000) ÷ 2 = $440,000.

# Practice Exercises

**1. (LO 2)** The comparative condensed balance sheets of Roadway Corporation are as follows.

*Prepare horizontal and vertical analyses.*

**Roadway Corporation**
**Condensed Balance Sheets**
**December 31**

| | 2022 | 2021 |
|---|---|---|
| **Assets** | | |
| Current assets | $ 76,000 | $ 80,000 |
| Property, plant, and equipment (net) | 99,000 | 90,000 |
| Intangibles | 25,000 | 40,000 |
| Total assets | $200,000 | $210,000 |
| **Liabilities and Stockholders' Equity** | | |
| Current liabilities | $ 40,800 | $ 48,000 |
| Long-term liabilities | 143,000 | 150,000 |
| Stockholders' equity | 16,200 | 12,000 |
| Total liabilities and stockholders' equity | $200,000 | $210,000 |

## Instructions

**a.** Prepare a horizontal analysis of the balance sheet data for Roadway Corporation using 2021 as a base.

**b.** Prepare a vertical analysis of the balance sheet data for Roadway Corporation in columnar form for 2022.

**Solution**

**1. a.**

### Roadway Corporation
### Condensed Balance Sheets
### December 31

| | 2022 | 2021 | Increase (Decrease) | Percent Change from 2021 |
|---|---|---|---|---|
| **Assets** | | | | |
| Current assets | $ 76,000 | $ 80,000 | $ (4,000) | (5.0%) |
| Property, plant, and equipment (net) | 99,000 | 90,000 | 9,000 | 10.0% |
| Intangibles | 25,000 | 40,000 | (15,000) | (37.5%) |
| Total assets | $200,000 | $210,000 | $(10,000) | (4.8%) |
| **Liabilities and Stockholders' Equity** | | | | |
| Current liabilities | $ 40,800 | $ 48,000 | $ (7,200) | (15.0%) |
| Long-term liabilities | 143,000 | 150,000 | (7,000) | (4.7%) |
| Stockholders' equity | 16,200 | 12,000 | 4,200 | 35.0% |
| Total liabilities and stockholders' equity | $200,000 | $210,000 | $(10,000) | (4.8%) |

**b.**

### Roadway Corporation
### Condensed Balance Sheet
### December 31, 2022

| | Amount | Percent |
|---|---|---|
| **Assets** | | |
| Current assets | $ 76,000 | 38.0% |
| Property, plant, and equipment (net) | 99,000 | 49.5% |
| Intangibles | 25,000 | 12.5% |
| Total assets | $200,000 | 100.0% |
| **Liabilities and Stockholders' Equity** | | |
| Current liabilities | $ 40,800 | 20.4% |
| Long-term liabilities | 143,000 | 71.5% |
| Stockholders' equity | 16,200 | 8.1% |
| Total liabilities and stockholders' equity | $200,000 | 100.0% |

*Compute ratios.*

**2. (LO 3)** Rondo Corporation's comparative balance sheets are presented here.

### Rondo Corporation
### Balance Sheets
### December 31

| | 2022 | 2021 |
|---|---|---|
| Cash | $ 5,300 | $ 3,700 |
| Accounts receivable | 21,200 | 23,400 |
| Inventory | 9,000 | 7,000 |
| Land | 20,000 | 26,000 |
| Buildings | 70,000 | 70,000 |
| Accumulated depreciation—buildings | (15,000) | (10,000) |
| Total | $110,500 | $120,100 |
| Accounts payable | $ 10,370 | $ 31,100 |
| Common stock | 75,000 | 69,000 |
| Retained earnings | 25,130 | 20,000 |
| Total | $110,500 | $120,100 |

Rondo's 2022 income statement included net sales of $120,000, cost of goods sold of $70,000, and net income of $14,000.

**Instructions**

Compute the following ratios for 2022.

a. Current ratio.

b. Accounts receivable turnover.

c. Inventory turnover.

d. Profit margin.

e. Asset turnover.

f. Return on assets.

g. Return on common stockholders' equity.

h. Debt to assets ratio.

**Solution**

2. **a.** ($5,300 + $21,200 + $9,000) ÷ $10,370 = 3.42:1

   **b.** $120,000 ÷ [($21,200 + $23,400) ÷ 2] = 5.38 times

   **c.** $70,000 ÷ [($9,000 + $7,000) ÷ 2] = 8.8 times

   **d.** $14,000 ÷ $120,000 = 11.7%

   **e.** $120,000 ÷ [($110,500 + $120,100) ÷ 2] = 1.04 times

   **f.** $14,000 ÷ [($110,500 + $120,100) ÷ 2] = 12.1%

   **g.** $14,000 ÷ [($100,130 + $89,000) ÷ 2] = 14.8%

   **h.** $10,370 ÷ $110,500 = 9.4%

## Practice Problem

**(LO 1)** The events and transactions of Dever Corporation for the year ending December 31, 2022, resulted in the following data.

*Prepare an income statement and a statement of comprehensive income.*

| | |
|---|---|
| Cost of goods sold | $2,600,000 |
| Net sales | 4,400,000 |
| Other expenses and losses | 9,600 |
| Other revenues and gains | 5,600 |
| Selling and administrative expenses | 1,100,000 |
| Income from operations of plastics division | 70,000 |
| Gain from disposal of plastics division | 500,000 |
| Unrealized loss on available-for-sale securities | 60,000 |

Analysis reveals the following:

1. All items are before the applicable income tax rate of 30%.

2. The plastics division was sold on July 1.

3. All operating data for the plastics division have been segregated.

**Instructions**

Prepare an income statement and a statement of comprehensive income for the year.

**Solution**

### Dever Corporation
#### Income Statement
#### For the Year Ended December 31, 2022

| | |
|---|---|
| Net sales | $4,400,000 |
| Cost of goods sold | 2,600,000 |
| Gross profit | 1,800,000 |
| Selling and administrative expenses | 1,100,000 |
| Income from operations | 700,000 |

| | | |
|---|---:|---:|
| Other revenues and gains | | 5,600 |
| Other expenses and losses | | 9,600 |
| Income before income taxes | | 696,000 |
| Income tax expense ($696,000 × 30%) | | 208,800 |
| Income from continuing operations | | 487,200 |
| Discontinued operations | | |
| Income from operation of plastics division, net of $21,000 | | |
| income taxes ($70,000 × 30%) | $ 49,000 | |
| Gain from disposal of plastics division, net of $150,000 | | |
| income taxes ($500,000 × 30%) | 350,000 | 399,000 |
| Net income | | $886,200 |

### Dever Corporation
### Statement of Comprehensive Income
### For the Year Ended December 31, 2022

| | |
|---|---:|
| Net income | $886,200 |
| Unrealized loss on available-for-sale securities, net of $18,000 | |
| income tax savings ($60,000 × 30%) | 42,000 |
| Comprehensive income | $844,200 |

# WileyPLUS

Brief Exercises, DO IT! Exercises, Exercises, Problems, and many additional resources are available for practice in WileyPLUS.

## Questions

**1.** Explain sustainable income. What relationship does this concept have to the treatment of discontinued operations on the income statement?

**2.** Hogan Inc. reported 2021 earnings per share of $3.26 and had no discontinued operations. In 2022, earnings per share on income from continuing operations was $2.99, and earnings per share on net income was $3.49. Do you consider this trend to be favorable? Why or why not?

**3.** Moosier Inc. has been in operation for 3 years and uses the FIFO method of pricing inventory. During the fourth year, Moosier changes to the average-cost method for all its inventory. How will Moosier report this change?

**4.** What amount did **Apple** report as "Other comprehensive earnings" in its consolidated statement of comprehensive income ending September 29, 2018? By what percentage did Apple's "Comprehensive income" differ from its "Net income"?

**5.** Identify and explain factors that affect quality of earnings.

**6.** Explain how the choice of one of the following accounting methods over the other raises or lowers a company's net income during a period of continuing inflation.

  **a.** Use of FIFO instead of LIFO for inventory costing.

  **b.** Use of a 6-year life for machinery instead of a 9-year life.

  **c.** Use of straight-line depreciation instead of declining-balance depreciation.

**7.** Two popular methods of financial statement analysis are horizontal analysis and vertical analysis. Explain the difference between these two methods.

**8.** **a.** If Erin Company had net income of $300,000 in 2021 and it experienced a 24.5% increase in net income for 2022, what is its net income for 2022?

  **b.** If 6 cents of every dollar of Erin's revenue is net income in 2021, what is the dollar amount of 2021 revenue?

**9.** **a.** Gina Jaimes believes that the analysis of financial statements is directed at two characteristics of a company: liquidity and profitability. Is Gina correct? Explain.

  **b.** Are short-term creditors, long-term creditors, and stockholders interested in primarily the same characteristics of a company? Explain.

**10. a.** Distinguish among the following bases of comparison: intra-company, intercompany, and industry averages.

   **b.** Give the principal value of using each of the three bases of comparison.

**11.** Name the major ratios useful in assessing (a) liquidity and (b) solvency.

**12.** Vern Thoms is puzzled. His company had a profit margin of 10% in 2022. He feels that this is an indication that the company is doing well. Tina Amos, his accountant, says that more information is needed to determine the company's financial well-being. Who is correct? Why?

**13.** What does each type of ratio measure?

   **a.** Liquidity ratios.

   **b.** Solvency ratios.

   **c.** Profitability ratios.

**14.** What is the difference between the current ratio and working capital?

**15.** Handi Mart, a retail store, has an accounts receivable turnover of 4.5 times. The industry average is 12.5 times. Does Handi Mart have a collection problem with its receivables?

**16.** Which ratios should be used to help answer each of these questions?

   **a.** How efficient is a company in using its assets to produce sales?

   **b.** How near to sale is the inventory on hand?

   **c.** How many dollars of net income were earned for each dollar invested by the owners?

   **d.** How able is a company to meet interest charges as they fall due?

**17.** At year-end, the price-earnings ratio of **General Motors** was 11.3, and the price-earnings ratio of **Microsoft** was 28.14. Which company did the stock market favor? Explain.

**18.** What is the formula for computing the payout ratio? Do you expect this ratio to be high or low for a growth company?

**19.** Holding all other factors constant, indicate whether each of the following changes generally signals good or bad news about a company.

   **a.** Increase in profit margin.

   **b.** Decrease in inventory turnover.

   **c.** Increase in current ratio.

   **d.** Decrease in earnings per share.

   **e.** Increase in price-earnings ratio.

   **f.** Increase in debt to assets ratio.

   **g.** Decrease in times interest earned.

**20.** The return on assets for Ayala Corporation is 7.6%. During the same year, Ayala's return on common stockholders' equity is 12.8%. What is the explanation for the difference in the two rates?

**21.** Which two ratios do you think should be of greatest interest in each of the following cases?

   **a.** A pension fund considering the purchase of 20-year bonds.

   **b.** A bank contemplating a short-term loan.

   **c.** A common stockholder.

**22.** Keanu Inc. has net income of $200,000, average shares of common stock outstanding of 40,000, and preferred dividends for the period of $20,000. What is Keanu's earnings per share of common stock? Fred Tyme, the president of Keanu, believes that the computed EPS of the company is high. Comment.

## Brief Exercises

**BE10.1 (LO 1), AP** On June 30, Flores Corporation discontinued its operations in Mexico. During the year, the operating income was $200,000 before taxes. On September 1, Flores disposed of the Mexico facility at a pretax loss of $640,000. The applicable tax rate is 25%. Show the discontinued operations section of Flores's income statement.

*Prepare a discontinued operations section of an income statement.*

**BE10.2 (LO 1), AP** An inexperienced accountant for Silva Corporation showed the following in the income statement: net income $337,500 and unrealized gain on available-for-sale securities (before taxes) $70,000. The unrealized gain on available-for-sale securities is subject to a 25% tax rate. Prepare a correct statement of comprehensive income.

*Prepare a statement of comprehensive income including unusual items.*

**BE10.3 (LO 1), C** On January 1, 2022, Bryce Inc. changed from the LIFO method of inventory pricing to the FIFO method. Explain how this change in accounting principle should be treated in the company's financial statements.

*Indicate how a change in accounting principle is reported.*

**BE10.4 (LO 2), AP** Using these data from the comparative balance sheet of Rollaird Company, perform horizontal analysis.

*Prepare horizontal analysis.*

|                      | December 31, 2022 | December 31, 2021 |
|----------------------|-------------------|-------------------|
| Accounts receivable  | $ 460,000         | $ 400,000         |
| Inventory            | 780,000           | 650,000           |
| Total assets         | 3,164,000         | 2,800,000         |

**BE10.5 (LO 2), AP** Using these data from the comparative balance sheet of Rollaird Company, perform vertical analysis.

*Prepare vertical analysis.*

|                      | December 31, 2022 | December 31, 2021 |
|----------------------|-------------------|-------------------|
| Accounts receivable  | $ 460,000         | $ 400,000         |
| Inventory            | 780,000           | 650,000           |
| Total assets         | 3,164,000         | 2,800,000         |

*Calculate percentage of change.*

**BE10.6 (LO 2), AP** Net income was $500,000 in 2020, $485,000 in 2021, and $518,400 in 2022. What is the percentage of change (a) from 2020 to 2021, and (b) from 2021 to 2022? Is the change an increase or a decrease?

*Calculate net income.*

**BE10.7 (LO 2), AP** If Coho Company had net income of $382,800 in 2022 and it experienced a 16% increase in net income over 2021, what was its 2021 net income?

*Analyze change in net income.*

**BE10.8 (LO 2), AP** Vertical analysis (common-size) percentages for Palau Company's sales revenue, cost of goods sold, and expenses are listed here.

| Vertical Analysis | 2022 | 2021 | 2020 |
| --- | --- | --- | --- |
| Sales revenue | 100.0% | 100.0% | 100.0% |
| Cost of goods sold | 60.5 | 62.9 | 64.8 |
| Expenses | 26.0 | 26.6 | 27.5 |

Did Palau's net income as a percent of sales increase, decrease, or remain unchanged over the 3-year period? Provide numerical support for your answer.

*Analyze change in net income.*

**BE10.9 (LO 2), AP** Writing Horizontal analysis (trend analysis) percentages for Phoenix Company's sales revenue, cost of goods sold, and expenses are listed here.

| Horizontal Analysis | 2022 | 2021 | 2020 |
| --- | --- | --- | --- |
| Sales revenue | 96.2% | 104.8% | 100.0% |
| Cost of goods sold | 101.0 | 98.0 | 100.0 |
| Expenses | 105.6 | 95.4 | 100.0 |

Explain whether Phoenix's net income increased, decreased, or remained unchanged over the 3-year period.

*Calculate current ratio.*

**BE10.10 (LO 3), AP** Suppose these selected condensed data are taken from recent balance sheets of **Bob Evans Farms** (in thousands).

| | 2022 | 2021 |
| --- | --- | --- |
| Cash | $ 13,606 | $ 7,669 |
| Accounts receivable | 23,045 | 19,951 |
| Inventory | 31,087 | 31,345 |
| Other current assets | 12,522 | 11,909 |
| Total current assets | $ 80,260 | $ 70,874 |
| Total current liabilities | $245,805 | $326,203 |

Compute the current ratio for each year and comment on your results.

*Evaluate collection of accounts receivable.*

**BE10.11 (LO 3), AN** Writing The following data are taken from the financial statements of Colby Company.

| | 2022 | 2021 |
| --- | --- | --- |
| Accounts receivable (net), end of year | $ 550,000 | $ 540,000 |
| Net sales on account | 4,300,000 | 4,000,000 |
| Terms for all sales are 1/10, n/45 | | |

Compute for each year (a) the accounts receivable turnover and (b) the average collection period. What conclusions about the management of accounts receivable can be drawn from these data? At the end of 2020, accounts receivable was $520,000.

*Evaluate management of inventory.*

**BE10.12 (LO 3), AN** Writing The following data were taken from the income statements of Mydorf Company.

| | 2022 | 2021 |
| --- | --- | --- |
| Sales revenue | $6,420,000 | $6,240,000 |
| Beginning inventory | 960,000 | 840,000 |
| Purchases | 4,840,000 | 4,661,000 |
| Ending inventory | 1,020,000 | 960,000 |

Compute for each year (a) the inventory turnover and (b) days in inventory. What conclusions concerning the management of the inventory can be drawn from these data?

*Calculate profitability ratios.*

**BE10.13 (LO 3), AN Staples, Inc.** is one of the largest suppliers of office products in the United States. Suppose it had net income of $738.7 million and sales of $24,275.5 million in 2022. Its total assets were $13,073.1 million at the beginning of the year and $13,717.3 million at the end of the year. What is Staples, Inc.'s (a) asset turnover and (b) profit margin? (Round to two decimals.) Provide a brief interpretation of your results.

**BE10.14 (LO 3), AN** Hollie Company has stockholders' equity of $400,000 and net income of $72,000. It has a payout ratio of 18% and a return on assets of 20%. How much did Hollie pay in cash dividends, and what were its average total assets?

*Calculate profitability ratios.*

**BE10.15 (LO 3), AN** Selected data taken from a recent year's financial statements of trading card company **Topps Company, Inc.** are as follows (in millions).

*Calculate and analyze free cash flow.*

| | |
|---|---|
| Net sales | $326.7 |
| Current liabilities, beginning of year | 41.1 |
| Current liabilities, end of year | 62.4 |
| Net cash provided by operating activities | 10.4 |
| Total liabilities, beginning of year | 65.2 |
| Total liabilities, end of year | 73.2 |
| Capital expenditures | 3.7 |
| Cash dividends | 6.2 |

Compute the free cash flow. Provide a brief interpretation of your results.

## DO IT! Exercises

**DO IT! 10.1 (LO 1), AP** In its proposed 2022 income statement, Hrabik Corporation reports income before income taxes $500,000, income taxes $100,000 (not including unusual items), loss on operation of discontinued music division $60,000, gain on disposal of discontinued music division $40,000, and unrealized loss on available-for-sale securities $150,000. The income tax rate is 20%. Prepare a correct partial income statement, beginning with income before income taxes, and a statement of comprehensive income.

*Prepare a partial income statement and a statement of comprehensive income.*

**DO IT! 10.2 (LO 2), AP** Summary financial information for Gandaulf Company is as follows.

*Prepare horizontal analysis.*

| | Dec. 31, 2022 | Dec. 31, 2021 |
|---|---|---|
| Current assets | $ 200,000 | $ 220,000 |
| Plant assets | 1,040,000 | 780,000 |
| Total assets | $1,240,000 | $1,000,000 |

Compute the amount and percentage changes in 2022 using horizontal analysis, assuming 2021 is the base year.

**DO IT! 10.3 (LO 3), AP** The condensed financial statements of Murawski Company for the years 2021 and 2022 are presented as follows. (Amounts in thousands.)

*Compute ratios.*

### Murawski Company
### Balance Sheets
### December 31

| | 2022 | 2021 |
|---|---|---|
| **Current assets** | | |
| Cash and cash equivalents | $ 330 | $ 360 |
| Accounts receivable (net) | 470 | 400 |
| Inventory | 460 | 390 |
| Prepaid expenses | 120 | 160 |
| Total current assets | 1,380 | 1,310 |
| Investments | 10 | 10 |
| Property, plant, and equipment | 420 | 380 |
| Intangibles and other assets | 530 | 510 |
| Total assets | $2,340 | $2,210 |
| Current liabilities | $ 900 | $ 790 |
| Long-term liabilities | 410 | 380 |
| Stockholders' equity—common | 1,030 | 1,040 |
| Total liabilities and stockholders' equity | $2,340 | $2,210 |

| | Murawski Company<br>**Income Statements**<br>**For the Years Ended December 31** | | |
|---|---|---|---|
| | | **2022** | **2021** |
| Sales revenue | | $3,800 | $3,460 |
| Costs and expenses | | | |
| Cost of goods sold | | 955 | 890 |
| Selling & administrative expenses | | 2,400 | 2,330 |
| Interest expense | | 25 | 20 |
| Total costs and expenses | | 3,380 | 3,240 |
| Income before income taxes | | 420 | 220 |
| Income tax expense | | 126 | 66 |
| Net income | | $ 294 | $ 154 |

Compute the following ratios for 2022 and 2021.

a. Current ratio.

b. Inventory turnover. (Inventory on 12/31/20 was $340.)

c. Profit margin.

d. Return on assets. (Assets on 12/31/20 were $1,900.)

e. Return on common stockholders' equity. (Stockholders' equity on 12/31/20 was $900.)

f. Debt to assets ratio.

g. Times interest earned.

# Exercises

*Prepare a correct partial income statement.*

**E10.1 (LO 1), AN** **Writing** For its fiscal year ending October 31, 2022, Haas Corporation reports the following partial data.

| | |
|---|---|
| Income before income taxes | $540,000 |
| Income tax expense (20% × $420,000) | 84,000 |
| Income from continuing operations | 456,000 |
| Loss on discontinued operations | 120,000 |
| Net income | $336,000 |

The loss on discontinued operations was comprised of a $50,000 loss from operations and a $70,000 loss from disposal. The income tax rate is 20% on all items.

**Instructions**

a. Prepare a correct partial income statement, beginning with income before income taxes.

b. Explain in memo form why the income statement data are misleading.

*Prepare a partial income statement and a statement of comprehensive income.*

**E10.2 (LO 1), AP** Trayer Corporation has income from continuing operations of $290,000 for the year ended December 31, 2022. It also has the following items (before considering income taxes).

1. An unrealized loss of $80,000 on available-for-sale securities.

2. A gain of $30,000 on the discontinuance of a division (comprised of a $10,000 loss from operations and a $40,000 gain on disposal).

Assume all items are subject to income taxes at a 20% tax rate.

**Instructions**

Prepare a partial income statement, beginning with income from continuing operations, and a statement of comprehensive income.

**E10.3 (LO 2), AP** Here is financial information for Glitter Inc.

*Prepare horizontal analysis.*

| | December 31, 2022 | December 31, 2021 |
|---|---|---|
| Current assets | $106,000 | $ 90,000 |
| Plant assets (net) | 400,000 | 350,000 |
| Current liabilities | 99,000 | 65,000 |
| Long-term liabilities | 122,000 | 90,000 |
| Common stock, $1 par | 130,000 | 115,000 |
| Retained earnings | 155,000 | 170,000 |

**Instructions**

Prepare a schedule showing a horizontal analysis for 2022, using 2021 as the base year.

**E10.4 (LO 2), AP** Operating data for Joshua Corporation are presented as follows.

*Prepare vertical analysis.*

| | 2022 | 2021 |
|---|---|---|
| Sales revenue | $800,000 | $600,000 |
| Cost of goods sold | 520,000 | 408,000 |
| Selling expenses | 120,000 | 72,000 |
| Administrative expenses | 60,000 | 48,000 |
| Income tax expense | 30,000 | 24,000 |
| Net income | 70,000 | 48,000 |

**Instructions**

Prepare a schedule showing a vertical analysis for 2022 and 2021.

**E10.5 (LO 2), AP** Hypothetical comparative condensed balance sheets of **Nike, Inc.** are presented here.

*Prepare horizontal and vertical analyses.*

**Nike, Inc.**
**Condensed Balance Sheets**
**May 31**
**($ in millions)**

| | 2022 | 2021 |
|---|---|---|
| **Assets** | | |
| Current assets | $ 9,734 | $ 8,839 |
| Property, plant, and equipment (net) | 1,958 | 1,891 |
| Other assets | 1,558 | 1,713 |
| Total assets | $13,250 | $12,443 |
| **Liabilities and Stockholders' Equity** | | |
| Current liabilities | $ 3,277 | $ 3,322 |
| Long-term liabilities | 1,280 | 1,296 |
| Stockholders' equity | 8,693 | 7,825 |
| Total liabilities and stockholders' equity | $13,250 | $12,443 |

**Instructions**

a. Prepare a horizontal analysis of the balance sheet data for Nike, using 2021 as a base. (Show the amount of increase or decrease as well.)

b. Prepare a vertical analysis of the balance sheet data for Nike for 2022.

**E10.6 (LO 2), AP** Here are the comparative condensed income statements of Delaney Corporation.

*Prepare horizontal and vertical analyses.*

**Delaney Corporation**
**Condensed Income Statements**
**For the Years Ended December 31**

| | 2022 | 2021 |
|---|---|---|
| Net sales | $598,000 | $500,000 |
| Cost of goods sold | 477,000 | 420,000 |
| Gross profit | 121,000 | 80,000 |
| Operating expenses | 80,000 | 44,000 |
| Net income | $ 41,000 | $ 36,000 |

**Instructions**

a. Prepare a horizontal analysis of the income statement data for Delaney Corporation, using 2021 as a base. (Show the amounts of increase or decrease.)

b. Prepare a vertical analysis of the income statement data for Delaney Corporation for both years.

*Compute liquidity ratios.*

**E10.7 (LO 3), AP Nordstrom, Inc.** operates department stores in numerous states. Selected hypothetical financial statement data (in millions) for 2022 are presented below.

|  | End of Year | Beginning of Year |
|---|---|---|
| Cash and cash equivalents | $ 795 | $ 72 |
| Accounts receivable (net) | 2,035 | 1,942 |
| Inventory | 898 | 900 |
| Other current assets | 326 | 303 |
| Total current assets | $4,054 | $3,217 |
| Total current liabilities | $2,014 | $1,601 |

For the year, net credit sales were $8,258 million, cost of goods sold was $5,328 million, and net cash provided by operating activities was $1,251 million.

**Instructions**

Compute the current ratio, accounts receivable turnover, average collection period, inventory turnover, and days in inventory at the end of the current year.

*Perform current ratio analysis.*

**E10.8 (LO 3), AP** Gwynn Incorporated had the following transactions involving current assets and current liabilities during February 2022.

| Feb. | 3 | Collected accounts receivable of $15,000. |
|---|---|---|
|  | 7 | Purchased equipment for $23,000 cash. |
|  | 11 | Paid $3,000 for a 1-year insurance policy. |
|  | 14 | Paid accounts payable of $12,000. |
|  | 18 | Declared cash dividends, $4,000. |

Additional information:
As of February 1, 2022, current assets were $120,000 and current liabilities were $40,000.

**Instructions**

Compute the current ratio as of the beginning of the month and after each transaction.

*Compute selected ratios.*

**E10.9 (LO 3), AP** Lendell Company has these comparative balance sheet data:

**Lendell Company**
**Balance Sheets**
**December 31**

|  | 2022 | 2021 |
|---|---|---|
| Cash | $ 15,000 | $ 30,000 |
| Accounts receivable (net) | 70,000 | 60,000 |
| Inventory | 60,000 | 50,000 |
| Plant assets (net) | 200,000 | 180,000 |
|  | $345,000 | $320,000 |
| Accounts payable | $ 50,000 | $ 60,000 |
| Mortgage payable (15%) | 100,000 | 100,000 |
| Common stock, $10 par | 140,000 | 120,000 |
| Retained earnings | 55,000 | 40,000 |
|  | $345,000 | $320,000 |

Additional information for 2022:

1. Net income was $25,000.

2. Sales on account were $375,000. Sales returns and allowances amounted to $25,000.

3. Cost of goods sold was $198,000.

4. Net cash provided by operating activities was $48,000.

5. Capital expenditures were $25,000, and cash dividends were $10,000.

**Instructions**

Compute the following ratios at December 31, 2022.

a. Current ratio.

b. Accounts receivable turnover.

c. Average collection period.

d. Inventory turnover.

e. Days in inventory.

f. Free cash flow.

**E10.10 (LO 3), AP** Selected hypothetical comparative statement data for the giant bookseller **Barnes & Noble** are presented here. All balance sheet data are as of the end of the fiscal year (in millions).

*Compute selected ratios.*

|  | 2022 | 2021 |
|---|---|---|
| Net sales | $5,121.8 | $5,286.7 |
| Cost of goods sold | 3,540.6 | 3,679.8 |
| Net income | 75.9 | 135.8 |
| Accounts receivable | 81.0 | 107.1 |
| Inventory | 1,203.5 | 1,358.2 |
| Total assets | 2,993.9 | 3,249.8 |
| Total common stockholders' equity | 921.6 | 1,074.7 |

**Instructions**

Compute the following ratios for 2022.

a. Profit margin.

b. Asset turnover.

c. Return on assets.

d. Return on common stockholders' equity.

e. Gross profit rate.

**E10.11 (LO 3), AP** Here is the income statement for Myers, Inc.

*Compute selected ratios.*

**Myers, Inc.**
**Income Statement**
**For the Year Ended December 31, 2022**

| | |
|---|---|
| Sales revenue | $400,000 |
| Cost of goods sold | 230,000 |
| Gross profit | 170,000 |
| Expenses (including $16,000 interest and $24,000 income taxes) | 98,000 |
| Net income | $ 72,000 |

Additional information:

1. Common stock outstanding January 1, 2022, was 32,000 shares, and 40,000 shares were outstanding at December 31, 2022.

2. The market price of Myers stock was $14 in 2022.

3. Cash dividends of $21,000 were declared and paid, $5,000 of which were to preferred stockholders.

**Instructions**

Compute the following measures for 2022.

a. Earnings per share.

b. Price-earnings ratio.

c. Payout ratio.

d. Times interest earned.

**E10.12 (LO 3), AP** Panza Corporation experienced a fire on December 31, 2022, in which its financial records were partially destroyed. It has been able to salvage some of the records and has ascertained the following balances.

*Compute amounts from ratios.*

|  | December 31, 2022 | December 31, 2021 |
|---|---|---|
| Cash | $ 30,000 | $ 10,000 |
| Accounts receivable (net) | 72,500 | 126,000 |
| Inventory | 200,000 | 180,000 |
| Accounts payable | 50,000 | 90,000 |
| Notes payable | 30,000 | 60,000 |
| Common stock, $100 par | 400,000 | 400,000 |
| Retained earnings | 113,500 | 101,000 |

Additional information:

1. The inventory turnover is 3.8 times.
2. The return on common stockholders' equity is 22%. The company had no additional paid-in capital.
3. The accounts receivable turnover is 11.2 times.
4. The return on assets is 18%.
5. Total assets at December 31, 2021, were $605,000.

### Instructions

Compute the following for Panza Corporation.

a. Cost of goods sold for 2022.

b. Net credit sales for 2022.

c. Net income for 2022.

d. Total assets at December 31, 2022.

*Compute ratios.*

**E10.13 (LO 3), AP** The condensed financial statements of Ness Company for the years 2021 and 2022 are as follows.

**Ness Company**
**Balance Sheets**
**December 31 (in thousands)**

|  | 2022 | 2021 |
|---|---|---|
| Current assets |  |  |
| Cash and cash equivalents | $ 330 | $ 360 |
| Accounts receivable (net) | 470 | 400 |
| Inventory | 460 | 390 |
| Prepaid expenses | 130 | 160 |
| Total current assets | 1,390 | 1,310 |
| Investments | 10 | 10 |
| Property, plant, and equipment (net) | 410 | 380 |
| Intangibles and other assets | 530 | 510 |
| Total assets | $2,340 | $2,210 |
| Current liabilities | $ 820 | $ 790 |
| Long-term liabilities | 480 | 380 |
| Stockholders' equity—common | 1,040 | 1,040 |
| Total liabilities and stockholders' equity | $2,340 | $2,210 |

**Ness Company**
**Income Statements**
**For the Year Ended December 31 (in thousands)**

|  | 2022 | 2021 |
|---|---|---|
| Sales revenue | $3,800 | $3,460 |
| Costs and expenses |  |  |
| Cost of goods sold | 970 | 890 |
| Selling & administrative expenses | 2,400 | 2,330 |
| Interest expense | 10 | 20 |
| Total costs and expenses | 3,380 | 3,240 |
| Income before income taxes | 420 | 220 |
| Income tax expense | 168 | 88 |
| Net income | $ 252 | $ 132 |

Compute the following ratios for 2022 and 2021.

a. Current ratio.

b. Inventory turnover. (Inventory on December 31, 2020, was $340.)

c. Profit margin.

d. Return on assets. (Assets on December 31, 2020, were $1,900.)

e. Return on common stockholders' equity. (Equity on December 31, 2020, was $900.)

f. Debt to assets ratio.

g. Times interest earned.

# Problems

P10.1 **(LO 2, 3), AN** **Writing** Here are comparative statement data for Duke Company and Lord Company, two competitors. All balance sheet data are as of December 31, 2022, and December 31, 2021.

*Prepare vertical analysis and comment on profitability.*

| | Duke Company | | Lord Company | |
|---|---|---|---|---|
| | **2022** | **2021** | **2022** | **2021** |
| Net sales | $1,849,000 | | $546,000 | |
| Cost of goods sold | 1,063,200 | | 289,000 | |
| Operating expenses | 240,000 | | 82,000 | |
| Interest expense | 6,800 | | 3,600 | |
| Income tax expense | 62,000 | | 28,000 | |
| Current assets | 325,975 | $312,410 | 83,336 | $ 79,467 |
| Plant assets (net) | 526,800 | 500,000 | 139,728 | 125,812 |
| Current liabilities | 66,325 | 75,815 | 35,348 | 30,281 |
| Long-term liabilities | 113,990 | 90,000 | 29,620 | 25,000 |
| Common stock, $10 par | 500,000 | 500,000 | 120,000 | 120,000 |
| Retained earnings | 172,460 | 146,595 | 38,096 | 29,998 |

## Instructions

**a.** Prepare a vertical analysis of the 2022 income statement data for Duke Company and Lord Company.

**b.** Comment on the relative profitability of the companies by computing the 2022 return on assets and the return on common stockholders' equity for both companies.

P10.2 **(LO 3), AP** The comparative statements of Wahlberg Company are presented here.

*Compute ratios from balance sheets and income statements.*

**Wahlberg Company**
**Income Statements**
**For the Years Ended December 31**

| | **2022** | **2021** |
|---|---|---|
| Net sales | $1,890,540 | $1,750,500 |
| Cost of goods sold | 1,058,540 | 1,006,000 |
| Gross profit | 832,000 | 744,500 |
| Selling and administrative expenses | 500,000 | 479,000 |
| Income from operations | 332,000 | 265,500 |
| Other expenses and losses | | |
|    Interest expense | 22,000 | 20,000 |
| Income before income taxes | 310,000 | 245,500 |
| Income tax expense | 92,000 | 73,000 |
| Net income | $ 218,000 | $ 172,500 |

**Wahlberg Company**
**Balance Sheets**
**December 31**

| | **2022** | **2021** |
|---|---|---|
| **Assets** | | |
| Current assets | | |
|    Cash | $    60,100 | $ 64,200 |
|    Debt investments (short-term) | 74,000 | 50,000 |
|    Accounts receivable | 117,800 | 102,800 |
|    Inventory | 126,000 | 115,500 |
|      Total current assets | 377,900 | 332,500 |
| Plant assets (net) | 649,000 | 520,300 |
| Total assets | $1,026,900 | $852,800 |

| | 2022 | 2021 |
|---|---|---|
| **Liabilities and Stockholders' Equity** | | |
| Current liabilities | | |
| Accounts payable | $ 160,000 | $145,400 |
| Income taxes payable | 43,500 | 42,000 |
| Total current liabilities | 203,500 | 187,400 |
| Bonds payable | 220,000 | 200,000 |
| Total liabilities | 423,500 | 387,400 |
| Stockholders' equity | | |
| Common stock ($5 par) | 290,000 | 300,000 |
| Retained earnings | 313,400 | 165,400 |
| Total stockholders' equity | 603,400 | 465,400 |
| Total liabilities and stockholders' equity | $1,026,900 | $852,800 |

All sales were on account. Net cash provided by operating activities for 2022 was $220,000. Capital expenditures were $136,000, and cash dividends were $70,000.

### Instructions

Compute the following ratios for 2022.

**a.** Earnings per share.

**b.** Return on common stockholders' equity.

**c.** Return on assets.

**d.** Current ratio.

**e.** Accounts receivable turnover.

**f.** Average collection period.

**g.** Inventory turnover.

**h.** Days in inventory.

**i.** Times interest earned.

**j.** Asset turnover.

**k.** Debt to assets ratio.

**l.** Free cash flow.

*Perform ratio analysis, and discuss changes in financial position and operating results.*

**P10.3 (LO 3), AN** **Writing** Condensed balance sheet and income statement data for Jergan Corporation are presented here.

**Jergan Corporation**
**Balance Sheets**
**December 31**

| | 2022 | 2021 | 2020 |
|---|---|---|---|
| Cash | $ 30,000 | $ 20,000 | $ 18,000 |
| Accounts receivable (net) | 50,000 | 45,000 | 48,000 |
| Other current assets | 90,000 | 95,000 | 64,000 |
| Investments | 55,000 | 70,000 | 45,000 |
| Plant and equipment (net) | 500,000 | 370,000 | 358,000 |
| | $725,000 | $600,000 | $533,000 |
| | | | |
| Current liabilities | $ 85,000 | $ 80,000 | $ 70,000 |
| Long-term debt | 145,000 | 85,000 | 50,000 |
| Common stock, $10 par | 320,000 | 310,000 | 300,000 |
| Retained earnings | 175,000 | 125,000 | 113,000 |
| | $725,000 | $600,000 | $533,000 |

**Jergan Corporation**
**Income Statements**
**For the Years Ended December 31**

| | 2022 | 2021 |
|---|---|---|
| Sales revenue | $740,000 | $600,000 |
| Less: Sales returns and allowances | 40,000 | 30,000 |
| Net sales | 700,000 | 570,000 |
| Cost of goods sold | 425,000 | 350,000 |
| Gross profit | 275,000 | 220,000 |
| Operating expenses (including income taxes) | 180,000 | 150,000 |
| Net income | $ 95,000 | $ 70,000 |

Additional information:

1. The market price of Jergan's common stock was $7.00, $7.50, and $8.50 for 2020, 2021, and 2022, respectively.

2. You must compute dividends paid. All dividends were paid in cash.

**Instructions**

a. Compute the following ratios for 2021 and 2022.

    1. Profit margin.

    2. Gross profit rate.

    3. Asset turnover.

    4. Earnings per share.

    5. Price-earnings ratio.

    6. Payout ratio.

    7. Debt to assets ratio.

b. Based on the ratios calculated, discuss briefly the improvement or lack thereof in the financial position and operating results from 2021 to 2022 of Jergan Corporation.

**P10.4 (LO 3), AN** The following financial information is for Priscoll Company.         *Compute ratios; comment on overall liquidity and profitability.*

**Priscoll Company**
**Balance Sheets**
**December 31**

| | 2022 | 2021 |
|---|---|---|
| **Assets** | | |
| Cash | $ 70,000 | $ 65,000 |
| Debt investments (short-term) | 55,000 | 40,000 |
| Accounts receivable | 104,000 | 90,000 |
| Inventory | 230,000 | 165,000 |
| Prepaid expenses | 25,000 | 23,000 |
| Land | 130,000 | 130,000 |
| Building and equipment (net) | 260,000 | 185,000 |
| Total assets | $874,000 | $698,000 |
| **Liabilities and Stockholders' Equity** | | |
| Notes payable | $170,000 | $120,000 |
| Accounts payable | 65,000 | 52,000 |
| Accrued liabilities | 40,000 | 40,000 |
| Bonds payable, due 2025 | 250,000 | 170,000 |
| Common stock, $10 par | 200,000 | 200,000 |
| Retained earnings | 149,000 | 116,000 |
| Total liabilities and stockholders' equity | $874,000 | $698,000 |

**Priscoll Company**
**Income Statements**
**For the Years Ended December 31**

| | 2022 | 2021 |
|---|---|---|
| Sales revenue | $882,000 | $790,000 |
| Cost of goods sold | 640,000 | 575,000 |
| Gross profit | 242,000 | 215,000 |
| Operating expenses | 190,000 | 167,000 |
| Net income | $ 52,000 | $ 48,000 |

Additional information:

1. Inventory at the beginning of 2021 was $115,000.

2. Accounts receivable (net) at the beginning of 2021 were $86,000.

3. Total assets at the beginning of 2021 were $660,000.

4. No common stock transactions occurred during 2021 or 2022.

5. All sales were on account.

## Instructions

**a.** Indicate, by using ratios, the change in liquidity and profitability of Priscoll Company from 2021 to 2022. (*Note:* Not all profitability ratios can be computed, nor can cash-basis ratios be computed.)

**b.** The following are three independent situations and a ratio that may be affected. For each situation, compute the affected ratio (1) as of December 31, 2022, and (2) as of December 31, 2023, after giving effect to the situation.

| Situation | Ratio |
|---|---|
| **1.** 18,000 shares of common stock were sold at par on July 1, 2023. Net income for 2023 was $54,000. | Return on common stockholders' equity |
| **2.** All of the notes payable were paid in 2023. All other liabilities remained at their December 31, 2022, levels. Total assets on December 31, 2023, were $900,000. | Debt to assets ratio |
| **3.** The market price of common stock was $9 and $12 on December 31, 2022 and 2023, respectively. Net income for 2023 was $54,000. | Price-earnings ratio |

*Compute selected ratios, and compare liquidity, profitability, and solvency for two companies.*

**P10.5 (LO 3), AN** Selected hypothetical financial data of **Target** and **Walmart** for 2022 are presented here (in millions).

| | Target Corporation | Walmart Inc. |
|---|---|---|
| **Income Statement Data for Year** | | |
| Net sales | $65,357 | $408,214 |
| Cost of goods sold | 45,583 | 304,657 |
| Selling and administrative expenses | 15,101 | 79,607 |
| Interest expense | 707 | 2,065 |
| Other income (expense) | (94) | (411) |
| Income tax expense | 1,384 | 7,139 |
| Net income | $ 2,488 | $ 14,335 |
| **Balance Sheet Data (End of Year)** | | |
| Current assets | $18,424 | $ 48,331 |
| Noncurrent assets | 26,109 | 122,375 |
| Total assets | $44,533 | $170,706 |
| Current liabilities | $11,327 | $ 55,561 |
| Long-term debt | 17,859 | 44,089 |
| Total stockholders' equity | 15,347 | 71,056 |
| Total liabilities and stockholders' equity | $44,533 | $170,706 |
| **Beginning-of-Year Balances** | | |
| Total assets | $44,106 | $163,429 |
| Total stockholders' equity | 13,712 | 65,682 |
| Current liabilities | 10,512 | 55,390 |
| Total liabilities | 30,394 | 97,747 |
| **Other Data** | | |
| Average net accounts receivable | $ 7,525 | $ 4,025 |
| Average inventory | 6,942 | 33,836 |
| Net cash provided by operating activities | 5,881 | 26,249 |
| Capital expenditures | 1,729 | 12,184 |
| Dividends | 496 | 4,217 |

## Instructions

**a.** For each company, compute the following ratios.

**1.** Current ratio.

**2.** Accounts receivable turnover.

**3.** Average collection period.

**4.** Inventory turnover.

**5.** Days in inventory.

**6.** Profit margin.

**7.** Asset turnover.

**8.** Return on assets.

**9.** Return on common stockholders' equity.

**11.** Times interest earned.

**10.** Debt to assets ratio.

**12.** Free cash flow.

**b.** Compare the liquidity, solvency, and profitability of the two companies.

# Expand Your Critical Thinking

## Financial Reporting Problem: Apple Inc.

**CT10.1** Your parents are considering investing in **Apple Inc.** common stock. They ask you, as an accounting expert, to make an analysis of the company for them. Financial statements of Apple are presented in Appendix A. The complete annual report, including the notes to its financial statements, is available at the company's website.

### Instructions

**a.** Make a 5-year trend analysis, using 2014 as the base year, of (1) net sales and (2) net income. Comment on the significance of the trend results.

**b.** Compute for 2018 and 2017 the (1) debt to assets ratio and (2) times interest earned. (See Note 3 for interest expense.) How would you evaluate Apple's long-term solvency?

**c.** Compute for 2018 and 2017 the (1) profit margin, (2) asset turnover, (3) return on assets, and (4) return on common stockholders' equity. How would you evaluate Apple's profitability? Total assets at September 24, 2016, were $321,686 million and total stockholders' equity at September 24, 2016, was $128,249 million.

**d.** What information outside the annual report may also be useful to your parents in making a decision about Apple?

## Comparative Analysis Problem: Columbia Sportswear Company vs. Under Armour, Inc.

**CT10.2** The financial statements of **Columbia Sportswear Company** are presented in Appendix B. Financial statements of **Under Armour, Inc.** are presented in Appendix C.

### Instructions

**a.** Based on the information in the financial statements, determine each of the following for each company:

**1.** The percentage increase (i) in net sales and (ii) in net income from 2017 to 2018.

**2.** The percentage increase (i) in total assets and (ii) in total stockholders' equity from 2017 to 2018.

**3.** The basic earnings per share for 2018.

**b.** What conclusions concerning the two companies can be drawn from these data?

## Interpreting Financial Statements

**CT10.3** **The Coca-Cola Company** and **PepsiCo, Inc.** provide refreshments to every corner of the world. Selected data from hypothetical consolidated financial statements for The Coca-Cola Company and for PepsiCo, Inc. are presented here (in millions).

|  | Coca-Cola | PepsiCo |
|---|---|---|
| Total current assets | $17,551 | $12,571 |
| Total current liabilities | 13,721 | 8,756 |
| Net sales | 30,990 | 43,232 |
| Cost of goods sold | 11,088 | 20,099 |
| Net income | 6,824 | 5,946 |
| Average (net) accounts receivable for the year | 3,424 | 4,654 |

|                                          | Coca-Cola | PepsiCo |
|------------------------------------------|-----------|---------|
| Average inventories for the year         | $ 2,271   | $ 2,570 |
| Average total assets                     | 44,595    | 37,921  |
| Average common stockholders' equity      | 22,636    | 14,556  |
| Average current liabilities              | 13,355    | 8,772   |
| Average total liabilities                | 21,960    | 23,466  |
| Total assets                             | 48,671    | 39,848  |
| Total liabilities                        | 23,872    | 23,044  |
| Income taxes                             | 2,040     | 2,100   |
| Interest expense                         | 355       | 397     |
| Net cash provided by operating activities| 8,186     | 6,796   |
| Capital expenditures                     | 1,993     | 2,128   |
| Cash dividends                           | 3,800     | 2,732   |

**Instructions**

a. Compute the following liquidity ratios for Coca-Cola and for PepsiCo and comment on the relative liquidity of the two competitors.

   1. Current ratio.
   2. Accounts receivable turnover.
   3. Average collection period.
   4. Inventory turnover.
   5. Days in inventory.

b. Compute the following solvency ratios for the two companies and comment on the relative solvency of the two competitors.

   1. Debt to assets ratio.
   2. Times interest earned.
   3. Free cash flow.

c. Compute the following profitability ratios for the two companies and comment on the relative profitability of the two competitors.

   1. Profit margin.
   2. Asset turnover.
   3. Return on assets.
   4. Return on common stockholders' equity.

## Real-World Focus

**CT10.4** You can use the Internet to employ comparative data and industry data to evaluate a company's performance and financial position.

**Instructions**

Identify two competing companies and then go to the **MarketWatch** website. Type in the company name in the search box (e.g., **Best Buy**) and then use the information from the Profile tab to answer the following questions.

a. Evaluate the company's liquidity relative to the industry averages and to the competitor that you chose.

b. Evaluate the company's solvency relative to the industry averages and to the competitor that you chose.

c. Evaluate the company's profitability relative to the industry averages and to the competitor that you chose.

**CT10.5** The April 25, 2012, edition of the *Wall Street Journal* contains an article by Spencer Jakab entitled "Amazon's Valuation Is Hard to Justify."

**Instructions**

Read the article and answer the following questions.

a. Explain what is meant by the statement that "On a split-adjusted basis, today's share price is the equivalent of $1,166."

b. The article says that **Amazon.com** nearly doubled its capital spending on items such as fulfillment centers (sophisticated warehouses where it finds, packages, and ships goods to customers). Discuss the implications that this spending would have on the company's return on assets in the short-term and in the long-term.

**c.** How does Amazon's P-E ratio compare to that of **Apple**, **Netflix**, and **Walmart**? What does this suggest about investors' expectations about Amazon's future earnings?

**d.** What factor does the article cite as a possible hurdle that might reduce Amazon's ability to raise its operating margin back to previous levels?

## Decision-Making Across the Organization

**CT10.6**  You are a loan officer for White Sands Bank of Taos. Paul Jason, president of P. Jason Corporation, has just left your office. He is interested in an 8-year loan to expand the company's operations. The borrowed funds would be used to purchase new equipment. As evidence of the company's debtworthiness, Jason provided you with the following facts.

|                      | 2022    | 2021     |
| -------------------- | ------- | -------- |
| Current ratio        | 3.1     | 2.1      |
| Asset turnover       | 2.8     | 2.2      |
| Net income           | Up 32%  | Down 8%  |
| Earnings per share   | $3.30   | $2.50    |

Jason is a very insistent (some would say pushy) man. When you told him that you would need additional information before making your decision, he acted offended and said, "What more could you possibly want to know?" You responded that, at a minimum, you would need complete, audited financial statements.

### Instructions

With the class divided into groups, answer the following.

**a.** Explain why you would want the financial statements to be audited.

**b.** Discuss the implications of the ratios provided for the lending decision you are to make. That is, does the information paint a favorable picture? Are these ratios relevant to the decision?

**c.** List three other ratios that you would want to calculate for this company, and explain why you would use each.

## Communication Activity

**CT10.7**  Larry Dundee is the chief executive officer of Palmer Electronics. Dundee is an expert engineer but a novice in accounting. Dundee asks you, as an accounting student, to explain (a) the bases for comparison in analyzing Palmer's financial statements and (b) the limitations, if any, in financial statement analysis.

### Instructions

Write a memo to Larry Dundee that explains the basis for comparison and the factors affecting quality of earnings.

## Ethics Case

**CT10.8**  René Kelly, president of RL Industries, wishes to issue a press release to bolster her company's image and maybe even its stock price, which has been gradually falling. As controller, you have been asked to provide a list of 20 financial ratios and other operating statistics for RL Industries' first-quarter financials and operations.

Two days after you provide the data requested, Erin Lourdes, the public relations director of RL, asks you to prove the accuracy of the financial and operating data contained in the press release written by the president and edited by Erin. In the news release, the president highlights the sales increase of 25% over last year's first quarter and the positive change in the current ratio from 1.5:1 last year to 3:1 this year. She also emphasizes that production was up 50% over the prior year's first quarter.

You note that the release contains only positive or improved ratios and none of the negative or deteriorated ratios. For instance, no mention is made that the debt to assets ratio has increased from 35% to 55%, that inventories are up 89%, and that although the current ratio improved, the accounts receivable turnover fell from 12 to 9. Nor is there any mention that the reported profit for the quarter would have been a loss had not the estimated lives of RL plant and machinery been increased by 30%. Erin emphasized, "The Pres wants this release by early this afternoon."

### Instructions

**a.**  Who are the stakeholders in this situation?

**b.**  Is there anything unethical in the president's actions?

**c.**  Should you as controller remain silent? Does Erin have any responsibility?

### All About You

**CT10.9** In this chapter, you learned how to use many tools for performing a financial analysis of a company. When making personal investments, however, it is most likely that you won't be buying stocks and bonds in individual companies. Instead, when most people want to invest in stock, they buy mutual funds. By investing in a mutual fund, you reduce your risk because the fund diversifies by buying the stock of a variety of different companies, bonds, and other investments, depending on the stated goals of the fund.

Before you invest in a fund, you will need to decide what type of fund you want. For example, do you want a fund that has the potential of high growth (but also high risk), or are you looking for lower risk and a steady stream of income? Do you want a fund that invests only in U.S. companies, or do you want one that invests globally? Many resources are available to help you with these types of decisions.

### Instructions

Do an Internet search on "Motley Fool Here's How to Determine Your Ideal Asset Allocation Strategy" and then complete the investment allocation questionnaire. Add up your total points to determine the type of investment fund that would be appropriate for you.

iNoppadol/Shutterstock.com

# Managerial Accounting

## Chapter Preview

This chapter focuses on issues illustrated in the following Feature Story about **Current Designs** and its parent company **Wenonah Canoe**. To succeed, the company needs to determine and control the costs of material, labor, and overhead, and understand the relationship between costs and profits. Managers often make decisions that determine their company's fate—and their own. Managers are evaluated on the results of their decisions. Managerial accounting provides tools to assist management in making decisions and evaluating the effectiveness of those decisions.

## Feature Story

### Just Add Water ... and Paddle

Mike Cichanowski grew up on the Mississippi River in Winona, Minnesota. At a young age, he learned to paddle a canoe so he could explore the river. Before long, Mike began crafting his own canoes from bent wood and fiberglass in his dad's garage. Then, when his canoe-making shop outgrew the garage, he moved it into an old warehouse. When that was going to be torn down, Mike came to a critical juncture in his life. He took out a bank loan and built his own small shop, giving birth to the company **Wenonah Canoe**.

Wenonah Canoe soon became known as a pioneer in developing techniques to get the most out of new materials such as plastics, composites, and carbon fibers—maximizing strength while minimizing weight.

In the 1990s, as kayaking became popular, Mike made another critical decision when he acquired **Current Designs**, a premier Canadian kayak manufacturer. This venture allowed Wenonah to branch out with new product lines while providing Current Designs with much-needed capacity expansion and manufacturing expertise. Mike moved Current Designs' headquarters to Minnesota and made a big (and potentially risky) investment in a new production facility. Today, the company's 90 employees produce about 12,000 canoes and kayaks per year. These are sold across the country and around the world.

Mike will tell you that business success is "a three-legged stool." The first leg is the knowledge and commitment to make a great product. Wenonah's canoes and Current Designs' kayaks are widely regarded as among the very best. The second leg is the ability to sell your product. Mike's company started off making great canoes, but it took a little longer to figure out how to sell them. The third leg is not something that most of you would immediately associate with entrepreneurial success. It is what goes on behind the scenes—accounting. Good accounting information is absolutely critical to the countless decisions, big and small, that ensure the survival and growth of the company.

Bottom line: No matter how good your product is, and no matter how many units you sell, if you don't have a firm grip on your numbers, you are up a creek without a paddle.

**Source:** www.wenonah.com.

# Chapter Outline

| LEARNING OBJECTIVES | REVIEW | PRACTICE |
|---|---|---|
| **LO 1** Identify the features of managerial accounting and the functions of management. | • Comparing managerial and financial accounting<br>• Management functions<br>• Organizational structure | **DO IT! 1** Managerial Accounting Overview |
| **LO 2** Describe the classes of manufacturing costs and the differences between product and period costs. | • Manufacturing costs<br>• Product vs. period costs<br>• Illustration of cost concepts | **DO IT! 2** Managerial Cost Concepts |
| **LO 3** Demonstrate how to compute cost of goods manufactured and prepare financial statements for a manufacturer. | • Income statement<br>• Cost of goods manufactured<br>• Cost of goods manufactured schedule<br>• Balance sheet | **DO IT! 3** Cost of Goods Manufactured |
| **LO 4** Discuss trends in managerial accounting. | • Service industries<br>• Value chain<br>• Balanced scorecard<br>• Business ethics<br>• Corporate social responsibility | **DO IT! 4** Trends in Managerial Accounting |

**Go to the Review and Practice section at the end of the chapter for a targeted summary and practice applications with solutions.**

**Visit WileyPLUS for additional tutorials and practice opportunities.**

# Managerial Accounting Basics

**Managerial accounting** provides economic and financial information for managers and other internal users. The skills that you learn in this course will be vital to your future success in business. You don't believe us? Let's look at examples of some of the crucial activities of employees at **Current Designs** and where those activities are addressed in this text.

- In order to know whether it is making a profit, Current Designs needs accurate information about the cost of each kayak (Chapters 11 and 12). To be profitable, Current Designs adjusts the number of kayaks it produces in response to changes in economic conditions and consumer tastes. It needs to understand how changes in the number of kayaks it produces impact its production costs and profitability (Chapter 13).

- Further, Current Designs' managers often consider alternative courses of action. For example, should the company accept a special order from a customer, produce a particular kayak component internally or outsource it, or continue or discontinue a particular product line (Chapter 14)?

- In order to plan for the future, Current Designs prepares budgets (Chapter 15), and it then compares its budgeted numbers with its actual results to evaluate performance and identify areas that need to change (Chapters 16 and 17).

- Finally, Current Designs sometimes needs to make substantial investment decisions, such as the building of a new plant or the purchase of new equipment (Chapter 18).

Someday, you are going to face decisions just like these. You may end up in sales, marketing, management, production, or finance. You may work for a company that provides medical care, produces software, or serves up mouth-watering meals. No matter what your position is and no matter what your product, the skills you acquire in this class will increase your chances of business success. Put another way, in business you can either guess or you can make an informed decision. As a CEO of **Microsoft** once noted: "If you're supposed to be making money in business and supposed to be satisfying customers and building market share, there are numbers that characterize those things. And if somebody can't speak to me quantitatively about it, then I'm nervous." This course gives you the skills you need to quantify information so you can make informed business decisions.

## Comparing Managerial and Financial Accounting

There are both similarities and differences between managerial and financial accounting.

- Each field of accounting deals with the economic events of a business. For example, *determining* the unit cost of manufacturing a product is part of managerial accounting. *Reporting* the total cost of goods manufactured and sold is part of financial accounting.

- Both managerial and financial accounting require that a company's economic events be quantified and communicated to interested parties.

**Illustration 11.1** summarizes the principal differences between financial accounting and managerial accounting.

**ILLUSTRATION 11.1** Differences between financial and managerial accounting

| Feature | Financial Accounting | Managerial Accounting |
|---|---|---|
| Primary Users of Reports | External users: stockholders, creditors, and regulators. | Internal users: officers and managers. |
| Types and Frequency of Reports | Financial statements. Quarterly and annually. | Internal reports. As frequently as needed. |
| Purpose of Reports | General-purpose. | Special-purpose for specific decisions. |
| Content of Reports | Pertains to business as a whole. Highly aggregated (condensed). Limited to accrual accounting and cost data. Generally accepted accounting principles. | Pertains to subunits of the business. Very detailed. Extends beyond accrual accounting to any relevant data. Evaluated based on relevance to decisions. |
| Verification Process | Audited by CPA. | No independent audits. |

# Management Functions

Managers' activities and responsibilities can be classified into three broad functions:

1. Planning.
2. Directing.
3. Controlling.

In performing these functions, managers make decisions that have a significant impact on the organization.

**Planning** requires managers to look ahead and to establish objectives.

- These objectives are often diverse: maximizing short-term profits and market share, maintaining a commitment to environmental protection, and contributing to social programs.
- A key objective of management is to **add value** to the business under its control. Value is usually measured by the price of the company's stock and by the potential selling price of the company.

For example, **Hewlett-Packard**, in an attempt to gain a stronger foothold in the computer industry, greatly reduced its prices to compete with **Dell**.

**Directing** involves coordinating a company's diverse activities and human resources to produce a smooth-running operation.

- This function relates to implementing planned objectives and providing necessary incentives to motivate employees.
- Directing also involves selecting executives, appointing managers and supervisors, and hiring and training employees.

For example, manufacturers such as **Campbell Soup Company**, **General Motors**, and **Dell** need to coordinate purchasing, manufacturing, warehousing, and selling. Service corporations such as **American Airlines**, **Federal Express**, and **AT&T** coordinate scheduling, sales, service, and acquisitions of equipment and supplies.

The third management function, **controlling**, is the process of keeping the company's activities on track.

- In controlling operations, managers determine whether planned goals are met.
- When there are deviations from targeted objectives, managers decide what changes are needed to get back on track.

Scandals at companies like **Enron**, **Lucent**, and **Xerox** attest to the fact that companies need adequate controls to ensure that the company develops and distributes accurate information.

How do managers achieve control? A smart manager in a very small operation can make personal observations, ask good questions, and know how to evaluate the answers. But using this approach in a larger organization would result in chaos. Imagine the president of **Current Designs** attempting to determine whether the company is meeting its planned objectives without some record of what has happened and what is expected to occur. Thus, large businesses typically use a formal system of evaluation. These systems include such features as budgets, responsibility centers, and performance evaluation reports—all of which are features of managerial accounting.

Decision-making is not a separate management function. Rather, it is the outcome of the exercise of good judgment in planning, directing, and controlling.

## Organizational Structure

Most companies prepare **organization charts** to show the interrelationships of activities and the delegation of authority and responsibility within the company. **Illustration 11.2** shows a typical organization chart.

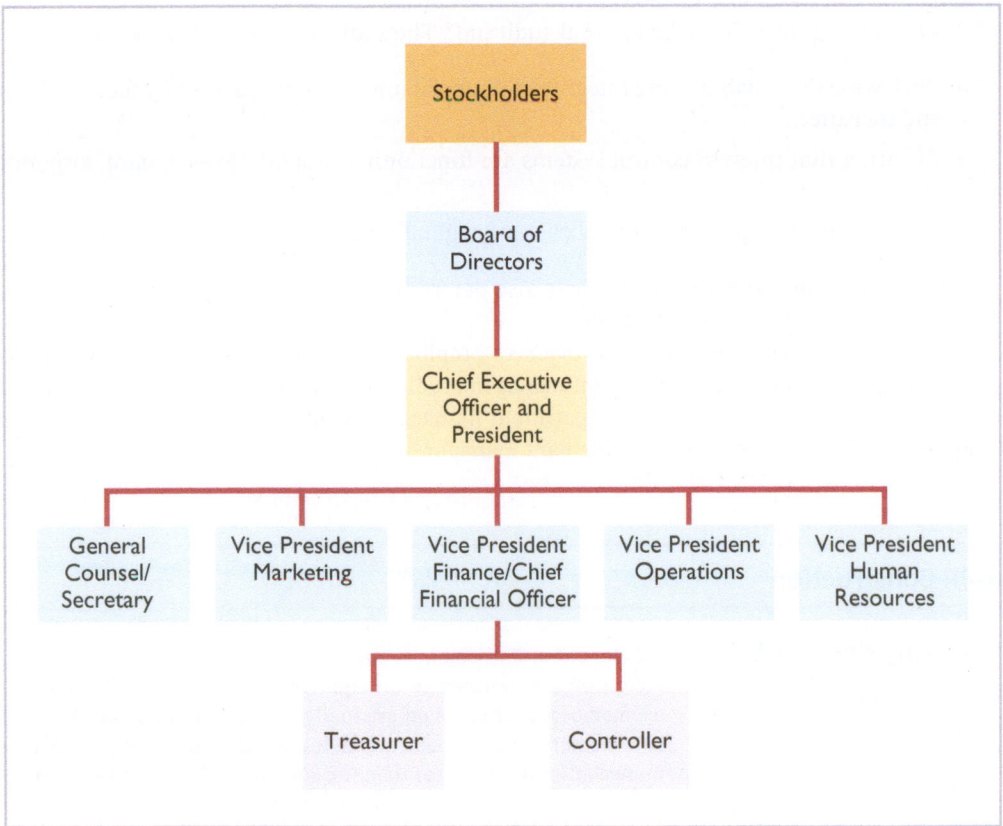

**ILLUSTRATION 11.2**

**A typical corporate organization chart**

Stockholders own the corporation, but they manage it indirectly through a **board of directors** they elect.

- The board formulates the operating policies for the company or organization.
- The board also selects officers, such as a president and one or more vice presidents, to execute policy and to perform daily management functions.

The **chief executive officer (CEO)** has overall responsibility for managing the business. As the organization chart shows, the CEO delegates responsibilities to other officers.

Responsibilities within the company are frequently classified as either line or staff positions.

- Employees with **line positions** are directly involved in the company's primary revenue-generating operating activities. Examples of line positions include the vice president of operations, vice president of marketing, plant managers, supervisors, and production personnel.
- Employees with **staff positions** are involved in activities that support the efforts of the line employees. In a company like **General Electric** or **Facebook**, employees in finance, legal, and human resources have staff positions.
- While activities of staff employees are vital to the company, these employees are nonetheless there to serve the line employees who engage in the company's primary operations.

The **chief financial officer (CFO)** is responsible for all of the accounting and finance issues the company faces. The CFO is supported by the **controller** and the **treasurer**. The controller's responsibilities include:

1. Maintaining the accounting records.
2. Ensuring an adequate system of internal control.
3. Preparing financial statements, tax returns, and internal reports.

The treasurer has custody of the corporation's funds and is responsible for maintaining the company's cash position.

Also serving the CFO is the internal audit staff. The staff's responsibilities include:

- Reviewing the reliability and integrity of financial information provided by the controller and treasurer.
- Ensuring that internal control systems are functioning properly to safeguard corporate assets.
- Investigating compliance with policies and regulations.

In many companies, these staff members also determine whether resources are used in the most economical and efficient fashion.

The vice president of operations oversees employees with line positions. For example, the company might have multiple plant managers, each of whom reports to the vice president of operations. Each plant also has department managers, such as fabricating, painting, and shipping, each of whom reports to the plant manager.

---

## Management Insight    DPR Construction

Sam Edwards/Caiaimage/
Getty Images

### Does a Company Need a CEO?

Can a company function without a person at the top? Nearly all companies have a CEO although some, such as **Oracle**, **Chipotle**, and **Whole Foods**, have operated with two people in the CEO position. **Samsung** even had three CEOs at the same time. On the other hand, **Abercrombie & Fitch** operated for more than two years without a CEO because its CEO unexpectedly quit and a suitable replacement was hard to find. In fact, some companies replace the CEO position with a management committee. These companies feel this structure improves decision-making and increases collaboration. For example, the 4,000 employees of **DPR Construction** are overseen by an eight-person committee. Committee members are rotated off gradually but then continue to advise current members. The company notes that this approach provides more continuity over time than the sometimes sudden and harsh changes that occur when CEOs are replaced.

**Source:** Rachel Feintzeig, "Companies Manage with No CEO," *Wall Street Journal* (December 13, 2016).

**What are some of the advantages cited by companies that choose a structure that lacks a CEO?** (Go to WileyPLUS for this answer and additional questions).

## DO IT! 1 | Managerial Accounting Overview

Indicate whether the following statements are true or false. If false, explain why.

1. Managerial accountants have a single role within an organization: collecting and reporting costs to management.

2. Financial accounting reports are general-purpose and intended for external users.

3. Managerial accounting reports are special-purpose and issued as frequently as needed.

4. Managers' activities and responsibilities can be classified into three broad functions: cost accounting, budgeting, and internal control.

5. Managerial accounting reports must now comply with generally accepted accounting principles (GAAP).

### ACTION PLAN

- Understand that managerial accounting is a field of accounting that provides economic and financial information for managers and other internal users.

- Understand that financial accounting provides information for external users.

- Analyze which users require which different types of information.

### Solution

1. False. Managerial accountants do determine product costs, but they are also responsible for evaluating how well the company employs its resources. As a result, when the company makes critical strategic decisions, managerial accountants serve as team members alongside personnel from production, marketing, and engineering.

2. True.

3. True.

4. False. Managers' activities are classified into three broad functions: planning, directing, and controlling. Planning requires managers to look ahead to establish objectives. Directing involves coordinating a company's diverse activities and human resources to produce a smooth-running operation. Controlling keeps the company's activities on track.

5. False. Managerial accounting reports are for internal use and thus do not have to comply with GAAP.

Related exercise material: **BE11.1, BE11.2, DO IT! 11.1, and E11.1.**

# Managerial Cost Concepts

### LEARNING OBJECTIVE 2

Describe the classes of manufacturing costs and the differences between product and period costs.

In order for managers at **Current Designs** to plan, direct, and control operations effectively, they need good information. One very important type of information relates to costs. Managers should ask questions such as the following.

1. What costs are involved in making a product or performing a service?

2. If we decrease production volume, will costs change?

3. What impact will automation have on total costs?

4. How can we best control costs?

To answer these questions, managers obtain and analyze reliable and relevant cost information. The first step is to understand the various cost categories that companies use.

# Manufacturing Costs

**Manufacturing** consists of activities and processes that convert raw materials into finished goods. Contrast this type of operation with merchandising, which sells products in the form in which they are purchased. Manufacturing costs incurred to produce a product are classified as direct materials, direct labor, and manufacturing overhead.

## Direct Materials

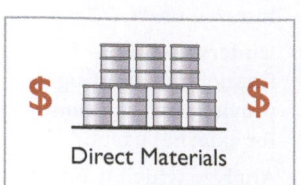

Direct Materials

To obtain the materials that will be converted into the finished product, the manufacturer purchases raw materials. **Raw materials** are the basic materials and parts used in the manufacturing process.

Raw materials that can be physically and directly associated with the finished product during the manufacturing process are **direct materials**. Examples include flour in the baking of bread, syrup in the bottling of soft drinks, and steel in the making of automobiles. A primary direct material of many Current Designs' kayaks is polyethylene powder. Some of its high-performance kayaks use Kevlar®.

Some raw materials cannot be easily associated with the finished product. These are called indirect materials. **Indirect materials** have one of two characteristics:

1. They do not physically become part of the finished product (such as polishing compounds used by Current Designs for the finishing touches on kayaks).

2. They are impractical to trace to the finished product because their physical association with the finished product is too small in terms of cost (such as cotter pins and lock washers used in kayak rudder assembly).

Companies account for indirect materials as part of **manufacturing overhead**.

## Direct Labor

Direct Labor

The work of factory employees that can be physically and directly associated with converting raw materials into finished goods is **direct labor**. Bottlers at **Coca-Cola**, bakers at **Sara Lee**, and equipment operators at **Current Designs** are employees whose activities are usually classified as direct labor. **Indirect labor** refers to the work of employees that has no physical association with the finished product or for which it is impractical to trace costs to the goods produced. Examples include wages of factory maintenance people, factory time-keepers, and factory supervisors. Like indirect materials, companies classify indirect labor as **manufacturing overhead**.

## Manufacturing Overhead

Manufacturing Overhead

**Manufacturing overhead** consists of costs that are indirectly associated with the manufacture of the finished product (see **Alternative Terminology**).

- Overhead costs also include manufacturing costs that cannot be classified as direct materials or direct labor.

- Manufacturing overhead includes indirect materials, indirect labor, depreciation on factory buildings and machines, and insurance, taxes, and maintenance on factory facilities.

**ALTERNATIVE TERMINOLOGY**

Some companies use terms such as *factory overhead, indirect manufacturing costs,* and *burden* instead of manufacturing overhead.

One study of manufactured goods found the following magnitudes of the three different product costs as a percentage of the total product cost: direct materials 54%, direct labor 13%, and manufacturing overhead 33%. Note that the direct labor component is the smallest. This component of product cost is dropping substantially because of automation. Companies are working hard to increase productivity by decreasing labor. In some companies, direct labor has become as little as 5% of the total cost.

Tracing direct materials and direct labor costs to specific products is fairly straightforward. Good recordkeeping can tell a company how much plastic it used in making each type of gear, or how many hours of factory labor it took to assemble a part. But allocating overhead costs to specific products presents problems. How much of the purchasing agent's salary is attributable to the hundreds of different products made in the same plant? What about the grease that keeps the machines running smoothly, or the computers that make sure paychecks are generated on time? Boiled down to its simplest form, the question becomes: Which products cause the incurrence of which costs? In subsequent chapters, we show various methods of allocating overhead to products.

## Product versus Period Costs

Each of the manufacturing cost components—direct materials, direct labor, and manufacturing overhead—are product costs. As the term suggests, **product costs** are costs that are a necessary and integral part of producing the finished product (see **Alternative Terminology**).

- Companies record product costs, when incurred, as an asset called inventory.
- These costs do not become expenses until the company sells the finished goods inventory.
- At that point, the company records the expense as cost of goods sold.

**Period costs** are costs that are matched with the revenue of a specific time period rather than included as part of the cost of a salable product.

- These are nonmanufacturing costs.
- Period costs include selling and administrative expenses.
- In order to determine net income, companies deduct these costs from revenues in the period in which they are incurred.

**Illustration 11.3** summarizes these relationships and cost terms. Our main concern in this chapter is with product costs.

**ALTERNATIVE TERMINOLOGY**
Product costs are also called *inventoriable* costs.

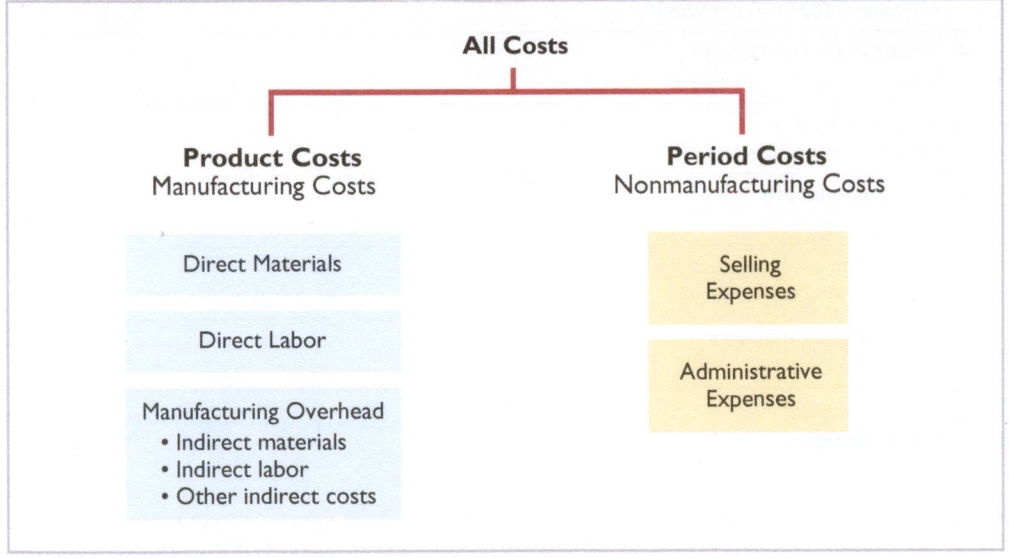

**ILLUSTRATION 11.3**
Product versus period costs

## Illustration of Cost Concepts

To improve your understanding of cost concepts, we illustrate them here through an extended example. Suppose you started your own snowboard factory, Terrain Park Boards. Think that's impossible? **Burton Snowboards** was started by Jake Burton Carpenter, when he was only 23 years old. Jake initially experimented with 100 different prototype designs before settling on a final design. Then Jake, along with two relatives and a friend, started making 50 boards per day in Londonderry, Vermont. Unfortunately, while they made a lot of boards in their first year, they were only able to sell 300 of them. To get by during those early years, Jake taught tennis and tended bar to pay the bills.

Here are some of the costs that your snowboard factory, Terrain Park Boards, would incur.

1. The materials cost of each snowboard (wood cores, fiberglass, resins, metal screw holes, metal edges, and ink) is $30.

2. The labor costs (for example, to trim and shape each board using jigsaws and band saws) are $40.

3. Depreciation on the factory building and equipment (for example, presses, grinding machines, and lacquer machines) used to make the snowboards is $25,000 per year.

4. Property taxes on the factory building (where the snowboards are made) are $6,000 per year.

5. Advertising costs (mostly online and catalog) are $60,000 per year.

6. Sales commissions related to snowboard sales are $20 per snowboard.

7. Salaries for factory maintenance employees are $45,000 per year.

8. The salary of the plant manager is $70,000.

9. The cost of shipping is $8 per snowboard.

**Illustration 11.4** shows how Terrain Park Boards would assign these manufacturing and selling costs to the various categories.

**ILLUSTRATION 11.4**

**Assignment of costs to cost categories**

**Terrain Park Boards**

| | Product Costs | | | Period Costs |
|---|---|---|---|---|
| Cost Item | Direct Materials | Direct Labor | Manufacturing Overhead | |
| 1. Material cost ($30 per board) | X | | | |
| 2. Labor costs ($40 per board) | | X | | |
| 3. Depreciation on factory equipment ($25,000 per year) | | | X | |
| 4. Property taxes on factory building ($6,000 per year) | | | X | |
| 5. Advertising costs ($60,000 per year) | | | | X |
| 6. Sales commissions ($20 per board) | | | | X |
| 7. Maintenance salaries (factory facilities, $45,000 per year) | | | X | |
| 8. Salary of plant manager ($70,000 per year) | | | X | |
| 9. Cost of shipping boards ($8 per board) | | | | X |

**Total manufacturing costs** are the sum of the **product costs**—direct materials, direct labor, and manufacturing overhead—incurred in the current period. If Terrain Park Boards produces 10,000 snowboards the first year, the total manufacturing costs would be $846,000, as shown in **Illustration 11.5**.

**ILLUSTRATION 11.5**

**Computation of total manufacturing costs**

| Cost Number and Item | Manufacturing Cost |
|---|---|
| 1. Material cost ($30 × 10,000) | $300,000 |
| 2. Labor cost ($40 × 10,000) | 400,000 |
| 3. Depreciation on factory equipment | 25,000 |
| 4. Property taxes on factory building | 6,000 |
| 7. Maintenance salaries (factory facilities) | 45,000 |
| 8. Salary of plant manager | 70,000 |
| **Total manufacturing costs** | **$846,000** |

Once it knows the total manufacturing costs, Terrain Park Boards can compute the manufacturing cost per unit. Assuming 10,000 units, the cost to produce one snowboard is $84.60 ($846,000 ÷ 10,000 units).

The cost concepts discussed in this chapter are used extensively in subsequent chapters. So study Illustration 11.4 carefully. If you do not understand any of these classifications, go back and reread the appropriate section.

---

## DO IT! 2 | Managerial Cost Concepts

A bicycle company has these costs: tires, salaries of employees who put tires on the wheels, factory building depreciation, advertising expenditures, factory machine lubricants, spokes, salary of factory manager, salary of accountant, handlebars, and salaries of factory maintenance employees. Classify each cost as direct materials, direct labor, overhead, or a period cost.

### Solution

**Direct materials:** Tires, spokes, and handlebars. **Direct labor:** Salaries of employees who put tires on the wheels. **Manufacturing overhead:** Factory building depreciation, factory machine lubricants, salary of factory manager, and salaries of factory maintenance employees. **Period costs:** Advertising expenditures and salary of accountant.

Related exercise material: **BE11.3, BE11.4, BE11.5, BE11.6, DO IT! 11.2, E11.2, E11.3, E11.4, E11.5, E11.6, and E11.7.**

**ACTION PLAN**

- **Direct materials: any raw materials physically and directly associated with the finished product.**
- **Direct labor: the work of factory employees directly associated with the finished product.**
- **Manufacturing overhead: any costs indirectly associated with the finished product.**
- **Costs that are not product costs are period costs.**

---

# Manufacturing Costs in Financial Statements

### LEARNING OBJECTIVE 3
Demonstrate how to compute cost of goods manufactured and prepare financial statements for a manufacturer.

The financial statements of a manufacturer are very similar to those of a merchandiser. For example, you will find many of the same sections and same accounts in the financial statements of **Procter & Gamble** that you find in the financial statements of **Dick's Sporting Goods**. The principal differences between their financial statements occur in two places:

1. The cost of goods sold section in the income statement.
2. The current assets section in the balance sheet.

## Income Statement

Under a periodic inventory system, the income statements of a merchandiser and a manufacturer differ in the cost of goods sold section.

- Merchandisers compute cost of goods sold by adding the beginning inventory to the **cost of goods purchased** and subtracting the ending inventory.
- Manufacturers compute cost of goods sold by adding the beginning finished goods inventory to the **cost of goods manufactured** and subtracting the ending finished goods inventory.

**Illustration 11.6**, which assumes a periodic inventory system, shows these different methods.

**ILLUSTRATION 11.6**

Cost of goods sold components

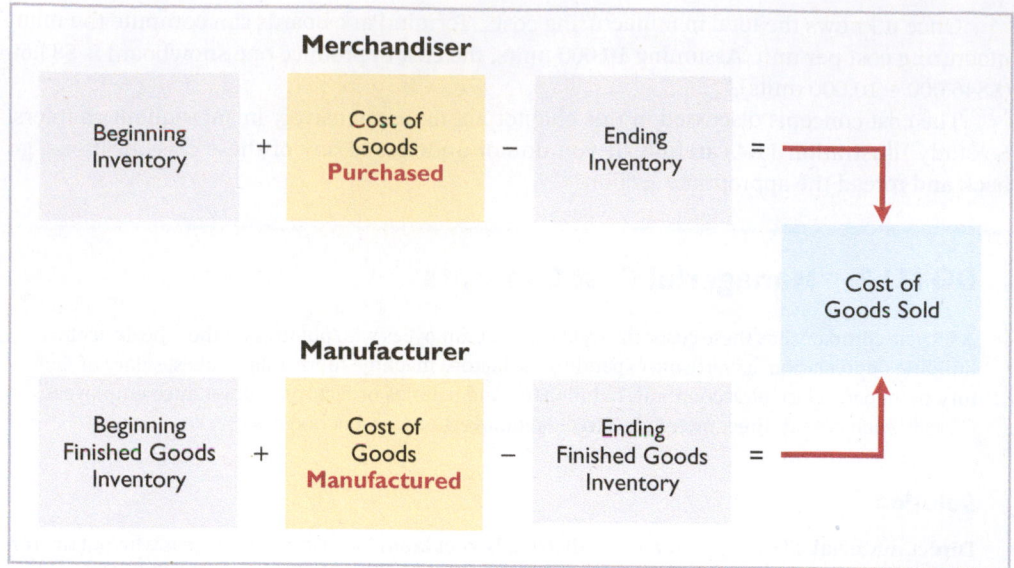

A number of accounts are involved in determining the cost of goods manufactured. To eliminate excessive detail, income statements typically show only the total cost of goods manufactured. A separate statement, called a Cost of Goods Manufactured Schedule, presents the details (see Illustration 11.9).

**Illustration 11.7** shows the different presentations of the cost of goods sold sections for merchandising and manufacturing companies. The other sections of an income statement are similar for merchandisers and manufacturers.

**ILLUSTRATION 11.7**   Cost of goods sold sections of merchandising and manufacturing income statements

| Merchandising Company | |
|---|---:|
| Income Statement (partial) | |
| For the Year Ended December 31, 2022 | |
| Cost of goods sold | |
| Inventory, Jan. 1 | $ 70,000 |
| Cost of goods purchased | 650,000 |
| Cost of goods available for sale | 720,000 |
| Less: Inventory, | |
| Dec. 31 | 400,000 |
| Cost of goods sold | $320,000 |

| Manufacturing Company | |
|---|---:|
| Income Statement (partial) | |
| For the Year Ended December 31, 2022 | |
| Cost of goods sold | |
| Finished goods inventory, Jan. 1 | $ 90,000 |
| Cost of goods manufactured | |
| (see Illustration 11.9) | 370,000 |
| Cost of goods available for sale | 460,000 |
| Less: Finished goods inventory, | |
| Dec. 31 | 80,000 |
| Cost of goods sold | $380,000 |

## Cost of Goods Manufactured

An example may help show how companies determine the cost of goods manufactured. Assume that on January 1, **Current Designs** has a number of kayaks in various stages of production. In total, these partially completed manufactured units are called **beginning work in process inventory**. These are kayaks that were worked on during the prior year but were not completed. As a result, these kayaks will be completed during the current year. The cost of beginning work in process inventory is based on the **manufacturing costs incurred in the prior period**.

Current Designs first incurs manufacturing costs in the current year to complete the kayaks that were in process on January 1. It then incurs manufacturing costs for production of new orders. The sum of the direct materials costs, direct labor costs, and manufacturing overhead incurred in the current year is the **total manufacturing costs** for the current period.

We now have two cost amounts:

1. The cost of the beginning work in process.
2. The total manufacturing costs for the current period.

The sum of these costs is the **total cost of work in process** for the year.

At the end of the year, Current Designs may have some kayaks that are only partially completed. The costs of these units become the cost of the **ending work in process inventory**. To find the **cost of goods manufactured**, we subtract this cost from the total cost of work in process. **Illustration 11.8** shows the formula for determining the cost of goods manufactured.

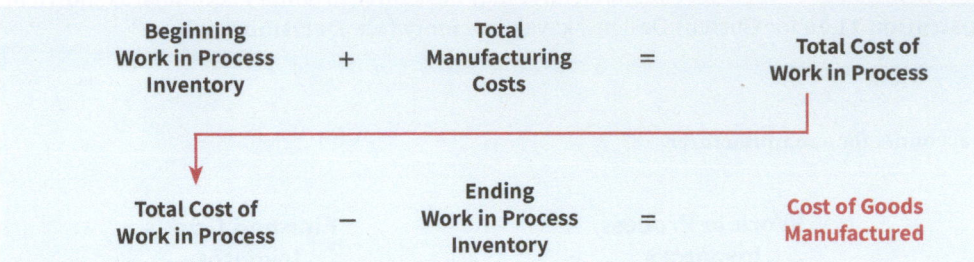

**ILLUSTRATION 11.8**

Cost of goods manufactured formula

# Cost of Goods Manufactured Schedule

The **cost of goods manufactured schedule** reports cost elements used in calculating cost of goods manufactured. **Illustration 11.9** shows the schedule for Current Designs (using assumed data). The schedule presents detailed data for direct materials and for manufacturing overhead (see **Decision Tools**).

You should be able to distinguish between "Total manufacturing costs" and "Cost of goods manufactured."

- As Illustration 11.9 shows, total manufacturing costs is the sum of all manufacturing costs (direct materials, direct labor, and manufacturing overhead) **incurred during the period**.

> **Decision Tools**
>
> The cost of goods manufactured schedule helps managers determine if the company is maintaining control over the costs of production.

**ILLUSTRATION 11.9**

Cost of goods manufactured schedule

| Current Designs | | |
|---|---:|---:|
| Cost of Goods Manufactured Schedule | | |
| for the Year Ended December 31, 2022 | | |
| **Work in process, January 1** | | $ 18,400 |
| **Direct materials** | | |
| Raw materials inventory, January 1 | $ 16,700 | |
| Raw materials purchases | 152,500 | |
| Total raw materials available for use | 169,200 | |
| Less: Raw materials inventory, December 31 | 22,800 | |
| Direct materials used | | $146,400* |
| **Direct labor** | | 175,600 |
| **Manufacturing overhead** | | |
| Indirect labor | 14,300 | |
| Factory repairs | 12,600 | |
| Factory utilities | 10,100 | |
| Factory depreciation | 9,440 | |
| Factory insurance | 8,360 | |
| Total manufacturing overhead | | 54,800 |
| **Total manufacturing costs** | | 376,800 |
| Total cost of work in process | | 395,200 |
| **Less: Work in process, December 31** | | 25,200 |
| **Cost of goods manufactured** | | $370,000 |

*Assumes all raw materials are direct materials.

- Cost of goods manufactured is the cost of those goods that were **completed during the period**.
- If we add beginning work in process inventory to the total manufacturing costs incurred during the period and then subtract the ending work in process inventory (the formula given in Illustration 11.8), we arrive at the cost of goods manufactured during the period.

# Balance Sheet

The balance sheet for a merchandising company shows just one category of inventory. In contrast, the balance sheet for a manufacturer may have three inventory accounts, as shown in **Illustration 11.10** for Current Designs' kayak inventory (see **Decision Tools**).

**ILLUSTRATION 11.10**   Inventory accounts for a manufacturer

| Raw Materials Inventory | Work in Process Inventory | Finished Goods Inventory |
|---|---|---|
| Shows the cost of raw materials on hand. | Shows the cost applicable to units that have been started into production but are only partially completed. | Shows the cost of completed goods on hand. |

Finished Goods Inventory is to a manufacturer what Inventory is to a merchandiser. Each of these classifications represents the goods that the company has available for sale. The current assets sections presented in **Illustration 11.11** contrast the presentations of inventories for merchandising and manufacturing companies. The remainder of the balance sheet is similar for the two types of companies.

**ILLUSTRATION 11.11**   Current assets sections of merchandising and manufacturing balance sheets

**Merchandising Company**
Balance Sheet
December 31, 2022

| Current assets | | |
|---|---:|---:|
| Cash | | $100,000 |
| Accounts receivable (net) | | 210,000 |
| Inventory | | 400,000 |
| Prepaid expenses | | 22,000 |
| Total current assets | | $732,000 |

**Manufacturing Company**
Balance Sheet
December 31, 2022

| Current assets | | |
|---|---:|---:|
| Cash | | $180,000 |
| Accounts receivable (net) | | 210,000 |
| Inventory | | |
| Finished goods | $80,000 | |
| Work in process | 25,200 | |
| Raw materials | 22,800 | 128,000 |
| Prepaid expenses | | 18,000 |
| Total current assets | | $536,000 |

Each step in the accounting cycle for a merchandiser applies to a manufacturer.

- For example, prior to preparing financial statements, manufacturers make adjustments.
- The adjustments are essentially the same as those of a merchandiser.

## DO IT! 3 | Cost of Goods Manufactured

The following information is available for Keystone Company.

|  | | March 1 | March 31 |
|---|---|---|---|
| Raw materials inventory | | $12,000 | $10,000 |
| Work in process inventory | | 2,500 | 4,000 |
| Materials purchased in March | $90,000 | | |
| Direct labor in March | 75,000 | | |
| Manufacturing overhead in March | 220,000 | | |

Prepare the cost of goods manufactured schedule for the month of March 2022.

### Solution

<table>
<tr><td colspan="4" align="center">Keystone Company<br>Cost of Goods Manufactured Schedule<br>For the Month Ended March 31, 2022</td></tr>
<tr><td>Work in process, March 1</td><td></td><td></td><td>$ 2,500</td></tr>
<tr><td>Direct materials</td><td></td><td></td><td></td></tr>
<tr><td>　Raw materials, March 1</td><td>$ 12,000</td><td></td><td></td></tr>
<tr><td>　Raw materials purchases</td><td>90,000</td><td></td><td></td></tr>
<tr><td>　Total raw materials available for use</td><td>102,000</td><td></td><td></td></tr>
<tr><td>　Less: Raw materials, March 31</td><td>10,000</td><td></td><td></td></tr>
<tr><td>　Direct materials used</td><td></td><td>$ 92,000</td><td></td></tr>
<tr><td>Direct labor</td><td></td><td>75,000</td><td></td></tr>
<tr><td>Manufacturing overhead</td><td></td><td>220,000</td><td></td></tr>
<tr><td>Total manufacturing costs</td><td></td><td></td><td>387,000</td></tr>
<tr><td>Total cost of work in process</td><td></td><td></td><td>389,500</td></tr>
<tr><td>Less: Work in process, March 31</td><td></td><td></td><td>4,000</td></tr>
<tr><td>Cost of goods manufactured</td><td></td><td></td><td>$385,500</td></tr>
</table>

Related exercise material: **BE11.7, BE11.8, BE11.9, BE11.10, DO IT! 11.3, E11.8, E11.9, E11.10, E11.11, E11.12, E11.13, E11.14, E11.15, E11.16, and E11.17.**

**ACTION PLAN**

- Start with beginning work in process as the first item in the cost of goods manufactured schedule.
- Sum direct materials used, direct labor, and manufacturing overhead to determine total manufacturing costs.
- Sum beginning work in process and total manufacturing costs to determine total cost of work in process.
- Cost of goods manufactured is the total cost of work in process less ending work in process.

# Managerial Accounting Today

### LEARNING OBJECTIVE 4

Discuss trends in managerial accounting.

The business environment never stands still. Regulations are always changing, global competition continues to intensify, and technology is a source of constant upheaval. In this rapidly changing world, managerial accounting needs to continue to innovate in order to provide managers with the information they need.

# Service Industries

Much of the U.S. economy has shifted toward an emphasis on services.

- Today, more than 50% of U.S. workers are employed by service companies.
- Airlines, marketing agencies, cable companies, and governmental agencies are just a few examples of service companies.
- Service companies differ from manufacturing companies in that services are consumed immediately by customers.

For example, when a restaurant produces a meal, that meal is not put in inventory but is instead consumed immediately. An airline uses special equipment to provide its product, but again, the output of that equipment is consumed immediately by the customer in the form of a flight. And a marketing agency performs services for its clients that are immediately consumed by the customer in the form of a marketing plan. In contrast, a manufacturing company like **Boeing** often has a long lead time before its airplane is used or consumed by the customer.

This chapter's examples feature manufacturing companies because accounting for the manufacturing environment requires the use of the broadest range of accounts. That is, the accounts used by service companies represent a subset of those used by manufacturers because service companies are not producing inventory. Neither the restaurant, the airline, nor the marketing agency discussed above produces an inventoriable product. However, just like a manufacturer, each needs to keep track of the costs of its services in order to know whether it is generating a profit (see **Ethics Note**). A successful restaurateur needs to know the cost of each offering on the menu, an airline needs to know the cost of flight service to each destination, and a marketing agency needs to know the cost to develop a marketing plan. Thus, the techniques shown in this chapter to accumulate manufacturing costs to determine manufacturing inventory are equally useful for determining the costs of performing services.

For example, let's consider the costs that **Hewlett-Packard (HP)** might incur on a consulting engagement.

- A significant portion of its costs would be salaries of consulting personnel. It might also incur travel costs, materials, software costs, and depreciation charges on equipment.
- In the same way that it needs to keep track of the cost of manufacturing its computers and printers, HP needs to know what its costs are on each consulting job.
- It could prepare a cost of services performed schedule similar to the cost of goods manufactured schedule in Illustration 11.9.
- The structure would be essentially the same as the cost of goods manufactured schedule, but section headings would be reflective of the costs of the particular service organization.

Many of the examples we present in subsequent chapters will be based on service companies, as well as some end-of-chapter materials.

**ETHICS NOTE**

**Do telecommunications companies have an obligation to provide service to remote or low-user areas for a fee that may be less than the cost of the service?**

---

## Service Company Insight    Allegiant Airlines

iStock.com/Stephen Strathdee

### Low Fares but Decent Profits

When other airlines were cutting flight service due to recession, **Allegiant Airlines** increased capacity by 21%. Sounds crazy, doesn't it? But it must have known something because while the other airlines were losing money, it was generating profits. In fact, it often has the industry's highest profit margins. Consider also that its average one-way fare is only $83. So how does it make money? As a low-budget airline, it focuses on controlling costs.

Allegiant purchases used planes for $3 million each rather than new planes for $40 million. It flies out of small towns, so wages are low and competition is nonexistent. It minimizes hotel

costs by having its flight crews finish their day in their home cities. The company also only flies a route if its 150-passenger planes are nearly full (it averages about 90% of capacity). The bottom line is that Allegiant knows its costs to the penny. Knowing what your costs are might not be glamorous, but it sure beats losing money.

**Sources:** Susan Carey, "For Allegiant, Getaways Mean Profits," *Wall Street Journal Online* (February 18, 2009); and Scott Mayerowitz, "Tiny Allegiant Air Thrives on Low Costs, High Fees," *http://bigstory.ap.org* (June 28, 2013).

**What are some of the line items that would appear in the cost of services performed schedule of an airline? (Go to WileyPLUS for this answer and additional questions.)**

# Focus on the Value Chain

The **value chain** refers to all business processes associated with providing a product or performing a service. **Illustration 11.12** depicts the value chain for a manufacturer. Many of the most significant business innovations in recent years have resulted either directly, or indirectly, from a focus on the value chain. For example, so-called **lean manufacturing**, originally pioneered by Japanese automobile manufacturer **Toyota** but now widely practiced, reviews all business processes in an effort to increase productivity and eliminate waste, all while continually trying to improve quality.

**ILLUSTRATION 11.12**    **A manufacturer's value chain**

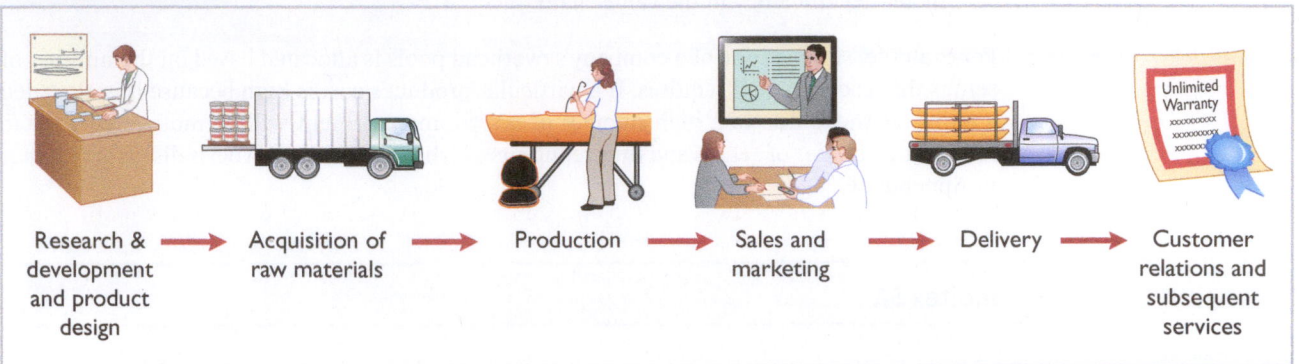

Research & development and product design → Acquisition of raw materials → Production → Sales and marketing → Delivery → Customer relations and subsequent services

**Just-in-time (JIT) inventory** methods, which have significantly lowered inventory levels and costs for many companies, are one innovation that resulted from the focus on the value chain.

- Under the JIT inventory method, goods are manufactured or purchased just in time for sale.
- However, JIT also necessitates increased emphasis on product quality. Because JIT companies do not have excess inventory on hand, they cannot afford to stop production because of defects or machine breakdowns. If they stop production, deliveries will be delayed and customers will be unhappy.

For example, **Dell** can produce and deliver a custom computer within 48 hours of a customer's order. However, a design flaw in an **Intel** computer chip was estimated to cost Dell $1 billion in repairs and reduced revenue.

As a consequence, many companies now focus on **total quality management (TQM)** to reduce defects in finished products, with the goal of zero defects. **Toyota** was one of the pioneers of TQM processes as early as the 1940s. Some of the largest companies in the world, including **Ford** and **ExxonMobil**, have benefitted from these practices.

Another innovation is the **theory of constraints**.

- This involves identification of "bottlenecks"—constraints within the value chain that limit a company's profitability.
- Once a major constraint has been identified and eliminated, the company moves on to fix the next most significant constraint.

**General Motors** found that by applying the theory of constraints to its distribution system, it could more effectively meet the demands of its dealers and minimize the amount of excess inventory in its distribution system. This also reduced its need for overtime labor.

Technology has played a big role in the focus on the value chain and the implementation of lean manufacturing. For example, **enterprise resource planning (ERP) systems**, such as those provided by **SAP**, provide a comprehensive, centralized, integrated source of information to manage all major business processes—from purchasing, to manufacturing, to sales, to human resources.

- ERP systems have, in some large companies, replaced as many as 200 individual software packages.
- In addition, the focus on improving efficiency in the value chain has also resulted in adoption of automated manufacturing processes.

- Many companies now use computer-integrated manufacturing, which often reduces the reliance on manual labor by using robotic equipment.
- This increases overhead costs as a percentage of total product costs.

As overhead costs have increased because of factory automation, the accuracy of overhead cost allocation to specific products has become more important. In response, managerial accountants devised an allocation approach called **activity-based costing (ABC)**.

- ABC allocates overhead based on each product's use of particular activities in making the product.
- In addition to providing more accurate product costing, ABC also can contribute to increased efficiency in the value chain.

For example, suppose one of a company's overhead pools is allocated based on the number of setups that each product requires. If a particular product's cost is high because it is allocated a lot of overhead due to a high number of setups, management will be motivated to try to reduce the number of setups and thus reduce its overhead allocation. ABC is discussed further in Appendix F.

---

## Management Insight    Inditex SA

Miguel Vidall/REUTERS/
Alamy Stock Photo

### Supplying Today's (Not Yesterday's) Fashions

In terms of total sales dollars, **Inditex SA** is the planet's largest fashion retailer. What does it do differently than its competitors? How did it double its sales over a recent seven-year period while competitors such as **Gap Inc**. stumbled badly? Inditex distinguishes itself in its value chain's ability to react quickly to constantly changing customer tastes. First, designers and commercial staff sit side by side in a massive, open workspace facility, taking direct input from sales staff around the world regarding new product ideas. Manufacturing facilities are located relatively near to company headquarters, allowing more direct input and oversight into production. Also, all goods (other than online sales) are shipped straight from the production facility to stores, rather than warehouses. As a result of its unique approach to how it designs, manufactures, and distributes its goods, Inditex can actually sometimes get a new product from initial idea to the store shelf in two weeks rather than the industry norm of two to eight months. And because Inditex provides customers with designs that competitors don't have yet, it can charge higher prices while also continuing to look for ways to increase efficiency and thus cut costs.

**Source:** Patricia Kowsmann, "Fast Fashion: How a Zara Coat Went from Design to Fifth Avenue in 25 Days," *Wall Street Journal* (December 6, 2016).

**What steps has Inditex taken that make its value chain unique? (Go to WileyPLUS for this answer and additional questions).**

---

# Balanced Scorecard

As companies implement various business practice innovations, managers sometimes focus too enthusiastically on the latest innovation, to the detriment of other areas of the business. For example, by focusing on total quality management, companies sometimes lose sight of cost/benefit considerations. Similarly, in focusing on reducing inventory levels through just-in-time inventory methods, companies sometimes lose sales due to inventory shortages. The **balanced scorecard** corrects for this limited perspective.

- This approach uses both financial and nonfinancial measures to evaluate all aspects of a company's operations in an integrated fashion.
- The performance measures are linked in a cause-and-effect fashion to ensure that they all tie to the company's overall objectives.

For example, to increase return on assets, the company could try to increase sales. To increase sales, the company could try to increase customer satisfaction. To increase customer satisfaction, the company could try to reduce product defects. Finally, to reduce product defects, the company could increase employee training. The balanced scorecard, which is discussed further in Chapter 17, is now used by many companies, including **Hilton Hotels, Walmart Inc.**, and **HP**.

# Business Ethics

All employees within an organization are expected to act ethically in their business activities. Given the importance of ethical behavior to corporations and their owners (stockholders), an increasing number of organizations provide codes of business ethics for their employees.

## Creating Proper Incentives

Companies like **Amazon.com**, **IBM**, and **Nike** use complex systems to monitor, control, and evaluate the actions of managers. Unfortunately, these systems and controls sometimes unwittingly create incentives for managers to take unethical actions.

- Because budgets are also used as an evaluation tool, some managers try to "game" the budgeting process by underestimating their division's predicted performance so that it will be easier to meet their performance targets.

- But, if budgets are set at unattainable levels, managers sometimes take unethical actions to meet the targets in order to receive higher compensation or, in some cases, to keep their jobs.

For example, at one time, airline manufacturer **Boeing** was plagued by a series of scandals including charges of over-billing, corporate espionage, and illegal conflicts of interest. Some long-time employees of Boeing blamed the decline in ethics on a change in the corporate culture that took place after Boeing merged with **McDonnell Douglas**. They suggested that evaluation systems implemented after the merger to evaluate employee performance gave employees the impression that they needed to succeed no matter what actions were required to do so.

In a recent example, the largest bank in the United States, **Wells Fargo**, admitted that it had fired 5,300 employees for opening more than 2 million accounts without customer approval or knowledge. According to the director of the Consumer Financial Protection Bureau, "Wells Fargo employees secretly opened unauthorized accounts to hit sales targets and receive bonuses."

## Code of Ethical Standards

In response to corporate scandals, the U.S. Congress enacted the **Sarbanes-Oxley Act (SOX)** to help prevent lapses in internal control.

- CEOs and CFOs are now required to certify that financial statements give a fair presentation of the company's operating results and its financial condition.

- Top managers must certify that the company maintains an adequate system of internal controls to safeguard the company's assets and ensure accurate financial reports.

- Companies now pay more attention to the composition of the board of directors. In particular, the audit committee of the board of directors must be comprised entirely of independent members (that is, non-employees) and must contain at least one financial expert.

- The law substantially increases the penalties for misconduct.

To provide guidance for managerial accountants, the Institute of Management Accountants (IMA) has developed a code of ethical standards, entitled *IMA Statement of Ethical Professional Practice*. Management accountants should not commit acts in violation of these standards. Nor should they condone such acts by others within their organizations. Throughout the text, we address various ethical issues managers face.

# Corporate Social Responsibility

The balanced scorecard attempts to take a broader, more inclusive view of corporate profitability measures. Many companies, however, have begun to evaluate not just corporate profitability but also **corporate social responsibility**.

- Corporate social responsibility considers a company's efforts to employ sustainable business practices with regard to its employees, society, and the environment.
- This is sometimes referred to as the **triple bottom line** because it evaluates a company's performance with regard to **people, planet, and profit**.
- Recent reports indicate that over 50% of the 500 largest U.S. companies provide sustainability reports.

Make no mistake, these companies are still striving to maximize profits—in a competitive world, they won't survive long if they don't. In fact, you might recognize a few of the names on a recent list (published by Corporate Knights) of the 100 most sustainable companies in the world. Are you surprised that **General Electric**, **adidas**, **BMW**, **Coca-Cola**, or **Apple** made the list? These companies have learned that with a long-term, sustainable approach, they can maximize profits while also acting in the best interest of their employees, their communities, and the environment. In fact, a monetary bonus was provided by 87% of the companies on the list to managers that met sustainability goals. At various points within this text, we discuss situations where real companies use the very skills that you are learning to evaluate decisions from a sustainable perspective, such as in the following Insight box.

## People, Planet, and Profit Insight  Phantom Tac

aabeele/Shutterstock.com

### People Matter

Many clothing factories in developing countries are known for unsafe buildings, poor working conditions, and wage and labor violations. One of the owners of **Phantom Tac**, a clothing manufacturer in Bangladesh, did make efforts to develop sustainable business practices. This owner, David Mayor, provided funding for a training program for female workers. He also developed a website to educate customers about the workers' conditions. But Phantom Tac also had to make a profit. Things got tight when one of its customers canceled orders because Phantom Tac failed a social compliance audit. The company had to quit funding the training program and the website.

Recently, Bangladesh's textile industry has seen some significant improvements in working conditions and safety standards. As Brad Adams, Asia director of **Human Rights Watch**, notes, "The (Dhaka) government has belatedly begun to register unions, which is an important first step, but it now needs to ensure that factory owners stop persecuting their leaders and actually allow them to function."

**Sources:** Jim Yardley, "Clothing Brands Sidestep Blame for Safety Lapses," *The New York Times Online* (December 30, 2013); and Palash Ghosh, "Despite Low Pay, Poor Work Conditions, Garment Factories Empowering Millions of Bangladeshi Women," *International Business Times* (March 25, 2014).

**What are some of the common problems for many clothing factories in developing countries?** (Go to WileyPLUS for this answer and additional questions.)

Sustainable business practices present numerous issues for management and managerial accountants.

1. Companies need to decide what items need to be measured, generally those that are of utmost importance to its stakeholders. For example, a particular company might be most concerned with minimizing water pollution or maximizing employee safety.

2. For each item identified, the company determines measurable attributes that provide relevant information regarding the company's performance with regard to that item, such as the amount of waste released into public waterways or the number of accidents per 1,000 hours worked.

3. The company needs to consider the materiality of the item, the cost of measuring these attributes, and the reliability of the measurements. If the company uses this information to make decisions, then accuracy is critical. Of particular concern is whether the measurements can be verified by an outside third party.

Unlike financial reporting, which is overseen by the Financial Accounting Standards Board (FASB), the reporting of sustainable business practices currently has no agreed-upon standard-setter. A number of organizations have, however, published guidelines. The guidelines published by the **Global Reporting Initiative** are among the most widely recognized and followed. **Illustration 11.13** provides a list of major categories provided by the Global Reporting Initiative for sustainability reporting and a sample of aspects that companies might consider within each category.

**ILLUSTRATION 11.13**    **Sample categories in Global Reporting Initiative guidelines**

| | | Social | | | |
|---|---|---|---|---|---|
| **Economic** | **Environmental** | **Labor Practices and Decent Work** | **Human Rights** | **Society** | **Product Responsibility** |
| Economic performance | Energy | Occupational health and safety | Non-discrimination | Anti-corruption | Customer health and safety |
| Market presence | Biodiversity | Training and education | Child labor | Anti-competitive behavior | Product and service labeling |
| Indirect economic impacts | Effluents and waste | Diversity and equal opportunity | Indigenous rights | Supplier assessment for impacts on society | Marketing communications |
| Procurement practices | Compliance | Labor practices grievance mechanisms | Supplier human rights assessment | Grievance mechanisms for impacts on society | Customer privacy |

**Source:** Global Reporting Initiative, *G4 Sustainability Reporting Guidelines*, p. 9. The full report is available at *www.globalreporting.org*.

---

## DO IT! 4 | Trends in Managerial Accounting

Match the descriptions that follow with the corresponding terms.

**Descriptions:**

1. _____ All activities associated with providing a product or performing a service.

2. _____ A method of allocating overhead based on each product's use of activities in making the product.

3. _____ Systems implemented to reduce defects in finished products with the goal of achieving zero defects.

4. _____ A performance-measurement approach that uses both financial and nonfinancial measures, tied to company objectives, to evaluate a company's operations in an integrated fashion.

5. _____ Inventory system in which goods are manufactured or purchased just as they are needed for use.

6. _____ A company's efforts to employ sustainable business practices with regards to its employees, society, and the environment.

7. _____ A code of ethical standards developed by the Institute of Management Accountants.

**Terms:**

a. Activity-based costing.

b. Balanced scorecard.

c. Corporate social responsibility.

d. Just-in-time (JIT) inventory.

e. Total quality management (TQM).

f. Statement of Ethical Professional Practice.

g. Value chain.

**ACTION PLAN**

- Develop a forward-looking view, in order to advise and provide information to various members of the organization.

- Understand current business trends and issues.

### Solution

**1.** g  **2.** a  **3.** e  **4.** b  **5.** d  **6.** c  **7.** f

Related exercise material: **BE11.11, DO IT! 11.4, and E11.18.**

## USING THE DECISION TOOLS | Current Designs

**Current Designs** faces many situations where it needs to apply the decision tools in this chapter, such as analyzing the balance sheet for optimal inventory levels. For example, assume that the market has responded enthusiastically to a new Current Designs' model, the Otter. As a result, the company has established a separate manufacturing facility to produce these kayaks. Now assume that the company produces 1,000 of these kayaks per month. Current Designs' monthly manufacturing costs and other data for the Otter are as follows.

| | | |
|---|---|---|
| 1. | Rent on manufacturing equipment (lease cost) | $2,000/month |
| 2. | Insurance on manufacturing building | $750/month |
| 3. | Raw materials (plastic, fiberglass, etc.) | $180/kayak |
| 4. | Utility costs for manufacturing facility | $1,000/month |
| 5. | Supplies for administrative office | $800/month |
| 6. | Wages for assembly-line workers in manufacturing facility | $130/kayak |
| 7. | Depreciation on administrative office equipment | $650/month |
| 8. | Miscellaneous manufacturing materials (lubricants, solders, etc.) | $12/kayak |
| 9. | Property taxes on manufacturing building | $24,000/year |
| 10. | Manufacturing supervisor's salary | $5,000/month |
| 11. | Advertising for the Otter | $30,000/year |
| 12. | Sales commissions | $30/kayak |
| 13. | Depreciation on manufacturing building | $4,000/month |

## Instructions

**a.** Prepare an answer sheet with the following column headings.

| | Product Costs | | | |
|---|---|---|---|---|
| Cost Item | Direct Materials | Direct Labor | Manufacturing Overhead | Period Costs |

Enter each cost item on your answer sheet, placing an "X" under the appropriate headings.

**b.** Compute total manufacturing costs for the month.

## Solution

**a.**

| | Product Costs | | | Period Costs |
|---|---|---|---|---|
| **Cost Item** | **Direct Materials** | **Direct Labor** | **Manufacturing Overhead** | |
| 1. Rent on manufacturing equipment ($2,000/month) | | | X | |
| 2. Insurance on manufacturing building ($750/month) | | | X | |
| 3. Raw materials ($180/kayak) | X | | | |
| 4. Manufacturing utilities ($1,000/month) | | | X | |
| 5. Office supplies ($800/month) | | | | X |
| 6. Wages for assembly workers ($130/kayak) | | X | | |
| 7. Depreciation on administrative office equipment ($650/month) | | | | X |
| 8. Miscellaneous manufacturing materials ($12/kayak) | | | X | |

| | Product Costs | | | |
| Cost Item | Direct Materials | Direct Labor | Manufacturing Overhead | Period Costs |
|---|---|---|---|---|
| 9. Property taxes on manufacturing building ($24,000/year) | | | X | |
| 10. Manufacturing supervisor's salary ($5,000/month) | | | X | |
| 11. Advertising cost ($30,000/year) | | | | X |
| 12. Sales commissions ($30/kayak) | | | | X |
| 13. Depreciation on manufacturing building ($4,000/month) | | | X | |

b.

| Cost Item | Manufacturing Cost |
|---|---|
| Rent on manufacturing equipment | $ 2,000 |
| Insurance on manufacturing building | 750 |
| Raw materials ($180 × 1,000) | 180,000 |
| Manufacturing utilities | 1,000 |
| Labor ($130 × 1,000) | 130,000 |
| Miscellaneous materials ($12 × 1,000) | 12,000 |
| Property taxes on manufacturing building ($24,000 ÷ 12) | 2,000 |
| Manufacturing supervisor's salary | 5,000 |
| Depreciation on manufacturing building | 4,000 |
| Total manufacturing costs | $336,750 |

Current Designs' monthly manufacturing cost to produce 1,000 Otters is $336,750.

# Review and Practice

## Learning Objectives Review

### 1 Identify the features of managerial accounting and the functions of management.

The *primary users* of managerial accounting reports, issued as frequently as needed, are internal users, who are officers, department heads, managers, and supervisors in the company. The purpose of these reports is to provide special-purpose information for a particular user for a specific decision. The content of managerial accounting reports pertains to subunits of the business. It may be very detailed, and may extend beyond the accrual accounting system. The reporting standard is relevance to the decision being made. No independent audits are required in managerial accounting.

The functions of management are planning, directing, and controlling. Planning requires management to look ahead and to establish objectives. Directing involves coordinating the diverse activities and human resources of a company to produce a smooth-running operation. Controlling is the process of keeping the activities on track.

### 2 Describe the classes of manufacturing costs and the differences between product and period costs.

Manufacturing costs are typically classified as either (1) direct materials, (2) direct labor, or (3) manufacturing overhead. Raw materials that can be physically and directly associated with the finished product during the manufacturing process are called direct materials. The work of factory employees that can be physically and directly associated with converting raw materials into finished goods is considered direct labor. Manufacturing overhead consists of costs that are indirectly associated with the manufacture of the finished product.

Product costs are costs that are a necessary and integral part of producing the finished product. Product costs are also called inventoriable costs. These costs do not become expenses until the company sells the finished goods inventory. Period costs are costs that are identified with a specific time period rather than with a salable product.

These costs relate to nonmanufacturing costs and therefore are not inventoriable costs.

---

**3** Demonstrate how to compute cost of goods manufactured and prepare financial statements for a manufacturer.

---

Companies add the cost of the beginning work in process to the total manufacturing costs for the current year to arrive at the total cost of work in process for the year. They then subtract the ending work in process from the total cost of work in process to arrive at the cost of goods manufactured.

The difference between a merchandising and a manufacturing income statement is in the cost of goods sold section. A manufacturing cost of goods sold section shows beginning and ending finished goods inventories and the cost of goods manufactured.

The difference between a merchandising and a manufacturing balance sheet is in the current assets section. The current assets section of a manufacturing company's balance sheet presents three inventory accounts: finished goods inventory, work in process inventory, and raw materials inventory.

---

**4** Discuss trends in managerial accounting.

---

Managerial accounting has experienced many changes in recent years, including a shift toward service companies as well as an emphasis on ethical behavior. Improved practices include a focus on managing the value chain through techniques such as just-in-time inventory, total quality management, activity-based costing, and theory of constraints. The balanced scorecard is now used by many companies in order to attain a more comprehensive view of the company's operations. Finally, companies are now evaluating their performance with regard to their corporate social responsibility.

## Decision Tools Review

| Decision Checkpoints | Info Needed for Decision | Tool to Use for Decision | How to Evaluate Results |
|---|---|---|---|
| Is the company maintaining control over the costs of production? | Cost of material, labor, and overhead | Cost of goods manufactured schedule | Compare the cost of goods manufactured to revenue expected from product sales. |
| What is the composition of a manufacturing company's inventory? | Amount of raw materials, work in process, and finished goods inventories | Balance sheet | Determine whether there are sufficient finished goods, raw materials, and work in process inventories to meet forecasted demand. |

## Glossary Review

**Activity-based costing (ABC)**   A method of allocating overhead based on each product's use of activities in making the product. (p. 11-18).

**Balanced scorecard**   A performance-measurement approach that uses both financial and nonfinancial measures, tied to company objectives, to evaluate a company's operations in an integrated fashion. (p. 11-18).

**Board of directors**   The group of officials elected by the stockholders of a corporation to formulate operating policies and select officers who will manage the company. (p. 11-5).

**Chief executive officer (CEO)**   Corporate officer who has overall responsibility for managing the business and delegates responsibilities to other corporate officers. (p. 11-6).

**Chief financial officer (CFO)**   Corporate officer who is responsible for all of the accounting and finance issues of the company. (p. 11-6).

**Controller**   Financial officer responsible for a company's accounting records, system of internal control, and preparation of financial statements, tax returns, and internal reports. (p. 11-6).

**Corporate social responsibility**   The efforts of a company to employ sustainable business practices with regard to its employees, society, and the environment. (p. 11-20).

**Cost of goods manufactured**   Total cost of work in process less the cost of the ending work in process inventory. (p. 11-13).

**Direct labor**   The work of factory employees that can be physically and directly associated with converting raw materials into finished goods. (p. 11-8).

**Direct materials**   Raw materials that can be physically and directly associated with manufacturing the finished product. (p. 11-8).

**Enterprise resource planning (ERP) system**   Software that provides a comprehensive, centralized, integrated source of information used to manage all major business processes. (p. 11-17).

**Indirect labor**   Work of factory employees that has no physical association with the finished product or for which it is impractical to trace the costs to the goods produced. (p. 11-8).

**Indirect materials**   Raw materials that do not physically become part of the finished product or for which it is impractical to trace to the finished product because their physical association with the finished product is too small. (p. 11-8).

**Just-in-time (JIT) inventory**   Inventory system in which goods are manufactured or purchased just in time for sale. (p. 11-17).

**Line positions**   Jobs that are directly involved in a company's primary revenue-generating operating activities. (p. 11-6).

**Managerial accounting**   A field of accounting that provides economic and financial information for managers and other internal users. (p. 11-3).

**Manufacturing overhead** Manufacturing costs that are indirectly associated with the manufacture of the finished product. (p. 11-8).

**Period costs** Costs that are matched with the revenue of a specific time period and charged to expense as incurred. (p. 11-9).

**Product costs** Costs that are a necessary and integral part of producing the finished product. (p. 11-9).

**Sarbanes-Oxley Act (SOX)** Law passed by Congress intended to reduce unethical corporate behavior. (p. 11-19).

**Staff positions** Jobs that support the efforts of line employees. (p. 11-6).

**Theory of constraints** A specific approach used to identify and manage constraints in order to achieve the company's goals. (p. 11-17).

**Total cost of work in process** Cost of the beginning work in process plus total manufacturing costs for the current period. (p. 11-13).

**Total manufacturing costs** The sum of direct materials, direct labor, and manufacturing overhead incurred in the current period. (p. 11-10).

**Total quality management (TQM)** Systems implemented to reduce defects in finished products with the goal of achieving zero defects. (p. 11-17).

**Treasurer** Financial officer responsible for custody of a company's funds and for maintaining its cash position. (p. 11-6).

**Triple bottom line** The evaluation of a company's social responsibility performance with regard to people, planet, and profit. (p. 11-20).

**Value chain** All business processes associated with providing a product or performing a service. (p. 11-17).

**Work in process inventory** Partially completed manufactured units. (p. 11-12).

## Practice Multiple-Choice Questions

1. **(LO 1)** Managerial accounting:
   a. is governed by generally accepted accounting principles.
   b. places emphasis on special-purpose information.
   c. pertains to the entity as a whole and is highly aggregated.
   d. is limited to cost data.

2. **(LO 1)** The management of an organization performs several broad functions. They are:
   a. planning, directing, and selling.
   b. planning, directing, and controlling.
   c. planning, manufacturing, and controlling.
   d. directing, manufacturing, and controlling.

3. **(LO 2)** Direct materials are a:

| | Product Cost | Manufacturing Overhead Cost | Period Cost |
|---|---|---|---|
| a. | Yes | Yes | No |
| b. | Yes | No | No |
| c. | Yes | Yes | Yes |
| d. | No | No | No |

4. **(LO 2)** Which of the following costs would a computer manufacturer include in manufacturing overhead?
   a. The cost of the disk drives.
   b. The wages earned by computer assemblers.
   c. The cost of the memory chips.
   d. Depreciation on testing equipment.

5. **(LO 2)** Which of the following is **not** an element of manufacturing overhead?
   a. Sales manager's salary.
   b. Plant manager's salary.
   c. Factory repairman's wages.
   d. Product inspector's salary.

6. **(LO 2)** Indirect labor is a:
   a. nonmanufacturing cost.   c. product cost.
   b. raw material cost.   d. period cost.

7. **(LO 2)** Which of the following costs are classified as a period cost?
   a. Wages paid to a factory custodian.
   b. Wages paid to a production department supervisor.
   c. Wages paid to a cost accounting department supervisor.
   d. Wages paid to an assembly worker.

8. **(LO 3)** For the year, Redder Company has cost of goods manufactured of $600,000, beginning finished goods inventory of $200,000, and ending finished goods inventory of $250,000. The cost of goods sold is:
   a. $450,000.   c. $550,000.
   b. $500,000.   d. $600,000.

9. **(LO 3)** Cost of goods available for sale is a step in the calculation of cost of goods sold of:
   a. a merchandising company but not a manufacturing company.
   b. a manufacturing company but not a merchandising company.
   c. a merchandising company and a manufacturing company.
   d. neither a manufacturing company nor a merchandising company.

10. **(LO 3)** A cost of goods manufactured schedule shows beginning and ending inventories for:
    a. raw materials and work in process only.
    b. work in process only.
    c. raw materials only.
    d. raw materials, work in process, and finished goods.

11. **(LO 3)** The formula to determine the cost of goods manufactured is:
    a. Beginning raw materials inventory + Total manufacturing costs − Ending work in process inventory.
    b. Beginning work in process inventory + Total manufacturing costs − Ending finished goods inventory.
    c. Beginning finished goods inventory + Total manufacturing costs − Ending finished goods inventory.
    d. Beginning work in process inventory + Total manufacturing costs − Ending work in process inventory.

**12. (LO 4)** After passage of the Sarbanes-Oxley Act:

a. reports prepared by managerial accountants must be audited by CPAs.

b. CEOs and CFOs must certify that financial statements give a fair presentation of the company's operating results.

c. the audit committee, rather than top management, is responsible for the company's financial statements.

d. reports prepared by managerial accountants must comply with generally accepted accounting principles (GAAP).

**13. (LO 4)** Which of the following managerial accounting techniques attempts to allocate manufacturing overhead in a more meaningful fashion?

a. Just-in-time inventory.　　c. Balanced scorecard.

b. Total quality management.　　d. Activity-based costing.

**14. (LO 4)** Corporate social responsibility refers to:

a. the practice by management of reviewing all business processes in an effort to increase productivity and eliminate waste.

b. an approach used to allocate overhead based on each product's use of activities.

c. the attempt by management to identify and eliminate constraints within the value chain.

d. efforts by companies to employ sustainable business practices with regard to employees and the environment.

## Solutions

**1. b.** Managerial accounting emphasizes special-purpose information. The other choices are incorrect because (a) financial accounting is governed by generally accepted accounting principles, (c) financial accounting pertains to the entity as a whole and is highly aggregated, and (d) cost accounting and cost data are a subset of management accounting.

**2. b.** Planning, directing, and controlling are the broad functions performed by the management of an organization. The other choices are incorrect because (a) selling is performed by the sales group in the organization, not by management; (c) manufacturing is performed by the manufacturing group in the organization, not by management; and (d) manufacturing is performed by the manufacturing group in the organization, not by management.

**3. b.** Direct materials are a product cost only. Therefore, choices (a), (c), and (d) are incorrect as direct materials are not manufacturing overhead or a period cost.

**4. d.** Depreciation on testing equipment would be included in manufacturing overhead because it is indirectly associated with the finished product. The other choices are incorrect because (a) disk drives would be direct materials, (b) computer assembler wages would be direct labor, and (c) memory chips would be direct materials.

**5. a.** The sales manager's salary is not directly or indirectly associated with the manufacture of the finished product. The other choices are incorrect because (b) the plant manager's salary, (c) the factory repairman's wages, and (d) the product inspector's salary are all elements of manufacturing overhead.

**6. c.** Indirect labor is a product cost because it is part of the effort required to produce a product. The other choices are incorrect because (a) indirect labor is a manufacturing cost because it is part of the effort required to produce a product, (b) indirect labor is not a raw material cost because raw material costs only include direct materials and indirect materials, and (d) indirect labor is not a period cost because it is part of the effort required to produce a product.

**7. c.** Wages paid to a cost accounting department supervisor would be included in administrative expenses and classified as a period cost. The other choices are incorrect because (a) factory custodian wages are indirect labor, which is manufacturing overhead and a product cost; (b) production department supervisor wages are indirect labor, which is manufacturing overhead and a product cost; and (d) assembly worker wages is direct labor and is a product cost.

**8. c.** Cost of goods sold is computed as Beginning finished goods inventory ($200,000) + Cost of goods manufactured ($600,000) − Ending finished goods inventory ($250,000), or $200,000 + $600,000 − $250,000 = $550,000. Therefore, choices (a) $450,000, (b) $500,000, and (d) $600,000 are incorrect.

**9. c.** Both a merchandising company and a manufacturing company use cost of goods available for sale to calculate cost of goods sold. Therefore, choices (a) only a merchandising company, (b) only a manufacturing company, and (d) neither a manufacturing company or a merchandising company are incorrect.

**10. a.** A cost of goods manufactured schedule shows beginning and ending inventories for raw materials and work in process only. Therefore, choices (b) work in process only and (c) raw materials only are incorrect. Choice (d) is incorrect because the schedule does not include finished goods.

**11. d.** The formula to determine the cost of goods manufactured is Beginning work in process inventory + Total manufacturing costs − Ending work in process inventory. The other choices are incorrect because (a) raw materials inventory, (b) ending finished goods inventory, and (c) beginning finished goods inventory and ending finished goods inventory are not part of the computation.

**12. b.** CEOs and CFOs must certify that financial statements give a fair presentation of the company's operating results. The other choices are incorrect because (a) reports prepared by financial (not managerial) accountants must be audited by CPAs; (c) SOX clarifies that top management, not the audit committee, is responsible for the company's financial statements; and (d) reports by financial (not managerial) accountants must comply with GAAP.

**13. d.** Activity-based costing attempts to allocate manufacturing overhead in a more meaningful fashion. Therefore, choices (a) just-in-time inventory, (b) total quality management, and (c) balanced scorecard are incorrect.

**14. d.** Corporate social responsibility refers to efforts by companies to employ sustainable business practices with regard to employees and the environment. The other choices are incorrect because (a) defines lean manufacturing, (b) refers to activity-based costing, and (c) describes the theory of constraints.

## Practice Brief Exercises

1. **(LO 1)** The following are selected data for Lopez Furniture.

| | |
|---|---|
| Utilities for manufacturing equipment | $120,000 |
| Wood | 850,000 |
| Depreciation on factory building | 220,000 |
| Wages for production workers | 391,000 |
| Fabric | 313,000 |
| Delivery expense | 144,000 |
| Property taxes on factory | 70,000 |

Using this selected data, determine total (a) direct materials, (b) direct labor, (c) manufacturing overhead, (d) product costs, and (e) period costs.

### Solution

1. **a.** Wood ($850,000) + Fabric ($313,000) = $1,163,000

   **b.** Wages for production workers, $391,000

   **c.** Utilities ($120,000) + Depreciation ($220,000) + Property taxes ($70,000) = $410,000

   **d.** Direct materials ($1,163,000) + Direct labor ($391,000) + Manufacturing overhead ($410,000) = $1,964,000

   **e.** Delivery expense, $144,000

2. **(LO 3)** Cody Cellular has the following data: direct labor $100,000, direct materials used $90,000, total manufacturing overhead $110,000, beginning work in process $15,000, and ending work-in-process $24,000. Compute (a) total manufacturing costs, (b) total cost of work in process, and (c) cost of goods manufactured.

### Solution

2. **a.**
| | |
|---|---|
| Direct materials use | $ 90,000 |
| Direct labor | 100,000 |
| Total manufacturing overhead | 110,000 |
| Total manufacturing costs | $300,000 |

   **b.**
| | |
|---|---|
| Beginning work in process | $ 15,000 |
| Total manufacturing costs | 300,000 |
| Total cost of work in process | $315,000 |

   **c.**
| | |
|---|---|
| Total cost of work in process | $315,000 |
| Less ending work in process | (24,000) |
| Cost of goods manufactured | $291,000 |

3. **(LO 3)** The following are current asset items in alphabetical order for Asche Company's balance sheet at December 31, 2022. Prepare the current assets section (including a complete heading).

| | |
|---|---|
| Accounts receivable | $100,000 |
| Cash | 29,000 |
| Finished goods | 47,000 |
| Prepaid expenses | 20,000 |
| Raw materials | 39,000 |
| Short-term investments | 51,000 |
| Work in process | 44,000 |

**Solution**

3.

|  | Asche Company | | |
|---|---|---|---|
|  | Balance Sheet | | |
|  | December 31, 2022 | | |
| Current assets | | | |
| Cash | | | $ 29,000 |
| Short-term investments | | | 51,000 |
| Accounts receivable | | | 100,000 |
| Inventories | | | |
| Finished goods | | $47,000 | |
| Work in process | | 44,000 | |
| Raw materials | | 39,000 | 130,000 |
| Prepaid expenses | | | 20,000 |
| Total current assets | | | $330,000 |

# Practice Exercises

*Determine the total amount of various types of costs.*

**1. (LO 2)** Fredricks Company reports the following costs and expenses in May.

| | | | |
|---|---|---|---|
| Factory utilities | $ 15,600 | Direct labor | $89,100 |
| Depreciation on factory | | Sales salaries | 46,400 |
|   equipment | 12,650 | Property taxes on factory | |
| Depreciation on delivery trucks | 8,800 |   building | 2,500 |
| Indirect factory labor | 48,900 | Repairs to office equipment | 2,300 |
| Indirect materials | 80,800 | Factory repairs | 2,000 |
| Direct materials used | 137,600 | Advertising | 18,000 |
| Factory manager's salary | 13,000 | Office supplies used | 5,640 |

**Instructions**

From the information, determine the total amount of:

a. Manufacturing overhead.

b. Product costs.

c. Period costs.

**Solution**

**1. a.** Factory utilities .......................................... $ 15,600
Depreciation on factory equipment ........... 12,650
Indirect factory labor ............................... 48,900
Indirect materials ...................................... 80,800
Factory manager's salary .......................... 13,000
Property taxes on factory building ............ 2,500
Factory repairs .......................................... 2,000
Manufacturing overhead .......................... $175,450

**b.** Direct materials ...................................... $137,600
Direct labor .............................................. 89,100
Manufacturing overhead .......................... 175,450
Product costs ............................................ $402,150

**c.** Depreciation on delivery trucks ............... $ 8,800
Sales salaries ............................................ 46,400
Repairs to office equipment ..................... 2,300
Advertising ............................................... 18,000
Office supplies used ................................. 5,640
Period costs .............................................. $ 81,140

**2. (LO 3)** Tommi Corporation incurred the following costs while manufacturing its product.

*Compute cost of goods manufactured and sold.*

| | | | |
|---|---|---|---|
| Direct materials used in production | $120,000 | Advertising expense | $45,000 |
| Depreciation on plant | 60,000 | Property taxes on plant | 19,000 |
| Property taxes on store | 7,500 | Delivery expense | 21,000 |
| Labor costs of assembly-line workers | 110,000 | Sales commissions | 35,000 |
| Factory supplies used | 25,000 | Salaries paid to sales clerks | 50,000 |

Work-in-process inventory was $10,000 at January 1 and $14,000 at December 31. Finished goods inventory was $60,500 at January 1 and $50,600 at December 31. (Assume all materials were direct.)

### Instructions

a. Compute cost of goods manufactured.

b. Compute cost of goods sold.

### Solution

**2. a.**

| | | | |
|---|---|---|---|
| Work-in-process, 1/1 | | | $ 10,000 |
| Direct materials used | | $120,000 | |
| Direct labor | | 110,000 | |
| Manufacturing overhead | | | |
| Depreciation on plant | $60,000 | | |
| Factory supplies used | 25,000 | | |
| Property taxes on plant | 19,000 | | |
| Total manufacturing overhead | | 104,000 | |
| Total manufacturing costs | | | 334,000 |
| Total cost of work-in-process | | | 344,000 |
| Less: Ending work-in-process | | | 14,000 |
| Cost of goods manufactured | | | $330,000 |

**b.**

| | |
|---|---|
| Finished goods, 1/1 | $ 60,500 |
| Cost of goods manufactured | 330,000 |
| Cost of goods available for sale | 390,500 |
| Less: Finished goods, 12/31 | 50,600 |
| Cost of goods sold | $339,900 |

## Practice Problem

**(LO 3)** Superior Company has the following cost and expense data for the year ending December 31, 2022.

*Prepare a cost of goods manufactured schedule, an income statement, and a partial balance sheet.*

| | | | |
|---|---|---|---|
| Raw materials, 1/1/22 | $ 30,000 | Property taxes, factory building | $ 6,000 |
| Raw materials, 12/31/22 | 20,000 | Sales revenue | 1,500,000 |
| Raw materials purchases | 205,000 | Delivery expenses | 100,000 |
| Work in process, 1/1/22 | 80,000 | Sales commissions | 150,000 |
| Work in process, 12/31/22 | 50,000 | Indirect labor | 105,000 |
| Finished goods, 1/1/22 | 110,000 | Factory machinery rent | 40,000 |
| Finished goods, 12/31/22 | 120,000 | Factory utilities | 65,000 |
| Direct labor | 350,000 | Depreciation, factory building | 24,000 |
| Factory manager's salary | 35,000 | Administrative expenses | 300,000 |
| Insurance, factory | 14,000 | | |

### Instructions

a. Prepare a cost of goods manufactured schedule for Superior Company for 2022. (Assume that all raw materials used were direct materials.)

b. Prepare an income statement for Superior Company for 2022.

c. Assume that Superior Company's accounting records show the balances of the following current asset accounts: Cash $17,000, Accounts Receivable (net) $120,000, Prepaid Expenses $13,000, and Short-Term Investments $26,000. Prepare the current assets section of the balance sheet for Superior Company as of December 31, 2022.

## Solution

**a.**

**Superior Company**
**Cost of Goods Manufactured Schedule**
**For the Year Ended December 31, 2022**

| | | | |
|---|---|---|---|
| Work in process, 1/1 | | | $ 80,000 |
| Direct materials | | | |
|   Raw materials inventory, 1/1 | $ 30,000 | | |
|   Raw materials purchases | 205,000 | | |
|   Total raw materials available for use | 235,000 | | |
|   Less: Raw materials inventory, 12/31 | 20,000 | | |
|   Direct materials used | | $215,000 | |
| Direct labor | | 350,000 | |
| Manufacturing overhead | | | |
|   Indirect labor | $105,000 | | |
|   Factory utilities | 65,000 | | |
|   Factory machinery rent | 40,000 | | |
|   Factory manager's salary | 35,000 | | |
|   Depreciation, factory building | 24,000 | | |
|   Insurance, factory | 14,000 | | |
|   Property taxes, factory building | 6,000 | | |
|   Total manufacturing overhead | | 289,000 | |
| Total manufacturing costs | | | 854,000 |
| Total cost of work in process | | | 934,000 |
| Less: Work in process, 12/31 | | | 50,000 |
| Cost of goods manufactured | | | $884,000 |

**b.**

**Superior Company**
**Income Statement**
**For the Year Ended December 31, 2022**

| | | |
|---|---|---|
| Sales revenue | | $1,500,000 |
| Cost of goods sold | | |
|   Finished goods inventory, January 1 | $110,000 | |
|   Cost of goods manufactured | 884,000 | |
|   Cost of goods available for sale | 994,000 | |
|   Less: Finished goods inventory, December 31 | 120,000 | |
|   Cost of goods sold | | 874,000 |
| Gross profit | | 626,000 |
| Operating expenses | | |
|   Administrative expenses | 300,000 | |
|   Sales commissions | 150,000 | |
|   Delivery expenses | 100,000 | |
|   Total operating expenses | | 550,000 |
| Net income | | $ 76,000 |

**c.**

**Superior Company**
**Balance Sheet (partial)**
**December 31, 2022**

| | | |
|---|---|---|
| Current assets | | |
|   Cash | | $ 17,000 |
|   Short-term investments | | 26,000 |
|   Accounts receivable (net) | | 120,000 |
|   Inventory | | |
|     Finished goods | $120,000 | |
|     Work in process | 50,000 | |
|     Raw materials | 20,000 | 190,000 |
|   Prepaid expenses | | 13,000 |
|   Total current assets | | $366,000 |

# WileyPLUS

Brief Exercises, DO IT! Exercises, Exercises, Problems, and many additional resources are available for practice in WileyPLUS.

## Questions

**1. a.** "Managerial accounting is a field of accounting that provides economic information for all interested parties." Do you agree? Explain.

**b.** Joe Delong believes that managerial accounting serves only manufacturing firms. Is Joe correct? Explain.

**2.** Distinguish between managerial and financial accounting as to (a) primary users of reports, (b) types and frequency of reports, and (c) purpose of reports.

**3.** How do the content of reports and the verification of reports differ between managerial and financial accounting?

**4.** Linda Olsen is studying for the next accounting mid-term examination. Summarize for Linda what she should know about management functions.

**5.** "Decision-making is management's most important function." Do you agree? Why or why not?

**6.** Explain the primary difference between line positions and staff positions, and give examples of each.

**7.** Jerry Lang is unclear as to the difference between the balance sheets of a merchandising company and a manufacturing company. Explain the difference to Jerry.

**8.** How are manufacturing costs classified?

**9.** Mel Finney claims that the distinction between direct and indirect materials is based entirely on physical association with the product. Is Mel correct? Why?

**10.** Tina Burke is confused about the differences between a product cost and a period cost. Explain the differences to Tina.

**11.** Identify the differences in the cost of goods sold section of an income statement between a merchandising company and a manufacturing company.

**12.** The determination of the cost of goods manufactured involves the following factors: (A) beginning work in process inventory, (B) total manufacturing costs, and (C) ending work in process inventory. Identify the meaning of x in the following formulas:

**a.** $A + B = x$          **b.** $A + B - C = x$

**13.** Sealy Company has beginning raw materials inventory $12,000, ending raw materials inventory $15,000, and raw materials purchases $170,000. What is the cost of direct materials used?

**14.** Tate Inc. has beginning work in process $26,000, direct materials used $240,000, direct labor $220,000, total manufacturing overhead $180,000, and ending work in process $32,000. What are the total manufacturing costs?

**15.** Tate Inc. has beginning work in process $26,000, direct materials used $240,000, direct labor $220,000, total manufacturing overhead $180,000, and ending work in process $32,000. What are (a) the total cost of work in process and (b) the cost of goods manufactured?

**16.** In what order should manufacturing inventories be listed in a balance sheet?

**17.** How does the output of manufacturing operations differ from that of service operations?

**18.** Discuss whether the product costing techniques discussed in this chapter apply equally well to manufacturers and service companies.

**19.** What is the value chain? Describe, in sequence, the main components of a manufacturer's value chain.

**20.** What is an enterprise resource planning (ERP) system? What are its primary benefits?

**21.** Why is product quality important for companies that implement a just-in-time inventory system?

**22.** Explain what is meant by "balanced" in the balanced scorecard approach.

**23.** In what ways can the budgeting process create incentives for unethical behavior?

**24.** What rules were enacted under the Sarbanes-Oxley Act to address unethical accounting practices?

**25.** What is activity-based costing, and what are its potential benefits?

## Brief Exercises

**BE11.1 (LO 1), C** Complete the following comparison table between managerial and financial accounting.   *Distinguish between managerial and financial accounting.*

|                         | **Financial Accounting** | **Managerial Accounting** |
| ----------------------- | ------------------------ | ------------------------- |
| Primary users of reports |                         |                           |
| Types of reports        |                          |                           |
| Frequency of reports    |                          |                           |
| Purpose of reports      |                          |                           |
| Content of reports      |                          |                           |
| Verification process    |                          |                           |

*Identify the three management functions.*

**BE11.2 (LO 1), C** Listed below are the three functions of the management of an organization.

1. Planning.     2. Directing.     3. Controlling.

Identify which of the following statements best describes each of the above functions.

a. _____ requires management to look ahead and to establish objectives. A key objective of management is to add value to the business.

b. _____ involves coordinating the diverse activities and human resources of a company to produce a smooth-running operation. This function relates to the implementation of planned objectives.

c. _____ is the process of keeping the activities on track. Management determines whether goals are being met and what changes are necessary when there are deviations.

*Classify manufacturing costs.*

**BE11.3 (LO 2), C** Determine whether each of the following costs should be classified as direct materials (DM), direct labor (DL), or manufacturing overhead (MO).

a. _____ Frames and tires used in manufacturing bicycles.

b. _____ Wages paid to production workers.

c. _____ Insurance on factory equipment and machinery.

d. _____ Depreciation on factory equipment.

*Classify manufacturing costs.*

**BE11.4 (LO 2), C** Indicate whether each of the following costs of an automobile manufacturer would be classified as direct materials, direct labor, or manufacturing overhead.

a. _____ Windshield.

b. _____ Engine.

c. _____ Wages of assembly-line worker.

d. _____ Depreciation of factory machinery.

e. _____ Factory machinery lubricants.

f. _____ Tires.

g. _____ Steering wheel.

h. _____ Salary of painting supervisor.

*Identify product and period costs.*

**BE11.5 (LO 2), C** Identify whether each of the following costs should be classified as product costs or period costs.

a. _____ Manufacturing overhead.

b. _____ Selling expenses.

c. _____ Administrative expenses.

d. _____ Advertising expenses.

e. _____ Direct labor.

f. _____ Direct materials.

*Classify manufacturing costs.*

**BE11.6 (LO 2), C** Presented here are Rook Company's monthly manufacturing cost data related to its tablet computer product.

a. Utilities for manufacturing equipment     $116,000

b. Raw materials (CPU, chips, etc.)     $ 85,000

c. Depreciation on manufacturing building     $880,000

d. Wages for production workers     $191,000

Enter each cost item in the following table, placing an "X" under the appropriate headings.

| | Product Costs | | |
| --- | --- | --- | --- |
| | Direct Materials | Direct Labor | Factory Overhead |
| a. | | | |
| b. | | | |
| c. | | | |
| d. | | | |

*Compute total manufacturing costs and total cost of work in process.*

**BE11.7 (LO 3), AP** Francum Company has the following data: direct labor $209,000, direct materials used $180,000, total manufacturing overhead $208,000, and beginning work in process $25,000. Compute (a) total manufacturing costs and (b) total cost of work in process.

*Prepare current assets section.*

**BE11.8 (LO 3), AP** In alphabetical order here are current asset items for Roland Company's balance sheet at December 31, 2022. Prepare the current assets section (including a complete heading).

| | |
| --- | --- |
| Accounts receivable | $200,000 |
| Cash | 62,000 |
| Finished goods | 91,000 |
| Prepaid expenses | 38,000 |
| Raw materials | 83,000 |
| Work in process | 87,000 |

**BE11.9 (LO 3), AP** The following are incomplete manufacturing cost data. Determine the missing amounts for three different situations.

*Determine missing amounts in computing total manufacturing costs.*

| | Direct Materials Used | Direct Labor Used | Factory Overhead | Total Manufacturing Costs |
|---|---|---|---|---|
| 1. | $40,000 | $61,000 | $ 50,000 | ? |
| 2. | ? | $75,000 | $140,000 | $296,000 |
| 3. | $55,000 | ? | $111,000 | $310,000 |

**BE11.10 (LO 3), AP** Use the same data from BE11.9 and the data that follow. Determine the missing amounts.

*Determine missing amounts in computing cost of goods manufactured.*

| | Total Manufacturing Costs | Work in Process (1/1) | Work in Process (12/31) | Cost of Goods Manufactured |
|---|---|---|---|---|
| 1. | ? | $120,000 | $82,000 | ? |
| 2. | $296,000 | ? | $98,000 | $331,000 |
| 3. | $310,000 | $463,000 | ? | $715,000 |

**BE11.11 (LO 4), C** The Sarbanes-Oxley Act (SOX) has important implications for the financial community. Explain two implications of SOX.

*Identify important regulatory changes.*

# DO IT! Exercises

**DO IT! 11.1 (LO 1), C** Indicate whether the following statements are true or false. If false, indicate how to correct the statement.

*Identify managerial accounting concepts.*

1. The board of directors has primary responsibility for daily management functions.

2. Financial accounting reports pertain to subunits of the business and are very detailed.

3. Managerial accounting reports must follow GAAP and are audited by CPAs.

4. Managers' activities and responsibilities can be classified into three broad functions: planning, directing, and controlling.

**DO IT! 11.2 (LO 2), C** A music company has these costs:

*Identify managerial cost classifications.*

| | |
|---|---|
| Advertising | Paper inserts for CD cases |
| Blank CDs | CD plastic cases |
| Depreciation of CD image burner | Salaries of sales representatives |
| Salary of factory manager | Salaries of factory maintenance employees |
| Factory supplies used | Salaries of employees who burn music onto CDs |

Classify each cost as a period or a product cost. Within the product cost category, indicate if the cost is part of direct materials (DM), direct labor (DL), or manufacturing overhead (MO).

**DO IT! 11.3 (LO 3), AP** The following information is available for Tomlin Company.

*Prepare cost of goods manufactured schedule.*

| | April 1 | April 30 |
|---|---|---|
| Raw materials inventory | $10,000 | $14,000 |
| Work in process inventory | 5,000 | 3,500 |

| | |
|---|---|
| Materials purchased in April | $ 98,000 |
| Direct labor in April | 80,000 |
| Manufacturing overhead in April | 160,000 |

Prepare the cost of goods manufactured schedule for the month of April.

**DO IT! 11.4 (LO 4), C** Match the descriptions that follow with the corresponding terms.

*Identify trends in managerial accounting.*

**Descriptions:**

1. _____ Inventory system in which goods are manufactured or purchased just as they are needed for sale.

2. _____ A method of allocating overhead based on each product's use of activities in making the product.

3. _____ Systems that are especially important to firms adopting just-in-time inventory methods.

4. _____ Provides guidelines for companies to describe their sustainable business practices to external parties.

5. _____ Part of the value chain for a manufacturing company.

6. _____ The U.S. economy is trending toward this.

7. _____ A performance-measurement approach that uses both financial and nonfinancial measures, tied to company objectives, to evaluate a company's operations in an integrated fashion.

8. _____ Requires that top managers certify that the company maintains an adequate system of internal controls.

**Terms:**

a. Activity-based costing.
b. Balanced scorecard.
c. Total quality management (TQM).
d. Research and development, and product design.

e. Service industries.
f. Just-in-time (JIT) inventory.
g. Sarbanes-Oxley Act (SOX).
h. Global Reporting Initiative.

# Exercises

*Identify distinguishing features of managerial accounting.*

**E11.1 (LO 1), C** Justin Bleeber has prepared the following list of statements about managerial accounting, financial accounting, and the functions of management.

1. Financial accounting focuses on providing information to internal users.
2. Staff positions are directly involved in the company's primary revenue-generating activities.
3. Preparation of budgets is part of financial accounting.
4. Managerial accounting applies only to merchandising and manufacturing companies.
5. Both managerial accounting and financial accounting deal with many of the same economic events.
6. Managerial accounting reports are prepared only quarterly and annually.
7. Financial accounting reports are general-purpose reports.
8. Managerial accounting reports pertain to subunits of the business.
9. Managerial accounting reports must comply with generally accepted accounting principles.
10. The company treasurer reports directly to the vice president of operations.

**Instructions**

Identify each statement as true or false. If false, indicate how to correct the statement.

*Classify costs into three classes of manufacturing costs.*

**E11.2 (LO 2), C** The following is a list of costs and expenses usually incurred by Barnum Corporation, a manufacturer of furniture, in its factory.

1. Salaries for product inspectors.
2. Insurance on factory machines.
3. Property taxes on the factory building.
4. Factory repairs.
5. Upholstery used in manufacturing furniture.
6. Wages paid to assembly-line workers.
7. Factory machinery depreciation.
8. Glue, nails, paint, and other small parts used in production.
9. Factory supervisors' salaries.
10. Wood used in manufacturing furniture.

**Instructions**

Classify these items into the following categories: (a) direct materials, (b) direct labor, and (c) manufacturing overhead.

**E11.3 (LO 2), C** Trak Corporation incurred the following costs while manufacturing its bicycles.

| | | | |
|---|---|---|---|
| Bicycle components | $100,000 | Advertising expense | $45,000 |
| Depreciation on plant | 60,000 | Property taxes on plant | 14,000 |
| Property taxes on store | 7,500 | Delivery expense | 21,000 |
| Labor costs of assembly-line workers | 110,000 | Sales commissions | 35,000 |
| Factory supplies used | 13,000 | Salaries paid to sales clerks | 50,000 |

*Identify types of cost and explain their accounting.*

**Instructions**

a. Identify each of the above costs as direct materials, direct labor, manufacturing overhead, or period costs.

b. Explain the basic difference in accounting for product costs and period costs.

**E11.4 (LO 2), AP** Knight Company reports the following costs and expenses in May.

| | | | |
|---|---|---|---|
| Factory utilities | $ 15,500 | Direct labor | $69,100 |
| Depreciation on factory | | Sales salaries | 46,400 |
| equipment | 12,650 | Property taxes on factory | |
| Depreciation on delivery trucks | 3,800 | building | 2,500 |
| Indirect factory labor | 48,900 | Repairs to office equipment | 1,300 |
| Indirect materials | 80,800 | Factory repairs | 2,000 |
| Direct materials used | 137,600 | Advertising | 15,000 |
| Factory manager's salary | 8,000 | Office supplies used | 2,640 |

*Determine the total amount of various types of costs.*

 **Excel**

**Instructions**

From the information, determine the total amount of:

a. Manufacturing overhead.

b. Product costs.

c. Period costs.

**E11.5 (LO 2), C** Gala Company is a manufacturer of laptop computers. Various costs and expenses associated with its operations are as follows.

*Classify various costs into different cost categories.*

1. Property taxes on the factory building.

2. Production superintendents' salaries.

3. Memory boards and chips used in assembling computers.

4. Depreciation on the factory equipment.

5. Salaries for quality control inspectors.

6. Sales commissions paid to sell laptop computers.

7. Electrical components used in assembling computers.

8. Wages of workers assembling laptop computers.

9. Soldering materials used on factory assembly lines.

10. Salaries for the night security guards for the factory building.

The company intends to classify these costs and expenses into the following categories: (a) direct materials, (b) direct labor, (c) manufacturing overhead, and (d) period costs.

**Instructions**

List the items (1) through (10). For each item, indicate the cost category to which it belongs.

**E11.6 (LO 2), C** Service The administrators of Crawford County's Memorial Hospital are interested in identifying the various costs and expenses that are incurred in producing a patient's X-ray. A list of such costs and expenses is presented here.

*Classify various costs into different cost categories.*

1. Salaries for the X-ray machine technicians.

2. Wages for the hospital janitorial personnel.

3. Film costs for the X-ray machines.

4. Property taxes on the hospital building.

5. Salary of the X-ray technicians' supervisor.

6. Electricity costs for the X-ray department.

7. Maintenance and repairs on the X-ray machines.

8. X-ray department supplies.

9. Depreciation on the X-ray department equipment.

10. Depreciation on the hospital building.

The administrators want these costs and expenses classified as (a) direct materials, (b) direct labor, or (c) service overhead.

**Instructions**

List the items (1) through (10). For each item, indicate the cost category to which the item belongs.

*Classify various costs into different cost categories.*

**E11.7 (LO 2), AP** Service National Express reports the following costs and expenses in June 2022 for its delivery service.

| | | | |
|---|---|---|---|
| Indirect materials | $ 6,400 | Drivers' salaries | $16,000 |
| Depreciation on delivery equipment | 11,200 | Advertising | 4,600 |
| Dispatcher's salary | 5,000 | Delivery equipment repairs | 300 |
| Property taxes on office building | 870 | Office supplies | 650 |
| CEO's salary | 12,000 | Office utilities | 990 |
| Gas and oil for delivery trucks | 2,200 | Repairs on office equipment | 180 |

**Instructions**

Determine the total amount of (a) delivery service (product) costs and (b) period costs.

*Compute cost of goods manufactured and sold.*

**E11.8 (LO 3), AP** Lopez Corporation incurred the following costs while manufacturing its product.

| | | | |
|---|---|---|---|
| Materials used in product | $120,000 | Advertising expense | $45,000 |
| Depreciation on plant | 60,000 | Property taxes on plant | 14,000 |
| Property taxes on store | 7,500 | Delivery expense | 21,000 |
| Labor costs of assembly-line workers | 110,000 | Sales commissions | 35,000 |
| Factory supplies used | 23,000 | Salaries paid to sales clerks | 50,000 |

Work in process inventory was $12,000 at January 1 and $15,500 at December 31. Finished goods inventory was $60,000 at January 1 and $45,600 at December 31.

**Instructions**

a. Compute cost of goods manufactured.

b. Compute cost of goods sold.

*Determine missing amounts in cost of goods manufactured schedule.*

**E11.9 (LO 3), AP** An incomplete cost of goods manufactured schedule is presented here.

**Hobbit Company**
**Cost of Goods Manufactured Schedule**
**For the Year Ended December 31, 2022**

| | | | |
|---|---|---|---|
| Work in process (1/1) | | | $210,000 |
| Direct materials | | | |
| Raw materials inventory (1/1) | $  ? | | |
| Add: Raw materials purchases | 158,000 | | |
| Total raw materials available for use | ? | | |
| Less: Raw materials inventory (12/31) | 22,500 | | |
| Direct materials used | | $180,000 | |
| Direct labor | | ? | |
| Manufacturing overhead | | | |
| Indirect labor | 18,000 | | |
| Factory depreciation | 36,000 | | |
| Factory utilities | 68,000 | | |
| Total overhead | | 122,000 | |
| Total manufacturing costs | | | ? |
| Total cost of work in process | | | ? |
| Less: Work in process (12/31) | | | 81,000 |
| Cost of goods manufactured | | | $540,000 |

**Instructions**

Complete the cost of goods manufactured schedule for Hobbit Company. Assume all raw materials are direct materials.

**E11.10 (LO 3), AN** Manufacturing cost data for Copa Company are presented as follows.

*Determine the missing amount of different cost items.*

|  | Case A | Case B | Case C |
|---|---|---|---|
| Direct materials used | $ (a) | $68,400 | $130,000 |
| Direct labor | 57,000 | 86,000 | (g) |
| Manufacturing overhead | 46,500 | 81,600 | 102,000 |
| Total manufacturing costs | 195,650 | (d) | 253,700 |
| Work in process 1/1/22 | (b) | 16,500 | (h) |
| Total cost of work in process | 221,500 | (e) | 337,000 |
| Work in process 12/31/22 | (c) | 11,000 | 70,000 |
| Cost of goods manufactured | 185,275 | (f) | (i) |

**Instructions**

Indicate the missing amount for each letter (a) through (i).

**E11.11 (LO 3), AN** Incomplete manufacturing cost data for Horizon Company for 2022 are presented as follows for four different situations.

*Determine the missing amount of different cost items, and prepare a condensed cost of goods manufactured schedule.*

|  | Direct Materials Used | Direct Labor Used | Manufac- turing Overhead | Total Manufac- turing Costs | Work in Process 1/1 | Work in Process 12/31 | Cost of Goods Manufac- tured |
|---|---|---|---|---|---|---|---|
| (1) | $117,000 | $140,000 | $ 87,000 | $ (a) | $33,000 | $ (b) | $360,000 |
| (2) | (c) | 200,000 | 132,000 | 450,000 | (d) | 40,000 | 470,000 |
| (3) | 80,000 | 100,000 | (e) | 265,000 | 60,000 | 80,000 | (f) |
| (4) | 70,000 | (g) | 75,000 | 288,000 | 45,000 | (h) | 270,000 |

**Instructions**

a. Indicate the missing amount for each letter.

b. Prepare a condensed cost of goods manufactured schedule for situation (1) for the year ended December 31, 2022.

**E11.12 (LO 3), AP** Cepeda Corporation has the following cost records for June 2022.

*Prepare a cost of goods manufactured schedule and a partial income statement.*

| | | | |
|---|---|---|---|
| Indirect factory labor | $ 4,500 | Factory utilities | $ 400 |
| Direct materials used | 20,000 | Depreciation, factory equipment | 1,400 |
| Work in process, 6/1/22 | 3,000 | Direct labor | 40,000 |
| Work in process, 6/30/22 | 3,800 | Maintenance, factory equipment | 1,800 |
| Finished goods, 6/1/22 | 5,000 | Indirect materials | 2,200 |
| Finished goods, 6/30/22 | 7,500 | Factory manager's salary | 3,000 |

**Instructions**

a. Prepare a cost of goods manufactured schedule for June 2022.

b. Prepare an income statement through gross profit for June 2022 assuming sales revenue is $92,100.

**E11.13 (LO 2, 3), AP** **Service** Keisha Tombert, the bookkeeper for Washington Consulting, a political consulting firm, has recently completed a managerial accounting course at her local college. One of the topics covered in the course was the cost of goods manufactured schedule. Keisha wondered if such a schedule could be prepared for her firm. She realized that, as a service-oriented company, it would have no work in process inventory to consider.

*Classify various costs into different categories and prepare cost of services performed schedule.*

Listed here are the costs her firm incurred for the month ended August 31, 2022.

| | |
|---|---|
| Supplies used on consulting contracts | $ 1,700 |
| Supplies used in the administrative offices | 1,500 |
| Depreciation on equipment used for contract work | 900 |
| Depreciation used on administrative office equipment | 1,050 |
| Salaries of professionals working on contracts | 15,600 |
| Salaries of administrative office personnel | 7,700 |
| Janitorial services for professional offices | 700 |
| Janitorial services for administrative offices | 500 |
| Insurance on contract operations | 800 |
| Insurance on administrative operations | 900 |
| Utilities for contract operations | 1,400 |
| Utilities for administrative offices | 1,300 |

**Instructions**

a. Prepare a schedule of cost of contract services performed (similar to a cost of goods manufactured schedule) for the month.

b. For those costs not included in (a), explain how they would be classified and reported in the financial statements.

*Prepare a cost of goods manufactured schedule and a partial income statement.*

**E11.14 (LO 3), AP** The following information is available for Aikman Company.

| | January 1, 2022 | 2022 | December 31, 2022 |
|---|---|---|---|
| Raw materials inventory | $21,000 | | $30,000 |
| Work in process inventory | 13,500 | | 17,200 |
| Finished goods inventory | 27,000 | | 21,000 |
| Materials purchased | | $150,000 | |
| Direct labor | | 220,000 | |
| Manufacturing overhead | | 180,000 | |
| Sales revenue | | 910,000 | |

**Instructions**

a. Compute cost of goods manufactured.

b. Prepare an income statement through gross profit.

c. Show the presentation of the ending inventories on the December 31, 2022, balance sheet.

d. How would the income statement and balance sheet of a merchandising company be different from Aikman's financial statements?

*Indicate in which schedule or financial statement(s) different cost items will appear.*

**E11.15 (LO 3), C** University Company produces collegiate apparel. From its accounting records, it prepares the following schedule and financial statements on a yearly basis.

a. Cost of goods manufactured schedule.

b. Income statement.

c. Balance sheet.

The following items are found in the company's accounting records and accompanying data.

1. Direct labor.

2. Raw materials inventory, 1/1.

3. Work in process inventory, 12/31.

4. Finished goods inventory, 1/1.

5. Indirect labor.

6. Depreciation on factory machinery.

7. Work in process, 1/1.

8. Finished goods inventory, 12/31.

9. Factory maintenance salaries.

10. Cost of goods manufactured.

11. Depreciation on delivery equipment.

12. Cost of goods available for sale.

13. Direct materials used.

14. Heat and electricity for factory.

15. Repairs to roof of factory building.

16. Cost of raw materials purchases.

**Instructions**

List the items (1)–(16). For each item, indicate by using the appropriate letter or letters, the schedule and/or financial statement(s) in which the item will appear.

*Prepare a cost of goods manufactured schedule, and present the ending inventories on the balance sheet.*

**E11.16 (LO 3), AP** An analysis of the accounts of Roberts Company reveals the following manufacturing cost data for the month ended June 30, 2022.

| Inventory | Beginning | Ending |
|---|---|---|
| Raw materials | $9,000 | $13,100 |
| Work in process | 5,000 | 7,000 |
| Finished goods | 9,000 | 8,000 |

Costs incurred: raw materials purchases $54,000, direct labor $47,000, manufacturing overhead $19,900. The specific overhead costs were: indirect labor $5,500, factory insurance $4,000, machinery depreciation $4,000, machinery repairs $1,800, factory utilities $3,100, and miscellaneous factory costs $1,500. Assume that all raw materials used were direct materials.

**Instructions**

a. Prepare the cost of goods manufactured schedule for the month ended June 30, 2022.

b. Show the presentation of the ending inventories on the June 30, 2022, balance sheet.

**E11.17 (LO 3), AP** Writing McQueen Motor Company manufactures automobiles. During September 2022, the company purchased 5,000 head lamps at a cost of $15 per lamp. Fifty of these lamps were used to replace the head lamps in autos used by traveling sales staff, and 4,600 lamps were put in autos manufactured during the month.

*Determine the amount of cost to appear in various accounts, and indicate in which financial statements these accounts would appear.*

Of the autos put into production during September 2022, 90% were completed and transferred to the company's storage lot. Of the cars completed during the month, 70% were sold by September 30.

**Instructions**

a. Determine the cost of head lamps that would appear in each of the following accounts at September 30, 2022: Raw Materials, Work in Process, Finished Goods, Cost of Goods Sold, and Selling Expenses.

b. Write a short memo to the chief accountant, indicating whether and where each of the accounts in (a) would appear on the income statement or on the balance sheet at September 30, 2022.

**E11.18 (LO 4), C** The following is a list of terms related to managerial accounting practices.

*Identify various managerial accounting practices.*

1. Activity-based costing.

2. Just-in-time inventory.

3. Balanced scorecard.

4. Value chain.

**Instructions**

Match each of the terms with the statement below that best describes the term.

a. _____ A performance-measurement technique that attempts to consider and evaluate all aspects of performance using financial and nonfinancial measures in an integrated fashion.

b. _____ The group of activities associated with providing a product or performing a service.

c. _____ An approach used to reduce the cost associated with handling and holding inventory by reducing the amount of inventory on hand.

d. _____ A method used to allocate overhead to products based on each product's use of the activities that cause the incurrence of the overhead cost.

## Problems

**P11.1 (LO 2), AP** Ohno Company specializes in manufacturing a unique model of bicycle helmet. The model is well accepted by consumers, and the company has enough orders to keep the factory production at 10,000 helmets per month (80% of its full capacity). Ohno's monthly manufacturing cost and other expense data are as follows.

*Classify manufacturing costs into different categories and compute the unit cost.*

| | |
|---|---|
| Rent on factory equipment | $11,000 |
| Insurance on factory building | 1,500 |
| Raw materials (plastics, polystyrene, etc.) | 75,000 |
| Utility costs for factory | 900 |
| Supplies for general office | 300 |
| Wages for assembly-line workers | 58,000 |
| Depreciation on office equipment | 800 |
| Miscellaneous materials (glue, thread, etc.) | 1,100 |
| Factory manager's salary | 5,700 |
| Property taxes on factory building | 400 |
| Advertising for helmets | 14,000 |
| Sales commissions | 10,000 |
| Depreciation on factory building | 1,500 |

## Instructions

a. DM          $75,000
   DL          $58,000
   MO          $22,100
   PC          $25,100

**a.** Prepare an answer sheet with the following column headings.

| Cost Item | Product Costs | | | Period Costs |
| | Direct Materials | Direct Labor | Manufacturing Overhead | |
| --- | --- | --- | --- | --- |

Enter each cost item on your answer sheet, placing the dollar amount under the appropriate headings. Total the dollar amounts in each of the columns.

**b.** Compute the cost to produce one helmet.

*Classify manufacturing costs into different categories and compute the unit cost.*

**P11.2 (LO 2), AP** Bell Company, a manufacturer of audio systems, started its production in October 2022. For the preceding 3 years, Bell had been a retailer of audio systems. After a thorough survey of audio system markets, Bell decided to turn its retail store into an audio equipment factory.

Raw material costs for an audio system will total $74 per unit. Workers on the production lines are on average paid $12 per hour. An audio system usually takes 5 hours to complete. In addition, the rent on the equipment used to assemble audio systems amounts to $4,900 per month. Indirect materials cost $5 per system. A supervisor was hired to oversee production; her monthly salary is $3,000.

Factory janitorial costs are $1,300 monthly. Advertising costs for the audio system will be $9,500 per month. The factory building depreciation expense is $7,800 per year. Property taxes on the factory building will be $9,000 per year.

## Instructions

a. DM          $111,000
   DL          $ 90,000
   MO          $ 18,100
   PC          $ 9,500

**a.** Prepare an answer sheet with the following column headings.

| Cost Item | Product Costs | | | Period Costs |
| | Direct Materials | Direct Labor | Manufacturing Overhead | |
| --- | --- | --- | --- | --- |

Assuming that Bell manufactures, on average, 1,500 audio systems per month, enter each cost item on your answer sheet, placing the dollar amount per month under the appropriate headings. Total the dollar amounts in each of the columns.

**b.** Compute the cost to produce one audio system.

*Indicate the missing amount of different cost items, and prepare a condensed cost of goods manufactured schedule, an income statement, and a partial balance sheet.*

**P11.3 (LO 3), AN** Incomplete manufacturing costs, expenses, and selling data for two different cases are as follows.

| | Case | |
| | 1 | 2 |
| --- | --- | --- |
| Direct materials used | $ 9,600 | $ (g) |
| Direct labor | 5,000 | 8,000 |
| Manufacturing overhead | 8,000 | 4,000 |
| Total manufacturing costs | (a) | 16,000 |
| Beginning work in process inventory | 1,000 | (h) |
| Ending work in process inventory | (b) | 3,000 |
| Sales revenue | 24,500 | (i) |
| Sales discounts | 2,500 | 1,400 |
| Cost of goods manufactured | 17,000 | 24,000 |
| Beginning finished goods inventory | (c) | 3,300 |
| Cost of goods available for sale | 22,000 | (j) |
| Cost of goods sold | (d) | (k) |
| Ending finished goods inventory | 3,400 | 2,500 |
| Gross profit | (e) | 7,000 |
| Operating expenses | 2,500 | (l) |
| Net income | (f) | 5,000 |

## Instructions

**a.** Indicate the missing amount for each letter.

b. Ending WIP    $ 6,600
c. Current assets $29,000

**b.** Prepare a condensed cost of goods manufactured schedule for Case 1.

**c.** Prepare an income statement and the current assets section of the balance sheet for Case 1. Assume that in Case 1 the other items in the current assets section are as follows: Cash $3,000, Receivables (net) $15,000, Raw Materials $600, and Prepaid Expenses $400.

**P11.4 (LO 3), AP** The following data were taken from the records of Clarkson Company for the fiscal year ended June 30, 2022.

*Prepare a cost of goods manufactured schedule, a partial income statement, and a partial balance sheet.*

| | | | |
|---|---|---|---|
| Raw Materials | | Accounts Receivable | $ 27,000 |
| Inventory 7/1/21 | $ 48,000 | Factory Insurance | 4,600 |
| Raw Materials | | Factory Machinery | |
| Inventory 6/30/22 | 39,600 | Depreciation | 16,000 |
| Finished Goods | | Factory Utilities | 27,600 |
| Inventory 7/1/21 | 96,000 | Office Utilities Expense | 8,650 |
| Finished Goods | | Sales Revenue | 534,000 |
| Inventory 6/30/22 | 75,900 | Sales Discounts | 4,200 |
| Work in Process | | Plant Manager's Salary | 58,000 |
| Inventory 7/1/21 | 19,800 | Factory Property Taxes | 9,600 |
| Work in Process | | Factory Repairs | 1,400 |
| Inventory 6/30/22 | 18,600 | Raw Materials Purchases | 96,400 |
| Direct Labor | 139,250 | Cash | 32,000 |
| Indirect Labor | 24,460 | | |

**Instructions**

a. Prepare a cost of goods manufactured schedule. (Assume all raw materials used were direct materials.)

b. Prepare an income statement through gross profit.

c. Prepare the current assets section of the balance sheet at June 30, 2022.

a. CGM $386,910
b. Gross profit $122,790
c. Current assets $193,100

**P11.5 (LO 3), AN** Empire Company is a manufacturer of smart phones. Its controller resigned in October 2022. An inexperienced assistant accountant has prepared the following income statement for the month of October 2022.

*Prepare a cost of goods manufactured schedule and a correct income statement.*

**Empire Company**
**Income Statement**
**For the Month Ended October 31, 2022**

| | | |
|---|---|---|
| Sales revenue | | $780,000 |
| Less: Operating expenses | | |
| Raw materials purchases | $264,000 | |
| Direct labor cost | 190,000 | |
| Advertising expense | 90,000 | |
| Selling and administrative salaries | 75,000 | |
| Rent on factory facilities | 60,000 | |
| Depreciation on sales equipment | 45,000 | |
| Depreciation on factory equipment | 31,000 | |
| Indirect labor cost | 28,000 | |
| Utilities expense | 12,000 | |
| Insurance expense | 8,000 | 803,000 |
| Net loss | | $ (23,000) |

Prior to October 2022, the company had been profitable every month. The company's president is concerned about the accuracy of the income statement. As her friend, you have been asked to review the income statement and make necessary corrections. After examining other manufacturing cost data, you have acquired additional information as follows.

1. Inventory balances at the beginning and end of October were:

| | October 1 | October 31 |
|---|---|---|
| Raw materials | $18,000 | $29,000 |
| Work in process | 20,000 | 14,000 |
| Finished goods | 30,000 | 50,000 |

2. Only 75% of the utilities expense and 60% of the insurance expense apply to factory operations. The remaining amounts should be charged to selling and administrative activities.

**Instructions**

a. Prepare a schedule of cost of goods manufactured for October 2022.

b. Prepare a correct income statement for October 2022.

a. CGM $581,800
b. NI $2,000

## Continuing Cases

Chapters 11–18 include a hypothetical case featuring **Current Designs**, the company described at the beginning of this chapter. Students can also work through this case following an **Excel tutorial** available in **WileyPLUS**. Each chapter's tutorial focuses on a different Excel function or feature.

### Current Designs

**CD11** Mike Cichanowski founded **Wenonah Canoe** and later purchased **Current Designs**, a company that designs and manufactures kayaks. The kayak-manufacturing facility is located just a few minutes from the canoe company's headquarters in Winona, Minnesota.

Current Designs makes kayaks using two different processes. The rotational molding process uses high temperature to melt polyethylene powder in a closed rotating metal mold to produce a complete kayak hull and deck in a single piece. These kayaks are less labor-intensive and less expensive for the company to produce and sell.

Its other kayaks use the vacuum-bagged composite lamination process (which we will refer to as the composite process). Layers of fiberglass or Kevlar® are carefully placed by hand in a mold and are bonded with resin. Then, a high-pressure vacuum is used to eliminate any excess resin that would otherwise add weight and reduce strength of the finished kayak. These kayaks require a great deal of skilled labor as each boat is individually finished. The exquisite finish of the vacuum-bagged composite kayaks gave rise to Current Designs' tag line, "A work of art, made for life."

Current Designs has the following managers:

Mike Cichanowski, CEO
Diane Buswell, Controller
Deb Welch, Purchasing Manager
Bill Johnson, Sales Manager
Dave Thill, Kayak Plant Manager
Rick Thrune, Production Manager for Composite Kayaks

| | | Product Costs | | | Period Costs | Amount |
|---|---|---|---|---|---|---|
| Payee | Purpose | Direct Materials | Direct Labor | Manufacturing Overhead | | |
| Winona Agency | Property insurance for the manufacturing plant | | | | | 3,200 |
| Bill Johnson (sales manager) | Payroll check—payment to sales manager | | | | | 1,700 |
| Xcel Energy | Electricity for manufacturing plant | | | | | 450 |
| Winona Printing | Price lists for salespeople | | | | | 85 |
| Jim Kaiser (sales representative) | Sales commissions | | | | | 1,250 |
| Dave Thill (plant manager) | Payroll check—payment to plant manager | | | | | 1,450 |
| Dana Schultz (kayak assembler) | Payroll check—payment to kayak assembler | | | | | 760 |
| Composite One | Bagging film used when kayaks are assembled; it is discarded after use | | | | | 260 |
| Fastenal | Shop supplies—brooms, paper towels, etc. | | | | | 890 |
| Ravago | Polyethylene powder which is the main ingredient for the rotational molded kayaks | | | | | 3,170 |
| Winona County | Property taxes on manufacturing plant | | | | | 5,480 |
| North American Composites | Kevlar® fabric for composite kayaks | | | | | 4,930 |
| Waste Management | Trash disposal for the company office building | | | | | 660 |
| None | Record depreciation of manufacturing equipment | | | | | 4,540 |

## Instructions

**a.** What are the primary information needs of each manager?

**b.** Name one special-purpose management accounting report that could be designed for each manager. Include the name of the report, the information it would contain, and how frequently it should be issued.

**c.** When Diane Buswell, controller for Current Designs, reviewed the accounting records for a recent period, she noted the cost items and amounts shown above (amounts are assumed). Enter the amount for each item in the appropriate cost category. Then sum the amounts in each cost category column.

## Waterways Corporation

The **Waterways case** starts in this chapter and continues in every remaining chapter. You will find the complete case for each chapter in **WileyPLUS**.

**WC11** Waterways Corporation is a private corporation formed for the purpose of providing the products and the services needed to irrigate farms, parks, commercial projects, and private lawns. It has a centrally located factory in a U.S. city that manufactures the products it markets to retail outlets across the nation. It also maintains a division that performs installation and warranty servicing in six metropolitan areas.

The mission of Waterways is to manufacture quality parts that can be used for effective irrigation projects that also conserve water. By that effort, the company hopes to satisfy its customers, perform rapid and responsible service, and serve the community and the employees who represent them in each community.

The company has been growing rapidly, so management is considering new ideas to help the company continue its growth and maintain the high quality of its products.

Waterways was founded by Will Winkman, who is the company president and chief executive officer (CEO). Working with him from the company's inception is Will's brother, Ben, whose sprinkler designs and ideas about the installation of proper systems have been a major basis of the company's success. Ben is the vice president who oversees all aspects of design and production in the company.

The factory itself is managed by Todd Senter who hires his line managers to supervise the factory employees. The factory makes all of the parts for the irrigation systems. The purchasing department is managed by Helen Hines.

The installation and training division is overseen by vice president Henry Writer, who supervises the managers of the six local installation operations. Each of these local managers hires his or her own local service people. These service employees are trained by the home office under Henry Writer's direction because of the uniqueness of the company's products.

There is a small human resources department under the direction of Sally Fenton, a vice president who handles the employee paperwork, though hiring is actually performed by the separate departments. Teresa Totter is the vice president who heads the sales and marketing area; she oversees 10 well-trained salespeople.

The accounting and finance division of the company is run by Ann Headman, who is the chief financial officer (CFO) and a company vice president. She is a member of the Institute of Management Accountants and holds a certificate in management accounting. She has a small staff of accountants, including a controller and a treasurer, and a staff of accounting input operators who maintain the financial records.

A partial list of Waterways' accounts and their balances for the month of November follows.

| | |
|---|---:|
| Accounts Receivable | $ 275,000 |
| Advertising Expenses | 54,000 |
| Cash | 260,000 |
| Depreciation—Factory Equipment | 16,800 |
| Depreciation—Office Equipment | 2,400 |
| Direct Labor | 42,000 |
| Factory Supplies Used | 16,800 |
| Factory Utilities | 10,200 |
| Finished Goods Inventory, November 30 | 68,800 |
| Finished Goods Inventory, October 31 | 72,550 |
| Indirect Labor | 48,000 |
| Office Supplies Expense | 1,600 |
| Other Administrative Expenses | 72,000 |
| Prepaid Expenses | 41,250 |
| Raw Materials Inventory, November 30 | 52,700 |
| Raw Materials Inventory, October 31 | 38,000 |
| Raw Materials Purchases | 184,500 |
| Rent—Factory Equipment | 47,000 |

| Repairs—Factory Equipment | $    4,500 |
| Salaries | 325,000 |
| Sales Revenue | 1,350,000 |
| Sales Commissions | 40,500 |
| Work in Process Inventory, October 31 | 52,700 |
| Work in Process Inventory, November 30 | 42,000 |

### Instructions

a. Based on the information given, construct an organizational chart of Waterways Corporation.

b. A list of accounts and their values are given above. From this information, prepare a cost of goods manufactured schedule, an income statement, and a partial balance sheet for Waterways Corporation for the month of November.

# Expand Your Critical Thinking

## Decision-Making Across the Organization

**CT11.1** Wendall Company specializes in producing fashion outfits. On July 31, 2022, a tornado touched down at its factory and general office. The inventories in the warehouse and the factory were completely destroyed, as was the general office nearby. However, after a careful search of the disaster site the next morning, Bill Francis, the company's controller, and Elizabeth Walton, the cost accountant, were able to recover a small part of the manufacturing cost data for the current month.

"What a horrible experience," sighed Bill. "And the worst part is that we may not have enough records to use in filing an insurance claim."

"It was terrible," replied Elizabeth. "However, I managed to recover some of the manufacturing cost data that I was working on yesterday afternoon. The data indicate that our direct labor cost in July totaled $250,000 and that we had purchased $365,000 of raw materials. Also, I recall that the amount of raw materials used for July was $350,000. But I'm not sure this information will help. The rest of our records are blown away."

"Well, not exactly," said Bill. "I was working on the year-to-date income statement when the tornado warning was announced. My recollection is that our sales in July were $1,240,000 and our gross profit ratio has been 40% of sales. Also, I can remember that our cost of goods available for sale was $770,000 for July."

"Maybe we can work something out from this information!" exclaimed Elizabeth. "My experience tells me that our manufacturing overhead is usually 60% of direct labor."

"Hey, look what I just found," cried Elizabeth. "It's a copy of this June's balance sheet, and it shows that our inventories as of June 30 are Finished goods $38,000, Work in process $25,000, and Raw materials $19,000."

"Super," yelled Bill. "Let's go work something out."

In order to file an insurance claim, Wendall Company needs to determine the amount of its inventories as of July 31, 2022, the date of the tornado touchdown.

### Instructions

With the class divided into groups, determine the amount of cost in the Raw Materials, Work in Process, and Finished Goods inventory accounts as of the date of the tornado touchdown.

## Managerial Analysis

**CT11.2** Tenrack is a fairly large manufacturing company located in the southern United States. The company manufactures tennis rackets, tennis balls, tennis clothing, and tennis shoes, all bearing the company's distinctive logo, a large green question mark on a white flocked tennis ball. The company's sales have been increasing over the past 10 years.

The tennis racket division has recently implemented several advanced manufacturing techniques. Robot arms hold the tennis rackets in place while glue dries, and machine vision systems check for defects. The engineering and design team uses computerized drafting and testing of new products. The following managers work in the tennis racket division:

Jason Dennis, Sales Manager (supervises all sales representatives)
Peggy Groneman, Technical Specialist (supervises computer programmers)
Dave Marley, Cost Accounting Manager (supervises cost accountants)
Kevin Carson, Production Supervisor (supervises all manufacturing employees)
Sally Renner, Engineer (supervises all new-product design teams)

### Instructions

a. What are the primary information needs of each manager?

b. Which, if any, financial accounting report(s) is each likely to use?

c. Name one special-purpose management accounting report that could be designed for each manager. Include the name of the report, the information it would contain, and how frequently it should be issued.

## Real-World Focus

**CT11.3** The **Institute of Management Accountants** (IMA) is an organization dedicated to excellence in the practice of management accounting and financial management.

### Instructions

Go to the IMA's website to locate the answers to the following questions.

a. How many members does the IMA have, and what are their job titles?

b. What are some of the benefits of joining the IMA as a student?

c. Use the chapter locator function to locate the IMA chapter nearest you, and find the name of the chapter president.

## Communication Activity

**CT11.4** Refer to P11.5 and add the following requirement.
Prepare a letter to the president of the company, Shelly Phillips, describing the changes you made. Explain clearly why net income is different after the changes. Keep the following points in mind as you compose your letter.

1. This is a letter to the president of a company, who is your friend. The style should be generally formal, but you may relax some requirements. For example, you may call the president by her first name.

2. Executives are very busy. Your letter should tell the president your main results first (for example, the amount of net income).

3. You should include brief explanations so that the president can understand the changes you made in the calculations.

## Ethics Case

**CT11.5** Steve Morgan, controller for Newton Industries, was reviewing production cost reports for the year. One amount in these reports continued to bother him—advertising. During the year, the company had instituted an expensive advertising campaign to sell some of its slower-moving products. It was still too early to tell whether the advertising campaign was successful.

There had been much internal debate as how to report advertising cost. The vice president of finance argued that advertising costs should be reported as a cost of production, just like direct materials and direct labor. He therefore recommended that this cost be identified as manufacturing overhead and reported as part of inventory costs until sold. Others disagreed. Morgan believed that this cost should be reported as an expense of the current period, so as not to overstate net income. Others argued that it should be reported as prepaid advertising and reported as a current asset.

The president finally had to decide the issue. He argued that these costs should be reported as inventory. His arguments were practical ones. He noted that the company was experiencing financial difficulty and that expensing this amount in the current period might jeopardize a planned bond offering. Also, by reporting the advertising costs as inventory rather than as prepaid advertising, less attention would be directed to it by the financial community.

### Instructions

a. Who are the stakeholders in this situation?

b. What are the ethical issues involved in this situation?

c. What would you do if you were Steve Morgan?

## All About You

**CT11.6** The primary purpose of managerial accounting is to provide information useful for management decisions. Many of the managerial accounting techniques that you learn in this course will be useful for decisions you make in your everyday life.

**Instructions**

For each of the following managerial accounting techniques, read the definition provided and then provide an example of a personal situation that would benefit from use of this technique.

**a.** Break-even point (Chapter 13).

**b.** Budget (Chapter 15).

**c.** Balanced scorecard (Chapter 17).

**d.** Capital budgeting (Chapter 18).

## Considering Your Costs and Benefits

**CT11.7** As noted in this chapter, because of global competition, companies have become increasingly focused on reducing costs. To reduce costs and remain competitive, many companies are turning to outsourcing. Outsourcing means hiring an outside supplier to provide elements of a product or service rather than producing them internally.

Suppose you are the managing partner in a CPA firm with 30 full-time staff. Larger firms in your community have begun to outsource basic tax-return preparation work to India. Should you outsource your basic tax-return work to India as well? You estimate that you would have to lay off six staff members if you outsource the work. The basic arguments for and against are as follows.

**YES:** The wages paid to Indian accountants are very low relative to U.S. wages. You will not be able to compete unless you outsource.

**NO:** Tax-return data are highly sensitive. Many customers will be upset to learn that their data are being emailed around the world.

**Instructions**

Write a response indicating your position regarding this situation. Provide support for your view.

# Job Order Costing

## Chapter Preview

The following Feature Story about **Disney** describes how important accurate costing is to movie studios. In order to submit accurate bids on new film projects and to know whether it profited from past films, the company needs a good costing system. This chapter illustrates how costs are assigned to specific jobs, such as the production of the most recent *Star Wars* movie. We begin the discussion in this chapter with an overview of the flow of costs in a job order cost accounting system. We then use a case study to explain and illustrate the documents, cost accumulation and assignment, and accounts in this type of cost accounting system.

## Feature Story

### Profiting from the Silver Screen

Have you ever had the chance to tour a movie studio? There's a lot going on! Lots of equipment and lots of people with a variety of talents. Running a film studio, whether as an independent company or part of a major corporation, is a complex and risky business. Consider **Disney**, which has produced such classics as *Snow White and the Seven Dwarfs* and such colossal successes as *Frozen*. The movie studio has, however, also seen its share of losses. Disney's *Lone Ranger* movie brought in revenues of $260 million, but its production and marketing costs were a combined $375 million—a loss of $115 million.

Every time Disney or another movie studio makes a new movie, it is creating a unique product. Ideally, each new movie should be able to stand on its own, that is, the film should generate revenues that exceed its costs. In order to know whether a particular movie is profitable, the studio must keep track of all of the costs incurred to make and market the film. These costs include such items as salaries of the writers, actors, director, producer, and production team (e.g., film crew); licensing costs; depreciation on equipment; music; studio rental; and marketing and distribution costs. If you've ever watched the credits at the end of a movie, you know the list goes on and on.

The movie studio isn't the only one with an interest in knowing a particular project's profitability. Many of the people involved in making the movie, such as the screenwriters, actors, and producers, have at least part of their compensation tied to its profitability. As such, complaints about inaccurate accounting are common in the movie industry.

In particular, a few well-known and widely attended movies reported low profits, or even losses, once the accountants got done with them. How can this be? The issue is that a large portion of a movie's costs are overhead costs that can't be directly traced to a film, such as depreciation of film equipment and sets, facility maintenance costs, and executives' salaries. Actors and others often complain that these overhead costs are overallocated to their movie and therefore negatively affect their compensation.

To reduce the risk of financial flops, many of the big studios now focus on making sequels of previous hits. This might explain why, shortly after losing money on the *Lone Ranger*, Disney announced plans to make another *Star Wars* movie—a much safer bet.

# Chapter Outline

| LEARNING OBJECTIVES | REVIEW | PRACTICE |
|---|---|---|
| **LO 1** Describe cost systems and the flow of costs in a job order system. | • Process cost system<br>• Job order cost system<br>• Job order cost flow<br>• Accumulating manufacturing costs | **DO IT! 1** Accumulating Manufacturing Costs |
| **LO 2** Use a job cost sheet to assign costs to work in process. | • Raw materials costs<br>• Factory labor costs | **DO IT! 2** Work in Process |
| **LO 3** Demonstrate how to determine and use the predetermined overhead rate. | • Predetermined overhead rate<br>• Applying manufacturing overhead | **DO IT! 3** Predetermined Overhead Rate |
| **LO 4** Record manufacturing and service jobs completed and sold. | • Finished goods<br>• Cost of goods sold<br>• Summary of job order cost flows<br>• Job order for service companies<br>• Advantages and disadvantages of job order costing | **DO IT! 4** Completion and Sale of Jobs |
| **LO 5** Distinguish between under- and overapplied manufacturing overhead. | • Cost of goods manufactured schedule<br>• Under- or overapplied manufacturing overhead | **DO IT! 5** Applied Manufacturing Overhead |

**Go to the Review and Practice section at the end of the chapter for a targeted summary and practice applications with solutions.**

**Visit WileyPLUS for additional tutorials and practice opportunities.**

# Cost Accounting Systems

**Cost accounting** involves measuring, recording, and reporting product and service costs. Companies determine both the total cost and the unit cost of each product.

- The accuracy of the product cost information is critical to the success of the company.
- Companies use this information to determine which products to produce, what prices to charge, and how many units to produce.
- Accurate product cost information is also vital for effective evaluation of employee performance.

A **cost accounting system** consists of accounts for the various manufacturing and service costs. These accounts are fully integrated into the accounting records of a company. An important feature of a cost accounting system is the use of **a perpetual inventory system**. Such a system **provides immediate, up-to-date information on the cost of a product**.

There are two basic types of cost accounting systems:

1. A process cost system.
2. A job order cost system.

Although cost accounting systems differ widely from company to company, most involve one of these two traditional product costing systems.

## Process Cost System

A company uses a **process cost system** when it manufactures a large volume of similar products. Production is continuous. Examples of a process cost system are the manufacture of cereal by **Kellogg**, the refining of petroleum by **ExxonMobil**, and the production of ice cream by **Ben & Jerry's**.

- Process costing accumulates product-related costs **for a period of time** (such as a week or a month) instead of assigning costs to specific products or job orders.
- In process costing, companies assign the costs to departments or processes for the specified period of time.

**Illustration 12.1** shows an example of the use of a process cost system.

**ILLUSTRATION 12.1** Process cost system

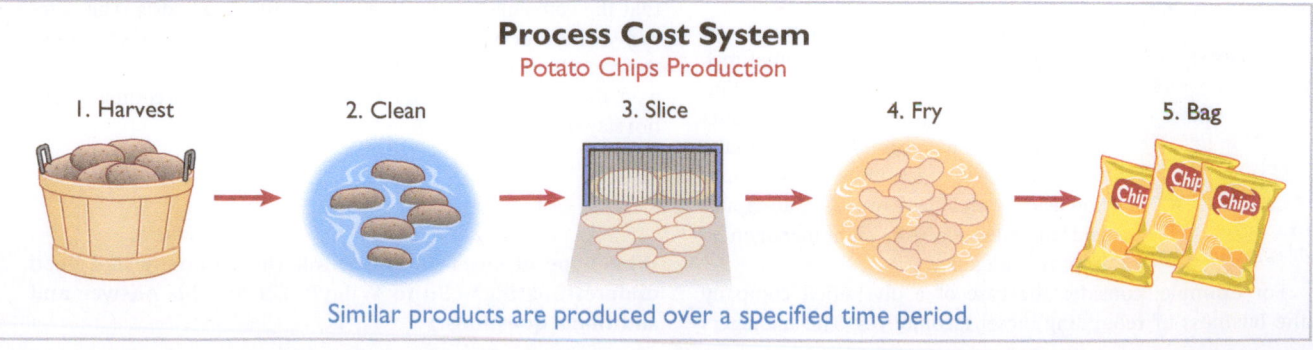

**Process Cost System**
Potato Chips Production

1. Harvest    2. Clean    3. Slice    4. Fry    5. Bag

Similar products are produced over a specified time period.

# Job Order Cost System

Under a **job order cost system**, the company assigns costs to each **job** or to each **batch** of goods. An example of a job is the manufacture of a jet by **Boeing**, the production of a movie by **Disney**, or the making of a fire truck by **Pierce Manufacturing**. An example of a batch is the printing of 225 wedding invitations by a local print shop, or the printing of a weekly issue of *Fortune* magazine by a high-tech printer such as **Quad Graphics**.

- An important feature of job order costing is that each job or batch has its own distinguishing characteristics. For example, each house is custom built, each consulting engagement by a CPA firm is unique, and each printing job is different.
- **The objective is to compute the cost per job.** At each point in manufacturing a product or performing a service, the company can identify the job and its associated costs.
- A job order cost system measures costs for each completed job, rather than for set time periods.

**Illustration 12.2** shows the recording of costs in a job order cost system for Disney as it produced two different films at the same time: an animated film and an action thriller.

**ILLUSTRATION 12.2**

**Job order cost system for Disney**

**Job Order Cost System**
Two Jobs: Animated Film and Action Thriller

- Computer programmers
- Musical composers
- Voice-over talent
- Animation talent

Job #9501

- Actors
- Stuntpeople
- Set design
- Food caterers
- Stuntperson insurance
- Location fees

Job #9502

Each job has distinguishing characteristics and related costs.

Can a company use both job order and process cost systems? Yes. For example, **General Motors** uses process cost accounting for its standard model cars, such as Malibu and Corvettes, and job order cost accounting for a custom-made limousine for the president of the United States.

The objective of both cost accounting systems is to provide unit cost information for product pricing, cost control, inventory valuation, and financial statement presentation.

## Management Insight

iStock.com/Tony Tremblay

### Jobs Won, Money Lost

Many companies suffer from poor cost accounting. As a result, they sometimes make products they should not be selling at all, or they buy product components that they could more profitably make themselves. Also, inaccurate cost information leads companies to misallocate capital and frustrates efforts by plant managers to improve efficiency.

For example, consider the case of a diversified company in the business of rebuilding diesel locomotives. The managers thought they were making money, but a consulting firm found that the company had seriously underestimated costs. The company bailed out of the business and not a moment too soon. Says the consultant who advised the company, "The more contracts it won, the more money it lost." Given that situation, a company cannot stay in business very long!

**What type of costs do you think the company had been underestimating? (Go to WileyPLUS for this answer and additional questions.)**

# Job Order Cost Flow

We first address the flow of costs for a manufacturer (service company costs are addressed in a later section). The flow of costs (direct materials, direct labor, and manufacturing overhead) in job order cost accounting parallels the physical flow of the materials as they are converted into finished goods and then sold (see **Illustration 12.3**).

1. Companies first accumulate manufacturing costs in the form of raw materials, factory labor, or manufacturing overhead.
2. They then **assign** manufacturing costs to the Work in Process Inventory account.
3. When a job is completed, the company transfers the cost of the job to Finished Goods Inventory.
4. Later, when the goods are sold, the company transfers their cost to Cost of Goods Sold.

**ILLUSTRATION 12.3**   **Flow of costs in job order costing**

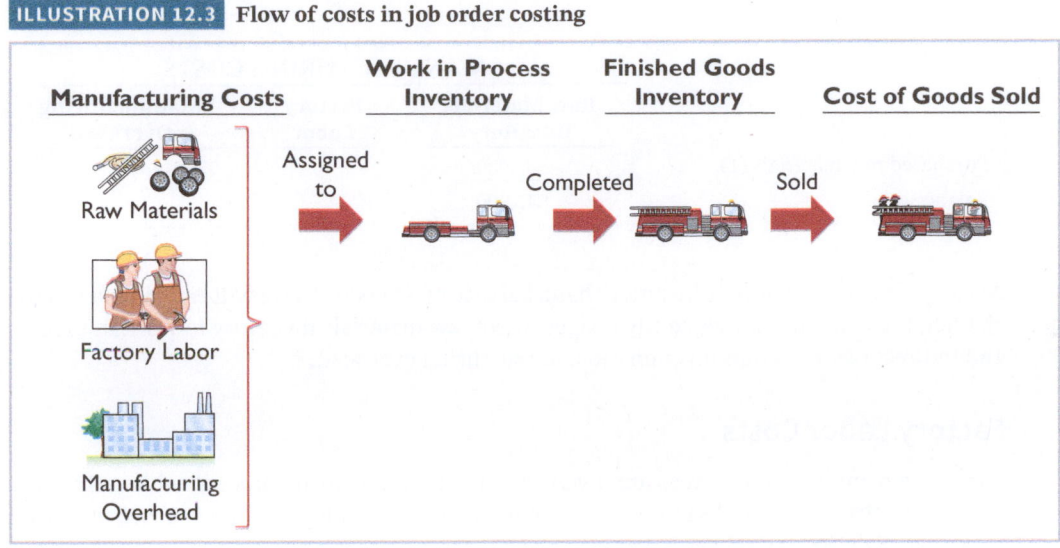

Illustration 12.3 provides a basic overview of the flow of costs in a manufacturing setting for production of a fire truck. (A more detailed presentation of the flow of costs is provided near the end of this chapter in Illustration 12.24.) There are two major steps in the flow of costs:

1. *Accumulating* the manufacturing costs incurred.
2. *Assigning* the accumulated costs to the work done.

The following discussion shows that the company accumulates manufacturing costs incurred by increases to Raw Materials Inventory, Factory Labor, and Manufacturing Overhead. When the company initially incurs these costs, it does not attempt to associate the costs with specific jobs. It later assigns manufacturing costs incurred to specific jobs as work is performed on them. In the remainder of this chapter, we will use a case study to explain how a job order cost system operates.

# Accumulating Manufacturing Costs

To illustrate a job order cost system, we will use the January transactions of Wallace Company, which makes custom electronic sensors for corporate safety applications (such as fire and carbon monoxide) and security applications (such as theft and corporate espionage).

## Raw Materials Costs

When Wallace receives the raw materials (both direct and indirect) it has purchased from a supplier, **it records the cost of the materials as Raw Materials Inventory**.

- The company increases this account for the invoice cost of the raw materials and freight costs chargeable to the purchaser.
- It reduces the account for purchase discounts taken and purchase returns and allowances.
- Wallace makes **no effort at this point to associate the cost of materials with specific jobs or orders**.

To illustrate, assume that Wallace purchases 2,000 lithium batteries (Stock No. AA2746) at $5 per unit ($10,000) and 800 electronic modules (Stock No. AA2850) at $40 per unit ($32,000) for a total cost of $42,000 ($10,000 + $32,000). This purchase increases Raw Materials Inventory as shown in **Illustration 12.4**.

**ILLUSTRATION 12.4**

Recording purchase of raw materials

| | MANUFACTURING COSTS | | |
| --- | --- | --- | --- |
| | Raw Materials Inventory | Factory Labor | Manufacturing Overhead |
| Purchased raw materials (1) | +$42,000 | | |
| Balance | $42,000 | | |

At this point, Raw Materials Inventory has a balance of $42,000. As we will explain later in the chapter, the company subsequently assigns direct raw materials inventory to work in process and indirect raw materials inventory to manufacturing overhead.

## Factory Labor Costs

Some of a company's employees are involved in the manufacturing process, while others are not. Recall that wages and salaries of nonmanufacturing employees are expensed as period costs (e.g., Salaries and Wages Expense).

- Costs related to manufacturing employees are accumulated in Factory Labor to ensure their treatment as product costs.
- Factory labor consists of three costs:

  1. Gross earnings of factory workers.
  2. Employer payroll taxes on these earnings.
  3. Fringe benefits (such as sick pay, pensions, and vacation pay) incurred by the employer.

- **Companies record labor costs as Factory Labor as they incur those costs.**

To illustrate, assume that Wallace incurs $32,000 of factory labor costs (both direct and indirect). This transaction increases Factory Labor as shown in **Illustration 12.5**.

**ILLUSTRATION 12.5**

Recording factory labor costs

| | MANUFACTURING COSTS | | |
| --- | --- | --- | --- |
| | Raw Materials Inventory | Factory Labor | Manufacturing Overhead |
| Purchased raw materials (1) | +$42,000 | | |
| Incurred factory labor (2) | | +$32,000 | |
| Balance | $42,000 | $32,000 | |

At this point, Factory Labor has a balance of $32,000. The company subsequently assigns direct factory labor to work in process and indirect factory labor to manufacturing overhead.

## Manufacturing Overhead Costs

A company has many types of overhead costs.

- If these overhead costs, such as property taxes, depreciation, insurance, and repairs, relate to overhead costs of a nonmanufacturing facility, such as an office building, then these costs are expensed as period costs (e.g., Property Tax Expense, Depreciation Expense, Insurance Expense, and Maintenance and Repairs Expense).
- If the costs relate to the manufacturing process, then they are accumulated in Manufacturing Overhead to ensure their treatment as product costs.

Using assumed data, Wallace Company incurs the following costs (other than indirect materials and indirect labor) that increase Manufacturing Overhead as shown in **Illustration 12.6**.

| | MANUFACTURING COSTS | | |
| --- | --- | --- | --- |
| | Raw Materials Inventory | Factory Labor | Manufacturing Overhead |
| Purchased raw materials (1) | +$42,000 | | |
| Incurred factory labor (2) | | +$32,000 | |
| Factory utilities (3) | | | +$4,800 |
| Factory insurance (3) | | | +2,000 |
| Factory repairs (3) | | | +2,600 |
| Factory depreciation (3) | | | +3,000 |
| Factory property taxes (3) | | | +1,400 |
| Balance | $42,000 | $32,000 | $13,800 |

**ILLUSTRATION 12.6**

Recording manufacturing costs

At this point, Manufacturing Overhead has a balance of $13,800. The company subsequently assigns manufacturing overhead to work in process.

## DO IT! 1 | Accumulating Manufacturing Costs

During the current month, Ringling Company incurs the following manufacturing costs:

a. Raw material purchases of $4,200.

b. Factory labor of $18,000. Of that amount, $15,000 relates to wages and $3,000 relates to payroll taxes.

c. Factory utilities of $2,200 are incurred, prepaid factory insurance of $1,800 has expired, and depreciation on the factory building is $3,500.

Using the format shown in Illustration 12.6, record the company's manufacturing costs in its job order costing system.

**ACTION PLAN**

- In accumulating manufacturing costs, increase at least one of three accounts: Raw Materials Inventory, Factory Labor, and Manufacturing Overhead.
- Manufacturing overhead costs may be recognized daily. Or, manufacturing overhead may be recorded periodically.

### Solution

| | MANUFACTURING COSTS | | |
| --- | --- | --- | --- |
| | Raw Materials Inventory | Factory Labor | Manufacturing Overhead |
| a. | +$4,200 | | |
| b. | | +$18,000 | |
| c. | | | +$2,200 |
| c. | | | +1,800 |
| c. | | | +3,500 |

Related exercise material: **BE12.1, BE12.2, DO IT! 12.1, E12.1, and E12.11.**

# Assigning Manufacturing Costs

### LEARNING OBJECTIVE 2
Use a job cost sheet to assign costs to work in process.

Assigning manufacturing costs to work in process results in:

1. **Increases** to Work in Process Inventory.
2. **Decreases** to Raw Materials Inventory, Factory Labor, and Manufacturing Overhead.

An essential accounting record in assigning costs to jobs is a **job cost sheet**, as shown in **Illustration 12.7**. A **job cost sheet** is a form used to record the costs chargeable to a specific job and to determine the total and unit costs of the completed job (see **Decision Tools**).

**ILLUSTRATION 12.7**

**Job cost sheet**

**Job Cost Sheet**

Job No. _____  Quantity _____
Item _____  Date Requested _____
For _____  Date Completed _____

| Date | Direct Materials | Direct Labor | Manufacturing Overhead |
|------|------------------|--------------|------------------------|
|      |                  |              |                        |
|      |                  |              |                        |

Cost of completed job
   Direct materials     $ _____
   Direct labor
   Manufacturing overhead     _____
Total cost     $ _____
Unit cost (total cost ÷ quantity)     $ _____

Companies keep a separate job cost sheet for each job, typically as a computer file.

- The job cost sheets constitute the subsidiary ledger for the Work in Process Inventory control account in the general ledger. A **subsidiary ledger** consists of individual records for each individual item—in this case, each job.
- The Work in Process account is referred to as a **control account** because it summarizes the detailed data regarding specific jobs contained in the job cost sheets.
- **Each increase or decrease to Work in Process Inventory must be accompanied by a corresponding posting to one or more job cost sheets.**

## Raw Materials Costs

**Companies assign raw materials costs to jobs when their materials storeroom issues the materials in response to requests.** Requests for issuing raw materials are made by production department personnel on a prenumbered **materials requisition slip**. The materials issued may be used directly on a job, or they may be considered indirect materials.

**ETHICS NOTE**

Approvals are an important internal control feature of a requisition slip because they establish individual accountability over inventory.

- As **Illustration 12.8** shows, the requisition should indicate the quantity and type of materials withdrawn and the account to be charged (see **Ethics Note**).
- Note also in Illustration 12.8 the specific job (in this case, Job No. 101) to be charged. The materials requisition slip also is an example of the internal control principle of documentation (in this case, prenumbering).
- The company will charge direct materials to Work in Process Inventory, and indirect materials to Manufacturing Overhead.

**ILLUSTRATION 12.8**
**Materials requisition slip**

### Wallace Company
### Materials Requisition Slip

| Deliver to: | Assembly Department | | Req. No. | R247 |
|---|---|---|---|---|
| Charge to: | **Work in Process—Job No. 101** | | Date: | 1/6/22 |

| Quantity | Description | Stock No. | Cost per Unit | Total |
|---|---|---|---|---|
| 200 | Lithium batteries | AA2746 | $5.00 | $1,000 |

Requested by *Bruce Howart*    Received by *Herb Crowley*

Approved by *Kap Shin*    Costed by *Heather Remmers*

The company may use any of the inventory costing methods (FIFO, LIFO, or average-cost) in costing the requisitions **to the individual job cost sheets**. In an automated system, the requisition is entered electronically. Once approved and delivered to production, the materials are charged automatically to an electronic job cost record.

Periodically, the company records the requisitions. For example, if Wallace uses $24,000 of direct materials and $6,000 of indirect materials in January, it will reduce Raw Materials Inventory by $30,000 and increase Work in Process Inventory by $24,000 as the direct materials are assigned to jobs, and increase Manufacturing Overhead by $6,000 as shown in **Illustration 12.9**.

**ILLUSTRATION 12.9**
**Recording of direct and indirect materials**

| | MANUFACTURING COSTS | | | WORK IN PROCESS INVENTORY |
|---|---|---|---|---|
| | Raw Materials Inventory | Factory Labor | Manufacturing Overhead | |
| Balance | $42,000 | $32,000 | $13,800 | |
| Direct materials (4) | −24,000 | | | +$24,000 |
| Indirect materials (4) | −6,000 | | +6,000 | |
| Balance | $12,000 | $32,000 | $19,800 | $24,000 |

**HELPFUL HINT**

Companies post to control accounts monthly, and post to job cost sheets daily.

**Illustration 12.10** shows the posting of requisition slip R247 to Job No. 101 and other assumed postings to the job cost sheets for materials (see **Helpful Hint**). The requisition slips provide the basis for total direct materials costs of $12,000 for Job No. 101, $7,000 for Job No. 102, and $5,000 for Job No. 103. After the company has completed all postings, the sum of the direct materials columns of the job cost sheets (the **subsidiary** account amounts of $12,000, $7,000, and $5,000) should equal the direct materials recorded to Work in Process Inventory (the **control** account amount of $24,000).

**ILLUSTRATION 12.10**   **Job cost sheets—posting of direct materials**

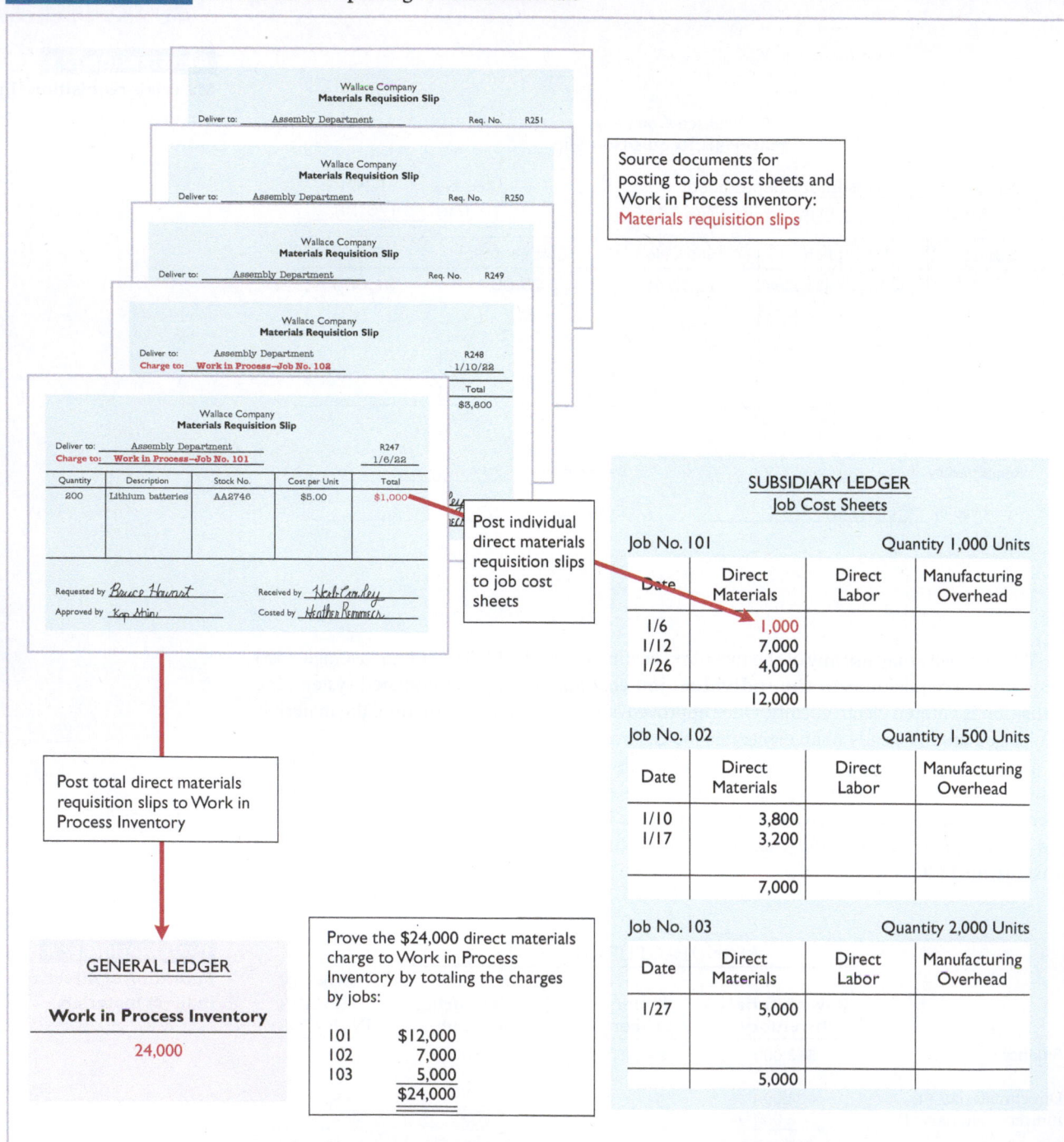

---

**Management Insight**    IHS

iStock.com/TommL

### The Cost of an iPhone? Just Tear One Apart

All companies need to know what it costs to make their own products—but a lot of companies would also like to know the cost of their competitors' products as well. That's where IHS steps in. IHS tears apart sophisticated electronic devices to tell you what it would cost to replicate.

In the case of smartphones, which often have more than 1,000 tiny components, that is no small feat. For example, consider that the components of a recent iPhone model cost about $221.

Assembly adds only about another $5. However, the difference between what you pay (almost triple the total component cost) and the "cost" is not all profit. You also have to consider the additional nonproduction costs of research, design, marketing, patent fees, and selling costs.

**Source:** 2016 IHS Markit; *https://9to5mac.com/2016/09/20/649-iphone-7-estimated-to-cost-apple-220-heres-the-component-break down.*

**What type of costs are marketing and selling costs, and how are they treated for accounting purposes? (Go to WileyPLUS for this answer and additional questions.)**

---

## Factory Labor Costs

**Companies assign factory labor costs to jobs on the basis of time tickets prepared when the work is performed.**

- The **time ticket** indicates the employee, the hours worked, the account and job to be charged, and the total labor cost.
- Many companies accumulate these data through the use of bar coding and scanning devices.

When they start and end work, employees scan bar codes on their identification badges and bar codes associated with each job they work on. When direct labor is involved, the time ticket must indicate the job number, as shown in **Illustration 12.11**. The employee's supervisor should approve all time tickets.

**ILLUSTRATION 12.11**
**Time ticket**

**Wallace Company**
**Time Ticket**

| Employee | John Nash | | Date: | 1/6/22 |
| | | | Employee No. | 124 |
| **Charge to:** | **Work in Process** | | **Job No.** | **101** |

| Time | | | Hourly Rate | Total Cost |
|---|---|---|---|---|
| Start | Stop | Total Hours | | |
| 0800 | 1200 | 4 | 10.00 | 40.00 |

Approved by  *Bob Kadler*          Costed by  *M. Chen*

In an automated system:

1. After factory employees scan their identification codes, labor costs are automatically posted to specific jobs at the appropriate pay scale.
2. The time tickets are later sent to the payroll department, which applies the employee's hourly wage rate plus fringe benefits and computes the total labor cost.

**3.** Finally, the company records the time tickets. It increases the account Work in Process Inventory for direct labor and increases Manufacturing Overhead for indirect labor.

For example, if the $32,000 total factory labor cost consists of $28,000 of direct labor and $4,000 of indirect labor, Wallace reduces Factory Labor by $32,000 so it has a zero balance, and labor costs are assigned to the appropriate manufacturing accounts. This increases Work in Process Inventory by $28,000 and increases Manufacturing Overhead by $4,000 as shown in **Illustration 12.12**.

**ILLUSTRATION 12.12**

**Recording factory labor**

| | MANUFACTURING COSTS | | | WORK IN PROCESS INVENTORY |
|---|---|---|---|---|
| | Raw Materials Inventory | Factory Labor | Manufacturing Overhead | |
| Balance | $12,000 | $32,000 | $19,800 | $24,000 |
| Direct labor (5) | | −28,000 | | +28,000 |
| Indirect labor (5) | | −4,000 | +4,000 | |
| Balance | $12,000 | $   0 | $23,800 | $52,000 |

Let's assume that the labor costs chargeable to Wallace's three jobs are $15,000, $9,000, and $4,000. **Illustration 12.13** shows the Work in Process Inventory and job cost sheets after posting.

- As in the case of direct materials, the sum of the postings to the direct labor columns of the job cost sheets (subsidiary accounts Job 101 $15,000, Job 102 $9,000, and Job 103 $4,000) should equal the posting of direct labor to the Work in Process Inventory control account ($28,000).

- Also, time ticket and job ticket hours should be periodically reconciled as an internal control.

**ILLUSTRATION 12.13**    **Job cost sheets—direct labor**

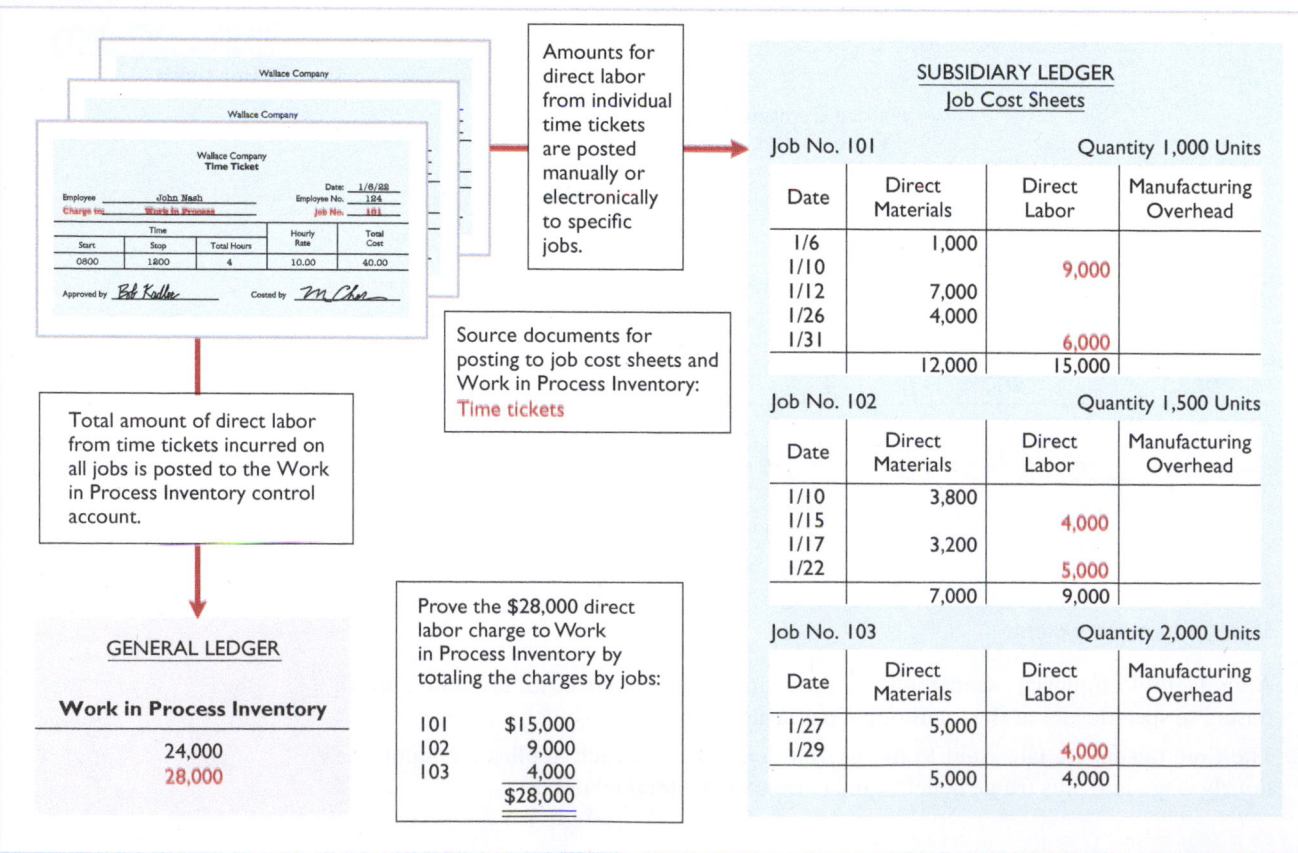

## DO IT! 2 | Work in Process

Danielle Company is working on two job orders. The job cost sheets show the following:

> Direct materials—Job 120 $6,000; Job 121 $3,600
> Direct labor—Job 120 $4,000; Job 121 $2,000

Using the format shown in Illustration 12.12, record the assignment of costs to Work in Process from the data on the job cost sheets.

### Solution

| | MANUFACTURING COSTS | | | |
|---|---|---|---|---|
| | Raw Materials Inventory | Factory Labor | Manufacturing Overhead | WORK IN PROCESS INVENTORY |
| Direct materials | −$9,600 | | | +$9,600 |
| Direct labor | | −$6,000 | | +6,000 |

Related exercise material: **BE12.3, BE12.4, BE12.5, DO IT! 12.2, E12.1, E12.7,** and **E12.8.**

**ACTION PLAN**

- Recognize that Work in Process Inventory is the control account for all unfinished job cost sheets.
- Increase Work in Process Inventory for the materials and labor charged to the job cost sheets.
- Decrease the accounts that were increased when the manufacturing costs were accumulated.

# Predetermined Overhead Rates

### LEARNING OBJECTIVE 3
Demonstrate how to determine and use the predetermined overhead rate.

Companies charge the actual costs of direct materials and direct labor to specific jobs because these costs can be directly traced to specific jobs. In contrast, manufacturing **overhead** relates to production operations **as a whole**.

- As a result, overhead costs cannot be assigned to specific jobs on the basis of actual costs incurred because overhead cannot be traced to (identified with) specific jobs.
- Instead, companies assign manufacturing overhead to work in process and to specific jobs **on an estimated basis through the use of a predetermined overhead rate**.
- The **predetermined overhead rate** is based on the relationship between estimated annual overhead costs and estimated annual operating activity, expressed in terms of a common **activity base**.
- The company may state the activity in terms of direct labor costs, direct labor hours, machine hours, or any other measure that will provide an equitable basis for applying overhead costs to jobs.

Companies establish the predetermined overhead rate at the beginning of the year. Small companies often use a single, company-wide predetermined overhead rate. Large companies often use rates that vary from department to department. **Illustration 12.14** presents the formula for the predetermined overhead rate.

| Estimated Annual Overhead Costs | ÷ | Estimated Annual Operating Activity | = | Predetermined Overhead Rate |
|---|---|---|---|---|

**ILLUSTRATION 12.14**

Formula for predetermined overhead rate

Overhead consists of indirect costs and relates to production operations as a whole. To know what "the whole" is, it might seem that the logical thing is to wait until the end of the year's operations. At that time, the company knows all of its actual costs for the period. As a practical matter, though, managers cannot wait until the end of the year.

- To price products effectively as they are completed, managers need information about product costs of specific jobs completed during the year.
- Using an estimated predetermined overhead rate enables a cost to be determined for the job immediately.

**Illustration 12.15** indicates how manufacturing overhead is assigned to work in process.

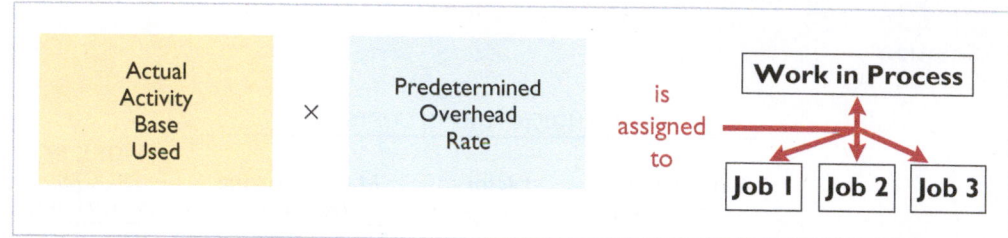

Wallace Company uses direct labor cost as the activity base. Assuming that the company expects annual overhead costs to be $280,000 and direct labor costs for the year to be $350,000, the overhead rate is 80%, computed as shown in **Illustration 12.16**.

| Estimated Annual Overhead Costs | ÷ | Estimated Direct Labor Cost | = | Predetermined Overhead Rate |
|---|---|---|---|---|
| $280,000 | ÷ | $350,000 | = | 80% |

This means that for every dollar of direct labor, Wallace will assign 80 cents of manufacturing overhead to a job. The use of a predetermined overhead rate enables the company to determine the approximate total cost of each job **when it completes the job**.

Historically, companies used direct labor costs or direct labor hours as the activity base. The reason was the relatively high correlation between direct labor and manufacturing overhead.

- Today, more companies are using **machine hours as the activity base, due to increased reliance on automation in manufacturing operations**.
- Alternatively, many companies now use activity-based costing to more accurately assign overhead costs based on the activities that give rise to the costs.
- A company may use more than one activity base.

For example, if a job is manufactured in more than one factory department, each department may have its own overhead rate. A company might use two bases in assigning overhead to jobs: direct materials dollars for indirect materials, and direct labor hours for such costs as insurance and supervisor salaries.

Wallace Company applies manufacturing overhead to work in process after it assigns direct labor costs. It also applies manufacturing overhead to specific jobs at that time. For January, Wallace applied overhead of $22,400 in response to its assignment of $28,000 of direct labor costs (direct labor cost of $28,000 × 80%). This reduces the balance in Manufacturing Overhead and increases Work in Process Inventory by $22,400 as shown in **Illustration 12.17**.

| | MANUFACTURING COSTS | | | WORK IN PROCESS INVENTORY |
|---|---|---|---|---|
| | Raw Materials Inventory | Factory Labor | Manufacturing Overhead | |
| Balance | $12,000 | $0 | $23,800 | $52,000 |
| Assigned manufacturing overhead (6) | | | −22,400 | +22,400 |
| Balance | $12,000 | $0 | $ 1,400 | $74,400 |

The overhead that Wallace applies to each job will be 80% of the direct labor cost of the job for the month. **Illustration 12.18** shows the Work in Process Inventory account and the job cost sheets after posting. Note that the increase of $22,400 to Work in Process Inventory equals the sum of the overhead applied to jobs: Job No. 101 $12,000 + Job No. 102 $7,200 + Job No. 103 $3,200.

**ILLUSTRATION 12.18** Job cost sheets—manufacturing overhead applied

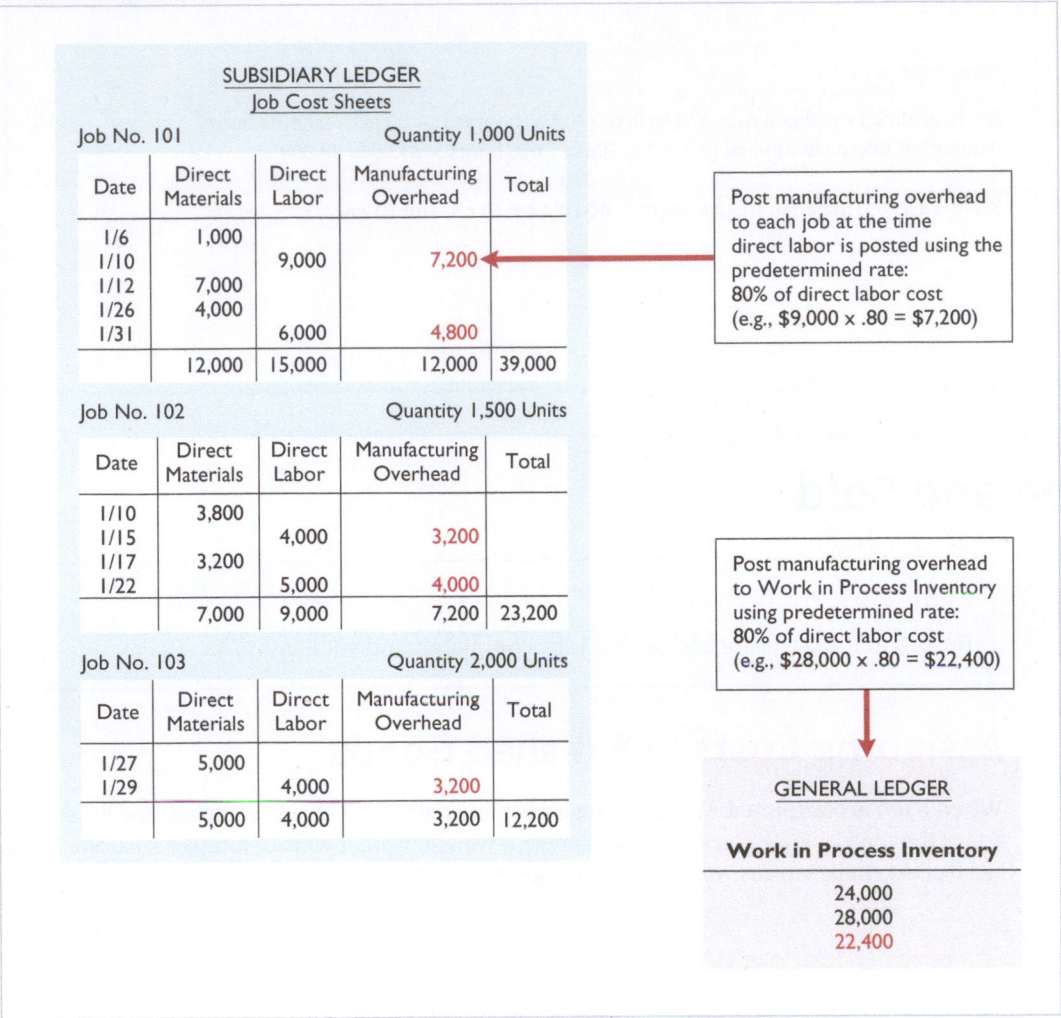

Notice that after posting the decrease of $22,400 to manufacturing overhead, a positive balance of $1,400 remains.

- This means that the overhead applied to jobs using the predetermined rate was $1,400 less than the actual amount of overhead incurred during the period.
- This situation is referred to as underapplied overhead.

We address the treatment of under- and overapplied overhead in a later section.

At the end of each month, the **balance in Work in Process Inventory should equal the sum of the costs shown on the job cost sheets of unfinished jobs**. **Illustration 12.19** presents proof of the agreement of the control and subsidiary accounts for Wallace. (It assumes that all jobs are still in process.)

| Work in Process Inventory | Job Cost Sheets | |
|---|---|---|
| $ 24,000 | No. 101 | $ 39,000 |
| 28,000 | 102 | 23,200 |
| 22,400 | 103 | 12,200 |
| **$ 74,400** ← | ← | **$74,400** |

**ACTION PLAN**

- The predetermined overhead rate is estimated annual overhead cost divided by estimated annual operating activity.
- Assignment of overhead to jobs is determined by multiplying the actual activity base used by the predetermined overhead rate.
- Record the assignment of overhead by transferring an amount out of Manufacturing Overhead into Work in Process Inventory.

## DO IT! 3 | Predetermined Overhead Rate

Stanley Company produces specialized safety devices. For the year, manufacturing overhead costs are estimated to be $160,000. Estimated machine usage is 40,000 hours. The company applies overhead based on machine hours. Job No. 302 used 2,000 machine hours.

Compute the predetermined overhead rate and determine the amount of overhead to apply to Job No. 302.

### Solution

Predetermined overhead rate = $160,000 ÷ 40,000 hours = $4.00 per machine hour
Amount of overhead applied to Job No. 302 = 2,000 hours × $4.00 = $8,000

Related exercise material: **BE12.6, BE12.7, DO IT! 12.3, E12.5, and E12.6.**

# Jobs Completed and Sold

**LEARNING OBJECTIVE 4**

Record manufacturing and service jobs completed and sold.

## Assigning Costs to Finished Goods

**When a job is completed**, Wallace Company summarizes the costs and completes the lower portion of the applicable job cost sheet. For example, if we assume that Wallace completes Job No. 101, a batch of electronic sensors, on January 31, the job cost sheet appears as shown in **Illustration 12.20**.

**ILLUSTRATION 12.20**

**Completed job cost sheet**

**Job Cost Sheet**

Job No. _____ 101 _____    Quantity _____ 1,000 _____
Item ____ Electronic Sensors ____    Date Requested ____ January 5 ____
For _____ Tanner Company _____    Date Completed ____ January 31 ____

| Date | Direct Materials | Direct Labor | Manufacturing Overhead |
|---|---|---|---|
| 1/6 | $ 1,000 | | |
| 1/10 | | $ 9,000 | $ 7,200 |
| 1/12 | 7,000 | | |
| 1/26 | 4,000 | | |
| 1/31 | | 6,000 | 4,800 |
| | $12,000 | $15,000 | $12,000 |

| Cost of completed job | | |
|---|---|---|
| Direct materials | $ | 12,000 |
| Direct labor | | 15,000 |
| Manufacturing overhead | | 12,000 |
| Total cost | $ | 39,000 |
| Unit cost ($39,000 ÷ 1,000) | $ | 39.00 |

When a job is finished, Wallace transfers its total cost to finished goods inventory. This increases Finished Goods Inventory and reduces Work in Process Inventory by $39,000 as shown in **Illustration 12.21**.

| | MANUFACTURING COSTS | | | WORK IN PROCESS INVENTORY | FINISHED GOODS INVENTORY |
|---|---|---|---|---|---|
| | Raw Materials Inventory | Factory Labor | Manuf. Overhead | | |
| Balance | $12,000 | $0 | $1,400 | $74,400 | |
| Completion of Job No. 101 (7) | | | | −39,000 | +$39,000 |
| Balance | $12,000 | $0 | $1,400 | $35,400 | $39,000 |

**ILLUSTRATION 12.21**
**Recording finished jobs**

**Finished Goods Inventory is a control account. It controls individual finished goods records** in a finished goods subsidiary ledger.

## Assigning Costs to Cost of Goods Sold

Companies recognize cost of goods sold when each sale occurs. For example, assume that on January 31 Wallace Company sells on account Job No. 101. The job cost $39,000. This increases Cost of Goods Sold and reduces Finished Goods Inventory by $39,000 as shown in **Illustration 12.22**.

| | MANUFACTURING COSTS | | | WORK IN PROCESS INVENTORY | FINISHED GOODS INVENTORY | COST OF GOODS SOLD |
|---|---|---|---|---|---|---|
| | Raw Materials Inventory | Factory Labor | Manuf. Overhead | | | |
| Balance | $12,000 | $0 | $1,400 | $35,400 | $39,000 | |
| Sale of Job 101 (8) | | | | | −39,000 | +$39,000 |
| Balance | $12,000 | $0 | $1,400 | $35,400 | $ 0 | $39,000 |

**ILLUSTRATION 12.22**
**Assigning cost of goods sold**

## Summary of Job Order Cost Flows

**Illustration 12.23** summarizes the flow of documents in a job order cost system.

**ILLUSTRATION 12.23**  **Flow of documents in a job order cost system**

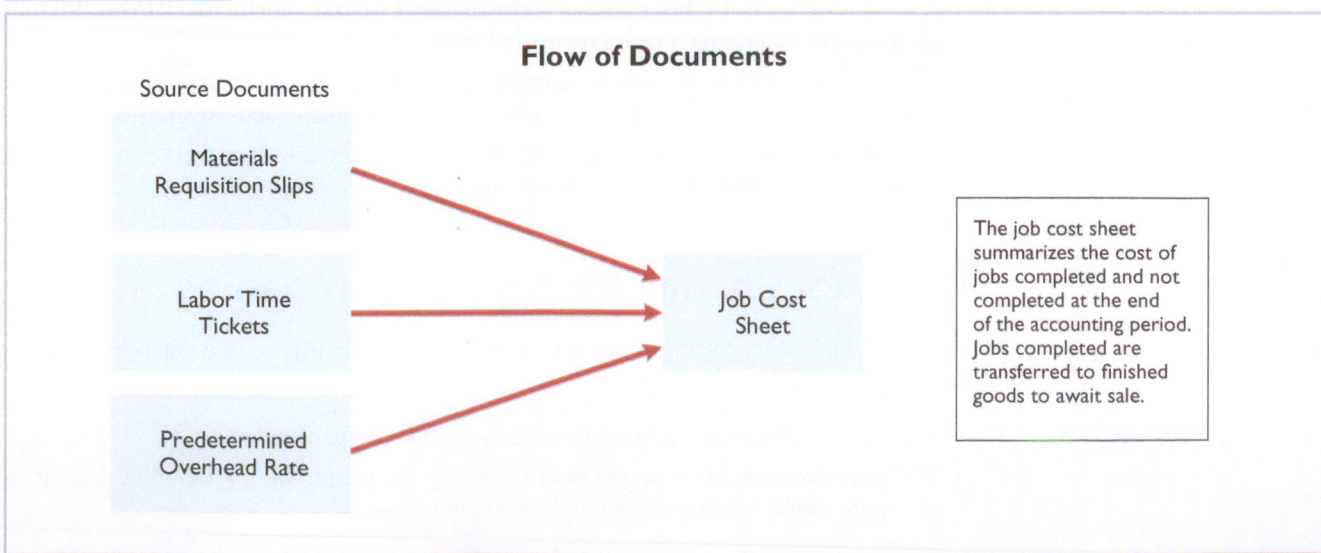

**Flow of Documents**

Source Documents

Materials Requisition Slips

Labor Time Tickets

Predetermined Overhead Rate

Job Cost Sheet

The job cost sheet summarizes the cost of jobs completed and not completed at the end of the accounting period. Jobs completed are transferred to finished goods to await sale.

**Illustration 12.24** diagrams the flow of costs for a job order cost accounting system. All postings are keyed to items 1–8 in the example presented in the previous pages for Wallace Company.

**ILLUSTRATION 12.24** Flow of costs in a job order cost system

**Flow of Costs**

|  | **MANUFACTURING COSTS** | | | **WORK IN PROCESS INVENTORY** | **FINISHED GOODS INVENTORY** | **COST OF GOODS SOLD** |
|---|---|---|---|---|---|---|
|  | **Raw Materials Inventory** | **Factory Labor** | **Manuf. Overhead** |  |  |  |
| (1) | +$42,000 |  |  |  |  |  |
| (2) |  | +$32,000 |  |  |  |  |
| (3) |  |  | +$4,800 |  |  |  |
| (3) |  |  | +2,000 |  |  |  |
| (3) |  |  | +2,600 |  |  |  |
| (3) |  |  | +3,000 |  |  |  |
| (3) |  |  | +1,400 |  |  |  |
| (4) | −24,000 |  |  | +$24,000 |  |  |
| (4) | −6,000 |  | +6,000 |  |  |  |
| (5) |  | −28,000 |  | +28,000 |  |  |
| (5) |  | −4,000 | +4,000 |  |  |  |
| (6) |  |  | −22,400 | +22,400 |  |  |
| (7) |  |  |  | −39,000 | +$39,000 |  |
| (8) |  |  |  |  | −39,000 | +$39,000 |
| Ending balance | $12,000 | $   0 | $1,400 | $35,400 | $   0 | $39,000 |

**Accumulation**
1. Purchase raw materials
2. Incur factory labor
3. Incur manufacturing overhead

**Assignment**
4. Raw materials are used
5. Factory labor is used
6. Overhead is applied
7. Completed goods are recognized
8. Cost of goods sold is recognized

The cost flows in the diagram can be categorized as one of four types:

- **Accumulation.** The company first accumulates costs by (1) purchasing raw materials, (2) incurring labor costs, and (3) incurring manufacturing overhead costs.
- **Assignment to jobs.** Once the company has incurred manufacturing costs, it must assign them to specific jobs. For example, as it uses raw materials on specific jobs (4), the company assigns them to work in process or treats them as manufacturing overhead if the raw materials cannot be associated with a specific job. Similarly, the company either assigns factory labor (5) to work in process or treats it as manufacturing overhead if the factory labor cannot be associated with a specific job. Finally, the company assigns manufacturing overhead (6) to work in process using a *predetermined overhead rate*. This deserves emphasis: **Do not assign overhead using actual overhead costs but instead apply overhead using a predetermined rate.**
- **Completion of jobs.** As jobs are completed (7), the company transfers the cost of the completed job out of work in process inventory into finished goods inventory.
- **Sale of jobs.** As specific items are sold (8), the company transfers their cost out of finished goods inventory into cost of goods sold.

# Job Order Costing for Service Companies

Our extended job order costing example focuses on a manufacturer so that you see the flow of costs through the inventory accounts.

- Job order costing is also commonly used by service companies.
- While service companies do not have inventory, the techniques of job order costing are still quite useful in many service-industry environments.

Consider, for example, the **Mayo Clinic** (healthcare), **PricewaterhouseCoopers** (accounting), and **Goldman Sachs** (investment banking). These companies need to keep track of the cost of jobs performed for specific customers to evaluate the profitability of medical treatments, audits, or investment banking engagements.

Many service organizations bill their customers using cost-plus contracts.

- Cost-plus contracts mean that the customer's bill is the sum of the costs incurred on the job, plus a profit amount that is calculated as a percentage of the costs incurred.

- In order to minimize conflict with customers and reduce potential contract disputes, service companies that use cost-plus contracts must maintain accurate and up-to-date costing records.

Up-to-date cost records enable a service company to immediately notify a customer of cost overruns due to customer requests for changes to the original plan or unexpected complications. Timely recordkeeping allows the contractor and customer to consider alternatives before it is too late.

A service company that uses a job order cost system does not have inventory accounts. It does, however, use an account similar to Work in Process Inventory, referred to here as Service Contracts in Process, to record job costs prior to completion. For example, consider the following transactions for Dorm Decor, an interior design company.

1. Assignment of $9,000 of supplies to projects ($7,000 direct and $2,000 indirect).

2. Assignment of service salaries and wages of $100,000 ($84,000 direct and $16,000 indirect).

3. Dorm Decor applies operating overhead at a rate of 50% of direct labor costs (direct labor cost is $84,000), which is $42,000 ($84,000 × 50%).

4. Upon completion of a design project for State University, the job cost sheet shows a total cost of $34,000 as shown in **Illustration 12.25**.

**ILLUSTRATION 12.25**

**Recording service job costs**

|  | SERVICE CONTRACT COSTS | | | | |
|---|---|---|---|---|---|
|  | **Supplies** | **Service Salaries and Wages** | **Operating Overhead** | SERVICE CONTRACTS IN PROCESS | COST OF COMPLETED SERVICE CONTRACTS |
| Beginning balances | $16,000 | $100,000 | $40,000 | | |
| Assign supplies to projects (1) | −9,000 | | +2,000 | +$ 7,000 | |
| Assign personnel costs to projects (2) | | −100,000 | +16,000 | +84,000 | |
| Assign operating overhead to projects (3) | | | −42,000 | +42,000 | |
| Completion of State University project (4) | | | | −34,000 | +$34,000 |
| Balance | $ 7,000 | $ 0 | $16,000 | $99,000 | $34,000 |

Job cost sheets for a service company keep track of materials, labor, and overhead used on a particular job, similar to a manufacturer. Several exercises at the end of this chapter apply job order costing to service companies.

iStock.com/Christian Lagereek

### Sales Are Nice, but Service Revenue Pays the Bills

Jet engines are one of the many products made by the industrial operations division of **General Electric (GE)**. At prices as high as $30 million per engine, you can bet that GE does its best to keep track of costs. It might surprise you that GE doesn't make much profit on the sale of each engine. So why does it bother making them? For the service revenue. During one recent year, about 75% of the division's revenues came from servicing its own products. One estimate is that the $13 billion in aircraft engines sold during a recent 3-year period will generate about $90 billion in service revenue over the 30-year life of the engines. GE hopes to have 44,000 engines in service in the near future.

Because of the high product costs, both the engines themselves and the subsequent service are most likely accounted for using job order costing. Accurate service cost records are important because GE needs to generate high profit margins (estimated to be 30%) on its service jobs to make up for the low margins on the original sale. It also needs good cost records for its service jobs in order to control its costs. Otherwise, a competitor, such as **Pratt & Whitney**, might submit lower bids for service contracts and take lucrative service jobs away from GE.

**Sources:** Paul Glader, "GE's Focus on Services Faces Test," *Wall Street Journal Online* (March 3, 2009); and Steve Heller, "General Electric's Untapped Opportunity in Aviation," *The Motley Fool* (August 27, 2016).

**Explain why GE would use job order costing to keep track of the cost of repairing a malfunctioning engine for a major airline. (Go to WileyPLUS for this answer and additional questions.)**

# Advantages and Disadvantages of Job Order Costing

Job order costing is more precise in the assignment of costs to projects than process costing. For example, assume that a construction company, Juan Company, builds 10 custom homes a year at a total cost of $2,000,000. One way to determine the cost of the homes is to divide the total construction cost incurred during the year by the number of homes produced during the year. For Juan Company, an average cost of $200,000 ($2,000,000 ÷ 10) is computed. If the homes are nearly identical, then this approach is adequate for purposes of determining profit per home.

- But if the homes vary in terms of size, style, and material types, using the average cost of $200,000 to determine profit per home is inappropriate.
- Instead, Juan Company should use a job order cost system to determine the specific cost incurred to build each home and the amount of profit made on each.
- Thus, job order costing provides more useful information for determining the profitability of particular projects and for estimating costs when preparing bids on future jobs.

However, job order costing requires a significant amount of data entry. For Juan Company, it is much easier to simply keep track of total costs incurred during the year than it is to keep track of the costs incurred on each job (home built). Recording this information is time-consuming, and if the data is not entered accurately, then the product costs are incorrect.

- In recent years, technological advances, such as bar-coding devices for both labor costs and materials, have increased the accuracy and reduced the effort needed to record costs on specific jobs.
- These innovations expand the opportunities to apply job order costing in a wider variety of business settings, thus improving management's ability to control costs and make better informed decisions.

A common problem of all costing systems is how to assign overhead to the finished product. Overhead often represents more than 50% of a product's cost, and this cost is often difficult to assign meaningfully to the product. How, for example, is the salary of a project manager at Juan Company assigned to the various homes, which may differ in size, style, and cost of materials used?

- The accuracy of the job order cost system is largely dependent on the accuracy of the overhead allocation process.
- Even if the company does a good job of keeping track of the specific amounts of materials and labor used on each job, if the overhead costs are not assigned to individual jobs in a meaningful way, the product costing information is not useful.

---

## DO IT! 4 | Completion and Sale of Jobs

During the current month, Onyx Corporation completed Job 109 and Job 112. Job 109 cost $19,000 and Job 112 cost $27,000. Job 112 was sold on account for $42,000. Using the format shown in Illustration 12.24, record the completion of the two jobs and the sale of Job 112 in the company's job order cost system.

### ACTION PLAN

- Increase Finished Goods Inventory for the cost of completed jobs.
- Increase Cost of Goods Sold for the cost of jobs sold.

### Solution

| | WORK IN PROCESS INVENTORY | FINISHED GOODS INVENTORY | COST OF GOODS SOLD |
|---|---|---|---|
| Completed Job 109 | –$19,000 | +$19,000 | |
| Completed Job 112 | –27,000 | +27,000 | |
| Sold Job 112 | | –27,000 | +$27,000 |

Related exercise material: **BE12.8, DO IT! 12.4, E12.2, E12.6, E12.7, and E12.10.**

---

# Applied Manufacturing Overhead

### LEARNING OBJECTIVE 5
Distinguish between under- and overapplied manufacturing overhead.

## Cost of Goods Manufactured Schedule

At the end of a period, companies prepare financial statements that present aggregate data on all jobs manufactured and sold.

- The cost of goods manufactured schedule in job order costing is the same as presented in Chapter 11 but with one exception: **The schedule shows manufacturing overhead applied, rather than actual overhead costs.**
- **The company adds this amount to direct materials and direct labor to determine total manufacturing costs.**
- Companies prepare the cost of goods manufactured schedule directly from the Work in Process Inventory account (see **Helpful Hint**).

### HELPFUL HINT

Companies usually prepare monthly financial statements for management use only.

**Illustration 12.26** shows a condensed schedule for Wallace Company for January.

| Wallace Company | | |
|---|---|---|
| **Cost of Goods Manufactured Schedule** | | |
| **For the Month Ending January 31, 2022** | | |
| Work in process, January 1 | | $  —0— |
| Direct materials used | $ 24,000 | |
| Direct labor | 28,000 | |
| **Manufacturing overhead applied** | **22,400** | |
| Total manufacturing costs | | 74,400 |
| Total cost of work in process | | 74,400 |
| Less: Work in process, January 31 | | 35,400 |
| Cost of goods manufactured | | $39,000 |

Note that the cost of goods manufactured ($39,000) agrees with the amount transferred from Work in Process Inventory to Finished Goods Inventory in item No. 7 in Illustration 12.24.

# Under- or Overapplied Manufacturing Overhead

Recall that overhead is applied based on an estimate of total annual overhead costs. This estimate will rarely be exactly equal to actual overhead incurred. Therefore, at the end of the year, after overhead has been applied to specific jobs, the Manufacturing Overhead account will likely have a remaining balance (see **Decision Tools**).

- When Manufacturing Overhead has a **positive balance**, overhead is said to be underapplied.
- **Underapplied overhead** means that the overhead applied to work in process is less than the overhead incurred.
- Conversely, when manufacturing overhead has a **negative balance**, overhead is overapplied.
- **Overapplied overhead** means that the overhead applied to work in process is greater than the overhead incurred.

## Year-End Balance

At the end of the year, all manufacturing overhead transactions are complete. There is no further opportunity for offsetting events to occur. At this point, Wallace Company eliminates any remaining balance in Manufacturing Overhead by an adjustment, and either increases or decreases Cost of Goods Sold. It considers under- or overapplied overhead to be an **adjustment to cost of goods sold**.

- If Manufacturing Overhead has a positive balance, it increases Cost of Goods Sold by the amount of underapplied overhead.
- If Manufacturing Overhead has a negative balance, it decreases Cost of Goods Sold by the amount of overapplied overhead.

To illustrate, as shown in Illustration 12.17 and repeated in **Illustration 12.27**, after applying overhead of $22,400 Wallace has a $1,400 positive balance in Manufacturing Overhead at December 31. This occurred because the amount of overhead applied was less than the amount incurred during the period. This means it was underapplied.

| | Manufacturing Overhead | |
|---|---|---|
| Incurred | $ 13,800 | |
| | 6,000 | |
| | 4,000 | |
| Applied | −22,400 | |
| Underapplied balance | $  1,400 | |

Since Wallace's overhead is underapplied, we will decrease the overhead account and increase cost of goods sold by $1,400 as shown in **Illustration 12.28**. This results in a zero balance in Manufacturing Overhead and an adjusted Cost of Goods Sold balance of $40,400.

|  | Manufacturing Overhead | Cost of Goods Sold |
|---|---|---|
| Unadjusted balance | $1,400 | $39,000 |
| Adjustment | −1,400 | +1,400 |
| Adjusted balance | $   0 | $40,400 |

**ILLUSTRATION 12.28**

**Adjusting Manufacturing Overhead and Cost of Goods Sold**

**Illustration 12.29** presents an income statement for Wallace after adjusting for the $1,400 of underapplied overhead (assuming the goods were sold for $50,000).

**ILLUSTRATION 12.29**

**Partial income statement**

### Wallace Company
#### Income Statement (partial)
#### For the Month Ending January 31, 2022

| | | |
|---|---|---|
| Sales revenue | | $50,000 |
| Cost of goods sold | | |
| Finished goods inventory, January 1 | $   -0- | |
| **Cost of goods manufactured (see Illustration 12.26)** | **39,000** | |
| Cost of goods available for sale | 39,000 | |
| Less: Finished goods inventory, January 31 | -0- | |
| Cost of goods sold—unadjusted | 39,000 | |
| Add: Adjustment for underapplied overhead | 1,400 | |
| Cost of goods sold—adjusted | | 40,400 |
| Gross profit | | $ 9,600 |

For more accurate costing, significant under- or overapplied overhead at the end of the year should be allocated among ending work in process, finished goods, and cost of goods sold. The discussion of this allocation approach is left to more advanced courses.

---

## DO IT! 5 | Applied Manufacturing Overhead

For Karr Company, the predetermined overhead rate is 140% of direct labor cost. During the month, Karr incurred $90,000 of factory labor costs, of which $80,000 is direct labor and $10,000 is indirect labor. Actual overhead incurred (including indirect labor) was $119,000.

Compute the amount of manufacturing overhead applied during the month. Determine the amount of under- or overapplied manufacturing overhead.

### Solution

Manufacturing overhead applied = (140% × $80,000) = $112,000
Underapplied manufacturing overhead = ($119,000 − $112,000) = $7,000

Related exercise material: **BE12.10, DO IT! 12.5, E12.4, E12.5, E12.9, and E12.13.**

**ACTION PLAN**

• **Calculate the amount of overhead applied by multiplying the predetermined overhead rate by actual activity.**

• **If applied overhead is less than actual, overhead is underapplied.**

• **If applied overhead is greater than actual, overhead is overapplied.**

## USING THE DECISION TOOLS | Disney

**Disney** faces many situations where it needs to apply the decision tools learned in this chapter, such as using a job cost sheet to determine a film's profitability. For example, assume Disney uses a job order cost system and applies overhead to production of its films on the basis of direct labor cost. In computing a predetermined overhead rate for the year 2022, the company estimated film production overhead to be $24 million and direct labor costs to be $20 million. In addition, it developed the following information.

**Actual Costs Incurred During 2022**

| | |
|---|---|
| Direct materials used | $30,000,000 |
| Direct labor cost incurred | 21,000,000 |
| Insurance, studio | 500,000 |
| Indirect labor | 7,500,000 |
| Studio maintenance | 1,000,000 |
| Rent on studio building | 11,000,000 |
| Depreciation on studio equipment | 2,000,000 |

## Instructions

Answer each of the following.

**a.** Why is Disney using a job order cost system?

**b.** On what basis does Disney apply its film production overhead? Compute the predetermined overhead rate for 2022.

**c.** Compute the amount of the under- or overapplied overhead for 2022.

**d.** Disney had balances in the beginning and ending films in process and finished films accounts as follows.

| | 1/1/22 | 12/31/22 |
|---|---|---|
| Films in process | $ 5,000,000 | $ 4,000,000 |
| Finished films | 13,000,000 | 11,000,000 |

Determine the (1) cost of films produced and (2) cost of films sold for Disney during 2022. Assume that any under- or overapplied overhead should be included in the cost of films sold.

**e.** During 2022, Film G408 (a short documentary film produced for a customer) was started and completed. Its cost sheet showed a total cost of $100,000, and Disney prices its film at 50% above its cost. What is the price to the customer if the company follows this pricing strategy?

## Solution

**a.** Disney is using a job order cost system because it produces films. Each film is unique, with its own distinguishing characteristics.

**b.** Disney applies its overhead on the basis of direct labor cost. The predetermined overhead rate is 120%, computed as follows: $24,000,000 ÷ $20,000,000 = 120%.

**c.**

| | | |
|---|---|---|
| Actual film production overhead | | $ 22,000,000* |
| Applied overhead cost ($21,000,000 × 120%) | | 25,200,000 |
| Overapplied overhead | | $ 3,200,000 |

*$500,000 + $7,500,000 + $1,000,000 + $11,000,000 + $2,000,000

**d. 1.**

| | | |
|---|---|---|
| Films in process, 1/1/22 | | $ 5,000,000 |
| Direct materials used | $30,000,000 | |
| Direct labor | 21,000,000 | |
| Film production overhead applied | 25,200,000 | |
| Total film production costs | | 76,200,000 |
| Total cost of films in process | | 81,200,000 |
| Less: Films in process, 12/31/22 | | 4,000,000 |
| Cost of films produced | | $77,200,000 |

| | | |
|---|---|---|
| **2.** Finished films, 1/1/22 | | $13,000,000 |
| Cost of films produced (see above) | | 77,200,000 |
| Cost of films available for sale | | 90,200,000 |
| Finished films, 12/31/22 | | 11,000,000 |
| Cost of films sold (unadjusted) | | 79,200,000 |
| Less: Overapplied overhead | | 3,200,000 |
| Cost of films sold | | $76,000,000 |
| | | |
| **e.** Film G408 cost | $ | 100,000 |
| Markup percentage | | × 50% |
| Markup | $ | 50,000 |

Price to customer: $150,000 ($100,000 + $50,000)

# Review and Practice

## Learning Objectives Review

### 1  Describe cost systems and the flow of costs in a job order system.

Cost accounting involves the procedures for measuring, recording, and reporting product and service costs. From the data accumulated, companies determine the total cost and the unit cost of each product. The two basic types of cost accounting systems are process cost and job order cost.

In job order costing, companies first accumulate manufacturing costs in three accounts: Raw Materials Inventory, Factory Labor, and Manufacturing Overhead. They then assign the accumulated costs to Work in Process Inventory and eventually to Finished Goods Inventory and Cost of Goods Sold.

### 2  Use a job cost sheet to assign costs to work in process.

A job cost sheet is a form used to record the costs chargeable to a specific job and to determine the total and unit costs of the completed job. Job cost sheets constitute the subsidiary ledger for the Work in Process Inventory control account.

### 3  Demonstrate how to determine and use the predetermined overhead rate.

The predetermined overhead rate is based on the relationship between estimated annual overhead costs and estimated annual operating activity. This is expressed in terms of a common activity base, such as direct labor cost. Companies use this rate to assign overhead costs to work in process and to specific jobs.

### 4  Record manufacturing and service jobs completed and sold.

When jobs are completed, companies add the cost to Finished Goods Inventory and remove it from Work in Process Inventory. When a job is sold, a company increases Cost of Goods Sold and decreases Finished Goods Inventory for the cost of the goods.

### 5  Distinguish between under- and overapplied manufacturing overhead.

Underapplied manufacturing overhead indicates that the overhead assigned to work in process is less than the overhead incurred. Overapplied overhead indicates that the overhead assigned to work in process is greater than the overhead incurred.

## Decision Tools Review

| Decision Checkpoints | Info Needed for Decision | Tool to Use for Decision | How to Evaluate Results |
|---|---|---|---|
| What is the cost of a job? | Cost of material, labor, and overhead assigned to a specific job | Job cost sheet | Compare costs to those of previous periods to ensure that costs are in line. Compare costs to expected selling price or service fees charged to determine overall profitability. |
| Has the company over- or underapplied overhead for the period? | Actual overhead costs and overhead applied | Manufacturing Overhead account | If the account balance is negative, overhead applied exceeded actual overhead costs. If the account balance is positive, overhead applied was less than actual overhead costs. |

## Glossary Review

**Cost accounting** An area of accounting that involves measuring, recording, and reporting product and service costs. (p. 12-3).

**Cost accounting system** Manufacturing and service cost accounts that are fully integrated into the accounting records of a company. (p. 12-3).

**Job cost sheet** A form used to record the costs chargeable to a specific job and to determine the total and unit costs of the completed job. (p. 12-8).

**Job order cost system** A cost accounting system in which costs are assigned to each job or batch. (p. 12-4).

**Materials requisition slip** A document authorizing the issuance of raw materials from the storeroom to production. (p. 12-9).

**Overapplied overhead** A situation in which overhead applied to work in process is greater than the overhead incurred. (12-22).

**Predetermined overhead rate** A rate based on the relationship between estimated annual overhead costs and estimated annual operating activity, expressed in terms of a common activity base. (12-13).

**Process cost system** A cost accounting system used when a company manufactures a large volume of similar products. (p. 12-3).

**Time ticket** A document that indicates the employee, the hours worked, the account and job to be charged, and the total labor cost. (p. 12-11).

**Underapplied overhead** A situation in which overhead applied to work in process is less than the overhead incurred. (p. 12-22).

## Practice Multiple-Choice Questions

1. **(LO 1)** Cost accounting involves the measuring, recording, and reporting of:
   a. product and service costs.
   b. future costs.
   c. manufacturing processes.
   d. managerial accounting decisions.

2. **(LO 1)** A company is more likely to use a job order cost system if:
   a. it manufactures a large volume of similar products.
   b. its production is continuous.
   c. it manufactures products with unique characteristics.
   d. it uses a periodic inventory system.

3. **(LO 1)** In accumulating raw materials costs, companies add the cost of raw materials purchased in a perpetual system to:
   a. Raw Materials Purchases.
   b. Raw Materials Inventory.
   c. Purchases.
   d. Work in Process.

4. **(LO 1)** When incurred, factory labor costs are added to:
   a. Work in Process.
   b. Factory Wages Expense.
   c. Factory Labor.
   d. Finished Goods.

5. **(LO 1)** The flow of costs in job order costing:
   a. begins with work in process inventory and ends with finished goods inventory.
   b. begins as soon as a sale occurs.
   c. parallels the physical flow of materials as they are converted into finished goods.
   d. is necessary to prepare the cost of goods manufactured schedule.

6. **(LO 2)** Raw materials are assigned to a job when:
   a. the job is sold.
   b. the materials are purchased.
   c. the materials are received from the vendor.
   d. the materials are issued by the materials storeroom.

**7. (LO 2)** The sources of information for assigning costs to job cost sheets are:

    **a.** invoices, time tickets, and the predetermined overhead rate.

    **b.** materials requisition slips, time tickets, and the actual overhead costs.

    **c.** materials requisition slips, payroll register, and the predetermined overhead rate.

    **d.** materials requisition slips, time tickets, and the predetermined overhead rate.

**8. (LO 2)** In recording the issuance of raw materials in a job order cost system, it would be **incorrect** to:

    **a.** increase Work in Process Inventory.

    **b.** increase Finished Goods Inventory.

    **c.** increase Manufacturing Overhead.

    **d.** decrease Raw Materials Inventory.

**9. (LO 2)** When direct factory labor is assigned to jobs, there is an increase to:

    **a.** Work in Process Inventory and a decrease to Factory Labor.

    **b.** Manufacturing Overhead and a decrease to Factory Labor.

    **c.** Factory Labor and a decrease to Manufacturing Overhead.

    **d.** Factory Labor and a decrease to Work in Process Inventory.

**10. (LO 3)** The formula for computing the predetermined manufacturing overhead rate is estimated annual overhead costs divided by estimated annual operating activity, expressed as:

    **a.** direct labor cost.

    **b.** direct labor hours.

    **c.** machine hours.

    **d.** Any of the answer choices is correct.

**11. (LO 3)** In Crawford Company, the predetermined overhead rate is 80% of direct labor cost. During the month, Crawford incurs $210,000 of factory labor costs, of which $180,000 is direct labor and $30,000 is indirect labor. Actual overhead incurred was $200,000. The amount of overhead added to Work in Process Inventory should be:

    **a.** $200,000.

    **b.** $144,000.

    **c.** $168,000.

    **d.** $160,000.

**12. (LO 4)** Mynex Company completes Job No. 26 at a cost of $4,500 and later sells it for $7,000 cash. A **correct** recording is:

    **a.** increase Finished Goods Inventory $7,000 and decrease Work in Process Inventory $7,000.

    **b.** increase Cost of Goods Sold $7,000 and decrease Finished Goods Inventory $7,000.

    **c.** increase Finished Goods Inventory $4,500 and decrease Work in Process Inventory $4,500.

    **d.** increase Accounts Receivable $7,000 and increase Sales Revenue $7,000.

**13. (LO 5)** At the end of an accounting period, a company using a job order cost system calculates the cost of goods manufactured:

    **a.** from the job cost sheet.

    **b.** from the Work in Process Inventory account.

    **c.** by adding direct materials used, direct labor incurred, and manufacturing overhead incurred.

    **d.** from the Cost of Goods Sold account.

**14. (LO 4)** Which of the following statements is **true**?

    **a.** Job order costing requires less data entry than process costing.

    **b.** Allocation of overhead is easier under job order costing than process costing.

    **c.** Job order costing provides more precise costing for custom jobs than process costing.

    **d.** The use of job order costing has declined because more companies have adopted automated accounting systems.

**15. (LO 5)** At end of the year, a company has a $1,200 positive balance in Manufacturing Overhead. The company:

    **a.** makes an adjustment by increasing Manufacturing Overhead Applied for $1,200 and decreasing Manufacturing Overhead for $1,200.

    **b.** makes an adjustment by increasing Manufacturing Overhead Expense for $1,200 and decreasing Manufacturing Overhead for $1,200.

    **c.** makes an adjustment by increasing Cost of Goods Sold for $1,200 and decreasing Manufacturing Overhead for $1,200.

    **d.** makes no adjustment because differences between actual overhead and the amount applied are a normal part of job order costing and will average out over the next year.

**16. (LO 5)** Manufacturing overhead is underapplied if:

    **a.** actual overhead is less than applied.

    **b.** actual overhead is greater than applied.

    **c.** the predetermined rate equals the actual rate.

    **d.** actual overhead equals applied overhead.

## Solutions

**1. a.** Cost accounting involves the measuring, recording, and reporting of product and service costs, not (b) future costs, (c) manufacturing processes, or (d) managerial accounting decisions.

**2. c.** A job costing system is more likely for products with unique characteristics. The other choices are incorrect because a process cost system is more likely for (a) large volumes of similar products or (b) if production is continuous. (d) is incorrect because the choice of a costing system is not dependent on whether a periodic or perpetual inventory system is used.

**3. b.** In a perpetual system, purchases of raw materials increase Raw Materials Inventory, not (a) Raw Materials Purchases, (c) Purchases, or (d) Work in Process.

**4. c.** When factory labor costs are incurred, they are added to Factory Labor, not (a) Work in Process, (b) Factory Wages Expense, or (d) Finished Goods.

**5. c.** Job order costing parallels the physical flow of materials as they are converted into finished goods. The other choices are incorrect because job order costing begins (a) with raw materials, not work in process, and ends with cost of goods sold; and (b) as soon as raw materials are purchased, not when the sale occurs. Choice (d) is incorrect because the cost of goods manufactured schedule is prepared from the Work in Process account and is only a portion of the costs in a job order system.

**6. d.** Raw materials are assigned to a job when the materials are issued by the materials storeroom, not when (a) the job is sold, (b) the materials are purchased, or (c) the materials are received from the vendor.

**7. d.** Materials requisition slips are used to assign direct materials, time tickets are used to assign direct labor, and the predetermined overhead rate is used to assign manufacturing overhead to job cost sheets. The other choices are incorrect because (a) materials requisition slips, not invoices, are used to assign direct materials; (b) the predetermined overhead rate, not the actual overhead costs, is used to assign manufacturing overhead; and (c) time tickets, not the payroll register, are used to assign direct labor.

**8. b.** Finished Goods Inventory is increased when goods are transferred from work in process to finished goods, not when raw materials are issued for a job. Choices (a), (c), and (d) are true statements.

**9. a.** When direct factory labor is assigned to jobs, the result is an increase to Work in Process Inventory and a decrease to Factory Labor. The other choices are incorrect because (b) Work in Process Inventory, not Manufacturing Overhead, is increased; (c) Work in Process Inventory, not Factory Labor, is increased and Factory Labor, not Manufacturing Overhead, is decreased; and (d) Work in Process Inventory, not Factory Labor, is increased and Factory Labor, not Work in Process Inventory, is decreased.

**10. d.** Any of the activity measures mentioned can be used in computing the predetermined manufacturing overhead rate. Choices (a) direct labor cost, (b) direct labor hours, and (c) machine hours can all be used in computing the predetermined manufacturing overhead rate, but (d) is a better answer.

**11. b.** Work in Process Inventory should be increased $144,000 ($180,000 × 80%), the amount of manufacturing overhead applied, not (a) $200,000, (c) $168,000, or (d) $160,000.

**12. c.** When a job costing $4,500 is completed, Finished Goods Inventory is increased and Work in Process Inventory is decreased for

$4,500. Choices (a) and (b) are incorrect because the amounts should be for the cost of the job ($4,500), not the sale amount ($7,000). Choice (d) is incorrect because the increase should be to Cash, not Accounts Receivable.

**13. b.** At the end of an accounting period, a company using a job costing system prepares the cost of goods manufactured from the Work in Process Inventory account, not (a) from the job cost sheet; (c) by adding direct materials used, direct labor incurred, and manufacturing overhead incurred; or (d) from the Cost of Goods Sold account.

**14. c.** Job order costing provides more precise costing for custom jobs than process costing. The other choices are incorrect because (a) job order costing often requires significant data entry, (b) overhead allocation is a problem for all costing systems, and (d) the use of job order costing has increased due to automated accounting systems.

**15. c.** The company would make an adjustment for the underapplied overhead by increasing Cost of Goods Sold for $1,200 and decreasing Manufacturing Overhead for $1,200, not by increasing (a) Manufacturing Overhead Applied for $1,200 or (b) Manufacturing Overhead Expense for $1,200. Choice (d) is incorrect because at the end of the year, a company makes an adjustment to eliminate any balance in Manufacturing Overhead.

**16. b.** Manufacturing overhead is underapplied if actual overhead is greater than applied overhead. The other choices are incorrect because (a) if actual overhead is less than applied, then manufacturing overhead is overapplied; (c) if the predetermined rate equals the actual rate, the actual overhead costs incurred equal the overhead costs applied, neither over- nor underapplied; and (d) if the actual overhead equals the applied overhead, neither over- nor underapplied occurs.

---

## Practice Brief Exercises

*Record the assignment of raw materials costs.*

**1. (LO 2)** During January, its first month of operations, Derse Company accumulated the following manufacturing costs: raw materials purchased $5,500, factory labor $6,600, and utilities payable $2,000. In January, requisitions of raw materials for production are as follows: Job 1 $1,000, Job 2 $800, Job 3, $1,300, and general factory use $700. Using the format shown in Illustration 12.9, record raw materials used.

### Solution

1.

| | MANUFACTURING COSTS | | | |
| | Raw Materials Inventory | Factory Labor | Manufacturing Overhead | WORK IN PROCESS INVENTORY |
|---|---|---|---|---|
| Balance | $5,500 | $6,600 | $2,000 | |
| Direct materials | −3,100 | | | +$3,100 |
| Indirect materials | −700 | | +700 | |
| Balance | $1,700 | $6,600 | $2,700 | $3,100 |

*Assign manufacturing overhead to production.*

**2. (LO 3)** Bogut Company estimates that annual manufacturing overhead costs will be $1,500,000. Estimated annual operating activity bases are direct labor cost $300,000, direct labor hours 15,000, and machine hours 50,000. Compute predetermined overhead rate for each activity base.

### Solution

2. Overhead rate per direct labor cost is 500% ($1,500,000 ÷ $300,000 DLC).

Overhead rate per direct labor hour is $100 ($1,500,000 ÷ 15,000 DLH).

Overhead rate per machine hour is $30 ($1,500,000 ÷ 50,000 MH).

**3. (LO 4)** In June, Rafael Company completes Job 15 for $70,000 and Job 16 for $35,000. On June 30, Job 15 is sold to a customer for $72,000. Using the format shown in Illustration 12.24, record the completion of the two jobs and the sale of Job 15.

*Record completion and sale of completed jobs.*

**Solution**

3.

| | MANUFACTURING COSTS | | | WORK IN PROCESS INVENTORY | FINISHED GOODS INVENTORY | COST OF GOODS SOLD |
|---|---|---|---|---|---|---|
| | **Raw Materials Inventory** | **Factory Labor** | **Operating Manufacturing Overhead** | | | |
| Balance | | | | +$105,000 | | |
| Completion of Jobs: | | | | | | |
| Job 15 | | | | −70,000 | +$70,000 | |
| Job 16 | | | | −35,000 | +35,000 | |
| Job Sold: | | | | | | |
| Job 15 | | | | | −70,000 | +$70,000 |
| Balance | | | | $    0 | $35,000 | $70,000 |

**4. (LO 5)** At December 31, the balance in Manufacturing Overhead for Alex Company is a negative $2,200 and for Katz Company a positive $1,900. Assuming the December 31 adjustment is made to cost of goods sold, indicate the effect that each company's adjustment has on its cost of goods sold.

*Prepare adjustments for under- and overapplied overhead.*

**Solution**

4. **Alex Company:** The adjustment will decrease Cost of Goods Sold and increase Manufacturing Overhead.

**Katz Company:** The adjustment will increase Cost of Goods Sold and decrease Manufacturing Overhead.

# Practice Exercises

**1. (LO 1, 2, 3)** A job order cost sheet for Michaels Company is shown here.

*Analyze a job cost sheet.*

| Job No. 92 | | | For 2,000 Units | |
|---|---|---|---|---|
| Date | | Direct Materials | Direct Labor | Manufacturing Overhead |
| Beg. bal. Jan. | 1 | $ 3,925 | $ 6,000 | $ 4,200 |
| | 8 | 6,000 | | |
| | 12 | | 8,500 | 6,375 |
| | 25 | 2,000 | | |
| | 27 | | 4,000 | 3,000 |
| | | $11,925 | $18,500 | $13,575 |

| Cost of completed job: | |
|---|---|
| Direct materials | $11,925 |
| Direct labor | 18,500 |
| Manufacturing overhead | 13,575 |
| Total cost | $44,000 |
| Unit cost ($44,000 ÷ 2,000) | $ 22.00 |

**Instructions**

Answer the following questions.

a. What was the balance in Work in Process Inventory on January 1 if this was the only unfinished job?

b. If manufacturing overhead is applied on the basis of direct labor cost, what overhead rate was used in each year?

**Solution**

1. a. $14,125, or ($3,925 + $6,000 + $4,200).

b. Last year 70%, or ($4,200 ÷ $6,000); this year 75% (either $6,375 ÷ $8,500 or $3,000 ÷ $4,000).

*Compute the overhead rate and under- or overapplied overhead.*

2. **(LO 3, 5)** Kwik Kopy Company applies operating overhead to photocopying jobs on the basis of machine hours used. Overhead costs are estimated to total $290,000 for the year, and machine usage is estimated at 125,000 hours.

For the year, $295,000 of overhead costs are incurred and 130,000 hours are used.

**Instructions**

a. Compute the service overhead rate for the year.

b. What is the amount of under- or overapplied overhead at December 31?

c. Assuming the under- or overapplied overhead for the year is not allocated to inventory accounts, indicate the effect that the year-end adjustment will have on Cost of Completed Service Contracts.

**Solution**

2. a. $2.32 per machine hour ($290,000 ÷ 125,000).

b. $295,000 − ($2.32 × 130,000 machine hours)

$295,000 − $301,600 = $6,600 overapplied

c. The year-end adjustment will decrease Cost of Completed Service Contracts by $6,600.

# Practice Problem

*Compute predetermined overhead rate, apply overhead, and calculate under- or overapplied overhead.*

**(LO 3, 5)** Cardella Company applies overhead on the basis of direct labor costs. The company estimates annual overhead costs will be $760,000 and annual direct labor costs will be $950,000. During February, Cardella works on two jobs: A16 and B17. Summary data concerning these jobs are as follows.

**Manufacturing Costs Incurred**

Purchased $54,000 of raw materials on account.
Factory labor $80,000.
Manufacturing overhead incurred exclusive of indirect materials and indirect labor $59,800.

**Assignment of Costs**

Direct materials:     Job A16 $27,000, Job B17 $21,000
Indirect materials:  $3,000
Direct labor:          Job A16 $52,000, Job B17 $26,000
Indirect labor:       $2,000

By the end of February, the company completed Job A16 and sold it. Job B17 was only partially completed.

**Instructions**

a. Compute the predetermined overhead rate.

b. Record the February transactions in the format and sequence followed in Illustration 12.24.

c. What was the amount of under- or overapplied manufacturing overhead?

**Solution**

a.

| Estimated annual overhead costs | ÷ | Estimated annual operating activity | = | Predetermined overhead rate |
|---|---|---|---|---|
| $760,000 | ÷ | $950,000 | = | 80% |

b.

| | MANUFACTURING COSTS | | | WORK IN PROCESS INVENTORY | FINISHED GOODS INVENTORY | COST OF GOODS SOLD |
|---|---|---|---|---|---|---|
| | **Raw Materials Inventory** | **Factory Labor** | **Manuf. Overhead** | | | |
| Purchased raw materials (1) | +$54,000 | | | | | |
| Incurred factory labor (2) | | +$80,000 | | | | |
| Incurred manuf. overhead (3) | | | +$59,800 | | | |
| Direct materials (4) | −48,000 | | | +$48,000 | | |
| Indirect materials (4) | −3,000 | | +3,000 | | | |
| Direct labor (5) | | −78,000 | | +78,000 | | |
| Indirect labor (5) | | −2,000 | +2,000 | | | |
| Assigned manuf. overhead (80% × $78,000) (6) | | | −62,400 | +62,400 | | |
| Completed Job A16 (7) | | | | −120,600* | +$120,600 | |
| Sold Job A16 (8) | | | | | −120,600 | +$120,600 |
| Ending balance | $3,000 | $   0 | $ 2,400 | $67,800 | $   0 | $120,600 |

*$27,000 + $52,000 + ($52,000 × 80%)

c. Manufacturing Overhead has a positive balance of $2,400 as shown below.

| | Manufacturing Overhead |
|---|---|
| (3) | +$59,800 |
| (4) | +3,000 |
| (5) | +2,000 |
| (6) | −62,400 |
| Balance | $ 2,400 |

Thus, manufacturing overhead is underapplied for the month.

# WileyPLUS

Brief Exercises, DO IT! Exercises, Exercises, Problems, and many additional resources are available for practice in WileyPLUS.

## Questions

1. a. Mary Barett is not sure about the difference between cost accounting and a cost accounting system. Explain the difference to Mary.

   b. What is an important feature of a cost accounting system?

2. a. Distinguish between the two types of cost accounting systems.

   b. Can a company use both types of cost accounting systems?

3. What type of industry is likely to use a job order cost system? Give some examples.

4. What type of industry is likely to use a process cost system? Give some examples.

5. Your roommate asks your help in understanding the major steps in the flow of costs in a job order cost system. Identify the steps for your roommate.

6. There are three inventory control accounts in a job order system. Identify the control accounts and their subsidiary ledgers.

7. What source documents are used in accumulating direct labor costs?

8. "Updates to Manufacturing Overhead normally are made daily." Do you agree? Explain.

9. Stan Kaiser is confused about the source documents used in assigning materials and labor costs. Identify the documents and indicate how each is assigned.

10. What is the purpose of a job cost sheet?

11. Indicate the source documents that are used in charging costs to specific jobs.

12. Explain the purpose and use of a "materials requisition slip" as used in a job order cost system.

13. Sam Bowden believes actual manufacturing overhead should be charged to jobs. Do you agree? Why or why not?

14. What elements are involved in computing a predetermined overhead rate?

15. How can the agreement of Work in Process Inventory and job cost sheets be verified?

16. Matt Litkee is confused about under- and overapplied manufacturing overhead. Define the terms for Matt, and indicate if the balance in the manufacturing overhead account applicable to each term is positive or negative.

17. "At the end of the year, under- or overapplied overhead is eliminated by adjusting cost sheets." Is this correct? If not, indicate the customary treatment of this amount.

## Brief Exercises

*Prepare a diagram of a job order cost accounting system and identify transactions.*

**BE12.1 (LO 1), C** Dieker Company begins operations on January 1. Because all work is done to customer specifications, the company decides to use a job order cost system. Prepare a chart of a typical job order cost system showing the increases and decreases that result from the eight transactions illustrated in the chapter. Use Illustration 12.24 as a reference.

*Record the accumulation of manufacturing costs.*

**BE12.2 (LO 1), AP** During January, its first month of operations, Dieker Company accumulated the following manufacturing costs: raw materials purchased $4,000 on account, factory labor $6,000, and utilities payable $2,000. Using the format shown in Illustration 12.6, record the company's manufacturing costs in its job order costing system.

*Record the assignment of raw materials costs.*

**BE12.3 (LO 2), AP** During January, its first month of operations, Dieker Company accumulated the following manufacturing costs: raw materials purchased $4,000 on account, factory labor $6,000, and utilities payable $2,000. In January, requisitions of raw materials for production are as follows: Job 1 $900, Job 2 $1,200, Job 3 $700, and general factory use $600. Using the format shown in Illustration 12.9, record raw materials used.

*Record the assignment of factory labor costs.*

**BE12.4 (LO 2), AP** Manufacturing information for Dieker Company is given in BE12.3. During January, time tickets show that the factory labor of $6,000 was used as follows: Job 1 $2,200, Job 2 $1,600, Job 3 $1,400, and general factory use $800. Using the format shown in Illustration 12.12, record factory labor used.

*Prepare job cost sheets.*

**BE12.5 (LO 2), AP** Data pertaining to job cost sheets for Dieker Company are given in BE12.3 and BE12.4. Prepare the job cost sheets for each of the three jobs. (*Note:* You may omit the column for Manufacturing Overhead.)

*Compute predetermined overhead rates.*

**BE12.6 (LO 3), AP** Marquis Company estimates that annual manufacturing overhead costs will be $900,000. Estimated annual operating activity bases are direct labor cost $500,000, direct labor hours 50,000, and machine hours 100,000. Compute the predetermined overhead rate for each activity base.

*Assign manufacturing overhead to production.*

**BE12.7 (LO 3), AP** During the first quarter, Francum Company incurs the following direct labor costs: January $40,000, February $30,000, and March $50,000. For each month, indicate the amount of overhead assigned to production using a predetermined rate of 70% of direct labor cost.

*Record completion and sale of completed jobs.*

**BE12.8 (LO 4), AP** On March 1, Stinson Company has a beginning balance of $50,000 in its Work in Progress Inventory account. In March, Stinson Company completes its only two jobs in process, Jobs 10 and 11. Job 10 cost $20,000 and Job 11 $30,000. On March 31, Job 10 is sold. Using the format shown in Illustration 12.24, enter the balance for Work in Process, record the completion of the two jobs and the sale of Job 10.

*Record service salaries and wages and operating overhead.*

**BE12.9 (LO 4), AP** Ruiz Engineering Contractors incurred service salaries and wages of $36,000 ($28,000 direct and $8,000 indirect) on an engineering project. The company applies overhead at a rate of 25% of direct labor. Using the format shown in the chapter, assign service salaries and wages and apply overhead.

*Prepare adjustments for under- and overapplied overhead.*

**BE12.10 (LO 5), AP** At December 31, balances in Manufacturing Overhead are Shimeca Company—$1,200 positive, Garcia Company—$900 negative. Assuming the December 31 adjustment is made to cost of goods sold, indicate the effect that each company's adjustment has on its cost of goods sold.

## DO IT! Exercises

**DO IT! 12.1 (LO 1), AP** During the current month, Wacholz Company incurs the following manufacturing costs.

  a. Purchased raw materials of $18,000 on account.

  b. Incurred factory labor of $40,000.

  c. Factory utilities of $3,100 are payable, prepaid factory property taxes of $2,700 have expired, and depreciation on the factory building is $9,500.

Using the format shown in Illustration 12.6, record the company's manufacturing costs in its job order costing system.

*Record manufacturing costs.*

**DO IT! 12.2 (LO 2), AP** Milner Company is working on two job orders. The job cost sheets show the following.

*Assign costs to work in process.*

|  | Job 201 | Job 202 |
|---|---|---|
| Direct materials | $7,200 | $9,000 |
| Direct labor | 4,000 | 8,000 |

Using the format shown in Illustration 12.9, record the assignment of costs to Work in Process from the data on the job cost sheets.

**DO IT! 12.3 (LO 3), AP** Washburn Company produces earbuds. During the year, manufacturing overhead costs are estimated to be $200,000. Estimated machine usage is 2,500 hours. The company assigns overhead based on machine hours. Job No. 551 used 90 machine hours. Compute the predetermined overhead rate and determine the amount of overhead to apply to Job No. 551.

*Compute the predetermined overhead rate.*

**DO IT! 12.4 (LO 4), AP** During the current month, Standard Corporation completed Job 310 and Job 312. Job 310 cost $70,000 and Job 312 cost $50,000. Job 312 was sold. Using the format shown in Illustration 12.24, record the completion of the two jobs and the sale of Job 312.

*Record completion and sale of jobs.*

**DO IT! 12.5 (LO 5), AP** For Eckstein Company, the predetermined overhead rate is 130% of direct labor cost. During the month, Eckstein incurred $100,000 of factory labor costs, of which $85,000 is direct labor and $15,000 is indirect labor. Actual overhead incurred was $115,000. Compute the amount of manufacturing overhead applied during the month. Determine the amount of under- or overapplied manufacturing overhead.

*Apply manufacturing overhead and determine under- or overapplication.*

## Exercises

**E12.1 (LO 1, 2), AP** The gross earnings of the factory workers for Larkin Company during the month of January are $90,000. Of the total accumulated cost of factory labor, 85% is related to direct labor and 15% is attributable to indirect labor.

*Record factory labor.*

### Instructions

Using the format shown in Illustration 12.12:

  a. Record the factory labor costs for the month of January.

  b. Assign factory labor to production.

**E12.2 (LO 1, 2, 3, 4), AP** Stine Company uses a job order cost system. On May 1, the company has balances in Raw Materials Inventory of $15,000 and Work in Process Inventory of $3,500 and two jobs in process: Job No. 429 $2,000, and Job No. 430 $1,500. During May, the company incurred factory labor of $13,700. A summary of source documents reveals the following.

*Record manufacturing costs.*

| Job Number | Materials Requisition Slips | | Labor Time Tickets | |
|---|---|---|---|---|
| 429 | $2,500 | | $1,900 | |
| 430 | 3,500 | | 3,000 | |
| 431 | 4,400 | $10,400 | 7,600 | $12,500 |
| General use | | 800 | | 1,200 |
| | | $11,200 | | $13,700 |

Stine Company applies manufacturing overhead to jobs at an overhead rate of 60% of direct labor cost. Job No. 429 is completed during the month.

**Instructions**

Using the format shown in Illustration 12.24:

a. Record the May 1 inventory balances and the factory labor incurred.

b. Record (1) material usage from requisition slips, (2) factory labor usage from time tickets, (3) the assignment of manufacturing overhead to jobs, and (4) the completion of Job No. 429.

c. Prove the agreement of the Work in Process Inventory control account with the job cost sheets.

*Analyze a job cost sheet.*

**E12.3 (LO 1, 2, 3, 4), AP** A job order cost sheet for Ryan Company is as follows.

| Job No. 92 | | | | For 2,000 Units |
|---|---|---|---|---|
| Date | | Direct Materials | Direct Labor | Manufacturing Overhead |
| Beg. bal. Jan. | 1 | $ 5,000 | $ 6,000 | $ 4,200 |
| | 8 | 6,000 | | |
| | 12 | | 8,000 | 6,400 |
| | 25 | 2,000 | | |
| | 27 | | 4,000 | 3,200 |
| | | $13,000 | $18,000 | $13,800 |

| Cost of completed job: | |
|---|---|
| Direct materials | $13,000 |
| Direct labor | 18,000 |
| Manufacturing overhead | 13,800 |
| Total cost | $44,800 |
| Unit cost ($44,800 ÷ 2,000) | $22.40 |

**Instructions**

On the basis of this data, answer the following questions.

a. What was the balance in Work in Process Inventory on January 1 if this was the only unfinished job?

b. If manufacturing overhead is applied on the basis of direct labor cost, what overhead rate was used in each year?

*Analyze costs of manufacturing and determine missing amounts.*

**E12.4 (LO 1, 5), AN** Manufacturing cost data for Orlando Company, which uses a job order cost system, are presented here.

| | Case A | Case B | Case C |
|---|---|---|---|
| Direct materials used | $  (a) | $ 83,000 | $ 63,150 |
| Direct labor | 50,000 | 140,000 | (h) |
| Manufacturing overhead applied | 42,500 | (d) | (i) |
| Total manufacturing costs | 145,650 | (e) | 213,000 |
| Work in process 1/1/22 | (b) | 15,500 | 18,000 |
| Total cost of work in process | 201,500 | (f) | (j) |
| Work in process 12/31/22 | (c) | 11,800 | (k) |
| Cost of goods manufactured | 192,300 | (g) | 222,000 |

**Instructions**

Indicate the missing amount for each letter. Assume that in all cases manufacturing overhead is applied on the basis of direct labor cost and the rate is the same.

*Compute the manufacturing overhead rate and under- or overapplied overhead.*

→ Excel

**E12.5 (LO 3, 5), AN** Ikerd Company applies manufacturing overhead to jobs on the basis of machine hours used. Overhead costs are estimated to total $300,000 for the year, and machine usage is estimated at 125,000 hours.

For the year, $322,000 of overhead costs are incurred and 130,000 hours are used.

**Instructions**

a. Compute the manufacturing overhead rate for the year.

b. What is the amount of under- or overapplied overhead at December 31?

c. Indicate the effect of the adjustment to assign the under- or overapplied overhead for the year to cost of goods sold.

**E12.6 (LO 1, 2, 3, 4), AP** A job cost sheet of Sandoval Company is given here.

*Analyze job cost sheet.*

| | | | | |
|---|---|---|---|---|
| **Job Cost Sheet** | | | | |

JOB NO.   469                                              Quantity   2,500

ITEM   White Lion Cages                            Date Requested   7/2

FOR   Todd Company                                  Date Completed   7/31

| Date | Direct Materials | Direct Labor | Manufacturing Overhead |
|---|---|---|---|
| 7/10 | $  690 | | |
| 12 | 900 | | |
| 15 | | $440 | $550 |
| 22 | | 380 | 475 |
| 24 | 1,600 | | |
| 27 | 1,500 | | |
| 31 | | 540 | 675 |

Cost of completed job:
   Direct materials        _____
   Direct labor             _____
   Manufacturing overhead   _____
Total cost                ══════

Unit cost                 ══════

**Instructions**

Answer the following questions.

   **a.** What are the source documents for direct materials, direct labor, and manufacturing overhead costs assigned to this job?

   **b.** What is the predetermined manufacturing overhead rate?

   **c.** What are the total cost and the unit cost of the completed job?

**E12.7 (LO 1, 2, 3, 4), AP** Crawford Corporation incurred the following transactions.

*Record manufacturing and nonmanufacturing costs.*

   **1.** Purchased raw materials on account $46,300.

   **2.** Raw materials of $36,000 were requisitioned to the factory. An analysis of the materials requisition slips indicated that $6,800 was classified as indirect materials.

   **3.** Factory labor costs incurred were $59,900.

   **4.** Time tickets indicated that $54,000 was direct labor and $5,900 was indirect labor.

   **5.** Manufacturing overhead costs incurred on account were $80,500.

   **6.** Manufacturing overhead was applied at the rate of 150% of direct labor cost.

   **7.** Goods costing $88,000 were completed and transferred to finished goods.

   **8.** Finished goods costing $75,000 to manufacture were sold.

**Instructions**

Using the format shown in Illustration 12.24, record the transactions.

**E12.8 (LO 1, 2, 3, 4), AP** Enos Printing Corp. uses a job order cost system. The following data summarize the operations related to the first quarter's production.

*Record manufacturing and nonmanufacturing costs.*

   **1.** Materials purchased on account $192,000, and factory wages incurred $87,300.

   **2.** Materials requisitioned and factory labor used by job:

| Job Number | Materials | Factory Labor |
|---|---|---|
| A20 | $ 35,240 | $18,000 |
| A21 | 42,920 | 22,000 |
| A22 | 36,100 | 15,000 |
| A23 | 39,270 | 25,000 |
| General factory use | 4,470 | 7,300 |
| | $158,000 | $87,300 |

3. Manufacturing overhead costs incurred on account $49,500.

4. Depreciation on factory equipment $14,550.

5. Manufacturing overhead rate is 90% of direct labor cost.

6. Jobs completed during the quarter: A20, A21, and A23.

**Instructions**

Using the format shown in Illustration 12.24, record the operations summarized above. Prepare a schedule showing the individual cost elements and total cost for each job in item 6.

*Prepare a cost of goods manufactured schedule and partial financial statements.*

**E12.9 (LO 1, 5), AP** At May 31, 2022, the accounts of Lopez Company show the following.

1. May 1 inventories—finished goods $12,600, work in process $14,700, and raw materials $8,200.

2. May 31 inventories—finished goods $9,500, work in process $15,900, and raw materials $7,100.

3. Increases to work in process were direct materials $62,400, direct labor $50,000, and manufacturing overhead applied $40,000.

4. Sales revenue totaled $215,000.

**Instructions**

a. Prepare a condensed cost of goods manufactured schedule for May 2022.

b. Prepare an income statement for May 2022 through gross profit.

c. Indicate the balance sheet presentation of the manufacturing inventories at May 31, 2022.

*Compute work in process and finished goods from job cost sheets.*

**E12.10 (LO 2, 4), AP** Tierney Company begins operations on April 1. Information from job cost sheets shows the following.

| Job Number | Manufacturing Costs Assigned | | | Month Completed |
|---|---|---|---|---|
| | April | May | June | |
| 10 | $5,200 | $4,400 | | May |
| 11 | 4,100 | 3,900 | $2,000 | June |
| 12 | 1,200 | | | April |
| 13 | | 4,700 | 4,500 | June |
| 14 | | 5,900 | 3,600 | Not complete |

Job 12 was completed in April. Job 10 was completed in May. Jobs 11 and 13 were completed in June. Each job was sold for 25% above its cost in the month following completion.

**Instructions**

a. What is the balance in Work in Process Inventory at the end of each month?

b. What is the balance in Finished Goods Inventory at the end of each month?

c. What is the gross profit for May, June, and July?

*Record costs of services provided.*

**E12.11 (LO 1, 3, 4), AP** Service The law firm of Colaw Associates uses a job order cost system. Cost data for the month of March follow.

1. Purchased supplies on account $1,800.

2. Issued supplies $1,200 (60% direct and 40% indirect).

3. Assigned labor costs based on time tickets for the month which indicated labor costs of $70,000 (80% direct and 20% indirect).

4. Operating overhead costs incurred for cash totaled $40,000.

5. Operating overhead is applied at a rate of 90% of direct labor cost.

6. Work completed totaled $75,000.

**Instructions**

Using the format shown in Illustration 12.25:

a. Record the transactions for March.

b. Determine the balance of the Service Contracts in Process account.

**E12.12 (LO 2, 3, 4), AP** Service Don Lieberman and Associates, a CPA firm, uses job order costing to capture the costs of its audit jobs. There were no audit jobs in process at the beginning of November. The following data concern the three audit jobs conducted during November.

*Determine cost of jobs and ending balance in work in process and overhead accounts.*

|                      | Waters Inc. | Renolds Inc. | Bayfield Inc. |
|----------------------|-------------|--------------|---------------|
| Direct materials     | $600        | $400         | $200          |
| Auditor labor costs  | $5,400      | $6,600       | $3,375        |
| Auditor hours        | 72          | 88           | 45            |

Overhead costs are applied to jobs on the basis of auditor hours, and the predetermined overhead rate is $50 per auditor hour. The Waters Inc. job is the only incomplete job at the end of November. Actual overhead for the month was $11,000.

**Instructions**

a.  Determine the cost of each job.

b.  Indicate the balance of the Service Contracts in Process account at the end of November.

c.  Calculate the ending balance of the Operating Overhead account for November.

**E12.13 (LO 3, 5), AP** Service Tombert Decorating uses a job order cost system to collect the costs of its interior decorating business. Each client's consultation is treated as a separate job. Overhead is applied to each job based on the number of decorator hours incurred. The following data are for the current year.

*Determine predetermined overhead rate, apply overhead, and determine whether balance is under- or overapplied.*

| Estimated overhead       | $960,000 |
|--------------------------|----------|
| Actual overhead          | $982,800 |
| Estimated decorator hours | 40,000   |
| Actual decorator hours   | 40,500   |

The company uses Operating Overhead in place of Manufacturing Overhead.

**Instructions**

a.  Compute the predetermined overhead rate.

b.  Determine the amount of overhead to apply for the year.

c.  Determine whether the overhead was under- or overapplied and by how much.

## Problems

**P12.1 (LO 1, 2, 3, 4, 5), AP** Lott Company uses a job order cost system and applies overhead to production on the basis of direct labor costs. On January 1, 2022, Job 50 was the only job in process. The costs incurred prior to January 1 on this job were as follows: direct materials $20,000, direct labor $12,000, and manufacturing overhead $16,000. As of January 1, Job 49 had been completed at a cost of $90,000 and was part of finished goods inventory. There was a $15,000 balance in the Raw Materials Inventory account.

*Record transactions in a job order cost system and job cost sheets.*

During the month of January, Lott Company began production on Jobs 51 and 52, and completed Jobs 50 and 51. Jobs 49 and 50 were sold during the month. The following additional events occurred during the month.

1.  Purchased additional raw materials of $90,000 on account.

2.  Incurred factory labor costs of $70,000.

3.  Incurred manufacturing overhead costs as follows: indirect materials $17,000, indirect labor $20,000, depreciation expense on equipment $12,000, and various other manufacturing overhead costs on account $16,000.

4.  Assigned direct materials and direct labor to jobs as follows.

| Job No. | Direct Materials | Direct Labor |
|---------|------------------|--------------|
| 50      | $10,000          | $ 5,000      |
| 51      | 39,000           | 25,000       |
| 52      | 30,000           | 20,000       |

## Instructions

a. Calculate the predetermined overhead rate for 2022, assuming Lott Company estimates total manufacturing overhead costs of $840,000, direct labor costs of $700,000, and direct labor hours of 20,000 for the year.

b. Open job cost sheets for Jobs 50, 51, and 52. Enter the January 1 balances on the job cost sheet for Job 50.

c. Using the format shown in Illustration 12.24, record the purchase of raw materials, the factory labor costs incurred, and the manufacturing overhead costs incurred during the month of January.

d. Using the format shown in Illustration 12.24, record the assignment of direct materials, direct labor, and manufacturing overhead costs to production. In assigning manufacturing overhead costs, use the overhead rate calculated in (a). Post all costs to the job cost sheets as necessary.

e. Job 50, $69,000
   Job 51, $94,000

e. Total the job cost sheets for any job(s) completed during the month. Using the format shown in Illustration 12.24, record the completion of any job(s) during the month.

f. Using the format shown in Illustration 12.24, record the sale of any job(s) during the month.

g. What is the balance in the Finished Goods Inventory account at the end of the month? What does this balance consist of?

h. What is the amount of over- or underapplied overhead?

*Record transactions in a job order cost system and prepare partial income statement.*

**P12.2 (LO 1, 2, 3, 4, 5), AP** For the year ended December 31, 2022, the job cost sheets of Cinta Company contained the following data.

| Job Number | Explanation | Direct Materials | Direct Labor | Manufacturing Overhead | Total Costs |
|---|---|---|---|---|---|
| 7640 | Balance 1/1 | $25,000 | $24,000 | $28,800 | $ 77,800 |
| | Current year's costs | 30,000 | 36,000 | 43,200 | 109,200 |
| 7641 | Balance 1/1 | 11,000 | 18,000 | 21,600 | 50,600 |
| | Current year's costs | 43,000 | 48,000 | 57,600 | 148,600 |
| 7642 | Current year's costs | 58,000 | 55,000 | 66,000 | 179,000 |

Other data:

1. Raw materials inventory totaled $15,000 on January 1. During the year, $140,000 of raw materials were purchased on account. Factory labor incurred was $157,000.

2. Finished goods on January 1 consisted of Job No. 7638 for $87,000 and Job No. 7639 for $92,000.

3. Job No. 7640 and Job No. 7641 were completed during the year.

4. Job Nos. 7638, 7639, and 7641 were sold.

5. Manufacturing overhead incurred on account totaled $120,000.

6. Other manufacturing overhead consisted of indirect materials $14,000, indirect labor $18,000, and depreciation on factory machinery $8,000.

## Instructions

a. Using the format shown in Illustration 12.24 and the information provided above:

   1. Enter January 1 balances in Raw Materials Inventory, Work in Process Inventory, and Finished Goods Inventory.

   2. Record the 2022 transactions.

b. $179,000; Job 7642: $179,000

b. Prove the agreement of Work in Process Inventory with job cost sheets pertaining to unfinished work.

c. Amount = $6,800

c. Record the adjustment for over- or underapplied manufacturing overhead, assuming the balance is allocated entirely to Cost of Goods Sold.

d. $158,600

d. Determine the gross profit to be reported for 2022. Sales were $530,000.

*Record transactions in a job order cost system and prepare cost of goods manufactured schedule.*

**P12.3 (LO 1, 2, 3, 4, 5), AP** Case Inc. is a construction company specializing in custom patios. The patios are constructed of concrete, brick, fiberglass, and lumber, depending upon customer preference. On June 1, 2022, accounting records for Case Inc. contain the following data.

| Raw Materials Inventory | $4,200 | | Manufacturing Overhead Applied | $32,640 |
|---|---|---|---|---|
| Work in Process Inventory | 5,540 | | Manufacturing Overhead Incurred | 31,650 |

Subsidiary data for Work in Process Inventory on June 1 are as follows.

**Job Cost Sheets**

| | Customer Job | | |
|---|---|---|---|
| **Cost Element** | **Rodgers** | **Stevens** | **Linton** |
| Direct materials | $ 600 | $ 800 | $ 900 |
| Direct labor | 320 | 540 | 580 |
| Manufacturing overhead | 400 | 675 | 725 |
| | $1,320 | $2,015 | $2,205 |

During June, raw materials purchased on account were $4,900, and all wages were paid. Additional overhead costs consisted of depreciation on equipment $900 and miscellaneous costs of $400 incurred on account.

A summary of materials requisition slips and time tickets for June shows the following.

| Customer Job | Materials Requisition Slips | Time Tickets |
|---|---|---|
| Rodgers | $ 800 | $ 850 |
| Koss | 2,000 | 800 |
| Stevens | 500 | 360 |
| Linton | 1,300 | 1,200 |
| Rodgers | 300 | 390 |
| | 4,900 | 3,600 |
| General use | 1,500 | 1,200 |
| | $6,400 | $4,800 |

Overhead was charged to jobs at the rate of $1.25 per dollar of direct labor cost. The patios for customers Rodgers, Stevens, and Linton were completed during June and sold. Each customer paid in full.

**Instructions**

a. Using the format shown in Illustration 12.24, record the June transactions: (1) for purchase of raw materials, factory labor costs incurred, and manufacturing overhead costs incurred; (2) assignment of direct materials, labor, and overhead to production; and (3) completion of jobs and sale of goods.

b. Reconcile the balance in Work in Process Inventory with the costs of unfinished jobs.

c. Prepare a cost of goods manufactured schedule for June.

*c. Cost of goods manufactured $14,740*

**P12.4 (LO 3, 5), AP** Agassi Company uses a job order cost system in each of its three manufacturing departments. Manufacturing overhead is applied to jobs on the basis of direct labor cost in Department D, direct labor hours in Department E, and machine hours in Department K.

In establishing the predetermined overhead rates for 2022, the following estimates were made for the year.

*Compute predetermined overhead rates, apply overhead, and calculate under- or overapplied overhead.*

| | Department | | |
|---|---|---|---|
| | **D** | **E** | **K** |
| Manufacturing overhead | $1,200,000 | $1,500,000 | $900,000 |
| Direct labor costs | $1,500,000 | $1,250,000 | $450,000 |
| Direct labor hours | 100,000 | 125,000 | 40,000 |
| Machine hours | 400,000 | 500,000 | 120,000 |

During January, the job cost sheets showed the following costs and production data.

| | Department | | |
|---|---|---|---|
| | **D** | **E** | **K** |
| Direct materials used | $140,000 | $126,000 | $78,000 |
| Direct labor costs | $120,000 | $110,000 | $37,500 |
| Manufacturing overhead incurred | $ 99,000 | $124,000 | $79,000 |
| Direct labor hours | 8,000 | 11,000 | 3,500 |
| Machine hours | 34,000 | 45,000 | 10,400 |

## Instructions

a. 80%, $12, $7.50

b. $356,000, $368,000, $193,500

c. $3,000, $(8,000), $1,000

**a.** Compute the predetermined overhead rate for each department.

**b.** Compute the total manufacturing costs assigned to jobs in January in each department.

**c.** Compute the under- or overapplied overhead for each department at January 31.

*Analyze manufacturing accounts and determine missing amounts.*

 Excel

**P12.5 (LO 1, 2, 3, 4, 5), AN** Phillips Corporation's fiscal year ends on November 30. A partially completed table for the flow of costs in its job order cost accounting system for the first month of the new fiscal year is shown here.

| | MANUFACTURING COSTS | | | | | |
|---|---|---|---|---|---|---|
| | Raw Materials Inventory | Factory Labor | Manufact. Overhead | WORK IN PROCESS INVENTORY | FINISHED GOODS INVENTORY | COST OF GOODS SOLD |
| Beginning balance | (a) | | | (b) | (g) | |
| Purchase raw materials | $17,225 | | | | | |
| Incur factory labor | | $12,025 | | | | |
| Raw materials are used | −16,850 | | $2,900 | (c) | | |
| Factory labor is used | | (k) | (l) | $8,400 | | |
| Incur manufacturing overhead | | | +1,245 | | | |
| Assign manufacturing overhead | | | (m) | (d) | | |
| Complete jobs | | | | (f) | (h) | |
| Sell jobs | | | | | (i) | (o) |
| Ending balance | $7,975 | | (n) | (e) | (j) | (p) |

Other data:

1. On December 1, two jobs were in process: Job No. 154 and Job No. 155. These jobs had combined direct materials costs of $9,750 and direct labor costs of $15,000. Overhead is applied at a rate of 75% of direct labor cost.

2. During December, Job Nos. 156, 157, and 158 were started. On December 31, Job No. 158 was unfinished. This job had charges for direct materials $3,800 and direct labor $4,800, plus manufacturing overhead. All jobs, except for Job No. 158, were completed in December.

3. On December 1, Job No. 153 was in the finished goods warehouse. It had a total cost of $5,000. On December 31, Job No. 157 was the only job finished that was not sold. It had a cost of $4,000.

4. Manufacturing overhead was $1,470 underapplied in December.

c. $13,950

f. $52,450

i. $53,450

## Instructions

List the letters (a) through (p) and indicate the amount pertaining to each letter.

# Continuing Cases

 Excel

### Current Designs

**CD12** Huegel Hollow Resort has ordered 20 rotomolded kayaks from **Current Designs**. Each kayak will be formed in the rotomolded oven, cooled, and then have the excess plastic trimmed away. Then, the hatches, seat, ropes, and bungees will be attached to the kayak.

Dave Thill, the kayak plant manager, knows that manufacturing each kayak requires 54 pounds of polyethylene powder and a finishing kit (rope, seat, hardware, etc.). The polyethylene powder used in these kayaks costs $1.50 per pound, and the finishing kits cost $170 each. Each kayak will use two kinds of labor: 2 hours of more-skilled type I labor from people who run the oven and trim the plastic, and 3 hours of less-skilled type II labor from people who attach the hatches and seat and other hardware. The type I employees are paid $15 per hour, and the type II employees are paid $12 per hour. For purposes of this problem, assume that overhead is applied to all jobs at a rate of 150% of direct labor costs.

**Instructions**

Determine the total cost of the Huegel Hollow order and the cost of each individual kayak in the order. Identify costs as direct materials, direct labor, or manufacturing overhead.

## Waterways Corporation

(*Note:* This is a continuation of the Waterways case from Chapter 11.)

**WC12** Waterways has two major public-park projects to provide with comprehensive irrigation in one of its service locations this month. Job J57 and Job K52 involve 15 acres of landscaped terrain which will require special-order sprinkler heads to meet the specifications of the project. This problem asks you to help Waterways use a job order cost system to account for production of these parts.

*Go to WileyPLUS for complete case details and instructions.*

## Comprehensive Case

**CC12** Greetings Inc., a nationally recognized retailer of greeting cards and small gift items, decides to employ Internet technology to expand its sales opportunities. For this case, you will employ traditional job order costing techniques and then evaluate the resulting product costs.

*Go to WileyPLUS for complete case details and instructions.*

**Comprehensive Cases** present realistic business situations that require students to apply topics learned in this and previous chapters.

## Expand Your Critical Thinking

### Decision-Making Across the Organization

**CT12.1** Khan Products Company uses a job order cost system. For a number of months, there has been an ongoing rift between the sales department and the production department concerning a special-order product, TC-1. TC-1 is a seasonal product that is manufactured in batches of 1,000 units. TC-1 is sold at cost plus a markup of 40% of cost.

The sales department is unhappy because fluctuating unit production costs significantly affect selling prices. Sales personnel complain that this has caused excessive customer complaints and the loss of considerable orders for TC-1.

The production department maintains that each job order must be fully costed on the basis of the costs incurred during the period in which the goods are produced. Production personnel maintain that the only real solution is for the sales department to increase sales in the slack periods.

Andrea Parley, president of the company, asks you as the company accountant to collect quarterly data for the past year on TC-1. From the cost accounting system, you accumulate the following production quantity and cost data.

| | | | Quarter | |
| Costs | 1 | 2 | 3 | 4 |
| --- | --- | --- | --- | --- |
| Direct materials | $100,000 | $220,000 | $ 80,000 | $200,000 |
| Direct labor | 60,000 | 132,000 | 48,000 | 120,000 |
| Manufacturing overhead | 105,000 | 153,000 | 97,000 | 125,000 |
| Total | $265,000 | $505,000 | $225,000 | $445,000 |
| Production in batches | 5 | 11 | 4 | 10 |
| Unit cost (per batch) | $ 53,000 | $ 45,909 | $ 56,250 | $ 44,500 |

**Instructions**

With the class divided into groups, answer the following questions.

**a.** What manufacturing cost element is responsible for the fluctuating unit costs? Why?

**b.** What is your recommended solution to the problem of fluctuating unit cost?

**c.** Restate the quarterly data on the basis of your recommended solution.

## Managerial Analysis

**CT12.2** In the course of routine checking of all transactions prior to preparing year-end reports, Betty Eller discovered several strange items. She recalled that the president's son Joe had come in to help out during an especially busy time and that he had recorded some transactions. She was relieved that there were only a few that he had completed, and even more relieved that he had included rather lengthy explanations. Joe recorded the following transactions.

1. An increase to Work in Process Inventory for $25,000 and a decrease to Cash for $25,000.
   (This is for materials put into process. I don't find the record that we paid for these, so I'm decreasing Cash because I know we'll have to pay for them sooner or later.)

2. An increase to Manufacturing Overhead for $12,000 and a decrease to Cash for $12,000.
   (This is for bonuses paid to salespeople. I know they're part of overhead, and I can't find an account called "Non-Factory Overhead" or "Other Overhead" so I'm putting it in Manufacturing Overhead. I have the check stubs, so I know we paid these.)

3. An increase to Wages Expense for $120,000 and a decrease to Cash for $120,000.
   (This is for the factory workers' wages that have not been paid.)

4. An increase to Work in Process Inventory for $3,000 and a decrease to Raw Materials Inventory for $3,000.
   (This is for the glue used in the factory. I know we used this to make the products, even though we didn't use very much on any one of the products. I got it out of inventory, so I decreased an inventory account.)

### Instructions

How should Joe have recorded each of the four events?

## Real-World Focus

**CT12.3** The **Institute of Management Accountants (IMA)** sponsors a certification for management accountants, allowing them to obtain the title of Certified Management Accountant.

### Instructions

Go to the IMA website. Choose **CMA Certification**, then **Getting Started**, and then answer part (a) below. Next, choose **CMA Certification**, then **Current CMAs**, then **Maintain Your Certification**, and then click on **Download the CPE Requirements and Rules**. Answer part (b) below.

a. What is the experience qualification requirement?

b. How many hours of continuing education are required, and what types of courses qualify?

## Communication Activity

**CT12.4** You are the management accountant for Williams Company. Your company does custom carpentry work and uses a job order cost system. Williams sends detailed job cost sheets to its customers, along with an invoice. The job cost sheets show the date materials were used, the dollar cost of materials, and the hours and cost of labor. A predetermined overhead application rate is used, and the total overhead applied is also listed.

Nancy Kopay is a customer who recently had custom cabinets installed. Along with her check in payment for the work done, she included a letter. She thanked the company for including the detailed cost information but questioned why overhead was estimated. She stated that she would be interested in knowing exactly what costs were included in overhead, and she thought that other customers would, too.

### Instructions

Prepare a letter to Ms. Kopay (address: 123 Cedar Lane, Altoona, KS 66651) and tell her why you did not send her information on exact costs of overhead included in her job. Respond to her suggestion that you provide this information.

## Ethics Case

**CT12.5** Service  LRF Printing provides printing services to many different corporate clients. Although LRF bids most jobs, some jobs, particularly new ones, are negotiated on a "cost-plus" basis. Cost-plus means that the buyer is willing to pay the actual cost plus a return (profit) on these costs to LRF.

Alice Reiley, controller for LRF, has recently returned from a meeting where LRF's president stated that he wanted her to find a way to charge more costs to any project that was on a cost-plus basis. The president noted that the company needed more profits to meet its stated goals this period. By charging more costs to the cost-plus projects and therefore fewer costs to the jobs that were bid, the company should be able to increase its profit for the current year.

Alice knew why the president wanted to take this action. Rumors were that he was looking for a new position and if the company reported strong profits, the president's opportunities would be enhanced. Alice also recognized that she could probably increase the cost of certain jobs by changing the basis used to assign manufacturing overhead.

### Instructions

    **a.** Who are the stakeholders in this situation?

    **b.** What are the ethical issues in this situation?

    **c.** What would you do if you were Alice Reiley?

## All About You

**CT12.6**  Many of you will work for a small business. Some of you will even own your own business. In order to operate a small business, you will need a good understanding of managerial accounting, as well as many other skills. Much information is available to assist people who are interested in starting a new business. A great place to start is the website provided by the **Small Business Administration (SBA)**, which is an agency of the federal government whose purpose is to support small businesses.

### Instructions

Go to the SBA website, click on **10 steps to get started**, and then list the top 10 steps to starting a business.

## Considering Your Costs and Benefits

**CT12.7**  After graduating, you might decide to start a small business. As discussed in this chapter, owners of any business need to know how to calculate the cost of their products. In fact, many small businesses fail because they don't accurately calculate their product costs, so they don't know if they are making a profit or losing money—until it's too late.

Suppose that you decide to start a landscape business. You use an old pickup truck that you've fully paid for. You store the truck and other equipment in your parents' barn, and you store trees and shrubs on their land. Your parents will not charge you for the use of these facilities for the first two years, but beginning in the third year they will charge a reasonable rent. Your mother helps you by answering phone calls and providing customers with information. She doesn't charge you for this service, but she plans on doing it for only your first two years in business. In pricing your services, should you include charges for the truck, the barn, the land, and your mother's services when calculating your product cost? The basic arguments for and against are as follows.

    **YES:** If you don't include charges for these costs, your costs are understated and your profitability is overstated.

    **NO:** At this point, you are not actually incurring costs related to these activities; therefore, you shouldn't record charges.

### Instructions

Write a response indicating your position regarding this situation. Provide support for your view.

iStock.com/Eric Gerrard

# Cost-Volume-Profit

## Chapter Preview

As the following Feature Story indicates, to manage any size business you must understand how costs respond to changes in sales volume and the effect of costs and revenues on profits. A prerequisite to understanding cost-volume-profit (CVP) relationships is knowledge of how costs behave. In this chapter, we first explain the considerations involved in cost behavior analysis. Then, we discuss and illustrate CVP analysis.

## Feature Story

### Don't Worry—Just Get Big

It wasn't that Jeff didn't have a good job. He was a vice president at a Wall Street firm. But, despite his good position, he quit his job, moved to Seattle, and started an online retailer, which he named **Amazon.com**. Like any good entrepreneur, Jeff Bezos strove to keep his initial investment small. Operations were run out of his garage. And, to avoid the need for a warehouse, he took orders for books and had them shipped from other distributors' warehouses.

By its fourth month, Amazon was selling 100 books a day. In its first full year, it had $15.7 million in sales. The next year, sales increased eightfold. Two years later, sales were $1.6 billion.

Although its sales growth was impressive, Amazon's ability to lose money was equally amazing. One analyst nick-named it *Amazon.bomb*, while another, predicting its demise, called it *Amazon.toast*. Why was it losing money? The company used every available dollar to reinvest in itself. It built massive warehouses and bought increasingly sophisticated (and expensive) computers and equipment to improve its distribution system. This desire to grow as fast as possible was captured in a T-shirt slogan at its company picnic, which read

"Eat another hot dog, get big fast." This buying binge was increasing the company's fixed costs at a rate that exceeded its sales growth. Skeptics predicted that Amazon would soon run out of cash. It didn't.

At the end of one year, even as it announced record profits, Amazon's share price fell by 9%. Why? Because although the company was predicting that its sales revenue in the next quarter would increase by at least 28%, it predicted that its operating profit would fall by at least 2% and perhaps by as much as 34%. The company made no apologies. It explained that it was in the process of expanding from 39 distribution centers to 52. As Amazon's finance chief noted, "You're not as productive on those assets for some time. I'm very pleased with the investments we're making and we've shown over our history that we've been able to make great returns on the capital we invest in." In other words, eat another hot dog.

**Sources:** Christine Frey and John Cook, "How Amazon.com Survived, Thrived and Turned a Profit," *Seattle Post* (January 28, 2008); Stu Woo, "Sticker Shock Over Amazon Growth," *Wall Street Journal* (January 28, 2011); and Miriam Guttfried, "Amazon's Never-Ending Story," *Wall Street Journal* (April 25, 2014).

## Chapter Outline

| LEARNING OBJECTIVES | REVIEW | PRACTICE |
|---|---|---|
| **LO 1** Explain variable, fixed, and mixed costs and the relevant range. | • Variable costs<br>• Fixed costs<br>• Relevant range<br>• Mixed costs | **DO IT! 1** Types of Costs |
| **LO 2** Apply the high-low method to determine the components of mixed costs. | • High-low method<br>• Identifying variable and fixed costs | **DO IT! 2** High-Low Method |
| **LO 3** Prepare a CVP income statement to determine contribution margin. | • Basic components<br>• CVP income statement | **DO IT! 3** CVP Income Statement |
| **LO 4** Compute the break-even point using three approaches. | • Mathematical equation<br>• Contribution margin technique<br>• Graphic presentation | **DO IT! 4** Break-Even Analysis |
| **LO 5** Determine the sales required to earn target net income and determine margin of safety. | • Target net income<br>• Margin of safety | **DO IT! 5** Break-Even, Margin of Safety, and Target Net Income |

**Go to the Review and Practice section at the end of the chapter for a targeted summary and practice applications with solutions.**

**Visit WileyPLUS for additional tutorials and practice opportunities.**

# Cost Behavior Analysis

### LEARNING OBJECTIVE 1
Explain variable, fixed, and mixed costs and the relevant range.

**Cost behavior analysis** is the study of how specific costs respond to changes in the level of business activity.

- Some costs change when activity changes and others remain the same. For example, for an airline company such as **Southwest** or **United**, the longer the flight, the higher the fuel costs. On the other hand, **Massachusetts General Hospital**'s costs to staff the emergency room on any given night are relatively constant regardless of the number of patients treated.

- A knowledge of cost behavior helps management plan operations and decide between alternative courses of action.

- Cost behavior analysis applies to all types of entities.

The starting point in cost behavior analysis is measuring the key business activities. Activity levels may be expressed in terms of sales dollars (in a retail company), miles driven (in a trucking company), room occupancy (in a hotel), or dance classes taught (by a dance studio). Many companies use more than one measurement base. A manufacturer, for example, may use direct labor hours or units of output for manufacturing costs, and sales revenue or units sold for selling expenses.

For an activity level to be useful in cost behavior analysis, changes in the level or volume of activity should be correlated with changes in costs.

- The activity level selected is referred to as the activity index or driver.

- The **activity index** identifies the activity that causes changes in the behavior of costs.

- With an appropriate activity index, companies can classify the behavior of costs in response to changes in activity levels into three categories: variable, fixed, or mixed.

# Variable Costs

**Variable costs** are costs that vary **in total** directly and proportionately with changes in the activity level.

- If the level increases 10%, total variable costs will increase 10%. If the level of activity decreases by 25%, variable costs will decrease 25%.

- Examples of variable costs include direct materials and direct labor for a manufacturer; cost of goods sold, sales commissions, and freight-out for a merchandiser; and gasoline in airline and trucking companies.

- A variable cost may also be defined as a cost that **remains the same *per unit* at every level of activity**.

To illustrate the behavior of a variable cost, assume that Damon Company manufactures tablet computers that contain cameras that cost $10. The activity index is the number of tablet computers produced. As Damon manufactures each tablet, the total cost of cameras installed in tablets increases by $10. As part (a) of **Illustration 13.1** shows, total cost of the cameras

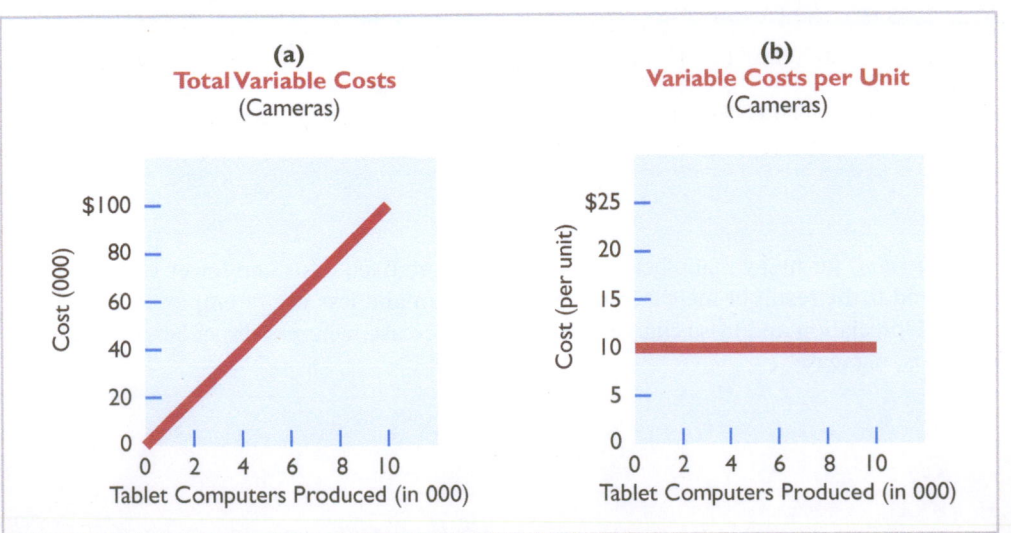

**ILLUSTRATION 13.1**

Behavior of total and unit variable costs; variable costs per unit remain constant

will be $20,000 (2,000 × $10) if Damon produces 2,000 tablets, and $100,000 when it produces 10,000 tablets. We also can see that a variable cost remains the same per unit as the level of activity changes. As part (b) of Illustration 13.1 shows, the unit cost of $10 for the cameras is the same whether Damon produces 2,000 or 10,000 tablets.

Companies that rely heavily on labor either to manufacture a product or perform a service, such as **Hilton** or **Marriott**, are likely to have a high percentage of variable costs. In contrast, companies that use a high proportion of machinery and equipment in producing revenue, such as **AT&T** or **Duke Energy**, may have a lower percentage of variable costs.

## Fixed Costs

**Fixed costs** are costs that **remain the same in total** regardless of changes in the activity level.

- Examples include property taxes, insurance, rent, supervisory salaries, and depreciation on buildings and equipment.
- Because total fixed costs remain constant as activity changes, it follows that **fixed costs *per unit* vary inversely with activity: As volume increases, unit cost declines, and vice versa**.

To illustrate the behavior of fixed costs, assume that Damon Company leases its productive facilities at a cost of $10,000 per month. Total fixed costs of the facilities remain a constant $10,000 at every level of activity, as part (a) of **Illustration 13.2** shows. But, **on a per unit basis, the cost of rent declines as activity increases**, as part (b) of Illustration 13.2 shows. At 2,000 units, the unit cost per tablet computer is $5 ($10,000 ÷ 2,000). When Damon produces 10,000 tablets, the unit cost of the rent is only $1 per tablet ($10,000 ÷ 10,000).

**ILLUSTRATION 13.2**

**Behavior of total and unit fixed costs**

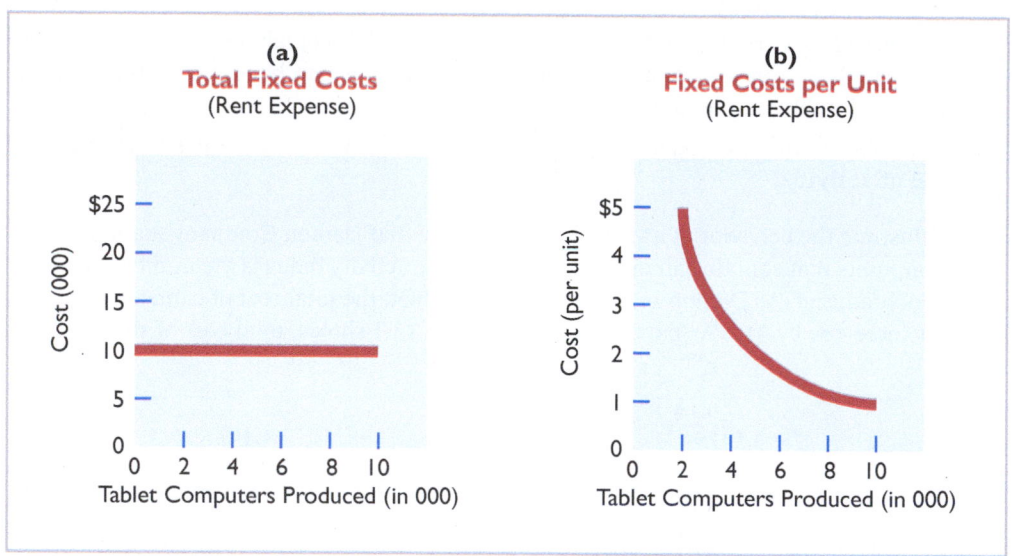

The trend for many manufacturers is to have more fixed costs and fewer variable costs. This trend is the result of increased use of automation and less use of employee labor. As a result, depreciation and lease charges (fixed costs) increase, whereas direct labor costs (variable costs) decrease.

## People, Planet, and Profit Insight   BrightFarms

### Gardens in the Sky

Because of population increases, the United Nations' Food and Agriculture Organization estimates that food production will need to increase by 70% by 2050. Also, by 2050, roughly 70% of people will live in cities, which means more food needs to be hauled farther to get it to the consumer. To address the lack of farmable land and reduce the cost of transporting produce, some companies, such as New York-based **BrightFarms**, are building urban greenhouses.

iStock.com/Jani Bryson

This sounds great, but do the numbers work? Some variable costs would be reduced. For example, the use of pesticides, herbicides, fuel costs for shipping, and water would all drop. Soil erosion would be a non-issue since plants would be grown hydroponically (in a solution of water and minerals), and land

requirements would be reduced because of vertical structures. But, other costs would be higher. First, there is the cost of the building. Also, any multistory building would require artificial lighting for plants on lower floors.

Until these cost challenges can be overcome, it appears that these urban greenhouses may not break even. On the other hand, rooftop greenhouses on existing city structures already appear financially viable. For example, a 15,000 square-foot rooftop greenhouse in Brooklyn already produces roughly 30 tons of vegetables per year for local residents.

**Sources:** "Vertical Farming: Does It Really Stack Up?" *The Economist* (December 9, 2010); and Jane Black, "BrightFarms Idea: Greenhouses That Cut Short the Path from Plant to Grocery Shelf," *The Washington Post* (May 7, 2013).

**What are some of the variable and fixed costs that are impacted by hydroponic farming? (Go to WileyPLUS for this answer and additional questions.)**

# Relevant Range

In Illustration 13.1 part (a), a straight line is drawn throughout the entire range of the activity index for total variable costs. In essence, the assumption is that the costs are **linear**. If a relationship is linear (that is, straight-line), then changes in the activity index will result in a direct, proportional change in the total variable cost. For example, if the activity level doubles, the cost doubles.

It is now necessary to ask: Is the straight-line relationship realistic? In most business situations, a straight-line relationship **does not exist** for variable costs throughout the entire range of possible activity.

- At abnormally low levels of activity, it may be impossible to be cost-efficient. Small-scale operations may not allow the company to obtain quantity discounts for raw materials or to use specialized labor.

- At abnormally high levels of activity, labor costs may increase sharply because of overtime pay. Also, at high activity levels, materials costs may jump significantly because of excess spoilage caused by worker fatigue.

As a result, in the real world, the relationship between the behavior of a variable cost and changes in the activity level is often **curvilinear**, as shown in part (a) of **Illustration 13.3**.

**ILLUSTRATION 13.3**

**Nonlinear behavior of variable and fixed costs**

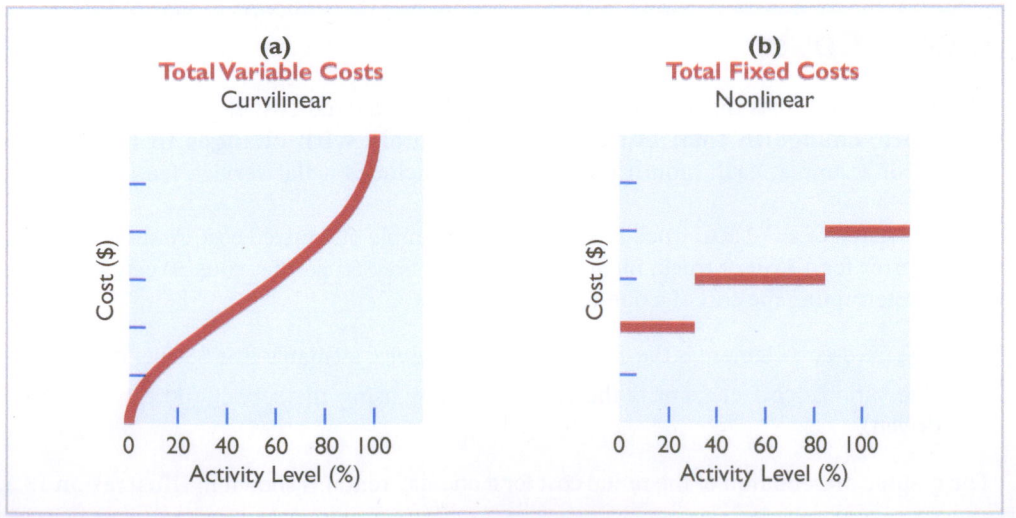

In the curved sections of the line, a change in the activity index will not result in a direct, proportional change in the variable cost. That is, a doubling of the activity index will not result in an exact doubling of the variable cost. The variable cost may be more than double, or it may be less than double.

Total fixed costs also do not have a straight-line relationship over the entire range of activity. Some fixed costs will not change. But it is possible for management to change other fixed costs (see **Helpful Hint**). For example, in some instances, salaried employees (fixed) are replaced with freelance workers (variable). Some costs are step costs. For example, once a company exceeds certain levels of activity, it may have to add an additional warehouse. Illustration 13.3, part (b), shows an example of step-cost behavior of total fixed costs through all potential levels of activity.

For most companies, operating at almost zero or at 100% capacity is the exception rather than the rule. Instead, companies often operate over a somewhat narrower range, such as 40–80% of capacity.

- The range over which a company expects to operate during a year is called the **relevant range** of the activity index (see **Alternative Terminology**).
- Within the relevant range, as both diagrams in **Illustration 13.4** show, a straight-line relationship generally exists for both variable and fixed costs between 40 and 80% of capacity.

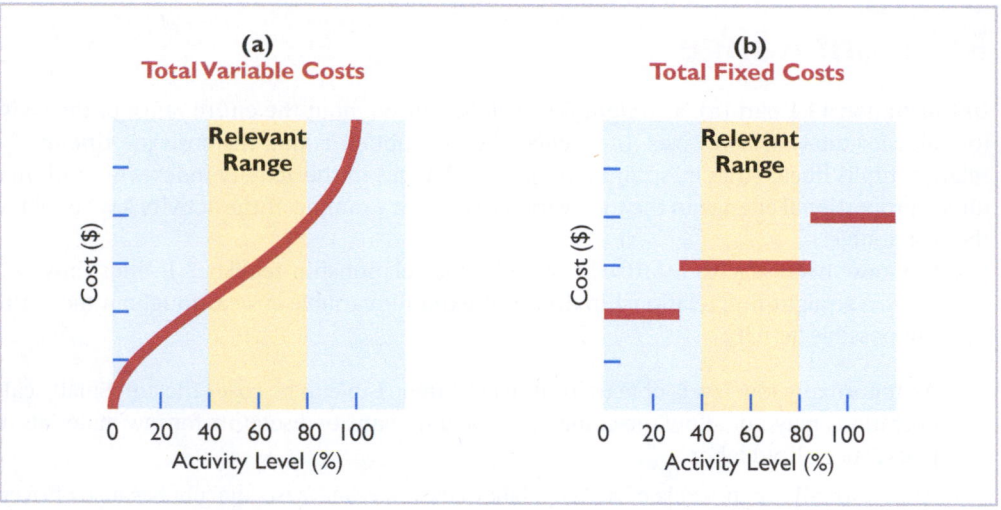

As you can see, although the linear (straight-line) relationship may not be completely realistic, **the linear assumption produces useful data for CVP analysis as long as the level of activity remains within the relevant range**.

## Mixed Costs

**Mixed costs** are costs that contain both a variable- and a fixed-cost element. **Mixed costs, therefore, change in total but not proportionately with changes in the activity level.** For example, each month the electric bill includes a flat service fee plus a usage charge.

The rental of a **U-Haul** truck is another good example of a mixed cost. Assume that local rental terms for a 17-foot truck, including insurance, are $50 per day plus 50 cents per mile. When determining the cost of a one-day rental:

- The fixed-cost element is the cost of having the service available (the $50 per day charge).
- The variable-cost element is the cost of actually using the service (50 cents per mile driven).

The graphic presentation of the rental cost for a one-day rental is shown in **Illustration 13.5**.

**ILLUSTRATION 13.5**
**Behavior of a mixed cost**

---

## DO IT! 1 | Types of Costs

Helena Company reports the following total costs at two levels of production.

| | 10,000 Units | 20,000 Units |
|---|---|---|
| Direct materials | $20,000 | $40,000 |
| Maintenance | 8,000 | 10,000 |
| Direct labor | 17,000 | 34,000 |
| Indirect materials | 1,000 | 2,000 |
| Depreciation | 4,000 | 4,000 |
| Utilities | 3,000 | 5,000 |
| Rent | 6,000 | 6,000 |

Classify each cost as variable, fixed, or mixed.

### Solution

Direct materials, direct labor, and indirect materials are variable costs because the total cost doubles with the doubling in activity.

Depreciation and rent are fixed costs because the total cost does not vary with the change in activity.

Maintenance and utilities are mixed costs because the total cost changes, but the change is not proportional to the change in activity.

Related exercise material: **BE13.1, BE13.2, BE13.3, DO IT! 13.1, E13.1, E13.2, E13.4,** and **E13.6.**

**ACTION PLAN**

- **Recall that a variable cost varies in total directly and proportionately with each change in activity level.**

- **Recall that a fixed cost remains the same in total with each change in activity level.**

- **Recall that a mixed cost changes in total but not proportionately with each change in activity level.**

---

# Mixed Costs Analysis

**LEARNING OBJECTIVE 2**

Apply the high-low method to determine the components of mixed costs.

For purposes of cost-volume-profit analysis, **mixed costs must be classified into their fixed and variable elements.** How does management make the classification?

- One possibility is to determine the variable and fixed components each time a mixed cost is incurred. But because of time and cost constraints, this approach is rarely followed.
- Instead, the usual approach is to collect data on the behavior of the mixed costs at various levels of activity.
- Analysts then identify the fixed- and variable-cost components.

Companies use various types of analysis. One type of analysis, called the **high-low method**, is discussed next.

## High-Low Method

The **high-low method** uses the total costs incurred at the high and low levels of activity to classify mixed costs into fixed and variable components. The difference in costs between the high and low levels represents variable costs, since only the variable-cost element can change as activity levels change.

The steps in computing fixed and variable costs under this method are as follows.

1. **Determine variable cost per unit from the formula shown in Illustration 13.6.** This is the slope of the cost function.

**ILLUSTRATION 13.6**

Formula for variable cost per unit using high-low method

| Change in Total Costs at High versus Low Activity Level | ÷ | High minus Low Activity Level | = | Variable Cost per Unit |
|---|---|---|---|---|

To illustrate, assume that Metro Transit Company has the maintenance costs and mileage data for its fleet of buses over a six-month period shown in **Illustration 13.7**.

**ILLUSTRATION 13.7**

Assumed maintenance costs and mileage data

| Month | Miles Driven | Total Cost | Month | Miles Driven | Total Cost |
|---|---|---|---|---|---|
| January | 20,000 | $30,000 | April | 50,000 | $63,000 |
| February | 40,000 | 48,000 | May | 30,000 | 42,000 |
| March | 35,000 | 49,000 | June | 43,000 | 61,000 |

The high and low levels of activity are 50,000 miles in April and 20,000 miles in January. The maintenance costs at these two levels are $63,000 and $30,000, respectively. The difference in maintenance costs is $33,000 ($63,000 − $30,000), and the difference in miles is 30,000 (50,000 − 20,000). Therefore, for Metro Transit, variable cost per unit is $1.10, computed as follows.

$$\$33,000 \div 30,000 = \$1.10$$

2. **Determine the total fixed costs by subtracting the total variable costs at either the high or the low activity level from the total cost at that activity level.**

**Illustration 13.8** shows the computations for Metro Transit.

**ILLUSTRATION 13.8**

High-low method computation of fixed costs

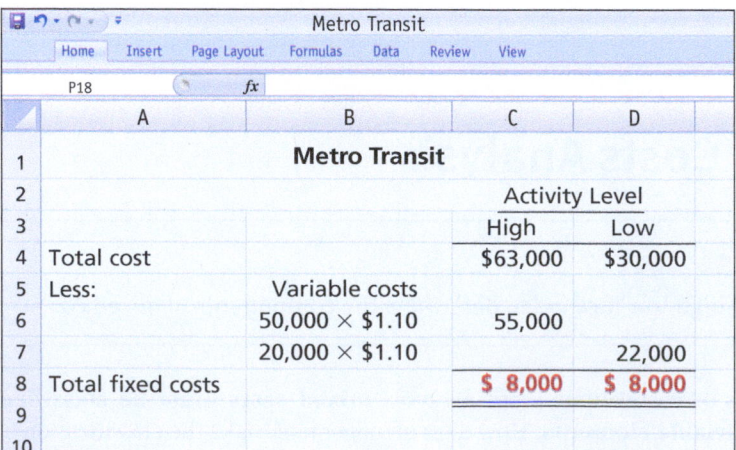

**Maintenance costs are therefore $8,000 per month of fixed costs plus $1.10 per mile of variable costs.** This is represented by the following formula, referred to as the total cost equation.

Maintenance costs = $8,000 + ($1.10 × Miles driven)

For example, at 45,000 miles, estimated maintenance costs would be $8,000 fixed and $49,500 variable ($1.10 × 45,000) for a total of $57,500.

The graph in **Illustration 13.9** plots the six-month data for Metro Transit Company.

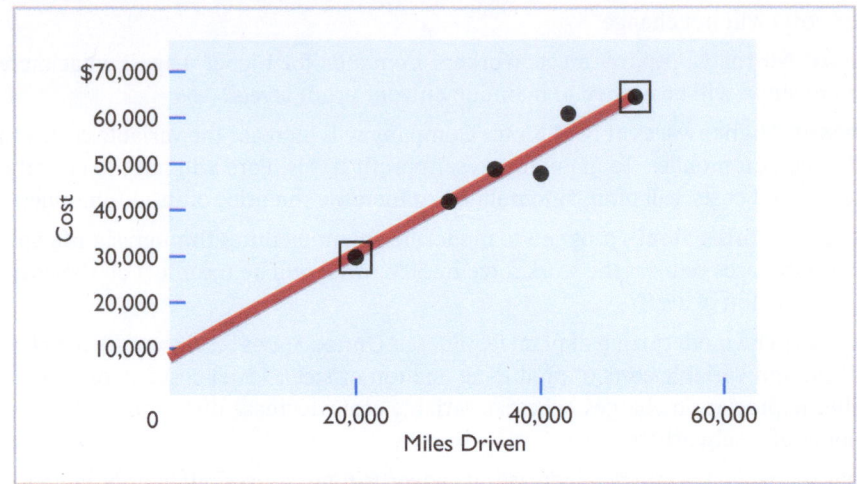

**ILLUSTRATION 13.9**

**Scatter plot for Metro Transit Company**

- The red line drawn in the graph connects the high and low data points (in squares) and therefore represents the equation that we just solved using the high-low method.

- The red, "high-low" line intersects the y-axis at $8,000 (the fixed-cost level), and it rises by its slope of $1.10 per unit (the variable cost per unit).

- Note that a completely different line would result if we chose any two of the other data points. That is, by choosing any two other data points, we would end up with a different estimate of fixed costs and a different variable cost per unit.

- Thus, from this scatter plot, we can see that while the high-low method is simple, the result is rather arbitrary.

A better approach, which uses information from all the data points to estimate fixed and variable costs, is called *regression analysis*. A discussion of regression analysis is provided in Appendix 13A as well as in the Excel video available in WileyPLUS.

---

## Management Insight   Kroger

tiero/iStock/
Getty Images

### Are Robotic Workers More Humane?

Warehouse distribution centers for large retailers and grocers employ more than 800,000 people in the United States. But many companies, such as grocer **Kroger**, have a hard time finding and retaining warehouse workers. One reason? Studies have shown that some warehouse workers walk up to 20 miles and lift 50,000 pounds during a single day. As a result, as the needs for storage increases and companies are faced with the proposition of building massive new warehouses, some are choosing instead to invest in robotic warehousing systems.

Robots can provide many advantages over their human counterparts. Robots need aisles that are less than 30 inches wide, as opposed to traditional warehouse aisles that are 10 to 12 feet wide. Moving at speeds of up to 25 miles per hour, robots can drop off and retrieve warehouse cases about five times as fast as a human. Robotic systems cut labor costs by about 80%, and they cut warehouse size anywhere from 25% to 40%. However, a fully automated system costs between $40 to $80 million, so the switch to robotic systems is not a trivial decision.

**Source:** Robbie Whelan, "Fully Autonomous Robots: The Warehouse Workers of the Near Future," *Wall Street Journal* (September 20, 2016).

**How would a company's variable and fixed costs change if it adopts a robotic system? (Go to WileyPLUS for this answer and additional questions).**

# Importance of Identifying Variable and Fixed Costs

Why is it important to segregate mixed costs into variable and fixed elements? The answer may become apparent if we look at the following four business decisions.

1. If **American Airlines** is to make a profit when it reduces all domestic fares by 30%, what reduction in costs or increase in passengers will be required?

   **Answer**: To make a profit when it cuts domestic fares by 30%, American Airlines will have to increase the number of passengers or cut its variable costs for those flights. Its fixed costs will not change.

2. If **Ford Motor Company** meets workers' demands for higher wages, what increase in sales revenue will be needed to maintain current profit levels?

   **Answer**: Higher wages at Ford Motor Company will increase the variable costs of manufacturing automobiles. To maintain present profit levels, Ford will have to cut other variable or fixed costs, sell more automobiles, or increase the price of its automobiles.

3. If **United States Steel**'s program to modernize plant facilities through significant equipment purchases reduces the work force by 50%, what will be the effect on the cost of producing one ton of steel?

   **Answer**: The modernizing of plant facilities at United States Steel changes the proportion of fixed and variable costs of producing one ton of steel. Fixed costs increase because of higher depreciation charges, whereas variable costs decrease due to the reduction in the number of steelworkers.

4. What happens if **Kellogg's** increases its advertising expenses but cannot increase prices because of competitive pressure?

   **Answer**: Sales volume must be increased to cover the increase in fixed advertising costs.

---

**ACTION PLAN**

- Determine the highest and lowest levels of activity.
- Compute variable cost per unit as Change in total costs ÷ (High − low activity level) = Variable cost per unit.
- Compute fixed cost as Total cost − (Variable cost per unit × Units produced) = Total fixed cost.

## DO IT! 2 | High-Low Method

Byrnes Company accumulates the following data concerning a mixed cost, using units produced as the activity level.

|  | **Units Produced** | **Total Cost** |
|---|---|---|
| March | 9,800 | $14,740 |
| April | 8,500 | 13,250 |
| May | 7,000 | 11,100 |
| June | 7,600 | 12,000 |
| July | 8,100 | 12,460 |

a. Compute the variable-cost and fixed-cost elements using the high-low method.

b. Using the information from your answer to part (a), write the cost formula.

c. Estimate the total cost if the company produces 8,000 units.

### Solution

a. Variable cost: ($14,740 − $11,100) ÷ (9,800 − 7,000) = $1.30 per unit

   Fixed cost: $14,740 − ($1.30 × 9,800 units) = $2,000
   *OR* $11,100 − ($1.30 × 7,000 units) = $2,000

b. Cost = $2,000 + ($1.30 × units produced)

c. Total cost to produce 8,000 units: $2,000 + $10,400 ($1.30 × 8,000 units) = $12,400

Related exercise material: **BE13.4, BE13.5, DO IT! 13.2, E13.3, and E13.5.**

# Cost-Volume-Profit Analysis

**Cost-volume-profit (CVP) analysis** is the study of the effects of changes in costs and volume on a company's profits.

- CVP analysis is important in profit planning.
- It also is a critical factor in such management decisions as setting selling prices, determining product mix, and maximizing use of production facilities.

## Basic Components

CVP analysis considers the interrelationships among the components shown in **Illustration 13.10**.

**ILLUSTRATION 13.10**    **Components of CVP analysis**

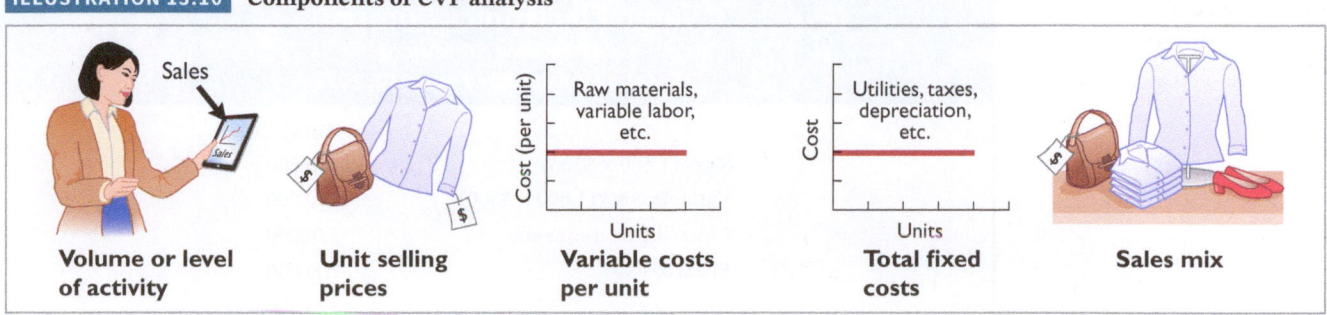

| Volume or level of activity | Unit selling prices | Variable costs per unit | Total fixed costs | Sales mix |

The following assumptions underlie each CVP analysis.

1. The behavior of both costs and revenues is linear throughout the relevant range of the activity index.
2. Costs can be classified accurately as either variable or fixed.
3. Changes in activity are the only factors that affect costs.
4. All units produced are sold.
5. When more than one type of product is sold, the sales mix will remain constant. That is, the percentage that each product represents of total sales will stay the same. Sales mix complicates CVP analysis because different products will have different cost relationships. In this chapter, we assume a single product. In Appendix G, however, we examine the sales mix more closely.

When these assumptions are not valid, the CVP analysis may be inaccurate.

## CVP Income Statement

Because CVP is so important for decision-making, management often wants this information reported in a **cost-volume-profit (CVP) income statement** format for internal use.

- The CVP income statement classifies costs as variable or fixed and computes a contribution margin.

- **Contribution margin (CM)** is the amount of revenue remaining after deducting variable costs. It is often stated both as a total amount and on a per unit basis.

We use Vargo Electronics Company to illustrate a CVP income statement. Vargo Electronics produces cell phones. **Illustration 13.11** presents relevant data for the cell phones sold by this company in June 2022.

**ILLUSTRATION 13.11**

**Assumed selling and cost data for Vargo Electronics**

| | |
|---|---|
| Unit selling price of cell phone | $500 |
| Unit variable costs* | $300 |
| Total monthly fixed costs** | $200,000 |
| Units sold | 1,600 |

*Includes variable manufacturing costs and variable selling and administrative expenses.
**Includes fixed manufacturing costs and fixed selling and administrative expenses.

Note that in Illustration 13.11, as well as in the applications and assignment material of CVP analysis that follow, **we assume that the term "cost" includes all costs and expenses related to production and sale of the product. That is, cost includes manufacturing costs plus selling and administrative expenses.**

The CVP income statement for Vargo would therefore be reported as shown in **Illustration 13.12**.

**ILLUSTRATION 13.12**

**CVP income statement, with net income**

### Vargo Electronics Company
#### CVP Income Statement
#### For the Month Ended June 30, 2022

| | Total |
|---|---|
| Sales (1,600 × $500) | $800,000 |
| Variable costs (1,600 × $300) | 480,000 |
| **Contribution margin** | **320,000** |
| Fixed costs | 200,000 |
| **Net income** | **$120,000** |

A traditional income statement and a CVP income statement both report the same net income of $120,000.

- However, a traditional income statement does not classify costs as variable or fixed, and therefore it does not report a contribution margin.
- In addition, sometimes per unit amounts and percentage of sales amounts are shown in separate columns on a CVP income statement to facilitate CVP analysis. *Homework assignments specify which columns to present.*

## Unit Contribution Margin

**Illustration 13.13** shows the formula for **unit contribution margin** and the computation for Vargo Electronics.

**ILLUSTRATION 13.13**

**Formula for unit contribution margin**

| Unit Selling Price | − | Unit Variable Costs | = | Unit Contribution Margin |
|---|---|---|---|---|
| $500 | − | $300 | = | $200 |

Unit contribution margin indicates that for every cell phone sold, the selling price exceeds the variable costs by $200.

- Vargo generates $200 per unit sold to cover fixed costs and contribute to net income.
- Because Vargo has fixed costs of $200,000, it must sell 1,000 cell phones ($200,000 ÷ $200) to cover its fixed costs.

- At the point where total contribution margin exactly equals fixed costs (sale of 1,000 cell phones), Vargo will report net income of zero.
- At this point, referred to as the **break-even point**, total costs (variable plus fixed) exactly equal total revenue.

**Illustration 13.14** shows Vargo's CVP income statement at the point where net income equals zero. It shows a contribution margin of $200,000, and a unit contribution margin of $200 ($500 − $300).

| Vargo Electronics Company | | |
|---|---|---|
| CVP Income Statement | | |
| For the Month Ended June 30, 2022 | | |
| | **Total** | **Per Unit** |
| Sales (1,000 × $500) | $500,000 | $500 |
| Variable costs (1,000 × $300) | 300,000 | 300 |
| **Contribution margin** | **200,000** | **$200** |
| Fixed costs | 200,000 | |
| **Net income** | **$ –0–** | |

ILLUSTRATION 13.14

CVP income statement, with zero net income

**Decision Tools**

The unit contribution margin indicates the increase in income that results from every additional unit sold after the break-even point.

It follows that for every cell phone sold above the break-even point of 1,000 units, **net income increases by the amount of the unit contribution margin, $200** (see **Decision Tools**). For example, assume that Vargo sold one more cell phone, for a total of 1,001 cell phones sold. In this case, Vargo reports net income of $200, as shown in **Illustration 13.15**.

| Vargo Electronics Company | | |
|---|---|---|
| CVP Income Statement | | |
| For the Month Ended June 30, 2022 | | |
| | **Total** | **Per Unit** |
| Sales (1,001 × $500) | $500,500 | $500 |
| Variable costs (1,001 × $300) | 300,300 | 300 |
| **Contribution margin** | **200,200** | **$200** |
| Fixed costs | 200,000 | |
| **Net income** | **$ 200** | |

ILLUSTRATION 13.15

CVP income statement, with net income and per unit data

## Contribution Margin Ratio

Some managers prefer to use a contribution margin ratio in CVP analysis. The contribution margin ratio is the contribution margin expressed as a percentage of sales. Vargo Electronics has a contribution margin ratio of 40% (contribution margin of $200,200 divided by sales of $500,500), as shown in the percent of sales column in **Illustration 13.16**.

| Vargo Electronics Company | | |
|---|---|---|
| CVP Income Statement | | |
| For the Month Ended June 30, 2022 | | |
| | **Total** | **Percent of Sales** |
| Sales (1,001 × $500) | $500,500 | 100% |
| Variable costs (1,001 × $300) | 300,300 | 60 |
| **Contribution margin** | **200,200** | **40%** |
| Fixed costs | 200,000 | |
| **Net income** | **$ 200** | |

ILLUSTRATION 13.16

CVP income statement, with net income and percent of sales data

Alternatively, the **contribution margin ratio** can be determined by dividing the unit contribution margin by the unit selling price. **Illustration 13.17** shows the ratio for Vargo Electronics.

**ILLUSTRATION 13.17**

**Formula for contribution margin ratio**

| Unit Contribution Margin | ÷ | Unit Selling Price | = | Contribution Margin Ratio |
|---|---|---|---|---|
| $200 | ÷ | $500 | = | 40% |

**Decision Tools**

The contribution margin ratio indicates by how much every dollar of sales will increase income after the break-even point.

- The contribution margin ratio of 40% means that Vargo generates 40 cents of contribution margin with each dollar of sales. That is, $0.40 of each sales dollar (40% × $1) is available to apply to fixed costs and to contribute to net income (see **Decision Tools**).
- This expression of contribution margin is very helpful in determining the effect of changes in sales on net income. For example, if Vargo's sales increase $100,000, net income will increase $40,000 (40% × $100,000).
- Thus, by using the contribution margin ratio, managers can quickly determine increases in net income from any change in sales.

We can also see this effect through a CVP income statement. Assume that Vargo's current sales are $500,000 and it wants to know the effect of a $100,000 (200-unit) increase in sales. Vargo prepares the comparative CVP income statement analysis shown in **Illustration 13.18**.

**ILLUSTRATION 13.18** Comparative CVP income statements

### Vargo Electronics Company
#### CVP Income Statement
#### For the Month Ended June 30, 2022

| | No Change | | | With $100,000 Increase in Sales | | |
|---|---|---|---|---|---|---|
| | Total | Per Unit | Percent of Sales | Total | Per Unit | Percent of Sales |
| Sales | $500,000 | $500 | 100% | $600,000 | $500 | 100% |
| Variable costs | 300,000 | 300 | 60 | 360,000 | 300 | 60% |
| Contribution margin | 200,000 | $200 | 40% | 240,000 | $200 | 40% |
| Fixed costs | 200,000 | | | 200,000 | | |
| Net income | $ –0– | | | $ 40,000 | | |

The $40,000 increase in net income can be calculated on either a unit contribution margin basis (200 units × $200 per unit) or using the contribution margin ratio times the increase in sales dollars (40% × $100,000). Note that the unit contribution margin and contribution margin as a percentage of sales (that is, the contribution margin ratio) remain unchanged by the increase in sales.

Study these CVP income statements carefully. The concepts presented in these statements are used extensively in this and later chapters.

**ACTION PLAN**

- **Provide a heading with the name of the company, name of statement, and period covered.**
- **Subtract variable costs from sales to determine contribution margin. Subtract fixed costs from contribution margin to determine net income.**

## DO IT! 3 | CVP Income Statement

Ampco Industries produces and sells a cell phone-operated thermostat. Information regarding the costs and sales of thermostats during September 2022 are provided below.

| | |
|---|---|
| Unit selling price of thermostat | $85 |
| Unit variable costs | $32 |
| Total monthly fixed costs | $190,000 |
| Units sold | 4,000 |

Prepare a CVP income statement for Ampco Industries for the month of September. Provide per unit values and total values.

**Solution**

• Express sales, variable costs and contribution margin on a per unit basis.

| Ampco Industries | | |
|---|---|---|
| CVP Income Statement | | |
| For the Month Ended September 30, 2022 | | |
| | Total | Per Unit |
| Sales | $340,000 | $85 |
| Variable costs | 128,000 | 32 |
| Contribution margin | 212,000 | $53 |
| Fixed costs | 190,000 | |
| Net income | $ 22,000 | |

Related exercise material: **BE13.6, BE13.7, DO IT! 13.3, and E13.7.**

# Break-Even Analysis

**LEARNING OBJECTIVE 4**

Compute the break-even point using three approaches.

A key relationship in CVP analysis is the level of activity at which total revenues equal total costs (both fixed and variable)—the **break-even point**. At this volume of sales, the company will realize no income but will suffer no loss. The process of finding the break-even point is called **break-even analysis**. Knowledge of the break-even point is useful to management when it considers decisions such as whether to introduce new product lines, change sales prices on established products, or enter new market areas (see **Decision Tools**).

> **Decision Tools**
>
> Break-even analysis indicates the amount of sales units or sales dollars that a company needs to cover its costs.

The break-even point can be:

1. Computed from a mathematical equation.
2. Computed by using contribution margin.
3. Derived from a cost-volume-profit (CVP) graph.

The break-even point can be expressed either in **sales units** or **sales dollars**.

## Mathematical Equation

**Illustration 13.19** shows a common profit equation used as the basis for CVP analysis. This equation expresses net income as sales minus variable and fixed costs.

| Sales | − | Variable Costs | − | Fixed Costs | = | Net Income |
|---|---|---|---|---|---|---|
| $500Q | − | $300Q | − | $200,000 | = | $0 |

**ILLUSTRATION 13.19**

Profit equation

• Sales is expressed as the unit selling price ($500) times the number of units sold (Q).
• Variable costs are determined by multiplying the unit variable cost ($300) by the number of units sold (Q).
• When net income is set to zero, as it is in this illustration, this equation can be used to calculate the break-even point.

As shown in Illustration 13.14, net income equals zero when the contribution margin (sales minus variable costs) is equal to fixed costs. To reflect this, **Illustration 13.20** rewrites the equation with contribution margin (sales minus variable costs) on the left side, and fixed costs and net income of zero on the right. We can then compute the break-even point **in units** by **using unit selling prices** and **unit variable costs** and solving for the quantity (Q).

**ILLUSTRATION 13.20**

Computation of break-even point in units

| Sales | − | Variable Costs | − | Fixed Costs | = | Net Income |
|---|---|---|---|---|---|---|
| $500Q | − | $300Q | − | $200,000 | = | $0 |
| $500Q | − | $300Q | = | $200,000 | + | $0 |
| $200Q | = | $200,000 | | | | |

$$Q = \frac{\$200{,}000}{\$200} = \frac{\text{Fixed Costs}}{\text{Unit Contribution Margin}}$$

$$Q = 1{,}000 \text{ units}$$

where

| Q | = | number of units sold |
|---|---|---|
| $500 | = | unit selling price |
| $300 | = | unit variable costs |
| $200,000 | = | total fixed costs |

Thus, Vargo Electronics must sell 1,000 units to break even.

To find the amount of **sales dollars** required to break even, we multiply the units sold at the break-even point times the selling price per unit, as shown below.

$$1{,}000 \times \$500 = \$500{,}000 \text{ (break-even sales dollars)}$$

## Contribution Margin Technique

Many managers employ the contribution margin to compute the break-even point.

### Contribution Margin in Units

The final step in Illustration 13.20 divides fixed costs by the unit contribution margin (highlighted in red). Thus, rather than walk through all of the steps of the equation approach, we can simply employ this formula shown in **Illustration 13.21**.

**ILLUSTRATION 13.21**

Formula for break-even point in units using unit contribution margin

| Fixed Costs | ÷ | Unit Contribution Margin | = | Break-Even Point in Units |
|---|---|---|---|---|
| $200,000 | ÷ | $200 | = | 1,000 units |

Why does this formula work?

- The unit contribution margin is the net amount by which each sale exceeds the variable costs per unit.

- Every sale generates this much to cover fixed costs.

- Consequently, if we divide fixed costs by the unit contribution margin, we know how many units we need to sell to break even.

## Contribution Margin Ratio

When a company has numerous products, it is not practical to determine the unit contribution margin for each product. In this case, using the contribution margin ratio is very useful for determining the break-even point in total dollars (rather than units).

- Recall that the contribution margin ratio is the percentage of each dollar of sales that is available to cover fixed costs and generate net income.
- Therefore, **to determine the sales dollars needed to cover fixed costs,** we divide fixed costs by the contribution margin ratio, as shown in **Illustration 13.22**.

| Fixed Costs | ÷ | Contribution Margin Ratio | = | Break-Even Point in Dollars |
|:---:|:---:|:---:|:---:|:---:|
| $200,000 | ÷ | 40% | = | $500,000 |

**ILLUSTRATION 13.22**
**Formula for break-even point in dollars using contribution margin ratio**

To apply this formula to Vargo Electronics, consider that its 40% contribution margin ratio means that for every dollar sold, it generates 40 cents of contribution margin. The question is, how many dollars of sales does Vargo need in order to generate total contribution margin of $200,000 to pay off fixed costs? We divide the fixed costs of $200,000 by the 40 cents of contribution margin generated by each dollar of sales to arrive at $500,000 ($200,000 ÷ 40%). To prove this result, if we generate 40 cents of contribution margin for each dollar of sales, then the total contribution margin generated by $500,000 in sales is $200,000 ($500,000 × 40%).

---

### Service Company Insight   Flightserve

Bill Ling/Photodisc/
Getty Images

#### Charter Flights Offer a Good Deal

The Internet is wringing inefficiencies out of nearly every industry. While commercial aircraft spend roughly 4,000 hours a year in the air, chartered aircraft are flown only 500 hours annually. That means that they are sitting on the ground—not making any money—about 90% of the time.

One company, **Flightserve**, saw a business opportunity in that fact. For about the same cost as a first-class ticket, Flightserve matches up executives with charter flights in small "private jets."

The executive gets a more comfortable ride and avoids the hassle of big airports. Flightserve noted that the average charter jet has eight seats. When all eight seats are full, the company has an 80% profit margin. It breaks even at an average of 3.3 full seats per flight. Another company, **NetJets**, uses an alternative approach to increase utilization of jets and thus reduce fixed costs. It offers shared ownership in private jets.

**Sources:** "Jet Set Go," *The Economist* (March 18, 2000), p. 68; and Doug Gollan, "How NetJets' Private Jet Service Is Making Itself Whole Again," *Forbes* (June 3, 2015).

**How did Flightserve determine that it would break even with 3.3 seats full per flight? (Go to WileyPLUS for this answer and additional questions.)**

---

# Graphic Presentation

An effective way to find the break-even point is to prepare a break-even graph. Because this graph also shows costs, volume, and profits, it is referred to as a **cost-volume-profit (CVP) graph**.

- Sales volume is recorded along the horizontal axis.
- This axis should extend to the maximum level of expected sales.
- Both total revenues (sales) and total costs (fixed plus variable) are recorded on the vertical axis.

An example of a CVP graph is shown in **Illustration 13.23**.

**ILLUSTRATION 13.23**

**CVP graph**

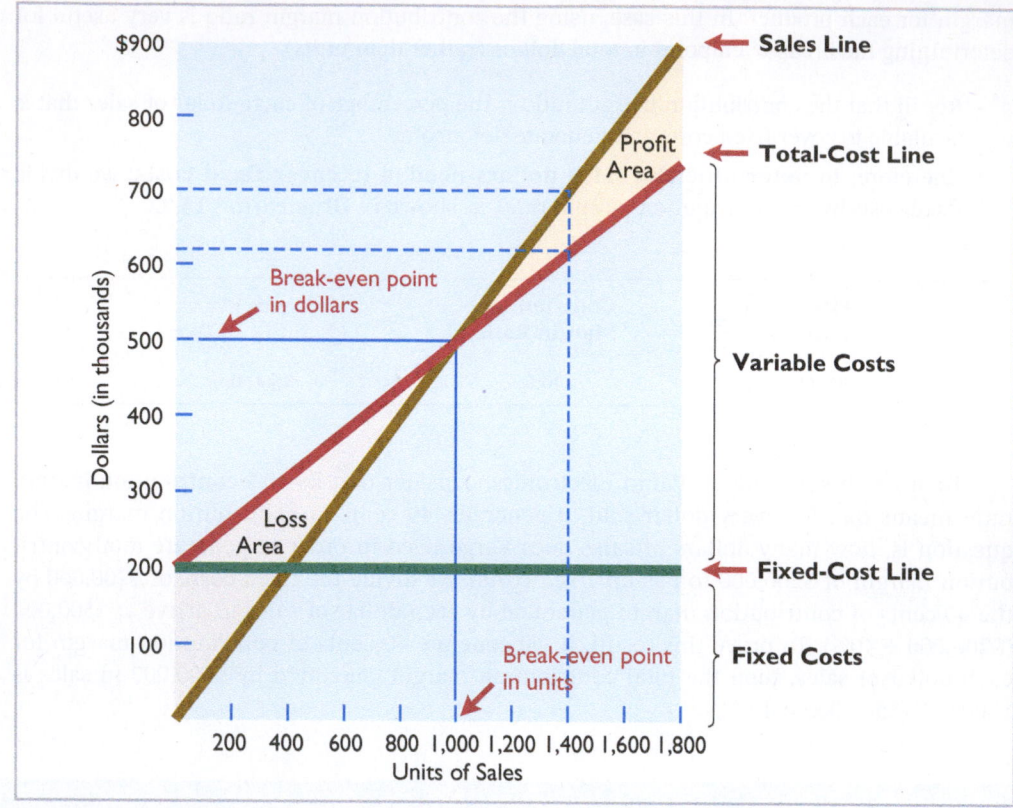

The construction of the graph, using the data for Vargo Electronics, is as follows.

1. Plot the sales line, starting at the zero activity level. For every cell phone sold, total revenue increases by $500. For example, at 200 units, sales are $100,000. At the upper level of activity (1,800 units), sales are $900,000. The revenue line is assumed to be linear through the full range of activity.

2. Plot the total fixed costs using a horizontal line. For the cell phones, this line is plotted at $200,000. The fixed costs are the same at every level of activity.

3. Plot the total-cost line. This starts at the fixed-cost line at zero activity. It increases by the variable costs at each level of activity. For each cell phone, variable costs are $300. Thus, at 200 units, total variable costs are $60,000 ($300 × 200) and the total cost is $260,000 ($60,000 + $200,000). At 1,800 units, total variable costs are $540,000 ($300 × 1,800) and total cost is $740,000 ($540,000 + $200,000). On the graph, the amount of the variable costs can be derived from the difference between the total-cost and fixed-cost lines at each level of activity.

4. Determine the break-even point from the intersection of the total-cost line and the sales line. The break-even point in dollars is found by drawing a horizontal line from the break-even point to the vertical axis. The break-even point in units is found by drawing a vertical line from the break-even point to the horizontal axis. For the cell phones, the break-even point is $500,000 of sales, or 1,000 units. At this sales level, Vargo will cover costs but make no profit.

The CVP graph also shows both the net income and net loss areas. Thus, the amount of income or loss at each level of sales can be derived from the sales and total-cost lines.

A CVP graph is useful because the effects of a change in any element in the CVP analysis can be quickly seen. For example, a 10% increase in selling price will change the location of the sales line. Likewise, the effects on total costs of wage increases can be quickly observed.

## DO IT! 4 | Break-Even Analysis

Lombardi Company has a unit selling price of $400, variable costs per unit of $240, and fixed costs of $180,000. Compute the break-even point in units using (a) a mathematical equation and (b) unit contribution margin.

### Solution

a. The equation is $400Q − $240Q − $180,000 = $0; ($400Q − $240Q) = $180,000. The break-even point in units is 1,125.

b. The unit contribution margin is $160 ($400 − $240). The formula therefore is $180,000 ÷ $160, and the break-even point in units is 1,125.

Related exercise material: **BE13.8, BE13.9, DO IT! 13.4, E13.8, E13.9, E13.10, E13.11, E13.12, and E13.13.**

**ACTION PLAN**

- Apply the profit equation: Sales − Variable costs − Fixed costs = Net income.

- Apply the break-even formula: Fixed costs ÷ Unit contribution margin = Break-even point in units.

# Target Net Income and Margin of Safety

**LEARNING OBJECTIVE 5**

Determine the sales required to earn target net income and determine margin of safety.

## Target Net Income

Rather than simply "breaking even," management usually sets an income objective often called **target net income**. It then determines the sales necessary to achieve this specified level of income by using one of the three approaches discussed earlier.

### Mathematical Equation

We know that at the break-even point no profit or loss results for the company. By adding an amount for target net income to the same basic equation, we obtain the formula shown in **Illustration 13.24** for determining required sales.

$$\text{Sales} \quad - \quad \begin{array}{c}\text{Variable} \\ \text{Costs}\end{array} \quad - \quad \begin{array}{c}\text{Fixed} \\ \text{Costs}\end{array} \quad = \quad \begin{array}{c}\text{Target Net} \\ \text{Income}\end{array}$$

**ILLUSTRATION 13.24**

Formula for sales to meet target net income

Recall that once the break-even point has been reached so that fixed costs are covered, each additional unit sold increases net income by the amount of the unit contribution margin. We can rewrite the equation with contribution margin (sales minus variable costs) on the left-hand side, and fixed costs and target net income on the right. Assuming that target net income is $120,000 for Vargo Electronics, the computation of required sales in units is as shown in **Illustration 13.25**.

**ILLUSTRATION 13.25**
**Computation of required sales**

| | Sales | − | Variable Costs | − | Fixed Costs | = | Target Net Income |
|---|---|---|---|---|---|---|---|
| | $500Q | − | $300Q | − | $200,000 | = | $120,000 |
| | $500Q | − | $300Q | = | $200,000 | + | $120,000 |

$$\$200Q = \$200,000 + \$120,000$$

$$Q = \frac{\$200,000 + \$120,000}{\$200} = \frac{\textbf{Fixed Costs + Target Net Income}}{\textbf{Unit Contribution Margin}}$$

$$Q = 1,600$$

where

$Q$ = number of units sold
$500 = unit selling price
$300 = unit variable costs
$200,000 = total fixed costs
$120,000 = target net income

Vargo must sell 1,600 units to achieve target net income of $120,000. The sales dollars required to achieve the target net income is found by multiplying the units sold by the unit selling price [(1,600 × $500) = $800,000].

## Contribution Margin Technique

As in the case of break-even sales, we can compute in either units or dollars the sales required to meet target net income. The formula to compute required sales in units for Vargo Electronics using the unit contribution margin can be seen in the final step of the equation approach in Illustration 13.25 (shown in red). We simply divide the sum of fixed costs and target net income by the unit contribution margin. **Illustration 13.26** shows this for Vargo.

**ILLUSTRATION 13.26**
**Formula for sales in units using unit contribution margin**

| $\begin{pmatrix} \textbf{Fixed Costs +} \\ \textbf{Target Net Income} \end{pmatrix}$ | ÷ | Unit Contribution Margin | = | Sales in Units |
|---|---|---|---|---|
| ($200,000 + $120,000) | ÷ | $200 | = | 1,600 units |

To achieve its desired target net income of $120,000, Vargo must sell 1,600 cell phones.

**Illustration 13.27** presents the formula to compute the required sales in dollars for Vargo using the contribution margin ratio.

**ILLUSTRATION 13.27**
**Formula for sales in dollars using contribution margin ratio**

| $\begin{pmatrix} \textbf{Fixed Costs +} \\ \textbf{Target Net Income} \end{pmatrix}$ | ÷ | Contribution Margin Ratio | = | Sales in Dollars |
|---|---|---|---|---|
| ($200,000 + $120,000) | ÷ | 40% | = | $800,000 |

To achieve its desired target net income of $120,000, Vargo must generate sales of $800,000.

## Graphic Presentation

We also can use the CVP graph in Illustration 13.23 to find the sales required to meet target net income.

- In the profit area of the graph, the distance between the sales line and the total-cost line at any point equals net income.
- We can find required sales by analyzing the differences between the two lines until the desired net income is found.

For example, suppose Vargo Electronics sells 1,400 cell phones. Illustration 13.23 shows that a vertical line drawn at 1,400 units intersects the sales line at $700,000 and the total-cost line at $620,000. The difference between the two amounts represents the net income (profit) of $80,000.

## Margin of Safety

**Margin of safety** is the difference between actual or expected sales and sales at the break-even point.

- It measures the "cushion" that a particular level of sales provides.
- It tells us how far sales could fall before the company begins operating at a loss.
- The margin of safety is expressed in dollars or as a ratio.

The formula for stating the **margin of safety in dollars** is actual (or expected) sales minus break-even sales. **Illustration 13.28** shows the computation for Vargo Electronics, assuming that actual (expected) sales are $750,000.

| Actual (Expected) Sales | − | Break-Even Sales | = | Margin of Safety in Dollars |
|---|---|---|---|---|
| $750,000 | − | $500,000 | = | $250,000 |

**ILLUSTRATION 13.28**

**Formula for margin of safety in dollars**

Vargo's margin of safety is $250,000. Its sales could fall $250,000 before it operates at a loss.

The **margin of safety ratio** is the margin of safety in dollars divided by actual (or expected) sales. **Illustration 13.29** shows the formula and computation for determining the margin of safety ratio.

| Margin of Safety in Dollars | ÷ | Actual (Expected) Sales | = | Margin of Safety Ratio |
|---|---|---|---|---|
| $250,000 | ÷ | $750,000 | = | 33% |

**ILLUSTRATION 13.29**

**Formula for margin of safety ratio**

This means that the company's sales could fall by 33% before it operates at a loss.

**The higher the margin of safety in dollars or the percentage, the lower the risk that the company will operate at a loss.** Management evaluates the adequacy of the margin of safety in terms of such factors as the vulnerability of the product to competitive pressures and to downturns in the economy.

---

### Service Company Insight   Rolling Stones

YAMIL LAGE/AFP/ Getty Images

#### How a Rolling Stones' Tour Makes Money

Computations of break-even and margin of safety are important for service companies. Consider how the promoter for the **Rolling Stones**' tour used the break-even point and margin of safety. For example, say one outdoor show should bring 70,000 individuals for ticket sales of $2.45 million. The promoter guarantees $1.2 million to the Rolling Stones. In addition, 20% of ticket sales goes to the stadium in which the performance is staged. Add another $400,000 for other expenses such as ticket takers, parking attendants, advertising, and so on. The promoter also shares in sales of T-shirts and memorabilia for which the promoter will net over $7 million during the tour. From a successful Rolling Stones' tour, the promoter could make $35 million!

**What amount of sales dollars are required for the promoter to break even?** (Go to WileyPLUS for this answer and additional questions.)

## DO IT! 5 | Break-Even, Margin of Safety, and Target Net Income

Zootsuit Inc. makes travel bags that sell for $56 each. For the coming year, management expects fixed costs to total $320,000 and variable costs to be $42 per unit. Compute the following: (a) break-even point in dollars using the contribution margin (CM) ratio; (b) the margin of safety and margin of safety ratio assuming actual sales are $1,382,400; and (c) the sales dollars required to earn net income of $410,000.

### Solution

a. Contribution margin ratio = [($56 − $42) ÷ $56] = 25%

   Break-even sales in dollars = $320,000 ÷ 25% = $1,280,000

b. Margin of safety = $1,382,400 − $1,280,000 = $102,400

   Margin of safety ratio = $102,400 ÷ $1,382,400 = 7.4%

c. Sales in dollars = ($320,000 + $410,000) ÷ 25% = $2,920,000

Related exercise material: **BE13.10, BE13.11, BE13.12, DO IT! 13.5, E13.14, E13.15, E13.16, and E13.17.**

## USING THE DECISION TOOLS | Amazon.com

**Amazon.com** faces many situations where it needs to apply the decision tools presented in this chapter, such as calculating the break-even point to determine a product's profitability. Amazon's dominance of the online retail space, selling other company's products, is well known. But not everyone may realize that Amazon also sells its own private-label electronics, including USB cables, mice, keyboards, and audio cables, under the brand name AmazonBasics. Assume that Amazon's management was provided with the following information regarding the production and sales of Bluetooth keyboards for tablet computers for 2022.

**Cost Schedules**

| | |
|---|---|
| Variable costs | |
|     Direct labor per keyboard | $ 8.00 |
|     Direct materials | 4.00 |
|     Variable overhead | 3.00 |
| Variable cost per keyboard | $15.00 |
| | |
| Fixed costs | |
|     Manufacturing | $ 25,000 |
|     Selling | 40,000 |
|     Administrative | 70,000 |
| Total fixed costs | $135,000 |
| | |
| Selling price per keyboard | $25.00 |
| Sales, 2022 (20,000 keyboards) | $500,000 |

### Instructions

(Ignore any income tax considerations.)

a. What is the operating income for 2022?

b. What is the unit contribution margin for 2022?

c. What is the break-even point in units for 2022?

d. Assume that management set the sales target for the year 2023 at a level of $550,000 (22,000 keyboards). Amazon's management believes that to attain the sales target in 2023, the company must incur an additional selling expense of $10,000 for advertising in 2023, with all other costs remaining constant. What will be the break-even point in sales dollars for 2023 if the company spends the additional $10,000?

e. If the company spends the additional $10,000 for advertising in 2023, what is the sales level in dollars required to equal 2022 operating income?

## Solution

**a.** Sales $500,000

Less:
    Variable costs (20,000 keyboards × $15)     300,000
    Fixed costs     135,000
Operating income     $ 65,000

**b.** Selling price per keyboard     $25
Variable cost per keyboard     15
Unit contribution margin     $10

**c.** Fixed costs ÷ Unit contribution margin = Break-even point in units: $135,000 ÷ $10 = 13,500 units

**d.** Fixed costs ÷ Contribution margin ratio = Break-even point in dollars: $145,000* ÷ 40%** = $362,500

    *Fixed costs     $135,000
     Additional advertising expense     10,000
     Revised fixed costs     $145,000

    **Contribution margin ratio = Unit contribution margin ÷ Unit selling price: 40% = $10 ÷ $25

**e.** Sales = (Fixed costs + Target net income) ÷ Contribution margin ratio

    $525,000 = ($145,000 + $65,000) ÷ 40%

---

| Appendix 13A | # Regression Analysis |
| --- | --- |

**LEARNING OBJECTIVE \*6**

Describe how regression analysis is used to classify mixed costs.

The high-low method is often used to estimate fixed and variable costs for a mixed-cost situation. An advantage of the high-low method is that it is easy to apply. But, how accurate and reliable is the estimated cost equation that it produces? For example, consider the example shown in **Illustration 13A.1**, which indicates the cost equation line produced by the high-low method for Metro Transit Company's maintenance costs. How well does the high-low method represent the relationship between miles driven and total cost? This line is close to, and in some cases bisects, nearly all of the data points. Therefore, in this case, the high-low method provides a cost equation that is a very good fit for this data set. It identifies fixed and variable costs in an accurate and reliable way.

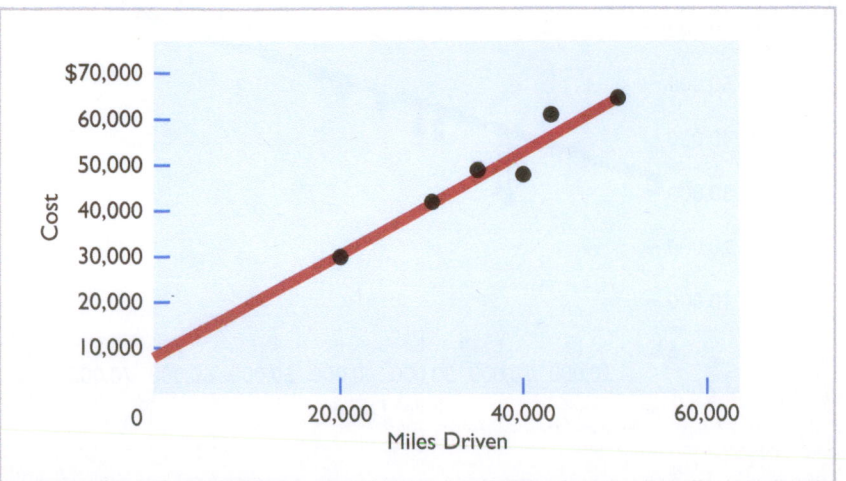

**ILLUSTRATION 13A.1**

**Scatter plot for Metro Transit Company**

While the high-low method works well for the Metro Transit data set, a weakness of this method is that it employs only two data points and ignores the rest.

- If those two data points are representative of the entire data set, then the high-low method provides reasonable results (as seen in Illustration 13A.1).
- But, if the high and low data points are not representative of the rest of the data set, then the results are misleading.

To illustrate, assume that Hanson Trucking Company has 12 months of maintenance cost data, as shown in **Illustration 13A.2**.

**ILLUSTRATION 13A.2**

**Maintenance costs and mileage data for Hanson Trucking Company**

| Month | Miles Driven | Total Cost | Month | Miles Driven | Total Cost |
|-------|-------------|-----------|-------|-------------|-----------|
| January | 20,000 | $30,000 | July | 15,000 | $39,000 |
| February | 40,000 | 49,000 | August | 28,000 | 41,000 |
| March | 35,000 | 46,000 | September | 60,000 | 72,000 |
| April | 50,000 | 63,000 | October | 55,000 | 67,000 |
| May | 30,000 | 42,000 | November | 19,000 | 29,000 |
| June | 43,000 | 52,000 | December | 65,000 | 63,000 |

The high and low activities are 65,000 miles in December and 15,000 miles in July. The maintenance costs at these two levels are $63,000 and $39,000, respectively. The difference in maintenance costs is $24,000 ($63,000 − $39,000), and the difference in miles is 50,000 (65,000 − 15,000). Therefore, for Hanson Trucking, variable cost per unit under the high-low method is $0.48 ($24,000 ÷ 50,000). To determine total variable cost, we multiply the number of miles by cost per mile. For example, at the low activity level of 15,000 miles, total variable cost is $7,200 (15,000 × $0.48). To determine fixed costs, we subtract total variable costs at the low activity level from the total cost at the low activity level ($39,000) as follows.

$$\text{Fixed costs} = \$39,000 - (\$0.48 \times 15,000) = \$31,800$$

Therefore, the cost equation based on the high-low method for this data produces the following formula:

| Maintenance costs | = | Intercept | + | Slope |
|-------------------|---|-----------|---|-------|
| | = | $31,800 | + | ($0.48 × Miles driven) |

**Illustration 13A.3** shows a scatter plot of the data with a line representing the high-low method cost equation.

**ILLUSTRATION 13A.3**

**Scatter plot for Hanson Trucking Company**

- Note that most of the data points for Hanson Trucking are a significant distance from the line.

- For example, at 19,000 miles, the observed maintenance cost is $29,000, but the equation predicts $40,920 [$31,800 + ($0.48 × 19,000)]. That is a difference of $11,920 ($40,920 − $29,000).

- In this case, the high-low method cost equation does not provide a good representation of the relationship between miles driven and maintenance costs.

To derive a more representative cost equation, the company should employ regression analysis. **Regression analysis** is a statistical approach that estimates the cost equation by employing information from all data points, not just the highest and lowest ones. While it involves mathematical analysis taught in statistics courses (which we will not address here), we can provide you with a basic understanding of how regression analysis works.

Consider Illustration 13A.3, which highlights the distance that each data point is from the high-low cost equation line. What regression analysis does is to find a cost equation that results in a cost equation line that minimizes the sum of the squared distances from the line to the data points.

Many software packages perform regression analysis. In **Illustration 13A.4**, we use the **Intercept** and **Slope** functions in Excel to estimate the regression equation for the Hanson Trucking Company data.[1] The Excel video provided in WileyPLUS demonstrates the use of the Intercept and Slope functions.

**ILLUSTRATION 13A.4**

**Excel spreadsheet for Hanson Trucking Company**

| | A | B | C | D |
|---|---|---|---|---|
| | | Hanson Trucking | | |
| | E2 | fx | | |
| 1 | Month | Miles Driven | Total Cost | |
| 2 | January | 20,000 | 30,000 | |
| 3 | February | 40,000 | 49,000 | |
| 4 | March | 35,000 | 46,000 | |
| 5 | April | 50,000 | 63,000 | |
| 6 | May | 30,000 | 42,000 | |
| 7 | June | 43,000 | 52,000 | |
| 8 | July | 15,000 | 39,000 | |
| 9 | August | 28,000 | 41,000 | |
| 10 | September | 60,000 | 72,000 | |
| 11 | October | 55,000 | 67,000 | |
| 12 | November | 19,000 | 29,000 | |
| 13 | December | 65,000 | 63,000 | |
| 14 | | | | |
| 15 | | Formula | | |
| 16 | Intercept | =INTERCEPT(C2:C13,B2:B13) | 18,502 | |
| 17 | Slope | =SLOPE(C2:C13,B2:B13) | 0.81 | |
| 18 | | | | |

The resulting cost equation is:

| Maintenance costs | = | Intercept | + | Slope |
|---|---|---|---|---|
| | = | $18,502 | + | ($0.81 × Miles driven) |

Compare this to the high-low cost equation:

| Maintenance costs | = | Intercept | + | Slope |
|---|---|---|---|---|
| | = | $31,800 | + | ($0.48 × Miles driven) |

[1] To use the Intercept and Slope functions in Excel, enter your data in two columns in an Excel spreadsheet. The first column should be your "X" variable (miles driven, cells B2 to B13 in our example). The second column should be your "Y" variable (maintenance costs, cells C2 to C13 in our example). Next, in a separate cell, choosing from Excel's statistical functions, enter =Intercept(C2:C13,B2:B13) and in a different cell enter =Slope(C2:C13,B2:B13).

As **Illustration 13A.5** shows, the intercept and slope differ significantly between the regression equation (green) and the high-low equation (red).[2]

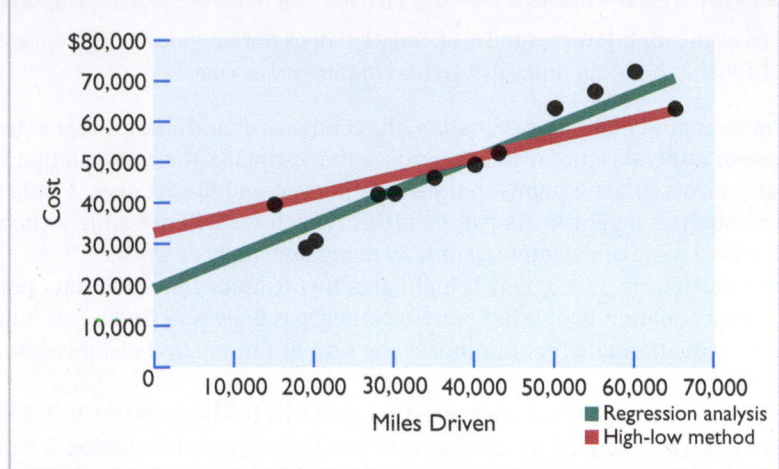

- The regression cost equation line does not bisect the high and low data points but instead follows a path that minimizes the cumulative distance from all of the data points.
- By doing so, it provides a cost equation that is more representative of the relationship between miles driven and total maintenance costs than the high-low method.

Why should managers care about the accuracy of the cost equation? Managers make many decisions that require that mixed costs be separated into fixed and variable components. Inaccurate classifications of these costs might cause a manager to make an inappropriate decision. For example, Hanson Trucking Company's break-even point differs significantly depending on which of these two cost equations was used. If Hanson Trucking relies on the high-low method, it would have a distorted view of the level of sales it would need in order to break even. In addition, misrepresentation for fixed and variable costs could result in inappropriate decisions, such as whether to discontinue a product line. It would also result in inaccurate product costing under activity-based costing.

While regression analysis usually provides more reliable estimates of the cost equation, it does have its limitations.

1. The regression approach that we applied above assumes a linear relationship between the variables (that is, an increase or decrease in one variable results in a proportional increase or decrease in the other). If the actual relationship differs significantly from linearity, then linear regression can provide misleading results. (Nonlinear regression is addressed in advanced statistics courses.)

2. Regression estimates can be severely influenced by "outliers"—data points that differ significantly from the rest of the observations. It is therefore good practice to plot data points in a scatter graph to identify outliers and then investigate the reasons why they differ. In some cases, outliers must be adjusted for or eliminated.

3. Regression estimation is most accurate when it is based on a large number of data points. However, collecting data can be time-consuming and costly. In some cases, there simply are not enough observable data points to arrive at a reliable estimate.

---

[2] To plot a scatter graph in Excel, highlight the data and then click on Scatter under the Insert tab. To draw the cost equation line, click on the scatter plot, then select Layout and Trendline. In order to get the cost equation line to intercept the Y axis, under Trendline Options in the Backward field, enter the lowest value of your X variable. For example, for Hanson Trucking, we entered 15,000.

# Review and Practice

## Learning Objectives Review

**1**   Explain variable, fixed, and mixed costs and the relevant range.

Variable costs are costs that vary in total directly and proportionately with changes in the activity index. Fixed costs are costs that remain the same in total regardless of changes in the activity index.

The relevant range is the range of activity in which a company expects to operate during a year. It is important in CVP analysis because the behavior of costs is assumed to be linear throughout the relevant range.

Mixed costs change in total but not proportionately with changes in the activity level. For purposes of CVP analysis, mixed costs must be classified into their fixed and variable elements.

**2**   Apply the high-low method to determine the components of mixed costs.

Determine the variable costs per unit by dividing the change in total costs at the highest and lowest levels of activity by the difference in activity at those levels. Then, determine fixed costs by subtracting total variable costs from the amount of total costs at either the highest or lowest level of activity.

**3**   Prepare a CVP income statement to determine contribution margin.

The five components of CVP analysis are (1) volume or level of activity, (2) unit selling prices, (3) variable costs per unit, (4) total fixed costs, and (5) sales mix. Contribution margin is the amount of revenue remaining after deducting variable costs. It is identified in a CVP income statement, which classifies costs as variable or fixed. It can be expressed as a total amount, as a per unit amount, or as a ratio.

**4**   Compute the break-even point using three approaches.

The break-even point can be (a) computed from a mathematical equation, (b) computed by using a contribution margin technique, and (c) derived from a CVP graph.

**5**   Determine the sales required to earn target net income and determine margin of safety.

The general formula for required sales is Sales − Variable costs − Fixed costs = Target net income. Two other formulas are (1) Sales in units = (Fixed costs + Target net income) ÷ Unit contribution margin, and (2) Sales in dollars = (Fixed costs + Target net income) ÷ Contribution margin ratio.

Margin of safety is the difference between actual or expected sales and sales at the break-even point. The formulas for margin of safety are (1) Actual (expected) sales − Break-even sales = Margin of safety in dollars, and (2) Margin of safety in dollars ÷ Actual (expected) sales = Margin of safety ratio.

**\*6**   Describe how regression analysis is used to classify mixed costs.

The high-low method provides a quick estimate of the cost equation for a mixed cost. However, the high-low method is based on only the highest and lowest data points. Regression analysis provides an estimate of the cost equation based on all data points. The cost equation line that results from regression analysis minimizes the sum of the (squared) distances of all of the data points from the cost equation line. Computer programs such as Excel enable easy estimation of the cost equation with regression.

## Decision Tools Review

| Decision Checkpoints | Info Needed for Decision | Tool to Use for Decision | | | How to Evaluate Results |
|---|---|---|---|---|---|
| What was the contribution toward fixed costs and income from each unit sold? | Selling price per unit and variable cost per unit | Unit contribution margin | = Unit selling price | − Unit variable cost | Every unit sold will increase income by the contribution margin. |
| What would be the increase in income as a result of an increase in sales? | Unit contribution margin and unit selling price | Contribution margin ratio | = Unit contribution margin | ÷ Unit selling price | Every dollar of sales will increase income by the contribution margin ratio. |

*(continues)*

*(continued)*

| Decision Checkpoints | Info Needed for Decision | Tool to Use for Decision | How to Evaluate Results |
|---|---|---|---|
| At what amount of sales does a company cover its costs? | Unit selling price, unit variable cost, and total fixed costs | Break-even point analysis<br><br>*In units:*<br><br>$$\text{Break-even point} = \frac{\text{Fixed costs}}{\text{Unit contribution margin}}$$<br><br>*In dollars:*<br><br>$$\text{Break-even point} = \frac{\text{Fixed costs}}{\text{Contribution margin ratio}}$$ | Below the break-even point, the company is unprofitable. |

## Glossary Review

**Activity index** The activity that causes changes in the behavior of costs. (p. 13-3).

**Break-even point** The level of activity at which total revenue equals total costs. (p. 13-13).

**Contribution margin (CM)** The amount of revenue remaining after deducting variable costs. (p. 13-12).

**Contribution margin ratio** The percentage of each dollar of sales that is available to apply to fixed costs and contribute to net income; calculated as unit contribution margin divided by unit selling price. (p. 13-14).

**Cost behavior analysis** The study of how specific costs respond to changes in the level of business activity. (p. 13-2).

**Cost-volume-profit (CVP) analysis** The study of the effects of changes in costs and volume on a company's profits. (p. 13-11).

**Cost-volume-profit (CVP) graph** A graph showing the relationship between costs, volume, and profits. (p. 13-17).

**Cost-volume-profit (CVP) income statement** A statement for internal use that classifies costs as fixed or variable and reports contribution margin in the body of the statement. (p. 13-11).

**Fixed costs** Costs that remain the same in total regardless of changes in the activity level. (p. 13-4).

**High-low method** A mathematical method that uses the total costs incurred at the high and low levels of activity to classify mixed costs into fixed and variable components. (p. 13-8).

**Margin of safety** The difference between actual or expected sales and sales at the break-even point. (p. 13-21).

**Mixed costs** Costs that contain both a variable- and a fixed-cost element and change in total but not proportionately with changes in the activity level. (p. 13-6).

**\*Regression analysis** A statistical approach that estimates the cost equation by employing information from all data points to find the cost equation line that minimizes the sum of the squared distances from the line to the data points. (p. 13-25).

**Relevant range** The range of the activity index over which the company expects to operate during the year. (p. 13-6).

**Target net income** The income objective set by management. (p. 13-19).

**Unit contribution margin** The amount of revenue remaining per unit after deducting variable costs; calculated as unit selling price minus unit variable costs. (p. 13-12).

**Variable costs** Costs that vary in total directly and proportionately with changes in the activity level. (p. 13-3).

## Practice Multiple-Choice Questions

1. **(LO 1)** Variable costs are costs that:
   a. vary in total directly and proportionately with changes in the activity level.
   b. remain the same per unit at every activity level.
   c. neither vary in total directly and proportionately with changes in the activity level nor remain the same per unit at every activity level.
   d. both vary in total directly and proportionately with changes in the activity level and remain the same per unit at every activity level.

2. **(LO 2)** The relevant range is:
   a. the range of activity in which variable costs will be curvilinear.
   b. the range of activity in which fixed costs will be curvilinear.
   c. the range over which the company expects to operate during a year.
   d. usually from zero to 100% of operating capacity.

3. **(LO 1, 2)** Mixed costs consist of a:
   a. variable-cost element and a fixed-cost element.
   b. fixed-cost element and a product-cost element.
   c. period-cost element and a product-cost element.
   d. variable-cost element and a period-cost element.

4. **(LO 1, 2)** Your cell phone service provider offers a plan that is classified as a mixed cost. The cost for 1,000 minutes in a month is $50. If you use 2,000 minutes this month, your cost will be:
   a. $50.
   b. $100.
   c. more than $100.
   d. between $50 and $100.

**5. (LO 2)** Kendra Corporation's total utility costs during the past year were $1,200 during its highest month and $600 during its lowest month. These costs corresponded with 10,000 units of production during the high month and 2,000 units during the low month. What are the fixed and variable components of its utility costs using the high-low method?

    **a.** $0.075 variable and $450 fixed.

    **b.** $0.120 variable and $0 fixed.

    **c.** $0.300 variable and $0 fixed.

    **d.** $0.060 variable and $600 fixed.

**6. (LO 3)** Which of the following is **not** involved in CVP analysis?

    **a.** Sales mix.     **c.** Fixed costs per unit.

    **b.** Unit selling prices.     **d.** Volume or level of activity.

**7. (LO 3)** When comparing a traditional income statement to a CVP income statement:

    **a.** net income will always be greater on the traditional statement.

    **b.** net income will always be less on the traditional statement.

    **c.** net income will always be identical on both.

    **d.** net income will be greater or less depending on the sales volume.

**8. (LO 3)** Contribution margin:

    **a.** is revenue remaining after deducting variable costs.

    **b.** may be expressed as unit contribution margin.

    **c.** is selling price less cost of goods sold.

    **d.** is revenue remaining after deducting variable costs and may be expressed as unit contribution margin.

**9. (LO 3)** Cournot Company sells 100,000 wrenches for $12 a unit. Fixed costs are $300,000, and net income is $200,000. What should be reported as variable expenses in the CVP income statement?

    **a.** $700,000.     **c.** $500,000.

    **b.** $900,000.     **d.** $1,000,000.

**10. (LO 4)** Gossen Company is planning to sell 200,000 pliers for $4 per unit. The contribution margin ratio is 25%. If Gossen will break even at this level of sales, what are the fixed costs?

    **a.** $100,000.     **c.** $200,000.

    **b.** $160,000.     **d.** $300,000.

**11. (LO 4)** Brownstone Company's contribution margin ratio is 30%. If Brownstone's sales revenue is $100 greater than its break-even sales in dollars, its net income:

    **a.** will be $100.

    **b.** will be $70.

    **c.** will be $30.

    **d.** cannot be determined without knowing fixed costs.

**12. (LO 5)** The mathematical equation for computing required sales to obtain target net income is:

    **a.** Variable costs + Target net income.

    **b.** Variable costs + Fixed costs + Target net income.

    **c.** Fixed costs + Target net income.

    **d.** No correct answer is given.

**13. (LO 5)** Margin of safety is computed as:

    **a.** Actual sales − Break-even sales.

    **b.** Contribution margin − Fixed costs.

    **c.** Break-even sales − Variable costs.

    **d.** Actual sales − Contribution margin.

**14. (LO 5)** Marshall Company had actual sales of $600,000 when break-even sales were $420,000. What is the margin of safety ratio?

    **a.** 25%.     **c.** $33\frac{1}{3}$%.

    **b.** 30%.     **d.** 45%.

## Solutions

**1. d.** Variable costs vary in total directly and proportionately with changes in the activity level and remain the same per unit at every activity level. Choices (a) and (b) are correct, but (d) is the better and more complete answer. Since (a) and (b) are both true statements, choice (c) is incorrect.

**2. c.** The relevant range is the range over which the company expects to operate during a year. The other choices are incorrect because the relevant range is the range over which (a) variable costs are expected to be linear, not curvilinear, and (b) the company expects fixed costs to remain the same. Choice (d) is incorrect because this answer does not specifically define relevant range.

**3. a.** Mixed costs consist of a variable-cost element and a fixed-cost element, not (b) a product-cost element, (c) a period-cost element or a product-cost element, or (d) a period-cost element.

**4. d.** Your cost will include the fixed-cost component (flat service fee), which does not increase, plus the variable cost (usage charge) for the additional 1,000 minutes, which will increase your cost to between $50 and $100. Therefore, choices (a) $50, (b) $100, and (c) more than $100 are incorrect.

**5. a.** Variable is $0.075 [($1,200 − $600) ÷ (10,000 − 2,000)] and fixed is $450 [($1,200 − ($0.075 × 10,000)]. Therefore, choices (b) $0.120 variable and $0 fixed, (c) $0.300 variable and $0 fixed, and (d) $0.060 variable and $600 fixed are incorrect.

**6. c.** Total fixed costs, not fixed costs per unit, are involved in CVP analysis. Choices (a) sales mix, (b) unit selling prices, and (d) volume or level of activity are all involved in CVP analysis.

**7. c.** Net income will always be identical on both a traditional income statement and a CVP income statement. Therefore, choices (a), (b), and (d) are incorrect statements.

**8. d.** Contribution margin is revenue remaining after deducting variable costs and it may be expressed on a per unit basis. Choices (a) and (b) are accurate, but (d) is a better answer. Choice (c) is incorrect because it defines gross margin, not contribution margin.

**9. a.** Contribution margin is equal to fixed costs plus net income ($300,000 + $200,000 = $500,000). Since variable expenses are the difference between total sales ($1,200,000) and contribution margin ($500,000), $700,000 must be the amount of variable expenses in the CVP income statement. Therefore, choices (b) $900,000, (c) $500,000, and (d) $1,000,000 are incorrect.

**10. c.** Unit contribution margin is $1 ($4 × 25%). Fixed costs ÷ Unit contribution margin = Break-even point in units. Solving for fixed costs, 200,000 units × $1 per unit = $200,000, not (a) $100,000, (b) $160,000, or (d) $300,000.

**11. c.** If Brownstone's sales revenue is $100 greater than its break-even sales in dollars, its net income will be $30 or ($100 × 30%), not (a) $100 or (b) $70. Choice (d) is incorrect because net income can be determined without knowing fixed costs.

**12. b.** The correct equation is Sales = Variable costs + Fixed costs + Target net income. The other choices are incorrect because (a) needs fixed costs added, (c) needs variable costs added, and (d) there is a correct answer given (b).

**13. a.** Margin of safety is computed as Actual sales − Break-even sales. Therefore, choices (b) Contribution margin − Fixed costs, (c) Break-even sales − Variable costs, and (d) Actual sales − Contribution margin are incorrect.

**14. b.** The margin of safety ratio is computed by dividing the margin of safety in dollars of $180,000 ($600,000 − $420,000) by actual sales of $600,000. The result is 30% ($180,000 ÷ $600,000), not (a) 25%, (c) $33\frac{1}{3}$%, or (d) 45%.

---

## Practice Brief Exercises

*Determine variable- and fixed-cost elements using the high-low method.*

**1. (LO 2)** Benji Company accumulates the following data concerning a mixed cost, using miles as the activity level.

| | Miles Driven | Total Cost | | Miles Driven | Total Cost |
|---|---|---|---|---|---|
| January | 7,500 | $20,000 | March | 8,500 | $22,000 |
| February | 8,200 | 21,100 | April | 8,300 | 21,750 |

Compute the variable- and fixed-cost elements using the high-low method.

### Solution

**1.**

| High | | Low | | Difference |
|---|---|---|---|---|
| $22,000 | − | $20,000 | = | $2,000 |
| 8,500 | − | 7,500 | = | 1,000 |

Variable cost per mile = $2,000 ÷ 1,000 = $2.00.

| | High | Low |
|---|---|---|
| Total cost | $22,000 | $20,000 |
| Less: Variable costs | | |
| 8,500 × $2.00 | 17,000 | |
| 7,500 × $2.00 | | 15,000 |
| Total fixed costs | $ 5,000 | $ 5,000 |

Mixed cost is $5,000 plus $2.00 per mile.

---

*Determine missing amounts for contribution margin.*

**2. (LO 3)** Determine the missing amounts.

| Unit Selling Price | Unit Variable Costs | Unit Contribution Margin | Contribution Margin Ratio |
|---|---|---|---|
| $800 | $520 | (a) | (b) |
| 500 | (c) | $200 | (d) |
| (e) | (f) | 450 | 45% |

### Solution

**2. a.** ($800 − $520) = $280

**b.** ($280 ÷ $800) = 35%

**c.** ($500 − $200) = $300

**d.** ($200 ÷ $500) = 40%

**e.** ($450 ÷ 45%) = $1,000

**f.** ($1,000 − $450) = $550

**3. (LO 4)** Jacob Company has a unit selling price of $600, variable costs per unit of $216, and fixed costs of $2,438,400. Compute the break-even point in units using (a) the mathematical equation and (b) unit contribution margin.

*Compute the break-even point.*

### Solution

3. **a.** $600Q − $216Q − $2,438,400 = $0

   $384Q = $2,438,400

   Q = 6,350 units

   **b.** Contribution margin per unit = ($600 − $216) = $384

   Unit contribution margin = $2,438,400 ÷ $384 = 6,350 units

**4. (LO 5)** For Posh Company, actual sales are $1,500,000, and break-even sales are $1,300,000. Compute (a) the margin of safety in dollars and (b) the margin of safety ratio.

*Compute the margin of safety and margin of safety ratio.*

### Solution

4. **a.** Margin of safety = $1,500,000 − $1,300,000 = $200,000

   **b.** Margin of safety ratio = $200,000 ÷ $1,500,000 = 13.3%

## Practice Exercises

**1. (LO 1, 2)** The controller of Teton Industries has collected the following monthly expense data for use in analyzing the cost behavior of maintenance costs.

*Determine fixed and variable costs using the high-low method and prepare graph.*

| Month | Total Maintenance Costs | Total Machine Hours |
|---|---|---|
| January | $2,900 | 300 |
| February | 3,000 | 400 |
| March | 3,600 | 600 |
| April | 4,300 | 790 |
| May | 3,200 | 500 |
| June | 4,500 | 800 |

### Instructions

**a.** Determine the fixed-cost and variable-cost components using the high-low method.

**b.** Prepare a graph showing the behavior of maintenance costs, and identify the fixed-cost and variable-cost elements. Use 200 unit increments and $1,000 cost increments.

### Solution

1. **a. Maintenance Costs:**

   $$\frac{\$4,500 − \$2,900}{800 − 300} = \frac{\$1,600}{500} = \$3.20 \text{ variable cost per machine hour}$$

| | 800 Machine Hours | 300 Machine Hours |
|---|---|---|
| Total costs | $4,500 | $2,900 |
| Less: Variable costs | | |
| 800 × $3.20 | 2,560 | |
| 300 × $3.20 | | 960 |
| Total fixed costs | $1,940 | $1,940 |

Thus, maintenance costs are $1,940 per month plus $3.20 per machine hour.

**b.**

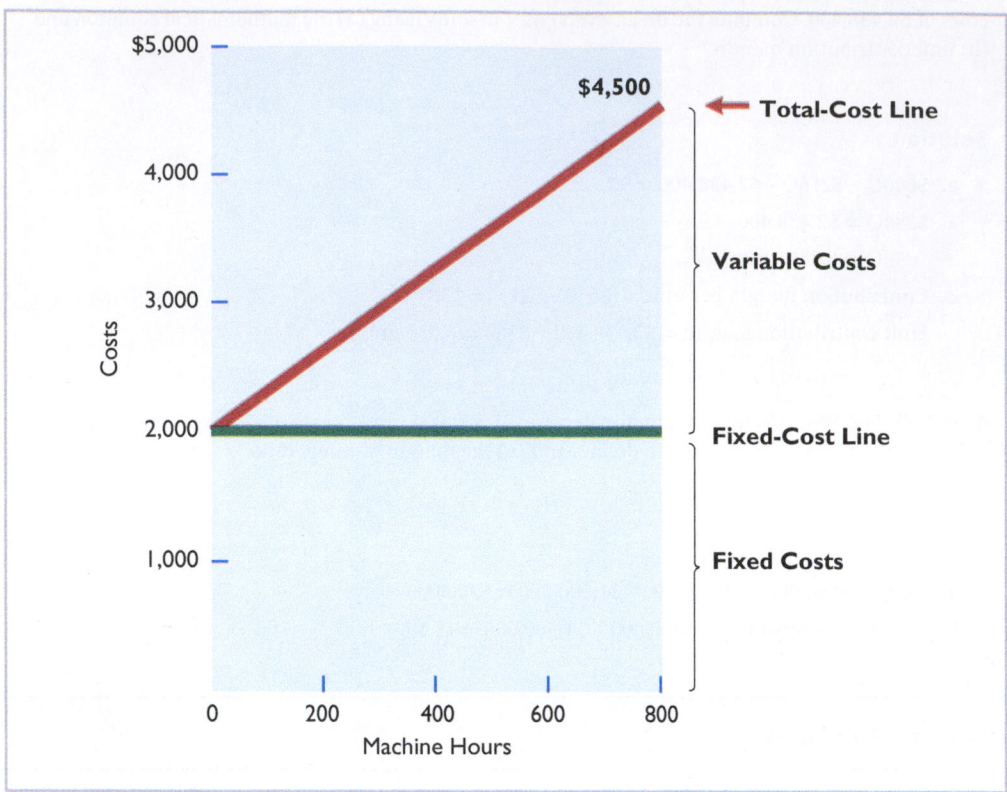

**2. (LO 3, 4, 5)** Zion Seating Co., a manufacturer of chairs, had the following data for 2022:

| | |
|---|---|
| Sales | 2,400 units |
| Sales price | $40 per unit |
| Variable costs | $15 per unit |
| Fixed costs | $19,500 |

**Instructions**

a. What is the contribution margin ratio?

b. What is the break-even point in dollars?

c. What is the margin of safety in dollars and the margin of safety ratio?

d. If the company wishes to increase its total dollar contribution margin by 40% in 2023, by how much will it need to increase its sales if variable costs per unit remain constant?

(CGA adapted)

**Solution**

**2. a.** Contribution margin ratio = Unit contribution margin ÷ Unit selling price
($40 − $15) ÷ $40 = 62.5%

**b.** Break-even in dollars: $19,500 ÷ 62.5% = $31,200

**c.** Margin of safety in dollars = (2,400 × $40) − $31,200 = $64,800
Margin of safety ratio = $64,800 ÷ (2,400 × $40) = 67.5%

**d.** Current contribution margin is $40 − $15 = $25
Total contribution margin is $25 × 2,400 = $60,000
40% increase in contribution margin is $60,000 × 40% = $24,000
Total increase in sales required is $24,000 ÷ 62.5% = $38,400

## Practice Problem

**(LO 4, 5)** Mabo Company makes calculators that sell for $20 each. For the coming year, management expects fixed costs to total $220,000 and variable costs to be $9 per unit.

*Compute break-even point, contribution margin ratio, margin of safety, and sales for target net income.*

### Instructions

a. Compute break-even point in units using the mathematical equation.

b. Compute break-even point in dollars using the contribution margin (CM) ratio.

c. Compute the margin of safety percentage assuming actual sales are $500,000.

d. Compute the sales required in dollars to earn net income of $165,000.

### Solution

a. Sales − Variable costs − Fixed costs = Net income

$$\$20Q - \$9Q - \$220{,}000 = \$0$$
$$\$11Q = \$220{,}000$$
$$Q = 20{,}000 \text{ units}$$

b. Unit contribution margin = Unit selling price − Unit variable costs

$$\$11 = \$20 - \$9$$

Contribution margin ratio = Unit contribution margin ÷ Unit selling price

$$55\% = \$11 \div \$20$$

Break-even point in dollars = Fixed costs ÷ Contribution margin ratio

$$= \$220{,}000 \div 55\%$$
$$= \$400{,}000$$

c. Margin of safety = $\dfrac{\text{Actual sales} - \text{Break-even sales}}{\text{Actual sales}}$

$$= \frac{\$500{,}000 - \$400{,}000}{\$500{,}000}$$
$$= 20\%$$

d. Sales − Variable costs − Fixed costs = Net income

$$\$20Q - \$9Q - \$220{,}000 = \$165{,}000$$
$$\$11Q = \$385{,}000$$
$$Q = 35{,}000 \text{ units}$$

35,000 units × $20 = $700,000 required sales

OR

(Fixed costs + Target net income) ÷ Contribution margin ratio = Sales in dollars

$$(\$220{,}000 + \$165{,}000) \div .55 = \$700{,}000$$

# WileyPLUS

Brief Exercises, DO IT! Exercises, Exercises, Problems, and many additional resources are available for practice in WileyPLUS.

*Note:* All asterisked Questions, Exercises, and Problems relate to material in the appendix to this chapter.

## Questions

1. a. What is cost behavior analysis?

   b. Why is cost behavior analysis important to management?

2. a. Scott Winter asks your help in understanding the term "activity index." Explain the meaning and importance of this term for Scott.

   b. State the two ways that variable costs may be defined.

3. Contrast the effects of changes in the activity level on total fixed costs and on unit fixed costs.

4. J. P. Alexander claims that the relevant range concept is important only for variable costs.

   a. Explain the relevant range concept.

   b. Do you agree with J. P.'s claim? Explain.

**5.** "The relevant range is indispensable in cost behavior analysis." Is this true? Why or why not?

**6.** Adam Antal is confused. He does not understand why rent on his apartment is a fixed cost and rent on a Hertz rental truck is a mixed cost. Explain the difference to Adam.

**7.** How should mixed costs be classified in CVP analysis? What approach is used to effect the appropriate classification?

**8.** At the high and low levels of activity during the month, direct labor hours are 90,000 and 40,000, respectively. The related costs are $165,000 and $100,000. What are the fixed and variable costs at each level of activity?

**9.** "Cost-volume-profit (CVP) analysis is based entirely on unit costs." Do you agree? Explain.

**10.** Faye Dunn defines contribution margin as the amount of profit available to cover operating expenses. Is there any truth in this definition? Discuss.

**11.** Marshall Company's GWhiz calculator sells for $40. Variable costs per unit are estimated to be $26. What are the unit contribution margin and the contribution margin ratio?

**12.** "Break-even analysis is of limited use to management because a company cannot survive by just breaking even." Do you agree? Explain.

**13.** Total fixed costs are $26,000 for Daz Inc. It has a unit contribution margin of $15, and a contribution margin ratio of 25%. Compute the break-even sales in dollars.

**14.** Peggy Turnbull asks your help in constructing a CVP graph. Explain to Peggy (a) how the break-even point is plotted, and (b) how the level of activity and dollar sales at the break-even point are determined.

**15.** Define the term "margin of safety." If Revere Company expects to sell 1,250 units of its product at $12 per unit, and break-even sales for the product are $13,200, what is the margin of safety ratio?

**16.** Huang Company's break-even sales are $500,000. Assuming fixed costs are $180,000, what sales volume is needed to achieve a target net income of $90,000?

**17.** The traditional income statement for Pace Company shows sales $900,000, cost of goods sold $600,000, and operating expenses $200,000. Assuming all costs and expenses are 70% variable and 30% fixed, prepare a CVP income statement through contribution margin.

*18. James Brooks estimated the variable and fixed components of his company's utility costs using the high-low method. He is concerned that the cost equation that resulted from the high-low method might not provide an accurate representation of his company's utility costs. What is the inherent weakness of the high-low method? What alternative approach might Brooks use, and what are its advantages?

*19. Mary Webster owns and manages a company that provides trenching services. Her clients are companies that need to lay power lines, gas lines, and fiber optic cable. Because trenching machines require considerable maintenance due to the demanding nature of the work, Mary has created a scatter plot that displays her monthly maintenance costs. If Mary were to estimate a cost equation line using regression analysis for the data in her scatter plot, what primary characteristic would that line display?

*20. What are some of the limitations of regression analysis?

# Brief Exercises

*Classify costs as variable, fixed, or mixed.*

**BE13.1 (LO 1), C** Monthly production costs in Dilts Company for two levels of production are as follows.

| Cost | 2,000 Units | 4,000 Units |
| --- | --- | --- |
| Indirect labor | $10,000 | $20,000 |
| Supervisory salaries | 5,000 | 5,000 |
| Maintenance | 4,000 | 6,000 |

Indicate which costs are variable, fixed, and mixed, and give the reason for each answer.

*Diagram the behavior of costs within the relevant range.*

**BE13.2 (LO 1), AN** For Lodes Company, the relevant range of production is 40–80% of capacity. At 40% of capacity, a variable cost is $4,000 and a fixed cost is $6,000. Diagram the behavior of each cost within the relevant range assuming the behavior is linear.

*Diagram the behavior of a mixed cost.*

**BE13.3 (LO 1), AN** For Wesland Company, a mixed cost is $15,000 plus $18 per direct labor hour. Diagram the behavior of the cost using increments of 500 hours up to 2,500 hours on the horizontal axis and increments of $15,000 up to $60,000 on the vertical axis.

*Determine variable- and fixed-cost elements using the high-low method.*

**BE13.4 (LO 2), AP** Bruno Company accumulates the following data concerning a mixed cost, using miles as the activity level.

| | Miles Driven | Total Cost | | Miles Driven | Total Cost |
| --- | --- | --- | --- | --- | --- |
| January | 8,000 | $14,150 | March | 8,500 | $15,000 |
| February | 7,500 | 13,500 | April | 8,200 | 14,490 |

Compute the variable- and fixed-cost elements using the high-low method.

*Determine variable- and fixed-cost elements using the high-low method.*

**BE13.5 (LO 2), AP** Markowis Corp. has collected the following data concerning its maintenance costs for the past 6 months.

| | Units Produced | Total Cost |
|---|---|---|
| July | 18,000 | $36,000 |
| August | 32,000 | 48,000 |
| September | 36,000 | 55,000 |
| October | 22,000 | 38,000 |
| November | 40,000 | 74,500 |
| December | 38,000 | 62,000 |

Compute the variable- and fixed-cost elements using the high-low method.

**BE13.6 (LO 3), AN** Determine the missing amounts.

*Determine missing amounts for contribution margin.*

| | Unit Selling Price | Unit Variable Costs | Unit Contribution Margin | Contribution Margin Ratio |
|---|---|---|---|---|
| 1. | $640 | $352 | (a) | (b) |
| 2. | $300 | (c) | $93 | (d) |
| 3. | (e) | (f) | $325 | 25% |

**BE13.7 (LO 3), AP** Russell Inc. had sales of $2,200,000 for the first quarter of 2022. In making the sales, the company incurred the following costs and expenses.

*Prepare CVP income statement.*

| | Variable | Fixed |
|---|---|---|
| Cost of goods sold | $920,000 | $440,000 |
| Selling expenses | 70,000 | 45,000 |
| Administrative expenses | 86,000 | 98,000 |

Prepare a CVP income statement for the quarter ended March 31, 2022.

**BE13.8 (LO 4), AP** Rice Company has a unit selling price of $520, variable costs per unit of $286, and fixed costs of $163,800. Compute the break-even point in units using (a) the mathematical equation and (b) unit contribution margin.

*Compute the break-even point.*

**BE13.9 (LO 4), AP** Presto Corp. had total variable costs of $180,000, total fixed costs of $110,000, and total revenues of $300,000. Compute the required sales in dollars to break even.

*Compute the break-even point.*

**BE13.10 (LO 5), AP** For Flynn Company, variable costs are 70% of sales, and fixed costs are $195,000. Management's net income goal is $75,000. Compute the required sales in dollars needed to achieve management's target net income of $75,000. (Use the contribution margin approach.)

*Compute sales for target net income.*

**BE13.11 (LO 5), AP** For Astoria Company, actual sales are $1,000,000, and break-even sales are $800,000. Compute (a) the margin of safety in dollars and (b) the margin of safety ratio.

*Compute the margin of safety and the margin of safety ratio.*

**BE13.12 (LO 5), AP** Deines Corporation has fixed costs of $480,000. It has a unit selling price of $6, unit variable costs of $4.40, and a target net income of $1,500,000. Compute the required sales in units to achieve its target net income.

*Compute the required sales in units for target net income.*

*BE13.13 (LO 6), AP** Stiever Corporation's maintenance costs are shown here.

*Compute variable and fixed cost elements using regression.*

| | Units Produced | Total Cost |
|---|---|---|
| July | 18,000 | $32,000 |
| August | 32,000 | 48,000 |
| September | 36,000 | 55,000 |
| October | 22,000 | 38,000 |
| November | 40,000 | 66,100 |
| December | 38,000 | 62,000 |

Compute the variable- and fixed-cost elements using regression analysis. Present your solution in the form of a cost equation. (We recommend that you use the Intercept and Slope functions in Excel.)

## DO IT! Exercises

**DO IT! 13.1 (LO 1), C** Amanda Company reports the following total costs at two levels of production.

*Classify types of costs.*

| | 5,000 Units | 10,000 Units |
|---|---|---|
| Indirect labor | $ 3,000 | $ 6,000 |
| Property taxes | 7,000 | 7,000 |
| Direct labor | 28,000 | 56,000 |
| Direct materials | 22,000 | 44,000 |
| Depreciation | 4,000 | 4,000 |
| Utilities | 5,000 | 8,000 |
| Maintenance | 9,000 | 11,000 |

Classify each cost as variable, fixed, or mixed.

*Compute costs using high-low method and estimate total cost.*

**DO IT! 13.2 (LO 2), AP** Westerville Company accumulates the following data concerning a mixed cost, using units produced as the activity level.

| | Units Produced | Total Cost |
|---|---|---|
| March | 10,000 | $18,000 |
| April | 9,000 | 16,650 |
| May | 10,500 | 18,580 |
| June | 8,800 | 16,200 |
| July | 9,500 | 17,100 |

a. Compute the variable- and fixed-cost elements using the high-low method.

b. Using the information from your answer to part (a), write the cost formula.

c. Estimate the total cost if the company produces 9,200 units.

*Prepare CVP income statement.*

**DO IT! 13.3 (LO 3), AP** Cedar Grove Industries produces and sells a cell phone-operated home security control. Information regarding the costs and sales of security controls during May 2022 is as follows.

| | |
|---|---|
| Unit selling price of security control | $45 |
| Unit variable costs | $22 |
| Total monthly fixed costs | $120,000 |
| Units sold | 8,000 |

Prepare a CVP income statement for Cedar Grove Industries for the month of May. Provide per unit values and total values.

*Compute break-even point in units.*

**DO IT! 13.4 (LO 4), AP** Snow Cap Company has a unit selling price of $250, variable costs per unit of $170, and fixed costs of $160,000. Compute the break-even point in units using (a) the mathematical equation and (b) unit contribution margin.

*Compute break-even point, margin of safety ratio, and sales for target net income.*

**DO IT! 13.5 (LO 4, 5), AP** Presto Company makes radios that sell for $30 each. For the coming year, management expects fixed costs to total $220,000 and variable costs to be $18 per unit.

a. Compute the break-even point in dollars using the contribution margin (CM) ratio.

b. Compute the margin of safety ratio assuming actual sales are $800,000.

c. Compute the sales dollars required to earn net income of $140,000.

# Exercises

*Define and classify variable, fixed, and mixed costs.*

**E13.1 (LO 1), C** Bonita Company manufactures a single product. Annual production costs incurred in the manufacturing process are shown here for two levels of production.

| | Costs Incurred | | | |
|---|---|---|---|---|
| **Production in Units** | **5,000** | | **10,000** | |
| | Total | Cost/ | Total | Cost/ |
| **Production Costs** | **Cost** | **Unit** | **Cost** | **Unit** |
| Direct materials | $8,000 | $1.60 | $16,000 | $1.60 |
| Direct labor | 9,500 | 1.90 | 19,000 | 1.90 |
| Utilities | 2,000 | 0.40 | 3,300 | 0.33 |
| Rent | 4,000 | 0.80 | 4,000 | 0.40 |
| Maintenance | 800 | 0.16 | 1,400 | 0.14 |
| Supervisory salaries | 1,000 | 0.20 | 1,000 | 0.10 |

**Instructions**

a. Define the terms variable costs, fixed costs, and mixed costs.

b. Classify each cost above as either variable, fixed, or mixed.

*Diagram cost behavior, determine relevant range, and classify costs.*

**E13.2 (LO 1), AP** Shingle Enterprises is considering manufacturing a new product. It projects the cost of direct materials and rent for a range of output as follows.

| Output in Units | Rent Expense | Direct Materials |
|---|---|---|
| 1,000 | $ 5,000 | $ 4,000 |
| 2,000 | 5,000 | 7,200 |
| 3,000 | 8,000 | 9,000 |
| 4,000 | 8,000 | 12,000 |
| 5,000 | 8,000 | 15,000 |
| 6,000 | 8,000 | 18,000 |
| 7,000 | 8,000 | 21,000 |
| 8,000 | 8,000 | 24,000 |
| 9,000 | 10,000 | 29,300 |
| 10,000 | 10,000 | 35,000 |
| 11,000 | 10,000 | 44,000 |

**Instructions**

a. Diagram the behavior of each cost for output ranging from 1,000 to 11,000 units.

b. Determine the relevant range of activity for this product.

c. Calculate the variable costs per unit within the relevant range.

d. Indicate the fixed cost within the relevant range.

**E13.3 (LO 1, 2), AN** The controller of Norton Industries has collected the following monthly expense data for use in analyzing the cost behavior of maintenance costs.

*Determine fixed and variable costs using the high-low method and prepare graph.*

| Month | Total Maintenance Costs | Total Machine Hours |
|---|---|---|
| January | $2,700 | 300 |
| February | 3,000 | 350 |
| March | 3,600 | 500 |
| April | 4,500 | 690 |
| May | 3,200 | 400 |
| June | 5,500 | 700 |

**Instructions**

a. Determine the fixed- and variable-cost components using the high-low method.

b. Prepare a graph showing the behavior of maintenance costs, and identify the fixed- and variable-cost elements. Use 100-hour increments and $1,000 cost increments.

**E13.4 (LO 1), C** Family Furniture Corporation incurred the following costs.

*Classify variable, fixed, and mixed costs.*

1. Wood used in the production of furniture.

2. Fuel used in delivery trucks.

3. Straight-line depreciation on factory building.

4. Screws used in the production of furniture.

5. Sales staff salaries.

6. Sales commissions.

7. Property taxes.

8. Insurance on buildings.

9. Hourly wages of furniture craftsmen.

10. Salaries of factory supervisors.

11. Utilities expense.

12. Telephone bill.

**Instructions**

Identify the costs above as variable, fixed, or mixed.

*Determine fixed and variable costs using the high-low method and prepare graph.*

**E13.5 (LO 1, 2), AP** The controller of Hall Industries has collected the following monthly expense data for use in analyzing the cost behavior of maintenance costs.

| Month | Total Maintenance Costs | Total Machine Hours |
|---|---|---|
| January | $2,640 | 3,500 |
| February | 3,000 | 4,000 |
| March | 3,600 | 6,000 |
| April | 4,500 | 7,900 |
| May | 3,200 | 5,000 |
| June | 4,620 | 8,000 |

### Instructions

a. Determine the fixed- and variable-cost components using the high-low method.

b. Prepare a graph showing the behavior of maintenance costs and identify the fixed- and variable-cost elements. Use 2,000-hour increments and $1,000 cost increments.

*Determine fixed, variable, and mixed costs.*

**E13.6 (LO 1), AP** PCB Corporation manufactures a single product. Monthly production costs incurred in the manufacturing process are shown below for the production of 3,000 units.

| Direct materials | $ 7,500 |
|---|---|
| Direct labor | 18,000 |
| Utilities | 2,100 |
| Property taxes | 1,000 |
| Indirect labor | 4,500 |
| Supervisory salaries | 1,900 |
| Maintenance | 1,100 |
| Depreciation | 2,400 |

The utilities and maintenance costs are mixed costs. The fixed portions of these costs are $300 and $200, respectively.

### Instructions

a. Identify the above costs as variable, fixed, or mixed.

b. Calculate the expected costs when production is 5,000 units.

*Explain assumptions underlying CVP analysis.*

**E13.7 (LO 3), K** **Writing** Marty Moser wants Moser Company to use CVP analysis to study the effects of changes in costs and volume on the company. Marty has heard that certain assumptions must be valid in order for CVP analysis to be useful.

### Instructions

Prepare a memo to Marty Moser concerning the assumptions that underlie CVP analysis.

*Compute break-even point in units and dollars.*

**E13.8 (LO 3, 4), AP** **Service** All That Blooms provides environmentally friendly lawn services for homeowners. Its operating costs are as follows.

| Depreciation | $1,400 per month |
|---|---|
| Advertising | $200 per month |
| Insurance | $2,000 per month |
| Weed and feed materials | $12 per lawn |
| Direct labor | $10 per lawn |
| Fuel | $2 per lawn |

All That Blooms charges $60 per treatment for the average single-family lawn.

### Instructions

Determine the company's break-even point in (a) number of lawns serviced per month and (b) dollars.

*Compute break-even point.*

Excel

**E13.9 (LO 3, 4), AP** **Service** The Palmer Acres Inn is trying to determine its break-even point during its off-peak season. The inn has 50 rooms that it rents at $60 a night. Operating costs are as follows.

| Salaries | $5,900 per month |
|---|---|
| Utilities | $1,100 per month |
| Depreciation | $1,000 per month |
| Maintenance | $100 per month |
| Maid service | $14 per room |
| Other costs | $28 per room |

## Instructions

Determine the inn's break-even point in (a) number of rented rooms per month and (b) dollars.

**E13.10 (LO 3, 4), AP** [Service] In the month of March, Style Salon serviced 560 clients at an average price of $120. During the month, fixed costs were $21,024 and variable costs were 60% of sales.

*Compute contribution margin and break-even point.*

### Instructions

a. Determine the total contribution margin in dollars, the per unit contribution margin, and the contribution margin ratio.

b. Using the contribution margin technique, compute the break-even point in dollars and in units.

**E13.11 (LO 3, 4), AP** [Service] Spencer Kars provides shuttle service between 4 hotels near a medical center and an international airport. Spencer Kars uses two 10-passenger vans to offer 12 round trips per day. A recent month's activity in the form of a cost-volume-profit income statement is as follows.

*Compute break-even point.*

| | | |
|---|---:|---:|
| Sales (1,500 passengers) | | $36,000 |
| Variable costs | | |
| Fuel | $ 5,040 | |
| Tolls and parking | 3,100 | |
| Maintenance | 860 | 9,000 |
| Contribution margin | | 27,000 |
| Fixed costs | | |
| Salaries | 15,700 | |
| Depreciation | 1,300 | |
| Insurance | 1,000 | 18,000 |
| Net income | | $ 9,000 |

### Instructions

a. Calculate the break-even point in (1) dollars and (2) number of passengers.

b. Without calculations, determine the contribution margin at the break-even point.

**E13.12 (LO 3, 4), AP** In 2021, Manhoff Company had a break-even point of $350,000 based on a selling price of $5 per unit and fixed costs of $112,000. In 2022, the selling price and the variable costs per unit did not change, but the break-even point increased to $420,000.

*Compute variable costs per unit, contribution margin ratio, and increase in fixed costs.*

### Instructions

a. Compute the variable costs per unit and the contribution margin ratio for 2021.

b. Compute the increase in fixed costs for 2022.

**E13.13 (LO 3, 4), AP** Billings Company has the following information available for September 2022.

*Prepare CVP income statements.*

| | |
|---|---:|
| Unit selling price of video game consoles | $400 |
| Unit variable costs | $280 |
| Total fixed costs | $54,000 |
| Units sold | 600 |

### Instructions

a. Compute the unit contribution margin.

b. Prepare a CVP income statement that shows both total and per unit amounts.

c. Compute Billings' break-even point in units.

d. Prepare a CVP income statement for the break-even point that shows both total and per unit amounts.

**E13.14 (LO 4, 5), AP** Naylor Company had $210,000 of net income in 2021 when the selling price per unit was $140, the variable costs per unit were $90, and the fixed costs were $570,000. Management expects per unit data and total fixed costs to remain the same in 2022. The president of Naylor Company is under pressure from stockholders to increase net income by $62,400 in 2022.

*Compute various components to derive target net income under different assumptions.*

### Instructions

a. Compute the number of units sold in 2021.

b. Compute the number of units that would have to be sold in 2022 to reach the stockholders' desired profit level.

c. Assume that Naylor Company sells the same number of units in 2022 as it did in 2021. What would the selling price have to be in order to reach the stockholders' desired profit level?

*Compute net income under different alternatives.*

**E13.15 (LO 5), AP** Yams Company reports the following operating results for the month of August: sales $400,000 (units 5,000), variable costs $240,000, and fixed costs $90,000. Management is considering the following independent courses of action to increase net income.

1. Increase selling price by 10% with no change in total variable costs or units sold.

2. Reduce variable costs to 55% of sales.

**Instructions**

Compute the net income to be earned under each alternative. Which course of action will produce the higher net income?

*Prepare a CVP graph and compute break-even point and margin of safety.*

**E13.16 (LO 4, 5), AP** Glacial Company estimates that variable costs will be 62.5% of sales, and fixed costs will total $600,000. The selling price of the product is $4.

**Instructions**

a. Compute the break-even point in (1) units and (2) dollars.

b. Prepare a CVP graph, assuming maximum sales of $3,200,000. (*Note:* Use $400,000 increments for sales and costs and 100,000 increments for units.)

c. Assuming actual sales are $2 million, compute the margin of safety in (1) dollars and (2) as a ratio.

*Determine contribution margin ratio, break-even point in dollars, and margin of safety.*

**E13.17 (LO 3, 4, 5), AP** Felde Bucket Co., a manufacturer of rain barrels, had the following data for 2021:

| | |
|---|---|
| Sales | 2,500 units |
| Sales price | $40 per unit |
| Variable costs | $24 per unit |
| Fixed costs | $19,500 |

**Instructions**

a. What is the contribution margin ratio?

b. What is the break-even point in dollars?

c. What is the margin of safety in dollars and as a ratio?

d. If the company wishes to increase its total dollar contribution margin by 30% in 2022, by how much will it need to increase its sales if all other factors remain constant?

(CGA adapted)

*Determine cost components using regression, prepare scatter plot, and estimate cost at particular level of activity.*

*E13.18 (LO 6), AP** The controller of Standard Industries has collected the following monthly expense data for analyzing the cost behavior of electricity costs.

| | Total Electricity Costs | Total Machine Hours |
|---|---|---|
| January | $2,500 | 300 |
| February | 3,000 | 350 |
| March | 3,600 | 500 |
| April | 4,500 | 690 |
| May | 3,200 | 400 |
| June | 4,900 | 700 |
| July | 4,100 | 650 |
| August | 3,800 | 520 |
| September | 5,100 | 680 |
| October | 4,200 | 630 |
| November | 3,300 | 350 |
| December | 6,100 | 720 |

**Instructions**

a. Determine the fixed- and variable-cost components using regression analysis (We recommend the use of Excel.)

b. Prepare a scatter plot using Excel. Present the cost equation line estimated in part (a).

c. What electricity cost does the cost equation estimate for a level of activity of 500 machine hours? By what amount does this differ from March's observed cost for 500 machine hours?

# Problems

**P13.1 (LO 1, 2), AP** The controller of Rather Production has collected the following monthly expense data for analyzing the cost behavior of electricity costs.

*Determine cost components using high-low method, and estimate cost at particular level of activity.*

| | Total Electricity Costs | Total Machine Hours |
|---|---|---|
| January | $2,500 | 300 |
| February | 3,000 | 350 |
| March | 3,600 | 500 |
| April | 4,500 | 690 |
| May | 3,200 | 400 |
| June | 4,900 | 700 |
| July | 4,100 | 650 |
| August | 3,800 | 520 |
| September | 5,100 | 680 |
| October | 4,200 | 630 |
| November | 3,300 | 350 |
| December | 5,860 | 720 |

### Instructions

a. Determine the fixed- and variable-cost components using the high-low method.

b. What electricity cost does the cost equation estimate for a level of activity of 500 machine hours? By what amount does this differ from March's observed cost for 500 machine hours?

c. What electricity cost does the cost equation estimate for a level of activity of 700 machine hours? By what amount does this differ from June's observed cost for 700 machine hours?

**P13.2 (LO 1, 2, 3, 4), AN** `Service` Vin Diesel owns the Fredonia Barber Shop. He employs four barbers and pays each a base rate of $1,250 per month. One of the barbers serves as the manager and receives an extra $500 per month. In addition to the base rate, each barber also receives a commission of $4.50 per haircut.

*Determine variable and fixed costs, compute break-even point, prepare a CVP graph, and determine net income.*

Other costs are as follows.

| | |
|---|---|
| Advertising | $200 per month |
| Rent | $1,100 per month |
| Barber supplies | $0.30 per haircut |
| Utilities | $175 per month plus $0.20 per haircut |
| Magazines | $25 per month |

Vin currently charges $10 per haircut.

### Instructions

a. Determine the variable costs per haircut and the total monthly fixed costs.

a. VC $5

b. Compute the break-even point in units and dollars.

c. Prepare a CVP graph, assuming a maximum of 1,800 haircuts in a month. Use increments of 300 haircuts on the horizontal axis and $3,000 on the vertical axis.

d. Determine net income, assuming 1,600 haircuts are given in a month.

**P13.3 (LO 3, 4, 5), AP** Jorge Company bottles and distributes B-Lite, a diet soft drink. The beverage is sold for 50 cents per 16-ounce bottle to retailers. For the year 2022, management estimates the following revenues and costs.

*Prepare a CVP income statement and compute break-even point, contribution margin ratio, margin of safety ratio, and sales for target net income.*

| | | | |
|---|---|---|---|
| Sales | $1,800,000 | Selling expenses—variable | $70,000 |
| Direct materials | 430,000 | Selling expenses—fixed | 65,000 |
| Direct labor | 360,000 | Administrative expenses— | |
| Manufacturing overhead— | | variable | 20,000 |
| variable | 380,000 | Administrative expenses— | |
| Manufacturing overhead— | | fixed | 60,000 |
| fixed | 280,000 | | |

**Instructions**

a. Prepare a CVP income statement for 2022 based on management's estimates. (Show column for total amounts only.)

b. (1) 2,700,000 units

b. Compute the break-even point in (1) units and (2) dollars.

c. CM ratio 30%

c. Compute the contribution margin ratio and the margin of safety ratio. (Round to nearest full percent.)

d. Determine the sales dollars required to earn net income of $180,000.

*Compute break-even point under alternative courses of action.*

**P13.4 (LO 4), E** Tanek Corp.'s sales slumped badly in 2022. For the first time in its history, it operated at a loss. The company's income statement showed the following results from selling 500,000 units of product: sales $2,500,000, total costs and expenses $2,590,000, and net loss $90,000. Costs and expenses consisted of the following amounts.

|  | Total | Variable | Fixed |
|---|---|---|---|
| Cost of goods sold | $2,140,000 | $1,590,000 | $550,000 |
| Selling expenses | 250,000 | 92,000 | 158,000 |
| Administrative expenses | 200,000 | 68,000 | 132,000 |
|  | $2,590,000 | $1,750,000 | $840,000 |

Management is considering the following independent alternatives for 2023.

1. Increase unit selling price 20% with no change in costs, expenses, and sales volume.

2. Change the compensation of salespersons from fixed annual salaries totaling $140,000 to total salaries of $60,000 plus a 5% commission on sales.

**Instructions**

a. Compute the break-even point in dollars for 2022.

b. Alternative 1 $2,000,000

b. Compute the break-even point in dollars under each of the alternative courses of action. (Round all ratios to nearest full percent.) Which course of action do you recommend?

*Compute break-even point and margin of safety ratio, and prepare a CVP income statement before and after changes in business environment.*

**P13.5 (LO 3, 4, 5), E** Mary Willis is the advertising manager for Bargain Shoe Store. She is currently working on a major promotional campaign. Her ideas include the installation of a new lighting system and increased display space that will add $29,000 in fixed costs to the $270,000 currently spent. In addition, Mary is proposing that a 5% price decrease ($40 to $38) will produce a 25% increase in sales volume (20,000 to 25,000). Variable costs will remain at $25 per pair of shoes. Management is impressed with Mary's ideas but concerned about the effects that these changes will have on the break-even point and the margin of safety.

**Instructions**

a. Compute the current break-even point in units, and compare it to the break-even point in units if Mary's ideas are used.

b. Current margin of safety ratio 10%

b. Compute the margin of safety ratio for current operations and after Mary's changes are introduced. (Round to nearest full percent.)

c. Prepare a CVP income statement for current operations and after Mary's changes are introduced. (Show column for total amounts only.) Would you make the changes suggested?

*Compute contribution margin, fixed costs, break-even point, sales for target net income, and margin of safety ratio.*

**P13.6 (LO 3, 4, 5), AN** Viejol Corporation has collected the following information after its first year of sales. Sales were $1,600,000 on 100,000 units, selling expenses $250,000 (40% variable and 60% fixed), direct materials $490,000, direct labor $290,000, administrative expenses $270,000 (20% variable and 80% fixed), and manufacturing overhead $380,000 (70% variable and 30% fixed). Top management has asked you to do a CVP analysis so that it can make plans for the coming year. It has projected that unit sales will increase by 10% next year.

**Instructions**

a. Compute (1) the contribution margin for the current year and the projected year, and (2) the fixed costs for the current year. (Assume that fixed costs will remain the same in the projected year.)

b. 120,000 units

b. Compute the break-even point in units and sales dollars for the current year.

c. The company has a target net income of $145,000. What is the required sales in dollars for the company to meet its target?

d. If the company meets its target net income number, by what percentage could its sales fall before it is operating at a loss? That is, what is its margin of safety ratio?

*Determine variable and fixed costs.*

**P13.7 (LO 1, 3, 5), E** Kaiser Industries carries no inventories. Its product is manufactured only when a customer's order is received. It is then shipped immediately after it is made. For its fiscal year ended October 31, 2022, Kaiser's break-even point was $1.3 million. On sales of $1.2 million, its income statement showed a gross profit of $180,000, direct materials cost of $400,000, and direct labor costs of $500,000. The contribution margin was $144,000, and variable manufacturing overhead was $50,000.

### Instructions

a. Calculate the following:

a. 2. $70,000

    1. Variable selling and administrative expenses.

    2. Fixed manufacturing overhead.

    3. Fixed selling and administrative expenses.

b. Ignoring your answer to part (a), assume that fixed manufacturing overhead was $100,000 and the fixed selling and administrative expenses were $80,000. The marketing vice president feels that if the company increased its advertising, sales could be increased by 25%. What is the maximum increased advertising cost the company can incur and still report the same income as before the advertising expenditure?

(CGA adapted)

## Continuing Cases

### Current Designs

**CD13** Bill Johnson, sales manager, and Diane Buswell, controller, at Current Designs are beginning to analyze the cost considerations for one of the composite models of the kayak division. They have provided the following production and operational costs necessary to produce one composite kayak.

| | A | B | C |
|---|---|---|---|
| 1 | Kevlar® | $250 per kayak | |
| 2 | Resin and supplies | $100 per kayak | |
| 3 | Finishing kit (seat, rudder, ropes, etc.) | $170 per kayak | |
| 4 | Labor | $420 per kayak | |
| 5 | Selling and administrative expenses—variable | $400 per kayak | |
| 6 | Selling and administrative expenses—fixed | $119,700 per year | |
| 7 | Manufacturing overhead—fixed | $240,000 per year | |
| 8 | | | |

Bill and Diane have asked you to provide a cost-volume-profit analysis, to help them finalize the budget projections for the upcoming year. Bill has informed you that the selling price of the composite kayak will be $2,000.

### Instructions

a. Calculate variable costs per unit.

b. Determine the unit contribution margin.

c. Using the unit contribution margin, determine the break-even point in units for this product line.

d. Assume that Current Designs plans to earn net income of $270,600 on this product line. Using the unit contribution margin, calculate the number of units that need to be sold to achieve this goal.

e. Based on the most recent sales forecast, Current Designs plans to sell 1,000 units of this model. Using your results from part (c), calculate the margin of safety in dollars and the margin of safety ratio.

### Waterways Corporation

(*Note:* This is a continuation of the Waterways case from Chapters 11–12.)

**WC13** The Vice President for Sales and Marketing at Waterways Corporation is planning for production needs to meet sales demand in the coming year. He is also trying to determine how the company's profits might be increased in the coming year. This problem asks you to use cost-volume-profit concepts to help Waterways understand contribution margins of some of its products and decide whether to mass-produce any of them.

*Go to WileyPLUS for complete case details and instructions.*

## Expand Your Critical Thinking

### Decision-Making Across the Organization

**CT13.1** Creative Ideas Company has decided to introduce a new product. The new product can be manufactured by either a capital-intensive method or a labor-intensive method. The manufacturing method will not affect the quality of the product. The estimated manufacturing costs by the two methods are as follows.

|  | Capital-Intensive | Labor-Intensive |
|---|---|---|
| Direct materials | $5 per unit | $5.50 per unit |
| Direct labor | $6 per unit | $8.00 per unit |
| Variable overhead | $3 per unit | $4.50 per unit |
| Fixed manufacturing costs | $2,524,000 | $1,550,000 |

Creative Ideas' market research department has recommended an introductory unit sales price of $32. The incremental selling expenses are estimated to be $502,000 annually plus $2 for each unit sold, regardless of manufacturing method.

#### Instructions

With the class divided into groups, answer the following.

a. Calculate the estimated break-even point in annual unit sales of the new product if Creative Ideas Company uses the:

 1. Capital-intensive manufacturing method.

 2. Labor-intensive manufacturing method.

b. Determine the annual unit sales volume at which Creative Ideas Company would be indifferent between the two manufacturing methods.

c. Explain the circumstance under which Creative Ideas should employ each of the two manufacturing methods.

(CMA adapted)

### Managerial Analysis

**CT13.2** The condensed income statement for the Peri and Paul partnership for 2022 is as follows.

**Peri and Paul Company**
**Income Statement**
**For the Year Ended December 31, 2022**

| | | |
|---|---|---|
| Sales (240,000 units) | | $1,200,000 |
| Cost of goods sold | | 800,000 |
| Gross profit | | 400,000 |
| Operating expenses | | |
| Selling | $300,000 | |
| Administrative | 152,500 | 452,500 |
| Net loss | | $  (52,500) |

A cost behavior analysis indicates that 75% of the cost of goods sold are variable and 40% of the selling expenses are variable. Administrative expenses are $92,500 fixed.

#### Instructions

(Round to nearest unit, cent, and percentage, where necessary. Use the CVP income statement format in computing profits.)

a. Compute the break-even point in total sales dollars and in units for 2022.

b. Peri has proposed a plan to get the partnership "out of the red" and improve its profitability. She feels that the quality of the product could be substantially improved by spending $0.32 more per unit on better raw materials. The selling price per unit could be increased to only $5.25 because of competitive pressures. Peri estimates that sales volume will increase by 25%. Compute net income under Peri's proposal and the break-even point in dollars.

**c.** Paul was a marketing major in college. He believes that sales volume can be increased only by intensive advertising and promotional campaigns. He therefore proposed the following plan as an alternative to Peri's: (1) increase variable selling expenses to $0.575 per unit, (2) lower the selling price per unit by $0.25, and (3) increase fixed selling expenses by $51,000. Paul quoted an old marketing research report that said that sales volume would increase by 60% if these changes were made. Compute net income under Paul's proposal and the break-even point in dollars.

**d.** Which plan should be accepted? Explain your answer.

## Real-World Focus

**CT13.3  The Coca-Cola Company** hardly needs an introduction. A line taken from the cover of a recent annual report says it all: If you measured time in servings of Coca-Cola, "a billion Coca-Cola's ago was yesterday morning." On average, every U.S. citizen drinks 363 8-ounce servings of Coca-Cola products each year. Coca-Cola's primary line of business is the making and selling of syrup to bottlers. These bottlers then sell the finished bottles and cans of Coca-Cola to retailers.

In the annual report of Coca-Cola, the following information was provided.

---

### The Coca-Cola Company
#### Management Discussion

Our gross margin declined to 61 percent this year from 62 percent in the prior year, primarily due to costs for materials such as sweeteners and packaging.

The increases [in selling expenses] in the last two years were primarily due to higher marketing expenditures in support of our Company's volume growth.

We measure our sales volume in two ways: (1) gallon shipments of concentrates and syrups and (2) unit cases of finished product (bottles and cans of Coke sold bottlers).

---

### Instructions

Answer the following questions.

**a.** Are sweeteners and packaging a variable cost or a fixed cost? What is the impact on the contribution margin of an increase in the per unit cost of sweeteners or packaging? What are the implications for profitability?

**b.** In your opinion, are Coca-Cola's marketing expenditures a fixed cost, variable cost, or mixed cost? Give justification for your answer.

**c.** Which of the two measures cited for measuring volume represents the activity index as defined in this chapter? Why might Coca-Cola use two different measures?

## Communication Activity

**CT13.4**  Your roommate asks for your help on the following questions about CVP analysis formulas.

**a.** How can the mathematical equation for break-even sales show both sales units and sales dollars?

**b.** How do the formulas differ for unit contribution margin and contribution margin ratio?

**c.** How can contribution margin be used to determine break-even sales in units and in dollars?

### Instructions

Write a memo to your roommate stating the relevant formulas and answering each question.

## Ethics Case

**CT13.5**  Scott Bestor is an accountant for Westfield Company. Early this year, Scott made a highly favorable projection of sales and profits over the next 3 years for Westfield's hot-selling computer PLEX. As a result of the projections Scott presented to senior management, the company decided to expand production in this area. This decision led to dislocations of some plant personnel, who were reassigned to one of the company's newer plants in another state. However, no one was fired, and in fact the company expanded its workforce slightly.

Unfortunately, Scott rechecked his projection computations a few months later and found that he had made an error that would have reduced his projections substantially. Luckily, sales of PLEX have exceeded projections so far, and management is satisfied with its decision. Scott, however, is not sure what to do. Should he confess his honest mistake and jeopardize his possible promotion? He suspects that no one will catch the error because PLEX sales have exceeded his projections, and it appears that profits will materialize close to his projections.

### Instructions

a. Who are the stakeholders in this situation?

b. Identify the ethical issues involved in this situation.

c. What are the possible alternative actions for Scott? What would you do in Scott's position?

## All About You

**CT13.6** Cost-volume-profit analysis can also be used in making personal financial decisions. For example, the purchase of a new car is one of your biggest personal expenditures. It is important that you carefully analyze your options.

Suppose that you are considering the purchase of a hybrid vehicle. Let's assume the following facts. The hybrid will initially cost an additional $4,500 above the cost of a traditional vehicle. The hybrid will get 40 miles per gallon of gas, and the traditional car will get 30 miles per gallon. Also, assume that the cost of gas is $3.60 per gallon.

### Instructions

Using the facts above, answer the following questions.

a. What is the variable gasoline cost of going one mile in the hybrid car? What is the variable cost of going one mile in the traditional car?

b. Using the information in part (a), if "miles" is your unit of measure, what is the "contribution margin" of the hybrid vehicle relative to the traditional vehicle? That is, express the variable cost savings on a per-mile basis.

c. How many miles would you have to drive in order to break even on your investment in the hybrid car?

d. What other factors might you want to consider?

# Incremental Analysis

## Chapter Preview

An important purpose of management accounting is to provide managers with relevant information for decision-making. Companies of all sorts must make product decisions. **Oral-B Laboratories** opted to produce a new, higher-priced toothbrush. **General Motors** announced the closure of its Oldsmobile Division. **Quaker Oats** decided to sell off a line of beverages, at a price more than $1 billion less than it paid for that product line only a few years before.

This chapter explains management's decision-making process and a decision-making approach called incremental analysis. The use of incremental analysis is demonstrated in a variety of situations.

## Feature Story

### Keeping It Clean

When you think of new, fast-growing, San Francisco companies, you probably think of fun products like smartphones, social networks, and game apps. You don't tend to think of soap. In fact, given that some of the biggest, most powerful companies in the world dominate the soap market (e.g., **Proctor & Gamble**, **Clorox**, and **Unilever**), starting a new soap company seems like an outrageously bad idea. But that didn't dissuade Adam Lowry and Eric Ryan from giving it a try. The long-time friends and former roommates combined their skills (Adam's chemical engineering and Eric's design and marketing) to start **Method Products**. Their goal: selling environmentally friendly soaps that actually remove dirt.

Within a year of its formation, the company had products on the shelves at **Target** stores. Within five years, Method was cited by numerous business publications as one of the fastest-growing companies in the country. It was easy—right? Wrong. Running a company is never easy, and given Method's commitment to sustainability, all of its business decisions are just a little more complex than usual. For example, the company wanted to use solar power to charge the batteries for the forklifts used in its factories. No problem, just put solar panels on the buildings. But because Method outsources its manufacturing, it doesn't actually own factory buildings. In fact, the company that does Method's manufacturing doesn't own the buildings either. Solution—Method parked old semi-trailers next to the factories and installed solar panels on those.

Since Method insists on using natural products and sustainable production practices, its production costs are higher than companies that don't adhere to these standards. Adam

and Eric insist, however, that this actually benefits them because they have to be far more careful about controlling costs and far more innovative in solving problems. Consider Method's most recently developed laundry detergent. It is eight times stronger than normal detergent, so it can be sold in a substantially smaller package. This reduces both its packaging and shipping costs. In fact, when the cost of the raw materials used for soap production recently jumped by as much as 40%, Method actually viewed it as an opportunity to grab market share. It determined that it could offset the cost increases in other places in its supply chain, thus absorbing the cost much easier than its big competitors.

In these and other instances, Adam and Eric identified their alternative courses of action, determined what was relevant to each choice and what wasn't, and then carefully evaluated the incremental costs of each alternative. When you are small and your competitors have some of the biggest marketing budgets in the world, you can't afford to make very many mistakes.

# Chapter Outline

| LEARNING OBJECTIVES | REVIEW | PRACTICE |
|---|---|---|
| **LO 1** Describe management's decision-making process and incremental analysis. | • Incremental analysis approach<br>• How incremental analysis works<br>• Qualitative factors<br>• Types of incremental analysis | **DO IT! 1** Incremental Analysis |
| **LO 2** Analyze the relevant costs in accepting an order at a special price. | • Special price<br>• Available capacity | **DO IT! 2** Special Orders |
| **LO 3** Analyze the relevant costs in a make-or-buy decision. | • Make or buy<br>• Opportunity cost | **DO IT! 3** Make or Buy |
| **LO 4** Analyze the relevant costs and revenues in determining whether to sell or process materials further. | • Single-product case<br>• Multiple-product case | **DO IT! 4** Sell or Process Further |
| **LO 5** Analyze the relevant costs to be considered in repairing, retaining, or replacing equipment. | • Repair, retain, or replace equipment<br>• Sunk costs | **DO IT! 5** Repair or Replace Equipment |
| **LO 6** Analyze the relevant costs in deciding whether to eliminate an unprofitable segment or product. | • Unprofitable segments<br>• Avoidable fixed costs<br>• Effect of contribution margin | **DO IT! 6** Unprofitable Segments |

**Go to the Review and Practice section at the end of the chapter for a targeted summary and practice applications with solutions.**

**Visit WileyPLUS for additional tutorials and practice opportunities.**

# Decision-Making and Incremental Analysis

**LEARNING OBJECTIVE 1**

Describe management's decision-making process and incremental analysis.

Making decisions is an important management function. Management's decision-making process does not always follow a set pattern because decisions vary significantly in their scope, urgency, and importance. It is possible, though, to identify some steps that are frequently involved in the process. These steps are shown in **Illustration 14.1**.

**ILLUSTRATION 14.1** **Management's decision-making process**

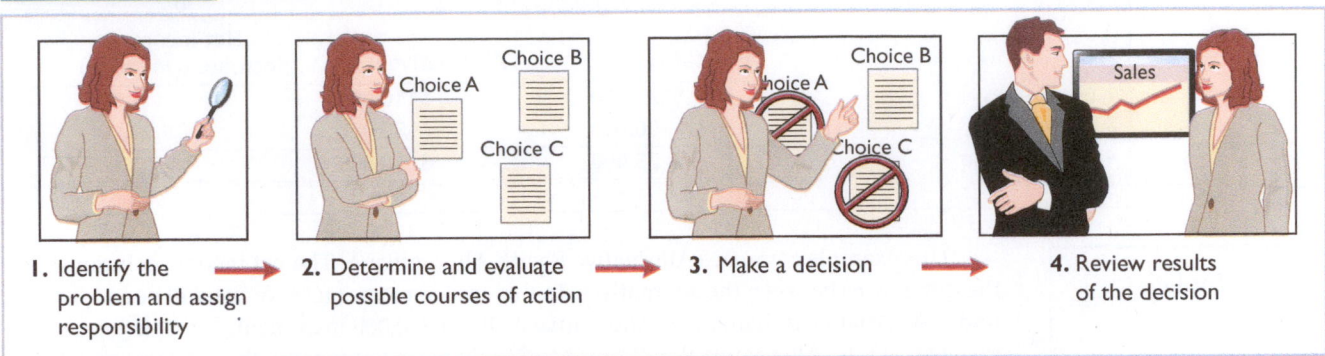

1. Identify the problem and assign responsibility
2. Determine and evaluate possible courses of action
3. Make a decision
4. Review results of the decision

Accounting's contribution to the decision-making process occurs primarily in Steps 2 and 4—evaluating possible courses of action and reviewing results.

- In Step 2, for each possible course of action, relevant revenue and cost data are provided. These show the expected overall effect on net income.
- In Step 4, internal reports are prepared that review the actual impact of the decision.

In making business decisions, management ordinarily considers both financial and non-financial information. **Financial** information is related to revenues and costs and their effect on the company's overall profitability. **Nonfinancial** information relates to such factors as the effect of the decision on employee turnover, the environment, or the overall image of the company in the community. (These are considerations that we touched on in our Chapter 11 discussion of corporate social responsibility.) Although nonfinancial information can be as important as financial information, we will focus primarily on financial information that is relevant to the decision.

## Incremental Analysis Approach

**Decisions involve a choice among alternative courses of action.** Suppose you face the personal financial decision of whether to purchase or lease a car. The financial data relate to the cost of leasing versus the cost of purchasing. For example, leasing involves periodic lease payments; purchasing requires "upfront" payment of the purchase price. In other words, the financial information relevant to the decision are the data that vary in the future among the possible alternatives.

- The process used to identify the financial data that change under alternative courses of action is called **incremental analysis** (see **Alternative Terminology**).
- In some cases, you will find that when you use incremental analysis, both costs **and** revenues vary.
- In other cases, only costs **or** revenues vary.

**ALTERNATIVE TERMINOLOGY**

Incremental analysis is also called *differential analysis* because the analysis focuses on differences.

Just as your decision to buy or lease a car affects your future financial situation, similar decisions, on a larger scale, affect a company's future. Incremental analysis identifies the probable effects of those decisions on future earnings. Such analysis inevitably involves estimates and uncertainty. Gathering data for incremental analyses may involve market analysts, engineers, and accountants. In quantifying the data, the accountant must produce the most reliable information available.

# How Incremental Analysis Works

The basic approach in incremental analysis is shown in **Illustration 14.2**.

**ILLUSTRATION 14.2** Basic approach in incremental analysis

| | A | B | C | D |
|---|---|---|---|---|
| | | Alternative A | Alternative B | Net Income Increase (Decrease) |
| 2 | Revenues | $125,000 | $110,000 | $ (15,000) |
| 3 | Costs | 100,000 | 80,000 | 20,000 |
| 4 | Net income | $ 25,000 | $ 30,000 | $ 5,000 |

---

**Decision Tools**

Incremental analysis helps managers choose the alternative that maximizes net income.

---

This example compares Alternative B with Alternative A. The net income column shows the differences between the alternatives. In this case, incremental revenue will be $15,000 less under Alternative B than under Alternative A. But a $20,000 incremental cost savings will be realized.[1] Thus, Alternative B will produce $5,000 more net income than Alternative A (see **Decision Tools**).

In the following pages, you will encounter three important cost concepts used in incremental analysis, as defined and discussed in **Illustration 14.3**.

**ILLUSTRATION 14.3** Key cost concepts in incremental analysis

- **Relevant cost and revenues** In incremental analysis, the only factors to be considered are those costs and revenues that differ across alternatives. Those factors are called **relevant costs and revenues**. Costs and revenues that do not differ across alternatives can be ignored when trying to choose between alternatives.

- **Opportunity cost** Often in choosing one course of action, the company must give up the opportunity to benefit from some other course of action. For example, if a machine is used to make one type of product, the benefit of making another type of product with that machine is lost. This lost potential benefit is referred to as **opportunity cost**.

- **Sunk cost** Costs that have already been incurred and will not be changed or avoided by any present or future decisions are referred to as **sunk costs**. For example, the amount you spent in the past to purchase or repair a laptop should have no bearing on your decision whether to buy a new laptop. **Sunk costs are not relevant costs.**

---

[1]Although income taxes are sometimes important in incremental analysis, they are ignored in the chapter for simplicity's sake.

Incremental analysis sometimes involves changes that at first glance might seem contrary to your intuition.

- Sometimes variable costs **do not change** under the alternative courses of action. For example, direct labor, normally a variable cost, is not a relevant cost in deciding between the acquisition of two new factory machines if each asset requires the same amount of direct labor.

- Sometimes fixed costs **do change**. For example, rent expense, normally a fixed cost, is a relevant cost in a decision whether to continue occupancy of a building or to purchase or lease a new building.

It is also important to understand that **the approaches to incremental analysis discussed in this chapter do not take into consideration the time value of money**. That is, amounts to be paid or received in future years are not discounted for the cost of interest in this chapter. Time value of money is addressed in Chapter 18 and Appendix E.

---

**Service Company Insight    American Express**

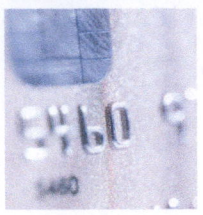

iStock.com/Jani Bryson

### That Letter from AmEx Might Not Be a Bill

No doubt every one of you has received an invitation from a credit card company to open a new account—some of you have probably received three in one day. But how many of you have received an offer of $300 to close out your credit card account? **American Express** decided to offer some of its customers $300 if they would give back their credit card. You could receive the $300 even if you hadn't paid off your balance yet, as long as you agreed to give up your credit card. Apparently, these customers cost more than they are worth.

**Source:** Aparajita Saha-Bubna and Lauren Pollock, "AmEx Offers Some Holders $300 to Pay and Leave," *Wall Street Journal Online* (February 23, 2009).

**What are the relevant costs that American Express would need to know in order to determine to whom to make this offer? (Go to WileyPLUS for this answer and additional questions.)**

---

## Qualitative Factors

In this chapter, we focus primarily on the quantitative factors that affect a decision—those attributes that can be easily expressed in terms of numbers or dollars. However, many of the decisions involving incremental analysis have important qualitative features. Though not easily measured, they should not be ignored.

- Consider, for example, the potential effects of the make-or-buy decision or of the decision to eliminate a line of business on existing employees and the community in which the plant is located.

- The cost savings that may be obtained from outsourcing or from eliminating a plant should be weighed against these qualitative attributes.

- One example would be the cost of lost morale that might result.

For example, Al "Chainsaw" Dunlap was a so-called "turnaround" artist who went into many companies, identified inefficiencies (using incremental analysis techniques), and tried to correct these problems to improve corporate profitability. Along the way, he laid off thousands of employees at numerous companies. As head of **Sunbeam**, it was Al Dunlap who lost his job because his Draconian approach failed to improve Sunbeam's profitability. It was reported that Sunbeam's employees openly rejoiced for days after his departure. Clearly, qualitative factors can matter.

## Types of Incremental Analysis

A number of different types of decisions involve incremental analysis. The more common types of decisions are whether to:

1. Accept an order at a special price.
2. Make or buy component parts or finished products.
3. Sell products or process them further.
4. Repair, retain, or replace equipment.
5. Eliminate an unprofitable business segment or product.

We consider each of these types of decisions in the following pages.

---

**ACTION PLAN**

- **Past costs that cannot be changed as a result of any present or future action are sunk costs.**

- **Benefits lost by choosing one option over another are opportunity costs.**

## DO IT! 1 | Incremental Analysis

Owen T Corporation is comparing two different options. The company currently operates under Option 1, with revenues of $80,000 per year, maintenance expenses of $5,000 per year, and operating expenses of $38,000 per year. Option 2 provides revenues of $80,000 per year, maintenance expenses of $12,000 per year, and operating expenses of $32,000 per year. Option 1 employs a piece of equipment that was upgraded 2 years ago at a cost of $22,000. If Option 2 is chosen, it will free up resources that will increase revenues by $3,000.

Complete the following table to show the change in income from choosing Option 2 versus Option 1. Designate any sunk costs with an "S."

|  | Option 1 | Option 2 | Net Income Increase (Decrease) | Sunk (S) |
|---|---|---|---|---|
| Revenues |  |  |  |  |
| Maintenance expenses |  |  |  |  |
| Operating expenses |  |  |  |  |
| Equipment upgrade |  |  |  |  |
| Opportunity cost |  |  |  |  |

### Solution

|  | Option 1 | Option 2 | Net Income Increase (Decrease) | Sunk (S) |
|---|---|---|---|---|
| Revenues | $80,000 | $80,000 | $ 0 |  |
| Maintenance expenses | 5,000 | 12,000 | (7,000) |  |
| Operating expenses | 38,000 | 32,000 | 6,000 |  |
| Equipment upgrade | 22,000 | 0 | 0 | S |
| Opportunity cost | 3,000 | 0 | 3,000 |  |
|  |  |  | $ 2,000 |  |

Related exercise material: **BE14.1, BE14.2, DO IT! 14.1, E14.1, and E14.18.**

---

# Special Orders

**LEARNING OBJECTIVE 2**

Analyze the relevant costs in accepting an order at a special price.

Sometimes a company has an opportunity to obtain additional business if it is willing to make a price concession to a specific customer. To illustrate, assume that Sunbelt Company produces 100,000 Smoothie blenders per month, which is 80% of plant capacity. Variable manufacturing costs are $8 per unit. Fixed manufacturing costs are $400,000, or $4 per unit. The Smoothie blenders are normally sold directly to retailers at $20 each. Sunbelt has an offer from

Kensington Co. (a foreign wholesaler) to purchase an additional 2,000 blenders at $11 per unit. Acceptance of the offer would not affect normal sales of the product, and the additional units can be manufactured without increasing plant capacity. What should management do?

If management makes its decision on the basis of the total cost per unit of $12 ($8 variable + $4 fixed), the order would be rejected because costs per unit ($12) exceed revenues per unit ($11) by $1 per unit. However, since the units can be produced within existing plant capacity, the special order **will not increase fixed costs**. Let's identify the relevant data for the decision.

- The variable manufacturing costs increase $16,000 ($8 × 2,000).
- The expected revenue increases $22,000 ($11 × 2,000).
- Thus, as shown in **Illustration 14.4**, Sunbelt increases its net income by $6,000 by accepting this special order (see **Helpful Hint**).

**HELPFUL HINT**

This is a good example of different costs for different purposes. In the long run all costs are relevant, but for this decision only costs that change are relevant.

**ILLUSTRATION 14.4** **Incremental analysis—accepting an order at a special price**

Incremental Analysis - Accepting an order at a special price

Home    Insert    Page Layout    Formulas    Data    Review    View

P18          fx

| | A | B | C | D |
|---|---|---|---|---|
| 1 | | Reject Order | Accept Order | Net Income Increase (Decrease) |
| 2 | Revenues | $0 | $22,000 | $ 22,000 |
| 3 | Costs | 0 | 16,000 | (16,000) |
| 4 | Net income | $0 | $ 6,000 | $ 6,000 |
| 5 | | | | |

Two points should be emphasized.

1. We assume that sales of the product in other markets **would not be affected by this special order**. If other sales were affected, then Sunbelt would have to consider the change in profit due to lost sales in making the decision.

2. If Sunbelt is operating **at full capacity**, it is likely that the special order would be rejected. Under such circumstances, the company would have to expand plant capacity. In that case, the special order would have to absorb these additional fixed manufacturing costs, as well as the variable manufacturing costs.

## DO IT! 2 | Special Orders

Cobb Company incurs costs of $28 per unit ($18 variable and $10 fixed) to make a product that normally sells for $42. A foreign wholesaler offers to buy 5,000 units at $25 each. The special order results in additional shipping costs of $1 per unit. Compute the increase or decrease in net income Cobb realizes by accepting the special order, assuming Cobb has excess operating capacity. Should Cobb Company accept the special order?

**ACTION PLAN**

- Identify all revenues that would change as a result of accepting the order.

- Identify all costs that would change as a result of accepting the order, and net this amount against the change in revenues.

### Solution

| | Reject | Accept | Net Income Increase (Decrease) |
|---|---|---|---|
| Revenues | $-0- | $125,000* | $125,000 |
| Costs | -0- | 95,000** | (95,000) |
| Net income | $-0- | $ 30,000 | $ 30,000 |

*5,000 × $25
**(5,000 × $18) + (5,000 × $1)

The analysis indicates net income increases by $30,000; therefore, Cobb Company should accept the special order.

Related exercise material: **BE14.3, DO IT! 14.2, E14.2, E14.3, and E14.4.**

# Make or Buy

---

**LEARNING OBJECTIVE 3**

Analyze the relevant costs in a make-or-buy decision.

---

When a manufacturer assembles component parts in producing a finished product, management must decide whether to make or buy the components. The decision to buy parts or services is often referred to as outsourcing. For example, as discussed in the Feature Story, a company such as **Method Products** may either make or buy the soaps used in its products. Similarly, **Hewlett-Packard Corporation** may make or buy the electronic circuitry, cases, and printer heads for its printers. **Boeing** recently sold some of its commercial aircraft factories in an effort to cut production costs and focus on engineering and final assembly rather than manufacturing. The decision to make or buy components should be made on the basis of incremental analysis.

Baron Company makes motorcycles and scooters. **Illustration 14.5** shows the annual costs it incurs in producing 25,000 ignition switches for scooters.

**ILLUSTRATION 14.5**

**Annual product cost data**

| | |
|---|---:|
| Direct materials | $ 50,000 |
| Direct labor | 75,000 |
| Variable manufacturing overhead | 40,000 |
| Fixed manufacturing overhead | 60,000 |
| Total manufacturing costs | $225,000 |
| **Total cost per unit ($225,000 ÷ 25,000)** | **$9.00** |

Instead of making its own switches at a cost of $9, Baron Company might purchase the ignition switches from Ignition, Inc. at a price of $8 per unit. Should management do this?

- A review of operations indicates that if the ignition switches are purchased from Ignition, Inc., *all* of Baron's variable costs but only $10,000 of its fixed manufacturing costs will be eliminated (avoided).

- Thus, $50,000 of the fixed manufacturing costs remain if the ignition switches are purchased.

- The relevant costs for incremental analysis, therefore, are as shown in **Illustration 14.6**.

**ILLUSTRATION 14.6** **Incremental analysis—make or buy**

Incremental Analysis - Make or buy

Home   Insert   Page Layout   Formulas   Data   Review   View

P18          fx

| | A | B | C | D |
|---|---|---:|---:|---:|
| 1 | | Make | Buy | Net Income Increase (Decrease) |
| 2 | Direct materials | $ 50,000 | $ 0 | $ 50,000 |
| 3 | Direct labor | 75,000 | 0 | 75,000 |
| 4 | Variable manufacturing costs | 40,000 | 0 | 40,000 |
| 5 | Fixed manufacturing costs | 60,000 | 50,000 | 10,000 |
| 6 | Purchase price (25,000 × $8) | 0 | 200,000 | (200,000) |
| 7 | Total annual cost | $225,000 | $250,000 | $ (25,000) |
| 8 | | | | |

This analysis indicates that Baron Company incurs $25,000 of additional costs by buying the ignition switches rather than making them. Therefore, Baron should continue to make the ignition switches even though the total manufacturing cost is $1 higher per unit than the purchase price. The primary cause of this result is that, even if the company purchases the ignition switches, it will still have fixed costs of $50,000 to absorb.

## Opportunity Cost

The foregoing make-or-buy analysis is complete only if it is assumed that the productive capacity used to make the ignition switches cannot be converted to another purpose. If there is an opportunity to use this productive capacity in some other manner, then this opportunity cost must be considered. As indicated earlier, **opportunity cost** is the lost potential benefit that could have been obtained by following an alternative course of action (see **Ethics Note**).

To illustrate, assume that through buying the switches, Baron Company can use the released productive capacity to generate additional income of $38,000 from producing a different product.

- This lost income is an additional cost of continuing to make the switches in the make-or-buy decision.
- This opportunity cost is therefore added to the "Make" column for comparison.
- As shown in **Illustration 14.7**, it is now advantageous to buy the ignition switches because the company's income would increase by $13,000.

**ILLUSTRATION 14.7** Incremental analysis—make or buy, with opportunity cost

| A | Make | Buy | Net Income Increase (Decrease) |
|---|---|---|---|
| Total annual cost | $225,000 | $250,000 | $(25,000) |
| Opportunity cost | 38,000 | 0 | 38,000 |
| Total cost | $263,000 | $250,000 | $ 13,000 |

The qualitative factors in this decision include the possible loss of jobs for employees who produce the ignition switches. In addition, management must assess the supplier's ability to satisfy the company's quality control standards at the quoted price per unit on a timely basis.

## Management Insight

Nerthuz/iStock/Getty Images Plus/Getty Images

### Batteries Are Included!

Top managers at every major car manufacturer face a massive "make or buy" decision. For example, consider the production of electric cars. By far, the most expensive component in an electric car is the battery, which costs about $7,500. The battery is critical to vehicle performance since it determines both the power and range of the vehicle. **Mercedes** and **Volkswagen** plan to make their own batteries, but **General Motors**, **BMW**, and **Renault** have decided to buy their batteries from suppliers such as Panasonic and Samsung.

It is not an easy decision. Battery production requires huge investments in plant assets and research and development. **Nissan** learned the hard way that making your own batteries can be a risky venture. It made a big investment in battery production for its electric car, the Leaf, but then suffered huge losses when sales of the Leaf were far below projections. Alternatively, **Tesla**, which only makes electric cars, has fully committed to making its own batteries. In fact, it often describes itself as a battery company.

**Source:** Stephen Wilmot, "Auto Companies: Better with Batteries Not Included," *Wall Street Journal* (December 19, 2016).

**What are the factors that companies must consider in deciding whether to make or to buy the batteries for their vehicles? (Go to WileyPLUS for this answer and additional questions.)**

## ACTION PLAN

- Look for the costs that change.
- Ignore the costs that do not change.
- Use the format in the chapter for your answer.
- Recognize that opportunity cost can make a difference.

## DO IT! 3 | Make or Buy

Juanita Company must decide whether to make or buy some of its components for the appliances it produces. The costs of producing 166,000 electrical cords for its appliances are as follows.

| | | | |
|---|---|---|---|
| Direct materials | $90,000 | Variable overhead | $32,000 |
| Direct labor | 20,000 | Fixed overhead | 24,000 |

Instead of making the electrical cords at an average cost per unit of $1.00 ($166,000 ÷ 166,000), the company has an opportunity to buy the cords at $0.90 per unit. If the company purchases the cords, all variable costs and one-fourth of the fixed costs are eliminated.

**a.** Prepare an incremental analysis showing whether the company should make or buy the electrical cords.

**b.** Will your answer be different if the released productive capacity of the production facility will generate additional income of $5,000?

## Solution

**a.**

| | Make | Buy | Net Income Increase (Decrease) |
|---|---|---|---|
| Direct materials | $ 90,000 | $ –0– | $ 90,000 |
| Direct labor | 20,000 | –0– | 20,000 |
| Variable manufacturing costs | 32,000 | –0– | 32,000 |
| Fixed manufacturing costs | 24,000 | 18,000* | 6,000 |
| Purchase price | –0– | 149,400** | (149,400) |
| Total cost | $166,000 | $167,400 | $ (1,400) |

\*$24,000 × .75
\*\*166,000 × $0.90

This analysis indicates that Juanita Company will incur $1,400 of additional costs if it buys the electrical cords rather than making them.

**b.**

| | Make | Buy | Net Income Increase (Decrease) |
|---|---|---|---|
| Total cost | $166,000 | $167,400 | $(1,400) |
| Opportunity cost | 5,000 | –0– | 5,000 |
| Total cost | $171,000 | $167,400 | $ 3,600 |

Yes, the answer is different. The analysis shows that net income increases by $3,600 if Juanita Company purchases the electrical cords rather than making them.

Related exercise material: **BE14.4, DO IT! 14.3, E14.5, E14.6, E14.7, and E14.8.**

# Sell or Process Further

**LEARNING OBJECTIVE 4**

Analyze the relevant costs and revenues in determining whether to sell or process materials further.

Many manufacturers have the option of selling products at a given point in the production cycle or continuing to process with the expectation of selling them at a later point at a higher price. For example, a bicycle manufacturer such as **Trek** could sell its bicycles to retailers either unassembled or assembled. A furniture manufacturer such as **IKEA** could sell its furniture to stores either unfinished or finished. The sell-or-process-further decision should be made on the basis of incremental analysis. The basic decision rule is: **Process further as long as the incremental revenue from such processing exceeds the incremental processing costs.**

# Single-Product Case

Assume, for example, that Woodmasters Inc. makes tables. It sells unfinished tables for $50. The cost to manufacture an unfinished table is $35, computed as shown in **Illustration 14.8**.

| | |
|---|---:|
| Direct materials | $15 |
| Direct labor | 10 |
| Variable manufacturing overhead | 6 |
| Fixed manufacturing overhead | 4 |
| **Manufacturing cost per unit** | **$35** |

**ILLUSTRATION 14.8**

**Per unit cost of unfinished table**

Woodmasters currently has unused productive capacity that is expected to continue indefinitely. Some of this capacity could be used to finish the tables and sell them at $60 per unit.

- For a finished table, direct materials will increase $2 and direct labor costs will increase $4.
- Variable manufacturing overhead costs will increase by $2.40 (60% of direct labor).
- No increase is anticipated in fixed manufacturing overhead.

Should the company sell the unfinished tables, or should it process them further (see **Helpful Hint**)? **Illustration 14.9** shows the incremental analysis on a per unit basis.

**HELPFUL HINT**

Current net income is known. Net income from processing further is an estimate. In making its decision, management could add a "risk" factor for the estimate.

**ILLUSTRATION 14.9**   **Incremental analysis—sell or process further**

| | A | B Sell Unfinished | C Process Further | D Net Income Increase (Decrease) |
|---|---|---|---|---|
| 1 | | $50.00 | $60.00 | $10.00 |
| 2 | Sales price per unit | $50.00 | $60.00 | $10.00 |
| 3 | Cost per unit | | | |
| 4 | Direct materials | 15.00 | 17.00 | (2.00) |
| 5 | Direct labor | 10.00 | 14.00 | (4.00) |
| 6 | Variable manufacturing overhead | 6.00 | 8.40 | (2.40) |
| 7 | Fixed manufacturing overhead | 4.00 | 4.00 | 0.00 |
| 8 | Total | 35.00 | 43.40 | (8.40) |
| 9 | Net income per unit | $15.00 | $16.60 | $ 1.60 |
| 10 | | | | |

It would be advantageous for Woodmasters to process the tables further. The incremental revenue of $10.00 from the additional processing is $1.60 higher than the incremental processing costs of $8.40.

# Multiple-Product Case

Sell-or-process-further decisions are particularly applicable to processes that produce multiple products simultaneously.

- In many industries, a number of end-products are produced from a single raw material and a common production process.
- These multiple end-products are commonly referred to as **joint products**.

For example, in the meat-packing industry, **Armour** processes a cow or pig into meat, internal organs, hides, bones, and fat products. In the petroleum industry, **ExxonMobil** refines crude oil to produce gasoline, lubricating oil, kerosene, paraffin, and ethylene.

**Illustration 14.10** presents a joint product situation for Marais Creamery involving a decision **to sell or process further** cream and skim milk. Cream and skim milk are joint products that result from the processing of raw milk.

ILLUSTRATION 14.10 | Joint production process—Creamery

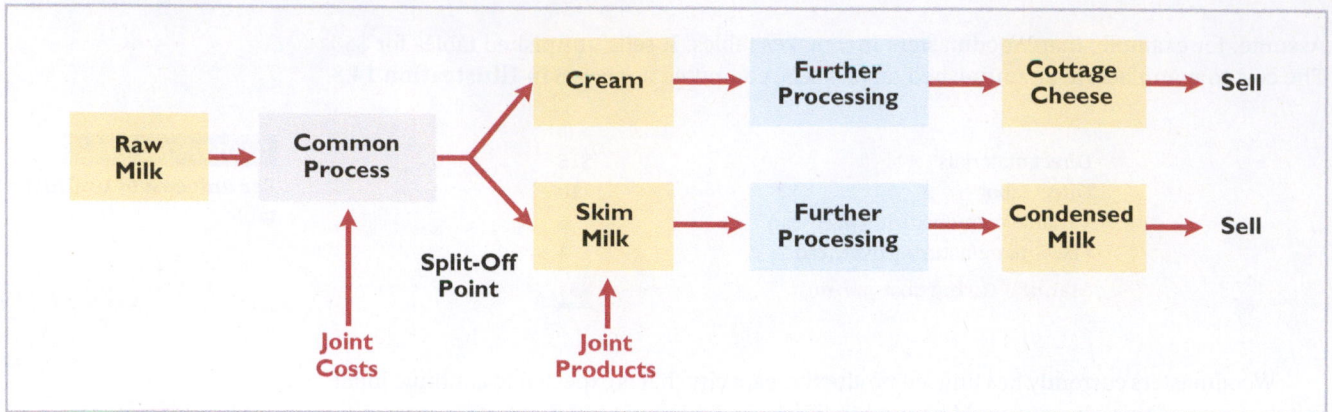

Marais incurs many costs prior to the manufacture of the cream and skim milk. All costs incurred prior to the point at which the two products are separately identifiable (the **split-off point**) are called **joint costs**.

- For purposes of determining the cost of each product, joint product costs must be allocated to the individual products.
- This is frequently done based on the relative sales value of the joint products.
- While this allocation is important for determination of product cost, **it is irrelevant for any sell-or-process-further decisions; joint product costs are sunk costs**. That is, they have already been incurred, and they cannot be changed or avoided by any subsequent decision.

**Illustration 14.11** provides the daily cost and revenue data for Marais Creamery related to cream and cottage cheese.

**ILLUSTRATION 14.11**

**Cost and revenue data per day for cream**

| Costs (per day) | |
| --- | --- |
| Joint cost allocated to cream | $ 9,000 |
| Cost to process cream into cottage cheese | 10,000 |
| **Revenues from Products (per day)** | |
| Cream | $19,000 |
| Cottage cheese | 27,000 |

From this information, we can determine whether the company should simply sell the cream or process it further into cottage cheese. **Illustration 14.12** shows the necessary analysis.

ILLUSTRATION 14.12 | Analysis of whether to sell cream or process into cottage cheese

Incremental Analysis - Sell or process further - Cream or cottage cheese

Home | Insert | Page Layout | Formulas | Data | Review | View

P18  fx

| | A | B | C | D |
| --- | --- | --- | --- | --- |
| 1 | | Sell | Process Further | Net Income Increase (Decrease) |
| 2 | Sales per day | $19,000 | $27,000 | $ 8,000 |
| 3 | Cost per day to process cream into cottage cheese | 0 | 10,000 | (10,000) |
| 4 | Net income per day | $19,000 | $17,000 | $ (2,000) |
| 5 | | | | |

- Note that the joint cost of $9,000 that is allocated to the cream is not included in this decision.
- It is not relevant to the decision because it is a sunk cost.
- It has been incurred in the past and will remain the same no matter whether the cream is subsequently processed into cottage cheese or not.

From this analysis, we can see that Marais should not process the cream further because it will sustain an incremental loss of $2,000.

**Illustration 14.13** provides the daily cost and revenue data for the company related to skim milk and condensed milk.

| Costs (per day) | |
|---|---:|
| Joint cost allocated to skim milk | $ 5,000 |
| Cost to process skim milk into condensed milk | 8,000 |
| **Revenues from Products (per day)** | |
| Skim milk | $11,000 |
| Condensed milk | 26,000 |

**ILLUSTRATION 14.13**

Cost and revenue data per day for skim milk

**Illustration 14.14** shows that Marais Company should process the skim milk into condensed milk, as it will increase net income by $7,000.

**ILLUSTRATION 14.14**  **Analysis of whether to sell skim milk or process into condensed milk**

Incremental Analysis - Sell or process further - Skim milk or condensed milk

Home   Insert   Page Layout   Formulas   Data   Review   View

P18            fx

| | A | B | C | D |
|---|---|---|---|---|
| 1 | | Sell | Process Further | Net Income Increase (Decrease) |
| 2 | Sales per day | $11,000 | $26,000 | $15,000 |
| 3 | Cost per day to process skim milk into condensed milk | 0 | 8,000 | (8,000) |
| 4 | Net income per day | $11,000 | $18,000 | $ 7,000 |
| 5 | | | | |

- Again, note that the $5,000 of joint cost allocated to the skim milk is irrelevant in deciding whether to sell or process further.
- The joint cost remains the same, whether or not further processing is performed.
- These decisions need to be reevaluated as market conditions change.

For example, if the price of skim milk increases relative to the price of condensed milk, it may become more profitable to sell the skim milk rather than process it into condensed milk. Consider also oil refineries. As market conditions change, the companies must constantly reassess which products to produce from the oil they receive at their plants.

## DO IT! 4 | Sell or Process Further

Easy Does It manufactures unpainted furniture for the do-it-yourself (DIY) market. It currently sells a child's rocking chair for $25. Production costs per unit are $12 variable and $8 fixed. Easy Does It is considering painting the rocking chair and selling it for $35. Variable costs to paint each chair are expected to be $9, and fixed costs are expected to be $2.

Prepare an analysis showing whether Easy Does It should sell unpainted or painted chairs.

**ACTION PLAN**

- **Identify the revenues that change as a result of painting the rocking chair.**
- **Identify all costs that change as a result of painting the rocking chair, and net the amount against the revenues.**

**Solution**

| | Sell | Process Further | Net Income Increase (Decrease) |
|---|---:|---:|---:|
| Revenues | $25 | $35 | $10 |
| Variable costs | 12 | 21[a] | (9) |
| Fixed costs | 8 | 10[b] | (2) |
| Net income | $ 5 | $ 4 | $(1) |

[a]$12 + $9;  [b]$8 + $2

The analysis indicates that the rocking chair should be sold unpainted because net income per chair will be $1 greater.

Related exercise material: **BE14.5, BE14.6, DO IT! 14.4, E14.9, E14.10, E14.11, and E14.12.**

# Repair, Retain, or Replace Equipment

> **LEARNING OBJECTIVE 5**
>
> Analyze the relevant costs to be considered in repairing, retaining, or replacing equipment.

Management often has to decide whether to continue using an asset, repair it, or replace it. For example, **Delta Airlines** must decide whether to replace old jets with new, more fuel-efficient ones. To illustrate, assume that Jeffcoat Company has a factory machine that originally cost $110,000. It has a balance in Accumulated Depreciation of $70,000, so the machine's book value is $40,000. It has a remaining useful life of four years. The company is considering replacing this machine with a new machine. A new machine is available that costs $120,000. It is expected to have zero salvage value at the end of its four-year useful life. If the new machine is acquired, variable manufacturing costs are expected to decrease from $160,000 to $125,000 annually, and the old unit could be sold for $5,000. **Illustration 14.15** shows the incremental analysis for the **four-year period**.

**ILLUSTRATION 14.15** Incremental analysis—retain or replace equipment

Incremental Analysis - Retain or replace equipment

| | Retain Equipment | | Replace Equipment | | Net Income Increase (Decrease) |
|---|---|---|---|---|---|
| Variable manufacturing costs | $640,000 | a | $500,000 | b | $140,000 |
| New machine cost | | | 120,000 | | (120,000) |
| Sale of old machine | | | (5,000) | | 5,000 |
| Total | $640,000 | | $615,000 | | $ 25,000 |

a4 years × $160,000
b4 years × $125,000

In this case, it would be to the company's advantage to replace the equipment.

- The lower variable manufacturing costs due to replacement more than offset the cost of the new equipment.
- Note that the $5,000 received from the sale of the old machine is relevant to the decision because it will only be received if the company chooses to replace its equipment.

In general, any trade-in allowance or cash disposal value of existing assets is relevant to the decision to retain or replace equipment.

One other point should be mentioned regarding Jeffcoat's decision: **The book value of the old machine does not affect the decision.**

- Book value is a **sunk cost**, which is a cost that cannot be changed by any present or future decision.
- **Sunk costs are not relevant in incremental analysis.**

In this example, if the asset is retained, book value will be depreciated over its remaining useful life. Or, if the new unit is acquired, book value will be recognized as a loss of the current period. Thus, the effect of book value on cumulative future earnings is the same regardless of the replacement decision.

Sometimes, decisions regarding whether to replace equipment are clouded by behavioral decision-making errors. For example, suppose a manager spent $90,000 repairing a machine two months ago. Suppose that the machine now breaks down again. The manager might be inclined to think that because the company recently spent a large amount of money to repair the machine, the machine should be repaired again rather than replaced. However, the amount spent in the past to repair the machine is irrelevant to the current decision. It is a sunk cost.

Similarly, suppose a manager spent $5,000,000 to purchase a machine. Six months later, a new machine comes on the market that is significantly more efficient than the one recently purchased. The manager might be inclined to think that he or she should not buy the new machine because of the recent purchase. In fact, the manager might fear that buying a different machine so quickly might call into question the merit of the previous decision. Again, the fact that the company recently bought a machine is not relevant. Instead, the manager should use incremental analysis to determine whether the savings generated by the efficiencies of the new machine would justify its purchase.

## DO IT! 5 | Repair or Replace Equipment

Rochester Roofing is faced with a decision. The company relies very heavily on the use of its 60-foot extension lift for work on large homes and commercial properties. Last year, the company spent $60,000 refurbishing the lift. It has just determined that another $40,000 of repair work is required. Alternatively, Rochester Roofing has found a newer used lift that is for sale for $170,000. The company estimates that both the old and new lifts would have useful lives of 6 years. However, the new lift is more efficient and thus would reduce operating expenses by about $20,000 per year. The company could also rent out the new lift for about $2,000 per year. The old lift is not suitable for rental. The old lift could currently be sold for $25,000 if the new lift is purchased. Prepare an incremental analysis that shows whether the company should repair or replace the equipment.

**ACTION PLAN**

- **Those costs and revenues that differ across the alternatives are relevant to the decision.**
- **Past costs that cannot be changed are sunk costs.**

### Solution

| | Retain Equipment | Replace Equipment | Net Income Increase (Decrease) |
|---|---|---|---|
| Operating expenses | $120,000* | | $120,000 |
| Repair costs | 40,000 | | 40,000 |
| Rental revenue | | $ (12,000)** | 12,000 |
| New machine cost | | 170,000 | (170,000) |
| Sale of old machine | | (25,000) | 25,000 |
| Total cost | $160,000 | $133,000 | $ 27,000 |

*6 years × $20,000
**6 years × $2,000

The analysis indicates that purchasing the new machine would increase net income for the 6-year period by $27,000.

Related exercise material: **BE14.7, DO IT! 14.5, E14.13, and E14.14.**

# Eliminate Unprofitable Segment or Product

**LEARNING OBJECTIVE 6**

Analyze the relevant costs in deciding whether to eliminate an unprofitable segment or product.

Management sometimes must decide whether to eliminate an unprofitable business segment or product. For example, in recent years, many airlines quit servicing certain cities or cut back on the number of flights. Goodyear quit producing several brands in the low-end tire market. Again, the key is to **focus on the relevant costs—the data that change under the** alternative courses of action (see **Helpful Hint**). To illustrate, assume that Venus Company manufactures tennis racquets in three models: Pro, Master, and Champ. Pro and Master are profitable lines. Champ (highlighted in red in the table below) operates at a loss. Condensed income statement data are as shown in **Illustration 14.16**.

**ILLUSTRATION 14.16**

**Segment income data**

|  | Pro | Master | Champ | Total |
|---|---|---|---|---|
| Sales | $800,000 | $300,000 | $100,000 | $1,200,000 |
| Variable costs | 520,000 | 210,000 | 90,000 | 820,000 |
| Contribution margin | 280,000 | 90,000 | 10,000 | 380,000 |
| Fixed costs | 80,000 | 50,000 | 30,000 | 160,000 |
| Net income | $200,000 | $ 40,000 | $ (20,000) | $ 220,000 |

You might think that total net income will increase by $20,000 to $240,000 if the unprofitable Champ line of racquets is eliminated. However, **net income may actually decrease if the Champ line is discontinued**.

- The reason is that the company's total fixed costs will be the same whether or not the Champ line is discontinued.
- That is, the fixed costs allocated to the Champ racquets cannot be eliminated, so they will have to be absorbed by the other products.

To illustrate, assume that the $30,000 of fixed costs applicable to the unprofitable segment are instead allocated $\frac{2}{3}$ to the Pro model and $\frac{1}{3}$ to the Master model if the Champ model is eliminated. Fixed costs will increase to $100,000 ($80,000 + $20,000) in the Pro line and to $60,000 ($50,000 + $10,000) in the Master line. **Illustration 14.17** shows the revised income statement.

**ILLUSTRATION 14.17**

**Income data after eliminating unprofitable product line**

|  | Pro | Master | Total |
|---|---|---|---|
| Sales | $800,000 | $300,000 | $1,100,000 |
| Variable costs | 520,000 | 210,000 | 730,000 |
| Contribution margin | 280,000 | 90,000 | 370,000 |
| Fixed costs | 100,000 | 60,000 | 160,000 |
| Net income | $180,000 | $ 30,000 | $ 210,000 |

Total net income would decrease $10,000 ($220,000 − $210,000). This result is also obtained in the incremental analysis of the Champ racquets shown in **Illustration 14.18**.

**ILLUSTRATION 14.18** **Incremental analysis—eliminating unprofitable segment with no reduction in fixed costs**

Incremental Analysis - Eliminating an unprofitable segment

Home   Insert   Page Layout   Formulas   Data   Review   View

P18        fx

|  | A | B | C | D |
|---|---|---|---|---|
| 1 |  | Continue | Eliminate | Net Income Increase (Decrease) |
| 2 | Sales | $100,000 | $ 0 | $(100,000) |
| 3 | Variable costs | 90,000 | 0 | 90,000 |
| 4 | Contribution margin | 10,000 | 0 | (10,000) |
| 5 | Fixed costs | 30,000 | 30,000 | 0 |
| 6 | Net income | $(20,000) | $(30,000) | $ (10,000) |
| 7 |  |  |  |  |

The loss in net income is attributable to the Champ line's $10,000 contribution margin ($220,000 − $210,000), which will not be realized if the segment is discontinued.

Assume the same facts as above, except now assume that $22,000 of the fixed costs attributed to the Champ line can be eliminated if the line is discontinued. **Illustration 14.19** presents the incremental analysis based on this revised assumption.

**ILLUSTRATION 14.19** Incremental analysis—eliminating unprofitable segment with reduction in fixed costs

| | Incremental Analysis - Eliminating an unprofitable segment | | |
|---|---|---|---|
| | Home   Insert   Page Layout   Formulas   Data   Review   View | | |
| | P18   *fx* | | |
| | A | B | C | D |
| 1 | | Continue | Eliminate | Net Income Increase (Decrease) |
| 2 | Sales | $100,000 | $    0 | $(100,000) |
| 3 | Variable costs | 90,000 | 0 | 90,000 |
| 4 | Contribution margin | 10,000 | 0 | (10,000) |
| 5 | Fixed costs | 30,000 | 8,000 | 22,000 |
| 6 | Net income | $ (20,000) | $(8,000) | $   12,000 |
| 7 | | | | |

In this case, because the company is able to eliminate some of its fixed costs by eliminating the division, it can increase its net income by $12,000. **This occurs because the $22,000 savings that results from the eliminated fixed costs exceeds the $10,000 in lost contribution margin by $12,000 ($22,000 − $10,000).**

In deciding on the future status of an unprofitable segment, management should consider the effect of elimination on related product lines.

- It may be possible for continuing product lines to obtain some or all of the sales lost by the discontinued product line.

- In some businesses, services or products may be linked—for example, free checking accounts at a bank, or coffee at a donut shop.

- In addition, management should consider the effect of eliminating the product line on employees who may have to be discharged or retrained.

---

## Service Company Insight   Amazon.com

### Giving Away the Store?

iStock.com/klenger

In an earlier chapter, we discussed Amazon.com's incredible growth. However, some analysts have questioned whether some of the methods that Amazon uses to increase its sales make good business sense. For example, a few years ago, Amazon initiated a "Prime" free-shipping subscription program. For an annual fee, Amazon's customers get free shipping on as many goods as they want to buy. At the time, CEO Jeff Bezos promised that the program would be costly in the short-term but benefit the company in the long-term. Six years later, it was true that Amazon's sales had grown considerably. It was also estimated that its Prime customers buy two to three times as much as non-Prime customers. But, its shipping costs rose from 2.8% of sales to 4% of sales, which is remarkably similar to the drop in its gross margin from 24% to 22.3%. Amazon's order fulfillment center uses 30,000 robots and more than 100 million square feet of space. It generates significant fees from merchants that sell on its site and rely on its fulfillment services.

**Sources:** Martin Peers, "Amazon's Prime Numbers," *Wall Street Journal Online* (February 3, 2011); and Evan Niu, "Ever Wonder How Amazon.com Pays for All of That Free Shipping?" *The Motley Fool* (October 26, 2015).

**What are the relevant revenues and costs that Amazon should consider relative to the decision whether to offer the Prime free-shipping subscription? (Go to WileyPLUS for this answer and additional questions.)**

---

## DO IT! 6  |  Unprofitable Segments

Lambert, Inc. manufactures several types of accessories. For the year, the knit hats and scarves line had sales of $400,000, variable expenses of $310,000, and fixed expenses of $120,000. Therefore, the knit hats and scarves line had a net loss of $30,000. If Lambert eliminates the knit hats and scarves line, $20,000 of fixed costs will remain. Prepare an analysis showing whether the company should eliminate the knit hats and scarves line.

**ACTION PLAN**

- **Identify the revenues that change as a result of eliminating a product line.**

- **Identify all costs that change as a result of eliminating a product line, and net the amount against the revenues.**

### Solution

| | Continue | Eliminate | Net Income Increase (Decrease) |
|---|---|---|---|
| Sales | $400,000 | $ 0 | $(400,000) |
| Variable costs | 310,000 | 0 | 310,000 |
| Contribution margin | 90,000 | 0 | (90,000) |
| Fixed costs | 120,000 | 20,000 | 100,000 |
| Net income | $(30,000) | $(20,000) | $ 10,000 |

The analysis indicates that Lambert should eliminate the knit hats and scarves line because net income will increase $10,000.

Related exercise material: **BE14.8, DO IT! 14.6, E14.15, E14.16, and E14.17.**

## USING THE DECISION TOOLS | Method Products

**Method Products** faces many situations where it needs to apply the decision tool learned in this chapter. For example, assume that in order to have control over the creative nature of its packaging, Method decides to manufacture (instead of outsourcing) some of its more creative soap dispensers. Suppose that the company has been approached by a plastic container manufacturer with a proposal to provide 500,000 Mickey and Minnie Mouse hand wash dispensers. Assume Method's cost of producing 500,000 of the dispensers is $110,000, broken down as follows.

| Direct materials | $60,000 | Variable manufacturing overhead | $12,000 |
|---|---|---|---|
| Direct labor | 30,000 | Fixed manufacturing overhead | 8,000 |

Instead of making the dispensers at an average cost per unit of $0.22 ($110,000 ÷ 500,000), Method has an opportunity to buy the dispensers at $0.215 per unit. If the dispensers are purchased, all variable costs and one-half of the fixed costs will be eliminated.

### Instructions

a. Prepare an incremental analysis showing whether Method should make or buy the dispensers.

b. Will your answer be different if the released productive capacity resulting from the purchase of the dispensers will generate additional income of $25,000?

c. What additional qualitative factors might Method need to consider?

### Solution
a.

| | Make | Buy | Net Income Increase (Decrease) |
|---|---|---|---|
| Direct materials | $ 60,000 | $ –0– | $ 60,000 |
| Direct labor | 30,000 | –0– | 30,000 |
| Variable manufacturing costs | 12,000 | –0– | 12,000 |
| Fixed manufacturing costs | 8,000 | 4,000* | 4,000 |
| Purchase price | –0– | 107,500** | (107,500) |
| Total cost | $110,000 | $111,500 | $ (1,500) |

*$8,000 × .50; **$0.215 × 500,000

This analysis indicates that Method will incur $1,500 of additional costs if it buys the dispensers. Method therefore would choose to make the dispensers.

b.

| | Make | Buy | Net Income Increase (Decrease) |
|---|---|---|---|
| Total cost | $110,000 | $111,500 | $(1,500) |
| Opportunity cost | 25,000 | –0– | 25,000 |
| Total cost | $135,000 | $111,500 | $23,500 |

Yes, the answer is different. The analysis shows that if additional capacity is released, net income will be increased by $23,500 if the dispensers are purchased. In this case, Method would choose to purchase the dispensers.

**c.** Method is very concerned about the image of its products. It charges a higher price for many of its products than those of its larger competitors. It therefore wants to ensure that the functionality of the dispenser, as well as the appearance, are up to its standards. Also, because of Method's commitment to sustainability, it would consider numerous qualitative issues. For example, is this supplier going to use sustainable manufacturing practices? Method currently requires that its suppliers meet its expectations regarding sustainability.

# Review and Practice

## Learning Objectives Review

**1  Describe management's decision-making process and incremental analysis.**

Management's decision-making process consists of (a) identifying the problem and assigning responsibility for the decision, (b) determining and evaluating possible courses of action, (c) making the decision, and (d) reviewing the results of the decision. Incremental analysis identifies financial data that change under alternative courses of action. These data are relevant to the decision because they vary across the possible alternatives.

**2  Analyze the relevant costs in accepting an order at a special price.**

The relevant costs are those that change if the order is accepted. The relevant information in accepting an order at a special price is the difference between the variable manufacturing costs to produce the special order and expected revenues. Any changes in fixed costs, opportunity cost, or other incremental costs or savings (such as additional shipping) should be considered.

**3  Analyze the relevant costs in a make-or-buy decision.**

In a make-or-buy decision, the relevant costs are (a) the variable manufacturing costs that will be saved as well as changes to fixed

manufacturing costs, (b) the purchase price, and (c) opportunity cost.

**4  Analyze the relevant costs and revenues in determining whether to sell or process materials further.**

The decision rule for whether to sell or process materials further is: Process further as long as the incremental revenue from processing exceeds the incremental processing costs.

**5  Analyze the relevant costs to be considered in repairing, retaining, or replacing equipment.**

The relevant costs to be considered in determining whether equipment should be repaired, retained, or replaced are the effects on variable costs and the cost of the new equipment. Also, any disposal value of the existing asset must be considered.

**6  Analyze the relevant costs in deciding whether to eliminate an unprofitable segment or product.**

In deciding whether to eliminate an unprofitable segment or product, the relevant costs are the variable costs that drive the contribution margin, if any, produced by the segment or product. Opportunity cost and reduction of fixed expenses must also be considered.

## Decision Tools Review

| Decision Checkpoints | Info Needed for Decision | Tool to Use for Decision | How to Evaluate Results |
|---|---|---|---|
| Which alternative should the company choose? | All relevant costs including opportunity cost | Compare the relevant cost of each alternative. | Choose the alternative that maximizes net income. |

## Glossary Review

**Incremental analysis** The process of identifying the financial data that change under alternative courses of action. (p. 14-3).

**Joint costs** For joint products, all costs incurred prior to the point at which the two products are separately identifiable (known as the split-off point). (p. 14-12).

**Joint products** Multiple end-products produced from a single raw material and a common production process. (p. 14-11).

**Opportunity cost** The potential benefit that is lost when one course of action is chosen rather than an alternative course of action. (p. 14-4).

**Relevant costs and revenues** Those costs and revenues that differ across alternatives. (p. 14-4).

**Sunk cost** A cost incurred in the past that cannot be changed or avoided by any present or future decision. (p. 14-4).

## Practice Multiple-Choice Questions

**1. (LO 1)** Three of the steps in management's decision-making process are (1) review results of decision, (2) determine and evaluate possible courses of action, and (3) make the decision. The steps are carried out in the following order:

a. (1), (2), (3).

b. (3), (2), (1).

c. (2), (1), (3).

d. (2), (3), (1).

**2. (LO 1)** Incremental analysis is the process of identifying the financial data that:

a. do not change under alternative courses of action.

b. change under alternative courses of action.

c. are mixed under alternative courses of action.

d. No correct answer is given.

**3. (LO 1)** In making business decisions, management ordinarily considers:

a. quantitative factors but not qualitative factors.

b. financial information only.

c. both financial and nonfinancial information.

d. relevant costs, opportunity cost, and sunk costs.

**4. (LO 1)** A company is considering the following alternatives:

| | Alternative A | Alternative B |
|---|---|---|
| Revenues | $50,000 | $50,000 |
| Variable costs | 24,000 | 24,000 |
| Fixed costs | 12,000 | 15,000 |

Which of the following are relevant in choosing between these alternatives?

a. Revenues, variable costs, and fixed costs.

b. Variable costs and fixed costs.

c. Variable costs only.

d. Fixed costs only.

**5. (LO 2)** It costs a company $14 of variable costs and $6 of fixed costs to produce product Z200, which sells for $30. A foreign buyer offers to purchase 3,000 units at $18 each. If the special offer is accepted and produced with unused capacity, net income will:

a. decrease $6,000.

b. increase $6,000.

c. increase $12,000.

d. increase $9,000.

**6. (LO 2)** It costs a company $14 of variable costs and $6 of fixed costs to produce product Z200. Product Z200 sells for $30. A buyer offers to purchase 3,000 units at $18 each. The seller will incur special shipping costs of $5 per unit. If the special offer is accepted and produced with unused capacity, net income will:

a. increase $3,000.

b. increase $12,000.

c. decrease $12,000.

d. decrease $3,000.

**7. (LO 3)** Jobart Company is currently operating at full capacity. It is considering buying a part from an outside supplier rather than making it in-house. If Jobart purchases the part, it can use the released productive capacity to generate additional income of $30,000 from producing a different product. When conducting incremental analysis in this make-or-buy decision, the company should:

a. ignore the $30,000.

b. add $30,000 to other costs in the "Make" column.

c. add $30,000 to other costs in the "Buy" column.

d. subtract $30,000 from the other costs in the "Make" column.

**8. (LO 3)** In a make-or-buy decision, relevant costs are:

a. manufacturing costs that will be saved.

b. the purchase price of the units.

c. the opportunity cost.

d. All of the answer choices are correct.

**9. (LO 3)** Derek is performing incremental analysis in a make-or-buy decision for Item X. If Derek buys Item X, he can use its released productive capacity to produce Item Z. Derek will sell Item Z for $12,000 and incur production costs of $8,000. Derek's incremental analysis should include an opportunity cost of:

a. $12,000.

b. $8,000.

c. $4,000.

d. $0.

**10. (LO 4)** The decision rule in a sell-or-process-further decision is: Process further as long as the incremental revenue from processing exceeds:

a. incremental processing costs.

b. variable processing costs.

c. fixed processing costs.

d. No correct answer is given.

**11. (LO 4)** Walton, Inc. makes an unassembled product that it currently sells for $55. Production costs are $20. Walton is considering assembling the product and selling it for $68. The cost to assemble the product is estimated at $12. What decision should Walton make?

a. Sell before assembly; net income per unit will be $12 greater.

b. Sell before assembly; net income per unit will be $1 greater.

c. Process further; net income per unit will be $13 greater.

d. Process further; net income per unit will be $1 greater.

**12. (LO 5)** In a decision to retain or replace equipment, the book value of the old equipment is a (an):

    **a.** opportunity cost.        **c.** incremental cost.

    **b.** sunk cost.            **d.** marginal cost.

**13. (LO 6)** If an unprofitable segment is eliminated:

    **a.** net income will always increase.

    **b.** variable costs of the eliminated segment will have to be absorbed by other segments.

    **c.** fixed costs allocated to the eliminated segment will have to be absorbed by other segments.

    **d.** net income will always decrease.

**14. (LO 6)** A segment of Hazard Inc. has the following data.

| | |
|---|---|
| Sales | $200,000 |
| Variable expenses | 140,000 |
| Fixed expenses | 100,000 |

If this segment is eliminated, what will be the effect on the remaining company? Assume that 50% of the fixed expenses will be eliminated and the rest will be allocated to the segments of the remaining company.

    **a.** $120,000 increase.

    **b.** $10,000 decrease.

    **c.** $50,000 increase.

    **d.** $10,000 increase.

## Solutions

**1. d.** The order of the steps in the decision process is (2) determine and evaluate possible courses of action, (3) make the decision, and (1) review the results of decision. Choices (a), (b), and (c) list the steps in the incorrect order.

**2. b.** Incremental analysis is the process of identifying the financial data that change under alternative courses of action, not the financial data that (a) do not change or (c) are mixed. Choice (d) is wrong as there is a correct answer given.

**3. c.** Management ordinarily considers both financial and nonfinancial information in making business decisions. The other choices are incorrect because they are all limited to financial data and do not consider nonfinancial information.

**4. d.** Fixed costs is the only relevant factor, that is, the only factor that differs across Alternatives A and B. The other choices are incorrect because they list either revenues, variable costs, or both, which are the same amounts for both alternatives.

**5. c.** If the special offer is accepted and produced with unused capacity, variable cost per unit = $14, income per unit = ($18 − $14), so net income will increase by $12,000 (3,000 × $4), not (a) decrease $6,000, (b) increase $6,000, or (d) increase $9,000.

**6. d.** If the special offer is accepted and produced with unused capacity, variable cost per unit = $19 ($14 variable + $5 shipping costs), income per unit = −$1 ($18 − $19), so net income will decrease by $3,000 (3,000 × −$1), not (a) increase $3,000, (b) increase $12,000, or (c) decrease $12,000.

**7. b.** Jobart Company should add $30,000 to other costs in the "Make" column as it represents lost income of continuing to make the part in-house. The other choices are incorrect because the $30,000 (a) should not be ignored as it is an opportunity cost, (c) represents potential lost income if the company continues to make the part instead of buying it so therefore should not be placed in the "Buy" column, and (d) should be added to, not subtracted from, the other costs in the "Make" column.

**8. d.** All the costs in choices (a), (b), and (c) are relevant in a make-or-buy decision. So although choices (a), (b), and (c) are true statements, choice (d) is a better answer.

**9. c.** Derek's opportunity cost in its make-or-buy decision is $12,000 (revenue for Item Z) − $8,000 (production costs for Item Z) = $4,000, not (a) $12,000, (b) $8,000, or (d) $0.

**10. a.** The decision rule in a sell-or-process-further decision is to process further as long as the incremental revenue from such processing exceeds incremental processing costs, not (b) variable processing costs or (c) fixed processing costs. Choice (d) is wrong as there is a correct answer given.

**11. d.** If Walton processes further, net income per unit will increase $13 ($68 − $55), which is $1 more than its additional production costs ($12). The other choices are therefore incorrect.

**12. b.** In the decision to retain or replace equipment, the book value of the old equipment is a sunk cost (it reflects the original cost less accumulated depreciation, neither of which is relevant to the decision), not (a) an opportunity cost, (c) an incremental cost, or (d) a marginal cost.

**13. c.** Even though the segment is eliminated, the fixed costs allocated to that segment will still have to be covered. This is done by having other segments absorb the fixed costs of that segment. Choices (a) and (d) are incorrect because net income can either increase or decrease if a segment is eliminated. Choice (b) is incorrect because when a segment is eliminated, the variable costs of that segment will also be eliminated and will not need to be absorbed by other segments.

**14. b.** If the segment continues, net income = −$40,000 ($200,000 − $140,000 − $100,000). If the segment is eliminated, the contribution margin will also be eliminated but $50,000 ($100,000 × .50) of the fixed costs will remain. Therefore, the effect of eliminating the segment will be a $10,000 decrease not (a) a $120,000 increase, (c) a $50,000 increase, or (d) a $10,000 increase.

## Practice Brief Exercises

**1. (LO 3)** Flavia Industries incurs unit costs of $24 ($18 variable and $6 fixed) in making an assembly part for its finished product. A supplier offers to make 20,000 units of the assembly part at $17 per unit. If the offer is accepted, Flavia will save all variable costs but no fixed costs. Prepare an analysis showing the total cost saving, if any, Flavia will realize by buying the part.

*Determine whether to make or buy a part.*

### Solution

**1.**

|  | Make | Buy | Net Income Increase (Decrease) |
|---|---|---|---|
| Variable manufacturing costs | $360,000 | $ –0– | $360,000 |
| Fixed manufacturing costs | 120,000 | 120,000 | –0– |
| Purchase price | –0– | 340,000 | (340,000) |
| Total annual cost | $480,000 | $460,000 | $ 20,000 |

The decision should be to buy the part.

*Determine whether to sell or process further.*

**2. (LO 4)** Fast Speed Bicycle Inc. makes parts for unfinished bicycles that it sells for $125. Production costs are $40 variable and $20 fixed. Because of unused capacity, Fast Speed is considering finishing the bicycles and selling them for $200. Additional variable finishing costs are expected to be $65 with no increase in fixed costs. Prepare an analysis on a per unit basis showing whether Fast Speed should sell unfinished or unfinished bicycles.

### Solution

**2.**

|  | Sell | Process Further | Net Income Increase (Decrease) |
|---|---|---|---|
| Sales price per unit | $125 | $200 | $75 |
| Cost per unit |  |  |  |
| Variable | 40 | 105 | (65) |
| Fixed | 20 | 20 | 0 |
| Total | 60 | 125 | (65) |
| Net income per unit | $ 65 | $ 75 | $10 |

The bicycles should be processed further because the incremental revenues exceed incremental costs by $10 per unit.

*Determine whether to eliminate an unprofitable segment.*

**3. (LO 6)** Hava Racquets Company manufactures pickleball racquets in four different models. For the year, the SoftNet line had a net loss of $40,000 from sales of $250,000, variable costs of $180,000, and fixed costs of $110,000. If the SoftNet line is eliminated, $30,000 of fixed costs will remain. Prepare an analysis showing whether the SoftNet Line should be eliminated.

### Solution

**3.**

|  | Continue | Eliminate | Net Income Increase (Decrease) |
|---|---|---|---|
| Sales | $250,000 | $ –0– | $(250,000) |
| Variable costs | 180,000 | –0– | 180,000 |
| Contribution margin | 70,000 | –0– | (70,000) |
| Fixed costs | 110,000 | 30,000 | 80,000 |
| Net income | $(40,000) | $(30,000) | $ 10,000 |

The SoftNet product line should be eliminated because $80,000 of fixed cost is eliminated whereas only $70,000 of contribution margin is realized if the line is continued. The $70,000 related to the contribution margin is lower than the $80,000 savings related to fixed costs and therefore a savings of $10,000 results by eliminating SoftNet.

## Practice Exercises

*Use incremental analysis for make-or-buy decision.*

**1. (LO 3)** Maningly Inc. has been manufacturing its own lampshades for its table lamps. The company is currently operating at 100% of capacity. Variable manufacturing overhead is charged to production at the rate of 50% of direct labor cost. The direct materials and direct labor cost per unit to make the lampshades are $4 and $6, respectively. Normal production is 50,000 table lamps per year.

A supplier offers to make the lampshades at a price of $13.50 per unit. If Maningly accepts the supplier's offer, all variable manufacturing costs will be eliminated. But, the $50,000 of fixed manufacturing overhead currently being charged to the lampshades will have to be absorbed by other products.

**Instructions**

a. Prepare the incremental analysis for the decision to make or buy the lampshades.

b. Should Maningly buy the lampshades?

c. Would your answer be different in (b) if the productive capacity released by not making the lampshades could be used to produce income of $40,000?

## Solution

**1. a.**

|  | Make | Buy | Net Income Increase (Decrease) |
|---|---|---|---|
| Direct materials (50,000 × $4.00) | $200,000 | $    -0- | $ 200,000 |
| Direct labor (50,000 × $6.00) | 300,000 | -0- | 300,000 |
| Variable manufacturing costs |  |  |  |
| ($300,000 × 50%) | 150,000 | -0- | 150,000 |
| Fixed manufacturing costs | 50,000 | 50,000 | -0- |
| Purchase price (50,000 × $13.50) | -0- | 675,000 | (675,000) |
| Total annual cost | $700,000 | $725,000 | $ (25,000) |

b. No, Maningly should not purchase the lampshades. As indicated by the incremental analysis, it would cost the company $25,000 more to purchase the lampshades.

c. Yes, by purchasing the lampshades, a total cost saving of $15,000 will result as shown below.

|  | Make | Buy | Net Income Increase (Decrease) |
|---|---|---|---|
| Total annual cost (from (a)) | $700,000 | $725,000 | $(25,000) |
| Opportunity cost | 40,000 | -0- | 40,000 |
| Total cost | $740,000 | $725,000 | $ 15,000 |

**2. (LO 4)** A company manufactures three products using the same production process. The costs incurred up to the split-off point are $200,000. These costs are allocated to the products on the basis of their sales value at the split-off point. The number of units produced, the selling prices per unit of the three products at the split-off point and after further processing, and the additional processing costs are as follows.

*Use incremental analysis for whether to sell or process materials further.*

| Product | Number of Units Produced | Selling Price at Split-Off | Selling Price after Processing | Additional Processing Costs |
|---|---|---|---|---|
| D | 3,000 | $11.00 | $15.00 | $14,000 |
| E | 6,000 | 12.00 | 16.20 | 16,000 |
| F | 2,000 | 19.40 | 24.00 | 9,000 |

**Instructions**

a. Which information is relevant to the decision on whether or not to process the products further? Explain why this information is relevant.

b. Which product(s) should be processed further and which should be sold at the split-off point?

c. Would your decision be different if the company was using the quantity of output to allocate joint costs? Explain.

(CGA adapted)

## Solution

**2. a.** The costs that are relevant in this decision are the incremental revenues and the incremental costs associated with processing the material past the split-off point. Any costs incurred up to the split-off point are sunk costs and therefore irrelevant to this decision.

**b.** Revenue after further processing:
Product D: $45,000 (3,000 units × $15.00 per unit)
Product E: $97,200 (6,000 units × $16.20 per unit)
Product F: $48,000 (2,000 units × $24.00 per unit)

Revenue at split-off:
Product D: $33,000 (3,000 units × $11.00 per unit)
Product E: $72,000 (6,000 units × $12.00 per unit)
Product F: $38,800 (2,000 units × $19.40 per unit)

| | D | E | F |
|---|---|---|---|
| Incremental revenue | $ 12,000[a] | $ 25,200[b] | $ 9,200[c] |
| Incremental cost | (14,000) | (16,000) | (9,000) |
| Increase (decrease) in profit | $ (2,000) | $ 9,200 | $ 200 |

[a]$45,000 − $33,000; [b]$97,200 − $72,000; [c]$48,000 − $38,800

Products E and F should be processed further, but Product D should not be processed further.

**c.** The decision would remain the same. It does not matter how the joint costs are allocated because joint costs are irrelevant to this decision.

*Use incremental analysis for retaining or replacing equipment.*

**3. (LO 5)** Tek Enterprises uses a computer to process its sales invoices. Lately, business has been so good that it takes an extra 3 hours per night, plus every third Saturday, to keep up with the volume of sales invoices. Management is considering updating its computer with a faster model that would eliminate all of the overtime processing.

| | Current Machine | New Machine |
|---|---|---|
| Original purchase cost | $15,000 | $25,000 |
| Accumulated depreciation | 6,000 | — |
| Estimated annual operating costs | 25,000 | 20,000 |
| Useful life | 6 years | 6 years |

If sold now, the current machine would have a salvage value of $5,000. If operated for the remainder of its useful life, the current machine would have zero salvage value. The new machine is expected to have zero salvage value after 6 years.

**Instructions**

Should the current machine be replaced? (Ignore the time value of money.)

**Solution**

**3.**

| | Retain Machine | Replace Machine | Net Income Increase (Decrease) |
|---|---|---|---|
| Operating costs | $150,000* | $120,000** | $30,000 |
| New machine cost | -0- | 25,000 | (25,000) |
| Salvage value (old) | -0- | (5,000) | 5,000 |
| Total | $150,000 | $140,000 | $10,000 |

*$25,000 × 6
**$20,000 × 6

The current machine should be replaced. The incremental analysis shows that net income for the 6-year period will be $10,000 higher by replacing the current machine.

*Use incremental analysis for elimination of division.*

**4. (LO 6)** Benai Lorenzo, a recent graduate of Bonita's accounting program, evaluated the operating performance of Wasson Company's six divisions. Benai made the following presentation to the Wasson board of directors and suggested the Ortiz Division be eliminated. "If the Ortiz Division is eliminated," she said, "our total profits would increase by $23,870."

| | The Other Five Divisions | Ortiz Division | Total |
|---|---|---|---|
| Sales | $1,664,200 | $ 96,200 | $1,760,400 |
| Cost of goods sold | 978,520 | 76,470 | 1,054,990 |
| Gross profit | 685,680 | 19,730 | 705,410 |
| Operating expenses | 527,940 | 43,600 | 571,540 |
| Net income | $ 157,740 | $(23,870) | $ 133,870 |

In the Ortiz Division, cost of goods sold is $70,000 variable and $6,470 fixed, and operating expenses are $15,000 variable and $28,600 fixed. None of the Ortiz Division's fixed costs will be eliminated if the division is discontinued.

### Instructions

Is Benai right about eliminating the Ortiz Division? Prepare an incremental analysis schedule to support your answer.

### Solution

4.

| | Continue | Eliminate | Net Income Increase (Decrease) |
|---|---|---|---|
| Sales | $ 96,200 | $      -0- | $(96,200) |
| Variable expenses | | | |
| Cost of goods sold | 70,000 | -0- | 70,000 |
| Operating expenses | 15,000 | -0- | 15,000 |
| Total variable | 85,000 | -0- | 85,000 |
| Contribution margin | 11,200 | -0- | (11,200) |
| Fixed expenses | | | |
| Cost of goods sold | 6,470 | 6,470 | -0- |
| Operating expenses | 28,600 | 28,600 | -0- |
| Total fixed | 35,070 | 35,070 | -0- |
| Net income (loss) | $(23,870) | $(35,070) | $(11,200) |

Benai is incorrect. The incremental analysis shows that net income will be $11,200 less if the Ortiz Division is eliminated. This amount equals the contribution margin that would be lost by discontinuing the division.

## Practice Problem

**(LO 2)** Walston Company produces kitchen cabinets for homebuilders across the western United States. The cost of producing 5,000 cabinets is as follows.

*Use incremental analysis for a special order.*

| | |
|---|---|
| Materials | $  500,000 |
| Labor | 250,000 |
| Variable overhead | 100,000 |
| Fixed overhead | 400,000 |
| Total | $1,250,000 |

Walston also incurs selling expenses of $20 per cabinet. Wellington Corp. has offered Walston $165 per cabinet for a special order of 1,000 cabinets. The cabinets would be sold to homebuilders in the eastern United States and thus would not conflict with Walston's current sales. Selling expenses per cabinet would be only $5 per cabinet. Walston has available capacity to do the work.

### Instructions

a. Prepare an incremental analysis for the special order.

b. Should Walston accept the special order? Why or why not?

### Solution

a. Relevant costs per unit would be:

| | |
|---|---|
| Materials | $500,000 ÷ 5,000 = $100 |
| Labor | 250,000 ÷ 5,000 =    50 |
| Variable overhead | 100,000 ÷ 5,000 =    20 |
| Selling expenses | 5 |
| Total relevant cost per unit | $175 |

| | Reject Order | Accept Order | Net Income Increase (Decrease) |
|---|---|---|---|
| Revenues | $-0- | $165,000* | $ 165,000 |
| Costs | -0- | 175,000** | (175,000) |
| Net income | $-0- | $(10,000) | $ (10,000) |

*$165 × 1,000; **$175 × 1,000

**b.** Walston should reject the offer. The incremental benefit of $165 per cabinet is less than the incremental cost of $175. By accepting the order, Walston's net income would actually decline by $10,000.

# WileyPLUS

Brief Exercises, DO IT! Exercises, Exercises, Problems, and many additional resources are available for practice in WileyPLUS.

## Questions

**1.** What steps are frequently involved in management's decision-making process?

**2.** Your roommate, Anna Polis, contends that accounting contributes to most of the steps in management's decision-making process. Is your roommate correct? Explain.

**3.** "Incremental analysis involves the accumulation of information concerning a single course of action." Do you agree? Why or why not?

**4.** Sydney Greene asks for your help concerning the relevance of variable and fixed costs in incremental analysis. Help Sydney with her problem.

**5.** What data are relevant in deciding whether to accept an order at a special price?

**6.** Emil Corporation has an opportunity to buy parts at $9 each that currently cost $12 to make. What manufacturing costs are relevant to this make-or-buy decision?

**7.** Define the term "opportunity cost." How may this cost be relevant in a make-or-buy decision?

**8.** What is the decision rule in deciding whether to sell a product or process it further?

**9.** What are joint products? What accounting issue results from the production process that creates joint products?

**10.** How are allocated joint costs treated when making a sell-or-process-further decision?

**11.** Your roommate, Gale Dunham, is confused about sunk costs. Explain to your roommate the meaning of sunk costs and their relevance to a decision to retain or replace equipment.

**12.** Huang Inc. has one product line that is unprofitable. What circumstances may cause overall company net income to be lower if the unprofitable product line is eliminated?

## Brief Exercises

*Identify the steps in management's decision-making process.*

**BE14.1 (LO 1), K** The steps in management's decision-making process are listed in random order below. Indicate the order in which the steps should be executed.

_____ Make a decision.
_____ Identify the problem and assign responsibility.
_____ Review results of the decision.
_____ Determine and evaluate possible courses of action.

*Determine incremental changes.*

**BE14.2 (LO 1), AP** Bogart Company is considering two alternatives. Alternative A will have revenues of $160,000 and costs of $100,000. Alternative B will have revenues of $180,000 and costs of $125,000. Compare Alternative A to Alternative B showing incremental revenues, costs, and net income.

*Determine whether to accept a special order.*

**BE14.3 (LO 2), AP** At Bargain Electronics, it costs $30 per unit ($20 variable and $10 fixed) to make an MP3 player that normally sells for $45. A foreign wholesaler offers to buy 3,000 units at $25 each. Bargain Electronics will incur special shipping costs of $3 per unit. Assuming that Bargain Electronics has excess operating capacity, indicate the net income (loss) Bargain Electronics would realize by accepting the special order.

*Determine whether to make or buy a part.*

**BE14.4 (LO 3), AP** Manson Industries incurs unit costs of $8 ($5 variable and $3 fixed) in making an assembly part for its finished product. A supplier offers to make 10,000 of the assembly part at $6 per unit. If the offer is accepted, Manson will save all variable costs but no fixed costs. Prepare an analysis showing the total cost saving, if any, that Manson will realize by buying the part.

**BE14.5 (LO 4), AP** Pine Street Inc. makes unfinished bookcases that it sells for $62. Production costs are $36 variable and $10 fixed. Because it has unused capacity, Pine Street is considering finishing the bookcases and selling them for $70. Variable finishing costs are expected to be $6 per unit with no increase in fixed costs. Prepare an analysis on a per unit basis showing whether Pine Street should sell unfinished or finished bookcases.

*Determine whether to sell or process further.*

**BE14.6 (LO 4), AP** Each day, Adama Corporation processes 1 ton of a secret raw material into two resulting products, AB1 and XY1. When it processes 1 ton of the raw material, the company incurs joint processing costs of $60,000. It allocates $25,000 of these costs to AB1 and $35,000 of these costs to XY1. The resulting AB1 can be sold for $100,000. Alternatively, it can be processed further to make AB2 at an additional processing cost of $45,000, and sold for $150,000. Each day's batch of XY1 can be sold for $95,000. Or, it can be processed further to create XY2, at an additional processing cost of $50,000, and sold for $130,000. Discuss what products Adama Corporation should make.

*Determine whether to sell or process further, joint products.*

**BE14.7 (LO 5), AP** Bryant Company has a factory machine with a book value of $90,000 and a remaining useful life of 5 years. It can be sold for $30,000. A new machine is available at a cost of $400,000. This machine will have a 5-year useful life with no salvage value. The new machine will lower annual variable manufacturing costs from $600,000 to $500,000. Prepare an analysis showing whether the old machine should be retained or replaced.

*Determine whether to retain or replace equipment.*

**BE14.8 (LO 6), AP** Lisah, Inc., manufactures golf clubs in three models. For the year, the Big Bart line has a net loss of $10,000 from sales $200,000, variable costs $180,000, and fixed costs $30,000. If the Big Bart line is eliminated, $20,000 of fixed costs will remain. Prepare an analysis showing whether the Big Bart line should be eliminated.

*Determine whether to eliminate an unprofitable segment.*

# DO IT! Exercises

**DO IT! 14.1 (LO 1), AN** Nathan T Corporation is comparing two different options. Nathan T currently uses Option 1, with revenues of $65,000 per year, maintenance expenses of $5,000 per year, and operating expenses of $26,000 per year. Option 2 provides revenues of $60,000 per year, maintenance expenses of $5,000 per year, and operating expenses of $22,000 per year. Option 1 employs a piece of equipment which was upgraded 2 years ago at a cost of $17,000. If Option 2 is chosen, it will free up resources that will bring in an additional $4,000 of revenue. Complete the following table to show the change in income from choosing Option 2 versus Option 1. Designate sunk costs with an "S."

*Determine incremental costs.*

|  | Option 1 | Option 2 | Net Income Increase (Decrease) | Sunk (S) |
|---|---|---|---|---|
| Revenues |  |  |  |  |
| Maintenance expenses |  |  |  |  |
| Operating expenses |  |  |  |  |
| Equipment upgrade |  |  |  |  |
| Opportunity cost |  |  |  |  |

**DO IT! 14.2 (LO 2), AN** Maize Company incurs a cost of $35 per unit, of which $20 is variable, to make a product that normally sells for $58. A foreign wholesaler offers to buy 6,000 units at $30 each. Maize will incur additional costs of $4 per unit to imprint a logo and to pay for shipping. Compute the increase or decrease in net income Maize will realize by accepting the special order, assuming Maize has sufficient excess operating capacity. Should Maize Company accept the special order?

*Evaluate special order.*

**DO IT! 14.3 (LO 3), AN** Wilma Company must decide whether to make or buy some of its components. The costs of producing 60,000 switches for its generators are as follows.

| | | | |
|---|---|---|---|
| Direct materials | $30,000 | Variable overhead | $45,000 |
| Direct labor | 42,000 | Fixed overhead | 60,000 |

*Evaluate make-or-buy opportunity.*

Instead of making the switches at an average cost of $2.95 ($177,000 ÷ 60,000), the company has an opportunity to buy the switches at $2.70 per unit. If the company purchases the switches, all the variable costs and one-fourth of the fixed costs will be eliminated. (a) Prepare an incremental analysis showing whether the company should make or buy the switches. (b) Would your answer be different if the released productive capacity will generate additional income of $34,000?

*Sell or process further.*

**DO IT! 14.4 (LO 4), AP** Mesa Verde manufactures unpainted furniture for the do-it-yourself (DIY) market. It currently sells a table for $75. Production costs per unit are $40 variable and $10 fixed. Mesa Verde is considering staining and sealing the table to sell it for $100. Variable costs per unit to finish each table are expected to be an additional $19 per unit, and fixed costs are expected to be an additional $3 per unit. Prepare an analysis showing whether Mesa Verde should sell stained or finished tables.

*Repair or replace equipment.*

**DO IT! 14.5 (LO 5), AP** Darcy Roofing is faced with a decision. The company relies very heavily on the use of its 60-foot extension lift for work on large homes and commercial properties. Last year, Darcy Roofing spent $60,000 refurbishing the lift. It has just determined that another $40,000 of repair work is required. Alternatively, it has found a newer used lift that is for sale for $170,000. The company estimates that both lifts would have useful lives of 6 years. The new lift is more efficient and thus would reduce operating expenses by about $20,000 per year. Darcy Roofing could also rent out the new lift for about $10,000 per year. The old lift is not suitable for rental. The old lift could currently be sold for $25,000 if the new lift is purchased. Prepare an incremental analysis showing whether the company should repair or replace the equipment.

*Analyze whether to eliminate unprofitable segment.*

**DO IT! 14.6 (LO 6), AP** Gator Corporation manufactures several types of accessories. For the year, the gloves and mittens line had sales of $500,000, variable expenses of $370,000, and fixed expenses of $150,000. Therefore, the gloves and mittens line had a net loss of $20,000. If Gator eliminates the line, $38,000 of fixed costs will remain. Prepare an analysis showing whether the company should eliminate the gloves and mittens line.

# Exercises

*Analyze statements about decision-making and incremental analysis.*

**E14.1 (LO 1), C** As a study aid, your classmate Pascal Adams has prepared the following list of statements about decision-making and incremental analysis.

1. The first step in management's decision-making process is, "Determine and evaluate possible courses of action."

2. The final step in management's decision-making process is to actually make the decision.

3. Accounting's contribution to management's decision-making process occurs primarily in evaluating possible courses of action and in reviewing the results.

4. In making business decisions, management ordinarily considers only financial information because it is objectively determined.

5. Decisions involve a choice among alternative courses of action.

6. The process used to identify the financial data that change under alternative courses of action is called incremental analysis.

7. Costs that are the same under all alternative courses of action sometimes affect the decision.

8. When using incremental analysis, some costs will always change under alternative courses of action, but revenues will not.

9. Variable costs will change under alternative courses of action, but fixed costs will not.

**Instructions**

Identify each statement as true or false. If false, indicate how to correct the statement.

*Use incremental analysis for special-order decision.*

**E14.2 (LO 2), AN** Gruden Company produces golf discs which it normally sells to retailers for $7 each. The cost of manufacturing 20,000 golf discs is:

| | |
|---|---|
| Materials | $ 10,000 |
| Labor | 30,000 |
| Variable overhead | 20,000 |
| Fixed overhead | 40,000 |
| Total | $100,000 |

Gruden also incurs 5% sales commission ($0.35) on each disc sold.

McGee Corporation offers Gruden $4.80 per disc for 5,000 discs. McGee would sell the discs under its own brand name in foreign markets not yet served by Gruden. If Gruden accepts the offer, its fixed overhead will increase from $40,000 to $46,000 due to the purchase of a new imprinting machine. No sales commission will result from the special order.

## Instructions

**a.** Prepare an incremental analysis for the special order.

**b.** Should Gruden accept the special order? Why or why not?

**c.** What assumptions underlie the decision made in part (b)?

**E14.3 (LO 2), AN** Moonbeam Company manufactures toasters. For the first 8 months of 2022, the company reported the following operating results while operating at 75% of plant capacity:

*Use incremental analysis for special order.*

| | |
|---|---|
| Sales (350,000 units) | $4,375,000 |
| Cost of goods sold | 2,600,000 |
| Gross profit | 1,775,000 |
| Operating expenses | 840,000 |
| Net income | $ 935,000 |

Cost of goods sold was 70% variable and 30% fixed; operating expenses were 80% variable and 20% fixed.

In September, Moonbeam receives a special order for 15,000 toasters at $7.60 each from Luna Company of Ciudad Juarez. Acceptance of the order would result in an additional $3,000 of shipping costs but no increase in fixed costs.

## Instructions

**a.** Prepare an incremental analysis for the special order.

**b.** Should Moonbeam accept the special order? Why or why not?

**E14.4 (LO 2), AN** Klean Fiber Company is the creator of Y-Go, a technology that weaves silver into its fabrics to kill bacteria and odor on clothing while managing heat. Y-Go has become very popular in undergarments for sports activities. Operating at capacity, the company can produce 1,000,000 Y-Go undergarments a year. The per unit and the total costs for an individual garment when the company operates at full capacity are as follows.

*Use incremental analysis for special order.*

| | Per Undergarment | Total |
|---|---|---|
| Direct materials | $2.00 | $2,000,000 |
| Direct labor | 0.75 | 750,000 |
| Variable manufacturing overhead | 1.00 | 1,000,000 |
| Fixed manufacturing overhead | 1.50 | 1,500,000 |
| Variable selling expenses | 0.25 | 250,000 |
| Totals | $5.50 | $5,500,000 |

The U.S. Army has approached Klean Fiber and expressed an interest in purchasing 250,000 Y-Go undergarments for soldiers in extremely warm climates. The Army would pay the unit cost for direct materials, direct labor, and variable manufacturing overhead costs. In addition, the Army has agreed to pay an additional $1 per undergarment to cover all other costs and provide a profit. Presently, Klean Fiber is operating at 70% capacity and does not have any other potential buyers for Y-Go. If Klean Fiber accepts the Army's offer, it will not incur any variable selling expenses related to this order.

## Instructions

Using incremental analysis, determine whether Klean Fiber should accept the Army's offer.

**E14.5 (LO 3), AN** Pottery Ranch Inc. has been manufacturing its own finials for its curtain rods. The company is currently operating at 100% of capacity, and variable manufacturing overhead is charged to production at the rate of 70% of direct labor cost. The direct materials and direct labor cost per unit to make a pair of finials are $4 and $5, respectively. Normal production is 30,000 curtain rods per year.

*Use incremental analysis for make-or-buy decision.*

A supplier offers to make a pair of finials at a price of $12.95 per unit. If Pottery Ranch accepts the supplier's offer, all variable manufacturing costs will be eliminated, but the $45,000 of fixed manufacturing overhead currently being charged to the finials will have to be absorbed by other products.

## Instructions

**a.** Prepare the incremental analysis for the decision to make or buy the finials.

**b.** Should Pottery Ranch buy the finials?

**c.** Would your answer be different in (b) if the productive capacity released by not making the finials could be used to produce income of $20,000?

**E14.6 (LO 3), E** Jobs, Inc. has recently started the manufacture of Tri-Robo, a three-wheeled robot that can scan a home for fires and gas leaks and then transmit this information to a smartphone. The cost structure to manufacture 20,000 Tri-Robos is as follows.

*Use incremental analysis for make-or-buy decision.*

| | Cost |
|---|---|
| Direct materials ($50 per robot) | $1,000,000 |
| Direct labor ($40 per robot) | 800,000 |
| Variable overhead ($6 per robot) | 120,000 |
| Allocated fixed overhead ($30 per robot) | 600,000 |
| Total | $2,520,000 |

Jobs is approached by Tienh Inc., which offers to make Tri-Robo for $115 per unit or $2,300,000.

**Instructions**

a. Using incremental analysis, determine whether Jobs should accept this offer under each of the following independent assumptions.

   1. Assume that $405,000 of the fixed overhead cost can be avoided.

   2. Assume that none of the fixed overhead can be avoided. However, if the robots are purchased from Tienh Inc., Jobs can use the released productive resources to generate additional income of $375,000.

b. Describe the qualitative factors that might affect the decision to purchase the robots from an outside supplier.

*Prepare incremental analysis for make-or-buy decision.*

**E14.7 (LO 3), E** Riggs Company purchases sails and produces sailboats. It currently produces 1,200 sailboats per year, operating at normal capacity, which is about 80% of full capacity. Riggs purchases sails at $250 each, but the company is considering using the excess capacity to manufacture the sails instead. The manufacturing cost per sail would be $100 for direct materials, $80 for direct labor, and $90 for overhead. The $90 overhead is based on $78,000 of annual fixed overhead that is allocated using normal capacity.

The president of Riggs has come to you for advice. "It would cost me $270 to make the sails," she says, "but only $250 to buy them. Should I continue buying them, or have I missed something?"

**Instructions**

a. Prepare a per unit analysis of the differential costs. Briefly explain whether Riggs should make or buy the sails.

b. If Riggs suddenly finds an opportunity to rent out the unused capacity of its factory for $77,000 per year, would your answer to part (a) change? Briefly explain.

c. Identify three qualitative factors that should be considered by Riggs in this make-or-buy decision.

(CGA adapted)

*Prepare incremental analysis concerning make-or-buy decision.*

**E14.8 (LO 3), E** Innova uses 1,000 units of the component IMC2 every month to manufacture one of its products. The unit costs incurred to manufacture the component are as follows.

| | |
|---|---|
| Direct materials | $ 65.00 |
| Direct labor | 45.00 |
| Overhead | 126.50 |
| Total | $236.50 |

Overhead costs include variable material handling costs of $6.50, which are applied to products on the basis of direct material costs. The remainder of the overhead costs are applied on the basis of direct labor dollars and consist of 60% variable costs and 40% fixed costs.

A vendor has offered to supply the IMC2 component at a price of $200 per unit.

**Instructions**

a. Should Innova purchase the component from the outside vendor if Innova's capacity remains idle?

b. Should Innova purchase the component from the outside vendor if it can use its facilities to manufacture another product? What information will Innova need to make an accurate decision? Show your calculations.

c. What are the qualitative factors that Innova will have to consider when making this decision?

(CGA adapted)

*Use incremental analysis for further processing of materials decision.*

**E14.9 (LO 4), AN** Anna Garden recently opened her own basketweaving studio. She sells finished baskets in addition to selling the raw materials needed by customers to weave baskets of their own. Unfortunately, owing to space limitations, Anna is unable to carry all the varieties of kits originally assembled and must choose between two basic packages.

The Basic Kit includes undyed, uncut reeds (with dye included) for weaving one basket. This basic package costs Anna $16 and sells for $30. The second kit, called Stage 2, includes cut reeds that have already been dyed. With this kit the customer need only soak the reeds and weave the basket. Anna produces the Stage 2 kit by using the materials included in the Basic Kit. Because she is more efficient at cutting and dying reeds than her average customer, Anna is able to produce two Stage 2 kits in one hour from one Basic Kit. (She values her time at $18 per hour.) The Stage 2 kit sells for $36.

### Instructions

Determine whether Anna's basketweaving studio should carry the Basic Kit with undyed and uncut reeds or the Stage 2 kit with reeds already dyed and cut. Prepare an incremental analysis to support your answer.

**E14.10 (LO 4), AN** Stahl Inc. produces three separate products from a common process costing $100,000. Each of the products can be sold at the split-off point or can be processed further and then sold for a higher price. Shown here are cost and selling price data for a recent period.

*Determine whether to sell or process further, joint products.*

| | Sales Value at Split-Off Point | Cost to Process Further | Sales Value after Further Processing |
|---|---|---|---|
| Product 10 | $60,000 | $100,000 | $190,000 |
| Product 12 | 15,000 | 30,000 | 35,000 |
| Product 14 | 55,000 | 150,000 | 215,000 |

### Instructions

a. Determine total net income if all products are sold at the split-off point.

b. Determine total net income if all products are sold after further processing.

c. Using incremental analysis, determine which products should be sold at the split-off point and which should be processed further.

d. Determine total net income using the results from (c) and explain why the net income is different from that determined in (b).

**E14.11 (LO 4), AN** Kirk Minerals processes materials extracted from mines. The most common raw material that it processes results in three joint products: Spock, Uhura, and Sulu. Each of these products can be sold as is, or each can be processed further and sold for a higher price. The company incurs joint costs of $180,000 to process one batch of the raw material that produces the three joint products. The following cost and sales information is available for one batch of each product.

*Determine whether to sell or process further, joint products.*

| | Sales Value at Split-Off Point | Allocated Joint Costs | Cost to Process Further | Sales Value of Processed Product |
|---|---|---|---|---|
| Spock | $210,000 | $40,000 | $110,000 | $300,000 |
| Uhura | 300,000 | 60,000 | 85,000 | 400,000 |
| Sulu | 455,000 | 80,000 | 250,000 | 800,000 |

### Instructions

Determine whether each of the three joint products should be sold as is, or processed further.

**E14.12 (LO 4), E** A company manufactures three products using the same production process. The costs incurred up to the split-off point are $200,000. These costs are allocated to the products on the basis of their sales value at the split-off point. The number of units produced, the selling prices per unit of the three products at the split-off point and after further processing, and the additional processing costs are as follows.

*Prepare incremental analysis for whether to sell or process materials further.*

| Product | Number of Units Produced | Selling Price at Split-Off | Selling Price after Processing | Additional Processing Costs |
|---|---|---|---|---|
| D | 4,000 | $10.00 | $15.00 | $14,000 |
| E | 6,000 | 11.60 | 16.20 | 20,000 |
| F | 2,000 | 19.40 | 22.60 | 9,000 |

### Instructions

a. Which information is relevant to the decision on whether or not to process the products further? Explain why this information is relevant.

**b.** Which product(s) should be processed further and which should be sold at the split-off point?

**c.** Would your decision be different if the company was using the quantity of output to allocate joint costs? Explain.

(CGA adapted)

*Use incremental analysis for retaining or replacing equipment decision.*

**E14.13 (LO 5), E** Service On January 2, 2021, Twilight Hospital purchased a $100,000 special radiology scanner from Bella Inc. The scanner had a useful life of 4 years and was estimated to have no disposal value at the end of its useful life. The straight-line method of depreciation is used on this scanner. Annual operating costs with this scanner are $105,000.

Approximately one year later, the hospital is approached by Dyno Technology salesperson, Jacob Cullen, who indicated that purchasing the scanner in 2021 from Bella Inc. was a mistake. He points out that Dyno has a scanner that will save Twilight Hospital $25,000 a year in operating expenses over its 3-year useful life. Jacob notes that the new scanner will cost $110,000 and has the same capabilities as the scanner purchased last year. The hospital agrees that both scanners are of equal quality. The new scanner will have no disposal value. Jacob agrees to buy the old scanner from Twilight Hospital for $50,000.

**Instructions**

**a.** If Twilight Hospital sells its old scanner on January 2, 2022, compute the gain or loss on the sale.

**b.** Using incremental analysis, determine if Twilight Hospital should purchase the new scanner on January 2, 2022.

**c.** Explain why Twilight Hospital might be reluctant to purchase the new scanner, regardless of the results indicated by the incremental analysis in (b).

*Use incremental analysis for retaining or replacing equipment decision.*

**E14.14 (LO 5), AN** Johnson Enterprises uses a computer to handle its sales invoices. Lately, business has been so good that it takes an extra 3 hours per night, plus every third Saturday, to keep up with the volume of sales invoices. Management is considering updating its computer with a faster model that would eliminate all of the overtime processing.

|  | Current Machine | New Machine |
|---|---|---|
| Original purchase cost | $15,000 | $25,000 |
| Accumulated depreciation | $ 6,000 | — |
| Estimated annual operating costs | $25,000 | $20,000 |
| Remaining useful life | 5 years | 5 years |

If sold now, the current machine would have a salvage value of $6,000. If operated for the remainder of its useful life, the current machine would have zero salvage value. The new machine is expected to have zero salvage value after 5 years.

**Instructions**

Prepare an incremental analysis to determine whether the current machine should be replaced.

*Use incremental analysis concerning elimination of division.*

**E14.15 (LO 6), AN** Veronica Mars, a recent graduate of Bell's accounting program, evaluated the operating performance of Dunn Company's six divisions. Veronica made the following presentation to Dunn's board of directors and suggested the Percy Division be eliminated. "If the Percy Division is eliminated," she said, "our total profits would increase by $26,000."

|  | The Other Five Divisions | Percy Division | Total |
|---|---|---|---|
| Sales | $1,664,200 | $100,000 | $1,764,200 |
| Cost of goods sold | 978,520 | 76,000 | 1,054,520 |
| Gross profit | 685,680 | 24,000 | 709,680 |
| Operating expenses | 527,940 | 50,000 | 577,940 |
| Net income | $ 157,740 | $(26,000) | $ 131,740 |

In the Percy Division, cost of goods sold is $61,000 variable and $15,000 fixed, and operating expenses are $30,000 variable and $20,000 fixed. None of the Percy Division's fixed costs will be eliminated if the division is discontinued.

**Instructions**

Is Veronica right about eliminating the Percy Division? Prepare a schedule to support your answer.

*Use incremental analysis for elimination of a product line.*

**E14.16 (LO 6), AN** Cawley Company makes three models of tasers. Information on the three products is given here.

| | Tingler | Shocker | Stunner |
|---|---|---|---|
| Sales | $300,000 | $500,000 | $200,000 |
| Variable expenses | 150,000 | 200,000 | 145,000 |
| Contribution margin | 150,000 | 300,000 | 55,000 |
| Fixed expenses | 120,000 | 230,000 | 95,000 |
| Net income | $ 30,000 | $ 70,000 | $(40,000) |

Fixed expenses consist of $300,000 of common costs allocated to the three products based on relative sales, as well as direct fixed expenses unique to each model of $30,000 (Tingler), $80,000 (Shocker), and $35,000 (Stunner). The common costs will be incurred regardless of how many models are produced. The direct fixed expenses would be eliminated if that model is phased out.

James Watt, an executive with the company, feels the Stunner line should be discontinued to increase the company's net income.

### Instructions

a. Compute current net income for Cawley Company.

b. Compute net income by product line and in total for Cawley Company if the company discontinues the Stunner product line. (*Hint:* Allocate the $300,000 common costs to the two remaining product lines based on their relative sales.)

c. Should Cawley eliminate the Stunner product line? Why or why not?

**E14.17 (LO 6), AN** Tharp Company operates a small factory in which it manufactures two products: C and D. Production and sales results for last year were as follows.

*Prepare incremental analysis concerning keeping or dropping a product to maximize operating income.*

| | C | D |
|---|---|---|
| Units sold | 9,000 | 20,000 |
| Selling price per unit | $95 | $75 |
| Variable cost per unit | 50 | 40 |
| Fixed cost per unit | 24 | 24 |

For purposes of simplicity, the firm averages total fixed costs over the total number of units of C and D produced and sold.

The research department has developed a new product (E) as a replacement for product D. Market studies show that Tharp Company could sell 10,000 units of E next year at a price of $115; the variable cost per unit of E is $45. The introduction of product E will lead to a 10% increase in demand for product C and discontinuation of product D. If the company does not introduce the new product, it expects next year's results to be the same as last year's.

### Instructions

Should Tharp Company introduce product E next year? Explain why or why not. Show calculations to support your decision.

(CMA-Canada adapted)

**E14.18 (LO 1, 2, 3, 4, 5, 6), C** The following costs relate to a variety of different decision situations.

*Identify relevant costs for different decisions.*

| Cost | Decision |
|---|---|
| 1. Unavoidable fixed overhead | Eliminate an unprofitable segment |
| 2. Direct labor | Make or buy |
| 3. Original cost of old equipment | Equipment replacement |
| 4. Joint production costs | Sell or process further |
| 5. Opportunity cost | Accepting a special order |
| 6. Segment manager's salary | Eliminate an unprofitable segment (manager will be terminated) |
| 7. Cost of new equipment | Equipment replacement |
| 8. Incremental production costs | Sell or process further |
| 9. Direct materials | Equipment replacement (the amount of materials required does not change) |
| 10. Rent expense | Purchase or lease a building |

### Instructions

For each cost listed above, indicate if it is relevant or not to the related decision. For those costs determined to be irrelevant, briefly explain why.

# Problems

*Use incremental analysis for special order and identify nonfinancial factors in the decision.*

**P14.1 (LO 2), E** Writing ThreePoint Sports Inc. manufactures basketballs for the Women's National Basketball Association (WNBA). For the first 6 months of 2022, the company reported the following operating results while operating at 80% of plant capacity and producing 120,000 units.

|  | Amount |
| --- | --- |
| Sales | $4,800,000 |
| Cost of goods sold | 3,600,000 |
| Selling and administrative expenses | 405,000 |
| Net income | $ 795,000 |

Fixed costs for the period were cost of goods sold $960,000, and selling and administrative expenses $225,000.

In July, normally a slack manufacturing month, ThreePoint Sports receives a special order for 10,000 basketballs at $28 each from the Greek Basketball Association (GBA). Acceptance of the order would increase variable selling and administrative expenses $0.75 per unit because of shipping costs but would not increase fixed costs and expenses.

### Instructions

**a.** NI increase $37,500

    **a.** Prepare an incremental analysis for the special order.

    **b.** Should ThreePoint Sports Inc. accept the special order? Explain your answer.

    **c.** What is the minimum selling price on the special order to produce net income of $5.00 per ball?

    **d.** What nonfinancial factors should management consider in making its decision?

*Use incremental analysis related to make or buy, consider opportunity cost, and identify nonfinancial factors.*

**P14.2 (LO 3), E** Writing The management of Shatner Manufacturing Company is trying to decide whether to continue manufacturing a part or to buy it from an outside supplier. The part, called CISCO, is a component of the company's finished product.

The following information was collected from the accounting records and production data for the year ending December 31, 2022.

    **1.** 8,000 units of CISCO were produced in the Machining Department.

    **2.** Variable manufacturing costs applicable to the production of each CISCO unit were: direct materials $4.80, direct labor $4.30, indirect labor $0.43, utilities $0.40.

    **3.** Fixed manufacturing costs applicable to the production of CISCO were:

| Cost Item | Direct | Allocated |
| --- | --- | --- |
| Depreciation | $2,100 | $ 900 |
| Property taxes | 500 | 200 |
| Insurance | 900 | 600 |
|  | $3,500 | $1,700 |

All variable manufacturing and direct fixed costs will be eliminated if CISCO is purchased. Allocated costs will not be eliminated if CISCO is purchased. So if CISCO is purchased, the fixed manufacturing costs allocated to CISCO will have to be absorbed by other production departments.

    **4.** The lowest quotation for 8,000 CISCO units from a supplier is $80,000.

    **5.** If CISCO units are purchased, freight and inspection costs would be $0.35 per unit, and receiving costs totaling $1,300 per year would be incurred by the Machining Department.

### Instructions

**a.** NI (decrease) $(1,160)

    **a.** Prepare an incremental analysis for CISCO. Your analysis should have columns for (1) Make CISCO, (2) Buy CISCO, and (3) Net Income Increase/(Decrease).

    **b.** Based on your analysis, what decision should management make?

**c.** NI increase $1,840

    **c.** Would the decision be different if Shatner Company has the opportunity to produce $3,000 of net income with the facilities currently being used to manufacture CISCO? Show computations.

    **d.** What nonfinancial factors should management consider in making its decision?

*Determine if product should be sold or processed further.*

**P14.3 (LO 4), AN** Thompson Industrial Products Inc. (TIPI) is a diversified industrial-cleaner processing company. The company's Dargan plant produces two products, a table cleaner and a floor cleaner, from

→ Excel

a common set of chemical inputs (CDG). Each week, 900,000 ounces of chemical input are processed at a cost of $210,000 into 600,000 ounces of floor cleaner and 300,000 ounces of table cleaner. The floor cleaner has no market value until it is converted into a polish with the trade name FloorShine. The additional processing costs for this conversion amount to $240,000.

FloorShine sells at $20 per 30-ounce bottle. The table cleaner can be sold for $17 per 25-ounce bottle. However, the table cleaner can be converted into two other products by adding 300,000 ounces of another compound (TCP) to the 300,000 ounces of table cleaner. This joint process will yield 300,000 ounces each of table stain remover (TSR) and table polish (TP). The additional processing costs for this process amount to $100,000. Both table products can be sold for $14 per 25-ounce bottle.

The company decided not to process the table cleaner into TSR and TP based on the following analysis.

|  | Table Cleaner | Process Further | | |
|---|---|---|---|---|
|  |  | Table Stain Remover (TSR) | Table Polish (TP) | Total |
| Production in ounces | 300,000 | 300,000 | 300,000 |  |
| Revenues | $204,000 | $168,000 | $168,000 | $336,000 |
| Costs: |  |  |  |  |
| CDG costs | 70,000* | 52,500 | 52,500 | 105,000** |
| TCP costs | -0- | 50,000 | 50,000 | 100,000 |
| Total costs | 70,000 | 102,500 | 102,500 | 205,000 |
| Weekly gross profit | $134,000 | $ 65,500 | $ 65,500 | $131,000 |

*If table cleaner is not processed further, it is allocated $\frac{1}{3}$ of the $210,000 of CDG cost, which is equal to $\frac{1}{3}$ of the total physical output.

**If table cleaner is processed further, total physical output is 1,200,000 ounces. TSR and TP combined account for 50% of the total physical output and are each allocated 25% of the CDG cost.

### Instructions

a. Determine if management made the correct decision to not process the table cleaner further by doing the following.

   1. Calculate the company's total weekly gross profit assuming the table cleaner is not processed further.

   2. Calculate the company's total weekly gross profit assuming the table cleaner is processed further.   *2. Gross profit $186,000*

   3. Compare the resulting net incomes and comment on management's decision.

b. Using incremental analysis, determine if the table cleaner should be processed further.

(CMA adapted)

**P14.4 (LO 5), S** `Service` `Writing`  At the beginning of last year (2021), Richter Condos installed a mechanized elevator for its tenants. The owner of the company, Ron Richter, recently returned from an industry equipment exhibition where he watched a computerized elevator demonstrated. He was impressed with the elevator's speed, comfort of ride, and cost efficiency. Upon returning from the exhibition, he asked his purchasing agent to collect price and operating cost data on the new elevator. In addition, he asked the company's accountant to provide him with cost data on the company's elevator. This information is presented here.   *Compute gain or loss, and determine if equipment should be replaced.*

|  | Old Elevator | New Elevator |
|---|---|---|
| Purchase price | $120,000 | $160,000 |
| Estimated salvage value | -0- | -0- |
| Estimated useful life | 5 years | 4 years |
| Depreciation method | Straight-line | Straight-line |
| Annual operating costs other than depreciation: |  |  |
| Variable | $35,000 | $10,000 |
| Fixed | 23,000 | 8,500 |

Annual revenues are $240,000, and selling and administrative expenses are $29,000, regardless of which elevator is used. If the old elevator is replaced now, at the beginning of 2022, Richter Condos will be able to sell it for $25,000.

## Instructions

**a.** Determine any gain or loss if the old elevator is replaced.

**b.** Prepare a 4-year summarized income statement for each of the following assumptions:

**1.** The old elevator is retained.

b. 2. NI $539,000

c. NI increase $23,000

**2.** The old elevator is replaced.

**c.** Using incremental analysis, determine if the old elevator should be replaced.

**d.** Write a memo to Ron Richter explaining why any gain or loss should be ignored in the decision to replace the old elevator.

*Prepare incremental analysis concerning elimination of divisions.*

**P14.5 (LO 6), AN** Brislin Company has four operating divisions. During the first quarter of 2022, the company reported aggregate income from operations of $213,000 and the following divisional results.

| | Division | | | |
| | I | II | III | IV |
|---|---|---|---|---|
| Sales | $250,000 | $200,000 | $500,000 | $450,000 |
| Cost of goods sold | 200,000 | 192,000 | 300,000 | 250,000 |
| Selling and administrative expenses | 75,000 | 60,000 | 60,000 | 50,000 |
| Income (loss) from operations | $(25,000) | $(52,000) | $140,000 | $150,000 |

Analysis reveals the following percentages of variable costs in each division.

| | I | II | III | IV |
|---|---|---|---|---|
| Cost of goods sold | 70% | 90% | 80% | 75% |
| Selling and administrative expenses | 40 | 60 | 50 | 60 |

Discontinuance of any division would save 50% of the fixed costs and expenses for that division.

Top management is very concerned about the unprofitable divisions (I and II). Consensus is that one or both of the divisions should be discontinued.

## Instructions

a. Contribution margin I $80,000

**a.** Compute the contribution margin for Divisions I and II.

**b.** Prepare an incremental analysis concerning the possible discontinuance of (1) Division I and (2) Division II. What course of action do you recommend for each division?

c. Income III $132,800

**c.** Prepare a columnar condensed income statement for Brislin Company, assuming Division II is eliminated. (Use the CVP format.) Division II's unavoidable fixed costs are allocated equally to the continuing divisions.

**d.** Reconcile the total income from operations ($213,000) with the total income from operations without Division II.

# Continuing Cases

## Current Designs

**CD14 Current Designs** faces a number of important decisions that require incremental analysis. Consider each of the following situations independently.

### Situation 1

Recently, Mike Cichanowski, owner and CEO of Current Designs, received a phone call from the president of a brewing company. He was calling to inquire about the possibility of Current Designs producing "floating coolers" for a promotion his company was planning. These coolers resemble a kayak but are about one-third the size. They are used to float food and beverages while paddling down the river on a weekend leisure trip. The company would be interested in purchasing 100 coolers for the upcoming summer. It is willing to pay $250 per cooler. The brewing company would pick up the coolers upon completion of the order.

Mike met with Diane Buswell, controller, to identify how much it would cost Current Designs to produce the coolers. After careful analysis, the following costs were identified.

| Direct materials | $80/unit | | Variable overhead | $20/unit |
|---|---|---|---|---|
| Direct labor | $60/unit | | Fixed overhead | $1,000 |

Current Designs would be able to modify an existing mold to produce the coolers. The cost of these modifications would be approximately $2,000.

### Instructions

a. Prepare an incremental analysis to determine whether Current Designs should accept this special order to produce the coolers.

b. Discuss additional factors that Mike and Diane should consider if Current Designs is currently operating at full capacity.

### Situation 2

Current Designs is always working to identify ways to increase efficiency while becoming more environmentally conscious. During a recent brainstorming session, one employee suggested to Diane Buswell, controller, that the company should consider replacing the current rotomold oven as a way to realize savings from reduced energy consumption. The oven operates on natural gas, using 17,000 therms of natural gas for an entire year. A new, energy-efficient rotomold oven would operate on 15,000 therms of natural gas for an entire year. After seeking out price quotes from a few suppliers, Diane determined that it would cost approximately $250,000 to purchase a new, energy-efficient rotomold oven. She determines that the expected useful life of the new oven would be 10 years, and it would have no salvage value at the end of its useful life. Current Designs would be able to sell the current oven for $10,000.

### Instructions

a. Prepare an incremental analysis to determine if Current Designs should purchase the new rotomold oven, assuming that the average price for natural gas over the next 10 years will be $0.65 per therm.

b. Diane is concerned that natural gas prices might increase at a faster rate over the next 10 years. If the company projects that the average natural gas price of the next 10 years could be as high as $0.85 per therm, discuss how that might change your conclusion in (a).

### Situation 3

One of Current Designs' competitive advantages is found in the ingenuity of its owner and CEO, Mike Cichanowski. His involvement in the design of kayak molds and production techniques has led to Current Designs being recognized as an industry leader in the design and production of kayaks. This ingenuity was evident in an improved design of one of the most important components of a kayak, the seat. The "Revolution Seating System" is a one-of-a-kind, rotating axis seat that gives unmatched, full-contact, under-leg support. It is quickly adjustable with a lever-lock system that allows for a customizable seat position that maximizes comfort for the rider.

Having just designed the "Revolution Seating System," Current Designs must now decide whether to produce the seats internally or buy them from an outside supplier. The costs for Current Designs to produce the seats are as follows.

| Direct materials | $20/unit | | Direct labor | $15/unit |
|---|---|---|---|---|
| Variable overhead | $12/unit | | Fixed overhead | $20,000 |

Current Designs will need to produce 3,000 seats this year; 25% of the fixed overhead will be avoided if the seats are purchased from an outside vendor. After soliciting prices from outside suppliers, the company determined that it will cost $50 to purchase a seat from an outside vendor.

### Instructions

a. Prepare an incremental analysis showing whether Current Designs should make or buy the "Revolution Seating System."

b. Would your answer in (a) change if the productive capacity released by not making the seats could be used to produce income of $20,000?

## Waterways Corporation

(*Note:* This is a continuation of the Waterways case from Chapters 11–13.)

**WC14** Waterways Corporation is considering various business opportunities. It wants to make the best use of its production facilities to maximize income. This problem asks you to help Waterways do incremental analysis on these various opportunities.

*Go to WileyPLUS for complete case details and instructions.*

# Expand Your Critical Thinking

## Decision-Making Across the Organization

**CT14.1** Aurora Company is considering the purchase of a new machine. The invoice price of the machine is $140,000, freight charges are estimated to be $4,000, and installation costs are expected to be $6,000. Salvage value of the new equipment is expected to be zero after a useful life of 5 years. Existing equipment could be retained and used for an additional 5 years if the new machine is not purchased. At that time, the salvage value of the equipment would be zero. If the new machine is purchased now, the existing machine would have to be scrapped. Aurora's accountant, Lisah Huang, has accumulated the following data regarding annual sales and expenses with and without the new machine.

1. Without the new machine, Aurora can sell 12,000 units of product annually at a per unit selling price of $100. If the new machine is purchased, the number of units produced and sold would increase by 10%, and the selling price would remain the same.

2. The new machine is faster than the old machine, and it is more efficient in its usage of materials. With the old machine the gross profit rate will be 25% of sales, whereas the rate will be 30% of sales with the new machine.

3. Annual selling expenses are $180,000 with the current equipment. Because the new equipment would produce a greater number of units to be sold, annual selling expenses are expected to increase by 10% if it is purchased.

4. Annual administrative expenses are expected to be $100,000 with the old machine, and $113,000 with the new machine.

5. The current book value of the existing machine is $36,000. Aurora uses straight-line depreciation.

### Instructions

With the class divided into groups, prepare an incremental analysis for the 5 years showing whether Aurora should keep the existing machine or buy the new machine. (Ignore income tax effects.)

## Managerial Analysis

**CT14.2** MiniTek manufactures private-label small electronic products, such as alarm clocks, calculators, kitchen timers, stopwatches, and automatic pencil sharpeners. Some of the products are sold as sets, and others are sold individually. Products are studied as to their sales potential, and then cost estimates are made. The Engineering Department develops production plans, and then production begins. The company has generally had very successful product introductions. Only two products introduced by the company have been discontinued.

One of the products currently sold is a multi-alarm clock. The clock has four alarms that can be programmed to sound at various times and for varying lengths of time. The company has experienced a great deal of difficulty in making the circuit boards for the clocks. The production process has never operated smoothly. The product is unprofitable at the present time, primarily because of warranty repairs and product recalls. Two models of the clocks were recalled, for example, because they sometimes caused an electric shock when the alarms were being shut off. The Engineering Department is attempting to revise the manufacturing process, but the revision will take another 6 months at least.

The clocks were very popular when they were introduced, and since they are private-label, the company has not suffered much from the recalls. Presently, the company has a very large order for several items from BigMart. The order includes 5,000 of the multi-alarm clocks. When the company suggested that BigMart purchase the clocks from another manufacturer, BigMart threatened to rescind the entire order unless the clocks were included.

The company has therefore investigated the possibility of having another company make the clocks for them. The clocks were bid for the BigMart order based on an estimated $6.90 cost to manufacture:

| | |
|---|---|
| Circuit board, 1 each @ $2.00 | $2.00 |
| Plastic case, 1 each @ $0.80 | 0.80 |
| Alarms, 4 @ $0.15 each | 0.60 |
| Labor, 15 minutes @ $12/hour | 3.00 |
| Overhead, $2.00 per labor hour | 0.50 |

MiniTek could purchase clocks to fill the BigMart order for $10 from Trans-Tech Asia, a Korean manufacturer with a very good quality record. Trans-Tech has offered to reduce the price to $7.50 after MiniTek has been a customer for 6 months, placing an order of at least 1,000 units per month. If MiniTek becomes a "preferred customer" by purchasing 15,000 units per year, the price would be reduced still further to $4.50.

Omega Products, a local manufacturer, has also offered to make clocks for MiniTek. They have offered to sell 5,000 clocks for $5 each. However, Omega Products has been in business for only 6 months. They have experienced significant turnover in their labor force, and the local press has reported that the owners may face tax evasion charges soon. The owner of Omega Products is an electronic engineer, however, and the quality of the clocks is likely to be good.

If MiniTek decides to purchase the clocks from either Trans-Tech or Omega, all the costs to manufacture could be avoided, except a total of $1,000 in overhead costs for machine depreciation. The machinery is fairly new, and has no alternate use.

### Instructions

a. What is the difference in profit under each of the alternatives if the clocks are to be sold for $14.50 each to BigMart?

b. What are the most important nonfinancial factors that MiniTek should consider when making this decision?

c. What do you think MiniTek should do in regard to the BigMart order? What should it do in regard to continuing to manufacture the multi-alarm clocks? Be prepared to defend your answer.

## Real-World Focus

**CT14.3** Founded in 1983 and foreclosed in 1996, **Beverly Hills Fan Company** was located in Woodland Hills, California. With 23 employees and sales of less than $10 million, the company was relatively small. Management felt that there was potential for growth in the upscale market for ceiling fans and lighting. They were particularly optimistic about growth in Mexican and Canadian markets.

Presented here is information from the president's letter in one of the company's last annual reports.

### Beverly Hills Fan Company
#### President's Letter

An aggressive product development program was initiated during the past year resulting in new ceiling fan models planned for introduction this year. Award winning industrial designer Ron Rezek created several new fan models for the Beverly Hills Fan and L.A. Fan lines, including a new Showroom Collection, designed specifically for the architectural and designer markets. Each of these models has received critical acclaim, and order commitments for this year have been outstanding. Additionally, our Custom Color and special order fans continued to enjoy increasing popularity and sales gains as more and more customers desire fans that match their specific interior decors. Currently, Beverly Hills Fan Company offers a product line of over 100 models of contemporary, traditional, and transitional ceiling fans.

### Instructions

a. What points did the company management need to consider before deciding to offer the special-order fans to customers?

b. How would have incremental analysis been employed to assist in this decision?

## Communication Activity

**CT14.4** Hank Jewell is a production manager at a metal fabricating plant. Last night, he read an article about a new piece of equipment that would dramatically reduce his division's costs. Hank was very excited about the prospect, and the first thing he did this morning was to bring the article to his supervisor, Preston Thiese, the plant manager. The following conversation occurred:

Hank: Preston, I thought you would like to see this article on the new PDD1130; they've made some fantastic changes that could save us millions of dollars.

Preston: I appreciate your interest, Hank, but I actually have been aware of the new machine for 2 months. The problem is that we just bought a new machine last year. We spent $2 million on that machine, and it was supposed to last us 12 years. If we replace it now, we would have to write its book value off of the books for a huge loss. If I go to top management now and say that I want a new machine, they will fire me. I think we should use our existing machine for a couple of years, and then when it becomes obvious that we have to have a new machine, I will make the proposal.

### Instructions

Hank just completed a course in managerial accounting, and he believes that Preston is making a big mistake. Write a memo from Hank to Preston explaining Preston's decision-making error.

## Ethics Case

**CT14.5** Blake Romney became chief executive officer of Peters Inc. 2 years ago. At the time, the company was reporting lagging profits, and Blake was brought in to "stir things up." The company has three divisions: electronics, fiber optics, and plumbing supplies. Blake has no interest in plumbing supplies, and one of the first things he did was to put pressure on his accountants to reallocate some of the company's fixed costs away from the other two divisions to the plumbing division. This had the effect of causing the plumbing division to report losses during the last 2 years; in the past it had always reported low, but acceptable, net income. Blake felt that this reallocation would shine a favorable light on him in front of the board of directors because it meant that the electronics and fiber optics divisions would look like they were improving. Given that these are "businesses of the future," he believed that the stock market would react favorably to these increases, while not penalizing the poor results of the plumbing division. Without this shift in the allocation of fixed costs, the profits of the electronics and fiber optics divisions would not have improved. But now the board of directors has suggested that the plumbing division be closed because it is reporting losses. This would mean that nearly 500 employees, many of whom have worked for Peters their whole lives, would lose their jobs.

### Instructions

   **a.** If a division is reporting losses, does that necessarily mean that it should be closed?

   **b.** Was the reallocation of fixed costs across divisions unethical?

   **c.** What should Blake do?

## All About You

**CT14.6** Managerial accounting techniques can be used in a wide variety of settings. As we have frequently pointed out, you can use them in many personal situations. They also can be useful in trying to find solutions for societal issues that appear to be hard to solve.

### Instructions

Read the *Fortune* article, "The Toughest Customers: How Hardheaded Business Metrics Can Help the Hard-Core Homeless," by Cait Murphy (do an Internet search on the title), and then answer the following questions.

   **a.** How does the article define "chronic" homelessness?

   **b.** In what ways does homelessness cost a city money? What are the estimated costs of a chronic homeless person to various cities?

   **c.** What are the steps suggested to address the problem?

   **d.** What is the estimated cost of implementing this program in New York? What results have been seen?

   **e.** In terms of incremental analysis, frame the relevant costs in this situation.

## Considering Your Costs and Benefits

**CT14.7** School costs money. Is this an expenditure that you should have avoided? On average, a year of tuition at a public four-year college costs about $10,000, and a year of tuition at a public two-year college costs about $5,000. If you did not go to college, you might avoid mountains of school-related debt. In fact, each year, about 600,000 students decide to drop out of school. Many of them never return. Suppose that you are working two jobs and going to college, and that you are not making ends meet. Your grades are suffering due to your lack of available study time. You feel depressed. Should you drop out of school?

   **YES:** You can always go back to school. If your grades are bad and you are depressed, what good is school doing you anyway?

   **NO:** Once you drop out, it is very hard to get enough momentum to go back. Dropping out will dramatically reduce your long-term opportunities. It is better to stay in school, even if you take only one class per semester. While you cannot go back and redo your initial decision, you can look at some facts to evaluate the wisdom of your decision.

### Instructions

Write a response indicating your position regarding this situation. Provide support for your view.

## CHAPTER 15

Deidre Schoo/The New York Times/Redux Pictures

# Budgetary Planning

## Chapter Preview

As the following Feature Story about **BabyCakes NYC** indicates, budgeting is critical to financial well-being. As a student, you budget your study time and your money. Families budget income and expenses. Governmental agencies budget revenues and expenditures. Businesses use budgets in planning and controlling their operations.

Our primary focus in this chapter is budgeting—specifically, how budgeting is used as a planning tool by management. Through budgeting, it should be possible for management to maintain enough cash to pay creditors as well as have sufficient raw materials to meet production requirements and adequate finished goods to meet expected sales.

## Feature Story

### What's in Your Cupcake?

The best business plans often result from meeting a basic human need. Many people would argue that cupcakes aren't necessarily essential to support life. But if you found out that

allergies were going to deprive you forever of cupcakes, you might view baked goods in a whole new light. Such was the dilemma faced by Erin McKenna. When she found that her wheat allergies prevented her from consuming most baked sweets, she decided to open a bakery that met her needs. Her vegan and kosher bakery, **BabyCakes NYC**, advertises that it is refined-sugar-free, gluten-free, wheat-free, soy-free, dairy-free, and egg-free. So if you're one of the more than 10 million Americans with a food allergy or some other dietary constraint, this is probably the bakery for you.

Those of you that have spent a little time in the kitchen might wonder what kind of ingredients BabyCakes uses. To avoid the gluten in wheat, the company uses **Bob's Red Mill** rice flour, a garbanzo/fava bean mix, or oat flours. How does BabyCakes get all those great frosting colors without artificial dyes? The company achieves pink with beets, green with chlorophyll, yellow with turmeric, and blue/purple with red cabbage. To eliminate dairy and soy, the bakers use rice and coconut milk. And finally, to accomplish over-the-top deliciousness without refined sugar, BabyCakes uses agave nectar (a sweetener derived from cactus) and evaporated cane juice (often referred to as organic or unrefined sugar).

With cupcakes priced at over $3 per item and a brisk business, you might think that making money is easy for BabyCakes. But all of these specialty ingredients don't come cheap. In addition, BabyCakes' shops are located in Manhattan, Los Angeles, and Orlando, so rent isn't exactly inexpensive either. Despite these costs, Erin's first store made a profit its first year and did even better in later years. To achieve this profitability, Erin relies on careful budgeting. First, she needs to estimate how many items she will sell. Then, she determines her needs for materials, labor, and overhead. Prices for raw materials can fluctuate significantly, so Erin needs to update her budget accordingly. Finally, she has to budget for other products such as her cookbooks, baking kits, and T-shirts. Without a budget, Erin's business might not be so sweet.

# Chapter Outline

| LEARNING OBJECTIVES | REVIEW | PRACTICE |
|---|---|---|
| **LO 1** State the essentials of effective budgeting and the components of the master budget. | • Budgeting and accounting<br>• Benefits of budgeting<br>• Effective budgeting essentials<br>• Master budget | **DO IT! 1** Budget Terminology |
| **LO 2** Prepare budgets for sales, production, and direct materials. | • Sales budget<br>• Production budget<br>• Direct materials budget | **DO IT! 2** Sales, Production, and Direct Materials Budgets |
| **LO 3** Prepare budgets for direct labor, manufacturing overhead, and selling and administrative expenses, and a budgeted income statement. | • Direct labor budget<br>• Manufacturing overhead budget<br>• Selling and administrative expense budget<br>• Budgeted income statement | **DO IT! 3** Budgeted Income Statement |
| **LO 4** Prepare a cash budget and a budgeted balance sheet. | • Cash budget<br>• Budgeted balance sheet | **DO IT! 4** Cash Budget |
| **LO 5** Apply budgeting principles to nonmanufacturing companies. | • Merchandisers<br>• Service companies<br>• Not-for-profit organizations | **DO IT! 5** Merchandise Purchases Budget |

**Go to the Review and Practice section at the end of the chapter for a targeted summary and practice applications with solutions.**

**Visit WileyPLUS for additional tutorials and practice opportunities.**

# Effective Budgeting and the Master Budget

**LEARNING OBJECTIVE 1**

State the essentials of effective budgeting and the components of the master budget.

Planning is one of management's major responsibilities. As explained in Chapter 11, **planning** is the process of establishing company-wide objectives. A successful organization makes both long-term and short-term plans. These plans establish the objectives of the company and the proposed approach to accomplish them.

A **budget** is a formal written statement of management's plans for a specified future time period, expressed in financial terms.

- It represents the primary method of communicating agreed-upon objectives throughout the organization.
- Once adopted, a budget becomes an important basis for evaluating performance.
- It promotes efficiency and serves as a deterrent to waste and inefficiency.

We consider the role of budgeting as a **control device** in Chapter 16.

## Budgeting and Accounting

Accounting information makes major contributions to the budgeting process. From the accounting records, companies obtain historical data on revenues, costs, and expenses. These data are helpful in formulating future budget goals.

Accountants are responsible for presenting management's budgeting goals in financial terms.

- Accountants translate management's plans and communicate the budget to employees throughout the company.
- They prepare periodic budget reports that provide the basis for measuring performance and comparing actual results with planned objectives.

The budget itself and the administration of the budget, however, are entirely management responsibilities.

## The Benefits of Budgeting

The primary benefits of budgeting are as follows.

1. It requires all levels of management to **plan ahead** and to formalize goals on a recurring basis.
2. It provides **definite objectives** for evaluating performance at each level of responsibility.
3. It creates an **early warning system** for potential problems so that management can make changes before things get out of hand.
4. It facilitates the **coordination of activities** within the business. It does this by correlating the goals of each segment with overall company objectives. Thus, the company can integrate production and sales promotion with expected sales.
5. It results in greater **management awareness** of the entity's overall operations and the impact on operations of external factors, such as economic trends.
6. It **motivates personnel** throughout the organization to meet planned objectives.

A budget is an aid to management; it is not a *substitute* for management. A budget cannot operate or enforce itself. Companies can realize the benefits of budgeting only when managers carefully administer budgets.

# Essentials of Effective Budgeting

Effective budgeting depends on a **sound organizational structure**. In such a structure, authority and responsibility for all phases of operations are clearly defined. Budgets based on **research and analysis** are more likely to result in realistic goals that will contribute to the growth and profitability of a company. And, the effectiveness of a budget program is directly related to its **acceptance by all levels of management**.

Once adopted, the budget is an important tool for evaluating performance. Managers should systematically and periodically review variations between actual and expected results to determine their cause(s). However, individuals should not be held responsible for variations that are beyond their control.

## Length of the Budget Period

The budget period is not necessarily one year in length. **A budget may be prepared for any period of time.** Various factors influence the length of the budget period:

- The type of budget.
- The nature of the organization.
- The need for periodic appraisal.
- Prevailing business conditions.

The budget period should be long enough to provide an attainable goal under normal business conditions. Ideally, the time period should minimize the impact of seasonal or cyclical fluctuations. On the other hand, the budget period should not be so long that reliable estimates are impossible.

The **most common budget period is one year**. The annual budget, in turn, is often supplemented by monthly and quarterly budgets. Many companies use **continuous 12-month budgets**. These budgets drop the month just ended and add a future month. One benefit of continuous budgeting is that it keeps management planning a full year ahead.

## Accounting Across the Organization

Thinkstock/Stockbyte/
Getty Images

### Businesses Often Feel Too Busy to Plan for the Future

A study by Willard & Shullman Group Ltd. found that fewer than 14% of businesses with less than 500 employees do an annual budget or have a written business plan. For many small businesses, the basic assumption is that, "As long as I sell as much as I can, and keep my employees paid, I'm doing OK." A few small business owners even say that they see no need for budgeting and planning. Most small business owners, though, say that they understand that budgeting and planning are critical for survival and growth. But given the long hours that they already work addressing day-to-day challenges, they also say that they are "just too busy to plan for the future."

**Describe a situation in which a business "sells as much as it can" but cannot "keep its employees paid." (Go to WileyPLUS for this answer and additional questions.)**

## The Budgeting Process

The development of the budget for the coming year generally starts several months before the end of the current year. The budgeting process usually begins with the collection of data from each organizational unit of the company. Past performance is often the starting point from which future budget goals are formulated.

The budget is developed within the framework of a **sales forecast**.

- This forecast shows potential sales for the industry and the company's expected share of such sales.
- Sales forecasting involves a consideration of various factors:

    1. General economic conditions.
    2. Industry trends.
    3. Market research studies.
    4. Anticipated advertising and promotion.

    5. Previous market share.
    6. Changes in prices.
    7. Technological developments.

- The input of sales personnel and top management is essential to the sales forecast.

In small companies like **BabyCakes NYC**, the budgeting process is often informal. In larger companies, a **budget committee** has responsibility for coordinating the preparation of the budget.

- The committee ordinarily includes the president, treasurer, chief accountant (controller), and management personnel from each of the major areas of the company, such as sales, production, and research.
- The budget committee serves as a review board where managers can defend their budget goals and requests. Differences are reviewed, modified if necessary, and reconciled.
- The budget is then put in its final form by the budget committee, approved, and distributed.

## Budgeting and Human Behavior

A budget can have a significant impact on human behavior. If done well, it can inspire managers to higher levels of performance. However, if done poorly, budgets can discourage additional effort and pull down the morale of managers. Why do these diverse effects occur? The answer is found in how the budget is developed and administered.

In developing the budget, each level of management should be invited to participate. This "bottom-to-top" approach is referred to as **participative budgeting**.

- One benefit of participative budgeting is that lower-level managers have more detailed knowledge of their specific area and thus are able to provide more accurate budgetary estimates.
- When lower-level managers participate in the budgeting process, they are more likely to perceive the resulting budget as fair.
- The overall goal is to reach agreement on a budget that the managers consider fair and achievable, but which also meets the corporate goals set by top management. When this goal is met, the budget will provide positive motivation for the managers.

In contrast, if managers view the budget as unfair and unrealistic, they may feel discouraged and uncommitted to budget goals. The risk of having unrealistic budgets is generally greater when the budget is developed from top management down to lower management than vice versa. **Illustration 15.1** shows the flow of budget data from bottom to top under participative budgeting.

For example, at one time, in an effort to revive its plummeting stock price, **WarnerMedia**'s top management determined and publicly announced bold new financial goals for the coming year. Unfortunately, these goals were not reached. The next year, the company got a new CEO who said the company would now actually set reasonable goals that it could meet. The new budgets were developed with each operating unit setting what it felt were optimistic but attainable goals. In the words of one manager, using this approach created a sense of teamwork.

**ILLUSTRATION 15.1** Flow of budget data under participative budgeting

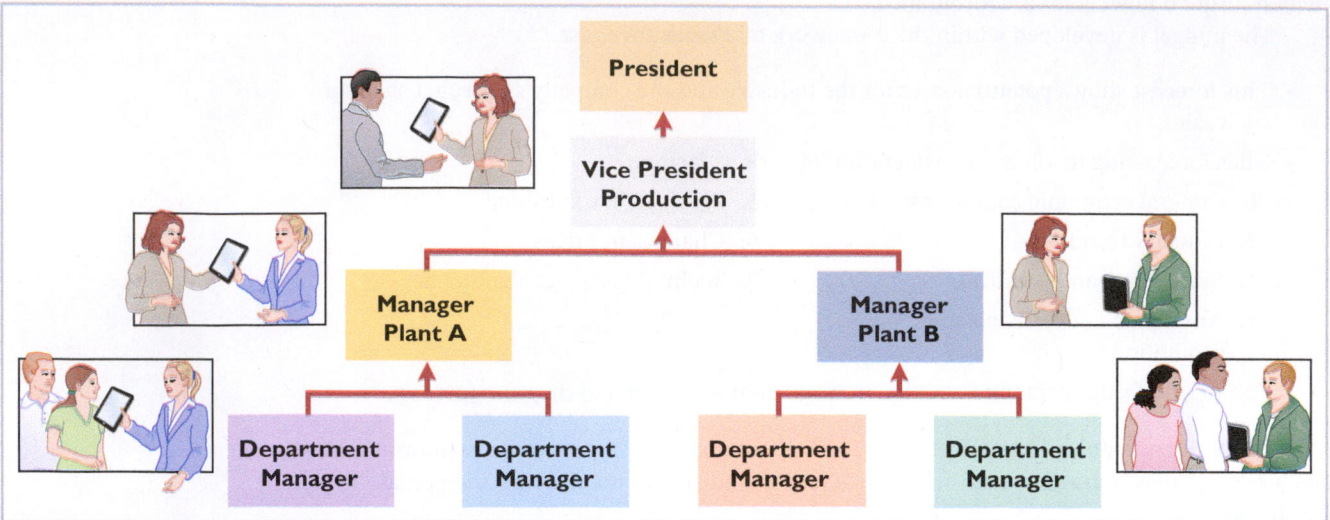

Participative budgeting does, however, have potential disadvantages.

1. The "give and take" of participative budgeting is time-consuming (and thus more costly). Under a "top-down" approach, the budget is simply developed by top management and then dictated to lower-level managers.

2. Participative budgeting can foster budgetary "gaming" through **budgetary slack**, which occurs when managers intentionally underestimate budgeted revenues or overestimate budgeted expenses in order to make it easier to achieve budgetary goals for their division.

To minimize budgetary slack, higher-level managers must carefully review and thoroughly question the budget projections provided to them by employees whom they supervise.

For the budget to be effective, top management must completely support the budget. The budget is an important tool for evaluating performance. It also can be used as a positive aid in achieving projected goals. The effect of an evaluation is positive when top management tempers criticism with advice and assistance. In contrast, a manager is likely to respond negatively if top management uses the budget exclusively to assess blame. A budget should not be used as a pressure device to force improved performance (see **Ethics Note**). In sum, a budget can be a manager's friend or foe.

**ETHICS NOTE**

**Unrealistic budgets can lead to unethical employee behavior such as cutting corners on the job or distorting internal financial reports.**

## Budgeting and Long-Range Planning

Budgeting and long-range planning have three significant differences:

**HELPFUL HINT**

**A budget has more detail and is more concerned with short-term goals than a long-range plan.**

1. **The time period involved**. The maximum length of a budget is usually one year, and budgets are often prepared for shorter periods of time, such as a month or a quarter. In contrast, long-range planning usually encompasses a period of at least five years (see **Helpful Hint**).

2. **Emphasis**. Budgeting focuses on achieving specific short-term goals, such as meeting annual profit objectives. **Long-range planning**, on the other hand:
   • Identifies long-term goals.
   • Selects strategies to achieve those goals.
   • Develops policies and plans to implement the strategies.

In long-range planning, management also considers anticipated trends in the economic and political environment and how the company should cope with them.

3. **The amount of detail presented**. Budgets, as you will see in this chapter, can be very detailed. Long-range plans contain considerably less detail as the data are intended more for a review of progress toward long-term goals than as a basis of control for achieving specific results. The primary objective of long-range planning is to develop the best strategy to maximize the company's performance over an extended future period.

# The Master Budget

The term "budget" is actually a shorthand term to describe a variety of budget documents. All of these documents are combined into a master budget. The **master budget** is a set of interrelated budgets that constitutes a plan of action for a specified time period (see **Decision Tools**).

The master budget contains two classes of budgets:

1. **Operating budgets**, which are the individual budgets that result in the preparation of the budgeted income statement. These budgets establish goals for the company's sales and production personnel.

2. **Financial budgets**, which focus primarily on the cash resources needed to fund expected operations and planned capital expenditures. Financial budgets include the capital expenditure budget, the cash budget, and the budgeted balance sheet.

**Illustration 15.2** shows the individual budgets included in a master budget, and the sequence in which they are prepared. The company first develops the operating budgets, beginning with the sales budget. Then, it prepares the financial budgets. We will explain and illustrate each budget shown in Illustration 15.2 except the capital expenditure budget. That budget is discussed under the topic of capital budgeting in Chapter 18.

> **Decision Tools**
>
> Managers use the master budget to determine if the company met its targets for such things as sales, production expenses, selling and administrative expenses, and net income.

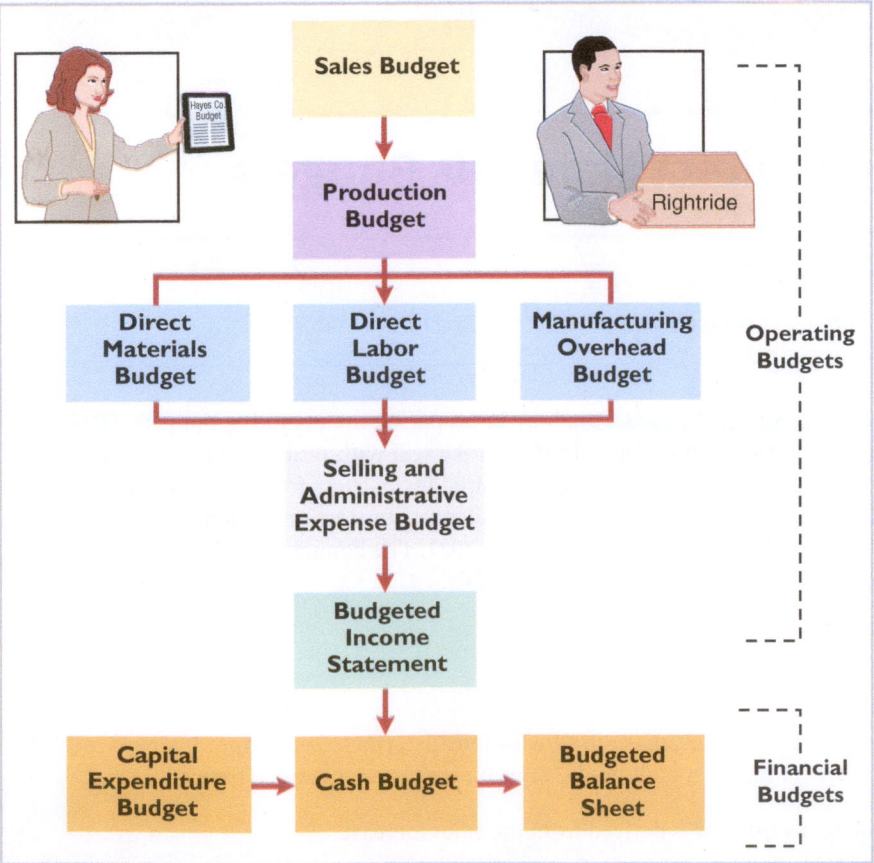

**ILLUSTRATION 15.2**

**Components of the master budget**

## DO IT! 1 | Budget Terminology

Use this list of terms to complete the sentences that follow.

| | |
|---|---|
| Long-range planning | Participative budgeting |
| Sales forecast | Operating budgets |
| Master budget | Financial budgets |

1. A _____ shows potential sales for the industry and a company's expected share of such sales.

2. _____ are used as the basis for the preparation of the budgeted income statement.

3. The _____ is a set of interrelated budgets that constitutes a plan of action for a specified time period.

4. _____ identifies long-term goals, selects strategies to achieve these goals, and develops policies and plans to implement the strategies.

5. Lower-level managers are more likely to perceive results as fair and achievable under a _____ approach.

6. _____ focus primarily on the cash resources needed to fund expected operations and planned capital expenditures.

### Solution

1. Sales forecast.
2. Operating budgets.
3. Master budget.
4. Long-range planning.
5. Participative budgeting.
6. Financial budgets.

Related exercise material: **BE15.1, DO IT! 15.1, and E15.1.**

# Sales, Production, and Direct Materials Budgets

**LEARNING OBJECTIVE 2**

Prepare budgets for sales, production, and direct materials.

We use a case study of Hayes Company in preparing the operating budgets. Hayes manufactures and sells an ergonomically designed bike seat with multiple customizable adjustments, called the Rightride. The budgets are prepared by quarters for the year ending December 31, 2022. Hayes Company begins its annual budgeting process on September 1, 2021, and it completes the budget for 2022 by December 1, 2021. The company begins by preparing the budgets for sales, production, and direct materials.

## Sales Budget

As shown in the master budget in Illustration 15.2, **the sales budget is prepared first**. Each of the other budgets depends on the sales budget (see **Helpful Hint**).

- The **sales budget** is derived from the sales forecast.
- It represents management's best estimate of sales revenue for the budget period.
- An inaccurate sales budget may adversely affect net income.

For example, an overly optimistic sales budget may result in excessive inventories that may have to be sold at reduced prices. In contrast, an unduly pessimistic sales budget may result in loss of sales revenue due to inventory shortages.

For example, at one time **Amazon.com** significantly underestimated demand for its e-book reader, the Kindle. As a consequence, it did not produce enough Kindles and was completely sold out well before the holiday shopping season. Not only did this represent a huge lost opportunity for Amazon, but it exposed the company to potential competitors, who were eager to provide customers with alternatives to the Kindle.

Forecasting sales is challenging. For example, consider the forecasting challenges faced by major sports arenas, whose revenues depend on the success of the home team. **Madison Square Garden**'s revenues from April to June were $193 million during a year when the New York Knicks made the NBA playoffs. But revenues were only $133.2 million a couple of years later when the team did not make the playoffs. Or, consider the challenges faced by Hollywood movie producers in predicting the complicated revenue stream produced by a new movie. Movie theater ticket sales represent only 20% of total revenue. The bulk of revenue comes from global sales, DVDs, video-on-demand, merchandising products, and videogames, all of which are difficult to forecast.

The sales budget is prepared by multiplying the expected unit sales volume for each product by its anticipated unit selling price. Hayes Company expects sales volume to be 3,000 units in the first quarter, with 500-unit increases in each succeeding quarter. **Illustration 15.3** shows the sales budget for the year, by quarter, based on a sales price of $60 per unit.

**ILLUSTRATION 15.3**

**Sales budget**

| | | Hayes Company Sales Budget | | | | |
|---|---|---|---|---|---|---|
| | **Home** Insert Page Layout Formulas Data Review View | | | | | |
| | P18 | *fx* | | | | |
| | A | B | C | D | E | F |
| 1 | | **Hayes Company** | | | | |
| 2 | | **Sales Budget** | | | | |
| 3 | | **For the Year Ending December 31, 2022** | | | | |
| 4 | | Quarter | | | | |
| 5 | | 1 | 2 | 3 | 4 | Year |
| 6 | Expected sales units | 3,000 | 3,500 | 4,000 | 4,500 | 15,000 |
| 7 | Unit selling price | × $60 | × $60 | × $60 | × $60 | × $60 |
| 8 | Total sales | $180,000 | $210,000 | $240,000 | $270,000 | $900,000 |

Some companies classify the anticipated sales revenue as cash or credit sales and by geographic regions, territories, or salespersons.

---

## Service Company Insight

MarsBars/iStock/Getty Images Plus/Getty Images

### The Implications of Budgetary Optimism

Companies aren't the only ones that have to estimate revenues. Governments at all levels (e.g., local, state or federal) prepare annual budgets. Most are required to submit balanced budgets, that is, estimated revenues are supposed to cover anticipated expenditures. Unfortunately, estimating government revenues can be as difficult as, or even more difficult than, estimating company revenues. For example, at one time, the median state government overestimated revenues by 10.2%, with four state governments missing by more than 25%.

What makes estimation so difficult for these governments? Most states rely on income taxes, which fluctuate widely with economic gyrations. Some states rely on sales taxes, which are problematic because the laws regarding sales taxes haven't adjusted for the shift from manufacturing to service companies and from brick-and-mortar stores to online sales.

**Source:** Conor Dougherty, "States Fumble Revenue Forecasts," *Wall Street Journal Online* (March 2, 2011).

**Why is it important that government budgets accurately estimate future revenues during economic downturns? (Go to WileyPLUS for this answer and additional questions.)**

## Production Budget

The **production budget** shows the number of units of a product to produce to meet anticipated sales demand. Production requirements are determined from the formula shown in **Illustration 15.4.**[1]

**ILLUSTRATION 15.4**
Production requirements
formula

| Expected Sales Units | + | Desired Ending Finished Goods Units | − | Beginning Finished Goods Units | = | Required Production Units |
|---|---|---|---|---|---|---|

**Illustration 15.5** shows the production budget for Hayes Company, which is based on the formula shown in Illustration 15.4.

**ILLUSTRATION 15.5**  Production budget

| | Hayes Company Production Budget | | | | | |
|---|---|---|---|---|---|---|
| | Home   Insert   Page Layout   Formulas   Data   Review   View | | | | | |
| | P18 | *fx* | | | | |
| | A | B | C | D | E | F |
| 1 | **Hayes Company** | | | | | |
| 2 | **Production Budget** | | | | | |
| 3 | **For the Year Ending December 31, 2022** | | | | | |
| 4 | | Quarter | | | | |
| 5 | | 1 | 2 | 3 | 4 | Year |
| 6 | Expected sales units (Illustration 15.3) | 3,000 | 3,500 | 4,000 | 4,500 | |
| 7 | Add: Desired ending finished goods units[a] | 700 | 800 | 900 | 1,000[b] | |
| 8 | Total required units | 3,700 | 4,300 | 4,900 | 5,500 | |
| 9 | Less: Beginning finished goods units[c] | 600 | 700 | 800 | 900 | |
| 10 | **Required production units** | **3,100** | **3,600** | **4,100** | **4,600** | **15,400** |
| 11 | | | | | | |
| 12 | [a]20% of next quarter's sales | | | | | |
| 13 | [b]Expected 2023 first-quarter sales, 5,000 units × .20 | | | | | |
| 14 | [c]20% of estimated first-quarter 2022 sales units | | | | | |

- In the first quarter, expected sales are 3,000 units.
- Hayes Company believes it can meet future sales requirements by maintaining an ending inventory equal to 20% of the next quarter's budgeted sales volume. The ending finished goods inventory for the first quarter is 700 units (.20 × anticipated second-quarter sales of 3,500 units).
- If we then subtract the beginning finished goods units of 600 units (20% of first-quarter sales), we arrive at required production of 3,100 units.

**A realistic estimate of ending inventory is essential in scheduling production requirements.** Excessive inventories in one quarter may lead to cutbacks in production and employee layoffs in a subsequent quarter. On the other hand, inadequate inventories may result either in added costs for overtime work or in lost sales.

The production budget, in turn, provides the basis for the budgeted costs for each manufacturing cost element, as explained in the following discussion.

## Direct Materials Budget

The **direct materials budget** shows both the quantity and cost of direct materials to be purchased. The first step toward computing the cost of direct materials purchases is to compute the direct materials units required for production. **Illustration 15.6** shows the formula for this amount.

---

[1] This formula ignores any work in process inventories, which are assumed to be nonexistent in Hayes Company.

| Units to Be Produced | × | Direct Materials Units per Unit of Unit Produced | = | Direct Materials Units Required for Production |
|---|---|---|---|---|

Employing this formula, Illustration 15.9 shows the following.

- For Hayes Company's first quarter of production, there are 3,100 units to be produced.
- Each unit produced requires two pounds of raw materials.
- Therefore, the units of direct materials required for production is 6,200 pounds (3,100 × 2).

Next we can compute the direct materials units to be purchased using the formula shown in **Illustration 15.7**.

| Direct Materials Units Required for Production | + | Desired Ending Direct Materials Units | − | Beginning Direct Materials Units | = | Direct Materials Units to Be Purchased |
|---|---|---|---|---|---|---|

Employing this formula, Illustration 15.9 shows the following.

- For Hayes Company's first quarter of production, the direct materials units required for production is 6,200 pounds (computed above).
- To that we add the desired ending direct materials units. For Hayes, this is assumed to be 10% of the next quarter's production requirements, or 720 pounds (.10 × 7,200).
- Then, we subtract the beginning direct materials units of 620 pounds (10% of this quarter's production requirements of 6,200) to arrive at the direct materials units to be purchased of 6,300 pounds.

Finally, to arrive at the cost of direct materials purchases, we employ the formula shown in **Illustration 15.8**.

| Direct Materials Units to Be Purchased | × | Cost per Direct Materials Unit | = | Cost of Direct Materials Purchases |
|---|---|---|---|---|

Employing this formula, **Illustration 15.9** shows that for Hayes Company's first quarter of production, the cost of direct materials purchases is computed by multiplying the units to be

**ILLUSTRATION 15.9**   **Direct materials budget**

Hayes Company Direct Materials Budget

| A | B | C | D | E | F |
|---|---|---|---|---|---|
| **Hayes Company** | | | | | |
| **Direct Materials Budget** | | | | | |
| **For the Year Ending December 31, 2022** | | | | | |
| | Quarter | | | | |
| | 1 | 2 | 3 | 4 | Year |
| Units to be produced (Illustration 15.5) | 3,100 | 3,600 | 4,100 | 4,600 | |
| Direct materials units per unit produced | × 2 | × 2 | × 2 | × 2 | |
| Direct materials units required for production | 6,200 | 7,200 | 8,200 | 9,200 | |
| Add: Desired ending direct materials (pounds)[a] | 720 | 820 | 920 | 1,020[c] | |
| Total materials required | 6,920 | 8,020 | 9,120 | 10,220 | |
| Less: Beginning direct materials (pounds) | 620[b] | 720 | 820 | 920 | |
| Direct materials units to be purchased (pounds) | 6,300 | 7,300 | 8,300 | 9,300 | |
| Cost per pound | × $4 | × $4 | × $4 | × $4 | |
| **Cost of direct materials purchases** | **$25,200** | **$29,200** | **$33,200** | **$37,200** | **$124,800** |
| | | | | | |
| [a]10% of next quarter's production requirements | | | | | |
| [b]10% of estimated first-quarter pounds needed for production | | | | | |
| [c]Total pounds needed for production is assumed to be 10,200 for the first quarter of 2023 | | | | | |

purchased of 6,300 pounds by the cost per direct materials unit of $4 per pound, to arrive at $25,200 (6,300 × $4).

**The desired ending inventory is again a key component in the budgeting process.** For example, inadequate inventories could result in temporary shutdowns of production. Because of its close proximity to suppliers, Hayes Company maintains an ending inventory of raw materials equal to 10% of the next quarter's production requirements.

---

## Management Insight

iStock.com/William Wang

### Betting That Prices Won't Fall

Sometimes things happen that cause managers to reevaluate their normal purchasing patterns. Consider, for example, the predicament that businesses faced when the price of many raw materials skyrocketed. Rubber, cotton, oil, corn, wheat, steel, copper, and spices—prices for seemingly everything were going straight up. Anticipating that prices might continue to go up, many managers decided to stockpile much larger quantities of raw materials to avoid paying

even higher prices in the future. For example, after cotton prices rose 92%, one manager of a printed T-shirt manufacturer decided to stockpile a huge supply of plain T-shirts in anticipation of additional price increases. While he normally has about 30 boxes of T-shirts in inventory, he purchased 2,500 boxes.

**Source:** Liam Pleven and Matt Wirz, "Companies Stock Up as Commodities Prices Rise," *Wall Street Journal Online* (February 3, 2011).

**What are the potential downsides of stockpiling a huge amount of raw materials? (Go to WileyPLUS for this answer and additional questions.)**

---

### ACTION PLAN
- Know the form and content of the sales budget.
- **Prepare the sales budget first, as the basis for the other budgets.**
- Determine the units that must be produced to meet anticipated sales.
- Know how to compute the beginning and ending finished goods units.
- Determine the materials required to meet production needs.
- Know how to compute the beginning and ending direct materials units.

## DO IT! 2 | Sales, Production, and Direct Materials Budgets

Soriano Company is preparing its master budget for 2022. Relevant data pertaining to its sales, production, and direct materials budgets are as follows.

*Sales.* Sales for the year are expected to total 1,200,000 units. Quarterly sales, as a percentage of total sales, are 20%, 25%, 30%, and 25%, respectively. The sales price is expected to be $50 per unit for the first three quarters and $55 per unit beginning in the fourth quarter. Sales in the first quarter of 2023 are expected to be 10% higher than the budgeted sales for the first quarter of 2022.

*Production.* Management desires to maintain the ending finished goods inventories at 25% of the next quarter's budgeted sales volume.

*Direct materials.* Each unit requires 3 pounds of raw materials at a cost of $5 per pound. Management desires to maintain raw materials inventories at 5% of the next quarter's production requirements. Assume the production requirements for the first quarter of 2023 are 810,000 pounds.

Prepare the sales, production, and direct materials budgets by quarters for 2022.

### Solution

| Soriano Company Sales Budget | | | | | |
|---|---|---|---|---|---|
| P18 | fx | | | | |
| | A | B | C | D | E | F |

| | A | B | C | D | E | F |
|---|---|---|---|---|---|---|
| 1 | | **Soriano Company** | | | | |
| 2 | | **Sales Budget** | | | | |
| 3 | | **For the Year Ending December 31, 2022** | | | | |
| 4 | | Quarter | | | | |
| 5 | | 1 | 2 | 3 | 4 | Year |
| 6 | Expected unit salesᵃ | 240,000 | 300,000 | 360,000 | 300,000 | 1,200,000 |
| 7 | Unit selling price | × $50 | × $50 | × $50 | × $55 | |
| 8 | **Total sales** | $12,000,000 | $15,000,000 | $18,000,000 | $16,500,000 | $61,500,000 |
| 9 | | | | | | |
| 10 | ᵃSpecified quarterly percentage times annual units, e.g., first quarter of .20 × 1,200,000 | | | | | |

**Soriano Company Production Budget**

Home   Insert   Page Layout   Formulas   Data   Review   View

P18          fx

### Soriano Company
### Production Budget
### For the Year Ending December 31, 2022

| | Quarter | | | | |
|---|---|---|---|---|---|
| | 1 | 2 | 3 | 4 | Year |
| Expected unit sales | 240,000 | 300,000 | 360,000 | 300,000 | |
| Add: Desired ending finished goods units[a] | 75,000 | 90,000 | 75,000 | 66,000[b] | |
| Total required units | 315,000 | 390,000 | 435,000 | 366,000 | |
| Less: Beginning finished goods units | 60,000[c] | 75,000 | 90,000 | 75,000 | |
| **Required production units** | **255,000** | **315,000** | **345,000** | **291,000** | **1,206,000** |

[a]25% of next quarter's unit sales
[b]Estimated first-quarter 2023 sales units: 240,000 + (240,000 × .10) = 264,000: 264,000 × .25
[c]25% of estimated first-quarter 2022 sales units (240,000 × .25)

**Soriano Company Direct Materials Budget**

Home   Insert   Page Layout   Formulas   Data   Review   View

P18          fx

### Soriano Company
### Direct Materials Budget
### For the Year Ending December 31, 2022

| | Quarter | | | | |
|---|---|---|---|---|---|
| | 1 | 2 | 3 | 4 | Year |
| Units to be produced | 255,000 | 315,000 | 345,000 | 291,000 | |
| Direct materials per unit | × 3 | × 3 | × 3 | × 3 | |
| Total pounds needed for production | 765,000 | 945,000 | 1,035,000 | 873,000 | |
| Add: Desired ending direct materials (pounds) | 47,250 | 51,750 | 43,650 | 40,500[a] | |
| Total materials required | 812,250 | 996,750 | 1,078,650 | 913,500 | |
| Less: Beginning direct materials (pounds) | 38,250[b] | 47,250 | 51,750 | 43,650 | |
| Direct materials purchases | 774,000 | 949,500 | 1,026,900 | 869,850 | |
| Cost per pound | × $5 | × $5 | × $5 | × $5 | |
| **Total cost of direct materials purchases** | **$3,870,000** | **$4,747,500** | **$5,134,500** | **$4,349,250** | **$18,101,250** |

[a]Estimated first-quarter 2023 production requirements: 810,000 × .05 = 40,500
[b]5% of estimated first-quarter pounds needed for production

Related exercise material: **BE15.2, BE15.3, BE15.4, DO IT! 15.2, E15.2, E15.3, E15.4, E15.5, E15.6, E15.7, and E15.8.**

# Direct Labor, Manufacturing Overhead, and S&A Expense Budgets

> **LEARNING OBJECTIVE 3**
> Prepare budgets for direct labor, manufacturing overhead, and selling and administrative expenses, and a budgeted income statement.

As shown in Illustration 15.2, the operating budgets culminate with preparation of the budgeted income statement. Before we can do that, we need to prepare budgets for direct labor, manufacturing overhead, and selling and administrative expenses.

## Direct Labor Budget

Like the direct materials budget, the **direct labor budget** contains the quantity (hours) and cost of direct labor necessary to meet production requirements. The total direct labor cost is derived from the formula shown in **Illustration 15.10**.

**ILLUSTRATION 15.10**
**Formula for direct labor cost**

$$\begin{array}{ccccccc} \text{Units} & & \text{Direct Labor} & & \text{Direct} & & \text{Total Direct} \\ \text{to Be} & \times & \text{Hours} & \times & \text{Labor Cost} & = & \text{Labor Cost} \\ \text{Produced} & & \text{per Unit} & & \text{per Hour} & & \end{array}$$

Direct labor hours are determined from the production budget. At Hayes Company, two hours of direct labor are required to produce each unit of finished goods. The anticipated hourly wage rate is $10. **Illustration 15.11** employs the formula in Illustration 15.10 using these data.

**ILLUSTRATION 15.11** Direct labor budget

| | | | | | | |
|---|---|---|---|---|---|---|
| | | Hayes Company Direct Labor Budget | | | | |
| | | A | B | C | D | E | F |

| | A | B | C | D | E | F |
|---|---|---|---|---|---|---|
| 1 | **Hayes Company** | | | | | |
| 2 | **Direct Labor Budget** | | | | | |
| 3 | **For the Year Ending December 31, 2022** | | | | | |
| 4 | | Quarter | | | | |
| 5 | | 1 | 2 | 3 | 4 | Year |
| 6 | Units to be produced (Illustration 15.5) | 3,100 | 3,600 | 4,100 | 4,600 | |
| 7 | Direct labor time (hours) per unit | × 2 | × 2 | × 2 | × 2 | |
| 8 | Total required direct labor hours | 6,200 | 7,200 | 8,200 | 9,200 | |
| 9 | Direct labor cost per hour | × $10 | × $10 | × $10 | × $10 | |
| 10 | **Total direct labor cost** | **$62,000** | **$72,000** | **$82,000** | **$92,000** | **$308,000** |
| 11 | | | | | | |

- In the first quarter, 3,100 units are to be produced requiring two hours of labor per unit, for a total of 6,200 hours (3,100 × $2).
- Each hour of labor costs $10, for a total cost of $62,000 (6,200 × $10).

The direct labor budget is critical in maintaining a labor force that can meet the expected levels of production (see **Helpful Hint**).

# Manufacturing Overhead Budget

The **manufacturing overhead budget** shows the expected manufacturing overhead costs for the budget period. As **Illustration 15.12** shows, **this budget distinguishes between variable and fixed overhead costs**.

**ILLUSTRATION 15.12**

Manufacturing overhead budget

Hayes Company Manufacturing Overhead Budget

| | | | | | | |
|---|---|---|---|---|---|---|
| | A | B | C | D | E | F |
| 1 | | **Hayes Company** | | | | |
| 2 | | **Manufacturing Overhead Budget** | | | | |
| 3 | | **For the Year Ending December 31, 2022** | | | | |
| 4 | | | | Quarter | | |
| 5 | | 1 | 2 | 3 | 4 | Year |
| 6 | Direct labor hours (Illustration 15.11) | 6,200 | 7,200 | 8,200 | 9,200 | 30,800 |
| 7 | Variable costs | | | | | |
| 8 | Indirect materials ($1.00/hour) | $ 6,200 | $ 7,200 | $ 8,200 | $ 9,200 | $ 30,800 |
| 9 | Indirect labor ($1.40/hour) | 8,680 | 10,080 | 11,480 | 12,880 | 43,120 |
| 10 | Utilities ($0.40/hour) | 2,480 | 2,880 | 3,280 | 3,680 | 12,320 |
| 11 | Maintenance ($0.20/hour) | 1,240 | 1,440 | 1,640 | 1,840 | 6,160 |
| 12 | Total variable costs | 18,600 | 21,600 | 24,600 | 27,600 | 92,400 |
| 13 | Fixed costs | | | | | |
| 14 | Supervisory salaries | 20,000 | 20,000 | 20,000 | 20,000 | 80,000 |
| 15 | Depreciation | 3,800 | 3,800 | 3,800 | 3,800 | 15,200 |
| 16 | Property taxes and insurance | 9,000 | 9,000 | 9,000 | 9,000 | 36,000 |
| 17 | Maintenance | 5,700 | 5,700 | 5,700 | 5,700 | 22,800 |
| 18 | Total fixed costs | 38,500 | 38,500 | 38,500 | 38,500 | 154,000 |
| 19 | Total manufacturing overhead | $57,100 | $60,100 | $63,100 | $66,100 | $246,400 |
| 20 | Manufacturing overhead rate per direct labor hour ($246,400 ÷ 30,800) | | | | | $8 |
| 21 | | | | | | |

- Hayes Company expects variable costs to fluctuate with production volume on the basis of the following rates per direct labor hour: indirect materials $1.00, indirect labor $1.40, utilities $0.40, and maintenance $0.20.

- Thus, for the 6,200 direct labor hours to produce 3,100 units, budgeted indirect materials are $6,200 (6,200 × $1), and budgeted indirect labor is $8,680 (6,200 × $1.40).

- Hayes also recognizes that some maintenance is fixed (the amounts reported for fixed costs are assumed for our example).

At Hayes Company, overhead is applied to production on the basis of direct labor hours. Thus, as Illustration 15.12 shows, the budgeted annual rate is $8 per hour ($246,400 ÷ 30,800).

# Selling and Administrative Expense Budget

Hayes Company combines its operating expenses into one budget, the **selling and administrative expense budget**. This budget projects anticipated selling and administrative expenses for the budget period. This budget (**Illustration 15.13**) also classifies expenses as either variable or fixed.

**ILLUSTRATION 15.13** Selling and administrative expense budget

Hayes Company Manufacturing Selling and Administrative Expense Budget

| | 1 | 2 | 3 | 4 | Year |
|---|---|---|---|---|---|
| | | | Quarter | | |
| Budgeted sales in units (Illustration 15.3) | 3,000 | 3,500 | 4,000 | 4,500 | 15,000 |
| **Variable expenses** | | | | | |
| Sales commissions ($3 per unit) | $ 9,000 | $10,500 | $12,000 | $13,500 | $ 45,000 |
| Freight-out ($1 per unit) | 3,000 | 3,500 | 4,000 | 4,500 | 15,000 |
| Total variable expenses | 12,000 | 14,000 | 16,000 | 18,000 | 60,000 |
| **Fixed expenses** | | | | | |
| Advertising | 5,000 | 5,000 | 5,000 | 5,000 | 20,000 |
| Sales salaries | 15,000 | 15,000 | 15,000 | 15,000 | 60,000 |
| Office salaries | 7,500 | 7,500 | 7,500 | 7,500 | 30,000 |
| Depreciation | 1,000 | 1,000 | 1,000 | 1,000 | 4,000 |
| Property taxes and insurance | 1,500 | 1,500 | 1,500 | 1,500 | 6,000 |
| Total fixed expenses | 30,000 | 30,000 | 30,000 | 30,000 | 120,000 |
| **Total selling and administrative expenses** | **$42,000** | **$44,000** | **$46,000** | **$48,000** | **$180,000** |

Heading: Hayes Company / Selling and Administrative Expense Budget / For the Year Ending December 31, 2022

- In this case, the variable expense rates per unit of sales are sales commissions $3 and freight-out $1.
- Variable expenses per quarter are based on the unit sales from the sales budget (see Illustration 15.3).

Because Hayes expects sales in the first quarter to be 3,000 units, sales commissions expense is therefore $9,000 (3,000 × $3), and freight-out is $3,000 (3,000 × $1) (fixed expenses are based on assumed data).

# Budgeted Income Statement

The **budgeted income statement** is the important end-product of the operating budgets.

- This budget indicates the expected profitability of operations for the budget period.
- The budgeted income statement provides the basis for evaluating company performance.

Budgeted income statements often act as a call to action. For example, a board member at **XM Satellite Radio** felt that budgeted costs were too high relative to budgeted revenues. When management refused to cut its marketing and programming costs, the board member resigned. He felt that without the cuts, the company risked financial crisis.

As you would expect, the budgeted income statement is prepared from the various operating budgets. For example, to find the cost of goods sold, Hayes Company must first determine the total unit cost of producing one Rightride bicycle seat, as shown in **Illustration 15.14**.

**ILLUSTRATION 15.14**
Computation of total unit cost

Cost of One Rightride

| Cost Element | Illustration | Quantity | Unit Cost | Total |
|---|---|---|---|---|
| Direct materials | 15.9 | 2 pounds | $ 4.00 | $ 8.00 |
| Direct labor | 15.11 | 2 hours | $10.00 | 20.00 |
| Manufacturing overhead | 15.12 | 2 hours | $ 8.00 | 16.00 |
| **Total unit cost** | | | | **$44.00** |

Hayes then determines cost of goods sold by multiplying the units sold by the unit cost. Its budgeted cost of goods sold is $660,000 (15,000 × $44). All data for the income statement come from the individual operating budgets except the following: (1) interest expense is expected to be $100, and (2) income taxes are estimated to be $12,000. **Illustration 15.15** shows the budgeted multiple-step income statement.

**ILLUSTRATION 15.15**

**Budgeted multiple-step income statement**

### Hayes Company
**Budgeted Income Statement**
**For the Year Ending December 31, 2022**

| | |
|---|---:|
| Sales (Illustration 15.3) | $900,000 |
| Cost of goods sold (15,000 × $44) | 660,000 |
| Gross profit | 240,000 |
| Selling and administrative expenses (Illustration 15.13) | 180,000 |
| Income from operations | 60,000 |
| Interest expense | 100 |
| Income before income taxes | 59,900 |
| Income tax expense | 12,000 |
| Net income | $ 47,900 |

## DO IT! 3 | Budgeted Income Statement

Soriano Company is preparing its budgeted income statement for 2022. Relevant data pertaining to its sales, production, and direct materials budgets can be found in **DO IT! 2**.

In addition, Soriano budgets 0.5 hours of direct labor per unit, labor costs at $15 per hour, and manufacturing overhead at $25 per direct labor hour. Its budgeted selling and administrative expenses for 2022 are $12,000,000.

**a.** Calculate the budgeted total unit cost.

**b.** Prepare the budgeted multiple-step income statement for 2022. (Ignore income taxes.)

**ACTION PLAN**

- **Recall that total unit cost consists of direct materials, direct labor, and manufacturing overhead.**
- **Recall that direct materials costs are included in the direct materials budget.**
- **Know the form and content of the income statement.**
- **Use the total unit sales information from the sales budget to compute annual sales and cost of goods sold.**

### Solution

**a.**

| Cost Element | Quantity | Unit Cost | Total |
|---|---|---|---:|
| Direct materials | 3.0 pounds | $ 5 | $15.00 |
| Direct labor | 0.5 hours | $15 | 7.50 |
| Manufacturing overhead | 0.5 hours | $25 | 12.50 |
| **Total unit cost** | | | **$35.00** |

**b.**

### Soriano Company
**Budgeted Income Statement**
**For the Year Ending December 31, 2022**

| | |
|---|---:|
| Sales (1,200,000 units from sales budget) | $61,500,000 |
| Cost of goods sold (1,200,000 × $35.00/unit) | 42,000,000 |
| Gross profit | 19,500,000 |
| Selling and administrative expenses | 12,000,000 |
| Net income | $ 7,500,000 |

Related exercise material: **BE15.8, DO IT! 15.3, E15.11, and E15.13**.

# Cash Budget and Budgeted Balance Sheet

> ## LEARNING OBJECTIVE 4
>
> Prepare a cash budget and a budgeted balance sheet.

As shown in Illustration 15.2, the financial budgets consist of the capital expenditure budget, the cash budget, and the budgeted balance sheet. We will discuss the capital expenditure budget in Chapter 18.

## Cash Budget

The **cash budget** shows anticipated cash flows.

- Because cash is so vital, this budget is often considered to be the most important financial budget (see **Decision Tools**).
- The cash budget contains three sections (cash receipts, cash disbursements, and financing) and the beginning and ending cash balances, as shown in **Illustration 15.16** (see **Helpful Hint**).

  1. The **cash receipts section** includes expected receipts from the company's principal source(s) of revenue. These are usually cash sales and collections from customers on credit sales. This section also shows anticipated receipts of interest and dividends, and proceeds from planned sales of investments, plant assets, and the company's capital stock.

  2. The **cash disbursements section** shows expected cash payments. Such payments include direct materials, direct labor, manufacturing overhead, and selling and administrative expenses. This section also includes projected payments for income taxes, dividends, investments, and plant assets.

  3. The **financing section** shows expected borrowings and the repayment of the borrowed funds plus interest. Companies need this section when there is a cash deficiency or when the cash balance is below management's minimum required balance.

**ILLUSTRATION 15.16**

**Basic form of a cash budget**

**HELPFUL HINT**

The cash budget is prepared after the other budgets because the information generated by the other budgets dictates the expected inflows and outflows of cash.

| | **Any Company** **Cash Budget** | B | C |
| --- | --- | --- | --- |
| 3 | Beginning cash balance | $X,XXX | |
| 4 | **Add: Cash receipts** (itemized) | X,XXX | |
| 5 | Total available cash | X,XXX | |
| 6 | **Less: Cash disbursements** (itemized) | X,XXX | |
| 7 | Excess (deficiency) of available cash over cash disbursements | X,XXX | |
| 8 | **Financing** | X,XXX | |
| 9 | Ending cash balance | $X,XXX | |

Data in the cash budget are prepared in sequence. The ending cash balance of one period becomes the beginning cash balance for the next period. Companies obtain data for preparing the cash budget from other budgets and from information provided by management. In practice, cash budgets are often prepared for the year on a monthly basis.

To minimize detail, we assume that Hayes Company prepares an annual cash budget by quarters. To prepare the cash budget, it is useful to prepare a schedule for collections from customers. This schedule is based on the following assumption:

Sales (Illustration 15.3): 60% are collected in the quarter sold and 40% are collected in the following quarter. Accounts receivable of $60,000 at December 31, 2021, are expected to be collected in full in the first quarter of 2022.

The schedule of cash collections from customers in **Illustration 15.17** applies this assumption.

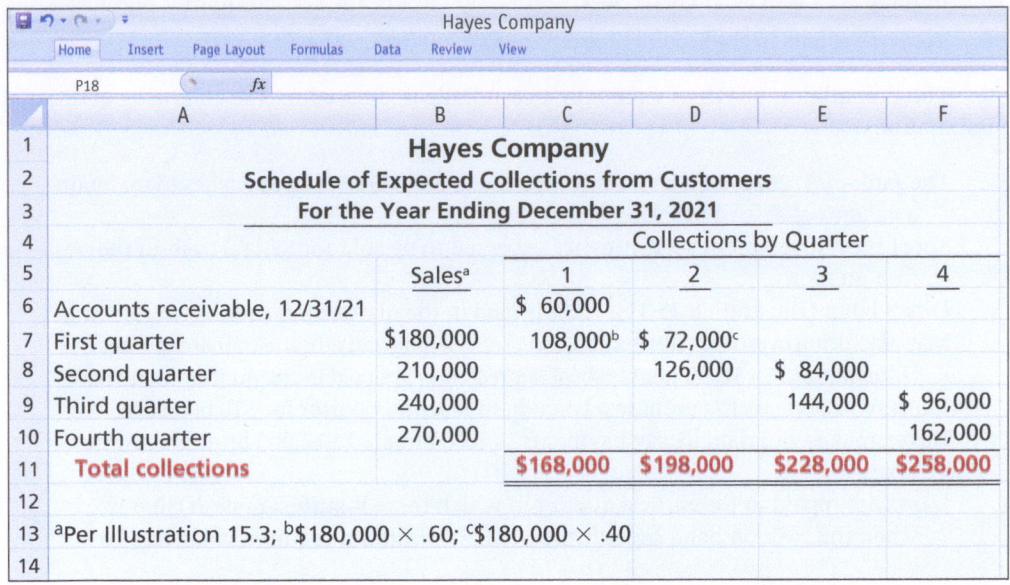

**ILLUSTRATION 15.17**

**Collections from customers**

**Hayes Company**

**Schedule of Expected Collections from Customers**

**For the Year Ending December 31, 2021**

| | Sales[a] | Collections by Quarter | | | |
|---|---|---|---|---|---|
| | | 1 | 2 | 3 | 4 |
| Accounts receivable, 12/31/21 | | $ 60,000 | | | |
| First quarter | $180,000 | 108,000[b] | $ 72,000[c] | | |
| Second quarter | 210,000 | | 126,000 | $ 84,000 | |
| Third quarter | 240,000 | | | 144,000 | $ 96,000 |
| Fourth quarter | 270,000 | | | | 162,000 |
| **Total collections** | | **$168,000** | **$198,000** | **$228,000** | **$258,000** |

[a]Per Illustration 15.3; [b]$180,000 × .60; [c]$180,000 × .40

- In the first quarter, Hayes collects the $60,000 that was outstanding at the beginning of the quarter, as well as an additional $108,000 (.60 × $180,000), which is 60% of the first-quarter sales of $180,000.

- Total receipts in the first quarter are $168,000 ($60,000 + $108,000).

- In the second quarter, the company collects the remaining 40% of first-quarter sales of $72,000 (.40 × $180,000) as well as $126,000 (.60 × $210,000), which is 60% of second-quarter sales of $210,000.

- Second-quarter receipts are $198,000 ($72,000 + $126,000).

Next, it is useful to prepare a schedule of expected cash payments for direct materials, based on this second assumption:

Direct materials (Illustration 15.9): 50% are paid in the quarter purchased and 50% are paid in the following quarter. Accounts payable of $10,600 at December 31, 2021, are expected to be paid in full in the first quarter of 2022.

The schedule of cash payments for direct materials in **Illustration 15.18** applies this second assumption.

**ILLUSTRATION 15.18**

**Payments for direct materials**

**Hayes Company**

**Schedule of Expected Payments for Direct Materials**

**For the Year Ending December 31, 2021**

| | Purchases[a] | Payments by Quarter | | | |
|---|---|---|---|---|---|
| | | 1 | 2 | 3 | 4 |
| Accounts payable, 12/31/21 | | $10,600 | | | |
| First quarter | $25,200 | 12,600[b] | $12,600[c] | | |
| Second quarter | 29,200 | | 14,600 | $14,600 | |
| Third quarter | 33,200 | | | 16,600 | $16,600 |
| Fourth quarter | 37,200 | | | | 18,600 |
| **Total payments** | | **$23,200** | **$27,200** | **$31,200** | **$35,200** |

[a]Per Illustration 15.9; [b]$25,200 × .50; [c]$25,200 × .50

- In the first quarter, Hayes pays the balance of its beginning accounts payable balance of $10,600 as well as pays $12,600, which is 50% of its first-quarter purchases of $25,200.

- The total payments in the first quarter are $23,200 ($10,600 + $12,600).

- In the second quarter, it pays $12,600 (.50 × $25,200) for the remaining 50% of its first-quarter purchases as well as $14,600 (.50 × $29,200) for 50% of the second-quarter purchases.

- Total payments in the second quarter are $27,200 ($12,600 + $14,600).

The preparation of Hayes Company's cash budget is based on the following additional assumptions.

> The January 1, 2022, cash balance is expected to be $38,000. Hayes wishes to maintain a balance of at least $15,000.
>
> Short-term investment securities are expected to be sold for $2,000 cash in the first quarter.
>
> Direct labor (Illustration 15.11): 100% is paid in the quarter incurred.
>
> Manufacturing overhead (Illustration 15.12) and selling and administrative expenses (Illustration 15.13): All items except depreciation are paid in the quarter incurred.
>
> Management plans to purchase a truck in the second quarter for $10,000 cash.
>
> Hayes makes equal quarterly payments of its estimated $12,000 annual income taxes.
>
> Loans are repaid in the earliest quarter in which there is sufficient cash (that is, when the cash on hand exceeds the $15,000 minimum required balance).

**Illustration 15.19** shows the cash budget for Hayes Company. The budget indicates that Hayes will need $3,000 of financing in the second quarter to maintain a minimum cash balance of $15,000. Since there is an excess of available cash over disbursements of $22,500 at the end of the third quarter, the borrowing, plus $100 interest, is repaid in this quarter.

**A cash budget contributes to more effective cash management.** It shows managers when additional financing is necessary well before the actual need arises. And, it indicates when excess cash is available for investments or other purposes.

---

## Management Insight    Kraft Heinz

Violka08/iStock/Getty Images Plus/Getty Images

### Starting from Scratch

Recently an increasing number of companies, including the giant food company **Kraft Heinz**, have adopted "zero-based budgeting." This budgeting approach requires that the budgeting process starts from scratch, rather than using the previous year's budget as a starting point. Every proposed cost must be justified and not just the large expenses. For example, **Pilgrim's Pride Corp.**, "scrutinized how much paper it used to print documents, how much soap employees used to wash their hands, and how much Gatorade hourly employees at one processing facility drank during breaks." The move toward zero-based budgeting is due in part to pressure by shareholders to increase company performance, as well as management fear that if a company's operations aren't lean, it will be taken over by outside investors. Proponents point toward zero-based budgeting's ability to reduce wasteful spending practices such as first-class plane flights. But critics suggest that it often results in significant layoffs, destroys employee morale, and potentially reduces a company's ability to pursue growth opportunities. **Coca-Cola** recently implemented zero-based budgeting but calls it "zero-based work" to try to disassociate its efforts from some of the negative connotations associated with zero-based budgeting.

**Source:** David Kesmodel and Annie Gasparro, "Kraft-Heinz Deal Shows Brazilian Buyout Firm's Cost-Cutting Recipe," *Wall Street Journal* (March 2015).

**What are some of the pros and cons of zero-based budgeting? (Go to WileyPLUS for this answer and additional questions.)**

---

## Budgeted Balance Sheet

The **budgeted balance sheet** is a projection of financial position at the end of the budget period. This budget is developed from the budgeted balance sheet for the preceding year and the budgets for the current year. Pertinent data from the budgeted balance sheet at December 31, 2021, are as follows.

| | | | |
|---|---|---|---|
| Buildings and equipment | $182,000 | Common stock | $225,000 |
| Accumulated depreciation | 28,800 | Retained earnings | 46,480 |

**ILLUSTRATION 15.19**   **Cash budget**

| | | Hayes Company Cash Budget | | | | |
|---|---|---|---|---|---|---|

| Home | Insert | Page Layout | Formulas | Data | Review | View |
|---|---|---|---|---|---|---|

P18    *fx*

| | A | B | C | D | E | F |
|---|---|---|---|---|---|---|
| 1 | | | **Hayes Company** | | | |
| 2 | | | **Cash Budget** | | | |
| 3 | | | **For the Year Ending December 31, 2022** | | | |
| 4 | | | Quarter | | | |
| 5 | | Assumption | 1 | 2 | 3 | 4 |
| 6 | Beginning cash balance | 3 | $ 38,000 | $ 25,500 | $ 15,000 | $ 19,400 |
| 7 | **Add: Receipts** | | | | | |
| 8 | Collections from customers | 1 | 168,000 | 198,000 | 228,000 | 258,000 |
| 9 | Sale of investment securities | 4 | 2,000 | 0 | 0 | 0 |
| 10 | Total receipts | | 170,000 | 198,000 | 228,000 | 258,000 |
| 11 | Total available cash | | 208,000 | 223,500 | 243,000 | 277,400 |
| 12 | **Less: Disbursements** | | | | | |
| 13 | Direct materials | 2 | 23,200 | 27,200 | 31,200 | 35,200 |
| 14 | Direct labor | 5 | 62,000 | 72,000 | 82,000 | 92,000 |
| 15 | Manufacturing overhead | 6 | 53,300[a] | 56,300 | 59,300 | 62,300 |
| 16 | Selling and administrative expenses | 6 | 41,000[b] | 43,000 | 45,000 | 47,000 |
| 17 | Purchase of truck | 7 | 0 | 10,000 | 0 | 0 |
| 18 | Income tax expense | 8 | 3,000 | 3,000 | 3,000 | 3,000 |
| 19 | Total disbursements | | 182,500 | 211,500 | 220,500 | 239,500 |
| 20 | Excess (deficiency) of available cash over cash disbursements | | 25,500 | 12,000 | 22,500 | 37,900 |
| 21 | **Financing** | | | | | |
| 22 | Add: Borrowings | | 0 | **3,000** | 0 | 0 |
| 23 | Less: Repayments including interest | 9 | 0 | 0 | **3,100** | 0 |
| 24 | Ending cash balance | 3 | $ 25,500 | $ 15,000 | $ 19,400 | $ 37,900 |
| 25 | | | | | | |
| 26 | [a]$57,100 − $3,800 depreciation; [b]$42,000 − $1,000 depreciation | | | | | |
| 27 | | | | | | |

Illustration 15.20 shows Hayes Company's budgeted classified balance sheet at December 31, 2022.

**ILLUSTRATION 15.20**

**Budgeted classified balance sheet**

### Hayes Company
### Budgeted Balance Sheet
### December 31, 2022

**Assets**

| | | |
|---|---|---|
| Current assets | | |
| Cash | | $ 37,900 |
| Accounts receivable | | 108,000 |
| Finished goods inventory | | 44,000 |
| Raw materials inventory | | 4,080 |
| Total current assets | | 193,980 |
| Property, plant, and equipment | | |
| Buildings and equipment | $192,000 | |
| Less: Accumulated depreciation | 48,000 | 144,000 |
| Total assets | | $337,980 |

**ILLUSTRATION 15.20**

*(continued)*

| **Liabilities and Stockholders' Equity** | | |
|---|---|---|
| Liabilities | | |
| Accounts payable | | $ 18,600 |
| Stockholders' equity | | |
| Common stock | $225,000 | |
| Retained earnings | 94,380 | |
| Total stockholders' equity | | 319,380 |
| Total liabilities and stockholders' equity | | $337,980 |

The computations and sources of the amounts are explained as follows.

- **Cash:** Ending cash balance $37,900, shown in the cash budget (Illustration 15.19).
- **Accounts receivable:** 40% of fourth-quarter sales $270,000, shown in the schedule of expected collections from customers (Illustration 15.17).
- **Finished goods inventory:** Desired ending inventory 1,000 units, shown in the production budget (Illustration 15.5) times the total unit cost $44 (shown in Illustration 15.14).
- **Raw materials inventory:** Desired ending inventory 1,020 pounds, times the cost per pound $4, shown in the direct materials budget (Illustration 15.9).
- **Buildings and equipment:** December 31, 2021, balance $182,000, plus purchase of truck for $10,000 (Illustration 15.19).
- **Accumulated depreciation:** December 31, 2021, balance $28,800, plus $15,200 depreciation shown in manufacturing overhead budget (Illustration 15.12) and $4,000 depreciation shown in selling and administrative expense budget (Illustration 15.13).
- **Accounts payable:** 50% of fourth-quarter purchases $37,200, shown in schedule of expected payments for direct materials (Illustration 15.18).
- **Common stock:** Unchanged from the beginning of the year.
- **Retained earnings:** December 31, 2021, balance $46,480, plus net income $47,900, shown in budgeted income statement (Illustration 15.15).

After budget data are entered into the computer, Hayes prepares the various budgets (sales, cash, etc.), as well as the budgeted financial statements. Using spreadsheets, management can also perform "what if" (sensitivity) analyses based on different hypothetical assumptions. For example, suppose that sales managers project that sales will be 10% higher in the coming quarter. What impact does this change have on the rest of the budgeting process and the financing needs of the business? The impact of the various assumptions on the budget is quickly determined by the spreadsheet. Armed with these analyses, managers make more informed decisions about the impact of various projects. They also anticipate future problems and business opportunities. As seen in this chapter, budgeting is an excellent use of computer spreadsheets.

### DO IT! 4 | Cash Budget

Martian Company management wants to maintain a minimum monthly cash balance of $15,000. At the beginning of March, the cash balance is $16,500, expected cash receipts for March are $210,000, and cash disbursements are expected to be $220,000. How much cash, if any, must be borrowed to maintain the desired minimum monthly balance?

### Solution

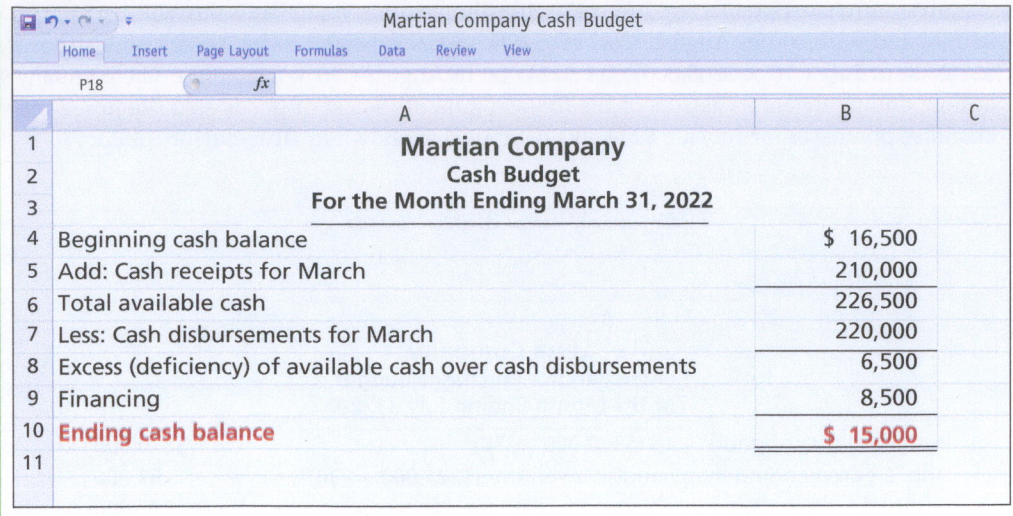

**ACTION PLAN**

- Write down the basic form of the cash budget, starting with the beginning cash balance, adding cash receipts for the period, deducting cash disbursements, and identifying the needed financing to achieve the desired minimum ending cash balance.
- Insert the data given into the outlined form of the cash budget.

To maintain the desired minimum cash balance of $15,000, Martian Company must borrow $8,500 of cash.

Related exercise material: **BE15.9, DO IT! 15.4, E15.14, E15.15, and E15.16.**

---

# Budgeting in Nonmanufacturing Companies

**LEARNING OBJECTIVE 5**

Apply budgeting principles to nonmanufacturing companies.

Budgeting is not limited to manufacturers. Budgets are also used by merchandisers, service companies, and not-for-profit organizations.

## Merchandisers

As in manufacturing operations, the sales budget for a merchandiser is both the starting point and the key factor in the development of the master budget. The major differences between the master budgets of a merchandiser and a manufacturer are as follows.

1. A merchandiser **uses a merchandise purchases budget instead of a production budget**.

2. A merchandiser **does not use the manufacturing budgets (direct materials, direct labor, and manufacturing overhead)**.

The **merchandise purchases budget** shows the estimated cost of goods to be purchased to meet expected sales. The formula for determining budgeted merchandise purchases is as shown in **Illustration 15.21**.

| Budgeted Cost of Goods Sold | + | Desired Ending Merchandise Inventory | − | Beginning Merchandise Inventory | = | Required Merchandise Purchases |
|---|---|---|---|---|---|---|

**ILLUSTRATION 15.21**

Merchandise purchases formula

To illustrate, assume that the budget committee of Lima Company is preparing the merchandise purchases budget for July 2022. It estimates that budgeted sales will be $300,000 in July and $320,000 in August. Cost of goods sold is expected to be 70% of sales—that is, $210,000 in July (.70 × $300,000) and $224,000 in August (.70 × $320,000). The company's desired ending inventory is 30% of the following month's cost of goods sold. Required merchandise purchases for July are $214,200, computed as shown in **Illustration 15.22**.

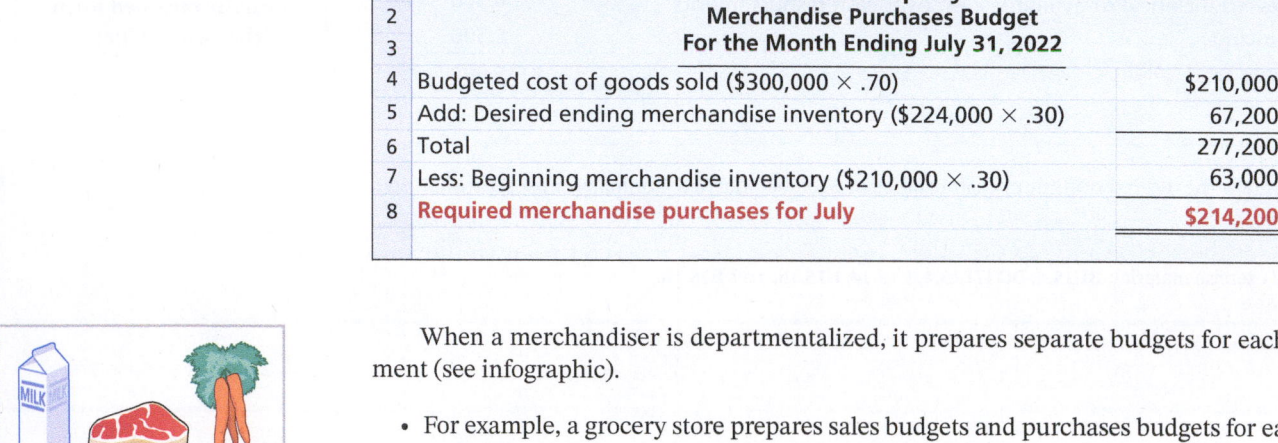

**ILLUSTRATION 15.22**

**Merchandise purchases budget**

| | A | B | C |
|---|---|---|---|
| 1 | **Lima Company** | | |
| 2 | **Merchandise Purchases Budget** | | |
| 3 | **For the Month Ending July 31, 2022** | | |
| 4 | Budgeted cost of goods sold ($300,000 × .70) | $210,000 | |
| 5 | Add: Desired ending merchandise inventory ($224,000 × .30) | 67,200 | |
| 6 | Total | 277,200 | |
| 7 | Less: Beginning merchandise inventory ($210,000 × .30) | 63,000 | |
| 8 | **Required merchandise purchases for July** | **$214,200** | |

When a merchandiser is departmentalized, it prepares separate budgets for each department (see infographic).

- For example, a grocery store prepares sales budgets and purchases budgets for each of its major departments, such as meats, dairy, and produce.
- The store then combines these budgets into a master budget for the store.

When a retailer has branch stores, it prepares a separate master budget for each store. Then, it incorporates these budgets into master budgets for the company as a whole.

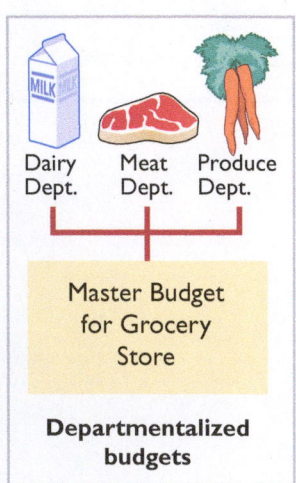

**Departmentalized budgets**

# Service Companies

In a service company, such as a public accounting firm, a law office, or a medical practice, the critical factor in budgeting is **coordinating professional staff needs with anticipated services**.

- If a firm is overstaffed, labor costs may be disproportionately high, profits may be lower because of the additional salaries, and staff turnover sometimes increases because of lack of challenging work.

- If a service company is understaffed, it may lose revenue because existing and prospective client needs for service cannot be met, and professional staff may seek other jobs because of excessive workloads.

Suppose that Stephan Lawn and Plowing Service estimates that it will service 300 small lawns, 200 medium lawns, and 100 large lawns during the month of July. It estimates its direct labor needs as 1 hour per small lawn, 1.75 hours for a medium lawn, and 2.75 hours for a large lawn. Its average cost for direct labor is $15 per hour. Stephan prepares a direct labor budget as shown in **Illustration 15.23**.

Service companies can obtain budget data for service revenue from **expected output** or **expected input**.

- When output is used, it is necessary to determine the expected billings of clients for services performed. In a public accounting firm, for example, output is the sum of its billings in auditing, tax, and consulting services.

- When input data are used, each professional staff member projects his or her billable time. The firm then applies billing rates to billable time to produce expected service revenue.

| Stephan Lawn and Plowing Service Direct Labor Budget | | | | |
| --- | --- | --- | --- | --- |
| Home   Insert   Page Layout   Formulas   Data   Review   View | | | | |
| P18 | | $fx$ | | |
| A | B | C | D | E |
| 1 | **Stephan Lawn and Plowing Service** | | | |
| 2 | **Direct Labor Budget** | | | |
| 3 | **For the Month Ending July 31, 2022** | | | |
| 4 | Small | Medium | Large | Total |
| 5  Lawns to be serviced | 300 | 200 | 100 | |
| 6  Direct labor time (hours) per lawn | × 1 | × 1.75 | × 2.75 | |
| 7  Total required direct labor hours | 300 | 350 | 275 | |
| 8  Direct labor cost per hour | × $15 | × $15 | × $15 | |
| 9  **Total direct labor cost** | **$4,500** | **$5,250** | **$4,125** | **$13,875** |

**ILLUSTRATION 15.23**
**Direct labor budget for service company**

# Not-for-Profit Organizations

Budgeting is just as important for not-for-profit organizations as for profit-oriented businesses. The budget process, however, is different. In most cases, not-for-profit entities budget **on the basis of cash flows (expenditures and receipts), rather than on a revenue and expense basis**.

- The starting point in the process is usually expenditures, not receipts. Management's task generally is to find the receipts needed to support the planned expenditures.

- The activity index is also likely to be significantly different. For example, in a not-for-profit entity, such as a university, budgeted faculty positions may be based on full-time equivalent students or credit hours expected to be taught in a department.

For some governmental units, voters approve the budget. In other cases, such as state governments and the federal government, legislative approval is required. After the budget is adopted, it must be followed. Overspending is often illegal. In governmental budgets, authorizations tend to be on a line-by-line basis. That is, the budget for a municipality may have a specified authorization for police and fire protection, garbage collection, street paving, and so on. The line-item authorization of governmental budgets significantly limits the amount of discretion management can exercise. The city manager often cannot use savings from one line item, such as street paving, to cover increased spending in another line item, such as snow removal.

## ACTION PLAN

- Begin with budgeted cost of goods sold.
- Add desired ending merchandise inventory.
- Subtract beginning merchandise inventory.

## DO IT! 5 | Merchandise Purchases Budget

Becker Company estimates that 2022 sales will be $15,000 in quarter 1, $20,000 in quarter 2, and $25,000 in quarter 3. Cost of goods sold is 80% of sales. Management desires to have ending finished goods inventory equal to 15% of the next quarter's expected cost of goods sold. Prepare a merchandise purchases budget by quarter for the first six months of 2022.

### Solution

| Becker Company Merchandise Purchases Budget | | | |
|---|---|---|---|

|  | A | B | C | D |
|---|---|---|---|---|
| 1 | **Becker Company** | | | |
| 2 | **Merchandise Purchases Budget** | | | |
| 3 | **For the Six Months Ending June 30, 2022** | | | |
| 4 | | Quarter | | |
| 5 | | 1 | 2 | Six Months |
| 6 | Budgeted cost of goods sold (sales × .80) | $12,000 | $16,000 | |
| 7 | Add: Desired ending merchandise inventory (15% of next quarter's cost of goods sold) | 2,400 | 3,000 | |
| 8 | Total | 14,400 | 19,000 | |
| 9 | Less: Beginning merchandise inventory (15% this quarter's cost of goods sold) | 1,800 | 2,400 | |
| 10 | **Required merchandise purchases** | **$12,600** | **$16,600** | **$29,200** |

Related exercise material: **BE15.10, DO IT! 15.5, E15.19, E15.20, and E15.21**.

## USING THE DECISION TOOLS | BabyCakes NYC

As discussed in the Feature Story, **BabyCakes NYC** relies on budgeting to aid in the management of its cupcake operations. Assume that BabyCakes prepares monthly cash budgets. Relevant data from assumed operating budgets for 2022 are as follows.

|  | January | February |
|---|---|---|
| Sales | $460,000 | $412,000 |
| Direct materials purchases | 185,000 | 210,000 |
| Direct labor | 70,000 | 85,000 |
| Manufacturing overhead | 50,000 | 65,000 |
| Selling and administrative expenses | 85,000 | 95,000 |

Assume that BabyCakes sells its cupcakes in its own shops as well as to other stores. Collections are expected to be 75% in the month of sale, and 25% in the month following sale. BabyCakes pays 60% of direct materials purchases in cash in the month of purchase, and the balance due in the month following the purchase. All other items above are paid in the month incurred. (Depreciation has been excluded from manufacturing overhead and selling and administrative expenses.)

Other data:

1. Sales: December 2021, $320,000
2. Purchases of direct materials: December 2021, $175,000
3. Other receipts: January—Donation received, $2,000
   February—Sale of used equipment, $4,000

4. Other disbursements: February—Purchased equipment, $10,000

5. Repaid debt: January, $30,000

The company's cash balance on January 1, 2022, is expected to be $50,000. The company wants to maintain a minimum cash balance of $45,000.

## Instructions

a. Prepare schedules for (1) expected collections from customers and (2) expected payments for direct materials purchases for January and February.

b. Prepare a cash budget for January and February in columnar form.

## Solution

a. 1.

**Expected Collections from Customers**

|  | Sales | January | February |
|---|---|---|---|
| December | $320,000 | $ 80,000 | $     0 |
| January | 460,000 | 345,000 | 115,000 |
| February | 412,000 | 0 | 309,000 |
| Totals |  | $425,000 | $424,000 |

2.

**Expected Payments for Direct Materials**

|  | Purchases | January | February |
|---|---|---|---|
| December | $175,000 | $ 70,000 | $     0 |
| January | 185,000 | 111,000 | 74,000 |
| February | 210,000 | 0 | 126,000 |
| Totals |  | $181,000 | $200,000 |

b.

**BabyCakes NYC**
**Cash Budget**
**For the Two Months Ending February 28, 2022**

|  | January | February |
|---|---|---|
| Beginning cash balance | $ 50,000 | $ 61,000 |
| Add: Receipts |  |  |
| Collections from customers | 425,000 | 424,000 |
| Donations received | 2,000 | 0 |
| Sale of used equipment | 0 | 4,000 |
| Total receipts | 427,000 | 428,000 |
| Total available cash | 477,000 | 489,000 |
| Less: Disbursements |  |  |
| Direct materials | 181,000 | 200,000 |
| Direct labor | 70,000 | 85,000 |
| Manufacturing overhead | 50,000 | 65,000 |
| Selling and administrative expenses | 85,000 | 95,000 |
| Purchase of equipment | 0 | 10,000 |
| Total disbursements | 386,000 | 455,000 |
| Excess (deficiency) of available cash over cash disbursements | 91,000 | 34,000 |
| Financing |  |  |
| Add: Borrowings | 0 | 11,000 |
| Less: Repayments | 30,000 | 0 |
| Ending cash balance | $ 61,000 | $ 45,000 |

# Review and Practice

## Learning Objectives Review

### 1 State the essentials of effective budgeting and the components of the master budget.

The primary benefits of budgeting are that it (a) requires management to plan ahead, (b) provides definite objectives for evaluating performance, (c) creates an early warning system for potential problems, (d) facilitates coordination of activities, (e) results in greater management awareness, and (f) motivates personnel to meet planned objectives. The essentials of effective budgeting are (a) sound organizational structure, (b) research and analysis, and (c) acceptance by all levels of management.

The master budget consists of the following budgets: (a) sales, (b) production, (c) direct materials, (d) direct labor, (e) manufacturing overhead, (f) selling and administrative expense, (g) budgeted income statement, (h) capital expenditure budget, (i) cash budget, and (j) budgeted balance sheet.

### 2 Prepare budgets for sales, production, and direct materials.

The sales budget is derived from sales forecasts. The production budget starts with budgeted sales units, adds desired ending finished goods inventory, and subtracts beginning finished goods inventory to arrive at the required number of units to be produced. The direct materials budget starts with the direct materials units (e.g., pounds) required for budgeted production, adds desired ending direct materials units, and subtracts beginning direct materials units to arrive at required direct materials units to be purchased. This amount is multiplied by the direct materials cost (e.g., cost per pound) to arrive at the total cost of direct materials purchases.

### 3 Prepare budgets for direct labor, manufacturing overhead, and selling and administrative expenses, and a budgeted income statement.

The direct labor budget starts with the units to be produced as determined in the production budget. This amount is multiplied by the direct labor hours per unit and the direct labor cost per hour to arrive at the total direct labor cost. The manufacturing overhead budget lists all of the individual types of overhead costs, distinguishing between fixed and variable costs. The selling and administrative expense budget lists all of the individual types of selling and administrative expense items, distinguishing between fixed and variable costs. The budgeted income statement is prepared from the various operating budgets. Cost of goods sold is determined by calculating the budgeted cost to produce one unit, then multiplying this amount by the number of units sold.

### 4 Prepare a cash budget and a budgeted balance sheet.

The cash budget has three sections (receipts, disbursements, and financing) and the beginning and ending cash balances. Receipts and payments sections are determined after preparing separate schedules for collections from customers and payments to suppliers. The budgeted balance sheet is developed from the budgeted balance sheet from the preceding year and the various budgets for the current year.

### 5 Apply budgeting principles to nonmanufacturing companies.

Budgeting may be used by merchandisers for development of a merchandise purchases budget. In service companies, budgeting is a critical factor in coordinating staff needs with anticipated services. In not-for-profit organizations, the starting point in budgeting is usually expenditures, not receipts.

## Decision Tools Review

| Decision Checkpoints | Info Needed for Decision | Tool to Use for Decision | How to Evaluate Results |
| --- | --- | --- | --- |
| Has the company met its targets for sales, production expenses, selling and administrative expenses, and net income? | Sales forecasts, inventory levels, projected materials, labor, overhead, and selling and administrative requirements | Master budget—a set of interrelated budgets including sales, production, materials, labor, overhead, and selling and administrative expense budgets | Results are favorable if revenues exceed budgeted amounts, or if expenses are less than budgeted amounts. |
| Is the company going to need to borrow funds in the coming period? | Beginning cash balance, cash receipts, cash disbursements, and desired ending cash balance | Cash budget | The company will need to borrow money if the cash budget indicates a projected cash deficiency. |

## Glossary Review

**Budget**   A formal written statement of management's plans for a specified future time period, expressed in financial terms. (p. 15-3).

**Budgetary slack**   The amount by which a manager intentionally underestimates budgeted revenues or overestimates budgeted expenses in order to make it easier to achieve budgetary goals. (p. 15-6).

**Budget committee**   A group responsible for coordinating the preparation of the budget. (p. 15-5).

**Budgeted balance sheet**   A projection of financial position at the end of the budget period. (p. 15-20).

**Budgeted income statement**   An estimate of the expected profitability of operations for the budget period. (p. 15-16).

**Cash budget**   A projection of anticipated cash flows. (p. 15-18).

**Direct labor budget**   A projection of the quantity and cost of direct labor necessary to meet production requirements. (p. 15-14).

**Direct materials budget**   An estimate of the quantity and cost of direct materials to be purchased. (p. 15-10).

**Financial budgets**   Individual budgets that focus primarily on the cash resources needed to fund expected operations and planned capital expenditures. (p. 15-7).

**Long-range planning**   A formalized process of identifying long-term goals, selecting strategies to achieve those goals, and developing policies and plans to implement the strategies. (p. 15-6).

**Manufacturing overhead budget**   An estimate of expected manufacturing overhead costs for the budget period. (p. 15-15).

**Master budget**   A set of interrelated budgets that constitutes a plan of action for a specific time period. (p. 15-7).

**Merchandise purchases budget**   The estimated cost of goods to be purchased by a merchandiser to meet expected sales. (p. 15-23).

**Operating budgets**   Individual budgets that result in a budgeted income statement. (p. 15-7).

**Participative budgeting**   A budgetary approach that starts with input from lower-level managers and works upward so that managers at all levels participate. (p. 15-5).

**Production budget**   A projection of the units that must be produced to meet anticipated sales. (p. 15-10).

**Sales budget**   An estimate of expected sales revenue for the budget period. (p. 15-8).

**Sales forecast**   The projection of potential sales for the industry and the company's expected share of such sales. (p. 15-5).

**Selling and administrative expense budget**   A projection of anticipated selling and administrative expenses for the budget period. (p. 15-15).

## Practice Multiple-Choice Questions

1. **(LO 1)** Which of the following is **not** a benefit of budgeting?
   a. Management can plan ahead.
   b. An early warning system is provided for potential problems.
   c. It enables disciplinary action to be taken at every level of responsibility.
   d. The coordination of activities is facilitated.

2. **(LO 1)** A budget:
   a. is the responsibility of management accountants.
   b. is the primary method of communicating agreed-upon objectives throughout an organization.
   c. ignores past performance because it represents management's plans for a future time period.
   d. may promote efficiency but has no role in evaluating performance.

3. **(LO 1)** The essentials of effective budgeting do **not** include:
   a. top-down budgeting.
   b. management acceptance.
   c. research and analysis.
   d. sound organizational structure.

4. **(LO 1)** Compared to budgeting, long-range planning generally has the:
   a. same amount of detail.   c. same emphasis.
   b. longer time period.   d. same time period.

5. **(LO 2)** A sales budget is:
   a. derived from the production budget.
   b. management's best estimate of sales revenue for the year.

   c. not the starting point for the master budget.
   d. prepared only for credit sales.

6. **(LO 2)** The formula for the production budget is budgeted sales in units plus:
   a. desired ending merchandise inventory less beginning merchandise inventory.
   b. beginning finished goods units less desired ending finished goods units.
   c. desired ending direct materials units less beginning direct materials units.
   d. desired ending finished goods units less beginning finished goods units.

7. **(LO 2)** Direct materials inventories are kept in pounds in Byrd Company, and the total pounds of direct materials needed for production is 9,500. If the beginning inventory is 1,000 pounds and the desired ending inventory is 2,200 pounds, the total number of pounds to be purchased is:
   a. 9,400.
   b. 9,500.
   c. 9,700.
   d. 10,700.

8. **(LO 3)** The formula for computing the direct labor budget is to multiply the direct labor cost per hour by the:
   a. total required direct labor hours.
   b. physical units to be produced.
   c. equivalent units to be produced.
   d. No correct answer is given.

**9. (LO 3)** Each of the following budgets is used in preparing the budgeted income statement **except** the:

    **a.** sales budget.

    **b.** selling and administrative expense budget.

    **c.** capital expenditure budget.

    **d.** direct labor budget.

**10. (LO 3)** The budgeted income statement is:

    **a.** the end-product of the operating budgets.

    **b.** the end-product of the financial budgets.

    **c.** the starting point of the master budget.

    **d.** dependent on cash receipts and cash disbursements.

**11. (LO 4)** The budgeted balance sheet is:

    **a.** developed from the budgeted balance sheet for the preceding year and the budgets for the current year.

    **b.** the last operating budget prepared.

    **c.** used to prepare the cash budget.

    **d.** All of the answer choices are correct.

**12. (LO 4)** The format of a cash budget is:

    **a.** Beginning cash balance + Cash receipts + Cash from financing − Cash disbursements = Ending cash balance.

    **b.** Beginning cash balance + Cash receipts − Cash disbursements +/− Financing = Ending cash balance.

    **c.** Beginning cash balance + Net income − Cash dividends = Ending cash balance.

    **d.** Beginning cash balance + Cash revenues − Cash expenses = Ending cash balance.

**13. (LO 4)** Expected direct materials purchases in Read Company are $70,000 in the first quarter and $90,000 in the second quarter. Forty percent of the purchases are paid in cash as incurred, and the balance is paid in the following quarter. The budgeted cash payments for purchases in the second quarter are:

    **a.** $96,000.        **c.** $78,000.

    **b.** $90,000.        **d.** $72,000.

**14. (LO 5)** The budget for a merchandiser differs from a budget for a manufacturer because:

    **a.** a merchandise purchases budget replaces the production budget, and the other manufacturing budgets are not used.

    **b.** the manufacturing budgets are not applicable, except the production budget is still used.

    **c.** a merchandise purchases budget replaces the production budget (and the other manufacturing budgets are not used), and the manufacturing budgets are not applicable (except the production budget is still used).

    **d.** None of the answer choices is correct.

**15. (LO 5)** In most cases, not-for-profit entities:

    **a.** prepare budgets using the same steps as those used by profit-oriented businesses.

    **b.** know budgeted cash receipts at the beginning of a time period, so they budget only for expenditures.

    **c.** begin the budgeting process by budgeting expenditures rather than receipts.

    **d.** can ignore budgets because they are not expected to generate net income.

## Solutions

**1. c.** Budgeting does not necessarily enable disciplinary action to be taken at every level of responsibility. The other choices are all benefits of budgeting.

**2. b.** A budget is the primary method of communicating agreed-upon objectives throughout an organization. The other choices are incorrect because (a) a budget is the responsibility of all levels of management, not management accountants; (c) past performance is not ignored in the budgeting process but instead is the starting point from which future budget goals are formulated; and (d) the budget not only may promote efficiency but is an important tool for evaluating performance.

**3. a.** Top-down budgeting is not one of the essentials of effective budgeting. The other choices are true statements.

**4. b.** Long-range planning generally encompasses a period of at least 5 years whereas budgeting usually covers a period of 1 year. The other choices are incorrect because budgeting and long-range planning (a) do not have the same amount of detail, (c) do not have the same emphasis, and (d) do not cover the same time period.

**5. b.** A sales budget is management's best estimate of sales revenue for the year. The other choices are incorrect because a sales budget (a) is the first budget prepared and is the one budget that is not derived from any other budget, (c) is the starting point for the master budget, and (d) is prepared for both cash and credit sales.

**6. d.** The formula for the production budget is budgeted sales in units plus desired ending finished goods units less beginning finished goods units. The other choices are therefore incorrect.

**7. d.** Pounds to be purchased = Amount needed for production (9,500) + Desired ending inventory (2,200) − Beginning inventory (1,000) = 10,700, not (a) 9,400, (b) 9,500, or (c) 9,700.

**8. a.** Direct labor cost = Direct labor cost per hour × Total required direct labor hours. The other choices are therefore incorrect.

**9. c.** The capital expenditure budget is not used in preparing the budgeted income statement. The other choices are true statements.

**10. a.** The budgeted income statement is the end-product of the operating budgets, not (b) the end-product of the financial budgets, (c) the starting point of the master budget, or (d) dependent on cash receipts and cash disbursements.

**11. a.** The budgeted balance sheet is developed from the budgeted balance sheet for the preceding year and the budgets for the current year. The other choices are therefore incorrect.

**12. b.** The format of a cash budget is Beginning cash balance + Cash receipts − Cash disbursements +/− Financing = Ending cash balance. The other choices are therefore incorrect.

**13. c.** Budgeted cash payments for the second quarter = Purchases for the first quarter ($42,000; $70,000 × .60) + 40% of the purchases for the second quarter ($36,000; $90,000 × .40) = $78,000, not (a) $96,000, (b) $90,000, or (d) $72,000.

**14. a.** The budget for a merchandiser uses a merchandise purchases budget in place of a production budget, and the other manufacturing budgets are not used. It is true the manufacturing budgets are not applicable for a merchandiser, but it is not true the production budget is still used, so choice (b) is not correct.

**15. c.** In most cases, not-for-profit entities begin the budgeting process by budgeting expenditures rather than receipts. The other choices are incorrect because in most cases not-for-profit entities (a) prepare budgets using different, not the same, steps as those used by profit-oriented enterprises; (b) budget for both expenditures and receipts; and (d) cannot ignore budgets.

# Practice Brief Exercises

**1. (LO 2)** Romana Company estimates that unit sales will be 20,000 in quarter 1, 24,000 in quarter 2, 27,000 in quarter 3, and 33,000 in quarter 4. Management desires to have an ending finished goods inventory equal to 20% of the next quarter's expected unit sales. Prepare a production budget by quarters for the first 6 months of 2022.

*Prepare a production budget for two quarters.*

**Solution**

1.

**Romana Company**
**Production Budget**
**For the Six Months Ending June 30, 2022**

| | Quarter | | Six |
| --- | --- | --- | --- |
| | **1** | **2** | **Months** |
| Expected unit sales | 20,000 | 24,000 | |
| Add: Desired ending finished goods | 4,800[a] | 5,400[c] | |
| Total required units | 24,800 | 29,400 | |
| Less: Beginning finished goods inventory | 4,000[b] | 4,800 | |
| Required production units | 20,800 | 24,600 | 45,400 |

[a]24,000 × .2; [b]20,000 × .2; [c]27,000 × .2

**2. (LO 3)** For Jovanka Company, units to be produced are 7,000 in quarter 1 and 9,800 in quarter 2. It takes 2.2 hours to make a finished unit, and the expected hourly wage rate is $20 per hour. Prepare a direct labor budget by quarters for the 6 months ending June 30, 2022.

*Prepare a direct labor budget for 2 quarters.*

**Solution**

2.

**Jovanka Company**
**Direct Labor Budget**
**For the Six Months Ending June 30, 2022**

| | Quarter | | Six |
| --- | --- | --- | --- |
| | **1** | **2** | **Months** |
| Units to be produced | 7,000 | 9,800 | |
| Direct labor time (hours) per unit | × 2.2 | × 2.2 | |
| Total required direct labor hours | 15,400 | 21,560 | |
| Direct labor cost per hour | × $20 | × $20 | |
| Total direct labor cost | $308,000 | $431,200 | $739,200 |

**3. (LO 4)** Vislor Industries expects credit sales for January, February, and March to be $165,000, $200,000, and $220,000, respectively. It is expected that 70% of the sales will be collected in the month of sale, and 30% will be collected in the following month. Compute cash collections from customers for each month.

*Prepare data for a cash budget.*

**Solution**

3.

| | Collections from Customers | | |
| --- | --- | --- | --- |
| **Credit Sales** | **January** | **February** | **March** |
| January, $165,000 | $115,500 | $ 49,500 | |
| February, $200,000 | | 140,000 | $ 60,000 |
| March, $220,000 | | | 154,000 |
| | $115,500 | $189,500 | $214,000 |

**4. (LO 5)** Turlough Wholesalers is preparing its merchandise purchases budget. Budgeted sales are $300,000 for June and $380,000 for July. Cost of goods sold is expected to be 60% of sales. The company's desired ending inventory is 25% of the following month's cost of goods sold. Compute the required purchases for June.

*Determine required merchandise purchases for 1 month.*

**Solution**

4.

| | |
|---|---:|
| Budgeted cost of goods sold ($300,000 × 60%) | $180,000 |
| Add: Desired ending inventory ($380,000 × 60% × 25%) | 57,000 |
| Total inventory required | 237,000 |
| Less: Beginning inventory ($300,000 × 60% × 25%) | 45,000 |
| Required merchandise purchases for June | $192,000 |

## Practice Exercises

*Prepare production and direct materials budgets by quarter for 6 months.*

**1. (LO 2)** On January 1, 2022, the Heche Company budget committee has reached agreement on the following data for the 6 months ending June 30, 2022.

| | |
|---|---|
| Sales units: | First quarter 5,000; second quarter 6,000; third quarter 7,000 |
| Ending raw materials inventory: | 40% of the next quarter's production requirements |
| Ending finished goods inventory: | 30% of the next quarter's expected sales units |
| Third-quarter 2022 production: | 7,500 units |

The ending raw materials and finished goods inventories at December 31, 2021, follow the same percentage relationships to production and sales that are desired for 2022. Two pounds of raw materials are required to make each unit of finished goods. Raw materials purchased are expected to cost $5 per pound.

### Instructions

**a.** Prepare a production budget by quarters for the 6-month period ended June 30, 2022.
**b.** Prepare a direct materials budget by quarters for the 6-month period ended June 30, 2022.

**Solution**

**1. a.**

Heche Company Production Budget

Home | Insert | Page Layout | Formulas | Data | Review | View

P18    *fx*

| | A | B | C | D |
|---|---|---|---|---|
| 1 | **Heche Company** | | | |
| 2 | **Production Budget** | | | |
| 3 | **For the Six Months Ending June 30, 2022** | | | |
| 4 | | | Quarter | |
| 5 | | 1 | 2 | Six Months |
| 6 | Expected unit sales | 5,000 | 6,000 | |
| 7 | Add: Desired ending finished goods units | 1,800[(1)] | 2,100[(2)] | |
| 8 | Total required units | 6,800 | 8,100 | |
| 9 | Less: Beginning finished goods units | 1,500[(3)] | 1,800 | |
| 10 | **Required production units** | **5,300** | **6,300** | **11,600** |
| 11 | | | | |
| 12 | [(1)].30 × 6,000; [(2)].30 × 7,000; [(3)].30 × 5,000 | | | |

**b.**

Heche Company Direct Materials Budget

Home | Insert | Page Layout | Formulas | Data | Review | View

P18    *fx*

| | A | B | C | D |
|---|---|---|---|---|
| 1 | **Heche Company** | | | |
| 2 | **Direct Materials Budget** | | | |
| 3 | **For the Six Months Ending June 30, 2022** | | | |
| 4 | | | Quarter | |
| 5 | | 1 | 2 | Six Months |
| 6 | Units to be produced | 5,300 | 6,300 | |
| 7 | Direct materials per unit | × 2 | × 2 | |
| 8 | Total pounds needed for production | 10,600 | 12,600 | |
| 9 | Add: Desired ending direct materials (pounds) | 5,040[(1)] | 6,000[(2)] | |
| 10 | Total materials required | 15,640 | 18,600 | |
| 11 | Less: Beginning direct materials (pounds) | 4,240[(3)] | 5,040 | |
| 12 | Direct materials purchase | 11,400 | 13,560 | |
| 13 | Cost per pound | × $5 | × $5 | |
| 14 | **Total cost of direct materials purchase** | **$57,000** | **$67,800** | **$124,800** |
| 15 | | | | |
| 16 | [(1)].40 × 12,600; [(2)].40 × (7,500 × 2); [(3)].40 × 10,600 | | | |
| 17 | | | | |

**2. (LO 4)** Jake Company expects to have a cash balance of $45,000 on January 1, 2022. Relevant monthly budget data for the first 2 months of 2022 are as follows.

*Prepare a cash budget for 2 months.*

Collections from customers: January $100,000, February $160,000.
Payments for direct materials: January $60,000, February $80,000.
Direct labor: January $30,000, February $45,000. Wages are paid in the month they are incurred.
Manufacturing overhead: January $26,000, February $31,000. These costs include depreciation of $1,000 per month. All other overhead costs are paid as incurred.
Selling and administrative expenses: January $15,000, February $20,000. These costs are exclusive of depreciation. They are paid as incurred.

Sales of marketable securities in January are expected to realize $10,000 in cash. Jake Company has a line of credit at a local bank that enables it to borrow up to $25,000. The company wants to maintain a minimum monthly cash balance of $25,000.

### Instructions

Prepare a cash budget for January and February.

### Solution

2.

| | Jake Company Cash Budget | | |
|---|---|---|---|
| | **Jake Company** | | |
| | **Cash Budget** | | |
| | **For the Two Months Ending February 28, 2022** | | |
| | | January | February |
| Beginning cash balance | | $ 45,000 | $ 25,000 |
| Add: Receipts | | | |
|     Collections from customers | | 100,000 | 160,000 |
|     Sale of marketable securities | | 10,000 | 0 |
|        Total receipts | | 110,000 | 160,000 |
| Total available cash | | 155,000 | 185,000 |
| Less: Disbursements | | | |
|     Direct materials | | 60,000 | 80,000 |
|     Direct labor | | 30,000 | 45,000 |
|     Manufacturing overhead | | 25,000* | 30,000 |
|     Selling and administrative expenses | | 15,000 | 20,000 |
|        Total disbursements | | 130,000 | 175,000 |
| Excess (deficiency) of available cash over cash | | | |
|     Disbursements | | 25,000 | 10,000 |
| Financing | | | |
|     Borrowings | | 0 | 15,000 |
|     Repayments | | 0 | 0 |
| **Ending cash balance** | | **$ 25,000** | **$ 25,000** |
| | | | |
| *$26,000 – $1,000 | | | |

## Practice Problems

**1. (LO 2)** Asheville Company is preparing its master budget for 2022. Relevant data pertaining to its sales and production budgets are as follows.

*Prepare sales and production budgets.*

**Sales.**   Sales for the year are expected to total 2,100,000 units. Quarterly sales, as a percentage of total sales, are 15%, 25%, 35%, and 25%, respectively. The sales price is expected to be $70 per unit for the first three quarters and $75 per unit beginning in the fourth quarter. Sales in the first quarter of 2023 are expected to be 10% higher than the budgeted sales volume for the first quarter of 2022.

**Production.**  Management desires to maintain ending finished goods inventories at 20% of the next quarter's budgeted sales volume.

### Instructions

Prepare the sales budget and production budget by quarters for 2022.

### Solution

1.

Asheville Company Sales Budget and Production Budget

| | Home | Insert | Page Layout | Formulas | Data | Review | View | | |

P18  fx

| | A | B | C | D | E | F |
|---|---|---|---|---|---|---|
| | | **Asheville Company** | | | | |
| 1 | | | | | | |
| 2 | | **For the Year Ending December 31, 2022** | | | | |
| 3 | | **Sales Budget** | | | | |
| 4 | | Quarter | | | | |
| 5 | | 1 | 2 | 3 | 4 | Year |
| 6 | Expected unit sales[a] | 315,000 | 525,000 | 735,000 | 525,000 | 2,100,000 |
| 7 | Unit selling price | × $70 | × $70 | × $70 | × $75 | |
| 8 | Total sales | $22,050,000 | $36,750,000 | $51,450,000 | $39,375,000 | $149,625,000 |
| 9 | | | | | | |
| 10 | | **Production Budget** | | | | |
| 11 | Expected unit sales | 315,000 | 525,000 | 735,000 | 525,000 | |
| 11 | Add: Desired ending finished goods units | 105,000 | 147,000 | 105,000 | 69,300[b] | |
| 12 | Total required units | 420,000 | 672,000 | 840,000 | 594,300 | |
| 12 | Less: Beginning finished | | | | | |
| 13 | goods units | 63,000[c] | 105,000 | 147,000 | 105,000 | |
| 14 | **Required production units** | **357,000** | **567,000** | **693,000** | **489,300** | **2,106,300** |
| 15 | | | | | | |

16 [a]Expected first-quarter unit sales 2,100,000 × .15; second and fourth quarters 2,100,000 × .25;
17   third quarter 2,100,000 × .35
18 [b]Estimated first-quarter 2023 sales volume 315,000 + (315,000 × .10) = 346,500; 346,500 × .20
19 [c]20% of estimated first-quarter 2022 sales units (315,000 × .20)

*Prepare budgeted cost of goods sold, income statement, and balance sheet.*

**2. (LO 3, 4)** Barrett Company has completed all operating budgets other than the income statement for 2022. Selected data from these budgets follow.

Sales: $300,000
Purchases of raw materials: $145,000
Ending inventory of raw materials: $15,000
Direct labor: $40,000
Manufacturing overhead: $73,000, including $3,000 of depreciation expense
Selling and administrative expenses: $36,000 including depreciation expense of $1,000
Interest expense: $1,000
Principal payment on note: $2,000
Dividends declared: $2,000
Income tax rate: 30%

Other information:

Assume that there are no work-in-process or finished goods inventories.
Year-end accounts receivable: 4% of 2022 sales.
Year-end accounts payable: 50% of ending inventory of raw materials.
Interest, direct labor, manufacturing overhead, and selling and administrative expenses other than depreciation are paid as incurred.
Dividends declared and income taxes for 2022 will not be paid until 2023.

---

**Barrett Company**
**Balance Sheet**
**December 31, 2021**

**Assets**

| | | |
|---|---|---|
| Current assets | | |
| Cash | | $20,000 |
| Raw materials inventory | | 10,000 |
| Total current assets | | 30,000 |
| Property, plant, and equipment | | |
| Equipment | $40,000 | |
| Less: Accumulated depreciation | 4,000 | 36,000 |
| Total assets | | $66,000 |

**Liabilities and Stockholders' Equity**

| | | |
|---|---|---|
| Liabilities | | |
| Accounts payable | $ 5,000 | |
| Notes payable | 22,000 | |
| Total liabilities | | $27,000 |
| Stockholders' equity | | |
| Common stock | 25,000 | |
| Retained earnings | 14,000 | |
| Total stockholders' equity | | 39,000 |
| Total liabilities and stockholders' equity | | $66,000 |

## Instructions

a. Calculate budgeted cost of goods sold.

b. Prepare a budgeted multiple-step income statement for the year ending December 31, 2022.

c. Prepare a budgeted classified balance sheet as of December 31, 2022.

## Solution

2. a. Beginning raw materials + Purchases − Ending raw materials = Cost of direct materials used
   ($10,000 + $145,000 − $15,000 = $140,000)
   Direct materials used + Direct labor + Manufacturing overhead = Cost of goods sold ($140,000 + $40,000 + $73,000 = $253,000)

b.

---

**Barrett Company**
**Budgeted Income Statement**
**For the Year Ending December 31, 2022**

| | |
|---|---|
| Sales | $300,000 |
| Cost of goods sold | 253,000 |
| Gross profit | 47,000 |
| Selling and administrative expenses | 36,000 |
| Income from operations | 11,000 |
| Interest expense | 1,000 |
| Income before income tax expense | 10,000 |
| Income tax expense (30%) | 3,000* |
| Net income | $   7,000 |

*$10,000 × .30

c.

**Barrett Company**
**Budgeted Balance Sheet**
**December 31, 2022**

### Assets

| | | |
|---|---:|---:|
| Current assets | | |
| Cash[(1)] | | $17,500 |
| Accounts receivable (.04 × $300,000) | | 12,000 |
| Raw materials inventory | | 15,000 |
| Total current assets | | 44,500 |
| Property, plant, and equipment | | |
| Equipment | $40,000 | |
| Less: Accumulated depreciation[(2)] | 8,000 | 32,000 |
| Total assets | | $76,500 |

### Liabilities and Stockholders' Equity

| | | |
|---|---:|---:|
| Liabilities | | |
| Accounts payable (.50 × $15,000) | $ 7,500 | |
| Income taxes payable (see income statement) | 3,000 | |
| Dividends payable | 2,000 | |
| Note payable ($22,000 − $2,000) | 20,000 | |
| Total liabilities | | $32,500 |
| Stockholders' equity | | |
| Common stock | 25,000 | |
| Retained earnings[(3)] | 19,000 | |
| Total stockholders' equity | | 44,000 |
| Total liabilities and stockholders' equity | | $76,500 |

| | | |
|---|---:|---:|
| [(1)]Beginning cash balance | | $ 20,000 |
| Add: Receipts | | |
| Collections from customers [(1 − .04) × $300,000 sales)] | | 288,000 |
| Total available cash | | 308,000 |
| Less: Disbursements | | |
| Direct materials ($5,000 + $145,000 − $7,500) | $142,500 | |
| Direct labor | 40,000 | |
| Manufacturing overhead ($73,000 − $3,000) | 70,000 | |
| Selling and administrative expenses ($36,000 − $1,000) | 35,000 | |
| Total disbursements | | 287,500 |
| Excess of available cash over cash disbursements | | 20,500 |
| Financing | | |
| Less: Repayment of principal and interest | | 3,000 |
| Ending cash balance | | $ 17,500 |

[(2)]$4,000 + $3,000 + $1,000

[(3)]Beginning retained earnings + Net income − Dividends declared = Ending retained earnings ($14,000 + $7,000 − $2,000 = $19,000)

# WileyPLUS

Brief Exercises, DO IT! Exercises, Exercises, Problems, and many additional resources are available for practice in WileyPLUS.

## Questions

**1. a.** What is a budget?

**b.** How does a budget contribute to good management?

**2.** Kate Cey and Joe Coulter are discussing the benefits of budgeting. They ask you to identify the primary benefits of budgeting. Comply with their request.

3. Jane Gilligan asks your help in understanding the essentials of effective budgeting. Identify the essentials for Jane.

4. **a.** "Accounting plays a relatively unimportant role in budgeting." Do you agree? Explain.

   **b.** What responsibilities does management have in budgeting?

5. What criteria are helpful in determining the length of the budget period? What is the most common budget period?

6. Lori Wilkins maintains that the only difference between budgeting and long-range planning is time. Do you agree? Why or why not?

7. What is participative budgeting? What are its potential benefits? What are its potential disadvantages?

8. What is budgetary slack? What incentive do managers have to create budgetary slack?

9. Distinguish between a master budget and a sales forecast.

10. What budget is the starting point in preparing the master budget? What may result if this budget is inaccurate?

11. "The production budget shows both unit production data and unit cost data." Is this true? Explain.

12. Alou Company has 20,000 beginning finished goods units. Budgeted sales units are 160,000. If management desires 15,000 ending finished goods units, what are the required units of production?

13. In preparing the direct materials budget for Quan Company, management concludes that required purchases are 64,000 units. If 52,000 direct materials units are required in production and there are 9,000 units of beginning direct materials, what are the desired units of ending direct materials?

14. The production budget of Justus Company calls for 80,000 units to be produced. If it takes 45 minutes to make one unit and the

direct labor rate is $16 per hour, what is the total budgeted direct labor cost?

15. Ortiz Company's manufacturing overhead budget shows total variable costs of $198,000 and total fixed costs of $162,000. Total production in units is expected to be 150,000. It takes 20 minutes to make one unit, and the direct labor rate is $15 per hour. Express the manufacturing overhead rate as (a) a percentage of direct labor cost, and (b) an amount per direct labor hour.

16. Everly Company's variable selling and administrative expenses are 12% of net sales. Fixed expenses are $50,000 per quarter. The sales budget shows expected sales of $200,000 and $240,000 in the first and second quarters, respectively. What are the total budgeted selling and administrative expenses for each quarter?

17. For Goody Company, the budgeted cost for one unit of product is direct materials $10, direct labor $20, and manufacturing overhead 80% of direct labor cost. If 25,000 units are expected to be sold at $65 each, what is the budgeted gross profit?

18. Indicate the supporting schedules used in preparing a budgeted income statement through gross profit for a manufacturer.

19. Identify the three sections of a cash budget. What balances are also shown in this budget?

20. Noterman Company has credit sales of $600,000 in January. Past experience suggests that 40% is collected in the month of sale, 50% in the month following the sale, and 10% in the second month following the sale. Compute the cash collections from January sales in January, February, and March.

21. What is the formula for determining required merchandise purchases for a merchandiser?

22. How might expected revenues in a service company be computed?

## Brief Exercises

**BE15.1 (LO 1), AN** Maris Company uses the following budgets: balance sheet, capital expenditure, cash, direct labor, direct materials, income statement, manufacturing overhead, production, sales, and selling and administrative expense. Prepare a diagram of the interrelationships of the budgets in the master budget. Indicate whether each budget is an operating or a financial budget.

*Prepare a diagram of a master budget.*

**BE15.2 (LO 2), AP** Paige Company estimates that unit sales will be 10,000 in quarter 1, 14,000 in quarter 2, 15,000 in quarter 3, and 18,000 in quarter 4. Using a sales price of $70 per unit, prepare the sales budget by quarters for the year ending December 31, 2022.

*Prepare a sales budget.*

**BE15.3 (LO 2), AP** Paige Company estimates that unit sales will be 10,000 in quarter 1, 14,000 in quarter 2, 15,000 in quarter 3, and 18,000 in quarter 4. The sales price is $70 per unit. Management desires to have an ending finished goods inventory equal to 25% of the next quarter's expected unit sales. Prepare a production budget by quarters for the first 6 months of 2022.

*Prepare a production budget for 2 quarters.*

**BE15.4 (LO 2), AP** Perine Company has 2,000 pounds of raw materials in its December 31, 2021, ending inventory. Required production for January and February of 2022 are 4,000 and 5,000 units, respectively. Two pounds of raw materials are needed for each unit, and the estimated cost per pound is $6. Management desires an ending inventory equal to 25% of next month's materials requirements. Prepare the direct materials budget for January.

*Prepare a direct materials budget for 1 month.*

**BE15.5 (LO 3), AP** For Gundy Company, units to be produced are 5,000 in quarter 1 and 7,000 in quarter 2. It takes 1.6 hours to make a finished unit, and the expected hourly wage rate is $15 per hour. Prepare a direct labor budget by quarters for the 6 months ending June 30, 2022.

*Prepare a direct labor budget for 2 quarters.*

**BE15.6 (LO 3), AP** For Roche Inc., variable manufacturing overhead costs are expected to be $20,000 in the first quarter of 2022, with $5,000 increments in each of the remaining three quarters. Fixed overhead costs are estimated to be $40,000 in each quarter. Prepare the manufacturing overhead budget by quarters and in total for the year.

*Prepare a manufacturing overhead budget.*

*Prepare a selling and administrative expense budget.*

**BE15.7 (LO 3), AP** Elbert Company classifies its selling and administrative expense budget into variable and fixed components. Variable expenses are expected to be $24,000 in the first quarter, and $4,000 increments are expected in the remaining quarters of 2022. Fixed expenses are expected to be $40,000 in each quarter. Prepare the selling and administrative expense budget by quarters and in total for 2022.

*Prepare a budgeted income statement for the year.*

**BE15.8 (LO 3), AP** North Company has completed all of its operating budgets. The sales budget for the year shows 50,000 units and total sales of $2,250,000. The total cost of producing one unit is $25. Selling and administrative expenses are expected to be $300,000. Interest is estimated to be $10,000. Income taxes are estimated to be $200,000. Prepare a budgeted multiple-step income statement for the year ending December 31, 2022.

*Prepare data for a cash budget.*

**BE15.9 (LO 4), AP** Kaspar Industries expects credit sales for January, February, and March to be $220,000, $260,000, and $300,000, respectively. It is expected that 75% of the sales will be collected in the month of sale, and 25% will be collected in the following month. Compute cash collections from customers for each month.

*Determine required merchandise purchases for 1 month.*

**BE15.10 (LO 5), AP** Moore Wholesalers is preparing its merchandise purchases budget. Budgeted sales are $400,000 for April and $480,000 for May. Cost of goods sold is expected to be 65% of sales. The company's desired ending inventory is 20% of the following month's cost of goods sold. Compute the required purchases for April.

# DO IT! Exercises

*Identify budget terminology.*

**DO IT! 15.1 (LO 1), K** Use this list of terms to complete the sentences that follow.

| | |
|---|---|
| Long-range plans | Participative budgeting |
| Sales forecast | Operating budgets |
| Master budget | Financial budgets |

1. _____ establish goals for the company's sales and production personnel.

2. The _____ is a set of interrelated budgets that constitutes a plan of action for a specified time period.

3. _____ reduces the risk of having unrealistic budgets.

4. _____ include the cash budget and the budgeted balance sheet.

5. The budget is formed within the framework of a _____.

6. _____ contain considerably less detail than budgets.

*Prepare sales, production, and direct materials budgets.*

**DO IT! 15.2 (LO 2), AP** Pargo Company is preparing its master budget for 2022. Relevant data pertaining to its sales, production, and direct materials budgets are as follows.

**Sales.** Sales for the year are expected to total 1,000,000 units. Quarterly sales are 20%, 25%, 25%, and 30%, respectively. The sales price is expected to be $40 per unit for the first three quarters and $45 per unit beginning in the fourth quarter. Sales in the first quarter of 2023 are expected to be 20% higher than the budgeted sales for the first quarter of 2022.

**Production.** Management desires to maintain the ending finished goods inventories at 25% of the next quarter's budgeted sales volume.

**Direct materials.** Each unit requires 2 pounds of raw materials at a cost of $12 per pound. Management desires to maintain raw materials inventories at 10% of the next quarter's production requirements. Assume the production requirements for first quarter of 2023 are 450,000 pounds.

Prepare the sales, production, and direct materials budgets by quarters for 2022.

*Calculate budgeted total unit cost and prepare budgeted income statement.*

**DO IT! 15.3 (LO 3), AP** Pargo Company is preparing its budgeted income statement for 2022. Relevant data pertaining to its sales, production, and direct materials budgets can be found in **DO IT! 15.2**.

In addition, Pargo budgets 0.3 hours of direct labor per unit, labor costs at $15 per hour, and manufacturing overhead at $20 per direct labor hour. Its budgeted selling and administrative expenses for 2022 are $6,000,000.

a. Calculate the budgeted total unit cost.

b. Prepare the budgeted multiple-step income statement for 2022. (Ignore income taxes.)

*Determine amount of financing needed.*

**DO IT! 15.4 (LO 4), AP** Batista Company management wants to maintain a minimum monthly cash balance of $25,000. At the beginning of April, the cash balance is $25,000, expected cash receipts for

April are $245,000, and cash disbursements are expected to be $255,000. How much cash, if any, must be borrowed to maintain the desired minimum monthly balance?

**DO IT! 15.5  (LO 5), AP**  Zeller Company estimates that 2022 sales will be $40,000 in quarter 1, $48,000 in quarter 2, and $58,000 in quarter 3. Cost of goods sold is 50% of sales. Management desires to have ending merchandise inventory equal to 10% of the next quarter's expected cost of goods sold. Prepare a merchandise purchases budget by quarter for the first 6 months of 2022.

*Prepare merchandise purchases budget.*

# Exercises

**E15.1  (LO 1), C**  **Writing**  Trusler Company has always done some planning for the future, but the company has never prepared a formal budget. Now that the company is growing larger, it is considering preparing a budget.

*Explain the concept of budgeting.*

**Instructions**

Write a memo to Jim Dixon, the president of Trusler Company, in which you define budgeting, identify the budgets that comprise the master budget, identify the primary benefits of budgeting, and discuss the essentials of effective budgeting.

**E15.2  (LO 2), AP**  Edington Electronics Inc. produces and sells two models of calculators, XQ-103 and XQ-104. The calculators sell for $15 and $25, respectively. Because of the intense competition Edington faces, management budgets sales semiannually. Its projections for the first 2 quarters of 2022 are as follows.

*Prepare a sales budget for 2 quarters.*

 Excel

|  | Unit Sales | |
| --- | --- | --- |
| **Product** | **Quarter 1** | **Quarter 2** |
| XQ-103 | 20,000 | 22,000 |
| XQ-104 | 12,000 | 15,000 |

No changes in selling prices are anticipated.

**Instructions**

Prepare a sales budget for the 2 quarters ending June 30, 2022. List the products and show units, selling price, and total sales by product and in total for each quarter and for the 6 months.

**E15.3  (LO 2), AP**  **Service**  Thome and Crede, CPAs, are preparing their service revenue (sales) budget for the coming year (2022). The practice is divided into three departments: auditing, tax, and consulting. Billable hours for each department, by quarter, are provided here.

*Prepare a sales budget for 4 quarters.*

| **Department** | **Quarter 1** | **Quarter 2** | **Quarter 3** | **Quarter 4** |
| --- | --- | --- | --- | --- |
| Auditing | 2,300 | 1,600 | 2,000 | 2,400 |
| Tax | 3,000 | 2,200 | 2,000 | 2,500 |
| Consulting | 1,500 | 1,500 | 1,500 | 1,500 |

Average hourly billing rates are auditing $80, tax $90, and consulting $110.

**Instructions**

Prepare the service revenue (sales) budget for 2022 by listing the departments and showing billable hours, billable rate, and total revenue for each quarter and the year in total.

**E15.4  (LO 2), AP**  Turney Company produces and sells automobile batteries, the heavy-duty HD-240. The 2022 sales forecast is as follows.

*Prepare quarterly production budgets.*

 Excel

| **Quarter** | **HD-240** |
| --- | --- |
| 1 | 5,000 |
| 2 | 7,000 |
| 3 | 8,000 |
| 4 | 10,000 |

The January 1, 2022, inventory of HD-240 is 2,000 units. Management desires an ending inventory each quarter equal to 40% of the next quarter's sales. Sales in the first quarter of 2023 are expected to be 25% higher than sales in the same quarter in 2022.

**Instructions**

Prepare quarterly production budgets for each quarter and in total for 2022.

*Prepare a direct materials purchases budget.*

**E15.5 (LO 2), AP** DeWitt Industries has adopted the following production budget for the first 4 months of 2022.

| Month | Units | Month | Units |
|---|---|---|---|
| January | 10,000 | March | 5,000 |
| February | 8,000 | April | 4,000 |

Each unit requires 2 pounds of raw materials costing $3 per pound. On December 31, 2021, the ending raw materials inventory was 4,000 pounds. Management wants to have a raw materials inventory at the end of the month equal to 20% of next month's production requirements.

**Instructions**

Prepare a direct materials purchases budget by month for the first quarter.

*Prepare production and direct materials budgets by quarters for 6 months.*

**E15.6 (LO 2), AP** On January 1, 2022, the Hardin Company budget committee has reached agreement on the following data for the 6 months ending June 30, 2022.

Sales units: First quarter 5,000; second quarter 6,000; third quarter 7,000.

Ending raw materials inventory: 40% of the next quarter's production requirements.

Ending finished goods inventory: 25% of the next quarter's expected sales units.

Third-quarter production: 7,200 units.

The ending raw materials and finished goods inventories at December 31, 2021, follow the same percentage relationships to production and sales that occur in 2022. Three pounds of raw materials are required to make each unit of finished goods. Raw materials purchased are expected to cost $4 per pound.

**Instructions**

a. Prepare a production budget by quarters for the 6-month period ended June 30, 2022.

b. Prepare a direct materials budget by quarters for the 6-month period ended June 30, 2022.

*Calculate raw materials purchases in dollars.*

**E15.7 (LO 2), AP** Rensing Ltd. estimates sales for the second quarter of 2022 will be as follows.

| Month | Units |
|---|---|
| April | 2,550 |
| May | 2,675 |
| June | 2,390 |

The target ending inventory of finished products is as follows.

| March 31 | 2,000 |
|---|---|
| April 30 | 2,230 |
| May 31 | 2,200 |
| June 30 | 2,310 |

Two units of materials are required for each unit of finished product. Production for July is estimated at 2,700 units to start building inventory for the fall sales period. Rensing's policy is to have an inventory of raw materials at the end of each month equal to 50% of the following month's production requirements. Raw materials are expected to cost $4 per unit throughout the period.

**Instructions**

Calculate the May raw materials purchases in dollars.

(CGA adapted)

*Prepare a production and a direct materials budget.*

**E15.8 (LO 2), AP** Fuqua Company's sales budget projects unit sales of part 198Z of 10,000 units in January, 12,000 units in February, and 13,000 units in March. Each unit of part 198Z requires 4 pounds of materials, which cost $2 per pound. Fuqua Company desires its ending raw materials inventory to equal 40% of the next month's production requirements, and its ending finished goods inventory to equal 20% of the next month's expected unit sales. These goals were met at December 31, 2021.

**Instructions**

   a. Prepare a production budget for January and February 2022.

   b. Prepare a direct materials budget for January 2022.

**E15.9 (LO 3), AP** Rodriguez, Inc., is preparing its direct labor budget for 2022 from the following production budget based on a calendar year.

*Prepare a direct labor budget.*

| Quarter | Units | Quarter | Units |
|---------|-------|---------|-------|
| 1 | 20,000 | 3 | 35,000 |
| 2 | 25,000 | 4 | 30,000 |

Each unit requires 1.5 hours of direct labor.

**Instructions**

Prepare a direct labor budget for 2022. Wage rates are expected to be $16 for the first 2 quarters and $18 for quarters 3 and 4.

**E15.10 (LO 2, 3), AP** Lowell Company makes and sells artistic frames for pictures. The controller is responsible for preparing the master budget and has accumulated the following information for 2022.

*Prepare production and direct labor budgets.*

| | January | February | March | April | May |
|---|---------|----------|-------|-------|-----|
| Estimated unit sales | 12,000 | 14,000 | 13,000 | 11,000 | 11,000 |
| Sales price per unit | $50.00 | $47.50 | $47.50 | $47.50 | $47.50 |
| Direct labor hours per unit | 2.0 | 2.0 | 1.5 | 1.5 | 1.5 |
| Wage per direct labor hour | $8.00 | $8.00 | $8.00 | $9.00 | $9.00 |

Lowell has a labor contract that calls for a wage increase to $9.00 per hour on April 1. New labor-saving machinery has been installed and will be fully operational by March 1.

   Lowell expects to begin the year with 17,600 frames on hand and has a policy of carrying an end-of-month inventory of 100% of the following month's sales, plus 40% of the second following month's sales.

**Instructions**

Prepare a production budget and a direct labor budget for Lowell Company by month and for the first quarter of the year. The direct labor budget should include direct labor hours.

(CMA-Canada adapted)

**E15.11 (LO 3), AP** Atlanta Company is preparing its manufacturing overhead budget for 2022. Relevant data consist of the following.

*Prepare a manufacturing overhead budget for the year.*

 Excel

   Units to be produced (by quarters): 10,000, 12,000, 14,000, 16,000.

   Direct labor: time is 1.5 hours per unit.

   Variable overhead costs per direct labor hour: indirect materials $0.80; indirect labor $1.20; and maintenance $0.50.

   Fixed overhead costs per quarter: supervisory salaries $41,250; depreciation $15,000; and maintenance $12,000.

**Instructions**

Prepare the manufacturing overhead budget for the year, showing quarterly data.

**E15.12 (LO 3), AP** Kirkland Company combines its operating expenses for budget purposes in a selling and administrative expense budget. For the first 6 months of 2022, the following data are available.

*Prepare a selling and administrative expense budget for 2 quarters.*

   1. Sales: 20,000 units quarter 1; 22,000 units quarter 2.

   2. Variable costs per dollar of sales: sales commissions 5%, delivery expense 2%, and advertising 3%.

   3. Fixed costs per quarter: sales salaries $12,000, office salaries $8,000, depreciation $4,200, insurance $1,500, utilities $800, and repairs expense $500.

   4. Unit selling price: $20.

**Instructions**

Prepare a selling and administrative expense budget by quarters for the first 6 months of 2022.

*Prepare a budgeted income statement for the year.*

**E15.13 (LO 3), AP** Fultz Company has accumulated the following budget data for the year 2022.

1. Sales: 30,000 units, unit selling price $85.

2. Cost of one unit of finished goods: direct materials 1 pound at $5 per pound, direct labor 3 hours at $15 per hour, and manufacturing overhead $5 per direct labor hour.

3. Inventories (raw materials only): beginning, 10,000 pounds; ending, 15,000 pounds.

4. Selling and administrative expenses: $170,000; interest expense: $30,000.

5. Income taxes: 20% of income before income taxes.

**Instructions**

a. Prepare a schedule showing the computation of cost of goods sold for 2022.

b. Prepare a budgeted multiple-step income statement for 2022.

*Prepare a cash budget for 2 months.*

**E15.14 (LO 4), AP** Danner Company expects to have a cash balance of $45,000 on January 1, 2022. Relevant monthly budget data for the first 2 months of 2022 are as follows.

Collections from customers: January $85,000, February $150,000.

Payments for direct materials: January $50,000, February $75,000.

Direct labor: January $30,000, February $45,000. Wages are paid in the month they are incurred.

Manufacturing overhead: January $21,000, February $25,000. These costs include depreciation of $1,500 per month. All other overhead costs are paid as incurred.

Selling and administrative expenses: January $15,000, February $20,000. These costs are exclusive of depreciation. They are paid as incurred.

Sales of marketable securities in January are expected to realize $12,000 in cash. Danner Company has a line of credit at a local bank that enables it to borrow up to $25,000. The company wants to maintain a minimum monthly cash balance of $20,000.

**Instructions**

Prepare a cash budget for January and February.

*Prepare a cash budget.*

**E15.15 (LO 4), AP** Deitz Corporation is projecting a cash balance of $30,000 in its December 31, 2021, balance sheet. Deitz's schedule of expected collections from customers for the first quarter of 2022 shows total collections of $185,000. The schedule of expected payments for direct materials for the first quarter of 2022 shows total payments of $43,000. Other information gathered for the first quarter of 2022 is sale of equipment $3,000, direct labor $70,000, manufacturing overhead $35,000, selling and administrative expenses $45,000, and purchase of securities $14,000. Deitz wants to maintain a balance of at least $25,000 cash at the end of each quarter.

**Instructions**

Prepare a cash budget for the first quarter.

*Prepare cash budget for a month.*

**E15.16 (LO 4), AN** The controller of Trenshaw Company wants to improve the company's control system by preparing a month-by-month cash budget. The following information is for the month ending July 31, 2022.

| | |
|---|---|
| June 30, 2022, cash balance | $45,000 |
| Dividends to be declared on July 15* | 12,000 |
| Cash expenditures to be paid in July for operating expenses | 40,800 |
| Amortization expense in July | 4,500 |
| Cash collections to be received in July | 90,000 |
| Merchandise purchases to be paid in cash in July | 56,200 |
| Equipment to be purchased for cash in July | 20,000 |

*Dividends are payable 30 days after declaration to shareholders of record on the declaration date.

Trenshaw Company wants to keep a minimum cash balance of $25,000.

**Instructions**

a. Prepare a cash budget for the month ended July 31, 2022, and indicate how much money, if any, Trenshaw Company will need to borrow to meet its minimum cash requirement.

b. Explain how cash budgeting can reduce the cost of short-term borrowing.

(CGA adapted)

**E15.17 (LO 4), AP** Nieto Company's budgeted sales and direct materials purchases are as follows.

*Prepare schedules of expected collections and payments.*

|  | **Budgeted Sales** | **Budgeted D.M. Purchases** |
|---|---|---|
| January | $200,000 | $30,000 |
| February | 220,000 | 36,000 |
| March | 250,000 | 38,000 |

Nieto's sales are 30% cash and 70% credit. Credit sales are collected 10% in the month of sale, 50% in the month following sale, and 36% in the second month following sale; 4% are uncollectible. Nieto's purchases are 50% cash and 50% on account. Purchases on account are paid 40% in the month of purchase, and 60% in the month following purchase.

**Instructions**

  **a.** Prepare a schedule of expected collections from customers for March.

  **b.** Prepare a schedule of expected payments for direct materials for March.

**E15.18 (LO 4, 5), AP** **Service** Green Landscaping Inc. is preparing its budget for the first quarter of 2022. The next step in the budgeting process is to prepare a cash receipts schedule and a cash payments schedule. To that end, the following information has been collected.

*Prepare schedules for cash receipts and cash payments, and determine ending balances for balance sheet.*

  Clients usually pay 60% of their fee in the month that service is performed, 30% the month after, and 10% the second month after receiving service.

  Actual service revenue for 2021 and expected service revenues for 2022 are November 2021, $80,000; December 2021, $90,000; January 2022, $100,000; February 2022, $120,000; and March 2022, $140,000.

  Purchases of landscaping supplies (direct materials) are paid 60% in the month of purchase and 40% the following month. Actual purchases for 2021 and expected purchases for 2022 are December 2021, $14,000; January 2022, $12,000; February 2022, $15,000; and March 2022, $18,000.

**Instructions**

  **a.** Prepare the following schedules for each month in the first quarter of 2022 and for the quarter in total:

    **1.** Expected collections from clients.

    **2.** Expected payments for landscaping supplies.

  **b.** Determine the following balances at March 31, 2022:

    **1.** Accounts receivable.

    **2.** Accounts payable.

**E15.19 (LO 4, 5), AP** **Service** Pletcher Dental Clinic is a medium-sized dental service specializing in family dental care. The clinic is currently preparing the master budget for the first 2 quarters of 2022. All that remains in this process is the cash budget. The following information has been collected from other portions of the master budget and elsewhere.

*Prepare a cash budget for 2 quarters.*

| | |
|---|---|
| Beginning cash balance | $ 30,000 |
| Required minimum cash balance | 25,000 |
| Payment of income taxes (2nd quarter) | 4,000 |
| Professional salaries: | |
|    1st quarter | 140,000 |
|    2nd quarter | 140,000 |
| Interest from investments (2nd quarter) | 7,000 |
| Overhead costs: | |
|    1st quarter | 77,000 |
|    2nd quarter | 100,000 |
| Selling and administrative costs, including | |
| $2,000 depreciation: | |
|    1st quarter | 50,000 |
|    2nd quarter | 70,000 |
| Purchase of equipment (2nd quarter) | 50,000 |
| Sale of equipment (1st quarter) | 12,000 |
| Collections from patients: | |
|    1st quarter | 235,000 |
|    2nd quarter | 380,000 |
| Interest payments (2nd quarter) | 200 |

**Instructions**

Prepare a cash budget for each of the first two quarters of 2022.

*Prepare a purchases budget and budgeted income statement for a merchandiser.*

**E15.20 (LO 5), AP** Service In May 2022, the budget committee of Grand Stores assembles the following data in preparation of budgeted merchandise purchases for the month of June.

1. Expected sales: June $500,000, July $600,000.

2. Cost of goods sold is expected to be 75% of sales.

3. Desired ending merchandise inventory is 30% of the following (next) month's cost of goods sold.

4. The beginning inventory at June 1 will be the desired amount.

**Instructions**

a. Compute the budgeted merchandise purchases for June.

b. Prepare the budgeted multiple-step income statement for June through gross profit.

*Prepare a direct labor budget for a service company.*

**E15.21 (LO 5), AP** Emeric and Ellie's Painting Service estimates that it will paint 10 small homes, 5 medium homes, and 2 large homes during the month of June 2022. The company estimates its direct labor needs as 40 hours per small home, 70 hours for a medium home, and 120 hours for a large home. Its average cost for direct labor is $18 per hour.

**Instructions**

Prepare a direct labor budget for Emeric and Ellie's Painting Service for June 2022.

# Problems

*Prepare budgeted income statement and supporting budgets.*

**P15.1 (LO 2, 3), AP** Cook Farm Supply Company manufactures and sells a pesticide called Snare. The following data are available for preparing budgets for Snare for the first 2 quarters of 2022.

1. Sales: quarter 1, 40,000 bags; quarter 2, 56,000 bags. Selling price is $60 per bag.

2. Direct materials: each bag of Snare requires 4 pounds of Gumm at a cost of $3.80 per pound and 6 pounds of Tarr at $1.50 per pound.

3. Desired inventory levels:

| Type of Inventory | January 1 | April 1 | July 1 |
|---|---|---|---|
| Snare (bags) | 8,000 | 15,000 | 18,000 |
| Gumm (pounds) | 9,000 | 10,000 | 13,000 |
| Tarr (pounds) | 14,000 | 20,000 | 25,000 |

4. Direct labor: direct labor time is 15 minutes per bag at an hourly rate of $16 per hour.

5. Selling and administrative expenses are expected to be 15% of sales plus $175,000 per quarter.

6. Interest expense is $100,000 for the 2 quarters.

7. Income taxes are expected to be 20% of income before income taxes.

Your assistant has prepared two budgets: (1) the manufacturing overhead budget shows expected costs to be 125% of direct labor cost, and (2) the direct materials budget for Tarr shows the cost of Tarr purchases to be $297,000 in quarter 1 and $439,500 in quarter 2.

**Instructions**

*Net income $1,007,040*
*Cost per bag $33.20*

Prepare the budgeted multiple-step income statement for the first 6 months and all required operating budgets by quarters. (*Note:* Use variable and fixed in the selling and administrative expense budget.) Do not prepare the manufacturing overhead budget or the direct materials budget for Tarr.

*Prepare sales, production, direct materials, direct labor, and income statement budgets.*

**P15.2 (LO 2, 3), AP** Deleon Inc. is preparing its annual budgets for the year ending December 31, 2022. Accounting assistants furnish the following data.

| | Product JB 50 | Product JB 60 |
|---|---|---|
| Sales budget: | | |
| Anticipated volume in units | 400,000 | 200,000 |
| Unit selling price | $20 | $25 |
| Production budget: | | |
| Desired ending finished goods units | 30,000 | 15,000 |
| Beginning finished goods units | 25,000 | 10,000 |

Direct materials budget:

| | 2 | 3 |
|---|---|---|
| Direct materials per unit (pounds) | 2 | 3 |
| Desired ending direct materials pounds | 30,000 | 10,000 |
| Beginning direct materials pounds | 40,000 | 15,000 |
| Cost per pound | $3 | $4 |
| Direct labor budget: | | |
| Direct labor time per unit | 0.4 | 0.6 |
| Direct labor rate per hour | $12 | $12 |
| Budgeted income statement: | | |
| Total unit cost | $13 | $20 |

An accounting assistant has prepared the detailed manufacturing overhead budget and the selling and administrative expense budget. The latter shows selling expenses of $560,000 for product JB 50 and $360,000 for product JB 60, and administrative expenses of $540,000 for product JB 50 and $340,000 for product JB 60. Interest expense is $150,000 (not allocated to products). Income taxes are expected to be 20%.

### Instructions

Prepare the following budgets for the year. Show data for each product. Quarterly budgets should not be prepared.

a. Sales.

b. Production.

c. Direct materials.

d. Direct labor.

e. Multiple-step income statement (*Note:* income taxes are not allocated to the products).

*a. Total sales $13,000,000*
*b. Required production units:*
*   JB 50, 405,000*
*   JB 60, 205,000*
*c. Total cost of direct materials*
*   purchases $4,840,000*
*d. Total direct labor cost*
*   $3,420,000*
*e. Net income $1,480,000*

**P15.3 (LO 2), E** Hill Industries had sales in 2021 of $6,800,000 and gross profit of $1,100,000. Management is considering two alternative budget plans to increase its gross profit in 2022.

Plan A would increase the selling price per unit from $8.00 to $8.40. Sales volume would decrease by 125,000 units from its 2021 level. Plan B would decrease the selling price per unit by $0.50. The marketing department expects that the sales volume would increase by 130,000 units.

At the end of 2021, Hill has 40,000 units of inventory on hand. If Plan A is accepted, the 2022 ending inventory should be 35,000 units. If Plan B is accepted, the ending inventory should be 60,000 units. Each unit produced will cost $1.50 in direct labor, $1.30 in direct materials, and $1.20 in variable overhead. The fixed overhead for 2022 should be $1,895,000.

*Prepare sales and production budgets and compute cost per unit under two plans.*

### Instructions

a. Prepare a sales budget for 2022 under each plan.

b. Prepare a production budget for 2022 under each plan.

c. Compute the production cost per unit under each plan. Why is the cost per unit different for each of the two plans? (Round to two decimals.)

d. Which plan should be accepted? (*Hint:* Compute the gross profit under each plan.)

*c. Unit cost: Plan A $6.63*
*   Plan B $5.90*
*d. Gross profit:*
*   Plan A $1,283,250*
*   Plan B $1,568,500*

**P15.4 (LO 4), AP** Colter Company prepares monthly cash budgets. Relevant data from operating budgets for 2022 are as follows.

*Prepare cash budget for 2 months.*

| | January | February |
|---|---|---|
| Sales | $360,000 | $400,000 |
| Direct materials purchases | 120,000 | 125,000 |
| Direct labor | 90,000 | 100,000 |
| Manufacturing overhead | 70,000 | 75,000 |
| Selling and administrative expenses | 79,000 | 85,000 |

All sales are on account. Collections are expected to be 50% in the month of sale, 30% in the first month following the sale, and 20% in the second month following the sale. Sixty percent (60%) of direct materials purchases are paid in cash in the month of purchase, and the balance due is paid in the month following the purchase. All other items above are paid in the month incurred except for selling and administrative expenses, which include $1,000 of depreciation per month.

Other data:

1. Credit sales: November 2021, $250,000; December 2021, $320,000.

2. Purchases of direct materials: December 2021, $100,000.

3. Other receipts: January—collection of December 31, 2021, notes receivable $15,000; February—proceeds from sale of securities $6,000.

4. Other disbursements: February—payment of $6,000 cash dividend.

The company's cash balance on January 1, 2022, is expected to be $60,000. The company wants to maintain a minimum cash balance of $50,000.

*a. January: collections $326,000; payments $112,000*

*b. Ending cash balance: January $51,000 February $50,000*

**Instructions**

a. Prepare schedules for (1) expected collections from customers and (2) expected payments for direct materials purchases for January and February.

b. Prepare a cash budget for January and February in columnar form.

*Prepare purchases and income statement budgets for a merchandiser.*

**P15.5 (LO 5), AP** The budget committee of Suppar Company collects the following data for its San Miguel Store in preparing budgeted income statements for May and June 2022.

1. Sales for May are expected to be $800,000. Sales in June and July are expected to be 5% higher than the preceding month.

2. Cost of goods sold is expected to be 75% of sales.

3. Company policy is to maintain ending merchandise inventory at 10% of the following month's cost of goods sold.

4. Operating expenses are estimated to be as follows:

| | |
|---|---|
| Sales salaries | $35,000 per month |
| Advertising | 6% of monthly sales |
| Delivery expense | 2% of monthly sales |
| Sales commissions | 5% of monthly sales |
| Rent expense | $5,000 per month |
| Depreciation | $800 per month |
| Utilities | $600 per month |
| Insurance | $500 per month |

5. Interest expense is $2,000 per month. Income taxes are estimated to be 20% of income before income taxes.

**Instructions**

a. Prepare the merchandise purchases budget for each month in columnar form.

b. Prepare budgeted multiple-step income statements for each month in columnar form. Show in the statements the details of cost of goods sold.

*a. Purchases: May $603,000 June $633,150*

*b. Net income: May $41,680 June $45,520*

*Prepare budgeted cost of goods sold, income statement, retained earnings, and balance sheet.*

**P15.6 (LO 3, 4), AP** Krause Industries' balance sheet at December 31, 2021, is presented here.

**Krause Industries**
**Balance Sheet**
**December 31, 2021**

**Assets**

| | | |
|---|---|---|
| Current assets | | |
| Cash | | $ 7,500 |
| Accounts receivable | | 73,500 |
| Finished goods inventory (1,500 units) | | 24,000 |
| Total current assets | | 105,000 |
| Property, plant, and equipment | | |
| Equipment | $40,000 | |
| Less: Accumulated depreciation | 10,000 | 30,000 |
| Total assets | | $135,000 |

**Liabilities and Stockholders' Equity**

| | | |
|---|---|---|
| Liabilities | | |
| Notes payable | | $ 25,000 |
| Accounts payable | | 45,000 |
| Total liabilities | | 70,000 |
| Stockholders' equity | | |
| Common stock | $40,000 | |
| Retained earnings | 25,000 | |
| Total stockholders' equity | | 65,000 |
| Total liabilities and stockholders' equity | | $135,000 |

Budgeted data for the year 2022 include the following.

| | 2022 | |
| --- | --- | --- |
| | Quarter 4 | Total |
| Sales budget (8,000 units at $32) | $76,800 | $256,000 |
| Direct materials used | 17,000 | 62,500 |
| Direct labor | 12,500 | 50,900 |
| Manufacturing overhead applied | 10,000 | 48,600 |
| Selling and administrative expenses | 18,000 | 75,000 |

To meet sales requirements and to have 2,500 units of finished goods on hand at December 31, 2022, the production budget shows 9,000 required units of output. The total unit cost of production is expected to be $18. Krause uses the first-in, first-out (FIFO) inventory costing method. Interest expense is expected to be $3,500 for the year. Income taxes are expected to be 20% of income before income taxes. In 2022, the company expects to declare and pay an $8,000 cash dividend.

The company's cash budget shows an expected cash balance of $13,180 at December 31, 2022. All sales and purchases are on account. It is expected that 60% of quarterly sales are collected in cash within the quarter and the remainder is collected in the following quarter. Direct materials purchased from suppliers are paid 50% in the quarter incurred and the remainder in the following quarter. Purchases in the fourth quarter were the same as the materials used. In 2022, the company expects to purchase additional equipment costing $9,000. A total of $4,000 of depreciation expense on equipment is included in the budget data and split equally between manufacturing overhead and selling and administrative expenses. Krause expects to pay $8,000 on the outstanding notes payable balance plus all interest due and payable to December 31 (included in interest expense $3,500, above). Accounts payable at December 31, 2022, includes amounts due suppliers (see above) plus other accounts payable relating to manufacturing overhead of $7,200. Unpaid income taxes at December 31 will be $5,000.

### Instructions

Prepare a budgeted statement of cost of goods sold, budgeted multiple-step income statement, and retained earnings statement for 2022, and a budgeted classified balance sheet at December 31, 2022.

Net income $29,200
Total assets $123,900

## Continuing Cases

### Current Designs

**CD15** Diane Buswell is preparing the 2022 budget for one of **Current Designs'** rotomolded kayaks. Extensive meetings with members of the sales department and executive team have resulted in the following unit sales projections for 2022.

| Quarter 1 | 1,000 kayaks |
| --- | --- |
| Quarter 2 | 1,500 kayaks |
| Quarter 3 | 750 kayaks |
| Quarter 4 | 750 kayaks |

Current Designs' policy is to have finished goods ending inventory in a quarter equal to 20% of the next quarter's anticipated sales. Preliminary sales projections for 2023 are 1,100 units for the first quarter and 1,500 units for the second quarter. Ending inventory of finished goods at December 31, 2021, will be 200 rotomolded kayaks.

Production of each kayak requires 54 pounds of polyethylene powder and a finishing kit (rope, seat, hardware, etc.). Company policy is that the ending inventory of polyethylene powder should be 25% of the amount needed for production in the next quarter. Assume that the ending inventory of polyethylene powder on December 31, 2021, is 19,400 pounds. The finishing kits can be assembled as they are needed. As a result, Current Designs does not maintain a significant inventory of the finishing kits.

The polyethylene powder used in these kayaks costs $1.50 per pound, and the finishing kits cost $170 each. Production of a single kayak requires 2 hours of time by more experienced, type I employees and 3 hours of finishing time by type II employees. The type I employees are paid $15 per hour, and the type II employees are paid $12 per hour.

Selling and administrative expenses for this line are expected to be $45 per unit sold plus $7,500 per quarter. Manufacturing overhead is assigned at 150% of labor costs.

### Instructions

Prepare the production budget, direct materials budget, direct labor budget, manufacturing overhead budget, and selling and administrative budget for this product line by quarter and in total for 2022.

### Waterways Corporation

(*Note:* This is a continuation of the Waterways case from Chapters 11–14.)

**WC15**  Waterways Corporation is preparing its budget for the coming year, 2022. The first step is to plan for the first quarter of that coming year. The company has gathered information from its managers in preparation of the budgeting process. This problem asks you to prepare the various budgets that comprise the master budget for 2022.

*Go to WileyPLUS for complete case details and instructions.*

## Comprehensive Cases

**CC15.1**  **Service**  Auburn Circular Club is planning a major fundraiser that it hopes will become a successful annual event: sponsoring a professional rodeo. For this case, you will encounter many managerial accounting issues that would be common for a start-up business, such as CVP analysis (Chapter 11), incremental analysis (Chapter 14), and budgetary planning (Chapter 15).

**CC15.2**  Sweats Galore is a new business venture that will make custom sweatshirts using a silk-screen process. In helping the company's owner, Michael Woods, set up his business, you will have the opportunity to apply your understanding of CVP relationships (Chapter 13) and budgetary planning (Chapter 15).

*Go to WileyPLUS for complete details and instructions for both cases.*

## Expand Your Critical Thinking

### Decision-Making Across the Organization

**CT15.1**  Palmer Corporation operates on a calendar-year basis. It begins the annual budgeting process in late August when the president establishes targets for the total dollar sales and net income before taxes for the next year.

The sales target is given first to the marketing department. The marketing manager formulates a sales budget by product line in both units and dollars. From this budget, sales quotas by product line in units and dollars are established for each of the corporation's sales districts. The marketing manager also estimates the cost of the marketing activities required to support the target sales volume and prepares a tentative marketing expense budget.

The executive vice president uses the sales and profit targets, the sales budget by product line, and the tentative marketing expense budget to determine the dollar amounts that can be devoted to manufacturing and corporate office expense. The executive vice president prepares the budget for corporate expenses. She then forwards to the production department the product-line sales budget in units and the total dollar amount that can be devoted to manufacturing.

The production manager meets with the factory managers to develop a manufacturing plan that will produce the required units when needed within the cost constraints set by the executive vice president. The budgeting process usually comes to a halt at this point because the production department does not consider the financial resources allocated to be adequate.

When this standstill occurs, the vice president of finance, the executive vice president, the marketing manager, and the production manager meet together to determine the final budgets for each of the areas. This normally results in a modest increase in the total amount available for manufacturing costs and cuts in the marketing expense and corporate office expense budgets. The total sales and net income figures proposed by the president are seldom changed. Although the participants are seldom pleased with the compromise, these budgets are final. Each executive then develops a new detailed budget for the operations in his or her area.

None of the areas has achieved its budget in recent years. Sales often run below the target. When budgeted sales are not achieved, each area is expected to cut costs so that the president's profit target can be met. However, the profit target is seldom met because costs are not cut enough. In fact, costs often run above the original budget in all functional areas (marketing, production, and corporate office).

The president is disturbed that Palmer has not been able to meet the sales and profit targets. He hires a consultant with considerable experience with companies in Palmer's industry. The consultant reviews the budgets for the past 4 years. He concludes that the product line sales budgets were reasonable and that the cost and expense budgets were adequate for the budgeted sales and production levels.

**Instructions**

With the class divided into groups, answer the following.

**a.** Discuss how the budgeting process employed by Palmer Corporation contributes to the failure to achieve the president's sales and profit targets.

**b.** Suggest how Palmer Corporation's budgeting process could be revised to correct the problems.

**c.** Should the functional areas be expected to cut their costs when sales volume falls below budget? Explain your answer.

(CMA adapted)

## Managerial Analysis

**CT15.2** Elliot & Hesse Inc. manufactures ergonomic devices for computer users. Some of its more popular products include anti-glare filters and privacy filters (for computer monitors) and keyboard stands with wrist rests. Over the past 5 years, it experienced rapid growth, with sales of all products increasing 20% to 50% each year.

Last year, some of the primary manufacturers of computers began introducing new products with some of the ergonomic designs, such as anti-glare filters and wrist rests, already built in. As a result, sales of Elliot & Hesse's accessory devices have declined somewhat. The company believes that the privacy filters will probably continue to show growth, but that the other products will probably continue to decline. When the next year's budget was prepared, increases were built into research and development so that replacement products could be developed or the company could expand into some other product line. Some product lines being considered are general-purpose ergonomic devices including back supports, foot rests, and sloped writing pads.

The most recent results have shown that sales decreased more than was expected for the anti-glare filters. As a result, the company may have a shortage of funds. Top management has therefore asked that all expenses be reduced 10% to compensate for these reduced sales. Summary budget information is as follows.

| | |
|---|---|
| Direct materials | $240,000 |
| Direct labor | 110,000 |
| Insurance | 50,000 |
| Depreciation | 90,000 |
| Machine repairs | 30,000 |
| Sales salaries | 50,000 |
| Office salaries | 80,000 |
| Factory salaries (indirect labor) | 50,000 |
| Total | $700,000 |

**Instructions**

Using the information above, answer the following questions.

**a.** What are the implications of reducing each of the costs? For example, if the company reduces direct materials costs, it may have to do so by purchasing lower-quality materials. This may affect sales in the long run.

**b.** Based on your analysis in (a), what do you think is the best way to obtain the $70,000 in cost savings requested? Be specific. Are there any costs that cannot or should not be reduced? Why?

## Real-World Focus

**CT15.3** Information regarding many approaches to budgeting can be found online. The following activity investigates the merits of "zero-based" budgeting, as discussed by Michael LaFaive, Director of Fiscal Policy of the **Mackinac Center for Public Policy**.

**Instructions**

Read the article at the Mackinac website and answer the following questions.

**a.** How does zero-based budgeting differ from standard budgeting procedures?

**b.** What are some potential advantages of zero-based budgeting?

**c.** What are some potential disadvantages of zero-based budgeting?

**d.** How often do departments in Oklahoma undergo zero-based budgeting?

## Communication Activity

**CT15.4** `Service` In order to better serve their rural patients, Drs. Joe and Rick Parcells (brothers) began giving safety seminars. Especially popular were their "emergency-preparedness" talks given to farmers. Many people asked whether the "kit" of materials the doctors recommended for common farm emergencies was commercially available.

After checking with several suppliers, the doctors realized that no other company offered the supplies they recommended in their seminars, packaged in the way they described. Their wives, Megan and Sue, agreed to make a test package by ordering supplies from various medical supply companies and assembling them into a "kit" that could be sold at the seminars. When these kits proved a runaway success, the sisters-in-law decided to market them. At the advice of their accountant, they organized this venture as a separate company, called Life Protection Products (LPP), with Megan Parcells as CEO and Sue Parcells as Secretary-Treasurer.

LPP soon started receiving requests for the kits from all over the country, as word spread about their availability. Even without advertising, LPP was able to sell its full inventory every month. However, the company was becoming financially strained. Megan and Sue had about $100,000 in savings, and they invested about half that amount initially. They believed that this venture would allow them to make money. However, at the present time, only about $30,000 of the cash remains, and the company is constantly short of cash.

Megan has come to you for advice. She does not understand why the company is having cash flow problems. She and Sue have not even been withdrawing salaries. However, they have rented a local building and have hired two more full-time workers to help them cope with the increasing demand. They do not think they could handle the demand without this additional help.

Megan is also worried that the cash problems mean that the company may not be able to support itself. She has prepared the cash budget shown below. All seminar customers pay for their products in full at the time of purchase. In addition, several large companies have ordered the kits for use by employees who work in remote sites. They have requested credit terms and have been allowed to pay in the month following the sale. These large purchasers amount to about 25% of the sales at the present time. LPP purchases the materials for the kits about 2 months ahead of time. Megan and Sue are considering slowing the growth of the company by simply purchasing less materials, which will mean selling fewer kits.

The workers are paid weekly. Megan and Sue need about $15,000 cash on hand at the beginning of the month to pay for purchases of raw materials. Right now they have been using cash from their savings, but as noted, only $30,000 is left.

**Life Protection Products**
**Cash Budget**
**For the Quarter Ending June 30, 2022**

| | April | May | June |
|---|---|---|---|
| Cash balance, beginning | $15,000 | $15,000 | $15,000 |
| Cash received | | | |
|   From prior month sales | 5,000 | 7,500 | 12,500 |
|   From current sales | 15,000 | 22,500 | 37,500 |
| Total cash on hand | 35,000 | 45,000 | 65,000 |
| Cash payments | | | |
|   To employees | 3,000 | 3,000 | 3,000 |
|   For products | 25,000 | 35,000 | 45,000 |
|   Miscellaneous expenses | 5,000 | 6,000 | 7,000 |
|   Postage | 1,000 | 1,000 | 1,000 |
| Total cash payments | 34,000 | 45,000 | 56,000 |
| Cash balance | $ 1,000 | $ 0 | $ 9,000 |
| Borrow from savings | $14,000 | $15,000 | $ 1,000 |
| Borrow from bank? | $ 0 | $ 0 | $ 5,000 |

### Instructions

Write a response to Megan Parcells. Explain why LPP is short of cash. Will this company be able to support itself? Explain your answer. Make any recommendations you deem appropriate.

## Ethics Case

**CT15.5** You are an accountant in the budgetary, projections, and special projects department of Fernetti Conductor, Inc., a large manufacturing company. The president, Richard Brown, asks you on very short notice to prepare some sales and income projections covering the next 2 years of the company's much-heralded new product lines. He wants these projections for a series of speeches he is making while on a 2-week trip to eight East Coast brokerage firms. The president hopes to bolster Fernetti's stock sales and price.

You work 23 hours in 2 days to compile the projections, hand-deliver them to the president, and are swiftly but graciously thanked as he departs. A week later, you find time to go over some of your computations and discover a miscalculation that makes the projections grossly overstated. You quickly inquire about the president's itinerary and learn that he has made half of his speeches and has half yet to make. You are in a quandary as to what to do.

### Instructions

**a.** What are the consequences of telling the president of your gross miscalculations?

**b.** What are the consequences of not telling the president of your gross miscalculations?

**c.** What are the ethical considerations to you and the president in this situation?

## All About You

**CT15.6** In order to get your personal finances under control, you need to prepare a personal budget. Assume that you have compiled the following information regarding your expected cash flows for a typical month.

| | | | |
|---|---|---|---|
| Rent payment | $ 500 | Miscellaneous costs | $210 |
| Interest income | 50 | Savings | 50 |
| Income tax withheld | 300 | Eating out | 150 |
| Electricity bill | 85 | Telephone and Internet costs | 125 |
| Groceries | 100 | Student loan payments | 375 |
| Wages earned | 2,500 | Entertainment costs | 250 |
| Insurance | 100 | Transportation costs | 150 |

### Instructions

Using the information above, prepare a personal budget. In preparing this budget, use the format included in the "Steps to Creating a Household Budget" article available at **the balance**'s website (go to the site and do a search for the article). Just skip any unused line items.

## Considering Your Costs and Benefits

**CT15.7** You might hear people say that they "need to learn to live within a budget." The funny thing is that most people who say this haven't actually prepared a personal budget, nor do they intend to. Instead, what they are referring to is a vaguely defined, poorly specified collection of rough ideas of how much they should spend on various aspects of their lives. However, you can't live within or even outside of something that doesn't exist. With that in mind, let's take a look at one aspect of personal-budget templates.

Many personal-budget worksheet templates that are provided for college students treat student loans as an income source. See, for example, the template included in the "Steps to Creating a Household Budget" article available at **the balance**'s website. Based on your knowledge of accounting, is this correct?

**YES:** Student loans provide a source of cash, which can be used to pay costs. As the saying goes, "It all spends the same." Therefore, student loans are income.

**NO:** Student loans must eventually be repaid; therefore, they are not income. As the name indicates, they are loans.

### Instructions

Write a response indicating your position regarding this situation. Provide support for your view.

# Budgetary Control and Responsibility Accounting

## Chapter Preview

In Chapter 15, we discussed the use of budgets for planning. We now consider how budgets are used by management to control operations. In the following Feature Story on **The Roxy Hotel Tribeca**, we see that management uses the budget to adapt to the business environment. This chapter focuses on two aspects of management control: (1) budgetary control and (2) responsibility accounting.

## Feature Story

### Pumpkin Madeleines and a Movie

Perhaps no place in the world has a wider variety of distinctive, high-end accommodations than New York City. It's tough to set yourself apart in the Big Apple, but unique is what **The Roxy Hotel Tribeca** is all about.

When you walk through the doors of this triangular-shaped building, nestled in one of Manhattan's most affluent neighborhoods, you immediately encounter a striking eight-story atrium. Although the hotel was completely renovated, it still maintains its funky mid-century charm. Just consider the always hip hotel bar. Besides serving up cocktails until 2 A.M., the bar also provides food. These are not the run-of-the-mill, chain-hotel, borderline edibles. The chef is famous for tantalizing delectables such as duck rillettes, sea salt baked branzino, housemade pappardelle, and pumpkin madeleines.

Another thing that really sets the hotel apart is its private screening room. As a guest, you can enjoy plush leather seating, state-of-the-art projection, and digital surround sound, all while viewing a cult classic from the hotel's film series. In fact, on Sundays, free screenings are available to guests and non-guests alike on a first-come-first-served basis.

To attract and satisfy a discerning clientele, The Roxy Hotel Tribeca's management incurs higher and more unpredictable costs than those of a standard hotel. As fun as it might be to run a high-end hotel, management cannot be cavalier about spending money. To maintain profitability, management closely monitors costs and revenues to make sure that they track with budgeted amounts. Further, because of unexpected fluctuations in demand for rooms (think hurricanes or bitterly cold winter weather), management must sometimes revise forecasts and budgets and adapt quickly. To evaluate performance and identify when changes need to be made, the budget needs to be flexible.

# Chapter Outline

| LEARNING OBJECTIVES | REVIEW | PRACTICE |
|---|---|---|
| **LO 1** Describe budgetary control and static budget reports. | • Budgetary control<br>• Static budget reports | **DO IT! 1** Static Budget Reports |
| **LO 2** Prepare flexible budget reports. | • Why flexible budgets?<br>• Developing the flexible budget<br>• Flexible budget—a case study<br>• Flexible budget reports | **DO IT! 2** Flexible Budgets |
| **LO 3** Apply responsibility accounting to cost and profit centers. | • Controllable vs. noncontrollable revenues and costs<br>• Principles of performance evaluation<br>• Responsibility reporting system<br>• Types of responsibility centers | **DO IT! 3** Profit Center Responsibility Report |
| **LO 4** Evaluate performance in investment centers. | • Return on investment (ROI)<br>• Responsibility report<br>• Judgmental factors in ROI<br>• Improving ROI | **DO IT! 4** Performance Evaluation |

**Go to the Review and Practice section at the end of the chapter for a targeted summary and practice applications with solutions.**

**Visit WileyPLUS for additional tutorials and practice opportunities.**

# Budgetary Control and Static Budget Reports

**LEARNING OBJECTIVE 1**
Describe budgetary control and static budget reports.

## Budgetary Control

One of management's responsibilities is to control company operations. Control consists of the steps taken by management to see that planned objectives are met. We now ask: How do budgets contribute to control of operations?

The use of budgets in controlling operations is known as **budgetary control**.

- Such control takes place by means of **budget reports** that compare actual results with planned objectives.
- The use of budget reports is based on the belief that planned objectives lose much of their potential value without some monitoring of progress along the way.
- Just as your professors give midterm exams to evaluate your progress, top management requires periodic reports on the progress of department managers toward their planned objectives.

Budget reports provide management with feedback on operations and are prepared as frequently as needed.

- The feedback for a crucial objective, such as having enough cash on hand to pay bills, may be made daily.
- For other objectives, such as meeting budgeted annual sales and operating expenses, monthly budget reports may suffice.

From these reports, management analyzes any differences between actual and planned results and determines their causes. Management then takes corrective action, or it decides to modify future plans. Budgetary control involves the activities shown in **Illustration 16.1**.

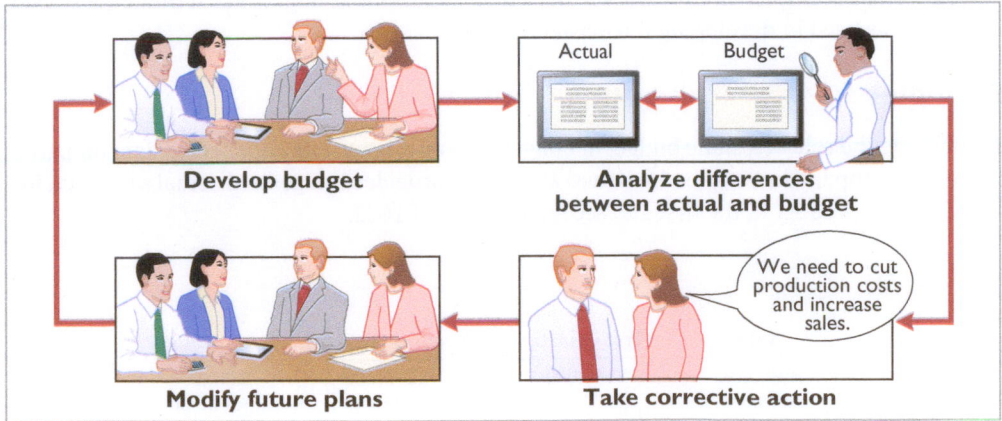

Develop budget

Analyze differences between actual and budget

Take corrective action

We need to cut production costs and increase sales.

Modify future plans

**ILLUSTRATION 16.1**
**Budgetary control activities**

Budgetary control works best when a company has a formalized reporting system. The reporting system does the following.

1. Identifies the name of the budget report, such as the sales budget or the manufacturing overhead budget.
2. States the frequency of the report, such as weekly or monthly.
3. Specifies the purpose of the report.
4. Indicates the primary recipient(s) of the report.

**Illustration 16.2** provides a partial budgetary control system for a manufacturing company. Note the frequency of the reports and their emphasis on control. For example, there is a daily report on scrap and a weekly report on labor.

**ILLUSTRATION 16.2** Budgetary control reporting system

| Name of Report | Frequency | Purpose | Primary Recipient(s) |
|---|---|---|---|
| Sales | Weekly | Determine whether sales goals are met | Top management and sales manager |
| Labor | Weekly | Control direct and indirect labor costs | Vice president of production and production department managers |
| Scrap | Daily | Determine efficient use of materials | Production manager |
| Departmental overhead costs | Monthly | Control overhead costs | Department manager |
| Selling expenses | Monthly | Control selling expenses | Sales manager |
| Income statement | Monthly and quarterly | Determine whether income goals are met | Top management |

## Static Budget Reports

You learned in Chapter 15 that the master budget formalizes management's planned objectives for the coming year. When used in budgetary control, each budget included in the master budget is considered to be static.

- A **static budget** is a projection of budget data **at a single level of activity before actual activity occurs**.
- These budgets do not consider data for different levels of activity.
- As a result, companies always compare actual results with budget data at the activity level that was used in developing the master budget.

### Examples

To illustrate the role of a static budget in budgetary control, we will use selected data prepared for Hayes Company in Chapter 15. **Illustration 16.3** provides budget and actual sales data for the Rightride product in the first and second quarters of 2022.

**ILLUSTRATION 16.3**

Budget and actual sales data

| Sales | First Quarter | Second Quarter | Total |
|---|---|---|---|
| Budgeted | $180,000 | $210,000 | $390,000 |
| Actual | 179,000 | 199,500 | 378,500 |
| Difference | $  1,000 | $ 10,500 | $ 11,500 |

**ALTERNATIVE TERMINOLOGY**

The difference between budget and actual is sometimes called a *budget variance.*

The sales budget report for Hayes' first quarter is shown in **Illustration 16.4**. The rightmost column reports the difference between the budgeted and actual amounts (see **Alternative Terminology**).

**ILLUSTRATION 16.4**

Sales budget report—first quarter

**Hayes Company Sales Budget Report**

| | A | B | C | D |
|---|---|---|---|---|
| 1 | | **Hayes Company** | | |
| 2 | | **Sales Budget Report** | | |
| 3 | | **For the Quarter Ended March 31, 2022** | | |
| 4 | | | | Difference |
| 5 | | | | Favorable F |
| 6 | Product Line | Budget | Actual | Unfavorable U |
| 7 | Rightride[a] | $180,000 | $179,000 | **$1,000 U** |
| 8 | | | | |
| 9 | [a]In practice, each product line would be included in the report. | | | |

The report shows that sales are $1,000 under budget—an unfavorable result.

- This difference is less than 1% of budgeted sales ($1,000 ÷ $180,000 = .0056).
- Top management's reaction to differences is often influenced by the materiality (significance) of the difference.
- Since the difference of $1,000 is immaterial in this case, we assume that Hayes management takes no specific corrective action.

**Illustration 16.5** shows the sales budget report for the second quarter. It contains one new feature: cumulative year-to-date information. This report indicates that sales for the second quarter are $10,500 below budget. This is 5% of budgeted sales ($10,500 ÷ $210,000). Top management may now conclude that the difference between budgeted and actual sales requires investigation.

**ILLUSTRATION 16.5**  **Sales budget report—second quarter**

**Hayes Company Sales Budget Report**

| | A | B | C | D | E | F | G | H |
|---|---|---|---|---|---|---|---|---|
| 1 | | | | **Hayes Company** | | | | |
| 2 | | | | **Sales Budget Report** | | | | |
| 3 | | | | **For the Quarter Ended June 30, 2022** | | | | |
| 4 | | | Second Quarter | | | | Year-to-Date | |
| 5 | | | | Difference | | | | Difference |
| 6 | | | | Favorable F | | | | Favorable F |
| 7 | Product Line | Budget | Actual | Unfavorable U | | Budget | Actual | Unfavorable U |
| 8 | Rightride | $210,000 | $199,500 | **$10,500 U** | | $390,000 | $378,500 | **$11,500 U** |
| 9 | | | | | | | | |

Management's analysis should start by:
- Asking the sales manager the cause(s) of the shortfall.
- Considering the need for corrective action.

For example, management may attempt to increase sales by offering sales incentives to customers or by increasing the advertising of Rightrides. Or, if management concludes that a downturn in the economy is responsible for the lower sales, it may modify planned sales and profit goals for the remainder of the year.

## Uses and Limitations

From these examples, you can see that a master sales budget is useful in evaluating the performance of a sales manager. It is now necessary to ask: Is the master budget appropriate for evaluating a manager's performance in controlling costs? Recall that in a static

**Static budgets report a single level of activity**

budget, data are not modified or adjusted, regardless of changes in activity. It follows, then, that a static budget is appropriate in evaluating a manager's effectiveness in controlling costs when:

1. The actual level of activity closely approximates the master budget activity level, and/or
2. The behavior of the costs in response to changes in activity is fixed.

A static budget report is, therefore, appropriate for **fixed manufacturing costs** and for **fixed selling and administrative expenses**. But, as you will see shortly, static budget reports may not be a proper basis for evaluating a manager's performance in controlling variable costs.

**ACTION PLAN**

- **Classify each cost as variable or fixed**
- **Determine the difference as favorable or unfavorable.**
- **Determine the difference in total variable costs, total fixed costs, and total costs.**

## DO IT! 1 | Static Budget Reports

Lawler Company expects to produce 5,000 units of product CV93 during the current month. Budgeted variable manufacturing costs per unit are direct materials $6, direct labor $15, and overhead $24. Monthly budgeted fixed manufacturing overhead costs are $10,000 for depreciation and $5,000 for supervision.

In the current month, Lawler actually produced 5,500 units and incurred the following costs: direct materials $33,900, direct labor $74,200, variable overhead $120,500, depreciation $10,000, and supervision $5,000.

Prepare a static budget report. (*Hint:* The Budget column is based on estimated production of 5,000 units while the Actual column is the actual costs incurred during the period.) Were costs controlled? Discuss limitations of this budget.

### Solution

**Lawler Company**

|  | | A | B | C | D | |
|---|---|---|---|---|---|---|
| 1 | | | | | Difference | |
| 2 | | | | | Favorable - F | |
| 3 | | | Budget | Actual | Unfavorable - U | |
| 4 | | Production in units | 5,000 | 5,500 | | |
| 5 | | | | | | |
| 6 | | Variable costs | | | | |
| 7 | | Direct materials ($6) | $ 30,000 | $ 33,900 | $3,900 | U |
| 8 | | Direct labor ($15) | 75,000 | 74,200 | 800 | F |
| 9 | | Overhead ($24) | 120,000 | 120,500 | 500 | U |
| 10 | | Total variable costs | 225,000 | 228,600 | 3,600 | U |
| 11 | | | | | | |
| 12 | | Fixed costs | | | | |
| 13 | | Depreciation | 10,000 | 10,000 | 0 | |
| 14 | | Supervision | 5,000 | 5,000 | 0 | |
| 15 | | Total fixed costs | 15,000 | 15,000 | 0 | |
| 16 | | Total costs | $240,000 | $243,600 | $3,600 | U |
| 17 | | | | | | |
| 18 | | | | | | |

The static budget indicates that actual variable costs exceeded budgeted amounts by $3,600. Fixed costs were exactly as budgeted. The static budget gives the impression that the company did not control its variable costs. However, the static budget does not give consideration to the fact that the company produced 500 more units than planned. As a result, the static budget is not a good tool to evaluate variable costs. It is, however, a good tool to evaluate fixed costs as those should not vary with changes in production volume.

Related exercise material: **BE16.1, BE16.2, DO IT! 16.1, and E16.2.**

# Flexible Budget Reports

In contrast to a static budget, which is based on one level of activity, a **flexible budget** projects budget data for various levels of activity.

- In essence, **the flexible budget is a series of static budgets at different levels of activity**.
- The flexible budget recognizes that the budgetary process is more useful if it is adaptable to changed operating conditions.

Flexible budgets can be prepared for each of the types of budgets included in the master budget. For example, **Marriott Hotels** can budget revenues and net income on the basis of 60%, 80%, and 100% of room occupancy. Similarly, **American Van Lines** can budget its operating expenses on the basis of various levels of truck-miles driven. **Duke Energy** can budget revenue and net income on the basis of estimated billions of kwh (kilowatt hours) of residential, commercial, and industrial electricity generated. In the following pages, we will illustrate a flexible budget for manufacturing overhead.

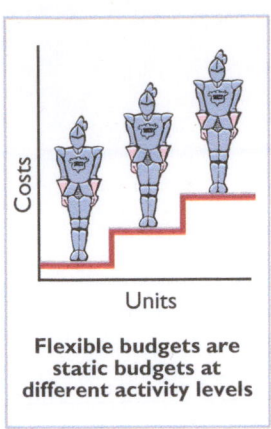

**Flexible budgets are static budgets at different activity levels**

## Why Flexible Budgets?

Assume that you are the manager in charge of manufacturing overhead in the Assembly Department of Barton Robotics. In preparing the manufacturing overhead budget for 2022, you prepare the static budget shown in **Illustration 16.6** based on a production volume of 10,000 units of robotic controls (see **Helpful Hint**).

**HELPFUL HINT**
The master budget described in Chapter 15 is based on a static budget.

**ILLUSTRATION 16.6**
**Static overhead budget**

| Barton Robotics | |
|---|---|
| Home    Insert    Page Layout    Formulas    Data    Review    View | |
| P18          *fx* | |
| **A** | **B** |
| 1    **Barton Robotics** | |
| 2    **Manufacturing Overhead Budget (Static)** | |
| 3    **Assembly Department** | |
| 4    **For the Year Ended December 31, 2022** | |
| 5    Budgeted production in units (robotic controls) | 10,000 |
| 6 | |
| 7    Budgeted costs | |
| 8      Indirect materials | $  250,000 |
| 9      Indirect labor | 260,000 |
| 10    Utilities | 190,000 |
| 11    Depreciation | 280,000 |
| 12    Property taxes | 70,000 |
| 13    Supervision | 50,000 |
| 14 | $1,100,000 |
| 15 | |

Fortunately for the company, the demand for robotic controls has increased, and Barton produces and sells 12,000 units during the year rather than 10,000. You are elated! Increased sales means increased profitability, which should mean a bonus or a raise for you and the employees in your department. Unfortunately, a comparison of Assembly Department actual and budgeted costs has put you on the spot. **Illustration 16.7** shows the budget report.

**ILLUSTRATION 16.7**

Overhead static budget report

| | Barton Robotics | | | |
|---|---|---|---|---|
| Home  Insert  Page Layout  Formulas  Data  Review  View | | | | |
| P18 | | *fx* | | |
| | A | B | C | D | E |
| 1 | | **Barton Robotics** | | | |
| 2 | | **Manufacturing Overhead Static Budget Report** | | | |
| 3 | | **For the Year Ended December 31, 2022** | | | |
| 4 | | | | Difference | |
| 5 | | Budget | Actual | Favorable - F Unfavorable - U | |
| 6 | Production in units | 10,000 | 12,000 | | |
| 7 | | | | | |
| 8 | Costs | | | | |
| 9 | Indirect materials | $ 250,000 | $ 295,000 | $ 45,000 | U |
| 10 | Indirect labor | 260,000 | 312,000 | 52,000 | U |
| 11 | Utilities | 190,000 | 225,000 | 35,000 | U |
| 12 | Depreciation | 280,000 | 280,000 | 0 | |
| 13 | Property taxes | 70,000 | 70,000 | 0 | |
| 14 | Supervision | 50,000 | 50,000 | 0 | |
| 15 | | $1,100,000 | $1,232,000 | $132,000 | U |
| 16 | | | | | |

This comparison uses budgeted cost data based on the original activity level (10,000 robotic controls).

- It indicates that the costs incurred by the Assembly Department are significantly **over budget** for three of the six overhead costs.
- There is a total unfavorable difference of $132,000, which is 12% over budget ($132,000 ÷ $1,100,000).

Your supervisor is very unhappy. Instead of sharing in the company's success, you may find yourself looking for another job. What went wrong?

When you calm down and carefully examine the manufacturing overhead budget, you identify the problem: The budget data are not relevant!

**HELPFUL HINT**

A static budget is not useful for performance evaluation if a company has substantial variable costs.

- At the time the budget was developed, the company anticipated that only 10,000 units would be produced. Instead, 12,000 units were actually produced.
- Comparing actual costs incurred at a production level of 12,000 units with budgeted variable costs at an expected production level of 10,000 units is meaningless (see **Helpful Hint**).
- As production increases, the budget allowances for variable costs should increase proportionately. The variable costs in this example are indirect materials, indirect labor, and utilities.

Analyzing the budget data for these costs at 10,000 units, you arrive at the per unit results shown in **Illustration 16.8**.

**ILLUSTRATION 16.8**

Variable costs per unit

| Item | Total Cost | Per Unit |
|---|---|---|
| Indirect materials | $250,000 | $25 |
| Indirect labor | 260,000 | 26 |
| Utilities | 190,000 | 19 |
| | $700,000 | $70 |

Using these per unit costs, **Illustration 16.9** calculates the budgeted variable costs at 12,000 units.

| Item | Computation | Total |
|---|---|---|
| Indirect materials | $25 × 12,000 | $300,000 |
| Indirect labor | 26 × 12,000 | 312,000 |
| Utilities | 19 × 12,000 | 228,000 |
| | | $840,000 |

ILLUSTRATION 16.9
**Budgeted variable costs, 12,000 units**

Because fixed costs do not change in total as activity changes, the budgeted amounts for these costs remain the same. **Illustration 16.10** shows the budget report based on the flexible budget for **12,000 units** of production. (Compare this with Illustration 16.7.)

**ILLUSTRATION 16.10**
**Overhead flexible budget report**

**Barton Robotics**
**Manufacturing Overhead Flexible Budget Report**
**For the Year Ended December 31, 2022**

| | Budget | Actual | Difference Favorable - F Unfavorable - U | |
|---|---|---|---|---|
| Production in units | 12,000 | 12,000 | | |
| **Variable costs** | | | | |
| Indirect materials ($25) | $ 300,000 | $ 295,000 | $5,000 | F |
| Indirect labor ($26) | 312,000 | 312,000 | 0 | |
| Utilities ($19) | 228,000 | 225,000 | 3,000 | F |
| Total variable costs | 840,000 | 832,000 | 8,000 | F |
| **Fixed costs** | | | | |
| Depreciation | 280,000 | 280,000 | 0 | |
| Property taxes | 70,000 | 70,000 | 0 | |
| Supervision | 50,000 | 50,000 | 0 | |
| Total fixed costs | 400,000 | 400,000 | 0 | |
| Total costs | $1,240,000 | $1,232,000 | $8,000 | F |

This flexible budget report indicates that the Assembly Department's costs are **under budget**—a favorable difference. Instead of worrying about being fired, you may be in line for a bonus or a raise after all! As this analysis shows, the only appropriate comparison is between actual costs at 12,000 units of production and budgeted costs at 12,000 units. Flexible budget reports provide this comparison (see **Decision Tools**).

**Decision Tools**
The flexible budget helps management evaluate whether cost changes resulting from different production volumes are reasonable.

## Developing the Flexible Budget

The flexible budget uses the master budget as its basis. To develop the flexible budget, management uses the following steps.

1. Identify the activity index and the relevant range of activity.
2. Identify the variable costs, and determine the budgeted variable cost per unit of activity for each cost.
3. Identify the fixed costs, and determine the budgeted amount for each cost.
4. Prepare the budget for selected increments of activity within the relevant range.

The activity index chosen should significantly influence the costs being budgeted. For manufacturing overhead costs, for example, the activity index is usually the same as the index used in developing the predetermined overhead rate—that is, direct labor hours or machine hours. For selling and administrative expenses, the activity index usually is sales or net sales.

The choice of the increment of activity is largely a matter of judgment. For example, if the relevant range is 8,000 to 12,000 direct labor hours, increments of 1,000 hours may be selected. The flexible budget is then prepared for each increment within the relevant range.

---

## Service Company Insight  NBCUniversal

Fox Broadcasting Company/Album/ Newscom

### Just What the Doctor Ordered?

Nobody is immune from the effects of declining revenues—not even movie stars. When the number of viewers of the television show "House," a medical drama, declined by almost 20%, **Fox Broadcasting** said it wanted to cut the license fee that it paid to **NBCUniversal** by 20%. What would NBCUniversal do in response? It might cut the size of the show's cast, which would reduce the payroll costs associated with the show. Or, it could reduce the number of episodes that take advantage of the full cast. Alternatively, it might threaten to quit providing the show to Fox altogether and instead present the show on its own NBC-affiliated channels.

**Source:** Sam Schechner, "Media Business Shorts: NBCU, Fox Taking Scalpel to 'House'," *Wall Street Journal Online* (April 17, 2011).

**Explain how the use of flexible budgets might help to identify the best solution to this problem. (Go to WileyPLUS for this answer and additional questions.)**

---

# Flexible Budget—A Case Study

To illustrate the flexible budget, we use Fox Company. Fox's management uses a **flexible budget for monthly comparisons** of actual and budgeted manufacturing overhead costs of the Finishing Department. The master budget for the year ending December 31, 2022, shows expected **annual** operating capacity of 120,000 direct labor hours and the overhead costs shown in **Illustration 16.11**.

**ILLUSTRATION 16.11**

**Master budget data**

| Variable Costs | | Fixed Costs | |
| --- | --- | --- | --- |
| Indirect materials | $180,000 | Depreciation | $180,000 |
| Indirect labor | 240,000 | Supervision | 120,000 |
| Utilities | 60,000 | Property taxes | 60,000 |
| Total | $480,000 | Total | $360,000 |

The four steps for developing the flexible budget are applied as follows.

**Step 1  Identify the activity index and the relevant range of activity.** The activity index is direct labor hours. The relevant range is 8,000–12,000 direct labor hours per **month**.

**Step 2  Identify the variable costs, and determine the budgeted variable cost per unit of activity for each cost.** A cost is variable if total costs vary directly as a result of a change in the activity index, which is direct labor in this case. In this example, indirect materials, indirect labor, and utilities are variable costs. The variable cost per unit is found by dividing each total budgeted cost by the direct labor hours used in preparing the annual master budget (120,000 hours). **Illustration 16.12** shows the computations for Fox Company.

**ILLUSTRATION 16.12**

**Computation of variable cost per direct labor hour**

| Variable Costs | Computation | Variable Cost per Direct Labor Hour |
| --- | --- | --- |
| Indirect materials | $180,000 ÷ 120,000 | $1.50 |
| Indirect labor | $240,000 ÷ 120,000 | 2.00 |
| Utilities | $60,000 ÷ 120,000 | 0.50 |
| Total | | $4.00 |

**Step 3  Identify the fixed costs, and determine the budgeted amount for each cost.** A cost is fixed if the total cost does not vary as a result of changes in the activity index. In this example, depreciation, supervision, and property taxes are fixed costs. Since Fox desires **monthly budget data**, it divides each annual budgeted cost by 12 to find the monthly amounts. Therefore, the monthly budgeted fixed costs are depreciation $15,000, supervision $10,000, and property taxes $5,000.

**Step 4  Prepare the budget for selected increments of activity within the relevant range.** Management prepares the budget in increments of 1,000 direct labor hours.
**Illustration 16.13** shows Fox's flexible budget.

**ILLUSTRATION 16.13**

Monthly overhead flexible budget

**Fox Company**
**Monthly Manufacturing Overhead Flexible Budget**
**Finishing Department**
**For Months During the Year 2022**

| Activity level | | | | | |
|---|---|---|---|---|---|
| Direct labor hours | 8,000 | 9,000 | 10,000 | 11,000 | 12,000 |
| **Variable costs** | | | | | |
| Indirect materials ($1.50)[a] | $12,000[b] | $13,500 | $15,000 | $16,500 | $18,000 |
| Indirect labor ($2.00)[a] | 16,000[c] | 18,000 | 20,000 | 22,000 | 24,000 |
| Utilities ($0.50)[a] | 4,000[d] | 4,500 | 5,000 | 5,500 | 6,000 |
| Total variable costs | 32,000 | 36,000 | 40,000 | 44,000 | 48,000 |
| **Fixed costs** | | | | | |
| Depreciation | 15,000 | 15,000 | 15,000 | 15,000 | 15,000 |
| Supervision | 10,000 | 10,000 | 10,000 | 10,000 | 10,000 |
| Property taxes | 5,000 | 5,000 | 5,000 | 5,000 | 5,000 |
| Total fixed costs | 30,000 | 30,000 | 30,000 | 30,000 | 30,000 |
| Total costs | $62,000 | $66,000 | $70,000 | $74,000 | $78,000 |

[a]Cost per direct labor hour; [b]8,000 x $1.50; [c]8,000 x $2.00; [d]8,000 x $0.50

Fox uses the cost equation shown in **Illustration 16.14** to determine total budgeted costs at any level of activity.

**ILLUSTRATION 16.14**

Cost equation for total budgeted costs

$$\text{Fixed Costs} + \text{Variable Costs*} = \text{Total Budgeted Costs}$$

*Total variable cost per unit of activity × Activity level.

For Fox, fixed costs are $30,000 per month, and total variable cost per direct labor hour is $4 ($1.50 + $2.00 + $0.50).

- At 9,000 direct labor hours, total budgeted costs are $66,000 [$30,000 + ($4 × 9,000)].
- At 8,622 direct labor hours, total budgeted costs are $64,488 [$30,000 + ($4 × 8,622)] (see **Helpful Hint**).

Total budgeted costs can also be shown graphically, as in **Illustration 16.15**.

**HELPFUL HINT**

Using the data given for Fox, the amount of total costs to be budgeted for 10,600 direct labor hours would be $30,000 fixed + $42,400 variable (10,600 × $4) = $72,400 total.

**ILLUSTRATION 16.15**
**Graphic flexible budget data highlighting 10,000 and 12,000 activity levels**

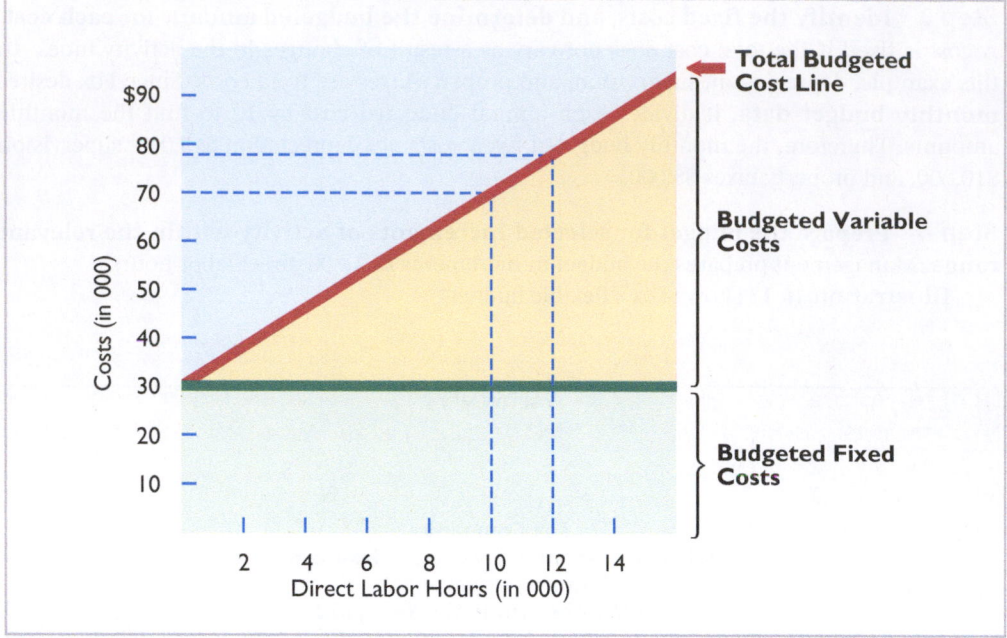

- In the graph, the horizontal axis represents the activity index, and costs are indicated on the vertical axis.
- The graph highlights two activity levels (10,000 and 12,000).
- As shown, total budgeted costs at these activity levels are $70,000 [$30,000 + ($4 × 10,000)] and $78,000 [$30,000 + ($4 × 12,000)], respectively.

## Flexible Budget Reports

Flexible budget reports are another type of internal report. The flexible budget report consists of two sections:

1. Production data for a selected activity index, such as direct labor hours.
2. Cost data for variable and fixed costs.

The report provides a basis for evaluating a manager's performance in two areas: production control and cost control. Flexible budget reports are widely used in production and service departments.

**Illustration 16.16** shows a flexible budget report for the Finishing Department of Fox Company for the month of January. In this month, 9,000 hours are worked. The budget data are therefore based on the flexible budget for 9,000 hours in Illustration 16.13. The actual cost data are assumed.

How appropriate is this report in evaluating the Finishing Department manager's performance in controlling overhead costs? The report clearly provides a reliable basis.

- Both actual and budget costs are based on the activity level worked during January.
- Since variable costs generally are incurred directly by the department, the difference between the budget allowance for those hours and the actual costs is the responsibility of the department manager.

| | Fox Company | | | |
|---|---|---|---|---|

**Fox Company**
**Manufacturing Overhead Flexible Budget Report**
**Finishing Department**
**For the Month Ended January 31, 2022**

| | Budget at 9,000 DLH | Actual costs at 9,000 DLH | Difference Favorable - F Unfavorable - U | |
|---|---|---|---|---|
| Direct labor hours (DLH) | | | | |
| **Variable costs** | | | | |
| Indirect materials ($1.50)[a] | $13,500 | $14,000 | $  500 | U |
| Indirect labor ($2.00)[a] | 18,000 | 17,000 | 1,000 | F |
| Utilities ($0.50)[a] | 4,500 | 4,600 | 100 | U |
| Total variable costs | 36,000 | 35,600 | 400 | F |
| | | | | |
| **Fixed costs** | | | | |
| Depreciation | 15,000 | 15,000 | 0 | |
| Supervision | 10,000 | 10,000 | 0 | |
| Property taxes | 5,000 | 5,000 | 0 | |
| Total fixed costs | 30,000 | 30,000 | 0 | |
| Total costs | $66,000 | $65,600 | $  400 | F |
| | | | | |
| [a]Cost per direct labor hour | | | | |

In subsequent months, Fox Company will prepare other flexible budget reports. For each month, the budget data are based on the actual activity level attained. In February, that level may be 11,000 direct labor hours, in July 10,000, and so on.

Note that this flexible budget is based on a single cost driver. A more accurate budget often can be developed using activity-based costing (see Appendix F).

---

## Service Company Insight    San Diego Zoo

iStock.com/Eric Isselée

### Budgets and the Exotic Newcastle Disease

Exotic Newcastle Disease, one of the most infectious bird diseases in the world, kills so swiftly that many victims die before any symptoms appear. When it broke out in Southern California, it could have spelled disaster for the **San Diego Zoo**. "We have one of the most valuable collections of birds in the world, if not *the* most valuable," says Paula Brock, CFO of the Zoological Society of San Diego, which operates the zoo.

Bird exhibits were closed to the public for several months (the disease, which is harmless to humans, can be carried on clothes and shoes). The tires of arriving delivery trucks were sanitized, as were the shoes of anyone visiting the zoo's nonpublic areas. Zoo-keeper uniforms had to be changed and cleaned daily. And ultimately, the zoo, with $150 million in revenues, spent almost half a million dollars on quarantine measures.

It worked: No birds got sick. Better yet, the damage to the rest of the zoo's budget was minimized by another protective measure: the monthly budget reforecast. "When we get a hit like this, we still have to find a way to make our bottom line," says Brock. Thanks to a new planning process Brock had introduced a year earlier, the zoo's scientists were able to raise the financial alarm as they redirected resources to ward off the disease. "Because we had timely awareness," she says, "we were able to make adjustments to weather the storm."

**Source:** Tim Reason, "Budgeting in the Real World," *CFO Magazine* (July 12, 2005), *www.cfodirect.com/cfopublic.nsf/vContentPrint /649A82C8FF8AB06B85257037004* (accessed July 2005).

**What is the major benefit of tying a budget to the overall goals of the company? (Go to WileyPLUS for this answer and additional questions.)**

## DO IT! 2 | Flexible Budgets

In Strassel Company's flexible budget graph, the fixed cost line and the total budgeted cost line intersect the vertical axis at $36,000. The total budgeted cost line is $186,000 at an activity level of 50,000 direct labor hours. Compute total budgeted costs at 30,000 direct labor hours.

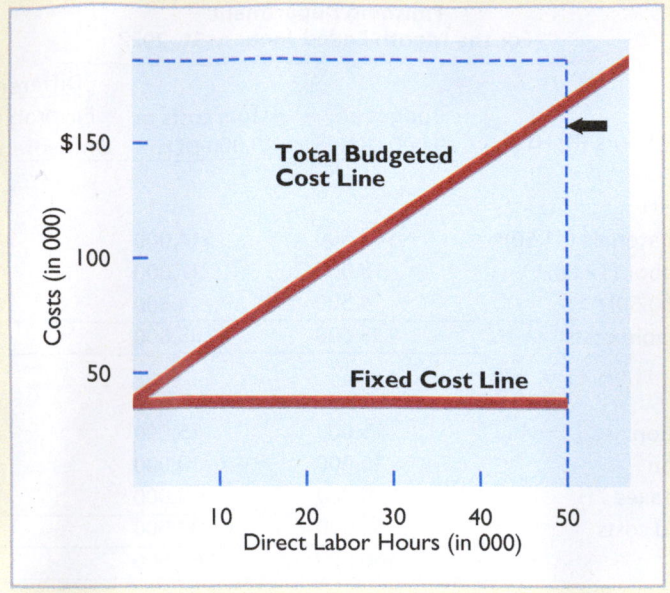

### Solution

Using the graph, fixed costs are $36,000, and variable costs are $3 per direct labor hour [($186,000 − $36,000) ÷ 50,000]. Thus, at 30,000 direct labor hours, total budgeted costs are $126,000 [$36,000 + ($3 × 30,000)].

Related exercise material: **BE16.4, DO IT! 16.2, E16.3, and E16.5.**

# Responsibility Accounting and Responsibility Centers

**LEARNING OBJECTIVE 3**

Apply responsibility accounting to cost and profit centers.

Like budgeting, responsibility accounting is an important part of management accounting.

- **Responsibility accounting** involves identifying and reporting costs (and revenues, where relevant) on the basis of the manager who has the authority to make the day-to-day decisions about the items.

- Under responsibility accounting, a manager's performance is evaluated on matters directly under that manager's control.

Responsibility accounting can be used at every level of management in which the following conditions exist.

1. Costs and revenues can be directly associated with the specific level of management responsibility.

2. The costs and revenues can be controlled by employees at the level of responsibility with which they are associated.

3. Budget data can be developed for evaluating the manager's effectiveness in controlling the costs and revenues.

**Illustration 16.17** depicts levels of responsibility for controlling costs.

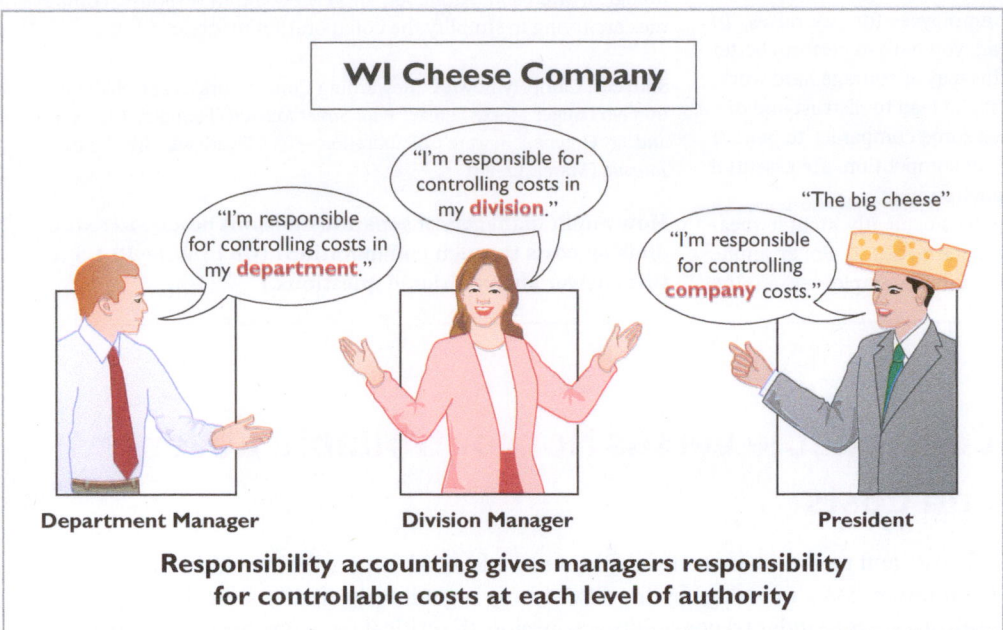

**ILLUSTRATION 16.17**
**Responsibility for controllable costs at varying levels of management**

Under responsibility accounting, any individual who controls a specified set of activities can be a responsibility center. Thus, responsibility accounting may extend from the lowest level of control to the top strata of management. Once responsibility is established, the company first measures and reports the effectiveness of the individual's performance for the specified activity. It then reports that measure upward throughout the organization (see **Helpful Hint**).

Responsibility accounting is especially valuable in a decentralized company.

- **Decentralization** means that the control of operations is delegated to many managers throughout the organization.
- The term **segment** (or **division**) is sometimes used to identify an area of responsibility in decentralized operations.

Under responsibility accounting, companies prepare segment reports periodically, such as monthly, quarterly, and annually, to evaluate managers' performance.

Responsibility accounting is an essential part of any effective system of budgetary control. The reporting of costs and revenues under responsibility accounting differs from budgeting in two respects:

1. A distinction is made between controllable and noncontrollable items.

2. Performance reports either emphasize or include only items controllable by the individual manager.

Responsibility accounting applies to both profit and not-for-profit entities. For-profit entities seek to maximize net income. Not-for-profit entities wish to provide services as efficiently as possible.

**HELPFUL HINT**

All companies use responsibility accounting. Without some form of responsibility accounting, there would be chaos in discharging management's control function.

---

### Management Insight    Procter & Gamble

iStock.com/Khuong Hoang

#### Competition versus Collaboration

Many compensation and promotion programs encourage competition among employees for pay raises. To get ahead, you have to perform better than your fellow employees. While this may encourage hard work, it does not foster collaboration, and it can lead to distrust and disloyalty. Such negative effects have led some companies to believe that cooperation and collaboration, not competition, are essential in order to succeed in today's work environment.

As a consequence, many companies explicitly include measures of collaboration in their performance measures. For example, **Procter & Gamble** measures collaboration in employees' annual performance reviews. At **Cisco Systems**, the assessment of an employee's teamwork can affect the annual bonus by as much as 20%. A recent concern is that employees have become swamped in a confusing array of collaboration tools from Box Inc., Slack Technologies, Microsoft, Alphabet, and Facebook. In response, companies are trying to simplify the collaboration process.

**Sources:** Carol Hymowitz, "Rewarding Competitors Over Collaboration No Longer Makes Sense," *Wall Street Journal* (February 13, 2006); and Jay Greene, "Beware Collaboration—Tool Overload," *Wall Street Journal* (March 12, 2017).

**How might managers of separate divisions be able to reduce division costs through collaboration? (Go to WileyPLUS for this answer and additional questions.)**

---

## Controllable versus Noncontrollable Revenues and Costs

> **HELPFUL HINT**
>
> **There are more, not fewer, controllable costs as you move to higher levels of management.**

All costs and revenues are controllable at some level of responsibility within a company. This truth underscores the adage by the CEO of any organization that "the buck stops here" (see **Helpful Hint**). Under responsibility accounting, the critical issue is **whether the cost or revenue is controllable at the level of responsibility with which it is associated**. A cost over which a manager has control is called a **controllable cost**. From this definition, it follows that:

1. All costs are controllable by top management because of the broad range of its authority.
2. Fewer costs are controllable as one moves down to each lower level of managerial responsibility because of the manager's decreasing authority.

> **HELPFUL HINT**
>
> **The longer the time span, the more likely that the cost becomes controllable.**

In general, **costs incurred directly by a level of responsibility are controllable at that level** (see **Helpful Hint**). In contrast, costs incurred indirectly and allocated to a responsibility level are **noncontrollable costs** at that level.

## Principles of Performance Evaluation

Performance evaluation is at the center of responsibility accounting. It is a management function that compares actual results with budget goals. It involves both behavioral and reporting principles.

### Management by Exception

**Management by exception** means:

- Top management's review of a budget report is focused either entirely or primarily on significant differences between actual results and planned objectives.
- This approach enables top management to focus on problem areas.

For example, many companies now use online reporting systems for employees to file their travel and entertainment expense reports. In addition to cutting reporting time in half, the online system enables managers to quickly analyze variances from travel budgets. This cuts down on expense account "padding" such as spending too much on meals or falsifying documents for costs that were never actually incurred.

Under management by exception, top management does not investigate every difference. For this approach to be effective, there must be guidelines for identifying which differences to investigate. The usual criteria are materiality and controllability.

**Materiality**   Without quantitative guidelines, management would have to investigate every budget difference regardless of the amount.

- Materiality is usually expressed as a percentage difference from budget. For example, management may set the percentage difference at 5% for important items and 10% for other items.
- Managers will investigate all differences either over or under budget by the specified percentage. Costs over budget warrant investigation to determine why they were not controlled. Likewise, costs under budget merit investigation to determine whether costs critical to profitability are being curtailed.

For example, if maintenance costs are budgeted at $80,000 but only $40,000 is spent, major unexpected breakdowns in productive facilities may occur in the future. Alternatively, as discussed in Chapter 15, cost might be under budget due to budgetary slack.

Alternatively, a company may specify a single percentage difference from budget for all items and supplement this guideline with a minimum dollar limit. For example, the exception criteria may be stated at 5% of budget or more than $10,000.

**Controllability of the Item**   Exception guidelines are more restrictive for controllable items than for items the manager cannot control.

- In fact, there may be no guidelines for noncontrollable items.
- For example, a large unfavorable difference between actual and budgeted property tax expense may not be flagged for investigation because the only possible causes are an unexpected increase in the tax rate or in the assessed value of the property.
- An investigation into the difference would be useless: The manager cannot control either cause.

## Behavioral Principles

The human factor is critical in evaluating performance. Behavioral principles include the following.

1. **Managers of responsibility centers should have direct input into the process of establishing budget goals of their area of responsibility.** Without such input, managers may view the goals as unrealistic or arbitrarily set by top management. Such views adversely affect the managers' motivation to meet the targeted objectives.

2. **The evaluation of performance should be based entirely on matters that are controllable by the manager being evaluated.** Criticism of a manager on matters outside his or her control reduces the effectiveness of the evaluation process. It leads to negative reactions by a manager and to doubts about the fairness of the company's evaluation policies.

3. **Top management should support the evaluation process.** As explained earlier, the evaluation process begins at the lowest level of responsibility and extends upward to the highest level of management. Managers quickly lose faith in the process when top management ignores, overrules, or bypasses established procedures for evaluating a manager's performance.

4. **The evaluation process must allow managers to respond to their evaluations.** Evaluation is not a one-way street. Managers should have the opportunity to defend their performance. Evaluation without feedback is both impersonal and ineffective.

5. **The evaluation should identify both good and poor performance.** Praise for good performance is a powerful motivating factor for a manager. This is especially true when a manager's compensation includes rewards for meeting budget goals.

### Reporting Principles

Performance evaluation under responsibility accounting should be based on certain reporting principles. These principles pertain primarily to the internal reports that provide the basis for evaluating performance. Performance reports should:

- Contain only data that are controllable by the manager of the responsibility center.
- Provide accurate and reliable budget data to measure performance.
- Highlight significant differences between actual results and budget goals.
- Be tailor-made for the intended evaluation by ensuring only controllable costs are included.
- Be prepared at reasonable time intervals.

In recent years, companies have come under increasing pressure from influential shareholder groups to do a better job of linking executive pay to corporate performance. For example, software maker **Siebel Systems** unveiled an incentive plan after lengthy discussions with the California Public Employees' Retirement System. One unique feature of the plan is that managers' targets will be publicly disclosed at the beginning of each year for investors to evaluate.

---

**Management Insight**     Honda

AP Images/Kyodo

#### Flexible Manufacturing Requires Flexible Accounting

Flexible budgeting is useful because it enables managers to evaluate performance in light of changing conditions. But the ability to react quickly to changing conditions is even more important. Among automobile manufacturing facilities in the U.S., few plants are more flexible than **Honda**.

The manufacturing facilities of some auto companies can make slight alterations to the features of a vehicle in response to changes in demand for particular features. But for most plants, to switch from production of one type of vehicle to a completely different one typically takes months and costs hundreds of millions of dollars. At the Honda plant, however, the switch takes minutes. For example, it takes about five minutes to install different hand-like parts on the robots so they can switch from making Civic compacts to the longer, taller CR-V crossover. This ability to adjust quickly to changing demand gave Honda a huge advantage when gas prices surged and demand for more fuel-efficient cars increased quickly.

**Source:** Kate Linebaugh, "Honda's Flexible Plants Provide Edge," *Wall Street Journal Online* (September 23, 2008).

**What implications do these improvements in production capabilities have for management accounting information and performance evaluation within the organization? (Go to WileyPLUS for this answer and additional questions.)**

---

# Responsibility Reporting System

**Decision Tools**

Responsibility reports help to hold individual managers accountable for the costs and revenues under their control.

A **responsibility reporting system** involves the preparation of a report for each level of responsibility in the company's organization chart (see **Decision Tools**). To illustrate such a system, we use the partial organization chart and production departments of Francis Chair Company in **Illustration 16.18**.

The responsibility reporting system begins with the lowest level of responsibility for controlling costs and moves upward to each higher level. (Illustration 16.19 details the connections between levels). A brief description of the four reports for Francis Chair is as follows.

1. **Report D** is typical of reports that go to department managers. Similar reports are prepared for the managers of the Assembly and Enameling Departments.
2. **Report C** is an example of reports that are sent to plant managers. It shows the costs of the Chicago plant that are controllable at the second level of responsibility. In addition, Report C shows summary data for each department that is controlled by the plant manager. Similar reports are prepared for the Detroit and St. Louis plant managers.
3. **Report B** illustrates the reports at the third level of responsibility. It shows the controllable costs of the vice president of production and summary data on the three assembly

**ILLUSTRATION 16.18**   Partial organization chart

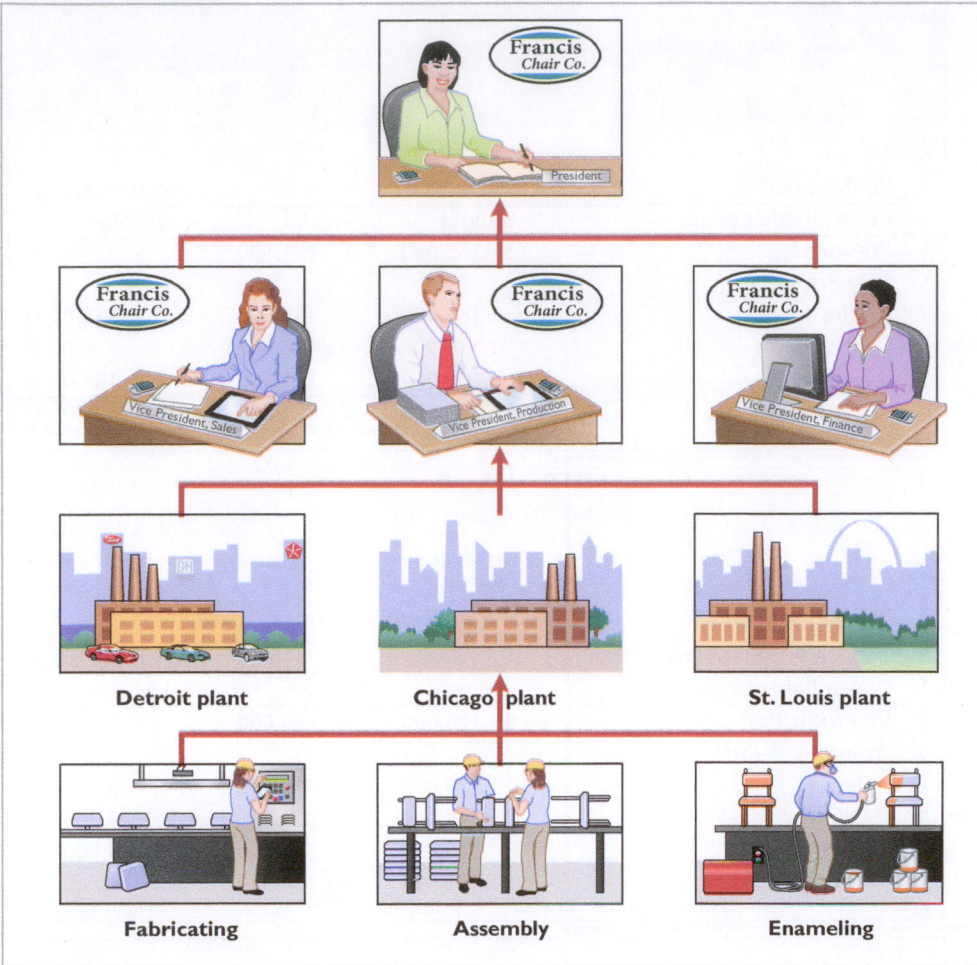

**Report A**
President sees summary data of vice presidents.

**Report B**
Vice president sees summary of controllable costs in his/her functional area.

**Report C**
Plant manager sees summary of controllable costs for each department in the plant.

**Report D**
Department manager sees controllable costs of his/her department.

plants for which this officer is responsible. Similar reports are prepared for the vice presidents of sales and finance.

4. **Report A** is typical of reports that go to the top level of responsibility—the president. It shows the controllable costs and expenses of this office and summary data on the vice presidents that are accountable to the president.

A responsibility reporting system permits management by exception at each level of responsibility. And, each higher level of responsibility can obtain the detailed report for each lower level of responsibility. For example, the vice president of production in Francis Chair may request the Chicago plant manager's report because this plant is $5,300 over budget.

This type of reporting system also permits comparative evaluations. In **Illustration 16.19**, the Chicago plant manager can easily rank the department managers' effectiveness in controlling manufacturing costs. Comparative rankings provide further incentive for a manager to control costs.

# Types of Responsibility Centers

There are three basic types of responsibility centers: cost centers, profit centers, and investment centers. These classifications indicate the degree of responsibility the manager has for the performance of the center.

1. A **cost center** incurs costs (and expenses) but does not directly generate revenues.
   - Managers of cost centers have the authority to incur costs.
   - They are evaluated on their ability to control costs.

**ILLUSTRATION 16.19** **Responsibility reporting system**

**Report A**
President sees summary data of vice presidents.

**Report B**
Vice president sees summary of controllable costs in his/her functional area.

**Report C**
Plant manager sees summary of controllable costs for each department in the plant.

**Report D**
Department manager sees controllable costs of his/her department.

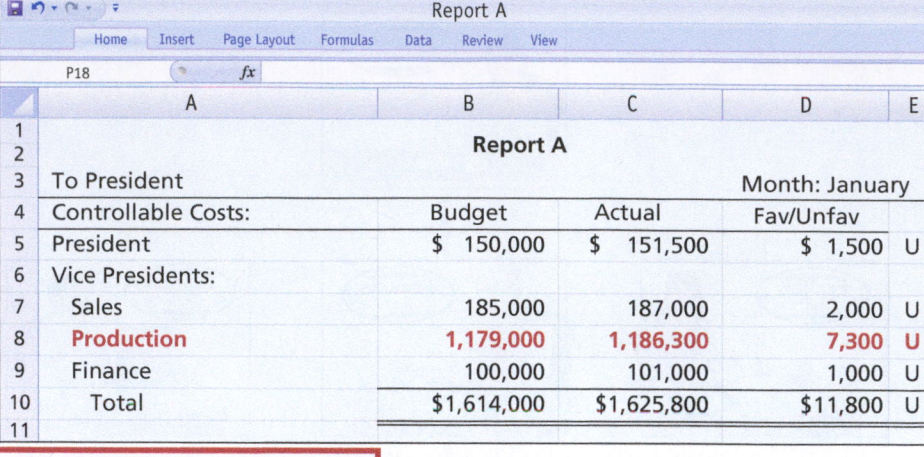

**Report A**

| To President | | | Month: January | |
|---|---|---|---|---|
| Controllable Costs: | Budget | Actual | Fav/Unfav | |
| President | $ 150,000 | $ 151,500 | $ 1,500 | U |
| Vice Presidents: | | | | |
| Sales | 185,000 | 187,000 | 2,000 | U |
| Production | 1,179,000 | 1,186,300 | 7,300 | U |
| Finance | 100,000 | 101,000 | 1,000 | U |
| Total | $1,614,000 | $1,625,800 | $11,800 | U |

**Report B**

| To Vice President Production | | | Month: January | |
|---|---|---|---|---|
| Controllable Costs: | Budget | Actual | Fav/Unfav | |
| VP Production | $ 125,000 | $ 126,000 | $ 1,000 | U |
| Assembly Plants: | | | | |
| Detroit | 420,000 | 418,000 | 2,000 | F |
| Chicago | 304,000 | 309,300 | 5,300 | U |
| St. Louis | 330,000 | 333,000 | 3,000 | U |
| Total | $1,179,000 | $1,186,300 | $ 7,300 | U |

**Report C**

| To Plant Manager-Chicago | | | Month: January | |
|---|---|---|---|---|
| Controllable Costs: | Budget | Actual | Fav/Unfav | |
| Chicago Plant | $110,000 | $113,000 | $3,000 | U |
| Departments: | | | | |
| Fabricating | 84,000 | 85,300 | 1,300 | U |
| Enameling | 62,000 | 64,000 | 2,000 | U |
| Assembly | 48,000 | 47,000 | 1,000 | F |
| Total | $304,000 | $309,300 | $5,300 | U |

**Report D**

| To Fabricating Dept. Manager | | | Month: January | |
|---|---|---|---|---|
| Controllable Costs: | Budget | Actual | Fav/Unfav | |
| Direct Materials | $20,000 | $20,500 | $ 500 | U |
| Direct Labor | 40,000 | 41,000 | 1,000 | U |
| Overhead | 24,000 | 23,800 | 200 | F |
| Total | $84,000 | $85,300 | $1,300 | U |

- **Cost centers are usually either production departments or service departments.**

Production departments participate directly in making the product. Service departments provide only support services. In a **Ford Motor Company** automobile plant, the welding, painting, and assembling departments are production departments. Ford's maintenance and human resources departments are service departments. All of them are cost centers.

2. A **profit center** incurs costs (and expenses) and also generates revenues.

- Managers of profit centers are judged on the profitability of their centers.

- Examples of profit centers include the individual departments of a retail store, such as clothing, furniture, and automotive products, and branch offices of banks (see **Helpful Hint**).

3. Like a profit center, an **investment center** incurs costs (and expenses) and generates revenues. In addition, an investment center has control over decisions regarding the assets available for use.

- Investment center managers are evaluated on both the profitability of the center and the rate of return earned on the assets used.

- Investment centers are often associated with subsidiary companies.

Utility company **Duke Energy** has operating divisions such as electric utility, energy trading, and natural gas. Investment center managers control or significantly influence investment decisions related to such matters as plant expansion and entry into new market areas.

**Illustration 16.20** depicts the three types of responsibility centers.

**ILLUSTRATION 16.20** **Types of responsibility centers**

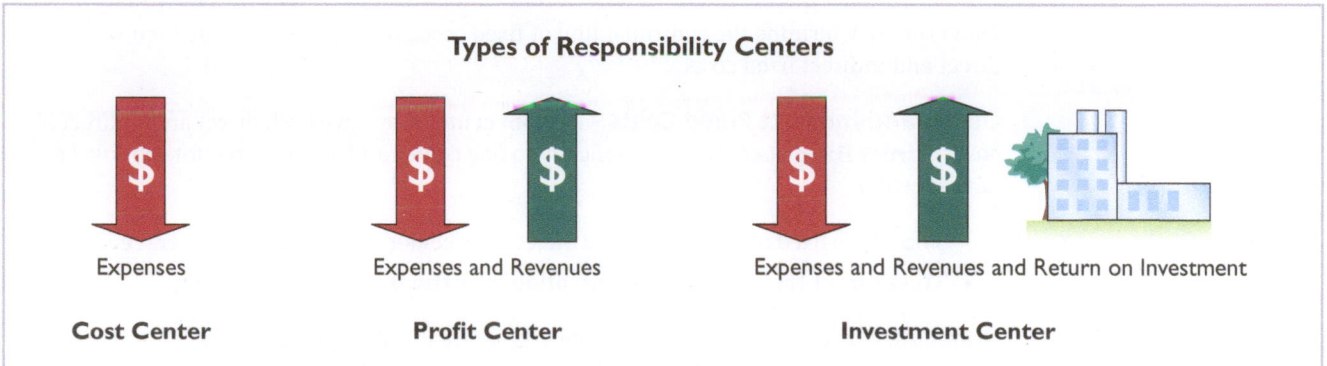

**Types of Responsibility Centers**

| Expenses | Expenses and Revenues | Expenses and Revenues and Return on Investment |
| :---: | :---: | :---: |
| **Cost Center** | **Profit Center** | **Investment Center** |

## Responsibility Accounting for Cost Centers

The evaluation of a manager's performance for cost centers is based on his or her ability to meet budgeted goals for controllable costs. **Responsibility reports for cost centers compare actual controllable costs with flexible budget data.**

**Illustration 16.21** shows a responsibility report. The report is adapted from the flexible budget report for Fox Company in Illustration 16.16. It assumes that the Finishing Department manager is able to control all manufacturing overhead costs except depreciation, property taxes, and his own monthly salary of $6,000. The remaining $4,000 ($10,000 − $6,000) of supervision costs are assumed to apply to other supervisory personnel within the Finishing Department, whose salaries are controllable by the manager.

- The report in Illustration 16.21 includes **only controllable costs,** and no distinction is made between variable and fixed costs.

- The responsibility report continues the concept of management by exception.

- In this case, top management may request an explanation of the $1,000 favorable difference in indirect labor and/or the $500 unfavorable difference in indirect materials if considered significant.

ILLUSTRATION 16.21

Responsibility report for a cost center

| | Fox Company Finishing Department Responsibility Report For the Month Ended January 31, 2022 | | | |
|---|---|---|---|---|
| Controllable Costs | Budget | Actual | Difference Favorable - F Unfavorable - U | |
| Indirect materials | $13,500 | $14,000 | $  500 | U |
| Indirect labor | 18,000 | 17,000 | 1,000 | F |
| Utilities | 4,500 | 4,600 | 100 | U |
| Supervision | 4,000 | 4,000 | 0 | |
| Total | $40,000 | $39,600 | $  400 | F |

## Responsibility Accounting for Profit Centers

To evaluate the performance of a profit center manager, upper management needs detailed information about both controllable revenues and controllable costs.

- The operating revenues earned by a profit center, such as sales, are controllable by the manager.
- All variable costs (and expenses) incurred by the center are also controllable by the manager because they vary with sales.

However, to determine the controllability of fixed costs, it is necessary to distinguish between direct and indirect fixed costs.

### Direct and Indirect Fixed Costs
A profit center may have both direct and indirect fixed costs. **Direct fixed costs** relate specifically to one center and are incurred for the sole benefit of that center.

- Since these fixed costs can be traced directly to a center, they are also called **traceable costs**.
- **Most direct fixed costs are controllable by the profit center manager**.

Examples of direct fixed costs include the salaries established by the profit center manager for supervisory personnel and the cost of a timekeeping department for the center's employees.

In contrast, **indirect fixed costs** pertain to a company's overall operating activities and are incurred for the benefit of more than one profit center.

- Management allocates indirect fixed costs to profit centers on some type of equitable basis.
- Because these fixed costs apply to more than one center, they are also called **common costs**.
- **Most indirect fixed costs are not controllable by the profit center manager**.

For example, property taxes on a building occupied by more than one center may be allocated on the basis of square feet of floor space used by each center. Or, the costs of a company's human resources department may be allocated to profit centers on the basis of the number of employees in each center.

### Responsibility Report
The responsibility report for a profit center shows budgeted and actual **controllable revenues and costs**. The report is prepared using the cost-volume-profit income statement explained in Chapter 13 (see **Helpful Hint**). In the report:

1. Controllable fixed costs are deducted from contribution margin.
2. The excess of contribution margin over controllable fixed costs is identified as **controllable margin**.
3. Noncontrollable fixed costs are not reported.

> **HELPFUL HINT**
>
> Recognize that we are emphasizing *financial* measures of performance. Companies are now making an effort to also stress *nonfinancial* performance measures such as product quality, labor productivity, market growth, materials' yield, manufacturing flexibility, and technological capability.

**Illustration 16.22** shows the responsibility report for the manager of the Marine Division, a profit center of Mantle Company. For the year, the Marine Division also had $60,000 of indirect fixed costs that were not controllable by the profit center manager and therefore were omitted from the report.

ILLUSTRATION 16.22

**Responsibility report for profit center**

**Mantle Company**
**Marine Division**
**Responsibility Report**
**For the Year Ended December 31, 2022**

| | Budget | Actual | Difference<br>Favorable - F<br>Unfavorable - U | |
|---|---|---|---|---|
| Sales | $1,200,000 | $1,150,000 | $50,000 | U |
| Variable costs | | | | |
|   Cost of goods sold | 500,000 | 490,000 | 10,000 | F |
|   Selling and administrative | 160,000 | 156,000 | 4,000 | F |
|   Total | 660,000 | 646,000 | 14,000 | F |
| Contribution margin | 540,000 | 504,000 | 36,000 | U |
| **Controllable fixed costs** | | | | |
|   Cost of goods sold | 100,000 | 100,000 | 0 | |
|   Selling and administrative | 80,000 | 80,000 | 0 | |
|   Total | 180,000 | 180,000 | 0 | |
| **Controllable margin** | **$ 360,000** | **$ 324,000** | **$36,000** | U |

Controllable margin is considered to be the best measure of the manager's performance **in controlling revenues and costs**.

- The report in Illustration 16.22 shows that the manager's performance was below budgeted expectations by 10% ($36,000 ÷ $360,000) of the budgeted controllable margin.
- Top management would likely investigate the causes of this unfavorable result.
- Note that the responsibility report for the division manager does not show the Marine Division's noncontrollable indirect fixed costs of $60,000 because the manager cannot control these costs.

Management also may choose to see **monthly** responsibility reports for profit centers. In addition, responsibility reports may include cumulative year-to-date results.

---

**DO IT! 3 | Profit Center Responsibility Report**

Midwest Division operates as a profit center. It reports the following for the year:

| | Budget | Actual |
|---|---|---|
| Sales | $1,500,000 | $1,700,000 |
| Variable costs | 700,000 | 800,000 |
| Controllable fixed costs | 400,000 | 400,000 |
| Noncontrollable fixed costs | 200,000 | 200,000 |

Prepare a responsibility report for the Midwest Division for December 31, 2022.

**ACTION PLAN**

- Deduct variable costs from sales to show contribution margin.
- Deduct controllable fixed costs from the contribution margin to show controllable margin.
- Do not report noncontrollable fixed costs.

**Solution**

| | Midwest Division Responsibility Report | | | |
|---|---|---|---|---|
| | Home  Insert  Page Layout  Formulas  Data  Review  View | | | |
| | P18  *fx* | | | |
| | A | B | C | D | E |
| 1 | **Midwest Division** | | | | |
| 2 | **Responsibility Report** | | | | |
| 3 | **For the Year Ended December 31, 2022** | | | | |
| 4 | | | | Difference | |
| 5 | | Budget | Actual | Favorable F Unfavorable U | |
| 6 | Sales | $1,500,000 | $1,700,000 | $200,000 | F |
| 7 | Variable costs | 700,000 | 800,000 | 100,000 | U |
| 8 | Contribution margin | 800,000 | 900,000 | 100,000 | F |
| 9 | Controllable fixed costs | 400,000 | 400,000 | 0 | |
| 10 | **Controllable margin** | $  400,000 | $  500,000 | $100,000 | F |
| 11 | | | | | |

Related exercise material: **BE16.7, DO IT! 16.3, and E16.15.**

# Investment Centers

**LEARNING OBJECTIVE 4**

Evaluate performance in investment centers.

As explained earlier, an investment center manager can control or significantly influence the investment funds available for use.

- Thus, the primary basis for evaluating the performance of a manager of an investment center is **return on investment (ROI)**.
- The return on investment is considered to be a useful performance measurement because it shows the **effectiveness of the manager in utilizing the assets at his or her disposal**.

## Return on Investment (ROI)

The formula for computing ROI for an investment center, together with assumed illustrative data, is shown in **Illustration 16.23**.

**ILLUSTRATION 16.23**

**ROI formula**

| Controllable Margin | ÷ | Average Operating Assets | = | Return on Investment (ROI) |
|---|---|---|---|---|
| $1,000,000 | ÷ | $5,000,000 | = | 20% |

**Decision Tools**

The ROI formula helps managers determine if the investment center has used its assets effectively.

Both factors in the formula are controllable by the investment center manager (see **Decision Tools**).

- Operating assets consist of current assets and plant assets used in operations by the center and controlled by the manager.
- Nonoperating assets such as idle plant assets and land held for future use are excluded.

- Average operating assets are usually based on the cost or book value of the assets at the beginning and end of the year.

Based on these assigned values, the ROI of 20% indicates that, on average, the segment generates 20 cents of profit for every dollar invested in assets.

# Responsibility Report

The scope of the investment center manager's responsibility significantly affects the content of the performance report.

- Since an investment center is an independent entity for operating purposes, **all fixed costs are controllable by its manager**. For example, the manager is responsible for depreciation on investment center assets.
- Therefore, more fixed costs are identified as controllable in the performance report for an investment center manager than in a performance report for a profit center manager.
- The report also shows budgeted and actual ROI below controllable margin.

To illustrate this responsibility report, we will now assume that the Marine Division of Mantle Company is an investment center. It has budgeted and actual average operating assets of $2,000,000. The manager can control $60,000 of additional fixed costs that were not controllable when the division was a profit center. **Illustration 16.24** shows the division's responsibility report.

**ILLUSTRATION 16.24**

**Responsibility report for investment center**

| | Budget | Actual | Difference Favorable - F Unfavorable - U | |
|---|---|---|---|---|
| **Mantle Company** **Marine Division** **Responsibility Report** **For the Year Ended December 31, 2022** | | | | |
| Sales | $ 1,200,000 | $ 1,150,000 | $ 50,000 | U |
| Variable costs | | | | |
| Cost of goods sold | 500,000 | 490,000 | 10,000 | F |
| Selling and administrative | 160,000 | 156,000 | 4,000 | F |
| Total | 660,000 | 646,000 | 14,000 | F |
| Contribution margin | 540,000 | 504,000 | 36,000 | U |
| **Controllable fixed costs** | | | | |
| Cost of goods sold | 100,000 | 100,000 | 0 | |
| Selling and administrative | 80,000 | 80,000 | 0 | |
| **Other fixed costs** | **60,000** | **60,000** | **0** | |
| Total | 240,000 | 240,000 | 0 | |
| **Controllable margin** | $ 300,000 | $ 264,000 | $ 36,000 | U |
| **Return on investment** | 15.0% | 13.2% | 1.8% | U |
| | (a) | (b) | (c) | |

$$\text{(a)} \ \frac{\$ \ 300,000}{\$ \ 2,000,000} \qquad \text{(b)} \ \frac{\$ \ 264,000}{\$ \ 2,000,000} \qquad \text{(c)} \ \frac{\$ \ 36,000}{\$ \ 2,000,000}$$

The report shows that the manager's performance based on ROI was below budget expectations by 1.8% (15.0% versus 13.2%). Top management would likely want explanations for this unfavorable result.

# Judgmental Factors in ROI

The return on investment approach is sometimes computed using alternative inputs in the denominator and numerator.

1. **Valuation of operating assets.**
   - Operating assets may be valued at acquisition cost, book value, appraised value, or fair value. The first two bases are readily available from the accounting records.
   - Each of the alternative values for operating assets can provide a reliable basis for evaluating a manager's performance as long as it is consistently applied between reporting periods.

2. **Margin (income) measure.**
   - Possible options for this measure might be controllable margin, income from operations, or net income.
   - When computing ROI for a responsibility report, the best option is to use controllable margin since it is computed using only controllable costs. Income from operations and net income include noncontrollable costs in their computation.

# Improving ROI

The manager of an investment center can improve ROI by increasing controllable margin, and/or reducing average operating assets. To illustrate, we use the assumed data for the Laser Division of Berra Company shown in **Illustration 16.25**.

**ILLUSTRATION 16.25**

**Assumed data for Laser Division**

| | |
|---|---:|
| Sales | $2,000,000 |
| Variable costs | 1,100,000 |
| Contribution margin (45%) | 900,000 |
| Controllable fixed costs | 300,000 |
| Controllable margin (a) | $ 600,000 |
| Average operating assets (b) | $5,000,000 |
| Return on investment (a) ÷ (b) | 12% |

## Increasing Controllable Margin

Controllable margin can be increased by increasing sales or by reducing variable and controllable fixed costs as follows.

1. **Increase sales 10%.** Sales will increase $200,000 ($2,000,000 × .10). Assuming no change in the contribution margin percentage of 45% ($900,000 ÷ $2,000,000), contribution margin will increase $90,000 ($200,000 × .45). Controllable margin will increase by the same amount because controllable fixed costs will not change. Thus, controllable margin becomes $690,000 ($600,000 + $90,000). The new ROI is 13.8%, computed as shown in **Illustration 16.26**.

**ILLUSTRATION 16.26**

**ROI computation—increase in sales**

$$\text{ROI} = \frac{\text{Controllable margin}}{\text{Average operating assets}} = \frac{\$690,000}{\$5,000,000} = 13.8\%$$

   - An increase in sales benefits both the investment center and the company if it results in new business.
   - It would not benefit the company if the increase was achieved at the expense of other investment centers.

2. **Decrease variable and fixed costs 10%.** Total costs decrease $140,000 [($1,100,000 + $300,000) × .10]. This reduction results in a corresponding increase in controllable margin. Thus, controllable margin becomes $740,000 ($600,000 + $140,000). The new ROI is 14.8%, computed as shown in **Illustration 16.27**.

$$ROI = \frac{\text{Controllable margin}}{\text{Average operating assets}} = \frac{\$740,000}{\$5,000,000} = 14.8\%$$

**ILLUSTRATION 16.27**

**ROI computation—decrease in costs**

- This course of action is clearly beneficial when the reduction in costs is the result of eliminating waste and inefficiency.
- But, a reduction in costs that results from cutting expenditures on vital activities, such as required maintenance and inspections, is not likely to be acceptable to top management.

## Reducing Average Operating Assets

Assume that average operating assets are reduced 10% or $500,000 ($5,000,000 × .10). Average operating assets become $4,500,000 ($5,000,000 − $500,000). Since controllable margin remains unchanged at $600,000, the new ROI is 13.3%, computed as shown in **Illustration 16.28**.

$$ROI = \frac{\text{Controllable margin}}{\text{Average operating assets}} = \frac{\$600,000}{\$4,500,000} = 13.3\%$$

**ILLUSTRATION 16.28**

**ROI computation—decrease in operating assets**

Reductions in operating assets may or may not be prudent.

- It is beneficial to eliminate overinvestment in inventories and to dispose of excessive plant assets.
- However, it is unwise to reduce inventories below expected needs or to dispose of essential plant assets.

## Management Insight

### Is Your Job a Game?

PeopleImages/E+/ Getty Images

As discussed in this chapter, the things you are held accountable for depend on your job responsibilities. Similarly, the form of a company's incentive and compensation structure varies depending on your level within the organization. If you are the chief executive officer (CEO), it is likely that a significant portion of your pay (about 30%) will be in the form of a stock-based bonus. This bonus is usually tied to overall company performance, typically measured by earnings per share and shareholder returns. But if you are a lower-level employee, your raises and bonuses might be structured similar to the incentives in video games. This so-called "gamification" has the ability to incentivize not just the most obvious aspect of your job but also many of the other functions that your manager deems important. For example, rather than just reward you for total sales made, your bonus under gamification might change if you "accurately enter their client's information into a sales tracker, assess the quality of sales leads or track how often they are going to sales meetings." It can also provide "points" for things like whether you lead a healthy lifestyle, collaborate with co-workers, and improve interpersonal skills.

**Sources:** Scott Thurm, "CEO Pay More Closely Matches Firms' Results," *Wall Street Journal* (September 11, 2013); and Farhad Manjoo, "The Gamification of the Office Approaches," *Wall Street Journal* (January 12, 2014).

**Why is the reward system of top managers tied to different types of measures than those of lower-level managers?** (Go to WileyPLUS for this answer and additional questions.)

## DO IT! 4 | Performance Evaluation

Metro Industries reported the following results for 2022.

| | |
|---|---|
| Sales | $400,000 |
| Variable costs | 320,000 |
| Controllable fixed costs | 40,800 |
| Average operating assets | 280,000 |

Management is considering the following independent courses of action in 2023 in order to maximize the return on investment for this division.

**ACTION PLAN**

Recall key formulas:
- **Sales − Variable costs = Contribution margin.**
- **Contribution margin − Controllable fixed costs = Controllable margin.**
- **Return on investment = Controllable margin ÷ Average operating assets.**

1. Reduce average operating assets by $80,000, with no change in controllable margin.
2. Increase sales $80,000, with no change in the contribution margin percentage.
a. Compute the controllable margin and the return on investment for 2022.
b. Compute the controllable margin and the expected return on investment for 2023 for each proposed alternative.

### Solution

a. Return on investment for 2022:

| | |
|---|---:|
| Sales | $400,000 |
| Variable costs | 320,000 |
| Contribution margin | 80,000 |
| Controllable fixed costs | 40,800 |
| Controllable margin | $ 39,200 |

$$\text{Return on investment} \quad \frac{\$39,200}{\$280,000} = 14\%$$

b. Expected return on investment for alternative 1:

$$\frac{\$39,200}{\$280,000 - \$80,000} = 19.6\%$$

Expected return on investment for alternative 2:

| | |
|---|---:|
| Sales ($400,000 + $80,000) | $480,000 |
| Variable costs ($320,000 ÷ $400,000 × $480,000) | 384,000 |
| Contribution margin | 96,000 |
| Controllable fixed costs | 40,800 |
| Controllable margin | $ 55,200 |

$$\text{Return on investment} \quad \frac{\$55,200}{\$280,000} = 19.7\%$$

Related exercise material: **BE16.8, BE16.9, BE16.10, DO IT! 16.4, E16.16, and E16.17.**

---

## USING THE DECISION TOOLS | The Roxy Hotel Tribeca

**The Roxy Hotel Tribeca**, which was discussed in the Feature Story, faces many situations where it needs to apply the decision tools learned in this chapter. For example, assume that the hotel's housekeeping budget contains the following items.

| Variable costs | |
|---|---:|
| Direct labor | $37,000 |
| Laundry service | 10,000 |
| Supplies | 6,000 |
| Total variable | $53,000 |

| Fixed costs | |
|---|---:|
| Supervision | $17,000 |
| Inspection costs | 1,000 |
| Insurance expenses | 2,000 |
| Depreciation | 15,000 |
| Total fixed | $35,000 |

The budget was based on an estimated 4,000-room rental for the month. During November, 3,000 rooms were actually rented, with the following costs incurred.

| | |
|---|---:|
| Variable costs | |
| Direct labor | $38,700 |
| Laundry service | 8,200 |
| Supplies | 5,100 |
| Total variable | $52,000 |
| | |
| Fixed costs | |
| Supervision | $19,300 |
| Inspection costs | 1,200 |
| Insurance expenses | 2,200 |
| Depreciation | 14,700 |
| Total fixed | $37,400 |

## Instructions

a. Determine which items would be controllable by the housekeeping manager. (Assume "supervision" excludes the housekeeping manager's own salary.)

b. How much should have been spent during the month for providing rental of 3,000 rooms?

c. Prepare a flexible housekeeping budget report for the housekeeping manager.

d. Prepare a responsibility report. Include only the costs that would have been controllable by the housekeeping manager.

## Solution

a. The housekeeping manager should be able to control all the variable costs and the fixed costs of supervision and inspection. Insurance and depreciation ordinarily are not the responsibility of the housekeeping manager.

b. The total variable cost per unit is $13.25 ($53,000 ÷ 4,000). The total budgeted cost during the month to provide 3,000 room rentals is variable costs $39,750 (3,000 × $13.25) plus fixed costs ($35,000), for a total of $74,750 ($39,750 + $35,000).

c.

**The Roxy Hotel Tribeca**
**Housekeeping Department**
**Housekeeping Budget Report (Flexible)**
**For the Month Ended November 30, 2022**

| | Budget at 3,000 Rooms | Actual at 3,000 Rooms | Difference Favorable F Unfavorable U |
|---|---:|---:|---:|
| Variable costs | | | |
| Direct labor ($9.25)* | $27,750 | $38,700 | $10,950 U |
| Laundry service ($2.50) | 7,500 | 8,200 | 700 U |
| Supplies ($1.50) | 4,500 | 5,100 | 600 U |
| Total variable ($13.25) | 39,750 | 52,000 | 12,250 U |
| | | | |
| Fixed costs | | | |
| Supervision | 17,000 | 19,300 | 2,300 U |
| Inspection | 1,000 | 1,200 | 200 U |
| Insurance | 2,000 | 2,200 | 200 U |
| Depreciation | 15,000 | 14,700 | 300 F |
| Total fixed | 35,000 | 37,400 | 2,400 U |
| Total costs | $74,750 | $89,400 | $14,650 U |

*Original budgeted amount divided by original budgeted units, e.g., $37,000 ÷ 4,000

**d.** Because a housekeeping department is a cost center, the responsibility report should include only the costs that are controllable by the housekeeping manager. In this type of report, no distinction is made between variable and fixed costs. Budget data in the report should be based on the rooms actually rented.

**The Roxy Hotel Tribeca**
**Housekeeping Department**
**Housekeeping Responsibility Report**
**For the Month Ended November 30, 2022**

| Controllable Costs | Budget | Actual | Difference<br>Favorable F<br>Unfavorable U |
|---|---|---|---|
| Direct labor | $27,750 | $38,700 | $10,950 U |
| Laundry service | 7,500 | 8,200 | 700 U |
| Supplies | 4,500 | 5,100 | 600 U |
| Supervision | 17,000 | 19,300 | 2,300 U |
| Inspection | 1,000 | 1,200 | 200 U |
| Total | $57,750 | $72,500 | $14,750 U |

<table>
<tr><td>**Appendix 16A**</td><td></td></tr>
</table>

# ROI vs. Residual Income

**LEARNING OBJECTIVE *5**

Explain the difference between ROI and residual income.

Although most companies use ROI to evaluate investment performance, ROI has a significant disadvantage. To illustrate, let's look at the Electronics Division of Pujols Company. It has an ROI of 20%, computed as shown in **Illustration 16A.1**.

**ILLUSTRATION 16A.1**

**ROI formula**

| Controllable Margin | ÷ | Average Operating Assets | = | Return on Investment (ROI) |
|---|---|---|---|---|
| $1,000,000 | ÷ | $5,000,000 | = | 20% |

The Electronics Division is considering producing a new product, a GPS device (hereafter referred to as Tracker) for its boats. To produce Tracker, operating assets will have to increase $2,000,000. Tracker is expected to generate an additional $260,000 of controllable margin. **Illustration 16A.2** shows how Tracker will effect ROI.

**ILLUSTRATION 16A.2**

**ROI comparison**

| | Without Tracker | Tracker | With Tracker |
|---|---|---|---|
| Controllable margin (a) | $1,000,000 | $260,000 | $1,260,000 |
| Average operating assets (b) | $5,000,000 | $2,000,000 | $7,000,000 |
| Return on investment [(a) ÷ (b)] | 20% | 13% | 18% |

The investment in Tracker reduces ROI from 20% to 18%.

Let's suppose that you are the manager of the Electronics Division and must make the decision to produce or not produce Tracker.

- If you were evaluated using ROI, you probably would not produce Tracker because your ROI would drop from 20% to 18%.
- The problem with this ROI analysis is that it ignores an important variable: the minimum rate of return on a company's operating assets.
- The **minimum rate of return** is the rate at which the Electronics Division can cover its costs and earn a profit.

Assuming that the Electronics Division has a minimum rate of return of 10%, it should invest in Tracker because its ROI of 13% is greater than 10%.

## Residual Income Compared to ROI

To evaluate performance using the minimum rate of return, companies use the residual income approach. **Residual income** is the income that remains after subtracting from the controllable margin the minimum rate of return on a company's average operating assets. The residual income for Tracker would be computed as shown in **Illustration 16A.3**.

ILLUSTRATION 16A.3
**Residual income formula**

$$\text{Controllable Margin} - \left( \begin{array}{c} \text{Minimum Rate of Return} \\ \times \\ \text{Average Operating Assets} \end{array} \right) = \text{Residual Income}$$

$$\$260{,}000 \quad - \quad (10\% \times \$2{,}000{,}000) \quad = \quad \$60{,}000$$

As shown, the residual income related to the Tracker investment is $60,000. **Illustration 16A.4** indicates how residual income changes as the additional investment is made.

ILLUSTRATION 16A.4
**Residual income comparison**

| | Without Tracker | Tracker | With Tracker |
|---|---|---|---|
| Controllable margin (a) | $1,000,000 | $260,000 | $1,260,000 |
| Average operating assets × 10% (b) | 500,000 | 200,000 | 700,000 |
| Residual income [(a) − (b)] | $ 500,000 | $ 60,000 | $ 560,000 |

This example illustrates how performance evaluation based on ROI can be misleading and can even cause managers to reject projects that would actually increase income for the company. As a result, many companies such as **Coca-Cola**, **Briggs & Stratton**, **Eli Lilly**, and **Siemens AG** use residual income (or a variant often referred to as economic value added) to evaluate investment alternatives and measure company performance.

## Residual Income Weakness

It might appear from the above discussion that the goal of any company should be to maximize the total amount of residual income in each division. This goal, however, ignores the fact that one division might use substantially fewer assets to attain the same level of residual income as another division. For example, we know that to produce Tracker, the Electronics Division of Pujols Company used $2,000,000 of average operating assets to generate $260,000 of controllable margin. Now let's say a different division produced a product called SeaDog, which used $4,000,000 to generate $460,000 of controllable margin, as shown in **Illustration 16A.5**.

**Comparison of two products**

|  | Tracker | SeaDog |
|---|---|---|
| Controllable margin (a) | $260,000 | $460,000 |
| Average operating assets × 10% (b) | 200,000 | 400,000 |
| Residual income [(a) − (b)] | $ 60,000 | $ 60,000 |

If the performance of these two investments were evaluated using residual income, they would be considered equal:

- Both products have the same total residual income.
- This ignores, however, the fact that SeaDog required **twice** as many operating assets to achieve the same level of residual income.

# Review and Practice

## Learning Objectives Review

### 1 Describe budgetary control and static budget reports.

Budgetary control consists of (a) preparing periodic budget reports that compare actual results with planned objectives, (b) analyzing the differences to determine their causes, (c) taking appropriate corrective action, and (d) modifying future plans, if necessary.

Static budget reports are useful in evaluating the progress toward planned sales and profit goals. They are also appropriate in assessing a manager's effectiveness in controlling costs when (a) actual activity closely approximates the master budget activity level, and/or (b) the behavior of the costs in response to changes in activity is fixed.

### 2 Prepare flexible budget reports.

To develop the flexible budget it is necessary to: (a) Identify the activity index and the relevant range of activity. (b) Identify the variable costs, and determine the budgeted variable cost per unit of activity for each cost. (c) Identify the fixed costs, and determine the budgeted amount for each cost. (d) Prepare the budget for selected increments of activity within the relevant range. Flexible budget reports permit an evaluation of a manager's performance in controlling production and costs.

### 3 Apply responsibility accounting to cost and profit centers.

Responsibility accounting involves accumulating and reporting revenues and costs on the basis of the individual manager who has the authority to make the day-to-day decisions about the items. The evaluation of a manager's performance is based on the matters directly under the manager's control. In responsibility accounting, it is necessary to distinguish between controllable and noncontrollable fixed costs and to identify three types of responsibility centers: cost, profit, and investment.

Responsibility reports for cost centers compare actual costs with flexible budget data. The reports show only controllable costs, and no distinction is made between variable and fixed costs. Responsibility reports show contribution margin, controllable fixed costs, and controllable margin for each profit center.

### 4 Evaluate performance in investment centers.

The primary basis for evaluating performance in investment centers is return on investment (ROI). The formula for computing ROI for investment centers is Controllable margin ÷ Average operating assets.

### *5 Explain the difference between ROI and residual income.

ROI is controllable margin divided by average operating assets. Residual income is the income that remains after subtracting the minimum rate of return on a company's average operating assets. ROI sometimes provides misleading results because profitable investments are often rejected when the investment reduces ROI but increases overall profitability.

## Decision Tools Review

| Decision Checkpoints | Info Needed for Decision | Tool to Use for Decision | How to Evaluate Results |
| --- | --- | --- | --- |
| Are the cost changes resulting from changed production levels reasonable? | Variable costs projected at different levels of production | Flexible budget | After taking into account different production levels, results are favorable if actual expenses are less than budgeted amounts at the actual activity level. |
| Have the individual managers been held accountable for the costs and revenues under their control? | Relevant costs and revenues, where the individual manager has authority to make day-to-day decisions about the items | Responsibility reports focused on cost centers, profit centers, and investment centers as appropriate | Compare budget to actual costs and revenues for controllable items. |
| Has the investment center performed up to expectations? | Controllable margin (contribution margin minus controllable fixed costs), and average investment center operating assets | Return on investment | Compare actual ROI to expected ROI based on the company's minimum required rate of return. |

## Glossary Review

**Budgetary control** The use of budgets to control operations. (p. 16-3).

**Controllable cost** A cost over which a manager has control. (p. 16-16).

**Controllable margin** Contribution margin less controllable fixed costs. (p. 16-22).

**Cost center** A responsibility center that incurs costs but does not directly generate revenues. (p. 16-19).

**Decentralization** Control of operations is delegated to many managers throughout the organization. (p. 16-15).

**Direct fixed costs** Costs that relate specifically to a responsibility center and are incurred for the sole benefit of the center. (p. 16-22).

**Flexible budget** A projection of budget data for various levels of activity. (p. 16-7).

**Indirect fixed costs** Costs that are incurred for the benefit of more than one profit center. (p. 16-22).

**Investment center** A responsibility center that incurs costs, generates revenues, and has control over decisions regarding the assets available for use. (p. 16-21).

**Management by exception** The review of budget reports by top management focused entirely or primarily on significant differences between actual results and planned objectives. (p. 16-16).

**Noncontrollable costs** Costs incurred indirectly and allocated to a responsibility level that are not controllable at that level. (p. 16-16).

**Profit center** A responsibility center that incurs costs and also generates revenues. (p. 16-21).

**\*Residual income** The income that remains after subtracting from the controllable margin the minimum rate of return on a company's average operating assets. (p. 16-31).

**Responsibility accounting** A part of management accounting that involves identifying and reporting revenues and costs on the basis of the manager who has the authority to make the day-to-day decisions about the items. (p. 16-14).

**Responsibility reporting system** The preparation of reports for each level of responsibility in the company's organization chart. (p. 16-18).

**Return on investment (ROI)** A measure of management's effectiveness in utilizing assets at its disposal in an investment center. (p. 16-24).

**Segment (or division)** An area of responsibility in decentralized operations. (p. 16-15).

**Static budget** A projection of budget data at one level of activity. (p. 16-4).

## Practice Multiple-Choice Questions

1. **(LO 1)** Budgetary control involves all but one of the following:
   a. modifying future plans.
   b. analyzing differences.
   c. using static budgets but **not** flexible budgets.
   d. determining differences between actual and planned results.

2. **(LO 1)** Depending on the nature of the report, budget reports are prepared:
   a. daily.
   b. weekly.
   c. monthly.
   d. All of the answer choices are correct.

**3.** (**LO 1**) A production manager in a manufacturing company would most likely receive a:

    **a.** sales report.

    **b.** income statement.

    **c.** scrap report.

    **d.** shipping department overhead report.

**4.** (**LO 1**) A static budget is:

    **a.** a projection of budget data at several levels of activity within the relevant range of activity.

    **b.** a projection of budget data at a single level of activity.

    **c.** compared to a flexible budget in a budget report.

    **d.** never appropriate in evaluating a manager's effectiveness in controlling costs.

**5.** (**LO 1**) A static budget is useful in controlling costs when cost behavior is:

    **a.** mixed.         **c.** variable.

    **b.** fixed.         **d.** linear.

**6.** (**LO 2**) At zero direct labor hours in a flexible budget graph, the total budgeted cost line intersects the vertical axis at $30,000. At 10,000 direct labor hours, a horizontal line drawn from the total budgeted cost line intersects the vertical axis at $90,000. Fixed and variable costs may be expressed as:

    **a.** $30,000 fixed plus $6 per direct labor hour variable.

    **b.** $30,000 fixed plus $9 per direct labor hour variable.

    **c.** $60,000 fixed plus $3 per direct labor hour variable.

    **d.** $60,000 fixed plus $6 per direct labor hour variable.

**7.** (**LO 2**) At 9,000 direct labor hours, the flexible budget for indirect materials (a variable cost) is $27,000. If $28,000 of indirect materials costs are incurred at 9,200 direct labor hours, the flexible budget report should show the following difference for indirect materials:

    **a.** $1,000 unfavorable.     **c.** $400 favorable.

    **b.** $1,000 favorable.      **d.** $400 unfavorable.

**8.** (**LO 3**) Under responsibility accounting, the evaluation of a manager's performance is based on matters that the manager:

    **a.** directly controls.

    **b.** directly and indirectly controls.

    **c.** indirectly controls.

    **d.** has shared responsibility for with another manager.

**9.** (**LO 3**) Responsibility centers include:

    **a.** cost centers.

    **b.** profit centers.

    **c.** investment centers.

    **d.** All of the answer choices are correct.

**10.** (**LO 3**) Responsibility reports for cost centers:

    **a.** distinguish between fixed and variable costs.

    **b.** use static budget data.

    **c.** include both controllable and noncontrollable costs.

    **d.** include only controllable costs.

**11.** (**LO 3**) The accounting department of a manufacturing company is an example of:

    **a.** a cost center.

    **b.** a profit center.

    **c.** an investment center.

    **d.** a contribution center.

**12.** (**LO 3**) To evaluate the performance of a profit center manager, upper management needs detailed information about:

    **a.** controllable costs.

    **b.** controllable revenues.

    **c.** controllable costs and revenues.

    **d.** controllable costs and revenues and average operating assets.

**13.** (**LO 3**) In a responsibility report for a profit center, controllable fixed costs are deducted from contribution margin to show:

    **a.** profit center margin.     **c.** net income.

    **b.** controllable margin.     **d.** income from operations.

**14.** (**LO 4**) In the formula for return on investment (ROI), the factors for controllable margin and operating assets are, respectively:

    **a.** controllable margin percentage and total operating assets.

    **b.** controllable margin dollars and average operating assets.

    **c.** controllable margin dollars and total assets.

    **d.** controllable margin percentage and average operating assets.

**15.** (**LO 4**) A manager of an investment center can improve ROI by:

    **a.** increasing average operating assets.

    **b.** reducing sales.

    **c.** increasing variable costs.

    **d.** reducing variable and/or controllable fixed costs.

## Solutions

**1. c.** Budgetary control involves using flexible budgets and sometimes static budgets. The other choices are all part of budgetary control.

**2. d.** Budget reports are prepared daily, weekly, or monthly. The other choices are correct, but choice (d) is the better answer.

**3. c.** A production manager in a manufacturing company would most likely receive a scrap report. The other choices are incorrect because (a) top management or a sales manager would most likely receive a sales report, (b) top management would most likely receive

an income statement, and (d) a department manager would most likely receive a shipping department overhead report.

**4. b.** A static budget is a projection of budget data at a single level of activity. The other choices are incorrect because a static budget (a) is a projection of budget data at a single level of activity, not at several levels of activity within the relevant range of activity; (c) is not compared to a flexible budget in a budget report; and (d) is appropriate in evaluating a manager's effectiveness in controlling fixed costs.

**5. b.** A static budget is useful for controlling fixed costs. The other choices are incorrect because a static budget is not useful for controlling (a) mixed costs, (c) variable costs, or (d) linear costs.

**6. a.** The intersection point of $90,000 is total budgeted costs, or budgeted fixed costs plus budgeted variable costs. Fixed costs are $30,000 (amount at zero direct labor hours), so budgeted variable costs are $60,000 [$90,000 (Total costs) − $30,000 (Fixed costs)]. Budgeted variable costs ($60,000) divided by total activity level (10,000 direct labor hours) gives the variable cost per unit of $6 per direct labor hour. The other choices are therefore incorrect.

**7. d.** Budgeted indirect materials per direct labor hour (DLH) is $3 ($27,000 ÷ 9,000). At an activity level of 9,200 direct labor hours, budgeted indirect materials are $27,600 (9,200 × $3 per DLH) but actual indirect materials costs are $28,000, resulting in a $400 unfavorable difference. The other choices are therefore incorrect.

**8. a.** The evaluation of a manager's performance is based only on matters that the manager directly controls. The other choices are therefore incorrect as they include indirect controls and shared responsibility.

**9. d.** Cost centers, profit centers, and investment centers are all responsibility centers. The other choices are correct, but choice (d) is the better answer.

**10. d.** Responsibility reports for cost centers report only controllable costs; they (a) do not distinguish between fixed and variable costs; (b) use flexible budget data, not static budget data; and (c) do not include noncontrollable costs.

**11. a.** The accounting department of a manufacturing company is an example of a cost center, not (b) a profit center, (c) an investment center, or (d) contribution center.

**12. c.** To evaluate the performance of a profit center manager, upper management needs detailed information about controllable costs and revenues, not just (a) controllable costs or (b) controllable revenues. Choice (d) is incorrect because upper management does not need information about average operating assets.

**13. b.** Contribution margin less controllable fixed costs is the controllable margin, not (a) the profit center margin, (c) net income, or (d) income from operations.

**14. b.** The factors in the formula for ROI are controllable margin dollars and average operating assets. The other choices are therefore incorrect.

**15. d.** Reducing variable or controllable fixed costs will cause the controllable margin to increase, which is one way a manager of an investment center can improve ROI. The other choices are incorrect because (a) increasing average operating assets will lower ROI; (b) reducing sales will cause contribution margin to go down, thereby decreasing controllable margin since there will be less contribution margin to cover controllable fixed costs and resulting in lower ROI; and (c) increasing variable costs will cause the contribution margin to be lower, thereby decreasing controllable margin and resulting in lower ROI.

## Practice Brief Exercises

**1. (LO 2)** Borusa Company expects to produce 600,000 units of its product Eldrad in 2022. Monthly production is expected to range from 40,000 to 60,000 units. Budgeted variable manufacturing costs per unit are direct materials $4, direct labor $5, and overhead $8. Budgeted fixed manufacturing costs per unit are $2 for depreciation and $1.50 for supervision. Prepare a flexible manufacturing budget for the relevant range value using 10,000-unit increments.

*Prepare a flexible budget for variable costs.*

### Solution

**1.**

**Borusa Company**
**Monthly Flexible Manufacturing Budget**
**For the Year 2022**

| Activity level | | | |
|---|---|---|---|
| Finished units | 40,000 | 50,000 | 60,000 |
| **Variable costs** | | | |
| Direct materials ($4) | $160,000 | $ 200,000 | $ 240,000 |
| Direct labor ($5) | 200,000 | 250,000 | 300,000 |
| Overhead ($8) | 320,000 | 400,000 | 480,000 |
| Total variable costs ($17) | $680,000 | $ 850,000 | $1,020,000 |
| **Fixed costs** | | | |
| Depreciation* | 100,000 | 100,000 | 100,000 |
| Supervision** | 75,000 | 75,000 | 75,000 |
| Total fixed costs | 175,000 | 175,000 | 175,000 |
| Total costs | $855,000 | $1,025,000 | $1,195,000 |

*($2 × 600,000) ÷ 12; **($1.50 × 600,000) ÷ 12

*Prepare a responsibility report for a profit center.*

**2. (LO 3)** Goth Company accumulates the following summary data for the year ending December 31, 2022, for its Chancellor Division, which it operates as a profit center: sales—$2,000,000 budget, $1,940,000 actual; variable costs—$1,000,000 budget, $980,000 actual; and controllable fixed costs—$300,000 budget, $317,000 actual. Prepare a responsibility report for the Chancellor Division.

### Solution

2.

**Goth Company**
**Chancellor Division**
**Responsibility Report**
**For the Year Ended December 31, 2022**

| | Budget | Actual | Difference<br>Favorable F<br>Unfavorable U |
|---|---|---|---|
| Sales | $2,000,000 | $1,940,000 | $ 60,000 U |
| Variable costs | 1,000,000 | 980,000 | 20,000 F |
| Contribution margin | 1,000,000 | 960,000 | 40,000 U |
| Controllable fixed costs | 300,000 | 317,000 | 17,000 U |
| Controllable margin | $ 700,000 | $ 643,000 | $ 57,000 U |

*Compute return on investment using the ROI formula.*

**3. (LO 4)** For its three investment centers, Usher Company accumulates the following data.

| | I | II | III |
|---|---|---|---|
| Sales | $2,000,000 | $4,000,000 | $4,000,000 |
| Controllable margin | 1,200,000 | 2,100,000 | 2,400,000 |
| Average operating assets | 4,000,000 | 7,000,000 | 9,600,000 |

Compute the return on investment (ROI) for each center.

### Solution

3.

I ($1,200,000 ÷ $4,000,000) = 30%
II ($2,100,000 ÷ $7,000,000) = 30%
III ($2,400,000 ÷ $9,600,000) = 25%

## Practice Exercises

*Prepare flexible manufacturing overhead budget.*

**1. (LO 2)** Felix Company uses a flexible budget for manufacturing overhead based on direct labor hours. Variable manufacturing overhead costs per direct labor hour are as follows.

| Indirect labor | $0.70 |
|---|---|
| Indirect materials | 0.50 |
| Utilities | 0.40 |

Budgeted fixed overhead costs per month are supervision $4,000, depreciation $3,000, and property taxes $800. The company believes it will normally operate in a range of 7,000–10,000 direct labor hours per month.

### Instructions

Prepare a monthly flexible manufacturing overhead budget for 2022 for the expected range of activity, using increments of 1,000 direct labor hours.

## Solution

**1.**

| Felix Company<br>Monthly Flexible Manufacturing Overhead Budget<br>For the Year 2022 | | | | |
|---|---|---|---|---|
| Activity level | | | | |
| Direct labor hours | 7,000 | 8,000 | 9,000 | 10,000 |
| Variable costs | | | | |
| Indirect labor ($.70) | $ 4,900 | $ 5,600 | $ 6,300 | $ 7,000 |
| Indirect materials ($.50) | 3,500 | 4,000 | 4,500 | 5,000 |
| Utilities ($.40) | 2,800 | 3,200 | 3,600 | 4,000 |
| Total variable costs ($1.60) | 11,200 | 12,800 | 14,400 | 16,000 |
| Fixed costs | | | | |
| Supervision | 4,000 | 4,000 | 4,000 | 4,000 |
| Depreciation | 3,000 | 3,000 | 3,000 | 3,000 |
| Property taxes | 800 | 800 | 800 | 800 |
| Total fixed costs | 7,800 | 7,800 | 7,800 | 7,800 |
| Total costs | $19,000 | $20,600 | $22,200 | $23,800 |

**2. (LO 4)** The White Division of Mesin Company reported the following data for the current year.

*Compute ROI for current year and for possible future changes.*

| | |
|---|---|
| Sales | $3,000,000 |
| Variable costs | 2,400,000 |
| Controllable fixed costs | 400,000 |
| Average operating assets | 5,000,000 |

Top management is unhappy with the investment center's return on investment (ROI). It asks the manager of the White Division to submit plans to improve ROI in the next year. The manager believes it is feasible to consider the following independent courses of action.

1. Increase sales by $300,000 with no change in the contribution margin percentage.

2. Reduce variable costs by $100,000.

3. Reduce average operating assets by 4%.

### Instructions

a. Compute the return on investment (ROI) for the current year.

b. Using the ROI formula, compute the ROI under each of the proposed courses of action. (Round to one decimal.)

## Solution

**2. a.** Controllable margin = ($3,000,000 − $2,400,000 − $400,000) = $200,000
   ROI = $200,000 ÷ $5,000,000 = 4%

**b. 1.** Contribution margin percentage is 20%, or [($3,000,000 − $2,400,000) ÷ $3,000,000]
   Increase in controllable margin = $300,000 × 20% = $60,000
   ROI = ($200,000 + $60,000) ÷ $5,000,000 = 5.2%

   **2.** ($200,000 + $100,000) ÷ $5,000,000 = 6%

   **3.** $200,000 ÷ [$5,000,000 − ($5,000,000 × .04)] = 4.2%

## Practice Problem

**(LO 2)** Glenda Company uses a flexible budget for manufacturing overhead based on direct labor hours. For 2022, the master overhead budget for the Packaging Department based on 300,000 direct labor hours was as follows.

*Prepare flexible budget report.*

| Variable Costs | | Fixed Costs | |
|---|---|---|---|
| Indirect labor | $360,000 | Supervision | $ 60,000 |
| Supplies and lubricants | 150,000 | Depreciation | 24,000 |
| Maintenance | 210,000 | Property taxes | 18,000 |
| Utilities | 120,000 | Insurance | 12,000 |
| | $840,000 | | $114,000 |

During July, 24,000 direct labor hours were worked. The company incurred the following variable costs in July: indirect labor $30,200, supplies and lubricants $11,600, maintenance $17,500, and utilities $9,200. Actual fixed overhead costs were the same as monthly budgeted fixed costs.

**Instructions**

Prepare a flexible budget report for the Packaging Department for July.

**Solution**

**Glenda Company**
**Manufacturing Overhead Budget Report (Flexible)**
**Packaging Department**
**For the Month Ended July 31, 2022**

| | | | Difference |
|---|---|---|---|
| | | **Actual** | |
| | **Budget** | **Costs** | **Favorable F** |
| **Direct labor hours (DLH)** | **24,000 DLH** | **24,000 DLH** | **Unfavorable U** |
| Variable costs | | | |
| Indirect labor ($1.20[a]) | $28,800 | $30,200 | $1,400 U |
| Supplies and lubricants ($0.50[a]) | 12,000 | 11,600 | 400 F |
| Maintenance ($0.70[a]) | 16,800 | 17,500 | 700 U |
| Utilities ($0.40[a]) | 9,600 | 9,200 | 400 F |
| Total variable | 67,200 | 68,500 | 1,300 U |
| Fixed costs | | | |
| Supervision | $ 5,000[b] | $ 5,000 | –0– |
| Depreciation | 2,000[b] | 2,000 | –0– |
| Property taxes | 1,500[b] | 1,500 | –0– |
| Insurance | 1,000[b] | 1,000 | –0– |
| Total fixed | 9,500 | 9,500 | –0– |
| Total costs | $76,700 | $78,000 | $1,300 U |

[a]$360,000 ÷ 300,000; $150,000 ÷ 300,000; $210,000 ÷ 300,000; $120,000 ÷ 300,000
[b]Annual cost divided by 12

# WileyPLUS

Brief Exercises, DO IT! Exercises, Exercises, Problems, and many additional resources are available for practice in WileyPLUS.

*Note:* All asterisked Questions, Exercises, and Problems relate to material in the appendix to the chapter.

## Questions

**1. a.** What is budgetary control?

**b.** Fred Barone is describing budgetary control. What steps should be included in Fred's description?

**2.** The following purposes are part of a budgetary reporting system: (a) Determine efficient use of materials. (b) Control overhead costs. (c) Determine whether income objectives are being met. For each purpose, indicate the name of the report, the frequency of the report, and the primary recipient(s) of the report.

**3.** How may a budget report for the second quarter differ from a budget report for the first quarter?

**4.** Ken Bay questions the usefulness of a master sales budget in evaluating sales performance. Is there justification for Ken's concern? Explain.

**5.** Under what circumstances may a static budget be an appropriate basis for evaluating a manager's effectiveness in controlling costs?

**6.** "A flexible budget is really a series of static budgets." Is this true? Why?

**7.** The static manufacturing overhead budget based on 40,000 direct labor hours shows budgeted indirect labor costs of $54,000. During March, the department incurs $64,000 of indirect labor while working 45,000 direct labor hours. Is this a favorable or unfavorable performance? Why?

**8.** A static overhead budget based on 40,000 direct labor hours shows Factory Insurance $6,500 as a fixed cost. At the 50,000 direct labor hours worked in March, factory insurance costs were $6,300. Is this a favorable or unfavorable performance? Why?

**9.** Megan Pedigo is confused about how a flexible budget is prepared. Identify the steps for Megan.

**10.** Cali Company has prepared a graph of flexible budget data. At zero direct labor hours, the total budgeted cost line intersects the vertical axis at $20,000. At 10,000 direct labor hours, the line drawn from the total budgeted cost line intersects the vertical axis at $85,000. How may the fixed and variable costs be expressed?

**11.** The flexible budget formula is fixed costs $50,000 plus variable costs of $4 per direct labor hour. What is the total budgeted cost at (a) 9,000 hours and (b) 12,345 hours?

**12.** What is management by exception? What criteria may be used in identifying exceptions?

**13.** What is responsibility accounting? Explain the purpose of responsibility accounting.

**14.** Eve Rooney is studying for an accounting examination. Describe for Eve what conditions are necessary for responsibility accounting to be used effectively.

**15.** Distinguish between controllable and noncontrollable costs.

**16.** How do responsibility reports differ from budget reports?

**17.** What is the relationship, if any, between a responsibility reporting system and a company's organization chart?

**18.** Distinguish among the three types of responsibility centers.

**19.** (a) What costs are included in a performance report for a cost center? (b) In the report, are variable and fixed costs identified?

**20.** How do direct fixed costs differ from indirect fixed costs? Are both types of fixed costs controllable?

**21.** Jane Nott is confused about controllable margin reported in an income statement for a profit center. How is this margin computed, and what is its primary purpose?

**22.** What is the primary basis for evaluating the performance of the manager of an investment center? Indicate the formula for this basis.

**23.** Explain the ways that ROI can be improved.

**24.** Indicate two behavioral principles that pertain to (a) the manager being evaluated and (b) top management.

**\*25.** What is a major disadvantage of using ROI to evaluate investment and company performance?

**\*26.** What is residual income, and what is one of its major weaknesses?

## Brief Exercises

**BE16.1 (LO 1), AP** For the quarter ended March 31, 2022, Croix Company accumulates the following sales data for its newest guitar, The Edge: $315,000 budget; $305,000 actual. Prepare a static budget report for the quarter.

*Prepare static budget report.*

**BE16.2 (LO 1), AP** For the quarter ended March 31, 2022, Croix Company accumulates the following sales data for its newest guitar, The Edge: $315,000 budget; $305,000 actual. In the second quarter, budgeted sales were $380,000, and actual sales were $384,000. Prepare a static budget report for the second quarter and for the year to date.

*Prepare static budget report for 2 quarters.*

**BE16.3 (LO 2), E** In Rooney Company, direct labor is $20 per hour. The company expects to operate at 10,000 direct labor hours each month. In January 2022, direct labor totaling $206,000 is incurred in working 10,400 hours. Prepare (a) a static budget report and (b) a flexible budget report. Evaluate the usefulness of each report.

*Show usefulness of flexible budgets in evaluating performance.*

**BE16.4 (LO 2), AP** Gundy Company expects to produce 1,200,000 units of Product XX in 2022. Monthly production is expected to range from 80,000 to 120,000 units. Budgeted variable manufacturing costs per unit are direct materials $5, direct labor $6, and overhead $8. Budgeted fixed manufacturing costs per unit for depreciation are $2 and for supervision are $1. Prepare a flexible manufacturing budget for the relevant range value using 20,000 unit increments.

*Prepare a flexible budget for variable costs.*

**BE16.5 (LO 2), AN** Gundy Company expects to produce 1,200,000 units of Product XX in 2022. Monthly production is expected to range from 80,000 to 120,000 units. Budgeted variable manufacturing costs per unit are direct materials $5, direct labor $6, and overhead $8. Budgeted fixed manufacturing costs per unit for depreciation are $2 and for supervision are $1. In March 2022, the company incurs the following costs in producing 100,000 units: direct materials $520,000, direct labor $596,000, and variable overhead $805,000. Actual fixed costs were equal to budgeted fixed costs. Prepare a flexible budget report for March. Were costs controlled?

*Prepare flexible budget report.*

*Prepare a responsibility report for a cost center.*

**BE16.6 (LO 3), AP** In the Assembly Department of Hannon Company, budgeted and actual manufacturing overhead costs for the month of April 2022 were as follows.

|  | Budget | Actual |
|---|---|---|
| Indirect materials | $16,000 | $14,300 |
| Indirect labor | 20,000 | 20,600 |
| Utilities | 10,000 | 10,850 |
| Supervision | 5,000 | 5,000 |

All costs are controllable by the department manager. Prepare a responsibility report for April for the cost center.

*Prepare a responsibility report for a profit center.*

**BE16.7 (LO 3), AP** Torres Company accumulates the following summary data for the year ending December 31, 2022, for its Water Division, which it operates as a profit center: sales—$2,000,000 budget, $2,080,000 actual; variable costs—$1,000,000 budget, $1,050,000 actual; and controllable fixed costs—$300,000 budget, $305,000 actual. Prepare a responsibility report for the Water Division for the year ending December 31, 2022.

*Prepare a responsibility report for an investment center.*

**BE16.8 (LO 4), AP** For the year ending December 31, 2022, Cobb Company accumulates the following data for the Plastics Division which it operates as an investment center: contribution margin—$700,000 budget, $710,000 actual; controllable fixed costs—$300,000 budget, $302,000 actual. Average operating assets for the year were $2,000,000. Prepare a responsibility report for the Plastics Division beginning with contribution margin for the year ending December 31, 2022.

*Compute return on investment using the ROI formula.*

**BE16.9 (LO 4), AP** For its three investment centers, Gerrard Company accumulates the following data:

|  | I | II | III |
|---|---|---|---|
| Sales | $2,000,000 | $4,000,000 | $ 4,000,000 |
| Controllable margin | 1,400,000 | 2,000,000 | 3,600,000 |
| Average operating assets | 5,000,000 | 8,000,000 | 10,000,000 |

Compute the return on investment (ROI) for each center.

*Compute return on investment under changed conditions.*

**BE16.10 (LO 4), AP** For its three investment centers, Gerrard Company accumulates the following data:

|  | I | II | III |
|---|---|---|---|
| Sales | $2,000,000 | $4,000,000 | $ 4,000,000 |
| Controllable margin | 1,400,000 | 2,000,000 | 3,600,000 |
| Average operating assets | 5,000,000 | 8,000,000 | 10,000,000 |

The company expects the following changes for investment centers I, II, and III in the next year: investment center I to increase sales 15%, investment center II to decrease controllable fixed costs $400,000, and investment center III to decrease average operating assets $400,000. Compute the expected return on investment (ROI) for each center. Assume investment center I has a contribution margin percentage of 70%.

*Compute ROI and residual income.*

**\*BE16.11 (LO 5), AP** Sterling, Inc. reports the following financial information for its sports clothing segment.

| | |
|---|---|
| Average operating assets | $3,000,000 |
| Controllable margin | $630,000 |
| Minimum rate of return | 10% |

Compute the return on investment and the residual income for the segment.

*Compute ROI and residual income.*

**\*BE16.12 (LO 5), AP** Presented here is information related to the Southern Division of Lumber, Inc.

| | |
|---|---|
| Contribution margin | $1,200,000 |
| Controllable margin | $800,000 |
| Average operating assets | $4,000,000 |
| Minimum rate of return | 15% |

Compute the Southern Division's return on investment and residual income.

# DO IT! Exercises

*Prepare and evaluate a static budget report.*

**DO IT! 16.1 (LO 1), AP** Wade Company estimates that it will produce 6,000 units of product IOA during the current month. Budgeted variable manufacturing costs per unit are direct materials $7, direct labor $13, and overhead $18. Monthly budgeted fixed manufacturing overhead costs are $8,000 for depreciation and $3,800 for supervision.

In the current month, Wade actually produced 6,500 units and incurred the following costs: direct materials $38,850, direct labor $76,440, variable overhead $116,640, depreciation $8,000, and supervision $4,000.

Prepare a static budget report. *Hint:* The Budget column is based on estimated production while the Actual column is the actual cost incurred during the period. (*Note:* You do not need to prepare the heading.) Were costs controlled? Discuss limitations of the budget.

**DO IT! 16.2 (LO 2), AP** In Pargo Company's flexible budget graph, the fixed cost line and the total budgeted cost line intersect the vertical axis at $90,000. The total budgeted cost line is $350,000 at an activity level of 50,000 direct labor hours. Compute total budgeted costs at 65,000 direct labor hours.

*Compute total budgeted costs in flexible budget.*

**DO IT! 16.3 (LO 3), AP** The Rockies Division operates as a profit center. It reports the following for the year ending December 31, 2022.

*Prepare a responsibility report.*

|  | **Budget** | **Actual** |
|---|---|---|
| Sales | $2,000,000 | $1,890,000 |
| Variable costs | 800,000 | 760,000 |
| Controllable fixed costs | 550,000 | 550,000 |
| Noncontrollable fixed costs | 250,000 | 250,000 |

Prepare a responsibility report for the Rockies Division at December 31, 2022.

**DO IT! 16.4 (LO 4), AP** The service division of Raney Industries reported the following results for 2022.

*Compute ROI and expected return on investments.*

| | |
|---|---|
| Sales | $500,000 |
| Variable costs | 300,000 |
| Controllable fixed costs | 75,000 |
| Average operating assets | 625,000 |

Management is considering the following independent courses of action in 2023 in order to maximize the return on investment for this division.

1. Reduce average operating assets by $125,000, with no change in controllable margin.
2. Increase sales $100,000, with no change in the contribution margin percentage.
a. Compute the controllable margin and the return on investment for 2022.
b. Compute the controllable margin and the expected return on investment for 2023 for each proposed alternative.

# Exercises

**E16.1 (LO 1, 2), K** Connie Rice has prepared the following list of statements about budgetary control.

*Understand the concept of budgetary control.*

1. Budget reports compare actual results with planned objectives.
2. All budget reports are prepared on a weekly basis.
3. Management uses budget reports to analyze differences between actual and planned results and to determine their causes.
4. As a result of analyzing budget reports, management may either take corrective action or modify future plans.
5. Budgetary control works best when a company has an informal reporting system.
6. The primary recipients of the sales report are the sales manager and the production supervisor.
7. The primary recipient of the scrap report is the production manager.
8. A static budget is a projection of budget data at a single level of activity.
9. Top management's reaction to unfavorable differences is not influenced by the materiality of the difference.
10. A static budget is not appropriate in evaluating a manager's effectiveness in controlling costs unless the actual activity level approximates the static budget activity level or the behavior of the costs is fixed.

## Instructions

Identify each statement as true or false. If false, indicate how to correct the statement.

*Prepare and evaluate static budget report.*

**E16.2 (LO 1), AN** Crede Company budgeted selling expenses of $30,000 in January, $35,000 in February, and $40,000 in March. Actual selling expenses were $31,200 in January, $34,525 in February, and $46,000 in March. The company considers any difference that is less than 5% of the budgeted amount to be immaterial.

**Instructions**

a. Prepare a selling expense report that compares budgeted and actual amounts by month and for the year to date.

b. What is the purpose of the report prepared in (a), and who would be the primary recipient?

c. What would be the likely result of management's analysis of the report?

*Prepare flexible manufacturing overhead budget.*

**E16.3 (LO 2), AP** Myers Company uses a flexible budget for manufacturing overhead based on direct labor hours. Variable manufacturing overhead costs per direct labor hour are as follows.

| | |
|---|---|
| Indirect labor | $1.00 |
| Indirect materials | 0.70 |
| Utilities | 0.40 |

Fixed overhead costs per month are supervision $4,000, depreciation $1,200, and property taxes $800. The company believes it will normally operate in a range of 7,000–10,000 direct labor hours per month.

**Instructions**

Prepare a monthly manufacturing overhead flexible budget for 2022 for the expected range of activity, using increments of 1,000 direct labor hours.

*Prepare flexible budget reports for manufacturing overhead costs, and comment on findings.*

**E16.4 (LO 2), AN** **Writing** Using the information in E16.3, assume that in July 2022, Myers Company incurs the following manufacturing overhead costs.

| **Variable Costs** | | **Fixed Costs** | |
|---|---|---|---|
| Indirect labor | $8,800 | Supervision | $4,000 |
| Indirect materials | 5,800 | Depreciation | 1,200 |
| Utilities | 3,200 | Property taxes | 800 |

**Instructions**

a. Prepare a flexible budget performance report, assuming that the company worked 9,000 direct labor hours during the month.

b. Prepare a flexible budget performance report, assuming that the company worked 8,500 direct labor hours during the month.

c. Comment on your findings.

*Prepare flexible selling expense budget.*

**E16.5 (LO 2), AP** Fallon Company uses flexible budgets to control its selling expenses. Monthly sales are expected to range from $170,000 to $200,000. Variable costs and their percentage relationship to sales are sales commissions 6%, advertising 4%, travel 3%, and delivery 2%. Fixed selling expenses will consist of sales salaries $35,000, depreciation on delivery equipment $7,000, and insurance on delivery equipment $1,000.

**Instructions**

Prepare a monthly selling expense flexible budget for each $10,000 increment of sales within the relevant range for the year ending December 31, 2022.

*Prepare flexible budget reports for selling expenses.*

**E16.6 (LO 2), AN** **Writing** The actual selling expenses incurred in March 2022 by Fallon Company are as follows.

| **Variable Expenses** | | **Fixed Expenses** | |
|---|---|---|---|
| Sales commissions | $11,000 | Sales salaries | $35,000 |
| Advertising | 6,900 | Depreciation | 7,000 |
| Travel | 5,100 | Insurance | 1,000 |
| Delivery | 3,450 | | |

**Instructions**

a. Prepare a flexible budget performance report for March using the budget data in E16.5, assuming that March sales were $170,000.

b. Prepare a flexible budget performance report, assuming that March sales were $180,000.

c. Comment on the importance of using flexible budgets in evaluating the performance of the sales manager.

**E16.7 (LO 2), AP** Appliance Possible Inc. (AP) is a manufacturer of toaster ovens. To improve control over operations, the president of AP wants to begin using a flexible budgeting system, rather than use only the current master budget. The following data are available for AP's expected costs at production levels of 90,000, 100,000, and 110,000 units.

*Prepare flexible budget.*

| | |
|---|---|
| Variable costs | |
| Manufacturing | $6 per unit |
| Administrative | $4 per unit |
| Selling | $3 per unit |
| Fixed costs | |
| Manufacturing | $160,000 |
| Administrative | $80,000 |

**Instructions**

a. Prepare a flexible budget for each of the possible production levels: 90,000, 100,000, and 110,000 units.

b. If AP sells the toaster ovens for $16 each, how many units will it have to sell to make a profit of $60,000 before taxes?

(CGA adapted)

**E16.8 (LO 1, 2), E** Service Writing Rensing Groomers is in the dog-grooming business. Its operating costs are described by the following formulas:

*Prepare flexible budget report; compare flexible and static budgets.*

| | |
|---|---|
| Grooming supplies (variable) | $y = \$0 + \$5x$ |
| Direct labor (variable) | $y = \$0 + \$14x$ |
| Overhead (mixed) | $y = \$10,000 + \$1x$ |

Milo, the owner, has determined that direct labor is the cost driver for all three categories of costs.

**Instructions**

a. Prepare a flexible budget for activity levels of 550, 600, and 700 direct labor hours.

b. Explain why the flexible budget is more informative than the static budget.

c. Calculate the total cost per direct labor hour at each of the activity levels specified in part (a).

d. The groomers at Rensing normally work a total of 650 direct labor hours during each month. Each grooming job normally takes a groomer 1.3 hours. Milo wants to earn a profit equal to 40% of the costs incurred. Determine what he should charge each pet owner for grooming.

(CGA adapted)

**E16.9 (LO 1, 2), E** As sales manager, Joe Batista was given the following static budget report for selling expenses in the Clothing Department of Soria Company for the month of October.

*Prepare flexible budget report, and answer question.*

**Soria Company**
**Clothing Department**
**Budget Report**
**For the Month Ended October 31, 2022**

| | Budget | Actual | Difference Favorable F Unfavorable U |
|---|---|---|---|
| Sales in units | 8,000 | 10,000 | 2,000 F |
| Variable expenses | | | |
| Sales commissions | $ 2,400 | $ 2,600 | $  200 U |
| Advertising expense | 720 | 850 | 130 U |
| Travel expense | 3,600 | 4,100 | 500 U |
| Free samples given out | 1,600 | 1,400 | 200 F |
| Total variable | 8,320 | 8,950 | 630 U |
| Fixed expenses | | | |
| Rent | 1,500 | 1,500 | –0– |
| Sales salaries | 1,200 | 1,200 | –0– |
| Office salaries | 800 | 800 | –0– |
| Depreciation—autos (sales staff) | 500 | 500 | –0– |
| Total fixed | 4,000 | 4,000 | –0– |
| Total expenses | $12,320 | $12,950 | $  630 U |

As a result of this budget report, Joe was called into the president's office and congratulated on his fine sales performance. He was reprimanded, however, for allowing his costs to get out of control. Joe knew something was wrong with the performance report that he had been given. However, he was not sure what to do, and comes to you for advice.

**Instructions**

a. Prepare a budget report based on flexible budget data to help Joe.

b. Should Joe have been reprimanded? Explain.

*Prepare flexible budget and responsibility report for manufacturing overhead.*

**E16.10 (LO 2, 3), AP** Chubbs Inc.'s manufacturing overhead budget for the first quarter of 2022 contained the following data.

| Variable Costs | | Fixed Costs | |
|---|---|---|---|
| Indirect materials | $12,000 | Supervisory salaries | $36,000 |
| Indirect labor | 10,000 | Depreciation | 7,000 |
| Utilities | 8,000 | Property taxes and insurance | 8,000 |
| Maintenance | 6,000 | Maintenance | 5,000 |

Actual variable costs were indirect materials $13,500, indirect labor $9,500, utilities $8,700, and maintenance $5,000. Actual fixed costs equaled budgeted costs except for property taxes and insurance, which were $8,300. The actual activity level equaled the budgeted level.

All costs are considered controllable by the production department manager except for depreciation, and property taxes and insurance.

**Instructions**

a. Prepare a manufacturing overhead flexible budget report for the first quarter.

b. Prepare a responsibility report for the first quarter.

*Prepare and discuss a responsibility report.*

**E16.11 (LO 2, 3), AP** **Service** **Writing** UrLink Company is a newly formed company specializing in high-speed Internet service for home and business. The owner, Lenny Kirkland, had divided the company into two segments: Home Internet Service and Business Internet Service. Each segment is run by its own supervisor, while basic selling and administrative services are shared by both segments.

Lenny has asked you to help him create a performance reporting system that will allow him to measure each segment's performance in terms of its profitability. To that end, the following information has been collected on the Home Internet Service segment for the first quarter of 2022.

| | Budget | Actual |
|---|---|---|
| Service revenue | $25,000 | $26,200 |
| Allocated portion of: | | |
| Building depreciation | 11,000 | 11,000 |
| Advertising | 5,000 | 4,200 |
| Billing | 3,500 | 3,000 |
| Property taxes | 1,200 | 1,000 |
| Material and supplies | 1,600 | 1,200 |
| Supervisory salaries | 9,000 | 9,500 |
| Insurance | 4,000 | 3,900 |
| Wages | 3,000 | 3,250 |
| Gas and oil | 2,800 | 3,400 |
| Equipment depreciation | 1,500 | 1,300 |

**Instructions**

a. Prepare a responsibility report for the first quarter of 2022 for the Home Internet Service segment.

b. Write a memo to Lenny Kirkland discussing the principles that should be used when preparing performance reports.

*State total budgeted cost formulas, and prepare flexible budget graph.*

**E16.12 (LO 2), AP** Venetian Company has two production departments, Fabricating and Assembling. At a department managers' meeting, the controller uses flexible budget graphs to explain total budgeted costs. Separate graphs based on direct labor hours are used for each department. The graphs show the following.

1. At zero direct labor hours, the total budgeted cost line and the fixed cost line intersect the vertical axis at $50,000 in the Fabricating Department and $40,000 in the Assembling Department.

2. At normal capacity of 50,000 direct labor hours, the line drawn from the total budgeted cost line intersects the vertical axis at $150,000 in the Fabricating Department, and $120,000 in the Assembling Department.

### Instructions

a. State the total budgeted cost formula for each department.

b. Compute the total budgeted cost for each department, assuming actual direct labor hours worked were 53,000 and 47,000, in the Fabricating and Assembling Departments, respectively.

c. Prepare the flexible budget graph for the Fabricating Department, assuming the maximum direct labor hours in the relevant range is 100,000. Use increments of 10,000 direct labor hours on the horizontal axis and increments of $50,000 on the vertical axis.

**E16.13 (LO 3), AP** Fey Company's organization chart includes the president; the vice president of production; three assembly plants—Dallas, Atlanta, and Tucson; and two departments within each plant—Machining and Finishing. Budget and actual manufacturing cost data for July 2022 are as follows.

*Prepare reports in a responsibility reporting system.*

*Finishing Department—Dallas:* direct materials $42,500 actual, $44,000 budget; direct labor $83,400 actual, $82,000 budget; manufacturing overhead $51,000 actual, $49,200 budget.

*Machining Department—Dallas:* total manufacturing costs $220,000 actual, $219,000 budget.

*Atlanta Plant:* total manufacturing costs $424,000 actual, $420,000 budget.

*Tucson Plant:* total manufacturing costs $494,200 actual, $496,500 budget.

The Dallas plant manager's office costs were $95,000 actual and $92,000 budget. The vice president of production's office costs were $132,000 actual and $130,000 budget. Office costs are not allocated to departments and plants.

### Instructions

Using the format shown in Illustration 16.19, prepare the reports in a responsibility system for:

a. The Finishing Department—Dallas.

b. The plant manager—Dallas.

c. The vice president of production.

**E16.14 (LO 3), AN** The Mixing Department manager of Malone Company is able to control all overhead costs except rent, property taxes, and salaries. Budgeted monthly overhead costs for the Mixing Department, in alphabetical order, are:

*Prepare a responsibility report for a cost center.*

| | | | |
|---|---|---|---|
| Indirect labor | $12,000 | Property taxes | $ 1,000 |
| Indirect materials | 7,700 | Rent | 1,800 |
| Lubricants | 1,675 | Salaries | 10,000 |
| Maintenance | 3,500 | Utilities | 5,000 |

Actual costs incurred for January 2022 are indirect labor $12,250, indirect materials $10,200, lubricants $1,650, maintenance $3,500, property taxes $1,100, rent $1,800, salaries $10,000, and utilities $6,400.

### Instructions

a. Prepare a responsibility report for January 2022.

b. What would be the likely result of management's analysis of the report?

**E16.15 (LO 3), AN** Horatio Inc. has three divisions which are operated as profit centers. Actual operating data for the divisions listed alphabetically are as follows.

*Compute missing amounts in responsibility reports for three profit centers, and prepare a report.*

| Operating Data | Women's Shoes | Men's Shoes | Children's Shoes |
|---|---|---|---|
| Contribution margin | $270,000 | (3) | $180,000 |
| Controllable fixed costs | 100,000 | (4) | (5) |
| Controllable margin | (1) | $ 90,000 | 95,000 |
| Sales | 600,000 | 450,000 | (6) |
| Variable costs | (2) | 320,000 | 250,000 |

### Instructions

a. Compute the missing amounts. Show computations.

b. Prepare a responsibility report for the Women's Shoes Division assuming (1) the data are for the month ended June 30, 2022, and (2) all data equal budget except variable costs which are $5,000 over budget.

*Prepare a responsibility report for a profit center, and compute ROI.*

**E16.16 (LO 3, 4), AP** The Sports Equipment Division of Harrington Company is operated as a profit center. Sales for the division were budgeted for 2022 at $900,000. The only variable costs budgeted for the division were cost of goods sold ($440,000) and selling and administrative ($60,000). Fixed costs were budgeted at $100,000 for cost of goods sold, $90,000 for selling and administrative, and $70,000 for non-controllable fixed costs. Actual results for these items were:

| | |
|---|---:|
| Sales | $880,000 |
| Cost of goods sold | |
|     Variable | 408,000 |
|     Fixed | 105,000 |
| Selling and administrative | |
|     Variable | 61,000 |
|     Fixed | 66,000 |
| Noncontrollable fixed | 90,000 |

**Instructions**

a. Prepare a responsibility report for the Sports Equipment Division for 2022.

b. Assume the division is an investment center, and average operating assets were $1,000,000. The noncontrollable fixed costs are controllable at the investment center level. Compute ROI using the actual amounts.

*Compute ROI for current year and for possible future changes.*

**E16.17 (LO 4), AP** The South Division of Wiig Company reported the following data for the current year.

| | |
|---|---:|
| Sales | $3,000,000 |
| Variable costs | 1,950,000 |
| Controllable fixed costs | 600,000 |
| Average operating assets | 5,000,000 |

Top management is unhappy with the investment center's return on investment (ROI). It asks the manager of the South Division to submit plans to improve ROI in the next year. The manager believes it is feasible to consider the following independent courses of action.

1. Increase sales by $300,000 with no change in the contribution margin percentage.

2. Reduce variable costs by $150,000.

3. Reduce average operating assets by 6.25%.

**Instructions**

a. Compute the return on investment (ROI) for the current year.

b. Using the ROI formula, compute the ROI under each of the proposed courses of action. (Round to one decimal.)

*Prepare a responsibility report for an investment center.*

**E16.18 (LO 4), AP** Service Writing The Dinkle and Frizell Dental Clinic provides both preventive and orthodontic dental services. The two owners, Reese Dinkle and Anita Frizell, operate the clinic as two separate investment centers: Preventive Services and Orthodontic Services. Each of them is in charge of one of the centers: Reese for Preventive Services and Anita for Orthodontic Services. Each month, they prepare an income statement for the two centers to evaluate performance and make decisions about how to improve the operational efficiency and profitability of the clinic.

Recently, they have been concerned about the profitability of the Preventive Services operations. For several months, it has been reporting a loss. The responsibility report for the month of May 2022 is shown here.

| | Actual | Difference from Budget |
|---|---:|---:|
| Service revenue | $40,000 | $1,000 F |
| Variable costs | | |
|     Filling materials | 5,000 | 100 U |
|     Novocain | 3,900 | 100 U |
|     Supplies | 1,900 | 350 F |
|     Dental assistant wages | 2,500 | –0– |
|     Utilities | 500 | 110 U |
| Total variable costs | 13,800 | 40 F |

| | Actual | Difference from Budget |
|---|---|---|
| Fixed costs | | |
| Allocated portion of receptionist's salary | $ 3,000 | $ 200 U |
| Dentist salary | 9,800 | 400 U |
| Equipment depreciation | 6,000 | –0– |
| Allocated portion of building depreciation | 15,000 | 1,000 U |
| Total fixed costs | 33,800 | 1,600 U |
| Operating income (loss) | $(7,600) | $ 560 U |

In addition, the owners know that the investment in operating assets at the beginning of the month was $82,400, and it was $77,600 at the end of the month. They have asked for your assistance in evaluating their current performance reporting system.

**Instructions**

a. Prepare an investment center responsibility report for the Preventative Services segment for May 2022.

b. Write a memo to the owners discussing the deficiencies of their current reporting system.

**E16.19 (LO 4), AN** Service The Ferrell Transportation Company uses a responsibility reporting system to measure the performance of its three investment centers: Planes, Taxis, and Limos. Segment performance is measured using a system of responsibility reports and return on investment calculations. The allocation of resources within the company and the segment managers' bonuses are based in part on the results shown in these reports.

*Prepare missing amounts in responsibility reports for three investment centers.*

Recently, the company was the victim of a computer virus that deleted portions of the company's accounting records. This was discovered when the current period's responsibility reports were being prepared. The printout of the actual operating results, with question marks for missing amounts, appeared as follows.

| | Planes | Taxis | Limos |
|---|---|---|---|
| Service revenue | $ ? | $500,000 | $ ? |
| Variable costs | 5,500,000 | ? | 300,000 |
| Contribution margin | ? | 250,000 | 480,000 |
| Controllable fixed costs | 1,500,000 | ? | ? |
| Controllable margin | ? | 80,000 | 210,000 |
| Average operating assets | 25,000,000 | ? | 1,500,000 |
| Return on investment | 12% | 10% | ? |

**Instructions**

Determine the missing pieces of information above.

**\*E16.20 (LO 5), AN** Presented here is selected information for three regional divisions of Medina Company.

*Compare ROI and residual income.*

| | Divisions | | |
|---|---|---|---|
| | North | West | South |
| Contribution margin | $300,000 | $500,000 | $400,000 |
| Controllable margin | $140,000 | $360,000 | $210,000 |
| Average operating assets | $1,000,000 | $2,000,000 | $1,500,000 |
| Minimum rate of return | 13% | 16% | 10% |

**Instructions**

a. Compute the return on investment for each division.

b. Compute the residual income for each division.

c. Assume that each division has an investment opportunity that would provide a rate of return of 16%.

1. If ROI is used to measure performance, which division or divisions will probably make the additional investment?

2. If residual income is used to measure performance, which division or divisions will probably make the additional investment?

*Fill in information related to ROI and residual income.*

*E16.21 (LO 5), AN** The following is selected financial information for two divisions of Samberg Brewing.

| | Lager | Lite Lager |
|---|---|---|
| Contribution margin | $500,000 | $300,000 |
| Controllable margin | 200,000 | (c) |
| Average operating assets | (a) | $1,200,000 |
| Minimum rate of return | (b) | 11% |
| Return on investment | 16% | (d) |
| Residual income | $100,000 | $156,000 |

**Instructions**

Supply the missing information for the lettered items.

## Problems

*Prepare flexible budget and budget report for manufacturing overhead.*

**P16.1 (LO 2), AN** **Writing** Bumblebee Company estimates that 300,000 direct labor hours will be worked during the coming year, 2022, in the Packaging Department. On this basis, the following budgeted manufacturing overhead cost data are computed for the year.

| Fixed Overhead Costs | | Variable Overhead Costs | |
|---|---|---|---|
| Supervision | $ 96,000 | Indirect labor | $126,000 |
| Depreciation | 72,000 | Indirect materials | 90,000 |
| Insurance | 30,000 | Repairs | 69,000 |
| Rent | 24,000 | Utilities | 72,000 |
| Property taxes | 18,000 | Lubricants | 18,000 |
| | $240,000 | | $375,000 |

It is estimated that direct labor hours worked each month will range from 27,000 to 36,000 hours.

During October, 27,000 direct labor hours were worked and the following overhead costs were incurred.

Fixed overhead costs: supervision $8,000, depreciation $6,000, insurance $2,460, rent $2,000, and property taxes $1,500.

Variable overhead costs: indirect labor $12,432, indirect materials $7,680, repairs $6,100, utilities $6,840, and lubricants $1,920.

**Instructions**

a. Total costs: DLH 27,000, $53,750; DLH 36,000, $65,000

b. Total $1,182 U

a. Prepare a monthly manufacturing overhead flexible budget for each increment of 3,000 direct labor hours over the relevant range for the year ending December 31, 2022.

b. Prepare a flexible budget report for October.

c. Comment on management's efficiency in controlling manufacturing overhead costs in October.

*Prepare flexible budget, budget report, and graph for manufacturing overhead.*

**P16.2 (LO 2), E** Zelmer Company manufactures tablecloths. Sales have grown rapidly over the past 2 years. As a result, the president has installed a budgetary control system for 2022. The following data were used in developing the master manufacturing overhead budget for the Ironing Department, which is based on an activity index of direct labor hours.

| Variable Costs | Rate per Direct Labor Hour | Annual Fixed Costs | |
|---|---|---|---|
| Indirect labor | $0.40 | Supervision | $48,000 |
| Indirect materials | 0.50 | Depreciation | 18,000 |
| Factory utilities | 0.30 | Insurance | 12,000 |
| Factory repairs | 0.20 | Rent | 30,000 |

The master overhead budget was prepared on the expectation that 480,000 direct labor hours will be worked during the year. In June, 41,000 direct labor hours were worked. At that level of activity, actual costs were as shown below.

Variable—per direct labor hour: indirect labor $0.44, indirect materials $0.48, factory utilities $0.32, and factory repairs $0.25.

Fixed: same as budgeted.

**Instructions**

a. Prepare a monthly manufacturing overhead flexible budget for the year ending December 31, 2022, assuming production levels range from 35,000 to 50,000 direct labor hours. Use increments of 5,000 direct labor hours.

b. Prepare a budget report for June comparing actual results with budget data based on the flexible budget.

c. Were costs effectively controlled? Explain.

d. State the formula for computing the total budgeted costs for the Ironing Department.

e. Prepare the flexible budget graph, showing total budgeted costs at 35,000 and 45,000 direct labor hours. Use increments of 5,000 direct labor hours on the horizontal axis and increments of $10,000 on the vertical axis.

a. Total costs: 35,000 DLH, $58,000; 50,000 DLH, $79,000

b. Budget $66,400
Actual $70,090

**P16.3 (LO 1, 2), AN** Ratchet Company uses budgets in controlling costs. The August 2022 budget report for the company's Assembling Department is as follows.

*State total budgeted cost formula, and prepare flexible budget reports for 2 time periods.*

**Ratchet Company**
**Budget Report**
**Assembling Department**
**For the Month Ended August 31, 2022**

| Manufacturing Costs | Budget | Actual | Difference<br>Favorable F<br>Unfavorable U |
|---|---|---|---|
| Variable costs | | | |
| Direct materials | $ 48,000 | $ 47,000 | $1,000 F |
| Direct labor | 54,000 | 51,200 | 2,800 F |
| Indirect materials | 24,000 | 24,200 | 200 U |
| Indirect labor | 18,000 | 17,500 | 500 F |
| Utilities | 15,000 | 14,900 | 100 F |
| Maintenance | 12,000 | 12,400 | 400 U |
| Total variable | 171,000 | 167,200 | 3,800 F |
| Fixed costs | | | |
| Rent | 12,000 | 12,000 | –0– |
| Supervision | 17,000 | 17,000 | –0– |
| Depreciation | 6,000 | 6,000 | –0– |
| Total fixed | 35,000 | 35,000 | –0– |
| Total costs | $206,000 | $202,200 | $3,800 F |

The monthly budget amounts in the report were based on an expected production of 60,000 units per month or 720,000 units per year. The Assembling Department manager is pleased with the report and expects a raise, or at least praise for a job well done. The company president, however, is unhappy with the results for August because only 58,000 units were produced.

**Instructions**

a. State the total monthly budgeted cost formula.

b. Prepare a budget report for August using flexible budget data. Why does this report provide a better basis for evaluating performance than the report based on static budget data?

c. In September, 64,000 units were produced. Prepare the budget report using flexible budget data, assuming (1) each variable cost was 10% higher than its actual cost in August, and (2) fixed costs were the same in September as in August.

b. Budget $200,300

c. Budget $217,400
Actual $218,920

**P16.4 (LO 3), AN** **Writing** Clarke Inc. operates the Patio Furniture Division as a profit center. Operating data for this division for the year ended December 31, 2022, are shown here.

*Prepare responsibility report for a profit center.*

| | Budget | Difference from Budget |
|---|---|---|
| Sales | $2,500,000 | $50,000 F |
| Cost of goods sold | | |
| Variable | 1,300,000 | 41,000 F |
| Controllable fixed | 200,000 | 3,000 U |
| Selling and administrative | | |
| Variable | 220,000 | 6,000 U |
| Controllable fixed | 50,000 | 2,000 U |
| Noncontrollable fixed costs | 70,000 | 4,000 U |

In addition, Clarke incurs $180,000 of indirect fixed costs that were budgeted at $175,000. Twenty percent (20%) of these costs are allocated to the Patio Furniture Division.

**Instructions**

*a. Contribution margin $85,000 F*
*Controllable margin $80,000 F*

a.  Prepare a responsibility report for the Patio Furniture Division for the year.

b.  Comment on the manager's performance in controlling revenues and costs.

c.  Identify any costs excluded from the responsibility report and explain why they were excluded.

*Prepare responsibility report for an investment center, and compute ROI.*

**P16.5 (LO 4), E**  Optimus Company manufactures a variety of tools and industrial equipment. The company operates through three divisions. Each division is an investment center. Operating data for the Home Division for the year ended December 31, 2022, and relevant budget data are as follows.

| | Actual | Comparison with Budget |
|---|---|---|
| Sales | $1,400,000 | $100,000 favorable |
| Variable cost of goods sold | 665,000 | 45,000 unfavorable |
| Variable selling and administrative expenses | 125,000 | 25,000 unfavorable |
| Controllable fixed cost of goods sold | 170,000 | On target |
| Controllable fixed selling and administrative expenses | 80,000 | On target |

Average operating assets for the year for the Home Division were $2,000,000 which was also the budgeted amount.

**Instructions**

*a. Controllable margin: Budget $330; Actual $360*

a.  Prepare a responsibility report (in thousands of dollars) for the Home Division.

b.  Evaluate the manager's performance. Which items will likely be investigated by top management?

c.  Compute the expected ROI in 2022 for the Home Division, assuming the following independent changes to actual data.

   1.  Variable selling and administrative expenses are decreased by 4%.

   2.  Average operating assets are decreased by 10%.

   3.  Sales are increased by $200,000, and this increase is expected to increase contribution margin by $80,000.

*Prepare reports for cost centers under responsibility accounting, and comment on performance of managers.*

**P16.6 (LO 3), AN**  Durham Company uses a responsibility reporting system. It has divisions in Denver, Seattle, and San Diego. Each division has three production departments: Cutting, Shaping, and Finishing. The responsibility for each department rests with a manager who reports to the division production manager. Each division manager reports to the vice president of production. There are also vice presidents for marketing and finance. All vice presidents report to the president.

In January 2022, controllable actual and budget manufacturing overhead cost data for the departments and divisions were as shown here.

| Manufacturing Overhead | Actual | Budget |
|---|---|---|
| Individual costs—Cutting Department—Seattle | | |
| Indirect labor | $ 73,000 | $ 70,000 |
| Indirect materials | 47,900 | 46,000 |
| Maintenance | 20,500 | 18,000 |
| Utilities | 20,100 | 17,000 |
| Supervision | 22,000 | 20,000 |
| | $183,500 | $171,000 |
| Total costs | | |
| Shaping Department—Seattle | $158,000 | $148,000 |
| Finishing Department—Seattle | 210,000 | 205,000 |
| Denver division | 678,000 | 673,000 |
| San Diego division | 722,000 | 715,000 |

Additional overhead costs were incurred as follows: Seattle division production manager—actual costs $52,500, budget $51,000; vice president of production—actual costs $65,000, budget $64,000; president—actual costs $76,400, budget $74,200. These expenses are not allocated.

The vice presidents who report to the president, other than the vice president of production, had the following expenses.

| Vice President | Actual | Budget |
|---|---|---|
| Marketing | $133,600 | $130,000 |
| Finance | 109,000 | 104,000 |

### Instructions

Using the format in Illustration 16.19, prepare the following responsibility reports.

**a.** Manufacturing overhead—Cutting Department manager—Seattle division.

**b.** Manufacturing overhead—Seattle division manager.

**c.** Manufacturing overhead—vice president of production.

**d.** Manufacturing overhead and expenses—president.

a. $12,500 U

b. $29,000 U

c. $42,000 U

d. $52,800 U

***P16.7  (LO 5), AN  Writing** Sentinel Industries has manufactured prefabricated houses for over 20 years. The houses are constructed in sections to be assembled on customers' lots. Sentinel expanded into the precut housing market when it acquired Jensen Company, one of its suppliers. In this market, various types of lumber are precut into the appropriate lengths, banded into packages, and shipped to customers' lots for assembly. Sentinel designated the Jensen Division as an investment center.

*Compare ROI and residual income.*

Sentinel uses return on investment (ROI) as a performance measure with investment defined as average operating assets. Management bonuses are based in part on ROI. All investments are expected to earn a minimum rate of return of 18%. Jensen's ROI has ranged from 20.1% to 23.5% since it was acquired. Jensen had an investment opportunity in 2022 that had an estimated ROI of 19%. Jensen management decided against the investment because it believed the investment would decrease the division's overall ROI.

Selected financial information for Jensen is presented here. The division's average operating assets were $12,300,000 for the year 2022.

**Sentinel Industries**
**Jensen Division**
**Selected Financial Information**
**For the Year Ended December 31, 2022**

| | |
|---|---|
| Sales | $24,000,000 |
| Contribution margin | 9,100,000 |
| Controllable margin | 2,460,000 |

### Instructions

**a.** Calculate the following performance measures for 2022 for the Jensen Division.

**1.** Return on investment (ROI).

**2.** Residual income.

**b.** Would the management of Jensen Division have been more likely to accept the investment opportunity it had in 2022 if residual income were used as a performance measure instead of ROI? Explain your answer.

(CMA adapted)

## Continuing Cases

 **Excel**

### Current Designs

**CD16** The **Current Designs** staff has prepared the annual manufacturing budget for the rotomolded line based on an estimated annual production of 4,000 kayaks during 2022. Each kayak will require 54 pounds of polyethylene powder and a finishing kit (rope, seat, hardware, etc.). The polyethylene powder used in these kayaks costs $1.50 per pound, and the finishing kits cost $170 each. Each kayak will use two kinds of labor—2 hours of type I labor from people who run the oven and trim the plastic, and 3 hours of work from type II workers who attach the hatches and seat and other hardware. The type I employees are paid $15 per hour, and the type II are paid $12 per hour.

Manufacturing overhead is budgeted at $396,000 for 2022, broken down as follows.

| | |
|---|---:|
| **Variable costs** | |
| Indirect materials | $ 40,000 |
| Manufacturing supplies | 53,800 |
| Maintenance and utilities | 88,000 |
| | 181,800 |
| | |
| **Fixed costs** | |
| Supervision | 90,000 |
| Insurance | 14,400 |
| Depreciation | 109,800 |
| | 214,200 |
| Total | $396,000 |

During the first quarter, ended March 31, 2022, 1,050 units were actually produced with the following costs.

| | |
|---|---:|
| Polyethylene powder | $ 87,000 |
| Finishing kits | 178,840 |
| Type I labor | 31,500 |
| Type II labor | 39,060 |
| Indirect materials | 10,500 |
| Manufacturing supplies | 14,150 |
| Maintenance and utilities | 26,000 |
| Supervision | 20,000 |
| Insurance | 3,600 |
| Depreciation | 27,450 |
| Total | $438,100 |

### Instructions

**a.** Prepare the annual manufacturing budget for 2022, assuming that 4,000 kayaks will be produced.

**b.** Prepare the flexible budget for manufacturing for the quarter ended March 31, 2022. Assume activity levels of 900, 1,000, and 1,050 units.

**c.** Assuming the rotomolded line is treated as a cost center, prepare a flexible budget report for manufacturing for the quarter ended March 31, 2022, when 1,050 units were produced.

## Waterways Corporation

(*Note:* This is a continuation of the Waterways case from Chapters 11–15.)

**WC16** Waterways Corporation is continuing its budget preparations. This problem gives you static budget information as well as actual overhead costs, and asks you to calculate amounts related to budgetary control and responsibility accounting.

*Go to WileyPLUS for complete case details and instructions.*

## Expand Your Critical Thinking

### Decision-Making Across the Organization

**CT16.1** Service Green Pastures is a 400-acre farm on the outskirts of the Kentucky Bluegrass, specializing in the boarding of broodmares and their foals. A recent economic downturn in the thoroughbred industry has made the boarding business extremely competitive. To meet the competition, Green Pastures planned in 2022 to entertain clients, advertise more extensively, and absorb expenses formerly paid by clients such as veterinary and blacksmith fees.

The budget report for 2022 follows. As shown, the static income statement budget for the year is based on an expected 21,900 boarding days at $25 per mare. The variable expenses per mare per day were budgeted: feed $5, veterinary fees $3, blacksmith fees $0.25, and supplies $0.55. All other budgeted expenses were either semifixed or fixed.

During the year, management decided not to replace a worker who quit in March, but it did issue a new advertising brochure and did more entertaining of clients.[1]

**Green Pastures**
**Static Budget Income Statement**
**For the Year Ended December 31, 2022**

| | Actual | Master Budget | Difference |
|---|---|---|---|
| Number of mares | 52 | 60 | 8 U |
| Number of boarding days | 19,000 | 21,900 | 2,900 U |
| Service revenue | $380,000 | $547,500 | $167,500 U |
| Less: Variable expenses | | | |
|   Feed | 104,390 | 109,500 | 5,110 F |
|   Veterinary fees | 58,838 | 65,700 | 6,862 F |
|   Blacksmith fees | 4,984 | 5,475 | 491 F |
|   Supplies | 10,178 | 12,045 | 1,867 F |
| Total variable expenses | 178,390 | 192,720 | 14,330 F |
| Contribution margin | 201,610 | 354,780 | 153,170 U |
| Less: Fixed expenses | | | |
|   Depreciation | 40,000 | 40,000 | –0– |
|   Insurance | 11,000 | 11,000 | –0– |
|   Utilities | 12,000 | 14,000 | 2,000 F |
|   Repairs and maintenance | 10,000 | 11,000 | 1,000 F |
|   Labor | 88,000 | 95,000 | 7,000 F |
|   Advertisement | 12,000 | 8,000 | 4,000 U |
|   Entertainment | 7,000 | 5,000 | 2,000 U |
| Total fixed expenses | 180,000 | 184,000 | 4,000 F |
| Net income | $ 21,610 | $170,780 | $149,170 U |

[1]Data for this case are based on Hans Sprohge and John Talbott, "New Applications for Variance Analysis," *Journal of Accountancy* (AICPA, New York), April 1989, pp. 137–141.

**Instructions**

With the class divided into groups, answer the following.

a. Based on the static budget report:
   1. What was the primary cause(s) of the decline in net income?
   2. Did management do a good, average, or poor job of controlling expenses?
   3. Were management's decisions to stay competitive sound?

b. Prepare a flexible budget report for the year.

c. Based on the flexible budget report, answer the three questions in part (a) above.

d. What course of action do you recommend for the management of Green Pastures?

## Managerial Analysis

**CT16.2** Lanier Company manufactures expensive watch cases sold as souvenirs. Three of its sales departments are Retail Sales, Wholesale Sales, and Outlet Sales. The Retail Sales Department is a profit center. The Wholesale Sales Department is a cost center. Its managers merely take orders from customers who purchase through the company's wholesale catalog. The Outlet Sales Department is an investment center because each manager is given full responsibility for an outlet store location. The manager can hire and discharge employees, purchase, maintain, and sell equipment, and in general is fairly independent of company control.

Mary Gammel is a manager in the Retail Sales Department. Stephen Flott manages the Wholesale Sales Department. Jose Gomez manages the Golden Gate Club outlet store in San Francisco. The following are the budget responsibility reports for each of the three departments.

| | Budget | | |
|---|---|---|---|
| | **Retail Sales** | **Wholesale Sales** | **Outlet Sales** |
| Sales | $ 750,000 | $ 400,000 | $200,000 |
| Variable costs | | | |
| Cost of goods sold | 150,000 | 100,000 | 25,000 |
| Advertising | 100,000 | 30,000 | 5,000 |
| Sales salaries | 75,000 | 15,000 | 3,000 |
| Printing | 10,000 | 20,000 | 5,000 |
| Travel | 20,000 | 30,000 | 2,000 |
| | | | |
| Fixed costs | | | |
| Rent | 50,000 | 30,000 | 10,000 |
| Insurance | 5,000 | 2,000 | 1,000 |
| Depreciation | 75,000 | 100,000 | 40,000 |
| Investment in assets | 1,000,000 | 1,200,000 | 800,000 |

| | Actual Results | | |
|---|---|---|---|
| | **Retail Sales** | **Wholesale Sales** | **Outlet Sales** |
| Sales | $ 750,000 | $ 400,000 | $200,000 |
| Variable costs | | | |
| Cost of goods sold | 192,000 | 122,000 | 26,500 |
| Advertising | 100,000 | 30,000 | 5,000 |
| Sales salaries | 75,000 | 15,000 | 3,000 |
| Printing | 10,000 | 20,000 | 5,000 |
| Travel | 14,000 | 21,000 | 1,500 |
| | | | |
| Fixed costs | | | |
| Rent | 40,000 | 50,000 | 12,300 |
| Insurance | 5,000 | 2,000 | 1,000 |
| Depreciation | 80,000 | 90,000 | 56,000 |
| Investment in assets | 1,000,000 | 1,200,000 | 800,000 |

**Instructions**

a. Determine which of the items should be included in the responsibility report for each of the three managers.

b. Compare the budgeted measures with the actual results. Decide which results should be called to the attention of each manager.

## Real-World Focus

**CT16.3 CA Technologies**, the world's leading business software company, delivers the end-to-end infrastructure to enable e-business through innovative technology, services, and education. Recently, CA Technologies had 19,000 employees worldwide and revenue of over $6 billion.

    The following information is from the company's annual report.

| CA Technologies |
|---|
| **Management Discussion** |
| The Company has experienced a pattern of business whereby revenue for its third and fourth fiscal quarters reflects an increase over first- and second-quarter revenue. The Company attributes this increase to clients' increased spending at the end of their calendar year budgetary periods and the culmination of its annual sales plan. Since the Company's costs do not increase proportionately with the third- and fourth-quarters' increase in revenue, the higher revenue in these quarters results in greater profit margins and income. Fourth-quarter profitability is traditionally affected by significant new hirings, training, and education expenditures for the succeeding year. |

### Instructions

**a.** Why don't the company's costs increase proportionately as the revenues increase in the third and fourth quarters?

**b.** What type of budgeting seems appropriate for the CA Technologies situation?

## Communication Activity

**CT16.4** The manufacturing overhead budget for Fleming Company contains the following items.

| Variable costs | | Fixed costs | |
|---|---|---|---|
| Indirect materials | $22,000 | Supervision | $17,000 |
| Indirect labor | 12,000 | Inspection costs | 1,000 |
| Maintenance expense | 10,000 | Insurance expense | 2,000 |
| Manufacturing supplies | 6,000 | Depreciation | 15,000 |
| Total variable | $50,000 | Total fixed | $35,000 |

The budget was based on an estimated 2,000 units being produced. During the past month, 1,500 units were produced, and the following costs incurred.

| Variable costs | | Fixed costs | |
|---|---|---|---|
| Indirect materials | $22,500 | Supervision | $18,400 |
| Indirect labor | 13,500 | Inspection costs | 1,200 |
| Maintenance expense | 8,200 | Insurance expense | 2,200 |
| Manufacturing supplies | 5,000 | Depreciation | 14,700 |
| Total variable | $49,200 | Total fixed | $36,500 |

### Instructions

**a.** Determine which items would be controllable by Fred Bedner, the production manager.

**b.** How much should have been spent during the month for the manufacture of the 1,500 units?

**c.** Prepare a flexible manufacturing overhead budget report for Mr. Bedner.

**d.** Prepare a responsibility report. Include only the costs that would have been controllable by Mr. Bedner. Assume that the supervision cost above includes Mr. Bedner's monthly salary of $10,000, both at budget and actual. In an attached memo, describe clearly for Mr. Bedner the areas in which his performance needs to be improved.

## Ethics Case

**CT16.5** American Products Corporation participates in a highly competitive industry. In order to meet this competition and achieve profit goals, the company has chosen the decentralized form of organization. Each manager of a decentralized investment center is measured on the basis of profit contribution, market penetration, and return on investment. Failure to meet the objectives established by corporate management for these measures has not been acceptable and usually has resulted in demotion or dismissal of an investment center manager.

An anonymous survey of managers in the company revealed that the managers feel the pressure to compromise their personal ethical standards to achieve the corporate objectives. For example, at certain plant locations there was pressure to reduce quality control to a level which could not assure that all unsafe products would be rejected. Also, sales personnel were encouraged to use questionable sales tactics to obtain orders, including gifts and other incentives to purchasing agents.

The chief executive officer is disturbed by the survey findings. In his opinion, such behavior cannot be condoned by the company. He concludes that the company should do something about this problem.

### Instructions

**a.** Who are the stakeholders (the affected parties) in this situation?

**b.** Identify the ethical implications, conflicts, or dilemmas in the above described situation.

**c.** What might the company do to reduce the pressures on managers and to decrease the ethical conflicts?

(CMA adapted)

## All About You

**CT16.6** It is one thing to prepare a personal budget; it is another thing to stick to it. Financial planners have suggested various mechanisms to provide support for enforcing personal budgets. One approach is called "envelope budgeting."

### Instructions

Do an Internet search on "envelope system money management" and then answer the following questions.

**a.** Summarize the process of envelope budgeting.

**b.** Evaluate whether you think you would benefit from envelope budgeting. What do you think are its strengths and weaknesses relative to your situation?

## Considering Your Costs and Benefits

**CT16.7** Preparing a personal budget is a great first step toward control over your personal finances. It is especially useful to prepare a budget when you face a big decision. For most people, the biggest decision they will ever make is whether to purchase a house. The percentage of people in the United States who own a home is high compared to many other countries. This is partially the result of U.S. government programs and incentives that encourage home ownership. For example, the interest on a home mortgage is tax-deductible, subject to some limitations.

Before purchasing a house, you should first consider whether buying it is the best choice for you. Suppose you just graduated from college and are moving to a new community. Should you immediately buy a new home?

**YES:** If I purchase a home, I am making my housing cost more like a "fixed cost," thus minimizing increases in my future housing costs. Also, I benefit from the appreciation in my home's value. Although recent turbulence in the economy has caused home prices in many communities to decline, I know that over the long term, home prices have increased across the country.

**NO:** I just moved to a new town, so I don't know the housing market. I am new to my job, so I don't know whether I will like it or my new community. Also, if my job does go well, it is likely that my income will increase in the next few years, so I will able to afford a better house if I wait. Therefore, the flexibility provided by renting is very valuable to me at this point in my life.

### Instructions

Write a response indicating your position regarding this situation. Provide support for your view.

## CHAPTER 17

JeffG/Alamy Stock Photo

# Standard Costs and Balanced Scorecard

## Chapter Preview

Standards are a fact of life. You met the admission standards for the school you are attending. The vehicle that you drive had to meet certain governmental emissions standards. The hamburgers and salads that you eat in a restaurant have to meet certain health and nutritional standards before they can be sold. As described in the following Feature Story, **Starbucks** has standards for the costs of its materials, labor, and overhead. The reason for standards in these cases is very simple: They help to ensure that overall product quality is high while keeping costs under control.

In this chapter, we continue the study of controlling costs. You will learn how to evaluate performance using standard costs and a balanced scorecard.

# Feature Story

## 80,000 Different Caffeinated Combinations

When Howard Schultz purchased a small Seattle coffee-roasting business in 1987, he set out to create a new kind of company. He thought the company should sell coffee by the cup in its store, in addition to the bags of roasted beans it already sold. He also saw the store as a place where you could order a beverage, custom-made to your unique tastes, in an environment that would give you the sense that you had escaped, if only momentarily, from the chaos we call life. Finally, Schultz believed that the company would prosper if employees shared in its success.

In a little more than 20 years, Howard Schultz's company, **Starbucks**, grew from that one store to over 17,000 locations in 54 countries. That is an incredible rate of growth, and it didn't happen by accident. While Starbucks does everything it can to maximize the customer's experience, behind the scenes it needs to control costs. Consider the almost infinite options of beverage combinations and variations at Starbucks. The company must determine the most efficient way to make each beverage, it must communicate these methods in the form of standards to its employees, and it must then evaluate whether those standards are being met.

Schultz's book, *Onward: How Starbucks Fought for Its Life Without Losing Its Soul*, describes a painful period in which Starbucks had to close 600 stores and lay off thousands of employees. However, when a prominent shareholder suggested that the company eliminate its employee healthcare plan, as so many other companies had done, Schultz refused. The healthcare plan represented one of the company's most tangible commitments to employee well-being as well as to corporate social responsibility. Schultz feels strongly that providing health care to the company's employees is an essential part of the standard cost of a cup of Starbucks' coffee.

# Chapter Outline

| LEARNING OBJECTIVES | REVIEW | PRACTICE |
|---|---|---|
| **LO 1** Describe standard costs. | • Distinguishing between standards and budgets <br> • Setting standard costs | **DO IT! 1** Standard Costs |
| **LO 2** Determine direct materials variances. | • Analyzing and reporting variances <br> • Calculating direct materials variances | **DO IT! 2** Direct Materials Variances |
| **LO 3** Determine direct labor and total manufacturing overhead variances. | • Direct labor variances <br> • Manufacturing overhead variances | **DO IT! 3** Labor and Manufacturing Overhead Variances |
| **LO 4** Prepare variance reports and balanced scorecards. | • Reporting variances <br> • Income statement presentation of variances <br> • Balanced scorecard | **DO IT! 4** Reporting Variances |

**Go to the Review and Practice section at the end of the chapter for a targeted summary and practice applications with solutions.**

**Visit WileyPLUS for additional tutorials and practice opportunities.**

# Overview of Standard Costs

Standards are common in business.

- Those imposed by government agencies are often called **regulations**. They include the Fair Labor Standards Act, the Equal Employment Opportunity Act, and a multitude of environmental standards.
- Standards established internally by a company may extend to personnel matters, such as employee absenteeism and ethical codes of conduct, quality control standards for products, and standard costs for goods and services.
- In managerial accounting, **standard costs** are predetermined unit costs, which companies use as measures of performance.

We focus on manufacturing operations in this chapter. But you should recognize that standard costs also apply to many types of service businesses as well. For example, a fast-food restaurant such as **McDonald's** knows the price it should pay for pickles, beef, buns, and other ingredients. It also knows how much time it should take an employee to flip hamburgers. If the company pays too much for pickles or if employees take too much time to prepare Big Macs, McDonald's notices the deviations from standards and takes corrective action. Not-for-profit entities, such as universities, charitable organizations, and governmental agencies, also may use standard costs as measures of performance.

Standard costs offer a number of advantages to an organization, as shown in **Illustration 17.1**.

**ILLUSTRATION 17.1**  **Advantages of standard costs**

### Advantages of Standard Costs

Facilitate management planning

Promote greater economy by making employees more "cost-conscious"

Useful in setting selling prices

Contribute to management control by providing basis for evaluation of cost control

Useful in highlighting variances in management by exception

Simplify costing of inventories and reduce clerical costs

- The organization will realize these advantages only when standard costs are carefully established and prudently used.
- Using standards solely as a way to place blame can have a negative effect on managers and employees.
- To minimize this effect, many companies offer wage incentives to those who meet the standards.

## Distinguishing Between Standards and Budgets

Both **standards** and **budgets** are predetermined costs, and both contribute to management planning and control. There is a difference, however, in the way the terms are expressed.

- A standard is a **unit** amount.
- A budget is a **total** amount.

Thus, it is customary to state that the **standard cost** of direct labor for a unit of product is, say, $10. If the company produces 5,000 units of the product, the $50,000 of direct labor is the **budgeted** labor cost. A standard is the budgeted **cost per unit** of product. A standard is therefore concerned with each individual cost component that makes up the entire budget.

There are important accounting differences between budgets and standards.

- Except in the application of manufacturing overhead to jobs and processes, budget data are not incorporated in cost accounting systems.
- A company may report its inventories at standard cost in its financial statements, but it would not report inventories at budgeted costs.

## Setting Standard Costs

The setting of standard costs to produce a unit of product is a difficult task. It requires input from all persons who have responsibility for costs and quantities.

- To determine the standard cost of direct materials, management consults purchasing agents, product managers, quality control engineers, and production supervisors.
- In setting the standard cost for direct labor, managers obtain pay rate data from the payroll department.
- Industrial engineers generally determine the labor time requirements.
- The managerial accountant provides important input for the standard-setting process by accumulating historical cost data and by knowing how costs respond to changes in activity levels.

To be effective in controlling costs, standard costs need to be current at all times. Thus, standards are under continuous review. They should change whenever managers determine that the existing standard is not a good measure of performance. Circumstances that warrant revision of a standard include changed wage rates resulting from a new union contract, a change in product specifications, or the implementation of a new manufacturing method.

### Ideal versus Normal Standards

Companies set standards at one of two levels: ideal or normal.

- **Ideal standards** represent optimum levels of performance under perfect operating conditions.
- **Normal standards** represent efficient levels of performance that are attainable under expected operating conditions.

Some managers believe ideal standards will stimulate workers to ever-increasing improvement. However, most managers believe that ideal standards lower the morale of the workforce because they are difficult, if not impossible, to meet (see **Ethics Note**). Very few companies use ideal standards.

Most companies that use standards set them at a normal level. Properly set, normal standards should be **rigorous but attainable**. Normal standards allow for rest periods, machine breakdowns, and other "normal" contingencies in the production process. In the remainder of this chapter, we will assume that standard costs are set at a normal level.

---

### Accounting Across the Organization    U.S. Navy

iStock.com/SpotX

#### How Do Standards Help a Business?

A number of organizations, including corporations, consultants, and governmental agencies, share information regarding performance standards in an effort to create a standard set of measures for thousands of business processes. The group, referred to as the Open Standards Benchmarking Collaborative, includes **IBM**, **Procter and Gamble**, the **U.S. Navy**, and the **World Bank**. Companies that are inter-

ested in participating can go to the group's website and enter their information.

**Source:** Becky Partida, "Benchmark Your Manufacturing Performance," *Control Engineering* (February 4, 2013).

**How will the creation of such standards help a business or organization? (Go to WileyPLUS for this answer and additional questions.)**

---

## A Case Study

To establish the standard cost of producing a product:

- It is necessary to establish standards for each manufacturing cost element—direct materials, direct labor, and manufacturing overhead.
- The standard for each element is derived from the standard price to be paid and the standard quantity to be used.

To illustrate, we use an extended example. Xonic Beverage Company uses standard costs to measure performance at the production facility of its caffeinated energy drink, Xonic Tonic. Xonic produces one-gallon containers of concentrated syrup that it sells to coffee and smoothie shops, and other retail outlets. The syrup is mixed with ice water or ice "slush" before serving. The potency of the beverage varies depending on the amount of concentrated syrup used.

**Direct Materials**   The **direct materials price standard** is the cost per finished unit of product of direct materials that should be incurred.

- This standard is based on the purchasing department's best estimate of the **cost of raw materials**.
- This cost is frequently based on current purchase prices.
- The price standard also includes an amount for related costs such as receiving, storing, and handling.

**Illustration 17.2** shows the materials price standard per pound of material for Xonic Tonic.

| Item | Price |
|---|---|
| Purchase price, net of discounts | $2.70 |
| Freight | 0.20 |
| Receiving and handling | 0.10 |
| **Standard direct materials price per pound** | **$3.00** |

**ILLUSTRATION 17.2**

**Setting direct materials price standard**

The **direct materials quantity standard** is the quantity of direct materials that management determines should be used per unit of finished goods.

- This standard is expressed as a physical measure, such as pounds, barrels, or board feet.
- In setting the standard, management considers both the quality and quantity of materials required to manufacture the product.
- The standard includes allowances for unavoidable waste and normal spoilage.

The standard quantity per unit for Xonic Tonic is shown in **Illustration 17.3**.

**ILLUSTRATION 17.3**

Setting direct materials quantity standard

| Item | Quantity (Pounds) |
|---|---|
| Required materials | 3.5 |
| Allowance for waste | 0.4 |
| Allowance for spoilage | 0.1 |
| **Standard direct materials quantity per unit** | **4.0** |

**The standard direct materials cost per unit is the standard direct materials price times the standard direct materials quantity.** For Xonic, the standard direct materials cost per gallon of Xonic Tonic is $12.00 ($3 × 4 pounds).

**Direct Labor**   The **direct labor price standard** is the rate per hour that should be incurred for direct labor (see **Alternative Terminology**).

**ALTERNATIVE TERMINOLOGY**

The direct labor price standard is also called the *direct labor rate standard.*

- This standard is based on current wage rates, adjusted for anticipated changes such as cost of living adjustments (COLAs).
- The price standard also generally includes employer payroll taxes and fringe benefits, such as paid holidays and vacations.

For Xonic, the direct labor price standard is as shown in **Illustration 17.4**.

**ILLUSTRATION 17.4**

Setting direct labor price standard

| Item | Price |
|---|---|
| Hourly wage rate | $12.50 |
| COLA | 0.25 |
| Payroll taxes | 0.75 |
| Fringe benefits | 1.50 |
| **Standard direct labor rate per hour** | **$15.00** |

**ALTERNATIVE TERMINOLOGY**

The direct labor quantity standard is also called the *direct labor efficiency standard.*

The **direct labor quantity standard** is the time that management determines should be required to make one unit of the product (see **Alternative Terminology**).

- This standard is especially critical in labor-intensive companies.
- Allowances should be made in this standard for rest periods, cleanup, machine setup, and machine downtime.

**Illustration 17.5** shows the direct labor quantity standard for Xonic.

**ILLUSTRATION 17.5**

Setting direct labor quantity standard

| Item | Quantity (Hours) |
|---|---|
| Actual production time | 1.5 |
| Rest periods and cleanup | 0.2 |
| Setup and downtime | 0.3 |
| **Standard direct labor hours per unit** | **2.0** |

**The standard direct labor cost per unit of finished product is the standard direct labor rate times the standard direct labor hours.** For Xonic, the standard direct labor cost per gallon is $30 ($15 × 2 hours).

**Manufacturing Overhead**   For manufacturing overhead, companies use a **standard predetermined overhead rate** in setting the standard.

- This overhead rate is determined by dividing budgeted overhead costs by an expected standard activity index.
- For example, the index may be standard direct labor hours or standard machine hours.

As discussed in Appendix F, many companies employ activity-based costing (ABC) to allocate overhead costs. Because ABC uses multiple activity indices to allocate overhead costs, it results in a better correlation between activities and costs incurred than do other methods. As a result, the use of ABC can significantly improve the usefulness of standard costing for management decision-making.

Xonic uses standard direct labor hours as the activity index. The company expects to produce 13,200 gallons of Xonic Tonic during the year at normal capacity. **Normal capacity** is the average activity output that a company should experience over the long run. Since it takes two direct labor hours for each gallon, total standard direct labor hours are 26,400 (13,200 gallons × 2 hours).

At normal capacity of 26,400 direct labor hours, overhead costs are budgeted to be $132,000. Of that amount, $79,200 are variable and $52,800 are fixed. **Illustration 17.6** shows computation of the standard predetermined overhead rates for Xonic.

| Budgeted Overhead Costs | Amount | ÷ | Standard Direct Labor Hours | = | Overhead Rate per Direct Labor Hour |
|---|---|---|---|---|---|
| Variable | $ 79,200 | | 26,400 | | $3.00 |
| Fixed | 52,800 | | 26,400 | | 2.00 |
| Total | $132,000 | | 26,400 | | **$5.00** |

**ILLUSTRATION 17.6**

Computing predetermined overhead rates

**The standard manufacturing overhead cost per unit is the predetermined overhead rate times the activity index quantity standard.** For Xonic, which uses direct labor hours as its activity index, the standard manufacturing overhead cost per gallon of Xonic Tonic is $10 ($5 × 2 hours).

**Total Standard Cost per Unit**   After a company has established the standard quantity and price per unit of finished product for each cost element, it can determine the total standard cost. The total standard cost per unit is the sum of the standard costs of direct materials, direct labor, and manufacturing overhead. The total standard cost per gallon of Xonic Tonic is $52, as the standard cost card in **Illustration 17.7** shows.

**Product: Xonic Tonic**                    **Unit Measure: Gallon**

| Manufacturing Cost Elements | Quantity | × | Price | = | Cost |
|---|---|---|---|---|---|
| Direct materials | 4 pounds | | $ 3.00 | | $12.00 |
| Direct labor | 2 hours | | $15.00 | | 30.00 |
| Manufacturing overhead | 2 hours | | $ 5.00 | | 10.00 |
| | | | | | $52.00 |

**ILLUSTRATION 17.7**

Standard cost per gallon of Xonic Tonic

The company prepares a standard cost card for each product. This card provides the basis for determining variances from standards.

**ACTION PLAN**

- Know that standard costs are predetermined unit costs.
- To establish the standard cost of producing a product, establish the standard for each manufacturing cost element—direct materials, direct labor, and manufacturing overhead.
- Compute the standard cost for each element from the standard price to be paid and the standard quantity to be used.

## DO IT! 1 | Standard Costs

Ridette Inc. accumulated the following standard cost data concerning product Cty31.

Direct materials per unit: 1.5 pounds at $4 per pound
Direct labor per unit: 0.25 hours at $13 per hour.
Manufacturing overhead: allocated based on direct labor hours at a predetermined rate of $15.60 per direct labor hour.

Compute the standard cost of one unit of product Cty31.

### Solution

| Manufacturing Cost Elements | Standard Quantity | × | Price | = | Cost |
|---|---|---|---|---|---|
| Direct materials | 1.5 pounds | | $ 4.00 | | $ 6.00 |
| Direct labor | 0.25 hours | | $13.00 | | 3.25 |
| Manufacturing overhead | 0.25 hours | | $15.60 | | 3.90 |
| Total | | | | | $13.15 |

Related exercise material: **BE17.2, BE17.3, DO IT! 17.1, E17.1, E17.2, and E17.3.**

# Direct Materials Variances

**LEARNING OBJECTIVE 2**
Determine direct materials variances.

**ALTERNATIVE TERMINOLOGY**

In business, the term *variance* is also used to indicate differences between total budgeted and total actual costs.

## Analyzing and Reporting Variances

One of the major management uses of standard costs is to identify variances from standards. **Variances** are the differences between total actual costs and total standard costs (see **Alternative Terminology**).

To illustrate, assume that in producing 1,000 gallons of Xonic Tonic in the month of June, Xonic incurred the costs listed in **Illustration 17.8**.

**ILLUSTRATION 17.8**

**Actual production costs**

| Direct materials | $13,020 |
|---|---|
| Direct labor | 31,080 |
| Variable overhead | 6,500 |
| Fixed overhead | 4,400 |
| Total actual costs | $55,000 |

Companies determine total standard costs by multiplying the units produced by the standard cost per unit. The total standard cost of Xonic Tonic is $52,000 (1,000 gallons × $52). Thus, the total variance is $3,000, as shown in **Illustration 17.9**.

**ILLUSTRATION 17.9**

**Computation of total variance**

| Actual costs | $55,000 |
|---|---|
| Less: Standard costs | 52,000 |
| **Total variance** | **$ 3,000** |

Note that the variance is expressed in total dollars, not on a per unit basis.

When actual costs exceed standard costs, the variance is **unfavorable**. The $3,000 variance in June for Xonic Tonic is unfavorable.

- An unfavorable variance has a negative connotation as it reduces profit.
- It suggests that the company paid too much for one or more of the manufacturing cost elements or that it used the elements inefficiently.

If actual costs are less than standard costs, the variance is **favorable**.

- A favorable variance has a positive connotation as it increases profit.
- It suggests efficiencies in incurring manufacturing costs and in using direct materials, direct labor, and manufacturing overhead.

However, be careful: A favorable variance could be obtained by using inferior materials. In printing wedding invitations, for example, a favorable variance could result from using an inferior grade of paper. Or, a favorable variance might be achieved in installing tires on an automobile assembly line by tightening only half of the lug bolts. A variance is not favorable if the company has sacrificed quality control standards.

- To interpret a variance, you must analyze its components.
- A variance can result from differences related to the cost of materials, labor, or overhead.

**Illustration 17.10** shows that the total variance is the sum of the materials, labor, and overhead variances.

| Materials Variance  +  Labor Variance  +  Overhead Variance  =  Total Variance |

**ILLUSTRATION 17.10**
**Components of total variance**

In the following discussion, you will see that the materials variance and the labor variance are the sum of variances resulting from price differences and quantity differences. **Illustration 17.11** shows a format for computing the price and quantity variances.

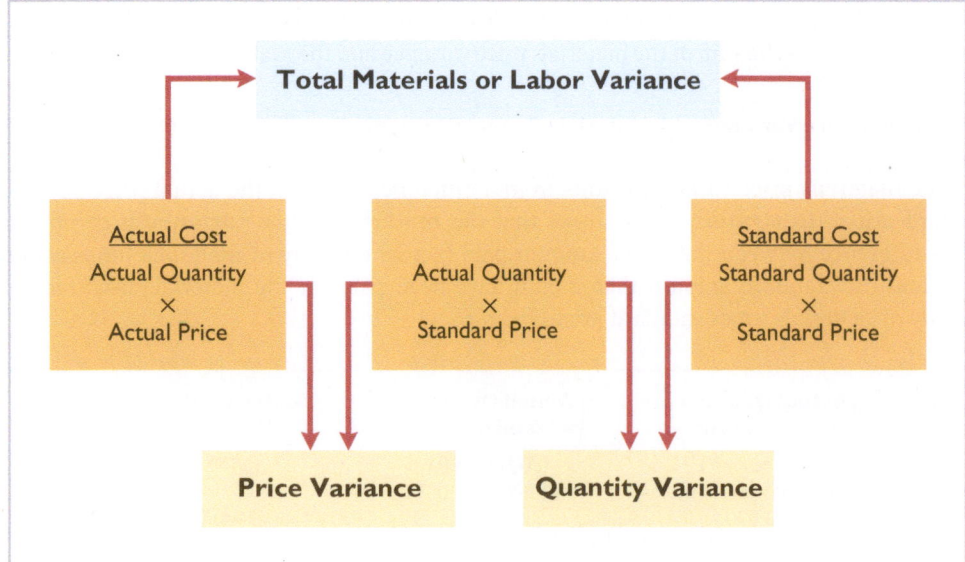

**ILLUSTRATION 17.11**
**Breakdown of materials or labor variance into price and quantity variances**

Note that the left side of the matrix is actual cost (actual quantity times actual price). The right hand is standard cost (standard quantity times standard price). The difference between these two amounts (shown in the blue box in Illustration 17.11) is the total materials or labor variance. The only additional element you need in order to compute the price and quantity variances is the middle element, the actual quantity at the standard price.

- To compute the price variance, we hold the quantity constant (at the actual quantity) but vary the price (actual versus standard).
- Similarly, to compute the quantity variance, we hold the price constant (at the standard price) but vary the quantity (actual versus standard).

## Calculating Direct Materials Variances

**Decision Tools**

The materials price and materials quantity variances help managers determine if they have met their price and quantity objectives regarding materials.

Part of Xonic's total variance of $3,000 is due to a materials variance (see **Decision Tools**).

- In completing the order for 1,000 gallons of Xonic Tonic, the company used 4,200 pounds of direct materials. From Illustration 17.3, we know that Xonic's standards require it to use 4 pounds of materials per gallon produced, so it should have only used 4,000 (4 × 1,000) pounds of direct materials to produce 1,000 gallons.
- The direct materials were purchased at a price of $3.10 per unit. Illustration 17.2 shows that the standard cost of each pound of direct materials is $3 instead of the $3.10 actually paid.

**Illustration 17.12** shows that the **total materials variance** is computed as the difference between the amount paid (actual quantity times actual price) and the amount that should have been paid based on standards (standard quantity times standard price of materials).

**ILLUSTRATION 17.12**
**Formula for total materials variance**

| (Actual Quantity × Actual Price) | – | (Standard Quantity × Standard Price) | = | Total Materials Variance |
|---|---|---|---|---|
| (AQ) × (AP) | | (SQ) × (SP) | | (TMV) |
| (4,200 × $3.10) | | (4,000* × $3.00) | | |
| $13,020 | – | $12,000 | = | $1,020 U |

*1,000 units × 4 pounds

Thus, for Xonic, the total materials variance is $1,020 ($13,020 – $12,000) unfavorable (abbreviated as "U"). It is unfavorable because the actual cost exceeded the standard cost.

The total materials variance could be caused by differences in the price paid for the materials or by differences in the amount of materials used. **Illustration 17.13** shows that the total materials variance is the sum of the materials price variance and the materials quantity variance.

**ILLUSTRATION 17.13**
**Components of total materials variance**

**Materials Price Variance + Materials Quantity Variance = Total Materials Variance**

The materials price variance results from a difference between the actual price and the standard price. **Illustration 17.14** shows that the **materials price variance** is computed as the difference between the actual amount paid (actual quantity of materials times actual price) and the standard amount that should have been paid for the materials used (actual quantity of materials times standard price).[1]

**ILLUSTRATION 17.14**
**Formula for materials price variance**

| (Actual Quantity × Actual Price) | – | (Actual Quantity × Standard Price) | = | Materials Price Variance |
|---|---|---|---|---|
| (AQ) × (AP) | | (AQ) × (SP) | | (MPV) |
| (4,200 × $3.10) | | (4,200 × $3.00) | | |
| $13,020 | – | $12,600 | = | $420 U |

For Xonic, the materials price variance is $420 ($13,020 – $12,600) unfavorable.

The price variance can also be computed by multiplying the actual quantity purchased by the difference between the actual and standard price per unit (see **Helpful Hint**). The computation in this case is 4,200 × ($3.10 – $3.00) = $420 U.

**HELPFUL HINT**

**The alternative formula is:**
AQ × AP – SP = MPV

[1]Assume that all materials purchased during the period are used in production and that no units remain in inventory at the end of the period.

As seen in Illustration 17.13, the other component of the materials variance is the quantity variance.

- The quantity variance results from differences between the amount of material actually used and the amount that should have been used.
- As shown in **Illustration 17.15**, the **materials quantity variance** is computed as the difference between the standard cost of the actual quantity (actual quantity times standard price) and the standard cost of the amount that should have been used (standard quantity times standard price for materials).

<table>
<tr><td>$\begin{pmatrix}\text{Actual Quantity} \\ \times \text{ Standard Price}\end{pmatrix}$</td><td>−</td><td>$\begin{pmatrix}\text{Standard Quantity} \\ \times \text{ Standard Price}\end{pmatrix}$</td><td>=</td><td>**Materials Quantity Variance**</td></tr>
<tr><td>(AQ) × (SP)</td><td></td><td>(SQ) × (SP)</td><td></td><td>(MQV)</td></tr>
<tr><td>(4,200 × $3.00)</td><td></td><td>(4,000 × $3.00)</td><td></td><td></td></tr>
<tr><td>$12,600</td><td>−</td><td>$12,000</td><td>=</td><td>$600 U</td></tr>
</table>

**ILLUSTRATION 17.15**

Formula for materials quantity variance

Thus, for Xonic, the materials quantity variance is $600 ($12,600 − $12,000) unfavorable.

The quantity variance can also be computed by applying the standard price to the difference between actual and standard quantities used (see **Helpful Hint**). The computation in this example is $3.00 × (4,200 − 4,000) = $600 U.

**Illustration 17.16** summarizes the total materials variance of $1,020 U.

**HELPFUL HINT**

The alternative formula is:
$$\boxed{SP} \times \boxed{AQ - SQ} = \boxed{MQV}$$

| | |
|---|---:|
| Materials price variance | $ 420 U |
| Materials quantity variance | 600 U |
| **Total materials variance** | **$1,020 U** |

**ILLUSTRATION 17.16**

Summary of materials variances

Companies sometimes use a matrix to analyze a variance.

- **When the matrix is used, a company computes the amounts using the formulas for each cost element first and then computes the variances.**
- The matrix provides a convenient structure for determining each variance.

**Illustration 17.17** shows the completed matrix for the direct materials variance for Xonic.

**ILLUSTRATION 17.17**   Matrix for direct materials variances

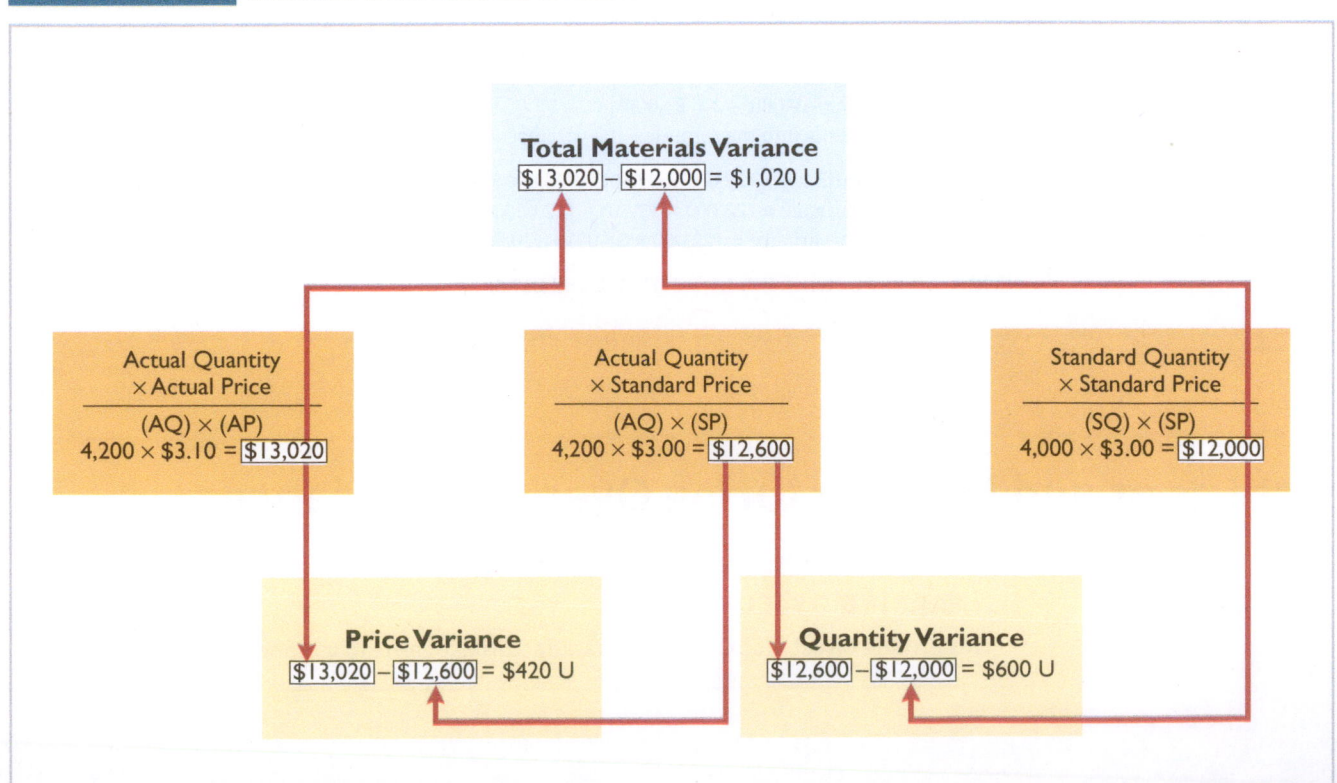

## Causes of Materials Variances

What are the causes of a variance? The causes may relate to both internal and external factors. The investigation of a **materials price variance usually begins in the purchasing department**.

- Many factors affect the price paid for raw materials, such as the availability of quantity and cash discounts, the quality of the materials requested, and the delivery method used.
- To the extent that these factors are considered in setting the price standard, the purchasing department is responsible for any variances.
- However, a variance may be beyond the control of the purchasing department. Sometimes, for example, prices may rise faster than expected, or actions by groups over which the company has no control, such as the OPEC nations' oil price increases, may cause an unfavorable variance.

For example, during a recent year, **Kraft Foods** and **Kellogg's** both experienced unfavorable materials price variances when the cost of dairy and wheat products jumped unexpectedly. There are also times when a production department may be responsible for the price variance. This may occur when a rush order forces the company to pay a higher price for the materials.

The starting point for determining the cause(s) of a significant **materials quantity variance is in the production department**.

- If the variances are due to inexperienced workers, faulty machinery, or carelessness, the production department is responsible.
- However, if the materials obtained by the purchasing department were of inferior quality, then the purchasing department is responsible.

---

### ACTION PLAN

- Use the formulas for computing each of the materials variances:
- Total materials variance = (AQ × AP) − (SQ × SP)
- Materials price variance = (AQ × AP) − (AQ × SP)
- Materials quantity variance = (AQ × SP) − (SQ × SP)

### DO IT! 2 | Direct Materials Variances

The standard cost of Wonder Walkers includes two units of direct materials at $8.00 per unit. During July, the company buys 22,000 units of direct materials at $7.50 and uses those materials to produce 10,000 Wonder Walkers. Compute the total, price, and quantity variances for materials.

#### Solution

Standard quantity = 10,000 × 2 = 20,000
Substituting amounts into the formulas, the variances are:

Total materials variance = (22,000 × $7.50) − (20,000 × $8.00) = $5,000 unfavorable
Materials price variance = (22,000 × $7.50) − (22,000 × $8.00) = $11,000 favorable
Materials quantity variance = (22,000 × $8.00) − (20,000 × $8.00) = $16,000 unfavorable

Related exercise material: **BE17.4, DO IT! 17.2, and E17.5**.

---

# Direct Labor and Manufacturing Overhead Variances

### LEARNING OBJECTIVE 3
Determine direct labor and total manufacturing overhead variances.

# Direct Labor Variances

**Decision Tools**

Labor price and labor quantity variances help managers to determine if they have met their price and quantity objectives regarding labor.

The process of determining direct labor variances is the same as for determining the direct materials variances (see **Decision Tools**). In completing the Xonic Tonic order, the company incurred 2,100 direct labor hours. The standard hours allowed for the units produced were 2,000 hours (1,000 gallons × 2 hours). The standard labor rate was $15 per hour, and the actual labor rate was $14.80.

- The total labor variance is the difference between the amount actually paid for labor versus the amount that should have been paid.
- **Illustration 17.18** shows that the **total labor variance** is computed as the difference between the amount actually paid for labor (actual hours times actual rate) and the amount that should have been paid (standard hours times standard rate for labor).

$$\begin{pmatrix} \text{Actual} \\ \text{Hours} \\ \times \text{Actual} \\ \text{Rate} \end{pmatrix} - \begin{pmatrix} \text{Standard} \\ \text{Hours} \\ \times \text{Standard} \\ \text{Rate} \end{pmatrix} = \begin{array}{c} \text{Total Labor} \\ \text{Variance} \end{array}$$

| (AH) × (AR) | | (SH) × (SR) | | (TLV) |
|---|---|---|---|---|
| (2,100 × $14.80) | | (2,000 × $15.00) | | |
| $31,080 | − | $30,000 | = | $1,080 U |

**ILLUSTRATION 17.18**

Formula for total labor variance

The total labor variance is $1,080 ($31,080 − $30,000) unfavorable.

The total labor variance is caused by differences in the labor rate or difference in labor hours. **Illustration 17.19** shows that the total labor variance is the sum of the labor price variance and the labor quantity variance.

| **Labor Price Variance** + **Labor Quantity Variance** = **Total Labor Variance** |
|---|

**ILLUSTRATION 17.19**

Components of total labor variance

- The labor price variance results from the difference between the rate paid to workers versus the rate that was supposed to be paid.
- **Illustration 17.20** shows that the **labor price variance** is computed as the difference between the actual amount paid (actual hours times actual rate) and the amount that should have been paid for the number of hours worked (actual hours times standard rate for labor).

$$\begin{pmatrix} \text{Actual Hours} \\ \times \text{Actual Rate} \end{pmatrix} - \begin{pmatrix} \text{Actual Hours} \\ \times \text{Standard Rate} \end{pmatrix} = \begin{array}{c} \text{Labor Price} \\ \text{Variance} \end{array}$$

| (AH) × (AR) | | (AH) × (SR) | | (LPV) |
|---|---|---|---|---|
| (2,100 × $14.80) | | (2,100 × $15.00) | | |
| $31,080 | − | $31,500 | = | $420 F |

**ILLUSTRATION 17.20**

Formula for labor price variance

For Xonic, the labor price variance is $420 ($31,080 − $31,500) favorable.

The labor price variance can also be computed by multiplying actual hours worked by the difference between the actual pay rate and the standard pay rate (see **Helpful Hint**). The computation in this example is 2,100 × ($15.00 − $14.80) = $420 F.

The other component of the total labor variance is the labor quantity variance.

**HELPFUL HINT**

The alternative formula is:
$$\boxed{\text{AH}} \times \boxed{\text{AR} - \text{SR}} = \boxed{\text{LPV}}$$

- The labor quantity variance results from the difference between the actual number of labor hours and the number of hours that should have been worked for the quantity produced.
- **Illustration 17.21** shows that the **labor quantity variance** is computed as the difference between the amount that should have been paid for the hours worked (actual hours times standard rate) and the amount that should have been paid for the amount of hours that should have been worked (standard hours times standard rate for labor).

**ILLUSTRATION 17.21**

**Formula for labor quantity variance**

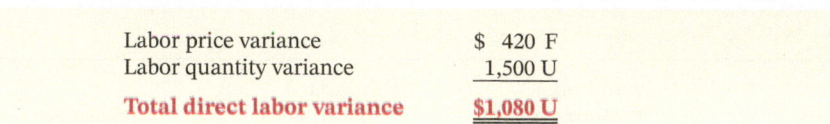

| $\begin{pmatrix} \text{Actual Hours} \\ \times \text{Standard Rate} \end{pmatrix}$ | − | $\begin{pmatrix} \text{Standard Hours} \\ \times \text{Standard Rate} \end{pmatrix}$ | = | **Labor Quantity Variance** |
|---|---|---|---|---|
| **(AH) × (SR)** | | **(SH) × (SR)** | | **(LQV)** |
| (2,100 × $15.00) | | (2,000 × $15.00) | | |
| $31,500 | − | $30,000 | = | $1,500 U |

**HELPFUL HINT**

The alternative formula is:

$$\boxed{SR} \times \boxed{AH \ - \ SH} = \boxed{LQV}$$

Thus, for Xonic, the labor quantity variance is $1,500 ($31,500 − $30,000) unfavorable.

The same result can be obtained by multiplying the standard rate by the difference between actual hours worked and standard hours allowed (see **Helpful Hint**). In this case, the computation is $15.00 × (2,100 − 2,000) = $1,500 U.

**Illustration 17.22** summarizes the total direct labor variance of $1,080 U.

**ILLUSTRATION 17.22**

**Summary of labor variances**

| Labor price variance | $ 420 F |
|---|---|
| Labor quantity variance | 1,500 U |
| **Total direct labor variance** | **$1,080 U** |

These results can also be obtained from the matrix in **Illustration 17.23**.

**ILLUSTRATION 17.23**  Matrix for direct labor variances

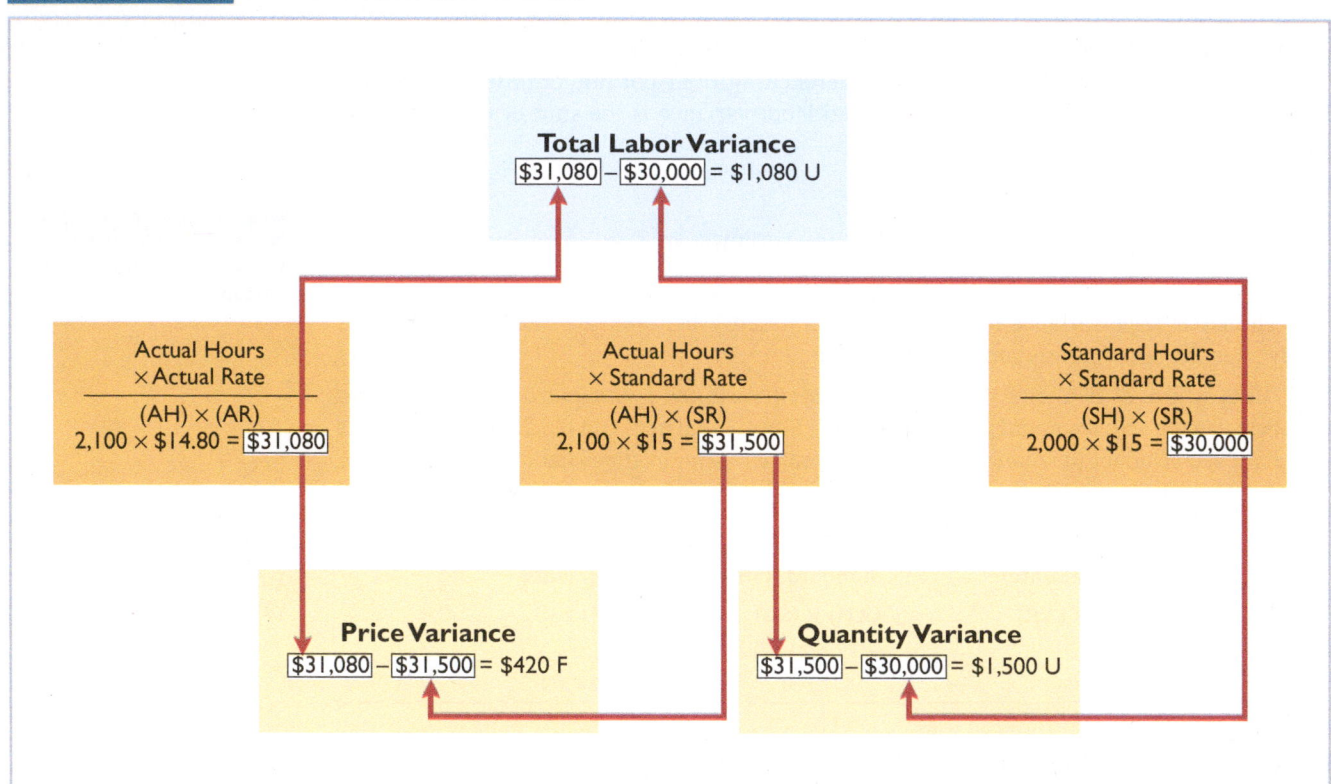

## Causes of Labor Variances

"What caused labor price variances?"

Personnel decisions

**Labor price variances** usually result from two factors:

1. Paying workers **different wages than expected.**

2. **Misallocation of workers.**

In companies where pay rates are determined by union contracts, labor price variances should be infrequent. When workers are not unionized, there is a much higher likelihood of such variances. The responsibility for these variances rests with the manager who authorized the wage change.

Misallocation of the workforce refers to using skilled workers in place of unskilled workers and vice versa.

- The use of an inexperienced worker instead of an experienced one will result in a favorable price variance because of the lower pay rate of the unskilled worker.
- An unfavorable price variance would result if a skilled worker were substituted for an inexperienced one.

The production department generally is responsible for labor price variances resulting from misallocation of the workforce.

**Labor quantity variances** relate to the **efficiency of workers**. The cause of a quantity variance generally can be traced to the production department.

"What caused labor quantity variances?"

Production Dept.

- The causes of an unfavorable variance may be poor training, worker fatigue, faulty machinery, or carelessness, the responsibility of the **production department**.
- However, if the excess time is due to inferior materials, the responsibility falls outside the production department and resides instead with the purchasing department.

# Manufacturing Overhead Variances

The **total overhead variance** is the difference between the actual overhead costs and overhead costs applied based on standard hours allowed for the amount of goods produced. As indicated in Illustration 17.8, Xonic incurred overhead costs of $10,900 to produce 1,000 gallons of Xonic Tonic in June. The computation of the actual overhead is comprised of a variable and a fixed component. **Illustration 17.24** shows this computation.

| | |
|---|---|
| Variable overhead | $ 6,500 |
| Fixed overhead | 4,400 |
| **Total actual overhead** | **$10,900** |

**ILLUSTRATION 17.24**
**Actual overhead costs**

To find the total overhead variance in a standard costing system, we determine the overhead costs applied based on standard hours allowed (see **Decision Tools**).

- **Standard hours allowed** are the hours that *should* have been worked for the units produced.
- Overhead costs for Xonic Tonic are applied based on direct labor hours. Because it takes two hours of direct labor to produce one gallon of Xonic Tonic, for the 1,000-gallon Xonic Tonic order, the standard hours allowed are 2,000 hours (1,000 gallons × 2 hours).
- We then apply the predetermined overhead rate to the 2,000 standard hours allowed.

**Decision Tools**

The total manufacturing overhead variance helps managers to determine if they have met their objectives regarding manufacturing overhead.

Recall from Illustration 17.6 that the amount of budgeted overhead costs at normal capacity of $132,000 was divided by normal capacity of 26,400 direct labor hours, to arrive at a predetermined overhead rate of $5 ($132,000 ÷ 26,400). The predetermined rate of $5 is then multiplied by the 2,000 standard hours allowed, to determine the overhead costs applied.

**Illustration 17.25** shows the formula for the total overhead variance and the calculation for Xonic for the month of June.

| Actual Overhead | − | Overhead Applied* | = | Total Overhead Variance |
|---|---|---|---|---|
| $10,900 | − | $10,000 | = | $900 U |
| ($6,500 + $4,400) | | ($5 × 2,000 hours) | | |

*Based on standard hours allowed.

**ILLUSTRATION 17.25**
**Formula for total overhead variance**

Thus, for Xonic, the total overhead variance is $900 unfavorable.

The overhead variance is generally analyzed through a price and a quantity variance. (These computations are discussed in more detail in advanced courses.)

- The name usually given to the price variance is the **overhead controllable variance**.
- The quantity variance is referred to as the **overhead volume variance**.

Appendix 17A discusses how the total overhead variance can be broken down into these two variances.

## Causes of Manufacturing Overhead Variances

One reason for an overhead variance relates to over- or underspending on overhead items. For example, overhead may include indirect labor for which a company paid wages higher than the standard labor price allowed. Or, the price of electricity to run the company's machines increased, and the company did not anticipate this additional cost.

- Companies should investigate any spending variances to determine whether they will continue in the future.
- Generally, the responsibility for these variances rests with the production department.

The overhead variance can also result from the inefficient use of overhead.

- For example, the flow of materials through the production process is impeded because of a lack of skilled labor to perform the necessary production tasks, due to a lack of planning.
- In this case, the production department is responsible for the cause of this variance.
- On the other hand, overhead can also be underutilized because of a lack of sales orders.
- When the cause is a lack of sales orders, the responsibility rests outside the production department and resides instead with the sales department.

For example, at one point **Chrysler** experienced a very significant unfavorable overhead variance because plant capacity was maintained at excessively high levels, due to overly optimistic sales forecasts.

---

## People, Planet, and Profit Insight    Starbucks

### What's Brewing at Starbucks?

ARCHER COLIN/SIPA/ Sipa Press/Manahattan New York United States/ Newscom

It's easy for a company to say it's committed to corporate social responsibility. But **Starbucks** actually spells out measurable goals. In its annual *Global Responsibility Report*, the company describes its goals, its achievements, and even its shortcomings related to corporate social responsibility. For example, Starbucks achieved its goal of getting more than 50% of its electricity from renewable sources. It also has numerous goals related to purchasing coffee from sources that are certified as responsibly grown and ethically traded; providing funds for loans to coffee farmers; and fostering partnerships with **Conservation International** to provide training to farmers on ecologically friendly growing.

The report also candidly explains that the company did not meet its goal to cut energy consumption by 25%. It also fell far short of its goal of getting customers to reuse their cups. In those instances where it didn't achieve its goals, Starbucks set new goals and described steps it would take to achieve them. You can view the company's *Global Responsibility Report* at the Starbucks website.

**Source:** "Starbucks Launches 10th Global Responsibility Report," *Business Wire* (April 18, 2011).

**What implications does Starbucks' commitment to corporate social responsibility have for the standard cost of a cup of coffee? (Go to WileyPLUS for this answer and additional questions.)**

### DO IT! 3 | Labor and Manufacturing Overhead Variances

The standard cost of Product YY includes 3 hours of direct labor at $12.00 per hour. The predetermined overhead rate is $20.00 per direct labor hour. During July, the company incurred 3,500 hours of direct labor at an average rate of $12.40 per hour and $71,300 of manufacturing overhead costs. It produced 1,200 units.

a. Compute the total, price, and quantity variances for labor.

b. Compute the total overhead variance.

#### Solution

Substituting amounts into the formulas, the variances are:

Total labor variance = $(3,500 \times \$12.40) - (3,600 \times \$12.00) = \$200$ unfavorable

Labor price variance = $(3,500 \times \$12.40) - (3,500 \times \$12.00) = \$1,400$ unfavorable

Labor quantity variance = $(3,500 \times \$12.00) - (3,600 \times \$12.00) = \$1,200$ favorable

Total overhead variance = $\$71,300 - \$72,000^* = \$700$ favorable

$^*(1,200 \times 3 \text{ hours}) \times \$20.00$

Related exercise material: **BE17.5, BE17.6, DO IT! 17.3, E17.4, E17.6, E17.7, E17.8, and E17.11.**

**ACTION PLAN**

Use the formulas for computing each of the variances.

- Total labor variance = $(AH \times AR) - (SH \times SR)$
- Labor price variance = $(AH \times AR) - (AH \times SR)$
- Labor quantity variance = $(AH \times SR) - (SH \times SR)$
- Total overhead variance = Actual overhead − Overhead applied*

*Based on standard hours allowed.

# Variance Reports and Balanced Scorecards

**LEARNING OBJECTIVE 4**

Prepare variance reports and balanced scorecards.

## Reporting Variances

All variances should be reported to appropriate levels of management as soon as possible. The sooner managers are informed, the sooner they can evaluate problems and take corrective action.

- The form, content, and frequency of variance reports vary considerably among companies.
- One approach is to prepare a weekly report for each department that has primary responsibility for cost control.
- Under this approach, materials price variances are reported to the purchasing department, and all other variances are reported to the production department that did the work.

The report for Xonic shown in **Illustration 17.26**, with the materials for the Xonic Tonic order listed first, illustrates this approach.

**ILLUSTRATION 17.26**

Materials price variance report

| Xonic | | | | | |
|---|---|---|---|---|---|
| Variance Report—Purchasing Department | | | | | |
| For the Week Ended June 8, 2022 | | | | | |
| Type of Materials | Quantity Purchased | Actual Price | Standard Price | Price Variance | Explanation |
| X100 | 4,200 lbs. | $3.10 | $3.00 | $420 U | Rush order |
| X142 | 1,200 units | 2.75 | 2.80 | 60 F | Quantity discount |
| A85 | 600 doz. | 5.20 | 5.10 | 60 U | Regular supplier on strike |
| **Total price variance** | | | | **$420 U** | |

The explanation column is completed after consultation with the purchasing department manager.

Variance reports facilitate the principle of "management by exception" explained in Chapter 16. For example, the vice president of purchasing can use the report shown above to evaluate the effectiveness of the purchasing department manager. Or, the vice president of production can use production department variance reports to determine how well each production manager is controlling costs.

- In using variance reports, top management normally looks for **significant variances**.
- These may be judged on the basis of some quantitative measure, such as more than 10% of the standard or more than $1,000.

# Income Statement Presentation of Variances

In income statements **prepared for management** under a standard cost accounting system, **cost of goods sold is stated at standard cost and the variances are disclosed separately**. Unfavorable variances increase cost of goods sold. Favorable variances decrease cost of goods sold, thus increasing gross profit. **Illustration 17.27** shows the presentation of variances in an income statement. This income statement is based on the production and sale of 1,000 units of Xonic Tonic at $70 per unit. It also assumes selling and administrative costs of $3,000. Observe that each variance is shown, as well as the total net variance. In this example, variations from standard costs reduced net income by $3,000.

**ILLUSTRATION 17.27**

**Variances in income statement for management**

| Xonic Income Statement For the Month Ended June 30, 2022 | | |
|---|---|---|
| Sales revenue | | $70,000 |
| Cost of goods sold (at standard) | | 52,000 |
| Gross profit (at standard) | | 18,000 |
| **Variances** | | |
| Materials price | $ 420 U | |
| Materials quantity | 600 U | |
| Labor price | 420 F | |
| Labor quantity | 1,500 U | |
| Overhead | 900 U | |
| Total variance unfavorable | | 3,000 |
| Gross profit (actual) | | 15,000 |
| Selling and administrative expenses | | 3,000 |
| Net income | | $12,000 |

Standard costs may be used in financial statements prepared for stockholders and other external users.

- The costing of inventories at standard costs is in accordance with generally accepted accounting principles when there are no significant differences between actual costs and standard costs. **Hewlett-Packard** and **Jostens, Inc.**, for example, report their inventories at standard costs.
- However, if there are significant differences between actual and standard costs, the financial statements must report inventories and cost of goods sold at actual costs.

It is also possible to show the variances in an income statement prepared in the variable costing (CVP) format. To do so, it is necessary to analyze the overhead variances into variable and fixed components. This type of analysis is explained in cost accounting texts.

# Balanced Scorecard

Financial measures (measurement in dollars), such as variance analysis and return on investment (ROI), are useful tools for evaluating performance. However, many companies now supplement these financial measures with nonfinancial measures to better assess performance and anticipate future results. For example, airlines like **Delta** and **United** use capacity utilization as an important measure to understand and predict future performance. Companies that publish the *New York Times* and the *Chicago Tribune* newspapers use circulation figures as another measure by which to assess performance. **Penske Automotive Group**, the owner of 300 dealerships, rewards executives for meeting employee retention targets. **Illustration 17.28** lists some key nonfinancial measures used in various industries.

**ILLUSTRATION 17.28**   **Nonfinancial measures used in various industries**

| Industry | Measure |
|---|---|
| **Automobiles** | Capacity utilization of plants.<br>Average age of key assets.<br>Impact of strikes.<br>Brand-loyalty statistics. |
| **Computer Systems** | Market profile of customer end-products.<br>Number of new products.<br>Employee stock ownership percentages.<br>Number of scientists and technicians used in R&D. |
| **Chemicals** | Customer satisfaction data.<br>Factors affecting customer product selection.<br>Number of patents and trademarks held.<br>Customer brand awareness. |
| **Regional Banks** | Number of ATMs by state.<br>Number of products used by average customer.<br>Percentage of customer service calls handled by<br>  interactive voice response units.<br>Personnel cost per employee.<br>Credit card retention rates. |

**Source:** Financial Accounting Standards Board, *Business Reporting: Insights into Enhancing Voluntary Disclosures* (Norwalk, Conn.: FASB, 2001).

Most companies recognize that both financial and nonfinancial measures can provide useful insights into what is happening in the company.

- As a result, many companies now use a broad-based measurement approach, called the **balanced scorecard**, to evaluate performance.
- The **balanced scorecard** incorporates financial and nonfinancial measures in an integrated system that links performance measurement with a company's strategic goals.

Nearly 50% of the largest companies in the United States, including **Unilever**, **Chase**, and **Walmart**, are using the balanced scorecard approach.

The balanced scorecard evaluates company performance from a series of "perspectives." The four most commonly employed perspectives are as follows.

1. The **financial perspective** is the most traditional view of the company. It employs financial measures of performance used by most firms.

2. The **customer perspective** evaluates the company from the viewpoint of those people who buy its products or services. This view compares the company to competitors in terms of price, quality, product innovation, customer service, and other dimensions.

3. The **internal process perspective** evaluates the internal operating processes critical to success. All critical aspects of the value chain—including product development, production, delivery, and after-sale service—are evaluated to ensure that the company is operating effectively and efficiently.

4. The **learning and growth perspective** evaluates how well the company develops and retains its employees. This would include evaluation of such things as employee skills, employee satisfaction, training programs, and information dissemination.

Within each perspective, the balanced scorecard identifies objectives that contribute to attainment of strategic goals. **Illustration 17.29** shows examples of objectives within each perspective.

**ILLUSTRATION 17.29** **Examples of objectives within the four perspectives of balanced scorecard**

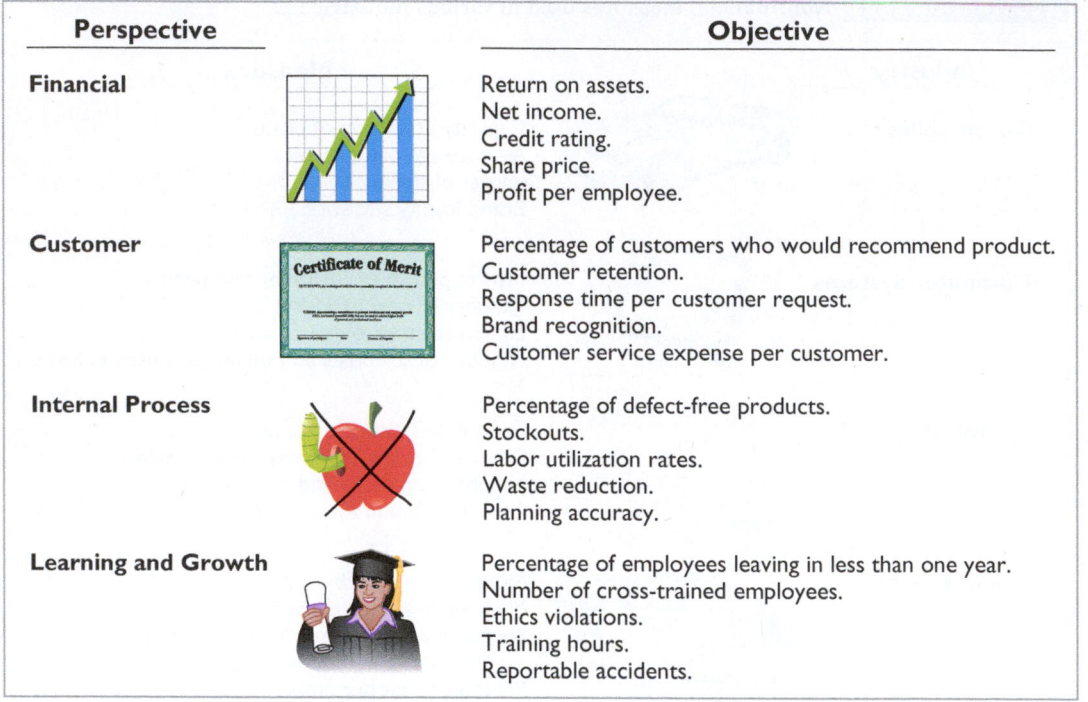

| Perspective | | Objective |
|---|---|---|
| Financial | | Return on assets. Net income. Credit rating. Share price. Profit per employee. |
| Customer | | Percentage of customers who would recommend product. Customer retention. Response time per customer request. Brand recognition. Customer service expense per customer. |
| Internal Process | | Percentage of defect-free products. Stockouts. Labor utilization rates. Waste reduction. Planning accuracy. |
| Learning and Growth | | Percentage of employees leaving in less than one year. Number of cross-trained employees. Ethics violations. Training hours. Reportable accidents. |

The objectives are linked across perspectives in order to tie performance measurement to company goals. The financial-perspective objectives are normally set first, and then objectives are set in the other perspectives in order to accomplish the financial goals.

For example, within the financial perspective, a common goal is to increase profit per dollars invested as measured by ROI.

- In order to increase ROI, a customer-perspective objective might be to increase customer satisfaction as measured by the percentage of customers who would recommend the product to a friend.

- In order to increase customer satisfaction, an internal-process-perspective objective might be to increase product quality as measured by the percentage of defect-free units.

- Finally, in order to increase the percentage of defect-free units, the learning-and-growth-perspective objective might be to reduce factory employee turnover as measured by the percentage of employees leaving in under one year.

**Illustration 17.30** illustrates this linkage across perspectives.

**ILLUSTRATION 17.30**

**Linked process across balanced scorecard perspectives**

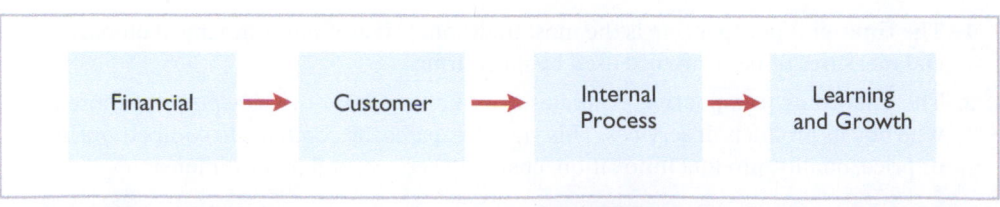

Through this linked process, the company can better understand how to achieve its goals and what measures to use to evaluate performance.

In summary, the balanced scorecard does the following:

1. Employs both **financial and nonfinancial measures**. (For example, ROI is a financial measure; employee turnover is a nonfinancial measure.)

2. **Creates linkages** so that high-level corporate goals can be communicated all the way down to the shop floor.

3. **Provides measurable objectives for nonfinancial measures** such as product quality, rather than vague statements such as "We would like to improve quality."

4. Integrates all of the company's goals into a single performance measurement system, so that **an inappropriate amount of weight will not be placed on any single goal.**

---

## Service Company Insight    United Airlines

Jack Hollingsworth/
Photodisc/Getty Images

### It May Be Time to Fly United Again

Many of the benefits of a balanced score-card approach are evident in the improved operations at **United Airlines**. At the time it filed for bankruptcy, United had a reputation for some of the worst service in the airline business. But when Glenn Tilton took over as United's chief executive officer, he recognized that things had to change.

He implemented an incentive program that allows all of United's 63,000 employees to earn a bonus of 2.5% or more of their wages if the company "exceeds its goals for on-time flight departures and for customer intent to fly United again." After instituting this program, the company's on-time departures were among the best, its customer complaints were reduced considerably, and the number of customers who said that they would fly United again was at its highest level ever. However, after a highly publicized incident where a traveler was injured as he was dragged off an overbooked flight, United must once again overcome a negative public image.

**Sources:** Susan Carey, "Friendlier Skies: In Bankruptcy, United Airlines Forges a Path to Better Service," *Wall Street Journal* (June 15, 2004); and Emre Serpen, "More to Maintain," *Airline Business* (November 2012), pp. 38–40.

**Which of the perspectives of a balanced scorecard were the focus of United's CEO? (Go to WileyPLUS for this answer and additional questions.)**

---

## DO IT! 4  |  Reporting Variances

Polar Vortex Corporation experienced the following variances: materials price $250 F, materials quantity $1,100 F, labor price $700 U, labor quantity $300 F, and overhead $800 F. Sales revenue was $102,700, and cost of goods sold (at standard) was $61,900. Determine the actual gross profit.

### Solution

| | | |
|---|---:|---:|
| Sales revenue | | $102,700 |
| Cost of goods sold (at standard) | | 61,900 |
| Standard gross profit | | 40,800 |
| Variances | | |
| Materials price | $  250 F | |
| Materials quantity | 1,100 F | |
| Labor price | 700 U | |
| Labor quantity | 300 F | |
| Overhead | 800 F | |
| Total variance favorable | | 1,750 |
| Gross profit (actual) | | $ 42,550 |

**ACTION PLAN**

- **Gross profit at standard is sales revenue less cost of goods sold at standard.**

- **Adjust standard gross profit by adding a net favorable variance or subtracting a net unfavorable variance.**

Related exercise material: **DO IT! 17.4, E17.10, E17.14, and E17.15.**

## USING THE DECISION TOOLS | Starbucks

**Starbucks** faces many situations where it needs to apply the decision tools learned in this chapter. Assume that during the past month, Starbucks produced 10,000 50-pound sacks of dark roast Sumatra coffee beans, with the standard cost for one 50-pound sack of dark roast Sumatra as follows.

| Manufacturing Cost Elements | Standard Quantity | × | Price | = | Cost |
|---|---|---|---|---|---|
| Direct materials (unroasted beans) | 60 lbs. | × | $ 2.00 | = | $120.00 |
| Direct labor | 0.25 hours | × | $16.00 | = | 4.00 |
| Overhead | 0.25 hours | × | $48.00 | = | 12.00 |
| | | | | | $136.00 |

During the month, the following transactions occurred in manufacturing the 10,000 50-pound sacks of Sumatra coffee.

1. Purchased 620,000 pounds of unroasted beans at a price of $1.90 per pound for a total cost of $1,178,000.

2. All materials purchased during the period were used to make coffee during the period.

3. 2,300 direct labor hours were worked at a total labor cost of $36,340 (an average hourly rate of $15.80).

4. Variable manufacturing overhead incurred was $34,600, and fixed overhead incurred was $84,000.

The manufacturing overhead rate of $48.00 is based on a normal capacity of 2,600 direct labor hours. The total overhead budget at this capacity is $83,980 fixed and $40,820 variable.

### Instructions

Determine whether Starbucks met its price and quantity objectives relative to materials, labor, and overhead.

### Solution

To determine whether Starbucks met its price and quantity objectives, compute the total variance and the variances for direct materials and direct labor, and calculate the total variance for manufacturing overhead.

**Total Variance**

| | |
|---|---|
| Actual cost incurred: | |
| Direct materials | $1,178,000 |
| Direct labor | 36,340 |
| Overhead | 118,600 |
| Total actual costs | 1,332,940 |
| Less: Standard cost (10,000 × $136.00) | 1,360,000 |
| Total variance | $ 27,060 F |

**Direct Materials Variances**

| | | | | | |
|---|---|---|---|---|---|
| Total | = $1,178,000 | − | $1,200,000 (600,000 × $2.00) | = | $22,000 F |
| Price | = $1,178,000 (620,000 × $1.90) | − | $1,240,000 (620,000 × $2.00) | = | $62,000 F |
| Quantity | = $1,240,000 (620,000 × $2.00) | − | $1,200,000 (600,000 × $2.00) | = | $40,000 U |

**Direct Labor Variances**

| | | | | | |
|---|---|---|---|---|---|
| Total | = $36,340 (2,300 × $15.80) | − | $40,000 (2,500* × $16.00) | = | $ 3,660 F |
| Price | = $36,340 (2,300 × $15.80) | − | $36,800 (2,300 × $16.00) | = | $ 460 F |
| Quantity | = $36,800 (2,300 × $16.00) | − | $40,000 (2,500* × $16.00) | = | $ 3,200 F |

*10,000 × .25

**Overhead Variance**

| | | | | | |
|---|---|---|---|---|---|
| Total | = $118,600 ($84,000 + $34,600) | − | $120,000 (2,500 × $48) | = | $ 1,400 F |

Starbucks' total variance was a favorable $27,060. The total materials, labor, and overhead variances were favorable. The company did have an unfavorable materials quantity variance, but this was outweighed by the favorable materials price variance.

| Appendix 17A | # Overhead Controllable and Volume Variances |
| --- | --- |

---

**LEARNING OBJECTIVE \*5**

Compute overhead controllable and volume variances.

---

As indicated in the chapter, the total overhead variance is generally analyzed through a price variance and a quantity variance. The name usually given to the price variance is the **overhead controllable variance**; the quantity variance is referred to as the **overhead volume variance**.

# Overhead Controllable Variance

The **overhead controllable variance** shows whether overhead costs are effectively controlled.

- To compute this variance, the company compares actual overhead costs incurred with budgeted costs for the **standard hours allowed**.
- The budgeted costs are determined from a flexible manufacturing overhead budget. (The concepts related to a flexible budget were discussed in Chapter 16.)

For Xonic, the budget formula for manufacturing overhead is variable manufacturing overhead cost of $3 per hour of labor plus fixed manufacturing overhead costs of $4,400 ($52,800 ÷ 12, per Illustration 17.6). **Illustration 17A.1** shows the monthly flexible budget for Xonic.

**ILLUSTRATION 17A.1**

**Flexible budget using standard direct labor hours**

| | A | B | C | D | E |
| --- | --- | --- | --- | --- | --- |
| 1 | | | Xonic | | |
| 2 | | Flexible Manufacturing Overhead Monthly Budget | | | |
| 3 | Activity Index | | | | |
| 4 | Standard direct labor hours | 1,800 | **2,000** | 2,200 | 2,400 |
| 5 | | | | | |
| 6 | Costs | | | | |
| 7 | Variable costs | | | | |
| 8 | Indirect materials | $1,800 | $ 2,000 | $ 2,200 | $ 2,400 |
| 9 | Indirect labor | 2,700 | 3,000 | 3,300 | 3,600 |
| 10 | Utilities | 900 | 1,000 | 1,100 | 1,200 |
| 11 | Total variable costs | 5,400 | 6,000 | 6,600 | 7,200 |
| 12 | | | | | |
| 13 | Fixed costs | | | | |
| 14 | Supervision | 3,000 | 3,000 | 3,000 | 3,000 |
| 15 | Depreciation | 1,400 | 1,400 | 1,400 | 1,400 |
| 16 | Total fixed costs | 4,400 | 4,400 | 4,400 | 4,400 |
| 17 | Total costs | $9,800 | $10,400 | $11,000 | $11,600 |

As shown, the budgeted costs for 2,000 standard hours are $10,400 ($6,000 variable and $4,400 fixed).

**Illustration 17A.2** shows the formula for the overhead controllable variance and the calculation for Xonic at 1,000 units of output (2,000 standard labor hours).

**ILLUSTRATION 17A.2**

**Formula for overhead controllable variance**

| Actual Overhead | − | Overhead Budgeted* | = | Overhead Controllable Variance |
|---|---|---|---|---|
| $10,900 ($6,500 + $4,400) | − | $10,400 ($6,000 + $4,400) | = | $500 U |

*Based on standard hours allowed.

The overhead controllable variance for Xonic is $500 unfavorable.

- Most controllable variances are associated with variable costs, which are controllable costs.
- Fixed costs are often known at the time the budget is prepared and are therefore not as likely to deviate from the budgeted amount.

In Xonic's case, all of the overhead controllable variance is due to the difference between the actual variable overhead costs ($6,500) and the budgeted variable costs ($6,000).

Management can compare actual and budgeted overhead for each manufacturing overhead cost that contributes to the controllable variance. In addition, management can develop cost and quantity variances for each overhead cost, such as indirect materials and indirect labor.

## Overhead Volume Variance

The **overhead volume variance** is the difference between normal capacity hours and standard hours allowed times the fixed overhead rate.

- The overhead volume variance relates to whether fixed costs were under- or overapplied during the year.
- For example, the overhead volume variance answers the question of whether Xonic effectively used its fixed costs.

If Xonic produces less Xonic Tonic than normal capacity would allow, an unfavorable variance results. Conversely, if Xonic produces more Xonic Tonic than what is considered normal capacity, a favorable variance results.

**Illustration 17A.3** provides the formula for computing the overhead volume variance.

**ILLUSTRATION 17A.3**

**Formula for overhead volume variance**

$$\text{Fixed Overhead Rate} \times \left( \begin{array}{c} \text{Normal} \\ \text{Capacity} \\ \text{Hours} \end{array} - \begin{array}{c} \text{Standard} \\ \text{Hours} \\ \text{Allowed} \end{array} \right) = \begin{array}{c} \text{Overhead} \\ \text{Volume} \\ \text{Variance} \end{array}$$

To illustrate the fixed overhead rate computation, recall that Xonic budgeted fixed overhead cost for the year of $52,800 (Illustration 17.6). At normal capacity, 26,400 standard direct labor hours are required. The fixed overhead rate is therefore $2 per hour ($52,800 ÷ 26,400 hours).

Xonic produced 1,000 units of Xonic Tonic in June. The standard hours allowed for the 1,000 gallons produced in June is 2,000 (1,000 gallons × 2 hours). For Xonic, normal capacity for June is 1,100, so standard direct labor hours for June at normal capacity is 2,200 (26,400 annual hours ÷ 12 months). The computation of the overhead volume variance in this case is as shown in **Illustration 17A.4**.

**ILLUSTRATION 17A.4**

**Computation of overhead volume variance for Xonic**

| Fixed Overhead Rate | × | Normal Capacity Hours | − | Standard Hours Allowed | = | Overhead Volume Variance |
|---|---|---|---|---|---|---|
| $2 | × | (2,200 | − | 2,000) | = | $400 U |

In Xonic's case, a $400 unfavorable volume variance results. The volume variance is unfavorable because Xonic produced only 1,000 gallons rather than the normal capacity of 1,100 gallons in the month of June. As a result, it underapplied fixed overhead for that period.

In computing the overhead variances, it is important to remember the following.

1. Standard hours allowed are used in each of the variances.
2. Budgeted costs for the controllable variance are derived from the flexible budget.
3. The controllable variance generally pertains to variable costs.
4. The volume variance pertains solely to fixed costs.

# Review and Practice

## Learning Objectives Review

### 1 Describe standard costs.

Both standards and budgets are predetermined costs. The primary difference is that a standard is a unit amount, whereas a budget is a total amount. A standard may be regarded as the budgeted cost per unit of product.

Standard costs offer a number of advantages. They (a) facilitate management planning, (b) promote greater economy, (c) are useful in setting selling prices, (d) contribute to management control, (e) permit "management by exception," and (f) simplify the costing of inventories and reduce clerical costs.

The direct materials price standard should be based on the delivered cost of raw materials plus an allowance for receiving and handling. The direct materials quantity standard should establish the required quantity plus an allowance for waste and spoilage.

The direct labor price standard should be based on current wage rates and anticipated adjustments such as COLAs. It also generally includes payroll taxes and fringe benefits. Direct labor quantity standards should be based on required production time plus an allowance for rest periods, cleanup, machine setup, and machine downtime.

For manufacturing overhead, a standard predetermined overhead rate is used. It is based on an expected standard activity index such as standard direct labor hours or standard machine hours.

### 2 Determine direct materials variances.

The formulas for the direct materials variances are as follows.

$$\begin{pmatrix} \text{Actual quantity} \\ \times \text{Actual price} \end{pmatrix} - \begin{pmatrix} \text{Standard quantity} \\ \times \text{Standard price} \end{pmatrix} = \begin{matrix} \text{Total} \\ \text{materials} \\ \text{variance} \end{matrix}$$

$$\begin{pmatrix} \text{Actual quantity} \\ \times \text{Actual price} \end{pmatrix} - \begin{pmatrix} \text{Actual quantity} \\ \times \text{Standard price} \end{pmatrix} = \begin{matrix} \text{Materials} \\ \text{price} \\ \text{variance} \end{matrix}$$

$$\begin{pmatrix} \text{Actual quantity} \\ \times \text{Standard price} \end{pmatrix} - \begin{pmatrix} \text{Standard quantity} \\ \times \text{Standard price} \end{pmatrix} = \begin{matrix} \text{Materials} \\ \text{quantity} \\ \text{variance} \end{matrix}$$

### 3 Determine direct labor and total manufacturing overhead variances.

The formulas for the direct labor variances are as follows.

$$\begin{pmatrix} \text{Actual hours} \\ \times \text{Actual rate} \end{pmatrix} - \begin{pmatrix} \text{Standard hours} \\ \times \text{Standard rate} \end{pmatrix} = \begin{matrix} \text{Total labor} \\ \text{variance} \end{matrix}$$

$$\begin{pmatrix} \text{Actual hours} \\ \times \text{Actual rate} \end{pmatrix} - \begin{pmatrix} \text{Actual hours} \\ \times \text{Standard rate} \end{pmatrix} = \begin{matrix} \text{Labor price} \\ \text{variance} \end{matrix}$$

$$\begin{pmatrix} \text{Actual hours} \\ \times \text{Standard rate} \end{pmatrix} - \begin{pmatrix} \text{Standard hours} \\ \times \text{Standard rate} \end{pmatrix} = \begin{matrix} \text{Labor quantity} \\ \text{variance} \end{matrix}$$

The formula for the total manufacturing overhead variance is as follows.

$$\begin{pmatrix} \text{Actual} \\ \text{overhead} \end{pmatrix} - \begin{pmatrix} \text{Overhead} \\ \text{applied at} \\ \text{standard hours} \\ \text{allowed} \end{pmatrix} = \begin{matrix} \text{Total overhead} \\ \text{variance} \end{matrix}$$

### 4 Prepare variance reports and balanced scorecards.

Variances are reported to management in variance reports. The reports facilitate management by exception by highlighting significant differences. Under a standard costing system, an income statement prepared for management will report cost of goods sold at standard cost and then disclose each variance separately.

The balanced scorecard incorporates financial and nonfinancial measures in an integrated system that links performance measurement and a company's strategic goals. It employs four perspectives: financial, customer, internal process, and learning and growth. Objectives are set within each of these perspectives that link to objectives within the other perspectives.

### *5 Compute overhead controllable and volume variances.

The total overhead variance is generally analyzed through a price variance and a quantity variance. The name usually given to the price variance is the overhead controllable variance. The quantity variance is referred to as the overhead volume variance.

## Decision Tools Review

| Decision Checkpoints | Info Needed for Decision | Tool to Use for Decision | How to Evaluate Results |
|---|---|---|---|
| Has management accomplished its price and quantity objectives regarding materials? | Actual cost and standard cost of materials | Materials price and materials quantity variances | Positive (favorable) variances suggest that price and quantity objectives have been met. |
| Has management accomplished its price and quantity objectives regarding labor? | Actual cost and standard cost of labor | Labor price and labor quantity variances | Positive (favorable) variances suggest that price and quantity objectives have been met. |
| Has management accomplished its objectives regarding manufacturing overhead? | Actual cost and standard cost of manufacturing overhead | Total manufacturing overhead variance | Positive (favorable) variances suggest that manufacturing overhead objectives have been met. |

## Glossary Review

**Balanced scorecard** An approach that incorporates financial and non-financial measures in an integrated system that links performance measurement and a company's strategic goals. (p. 17-19).

**Customer perspective** A viewpoint employed in the balanced scorecard to evaluate the company from the perspective of those people who buy and use its products or services. (p. 17-19).

**Direct labor price standard** The rate per hour that management determines should be incurred for direct labor to produce one unit of product. (p. 17-6).

**Direct labor quantity standard** The time that management determines should be required to produce one unit of product. (p. 17-6).

**Direct materials price standard** The cost per unit of direct materials that management determines should be incurred to produce one unit of product. (p. 17-5).

**Direct materials quantity standard** The quantity of direct materials that management determines should be used per unit of finished goods. (p. 17-6).

**Financial perspective** A viewpoint employed in the balanced scorecard to evaluate a company's performance using financial measures. (p. 17-19).

**Ideal standards** Standards based on the optimum level of performance under perfect operating conditions. (p. 17-4).

**Internal process perspective** A viewpoint employed in the balanced scorecard to evaluate the effectiveness and efficiency of a company's value chain, including product development, production, delivery, and after-sale service. (p. 17-20).

**Labor price variance** The difference between the actual hours times the actual rate and the actual hours times the standard rate for labor. (p. 17-13).

**Labor quantity variance** The difference between actual hours times the standard rate and standard hours times the standard rate for labor. (p. 17-13).

**Learning and growth perspective** A viewpoint employed in the balanced scorecard to evaluate how well a company develops and retains its employees. (p. 17-20).

**Materials price variance** The difference between the actual quantity times the actual price and the actual quantity times the standard price for materials. (p. 17-10).

**Materials quantity variance** The difference between the actual quantity times the standard price and the standard quantity times the standard price for materials. (p. 17-11).

**Normal capacity** The average activity output that a company should experience over the long run. (p. 17-7).

**Normal standards** Standards based on an efficient level of performance that are attainable under expected operating conditions. (p. 17-4).

*Overhead controllable variance** The difference between actual overhead incurred and overhead budgeted for the standard hours allowed. (p. 17-23).

*Overhead volume variance** The difference between normal capacity hours and standard hours allowed times the fixed overhead rate. (p. 17-24).

**Standard costs** Predetermined unit costs which companies use as measures of performance. (p. 17-3).

**Standard hours allowed** The hours that should have been worked for the units produced. (p. 17-15).

**Standard predetermined overhead rate** An overhead rate determined by dividing budgeted overhead costs by an expected standard activity index. (p. 17-7).

**Total labor variance** The difference between actual hours times the actual rate and standard hours times the standard rate for labor. (p. 17-13).

**Total materials variance** The difference between the actual quantity times the actual price and the standard quantity times the standard price of materials. (p. 17-10).

**Total overhead variance** The difference between actual overhead costs and overhead costs applied to work done, based on standard hours allowed. (p. 17-15).

**Variance** The difference between total actual costs and total standard costs. (p. 17-8).

## Practice Multiple-Choice Questions

1. **(LO 1)** Standards differ from budgets in that:

   a. budgets but not standards may be used in valuing inventories.

   b. budgets but not standards may be incorporated in cost accounting systems.

   c. budgets are a total amount and standards are a unit amount.

   d. only budgets contribute to management planning and control.

2. **(LO 1)** Standard costs:

   a. are imposed by governmental agencies.

   b. are predetermined unit costs which companies use as measures of performance.

   c. can be used by manufacturing companies but not by service or not-for-profit companies.

   d. All of the answer choices are correct.

3. **(LO 1)** The advantages of standard costs include all of the following **except**:

   a. management by exception may be used.

   b. management planning is facilitated.

   c. they may simplify the costing of inventories.

   d. management must use a static budget.

4. **(LO 1)** Normal standards:

   a. allow for rest periods, machine breakdowns, and setup time.

   b. represent levels of performance under perfect operating conditions.

   c. are rarely used because managers believe they lower workforce morale.

   d. are more likely than ideal standards to result in unethical practices.

5. **(LO 1)** The setting of standards is:

   a. a managerial accounting decision.

   b. a management decision.

   c. a worker decision.

   d. preferably set at the ideal level of performance.

6. **(LO 2)** Each of the following formulas is correct **except**:

   a. Labor price variance = (Actual hours × Actual rate) − (Actual hours × Standard rate).

   b. Total overhead variance = Actual overhead − Overhead applied.

   c. Materials price variance = (Actual quantity × Actual price) − (Standard quantity × Standard price).

   d. Labor quantity variance = (Actual hours × Standard rate) − (Standard hours × Standard rate).

7. **(LO 2)** In producing product AA, 6,300 pounds of direct materials were used at a cost of $1.10 per pound. The standard was 6,000 pounds at $1.00 per pound. The direct materials quantity variance is:

   a. $330 unfavorable.    c. $600 unfavorable.

   b. $300 unfavorable.    d. $630 unfavorable.

8. **(LO 3)** In producing product ZZ, 14,800 direct labor hours were used at a rate of $8.20 per hour. The standard was 15,000 hours at $8.00 per hour. Based on these data, the direct labor:

   a. quantity variance is $1,600 favorable.

   b. quantity variance is $1,600 unfavorable.

   c. price variance is $3,000 favorable.

   d. price variance is $3,000 unfavorable.

9. **(LO 3)** Which of the following is **correct** about the total overhead variance?

   a. Budgeted overhead and overhead applied are the same.

   b. Total actual overhead is composed of variable overhead, fixed overhead, and period costs.

   c. Standard hours actually worked are used in computing the variance.

   d. Standard hours allowed for the work done is the measure used in computing the variance.

10. **(LO 3)** The formula for computing the total overhead variance is:

    a. actual overhead less overhead applied.

    b. overhead budgeted less overhead applied.

    c. actual overhead less overhead budgeted.

    d. No correct answer is given.

11. **(LO 4)** Which of the following is **incorrect** about variance reports?

    a. They facilitate "management by exception."

    b. They should only be sent to the top level of management.

    c. They should be prepared as soon as possible.

    d. They may vary in form, content, and frequency among companies.

12. **(LO 4)** In using variance reports to evaluate cost control, management normally looks into:

    a. all variances.

    b. favorable variances only.

    c. unfavorable variances only.

    d. both favorable and unfavorable variances that exceed a predetermined quantitative measure such as a percentage or dollar amount.

13. **(LO 4)** Generally accepted accounting principles allow a company to:

    a. report inventory at standard cost but cost of goods sold must be reported at actual cost.

    b. report cost of goods sold at standard cost but inventory must be reported at actual cost.

    c. report inventory and cost of goods sold at standard cost as long as there are no significant differences between actual and standard cost.

    d. report inventory and cost of goods sold only at actual costs; standard costing is never permitted.

**14. (LO 4)** Which of the following would **not** be an objective used in the customer perspective of the balanced scorecard approach?

   **a.** Percentage of customers who would recommend product to a friend.

   **b.** Customer retention.

   **c.** Brand recognition.

   **d.** Earnings per share.

**\*15. (LO 5)** The formula to compute the overhead volume variance is:

   **a.** Fixed overhead rate × (Standard hours − Actual hours).

   **b.** Fixed overhead rate × (Normal capacity hours − Actual hours).

   **c.** Fixed overhead rate × (Normal capacity hours − Standard hours allowed).

   **d.** (Variable overhead rate + Fixed overhead rate) × (Normal capacity hours − Standard hours allowed).

## Solutions

**1. c.** Budgets are expressed in total amounts, and standards are expressed in unit amounts. The other choices are incorrect because (a) standards, not budgets, may be used in valuing inventories; (b) standards, not budgets, may be incorporated in cost accounting systems; and (d) both budgets and standards contribute to management planning and control.

**2. b.** Standard costs are predetermined units costs which companies use as measures of performance. The other choices are incorrect because (a) only those that are called regulations are imposed by governmental agencies, (c) standard costs can be used by all types of companies, and (d) choices (a) and (c) are incorrect.

**3. d.** Standard costs are separate from a static budget. The other choices are all advantages of using standard costs.

**4. a.** Normal standards allow for rest periods, machine breakdowns, and setup time. The other choices are incorrect because they describe ideal standards, not normal standards.

**5. b.** Standards are set by management. The other choices are incorrect because setting standards requires input from (a) managerial accountants and (c) sometimes workers, but the final decision is made by management. Choice (d) is incorrect because setting standards at the ideal level of performance is uncommon because of the perceived negative effect on worker morale.

**6. c.** Materials price variance = (Actual quantity × Actual price) − (Actual quantity (not Standard quantity) × Standard price). The other choices are correct formulas.

**7. b.** The direct materials quantity variance is $(6,300 \times \$1.00) - (6,000 \times \$1.00) = \$300$. This variance is unfavorable because more material was used than prescribed by the standard. The other choices are therefore incorrect.

**8. a.** The direct labor quantity variance is $(14,800 \times \$8) - (15,000 \times \$8) = \$1,600$. This variance is favorable because fewer labor hours were used than prescribed by the standard. The other choices are therefore incorrect.

**9. d.** Standard hours allowed for work done is the measure used in computing the variance. The other choices are incorrect because (a) budgeted overhead is used to calculate the predetermined overhead rate while overhead applied is equal to standard hours allowed times the predetermined overhead rate, (b) overhead is a product cost and does not include period costs, and (c) standard hours allowed, not hours actually worked, are used in computing the overhead variance.

**10. a.** Total overhead variance equals actual overhead less overhead applied. The other choices are therefore incorrect.

**11. b.** Variance reports should be sent to the level of management responsible for the area in which the variance occurred so it can be remedied as quickly as possible. The other choices are correct statements.

**12. d.** In using variance reports to evaluate cost control, management normally looks into both favorable and unfavorable variances that exceed a predetermined quantitative measure such as percentage or dollar amount. The other choices are therefore incorrect.

**13. c.** GAAP allows a company to report both inventory and cost of goods sold at standard cost as long as there are no significant differences between actual and standard cost. The other choices are therefore incorrect.

**14. d.** Earnings per share is not an objective used in the customer perspective of the balanced scorecard approach. The other choices are all true statements.

**\*15. c.** The formula to compute the overhead volume variance is Fixed overhead rate × (Normal capacity hours − Standard hours allowed). The other choices are therefore incorrect.

## Practice Brief Exercises

*Set direct materials standard.*

**1. (LO 1)** Castellen Company accumulates the following data concerning raw materials in making one quart of finished product. (1) Price—purchase price $3.00; terms 2/10, n/30; freight-in $0.25; and receiving and handling $0.10. (2) Quantity—required materials 2.7 pounds, allowance for waste and spoilage 0.3 pounds. Compute the following.

   **a.** Standard direct materials price per quart.

   **b.** Standard direct materials quantity per quart.

   **c.** Total standard materials cost per quart

## Solution

1.  **a.** Standard direct materials price per quart = ($3.00 − $0.06 + $0.25 + $0.10) = $3.29

    **b.** Standard direct materials quantity per quart = (2.7 + .3) = 3 pounds

    **c.** Standard materials cost per quart = ($3.29 × 3) = $9.87

---

**2. (LO 2)** Spandrell Company's standard materials cost per unit of output is $12 (3 pounds × $4). During July, the company purchases and uses 5,800 pounds of materials costing $22,910 in making 2,000 units of finished product. Compute the total, price, and quantity materials variances.

*Compute direct materials variances.*

## Solution

2.  Total materials variance = [(5,800 × $3.95*) − (6,000** × $4.00)] = $1,090 F

    Materials price variance = [(5,800 × $3.95) − (5,800 × $4.00)] = $290 F

    Materials quantity variance [(5,800 × $4.00) − (6,000 × $4.00)] = $800 F

    *$22,910 ÷ 5,800; **2,000 × 3

---

**3. (LO 3)** Timemore Company's standard labor cost per unit of output is $34 (2 hours × $17 per hour). During August, the company incurs 1,960 hours of direct labor at an hourly cost of $17.20 per hour in making 1,000 units of finished product. Compute the total, price, and quantity labor variances.

*Compute direct labor variances.*

## Solution

3.  Total labor variance = [(1,960 × $17.20) − (2,000 × $17.00)] = $288 F

    Labor price variance = [(1,960 × $17.20) − (1,960 × $17.00)] = $392 U

    Labor quantity variance = [(1,960 × $17.00) − (2,000 × $17.00)] = $680 F

---

# Practice Exercises

**1. (LO 2, 3)** Hector Inc., which produces a single product, has prepared the following standard cost sheet for one unit of the product.

*Compute materials and labor variances.*

| | |
|---|---|
| Direct materials (6 pounds at $2.50 per pound) | $15.00 |
| Direct labor (3.1 hours at $12.00 per hour) | $37.20 |

During the month of April, the company manufactures 250 units and incurs the following actual costs.

| | |
|---|---|
| Direct materials purchased and used (1,600 pounds) | $4,192 |
| Direct labor (760 hours) | $8,740 |

### Instructions

Compute the total, price, and quantity variances for materials and labor.

## Solution

1.  Total materials variance:

| (AQ × AP) | − | (SQ × SP) | = | TMV |
|---|---|---|---|---|
| (1,600 × $2.62*) | | (1,500** × $2.50) | | |
| $4,192 | − | $3,750 | = | $442 U |

*$4,192 ÷ 1,600; **250 × 6

Materials price variance:

| | (AQ × AP) | − | (AQ × SP) | = | MPV |
|---|---|---|---|---|---|
| | (1,600 × $2.62) | | (1,600 × $2.50) | | |
| | $4,192 | − | $4,000 | = | $192 U |

Materials quantity variance:

| | (AQ × SP) | − | (SQ × SP) | = | MQV |
|---|---|---|---|---|---|
| | (1,600 × $2.50) | | (1,500 × $2.50) | | |
| | $4,000 | − | $3,750 | = | $250 U |

Total labor variance:

| | (AH × AR) | − | (SH × SR) | = | TLV |
|---|---|---|---|---|---|
| | (760 × $11.50*) | | (775** × $12.00) | | |
| | $8,740 | − | $9,300 | = | $560 F |

*$8,740 ÷ 760; **250 × 3.1

Labor price variance:

| | (AH × AR) | − | (AH × SR) | = | LPV |
|---|---|---|---|---|---|
| | (760 × $11.50) | | (760 × $12.00) | | |
| | $8,740 | − | $9,120 | = | $380 F |

Labor quantity variance:

| | (AH × SR) | − | (SH × SR) | = | LQV |
|---|---|---|---|---|---|
| | (760 × $12.00) | | (775 × $12.00) | | |
| | $9,120 | − | $9,300 | = | $180 F |

*Compute overhead variances.*

**2. (LO 3)** Manufacturing overhead data for the production of Product H by Yamato Company are as follows.

| | |
|---|---|
| Overhead incurred for 35,000 actual direct labor hours worked | $140,000 |
| Overhead rate (variable $3; fixed $1) at normal capacity of 36,000 direct labor hours | $4 |
| Standard hours allowed for work done | 34,000 |

**Instructions**

Compute the total overhead variance.

**Solution**

2. Total overhead variance:

| | Actual Overhead | − | Overhead Applied | = | Overhead Variance |
|---|---|---|---|---|---|
| | $140,000 | − | $136,000 | = | $4,000 U |
| | | | (34,000 × $4) | | |

---

## Practice Problem

*Compute variances.*

**(LO 2, 3)** Manlow Company makes a cologne called Allure. The standard cost for one bottle of Allure is as follows.

| | Standard | | | |
|---|---|---|---|---|
| **Manufacturing Cost Elements** | **Quantity** | × **Price** | = | **Cost** |
| Direct materials | 6 oz. | × $ 0.90 | = | $ 5.40 |
| Direct labor | 0.5 hrs. | × $12.00 | = | 6.00 |
| Manufacturing overhead | 0.5 hrs. | × $ 4.80 | = | 2.40 |
| | | | | $13.80 |

During the month, the following transactions occurred in manufacturing 10,000 bottles of Allure.

1. 58,000 ounces of materials were purchased at $1.00 per ounce.

2. All the materials purchased were used to produce the 10,000 bottles of Allure.

3. 4,900 direct labor hours were worked at a total labor cost of $56,350.

4. Variable manufacturing overhead incurred was $15,000 and fixed overhead incurred was $10,400.

The manufacturing overhead rate of $4.80 is based on a normal capacity of 5,200 direct labor hours. The total budget at this capacity is $10,400 fixed and $14,560 variable.

### Instructions

a. Compute the total variance and the variances for direct materials and direct labor elements.

b. Compute the total variance for manufacturing overhead.

### Solution

**a.**

**Total Variance**

| | |
|---|---:|
| Actual costs incurred | |
| Direct materials | $ 58,000 |
| Direct labor | 56,350 |
| Manufacturing overhead | 25,400 |
| | 139,750 |
| Standard cost (10,000 × $13.80) | 138,000 |
| Total variance | $  1,750 U |

**Direct Materials Variances**

| | | | | | | |
|---|---|---|---|---|---|---|
| Total | = | $58,000 (58,000 × $1.00) | − | $54,000 (60,000* × $0.90) | = | $4,000 U |
| Price | = | $58,000 (58,000 × $1.00) | − | $52,200 (58,000 × $0.90) | = | $5,800 U |
| Quantity | = | $52,200 (58,000 × $0.90) | − | $54,000 (60,000 × $0.90) | = | $1,800 F |

*10,000 × 6

**Direct Labor Variances**

| | | | | | | |
|---|---|---|---|---|---|---|
| Total | = | $56,350 (4,900 × $11.50*) | − | $60,000 (5,000** × $12.00) | = | $3,650 F |
| Price | = | $56,350 (4,900 × $11.50) | − | $58,800 (4,900 × $12.00) | = | $2,450 F |
| Quantity | = | $58,800 (4,900 × $12.00) | − | $60,000 (5,000 × $12.00) | = | $1,200 F |

*56,350 ÷ 4,900; **10,000 × 0.5

**b.**

**Overhead Variance**

| | | | | | | |
|---|---|---|---|---|---|---|
| Total | = | $25,400 ($15,000 + $10,400) | − | $24,000 (5,000 × $4.80) | = | $1,400 U |

# WileyPLUS

Brief Exercises, DO IT! Exercises, Exercises, Problems, and many additional resources are available for practice in WileyPLUS.

*Note:* All asterisked Questions, Exercises, and Problems relate to material in the appendix to the chapter.

## Questions

1. a. "Standard costs are the expected total cost of completing a job." Is this correct? Explain.

   b. "A standard imposed by a governmental agency is known as a regulation." Do you agree? Explain.

2. a. Explain the similarities and differences between standards and budgets.

   b. Contrast the accounting for standards and budgets.

**3.** Standard costs facilitate management planning. What are the other advantages of standard costs?

**4.** Contrast the roles of the management accountant and management in setting standard costs.

**5.** Distinguish between an ideal standard and a normal standard.

**6.** What factors should be considered in setting (a) the direct materials price standard and (b) the direct materials quantity standard?

**7.** "The objective in setting the direct labor quantity standard is to determine the aggregate time required to make one unit of product." Do you agree? What allowances should be made in setting this standard?

**8.** How is the predetermined overhead rate determined when standard costs are used?

**9.** What is the difference between a favorable cost variance and an unfavorable cost variance?

**10.** In each of the following formulas, supply the words that should be inserted for each number in parentheses.

  **a.** (Actual quantity × (1)) − (Standard quantity × (2)) = Total materials variance

  **b.** ((3) × Actual price) − (Actual quantity × (4)) = Materials price variance

  **c.** (Actual quantity × (5)) − ((6) × Standard price) = Materials quantity variance

**11.** In the direct labor variance matrix, there are three factors: (1) Actual hours × Actual rate, (2) Actual hours × Standard rate, and (3) Standard hours × Standard rate. Using the numbers, indicate the formulas for each of the direct labor variances.

**12.** Mikan Company's standard predetermined overhead rate is $9 per direct labor hour. For the month of June, 26,000 actual hours were worked, and 27,000 standard hours were allowed. How much overhead was applied?

**13.** How often should variances be reported to management? What principle may be used with variance reports?

**14.** What circumstances may cause the purchasing department to be responsible for both an unfavorable materials price variance and an unfavorable materials quantity variance?

**15.** What are the four perspectives used in the balanced scorecard? Discuss the nature of each, and how the perspectives are linked.

**16.** Kerry James says that the balanced scorecard was created to replace financial measures as the primary mechanism for performance evaluation. He says that it uses only nonfinancial measures. Is this true?

**17.** What are some examples of nonfinancial measures used by companies to evaluate performance?

**18.** (a) How are variances reported in income statements prepared for management? (b) Can standard costs be used in preparing financial statements for stockholders? Explain.

**\*19.** Mikan Company's standard predetermined overhead rate is $9 per direct labor hour. For the month of June, 26,000 actual hours were worked, and 27,000 standard hours were allowed. If the $9 per hour overhead rate includes $5 variable, and actual overhead costs were $248,000, what is the overhead controllable variance for June? The normal capacity hours were 28,000. Is the variance favorable or unfavorable?

**\*20.** What is the purpose of computing the overhead volume variance? What is the basic formula for this variance?

**\*21.** Alma Ortiz does not understand why the overhead volume variance indicates that fixed overhead costs are under- or overapplied. Clarify this matter for Alma.

**\*22.** John Hsu is attempting to outline the important points about overhead variances on a class examination. List four points that John should include in his outline.

# Brief Exercises

*Distinguish between a standard and a budget.*

**BE17.1 (LO 1), AP** Lopez Company uses both standards and budgets. For the year, estimated production of Product X is 500,000 units. Total estimated cost for materials and labor are $1,400,000 and $1,700,000, respectively. Compute the estimates for (a) a standard cost and (b) a budgeted cost.

*Set direct materials standard.*

**BE17.2 (LO 1), AP** Tang Company accumulates the following data concerning raw materials in making its finished product. (1) Price per pound of raw materials is net purchase price $2.30, freight-in $0.20, and receiving and handling $0.10. (2) Quantity per gallon of finished product is required materials 3.6 pounds and allowance for waste and spoilage 0.4 pounds. Compute the following.

  **a.** Standard direct materials price per pound of raw materials.

  **b.** Standard direct materials quantity per gallon.

  **c.** Total standard materials cost per gallon.

*Set direct labor standard.*

**BE17.3 (LO 1), AP** Labor data for making one gallon of finished product in Bing Company are as follows. (1) Price—hourly wage rate $14.00, payroll taxes $0.80, and fringe benefits $1.20. (2) Quantity—actual production time 1.1 hours, rest periods and cleanup 0.25 hours, and setup and downtime 0.15 hours. Compute the following.

  **a.** Standard direct labor rate per hour.

  **b.** Standard direct labor hours per gallon.

  **c.** Standard labor cost per gallon.

**BE17.4 (LO 2), AP** Simba Company's standard materials cost per unit of output is $10 (2 pounds × $5). During July, the company purchases and uses 3,200 pounds of materials costing $16,192 in making 1,500 units of finished product. Compute the total, price, and quantity materials variances.

*Compute direct materials variances.*

**BE17.5 (LO 3), AP** Mordica Company's standard labor cost per unit of output is $22 (2 hours × $11 per hour). During August, the company incurs 2,150 hours of direct labor at an hourly cost of $10.80 per hour in making 1,000 units of finished product. Compute the total, price, and quantity labor variances.

*Compute direct labor variances.*

**BE17.6 (LO 3), AP** In October, Pine Company reports 21,000 actual direct labor hours, and it incurs $118,000 of manufacturing overhead costs. Standard hours allowed for the work done is 20,600 hours. The predetermined overhead rate is $6 per direct labor hour. Compute the total overhead variance.

*Compute total overhead variance.*

**BE17.7 (LO 4), C** The four perspectives in the balanced scorecard are (1) financial, (2) customer, (3) internal process, and (4) learning and growth. Match each of the following objectives with the perspective it is most likely associated with: (a) plant capacity utilization, (b) employee work days missed due to injury, (c) return on assets, and (d) brand recognition.

*Match balanced scorecard perspectives.*

**\*BE17.8 (LO 5), AP** In October, Pine Company reports 21,000 actual direct labor hours, and it incurs $118,000 of manufacturing overhead costs. Standard hours allowed for the work done is 20,600 hours. The predetermined overhead rate is $6 per direct labor hour. In addition, the flexible manufacturing overhead budget shows that budgeted costs are $4 variable per direct labor hour and $50,000 fixed. Compute the overhead controllable variance.

*Compute the overhead controllable variance.*

**\*BE17.9 (LO 5), AP** Using the data in BE17.8, compute the overhead volume variance. Normal capacity was 25,000 direct labor hours.

*Compute overhead volume variance.*

## DO IT! Exercises

**DO IT! 17.1 (LO 1), AP** Larkin Company accumulated the following standard cost data concerning product I-Tal.

*Compute standard cost.*

Direct materials per unit: 2 pounds at $5 per pound
Direct labor per unit: 0.2 hours at $16 per hour
Manufacturing overhead: Allocated based on direct labor hours at a predetermined rate of $20 per direct labor hour
Compute the standard cost of one unit of product I-Tal.

**DO IT! 17.2 (LO 2), AP** The standard cost of product 777 includes 2 units of direct materials at $6.00 per unit. During August, the company bought 29,000 units of materials at $6.30 and used those materials to produce 16,000 units. Compute the total, price, and quantity variances for materials.

*Compute materials variance.*

**DO IT! 17.3 (LO 3), AP** The standard cost of product 5252 includes 1.9 hours of direct labor at $14.00 per hour. The predetermined overhead rate is $22.00 per direct labor hour. During July, the company incurred 4,000 hours of direct labor at an average rate of $14.30 per hour and $81,300 of manufacturing overhead costs. It produced 2,000 units.

*Compute labor and manufacturing overhead variances.*

a. Compute the total, price, and quantity variances for labor.

b. Compute the total overhead variance.

**DO IT! 17.4 (LO 4), AP** Tropic Zone Corporation experienced the following variances: materials price $350 U, materials quantity $1,700 F, labor price $800 F, labor quantity $500 F, and total overhead $1,200 U. Sales revenue was $92,100, and cost of goods sold (at standard) was $51,600. Determine the actual gross profit.

*Prepare variance report.*

## Exercises

**E17.1 (LO 1), AP** **Writing** Parsons Company is planning to produce 2,000 units of product in 2022. Each unit requires 3 pounds of materials at $5 per pound and a half-hour of labor at $16 per hour. The overhead rate is 70% of direct labor.

*Compute budget and standard.*

**Instructions**

a. Compute the budgeted amounts for 2022 for direct materials to be used, direct labor, and applied overhead.

b. Compute the standard cost of one unit of product.

c. What are the potential advantages to a corporation of using standard costs?

*Compute standard materials costs.*

**E17.2 (LO 1), AP** Hank Itzek manufactures and sells homemade wine, and he wants to develop a standard cost per gallon. The following are required for production of a 50-gallon batch.

3,000 ounces of grape concentrate at $0.06 per ounce
54 pounds of granulated sugar at $0.30 per pound
60 lemons at $0.60 each
50 yeast tablets at $0.25 each
50 nutrient tablets at $0.20 each
2,600 ounces of water at $0.005 per ounce

Hank estimates that 4% of the grape concentrate is wasted, 10% of the sugar is lost, and 25% of the lemons cannot be used.

**Instructions**

Compute the standard cost of the ingredients for one gallon of wine. (Carry computations to two decimal places.)

*Compute standard cost per unit.*

**E17.3 (LO 1), AP** Stefani Company has gathered the following information about its product.

**Direct materials.** Each unit of product contains 4.5 pounds of materials. The average waste and spoilage per unit produced under normal conditions is 0.5 pounds. Materials cost $5 per pound, but Stefani always takes the 2% cash discount all of its suppliers offer. Freight costs average $0.25 per pound.

**Direct labor.** Each unit requires 2 hours of labor. Setup, cleanup, and downtime average 0.4 hours per unit. The average hourly pay rate of Stefani's employees is $12. Payroll taxes and fringe benefits are an additional $3 per hour.

**Manufacturing overhead.** Overhead is applied at a rate of $7 per direct labor hour.

**Instructions**

Compute Stefani's total standard cost per unit.

*Compute labor cost and labor quantity variance.*

**E17.4 (LO 1, 3), AP** **Service**  Monte Services, Inc. is trying to establish the standard labor cost of a typical brake repair. The following data have been collected from time and motion studies conducted over the past month.

| | |
|---|---|
| Actual time spent on the brake repair | 1.0 hour |
| Hourly wage rate | $12 |
| Payroll taxes | 10% of wage rate |
| Setup and downtime | 20% of actual labor time |
| Cleanup and rest periods | 30% of actual labor time |
| Fringe benefits | 25% of wage rate |

**Instructions**

a. Determine the standard direct labor hours per brake repair.

b. Determine the standard direct labor hourly rate.

c. Determine the standard direct labor cost per brake repair.

d. If a brake repair took 1.6 hours at the standard hourly rate, what was the direct labor quantity variance?

*Compute materials price and quantity variances.*

**E17.5 (LO 2), AP** The standard cost of Product B manufactured by Pharrell Company includes three units of direct materials at $5.00 per unit. During June, 29,000 units of direct materials are purchased at a cost of $4.70 per unit, and 29,000 units of direct materials are used to produce 9,400 units of Product B.

**Instructions**

a. Compute the total materials variance and the price and quantity variances.

b. Repeat (a), assuming the purchase price is $5.15 and the quantity purchased and used is 28,000 units.

*Compute labor price and quantity variances.*

**E17.6 (LO 3), AP** Lewis Company's standard labor cost of producing one unit of Product DD is 4 hours at the rate of $12.00 per hour. During August, 40,600 hours of labor are incurred at a cost of $12.15 per hour to produce 10,000 units of Product DD.

## Instructions

**a.** Compute the total labor variance.

**b.** Compute the labor price and quantity variances.

**c.** Repeat (b), assuming the standard is 4.1 hours of direct labor at $12.25 per hour.

**E17.7 (LO 2, 3), AP** Levine Inc., which produces a single product, has prepared the following standard cost sheet for one unit of the product.

| | |
|---|---|
| Direct materials (8 pounds at $2.50 per pound) | $20 |
| Direct labor (3 hours at $12.00 per hour) | $36 |

During the month of April, the company manufactures 230 units and incurs the following actual costs.

| | |
|---|---|
| Direct materials purchased and used (1,900 pounds) | $5,035 |
| Direct labor (700 hours) | $8,120 |

## Instructions

Compute the total, price, and quantity variances for materials and labor.

**E17.8 (LO 2, 3), AN** **Writing** The following direct materials and direct labor data pertain to the operations of Laurel Company for the month of August.

*Compute the materials and labor variances and list reasons for unfavorable variances.*

| Costs | | Quantities | |
|---|---|---|---|
| Actual labor rate | $13 per hour | Actual hours incurred and used | 4,150 hours |
| Actual materials price | $128 per ton | Actual quantity of materials purchased and used | 1,220 tons |
| Standard labor rate | $12.50 per hour | Standard hours used | 4,300 hours |
| Standard materials price | $130 per ton | Standard quantity of materials used | 1,200 tons |

## Instructions

**a.** Compute the total, price, and quantity variances for materials and labor.

**b.** Provide two possible explanations for each of the unfavorable variances calculated above, and suggest where responsibility for the unfavorable result might be placed.

**E17.9 (LO 2, 3), AN** You have been given the following information about the production of Usher Co., and are asked to provide the plant manager with information for a meeting with the vice president of operations.

*Determine amounts from variance report.*

| | Standard Cost Card |
|---|---|
| Direct materials (5 pounds at $4 per pound) | $20.00 |
| Direct labor (0.8 hours at $10) | 8.00 |
| Variable overhead (0.8 hours at $3 per hour) | 2.40 |
| Fixed overhead (0.8 hours at $7 per hour) | 5.60 |
| | $36.00 |

The following is a variance report for the most recent period of operations.

| | | Variances | |
|---|---|---|---|
| Costs | Total Standard Cost | Price | Quantity |
| Direct materials | $410,000 | $2,095 F | $ 9,000 U |
| Direct labor | 164,000 | 3,906 U | 22,000 U |

## Instructions

**a.** How many units were produced during the period?

**b.** How many pounds of raw materials were purchased and used during the period?

**c.** What was the actual cost per pound of raw materials?

**d.** How many actual direct labor hours were worked during the period?

**e.** What was the actual rate paid per direct labor hour?

(CGA adapted)

*Prepare a variance report for direct labor.*

**E17.10 (LO 3, 4), AP** During March 2022, Toby Tool & Die Company worked on four jobs. A review of direct labor costs reveals the following summary data.

| Job Number | Actual | | Standard | | Total |
|---|---|---|---|---|---|
| | Hours | Costs | Hours | Costs | Variance |
| A257 | 221 | $4,420 | 225 | $4,500 | $ 80 F |
| A258 | 450 | 9,450 | 430 | 8,600 | 850 U |
| A259 | 300 | 6,180 | 300 | 6,000 | 180 U |
| A260 | 116 | 2,088 | 110 | 2,200 | 112 F |
| Total variance | | | | | $838 U |

Analysis reveals that Job A257 was a repeat job. Job A258 was a rush order that required overtime work at premium rates of pay. Job A259 required a more experienced replacement worker on one shift. Work on Job A260 was done for one day by a new trainee when a regular worker was absent.

**Instructions**

Prepare a report for the plant supervisor on direct labor cost variances for March. The report should have columns for (1) Job No., (2) Actual Hours, (3) Standard Hours, (4) Quantity Variance, (5) Actual Rate, (6) Standard Rate, (7) Price Variance, and (8) Explanation.

*Compute overhead variance.*

**E17.11 (LO 3), AP** Manufacturing overhead data for the production of Product H by Shakira Company, assuming the company uses a standard cost system, are as follows.

| | |
|---|---|
| Overhead incurred for 52,000 actual direct labor hours worked | $263,000 |
| Overhead rate (variable $3; fixed $2) at normal capacity of 54,000 direct labor hours | $5 |
| Standard hours allowed for work done | 52,000 |

**Instructions**

Compute the total overhead variance.

*Compute overhead variances.*

**E17.12 (LO 3), AP** Byrd Company produces one product, a putter called GO-Putter. Byrd uses a standard cost system and determines that it should take one hour of direct labor to produce one GO-Putter. The normal production capacity for this putter is 100,000 units per year. The total budgeted overhead at normal capacity is $850,000 comprised of $250,000 of variable costs and $600,000 of fixed costs. Byrd applies overhead on the basis of direct labor hours.

During the current year, Byrd produced 95,000 putters, worked 94,000 direct labor hours, and incurred variable overhead costs of $256,000 and fixed overhead costs of $600,000.

**Instructions**

a. Compute the predetermined variable overhead rate and the predetermined fixed overhead rate.

b. Compute the applied overhead for Byrd for the year.

c. Compute the total overhead variance.

*Compute variances for materials.*

**E17.13 (LO 2, 3), AP** **Writing** Ceelo Company purchased (at a cost of $10,200) and used 2,400 pounds of materials during May. Ceelo's standard cost of materials per unit produced is based on 2 pounds per unit at a cost $5 per pound. Production in May was 1,050 units.

**Instructions**

a. Compute the total, price, and quantity variances for materials.

b. Assume Ceelo also had an unfavorable labor quantity variance. What is a possible scenario that would provide one cause for the variances computed in (a) and the unfavorable labor quantity variance?

*Prepare a variance report.*

**E17.14 (LO 2, 4), AP** **Service** Picard Landscaping plants grass seed as the basic landscaping for business campuses. During a recent month, the company worked on three projects (Remington, Chang, and Wyco). The company is interested in controlling the materials costs, namely the grass seed, for these plantings projects.

In order to provide management with useful cost control information, the company uses standard costs and prepares monthly variance reports. Analysis reveals that the purchasing agent mistakenly purchased poor-quality seed for the Remington project. The Chang project, however, received higher-than-standard-quality seed that was on sale. The Wyco project received standard-quality seed. However, the price had increased and a new employee was used to spread the seed.

Shown here are quantity and cost data for each project.

| Project | Actual Quantity | Actual Costs | Standard Quantity | Standard Costs | Total Variance |
|---|---|---|---|---|---|
| Remington | 500 lbs. | $1,200 | 460 lbs. | $1,150 | $ 50 U |
| Chang | 400 | 920 | 410 | 1,025 | 105 F |
| Wyco | 550 | 1,430 | 480 | 1,200 | 230 U |
| Total variance | | | | | $175 U |

### Instructions

**a.** Prepare a variance report for the purchasing department with the following columns: (1) Project, (2) Actual Pounds Purchased, (3) Actual Price per Pound, (4) Standard Price per Pound, (5) Price Variance, and (6) Explanation.

**b.** Prepare a variance report for the production department with the following columns: (1) Project, (2) Actual Pounds, (3) Standard Pounds, (4) Standard Price per Pound, (5) Quantity Variance, and (6) Explanation.

**E17.15 (LO 4), AN** Urban Corporation prepared the following variance report.

*Complete variance report.*

**Urban Corporation**
**Variance Report—Purchasing Department**
**For the Week Ended January 9, 2022**

| Type of Materials | Quantity Purchased | Actual Price | Standard Price | Price Variance | Explanation |
|---|---|---|---|---|---|
| Rogue11 | ? lbs. | $5.20 | $5.00 | $5,500 ? | Price increase |
| Storm17 | 7,000 oz. | ? | 3.30 | 1,050 U | Rush order |
| Beast29 | 22,000 units | 0.40 | ? | 660 F | Bought larger quantity |

### Instructions

Fill in the appropriate amounts or letters for the question marks in the report.

**E17.16 (LO 4), AP** Fisk Company uses a standard cost accounting system. During January, the company reported the following manufacturing variances.

*Prepare income statement for management.*

| | | | |
|---|---|---|---|
| Materials price variance | $1,200 U | Labor quantity variance | $750 U |
| Materials quantity variance | 800 F | Overhead variance | 800 U |
| Labor price variance | 550 U | | |

In addition, 8,000 units of product were sold at $8 per unit. Each unit sold had a standard cost of $5. Selling and administrative expenses were $8,000 for the month.

### Instructions

Prepare an income statement for management for the month ended January 31, 2022.

**E17.17 (LO 1, 4), C** The following is a list of terms related to performance evaluation.

*Identify performance evaluation terminology.*

1. Balanced scorecard
2. Variance
3. Learning and growth perspective
4. Nonfinancial measures
5. Customer perspective
6. Internal process perspective
7. Ideal standards
8. Normal standards

### Instructions

Match each of the following descriptions with one of the terms above.

**a.** The difference between total actual costs and total standard costs.

**b.** An efficient level of performance that is attainable under expected operating conditions.

**c.** An approach that incorporates financial and nonfinancial measures in an integrated system that links performance measurement and a company's strategic goals.

**d.** A viewpoint employed in the balanced scorecard to evaluate how well a company develops and retains its employees.

**e.** An evaluation tool that is not based on dollars.

**f.** A viewpoint employed in the balanced scorecard to evaluate the company from the perspective of those people who buy its products or services.

g. An optimum level of performance under perfect operating conditions.

h. A viewpoint employed in the balanced scorecard to evaluate the efficiency and effectiveness of the company's value chain.

*Identity balanced scorecard perspectives.*

**E17.18 (LO 4), C** Indicate which of the four perspectives in the balanced scorecard is most likely associated with the objectives that follow.

1. Percentage of repeat customers.
2. Number of suggestions for improvement from employees.
3. Contribution margin.
4. Brand recognition.
5. Number of cross-trained employees.
6. Amount of setup time.

*Identify balanced scorecard perspectives.*

**E17.19 (LO 4), C** Indicate which of the four perspectives in the balanced scorecard is most likely associated with the objectives that follow.

1. Ethics violations.
2. Credit rating.
3. Customer retention.
4. Stockouts.
5. Reportable accidents.
6. Brand recognition.

*Compute manufacturing overhead variances and interpret findings.*

**\*E17.20 (LO 5), AN** `Writing` The information shown below was taken from the annual manufacturing overhead cost budget of Connick Company.

| | |
|---|---|
| Variable manufacturing overhead costs | $34,650 |
| Fixed manufacturing overhead costs | $19,800 |
| Normal production level in labor hours | 16,500 |
| Normal production level in units | 4,125 |
| Standard labor hours per unit | 4 |

During the year, 4,050 units were produced, 16,100 hours were worked, and the actual manufacturing overhead was $55,500. Actual fixed manufacturing overhead costs equaled budgeted fixed manufacturing overhead costs. Overhead is applied on the basis of direct labor hours.

### Instructions

a. Compute the total, fixed, and variable predetermined manufacturing overhead rates.

b. Compute the total, controllable, and volume overhead variances.

c. Briefly interpret the overhead controllable and volume variances computed in (b).

*Compute overhead variances.*

**\*E17.21 (LO 5), AN** `Service` The loan department of Calgary Bank uses standard costs to determine the overhead cost of processing loan applications. During the current month, a fire occurred, and the accounting records for the department were mostly destroyed. The following data were salvaged from the ashes.

| | |
|---|---|
| Standard variable overhead rate per hour | $9 |
| Standard hours per application | 2 |
| Standard hours allowed | 2,000 |
| Standard fixed overhead rate per hour | $6 |
| Actual fixed overhead cost | $12,600 |
| Variable overhead budget based on standard hours allowed | $18,000 |
| Fixed overhead budget | $12,600 |
| Overhead controllable variance | $ 1,200 U |

### Instructions

a. Determine the following.

1. Total actual overhead cost.
2. Actual variable overhead cost.
3. Variable overhead costs applied.
4. Fixed overhead costs applied.
5. Overhead volume variance.

b. Determine how many loans were processed.

*E17.22 (LO 5), AP  Seacrest Company's overhead rate was based on estimates of $240,000 for overhead costs and 24,000 direct labor hours. Seacrest's standards allow 2 hours of direct labor per unit produced. Production in May was 900 units, and actual overhead incurred in May was $19,500. The overhead budgeted for 1,800 standard direct labor hours is $18,600 ($6,000 fixed and $12,600 variable).

*Compute variances.*

### Instructions

a. Compute the total, controllable, and volume variances for overhead.

b. What are possible causes of the variances computed in part (a)?

## Problems

**P17.1 (LO 2, 3), AP**  Rogen Corporation manufactures a single product. The standard cost per unit of product is shown here.

*Compute variances.*

| | |
|---|---:|
| Direct materials—1 pound plastic at $7.00 per pound | $ 7.00 |
| Direct labor—1.6 hours at $12.00 per hour | 19.20 |
| Variable manufacturing overhead | 12.00 |
| Fixed manufacturing overhead | 4.00 |
| Total standard cost per unit | $42.20 |

The predetermined manufacturing overhead rate is $10 per direct labor hour ($16.00 ÷ 1.6). It was computed from a master manufacturing overhead budget based on normal production of 8,000 direct labor hours (5,000 units) for the month. The master budget showed total variable costs of $60,000 ($7.50 per hour) and total fixed overhead costs of $20,000 ($2.50 per hour). Actual costs for October in producing 4,800 units were as follows.

| | |
|---|---:|
| Direct materials (5,100 pounds) | $ 36,720 |
| Direct labor (7,400 hours) | 92,500 |
| Variable overhead | 59,700 |
| Fixed overhead | 21,000 |
| Total manufacturing costs | $209,920 |

The purchasing department buys the quantities of raw materials that are expected to be used in production each month. Raw materials inventories, therefore, can be ignored.

### Instructions

a. Compute all of the materials and labor variances.

a. MPV $1,020 U

b. Compute the total overhead variance.

**P17.2 (LO 2, 3, 4), AP**  Ayala Corporation accumulates the following data relative to jobs started and finished during the month of June 2022.

*Compute variances, and prepare income statement.*

| Costs and Production Data | Actual | Standard |
|---|---:|---:|
| Raw materials unit cost | $2.25 | $2.10 |
| Raw materials units | 10,600 | 10,000 |
| Direct labor payroll | $120,960 | $120,000 |
| Direct labor hours | 14,400 | 15,000 |
| Manufacturing overhead incurred | $189,500 | |
| Manufacturing overhead applied | | $193,500 |
| Machine hours expected to be used at normal capacity | | 42,500 |
| Budgeted fixed overhead for June | | $55,250 |
| Variable overhead rate per machine hour | | $3.00 |
| Fixed overhead rate per machine hour | | $1.30 |

Overhead is applied on the basis of standard machine hours. Three hours of machine time are required for each direct labor hour. The jobs were sold for $400,000. Selling and administrative expenses were $40,000. Assume that the amount of raw materials purchased equaled the amount used.

### Instructions

**a.** Compute all of the variances for (1) direct materials and (2) direct labor.

**b.** Compute the total overhead variance.

**c.** Prepare an income statement for management. (Ignore income taxes.)

*Compute and identify significant variances.*

**P17.3 (LO 2, 3, 4), AN** **Writing** Rudd Clothiers is a small company that manufactures tall-men's suits. The company has used a standard cost accounting system. In May 2022, 11,250 suits were produced. The following standard and actual cost data applied to the month of May when normal capacity was 14,000 direct labor hours. All materials purchased were used.

| Cost Element | Standard (per unit) | Actual |
|---|---|---|
| Direct materials | 8 yards at $4.40 per yard | $375,575 for 90,500 yards ($4.15 per yard) |
| Direct labor | 1.2 hours at $13.40 per hour | $200,925 for 14,250 hours ($14.10 per hour) |
| Overhead | 1.2 hours at $6.10 per hour (fixed $3.50; variable $2.60) | $49,000 fixed overhead $37,000 variable overhead |

Overhead is applied on the basis of direct labor hours. At normal capacity, budgeted fixed overhead costs were $49,000, and budgeted variable overhead was $36,400.

### Instructions

**a.** Compute the total, price, and quantity variances for (1) materials and (2) labor.

**b.** Compute the total overhead variance.

**c.** Which of the materials and labor variances should be investigated if management considers a variance of more than 4% from standard to be significant?

*Answer questions about variances.*

**P17.4 (LO 2, 3), AN** Kansas Company uses a standard cost accounting system. In 2022, the company produced 28,000 units. Each unit took several pounds of direct materials and 1.6 standard hours of direct labor at a standard hourly rate of $12.00. Normal capacity was 50,000 direct labor hours. During the year, 117,000 pounds of raw materials were purchased at $0.92 per pound. All materials purchased were used during the year.

### Instructions

**a.** If the materials price variance was $3,510 favorable, what was the standard materials price per pound?

**b.** If the materials quantity variance was $4,750 unfavorable, what was the standard materials quantity per unit?

**c.** What were the standard hours allowed for the units produced?

**d.** If the labor quantity variance was $7,200 unfavorable, what were the actual direct labor hours worked?

**e.** If the labor price variance was $9,080 favorable, what was the actual rate per hour?

**f.** If total budgeted manufacturing overhead was $360,000 at normal capacity, what was the predetermined overhead rate?

**g.** What was the standard cost per unit of product?

**h.** How much overhead was applied to production during the year?

**i.** Using one or more answers above, what were the total costs assigned to work in process?

*Compute variances, prepare an income statement, and explain unfavorable variances*

**P17.5 (LO 2, 3, 4), AP** **Service** **Writing** Hart Labs, Inc. provides mad cow disease testing for both state and federal governmental agricultural agencies. Because the company's customers are governmental agencies, prices are strictly regulated. Therefore, Hart Labs must constantly monitor and control its testing costs. Shown here are the standard costs for a typical test.

| | |
|---|---:|
| Direct materials (2 test tubes @ $1.46 per tube) | $ 2.92 |
| Direct labor (1 hour @ $24 per hour) | 24.00 |
| Variable overhead (1 hour @ $6 per hour) | 6.00 |
| Fixed overhead (1 hour @ $10 per hour) | 10.00 |
| Total standard cost per test | $42.92 |

The lab does not maintain an inventory of test tubes. As a result, the tubes purchased each month are used that month. Actual activity for the month of November 2022, when 1,475 tests were conducted, resulted in the following.

| | |
|---|---|
| Direct materials (3,050 test tubes) | $ 4,270 |
| Direct labor (1,550 hours) | 35,650 |
| Variable overhead | 7,400 |
| Fixed overhead | 15,000 |

Monthly budgeted fixed overhead is $14,000. Revenues for the month were $75,000, and selling and administrative expenses were $5,000.

### Instructions

a. Compute the price and quantity variances for direct materials and direct labor.

b. Compute the total overhead variance.

c. Prepare an income statement for management.

d. Provide possible explanations for each unfavorable variance.

a. LQV $1,800 U

*P17.6 **(LO 5), AP** Using the information in P17.1, compute the overhead controllable variance and the overhead volume variance.

*Compute overhead controllable and volume variances.*

*P17.7 **(LO 5), AP** Using the information in P17.2, compute the overhead controllable variance and the overhead volume variance.

*Compute overhead controllable and volume variances.*

*P17.8 **(LO 5), AP** Using the information in P17.3, compute the overhead controllable variance and the overhead volume variance.

*Compute overhead controllable and volume variances.*

*P17.9 **(LO 5), AP** Using the information in P17.5, compute the overhead controllable variance and the overhead volume variance.

*Compute overhead controllable and volume variances.*

## Continuing Cases

### Current Designs

**CD17** The executive team at **Current Designs** has gathered to evaluate the company's operations for the last month. One of the topics on the agenda is the special order from Huegel Hollow, which was presented in CD12. Recall that Current Designs had a special order to produce a batch of 20 kayaks for a client, and you were asked to determine the cost of the order and the cost per kayak.

Mike Cichanowski asked the others if the special order caused any particular problems in the production process. Dave Thill, the production manager, made the following comments: "Since we wanted to complete this order quickly and make a good first impression on this new customer, we had some of our most experienced type I workers run the rotomold oven and do the trimming. They were very efficient and were able to complete that part of the manufacturing process even more quickly than the regular crew. However, the finishing on these kayaks required a different technique than what we usually use, so our type II workers took a little longer than usual for that part of the process."

Deb Welch, who is in charge of the purchasing function, said, "We had to pay a little more for the polyethylene powder for this order because the customer wanted a color that we don't usually stock. We also ordered a little extra since we wanted to make sure that we had enough to allow us to calibrate the equipment. The calibration was a little tricky, and we used all of the powder that we had purchased. Since the number of kayaks in the order was fairly small, we were able to use some rope and other parts that were left over from last year's production in the finishing kits. We've seen a price increase for these components in the last year, so using the parts that we already had in inventory cut our costs for the finishing kits."

### Instructions

a. Based on the comments above, predict whether each of the following variances will be favorable or unfavorable. If you don't have enough information to make a prediction, use "NEI" to indicate "Not Enough Information."

1. Quantity variance for polyethylene powder.

2. Price variance for polyethylene powder.

3. Quantity variance for finishing kits.

4. Price variance for finishing kits.

5. Quantity variance for type I workers.

6. Price variance for type I workers.

7. Quantity variance for type II workers.

8. Price variance for type II workers.

**b.** Diane Buswell examined some of the accounting records and reported that Current Designs purchased 1,200 pounds of pellets for this order at a total cost of $2,040. Twenty (20) finishing kits were assembled at a total cost of $3,240. The payroll records showed that the type I employees worked 38 hours on this project at a total cost of $570. The type II finishing employees worked 65 hours at a total cost of $796.25. A total of 20 kayaks were produced for this order.

The standards that had been developed for this model of kayak were used in CD12 and are reproduced here. For each kayak:

54 pounds of polyethylene powder at $1.50 per pound

1 finishing kit (rope, seat, hardware, etc.) at $170

2 hours of type I labor from people who run the oven and trim the plastic at a standard wage rate of $15 per hour

3 hours of type II labor from people who attach the hatches and seat and other hardware at a standard wage rate of $12 per hour.

Calculate the eight variances that are listed in part (a) of this problem.

## Waterways Corporation

(This is a continuation of the Waterways case from Chapters 11–16.)

**WC17** Waterways Corporation uses very stringent standard costs in evaluating its manufacturing efficiency. These standards are not "ideal" at this point, but management is working toward that as a goal. This problem asks you to calculate and evaluate the company's variances.

*Go to WileyPLUS for complete case details and instructions.*

# Expand Your Critical Thinking

## Decision-Making Across the Organization

**CT17.1** **Service** Milton Professionals, a management consulting firm, specializes in strategic planning for financial institutions. James Hahn and Sara Norton, partners in the firm, are assembling a new strategic planning model for use by clients. The model is designed for use on most personal computers and replaces a rather lengthy manual model currently marketed by the firm. To market the new model, James and Sara will need to provide clients with an estimate of the number of labor hours and computer time needed to operate the model. The model is currently being test-marketed at five small financial institutions. These financial institutions are listed here, along with the number of combined computer/labor hours used by each institution to run the model one time.

| Financial Institutions | Computer/Labor Hours Required |
| --- | --- |
| Midland National | 25 |
| First State | 45 |
| Financial Federal | 40 |
| Pacific America | 30 |
| Lakeview National | 30 |
| Total | 170 |
| Average | 34 |

Any company that purchases the new model will need to purchase user manuals for the system. User manuals will be sold to clients in cases of 20, at a cost of $320 per case. One manual must be used each time the model is run because each manual includes a nonreusable computer-accessed password for operating the system. Also required are specialized computer forms that are sold only by Milton. The specialized forms are sold in packages of 250, at a cost of $60 per package. One application of the model requires the use of 50 forms. This amount includes two forms that are generally wasted in each application due to printer alignment errors. The overall cost of the strategic planning model to clients is $12,000. Most clients will use the model four times annually.

Milton must provide its clients with estimates of ongoing costs incurred in operating the new planning model, and would like to do so in the form of standard costs.

### Instructions

With the class divided into groups, answer the following.

**a.** What factors should be considered in setting a standard for computer/labor hours?

**b.** What alternatives for setting a standard for computer/labor hours might be used?

**c.** What standard for computer/labor hours would you select? Justify your answer.

**d.** Determine the standard materials cost associated with the user manuals and computer forms for each application of the strategic planning model.

## Managerial Analysis

*CT17.2  Ana Carillo and Associates is a medium-sized company located near a large metropolitan area in the Midwest. The company manufactures cabinets of mahogany, oak, and other fine woods for use in expensive homes, restaurants, and hotels. Although some of the work is custom, many of the cabinets are a standard size.

One non-custom model is called Luxury Base Frame. Normal production is 1,000 units. Each unit has a direct labor hour standard of 5 hours. Overhead is applied to production based on standard direct labor hours. During the most recent month, only 900 units were produced; 4,500 direct labor hours were allowed for standard production, but only 4,000 hours were used. Standard and actual overhead costs were as follows.

|  | Standard (1,000 units) | Actual (900 units) |
|---|---|---|
| Indirect materials | $ 12,000 | $ 12,300 |
| Indirect labor | 43,000 | 51,000 |
| (Fixed) Manufacturing supervisors salaries | 22,500 | 22,000 |
| (Fixed) Manufacturing office employees salaries | 13,000 | 12,500 |
| (Fixed) Engineering costs | 27,000 | 25,000 |
| Computer costs | 10,000 | 10,000 |
| Electricity | 2,500 | 2,500 |
| (Fixed) Manufacturing building depreciation | 8,000 | 8,000 |
| (Fixed) Machinery depreciation | 3,000 | 3,000 |
| (Fixed) Trucks and forklift depreciation | 1,500 | 1,500 |
| Small tools | 700 | 1,400 |
| (Fixed) Insurance | 500 | 500 |
| (Fixed) Property taxes | 300 | 300 |
| Total | $144,000 | $150,000 |

### Instructions

**a.** Determine the overhead application rate.

**b.** Determine how much overhead was applied to production.

**c.** Calculate the total overhead variance, controllable variance, and volume variance.

**d.** Decide which overhead variances should be investigated.

**e.** Discuss causes of the overhead variances. What can management do to improve its performance next month?

## Real-World Focus

CT17.3  **Glassmaster Company** is organized as two divisions and one subsidiary. One division focuses on the manufacture of filaments such as fishing line and sewing thread; the other division manufactures antennas and specialty fiberglass products. Its subsidiary manufactures flexible steel wire controls and molded control panels.

The annual report of Glassmaster provides the following information.

## Glassmaster Company
### Management Discussion

Gross profit margins for the year improved to 20.9% of sales compared to last year's 18.5%. All operations reported improved margins due in large part to improved operating efficiencies as a result of cost reduction measures implemented during the second and third quarters of the fiscal year and increased manufacturing throughout due to higher unit volume sales. Contributing to the improved margins was a favorable materials price variance due to competitive pricing by suppliers as a result of soft demand for petrochemical-based products. This favorable variance is temporary and will begin to reverse itself as stronger worldwide demand for commodity products improves in tandem with the economy. Partially offsetting these positive effects on profit margins were competitive pressures on sales prices of certain product lines. The company responded with pricing strategies designed to maintain and/or increase market share.

### Instructions

a. Is it apparent from the information whether Glassmaster utilizes standard costs?

b. Do you think the price variance experienced should lead to changes in standard costs for the next fiscal year?

**CT17.4** **Service** The **Balanced Scorecard Institute** is a great resource for information about implementing the balanced scorecard. One item of interest provided at its website is an example of a balanced scorecard for a regional airline.

### Instructions

Go to the Balanced Scorecard Institute website, do a search on "Examples and Success Stories," scroll down to select the Regional Airline example under commercial organizations, and then answer the following questions.

a. What are the objectives identified for the airline for each perspective?

b. What measures are used for the objectives in the customer perspective?

c. What initiatives are planned to achieve the objective in the learning perspective?

## Communication Activity

**CT17.5** The setting of standards is critical to the effective use of standards in evaluating performance.

### Instructions

Explain the following in a memo to your instructor.

a. The comparative advantages and disadvantages of ideal versus normal standards.

b. The factors that should be included in setting the price and quantity standards for direct materials, direct labor, and manufacturing overhead.

## Ethics Case

**CT17.6** At Symond Company, production workers in the Painting Department are paid on the basis of productivity. The labor time standard for a unit of production is established through periodic time studies conducted by Douglas Management Consultants. In a time study, the actual time required to complete a specific task by a worker is observed. Allowances are then made for preparation time, rest periods, and cleanup time. Bill Carson is one of several veterans in the Painting Department.

Bill is informed by Douglas that he will be used in the time study for the painting of a new product. The findings will be the basis for establishing the labor time standard for the next 6 months. During the test, Bill deliberately slows his normal work pace in an effort to obtain a labor time standard that will be easy to meet. Because it is a new product, the Douglas representative who conducted the test is unaware that Bill did not give the test his best effort.

### Instructions

a. Who was benefited and who was harmed by Bill's actions?

b. Was Bill ethical in the way he performed the time study test?

c. What measure(s) might the company take to obtain valid data for setting the labor time standard?

## All About You

**CT17.7** From the time you first entered school many years ago, instructors have been measuring and evaluating you by imposing standards. In addition, many of you will pursue professions that administer professional examinations to attain recognized certification. A federal commission presented proposals suggesting all public colleges and universities should require standardized tests to measure their students' learning.

### Instructions

Do an Internet search on "Union Tribune U.S. panel endorses standards for college," read the **San Diego Union-Tribune** article, and then answer the following questions.

    **a.** What areas of concern did the panel's recommendations address?

    **b.** What are possible advantages of standard testing?

    **c.** What are possible disadvantages of standard testing?

    **d.** Would you be in favor of standardized tests?

## Considering Your Costs and Benefits

**CT17.8** **Writing** Do you think that standard costs are used only in making products like wheel bearings and hamburgers? Think again. Standards influence virtually every aspect of our lives. For example, the next time you call to schedule an appointment with your doctor, ask the receptionist how many minutes the appointment is scheduled for. Doctors are under increasing pressure to see more patients each day, which means the time spent with each patient is shorter. As insurance companies and employers push for reduced medical costs, every facet of medicine has been standardized and analyzed. Doctors, nurses, and other medical staff are evaluated in every part of their operations to ensure maximum efficiency. While keeping medical treatment affordable seems like a worthy goal, what are the potential implications for the quality of health care? Does a focus on the bottom line result in a reduction in the quality of health care?

A simmering debate has centered on a very basic question: To what extent should accountants, through financial measures, influence the type of medical care that you receive? Suppose that your local medical facility is in danger of closing because it has been losing money. Should the facility put in place incentives that provide bonuses to doctors if they meet certain standard-cost targets for the cost of treating specific ailments?

    **YES:** If the facility is in danger of closing, then someone should take steps to change the medical practices to reduce costs. A closed medical facility is of no use to me, my family, or the community.

    **NO:** I don't want an accountant deciding the right medical treatment for me. My family and I deserve the best medical care.

### Instructions

Write a response indicating your position regarding this situation. Provide support for your view.

## CHAPTER 18

Engel & Gielen/LOOK-foto/Getty Images

# Planning for Capital Investments

## Chapter Preview

Companies like **Holland America Line** (as discussed in the following Feature Story) must constantly determine how to invest their resources. Other examples: **Dell** announced plans to spend $1 billion on data centers for cloud computing. **ExxonMobil** announced that two wells off the Brazilian coast, which it had spent hundreds of millions of dollars to drill, would produce no oil. **Renault** and **Nissan** spent over $5 billion during a nearly 20-year period to develop electric cars, such as the Leaf.

The process of making such capital expenditure decisions is referred to as **capital budgeting**. Capital budgeting involves choosing among various capital projects to find those that will maximize a company's return on its financial investment. The purpose of this chapter is to discuss the various techniques used to make effective capital budgeting decisions.

# Feature Story

## Floating Hotels

Do you own a boat? Maybe you think it's a nice boat, but how many swimming pools, movie theaters, shopping malls, or restaurants does it have on board? If you are in the cruise-line business, like **Holland America Line**, you need all of these amenities and more just to stay afloat. Holland America Line is considered by many to be the leader of the premium luxury-liner segment.

**Carnival Corporation**, which owns Holland America Line and other cruise lines, is one of the largest vacation companies in the world. During one recent three-year period, Carnival spent more than $3 billion per year on capital expenditures. That's a big number, but keep in mind that Carnival estimates that at any given time there are 270,000 people (200,000 customers and 70,000 crew) on its 100 ships somewhere in the world.

The cruise industry is a tricky business. When times are good, customers are looking for ways to splurge. But when times get tough, people are more inclined to take a trip in a minivan than a luxury yacht. So, if you are a cruise-line executive, it's important to time your investments properly. For example, during one stretch of solid global economic growth, many cruise lines decided to add capacity. The industry built 14 new ships at a total price of $4.7 billion. (That's an average price of about $330 million.) But, it takes up to three years to build one of these giant vessels. Unfortunately, by the time the ships were completed, the economy was in a nosedive.

To maintain passenger numbers during the recession, cruise prices had to be cut by up to 40%. While the lower prices attracted lots of customers, that wasn't enough to offset an overall decline in revenue of 10%. The industry had added capacity at exactly the wrong time.

# Chapter Outline

| LEARNING OBJECTIVES | REVIEW | PRACTICE |
|---|---|---|
| **LO 1** Describe capital budgeting inputs and apply the cash payback technique. | • Cash flow information<br>• Cash payback | **DO IT! 1** Cash Payback Period |
| **LO 2** Use the net present value method. | • Equal annual cash flows<br>• Unequal annual cash flows<br>• Choosing a discount rate<br>• Simplifying assumptions<br>• Comprehensive example | **DO IT! 2** Net Present Value |
| **LO 3** Identify capital budgeting challenges and refinements. | • Intangible benefits<br>• Profitability index for mutually exclusive projects<br>• Risk analysis<br>• Post-audit of investment projects | **DO IT! 3** Profitability Index |
| **LO 4** Use the internal rate of return method. | • Comparing discounted cash flow methods | **DO IT! 4** Internal Rate of Return |
| **LO 5** Use the annual rate of return method. | • Based on accrual-accounting data | **DO IT! 5** Annual Rate of Return |

**Go to the Review and Practice section at the end of the chapter for a targeted summary and practice applications with solutions.**

**Visit WileyPLUS for additional tutorials and practice opportunities.**

# Capital Budgeting and Cash Payback

Many companies follow a carefully prescribed process for capital expenditure decisions, known as **capital budgeting**. **Illustration 18.1** shows this general process.

**ILLUSTRATION 18.1**   **Corporate capital budget authorization process**

1. Project proposals are requested from departments, plants, and authorized personnel.

2. Proposals are screened by a capital budget committee.

3. Company officers determine which projects are worthy of funding.

4. Board of directors approves capital budget.

The involvement of top management and the board of directors in the process demonstrates the importance of capital budgeting decisions.

- These decisions often have a significant impact on a company's future profitability.
- Poor capital budgeting decisions can cost a lot of money and have even led to the bankruptcy of some companies.

## Cash Flow Information

In this chapter, we look at several methods that help companies make effective capital budgeting decisions. Most of these methods employ **cash flow numbers**, rather than accrual accounting revenues and expenses.

- Remember from your financial accounting course that accrual accounting records **revenues** and **expenses**, rather than cash inflows and cash outflows. In fact, revenues and expenses measured during a period often differ significantly from their cash flow counterparts.
- Accrual accounting has advantages over cash accounting in many contexts.
- **For purposes of capital budgeting, though, estimated cash inflows and outflows are the preferred inputs.**
- Ultimately, the value of all financial investments is determined by the value of cash flows received and paid.

Sometimes cash flow information is not available. In this case, companies can make adjustments to accrual accounting numbers to estimate cash flow. Often, they estimate net annual cash flow by adding back depreciation expense to net income.

- Depreciation expense is added back because it is an expense that does not require an outflow of cash.
- By adding depreciation expense back to net income, companies approximate net annual cash flow.

Suppose, for example, that Reno Company's net income of $13,000 includes a charge for depreciation expense of $26,000. Its estimated net annual cash flow would be $39,000 ($13,000 + $26,000).

**Illustration 18.2** lists some typical cash outflows and inflows related to equipment purchase and replacement.

> **Cash Outflows**
>
> Initial investment
> Repairs and maintenance
> Increased operating costs
> Overhaul of equipment
>
> **Cash Inflows**
>
> Proceeds from sale of old equipment
> Increased cash received from customers
> Reduced cash outflows related to operating costs
> Salvage value of equipment

These cash flows are the inputs that are considered relevant in capital budgeting decisions.

The capital budgeting decision, under any technique, depends in part on a variety of considerations:

- **The availability of funds:** Does the company have unlimited funds, or will it have to ration capital investments?
- **Relationships among proposed projects:** Are proposed projects independent of each other, or does the acceptance or rejection of one depend on the acceptance or rejection of another?
- **The company's basic decision-making approach:** Does the company want to produce an accept-reject decision or a ranking of desirability among possible projects?
- **The risk associated with a particular project:** How certain are the projected returns? The certainty of estimates varies with such issues as market considerations or the length of time before returns are expected.

## Illustrative Data

To compare the results of the various capital budgeting techniques, we use a continuing example. Assume that Stewart Shipping Company is considering an investment of $130,000 in new equipment. The new equipment is expected to last 10 years. It is estimated to have a zero salvage value at the end of its useful life. The expected annual cash inflows are $200,000, and the annual cash outflows are $176,000. **Illustration 18.3** summarizes these data.

**ILLUSTRATION 18.3**

**Investment information for Stewart Shipping example**

| | |
|---|---|
| Initial investment | $130,000 |
| Estimated useful life | 10 years |
| Estimated salvage value | –0– |
| | |
| Estimated annual cash flows | |
|    Cash inflows from customers | $200,000 |
|    Cash outflows for operating costs | 176,000 |
| Net annual cash flow | $ 24,000 |

In the following two sections, we examine two popular techniques for evaluating capital investments: the cash payback technique and the net present value method.

# Cash Payback

The **cash payback technique** identifies the time period required to recover the cost of the capital investment from the net annual cash flow produced by the investment. **Illustration 18.4** presents the formula for computing the cash payback period assuming equal annual cash flows.

$$\text{Cost of Capital Investment} \div \text{Net Annual Cash Flow} = \text{Cash Payback Period}$$

**ILLUSTRATION 18.4**

Cash payback formula

The cash payback period in the Stewart Shipping example is 5.42 years, computed as follows (see **Helpful Hint**).

$$\$130,000 \div \$24,000 = 5.42 \text{ years}$$

**HELPFUL HINT**

Net annual cash flow can also be approximated by "Net cash provided by operating activities" from the statement of cash flows.

The evaluation of the payback period is often related to the expected useful life of the asset. For example, assume that at Stewart Shipping a project is unacceptable if the payback period is longer than 60% of the asset's expected useful life. The 5.42-year payback period is 54.2% (5.42 ÷ 10) of the project's expected useful life. Thus, the project is acceptable.

It follows that when the payback technique is used to decide among acceptable alternative projects, **the shorter the payback period, the more attractive the investment**. This is true for two reasons:

1. The earlier the investment is recovered, the sooner the company can use the cash funds for other purposes.

2. The risk of loss from obsolescence and changed economic conditions is less in a shorter payback period.

The preceding computation of the cash payback period assumes **equal** net annual cash flows in each year of the investment's life. In many cases, this assumption is not valid. In the case of **uneven** net annual cash flows, the company determines the cash payback period **when the cumulative net cash flows from the investment equal the cost of the investment**.

To illustrate, assume that Chen Company proposes an investment in a new website that is estimated to cost $300,000. **Illustration 18.5** shows the proposed investment cost, net annual cash flows, cumulative net cash flows, and the cash payback period.

| Year | Investment | Net Annual Cash Flow | Cumulative Net Cash Flow |
|------|------------|----------------------|--------------------------|
| 0 | **$300,000** | | |
| 1 | | $ 60,000 | $ 60,000 |
| 2 | | 90,000 | 150,000 |
| 3 | | 90,000 | 240,000 |
| 4 | | 120,000 | 360,000 |
| 5 | | 100,000 | 460,000 |

**Cash payback period = 3.5 years**

**ILLUSTRATION 18.5**

Computation of cash payback period—unequal cash flows

As Illustration 18.5 shows, at the end of year 3, cumulative net cash flow of $240,000 is less than the investment cost of $300,000, but at the end of year 4 the cumulative cash inflow of $360,000 exceeds the investment cost. The cash flow needed in year 4 to equal the investment cost is $60,000 ($300,000 − $240,000). Assuming the cash inflow occurred evenly during year 4, we divide $60,000 by the net annual cash flow in year 4 ($120,000) to determine the point during the year when the cash payback occurs. Thus, we get 0.50 ($60,000 ÷ $120,000), or half of the year, and the cash payback period is 3.5 years.

The cash payback technique may be useful as an initial screening tool. It may be the most critical factor in the capital budgeting decision for a company that desires a fast turnaround of its investment because of a weak cash position. It also is relatively easy to compute and understand.

However, cash payback should not ordinarily be the only basis for the capital budgeting decision.

- **It ignores the expected profitability of the project**. To illustrate, assume that Projects A and B have the same payback period, but Project A's useful life is double the useful life of Project B. Project A's earning power, therefore, is twice that of Project B's.
- A further—and major—disadvantage of this technique is that **it ignores the time value of money**. We address time value of money with the approach described in the next section.

---

**ACTION PLAN**

- **Annual cash inflows − Annual cash outflows = Net annual cash flow.**
- **Cash payback period = Cost of capital investment ÷ Net annual cash flow.**

### DO IT! 1 | Cash Payback Period

Watertown Paper Corporation is considering adding another machine for the manufacture of corrugated cardboard. The machine would cost $900,000. It would have an estimated life of 6 years and no salvage value. The company estimates that annual cash inflows would increase by $400,000 and that annual cash outflows would increase by $190,000. Compute the cash payback period.

#### Solution

| | |
|---|---:|
| Estimated annual cash inflows | $400,000 |
| Estimated annual cash outflows | 190,000 |
| Net annual cash flow | $210,000 |

Cash payback period = $900,000 ÷ $210,000 = 4.3 years

Related exercise material: **BE18.1 and DO IT! 18.1.**

---

# Net Present Value Method

### LEARNING OBJECTIVE 2
Use the net present value method.

The time value of money can have a significant impact on a capital budgeting decision. Cash flows that occur early in the life of an investment are worth more than those that occur later—because of the time value of money. Therefore, it is useful to recognize the timing of cash flows when evaluating projects.

Capital budgeting techniques that take into account both the time value of money and the estimated net cash flows from an investment are called **discounted cash flow techniques**.

- They are generally recognized as the most informative and best conceptual approaches to making capital budgeting decisions.
- The expected net cash flow used in discounting cash flows consists of the annual net cash flows plus the estimated liquidation proceeds (salvage value) when the asset is sold for salvage at the end of its useful life.

The primary discounted cash flow technique is the **net present value method**. A second method, discussed later in the chapter, is the **internal rate of return**. At this point, **we recommend that you examine Appendix E** to review the time value of money concepts upon which these methods are based. Also, the Excel tutorial provided in WileyPLUS for this chapter demonstrates the use of the NPV (net present value) and IRR (internal rate of return) functions in Excel.

The **net present value (NPV) method** involves discounting net cash flows to their present value and then comparing that present value with the capital outlay required by the investment (see **Decision Tools**).

- The difference between these two amounts is referred to as **net present value (NPV)**.
- Company management determines what interest rate to use in discounting the future net cash flows. This rate, often referred to as the **discount rate** or **required rate of return**, is management's minimum acceptable rate of return on investments (discussed in a later section).
- The NPV decision rule is this: **A proposal is acceptable when net present value is zero or positive**. A zero or positive NPV indicates that the rate of return on the investment equals or exceeds (respectively) the required rate of return. When net present value is negative, the project is unacceptable.

**Illustration 18.6** shows the net present value decision criteria.

**Decision Tools**

Using the net present value method helps companies to determine whether or not to invest in proposed projects.

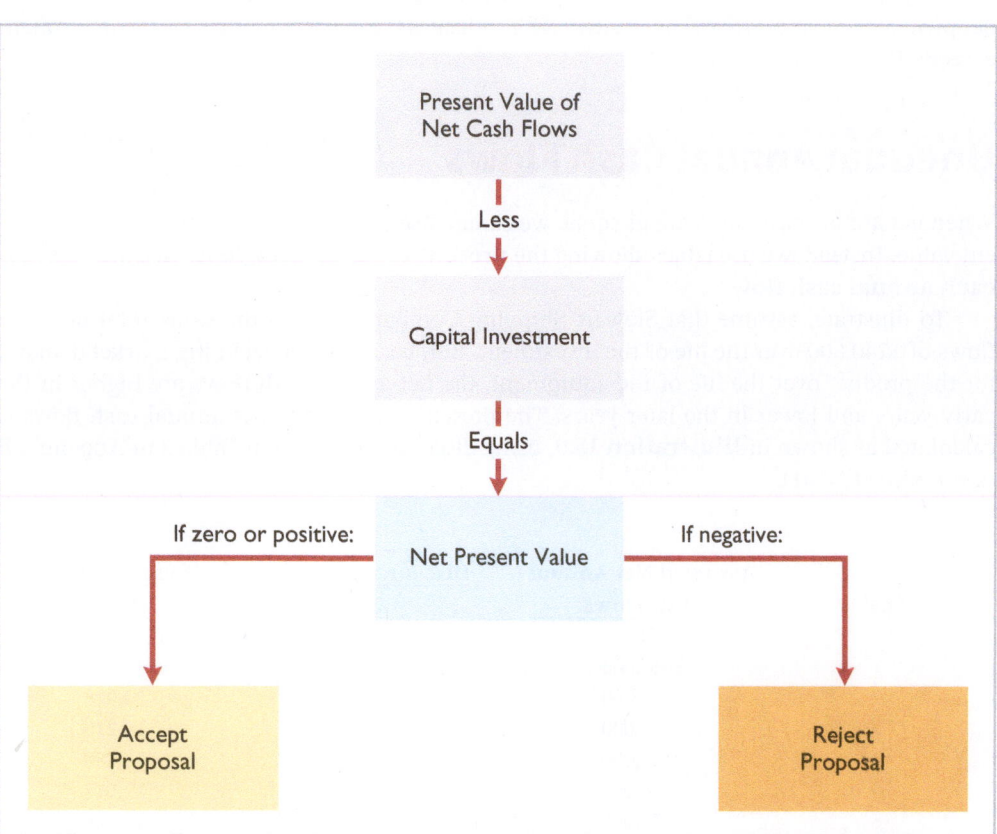

**ILLUSTRATION 18.6**

**Net present value decision criteria**

When making a selection among acceptable proposals, **the higher the positive net present value, the more attractive the investment**. The application of this method to two cases is described in the next two sections. In each case, we assume that the investment has no salvage value at the end of its useful life.

## Equal Annual Cash Flows

In our Stewart Shipping Company example, the company's net annual cash flows are $24,000. If we assume this amount **is uniform over the asset's useful life**, we can compute the present value of the net annual cash flows by using the present value of an annuity of 1 for 10 payments (from Table 4, Appendix E). Assuming a discount rate of 12%, the present value of net cash flows are as shown in **Illustration 18.7** (rounded to the nearest dollar) (see **Helpful Hint**).

**HELPFUL HINT**

The ABC Co. expects equal cash flows over an asset's 5-year useful life. The discount factor it should use in determining present values if management wants a 12% return is 3.60478 (using Table 4).

**ILLUSTRATION 18.7**

**Computation of present value of equal net annual cash flows**

| | Present Value at 12% |
|---|---|
| Discount factor for 10 periods | 5.65022 |
| Present value of net cash flows: | |
| $24,000 × 5.65022 | **$135,605** |

Illustration 18.8 shows the analysis of the proposal by the net present value method.

**ILLUSTRATION 18.8**

**Computation of net present value—equal net annual cash flows**

| | 12% |
|---|---|
| Present value of net cash flows | $135,605 |
| Less: Capital investment | 130,000 |
| **Net present value** | **$   5,605** |

The proposed capital expenditure is acceptable at a required rate of return of 12% because the net present value is positive. The positive NPV indicates the expected return on the investment exceeds 12%.

## Unequal Annual Cash Flows

When net annual cash flows are unequal, we cannot use annuity tables to calculate their present value. Instead, we use tables showing the **present value of a single future amount for each annual cash flow**.

To illustrate, assume that Stewart Shipping Company expects the same total net cash flows of $240,000 over the life of the investment. But, because of a declining market demand for the product over the life of the equipment, the net annual cash flows are higher in the early years and lower in the later years. The present value of the net annual cash flows is calculated as shown in **Illustration 18.9**, using discount factors from Table 3 in Appendix E (see **Helpful Hint**).

**HELPFUL HINT**

Appendix E demonstrates the use of a financial calculator to solve time value of money problems.

**ILLUSTRATION 18.9**

**Computation of present value of unequal annual cash flows**

| Year | Assumed Net Annual Cash Flows | Discount Factor 12% | Present Value 12% |
|---|---|---|---|
| | (1) | (2) | (1) × (2) |
| 1 | $ 34,000 | .89286 | $ 30,357 |
| 2 | 30,000 | .79719 | 23,916 |
| 3 | 27,000 | .71178 | 19,218 |
| 4 | 25,000 | .63552 | 15,888 |
| 5 | 24,000 | .56743 | 13,618 |
| 6 | 22,000 | .50663 | 11,146 |
| 7 | 21,000 | .45235 | 9,499 |
| 8 | 20,000 | .40388 | 8,078 |
| 9 | 19,000 | .36061 | 6,852 |
| 10 | 18,000 | .32197 | 5,795 |
| | **$240,000** | | **$144,367** |

Therefore, the analysis of the proposal by the net present value method is as shown in **Illustration 18.10**.

**ILLUSTRATION 18.10**

**Computation of net present value—unequal annual cash flows**

| | 12% |
|---|---|
| Present value of net cash flows | $144,367 |
| Less: Capital investment | 130,000 |
| **Net present value** | **$ 14,367** |

In this example, the present value of the net cash flows is greater than the $130,000 capital investment. Thus, the project is acceptable at a 12% required rate of return.

- The difference between the present values using the 12% rate under equal cash flows ($135,605) and unequal cash flows ($144,367) is due to the pattern of the flows.
- Since more money is received sooner under this particular uneven cash flow scenario, its present value is greater.

---

## Management Insight   Verizon

### Can You Hear Me—Better?

What's better than 4G wireless service? 5G. But the question for wireless service providers is whether customers will be willing to pay extra for that improvement. **Verizon** has spent billions on upgrading its networks in the past few years, and it now offers 4G LTE service to 97% of the nation. Verizon's investment in its 4G service certainly worked out better than its $23 billion investment in its FIOS fiber-wired network for TV and ultrahigh-speed Internet.

SchulteProductions/
iStock Editorial/
Getty Images

One analyst estimates that the present value of each FIOS customer is $800 less than the cost of the connection.

**Sources:** Martin Peers, "Investors: Beware Verizon's Generation GAP," *Wall Street Journal Online* (January 26, 2010); and Chad Fraser, "What Warren Buffett Sees in Verizon," *Investing Daily* (May 30, 2014).

**If customers had been slow to initially adopt 4G, how might the conclusions of a cash payback analysis of Verizon's 4G investment differ from a present value analysis? (Go to WileyPLUS for this answer and additional questions.)**

---

## Choosing a Discount Rate

Now that you understand how companies apply the net present value method, it is logical to ask a related question: How is a discount rate (required rate of return) determined in real capital budgeting decisions?

- In most instances, a company uses a required rate of return equal to its **cost of capital**—that is, the rate that it must pay to obtain funds from creditors and stockholders.
- The cost of capital is a weighted average of the rates paid on borrowed funds as well as on funds provided by investors in the company's common stock and preferred stock (see **Helpful Hint**).
- If management believes a project is riskier than the company's usual line of business, the discount rate should be increased.

That is, the discount rate has two elements, a cost of capital element and a risk element. Often, companies assume the risk element is equal to zero.

Using an incorrect discount rate can lead to incorrect capital budgeting decisions. Consider again the Stewart Shipping example in Illustration 18.8, where we used a discount rate of 12%. Suppose that this rate does not take into account the fact that this project is riskier than most of the company's investments. A more appropriate discount rate, given the risk, might be 15%. **Illustration 18.11** compares the net present values at the two rates. At the higher, more appropriate discount rate of 15%, the net present value is negative. The negative NPV indicates

> **HELPFUL HINT**
>
> Cost of capital is the rate that management expects to pay on all borrowed and equity funds. It does not relate to the cost of funding a *specific* project.

|  | Present Values at Different Discount Rates | |
|---|---|---|
|  | 12% | 15% |
| Discount factor for 10 payments | 5.65022 | 5.01877 |
| Present value of net cash flows: |  |  |
| $24,000 × 5.65022 | $135,605 |  |
| $24,000 × 5.01877 |  | $120,450 |
| Less: Capital investment | 130,000 | 130,000 |
| Positive (negative) net present value | $  5,605 | $ (9,550) |

> **ILLUSTRATION 18.11**
>
> Comparison of net present values at different discount rates

that the expected rate of return on the investment is less than the required rate of return of 15%. The company should reject the project (discount factors from Appendix E, Table 4).

The discount rate is often referred to by alternative names, including the **required rate of return**, the **hurdle rate**, and the **cutoff rate**. Determination of the cost of capital varies somewhat depending on whether the entity is a for-profit or not-for-profit business. Calculation of the cost of capital is discussed more fully in advanced accounting and finance courses.

## Simplifying Assumptions

In our examples of the net present value method, we made a number of simplifying assumptions:

- **All cash flows occur at the end of each year.** In reality, cash flows will occur at uneven intervals throughout the year. However, it is far simpler to assume that all cash flows come at the end (or in some cases the beginning) of the year. In fact, this assumption is frequently made in practice.

- **All cash flows are immediately reinvested in another project that has a similar return.** In most capital budgeting situations, companies receive cash flows during each year of a project's life. In order to determine the return on the investment, some assumption must be made about how the cash flows are reinvested in the year that they are received. It is customary to assume that cash flows received are reinvested in some other project of similar return until the end of the project's life.

- **All cash flows can be predicted with certainty.** The outcomes of business investments are full of uncertainty, as the Holland America Line Feature Story shows. There is no way of knowing how popular a new product will be, how long a new machine will last, or what competitors' reactions might be to changes in a product. But, in order to make investment decisions, analysts must estimate future outcomes. In this chapter, we have assumed that future amounts are known with certainty.[1] In reality, little is known with certainty. More advanced capital budgeting techniques deal with uncertainty by considering the probability that various outcomes will occur.

## Comprehensive Example

Best Taste Foods is considering investing in new equipment to produce fat-free snack foods. Management believes that although demand for fat-free foods has leveled off, fat-free foods are here to stay. The estimated costs, cost of capital, and cash flows shown in **Illustration 18.12** were determined in consultation with the marketing, production, and finance departments.

**ILLUSTRATION 18.12**

**Investment information for Best Taste Foods example**

| | |
|---|---|
| Initial investment | $1,000,000 |
| Cost of equipment overhaul in 5 years | $200,000 |
| Salvage value of equipment in 10 years | $20,000 |
| Cost of capital (discount rate) | 15% |
| Estimated annual cash flows | |
| Cash inflows received from sales | $500,000 |
| Cash outflows for cost of goods sold | $200,000 |
| Maintenance costs | $30,000 |
| Other direct operating costs | $40,000 |

- Remember that we are using cash flows in our analysis, not accrual revenues and expenses.
- Thus, for example, the direct operating costs would not include depreciation expense, since depreciation expense does not use cash.

**Illustration 18.13** presents the computation of the net annual cash flows of this project.

---

[1]One exception is a brief discussion of sensitivity analysis later in the chapter.

| | |
|---|---:|
| Cash inflows received from sales | $ 500,000 |
| Cash outflows for cost of goods sold | (200,000) |
| Maintenance costs | (30,000) |
| Other direct operating costs | (40,000) |
| **Net annual cash flow** | **$ 230,000** |

**ILLUSTRATION 18.13**

**Computation of net annual cash flow**

**Illustration 18.14** shows computation of the net present value for this proposed investment (discount factors from Appendix E, Tables 3 and 4).

| Event | Time Period | Cash Flow | × | 15% Discount Factor | = | Present Value |
|---|---|---|---|---|---|---|
| Net annual cash flow | 1–10 | $ 230,000 | | 5.01877 | | $1,154,317 |
| Salvage value | 10 | 20,000 | | .24719 | | 4,944 |
| Less: Equipment purchase | 0 | 1,000,000 | | 1.00000 | | 1,000,000 |
| Less: Equipment overhaul | 5 | 200,000 | | .49718 | | 99,436 |
| **Net present value** | | | | | | **$   59,825** |

**ILLUSTRATION 18.14**

**Computation of net present value for Best Taste Foods investment**

Because the net present value of the project is positive, Best Taste should accept the project.

## DO IT! 2 | Net Present Value

Watertown Paper Corporation is considering adding another machine for the manufacture of corrugated cardboard. The machine would cost $900,000. It would have an estimated life of 6 years and no salvage value. The company estimates that annual cash inflows would increase by $400,000 and that annual cash outflows would increase by $190,000. Management has a required rate of return of 9%. Calculate the net present value on this project and discuss whether it should be accepted.

### Solution

| | |
|---|---:|
| Estimated annual cash inflows | $400,000 |
| Estimated annual cash outflows | 190,000 |
| Net annual cash flow | $210,000 |

| | Cash Flow | × | 9% Discount Factor | = | Present Value |
|---|---|---|---|---|---|
| Present value of net annual cash flows | $210,000 | × | 4.48592[a] | = | $942,043 |
| Less: Capital investment | | | | | 900,000 |
| Net present value | | | | | $ 42,043 |

[a]Table 4, Appendix E, 9%, 6 years

Since the net present value is greater than zero, Watertown should accept the project.

Related exercise material: **BE18.2, BE18.3, DO IT! 18.2, E18.1, E18.2, and E18.3.**

**ACTION PLAN**

- Recall that Estimated annual cash inflows − Estimated annual cash outflows = Net annual cash flow.

- Use the NPV technique to calculate the difference between net cash flows and the initial investment.

- Accept the project if the net present value is positive.

# Capital Budgeting Challenges and Refinements

> ### LEARNING OBJECTIVE 3
> Identify capital budgeting challenges and refinements.

Now that you understand how the net present value method works, we can add some "additional wrinkles." Specifically, these are the impact of intangible benefits, a way to compare mutually exclusive projects, refinements that take risk into account, and the need to conduct post-audits of investment projects.

## Intangible Benefits

The NPV evaluation techniques employed thus far rely on tangible costs and benefits that can be relatively easily quantified. Some investment projects, especially high-tech projects, fail to make it through initial capital budget screens because only the project's tangible benefits are considered.

- **Intangible benefits** might include increased quality, improved safety, or enhanced employee loyalty.
- By ignoring intangible benefits, capital budgeting techniques might incorrectly eliminate projects that could be financially beneficial to the company.

To avoid rejecting projects that actually should be accepted, analysts suggest two possible approaches:

1. Calculate net present value ignoring intangible benefits. Then, if the NPV is negative, ask whether the project offers any intangible benefits that are worth at least the amount of the negative NPV.
2. Project conservative estimates of the value of the intangible benefits, and incorporate these values into the NPV calculation.

### Example

Assume that Berg Company is considering the purchase of a new mechanical robot to be used for soldering electrical connections. **Illustration 18.15** shows the estimates related to this proposed purchase (discount factor from Appendix E, Table 4).

| ILLUSTRATION 18.15 |
| :--- |
| **Investment information for Berg Company example** |

| | | | | |
| :--- | ---: | :---: | ---: | ---: |
| Initial investment | $200,000 | | | |
| Annual cash inflows | $ 50,000 | | | |
| Annual cash outflows | 20,000 | | | |
| **Net annual cash flow** | **$ 30,000** | | | |
| Estimated life of equipment | 10 years | | | |
| Discount rate | 12% | | | |

| | Cash Flows | | 12% Discount Factor | | Present Value |
| :--- | :---: | :---: | :---: | :---: | ---: |
| Present value of net annual cash flows | $30,000 | × | 5.65022 | = | $ 169,507 |
| Less: Initial investment | | | | | 200,000 |
| **Net present value** | | | | | **$ (30,493)** |

Based on the negative net present value of $30,493, the proposed project is not acceptable. This calculation, however, ignores important information.

- The company's engineers believe that purchasing this machine will improve the quality of electrical connections in the company's products. As a result, future warranty costs may be reduced.

- This higher quality may translate into higher future sales.
- The new machine will be safer than the current machine.

The managers at Berg Company do not have confidence in their ability to accurately estimate these potentially higher revenues and lower costs. But Berg can incorporate this new information into the capital budgeting decision in the two ways discussed earlier.

1. Management might simply ask whether the reduced warranty costs, increased sales, and improved safety benefits have an estimated total present value to the company of at least $30,493. If yes, then the project is acceptable.

2. Analysts can estimate the annual cash flows of these benefits. In our initial calculation, we assumed each of these benefits to have a value of zero. It seems likely that their actual values are much higher than zero. Given the difficulty of estimating these benefits, however, conservative values should be assigned to them. If, after using conservative estimates, the net present value is positive, Berg should accept the project.

To illustrate, assume that Berg estimates that improved sales will increase cash inflows by $10,000 annually as a result of an increase in perceived quality. Berg also estimates that annual cost outflows would be reduced by $5,000 as a result of lower warranty claims, reduced injury claims, and fewer missed work days. Consideration of the intangible benefits results in the revised NPV calculation shown in **Illustration 18.16** (discount factor from Appendix E, Table 4).

| | | | | |
|---|---|---|---|---|
| Initial investment | $200,000 | | | |
| Annual cash inflows (revised) | $ 60,000 ($50,000 + $10,000) | | | |
| Annual cash outflows (revised) | 15,000 ($20,000 − $5,000) | | | |
| **Net annual cash flow** | **$ 45,000** | | | |
| Estimated life of equipment | 10 years | | | |
| Discount rate | 12% | | | |

| | Cash Flows | | 12% Discount Factor | | Present Value |
|---|---|---|---|---|---|
| Present value of net annual cash flows | $45,000 | × | 5.65022 | = | $254,260 |
| Less: Initial investment | | | | | 200,000 |
| **Net present value** | | | | | **$ 54,260** |

**ILLUSTRATION 18.16**

**Revised investment information for Berg Company example, including intangible benefits**

Using these conservative estimates of the value of the additional benefits, Berg should accept the project.

## Ethics Insight

### It Need Not Cost an Arm and a Leg

Most manufacturers say that employee safety matters above everything else. But how many back up this statement with investments that improve employee safety? For example, a woodworking hobbyist, who also happens to be a patent attorney with a Ph.D. in physics, invented a mechanism that automatically shuts down a power saw when the saw blade comes in contact with human flesh. The blade stops so quickly that only minor injuries result.

Power saws injure 40,000 Americans each year, and 4,000 of those injuries are bad enough to require amputation. Therefore,

istock.com/cgering/E+/ Getty Images

you might think that power-saw companies would be lined up to incorporate this mechanism into their saws. But, in the words of one power-tool company, "Safety doesn't sell." Since existing saw manufacturers were unwilling to incorporate the device into their saws, the inventor eventually started his own company to build the devices and sell them directly to businesses that use power saws.

**Source:** Melba Newsome, "An Edgy New Idea," *Time: Inside Business* (May 2006), p. A16.

**In addition to the obvious humanitarian benefit of reducing serious injuries, how else might the manufacturer of this product convince potential customers of its worth? (Go to WileyPLUS for this answer and additional questions.)**

# Profitability Index for Mutually Exclusive Projects

In theory, companies should accept all projects with positive NPVs. However, companies rarely are able to adopt all positive-NPV proposals.

1. Proposals often are **mutually exclusive**.

   - This means that if the company adopts one proposal, it would be impossible or impractical to also adopt the other proposal.
   - For example, a company may be considering the purchase of a new packaging machine and is looking at various brands and models.
   - Once the company has determined which brand and model to purchase, the others will not be purchased—even though they also may have positive net present values.

2. Managers often must choose between various positive-NPV projects because of **limited resources**.

   - For example, the company might have ideas for two new lines of business, each of which has a projected positive NPV.
   - However, both of these proposals require skilled personnel, and the company determines that it will not be able to find enough skilled personnel to staff both projects.
   - Management will have to choose the project it thinks is a better option.

When choosing between alternative proposals, it is tempting simply to choose the project with the higher NPV. Consider the following example of two mutually exclusive projects. Each is assumed to have a 10-year life and a 12% discount rate (discount factors from Appendix E, Tables 3 and 4). **Illustration 18.17** shows the estimates for each project and the computation of the present value of the net cash flows.

**ILLUSTRATION 18.17**

Investment information for
mutually exclusive projects

| | Project A | Project B |
|---|---|---|
| Initial investment | $40,000 | $ 90,000 |
| Net annual cash inflow | 10,000 | 19,000 |
| Salvage value | 5,000 | 10,000 |
| Present value of net cash flows | | |
| ($10,000 × 5.65022) + ($5,000 × .32197) | 58,112 | |
| ($19,000 × 5.65022) + ($10,000 × .32197) | | 110,574 |

**Illustration 18.18** computes the net present values of Project A and Project B by subtracting the initial investment from the present value of the net cash flows.

**ILLUSTRATION 18.18**

Net present value
computation

| | Project A | Project B |
|---|---|---|
| Present value of net cash flows | $58,112 | $110,574 |
| Less: Initial investment | 40,000 | 90,000 |
| Net present value | $18,112 | $ 20,574 |

As Project B has the higher NPV, it would seem that the company should adopt it. However, Project B also requires more than twice the original investment of Project A. In choosing between the two projects, the company should also include in its calculations the amount of the original investment.

One relatively simple method of comparing alternative projects is the **profitability index**.

- This method takes into account both the size of the original investment and the discounted cash flows.
- The profitability index is calculated by dividing the present value of net cash flows that occur after the initial investment by the amount of the initial investment, as **Illustration 18.19** shows.

| Present Value of<br>Net Cash Flows | ÷ | Initial<br>Investment | = | Profitability<br>Index |
|---|---|---|---|---|

**ILLUSTRATION 18.19**

**Formula for profitability index**

- The profitability index allows comparison of the relative desirability of projects that require differing initial investments (see **Decision Tools**).
- Note that any project with a positive NPV will have a profitability index above 1.

The profitability index for each of the mutually exclusive projects is calculated in **Illustration 18.20**.

**Decision Tools**

The profitability index helps a company determine which investment proposal to accept.

$$\text{Profitability Index} = \frac{\text{Present Value of Net Cash Flows}}{\text{Initial Investment}}$$

| **Project A** | **Project B** |
|---|---|
| $\dfrac{\$58{,}112}{\$40{,}000} = 1.45$ | $\dfrac{\$110{,}574}{\$90{,}000} = 1.23$ |

**ILLUSTRATION 18.20**

**Calculation for profitability index**

In this case, the profitability index of Project A exceeds that of Project B. Thus, Project A is more desirable. Again, if these were not mutually exclusive projects and if resources were not limited, then the company should invest in both projects since both have positive NPVs. Additional considerations related to preference decisions are discussed in more advanced courses.

# Risk Analysis

A simplifying assumption made by many financial analysts is that projected results are known with certainty. In reality, projected results are only estimates based upon the forecaster's belief as to the most probable outcome.

- One approach for dealing with such uncertainty is **sensitivity analysis**.
- Sensitivity analysis uses a number of outcome estimates to get a sense of the variability among potential returns.

An example of sensitivity analysis was presented in Illustration 18.11, where we illustrated the impact on NPV of different discount rate assumptions. A higher-risk project would be evaluated using a higher discount rate.

Similarly, to take into account that more distant cash flows are often more uncertain, a higher discount rate can be used to discount more distant cash flows. Other techniques to address uncertainty are discussed in advanced courses.

## People, Planet, and Profit Insight

Elnur/Shutterstock.com

### Big Spenders

Investments in electricity production and transmission represent some of society's biggest capital budgeting decisions. For example, billionaire Philip Anschutz is backing a project to build a 3,000-megawatt Wyoming wind farm as well as a 730-mile transmission line that would efficiently transfer the electricity to Las Vegas, where it could then travel on existing lines to locations in California. Total cost: $9 billion. This would be the biggest wind farm in the United States except that an even bigger, 4,000-megawatt wind farm is being planned by a different group of investors. In the past, these investments were made by regulated utility companies which were allowed to pass on their costs to cus-

tomers and thus essentially guaranteed a steady revenue stream. Today, many of the biggest projects are instead being financed by private investors. These investors will be selling their electricity in energy markets driven by market demand. This provides for more potential upside on their investment but also more uncertainty regarding revenue flows.

**Source:** Russell Gold, "Investors Are Building Their Own Green-Power Lines," *Wall Street Journal* (April 6, 2017).

**How does the financing of today's big energy investments differ from big energy capital investments of the past, and what are the implications? (Go to WileyPLUS for this answer and additional questions.)**

# Post-Audit of Investment Projects

Any well-run organization should perform an evaluation, called a **post-audit**, of its investment projects after their completion. A post-audit is a thorough evaluation of how well a project's actual performance matches the original projections. An example of a post-audit is seen in a situation that occurred at **Campbell Soup**. The company made the original decision to invest in the Intelligent Quisine line based on management's best estimates of future cash flows. During the development phase of the project, Campbell hired an outside consulting firm to evaluate the project's potential for success. Because actual results during the initial years were far below the estimated results and because the future also did not look promising, the project was terminated.

Performing a post-audit is important for a variety of reasons.

1. If managers know that the company will compare their estimates to actual results, they will be more likely to submit reasonable and accurate data when they make investment proposals. This clearly is better for the company than for managers to submit overly optimistic estimates in an effort to get pet projects approved.

2. As seen with Campbell Soup, a post-audit provides a formal mechanism by which the company can determine whether existing projects should be supported or terminated.

3. Post-audits improve future investment proposals because, by evaluating past successes and failures, managers improve their estimation techniques.

A post-audit involves the same evaluation techniques used in making the original capital budgeting decision—for example, use of the NPV method. The difference is that, in the post-audit, analysts insert actual figures, where known, and they revise estimates of future amounts based on new information. The managers responsible for the estimates used in the original proposal must explain the reasons for any significant differences between their estimates and actual results.

Post-audits are not foolproof. In the case of Campbell Soup, some observers suggested that the company was too quick to abandon the project. Industry analysts suggested that with more time and more advertising expenditures, the company might have enjoyed success.

---

## ACTION PLAN

- Determine the present value of annual cash flows of each mutually exclusive project.
- Determine profitability index by dividing the present value of annual cash flows by the amount of the initial investment.
- Choose project with highest profitability index.

## DO IT! 3 | Profitability Index

Taz Corporation has decided to invest in renewable energy sources to meet part of its energy needs for production. It is considering solar power versus wind power. After considering cost savings as well as incremental revenues from selling excess electricity into the power grid, it has determined the following.

|  | Solar | Wind |
| --- | --- | --- |
| Present value of annual cash flows | $78,580 | $168,450 |
| Initial investment | $45,500 | $125,300 |

Determine the net present value and profitability index of each project. Which energy source should it choose?

### Solution

|  | Solar | Wind |
| --- | --- | --- |
| Present value of annual cash flows | $78,580 | $168,450 |
| Less: Initial investment | 45,500 | 125,300 |
| Net present value | $33,080 | $ 43,150 |
| Profitability index | 1.73* | 1.34** |

*$78,580 ÷ $45,500
**$168,450 ÷ $125,300

While the investment in wind power generates the higher net present value, it also requires a substantially higher initial investment. The profitability index favors solar power, which suggests that the additional net present value of wind is outweighed by the cost of the initial investment. The company should choose solar power.

Related exercise material: **BE18.5, DO IT! 18.3, and E18.4.**

# Internal Rate of Return

The **internal rate of return method** differs from the net present value method in that it finds the **interest yield of the potential investment**.

- The **internal rate of return (IRR)** is the interest rate that causes the present value of the proposed capital expenditure to equal the present value of the expected net annual cash flows (that is, NPV equal to zero).
- Because it recognizes the time value of money, the internal rate of return method is (like the NPV method) a discounted cash flow technique (see **Decision Tools**).

How do we determine the internal rate of return? One way is to use a financial calculator (see Appendix E) or electronic spreadsheet (see the Excel tutorial provided in WileyPLUS) to solve for this rate. Or, we can use a trial-and-error procedure.

To illustrate, assume that Stewart Shipping Company is considering the purchase of a new front-end loader at a cost of $244,371. Net annual cash flows from this loader are estimated to be $100,000 a year for three years. To determine the internal rate of return on this front-end loader, the company finds the discount rate that results in a net present value of zero. As **Illustration 18.21** shows, at a rate of return of 10%, Stewart Shipping has a positive net present value of $4,315. At a rate of return of 12%, it has a negative net present value of $4,188. At an 11% rate, the net present value is zero. Therefore, 11% is the internal rate of return for this investment (discount factors from Appendix E, Table 3).

> **Decision Tools**
> The IRR helps a company determine if it should invest in a proposed project.

**ILLUSTRATION 18.21**  **Estimation of internal rate of return**

| Year | Net Annual Cash Flows | Discount Factor 10% | Present Value 10% | Discount Factor 11% | Present Value 11% | Discount Factor 12% | Present Value 12% |
|---|---|---|---|---|---|---|---|
| 1 | $100,000 | .90909 | $ 90,909 | .90090 | $ 90,090 | .89286 | $ 89,286 |
| 2 | $100,000 | .82645 | 82,645 | .81162 | 81,162 | .79719 | 79,719 |
| 3 | $100,000 | .75132 | 75,132 | .73119 | 73,119 | .71178 | 71,178 |
| | | | 248,686 | | 244,371 | | 240,183 |
| Less: Initial investment | | | 244,371 | | 244,371 | | 244,371 |
| Net present value | | | $ 4,315 | | $ -0- | | $ (4,188) |

An easier approach to solving for the internal rate of return can be used if the net annual cash flows are **equal**, as in the Stewart Shipping example. In this special case, we can find the internal rate of return using the formula provided in **Illustration 18.22**.

| Capital Investment | ÷ | Net Annual Cash Flows | = | Internal Rate of Return Factor |
|---|---|---|---|---|

**ILLUSTRATION 18.22**
Formula for internal rate of return—even cash flows

Applying this formula to the Stewart Shipping example, we find:

$$\$244,371 \div 100,000 = 2.44371$$

We then look up the factor 2.44371 in Table 4 of Appendix E in the three-payment row and find it under 11%. Row 3 is reproduced here for your convenience.

| Table 4 Present Value of an Annuity of 1 | | | | | | | | | | |
|---|---|---|---|---|---|---|---|---|---|---|
| *(n)* Payments | 4% | 5% | 6% | 7% | 8% | 9% | 10% | 11% | 12% | 15% |
| 3 | 2.77509 | 2.72325 | 2.67301 | 2.62432 | 2.57710 | 2.53130 | 2.48685 | 2.44371 | 2.40183 | 2.28323 |

Recognize that if the cash flows are **uneven**, then a trial-and-error approach or a financial calculator or computerized spreadsheet must be used.

Once managers know the internal rate of return, they compare it to the company's required rate of return (the discount rate). The IRR decision rule is as follows:

- **Accept the project when the internal rate of return is equal to or greater than the required rate of return.**
- **Reject the project when the internal rate of return is less than the required rate of return.**

**Illustration 18.23** shows these relationships. The internal rate of return method is widely used in practice, largely because most managers find the internal rate of return easy to interpret.

**ILLUSTRATION 18.23**

**Internal rate of return decision criteria**

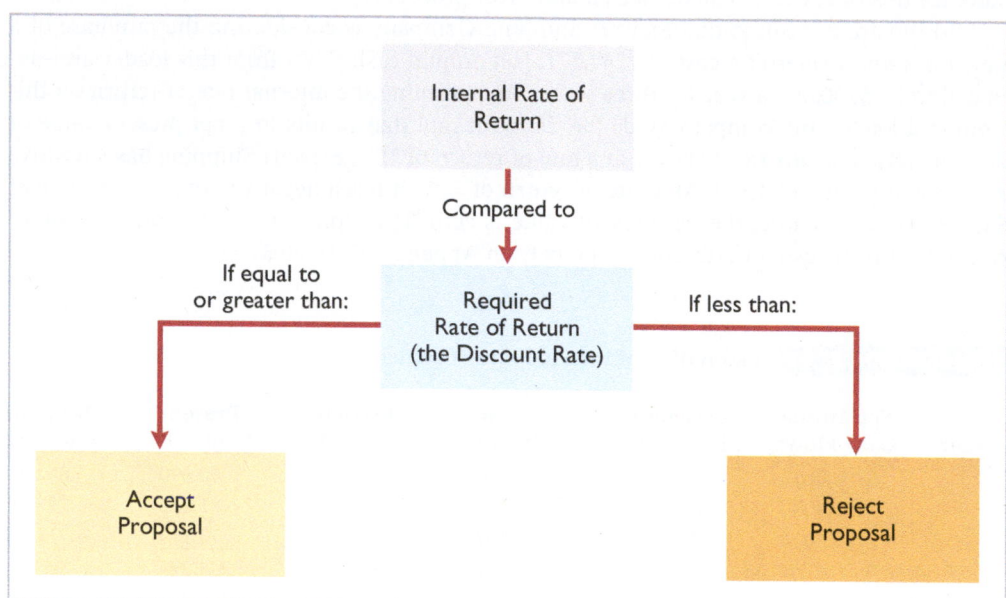

## Comparing Discounted Cash Flow Methods

**Illustration 18.24** compares the two discounted cash flow methods—net present value and internal rate of return. When properly used, either method will provide management with relevant quantitative data for making capital budgeting decisions.

**ILLUSTRATION 18.24**

**Comparison of discounted cash flow methods**

| | Net Present Value | Internal Rate of Return |
|---|---|---|
| 1. Objective | Compute net present value (a dollar amount). | Compute internal rate of return (a percentage). |
| 2. Decision Rule | If net present value is zero or positive, accept the proposal. | If internal rate of return is equal to or greater than the required rate of return, accept the proposal. |
| | If net present value is negative, reject the proposal. | If internal rate of return is less than the required rate of return, reject the proposal. |

## DO IT! 4 | Internal Rate of Return

Watertown Paper Corporation is considering adding another machine for the manufacture of corrugated cardboard. The machine would cost $900,000. It would have an estimated life of 6 years and no salvage value. The company estimates that annual cash inflows would increase by $400,000 and that annual cash outflows would increase by $190,000. Management has a required rate of return of 9%. Calculate the internal rate of return on this project and discuss whether it should be accepted.

### Solution

| | |
|---|---|
| Estimated annual cash inflows | $400,000 |
| Estimated annual cash outflows | 190,000 |
| Net annual cash flow | $210,000 |

$900,000 ÷ $210,000 = 4.285714. Using Table 4 of Appendix E and the factors that correspond with the six-payment row, 4.285714 is between the factors for 10% and 11%. Since the project has an internal rate that is greater than 10% and the required rate of return is only 9%, the project should be accepted.

Related exercise material: **BE18.7, BE18.8, DO IT! 18.4, E18.5, E18.6, and E18.7.**

**ACTION PLAN**

- **Estimated annual cash inflows − Estimated annual cash outflows = Net annual cash flow.**
- **Capital investment ÷ Net annual cash flows = Internal rate of return factor.**
- **Look up the factor in the present value of an annuity table to find the internal rate of return.**
- **Accept the project if the internal rate of return is equal to or greater than the required rate of return.**

# Annual Rate of Return

### LEARNING OBJECTIVE 5
Use the annual rate of return method.

The final capital budgeting technique we will look at is the **annual rate of return method**.

- It is based directly on accrual accounting data rather than on cash flows.
- It indicates **the profitability of a capital expenditure** by dividing expected annual net income by the average investment.

**Illustration 18.25** shows the formula for computing annual rate of return.

| Expected Annual Net Income | ÷ | Average Investment | = | Annual Rate of Return |
|---|---|---|---|---|

**ILLUSTRATION 18.25**

Annual rate of return formula

Assume that Reno Company is considering an investment of $130,000 in new equipment. The new equipment is expected to last five years and have zero salvage value at the end of its useful life. Reno uses the straight-line method of depreciation for accounting purposes. **Illustration 18.26** shows the expected annual revenues and costs of the new product that will be produced from the investment.

| | | |
|---|---|---|
| Sales | | $200,000 |
| Less: Costs and expenses | | |
| Manufacturing costs (exclusive of depreciation) | $132,000 | |
| Depreciation expense ($130,000 ÷ 5) | 26,000 | |
| Selling and administrative expenses | 22,000 | 180,000 |
| Income before income taxes | | 20,000 |
| Income tax expense | | 7,000 |
| Net income | | $ 13,000 |

**ILLUSTRATION 18.26**

Estimated annual net income from Reno Company's capital expenditure

Reno's expected annual net income is $13,000. Average investment is derived from the formula shown in **Illustration 18.27**.

**ILLUSTRATION 18.27**
Formula for computing average investment

$$\frac{\text{Original Investment} + \text{Value at End of Useful Life}}{2} = \text{Average Investment}$$

The value at the end of useful life is equal to the asset's salvage value, if any. For Reno, average investment is $65,000 [($130,000 + $0) ÷ 2]. The expected annual rate of return for Reno's investment in new equipment is therefore 20%, computed as follows.

$$\$13,000 \div \$65,000 = 20\%$$

Management then compares the annual rate of return with its **required rate of return** for investments of similar risk. The required rate of return is generally based on the company's cost of capital. The decision rule is:

- **A project is acceptable if its rate of return is greater than management's required rate of return**.
- **It is unacceptable when the reverse is true**.
- When companies use the rate of return technique in deciding among several acceptable projects, **the higher the rate of return for a given risk, the more attractive the investment**.

The principal advantages of this method are the simplicity of its calculation and management's familiarity with the accounting terms used in the computation. Two limitations of the annual rate of return method are:

**HELPFUL HINT**

A capital budgeting decision based on only one technique may be misleading. It is often wise to analyze an investment from a number of different perspectives.

1. It does not consider the time value of money. For example, no consideration is given as to whether cash inflows will occur early or late in the life of the investment. As explained in Appendix E, recognition of the time value of money can make a significant difference between the future value and the discounted present value of an investment.

2. This method relies on accrual accounting numbers rather than expected cash flows (see **Helpful Hint**).

---

**ACTION PLAN**

- Expected annual net income = Annual revenues − Annual expenses (including depreciation expense).
- Average investment = (Original investment + Value at end of useful life) ÷ 2.
- Annual rate of return = Expected annual net income ÷ Average investment.

## DO IT! 5 | Annual Rate of Return

Watertown Paper Corporation is considering adding another machine for the manufacture of corrugated cardboard. The machine would cost $900,000. It would have an estimated life of 6 years and no salvage value. The company estimates that annual revenues would increase by $400,000 and that annual expenses excluding depreciation would increase by $190,000. It uses the straight-line method to compute depreciation expense. Management has a required rate of return of 9%. Compute the annual rate of return.

### Solution

| | | |
|---|---:|---:|
| Revenues | | $400,000 |
| Less: | | |
| Expenses (excluding depreciation) | $190,000 | |
| Depreciation ($900,000 ÷ 6 years) | 150,000 | 340,000 |
| Annual net income | | $ 60,000 |

Average investment = ($900,000 + $0) ÷ 2 = $450,000
Annual rate of return = $60,000 ÷ $450,000 = 13.3%

Since the annual rate of return (13.3%) is greater than Watertown's required rate of return (9%), the proposed project is acceptable.

Related exercise material: **BE18.9, DO IT! 18.5, E18.8, E18.9, E18.10, and E18.11.**

## USING THE DECISION TOOLS | Holland America Line

As noted in the Feature Story, **Holland America Line** must continually make significant capital investments in ships. Some of these decisions require comparisons of strategic alternatives. For example, not all of the company's ships are the same size. Different-sized ships offer alternative advantages and disadvantages. Suppose the company engages in ferrying activities and is trying to decide between two investment options. It is weighing the purchase of three larger ships for a total of $2,500,000 versus five smaller ships for a total of $1,400,000. Information regarding these two alternatives is provided here.

| | Three Larger Ships | Five Smaller Ships |
|---|---|---|
| Initial investment | $2,500,000 | $1,400,000 |
| Estimated useful life | 20 years | 20 years |
| Annual revenues (accrual) | $500,000 | $380,000 |
| Annual expenses (accrual) | $200,000 | $180,000 |
| Annual cash inflows | $550,000 | $430,000 |
| Annual cash outflows | $222,250 | $206,350 |
| Estimated salvage value | $500,000 | $0 |
| Discount rate | 9% | 9% |

## Instructions

Evaluate each of these mutually exclusive proposals employing (a) cash payback, (b) net present value, (c) profitability index, (d) internal rate of return, and (e) annual rate of return. Discuss the implications of your findings.

## Solution

| | Three Larger Ships | Five Smaller Ships |
|---|---|---|
| a. Cash payback | $\dfrac{\$2,500,000}{\$327,750^*} = 7.63$ years | $\dfrac{\$1,400,000}{\$223,650^{**}} = 6.26$ years |

*$550,000 – $222,250; **$430,000 – $206,350

b. Net present value
   Present value of net cash flows

| | | Three Larger Ships | Five Smaller Ships |
|---|---|---|---|
| $327,750 × 9.12855 = | $2,991,882 | $223,650 × 9.12855 = $2,041,600 | |
| $500,000 × 0.17843 = | 89,215 | | |
| | 3,081,097 | | |
| Less: Initial investment | 2,500,000 | 1,400,000 | |
| Net present value | $ 581,097 | $ 641,600 | |

| | Three Larger Ships | Five Smaller Ships |
|---|---|---|
| c. Profitability index | $\dfrac{\$3,081,097}{\$2,500,000} = 1.23$ | $\dfrac{\$2,041,600}{\$1,400,000} = 1.46$ |

d. The internal rate of return can be approximated by experimenting with different discount rates to see which one comes the closest to resulting in a net present value of zero. Doing this, we find that the larger ships have an internal rate of return of approximately 12%, while the internal rate of return of the smaller ships is approximately 15% as shown below.

Internal rate of return

| Cash Flows | × | 12% Discount Factor | = | Present Value | Cash Flows | × | 15% Discount Factor | = | Present Value |
|---|---|---|---|---|---|---|---|---|---|
| $327,750 | × | 7.46944 | = | $2,448,109 | $223,650 | × | 6.25933 | = | $1,399,899 |
| $500,000 | × | 0.10367 | = | 51,835 | | | | | |
| | | | | $2,499,944 | | | | | |
| Less: Capital investment | | | | 2,500,000 | | | | | 1,400,000 |
| Net present value | | | | $ (56) | | | | | $ (101) |

e. Annual rate of return

| **Three Larger Ships** | **Five Smaller Ships** |
|---|---|

Average investment

$$\frac{(\$2,500,000 + \$500,000)}{2} = \$1,500,000 \qquad \frac{(\$1,400,000 + \$0)}{2} = \$700,000$$

$$\text{Annual rate of return } \frac{\$300,000^*}{\$1,500,000} = .20 = 20\% \qquad \frac{\$200,000^{**}}{\$700,000} = .286 = 28.6\%$$

*$500,000 − $200,000; **$380,000 − $180,000

Although the annual rate of return is higher for the smaller ships, annual rate of return has the disadvantage of ignoring time value of money, as well as using accrual numbers rather than cash flows. The cash payback of the smaller ships is also shorter, but this method also ignores the time value of money. Thus, while these two methods can be used for a quick assessment, neither should be relied upon as the sole evaluation tool.

From the net present value calculation, it would appear that the two alternatives are nearly identical in their acceptability. However, the profitability index indicates that the small-ship investment is far more desirable because it generates its cash flows with a much smaller initial investment. A similar result is found by using the internal rate of return. Overall, assuming that the company will select only one alternative, it would appear that the small-ship option should be chosen.

# Review and Practice

## Learning Objectives Review

### 1 Describe capital budgeting inputs and apply the cash payback technique.

Management gathers project proposals from each department; a capital budget committee screens the proposals and recommends worthy projects. Company officers decide which projects to fund, and the board of directors approves the capital budget. In capital budgeting, estimated cash inflows and outflows, rather than accrual-accounting numbers, are the preferred inputs.

The cash payback technique identifies the time period required to recover the cost of the investment. The formula when net annual cash flows are equal is: Cost of capital investment ÷ Estimated net annual cash flow = Cash payback period. The shorter the payback period, the more attractive the investment.

### 2 Use the net present value method.

The net present value method compares the present value of future cash inflows with the capital investment to determine net present value. The NPV decision rule is: Accept the project if net present value is zero or positive. Reject the project if net present value is negative.

### 3 Identify capital budgeting challenges and refinements.

Intangible benefits are difficult to quantify and thus are often ignored in capital budgeting decisions. This can result in incorrectly rejecting some projects. One method for considering intangible benefits is to calculate the NPV, ignoring intangible benefits. If the resulting NPV is below zero, evaluate whether the benefits are worth at least the amount of the negative net present value. Alternatively, intangible benefits can be incorporated into the NPV calculation, using conservative estimates of their value.

The profitability index is a tool for comparing the relative merits of alternative capital investment opportunities. It is computed as Present value of net cash flows ÷ Initial investment. The higher the index, the more desirable the project.

A post-audit is an evaluation of a capital investment's actual performance. Post-audits create an incentive for managers to make accurate estimates. Post-audits also are useful for determining whether a company should continue, expand, or terminate a project. Finally, post-audits provide feedback that is useful for improving estimation techniques.

### 4 Use the internal rate of return method.

The objective of the internal rate of return method is to find the interest yield of the potential investment, which is expressed as a percentage rate. The IRR decision rule is: Accept the project when the internal rate of return is equal to or greater than the required rate of return. Reject the project when the internal rate of return is less than the required rate of return.

### 5 Use the annual rate of return method.

The annual rate of return uses accrual accounting data to indicate the profitability of a capital investment. It is calculated as Expected annual net income ÷ Amount of the average investment. The higher the rate of return, the more attractive the investment.

## Decision Tools Review

| Decision Checkpoints | Info Needed for Decision | Tool to Use for Decision | How to Evaluate Results |
|---|---|---|---|
| Should the company invest in a proposed project? | Cash flow estimates, discount rate | Net present value = Present value of net cash flows less capital investment | The investment is financially acceptable if net present value is zero or positive. |
| Which investment proposal should a company accept? | Estimated cash flows and discount rate for each proposal | $\text{Profitability index} = \dfrac{\text{Present value of net cash flows}}{\text{Initial investment}}$ | The investment proposal with the highest profitability index should be accepted. |
| Should the company invest in a proposed project? | Estimated cash flows and the required rate of return (hurdle rate) | Internal rate of return = Interest rate that results in a net present value of zero | If the internal rate of return exceeds the required rate of return for the project, then the project is financially acceptable. |

## Glossary Review

**Annual rate of return method**  The determination of the profitability of a capital expenditure, computed by dividing expected annual net income by the average investment. (p. 18-19).

**Capital budgeting**  The process of making capital expenditure decisions in business. (p. 18-3).

**Cash payback technique**  A capital budgeting technique that identifies the time period required to recover the cost of a capital investment from the net annual cash flow produced by the investment. (p. 18-5).

**Cost of capital**  The weighted-average rate of return that the firm must pay to obtain funds from creditors and stockholders. (p. 18-9).

**Discounted cash flow technique**  A capital budgeting technique that considers both the estimated net cash flows from the investment and the time value of money. (p. 18-6).

**Discount rate**  The interest rate used in discounting the future net cash flows to determine present value. (p. 18-7).

**Internal rate of return (IRR)**  The interest rate that will cause the present value of the proposed capital expenditure to equal the present value of the expected net annual cash flows. (p. 18-17).

**Internal rate of return (IRR) method**  A method used in capital budgeting that results in finding the interest yield of the potential investment. (p. 18-17).

**Net present value (NPV)**  The difference that results when the original capital outlay is subtracted from the discounted net cash flows. (p. 18-7).

**Net present value (NPV) method**  A method used in capital budgeting in which net cash flows are discounted to their present value and then compared to the capital outlay required by the investment. (p. 18-7).

**Post-audit**  A thorough evaluation of how well a project's actual performance matches the original projections. (p. 18-16).

**Profitability index**  A method of comparing alternative projects that takes into account both the size of the investment and its discounted net cash flows. It is computed by dividing the present value of net cash flows by the initial investment. (p. 18-14).

**Required rate of return**  Management's minimum acceptable rate of return on investments, sometimes called the discount rate or cost of capital. (p. 18-7).

**Sensitivity analysis**  An approach that uses a number of outcome estimates to get a sense of the variability among potential returns. (p. 18-15).

## Practice Multiple-Choice Questions

**1. (LO 1)** Which of the following is **not** an example of a capital budgeting decision?

    **a.** Decision to build a new plant.

    **b.** Decision to renovate an existing facility.

    **c.** Decision to buy a piece of machinery.

    **d.** All of the answer choices are capital budgeting decisions.

**2. (LO 1)** What is the order of involvement of the following parties in the capital budgeting authorization process?

    **a.** Plant managers, officers, capital budget committee, board of directors.

    **b.** Board of directors, plant managers, officers, capital budget committee.

    **c.** Plant managers, capital budget committee, officers, board of directors.

    **d.** Officers, plant managers, capital budget committee, board of directors.

**3. (LO 1)** What is a weakness of the cash payback approach?

    **a.** It uses accrual-based accounting numbers.

    **b.** It ignores the time value of money.

    **c.** It ignores the useful life of alternative projects.

    **d.** It ignores both the time value of money and the useful life of alternative projects.

**4. (LO 1)** Siegel Industries is considering two capital budgeting projects. Project A requires an initial investment of $48,000. It is expected to produce net annual cash flows of $7,000. Project B requires an initial investment of $75,000 and is expected to produce net annual cash flows of $12,000. Using the cash payback technique to evaluate the two projects, Siegel should accept:

    **a.** Project A because it has a shorter cash payback period.

    **b.** Project B because it has a shorter cash payback period.

    **c.** Project A because it requires a smaller initial investment.

    **d.** Project B because it produces a larger net annual cash flow.

**5. (LO 2)** Which is a **true** statement regarding using a higher discount rate to calculate the net present value of a project?

    **a.** It will make it less likely that the project will be accepted.

    **b.** It will make it more likely that the project will be accepted.

    **c.** It is appropriate to use a higher rate if the project is perceived as being less risky than other projects being considered.

    **d.** It is appropriate to use a higher rate if the project will have a short useful life relative to other projects being considered.

**6. (LO 2)** A positive net present value means that the:

    **a.** project's rate of return is less than the cutoff rate.

    **b.** project's rate of return exceeds the required rate of return.

    **c.** project's rate of return equals the required rate of return.

    **d.** project is unacceptable.

**7. (LO 2)** Which of the following is **not** an alternative name for the discount rate?

    **a.** Hurdle rate.

    **b.** Required rate of return.

    **c.** Cutoff rate.

    **d.** All of the answer choices are alternative names for the discount rate.

**8. (LO 3)** If a project has intangible benefits whose value is hard to estimate, the best thing to do is:

    **a.** ignore these benefits, since any estimate of their value will most likely be wrong.

    **b.** include a conservative estimate of their value.

    **c.** ignore their value in your initial net present value calculation, but then estimate whether their potential value is worth at least the amount of the net present value deficiency.

    **d.** either include a conservative estimate of their value or ignore their value in your initial net present value calculation, but then estimate whether their potential value is worth at least the amount of the net present value deficiency.

**9. (LO 3)** An example of an intangible benefit provided by a capital budgeting project is:

    **a.** the salvage value of the capital investment.

    **b.** a positive net present value.

    **c.** a decrease in customer complaints regarding poor quality.

    **d.** an internal rate of return greater than zero.

**10. (LO 3)** The following information is available for a potential capital investment.

| | |
|---|---|
| Initial investment | $80,000 |
| Salvage value | 10,000 |
| Net annual cash flow | 14,820 |
| Present value of net annual cash flows | 98,112 |
| Net present value | 18,112 |
| Useful life | 10 years |

The potential investment's profitability index (rounded to two decimals) is:

    **a.** 5.40.         **c.** 1.23.

    **b.** 1.19.         **d.** 1.40.

**11. (LO 3)** A post-audit of an investment project should be performed:

    **a.** on all significant capital expenditure projects.

    **b.** on all projects that management feels might be financial failures.

    **c.** on randomly selected projects.

    **d.** only on projects that enjoy tremendous success.

**12. (LO 4)** A project should be accepted if its internal rate of return exceeds:

    **a.** zero.

    **b.** the rate of return on a government bond.

    **c.** the company's required rate of return.

    **d.** the rate the company pays on borrowed funds.

**13. (LO 4)** The following information is available for a potential capital investment.

| | |
|---|---|
| Initial investment | $60,000 |
| Net annual cash flow | 15,400 |
| Net present value | 3,143 |
| Useful life | 5 years |

The potential investment's internal rate of return is approximately:

    **a.** 5%.         **c.** 4%.

    **b.** 10%.        **d.** 9%.

**14. (LO 5)** Which of the following is **incorrect** about the annual rate of return technique?

    **a.** The calculation is simple.

    **b.** The accounting terms used are familiar to management.

    **c.** The timing of the cash inflows is not considered.

    **d.** The time value of money is considered.

**15. (LO 5)** The following information is available for a potential capital investment.

| | |
|---|---|
| Initial investment | $120,000 |
| Annual net income | 15,000 |
| Net annual cash flow | 27,500 |
| Salvage value | 20,000 |
| Useful life | 8 years |

The potential investment's annual rate of return is approximately:

    **a.** 21%.         **c.** 30%.

    **b.** 15%.         **d.** 39%.

## Solutions

**1. d.** Choices (a), (b), and (c) are all examples of capital budgeting decisions, so choice (d) is the best answer.

**2. c.** The process of authorizing capital budget expenditures starts with plant managers, moves on to the capital budgeting committee, goes next to the officers of the firm and finally is acted upon by the board of directors. The other choices are therefore incorrect.

**3. d.** Choices (b) and (c) are both correct; therefore, choice (d) is the best answer. Choice (a) is incorrect as the use of accrual-based accounting numbers is not a weakness of the cash payback approach.

**4. b.** Project B ($75,000 ÷ $12,000) has a shorter cash payback period than Project A ($48,000 ÷ $7,000). The other choices are therefore incorrect.

**5. a.** If a higher discount rate is used in calculating the net present value of a project, the resulting net present value will be lower and the project will be less likely to be accepted. The other choices are therefore incorrect.

**6. b.** A positive net present value means that the project's rate of return exceeds the required rate of return. The other choices are therefore incorrect.

**7. d.** Choices (a), (b), and (c) are all alternative names for the discount rate; therefore, choice (d) is the best answer.

**8. d.** Choices (b) and (c) are both reasonable approaches to including intangible benefits in the capital budgeting process; therefore, choice (d) is the best answer. Choice (a) is incorrect because even though these intangible benefits may be hard to quantify, they should not be ignored in the capital budgeting process.

**9. c.** A decrease in customer complaints regarding poor quality is one example of an intangible benefit provided by a capital budgeting project. The other choices are incorrect because (a) salvage value, (b) net present value, and (d) internal rate of return are all quantitative measures, i.e., tangible.

**10. c.** ($18,112 + $80,000) ÷ $80,000 = 1.23, not (a) 5.40, (b) 1.19, or (d) 1.40.

**11. a.** A post-audit should be performed on all significant capital expenditure projects, not just on (b) financial failures, (c) randomly selected projects, or (d) tremendous successes, because the feedback gained will help to improve the process in the future and also will give managers an incentive to be more realistic in preparing capital expenditure proposals.

**12. c.** A project should be accepted if its internal rate of return exceeds the company's required rate of return, not (a) zero, (b) the rate of return on a government bond, or (d) the rate the company pays on borrowed funds.

**13. d.** ($60,000 ÷ $15,400) equals 3.8961, which corresponds with approximately 9% in Table 4 of Appendix E, not (a) 5%, (b) 10%, or (c) 4%.

**14. d.** The time value of money is not considered when applying the annual rate of return method. The other choices are correct statements.

**15. a.** $15,000 ÷ [($120,000 + $20,000) ÷ 2] = 21%, not (b) 15%, (c) 30%, or (d) 39%.

## Practice Brief Exercises

**1. (LO 1)** Carson Company is considering purchasing new equipment for $600,000. Annual depreciation over the 8-year useful life of the equipment is $75,000. It is expected that the equipment will produce net annual cash inflows of $100,000 over its 8-year useful life. Compute the cash payback period.

*Compute the cash payback period for a capital investment.*

### Solution

**1.** Cash payback period = $600,000 ÷ $100,000 = 6 years

**2. (LO 2)** Hilred Company is considering two different, mutually exclusive capital expenditure proposals. Project A will cost $400,000, has an expected useful life of 8 years, a salvage value of zero, and is expected to increase net annual cash flows by $80,000. Project B will also cost $400,000, has an expected useful life of 8 years, a salvage value of $100,000, and is expected to increase net annual cash flows by $70,000. A discount rate of 10% is appropriate for both projects. Compute the net present value of each project. Which project should be accepted?

*Compute net present values.*

## Solution

**2.**

**Project A**

| | Cash Flows | × | 10% Discount Factor | = | Present Value |
|---|---|---|---|---|---|
| Present value of net annual cash flows | $ 80,000 | × | 5.33493 | = | $426,794 |
| Present value of salvage value | 0 | × | .46651 | = | 0 |
| | | | | | 426,794 |
| Less: Capital investment | | | | | 400,000 |
| Net present value | | | | | $ 26,794 |

**Project B**

| | Cash Flows | × | 10% Discount Factor | = | Present Value |
|---|---|---|---|---|---|
| Present value of net annual cash flows | $ 70,000 | × | 5.33493 | = | $373,445 |
| Present value of salvage value | 100,000 | × | .46651 | = | 46,651 |
| | | | | | 420,096 |
| Less: Capital investment | | | | | 400,000 |
| Net present value | | | | | $ 20,096 |

Project A has a higher net present value than Project B, and it should therefore be accepted.

*Calculate annual rate of return.*

**3. (LO 5)** King-Roken Company is considering investing in new automated equipment. It is expected that the equipment will increase annual revenues by $200,000 and annual expenses by $120,000 (including depreciation). The equipment will cost $540,000 and have a $20,000 salvage value at the end of its 10-year useful life. Calculate the annual rate of return.

## Solution

3. The annual rate of return is calculated by dividing expected annual income by the average investment. The company's expected annual income is:

$$\$200,000 - \$120,000 = \$80,000$$

Its average investment is:

$$\frac{\$540,000 + \$20,000}{2} = \$280,000$$

Therefore, its annual rate of return is:

$$\$80,000 \div \$280,000 = 28.6\%$$

# Practice Exercises

*Calculate payback period and internal rate of return, and apply decision rules.*

**1. (LO 1, 4)** BTMS Inc. wants to purchase a new machine for $30,000. Installation costs are $1,500. The old machine was bought 5 years ago and had an expected economic life of 10 years without salvage value. This old machine now has a book value of $2,000, and BTMS Inc. expects to sell it for that amount. The new machine would decrease operating costs by $8,000 each year of its economic life. The straight-line depreciation method would be used for the new machine, for a 5-year period with no salvage value.

## Instructions

a. Determine the cash payback period.

b. Determine the approximate internal rate of return.

c. Assuming the company has a required rate of return of 10%, state your conclusion on whether the new machine should be purchased.

(CGA adapted)

## Solution

1. **a.** Total net investment = $30,000 + $1,500 − $2,000 = $29,500

   Annual net cash flow = $8,000
   Payback period = $29,500 ÷ $8,000 = 3.7 years

   **b.** Net present value approximates zero when discount rate is 11%.

   | Item | Amount | Years | PV Factor | Present Value |
   |---|---|---|---|---|
   | Net annual cash flows | $8,000 | 1–5 | 3.69590 | $29,567 |
   | Less: Capital investment | | | | 29,500 |
   | Net present value | | | | $    67 |

   **c.** Because the approximate internal rate of return of 11% exceeds the required rate of return of 10%, the investment should be accepted.

2. **(LO 1, 2, 5)** MCA Corporation is reviewing an investment proposal. The initial cost is $105,000. Estimates of the book value of the investment at the end of each year, the net cash flows for each year, and the net income for each year are presented in the schedule below. All cash flows are assumed to take place at the end of the year. The salvage value of the investment at the end of each year is equal to its book value. There would be no salvage value at the end of the investment's life.

*Calculate payback, annual rate of return, and net present value*

### Investment Proposal

| Year | Book Value | Annual Cash Flows | Annual Net Income |
|---|---|---|---|
| 1 | $70,000 | $45,000 | $16,000 |
| 2 | 42,000 | 40,000 | 18,000 |
| 3 | 21,000 | 35,000 | 20,000 |
| 4 | 7,000 | 30,000 | 22,000 |
| 5 | 0 | 25,000 | 24,000 |

MCA Corporation uses a 15% target rate of return for new investment proposals.

### Instructions

**a.** What is the cash payback period for this proposal?

**b.** What is the annual rate of return for the investment?

**c.** What is the net present value of the investment?

(CMA-Canada adapted)

## Solution

2. **a.**

   | | Year | Amount | Balance |
   |---|---|---|---|
   | Initial investment | 0 | $(105,000) | $(105,000) |
   | Less: Cash flow | 1 | 45,000 | (60,000) |
   | | 2 | 40,000 | (20,000) |
   | | 3 | 35,000 | 15,000 |

   Payback period = 2 + ($20,000 ÷ $35,000) = 2.57 years

   **b.** Average annual net income = ($16,000 + $18,000 + $20,000 + $22,000 + $24,000) ÷ 5 = $20,000

   Average investment = ($105,000 + $0) ÷ 2 = $52,500

   Annual rate of return = $20,000 ÷ $52,500 = 38.10%

c.

| Year | Discount Factor, 15% | × Amount | = Present Value |
|---|---|---|---|
| Net cash flows 1 | 0.86957 | $45,000 | $ 39,131 |
| 2 | 0.75614 | 40,000 | 30,246 |
| 3 | 0.65752 | 35,000 | 23,013 |
| 4 | 0.57175 | 30,000 | 17,153 |
| 5 | 0.49718 | 25,000 | 12,430 |

Present value of cash inflows    121,973
Less: Initial investment    105,000
Net present value    $ 16,973

# Practice Problem

*Compute annual rate of return, cash payback, and net present value.*

**(LO 1, 2, 5)** Cornfield Company is considering a long-term capital investment project in laser equipment. This will require an investment of $280,000, and it will have a useful life of 5 years. Annual net income is expected to be $16,000 a year. Depreciation is computed by the straight-line method with no salvage value. The company's cost of capital is 10%, and it desires a cash payback of 60% of a project's useful life or less. (*Hint:* Assume cash flows can be computed by adding back depreciation expense.)

### Instructions

(Round all computations to two decimal places unless directed otherwise.)

a. Compute the cash payback period for the project.

b. Compute the net present value for the project. (Round to nearest dollar.)

c. Compute the annual rate of return for the project.

d. Should the project be accepted? Why or why not?

### Solution

a. $280,000 ÷ $72,000 ($16,000 + $56,000) = 3.89 years

b.

| | Present Value at 10% |
|---|---|
| Discount factor for 5 payments | 3.79079 |
| Present value of net cash flows: | |
|    $72,000 × 3.79079 | $272,937 |
| Less: Capital investment | 280,000 |
| Negative net present value | $ (7,063) |

c. $16,000 ÷ $140,000 ($280,000 ÷ 2) = 11.4%

d. The annual rate of return of 11.4% is reasonable. However, the cash payback period is 78% of the project's useful life, and net present value is negative. The recommendation is to reject the project.

# WileyPLUS

Brief Exercises, DO IT! Exercises, Exercises, Problems, and many additional resources are available for practice in WileyPLUS.

## Questions

**1.** Describe the process a company may use in screening and approving the capital expenditure budget.

**2.** What are the advantages and disadvantages of the cash payback technique?

**3.** Tom Wells claims the formula for the cash payback technique is the same as the formula for the annual rate of return technique. Is Tom correct? What is the formula for the cash payback technique?

**4.** Two types of present value tables may be used with the discounted cash flow techniques. Identify the tables and the circumstance(s) when each table should be used.

**5.** What is the decision rule under the net present value method?

**6.** Discuss the factors that determine the appropriate discount rate to use when calculating the net present value.

**7.** What simplifying assumptions were made in the chapter regarding the calculation of net present value?

**8.** What are some examples of potential intangible benefits of investment proposals? Why do these intangible benefits complicate the capital budgeting evaluation process? What might happen if intangible benefits are ignored in a capital budgeting decision?

**9.** What steps can be taken to incorporate intangible benefits into the capital budget evaluation process?

**10.** What advantages does the profitability index provide over direct comparison of net present value when comparing two projects?

**11.** What is a post-audit? What are the potential benefits of a post-audit?

**12.** Identify the steps required in using the internal rate of return method when the net annual cash flows are equal.

**13.** El Cajon Company uses the internal rate of return method. What is the decision rule for this method?

**14.** What are the strengths of the annual rate of return approach? What are its weaknesses?

**15.** Your classmate, Mike Dawson, is confused about the factors that are included in the annual rate of return technique. What is the formula for this technique?

**16.** Sveta Pace is trying to understand the term "cost of capital." Define the term and indicate its relevance to the decision rule under the internal rate of return technique.

## Brief Exercises

**BE18.1 (LO 1), AP** Rihanna Company is considering purchasing new equipment for $450,000. It is expected that the equipment will produce net annual cash flows of $60,000 over its 10-year useful life. Annual depreciation will be $45,000. Compute the cash payback period.

*Compute the cash payback period for a capital investment.*

**BE18.2 (LO 2), AN** Hsung Company accumulates the following data concerning a proposed capital investment: cash cost $215,000, net annual cash flows $40,000, and present value factor of cash inflows for 10 years is 5.65 (rounded). Determine the net present value, and indicate whether the investment should be made.

*Compute net present value of an investment.*

**BE18.3 (LO 2), AP** Thunder Corporation, an amusement park, is considering a capital investment in a new exhibit. The exhibit would cost $136,000 and have an estimated useful life of 5 years. It can be sold for $60,000 at the end of that time. (Amusement parks need to rotate exhibits to keep people interested.) It is expected to increase net annual cash flows by $25,000. The company's borrowing rate is 8%. Its cost of capital is 10%. Calculate the net present value of this project to the company.

*Compute net present value of an investment.*

**BE18.4 (LO 2, 3), AN** Caine Bottling Corporation is considering the purchase of a new bottling machine. The machine would cost $200,000 and has an estimated useful life of 8 years with zero salvage value. Management estimates that the new bottling machine will provide net annual cash flows of $34,000. Management also believes that the new bottling machine will save the company money because it is expected to be more reliable than other machines, and thus will reduce downtime. How much would the reduction in downtime have to be worth in order for the project to be acceptable? Assume a discount rate of 9%. (*Hint:* Calculate the net present value.)

*Compute net present value of an investment and consider intangible benefits.*

**BE18.5 (LO 2, 3), AN** McKnight Company is considering two different, mutually exclusive capital expenditure proposals. Project A will cost $400,000, has an expected useful life of 10 years, a salvage value of zero, and is expected to increase net annual cash flows by $70,000. Project B will cost $310,000, has an expected useful life of 10 years, a salvage value of zero, and is expected to increase net annual cash flows by $55,000. A discount rate of 9% is appropriate for both projects. Compute the net present value and profitability index of each project. Which project should be accepted?

*Compute net present value and profitability index.*

**BE18.6 (LO 3), AN** Quillen Company is performing a post-audit of a project completed one year ago. The initial estimates were that the project would cost $250,000, would have a useful life of 9 years, zero

*Perform a post-audit.*

salvage value, and would result in net annual cash flows of $46,000 per year. Now that the investment has been in operation for 1 year, revised figures indicate that it actually cost $260,000, will have a total useful life of 11 years (including the year just completed), and will produce net annual cash flows of $39,000 per year. Evaluate the success of the project. Assume a discount rate of 10%.

*Calculate internal rate of return.*

**BE18.7 (LO 4), AP** Kanye Company is evaluating the purchase of a rebuilt spot-welding machine to be used in the manufacture of a new product. The machine will cost $176,000, has an estimated useful life of 7 years, a salvage value of zero, and will increase net annual cash flows by $35,000. What is its approximate internal rate of return?

*Calculate internal rate of return.*

**BE18.8 (LO 4), AN** Viera Corporation is considering investing in a new facility. The estimated cost of the facility is $2,045,000. It will be used for 12 years, then sold for $716,000. The facility will generate annual cash inflows of $400,000 and will need new annual cash outflows of $150,000. The company has a required rate of return of 7%. Calculate the internal rate of return on this project, and discuss whether the project should be accepted.

*Compute annual rate of return.*

**BE18.9 (LO 5), AP** Swift Oil Company is considering investing in a new oil well. It is expected that the oil well will increase annual revenues by $130,000 and will increase annual expenses by $70,000 including depreciation. The oil well will cost $490,000 and will have a $10,000 salvage value at the end of its 10-year useful life. Calculate the annual rate of return.

# DO IT! Exercises

*Compute the cash payback period for an investment.*

**DO IT! 18.1 (LO 1), AP** Wayne Company is considering a long-term investment project called ZIP. ZIP will require an investment of $140,000. It will have a useful life of 4 years and no salvage value. Annual cash inflows would increase by $80,000, and annual cash outflows would increase by $40,000. Compute the cash payback period.

*Calculate net present value of an investment.*

**DO IT! 18.2 (LO 2), AN** Wayne Company is considering a long-term investment project called ZIP. ZIP will require an investment of $120,000. It will have a useful life of 4 years and no salvage value. Annual cash inflows would increase by $80,000, and annual cash outflows would increase by $40,000. The company's required rate of return is 12%. Calculate the net present value on this project and discuss whether it should be accepted.

*Compute profitability index.*

**DO IT! 18.3 (LO 3), AP** Ranger Corporation has decided to invest in renewable energy sources to meet part of its energy needs for production. It is considering solar power versus wind power. After considering cost savings as well as incremental revenues from selling excess electricity into the power grid, it has determined the following.

|  | **Solar** | **Wind** |
| --- | --- | --- |
| Present value of annual cash flows | $52,580 | $128,450 |
| Capital investment | $39,500 | $105,300 |

Determine the net present value and profitability index of each project. Which energy source should it choose?

*Calculate internal rate of return.*

**DO IT! 18.4 (LO 4), AN** Wayne Company is considering a long-term investment project called ZIP. ZIP will require an investment of $120,000. It will have a useful life of 4 years and no salvage value. Annual cash inflows would increase by $80,000, and annual cash outflows would increase by $40,000. The company's required rate of return is 12%. Calculate the internal rate of return on this project and discuss whether it should be accepted.

*Calculate annual rate of return.*

**DO IT! 18.5 (LO 5), AP** Wayne Company is considering a long-term investment project called ZIP. ZIP will require an investment of $120,000. It will have a useful life of 4 years and no salvage value. Annual revenues would increase by $80,000, and annual expenses (excluding depreciation) would increase by $41,000. Wayne uses the straight-line method to compute depreciation expense. The company's required rate of return is 12%. Compute the annual rate of return.

# Exercises

**E18.1 (LO 1, 2), AN** Linkin Corporation is considering purchasing a new delivery truck. The truck has many advantages over the company's current truck (not the least of which is that it runs). The new truck would cost $56,000. Because of the increased capacity, reduced maintenance costs, and increased fuel economy, the new truck is expected to generate cost savings of $8,000. At the end of 8 years, the company will sell the truck for an estimated $27,000. Traditionally the company has used a rule of thumb that a proposal should not be accepted unless it has a payback period that is less than 50% of the asset's estimated useful life. Larry Newton, a new manager, has suggested that the company should not rely solely on the payback approach, but should also employ the net present value method when evaluating new projects. The company's cost of capital is 8%.

*Compute cash payback and net present value.*

### Instructions

**a.** Compute the cash payback period and net present value of the proposed investment.

**b.** Does the project meet the company's cash payback criteria? Does it meet the net present value criteria for acceptance? Discuss your results.

**E18.2 (LO 1, 2), AN** Doug's Custom Construction Company is considering three new projects, each requiring an equipment investment of $22,000. Each project will last for 3 years and produce the following net annual cash flows.

*Compute cash payback period and net present value.*

| Year | AA | BB | CC |
|---|---|---|---|
| 1 | $ 7,000 | $10,000 | $13,000 |
| 2 | 9,000 | 10,000 | 12,000 |
| 3 | 12,000 | 10,000 | 11,000 |
| Total | $28,000 | $30,000 | $36,000 |

The equipment's salvage value is zero, and Doug uses straight-line depreciation. Doug will not accept any project with a cash payback period over 2 years. Doug's required rate of return is 12%.

### Instructions

**a.** Compute each project's payback period, indicating the most desirable project and the least desirable project using this method. (Round to two decimals and assume in your computations that cash flows occur evenly throughout the year.)

**b.** Compute the net present value of each project. Does your evaluation change? (Round to nearest dollar.)

**E18.3 (LO 2), AN** Hillsong Inc. manufactures snowsuits. Hillsong is considering purchasing a new sewing machine at a cost of $2.45 million. Its existing machine was purchased 5 years ago at a price of $1.8 million; 6 months ago, Hillsong spent $55,000 to keep it operational. The existing sewing machine can be sold today for $250,000. The new sewing machine would require a one-time, $85,000 training cost. Operating costs would decrease by the following amounts for years 1 to 7:

*Calculate net present value and apply decision rule.*

| Year | 1 | $390,000 |
|---|---|---|
| | 2 | 400,000 |
| | 3 | 411,000 |
| | 4 | 426,000 |
| | 5 | 434,000 |
| | 6 | 435,000 |
| | 7 | 436,000 |

The new sewing machine would be depreciated according to the declining-balance method at a rate of 20%. The salvage value is expected to be $400,000. This new equipment would require maintenance costs of $100,000 at the end of the fifth year. The cost of capital is 9%.

### Instructions

Use the net present value method to determine whether Hillsong should purchase the new machine to replace the existing machine, and state the reason for your conclusion.

(CGA adapted)

**E18.4 (LO 2, 3), AN** BAK Corp. is considering purchasing one of two new diagnostic machines. Either machine would make it possible for the company to bid on jobs that it currently isn't equipped to do. Estimates regarding each machine are provided here.

*Compute net present value and profitability index.*

|  | Machine A | Machine B |
|---|---|---|
| Original cost | $75,500 | $180,000 |
| Estimated life | 8 years | 8 years |
| Salvage value | –0– | –0– |
| Estimated annual cash inflows | $20,000 | $ 40,000 |
| Estimated annual cash outflows | $ 5,000 | $ 10,000 |

### Instructions

Calculate the net present value and profitability index of each machine. Assume a 9% discount rate. Which machine should be purchased?

*Determine internal rate of return.*

**E18.5 (LO 4), AN** Bruno Corporation is involved in the business of injection molding of plastics. It is considering the purchase of a new computer-aided design and manufacturing machine for $430,000. The company believes that with this new machine it will improve productivity and increase quality, resulting in an increase in net annual cash flows of $101,000 for the next 6 years. Management requires a 10% rate of return on all new investments.

### Instructions

Calculate the internal rate of return on this new machine. Should the investment be accepted?

*Calculate cash payback period and internal rate of return, and apply decision rules.*

**E18.6 (LO 1, 4), AN** BSU Inc. wants to purchase a new machine for $29,300, excluding $1,500 of installation costs. The old machine was purchased 5 years ago and had an expected economic life of 10 years with no salvage value. The old machine has a book value of $2,000, and BSU Inc. expects to sell it for that amount. The new machine will decrease operating costs by $7,000 each year of its economic life. The straight-line depreciation method will be used for the new machine for a 6-year period with no salvage value.

### Instructions

a. Determine the cash payback period.

b. Determine the approximate internal rate of return.

c. Assuming the company has a required rate of return of 10%, state your conclusion on whether the new machine should be purchased.

(CGA adapted)

*Determine internal rate of return.*

**E18.7 (LO 4), AN** Iggy Company is considering three capital expenditure projects. Relevant data for the projects are as follows.

| Project | Investment | Annual Income | Life of Project |
|---|---|---|---|
| 22A | $240,000 | $15,500 | 6 years |
| 23A | 270,000 | 20,600 | 9 years |
| 24A | 280,000 | 15,700 | 7 years |

Annual income is constant over the life of the project. Each project is expected to have zero salvage value at the end of the project. Iggy Company uses the straight-line method of depreciation.

### Instructions

a. Determine the internal rate of return for each project. Round the internal rate of return factor to three decimals.

b. If Iggy Company's required rate of return is 10%, which projects are acceptable?

*Calculate annual rate of return.*

**E18.8 (LO 5), AP** **Service** Pierre's Hair Salon is considering opening a new location in French Lick, California. The cost of building a new salon is $300,000. A new salon will normally generate annual revenues of $70,000, with annual expenses (including depreciation) of $41,500. At the end of 15 years, the salon will have a salvage value of $80,000.

### Instructions

Calculate the annual rate of return on the project.

*Compute cash payback period and annual rate of return.*

**E18.9 (LO 1, 5), AP** **Service** Legend Service Center just purchased an automobile hoist for $32,400. The hoist has an 8-year life and an estimated salvage value of $3,000. Installation costs and freight charges were $3,300 and $700, respectively. Legend uses straight-line depreciation.

The new hoist will be used to replace mufflers and tires on automobiles. Legend estimates that the new hoist will enable its mechanics to replace 5 extra mufflers per week. Each muffler sells for $72 installed. The cost of a muffler is $36, and the labor cost to install a muffler is $16.

**Instructions**

a. Compute the cash payback period for the new hoist.

b. Compute the annual rate of return for the new hoist. (Round to one decimal.)

**E18.10 (LO 1, 2, 5), AP** Vilas Company is considering a capital investment of $190,000 in additional productive facilities. The new machinery is expected to have a useful life of 5 years with no salvage value. Depreciation is by the straight-line method. During the life of the investment, annual net income and net annual cash flows are expected to be $12,000 and $50,000, respectively. Vilas has a 12% cost of capital rate, which is the required rate of return on the investment.

*Compute annual rate of return, cash payback period, and net present value.*

**Instructions**

(Round to two decimals.)

a. Compute (1) the cash payback period and (2) the annual rate of return on the proposed capital expenditure.

b. Using the discounted cash flow technique, compute the net present value.

**E18.11 (LO 1, 2, 5), AP** Drake Corporation is reviewing an investment proposal. The initial cost is $105,000. Estimates of the book value of the investment at the end of each year, the net cash flows for each year, and the net income for each year are presented in the following schedule. All cash flows are assumed to take place at the end of the year. The salvage value of the investment at the end of each year is assumed to equal its book value. There would be no salvage value at the end of the investment's life.

*Calculate payback, annual rate of return, and net present value.*

**Investment Proposal**

| Year | Book Value | Annual Cash Flows | Annual Net Income |
|------|-----------|-------------------|-------------------|
| 1 | $70,000 | $45,000 | $10,000 |
| 2 | 42,000 | 40,000 | 12,000 |
| 3 | 21,000 | 35,000 | 14,000 |
| 4 | 7,000 | 30,000 | 16,000 |
| 5 | 0 | 25,000 | 18,000 |

Drake Corporation uses an 11% target rate of return for new investment proposals.

**Instructions**

a. What is the cash payback period for this proposal?

b. What is the annual rate of return for the investment?

c. What is the net present value of the investment?

(CMA-Canada adapted)

# Problems

**P18.1 (LO 1, 2, 5), AN** U3 Company is considering three long-term capital investment proposals. Each investment has a useful life of 5 years. Relevant data on each project are as follows.

*Compute annual rate of return, cash payback, and net present value.*

|  | Project Bono | Project Edge | Project Clayton |
|--|-------------|--------------|-----------------|
| Capital investment | $160,000 | $175,000 | $200,000 |
| Annual net income: |  |  |  |
| Year 1 | 14,000 | 18,000 | 27,000 |
| 2 | 14,000 | 17,000 | 23,000 |
| 3 | 14,000 | 16,000 | 21,000 |
| 4 | 14,000 | 12,000 | 13,000 |
| 5 | 14,000 | 9,000 | 12,000 |
| Total | $ 70,000 | $ 72,000 | $ 96,000 |

Depreciation is computed by the straight-line method with no salvage value. The company's cost of capital is 15%. (Assume that cash flows occur evenly throughout the year.)

## Instructions

**a.** Compute the cash payback period for each project. (Round to two decimals.)

b. E $(7,312); C $2,163

**b.** Compute the net present value for each project. (Round to nearest dollar.)

**c.** Compute the annual rate of return for each project. (Round to two decimals.) (*Hint:* Use average annual net income in your computation.)

**d.** Rank the projects on each of the foregoing bases. Which project do you recommend?

*Compute annual rate of return, cash payback, and net present value.*

**P18.2 (LO 1, 2, 5), AN** Service Writing Lon Timur is an accounting major at a midwestern state university located approximately 60 miles from a major city. Many of the students attending the university are from the metropolitan area and visit their homes regularly on the weekends. Lon, an entrepreneur at heart, realizes that few good commuting alternatives are available for students doing weekend travel. He believes that a weekend commuting service could be organized and run profitably from several suburban and downtown shopping mall locations. Lon has gathered the following investment information.

1. Five used vans would cost a total of $75,000 to purchase and would have a 3-year useful life with negligible salvage value. Lon plans to use straight-line depreciation.

2. Ten drivers would have to be employed at a total payroll expense of $48,000.

3. Other annual out-of-pocket expenses associated with running the commuter service would include Gasoline $16,000, Maintenance $3,300, Repairs $4,000, Insurance $4,200, and Advertising $2,500.

4. Lon has visited several financial institutions to discuss funding. The best interest rate he has been able to negotiate is 15%. Use this rate for cost of capital.

5. Lon expects each van to make 10 round trips weekly and carry an average of 6 students each trip. The service is expected to operate 30 weeks each year, and each student will be charged $12.00 for a round-trip ticket.

## Instructions

a. (1) $5,000

b. (1) 2.5 years

**a.** Determine the annual (1) net income and (2) net annual cash flows for the commuter service.

**b.** Compute (1) the cash payback period and (2) the annual rate of return. (Round to two decimals.)

**c.** Compute the net present value of the commuter service. (Round to the nearest dollar.)

**d.** What should Lon conclude from these computations?

*Compute net present value, profitability index, and internal rate of return.*

**P18.3 (LO 2, 3, 4), AN** Service Brooks Clinic is considering investing in new heart-monitoring equipment. It has two options. Option A would have an initial lower cost but would require a significant expenditure for rebuilding after 4 years. Option B would require no rebuilding expenditure, but its maintenance costs would be higher. Since the Option B machine is of initial higher quality, it is expected to have a salvage value at the end of its useful life. The following estimates were made of the cash flows. The company's cost of capital is 8%.

|  | Option A | Option B |
|---|---|---|
| Initial cost | $160,000 | $227,000 |
| Annual cash inflows | $71,000 | $80,000 |
| Annual cash outflows | $30,000 | $31,000 |
| Cost to rebuild (end of year 4) | $50,000 | $0 |
| Salvage value | $0 | $8,000 |
| Estimated useful life | 7 years | 7 years |

## Instructions

a. (1) NPV A $16,709
   (3) IRR B 12%

**a.** Compute the (1) net present value, (2) profitability index, and (3) internal rate of return for each option. (*Hint:* To solve for internal rate of return, experiment with alternative discount rates to arrive at a net present value of zero.)

**b.** Which option should be accepted?

*Compute net present value considering intangible benefits.*

Excel

**P18.4 (LO 2, 3), E** Service Jane's Auto Care is considering the purchase of a new tow truck. The garage doesn't currently have a tow truck, and the $60,000 price tag for a new truck would represent a major expenditure. Jane Austen, owner of the garage, has compiled the following estimates in trying to determine whether the tow truck should be purchased.

| | |
|---|---|
| Initial cost | $60,000 |
| Estimated useful life | 8 years |
| Net annual cash flows from towing | $8,000 |
| Overhaul costs (end of year 4) | $6,000 |
| Salvage value | $12,000 |

Jane's good friend, Rick Ryan, stopped by. He is trying to convince Jane that the tow truck will have other benefits that Jane hasn't even considered. First, he says, cars that need towing need to be fixed. Thus, when Jane tows them to her facility, her repair revenues will increase. Second, he notes that the tow truck could have a plow mounted on it, thus saving Jane the cost of plowing her parking lot. (Rick will give her a used plow blade for free if Jane will plow Rick's driveway.) Third, he notes that the truck will generate goodwill; people who are rescued by Jane's tow truck will feel grateful and might be more inclined to use her service station in the future or buy gas there. Fourth, the tow truck will have "Jane's Auto Care" on its doors, hood, and back tailgate—a form of free advertising wherever the tow truck goes. Rick estimates that, at a minimum, these benefits would be worth the following.

| | |
|---|---|
| Additional annual net cash flows from repair work | $3,000 |
| Annual savings from plowing | 750 |
| Additional annual net cash flows from customer "goodwill" | 1,000 |
| Additional annual net cash flows resulting from free advertising | 750 |

The company's cost of capital is 9%.

### Instructions

**a.** Calculate the net present value, ignoring the additional benefits described by Rick. Should the tow truck be purchased?

*a. NPV $(13,950)*

**b.** Calculate the net present value, incorporating the additional benefits suggested by Rick. Should the tow truck be purchased?

*b. NPV $16,491*

**c.** Suppose Rick has been overly optimistic in his assessment of the value of the additional benefits. At a minimum, how much would the additional benefits have to be worth in order for the project to be accepted?

**P18.5 (LO 2, 3, 4), E** Service  Coolplay Corp. is thinking about opening a soccer camp in southern California. To start the camp, Coolplay would need to purchase land and build four soccer fields and a sleeping and dining facility to house 150 soccer players. Each year, the camp would be run for 8 sessions of 1 week each. The company would hire college soccer players as coaches. The camp attendees would be male and female soccer players ages 12–18. Property values in southern California have enjoyed a steady increase in value. It is expected that after using the facility for 20 years, Coolplay can sell the property for more than it was originally purchased for. The following amounts have been estimated.

*Compute net present value and internal rate of return with sensitivity analysis.*

| | |
|---|---|
| Cost of land | $300,000 |
| Cost to build soccer fields, dorm, and dining facility | $600,000 |
| Annual cash inflows assuming 150 players and 8 weeks | $920,000 |
| Annual cash outflows | $840,000 |
| Estimated useful life | 20 years |
| Salvage value | $1,500,000 |
| Discount rate | 8% |

### Instructions

**a.** Calculate the net present value of the project.

*a. NPV $207,277*

**b.** To gauge the sensitivity of the project to these estimates, assume that if only 125 players attend each week, annual cash inflows will be $805,000 and annual cash outflows will be $750,000. What is the net present value using these alternative estimates? Discuss your findings.

**c.** Assuming the original facts, what is the net present value if the project is actually riskier than first assumed and a 10% discount rate is more appropriate?

**d.** Assume that during the first 5 years, the annual net cash flows each year were only $40,000. At the end of the fifth year, the company is running low on cash, so management decides to sell the property for $1,332,000. What was the actual internal rate of return on the project? Explain how this return was possible given that the camp did not appear to be successful.

*d. IRR 12%*

## Continuing Cases

### Current Designs

**CD18** A company that manufactures recreational pedal boats has approached Mike Cichanowski to ask if he would be interested in using **Current Designs'** rotomold expertise and equipment to produce some of the pedal boat components. Mike is intrigued by the idea and thinks it would be an interesting way of complementing the present product line.

One of Mike's hesitations about the proposal is that the pedal boats are a different shape than the kayaks that Current Designs produces. As a result, the company would need to buy an additional roto-mold oven in order to produce the pedal boat components. This project clearly involves risks, and Mike wants to make sure that the returns justify the risks. In this case, since this is a new venture, Mike thinks that a 15% discount rate is appropriate to use to evaluate the project.

As an intern at Current Designs, Mike has asked you to prepare an initial evaluation of this proposal. To aid in your analysis, he has provided the following information and assumptions.

1. The new rotomold oven will have a cost of $256,000, a salvage value of $0, and an 8-year useful life. Straight-line depreciation will be used.

2. The projected revenues, costs, and results for each of the 8 years of this project are as follows.

| | | |
|---|---:|---:|
| Sales | | $220,000 |
| Less: | | |
|    Manufacturing costs | $140,000 | |
|    Depreciation | 32,000 | |
|    Shipping and administrative costs | 22,000 | 194,000 |
| Income before income taxes | | 26,000 |
| Income tax expense | | 10,800 |
| Net income | | $ 15,200 |

#### Instructions

a. Compute the annual rate of return. (Round to two decimal places.)

b. Compute the payback period. (Round to two decimal places.)

c. Compute the net present value using a discount rate of 9%. (Round to nearest dollar.) Should the proposal be accepted using this discount rate?

d. Compute the net present value using a discount rate of 15%. (Round to nearest dollar.) Should the proposal be accepted using this discount rate?

### Waterways Corporation

(*Note:* This is a continuation of the Waterways case from Chapters 11–17.)

**WC18** Waterways Corporation puts much emphasis on cash flow when it plans for capital investments. The company chose its discount rate of 8% based on the rate of return it must pay its owners and credi-tors. Using that rate, Waterways then uses different methods to determine the best decisions for making capital outlays. Waterways is considering buying five new backhoes to replace the backhoes it now has. This problem asks you to evaluate that decision, using various capital budgeting techniques.

*Go to WileyPLUS for complete case details and instructions.*

## Comprehensive Cases

**CC18.1** For this case, revisit the Greetings Inc. company presented in earlier chapters. The company is now searching for new opportunities for growth. This case will provide you with the opportunity to evalu-ate a proposal based on initial estimates as well as conduct sensitivity analysis. It also requires evaluation of the underlying assumptions used in the analysis.

**CC18.2** Armstrong Helmet Company needs to determine the cost for a given product. For this case, you will have the opportunity to explore cost-volume-profit relationships and prepare a set of budgets.

*Go to WileyPLUS for details and instructions for both cases.*

# Expand Your Critical Thinking

## Decision-Making Across the Organization

**CT18.1** Luang Company is considering the purchase of a new machine. Its invoice price is $122,000, freight charges are estimated to be $3,000, and installation costs are expected to be $5,000. Salvage value of the new machine is expected to be zero after a useful life of 4 years. Existing equipment could be retained and used for an additional 4 years if the new machine is not purchased. At that time, the salvage value of the equipment would be zero. If the new machine is purchased now, the existing machine would be scrapped. Luang's accountant, Lisa Hsung, has accumulated the following data regarding annual sales and expenses with and without the new machine.

1. Without the new machine, Luang can sell 10,000 units of product annually at a per unit selling price of $100. If the new unit is purchased, the number of units produced and sold would increase by 25%, and the selling price would remain the same.

2. The new machine is faster than the old machine, and it is more efficient in its usage of materials. With the old machine the gross profit rate will be 28.5% of sales, whereas the rate will be 30% of sales with the new machine. (*Note*: These gross profit rates do not include depreciation on the machines. For purposes of determining net income, treat depreciation expense as a separate line item.)

3. Annual selling expenses are $160,000 with the current equipment. Because the new equipment would produce a greater number of units to be sold, annual selling expenses are expected to increase by 10% if it is purchased.

4. Annual administrative expenses are expected to be $100,000 with the old machine, and $112,000 with the new machine.

5. The current book value of the existing machine is $40,000. Luang uses straight-line depreciation.

6. Luang's management has a required rate of return of 15% on its investment and a cash payback period of no more than 3 years.

### Instructions

With the class divided into groups, answer the following. (Ignore income tax effects.)

a. Calculate the annual rate of return for the new machine. (Round to two decimals.)

b. Compute the cash payback period for the new machine. (Round to two decimals.)

c. Compute the net present value of the new machine. (Round to the nearest dollar.)

d. On the basis of the foregoing data, would you recommend that Luang buy the machine? Why or why not?

## Managerial Analysis

**CT18.2** Hawke Skateboards is considering building a new plant. Bob Skerritt, the company's marketing manager, is an enthusiastic supporter of the new plant. Lucy Liu, the company's chief financial officer, is not so sure that the plant is a good idea. Currently, the company purchases its skateboards from foreign manufacturers. The following figures were estimated regarding the construction of a new plant.

| | | | | |
|---|---|---|---|---|
| Cost of plant | $4,000,000 | | Estimated useful life | 15 years |
| Annual cash inflows | 4,000,000 | | Salvage value | $2,000,000 |
| Annual cash outflows | 3,540,000 | | Discount rate | 11% |

Bob Skerritt believes that these figures understate the true potential value of the plant. He suggests that by manufacturing its own skateboards the company will benefit from a "buy American" patriotism that he believes is common among skateboarders. He also notes that the firm has had numerous quality problems with the skateboards manufactured by its suppliers. He suggests that the inconsistent quality has resulted in lost sales, increased warranty claims, and some costly lawsuits. Overall, he believes sales will be $200,000 higher than projected above, and that the savings from lower warranty costs and legal costs will be $60,000 per year. He also believes that the project is not as risky as assumed above, and that a 9% discount rate is more reasonable.

### Instructions

Answer each of the following.

    **a.** Compute the net present value of the project based on the original projections.

    **b.** Compute the net present value incorporating Bob's estimates of the value of the intangible benefits, but still using the 11% discount rate.

    **c.** Compute the net present value using the original estimates, but employing the 9% discount rate that Bob suggests is more appropriate.

    **d.** Comment on your findings.

## Real-World Focus

**CT18.3 Tecumseh Products Company** has its headquarters in Ann Arbor, Michigan. It describes itself as "a global multinational corporation producing mechanical and electrical components essential to industries creating end-products for health, comfort, and convenience." The following was excerpted from the management discussion and analysis section of a recent annual report.

### Tecumseh Products Company
#### Management Discussion and Analysis

The company has invested approximately $50 million in a scroll compressor manufacturing facility in Tecumseh, Michigan. After experiencing setbacks in developing a commercially acceptable scroll compressor, the Company is currently testing a new generation of scroll product. The Company is unable to predict when, or if, it will offer a scroll compressor for commercial sale, but it does anticipate that reaching volume production will require a significant additional investment. Given such additional investment and current market conditions, management is currently reviewing its options with respect to scroll product improvement, cost reductions, joint ventures and alternative new products.

### Instructions

Discuss issues the company should consider and techniques the company should employ to determine whether to continue pursuing this project.

**CT18.4 Campbell Soup Company** is an international provider of soup products. Management is very interested in continuing to grow the company in its core business, while "spinning off" those businesses that are not part of its core operation.

### Instructions

Go to the home page of Campbell Soup Company and access its current annual report. Review the financial statements and management's discussion and analysis, and answer the following questions.

    **a.** What was the total amount of capital expenditures in the current year, and how does this amount compare with the previous year? In your response, note what year you are using.

    **b.** What interest rate did the company pay on new borrowings in the current year?

    **c.** Assume that this year's capital expenditures are expected to increase cash flows by $60 million. What is the expected internal rate of return (IRR) for these capital expenditures? (Assume a 10-year period for the cash flows.)

## Communication Activity

**CT18.5** Refer to E18.9 to address the following.

### Instructions

Prepare a memo to Maria Fierro, your supervisor. Show your calculations from E18.9 (a) and (b). In one or two paragraphs, discuss important nonfinancial considerations. Make any assumptions you believe to be necessary. Make a recommendation based on your analysis.

### Ethics Case

**CT18.6** NuComp Company operates in a state where corporate taxes and workers' compensation insurance rates have recently doubled. NuComp's president has just assigned you the task of preparing an economic analysis and making a recommendation relative to moving the entire operation to Missouri. The president is slightly in favor of such a move because Missouri is his boyhood home and he also owns a fishing lodge there.

You have just completed building your dream house, moved in, and sodded the lawn. Your children are all doing well in school and sports and, along with your spouse, want no part of a move to Missouri. If the company does move, so will you because the town is a one-industry community and you and your spouse will have to move to have employment. Moving when everyone else does will cause you to take a big loss on the sale of your house. The same hardships will be suffered by your coworkers, and the town will be devastated.

In compiling the costs of moving versus not moving, you have latitude in the assumptions you make, the estimates you compute, and the discount rates and time periods you project. You are in a position to influence the decision singlehandedly.

#### Instructions

**a.** Who are the stakeholders in this situation?

**b.** What are the ethical issues in this situation?

**c.** What would you do in this situation?

### All About You

**CT18.7** Numerous articles have been written that identify early warning signs that you might be getting into trouble with your personal debt load. You can find many good articles on this topic on the Web.

#### Instructions

Find an article that identifies early warning signs of personal debt trouble. Write a summary of the article and bring your summary and the article to class to share.

### Considering Your Costs and Benefits

**CT18.8** The March 31, 2011, edition of the *Wall Street Journal* includes an article by Russell Gold entitled "Solar Gains Traction—Thanks to Subsidies."

#### Instructions

Read the article and then answer the following questions.

**a.** What was the total cost of the solar panels installed? What was the "out-of-pocket" cost to the couple?

**b.** Using the total annual electricity bill of $5,000 mentioned in the story, what is the cash payback of the project using the total cost? What is the cash payback based on the "out-of-pocket" cost?

**c.** Solar panel manufacturers estimate that solar panels can last up to 40 years with only minor maintenance costs. Assuming no maintenance costs, a 6% rate of interest, a more conservative 20-year life, and zero salvage value, what is the net present value of the project based on the total cost? What is the net present value of the project based on the "out-of-pocket" cost?

**d.** What was the wholesale price of panels per watt at the time the article was written? At what price per watt does the article say that subsidies will no longer be needed? Does this price appear to be achievable?

# Specimen Financial Statements:
# Apple Inc.

Once each year, a corporation communicates to its stockholders and other interested parties by issuing a complete set of audited financial statements. The **annual report**, as this communication is called, summarizes the financial results of the company's operations for the year and its plans for the future. Many annual reports are attractive, multicolored, glossy public relations pieces, containing pictures of corporate officers and directors as well as photos and descriptions of new products and new buildings. Yet the basic function of every annual report is to report financial information, almost all of which is a product of the corporation's accounting system.

The content and organization of corporate annual reports have become fairly standardized. Excluding the public relations part of the report (pictures, products, etc.), the following are the traditional financial portions of the annual report:

- Financial Highlights
- Letter to the Stockholders
- Management's Discussion and Analysis
- Financial Statements
- Notes to the Financial Statements
- Management's Responsibility for Financial Reporting
- Management's Report on Internal Control over Financial Reporting
- Report of Independent Registered Public Accounting Firm
- Selected Financial Data

The official SEC filing of the annual report is called a **Form 10-K**, which often omits the public relations pieces found in most standard annual reports. The following are **Apple Inc.**'s financial statements taken from the company's 2018 Form 10-K. The complete Form 10-K, including notes to the financial statements, is available at the company's website.

**Apple Inc.**
**CONSOLIDATED STATEMENTS OF OPERATIONS**
(In millions, except number of shares which are reflected in thousands and per share amounts)

| | Years ended | | |
| | September 29, 2018 | September 30, 2017 | September 24, 2016 |
| --- | ---: | ---: | ---: |
| Net sales | $ 265,595 | $ 229,234 | $ 215,639 |
| Cost of sales | 163,756 | 141,048 | 131,376 |
| Gross margin | 101,839 | 88,186 | 84,263 |
| | | | |
| Operating expenses: | | | |
| Research and development | 11,236 | 11,581 | 10,045 |
| Selling, general and administrative | 16,705 | 15,261 | 14,194 |
| Total operating expenses | 30,941 | 26,842 | 24,239 |
| | | | |
| Operating income | 70,898 | 61,344 | 60,024 |
| Other income/(expense), net | 2,005 | 2,745 | 1,348 |
| Income before provision for income taxes | 72,903 | 64,089 | 61,372 |
| Provision for income taxes | 13,372 | 15,738 | 15,685 |
| Net income | $ 59,531 | $ 48,351 | $ 45,687 |
| | | | |
| Earnings per share: | | | |
| Basic | $ 12.01 | $ 9.27 | $ 8.35 |
| Diluted | $ 11.91 | $ 9.21 | $ 8.31 |
| | | | |
| Shares used in computing earnings per share: | | | |
| Basic | 4,955,377 | 5,217,242 | 5,470,820 |
| Diluted | 5,000,109 | 5,251,692 | 5,500,281 |

See accompanying Notes to Consolidated Financial Statements.

**Apple Inc.**
**CONSOLIDATED STATEMENTS OF COMPREHENSIVE INCOME**
(In millions)

| | Years ended | | |
|---|---|---|---|
| | **September 29, 2018** | **September 30, 2017** | **September 24, 2016** |
| Net income | $59,531 | $48,351 | $45,687 |
| Other comprehensive income/(loss): | | | |
| Change in foreign currency translation, net of tax effects of $(1), $(77) and $8, respectively | (525) | 224 | 75 |
| Change in unrealized gains/losses on derivative instruments: | | | |
| Change in fair value of derivatives, net of tax benefit/(expense) of $(149), $(478) and $(7), respectively | 523 | 1,315 | 7 |
| Adjustment for net (gains)/losses realized and included in net income, net of tax expense/(benefit) of $(104), $475 and $131, respectively | 382 | (1,477) | (741) |
| Total change in unrealized gains/losses on derivative instruments, net of tax | 905 | (162) | (734) |
| Change in unrealized gains/losses on marketable securities: | | | |
| Change in fair value of marketable securities, net of tax benefit/ (expense) of $1,156, $425 and $(863), respectively | (3,407) | (782) | 1,582 |
| Adjustment for net (gains)/losses realized and included in net income, net of tax expense/(benefit) of $21, $35 and $(31), respectively | 1 | (64) | 56 |
| Total change in unrealized gains/losses on marketable securities, net of tax | (3,406) | (846) | 1,638 |
| Total other comprehensive income/(loss) | (3,026) | (784) | 979 |
| Total comprehensive income | $56,505 | $47,567 | $46,666 |

See accompanying Notes to Consolidated Financial Statements.

**Apple Inc.**
**CONSOLIDATED BALANCE SHEETS**
(In millions, except number of shares which are reflected in thousands and par value)

| | September 29, 2018 | September 30, 2017 |
|---|---|---|
| **ASSETS:** | | |
| Current assets: | | |
| Cash and cash equivalents | $ 25,913 | $ 20,289 |
| Marketable securities | 40,388 | 53,892 |
| Accounts receivable, net | 23,186 | 17,874 |
| Inventories | 3,956 | 4,855 |
| Vendor non-trade receivables | 25,809 | 17,799 |
| Other current assets | 12,087 | 13,936 |
| Total current assets | 131,339 | 128,645 |
| Non-current assets: | | |
| Marketable securities | 170,799 | 194,714 |
| Property, plant and equipment, net | 41,304 | 33,783 |
| Other non-current assets | 22,283 | 18,177 |
| Total non-current assets | 234,386 | 246,674 |
| Total assets | $365,725 | $375,319 |
| **LIABILITIES AND SHAREHOLDERS' EQUITY:** | | |
| Current liabilities: | | |
| Accounts payable | $ 55,888 | $ 44,242 |
| Other current liabilities | 32,687 | 30,551 |
| Deferred revenue | 7,543 | 7,548 |
| Commercial paper | 11,964 | 11,977 |
| Term debt | 8,784 | 6,496 |
| Total current liabilities | 116,866 | 100,814 |
| Non-current liabilities: | | |
| Deferred revenue | 2,797 | 2,836 |
| Term debt | 93,735 | 97,207 |
| Other non-current liabilities | 45,180 | 40,415 |
| Total non-current liabilities | 141,712 | 140,458 |
| Total liabilities | 258,578 | 241,272 |
| Commitments and contingencies | | |
| Shareholders' equity: | | |
| Common stock and additional paid-in capital, $0.00001 par value: 12,600,000 shares authorized; 4,754,986 and 5,126,201 shares issued and outstanding, respectively | 40,201 | 35,867 |
| Retained earnings | 70,400 | 98,330 |
| Accumulated other comprehensive income/(loss) | (3,454) | (150) |
| Total shareholders' equity | 107,147 | 134,047 |
| Total liabilities and shareholders' equity | $365,725 | $375,319 |

See accompanying Notes to Consolidated Financial Statements.

**Apple Inc.**
**CONSOLIDATED STATEMENTS OF SHAREHOLDERS' EQUITY**
(In millions, except number of shares which are reflected in thousands and per share amounts)

| | Common Stock and Additional Paid-In Capital | | Retained Earnings | Accumulated Other Comprehensive Income/(Loss) | Total Shareholders' Equity |
|---|---|---|---|---|---|
| | Shares | Amount | | | |
| Balances as of September 26, 2015 | 5,578,753 | $27,416 | $92,284 | $ (345) | $119,355 |
| Net income | — | — | 45,687 | — | 45,687 |
| Other comprehensive income/(loss) | — | — | — | 979 | 979 |
| Dividends and dividend equivalents declared at $2.18 per share or RSU | — | — | (12,188) | — | (12,188) |
| Repurchase of common stock | (279,609) | — | (29,000) | — | (29,000) |
| Share-based compensation | — | 4,262 | — | — | 4,262 |
| Common stock issued, net of shares withheld for employee taxes | 37,022 | (806) | (419) | — | (1,225) |
| Tax benefit from equity awards, including transfer pricing adjustments | — | 379 | — | — | 379 |
| Balances as of September 24, 2016 | 5,336,166 | 31,251 | 96,364 | 634 | 128,249 |
| Net income | — | — | 48,351 | — | 48,351 |
| Other comprehensive income/(loss) | — | — | — | (784) | (784) |
| Dividends and dividend equivalents declared at $2.40 per share or RSU | — | — | (12,803) | — | (12,803) |
| Repurchase of common stock | (246,496) | — | (33,001) | — | (33,001) |
| Share-based compensation | — | 4,909 | — | — | 4,909 |
| Common stock issued, net of shares withheld for employee taxes | 36,531 | (913) | (581) | — | (1,494) |
| Tax benefit from equity awards, including transfer pricing adjustments | — | 620 | — | — | 620 |
| Balances as of September 30, 2017 | 5,126,201 | 35,867 | 98,330 | (150) | 134,047 |
| Cumulative effect of change in accounting principle | — | — | 278 | (278) | — |
| Net income | — | — | 59,531 | — | 59,531 |
| Other comprehensive income/(loss) | — | — | — | (3,026) | (3,026) |
| Dividends and dividend equivalents declared at $2.72 per share or RSU | — | — | (13,735) | — | (13,735) |
| Repurchase of common stock | (405,549) | — | (73,056) | — | (73,056) |
| Share-based compensation | — | 5,443 | — | — | 5,443 |
| Common stock issued, net of shares withheld for employee taxes | 34,334 | (1,109) | (948) | — | (2,057) |
| Balances as of September 29, 2018 | 4,754,986 | $40,201 | $70,400 | $(3,454) | $107,147 |

See accompanying Notes to Consolidated Financial Statements.

**Apple Inc.**
**CONSOLIDATED STATEMENTS OF CASH FLOWS**
(In millions)

| | Years ended | | |
| --- | --- | --- | --- |
| | September 29, 2018 | September 30, 2017 | September 24, 2016 |
| Cash and cash equivalents, beginning of the year | $20,289 | $20,484 | $21,120 |
| Operating activities: | | | |
| Net income | 59,531 | 48,351 | 45,687 |
| Adjustments to reconcile net income to cash generated by operating activities: | | | |
| Depreciation and amortization | 10,903 | 10,157 | 10,505 |
| Share-based compensation expense | 5,340 | 4,840 | 4,210 |
| Deferred income tax expense/(benefit) | (62,590) | 5,966 | 4,938 |
| Other | (444) | (166) | 486 |
| Changes in operating assets and liabilities: | | | |
| Accounts receivable, net | (5,322) | (2,093) | 527 |
| Inventories | 828 | (2,723) | 217 |
| Vendor non-trade receivables | (8,010) | (4,254) | (51) |
| Other current and non-current assets | (423) | (5,318) | 1,055 |
| Accounts payable | 9,175 | 8,966 | 2,117 |
| Deferred revenue | (44) | (626) | (1,554) |
| Other current and non-current liabilities | 38,490 | 1,125 | (1,906) |
| Cash generated by operating activities | 77,434 | 64,225 | 66,231 |
| Investing activities: | | | |
| Purchases of marketable securities | (71,356) | (159,486) | (142,428) |
| Proceeds from maturities of marketable securities | 55,881 | 31,775 | 21,258 |
| Proceeds from sales of marketable securities | 47,838 | 94,564 | 90,536 |
| Payments for acquisition of property, plant and equipment | (13,313) | (12,451) | (12,734) |
| Payments made in connection with business acquisitions, net | (721) | (329) | (297) |
| Purchases of non-marketable securities | (1,871) | (521) | (1,388) |
| Proceeds from non-marketable securities | 353 | 126 | — |
| Other | (745) | (124) | (924) |
| Cash generated by/(used in) investing activities | 16,066 | (46,446) | (45,977) |
| Financing activities: | | | |
| Proceeds from issuance of common stock | 669 | 555 | 495 |
| Payments for taxes related to net share settlement of equity awards | (2.527) | (1,874) | (1,570) |
| Payments for dividends and dividend equivalents | (13,712) | (12,769) | (12,150) |
| Repurchases of common stock | (72,738) | (32,900) | (29,722) |
| Proceeds from issuance of term debt, net | 6,969 | 28,662 | 24,954 |
| Repayments of term debt | (6,500) | (3,500) | (2,500) |
| Change in commercial paper, net | (37) | 3,852 | (397) |
| Cash used in financing activities | (87,876) | (17,974) | (20,890) |
| Increase/(Decrease) in cash and cash equivalents | 5,624 | (195) | (636) |
| Cash and cash equivalents, end of the year | $25,913 | $20,289 | $20,484 |
| Supplemental cash flow disclosure: | | | |
| Cash paid for income taxes, net | $10,417 | $11,591 | $10,444 |
| Cash paid for interest | $ 3,022 | $ 2,092 | $ 1,316 |

See accompanying Notes to Consolidated Financial Statements.

# Specimen Financial Statements:
# Columbia Sportswear Company

**Columbia Sportswear Company** is a leader in outdoor sportswear. The following are Columbia's financial statements as presented in its 2018 annual report. Columbia's complete annual report, including notes to the financial statements, is available at the company's website.

**COLUMBIA SPORTSWEAR COMPANY**
**CONSOLIDATED STATEMENTS OF OPERATIONS**
**(In thousands, except per share amounts)**

| | Year Ended December 31, | | |
| --- | --- | --- | --- |
| | **2018** | **2017** | **2016** |
| Net sales | $2,802,326 | $2,466,105 | $2,377,045 |
| Cost of sales | 1,415,978 | 1,306,143 | 1,266,697 |
| Gross profit | 1,386,348 | 1,159,962 | 1,110,348 |
| Selling, general and administrative expenses | 1,051,152 | 910,894 | 864,084 |
| Net licensing income | 15,786 | 13,901 | 10,244 |
| Income from operations | 350,982 | 262,969 | 256,508 |
| Interest income, net | 9,876 | 4,515 | 2,003 |
| Interest expense on note payable to related party (Note 22) | — | (429) | (1,041) |
| Other non-operating expense | (141) | (321) | (572) |
| Income before income tax | 360,717 | 266,734 | 256,898 |
| Income tax expense (Note 11) | (85,769) | (154,419) | (58,459) |
| Net income | 274,948 | 112,315 | 198,439 |
| Net income attributable to non-controlling interest | 6,692 | 7,192 | 6,541 |
| Net income attributable to Columbia Sportswear Company | $ 268,256 | $ 105,123 | $ 191,898 |
| Earnings per share attributable to Columbia Sportswear Company (Note 17): | | | |
| Basic | $ 3.85 | $ 1.51 | $ 2.75 |
| Diluted | 3.81 | 1.49 | 2.72 |
| Weighted average shares outstanding (Note 17): | | | |
| Basic | 69,614 | 69,759 | 69,683 |
| Diluted | 70,401 | 70,453 | 70,632 |

See accompanying notes to consolidated financial statements

**COLUMBIA SPORTSWEAR COMPANY**
**CONSOLIDATED STATEMENTS OF COMPREHENSIVE INCOME**
**(In thousands)**

| | Year Ended December 31, | | |
| --- | --- | --- | --- |
| | **2018** | **2017** | **2016** |
| Net income | $274,948 | $112,315 | $198,439 |
| Other comprehensive income (loss): | | | |
| Unrealized holding losses on available-for-sale securities (net of tax effects of $17, $0, and $0, respectively) | (56) | — | (2) |
| Unrealized gains (losses) on derivative transactions (net of tax effects of $(7,782), $8,176, and ($1,922), respectively) | 24,262 | (18,005) | 843 |
| Foreign currency translation adjustments (net of tax effects of $1,557, $(4), and $347, respectively) | (18,079) | 34,160 | (4,485) |
| Other comprehensive income (loss) | 6,127 | 16,155 | (3,644) |
| Comprehensive income | 281,075 | 128,470 | 194,795 |
| Comprehensive income attributable to non-controlling interest | 7,480 | 9,617 | 4,678 |
| Comprehensive income attributable to Columbia Sportswear Company | $273,596 | $118,853 | $190,117 |

See accompanying notes to consolidated financial statements

**COLUMBIA SPORTWEAR COMPANY**
**CONSOLIDATED BALANCE SHEETS**
**(In thousands)**

| | December 31, | |
| --- | --- | --- |
| | **2018** | **2017** |
| **ASSETS** | | |
| Current Assets: | | |
| Cash and cash equivalents (Note 21) | $ 437,825 | $ 673,166 |
| Restricted cash (Note 22) | 13,970 | — |
| Short-term investments (Note 21) | 262,802 | 94,983 |
| Accounts receivable, net (Note 6) | 449,382 | 364,862 |
| Inventories | 521,827 | 457,927 |
| Prepaid expenses and other current assets | 79,500 | 58,559 |
| Total current assets | 1,765,306 | 1,649,497 |
| Property, plant, and equipment, net (Note 7) | 291,596 | 281,394 |
| Intangible assets, net (Note 8) | 126,575 | 129,555 |
| Goodwill (Note 8) | 68,594 | 68,594 |
| Deferred income taxes (Note 11) | 78,155 | 56,804 |
| Other non-current assets | 38,495 | 27,058 |
| Total assets | $2,368,721 | $2,212,902 |
| **LIABILITIES AND EQUITY** | | |
| Current Liabilities: | | |
| Accounts payable | $ 274,435 | $ 252,301 |
| Accrued liabilities (Note 10) | 275,684 | 182,228 |
| Income taxes payable (Note 11) | 22,763 | 19,107 |
| Total current liabilities | 572,882 | 453,636 |
| Other long-term liabilities (Notes 12, 13) | 45,214 | 48,735 |
| Income taxes payable (Note 11) | 50,791 | 58,104 |
| Deferred income taxes (Note 11) | 9,521 | 168 |
| Total liabilities | 678,408 | 560,643 |
| Commitment and contingencies (Note 14) | | |
| Shareholders' Equity: | | |
| Preferred stock; 10,000 shares authorized; none issued and outstanding | — | — |
| Common stock (no par value); 250,000 shares authorized; 68,246 and 69,995 issued and outstanding (Note 15) | — | 45,829 |
| Retained earnings | 1,677,920 | 1,585,009 |
| Accumulated other comprehensive loss (Note 18) | (4,063) | (8,887) |
| Total Columbia Sportswear Company shareholders' equity | 1,673,857 | 1,621,951 |
| Non-controlling interest (Note 5) | 16,456 | 30,308 |
| Total equity | 1,690,313 | 1,652,259 |
| Total liabilities and equity | $2,368,721 | $2,212,902 |

See accompanying notes to consolidated financial statements

## COLUMBIA SPORTSWEAR COMPANY
## CONSOLIDATED STATEMENTS OF CASH FLOWS
### (In thousands)

| | Year Ended December 31, | | |
| --- | --- | --- | --- |
| | 2018 | 2017 | 2016 |
| **Cash flows from operating activities:** | | | |
| Net income | $274,948 | $112,315 | $198,439 |
| Adjustments to reconcile net income to net cash provided by operating activities: | | | |
| Depreciation and amortization | 58,230 | 59,945 | 60,016 |
| Loss on disposal or impairment of property, plant, and equipment | 4,208 | 1,927 | 4,805 |
| Deferred income taxes | 1,462 | 44,851 | (19,178) |
| Stock-based compensation | 14,291 | 11,286 | 10,986 |
| Changes in operating assets and liabilities: | | | |
| Accounts receivable | (25,601) | (24,197) | 36,710 |
| Inventories | (94,716) | 46,662 | (18,777) |
| Prepaid expenses and other current assets | (9,771) | (19,241) | (5,452) |
| Other assets | (12,421) | 931 | (5,948) |
| Accounts payable | 19,384 | 30,568 | 1,483 |
| Accrued liabilities | 86,900 | 11,581 | 4,847 |
| Income taxes payable | (3,958) | 58,702 | 4,768 |
| Other liabilities | (3,387) | 5,798 | 2,468 |
| Net cash provided by operating activities | 289,569 | 341,128 | 275,167 |
| **Cash flows from investing activities:** | | | |
| Purchases of short-term investments | (518,755) | (130,993) | (21,263) |
| Sales and maturities of short-term investments | 352,127 | 36,282 | 21,263 |
| Capital expenditures | (65,622) | (53,352) | (49,987) |
| Proceeds from sale of property, plant, and equipment | 19 | 279 | 97 |
| Net cash used in investing activities | (232,231) | (147,784) | (49,890) |
| **Cash flows from financing activities:** | | | |
| Proceeds from credit facilities | 70,576 | 3,374 | 62,885 |
| Repayments on credit facilities | (70,576) | (3,374) | (64,825) |
| Proceeds from issuance of common stock related to stock-based compensation | 18,484 | 19,946 | 13,167 |
| Tax payments related to stock-based compensation | (4,285) | (3,662) | (5,117) |
| Repurchase of common stock | (201,600) | (35,542) | (11) |
| Cash dividends paid | (62,664) | (50,909) | (48,122) |
| Cash dividends paid to non-controlling interest | (19,949) | — | — |
| Payment of related party note payable | — | (14,236) | — |
| Net cash used in financing activities | (270,014) | (84,403) | (42,023) |
| **Net effect of exchange rate changes on cash** | (8,695) | 12,836 | (1,635) |
| **Net (decrease) increase in cash, cash equivalents and restricted cash** | (221,371) | 121,777 | 181,619 |
| **Cash, cash equivalents and restricted cash, beginning of period** | 673,166 | 551,389 | 369,770 |
| **Cash, cash equivalents and restricted cash, end of period** | $451,795 | $673,166 | $551,389 |
| **Supplemental disclosures of cash flow information:** | | | |
| Cash paid during the year for income taxes | $ 77,408 | $ 81,045 | $ 70,424 |
| Cash paid during the year for interest on note payable to related party | — | 685 | 1,049 |
| **Supplemental disclosures of non-cash investing activities:** | | | |
| Capital expenditures incurred but not yet paid | 11,831 | 3,188 | 2,710 |

See accompanying notes to consolidated financial statements

## COLUMBIA SPORTSWEAR COMPANY
## CONSOLIDATED STATEMENTS OF EQUITY
### (In thousands)

| | Common Stock | | | | | |
| | Shares Outstanding | Amount | Related Earnings | Accumulated Other Comprehensive Income (Loss) | Non-Controlling Interest | Total |
|---|---|---|---|---|---|---|
| **BALANCE, JANUARY 1, 2016** | 69,277 | $34,776 | $1,385,860 | $(20,836) | $16,013 | $1,415,813 |
| Net income | — | — | 191,898 | — | 6,541 | 198,439 |
| Other comprehensive income (loss): | | | | | | |
| Unrealized holding losses on available-for-sale securities, net | — | — | — | (2) | — | (2) |
| Unrealized holding gains on derivative transactions, net | — | — | — | 686 | 157 | 843 |
| Foreign currency translation adjustment, net | — | — | — | (2,465) | (2,020) | (14,485) |
| Cash dividends ($0.69 per share) | — | — | (48,122) | — | — | (48,122) |
| Issuance of common stock related to stock-based compensation, net | 596 | 8,050 | — | — | — | 8,050 |
| Stock-based compensation expense | — | 10,986 | — | — | — | 10,986 |
| Repurchase of common stock | | (11) | — | — | — | (11) |
| **BALANCE, DECEMBER 31, 2016** | 69,873 | 53,801 | 1,529,636 | (22,617) | 20,691 | 1,581,511 |
| Net income | — | — | 105,123 | — | 7,192 | 112,315 |
| Other comprehensive income (loss): | | | | | | |
| Unrealized holding gains (losses) on derivative transactions, net | — | — | 1,159 | (17,489) | (516) | (16,846) |
| Foreign currency translation adjustment, net | — | — | — | 31,219 | 2,941 | 34,160 |
| Cash dividends ($0.73 per share) | — | — | (50,909) | — | — | (50,909) |
| Issuance of common stock related to stock-based compensation, net | 787 | 16,284 | — | — | — | 16,284 |
| Stock-based compensation expense | — | 11,286 | — | — | — | 11,286 |
| Repurchase of common stock | (665) | (35,542) | — | — | — | (35,542) |
| **BALANCE, DECEMBER 31, 2017** | 69,995 | 45,829 | 1,585,009 | (8,887) | 30,308 | 1,652,259 |
| Net income | — | — | 268,256 | — | 6,692 | 274,948 |
| Other comprehensive income (loss): | | | | | | |
| Unrealized holding losses on available-for-sale securities, net | — | — | — | (56) | — | (56) |
| Unrealized holding gains on derivative transactions, net | — | — | — | 23,195 | 1,067 | 24,262 |
| Foreign currency translation adjustment, net | — | — | — | (17,800) | (279) | (18,079) |
| Cash dividends ($0.90 per share) | — | — | (62,664) | — | — | (62,664) |
| Dividends to non-controlling interest | — | — | — | — | (21,332) | (21,332) |
| Adoption of new accounting standards | — | — | 14,600 | (515) | — | 14,085 |
| Issuance of common stock related to stock-based compensation, net | 600 | 14,199 | — | — | — | 14,199 |
| Stock-based compensation expense | — | 14,291 | — | — | — | 14,291 |
| Repurchase of common stock | (2,349) | (74,319) | (127,281) | — | — | (201,600) |
| **BALANCE, DECEMBER 31, 2018** | 68,246 | $  — | $1,677,920 | $(4,063) | $16,456 | $1,690,313 |

See accompanying notes to consolidated financial statements

# Specimen Financial Statements:
# Under Armour, Inc.

**Under Armour, Inc.** is a leader in outdoor sportswear. The following are Under Armour's financial statements as presented in its 2018 annual report. Under Armour's complete annual report, including notes to the financial statements, is available at the company's website.

**Under Armour, Inc. and Subsidiaries**
**Consolidated Balance Sheets**
**(In thousands, except share data)**

|  | December 31, 2018 | December 31, 2017 |
|---|---|---|
| **Assets** | | |
| Current assets | | |
| Cash and cash equivalents | $ 557,403 | $ 312,483 |
| Accounts receivable, net | 652,546 | 609,670 |
| Inventories | 1,019,496 | 1,158,548 |
| Prepaid expenses and other current assets | 364,183 | 256,978 |
| Total current assets | 2,593,628 | 2,337,679 |
| Property and equipment, net | 826,868 | 885,774 |
| Goodwill | 546,494 | 555,674 |
| Intangible assets, net | 41,793 | 46,995 |
| Deferred income taxes | 112,420 | 82,801 |
| Other long term assets | 123,819 | 97,444 |
| Total assets | $4,245,022 | $4,006,367 |
| **Liabilities and Stockholders' Equity** | | |
| Current liabilities | | |
| Revolving credit facility, current | $ — | $ 125,000 |
| Accounts payable | 580,884 | 561,108 |
| Accrued expenses | 340,415 | 296,841 |
| Customer refund liability | 301,421 | — |
| Current maturities of long term debt | 25,000 | 27,000 |
| Other current liabilities | 88,257 | 50,426 |
| Total current liabilities | 1,315,977 | 1,060,375 |
| Long term debt, net of current maturities | 703,834 | 765,046 |
| Other long term liabilities | 208,340 | 162,304 |
| Total liabilities | 2,228,151 | 1,987,725 |

*(continues)*

|  | December 31, 2018 | December 31, 2017 |
|---|---|---|
| Commitments and contingencies (see Note 7) | | |
| **Stockholders' equity** | | |
| Class A Common Stock, $0.0003 1/3 par value; 400,000,000 shares authorized as of December 31, 2018, and 2017; 187,710,319 shares issued and outstanding as of December 31, 2018, and 185,257,423 shares issued and outstanding as of December 31, 2017. | 62 | 61 |
| Class B Convertible Common Stock, $0.0003 1/3 par value; 34,450,000 shares authorized, issued and outstanding as of December 31, 2018, and 2017. | 11 | 11 |
| Class C Common Stock, $0.0003 1/3 par value; 400,000,000 shares authorized as of December 31, 2018 and 2017; 226,421,963 shares issued and outstanding as of December 31, 2018, and 222,375,079 shares issued and outstanding as of December 31, 2017. | 75 | 74 |
| Additional paid-in capital | 916,628 | 872,266 |
| Retained earnings | 1,139,082 | 1,184,441 |
| Accumulated other comprehensive loss | (38,987) | (38,211) |
| Total stockholders' equity | 2,016,871 | 2,018,642 |
| Total liabilities and stockholders' equity | $4,245,022 | $4,006,367 |

See accompanying notes.

**Under Armour, Inc. and Subsidiaries**
**Consolidated Statements of Operations**
**(In thousands, except per share amounts)**

|  | Year Ended December 31, | | |
|---|---|---|---|
|  | 2018 | 2017 | 2016 |
| Net revenues | $5,193,185 | $4,989,244 | $4,833,338 |
| Cost of goods sold | 2,852,714 | 2,737,830 | 2,584,724 |
| Gross profit | 2,340,471 | 2,251,414 | 2,248,614 |
| Selling, general and administrative expenses | 2,182,339 | 2,099,522 | 1,831,143 |
| Restructuring and impairment charges | 183,149 | 124,049 | — |
| Income (loss) from operations | (25,017) | 27,843 | 417,471 |
| Interest expense, net | (33,568) | (34,538) | (26,434) |
| Other expense, net | (9,203) | (3,614) | (2,755) |
| Income (loss) before income taxes | (67,788) | (10,309) | 388,282 |
| Income tax expense (benefit) | (20,552) | 37,951 | 131,303 |
| Income from equity method investment | 934 | — | — |
| Net income (loss) | (46,302) | (48,260) | 256,979 |
| Adjustment payment to Class C capital stockholders | — | — | 59,000 |
| **Net income (loss) available to all stockholders** | $ (46,302) | $ (48,260) | $ 197,979 |
| Basic net income (loss) per share of Class A and B common stock | $ (0.10) | $ (0.11) | $ 0.45 |
| Basic net income (loss) per share of Class C common stock | $ (0.10) | $ (0.11) | $ 0.72 |
| Diluted net income (loss) per share of Class A and B common stock | $ (0.10) | $ (0.11) | $ 0.45 |
| Diluted net income (loss) per share of Class C common stock | $ (0.10) | $ (0.11) | $ 0.71 |
| **Weighted average common shares outstanding Class A and B common stock** | | | |
| Basic | 221,001 | 219,254 | 217,707 |
| Diluted | 221,001 | 219,254 | 221,944 |
| **Weighted average common shares outstanding Class C common stock** | | | |
| Basic | 224,814 | 221,475 | 218,623 |
| Diluted | 224,814 | 221,475 | 222,904 |

See accompanying notes.

**Under Armour, Inc. and Subsidiaries**
**Consolidated Statements of Comprehensive Income (Loss)**
**(In thousands)**

| | Year Ended December 31, | | |
| --- | --- | --- | --- |
| | **2018** | **2017** | **2016** |
| Net income (loss) | $(46,302) | $(48,260) | $256,979 |
| Other comprehensive income (loss): | | | |
| Foreign currency translation adjustment | (18,535) | 23,357 | (13,798) |
| Unrealized gain (loss) on cash flow hedge, net of tax benefit (expense) of $(7,936), $5,668 and $(3,346) for the years ended December 31, 2018, 2017, and 2016, respectively. | 22,800 | (16,624) | 9,084 |
| Gain (loss) on intra-entity foreign currency transactions | (5,041) | 7,199 | (2,416) |
| Total other comprehensive income (loss) | (776) | 13,932 | (7,130) |
| Comprehensive income (loss) | $(47,078) | $(34,328) | $249,849 |

See accompanying notes.

**Under Armour, Inc. and Subsidiaries**
**Consolidated Statements of Stockholders' Equity**
**(In thousands)**

| | Class A Common Stock | | Class B Convertible Common Stock | | Class C Common Stock | | Additional part-in-Capital | Retained Earnings | Accumulated Other Comprehensive Income | Total Equity |
| --- | --- | --- | --- | --- | --- | --- | --- | --- | --- | --- |
| | **Shares** | **Amount** | **Shares** | **Amount** | **Shares** | **Amount** | | | | |
| Balance as of December 31, 2015 | 181,630 | $61 | 34,450 | $11 | 216,080 | 72 | $636,558 | $1,076,533 | $(45,013) | $1,688,222 |
| Exercise of stock options | 792 | — | — | — | 971 | — | 6,203 | — | — | 6,203 |
| Shares withheld in consideration of employee tax, obligations relative to stock-based compensation arrangements | (199) | — | — | — | (276) | — | — | (15,098) | — | (15,098) |
| Issuance of Class A Common Stock, net forfeitures | 1,592 | — | — | — | — | — | 7,884 | — | — | 7,884 |
| Issuance of class C Common Stock, net forfeitures | — | — | — | — | 1,852 | 1 | 25,834 | — | — | 25,835 |
| Issuance of class C dividend | — | — | — | — | 1,547 | — | 56,073 | (59,000) | — | (2,927) |
| Stock-based compensation expenses | — | — | — | — | — | — | 46,149 | — | — | 46,149 |
| Net excess tax benefits from stock-based compensation arrangements | — | — | — | — | — | — | 44,783 | — | — | 44,783 |
| Comprehensive income (loss) | — | — | — | — | — | — | — | 256,979 | (7,130) | 249,849 |
| Balance as of 12/31/2016 | 183,815 | 61 | 34,450 | 11 | 220,174 | 73 | 823,484 | 1,259,414 | (52,143) | 2,030,900 |

*(continues)*

| | Class A Common Stock | | Class B Convertible Common Stock | | Class C Common Stock | | Additional part-in-Capital | Retained Earnings | Accumulated Other Comprehensive Income | Total Equity |
|---|---|---|---|---|---|---|---|---|---|---|
| | Shares | Amount | Shares | Amount | Shares | Amount | | | | |
| Exercise of stock options | 609 | — | — | — | 556 | — | 3,664 | — | — | 3,664 |
| Shares withheld in consideration of employee tax obligations relative to stock-based compensation arrangements | (65) | — | — | — | (78) | — | — | (2,781) | — | (2,781) |
| Issuance of Class A Common Stock, net of forfeitures | 896 | — | — | — | — | — | — | — | — | — |
| Issuance of Class C Common Stock, net of forfeitures | — | — | — | — | 1,723 | 1 | 7,852 | — | — | 7,853 |
| Impact of adoption of accounting standard updates | — | — | — | — | — | — | (2,686) | (23,932) | — | (26,596) |
| Stock-based compensation expanse | — | — | — | — | — | — | 39,932 | — | — | 39,932 |
| Comprehensive income (loss) | — | — | — | — | — | — | — | (48,260) | 13,932 | (34,328) |
| Balance as of December 31, 2017 | 185,257 | 61 | 34,450 | 11 | 222,375 | 74 | 872,266 | 1,184,441 | (38,211) | 2,018,642 |
| Exercise of stock options and warrants | 2,084 | 1 | — | — | 2,127 | — | 6,747 | — | — | 6,748 |
| Shares withheld in consideration of employee tax obligations relative to stock-based compensation arrangements | (23) | — | — | — | (140) | — | — | (2,564) | — | (2,564) |
| Issuance of Class A Common Stock, net of forfeitures | 392 | — | — | — | — | — | — | — | — | — |
| Issuance of Class C Common Stock, net of forfeitures | — | — | — | — | 2,060 | 1 | (4,168) | — | — | (4,167) |
| Impact of adoption of accounting standard updates | — | — | — | — | — | — | — | 3,507 | — | 3,507 |
| Stock-based compensation expense | — | — | — | — | — | — | 41,783 | — | — | 41,783 |
| Comprehensive income (loss) | — | — | — | — | — | — | — | (46,302) | (776) | (47,078) |
| Balance as of December 31, 2018 | 187,710 | $62 | 34,450 | $11 | 226,422 | $75 | $916,628 | $1,139,082 | $(38,987) | $ 2,016,871 |

See accompanying notes.

**Under Armour, Inc. and Subsidiaries**
**Consolidated Statements of Cash Flows**
**(In thousands)**

| | Year Ended December 31, | | |
| --- | --- | --- | --- |
| | **2018** | **2017** | **2016** |
| **Cash flows from operating activities** | | | |
| Net income (loss) | $ (46,302) | $ (48,260) | $ 256,979 |
| Adjustments to reconcile net income (loss) to net cash provided by operating activities | | | |
| Depreciation and amortization | 181,768 | 173,747 | 144,770 |
| Unrealized foreign currency exchange rate (gains) losses | 14,023 | (29,247) | 12,627 |
| Impairment charges | 9,893 | 71,378 | — |
| Amortization of bond premium | 254 | 254 | — |
| Loss on disposal of property and equipment | 4,256 | 2,313 | 1,580 |
| Stock-based compensation | 41,783 | 39,932 | 46,149 |
| Excess tax benefit (loss) from stock-based compensation arrangements | — | (75) | 44,783 |
| Deferred income taxes | (38,544) | 55,910 | (43,004) |
| Changes in reserves and allowances | (234,998) | 108,757 | 70,188 |
| Changes in operating assets and liabilities: | | | |
| Accounts receivable | 186,834 | (79,106) | (249,853) |
| Inventories | 109,919 | (222,391) | (148,055) |
| Prepaid expenses and other assets | (107,855) | (52,106) | (23,029) |
| Accounts payable | 26,413 | 145,695 | 202,446 |
| Accrued expenses and other liabilities | 134,594 | 109,823 | 67,754 |
| Customer refund liability | 305,141 | — | — |
| Income taxes payable and receivable | 41,051 | (39,164) | (16,712) |
| Net cash provided by operating activities | 628,230 | 237,460 | 366,623 |
| **Cash flows from investing activities** | | | |
| Purchases of property and equipment | (170,385) | (281,339) | (316,458) |
| Sale of property and equipment | 11,285 | — | — |
| Purchases of property and equipment from related parties | — | — | (70,288) |
| Purchase of equity method investment | (39,207) | — | — |
| Purchases of available-for-sale securities | — | — | (24,230) |
| Sales of available-for-sale securities | — | — | 30,712 |
| Purchases of other assets | (4,597) | (1,648) | (875) |
| Net cash used in investing activities | (202,904) | (282,987) | (381,139) |
| **Cash flows from financing activities** | | | |
| Proceeds from long term debt and revolving credit facility | 505,000 | 763,000 | 1,327,601 |
| Payments on long term debt and revolving credit facility | (695,000) | (665,000) | (1,170,750) |
| Employee taxes paid for shares withheld for income taxes | (2,743) | (2,781) | (15,098) |
| Proceeds from exercise of stock options and other stock issuances | 2,580 | 11,540 | 15,485 |
| Other financing fees | 306 | — | — |
| Payments of debt financing costs | (11) | — | (6,692) |
| Cash dividends paid | — | — | (2,927) |
| Contingent consideration payments for acquisitions | — | — | (1,505) |
| Net cash provided by (used in) financing activities | (189,868) | 106,759 | 146,114 |
| Effect of exchange rate changes on cash, cash equivalents and restricted cash | 12,467 | 4,178 | (8,725) |
| Net increase in cash, cash equivalents and restricted cash | 247,925 | 65,410 | 122,873 |

*(continues)*

| | Year Ended December 31, | | |
|---|---|---|---|
| | **2018** | **2017** | **2016** |
| **Cash, cash equivalents and restricted cash** | | | |
| Beginning of period | 318,135 | 252,725 | 129,852 |
| End of period | $ 566,060 | $ 318,315 | $ 252,725 |
| **Non-cash investing and financing activities** | | | |
| Change in accrual for property and equipment | $(14,611) | $10,580 | $16,973 |
| Non-cash dividends | — | — | (56,073) |
| **Other supplemental information** | | | |
| Cash paid for income taxes, net of refunds | (16,738) | 36,921 | 135,959 |
| Cash paid for interest, net of capitalized interest | 28,586 | 29,750 | 21,412 |

See accompanying notes.

# Double-Entry Accounting System

## Appendix Preview

In this text, we used tabular analysis to record business transactions. In this appendix, we introduce the double-entry accounting system. This system is the foundation of accounting systems, whether manual or computerized, used by companies to keep track of their finances. Tabular analysis is useful for instructional purposes since it highlights the effect of each transaction on the financial statements. In practice, however, companies actually employ double-entry accounting because it is more efficient for recording and accumulating large quantities of transactions.

## Appendix Outline

### LEARNING OBJECTIVES

| | |
|---|---|
| **1.** Explain how accounts, debits, and credits are used to record business transactions. | • Debits and credits <br> • Debit and credit procedures <br> • Summary of debit/credit rules |
| **2.** Indicate how a journal and ledger are used in the recording process. | • The recording process <br> • The journal <br> • The ledger <br> • Chart of accounts <br> • Posting <br> • The recording process illustrated |
| **3.** Prepare a trial balance. | • Purposes of a trial balance <br> • Procedures for preparing a trial balance |
| **4.** Prepare adjusting entries and an adjusted trial balance. | • The need for adjusting entries <br> • The adjusting process illustrated <br> • Preparing financial statements |

# Accounts, Debits, and Credits

**LEARNING OBJECTIVE 1**

Explain how accounts, debits, and credits are used to record business transactions.

Rather than using a tabular summary like the one in Illustration 3.6 for Sierra Corporation, an accounting information system uses accounts.

- An **account** is an individual accounting record of increases and decreases in a specific asset, liability, stockholders' equity, revenue, or expense item.
- For example, Sierra Corporation has separate accounts for Cash, Accounts Receivable, Accounts Payable, Service Revenue, Salaries and Wages Expense, and so on.
- Note that whenever we are referring to a specific account, we capitalize the name.

In its simplest form, an account consists of three parts:

1. The title of the account.
2. A left or debit side.
3. A right or credit side.

Because the alignment of these parts of an account resembles the letter **T**, it is referred to as a **T-account**. The basic form of an account is shown in **Illustration D.1**.

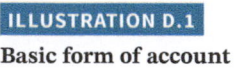

**ILLUSTRATION D.1**

**Basic form of account**

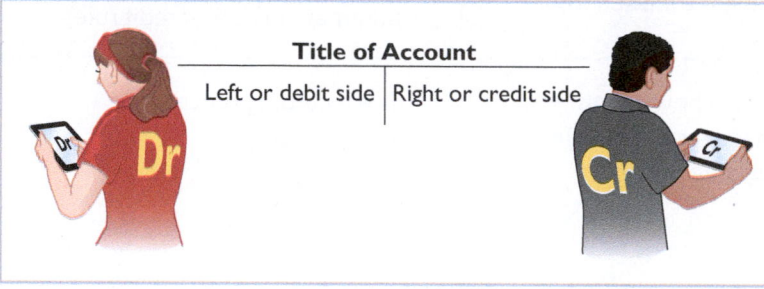

## Debits and Credits

The term **debit** indicates the left side of an account, and **credit** indicates the right side.

- They are commonly abbreviated as **Dr.** for debit and **Cr.** for credit.
- They **do not** mean increase or decrease, but instead describe **where** entries are made in accounts.
- The act of entering an amount on the left side of an account is called **debiting** the account; making an entry on the right side is **crediting** the account.

When comparing the totals of the two sides, an account shows a **debit balance** if the total of the debit amounts exceeds the credits. An account shows a **credit balance** if the credit amounts exceed the debits. Note the position of the debit side and credit side in **Illustration D.2**.

| Tabular Summary | | Account Form | | | |
|---|---|---|---|---|---|
| **Cash** | | | **Cash** | | |
| $10,000 | | (Debits) | 10,000 | (Credits) | 5,000 |
| 5,000 | | | 5,000 | | 900 |
| −5,000 | | | 1,200 | | 600 |
| 1,200 | | | 10,000 | | 500 |
| 10,000 | | | | | 4,000 |
| −900 | | Balance | 15,200 | | |
| −600 | | (Debit) | | | |
| −500 | | | | | |
| −4,000 | | | | | |
| $15,200 | | | | | |

The procedure of recording debits and credits in an account is shown in Illustration D.2 for the transactions affecting the Cash account of Sierra Corporation. The data are taken from the Cash column of the tabular summary in Illustration 3.6.

Every positive item in the tabular summary represents a receipt of cash; every negative amount represents a payment of cash. **Notice that in the account form, we record the increases in cash as debits and the decreases in cash as credits.** For example, the $10,000 receipt of cash (in blue) is debited to Cash, and the −$5,000 payment of cash (in red) is credited to Cash.

- Having increases on one side and decreases on the other reduces recording errors and helps in determining the totals of each side of the account as well as the account balance.
- The balance is determined by netting the two sides (subtracting one amount from the other).
- The account balance, a debit of $15,200, indicates that Sierra had $15,200 more increases than decreases in cash. That is, since it started with a balance of zero, it has $15,200 in its Cash account.

# Debit and Credit Procedures

Each transaction must affect two or more accounts to keep the basic accounting equation in balance. In other words, **for each transaction, debits must equal credits**. The equality of debits and credits provides the basis for the double-entry accounting system.

Under the **double-entry system**, the two-sided effect of each transaction is recorded in appropriate accounts.

- This system provides a logical method for recording transactions.
- If every transaction is recorded with equal debits and credits, then the sum of all the debits to the accounts must equal the sum of all the credits.
- The double-entry system for determining the equality of the accounting equation is much more efficient than the plus/minus procedure used in a tabular summary.

## Dr./Cr. Procedures for Assets and Liabilities

In Illustration D.2 for Sierra Corporation, increases in Cash—an asset—are entered on the left side, and decreases in Cash are entered on the right side. We know that both sides of the basic equation (Assets = Liabilities + Stockholders' Equity) must be equal. It therefore follows that increases and decreases in liabilities have to be recorded **opposite from** increases and decreases in assets. Thus, increases in liabilities are entered on the right or credit side, and decreases in liabilities are entered on the left or debit side.

- **Asset accounts normally show debit balances.** That is, debits to a specific asset account should exceed credits to that account.

- **Liability accounts normally show credit balances.** That is, credits to a liability account should exceed debits to that account.

The effects that debits and credits have on assets and liabilities and their **normal balances** may be diagrammed as shown in **Illustration D.3**.

**ILLUSTRATION D.3**

Normal balances—assets and liabilities

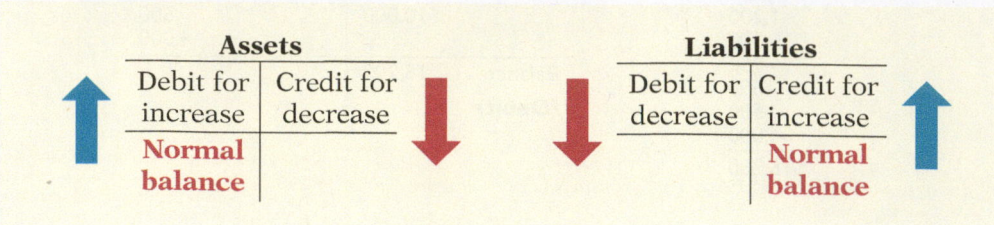

### Dr./Cr. Procedures for Stockholders' Equity

In Chapter 1, we indicated that stockholders' equity is comprised of two parts: common stock and retained earnings. You also learned that revenues, expenses, and the payment of dividends affect retained earnings. Therefore, the subdivisions of stockholders' equity are common stock, retained earnings, dividends, revenues, and expenses.

**Common Stock**   Common stock is issued to investors in exchange for the stockholders' investment.

- The Common Stock account is increased by credits and decreased by debits.
- For example, when cash is invested in the business, Cash is debited and Common Stock is credited.

The effects of debits and credits on the Common Stock account and its normal balance are shown in **Illustration D.4**.

**ILLUSTRATION D.4**

Normal balance—common stock

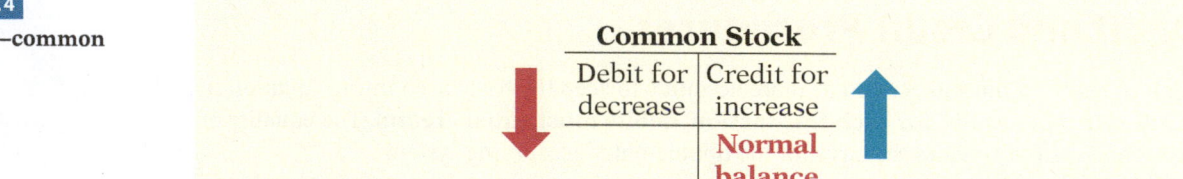

**Retained Earnings**   Retained earnings is net income that is retained in the business.

- It represents the portion of stockholders' equity that has been accumulated through the profitable operation of the company.
- Retained Earnings is increased by credits (for example, by net income) and decreased by debits (for example, by a net loss).

Retained Earnings has a normal credit balance as shown in **Illustration D.5**.

**ILLUSTRATION D.5**

Normal balance—retained earnings

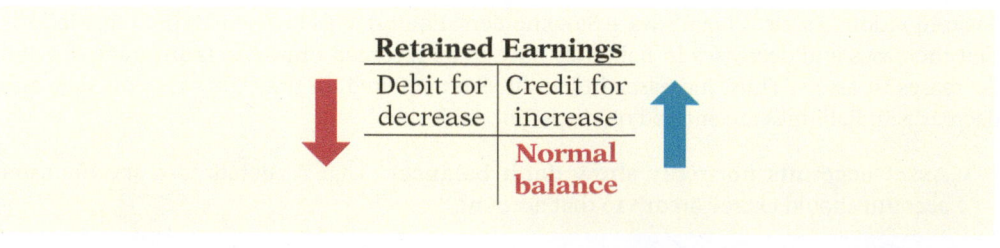

**Dividends**    A dividend is a distribution by a corporation to its stockholders.

- The most common form of distribution is a cash dividend.
- Dividends result in a reduction of the stockholders' claims on retained earnings.
- Because dividends reduce stockholders' equity, increases in the Dividends account are recorded with debits.

As shown in **Illustration D.6**, the Dividends account normally has a debit balance.

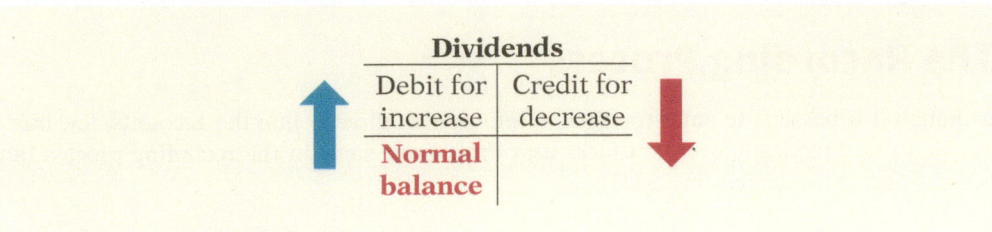

**ILLUSTRATION D.6**
**Normal balance—dividends**

**Revenues and Expenses**    Revenues and expenses affect stockholders' equity.

- When a company recognizes revenues, stockholders' equity is increased. Revenue accounts are increased by credits and decreased by debits.
- **Expenses decrease stockholders' equity.** Thus, expense accounts are increased by debits and decreased by credits.

The effects of debits and credits on revenues and expenses and their normal balances are shown in **Illustration D.7**.

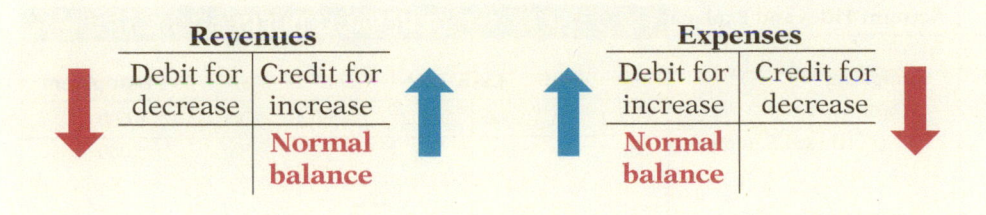

**ILLUSTRATION D.7**
**Normal balances—revenues and expenses**

# Summary of Debit/Credit Rules

**Illustration D.8** summarizes the debit/credit rules and effects on each type of account.

- **Study this diagram carefully.** It will help you understand the fundamentals of the double-entry system.
- No matter what the transaction, total debits must equal total credits in order to keep the accounting equation in balance.

**ILLUSTRATION D.8**    **Summary of debit/credit rules**

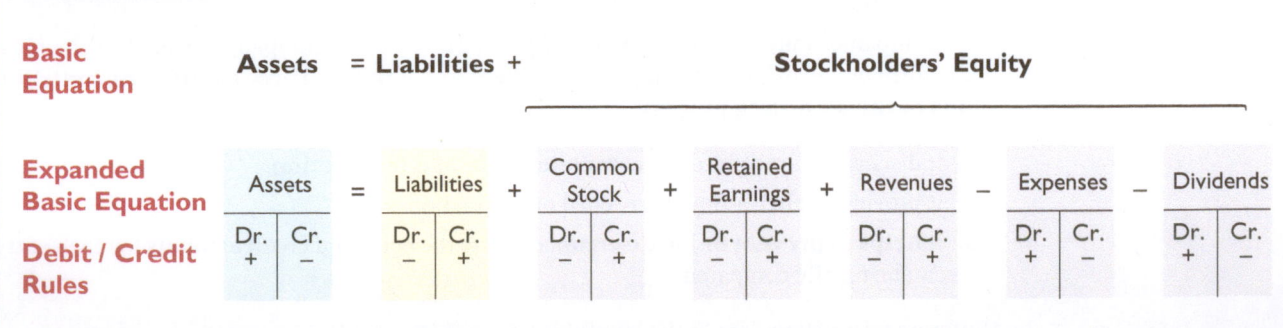

# Using a Journal and Ledger

## The Recording Process

Although it is possible to enter transaction information directly into the accounts, few businesses do so. Practically every business uses these basic steps in the recording process (an integral part of the accounting cycle):

1. Analyze each transaction in terms of its effect on the accounts.
2. Enter the transaction information in a journal.
3. Transfer the journal information to the appropriate accounts in the ledger.

The sequence of events in the recording process is shown in **Illustration D.9**.

**ILLUSTRATION D.9** **The recording process**

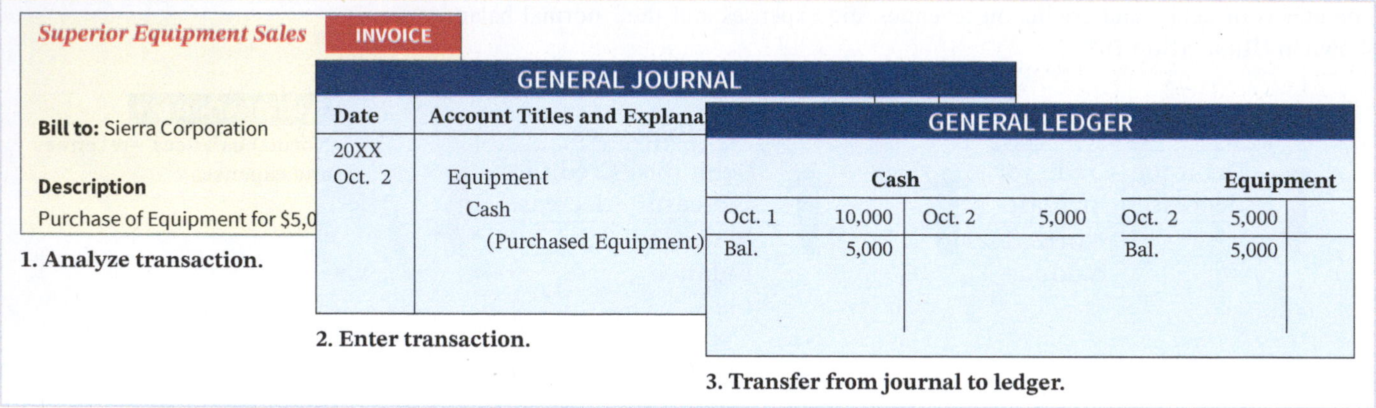

1. Analyze transaction.
2. Enter transaction.
3. Transfer from journal to ledger.

## The Journal

Transactions are initially recorded in chronological order in a **journal** before they are transferred to the accounts.

- For each transaction, the journal shows the debit and credit effects on specific accounts.
- In a computerized system, journals are kept as files, and accounts are recorded in computer databases.

Companies may use various kinds of journals, but every company has at least the most basic form of journal, a **general journal**. **The journal makes three significant contributions to the recording process:**

1. It discloses in one place the **complete effect of a transaction**.
2. It provides a **chronological record** of transactions.
3. It **helps to prevent or locate errors** because the debit and credit amounts for each entry can be readily compared.

Entering transaction data in the journal is known as **journalizing**.

# The Ledger

The entire group of accounts maintained by a company is referred to collectively as the **ledger**.

- The ledger provides the balance in each of the accounts as well as keeps track of changes in these balances.
- Companies may use various kinds of ledgers, but every company has a general ledger.
- A **general ledger** contains all the asset, liability, stockholders' equity, revenue, and expense accounts.

# Chart of Accounts

The number and type of accounts used differ for each company, depending on the size, complexity, and type of business. For example, the number of accounts depends on the amount of detail desired by management.

- Most companies list the accounts in a **chart of accounts**.
- They may create new accounts as needed during the life of the business.

**Illustration D.10** shows the chart of accounts for Sierra Corporation in the order that they are typically listed (assets, liabilities, stockholders' equity, revenues, and expenses).

**ILLUSTRATION D.10**  **Chart of accounts for Sierra Corporation**

### Sierra Corporation
#### Chart of Accounts

| Assets | Liabilities | Stockholders' Equity | Revenues | Expenses |
|---|---|---|---|---|
| Cash | Notes Payable | Common Stock | Service Revenue | Salaries and Wages Expense |
| Accounts Receivable | Accounts Payable | Retained Earnings | | Supplies Expense |
| Supplies | Interest Payable | Dividends | | Rent Expense |
| Prepaid Insurance | Unearned Service Revenue | Income Summary | | Insurance Expense |
| Equipment | Salaries and Wages Payable | | | Interest Expense |
| Accumulated Depreciation—Equipment | | | | Depreciation Expense |

# Posting

The procedure of transferring journal entry amounts to ledger accounts is called **posting**. **This phase of the recording process accumulates the effects of journalized transactions in the individual accounts.** Posting involves these steps:

1. In the ledger, enter in the appropriate columns of the debited account(s) the date and debit amount shown in the journal.
2. In the ledger, enter in the appropriate columns of the credited account(s) the date and credit amount shown in the journal.

# The Recording Process Illustrated

Chapter 3 described events that Sierra Corporation engaged in during its first month of operations. These events are summarized in **Illustration D.11**. We will use these events to illustrate the recording process.

ILLUSTRATION D.11
**October events for Sierra Corporation**

**Event (1): Investment of cash by stockholders.** On October 1, cash of $10,000 is invested in the business by investors in exchange for $10,000 of common stock.

**Event (2): Note issued for cash.** On October 1, Sierra borrowed $5,000 from Castle Bank by signing a 3-month, 12%, $5,000 note payable.

**Event (3): Purchase of equipment for cash.** On October 2, Sierra purchased equipment by paying $5,000 cash to Superior Equipment Sales Co.

**Event (4): Receipt of cash in advance from customer.** On October 2, Sierra received a $1,200 cash advance from R. Knox, a client.

**Event (5): Services performed for cash.** On October 3, Sierra received $10,000 in cash from Copa Company for guide services performed for a corporate event.

**Event (6): Payment of rent.** On October 3, Sierra paid its office rent for the month of October in cash, $900.

**Event (7): Purchase of insurance policy for cash.** On October 4, Sierra paid $600 for a one-year insurance policy that will expire next year on September 30.

**Event (8): Purchase of supplies on account.** On October 5, Sierra purchased an estimated three months of supplies on account from Aero Supply for $2,500.

**Event (9): Hiring of new employees.** On October 9, Sierra hired four new employees to begin work on October 15.

**Event (10): Payment of dividend.** On October 20, Sierra paid a $500 cash dividend.

**Event (11): Payment of cash for employee salaries.** Employees have worked two weeks, earning $4,000 in salaries, which were paid on October 26.

Recall from our earlier discussion that this process consists of three basic steps:

1. Analyze each transaction in terms of its effects on the accounts.
2. Enter the transaction information in a journal.
3. Transfer the journal information to the appropriate accounts in the ledger.

Note that a basic analysis and a debit–credit analysis precede the journalizing and posting of each transaction. **The purpose of transaction analysis is first to identify the type of account involved and then to determine whether a debit or a credit to the account is required.** Illustration D.12 provides a detailed example of each step in the recording process for Sierra's first event.

ILLUSTRATION D.12
**Investment of cash by stockholders**

Cash Flows
+10,000

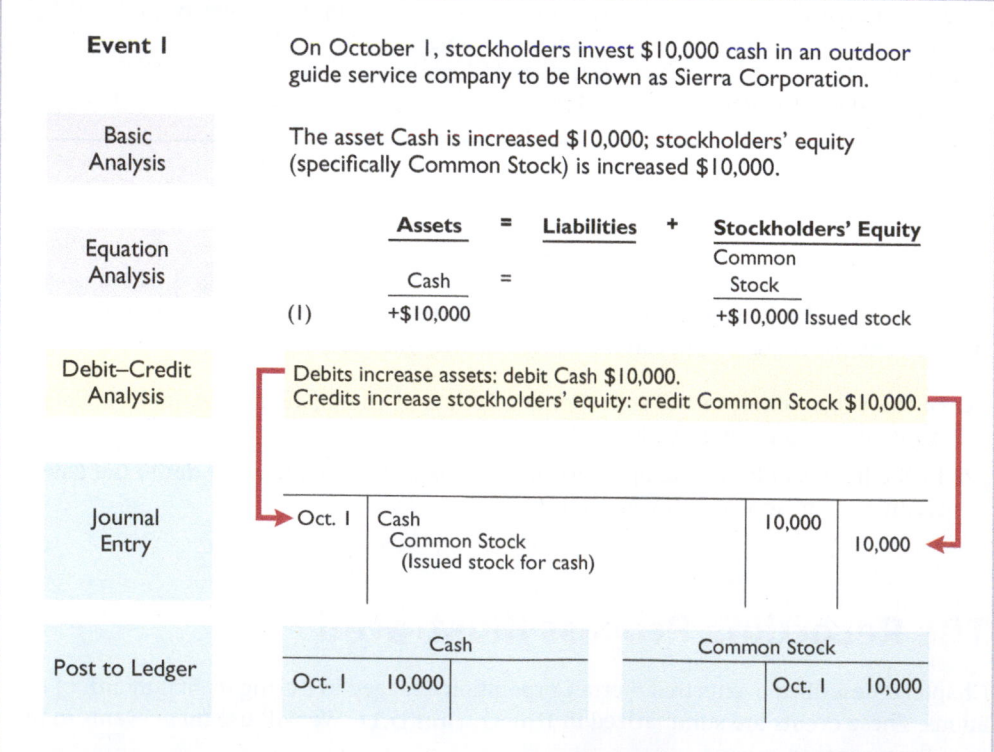

| **Event 1** | On October 1, stockholders invest $10,000 cash in an outdoor guide service company to be known as Sierra Corporation. |

Basic Analysis — The asset Cash is increased $10,000; stockholders' equity (specifically Common Stock) is increased $10,000.

Equation Analysis

| | **Assets** | **=** | **Liabilities** | **+** | **Stockholders' Equity** |
|---|---|---|---|---|---|
| | Cash | = | | | Common Stock |
| (1) | +$10,000 | | | | +$10,000 Issued stock |

Debit–Credit Analysis
- Debits increase assets: debit Cash $10,000.
- Credits increase stockholders' equity: credit Common Stock $10,000.

Journal Entry

| Oct. 1 | Cash | 10,000 | |
|---|---|---|---|
| | Common Stock | | 10,000 |
| | (Issued stock for cash) | | |

Post to Ledger

| Cash | | Common Stock | |
|---|---|---|---|
| Oct. 1  10,000 | | | Oct. 1  10,000 |

Journal entries and posting for the remaining events are summarized in **Illustrations D.13** and **D.14**.

**ILLUSTRATION D.13**

**General journal for Sierra Corporation**

| | GENERAL JOURNAL | | |
|---|---|---|---|
| **Date** | **Account Titles and Explanation** | **Debit** | **Credit** |
| 2022 | | | |
| Oct. 1 | Cash | 10,000 | |
| |    Common Stock | | 10,000 |
| |      (Issued stock for cash) | | |
| 1 | Cash | 5,000 | |
| |    Notes Payable | | 5,000 |
| |      (Issued 3-month, 12% note payable for cash) | | |
| 2 | Equipment | 5,000 | |
| |    Cash | | 5,000 |
| |      (Purchased equipment for cash) | | |
| 2 | Cash | 1,200 | |
| |    Unearned Service Revenue | | 1,200 |
| |      (Received advance from R. Knox for future service) | | |
| 3 | Cash | 10,000 | |
| |    Service Revenue | | 10,000 |
| |      (Received cash for services performed) | | |
| 3 | Rent Expense | 900 | |
| |    Cash | | 900 |
| |      (Paid cash for October office rent) | | |
| 4 | Prepaid Insurance | 600 | |
| |    Cash | | 600 |
| |      (Paid 1-year policy; effective date October 1) | | |
| 5 | Supplies | 2,500 | |
| |    Accounts Payable | | 2,500 |
| |      (Purchased supplies on account from Aero Supply) | | |
| 20 | Dividends | 500 | |
| |    Cash | | 500 |
| |      (Declared and paid a cash dividend) | | |
| 26 | Salaries and Wages Expense | 4,000 | |
| |    Cash | | 4,000 |
| |      (Paid salaries to date) | | |

*Note that Event (9) had no effect on the accounting equation so it is not journalized.

Note the following features of the journal entries in Illustration D.13:

1. The date of the transaction is entered in the Date column.
2. The account to be debited is entered first at the left. The account to be credited is then entered on the next line, indented under the line above. The indentation differentiates debits from credits and decreases the possibility of switching the debit and credit amounts.
3. The amounts for the debits are recorded in the Debit (left) column, and the amounts for the credits are recorded in the Credit (right) column.
4. A brief explanation of the transaction is given.

**ILLUSTRATION D.14**

**General ledger for Sierra Corporation**

| GENERAL LEDGER | | | | |
|---|---|---|---|---|

**Cash**

| | | | | | |
|---|---|---|---|---|---|
| Oct. | 1 | 10,000 | Oct. 2 | 5,000 | |
| | 1 | 5,000 | 3 | 900 | |
| | 2 | 1,200 | 4 | 600 | |
| | 3 | 10,000 | 20 | 500 | |
| | | | 26 | 4,000 | |
| Bal. | | 15,200 | | | |

**Unearned Service Revenue**

| | | | | |
|---|---|---|---|---|
| | | | Oct. 2 | 1,200 |
| | | | Bal. | 1,200 |

**Supplies**

| | | | |
|---|---|---|---|
| Oct. 5 | 2,500 | | |
| Bal. | 2,500 | | |

**Common Stock**

| | | | | |
|---|---|---|---|---|
| | | | Oct. 1 | 10,000 |
| | | | Bal. | 10,000 |

**Prepaid Insurance**

| | | | |
|---|---|---|---|
| Oct. 4 | 600 | | |
| Bal. | 600 | | |

**Dividends**

| | | | |
|---|---|---|---|
| Oct. 20 | 500 | | |
| Bal. | 500 | | |

**Equipment**

| | | | |
|---|---|---|---|
| Oct. 2 | 5,000 | | |
| Bal. | 5,000 | | |

**Service Revenue**

| | | | | |
|---|---|---|---|---|
| | | | Oct. 3 | 10,000 |
| | | | Bal. | 10,000 |

**Notes Payable**

| | | | |
|---|---|---|---|
| | | Oct. 1 | 5,000 |
| | | Bal. | 5,000 |

**Salaries and Wages Expense**

| | | | |
|---|---|---|---|
| Oct. 26 | 4,000 | | |
| Bal. | 4,000 | | |

**Accounts Payable**

| | | | |
|---|---|---|---|
| | | Oct. 5 | 2,500 |
| | | Bal. | 2,500 |

**Rent Expense**

| | | | |
|---|---|---|---|
| Oct. 3 | 900 | | |
| Bal. | 900 | | |

# The Trial Balance

**LEARNING OBJECTIVE 3**

Prepare a trial balance.

A **trial balance** lists accounts and their balances at a given time.

- A company usually prepares a trial balance at the end of an accounting period.
- The accounts are listed in the order in which they appear in the ledger.
- Debit balances are listed in the left column and credit balances in the right column; the totals of the two columns must be equal.

**The trial balance proves the mathematical equality of debits and credits after posting.** Under the double-entry system, this equality occurs when the sum of the debit account balances equals the sum of the credit account balances. **A trial balance may also uncover errors in journalizing and posting. In addition, a trial balance is useful in the preparation of financial statements.**

These are the procedures for preparing a trial balance:

1. List the account titles and their balances.
2. Total the debit column and total the credit column.
3. Verify the equality of the two columns.

   **Illustration D.15** presents the trial balance prepared from the ledger of Sierra Corporation. Note that the total debits, $28,700, equal the total credits, $28,700.

### Sierra Corporation
#### Trial Balance
#### October 31, 2022

|  | Debit | Credit |
| --- | --- | --- |
| Cash | $15,200 |  |
| Supplies | 2,500 |  |
| Prepaid Insurance | 600 |  |
| Equipment | 5,000 |  |
| Notes Payable |  | $ 5,000 |
| Accounts Payable |  | 2,500 |
| Unearned Service Revenue |  | 1,200 |
| Common Stock |  | 10,000 |
| Dividends | 500 |  |
| Service Revenue |  | 10,000 |
| Salaries and Wages Expense | 4,000 |  |
| Rent Expense | 900 |  |
|  | $28,700 | $28,700 |

# Adjusting Entries

**LEARNING OBJECTIVE 4**

Prepare adjusting entries and an adjusted trial balance.

## The Need for Adjusting Entries

Chapter 4 explained that in order for revenues to be recorded in the period in which the performance obligations are satisfied and for expenses to be recognized in the period in which they are incurred, companies make adjustments. **Adjusting entries ensure that the revenue recognition and expense recognition principles are followed.**

Adjusting entries are necessary because the **trial balance**—the first pulling together of the transaction data—may not contain up-to-date and complete data. This is true for several reasons:

1. Some events are not recorded daily because it is not efficient to do so. Examples are the use of supplies and the earning of wages by employees.
2. Some costs are not recorded during the accounting period because these costs expire with the passage of time rather than as a result of recurring daily transactions. Examples are charges related to the use of buildings and equipment, rent, and insurance.

3. Some items may be unrecorded. An example is a utility service bill that will not be received until the next accounting period.

**Adjusting entries are required every time a company prepares financial statements.** The company analyzes each account in the trial balance to determine whether it is complete and up-to-date for financial statement purposes. **Every adjusting entry will include one income statement account and one balance sheet account.**

# The Adjusting Process Illustrated

Recall from Chapter 4 that Sierra Corporation makes adjustments for the following items:

1. A physical count of the supply inventory at the close of business October 31 reveals that $1,000 of supplies are still on hand.
2. Insurance expires at the rate of $50 per month.
3. Depreciation expense is $40 per month.
4. Services related to unearned service revenue of $400 were performed.
5. Sierra performed guide services worth $200 that were not billed to clients on or before October 31.
6. Interest expense for the month of October is $50.
7. Accrued salaries at October 31 are $1,200.

**Illustrations D.16** and **D.17** show the journalizing and posting of adjusting entries for Sierra on October 31. The company then prepares an **adjusted trial balance**, which lists the accounts and their balances after all adjustments have been made, as shown in **Illustration D.18**.

**ILLUSTRATION D.16**

General journal showing adjusting entries

| | GENERAL JOURNAL | | |
|---|---|---|---|
| **Date** | **Account Titles and Explanation** | **Debit** | **Credit** |
| 2022 | *Adjusting Entries* | | |
| Oct. 31 | Supplies Expense | 1,500 | |
| |    Supplies | | 1,500 |
| |      (To record supplies used) | | |
| 31 | Insurance Expense | 50 | |
| |    Prepaid Insurance | | 50 |
| |      (To record insurance expired) | | |
| 31 | Depreciation Expense | 40 | |
| |    Accumulated Depreciation—Equipment | | 40 |
| |      (To record monthly depreciation) | | |
| 31 | Unearned Service Revenue | 400 | |
| |    Service Revenue | | 400 |
| |      (To record revenue for services performed) | | |
| 31 | Accounts Receivable | 200 | |
| |    Service Revenue | | 200 |
| |      (To record revenue for services performed) | | |
| 31 | Interest Expense | 50 | |
| |    Interest Payable | | 50 |
| |      (To record interest on notes payable) | | |
| 31 | Salaries and Wages Expense | 1,200 | |
| |    Salaries and Wages Payable | | 1,200 |
| |      (To record accrued salaries) | | |

**GENERAL LEDGER**

**ILLUSTRATION D.17**
General ledger after adjustments

### Cash

| Oct. 1 | 10,000 | Oct. 2 | 5,000 |
| 1 | 5,000 | 3 | 900 |
| 2 | 1,200 | 4 | 600 |
| 3 | 10,000 | 20 | 500 |
| | | 26 | 4,000 |
| Oct. 31 | Bal. 15,200 | | |

### Accounts Receivable

| Oct. 31 | 200 | | |
| Oct. 31 | Bal. 200 | | |

### Supplies

| Oct. 5 | 2,500 | Oct. 31 | 1,500 |
| Oct. 31 | Bal. 1,000 | | |

### Prepaid Insurance

| Oct. 4 | 600 | Oct. 31 | 50 |
| Oct. 31 | Bal. 550 | | |

### Equipment

| Oct. 2 | 5,000 | | |
| Oct. 31 | Bal. 5,000 | | |

### Accumulated Depreciation— Equipment

| | | Oct. 31 | 40 |
| | | Oct. 31 | Bal. 40 |

### Notes Payable

| | | Oct. 1 | 5,000 |
| | | Oct. 31 | Bal. 5,000 |

### Accounts Payable

| | | Oct. 5 | 2,500 |
| | | Oct. 31 | Bal. 2,500 |

### Interest Payable

| | | Oct. 31 | 50 |
| | | Oct. 31 | Bal. 50 |

### Unearned Service Revenue

| Oct. 31 | 400 | Oct. 2 | 1,200 |
| | | Oct. 31 | Bal. 800 |

### Salaries and Wages Payable

| | | Oct. 31 | 1,200 |
| | | Oct. 31 | Bal. 1,200 |

### Common Stock

| | | Oct. 1 | 10,000 |
| | | Oct. 31 | Bal. 10,000 |

### Retained Earnings

| | | Oct. 31 | Bal. 0 |

### Dividends

| Oct. 20 | 500 | | |
| Oct. 31 | Bal. 500 | | |

### Service Revenue

| | | Oct. 3 | 10,000 |
| | | 31 | 400 |
| | | 31 | 200 |
| | | Oct. 31 | Bal. 10,600 |

### Salaries and Wages Expense

| Oct. 26 | 4,000 | | |
| 31 | 1,200 | | |
| Oct. 31 | Bal. 5,200 | | |

### Supplies Expense

| Oct. 31 | 1,500 | | |
| Oct. 31 | Bal. 1,500 | | |

### Rent Expense

| Oct. 3 | 900 | | |
| Oct. 31 | Bal. 900 | | |

### Insurance Expense

| Oct. 31 | 50 | | |
| Oct. 31 | Bal. 50 | | |

### Interest Expense

| Oct. 31 | 50 | | |
| Oct. 31 | Bal. 50 | | |

### Depreciation Expense

| Oct. 31 | 40 | | |
| Oct. 31 | Bal. 40 | | |

# Preparing Financial Statements

**Companies can prepare financial statements directly from an adjusted trial balance.**

- Companies prepare the income statement from the revenue and expense accounts.
- They derive the retained earnings statement from the Retained Earnings account, the Dividends account, and the net income (or net loss) shown in the income statement.
- Companies then prepare the balance sheet from the asset, liability, and stockholders' equity accounts. They obtain the amount reported for retained earnings on the balance sheet from the ending balance in the retained earnings statements.

Note that Sierra Corporation financial statements are shown in Illustration 4.26.

**ILLUSTRATION D.18**

**Adjusted trial balance**

### Sierra Corporation
### Trial Balance
### October 31, 2022

| | Debit | Credit |
|---|---|---|
| Cash | $15,200 | |
| Accounts Receivable | 200 | |
| Supplies | 1,000 | |
| Prepaid Insurance | 550 | |
| Equipment | 5,000 | |
| Accumulated Depreciation—Equipment | | $ 40 |
| Notes Payable | | 5,000 |
| Accounts Payable | | 2,500 |
| Interest Payable | | 50 |
| Unearned Service Revenue | | 800 |
| Salaries and Wages Payable | | 1,200 |
| Common Stock | | 10,000 |
| Retained Earnings | | 0 |
| Dividends | 500 | |
| Service Revenue | | 10,600 |
| Salaries and Wages Expense | 5,200 | |
| Supplies Expense | 1,500 | |
| Rent Expense | 900 | |
| Insurance Expense | 50 | |
| Interest Expense | 50 | |
| Depreciation Expense | 40 | |
| | $30,190 | $30,190 |

# Review

## Learning Objective Review

**1 Explain how accounts, debits, and credits are used to record business transactions.**

An account is an individual accounting record of increases and decreases in specific asset, liability, and stockholders' equity items.

The terms debit and credit are synonymous with left and right. Assets, dividends, and expenses are increased by debits and decreased by credits. Liabilities, common stock, retained earnings, and revenues are increased by credits and decreased by debits.

**2 Indicate how a journal and ledger are used in the recording process.**

The basic steps in the recording process are (a) analyze each transaction in terms of its effect on the accounts, (b) enter the transaction information in a journal, and (c) transfer the journal information to the appropriate accounts in the ledger.

The initial accounting record of a transaction is entered in a journal before the data are entered in the accounts. A journal (a) discloses in one place the complete effect of a transaction, (b) provides a chronological record of transactions, and (c) prevents or locates errors because the debit and credit amounts for each entry can be readily compared.

The entire group of accounts maintained by a company is referred to collectively as a ledger. The ledger provides the balance in each of the accounts as well as keeps track of changes in these balances.

Posting is the procedure of transferring journal entries to the ledger accounts. This phase of the recording process accumulates the effects of journalized transactions in the individual accounts.

**3  Prepare a trial balance.**

A trial balance is a list of accounts and their balances at a given time. The primary purpose of the trial balance is to prove the mathematical equality of debits and credits after posting. A trial balance also uncovers errors in journalizing and posting and is useful in preparing financial statements.

**4  Prepare adjusting entries and an adjusted trial balance.**

Companies make adjusting entries at the end of the accounting period to ensure revenues and expenses are recorded in the proper period. An adjusted trial balance is a trial balance that shows the balances of all accounts, including those that have been adjusted, at the end of an accounting period. The purpose of an adjusted trial balance is to show the effects of all financial events that have occurred during the accounting period.

## Glossary Review

**Account**  An individual accounting record of increases and decreases in specific asset, liability, stockholders' equity, revenue, or expense items. (p. D-2).

**Adjusted trial balance**  A list of accounts and their balances after all adjustments have been made. (p. D-12).

**Chart of accounts**  A list of a company's accounts. (p. D-7).

**Credit**  The right side of an account. (p. D-2).

**Debit**  The left side of an account. (p. D-2).

**Double-entry system**  A system that records the two-sided effect of each transaction in appropriate accounts. (p. D-3).

**General journal**  The most basic form of journal. (p. D-6).

**General ledger**  A ledger that contains all asset, liability, stockholders' equity, revenue, and expense accounts. (p. D-7).

**Journal**  An accounting record in which transactions are initially recorded in chronological order. (p. D-6).

**Journalizing**  The procedure of entering transaction data in the journal. (p. D-6).

**Ledger**  The group of accounts maintained by a company. (p. D-7).

**Posting**  The procedure of transferring journal entry amounts to the ledger accounts. (p. D-7).

**T-account**  The basic form of an account. (p. D-2).

**Trial balance**  A list of accounts and their balances at a given time. (p. D-10).

# WileyPLUS

Many additional resources are available for practice in WileyPLUS.

## Questions

**1.**  Why is an account referred to as a T-account?

**2.**  The terms debit and credit mean "increase" and "decrease," respectively. Do you agree? Explain.

**3.**  Barry Barack, a fellow student, contends that the double-entry system means each transaction must be recorded twice. Is Barry correct? Explain.

**4.**  Misty Reno, a beginning accounting student, believes debit balances are favorable and credit balances are unfavorable. Is Misty correct? Discuss.

**5.**  State the rules of debit and credit as applied to (a) asset accounts, (b) liability accounts, and (c) the Common Stock account.

**6.**  What is the normal balance for each of these accounts?

  **a.**  Accounts Receivable.

  **b.**  Cash.

  **c.**  Dividends.

  **d.**  Accounts Payable.

  **e.**  Service Revenue.

  **f.**  Salaries and Wages Expense.

  **g.**  Common Stock.

**7.**  Indicate whether each account is an asset, a liability, or a stockholders' equity account, and whether it would have a normal debit or credit balance.

  **a.**  Accounts Receivable.    **d.**  Dividends.

  **b.**  Accounts Payable.    **e.**  Supplies.

  **c.**  Equipment.

**8.**  For the following transactions, indicate the account debited and the account credited.

  **a.**  Supplies are purchased on account.

  **b.**  Cash is received on signing a note payable.

  **c.**  Employees are paid salaries in cash.

**9.** For each account listed here, indicate whether it generally will have debit entries only, credit entries only, or both debit and credit entries.

   **a.** Cash.

   **b.** Accounts Receivable.

   **c.** Dividends.

   **d.** Accounts Payable.

   **e.** Salaries and Wages Expense.

   **f.** Service Revenue.

**10.** What are the basic steps in the recording process?

**11.** **a.** When entering a transaction in the journal, should the debit or credit be written first?

   **b.** Which should be indented, the debit or the credit?

**12.** **a.** Should accounting transaction debits and credits be recorded directly in the ledger accounts?

   **b.** What are the advantages of first recording transactions in the journal and then posting to the ledger?

**13.** Journalize these accounting transactions.

   **a.** Stockholders invested $12,000 in the business in exchange for common stock.

   **b.** Insurance of $800 is paid for the year.

   **c.** Supplies of $1,800 are purchased on account.

   **d.** Cash of $7,500 is received for services rendered.

**14.** **a.** What is a ledger?

   **b.** Why is a chart of accounts important?

**15.** What is a trial balance and what are its purposes?

**16.** Brad Tyler is confused about how accounting information flows through the accounting system. He believes information flows in this order:

   **a.** Debits and credits are posted to the ledger.

   **b.** Accounting transaction occurs.

   **c.** Information is entered in the journal.

   **d.** Financial statements are prepared.

   **e.** Trial balance is prepared.

Indicate to Brad the proper flow of the information.

**17.** Whistler Corp. performed services for a customer but has not received payment, nor has it recorded any entry related to the work. Which of the following types of accounts are involved in the adjusting entry: (a) asset, (b) liability, (c) revenue, or (d) expense? For the accounts selected, indicate whether they would be debited or credited in the entry.

**18.** A company fails to recognize an expense incurred but not paid. Indicate which of the following types of accounts is debited and which is credited in the adjusting entry: (a) asset, (b) liability, (c) revenue, or (d) expense.

**19.** One-half of the adjusting entry is given below. Indicate the account title for the other half of the entry.

   **a.** Salaries and Wages Expense is debited.

   **b.** Depreciation Expense is debited.

   **c.** Interest Payable is credited.

   **d.** Supplies is credited.

   **e.** Accounts Receivable is debited.

   **f.** Unearned Service Revenue is debited.

# Brief Exercises

*Indicate debit and credit effects.*

**BED.1 (LO 1), K** For each of the following accounts, indicate the effect of a debit or a credit on the account and the normal balance.

   **a.** Accounts Payable.

   **b.** Advertising Expense.

   **c.** Service Revenue.

   **d.** Accounts Receivable.

   **e.** Retained Earnings.

   **f.** Dividends.

*Identify accounts to be debited and credited.*

**BED.2 (LO 1), C** Transactions for Jayne Company for the month of June are as follows. Identify the accounts to be debited and credited for each transaction.

   June  1  Issues common stock to investors in exchange for $5,000 cash.

          2  Buys equipment on account for $1,100.

          3  Pays $740 to landlord for June rent.

        12  Sends Wil Wheaton a bill for $700 after completing welding work.

*Journalize transactions.*

**BED.3 (LO 2), AP** Journalize the following transactions for Jayne Company. (You may omit explanations.)

   June  1  Issues common stock to investors in exchange for $5,000 cash.

          2  Buys equipment on account for $1,100.

          3  Pays $740 to landlord for June rent.

        12  Sends Wil Wheaton a bill for $700 after completing welding work.

*Identify steps in the recording process.*

**BED.4 (LO 2), C** Rae Mohlee, a fellow student, is unclear about the basic steps in the recording process. Identify and briefly explain the steps in the order in which they occur.

**BED.5 (LO 2), AP** Selected transactions for Montes Company are presented below in journal form (without explanations). Post the transactions to T-accounts.

*Post journal entries to T-accounts.*

| Date | | Account Title | Debit | Credit |
|---|---|---|---|---|
| May | 5 | Accounts Receivable | 3,800 | |
| | | Service Revenue | | 3,800 |
| | 12 | Cash | 1,600 | |
| | | Accounts Receivable | | 1,600 |
| | 15 | Cash | 2,000 | |
| | | Service Revenue | | 2,000 |

**BED.6 (LO 3), AP** From the following ledger balances, prepare a trial balance for Peete Company at June 30, 2022. All account balances are normal.

*Prepare a trial balance.*

| | | | |
|---|---|---|---|
| Accounts Payable | $ 1,000 | Service Revenue | $8,600 |
| Cash | 5,400 | Accounts Receivable | 3,000 |
| Common Stock | 18,000 | Salaries and Wages Expense | 4,000 |
| Dividends | 1,200 | Rent Expense | 1,000 |
| Equipment | 13,000 | | |

**BED.7 (LO 4), AP** Lahey Advertising Company's trial balance at December 31 shows Supplies $8,800 and Supplies Expense $0. On December 31, there are $1,100 of supplies on hand. Prepare the adjusting entry at December 31 and, using T-accounts, enter the balances in the accounts, post the adjusting entry, and indicate the adjusted balance in each account.

*Prepare adjusting entry for supplies.*

**BED.8 (LO 4), AP** At the end of its first year, the trial balance of Rayburn Company shows Equipment $22,000 and zero balances in Accumulated Depreciation—Equipment and Depreciation Expense. Depreciation for the year is estimated to be $2,750. Prepare the annual adjusting entry for depreciation at December 31, post the adjustments to T-accounts, and indicate the balance sheet presentation of the equipment at December 31.

*Prepare adjusting entry for depreciation.*

**BED.9 (LO 4), AP** On July 1, 2022, Ling Co. pays $12,400 to Marsh Insurance Co. for a 2-year insurance contract. Both companies have fiscal years ending December 31. For Ling Co., journalize and post the entry on July 1 and the annual adjusting entry on December 31.

*Prepare adjusting entry for prepaid expense.*

**BED.10 (LO 4), AP** On July 1, 2022, Ling Co. pays $12,400 to Marsh Insurance Co. for a 2-year insurance contract. Both companies have fiscal years ending December 31. Journalize and post the entry on July 1 and the adjusting entry on December 31 for Marsh Insurance Co. Marsh uses the accounts Unearned Service Revenue and Service Revenue.

*Prepare adjusting entry for unearned revenue.*

**BED.11 (LO 4), AP** The bookkeeper for Tran Company asks you to prepare the following accrual adjusting entries at December 31. Use these account titles: Service Revenue, Accounts Receivable, Interest Expense, Interest Payable, Salaries and Wages Expense, and Salaries and Wages Payable.

*Prepare adjusting entries for accruals.*

a. Interest on notes payable of $300 is accrued.

b. Services performed but unbilled total $1,700.

c. Salaries of $780 earned by employees have not been recorded.

# Exercises

**ED.1 (LO 1), K** The following accounts, in alphabetical order, were selected from recent financial statements of **Krispy Kreme Doughnuts, Inc.**

*Identify normal account balance and corresponding financial statement.*

| | |
|---|---|
| Accounts Payable | Interest Income |
| Accounts Receivable | Inventories |
| Common Stock | Prepaid Expenses |
| Depreciation Expense | Property and Equipment |
| Interest Expense | Revenues |

### Instructions

For each account, indicate (a) whether the normal balance is a debit or a credit, and (b) the financial statement—balance sheet or income statement—where the account should be presented.

*Identify debits, credits, and normal balances and journalize transactions.*

**ED.2 (LO 1, 2), AP** Selected transactions for Front Room, an interior decorator corporation, in its first month of business, are as follows.

1. Issued stock to investors for $15,000 in cash.
2. Purchased used car for $10,000 cash for use in business.
3. Purchased supplies on account for $300.
4. Billed customers $3,700 for services performed.
5. Paid $200 cash for advertising at the start of the business.
6. Received $1,100 cash from customers billed in transaction (4).
7. Paid creditor $300 cash on account.
8. Paid dividends of $400 cash to stockholders.

### Instructions

a. For each transaction indicate (a) the basic type of account debited and credited (asset, liability, stockholders' equity); (b) the specific account debited and credited (Cash, Rent Expense, Service Revenue, etc.); (c) whether the specific account is increased or decreased; and (d) the normal balance of the specific account. Use the following format, in which transaction (1) is given as an example.

| | Account Debited | | | | Account Credited | | | |
|---|---|---|---|---|---|---|---|---|
| | (a) | (b) | (c) | (d) | (a) | (b) | (c) | (d) |
| Transaction | Basic Type | Specific Account | Effect | Normal Balance | Basic Type | Specific Account | Effect | Normal Balance |
| 1 | Asset | Cash | Increase | Debit | Stock-holders' equity | Common Stock | Increase | Credit |

b. Journalize the transactions. Do not provide explanations.

*Journalize a series of transactions.*

**ED.3 (LO 2), AP** The May transactions of Chulak Corporation were as follows.

| May | 4 | Paid $700 due for supplies previously purchased on account. |
|---|---|---|
| | 7 | Performed advisory services on account for $6,800. |
| | 8 | Purchased supplies for $850 on account. |
| | 9 | Purchased equipment for $1,000 in cash. |
| | 17 | Paid employees $530 in cash. |
| | 22 | Received bill for equipment repairs of $900. |
| | 29 | Paid $1,200 for 12 months of insurance policy. Coverage begins June 1. |

### Instructions

Journalize the transactions. Do not provide explanations.

*Journalize a series of transactions.*

**ED.4 (LO 2), AP** Selected transactions for Sophie's Dog Care are as follows during the month of March.

| March | 1 | Paid monthly rent of $1,200. |
|---|---|---|
| | 3 | Performed services for $140 on account. |
| | 5 | Performed services for cash of $75. |
| | 8 | Purchased equipment for $600. The company paid cash of $80 and the balance was on account. |
| | 12 | Received cash from customers billed on March 3. |
| | 14 | Paid wages to employees of $525. |
| | 22 | Paid utilities of $72. |
| | 24 | Borrowed $1,500 from Grafton State Bank by signing a note. |
| | 27 | Paid $220 to repair service for plumbing repairs. |
| | 28 | Paid balance amount owed from equipment purchase on March 8. |
| | 30 | Paid $1,800 for six months of insurance. |

### Instructions

Journalize the transactions. Do not provide explanations.

**ED.5 (LO 2), AP** On April 1, Adventures Travel Agency, Inc. began operations. The following transactions were completed during the month. *Record journal entries.*

1. Issued common stock for $24,000 cash.
2. Obtained a bank loan for $7,000 by issuing a note payable.
3. Paid $11,000 cash to buy equipment.
4. Paid $1,200 cash for April office rent.
5. Paid $1,450 for supplies.
6. Purchased $600 of advertising in the *Daily Herald,* on account.
7. Performed services for $18,000: cash of $2,000 was received from customers, and the balance of $16,000 was billed to customers on account.
8. Paid $400 cash dividend to stockholders.
9. Paid the utility bill for the month, $2,000.
10. Paid *Daily Herald* the amount due in transaction (6).
11. Paid $40 of interest on the bank loan obtained in transaction (2).
12. Paid employees' salaries, $6,400.
13. Received $12,000 cash from customers billed in transaction (7).
14. Paid income tax, $1,500.

**Instructions**

Journalize the transactions. Do not provide explanations.

**ED.6 (LO 2, 3), AN** The following T-accounts summarize the ledger of Salvador's Gardening Company, Inc. at the end of the first month of operations. *Journalize transactions from T-accounts and prepare a trial balance.*

| Cash | | | | | Unearned Service Revenue | | |
|---|---|---|---|---|---|---|---|
| Apr. | 1 | 15,000 | Apr. | 15 | 800 | Apr. 30 | 900 |
| | 12 | 700 | | 25 | 3,500 | | |
| | 29 | 800 | | | | | |
| | 30 | 900 | | | | | |

| Accounts Receivable | | | | | Common Stock | | |
|---|---|---|---|---|---|---|---|
| Apr. | 7 | 3,400 | Apr. | 29 | 800 | Apr. 1 | 15,000 |

| Supplies | | | Service Revenue | | |
|---|---|---|---|---|---|
| Apr. | 4 | 5,200 | Apr. | 7 | 3,400 |
| | | | | 12 | 700 |

| Accounts Payable | | | | | Salaries and Wages Expense | | |
|---|---|---|---|---|---|---|---|
| Apr. | 25 | 3,500 | Apr. | 4 | 5,200 | Apr. | 15 | 800 |

**Instructions**

a. Prepare the journal entries (including explanations) that resulted in the amounts posted to the accounts. Present them in the order they occurred.
b. Prepare a trial balance at April 30, 2022. (*Hint:* Compute ending balances of T-accounts first.)

**ED.7 (LO 2, 3), AP** Selected transactions from the journal of Baylee Inc. during its first month of operations are presented here. *Post journal entries and prepare a trial balance.*

| Date | | Account Titles | Debit | Credit |
|---|---|---|---|---|
| Aug. | 1 | Cash | 8,000 | |
| | | Common Stock | | 8,000 |
| | 10 | Cash | 1,700 | |
| | | Service Revenue | | 1,700 |
| | 12 | Equipment | 6,200 | |
| | | Cash | | 1,200 |
| | | Notes Payable | | 5,000 |
| | 25 | Accounts Receivable | 3,400 | |
| | | Service Revenue | | 3,400 |
| | 31 | Cash | 600 | |
| | | Accounts Receivable | | 600 |

**Instructions**

a. Post the transactions to T-accounts.

b. Prepare a trial balance at August 31, 2022.

*Journalize transactions, post transactions to T-accounts, and prepare trial balance.*

**ED.8 (LO 2, 3), AP** Beyers Corporation provides security services. Selected transactions for Beyers are presented here.

Oct. 1  Issued common stock in exchange for $66,000 cash from investors.

2  Hired part-time security consultant. Salary will be $2,000 per month. First day of work will be October 15.

4  Paid 1 month of rent for building for $2,000.

7  Purchased equipment for $18,000, paying $4,000 cash and the balance on account.

8  Paid $500 for advertising.

10  Received bill for equipment repair cost of $390.

12  Provided security services for event for $3,200 on account.

16  Purchased supplies for $410 on account.

21  Paid balance due from October 7 purchase of equipment.

24  Received and paid utility bill for $148.

27  Received payment from customer for October 12 services performed.

31  Paid employee salaries and wages of $5,100.

**Instructions**

a. Journalize the transactions. Do not provide explanations.

b. Post the transactions to T-accounts.

c. Prepare a trial balance at October 31, 2022. (*Hint:* Compute ending balances of T-accounts first.)

*Prepare a trial balance and financial statements.*

**ED.9 (LO 3), AP** The accounts in the ledger of Rapid Delivery Service contain the following balances on July 31, 2022.

| | | | |
|---|---|---|---|
| Accounts Receivable | $13,400 | Prepaid Insurance | $ 2,200 |
| Accounts Payable | 8,400 | Service Revenue | 15,500 |
| Cash | ? | Dividends | 700 |
| Equipment | 59,360 | Common Stock | 40,000 |
| Maintenance and | | Salaries and Wages Expense | 7,428 |
| Repairs Expense | 1,958 | Salaries and Wages Payable | 820 |
| Insurance Expense | 900 | Retained Earnings (July 1, 2022) | 5,200 |
| Notes Payable (due 2025) | 28,450 | | |

**Instructions**

a. Prepare a trial balance with the accounts arranged as illustrated in the appendix, and fill in the missing amount for Cash.

b. Prepare an income statement, a retained earnings statement, and a classified balance sheet for the month of July 2022.

*Identify types of adjustments and accounts before adjustment.*

**ED.10 (LO 2, 4), AN** Wang Company accumulates the following adjustment data at December 31.

a. Services performed but unbilled total $600.

b. Store supplies of $160 are on hand. The supplies account shows a $1,900 balance.

c. Utility expenses of $275 are unpaid.

d. Service performed of $490 collected in advance.

e. Salaries of $620 are unpaid.

f. Prepaid insurance totaling $400 has expired.

**Instructions**

For each item, indicate (1) the type of adjustment (prepaid expense, unearned revenue, accrued revenue, or accrued expense) and (2) the status of the accounts before adjustment (overstated or understand).

**ED.11 (LO 2, 4), AP** The ledger of Howard Rental Agency on March 31 of the current year includes the following selected accounts before adjusting entries have been prepared.

*Prepare adjusting entries from selected account data.*

|  | Debit | Credit |
|---|---|---|
| Supplies | $ 3,000 | |
| Prepaid Insurance | 3,600 | |
| Equipment | 25,000 | |
| Accumulated Depreciation—Equipment | | $ 8,400 |
| Notes Payable | | 20,000 |
| Unearned Rent Revenue | | 12,400 |
| Rent Revenue | | 60,000 |
| Salaries and Wages Expense | 14,000 | |

An analysis of the accounts shows the following.

1. The equipment depreciates $280 per month.

2. Half of the unearned rent revenue was earned during the quarter.

3. Interest of $400 is accrued on the notes payable.

4. Supplies on hand total $850.

5. Insurance expires at the rate of $400 per month.

**Instructions**

Prepare the adjusting entries at March 31, assuming that the adjusting entries are made quarterly. Additional accounts are Depreciation Expense, Insurance Expense, Interest Expense, Interest Payable, and Supplies Expense.

**ED.12 (LO 2, 4), AP** The ledger of Armour Lake Lumber Supply on July 31, 2022, includes the selected accounts shown here before adjusting entries have been prepared.

*Prepare adjusting entries from selected account data.*

|  | Debit | Credit |
|---|---|---|
| Notes Receivable | $ 20,000 | |
| Supplies | 24,000 | |
| Prepaid Rent | 3,600 | |
| Buildings | 250,000 | |
| Accumulated Depreciation—Buildings | | $140,000 |
| Unearned Service Revenue | | 11,500 |

An analysis of the company's accounts shows the following.

1. The investment in the notes receivable earns interest at a rate of 6% per year.

2. Supplies on hand at the end of the month totaled $18,600.

3. The balance in Prepaid Rent represents 4 months of rent costs.

4. Employees were owed $3,100 related to unpaid salaries and wages.

5. Depreciation on buildings is $6,000 per year.

6. During the month, services related to unearned service revenue of $4,700 were performed.

7. Unpaid maintenance and repairs costs were $2,300.

**Instructions**

Prepare the adjusting entries at July 31 assuming that adjusting entries are made monthly. Use additional accounts as needed.

# Problems

*Journalize a series of transactions.*

**PD.1 (LO 2), AP** Bradley's Miniature Golf and Driving Range Inc. was opened on March 1 by Bob Dean. These selected events and transactions occurred during March.

Mar. 1    Stockholders invested $50,000 cash in the business in exchange for common stock of the corporation.

3    Purchased Snead's Golf Land for $38,000 cash. The price consists of land $23,000, building $9,000, and equipment $6,000. (Record this in a single entry.)

5    Advertised the opening of the driving range and miniature golf course, paying advertising expenses of $1,200 cash.

6    Paid cash $2,400 for a 1-year insurance policy.

10    Purchased golf clubs and other equipment for $5,500 from Tahoe Company, payable in 30 days.

18    Received golf fees of $1,600 in cash from customers for golf services performed.

19    Sold 100 coupon books for $25 each in cash. Each book contains 10 coupons that enable the holder to play one round of miniature golf or to hit one bucket of golf balls. (*Hint:* The revenue should not be recognized until the customers use the coupons.)

25    Paid a $500 cash dividend.

30    Paid salaries of $800.

30    Paid Tahoe Company in full for equipment purchased on March 10.

31    Received $900 in cash from customers for golf services performed.

The company uses these accounts: Cash, Prepaid Insurance, Land, Buildings, Equipment, Accounts Payable, Unearned Service Revenue, Common Stock, Retained Earnings, Dividends, Service Revenue, Advertising Expense, and Salaries and Wages Expense.

## Instructions

Journalize the March transactions, including explanations. Bradley's records golf fees as service revenue.

*Journalize transactions, post, and prepare a trial balance.*

**PD.2 (LO 2, 3), AP** Ayala Architects incorporated as licensed architects on April 1, 2022. During the first month of the operation of the business, these events and transactions occurred:

Apr. 1    Stockholders invested $18,000 cash in exchange for common stock of the corporation.

1    Hired a secretary-receptionist at a salary of $375 per week, payable monthly.

2    Paid office rent for the month $900.

3    Purchased architectural supplies on account from Burmingham Company $1,300.

10    Completed blueprints on a carport and billed client $1,900 for services.

11    Received $700 cash advance from M. Jason to design a new home.

20    Received $2,800 cash for services completed and delivered to S. Melvin.

30    Paid secretary-receptionist for the month $1,500.

30    Paid $300 to Burmingham Company for accounts payable due.

The company uses these accounts: Cash, Accounts Receivable, Supplies, Accounts Payable, Unearned Service Revenue, Common Stock, Service Revenue, Salaries and Wages Expense, and Rent Expense.

## Instructions

a. Journalize the transactions, including explanations.

b. Post to the ledger T-accounts.

*(c) Cash    $18,800*

*Tot. trial balance    $24,400*

c. Prepare a trial balance on April 30, 2022.

**PD.3 (LO 2, 3), AP** This is the trial balance of Lacey Company on September 30.

*Journalize transactions, post, and prepare a trial balance.*

**Lacey Company**
**Trial Balance**
**September 30, 2022**

| | Debit | Credit |
|---|---|---|
| Cash | $19,200 | |
| Accounts Receivable | 2,600 | |
| Supplies | 2,100 | |
| Equipment | 8,000 | |
| Accounts Payable | | $ 4,800 |
| Unearned Service Revenue | | 1,100 |
| Common Stock | | 15,000 |
| Retained Earnings | | 11,000 |
| | $31,900 | $31,900 |

The October transactions were as follows.

Oct.  5  Received $1,300 in cash from customers for accounts receivable due.
     10  Billed customers for services performed $5,100.
     15  Paid employee salaries $1,200.
     17  Performed $600 of services in exchange for cash.
     20  Paid $1,900 to creditors for accounts payable due.
     29  Paid a $300 cash dividend.
     31  Paid utilities $400.

### Instructions

a. Prepare a general ledger using T-accounts. Enter the opening balances in the ledger accounts as of October 1. (*Hint:* The October 1 beginning amounts are the September 30 balances in the trial balance above.) Provision should be made for these additional accounts: Dividends, Service Revenue, Salaries and Wages Expense, and Utilities Expense.

b. Journalize the transactions, including explanations.

c. Post to the ledger accounts.

d. Prepare a trial balance on October 31, 2022.

(d) Cash                        $17,300
Tot. trial balance    $35,700

**PD.4 (LO 2, 4), AP** Len Kumar started his own consulting firm, Kumar Consulting, on June 1, 2022. The trial balance at June 30 is as follows.

*Prepare adjusting entries, post to ledger accounts, prepare adjusted trial balance.*

**Kumar Consulting**
**Trial Balance**
**June 30, 2022**

| | Debit | Credit |
|---|---|---|
| Cash | $ 6,850 | |
| Accounts Receivable | 7,000 | |
| Supplies | 2,000 | |
| Prepaid Insurance | 2,880 | |
| Equipment | 15,000 | |
| Accounts Payable | | $ 4,230 |
| Unearned Service Revenue | | 5,200 |
| Common Stock | | 22,000 |
| Service Revenue | | 8,300 |
| Salaries and Wages Expense | 4,000 | |
| Rent Expense | 2,000 | |
| | $39,730 | $39,730 |

In addition to those accounts listed on the trial balance, the chart of accounts for Kumar also contains the following accounts: Accumulated Depreciation—Equipment, Salaries and Wages Payable, Depreciation Expense, Insurance Expense, Utilities Expense, and Supplies Expense.

Other data:

1. Supplies on hand at June 30 total $720.
2. A utility bill for $180 has not been recorded and will not be paid until next month.

3. The insurance policy is for a year.

4. Services were performed for $4,100 of unearned service revenue by the end of the month.

5. Salaries of $1,250 are accrued at June 30.

6. The equipment has a 5-year life with no salvage value and is being depreciated at $250 per month for 60 months.

7. Invoices representing $3,900 of services performed during the month have not been recorded as of June 30.

### Instructions

a. Prepare the adjusting entries for the month of June.

b. Enter the totals from the trial balance as beginning account balances and then post the adjusting entries to the ledger accounts. (Use T-accounts.)

c. Prepare an adjusted trial balance at June 30, 2022.

*(b) Service rev.*    $16,300

*(c) Tot. trial balance*    $45,310

*Journalize transactions and follow through accounting cycle to preparation of financial statements.*

**PD.5 (LO 2, 3, 4), AP** On November 1, 2022, the following were the account balances of Soho Equipment Repair.

| | Debit | | Credit |
|---|---|---|---|
| Cash | $ 2,790 | Accumulated Depreciation—Equipment | $ 500 |
| Accounts Receivable | 2,910 | Accounts Payable | 2,300 |
| Supplies | 1,120 | Unearned Service Revenue | 400 |
| Equipment | 10,000 | Salaries and Wages Payable | 620 |
| | | Common Stock | 10,000 |
| | | Retained Earnings | 3,000 |
| | $16,820 | | $16,820 |

During November, the following summary transactions were completed.

Nov.   8   Paid $1,220 for salaries due employees, of which $600 is for November and $620 is for October salaries payable.

     10   Received $1,800 cash from customers in payment of account.

     12   Received $3,700 cash for services performed in November.

     15   Purchased store equipment on account $3,600.

     17   Purchased supplies on account $1,300.

     20   Paid creditors $2,500 of accounts payable due.

     22   Paid November rent $480.

     25   Paid salaries $1,000.

     27   Performed services on account worth $900 and billed customers.

     29   Received $750 from customers for services to be performed in the future.

Adjustment data:

1. Supplies on hand are valued at $1,100.

2. Accrued salaries payable are $480.

3. Depreciation for the month is $250.

4. Services were performed to satisfy $500 of unearned service revenue.

### Instructions

a. Enter the November 1 balances in the ledger accounts. (Use T-accounts.)

b. Journalize the November transactions. Use Service Revenue, Depreciation Expense, Supplies Expense, Salaries and Wages Expense, and Rent Expense.

c. Post to the ledger accounts.

d. Prepare a trial balance at November 30.

e. Journalize and post adjusting entries.

f. Prepare an adjusted trial balance.

g. Prepare an income statement and a retained earnings statement for November and a classified balance sheet at November 30.

*(f) Cash*    $3,840

*Tot. adj. trial balance*    $24,680

*(g) Net income*    $970

# Time Value of Money

## Appendix Preview

Would you rather receive $1,000 today or a year from now? You should prefer to receive the $1,000 today because you can invest the $1,000 and then earn interest on it. As a result, you will have more than $1,000 a year from now. What this example illustrates is the concept of the **time value of money**. Everyone prefers to receive money today rather than in the future because of the interest factor.

## Appendix Outline

### LEARNING OBJECTIVES

| | |
|---|---|
| **1.** Compute interest and future values. | • Nature of interest<br>• Future value of a single amount<br>• Future value of an annuity |
| **2.** Compute present values. | • Present value variables<br>• Present value of a single amount<br>• Present value of an annuity<br>• Time periods and discounting<br>• Present value of a long-term note or bond |
| **3.** Compute the present value in capital budgeting situations. | • Using alternative discount rates |
| **4.** Use a financial calculator to solve time value of money problems. | • Present value of a single sum<br>• Present value of an annuity<br>• Future value of a single sum<br>• Future value of an annuity<br>• Internal rate of return<br>• Useful financial calculator applications |

# Interest and Future Values

## Nature of Interest

**Interest** is payment for the use of another party's money.

- It is the difference between the amount borrowed or invested (called the **principal**) and the amount repaid or collected.
- The amount of interest to be paid or collected is usually stated as a rate over a specific period of time.
- The rate of interest is generally stated as an annual rate.

The amount of interest involved in any financing transaction is based on three elements:

1. **Principal ($p$):** The original amount borrowed or invested.
2. **Interest rate ($i$):** An annual percentage of the principal.
3. **Time ($n$):** The number of periods over which the principal is borrowed or invested.

## Simple Interest

**Simple interest** is computed on the principal amount only.

- It is the return on the principal for one period (we use an annual interest rate unless stated otherwise).
- Simple interest is usually expressed as shown in **Illustration E.1**.

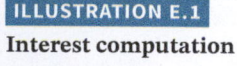

**ILLUSTRATION E.1**
Interest computation

| Interest | = | Principal $p$ | × | Rate $i$ | × | Time $n$ |
|----------|---|---------------|---|----------|---|----------|

For example, if you borrowed $5,000 for 2 years at a simple interest rate of 12% annually, you would pay $1,200 in total interest, computed as follows.

$$
\begin{aligned}
\text{Interest} &= p && \times && i && \times && n \\
&= \$5{,}000 && \times && .12 && \times && 2 \\
&= \$1{,}200
\end{aligned}
$$

## Compound Interest

**Compound interest** is computed on principal **and** on any interest earned that has not been paid or withdrawn.

- It is the return on (or growth of) the principal for two or more time periods.
- Compounding computes interest not only on the principal but also on the interest earned to date on that principal, assuming the interest is left on deposit.

To illustrate the difference between simple and compound interest, assume that you deposit $1,000 in Bank Two, where it will earn simple interest of 9% per year, and you deposit another $1,000 in Citizens Bank, where it will earn compound interest of 9% per year compounded annually. Also assume that in both cases you will not withdraw any cash until three years from the date of deposit. **Illustration E.2** shows the computation of interest to be received and the accumulated year-end balances.

**ILLUSTRATION E.2**  Simple versus compound interest

| Bank Two | | | | Citizens Bank | | |
|---|---|---|---|---|---|---|
| Simple Interest Calculation | Simple Interest | Accumulated Year-End Balance | | Compound Interest Calculation | Compound Interest | Accumulated Year-End Balance |
| Year 1  $1,000.00 × 9% | $  90.00 | $1,090.00 | | Year 1  $1,000.00 × 9% | $  90.00 | $1,090.00 |
| Year 2  $1,000.00 × 9% | 90.00 | $1,180.00 | | Year 2  $1,090.00 × 9% | 98.10 | $1,188.10 |
| Year 3  $1,000.00 × 9% | 90.00 | $1,270.00 | | Year 3  $1,188.10 × 9% | 106.93 | $1,295.03 |
| | $ 270.00 | | $25.03 Difference | | $ 295.03 | |

Note the following in Illustration E.2:

- Simple interest uses the initial principal of $1,000 to compute the interest in all three years.
- Compound interest uses the accumulated balance (principal plus interest to date) at each year-end to compute interest in the succeeding year—which explains why your compound interest account is larger.

Obviously, if you had a choice between investing your money at simple interest or at compound interest, you would choose compound interest, all other things—especially risk—being equal. In the example, compounding provides $25.03 of additional interest income. For practical purposes, compounding assumes that unpaid interest earned becomes a part of the principal, and the accumulated balance at the end of each year becomes the new principal on which interest is earned during the next year.

Most business situations use compound interest. Simple interest is generally applicable only to short-term situations of one year or less.

# Future Value of a Single Amount

The **future value of a single amount** is the value at a future date of a given amount invested, assuming compound interest. For example, in Illustration E.2, $1,295.03 is the future value of the $1,000 investment earning 9% for three years. The $1,295.03 is determined more easily by using the formula shown in **Illustration E.3**.

$$FV = p \times (1 + i)^n$$

**ILLUSTRATION E.3**

**Formula for future value**

where:

$FV$ = future value of a single amount
$p$ = principal (or present value; the value today)
$i$ = interest rate for one period
$n$ = number of periods

The $1,295.03 is computed as follows.

$$
\begin{aligned}
FV &= p \times (1 + i)^n \\
&= \$1,000 \times (1 + .09)^3 \\
&= \$1,000 \times 1.29503 \\
&= \$1,295.03
\end{aligned}
$$

The 1.29503 is computed by multiplying (1.09 × 1.09 × 1.09). The amounts in this example can be depicted in the time diagram shown in **Illustration E.4**.

ILLUSTRATION E.4 **Time Diagram**

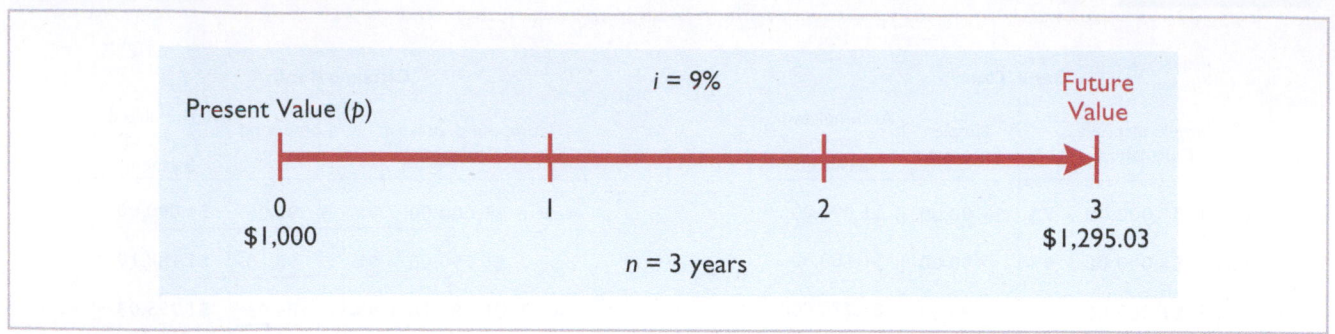

Another method used to compute the future value of a single amount involves a compound interest table. This table shows the future value of 1 for *n* periods. **Table 1** is such a table.

**TABLE 1** **Future Value of 1**

| (n) Periods | 4% | 5% | 6% | 7% | 8% | 9% | 10% | 11% | 12% | 15% |
|---|---|---|---|---|---|---|---|---|---|---|
| 0 | 1.00000 | 1.00000 | 1.00000 | 1.00000 | 1.00000 | 1.00000 | 1.00000 | 1.00000 | 1.00000 | 1.00000 |
| 1 | 1.04000 | 1.05000 | 1.06000 | 1.07000 | 1.08000 | 1.09000 | 1.10000 | 1.11000 | 1.12000 | 1.15000 |
| 2 | 1.08160 | 1.10250 | 1.12360 | 1.14490 | 1.16640 | 1.18810 | 1.21000 | 1.23210 | 1.25440 | 1.32250 |
| 3 | 1.12486 | 1.15763 | 1.19102 | 1.22504 | 1.25971 | 1.29503 | 1.33100 | 1.36763 | 1.40493 | 1.52088 |
| 4 | 1.16986 | 1.21551 | 1.26248 | 1.31080 | 1.36049 | 1.41158 | 1.46410 | 1.51807 | 1.57352 | 1.74901 |
| 5 | 1.21665 | 1.27628 | 1.33823 | 1.40255 | 1.46933 | 1.53862 | 1.61051 | 1.68506 | 1.76234 | 2.01136 |
| 6 | 1.26532 | 1.34010 | 1.41852 | 1.50073 | 1.58687 | 1.67710 | 1.77156 | 1.87041 | 1.97382 | 2.31306 |
| 7 | 1.31593 | 1.40710 | 1.50363 | 1.60578 | 1.71382 | 1.82804 | 1.94872 | 2.07616 | 2.21068 | 2.66002 |
| 8 | 1.36857 | 1.47746 | 1.59385 | 1.71819 | 1.85093 | 1.99256 | 2.14359 | 2.30454 | 2.47596 | 3.05902 |
| 9 | 1.42331 | 1.55133 | 1.68948 | 1.83846 | 1.99900 | 2.17189 | 2.35795 | 2.55803 | 2.77308 | 3.51788 |
| 10 | 1.48024 | 1.62889 | 1.79085 | 1.96715 | 2.15892 | 2.36736 | 2.59374 | 2.83942 | 3.10585 | 4.04556 |
| 11 | 1.53945 | 1.71034 | 1.89830 | 2.10485 | 2.33164 | 2.58043 | 2.85312 | 3.15176 | 3.47855 | 4.65239 |
| 12 | 1.60103 | 1.79586 | 2.01220 | 2.25219 | 2.51817 | 2.81267 | 3.13843 | 3.49845 | 3.89598 | 5.35025 |
| 13 | 1.66507 | 1.88565 | 2.13293 | 2.40985 | 2.71962 | 3.06581 | 3.45227 | 3.88328 | 4.36349 | 6.15279 |
| 14 | 1.73168 | 1.97993 | 2.26090 | 2.57853 | 2.93719 | 3.34173 | 3.79750 | 4.31044 | 4.88711 | 7.07571 |
| 15 | 1.80094 | 2.07893 | 2.39656 | 2.75903 | 3.17217 | 3.64248 | 4.17725 | 4.78459 | 5.47357 | 8.13706 |
| 16 | 1.87298 | 2.18287 | 2.54035 | 2.95216 | 3.42594 | 3.97031 | 4.59497 | 5.31089 | 6.13039 | 9.35762 |
| 17 | 1.94790 | 2.29202 | 2.69277 | 3.15882 | 3.70002 | 4.32763 | 5.05447 | 5.89509 | 6.86604 | 10.76126 |
| 18 | 2.02582 | 2.40662 | 2.85434 | 3.37993 | 3.99602 | 4.71712 | 5.55992 | 6.54355 | 7.68997 | 12.37545 |
| 19 | 2.10685 | 2.52695 | 3.02560 | 3.61653 | 4.31570 | 5.14166 | 6.11591 | 7.26334 | 8.61276 | 14.23177 |
| 20 | 2.19112 | 2.65330 | 3.20714 | 3.86968 | 4.66096 | 5.60441 | 6.72750 | 8.06231 | 9.64629 | 16.36654 |

- In Table 1, *n* is the number of compounding periods, the percentages are the periodic interest rates, and the five-digit decimal numbers in the respective columns are the future value of 1 factors.

- To use Table 1, you multiply the principal amount by the future value factor for the specified number of periods and interest rate. For example, the future value factor for two periods at 9% is 1.18810.

- Multiplying this factor by $1,000 equals $1,188.10—which is the accumulated balance at the end of year 2 in the Citizens Bank example in Illustration E.2.

- The $1,295.03 accumulated balance at the end of the third year is calculated from Table 1 by multiplying the future value factor for three periods (1.29503) by the $1,000.

The demonstration problem in **Illustration E.5** shows how to use Table 1.

ILLUSTRATION E.5  **Demonstration problem—Using Table 1 for *FV* of 1**

John and Mary Rich invested $20,000 in a savings account paying 6% interest at the time their son, Mike, was born. The money is to be used by Mike for his college education. On his 18th birthday, Mike withdraws the money from his savings account. How much did Mike withdraw from his account?

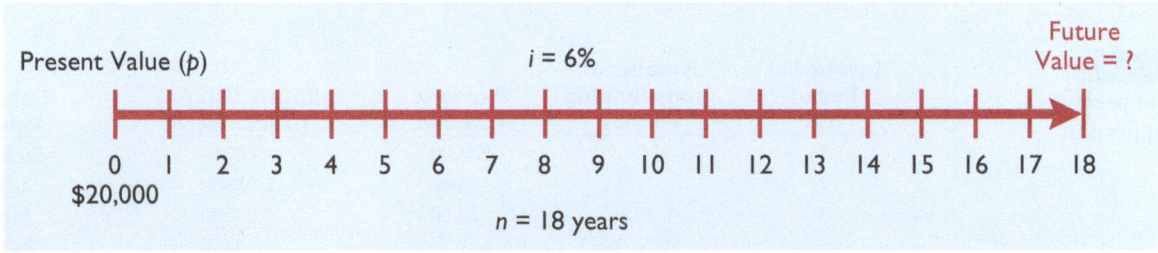

Present Value (p)          *i* = 6%          Future Value = ?

0  1  2  3  4  5  6  7  8  9  10  11  12  13  14  15  16  17  18
$20,000

*n* = 18 years

**Answer:** The future value factor from Table 1 is 2.85434 (18 periods at 6%). The future value of $20,000 earning 6% per year for 18 years is **$57,086.80** ($20,000 × 2.85434).

# Future Value of an Annuity

The preceding discussion involved the accumulation of only a single principal sum. Individuals and businesses frequently encounter situations in which a **series** of equal dollar amounts are to be paid or received at evenly spaced time intervals (periodically), such as loans or lease (rental) contracts.

- A series of payments or receipts of equal dollar amounts is referred to as an **annuity**.

- The **future value of an annuity** is the sum of all the payments (receipts) plus the accumulated compound interest on them.

- In computing the future value of an annuity, it is necessary to know:

  1. The interest rate.

  2. The number of payments (receipts).

  3. The amount of the periodic payments (receipts).

To illustrate the computation of the future value of an annuity, assume that you invest $2,000 at the end of each year for three years at 5% interest compounded annually. This situation is depicted in the time diagram in **Illustration E.6**.

**ILLUSTRATION E.6** Time diagram for a three-year annuity

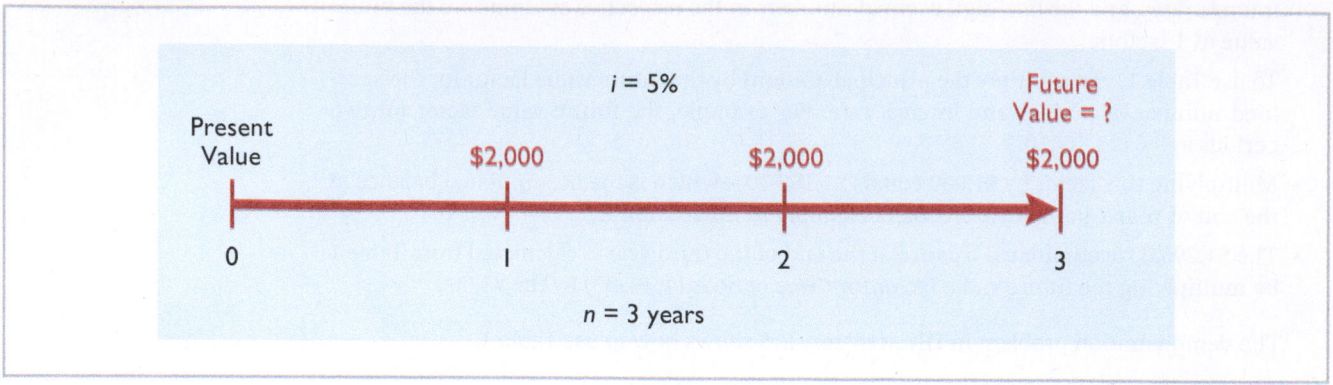

The $2,000 invested at the end of year 1 will earn interest for two years (years 2 and 3), and the $2,000 invested at the end of year 2 will earn interest for one year (year 3). However, the last $2,000 investment (made at the end of year 3) will not earn any interest. Using the future value factors from Table 1, the future value of these periodic payments is computed as shown in **Illustration E.7**.

**ILLUSTRATION E.7**

Future value of periodic payment computation

| Invested at End of Year | Number of Compounding Periods | Amount Invested | × | Future Value of 1 Factor at 5% | = | Future Value |
|---|---|---|---|---|---|---|
| 1 | 2 | $2,000 | | 1.10250 | | $2,205 |
| 2 | 1 | 2,000 | | 1.05000 | | 2,100 |
| 3 | 0 | 2,000 | | 1.00000 | | 2,000 |
| | | | | **3.15250** | | **$6,305** |

- The first $2,000 investment is multiplied by the future value factor for two periods (1.1025) because two years' interest will accumulate on it (in years 2 and 3).

- The second $2,000 investment will earn only one year's interest (in year 3) and therefore is multiplied by the future value factor for one year (1.0500).

- The final $2,000 investment is made at the end of the third year and will not earn any interest. Thus, $n = 0$ and the future value factor is 1.00000. Consequently, the future value of the last $2,000 invested is only $2,000 since it does not accumulate any interest.

Calculating the future value of each individual cash flow is required when the periodic payments or receipts are not equal in each period. However, when the periodic payments (receipts) are **the same in each period**, the future value can be computed by using a future value of an annuity of 1 table. **Table 2** is such a table.

**TABLE 2**   **Future Value of an Annuity of 1**

| (n) Payments | 4% | 5% | 6% | 7% | 8% | 9% | 10% | 11% | 12% | 15% |
|---|---|---|---|---|---|---|---|---|---|---|
| 1 | 1.00000 | 1.00000 | 1.00000 | 1.0000 | 1.00000 | 1.00000 | 1.00000 | 1.00000 | 1.00000 | 1.00000 |
| 2 | 2.04000 | 2.05000 | 2.06000 | 2.0700 | 2.08000 | 2.09000 | 2.10000 | 2.11000 | 2.12000 | 2.15000 |
| 3 | 3.12160 | 3.15250 | 3.18360 | 3.2149 | 3.24640 | 3.27810 | 3.31000 | 3.34210 | 3.37440 | 3.47250 |
| 4 | 4.24646 | 4.31013 | 4.37462 | 4.4399 | 4.50611 | 4.57313 | 4.64100 | 4.70973 | 4.77933 | 4.99338 |
| 5 | 5.41632 | 5.52563 | 5.63709 | 5.7507 | 5.86660 | 5.98471 | 6.10510 | 6.22780 | 6.35285 | 6.74238 |
| 6 | 6.63298 | 6.80191 | 6.97532 | 7.1533 | 7.33592 | 7.52334 | 7.71561 | 7.91286 | 8.11519 | 8.75374 |
| 7 | 7.89829 | 8.14201 | 8.39384 | 8.6540 | 8.92280 | 9.20044 | 9.48717 | 9.78327 | 10.08901 | 11.06680 |
| 8 | 9.21423 | 9.54911 | 9.89747 | 10.2598 | 10.63663 | 11.02847 | 11.43589 | 11.85943 | 12.29969 | 13.72682 |
| 9 | 10.58280 | 11.02656 | 11.49132 | 11.9780 | 12.48756 | 13.02104 | 13.57948 | 14.16397 | 14.77566 | 16.78584 |
| 10 | 12.00611 | 12.57789 | 13.18079 | 13.8164 | 14.48656 | 15.19293 | 15.93743 | 16.72201 | 17.54874 | 20.30372 |
| 11 | 13.48635 | 14.20679 | 14.97164 | 15.7836 | 16.64549 | 17.56029 | 18.53117 | 19.56143 | 20.65458 | 24.34928 |
| 12 | 15.02581 | 15.91713 | 16.86994 | 17.8885 | 18.97713 | 20.14072 | 21.38428 | 22.71319 | 24.13313 | 29.00167 |
| 13 | 16.62684 | 17.71298 | 18.88214 | 20.1406 | 21.49530 | 22.95339 | 24.52271 | 26.21164 | 28.02911 | 34.35192 |
| 14 | 18.29191 | 19.59863 | 21.01507 | 22.5505 | 24.21492 | 26.01919 | 27.97498 | 30.09492 | 32.39260 | 40.50471 |
| 15 | 20.02359 | 21.57856 | 23.27597 | 25.1290 | 27.15211 | 29.36092 | 31.77248 | 34.40536 | 37.27972 | 47.58041 |
| 16 | 21.82453 | 23.65749 | 25.67253 | 27.8881 | 30.32428 | 33.00340 | 35.94973 | 39.18995 | 42.75328 | 55.71747 |
| 17 | 23.69751 | 25.84037 | 28.21288 | 30.8402 | 33.75023 | 36.97351 | 40.54470 | 44.50084 | 48.88367 | 65.07509 |
| 18 | 25.64541 | 28.13238 | 30.90565 | 33.9990 | 37.45024 | 41.30134 | 45.59917 | 50.39593 | 55.74972 | 75.83636 |
| 19 | 27.67123 | 30.53900 | 33.75999 | 37.3790 | 41.44626 | 46.01846 | 51.15909 | 56.93949 | 63.43968 | 88.21181 |
| 20 | 29.77808 | 33.06595 | 36.78559 | 40.9955 | 45.76196 | 51.16012 | 57.27500 | 64.20283 | 72.05244 | 102.44358 |

- Table 2 shows the future value of 1 to be received periodically for a given number of payments. It assumes that each payment is made at the **end** of each period.
- We can see from Table 2 that the future value of an annuity of 1 factor for three payments at 5% is 3.15250.
- The future value factor is the total of the three individual future value factors shown in Illustration E.7. Multiplying this amount by the annual investment of $2,000 produces a future value of $6,305.

The demonstration problem in **Illustration E.8** shows how to use Table 2.

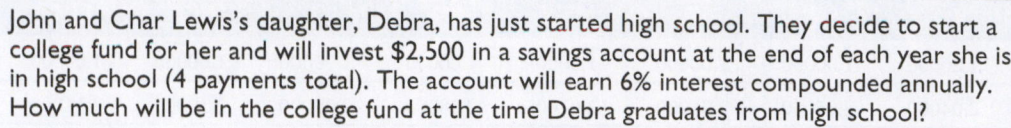

**ILLUSTRATION E.8**   Demonstration problem—Using Table 2 for *FV* of an annuity of 1

John and Char Lewis's daughter, Debra, has just started high school. They decide to start a college fund for her and will invest $2,500 in a savings account at the end of each year she is in high school (4 payments total). The account will earn 6% interest compounded annually. How much will be in the college fund at the time Debra graduates from high school?

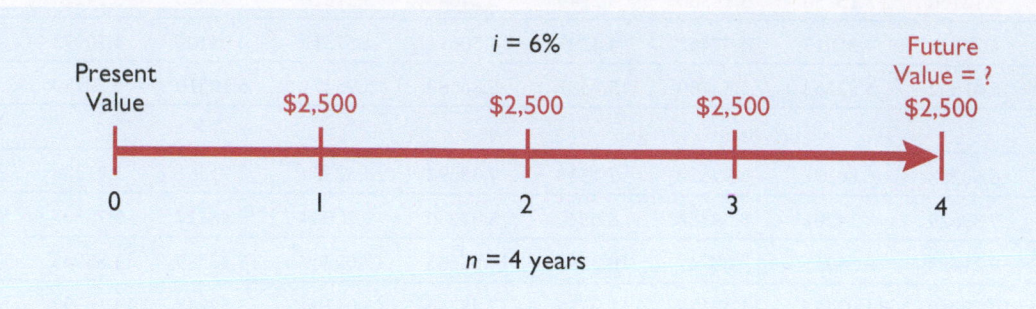

**Answer:** The future value factor from Table 2 is 4.37462 (4 payments at 6%). The future value of $2,500 invested each year for 4 years at 6% interest is **$10,936.55** ($2,500 × 4.37462).

# Present Values

**LEARNING OBJECTIVE 2**
Compute present values.

## Present Value Variables

The **present value** is the value now of a given amount to be paid or received in the future, assuming compound interest.

- The present value, like the future value, is based on three variables:
  1. The dollar amount to be received (future amount).
  2. The length of time until the amount is received (number of periods).
  3. The interest rate (the discount rate).
- The process of determining the present value is referred to as **discounting the future amount**.

Present value computations are used in measuring many items. For example, the present value of principal and interest payments is used to determine the market price of a bond. Determining the amount to be reported for notes payable and lease liabilities also involves present value computations. In addition, capital budgeting and other investment proposals are evaluated using present value computations. Finally, all rate of return and internal rate of return computations involve present value techniques.

# Present Value of a Single Amount

To illustrate present value, assume that you want to invest a sum of money today that will provide $1,000 at the end of one year. What amount would you need to invest today to have $1,000 one year from now? If you want a 10% rate of return, the investment or present value is $909.09 ($1,000 ÷ 1.10). The formula for calculating present value is shown in **Illustration E.9**.

**ILLUSTRATION E.9**
**Formula for present value**

$$\text{Present Value } (PV) = \text{Future Value } (FV) \div (1 + i)^n$$

The computation of $1,000 discounted at 10% for one year is as follows.

$$
\begin{aligned}
PV &= FV \div (1 + i)^n \\
&= \$1,000 \div (1 + .10)^1 \\
&= \$1,000 \div 1.10 \\
&= \$909.09
\end{aligned}
$$

The future amount ($1,000), the discount rate (10%), and the number of periods (1) are known. The variables in this situation are depicted in the time diagram in **Illustration E.10**.

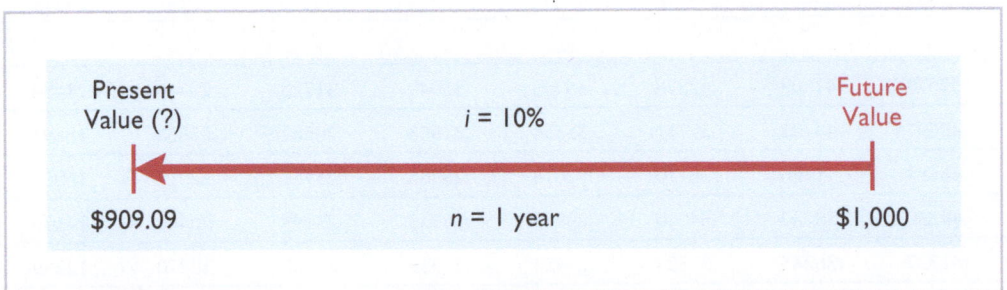

**ILLUSTRATION E.10**
**Finding present value if discounted for one period**

If the single amount of $1,000 is to be received **in two years** and discounted at 10%, the formula $PV = \$1,000 \div (1 + .10)^2$ is used, where $(1 + .10)^2$ is equal to 1.21 (1.10 × 1.10). Its present value is $826.45 ($1,000 ÷ 1.21), depicted in **Illustration E.11**.

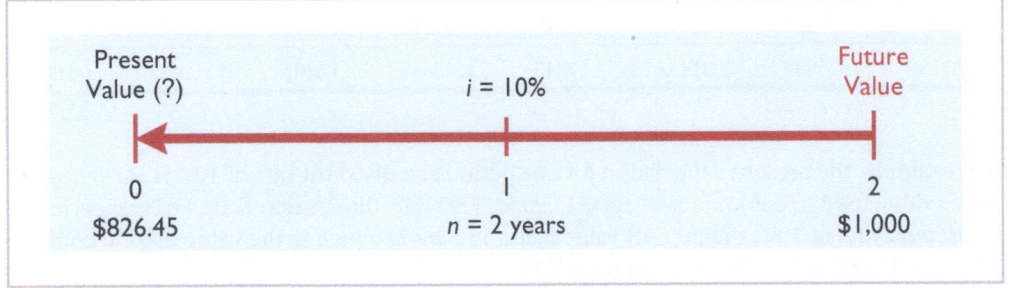

**ILLUSTRATION E.11**
**Finding present value if discounted for two periods**

The present value of 1 may also be determined through tables that show the present value of 1 for $n$ periods. In **Table 3**, $n$ is the number of discounting periods involved.

- The percentages are the periodic interest rates or discount rates, and the five-digit decimal numbers in the respective columns are the present value of 1 factors.
- When using Table 3, the future value is multiplied by the present value factor specified at the intersection of the number of periods and the discount rate.

**TABLE 3   Present Value of 1**

| (n) Periods | 4% | 5% | 6% | 7% | 8% | 9% | 10% | 11% | 12% | 15% |
|---|---|---|---|---|---|---|---|---|---|---|
| 1 | .96154 | .95238 | .94340 | .93458 | .92593 | .91743 | .90909 | .90090 | .89286 | .86957 |
| 2 | .92456 | .90703 | .89000 | .87344 | .85734 | .84168 | .82645 | .81162 | .79719 | .75614 |
| 3 | .88900 | .86384 | .83962 | .81630 | .79383 | .77218 | .75132 | .73119 | .71178 | .65752 |
| 4 | .85480 | .82270 | .79209 | .76290 | .73503 | .70843 | .68301 | .65873 | .63552 | .57175 |
| 5 | .82193 | .78353 | .74726 | .71299 | .68058 | .64993 | .62092 | .59345 | .56743 | .49718 |
| 6 | .79031 | .74622 | .70496 | .66634 | .63017 | .59627 | .56447 | .53464 | .50663 | .43233 |
| 7 | .75992 | .71068 | .66506 | .62275 | .58349 | .54703 | .51316 | .48166 | .45235 | .37594 |
| 8 | .73069 | .67684 | .62741 | .58201 | .54027 | .50187 | .46651 | .43393 | .40388 | .32690 |
| 9 | .70259 | .64461 | .59190 | .54393 | .50025 | .46043 | .42410 | .39092 | .36061 | .28426 |
| 10 | .67556 | .61391 | .55839 | .50835 | .46319 | .42241 | .38554 | .35218 | .32197 | .24719 |
| 11 | .64958 | .58468 | .52679 | .47509 | .42888 | .38753 | .35049 | .31728 | .28748 | .21494 |
| 12 | .62460 | .55684 | .49697 | .44401 | .39711 | .35554 | .31863 | .28584 | .25668 | .18691 |
| 13 | .60057 | .53032 | .46884 | .41496 | .36770 | .32618 | .28966 | .25751 | .22917 | .16253 |
| 14 | .57748 | .50507 | .44230 | .38782 | .34046 | .29925 | .26333 | .23199 | .20462 | .14133 |
| 15 | .55526 | .48102 | .41727 | .36245 | .31524 | .27454 | .23939 | .20900 | .18270 | .12289 |
| 16 | .53391 | .45811 | .39365 | .33873 | .29189 | .25187 | .21763 | .18829 | .16312 | .10687 |
| 17 | .51337 | .43630 | .37136 | .31657 | .27027 | .23107 | .19785 | .16963 | .14564 | .09293 |
| 18 | .49363 | .41552 | .35034 | .29586 | .25025 | .21199 | .17986 | .15282 | .13004 | .08081 |
| 19 | .47464 | .39573 | .33051 | .27615 | .23171 | .19449 | .16351 | .13768 | .11611 | .07027 |
| 20 | .45639 | .37689 | .31180 | .25842 | .21455 | .17843 | .14864 | .12403 | .10367 | .06110 |

For example, the present value factor for one period at a discount rate of 10% is .90909, which is the value used to compute $909.09 ($1,000 × .90909) in Illustration E.10. For two periods at a discount rate of 10%, the present value factor is .82645, which is the value used to compute $826.45 ($1,000 × .82645) in Illustration E.11.

- Note that a higher discount rate produces a smaller present value. For example, using a 15% discount rate, the present value of $1,000 due one year from now is $869.57 ($1,000 × .86957), versus $909.09 at 10%.

- Also note that the farther in the future that the future value is, the smaller the present value. For example, using the same discount rate of 10%, the present value of $1,000 due in **five years** at 10% is $620.92 ($1,000 × .62092). The present value of $1,000 due in **one year** is $909.09, a difference of $288.17.

The following two demonstration problems **(Illustrations E.12** and **E.13)** illustrate how to use Table 3.

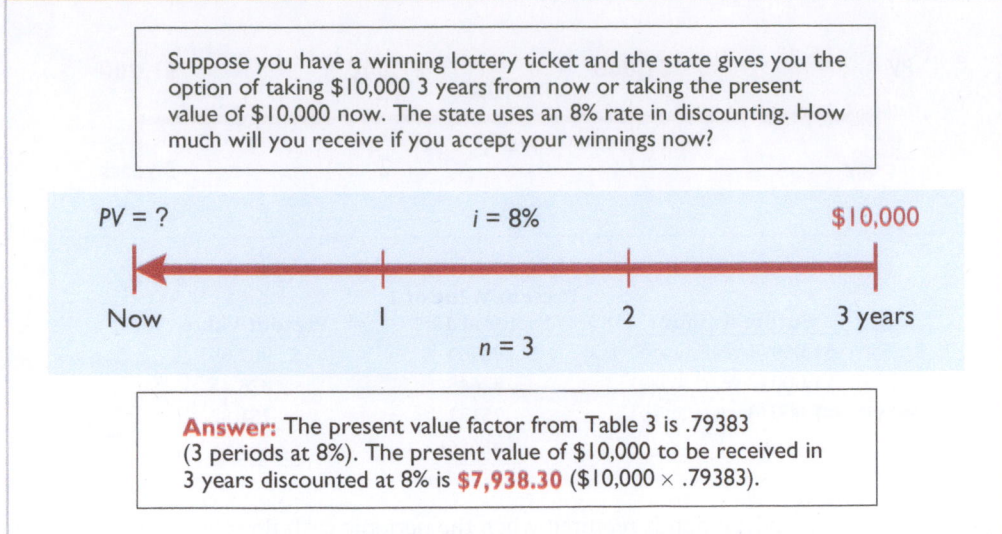

Suppose you have a winning lottery ticket and the state gives you the option of taking $10,000 3 years from now or taking the present value of $10,000 now. The state uses an 8% rate in discounting. How much will you receive if you accept your winnings now?

PV = ?          *i* = 8%          $10,000

Now          1          2          3 years

*n* = 3

**Answer:** The present value factor from Table 3 is .79383 (3 periods at 8%). The present value of $10,000 to be received in 3 years discounted at 8% is **$7,938.30** ($10,000 × .79383).

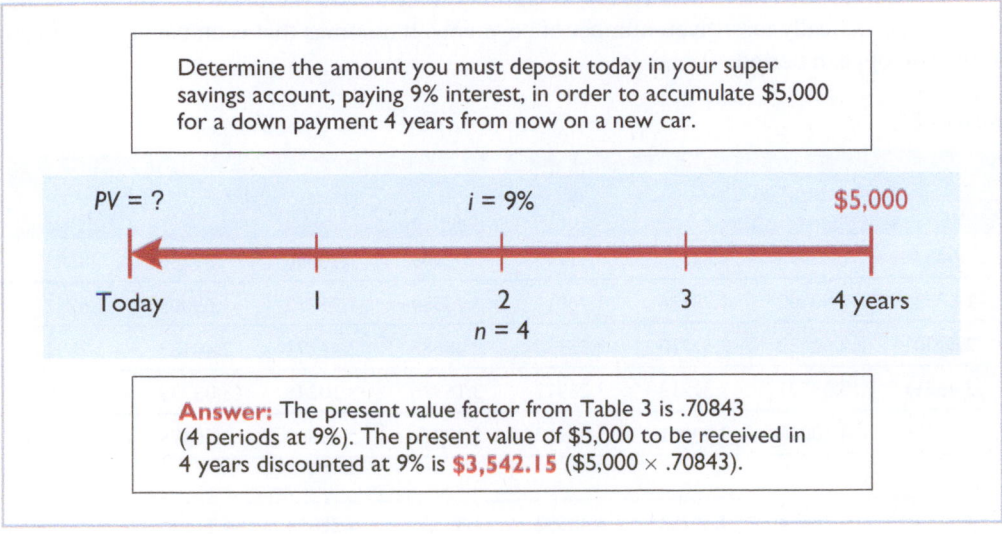

Determine the amount you must deposit today in your super savings account, paying 9% interest, in order to accumulate $5,000 for a down payment 4 years from now on a new car.

PV = ?          *i* = 9%          $5,000

Today          1          2          3          4 years

*n* = 4

**Answer:** The present value factor from Table 3 is .70843 (4 periods at 9%). The present value of $5,000 to be received in 4 years discounted at 9% is **$3,542.15** ($5,000 × .70843).

## Present Value of an Annuity

The preceding discussion involved the discounting of only a single future amount. Businesses and individuals frequently engage in transactions in which a series of equal dollar amounts are to be received or paid at evenly spaced time intervals (periodically). Examples of a series of periodic receipts or payments are loan agreements, installment sales, mortgage notes, lease (rental) contracts, and pension obligations. As discussed earlier, these periodic receipts or payments are **annuities**.

- The **present value of an annuity** is the value now of a series of future receipts or payments, discounted assuming compound interest.
- In computing the present value of an annuity, it is necessary to know:
  1. The discount rate.
  2. The number of payments (receipts).
  3. The amount of the periodic receipts or payments.

To illustrate the computation of the present value of an annuity, assume that you will receive $1,000 cash annually for three years at a time when the discount rate is 10%. This situation is depicted in the time diagram in **Illustration E.14**. **Illustration E.15** shows the computation of its present value in this situation.

**ILLUSTRATION E.14**

**Time diagram for a three-year annuity**

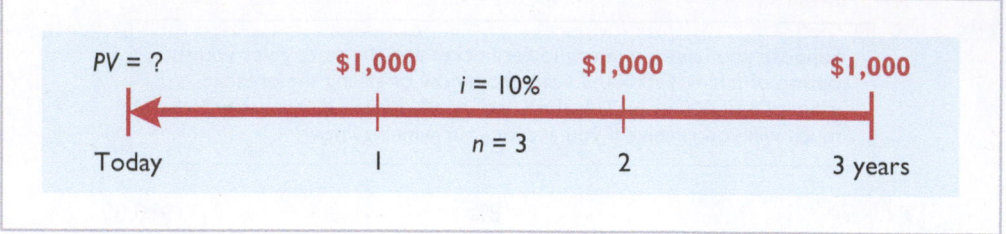

**ILLUSTRATION E.15**

**Present value of a series of future amounts computation**

| Future Amount | × | Present Value of 1 Factor at 10% | = | Present Value |
|---|---|---|---|---|
| $1,000 (1 year away) | | .90909 | | $   909.09 |
| 1,000 (2 years away) | | .82645 | | 826.45 |
| 1,000 (3 years away) | | .75132 | | 751.32 |
| | | **2.48686** | | **$2,486.86** |

This method of calculation is required when the periodic cash flows are not uniform in each period. However, when the future receipts are the same in each period, an annuity table can be used. As illustrated in **Table 4**, an annuity table shows the present value of 1 to be received periodically for a given number of payments. It assumes that each payment is made at the end of each period.

**TABLE 4    Present Value of an Annuity of 1**

| (n) Payments | 4% | 5% | 6% | 7% | 8% | 9% | 10% | 11% | 12% | 15% |
|---|---|---|---|---|---|---|---|---|---|---|
| 1 | .96154 | .95238 | .94340 | .93458 | .92593 | .91743 | .90909 | .90090 | .89286 | .86957 |
| 2 | 1.88609 | 1.85941 | 1.83339 | 1.80802 | 1.78326 | 1.75911 | 1.73554 | 1.71252 | 1.69005 | 1.62571 |
| 3 | 2.77509 | 2.72325 | 2.67301 | 2.62432 | 2.57710 | 2.53130 | 2.48685 | 2.44371 | 2.40183 | 2.28323 |
| 4 | 3.62990 | 3.54595 | 3.46511 | 3.38721 | 3.31213 | 3.23972 | 3.16986 | 3.10245 | 3.03735 | 2.85498 |
| 5 | 4.45182 | 4.32948 | 4.21236 | 4.10020 | 3.99271 | 3.88965 | 3.79079 | 3.69590 | 3.60478 | 3.35216 |
| 6 | 5.24214 | 5.07569 | 4.91732 | 4.76654 | 4.62288 | 4.48592 | 4.35526 | 4.23054 | 4.11141 | 3.78448 |
| 7 | 6.00205 | 5.78637 | 5.58238 | 5.38929 | 5.20637 | 5.03295 | 4.86842 | 4.71220 | 4.56376 | 4.16042 |
| 8 | 6.73274 | 6.46321 | 6.20979 | 5.97130 | 5.74664 | 5.53482 | 5.33493 | 5.14612 | 4.96764 | 4.48732 |
| 9 | 7.43533 | 7.10782 | 6.80169 | 6.51523 | 6.24689 | 5.99525 | 5.75902 | 5.53705 | 5.32825 | 4.77158 |
| 10 | 8.11090 | 7.72173 | 7.36009 | 7.02358 | 6.71008 | 6.41766 | 6.14457 | 5.88923 | 5.65022 | 5.01877 |
| 11 | 8.76048 | 8.30641 | 7.88687 | 7.49867 | 7.13896 | 6.80519 | 6.49506 | 6.20652 | 5.93770 | 5.23371 |
| 12 | 9.38507 | 8.86325 | 8.38384 | 7.94269 | 7.53608 | 7.16073 | 6.81369 | 6.49236 | 6.19437 | 5.42062 |
| 13 | 9.98565 | 9.39357 | 8.85268 | 8.35765 | 7.90378 | 7.48690 | 7.10336 | 6.74987 | 6.42355 | 5.58315 |
| 14 | 10.56312 | 9.89864 | 9.29498 | 8.74547 | 8.24424 | 7.78615 | 7.36669 | 6.98187 | 6.62817 | 5.72448 |
| 15 | 11.11839 | 10.37966 | 9.71225 | 9.10791 | 8.55948 | 8.06069 | 7.60608 | 7.19087 | 6.81086 | 5.84737 |
| 16 | 11.65230 | 10.83777 | 10.10590 | 9.44665 | 8.85137 | 8.31256 | 7.82371 | 7.37916 | 6.97399 | 5.95424 |
| 17 | 12.16567 | 11.27407 | 10.47726 | 9.76322 | 9.12164 | 8.54363 | 8.02155 | 7.54879 | 7.11963 | 6.04716 |
| 18 | 12.65930 | 11.68959 | 10.82760 | 10.05909 | 9.37189 | 8.75563 | 8.20141 | 7.70162 | 7.24967 | 6.12797 |
| 19 | 13.13394 | 12.08532 | 11.15812 | 10.33560 | 9.60360 | 8.95012 | 8.36492 | 7.83929 | 7.36578 | 6.19823 |
| 20 | 13.59033 | 12.46221 | 11.46992 | 10.59401 | 9.81815 | 9.12855 | 8.51356 | 7.96333 | 7.46944 | 6.25933 |

- Table 4 shows that the present value of an annuity of 1 factor for three payments at 10% is 2.48685.[1] This present value factor is the total of the three individual present value factors, as shown in Illustration E.15.
- Applying this amount to the annual cash flow of $1,000 produces a present value of $2,486.85.

The following demonstration problem (**Illustration E.16**) illustrates how to use Table 4.

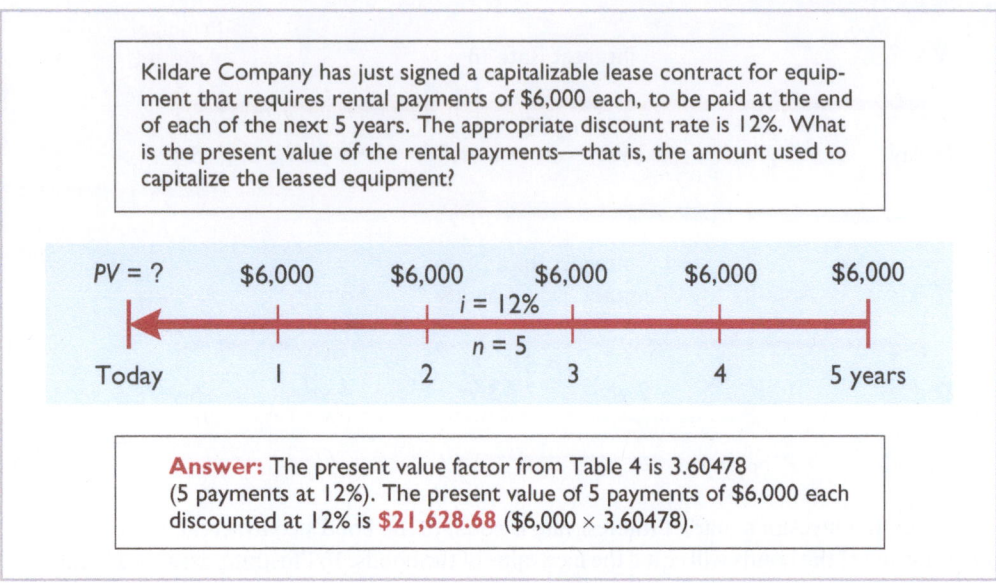

Kildare Company has just signed a capitalizable lease contract for equipment that requires rental payments of $6,000 each, to be paid at the end of each of the next 5 years. The appropriate discount rate is 12%. What is the present value of the rental payments—that is, the amount used to capitalize the leased equipment?

**Answer:** The present value factor from Table 4 is 3.60478 (5 payments at 12%). The present value of 5 payments of $6,000 each discounted at 12% is **$21,628.68** ($6,000 × 3.60478).

**ILLUSTRATION E.16**

**Demonstration problem—Using Table 4 for *PV* of an annuity of 1**

## Time Periods and Discounting

In the preceding calculations, the discounting was done on an annual basis using an annual interest rate. Discounting may also be done over shorter periods of time such as monthly, quarterly, or semiannually.

When the time frame is less than one year, it is necessary to convert the annual interest rate to the applicable time frame.

- Assume, for example, that the investor in Illustration E.14 received $500 **semiannually** for three years instead of $1,000 annually.
- In this case, the number of periods becomes six (3 × 2), the discount rate is 5% (10% ÷ 2), the present value factor from Table 4 is 5.07569 (6 periods at 5%), and the present value of the future cash flows is $2,537.85 (5.07569 × $500).

This amount is slightly higher than the $2,486.86 computed in Illustration E.15 because interest is computed twice during the same year. That is, during the second half of the year, interest is earned on the first half-year's interest. Each period's $1,000 is received and earns interest six months sooner.

## Present Value of a Long-Term Note or Bond

The present value (or market price) of a long-term note or bond is a function of three variables: (1) the payment amounts, (2) the length of time until the amounts are paid, and (3) the discount rate. Our example uses a five-year bond issue.

The first variable (dollars to be paid) is made up of two elements:

1. A series of interest payments (an annuity).
2. The principal amount (a single sum).

---

[1]The difference of .00001 between 2.48686 and 2.48685 is due to rounding.

To compute the present value of the bond, both the interest payments and the principal amount must be discounted—two different computations. The time diagrams for a bond due in five years are shown in **Illustration E.17**.

**ILLUSTRATION E.17** Time diagrams for the present value of a bond

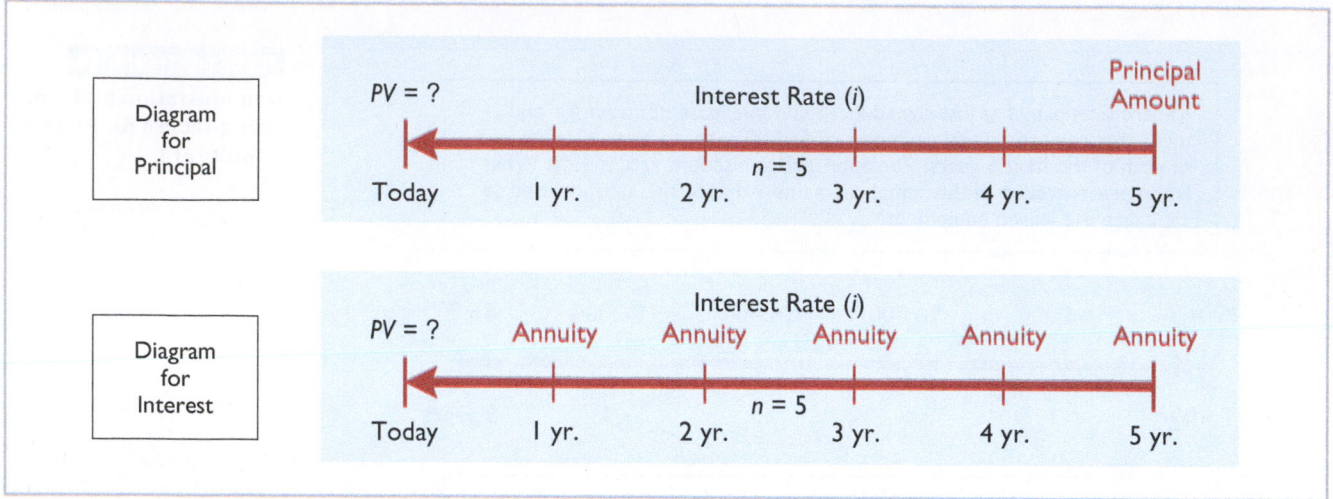

When the investor's market interest rate is equal to the bond's contractual interest rate, the present value of the bonds will equal the face value of the bonds. To illustrate, assume a bond issue of 5%, 10-year bonds with a face value of $100,000 with interest payable **annually** on January 1.

• If the discount rate is the same as the contractual rate, the bonds will sell at face value.
• In this case, the investor will receive:
  1. $100,000 at maturity.
  2. A series of 10 interest payments of $5,000 each ($100,000 × 5%) over the term of the bonds.
• The length of time is expressed in terms of interest periods—in this case, 10—and the discount rate per interest period, 5%.

The time diagram in **Illustration E.18** depicts the variables involved in this discounting situation.

**ILLUSTRATION E.18** Time diagram for present value of a 5%, 10-year bond paying interest annually

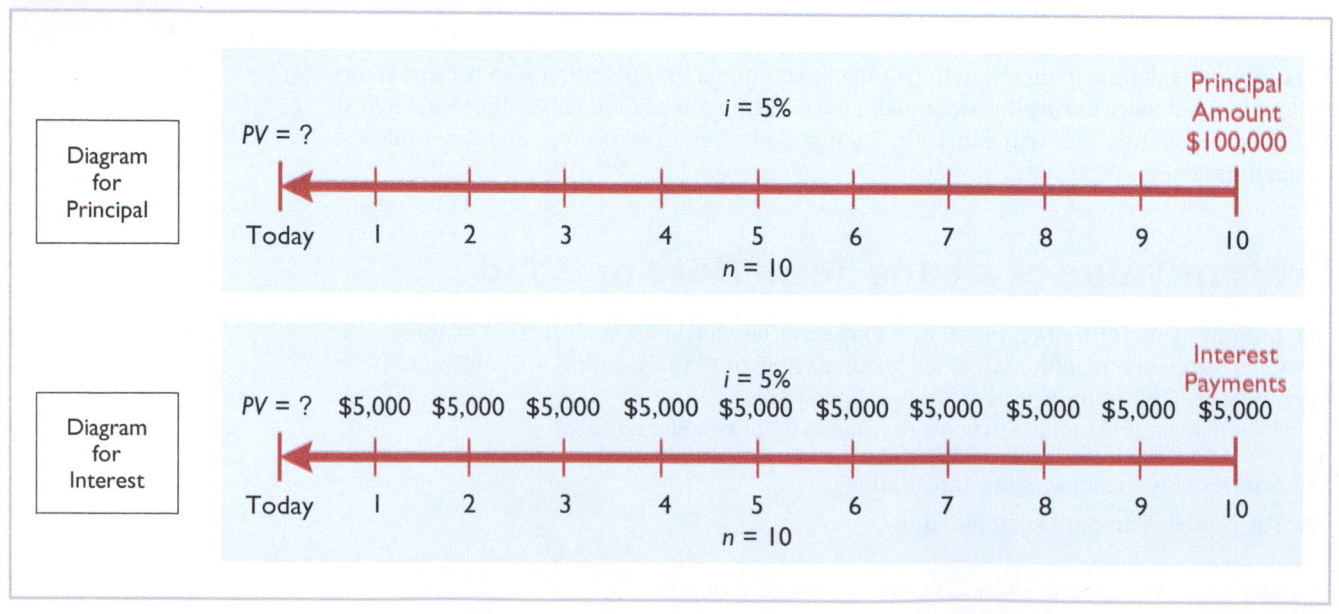

**Illustration E.19** shows the computation of the present value of these bonds.

| 5% Contractual Rate—5% Discount Rate | |
|---|---|
| **Present value of principal to be received at maturity** | |
| $100,000 × PV of 1 due in 10 periods at 5% | |
| $100,000 × .61391 (Table 3) | $ 61,391 |
| **Present value of interest to be received periodically over the term of the bonds** | |
| $5,000 × PV of 1 due periodically for 10 periods at 5% | |
| $5,000 × 7.72173 (Table 4) | 38,609* |
| **Present value of bonds** | **$100,000** |

*Rounded

Now assume that the investor's required rate of return is 6%, not 5%. The future amounts are again $100,000 and $5,000, respectively, but now a discount rate of 6% must be used. The present value of the bonds is $92,639, as computed in **Illustration E.20**.

| 5% Contractual Rate—6% Discount Rate | |
|---|---|
| **Present value of principal to be received at maturity** | |
| $100,000 × .55839 (Table 3) | $55,839 |
| **Present value of interest to be received periodically over the term of the bonds** | |
| $5,000 × 7.36009 (Table 4) | 36,800 |
| **Present value of bonds** | **$92,639** |

Conversely, if the discount rate is 4% and the contractual rate is 5%, the present value of the bonds is $108,111, computed as shown in **Illustration E.21**.

| 5% Contractual Rate—4% Discount Rate | |
|---|---|
| **Present value of principal to be received at maturity** | |
| $100,000 × .67556 (Table 3) | $ 67,556 |
| **Present value of interest to be received periodically over the term of the bonds** | |
| $5,000 × 8.11090 (Table 4) | 40,555* |
| **Present value of bonds** | **$108,111** |

*Rounded

The above discussion relied on present value tables in solving present value problems.

- Calculators, apps, and Excel spreadsheets may also be used to compute present values without the use of these tables.
- Many calculators, especially financial calculators, have present value (*PV*) functions that allow you to calculate present values by merely inputting the proper amount, discount rate, and periods, and then pressing the PV key. (We discuss the use of financial calculators in a later section.)

# Capital Budgeting Situations

The decision to make long-term capital investments is best evaluated using discounting techniques that recognize the time value of money. To do this, many companies calculate the present value of the cash flows involved in a capital investment.

To illustrate, Nagel-Siebert Trucking Company, a cross-country freight carrier in Montgomery, Illinois, is considering adding another truck to its fleet because of a purchasing opportunity. **Navistar International**, Nagel-Siebert's primary supplier of overland rigs, is overstocked and offers to sell its biggest rig for $154,000 cash payable upon delivery. Nagel-Siebert knows that the rig will produce a net cash flow per year of $40,000 for five years (received at the end of each year), at which time it will be sold for an estimated salvage value of $35,000. Nagel-Siebert's discount rate in evaluating capital expenditures is 10%. Should Nagel-Siebert commit to the purchase of this rig?

The cash flows that must be discounted to present value by Nagel-Siebert are as follows.

- Cash payable on delivery (today): $154,000.
- Net cash flow from operating the rig: $40,000 for five years (at the end of each year).
- Cash received from sale of rig at the end of five years: $35,000.

The time diagrams for the latter two cash flows are shown in **Illustration E.22**.

**ILLUSTRATION E.22**   **Time diagrams for Nagel-Siebert Trucking Company**

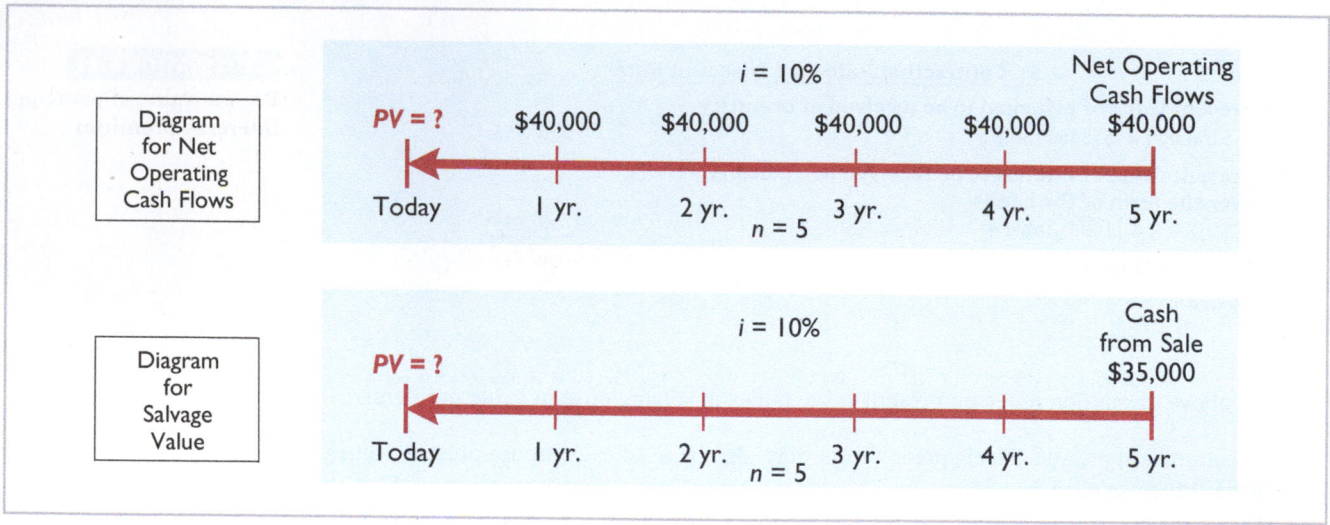

Notice from the diagrams that:

- Computing the present value of the net operating cash flows ($40,000 at the end of each year) is **discounting an annuity** (Table 4).
- Computing the present value of the $35,000 salvage value is **discounting a single sum** (Table 3).

The computation of these present values is shown in **Illustration E.23**.

**Present Values Using a 10% Discount Rate**

Present value of net operating cash flows received annually over 5 years

    $40,000 × PV of 1 received annually for 5 years at 10%

    $40,000 × 3.79079                           $151,631.60

Present value of salvage value (cash) to be received in 5 years

    $35,000 × PV of 1 received in 5 years at 10%

    $35,000 × .62092                              21,732.20

Present value of cash **inflows**                      173,363.80

Present value of cash **outflows** (purchase price due today at 10%)

    $154,000 × PV of 1 due today

    $154,000 × 1.00000                        (154,000.00)

Net present value                            **$ 19,363.80**

**ILLUSTRATION E.23**
**Present value computations at 10%**

- The present value of the cash receipts (inflows) of $173,363.80 ($151,631.60 + $21,732.20) exceeds the present value of the cash payments (outflows) of $154,000.00.
- The net present value of $19,363.80 is positive, and **the decision to invest should be accepted**.

Now assume that Nagel-Siebert uses a discount rate of 15%, not 10%, because it wants a greater return on its investments in capital assets. The cash receipts and cash payments by Nagel-Siebert are the same. The present values of these receipts and cash payments discounted at 15% are shown in **Illustration E.24**.

**Present Values Using a 15% Discount Rate**

Present value of net operating cash flows received annually

over 5 years at 15%

    $40,000 × 3.35216                           $134,086.40

Present value of salvage value (cash) to be received in 5 years at 15%

    $35,000 × .49718                              17,401.30

Present value of cash **inflows**                      $151,487.70

Present value of cash **outflows** (purchase price due today at 15%)

    $154,000 × 1.00000                        (154,000.00)

Net present value                            **$ (2,512.30)**

**ILLUSTRATION E.24**
**Present value computations at 15%**

- The present value of the cash payments (outflows) of $154,000.00 exceeds the present value of the cash receipts (inflows) of $151,487.70 ($134,086.40 + $17,401.30).
- The net present value of $2,512.30 is negative, and **the investment should be rejected**.

The above discussion relied on present value tables in solving present value problems. As we show in the next section, calculators may also be used to compute present values without the use of these tables. Financial calculators have present value (PV) functions that allow you to calculate present values by merely identifying the proper amount, discount rate, and periods, and then pressing the PV key.

# Using Financial Calculators

**LEARNING OBJECTIVE 4**

Use a financial calculator to solve time value of money problems.

Business professionals, once they have mastered the underlying time value of money concepts, often use a financial calculator to solve these types of problems. To use financial calculators, you enter the time value of money variables into the calculator. **Illustration E.25** shows the five most common keys used to solve time value of money problems.[2]

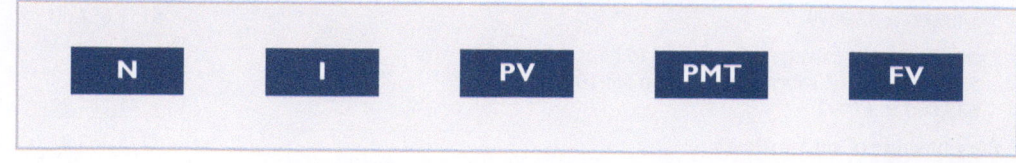

where:

| | | |
|---|---|---|
| N | = | number of periods |
| I | = | interest rate per period (some calculators use I/YR or i) |
| PV | = | present value (occurs at the beginning of the first period) |
| PMT | = | payment (all payments are equal, and none are skipped) |
| FV | = | future value (occurs at the end of the last period) |

In solving time value of money problems in this appendix, you will generally be given three of four variables and will have to solve for the remaining variable. The fifth key (the key not used) is given a value of zero to ensure that this variable is not used in the computation.

## Present Value of a Single Sum

To illustrate how to solve a present value problem using a financial calculator, assume that you want to know the present value of $84,253 to be received in five years, discounted at 11% compounded annually. **Illustration E.26** depicts this problem.

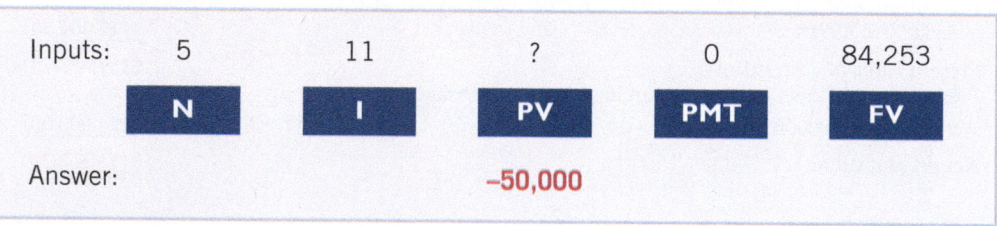

Illustration E.26 shows you the information (inputs) to enter into the calculator:

- N = 5, I = 11, PMT = 0, and FV = 84,253.
- You then press PV for the answer: −$50,000.
- As indicated, the PMT key was given a value of zero because a series of payments did not occur in this problem.

### Plus and Minus

The use of plus and minus signs in time value of money problems with a financial calculator can be confusing. Most financial calculators are programmed so that the positive and negative cash flows in any problem offset each other.

- In the present value problem above, we identified the $84,253 future value initial investment as a positive (inflow).
- The answer −$50,000 was shown as a negative amount, reflecting a cash outflow.
- If the 84,253 were entered as a negative, then the final answer would have been reported as a positive 50,000.

[2]On many calculators, these keys are actual buttons on the face of the calculator; on others, they appear on the display after the user accesses a present value menu.

Hopefully, the sign convention will not cause confusion. If you understand what is required in a problem, you should be able to interpret a positive or negative amount in determining the solution to the problem.

## Compounding Periods

In the problem above, we assumed that compounding occurs once a year.

- Some financial calculators have a default setting, which assumes that compounding occurs 12 times a year.
- You must determine what default period has been programmed into your calculator and change it as necessary to arrive at the proper compounding period.

## Rounding

Most financial calculators store and calculate using 12 decimal places. As a result, because compound interest tables generally have factors only up to five decimal places, a slight difference in the final answer can result. In most time value of money problems, the final answer will not include more than two decimal places.

# Present Value of an Annuity

To illustrate how to solve a present value of an annuity problem using a financial calculator, assume that you are asked to determine the present value of rental receipts of $6,000 each to be received at the end of each of the next five years, when discounted at 12%, as pictured in **Illustration E.27**.

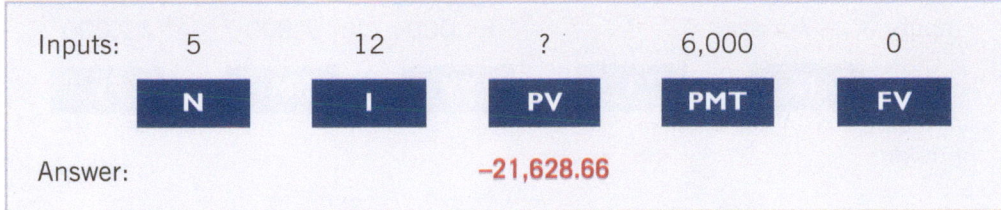

**ILLUSTRATION E.27**

**Calculator solution for present value of an annuity**

In this case, you enter N = 5, I = 12, PMT = 6,000, and FV = 0, and then press PV to arrive at the answer of −$21,628.66.

# Future Value of a Single Sum

Now let us look at an investment to illustrate how to solve a future value problem using a financial calculator. Assume that you will invest $20,000 today into a fund and you intend to leave it there for 15 years. The fund earns 7% interest. **Illustration E.28** shows how to compute the future value of the fund at the end of year 15.

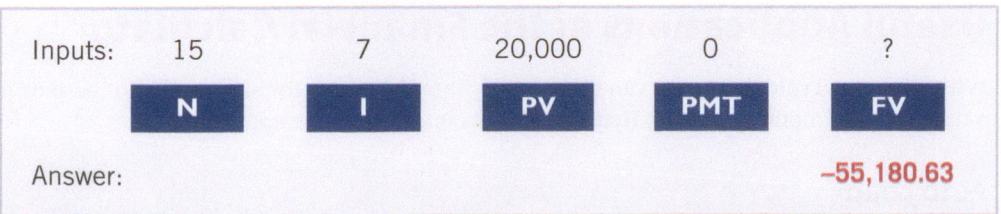

**ILLUSTRATION E.28**

**Calculator solution for future value of single sum**

In this case, you enter N = 15, I = 7, PV = 20,000, and PMT = 0, and then press FV to calculate the future value of −$55,180.63.

# Future Value of an Annuity

You can use a financial calculator to solve a future value of an annuity problem for an annuity investment. Assume that you will invest $8,000 into a fund at the end of each of the next eight years. The fund earns 9% interest. **Illustration E.29** shows how to compute the future value of the fund at the end of the eighth year.

**ILLUSTRATION E.29**

**Calculator solution for future value of an annuity**

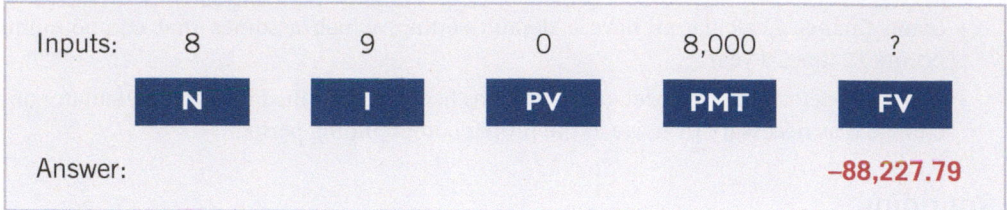

In this case, you enter N = 8, I = 9, PV = 0, and PMT = 8,000, and then press FV to determine the future value of −$88,227.79.

# Internal Rate of Return

You can also use these same calculator keys to compute the internal rate of return of an investment that has equal cash flows. Suppose that a purchase of a piece of equipment with a seven-year life requires an initial investment of $54,000, has positive cash flows of $7,800 per year, and has an estimated salvage value of $11,000. The computation is shown in **Illustration E.30**.

**ILLUSTRATION E.30**

**Calculator solution for internal rate of return**

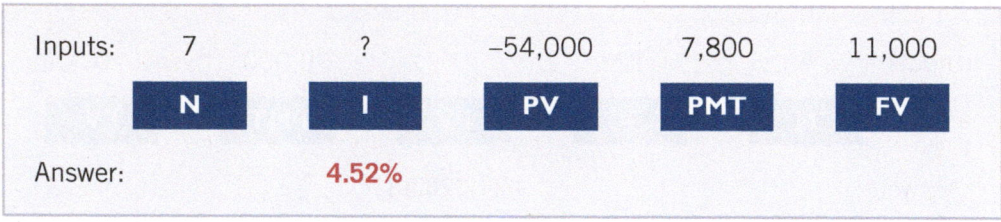

In this case, you enter N = 7, PV = −54,000 (we entered as a negative, since it is an outflow), PMT = 7,800, and FV = 11,000, and then press I to determine the answer of 4.52%.

- Notice that the advantage to this approach is that you arrive at a much more precise result, rather than the rough approximation provided by the present value tables.
- To determine the internal rate of return using your calculator for an investment with unequal cash flows, you need to employ the cash flow key (CF) and the internal rate of return key (IRR). (The use of these function keys varies across calculators, so you should consult the user manual for your calculator or the manufacturer's website for specific information.)

# Useful Applications of the Financial Calculator

With a financial calculator, you can solve for any interest rate or for any number of periods in a time value of money problem. Here are some examples of these applications.

## Auto Loan

Assume you are financing the purchase of a used car with a three-year loan. The loan has a 9.5% stated annual interest rate, compounded monthly. The price of the car is $6,000, and you want to determine the monthly payments, assuming that the payments start one month after the purchase. This problem is pictured in **Illustration E.31**.

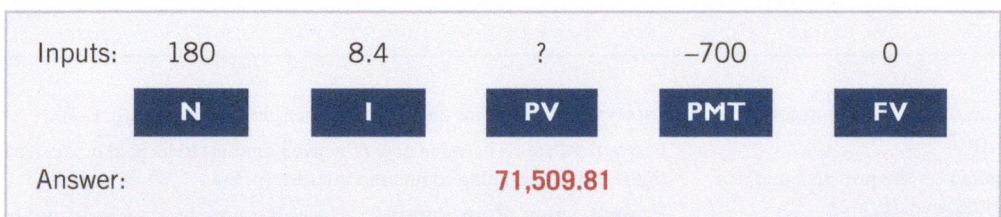

**Calculator solution for auto loan payments**

To solve this problem, you enter N = 36 (12 × 3), I = 9.5, PV = 6,000, and FV = 0, and then press PMT.

- You will find that the monthly payments will be $192.20.
- Note that the payment key is usually programmed for 12 payments per year. Thus, you must change the default (compounding period) if the payments are other than monthly.

## Mortgage Loan Amount

Say you are evaluating financing options for a loan on a house (a mortgage). You decide that the maximum mortgage payment you can afford is $700 per month. The annual interest rate is 8.4%. If you get a mortgage that requires you to make monthly payments over a 15-year period, what is the maximum home loan you can afford? **Illustration E.32** depicts this problem.

| Inputs: | 180 | 8.4 | ? | −700 | 0 |
|---------|-----|-----|---|------|---|
|         | N   | I   | PV | PMT | FV |
| Answer: |     |     | 71,509.81 | | |

**ILLUSTRATION E.32**
**Calculator solution for mortgage amount**

You enter N = 180 (12 × 15 years), I = 8.4, PMT = −700, and FV = 0, and then press PV.

- With the payments-per-year key set at 12, you find a present value of $71,509.81—the maximum home loan you can afford, given that you want to keep your mortgage payments at $700.
- Note that by changing any of the variables, you can quickly conduct "what-if" analyses for different situations.

# Review

## Learning Objectives Review

---

**1  Compute interest and future values.**

---

Simple interest is computed on the principal only, while compound interest is computed on the principal and any interest earned that has not been withdrawn.

To solve for future value of a single amount, prepare a time diagram of the problem. Identify the principal amount, the number of compounding periods, and the interest rate. Using the future value of 1 table, multiply the principal amount by the future value factor specified at the intersection of the number of periods and the interest rate.

To solve for future value of an annuity, prepare a time diagram of the problem. Identify the amount of the periodic payments (receipts), the number of payments (receipts), and the interest rate. Using the

future value of an annuity of 1 table, multiply the amount of the payments by the future value factor specified at the intersection of the number of periods and the interest rate.

---

**2  Compute present values.**

---

The following three variables are fundamental to solving present value problems: (1) the future amount, (2) the number of periods, and (3) the interest rate (the discount rate).

To solve for present value of a single amount, prepare a time diagram of the problem. Identify the future amount, the number of discounting periods, and the discount (interest) rate. Using the present value of a single amount table, multiply the future amount by the present value factor specified at the intersection of the number of periods and the discount rate.

To solve for present value of an annuity, prepare a time diagram of the problem. Identify the amount of future periodic receipts or payments (annuities), the number of payments (receipts), and the discount (interest) rate. Using the present value of an annuity of 1 table, multiply the amount of the annuity by the present value factor specified at the intersection of the number of payments and the interest rate.

To compute the present value of notes and bonds, determine the present value of the principal amount and the present value of the interest payments. Multiply the principal amount (a single future amount) by the present value factor (from the present value of 1 table) intersecting at the number of periods (number of interest payments) and the discount rate. To determine the present value of the series of interest payments, multiply the amount of the interest payment by the present value factor (from the present value of an annuity of 1 table) intersecting at the number of periods (number of interest payments) and the discount rate. Add the present value of the principal amount to the present value of the interest payments to arrive at the present value of the note or bond.

**3 Compute the present value in capital budgeting situations.**

Compute the present values of all cash inflows and all cash outflows related to the capital budgeting proposal (an investment-type decision). If the **net** present value is positive, accept the proposal (make the investment). If the **net** present value is negative, reject the proposal (do not make the investment).

**4 Use a financial calculator to solve time value of money problems.**

Financial calculators can be used to solve the same and additional problems as those solved with time value of money tables. Enter into the financial calculator the amounts for all of the known elements of a time value of money problem (periods, interest rate, payments, future or present value), and it solves for the unknown element. Particularly useful situations involve interest rates and compounding periods not presented in the tables.

## Glossary Review

**Annuity** A series of equal dollar amounts to be paid or received at evenly spaced time intervals (periodically). (p. E-5).

**Compound interest** The interest computed on the principal and any interest earned that has not been paid or withdrawn. (p. E-2).

**Discounting the future amount(s)** The process of determining present value. (p. E-8).

**Future value of an annuity** The sum of all the payments (receipts) plus the accumulated compound interest on them. (p. E-5).

**Future value of a single amount** The value at a future date of a given amount invested, assuming compound interest. (p. E-3).

**Interest** Payment for the use of another person's money. (p. E-2).

**Present value** The value now of a given amount to be paid or received in the future, assuming compound interest. (p. E-8).

**Present value of an annuity** The value now of a series of future receipts or payments, discounted assuming compound interest. (p. E-11).

**Principal** The amount borrowed or invested. (p. E-2).

**Simple interest** The interest computed on the principal only. (p. E-2).

# WileyPLUS

Many additional resources are available for practice in WileyPLUS.

## Brief Exercises

*(Use tables to solve exercises BEE.1 to BEE.23.)*

*Compute the future value of a single amount.*

**BEE.1 (LO 1), AP** Jozy Altidore invested $6,000 at 5% annual interest, and left the money invested without withdrawing any of the interest for 12 years. At the end of the 12 years, Jozy withdrew the accumulated amount of money. (a) What amount did Jozy withdraw, assuming the investment earns simple interest? (b) What amount did Jozy withdraw, assuming the investment earns interest compounded annually?

*Use future value tables.*

**BEE.2 (LO 1), AP** For each of the following cases, indicate (a) what interest rate columns and (b) what number of periods you would refer to in looking up the future value factor.

**1.** In Table 1 (future value of 1):

| | Annual Rate | Number of Years Invested | Compounded |
|---|---|---|---|
| Case A | 5% | 3 | Annually |
| Case B | 12% | 4 | Semiannually |

**2.** In Table 2 (future value of an annuity of 1):

|  | Annual Rate | Number of Years Invested | Compounded |
|---|---|---|---|
| Case A | 3% | 8 | Annually |
| Case B | 8% | 6 | Semiannually |

**BEE.3 (LO 1), AP** Liam Company signed a lease for an office building for a period of 12 years. Under the lease agreement, a security deposit of $9,600 is made. The deposit will be returned at the expiration of the lease with interest compounded at 4% per year. What amount will Liam receive at the time the lease expires?

*Compute the future value of a single amount.*

**BEE.4 (LO 1), AP** Bates Company issued $1,000,000, 10-year bonds. It agreed to make annual deposits of $78,000 to a fund (called a sinking fund), which will be used to pay off the principal amount of the bond at the end of 10 years. The deposits are made at the end of each year into an account paying 6% annual interest. What amount will be in the sinking fund at the end of 10 years?

*Compute the future value of an annuity.*

**BEE.5 (LO 1), AP** Andrew and Emma Garfield invested $8,000 in a savings account paying 5% annual interest when their daughter, Angela, was born. They also deposited $1,000 on each of her birthdays until she was 18 (including her 18th birthday). How much was in the savings account on her 18th birthday (after the last deposit)?

*Compute the future value of a single amount and of an annuity.*

**BEE.6 (LO 1), AP** Hugh Curtin borrowed $35,000 on July 1, 2022. This amount plus accrued interest at 8% compounded annually is to be repaid on July 1, 2027. How much will Hugh have to repay on July 1, 2027?

*Compute the future value of a single amount.*

**BEE.7 (LO 2), AP** For each of the following cases, indicate (a) what interest rate columns and (b) what number of periods you would refer to in looking up the discount rate.

*Use present value tables.*

**1.** In Table 3 (present value of 1):

|  | Annual Rate | Number of Years Invested | Discounts Per Year |
|---|---|---|---|
| Case A | 12% | 7 | Annually |
| Case B | 8% | 11 | Semiannually |
| Case C | 10% | 8 | Semiannually |

**2.** In Table 4 (present value of an annuity of 1):

|  | Annual Rate | Number of Years Involved | Number of Payments Involved | Frequency of Payments |
|---|---|---|---|---|
| Case A | 10% | 20 | 20 | Annually |
| Case B | 10% | 7 | 7 | Annually |
| Case C | 6% | 5 | 10 | Semiannually |

**BEE.8 (LO 2), AP** **a.** What is the present value of $25,000 due 9 periods from now, discounted at 10%?

**b.** What is the present value of $25,000 to be received at the end of each of 6 periods, discounted at 9%?

*Determine present values.*

**BEE.9 (LO 2), AP** Messi Company is considering an investment that will return a lump sum of $900,000 6 years from now. What amount should Messi Company pay for this investment to earn an 8% return?

*Compute the present value of a single amount investment.*

**BEE.10 (LO 2), AP** Lloyd Company earns 6% on an investment that will return $450,000 8 years from now. What is the amount Lloyd should invest now to earn this rate of return?

*Compute the present value of a single amount investment.*

**BEE.11 (LO 2), AP** Robben Company is considering investing in an annuity contract that will return $40,000 annually at the end of each year for 15 years. What amount should Robben Company pay for this investment if it earns an 8% return?

*Compute the present value of an annuity investment.*

**BEE.12 (LO 2), AP** Kaehler Enterprises earns 5% on an investment that pays back $80,000 at the end of each of the next 6 years. What is the amount Kaehler Enterprises invested to earn the 5% rate of return?

*Compute the present value of an annual investment.*

**BEE.13 (LO 2), AP** Dempsey Railroad Co. is about to issue $400,000 of 10-year bonds paying an 11% interest rate, with interest payable annually. The discount rate for such securities is 10%. How much can Dempsey expect to receive for the sale of these bonds?

*Compute the present value of bonds.*

*Compute the present value of bonds.*

**BEE.14 (LO 2), AP** Dempsey Railroad Co. is about to issue $400,000 of 10-year bonds paying an 11% interest rate, with interest payable annually. The discount rate is 12% (instead of 10% as in BEE.13). In this case, how much can Dempsey expect to receive from the sale of these bonds?

*Compute the present value of a note.*

**BEE.15 (LO 2), AP** Neymar Taco Company receives a $75,000, 6-year note bearing interest of 4% (paid annually) from a customer at a time when the discount rate is 6%. What is the present value of the note received by Neymar?

*Compute the present value of bonds.*

**BEE.16 (LO 2), AP** Gleason Enterprises issued 6%, 8-year, $2,500,000 par value bonds that pay interest annually on April 1. The bonds are dated April 1, 2022, and are issued on that date. The discount rate of interest for such bonds on April 1, 2022, is 8%. What cash proceeds did Gleason receive from issuance of the bonds?

*Compute the present value of a note.*

**BEE.17 (LO 2), AP** Frazier Company issues a 10%, 5-year mortgage note on January 1, 2022, to obtain financing for new equipment. Land is used as collateral for the note. The terms provide for semiannual installment payments of $48,850. What are the cash proceeds received from the issuance of the note?

*Compute the interest rate on a single amount.*

**BEE.18 (LO 2), AP** If Colleen Mooney invests $4,765.50 now and she will receive $12,000 at the end of 12 years, what annual rate of interest will Colleen earn on her investment? (*Hint:* Use Table 3.)

*Compute the number of periods of a single amount.*

**BEE.19 (LO 2), AP** Tim Howard has been offered the opportunity of investing $36,125 now. The investment will earn 11% per year and at the end of that time will return Tim $75,000. How many years must Tim wait to receive $75,000? (*Hint:* Use Table 3.)

*Compute the interest rate on an annuity.*

**BEE.20 (LO 2), AP** Joanne Quick made an investment of $10,271.38. From this investment, she will receive $1,200 annually for the next 15 years starting one year from now. What rate of interest will Joanne's investment be earning for her? (*Hint:* Use Table 4.)

*Compute the number of periods of an annuity.*

**BEE.21 (LO 2), AP** Kevin Morales invests $7,793.83 now for a series of $1,300 annual returns beginning one year from now. Kevin will earn a return of 9% on the initial investment. How many annual payments of $1,300 will Kevin receive? (*Hint:* Use Table 4.)

*Compute the present value of a machine for purposes of making a purchase decision.*

**BEE.22 (LO 3), AP** Barney Googal owns a garage and is contemplating purchasing a tire retreading machine for $12,820. After estimating costs and revenues, Barney projects a net cash inflow from the retreading machine of $2,700 annually for 7 years. Barney hopes to earn a return of 9% on such investments. What is the present value of the retreading operation? Should Barney Googal purchase the retreading machine?

*Compute the maximum price to pay for a machine.*

**BEE.23 (LO 3), AP** Snyder Company is considering purchasing equipment. The equipment will produce the following cash inflows: Year 1, $25,000; Year 2, $30,000; and Year 3, $40,000. Snyder requires a minimum rate of return of 11%. What is the maximum price Snyder should pay for this equipment?

*Determine interest rate.*

**BEE.24 (LO 4), AP** Carly Simon wishes to invest $18,000 on July 1, 2022, and have it accumulate to $50,000 by July 1, 2032. Use a financial calculator to determine at what exact annual rate of interest Carly must invest the $18,000.

*Determine interest rate.*

**BEE.25 (LO 4), AP** On July 17, 2021, Keith Urban borrowed $42,000 from his grandfather to open a clothing store. Starting July 17, 2022, Keith has to make 10 equal annual payments of $6,500 each to repay the loan. Use a financial calculator to determine what interest rate Keith is paying.

*Determine interest rate.*

**BEE.26 (LO 4), AP** As the purchaser of a new house, Carrie Underwood has signed a mortgage note to pay the Nashville National Bank and Trust Co. $8,400 every 6 months for 20 years, at the end of which time she will own the house. At the date the mortgage is signed, the purchase price was $198,000 and Underwood made a down payment of $20,000. The first payment will be made 6 months after the date the mortgage is signed. Using a financial calculator, compute the exact rate of interest earned on the mortgage by the bank.

*Various time value of money situations.*

**BEE.27 (LO 4), AP** Using a financial calculator, solve for the unknowns in each of the following situations.

a. On June 1, 2021, Jennifer Lawrence purchases lakefront property from her neighbor, Josh Hutcherson, and agrees to pay the purchase price in 7 payments of $16,000 each, the first payment to be payable June 1, 2022. (Assume that interest compounded at an annual rate of 7.35% is implicit in the payments.) What is the purchase price of the property?

b. On January 1, 2021, Gerrard Corporation purchased 200 of the $1,000 face value, 8% coupon, 10-year bonds of Sterling Inc. The bonds mature on January 1, 2031, and pay interest annually beginning January 1, 2022. Gerrard purchased the bonds to yield 10.65%. How much did Gerrard pay for the bonds?

**BEE.28 (LO 4), AP** Using a financial calculator, provide a solution to each of the following situations.   *Various time value of money situations.*

a. Lynn Anglin owes a debt of $42,000 from the purchase of her new sport utility vehicle. The debt bears annual interest of 7.8% compounded monthly. Lynn wishes to pay the debt and interest in equal monthly payments over 8 years, beginning one month hence. What equal monthly payments will pay off the debt and interest?

b. On January 1, 2022, Roger Molony offers to buy Dave Feeney's used snowmobile for $8,000, payable in five equal annual installments, which are to include 7.25% interest on the unpaid balance and a portion of the principal. If the first payment is to be made on December 31, 2022, how much will each payment be?

**BEE.29 (LO 4), AP** Renolds Corporation is considering two alternative investments in excavating   *Determine internal rate of return.* equipment. Investment A requires an initial investment of $184,000, has positive cash flows of $27,500 per year, and has an estimated salvage value of $21,000. Investment B requires an initial investment of $234,000, has positive cash flows of $32,800 per year, and has an estimated salvage value of $19,000. Each piece of equipment is expected to have a 12-year useful life. Use a financial calculator to determine the internal rate of return of each project to decide which is more desirable. (Round to two decimal places, e.g., 9.74%.)

# Company Index

# Subject Index

# RAPID REVIEW
## Chapter Content

### ACCOUNTING CONCEPTS (Chapters 2–4)

| Fundamental Qualities | Enhancing Qualities | Assumptions | Principles | Constraint |
|---|---|---|---|---|
| Relevance<br>Faithful representation | Comparability<br>Verifiability<br>Timeliness<br>Understandability | Monetary unit<br>Economic entity<br>Periodicity<br>Going concern | Historical cost<br>Fair value<br>Full disclosure<br>Revenue recognition<br>Expense recognition | Cost |

### BASIC ACCOUNTING EQUATION (Chapter 3)

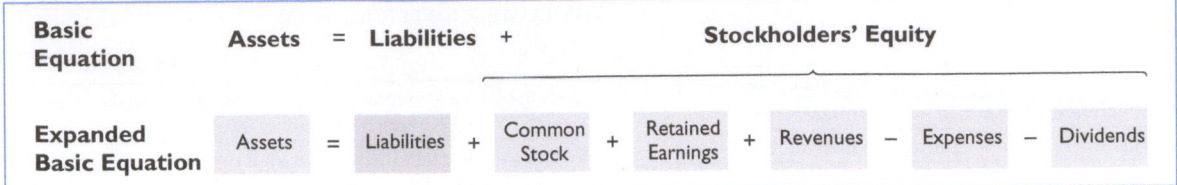

| | |
|---|---|
| **Basic Equation** | Assets = Liabilities + Stockholders' Equity |
| **Expanded Basic Equation** | Assets = Liabilities + Common Stock + Retained Earnings + Revenues − Expenses − Dividends |

### ADJUSTMENTS (Chapter 4)

| Type | | Adjustment | |
|---|---|---|---|
| | | Increase | Decrease |
| Deferrals | 1. Prepaid expenses | Expenses | Assets |
| | 2. Unearned revenues | Liabilities | Revenues |
| Accruals | 1. Accrued revenues | Assets | Revenues |
| | 2. Accrued expenses | Expenses | Liabilities |

*Note:* Each adjustment will affect one or more income statement accounts and one or more balance sheet accounts.

#### Interest Computation

Interest = Face value of note × Annual interest rate × Time in terms of one year

### FRAUD, INTERNAL CONTROL, AND CASH (Chapter 5)

Principles of Internal Control Activities

Establishment of responsibility
Segregation of duties
Documentation procedures
Physical controls
Independent internal verification
Human resource controls

The Fraud Triangle

Opportunity
Financial pressure
Rationalization

#### Bank Reconciliation

| Bank | Books |
|---|---|
| Balance per bank statement<br>Add: Deposits in transit<br>Deduct: Outstanding checks<br>Adjusted cash balance | Balance per books<br><br>Add: Unrecorded credit memoranda from bank statement<br>Deduct: Unrecorded debit memoranda from bank statement<br>Adjusted cash balance |

*Note:* 1. Errors should be offset (added or deducted) on the side that made the error.
2. Adjustments to accounts should only be made for items affecting books.

**Stop and Check:** Does the adjusted cash balance in the Cash account equal the reconciled balance?

### INVENTORY (Chapter 6)

Recording Inventory Under the Perpetual Inventory System

| Event | Effect on Accounts | |
|---|---|---|
| Purchase of goods | Inventory | Increase |
| | Cash | Decrease |
| Return of purchased goods | Cash | Increase |
| | Inventory | Decrease |
| Sale of goods | Cash | Increase |
| | Sales Revenue | Increase |
| | Cost of Goods Sold | Increase |
| | Inventory | Decrease |
| Return of sold goods | Sales Returns and Allowances | Increase |
| | Accounts Receivable | Decrease |
| | Inventory | Increase |
| | Cost of Goods Sold | Decrease |

#### Cost Flow Methods

- Specific identification
- First-in, first-out (FIFO)
- Weighted-average
- Last-in, first-out (LIFO)

### RECEIVABLES (Chapter 7)

Two Methods to Account for Uncollectible Accounts

| Direct write-off method | Record bad debt expense when the company determines a particular account to be uncollectible. |
|---|---|
| Allowance method | At the end of each period, estimate the amount of uncollectible receivables. Increase Bad Debt Expense and Allowance for Doubtful Accounts in an amount that results in a balance in the allowance account equal to the estimate of uncollectibles. As specific accounts become uncollectible, decrease Allowance for Doubtful Accounts and Accounts Receivable. |

Steps to Manage Accounts Receivable

1. Determine to whom to extend credit.
2. Establish a payment period.
3. Monitor collections.
4. Evaluate the receivables balance.
5. Accelerate cash receipts from receivables when necessary.

## PLANT ASSETS (Chapter 8)

Computation of Annual Depreciation Expense

| Straight-line | $\dfrac{\text{Cost} - \text{Salvage value}}{\text{Useful life (in years)}}$ |
| --- | --- |

*Note:* If depreciation is calculated for partial periods, the straight-line and declining-balance methods must be adjusted for the relevant proportion of the year. Multiply the annual depreciation expense by the number of months expired in the year divided by 12 months.

## BONDS (Chapter 9)

| Premium | Market interest rate < Contractual interest rate |
| --- | --- |
| Face Value | Market interest rate = Contractual interest rate |
| Discount | Market interest rate > Contractual interest rate |

Computation of Annual Bond Interest Expense

Interest expense = Interest paid (payable) + Amortization of discount
(OR − Amortization of premium)

## STOCKHOLDERS' EQUITY (Chapter 9)

No-Par Value vs. Par Value Stock

| No-Par Value | | Par Value | |
| --- | --- | --- | --- |
| Cash | Increase | Cash | Increase |
| Common | | Common Stock (par value) | Increase |
|   Stock | Increase | Paid-in Capital in Excess of | |
| | |   Par Value | Increase |

## FINANCIAL STATEMENT ANALYSIS (Chapter 10)

| Discontinued operations | Income statement (presented separately after "Income from continuing operations") |
| --- | --- |
| Changes in accounting principle | In most instances, use the new method in current period and restate previous years' results using new method. For changes in depreciation and amortization methods, use the new method in the current period but do not restate previous periods. |

## MANAGERIAL ACCOUNTING (Chapter 11)

Characteristics of Managerial Accounting

| Primary users | Internal users |
| --- | --- |
| Reports | Internal reports issued as needed |
| Purpose | Special purpose for a particular user |
| Content | Pertains to subunits, may be detailed, use of relevant data |
| Verification | No independent audits |

Types of Manufacturing Costs

| Direct materials | Raw materials directly associated with finished product |
| --- | --- |
| Direct labor | Work of employees directly associated with turning raw materials into finished product |
| Manufacturing overhead | Costs indirectly associated with manufacture of finished product |

## JOB ORDER COSTING (Chapter 12)

Job Order Cost Flow

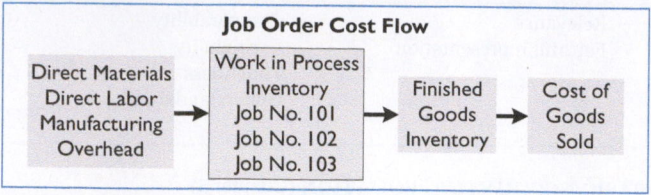

## COST-VOLUME-PROFIT (Chapter 13)

Types of Costs

| Variable costs | Vary in total directly and proportionately with changes in activity level |
| --- | --- |
| Fixed costs | Remain the same in total regardless of change in activity level |
| Mixed costs | Contain both a fixed and a variable element |

CVP Income Statement Format

| | Total | Per Unit |
| --- | --- | --- |
| Sales | $xx | $xx |
| Variable costs | xx | xx |
| Contribution margin | xx | $xx |
| Fixed costs | xx | |
| Net income | $xx | |

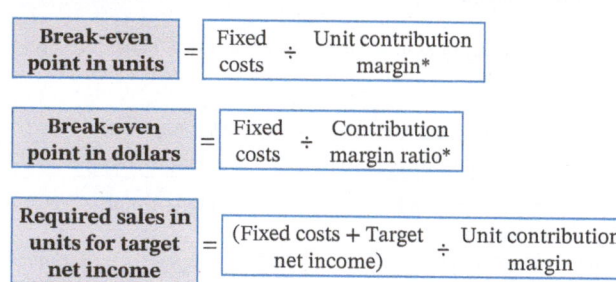

$$\text{Unit contribution margin} = \text{Unit selling price} - \text{Unit variable costs}$$

$$\text{Break-even point in units} = \text{Fixed costs} \div \text{Unit contribution margin}^*$$

$$\text{Break-even point in dollars} = \text{Fixed costs} \div \text{Contribution margin ratio}^*$$

$$\text{Required sales in units for target net income} = (\text{Fixed costs} + \text{Target net income}) \div \text{Unit contribution margin}$$

## INCREMENTAL ANALYSIS (Chapter 14)

1. Identify the relevant costs associated with each alternative. **Relevant costs** are those costs and revenues that differ across alternatives. Choose the alternative that maximizes net income.
2. **Opportunity costs** are those benefits that are given up when one alternative is chosen instead of another one. Opportunity costs are relevant costs.
3. **Sunk costs** have already been incurred and will not be changed or avoided by any future decision. Sunk costs are not relevant costs.

## BUDGETS (Chapter 15)

Components of the Master Budget

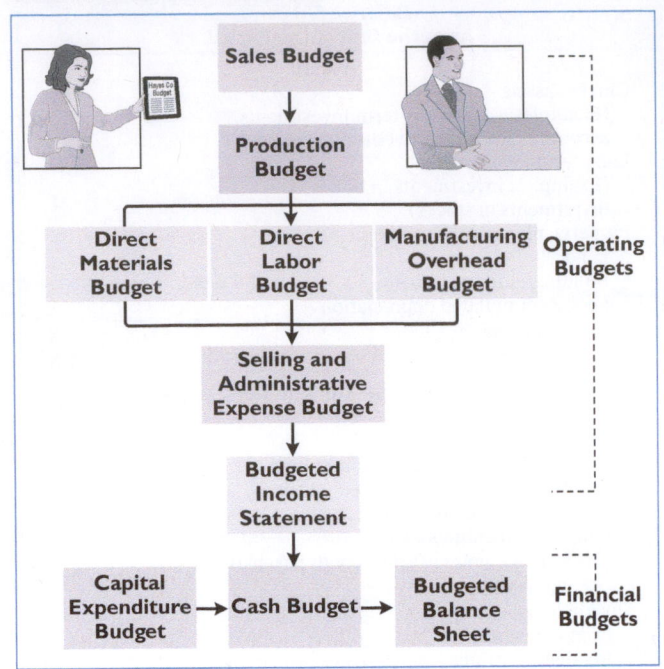

| Materials price variance | $= \boxed{AQ \times AP} - \boxed{AQ \times SP}$ |
|---|---|
| Materials quantity variance | $= \boxed{AH \times SR} - \boxed{SQ \times SP}$ |
| Labor price variance | $= \boxed{AH \times AR} - \boxed{AH \times SR}$ |
| Labor quantity variance | $= \boxed{AQ \times SP} - \boxed{SH \times SR}$ |
| * Overhead controllable variance | $= \boxed{\text{Actual overhead}} - \boxed{\text{Overhead budgeted}}$ |
| * Overhead volume variance | $= \boxed{\text{Fixed overhead rate}} \times \boxed{\text{Normal capacity hours} - \text{Standard hours allowed}}$ |

*Appendix coverage

Balanced Scorecard

**Linked process across perspectives:**

Financial → Customer → Internal Process → Learning and Growth

## RESPONSIBILITY ACCOUNTING (Chapter 16)

Types of Responsibility Centers

| Cost | Profit | Investment |
|---|---|---|
| Expenses only | Expenses and Revenues | Expenses and Revenues and ROI |

Return on Investment

| Return on investment (ROI) | $=$ Investment center controllable margin $\div$ Average investment center operating assets |
|---|---|

## STANDARD COSTS (Chapter 17)

Standard Cost Variances

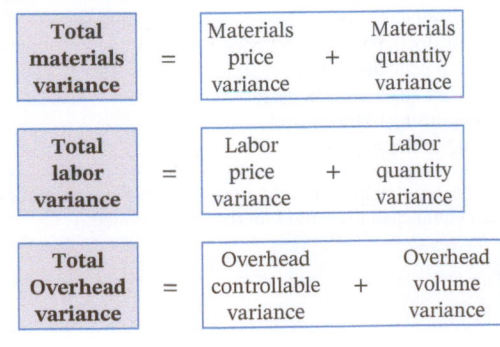

| Total materials variance | $=$ Materials price variance $+$ Materials quantity variance |
|---|---|

| Total labor variance | $=$ Labor price variance $+$ Labor quantity variance |
|---|---|

| Total Overhead variance | $=$ Overhead controllable variance $+$ Overhead volume variance |
|---|---|

## CAPITAL BUDGETING (Chapter 18)

Annual Rate of Return

| Annual rate of return | $=$ Expected annual net income $\div$ Average investment |
|---|---|

Cash Payback

| Cash payback period | $=$ Cost of capital investment $\div$ Annual cash inflow |
|---|---|

Discounted Cash Flow Approaches

| Net Present Value | Internal Rate of Return |
|---|---|
| Compute net present value (a dollar amount). If net present value is zero or positive, accept the proposal. If net present value is negative, reject the proposal. | Compute internal rate of return (a percentage). If internal rate of return is equal to or greater than the minimum required rate of return, accept the proposal. If internal rate of return is less than the minimum rate, reject the proposal. |

| Order of Preparation | Date |
|---|---|
| 1. Income statement | For the period ended |
| 2. Retained earnings statement | For the period ended |
| 3. Balance sheet | As of the end of the period |
| 4. Statement of cash flows | For the period ended |

# RAPID REVIEW
## Financial Statements

Income Statement

| Name of Company<br>Income Statement<br>For the Period Ended | | |
|---|---|---|
| Sales | | |
| Sales revenue | $ X | |
| Less: Sales returns and allowances | X | |
| Sales discounts | X | |
| Net sales | | $ X |
| Cost of goods sold | | X |
| Gross profit | | X |
| Operating expenses | | |
| (Examples: store salaries, advertising, delivery, rent, depreciation, utilities, insurance) | | X |
| Income from operations | | X |
| Other revenues and gains | | |
| (Examples: interest, gains) | X | |
| Other expenses and losses | | |
| (Examples: interest, losses) | X | X |
| Income before income taxes | | X |
| Income tax expense | | X |
| Net income | | $ X |

| Name of Company<br>Statement of Comprehensive Income<br>For the Period Ended | |
|---|---|
| Net income | $XX |
| Other comprehensive income | XX |
| Comprehensive income | $XX |

Retained Earnings Statement

| Name of Company<br>Retained Earnings Statement<br>For the Period Ended | |
|---|---|
| Retained earnings, beginning of period | $ X |
| Add: Net income (or deduct net loss) | X |
| | X |
| Deduct: Dividends | X |
| Retained earnings, end of period | $ X |

**Stop and Check:** Net income (loss) presented on the retained earnings statement must equal the net income (loss) presented on the income statement.

Balance Sheet

| Name of Company<br>Balance Sheet<br>As of the End of the Period | | | |
|---|---|---|---|
| **Assets** | | | |
| Current assets | | | |
| (Examples: cash, short-term investments, accounts receivable, inventory, prepaids) | | | $ X |
| Long-term investments | | | |
| (Examples: investments in bonds, investments in stocks) | | | X |
| Property, plant, and equipment | | | |
| Land | | $ X | |
| Buildings and equipment | $ X | | |
| Less: Accumulated depreciation | X | X | X |
| Intangible assets | | | X |
| Total assets | | | $ X |
| **Liabilities and Stockholders' Equity** | | | |
| Liabilities | | | |
| Current liabilities | | | |
| (Examples: notes payable, accounts payable, accruals, unearned revenues, current portion of notes payable) | | | $ X |
| Long-term liabilities | | | |
| (Examples: notes payable, bonds payable) | | | X |
| Total liabilities | | | X |
| Stockholders' equity | | | |
| Common stock | | | X |
| Retained earnings | | | X |
| Total liabilities and stockholders' equity | | | $ X |

**Stop and Check:** Total assets on the balance sheet must equal total liabilities plus stockholders' equity; and, ending retained earnings on the balance sheet must equal ending retained earnings on the retained earnings statement.

Statement of Cash Flows

| Name of Company<br>Statement of Cash Flows<br>For the Period Ended | |
|---|---|
| Cash flows from operating activities | |
| (*Note:* May be prepared using the direct or indirect method) | |
| Net cash provided (used) by operating activities | $ X |
| Cash flows from investing activities | |
| (Examples: purchase/sale of long-term assets) | |
| Net cash provided (used) by investing activities | X |
| Cash flows from financing activities | |
| (Examples: issue/repayment of long-term liabilities, issue of stock, payment of dividends) | |
| Net cash provided (used) by financing activities | X |
| Net increase (decrease) in cash | X |
| Cash, beginning of the period | X |
| Cash, end of the period | $ X |

**Stop and Check:** Cash, end of the period, on the statement of cash flows must equal cash presented on the balance sheet.

# Tools for Analysis

| Ratio | Formula | Purpose or Use |
|---|---|---|
| **Liquidity Ratios** | | |
| Working capital | Current assets – Current liabilities | Measures liquidity of assets. |
| Current ratio | $\dfrac{\text{Current assets}}{\text{Current liabilities}}$ | Measures short-term debt-paying ability. |
| Inventory turnover | $\dfrac{\text{Cost of goods sold}}{\text{Average inventory}}$ | Measures liquidity of inventory. |
| Days in inventory | $\dfrac{365}{\text{Inventory turnover}}$ | Measures the average number of days that inventory is held. |
| Accounts receivable turnover | $\dfrac{\text{Net credit sales}}{\text{Average net accounts receivable}}$ | Measures liquidity of receivables. |
| Average collection period | $\dfrac{365}{\text{Accounts receivable turnover}}$ | Measures the effectiveness of credit and collection policies. |
| **Solvency Ratios** | | |
| Debt to assets ratio | $\dfrac{\text{Total liabilities}}{\text{Total assets}}$ | Measures percentage of total assets provided by creditors. |
| Times interest earned | $\dfrac{\text{Net income} + \text{Interest expense} + \text{Income tax expense}}{\text{Interest expense}}$ | Measures ability to meet interest payments as they come due. |
| Free cash flow | Net cash provided by operating activities – Capital expenditures – Cash dividends | Measures the amount of cash generated during the current year that is available for the payment of additional dividends or for expansion. |
| **Profitability Ratios** | | |
| Earnings per share (EPS) | $\dfrac{\text{Net income} - \text{Preferred dividends}}{\text{Weighted-average common shares outstanding}}$ | Measures net income earned on each share of common stock. |
| Price-earnings (P-E) ratio | $\dfrac{\text{Market price per share of stock}}{\text{Earnings per share}}$ | Measures the ratio of the market price per share to earnings per share. |
| Gross profit rate | $\dfrac{\text{Gross profit}}{\text{Net sales}}$ | Measures the ability to maintain an adequate selling price above cost of goods sold. |
| Profit margin | $\dfrac{\text{Net income}}{\text{Net sales}}$ | Measures net income generated by each dollar of sales. |
| Return on assets | $\dfrac{\text{Net income}}{\text{Average total assets}}$ | Measures overall profitability of assets. |
| Asset turnover | $\dfrac{\text{Net sales}}{\text{Average total assets}}$ | Measures how efficiently assets are used to generate sales. |
| Payout ratio | $\dfrac{\text{Cash dividends declared on common stock}}{\text{Net income}}$ | Measures percentage of earnings distributed in the form of cash dividends. |
| Return on common stockholders' equity | $\dfrac{\text{Net income} - \text{Preferred dividends}}{\text{Average common stockholders' equity}}$ | Measures profitability of stockholders' investment. |

# NOTES

# NOTES

# NOTES